Lecture Notes in Artificial Intelligence 11839

Subseries of Lecture Notes in Computer Science

More information about this series at http://www.springer.com/series/1244

Jie Tang · Min-Yen Kan · Dongyan Zhao ·
Sujian Li · Hongying Zan (Eds.)

Natural Language Processing and Chinese Computing

8th CCF International Conference, NLPCC 2019 Dunhuang, China, October 9–14, 2019 Proceedings, Part II

Editors
Jie Tang
Tsinghua University
Beijing, China

Min-Yen Kan
National University of Singapore
Singapore, Singapore

Dongyan Zhao
Peking University
Beijing, China

Sujian Li
Peking University
Beijing, China

Hongying Zan
Zhengzhou University
Zhengzhou, China

ISSN 0302-9743 ISSN 1611-3349 (electronic)
Lecture Notes in Artificial Intelligence
ISBN 978-3-030-32235-9 ISBN 978-3-030-32236-6 (eBook)
https://doi.org/10.1007/978-3-030-32236-6

LNCS Sublibrary: SL7 – Artificial Intelligence

This Springer imprint is published by the registered company Springer Nature Switzerland AG
The registered company address is: Gewerbestrasse 11, 6330 Cham, Switzerland

Preface

Welcome to the proceedings of NLPCC 2019, the 8th CCF International Conference on Natural Language Processing and Chinese Computing. Following the success of previous iterations of the conference held in Beijing (2012), Chongqing (2013), Shenzhen (2014), Nanchang (2015), Kunming (2016), Dalian (2017), and Hohhot (2018), this year's NLPCC was held at Dunhuang, an oasis on China's ancient Silk Road. It is situated in the northwest region of China, where the Gobi Desert and the far eastern edge of the Taklamakan Desert meet in the Gansu Province. As a leading international conference on natural language processing and Chinese computing, organized by the CCF-TCCI (Technical Committee of Chinese Information, China Computer Federation), NLPCC 2019 serves as an important forum for researchers and practitioners from academia, industry, and government to share their ideas, research results and experiences, and to promote their research and technical innovations in the fields.

The fields of natural language processing (NLP) and Chinese computing (CC) have boomed in recent years, and the growing number of submissions to NLPCC is testament to this trend. After unfortunately having to reject over 50 submissions that did not meet the submission guidelines, we received a total of 492 valid submissions to the entire conference, inclusive of the main conference, Student Workshop, Evaluation Workshop and the special Explainable AI (XAI) Workshop. This represents a record 76% increase in the number of submissions compared with NLPCC 2018. Of the 451 valid submissions to the main conference, 343 were written in English and 108 were written in Chinese. Following NLPCC's tradition, we welcomed submissions in eight areas for the main conference: NLP Fundamentals, NLP Applications, Text Mining, Machine Translation, Machine Learning for NLP, Information Extraction/Knowledge Graph, Conversational Bot/Question Answering/Information Retrieval, and NLP for Social Networks. This year, we also adapted the call for papers to especially allow for papers addressing privacy and ethics as well, as this has become a key area of interest as NLP and CC deployments grow in industry. We adopted last year's innovation by inviting authors to submit their work to one of five categories, each which had a different review form.

Acceptance decisions were made during a hybrid virtual and physical scientific Program Committee (PC) meeting attended by the general, PC, and area chairs. After our deliberations for the main conference, 92 submissions were accepted as full papers (with 77 papers in English and 15 papers in Chinese) and 38 as short papers. Eight papers were nominated by the area chairs for the best paper award in both the English and Chinese tracks. An independent best paper award committee was formed to select the best paper from the shortlist. The proceedings include only the accepted English papers; the Chinese papers appear in *ACTA Scientiarum Naturalium Universitatis Pekinensis*. In addition to the main proceedings, four papers were accepted for the student workshop, 14 papers were accepted for the Evaluation Workshop, and nine papers were accepted to the special Explainable AI (XAI) Workshop.

We were honored to have four internationally renowned keynote speakers—Keh-Yih Su, Mark Liberman, Dawei Song, and Fei Xia—share their expert opinions on recent developments in NLP via their lectures "On Integrating Domain Knowledge into DNN," "Clinical Applications of Human Language Technology," "A Quantum Cognitive Perspective for Information Access and Retrieval," and "NLP Is Not Equal to NN."

The organization of NLPCC 2019 took place with the help of a great many people:

- We are grateful to the guidance and advice provided by General Co-chairs Kenneth Church and Qun Liu, and Organization Committee Co-chairs Dongyan Zhao, Hongzhi Yu, and Zhijun Sun. We especially thank Dongyan Zhao, as the central committee member who acted as a central adviser to both of us as PC chairs, in making sure all of the decisions were made on schedule.
- We would like to thank Student Workshop Co-chairs Yue Zhang and Jiajun Zhang, as well as Evaluation Co-chairs Weiwei Sun and Nan Duan, who undertook the difficult task of selecting the slate of accepted papers from the large pool of high-quality papers.
- We are indebted to the 17 area chairs and the 287 primary reviewers, for both the English and Chinese tracks. This year, with a record number of submissions, they operated under severe load, and completed their careful reviews, still under a month. We could not have met the various deadlines during the review process without their hard work.
- We thank ADL/Tutorial Co-chairs Xiaojun Wan, Qi Zhang, and Hua Wu for assembling a comprehensive tutorial program consisting of six tutorials covering a wide range of cutting-edge topics in NLP.
- We thank Sponsorship Co-chairs Ming Zhou and Tiejun Zhao for securing sponsorship for the conference.
- We also thank Publication Co-chairs Sujian Li and Hongying Zan for ensuring every little detail in the publication process was properly taken care of. Those who have done this form of service work know how excruciating it can be. On behalf of us and all of the authors, we thank them for their work, as they truly deserve a big applause.
- Above all, we thank everybody who chose to submit their work to NLPCC 2019. Without your support, we could not have put together a strong conference program.

September 2019

Jie Tang
Min-Yen Kan

Organization

NLPCC 2019 was organized by China Computer Federation, and hosted by Northwest Minzu University, Dunhuang Academy and the National State Key Lab of Digital Publishing Technology.

Organizing Committee

General Co-chairs

Kenneth Church — Baidu Inc.
Qun Liu — Huawei Noah's Ark Lab

Program Co-chairs

Min-Yen Kan — National University of Singapore, Singapore
Jie Tang — Tsinghua University, China

Area Chairs

Conversational Bot/QA

Yunhua Hu — Abitai.com
Wenjie Li — Hong Kong Polytechnic University, SAR China

Fundamentals of NLP

Yangfeng Ji — University of Virginia, USA
Meishan Zhang — Heilongjiang University, China

Knowledge Graph

Yangqiu Song — Hong Kong University of Science and Technology, SAR China
Haofen Wang — Gowild.cn, China

Machine Learning for NLP

Caiming Xiong — Salesforce Research
Xu Sun — Peking University, China

Machine Translation

Derek Wong — University of Macau, SAR China
Jiajun Zhang — Institute of Automation, Chinese Academy of Sciences, China

NLP Applications

Ping Luo — Institute of Computing Technology, Chinese Academy of Sciences, China
Xiang Ren — University of Southern California, USA

Text Mining

Michalis Vazirgiannis — Ecole Polytechnique, France
Jun Xu — Renmin University, China
Furu Wei — Microsoft Research Asia

Social Network

Wei Gao — Victoria University of Wellington, New Zealand
Chuan Shi — Beijing University of Posts and Telecommunications, China

Student Workshop Co-chairs

Yue Zhang — Westlake University, China
Jiajun Zhang — Institute of Automation, Chinese Academy of Sciences, China

Evaluation Co-chairs

Nan Duan — Microsoft Research Asia
Weiwei Sun — Peking University

ADL/Tutorial Co-chairs

Xiaojun Wan — Peking University, China
Qi Zhang — Fudan University, China
Hua Wu — Baidu Inc.

Publication Chairs

Sujian Li — Peking University, China
Hongying Zan — Zhengzhou University, China

Sponsorship Co-chairs

Ming Zhou — Microsoft Research Asia, China
Tiejun Zhao — Harbin Institute of Technology, China

Publicity Co-chairs

Ruifeng Xu — Harbin University of Technology (Shenzhen), China
Wanxiang Che — Harbin Institute of Technology, China

Organization Co-chairs

Dongyan Zhao — Peking University, China
Hongzhi Yu — Northwest Minzu University, China
Zhijun Sun — Dunhuang Academy, China

Program Committee

Qingyao Ai — University of Massachusetts, Amherst, USA
Xiang Ao — Institute of Computing Technology, Chinese Academy of Sciences, China
António Branco — University of Lisbon, Portugal
Deng Cai — The Chinese University of Hong Kong, SAR China

Hailong Cao	Harbin Institute of Technology, China
Kai Cao	New York University, USA
Yung-Chun Chang	Graduate Institute of Data Science, Taipei Medical University, China
Berlin Chen	National Taiwan Normal University, China
Boxing Chen	Alibaba, China
Chen Chen	Arizona State University, USA
Chengyao Chen	Wisers AI Lab, China
Hanjie Chen	University of Virginia, USA
Hongshen Chen	JD.com, China
Hsin-Hsi Chen	National Taiwan University, China
Muhao Chen	University of California Los Angeles, USA
Qingcai Chen	Harbin Institute of Technology Shenzhen Graduate School, China
Ruey-Cheng Chen	SEEK Ltd., China
Tao Chen	Google AI, USA
Wenliang Chen	Soochow University, China
Yidong Chen	Xiamen University, China
Yinfen Chen	Jiangxi Normal University, China
Yubo Chen	Institute of Automation, Chinese Academy of Sciences, China
Zhumin Chen	Shandong University, China
Gong Cheng	Nanjing University, China
Li Cheng	Xinjiang Technical Institute of Physics and Chemistry, Chinese Academy of Sciences, China
Yong Cheng	Google
Zhiyong Cheng	Shandong Artificial Intelligence Institute, China
Chenhui Chu	Osaka University, Japan
Hongliang Dai	Hong Kong University of Science and Technology, SAR China
Xinyu Dai	Nanjing University, China
Chenchen Ding	NICT, Japan
Xiao Ding	Harbin Institute of Technology, China
Li Dong	Microsoft Research Asia
Jiachen Du	Harbin Institute of Technology Shenzhen Graduate School, China
Jinhua Du	Dublin City University, Ireland
Junwen Duan	Harbin Institute of Technology, China
Nan Duan	Microsoft Research Asia
Xiangyu Duan	Soochow University, China
Miao Fan	BAIDU Research
Yixing Fan	Institute of Computing Technology, Chinese Academy of Sciences, China
Yang Feng	Institute of Computing Technology, Chinese Academy of Sciences, China
Guohong Fu	Heilongjiang University, China

Sheng Gao	Beijing University of Posts and Telecommunications, China
Wei Gao	Victoria University of Wellington, New Zealand
Yang Gao	Beijing Institute of Technology, China
Niyu Ge	IBM Research
Xiubo Geng	Microsoft
Yupeng Gu	Pinterest, USA
Lin Gui	University of Warwick, UK
Jiafeng Guo	Institute of Computing Technology, CAS, China
Jiang Guo	Massachusetts Institute of Technology, USA
Lifeng Han	Dublin City University, Ireland
Xianpei Han	Institute of Software, Chinese Academy of Sciences, China
Tianyong Hao	South China Normal University, China
Ji He	University of Washington, USA
Yanqing He	Institute of Scientific and Technical Information of China, China
Yifan He	Alibaba Group
Zhongjun He	Baidu, Inc.
Yu Hong	Soochow University, China
Hongxu Hou	Inner Mongolia University
Linmei Hu	School of Computer Science, Beijing University of Posts and Telecommunications, China
Yunhua Hu	Taobao, China
Dongyan Huang	UBTECH Robotics Corp., China
Guoping Huang	Tencent AI Lab, China
Jiangping Huang	Chongqing University of Posts and Telecommunications, China
Shujian Huang	National Key Laboratory for Novel Software Technology, Nanjing University, China
Xiaojiang Huang	Microsoft
Xuanjing Huang	Fudan University, China
Yangfeng Ji	University of Virginia, USA
Yuxiang Jia	Zhengzhou University, China
Shengyi Jiang	Guangdong University of Foreign Studies, China
Wenbin Jiang	Baidu Inc.
Yutong Jiang	Beijing Information and Technology University, China
Zhuoren Jiang	Sun Yat-sen University, China
Bo Jin	Dalian University of Technology, China
Peng Jin	Leshan Normal University, China
Xiaolong Jin	Institute of Computing Technology, Chinese Academy of Sciences, China
Min-Yen Kan	National University of Singapore, Singapore
Fang Kong	Soochow University, China
Lun-Wei Ku	Academia Sinica, China
Oi Yee Kwong	The Chinese University of Hong Kong, SAR China

Man Lan	East China Normal University, China
Yanyan Lan	Institute of Computing Technology, CAS, China
Yves Lepage	Waseda University, Japan
Bin Li	Nanjing Normal University, China
Chen Li	Tencent
Chenliang Li	Wuhan University, China
Fangtao Li	Google Research
Fei Li	UMASS Lowell, USA
Hao Li	Rensselaer Polytechnic Institute, USA
Junhui Li	Soochow University, China
Lei Li	Bytedance AI Lab
Maoxi Li	Jiangxi Normal University, China
Piji Li	Tencent AI Lab
Qiang Li	Northeastern University, China
Sheng Li	University of Georgia
Shoushan Li	Soochow University, China
Si Li	Beijing University of Posts and Telecommunications, China
Sujian Li	Peking University, China
Wenjie Li	The Hong Kong Polytechnic University, SAR China
Yaliang Li	Alibaba
Yuan-Fang Li	Monash University, Australia
Zhenghua Li	Soochow University, China
Shangsong Liang	Sun Yat-sen University, China
Shuailong Liang	Singapore University of Technology and Design, Singapore
Bill Yuchen Lin	University of Southern California, USA
Junyang Lin	Peking University, China
Jialu Liu	UIUC, USA
Jiangming Liu	University of Edinburgh, UK
Jie Liu	Nankai University, China
Lemao Liu	Tencent AI Lab
Pengfei Liu	Fudan University, China
Qi Liu	University of Science and Technology of China, China
Shenghua Liu	Institute of Computing Technology, CAS, China
Shujie Liu	Microsoft Research Asia, China
Xin Liu	Hong Kong University of Science and Technology, SAR China
Xuebo Liu	University of Macau, SAR China
Yang Liu	Shandong University, China
Yang Liu	Tsinghua University, China
Ye Liu	National University of Singapore, Singapore
Yijia Liu	Harbin Institute of Technology, China
Zhengzhong Liu	Carnegie Mellon University, USA
Zhiyuan Liu	Tsinghua University, China

Wei Lu	Singapore University of Technology and Design, Singapore
Cheng Luo	Tsinghua University, China
Fuli Luo	Peking University, China
Ping Luo	Institute of Computing Technology, CAS, China
Weihua Luo	Alibaba
Wencan Luo	Google
Zhunchen Luo	PLA Academy of Military Science, China
Chen Lyu	Guangdong University of Foreign Studies, China
Shuming Ma	Peking University, China
Wei-Yun Ma	Institute of Information Science, Academia Sinica, China
Yue Ma	Université Paris Sud, France
Cunli Mao	Kunming University of Science and Technology, China
Jiaxin Mao	Tsinghua University, China
Xian-Ling Mao	Beijing Institute of Technology, China
Haitao Mi	Ant Financial US
Lili Mou	University of Waterloo, Canada
Aldrian Obaja Muis	Carnegie Mellon University, USA
Toshiaki Nakazawa	The University of Tokyo, Japan
Giannis Nikolentzos	Athens University of Economics and Business, Greece
Nedjma Ousidhoum	The Hong Kong University of Science and Technology, SAR China
Liang Pang	ICT, China
Baolin Peng	The Chinese University of Hong Kong, SAR China
Longhua Qian	Soochow University, China
Tieyun Qian	Wuhan University, China
Yanxia Qin	Donghua University, China
Likun Qiu	Ludong University, China
Weiguang Qu	Nanjing Normal University, China
Feiliang Ren	Northeastern University
Xiang Ren	University of Southern California, USA
Yafeng Ren	Guangdong University of Foreign Studies, China
Zhaochun Ren	Shandong University, China
Lei Sha	Peking University, China
Chuan Shi	BUPT, China
Xiaodong Shi	Xiamen University, China
Guojie Song	Peking University, China
Wei Song	Capital Normal University, China
Yangqiu Song	The Hong Kong University of Science and Technology, SAR China
Jinsong Su	Xiamen University, China
Aixin Sun	Nanyang Technological University, Singapore
Chengjie Sun	Harbin Institute of Technology, China
Fei Sun	Alibaba Group
Weiwei Sun	Peking University, China

Xu Sun	Peking University, China
Jie Tang	Tsinghua University, China
Zhi Tang	Peking University, China
Zhiyang Teng	Westlake University, China
Fei Tian	Microsoft Research
Jin Ting	Hainan University, China
Ming-Feng Tsai	National Chengchi University, China
Yuen-Hsien Tseng	National Taiwan Normal University, China
Masao Utiyama	NICT, Japan
Michalis Vazirgiannis	Ecole Polytechnique, France
Shengxian Wan	Bytedance AI Lab
Xiaojun Wan	Peking University, China
Bin Wang	Institute of Information Engineering, Chinese Academy of Sciences, China
Bingning Wang	Sogou Search AI Group, China
Bo Wang	Tianjin University, China
Chuan-Ju Wang	Academia Sinica, China
Di Wang	Carnegie Mellon University, USA
Haofen Wang	Shenzhen Gowild Robotics Co. Ltd., China
Longyue Wang	Tencent AI Lab, China
Mingxuan Wang	Bytedance, China
Pidong Wang	Machine Zone Inc., China
Quan Wang	Baidu Inc., China
Rui Wang	NICT, Japan
Senzhang Wang	Nanjing University of Aeronautics and Astronautics, China
Wei Wang	Google Research, USA
Wei Wang	UNSW, Australia
Xiao Wang	Beijing University of Posts and Telecommunications, China
Xiaojie Wang	Beijing University of Posts and Telecommunications, China
Xin Wang	Tianjin University, China
Xuancong Wang	Institute for Infocomm Research, Singapore
Yanshan Wang	Mayo Clinic, USA
Yuan Wang	Nankai University, China
Zhongqing Wang	Soochow University, China
Ziqi Wang	Facebook
Furu Wei	Microsoft Research Asia
Wei Wei	Huazhong University of Science and Technology, China
Zhongyu Wei	Fudan University, China
Derek F. Wong	University of Macau, SAR China
Le Wu	Hefei University of Technology, China
Long Xia	JD.COM
Rui Xia	Nanjing University of Science and Technology, China

Yunqing Xia	Microsoft
Tong Xiao	Northeastern University, China
Yanghua Xiao	Fudan University, China
Xin Xin	Beijing Institute of Technology, China
Caiming Xiong	Salesforce
Deyi Xiong	Soochow University, China
Hao Xiong	Baidu Inc.
Jinan Xu	Beijing Jiaotong University, China
Jingjing Xu	Peking University, China
Jun Xu	Renmin University of China, China
Kun Xu	Tencent AI Lab
Ruifeng Xu	Harbin Institute of Technology (Shenzhen), China
Xiaohui Yan	Huawei, China
Zhao Yan	Tencent
Baosong Yang	University of Macau, SAR China
Jie Yang	Harvard University, USA
Liang Yang	Dalian University of Technology, China
Pengcheng Yang	Peking University, China
Zi Yang	Google
Dong Yu	Beijing Language and Cultural University, China
Heng Yu	Alibaba
Liang-Chih Yu	Yuan Ze University, China
Zhengtao Yu	Kunming University of Science and Technology, China
Yufeng Chen	Beijing Jiaotong University, China
Hongying Zan	Zhengzhou University, China
Ying Zeng	Peking University, China
Ziqian Zeng	The Hong Kong University of Science and Technology, SAR China
Feifei Zhai	Sogou, Inc.
Biao Zhang	University of Edinburgh, UK
Chengzhi Zhang	Nanjing University of Science and Technology, China
Dakun Zhang	SYSTRAN
Dongdong Zhang	Microsoft Research Asia
Fan Zhang	Google
Fuzheng Zhang	Meituan AI Lab, China
Hongming Zhang	The Hong Kong University of Science and Technology, SAR China
Jiajun Zhang	Institute of Automation Chinese Academy of Sciences, China
Meishan Zhang	Tianjin University, China
Min Zhang	Tsinghua University, China
Min Zhang	SooChow University, China
Peng Zhang	Tianjin University, China
Qi Zhang	Fudan University, China
Wei Zhang	Institute for Infocomm Research, Singapore
Wei-Nan Zhang	Harbin Institute of Technology, China

Organizers

Organized by

China Computer Federation, China

Hosted by

Northwest Minzu University

Dunhuang Academy

State Key Lab of Digital Publishing Technology

In Cooperation with

Lecture Notes in Computer Science

Springer

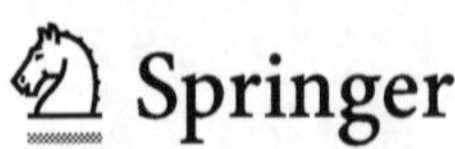

ACTA Scientiarum Naturalium Universitatis Pekinensis

Sponsoring Institutions

Diamond Sponsors

CMRI

Tencent AI Lab

JD AI

Gowild

Meituan Dianping

Miaobi

Platinum Sponsors

Microsoft

Baidu

GTCOM

Huawei

Xiaomi

Lenovo

ByteDance

Golden Sponsors

Keji Data

Gridsum

Sogou

Alibaba

Silver Sponsors

Speech Ocean

Niutrans

Contents – Part II

Text Mining

Short Papers

Explainable AI Workshop

Student Workshop

Evaluation Workshop

Contents – Part I

Knowledge Graph/IE

Machine Learning for NLP

Machine Translation

NLP Applications

NLP for Social Network

NLP Fundamentals

Text Mining

An Improved Class-Center Method for Text Classification Using Dependencies and WordNet

Xinhua Zhu[1], Qingting Xu[1], Yishan Chen[1,2(✉)], and Tianjun Wu[1]

[1] Guangxi Key Lab of Multi-Source Information Mining and Security, Guangxi Normal University, Guilin, China
zxh429@263.net, xat341126@163.com, GLCYS@163.com, 1035626809@qq.com

[2] International Business School, Guilin Tourism University, Guilin, China

Abstract. Automatic text classification is a research focus and core technology in natural language processing and information retrieval. The class-center vector method is an important text classification method, which has the advantages of less calculation and high efficiency. However, the traditional class-center vector method for text classification has the disadvantages that the class vector is large and sparse; its classification accuracy is not high and it lacks semantic information. To overcome these problems, this paper proposes an improved class-center method for text classification using dependencies and the WordNet dictionary. Experiments show that, compared with traditional text classification algorithms, the improved class-center vector method has lower time complexity and higher accuracy on a large corpus.

Keywords: Text classification · Dependency · Weight calculation · WordNet · Class-center vector

1 Introduction

With the rapid development of Internet technology, network information has exploded in an exponential manner. How to effectively organize and manage this text information becomes an urgent problem to be solved [1]. Text classification is one of the important research directions [2].

Common text classification algorithms include the Bayesian classification [3], *K*-nearest neighbor (KNN) [4], support vector machine (SVM) [5], and class-center vector algorithms [6]. Although the Bayesian algorithm is simple in principle and easy to implement, it is based on the hypothesis that the classification accuracy will be high only if the text dataset is independent of each other [7]. The classification accuracy of KNN is very high, but the classification efficiency is very low. SVM is widely used in small corpora because of its strong generalization ability, but it is not very effective in large corpora [8]. The main advantage of the class-center vector method is that the corpus is greatly reduced before its classification process [9]. Therefore, its classification process has a less calculation and high classification efficiency. However,

J. Tang et al. (Eds.): NLPCC 2019, LNAI 11839, pp. 3–15, 2019.
https://doi.org/10.1007/978-3-030-32236-6_1

the traditional class-center vector algorithms for text classification have the disadvantages that the class vector is large and sparse; classification accuracy is not high and lacks semantic information.

In terms of weight calculations for text vectors, in 1973, Salton et al. [10] combined the idea of Jones [11] to present a TFIDF (Frequency & Inverse Documentation Frequency Term) algorithm. The TFIDF algorithm has been highly favored by the relevant researchers [12–14] and many application fields, because of its easy understanding, simple operation, low time complexity, high accuracy and high recall rate. To further improve its performance, scholars have made continuous efforts. For example, How and Narayanan [12] put forward the Category Term Descriptor (CTD) to improve TFIDF in 2004. It solved the adverse effect of the number of documents in different categories on the TFIDF algorithm. Qu et al. [13] proposed a new approach for calculating text vector weights, which combined simple distance vector to traditional TFIDF algorithms and obtained the very good classification effect. In 2012, Wang et al. [14] proposed a new TFIDF algorithm based on information gain and information entropy. This method only considers the feature words with high information gain. The above methods have made some progress in improving the performance of TFIDF algorithm, but they all lack the combination of text semantics to understand the text content.

Principal Component Analysis (PCA) [15] and Non-negative Matrix Factorization (NMF) [16] are traditional techniques for dimensionality reduction. However, the PCA contains both positive and negative values in the decomposed matrices, the cost of PCA computation will be prohibitive when matrices become large. The NMF is distinguished from the PCA method by its non-negativity constraints. These constraints lead to a parts-based representation because they allow only additive, not subtractive, combinations. Besides, PCA and NMF are only suitable for vectors have the same order of magnitude, and both require dimensionality reduction. In this paper, the dimension of the class-center vector is much bigger than the classified text vector, and the order of magnitude is not equivalent. Therefore, neither PCA nor NMF is suitable for the dimensionality reduction of this paper.

To overcome the above problems, this paper proposes an improved class-center vector method for text classification based on dependencies and the semantic dictionary WordNet. The main contributions of this paper can be summarized as follows:

(1) Aiming at the semantic defects of the statistics-based TFIDF algorithm, we introduce dependencies and the synonyms in the WordNet dictionary to understand and optimize the text feature, and put forward an improved weight calculation algorithm based on TFIDF.
(2) We use the category nodes located in the 6-9 layers of WordNet to cluster feature words in the class-center vector and to significantly reduce the dimension of class-center vector, thereby realizing a new class-center vector for text classification using dependencies and the WordNet dictionary.
(3) Since the dimension of our clustered class-center vector is very different from that of the classified text vector, the similarity between them is not suitable to directly use the traditional cosine similarity method. This paper proposes a new vector similarity method for our clustered class-center vector, in which the similarity

between the class-center vector and the classified text vector is expressed as the ratio of the sum of the classified text feature weights matching with the class center vector and the sum of all the weights of the class center vectors. It can improve the accuracy of our class-center vector text classification.

2 Class-Center Vector Method

The basic idea of the class-center vector method [6] is to use the arithmetic average method to determine the class-center vector of each class, calculate the similarities between the classified text vector and each class-center vector according to the cosine similarity formula, and assign the classified text into the category with the highest similarity value. The detailed calculation steps are as follows:

(1) The arithmetic average formula is used to determine the class-center vector. The formula is as follows:

$$\mathbf{v}_{C_k} = \left\{ \left(t_{k,j}, w_{k,j}\right) \middle| j \in \{1, 2, \ldots, m\} \text{ and } w_{k,j} = \frac{1}{S_k} \sum_{i=1}^{S_k} w_{k_{i,j}} \right\} \tag{1}$$

where, m is the feature dimension of class-center vector; $\mathrm{t}_{k,j}$ represents the jth feature of the class-center vector of the kth class; $w_{k,j}$ is the weight value of the jth feature of the class-center vector of the kth class; S_k is the total number of text in the kth category in the training set; $w_{k_{i,j}}$ represents the weight value of the jth feature of the ith text in the kth category, and can be calculated by a feature weight algorithm (such as the TFIDF algorithm).

(2) The xth classified text is represented as a text feature vector $\mathbf{v}_{d_x}$:

$$\mathbf{v}_{d_x} = \left\{ \left(t_{x,j}, w_{x,j}\right) | j \in \{1, 2, \ldots, l\} \right\} \tag{2}$$

where, l is the dimension of the text feature vector; $\mathrm{t}_{x,j}$ denotes the jth feature of the xth classified text; $w_{x,j}$ is the weight value of the jth feature in the xth classified text, and can be calculated by the feature weight algorithm.

(3) Cosine similarity is generally used to calculate the similarity between the class-center vector and the classified text vector, and the formula is as follows:

$$Sim(\mathbf{v}_{C_k}, \mathbf{v}_{d_x}) = \frac{\langle \mathbf{v}_{C_k}, \mathbf{v}_{d_x} \rangle}{\|\mathbf{v}_{C_k}\| \times \|\mathbf{v}_{d_x}\|} \tag{3}$$

(4) All the calculated similarity values are sorted by their values, and the classified text is classified into the category with the largest similarity value.

3 Proposed Method

3.1 Preprocessing

To perform a text classification experiment, we first need to convert the text in the corpus into a form of data that the computer can directly process, and the preprocessing is the first step to complete the transformation. The preprocessing in this paper includes stemming and stop words deletion.

3.2 TFIDF Weight Improvement Based on Dependencies and WordNet

Syntactic analysis based on dependencies can reflect the semantic relationship between the components in a sentence, and is not affected by the physical location of the component [17]. Now it is widely used in the analysis of sentence structure. Firstly, according to the different dependencies between the word and the predicate in sentences, we determine the importance of the word to the sentence, the text and even the category, that is, determines the importance of the word to the text according to the sentence component represented by the word. Then, according to the importance of different components to the sentence, we divide the sentence components into eight levels (see Table 1), and propose an improved TFIDF method for text classification according to Table 1.

Table 1. Dependency levels

Sentence components	Dependencies	level
Subject	Subj (subject)	1
	Nsubj (noun subject)	
	Npsubj (passive subject)	
	Nsubjpass (passive noun subject)	
Object	Obj (object)	2
	Dobj (direct object)	
	Iobj (indirect object)	
Nominal modifier	Nmod (compound noun modification)	3
	Npadvmod (noun as adverbial)	
Predicate	Root (central word)	4
Attribute	Assmod (correlation modification)	5
	Numod (quantitative modification)	
Complement	Comp (complement)	6
	Acomp (adjective complement)	
	Tcomp (time complement)	
	Lccomp (location complement)	
Adverbial	Advmod (adverbial)	7
Other	Other dependencies	8

In a sentence, the subject, as the agent of the predicate, is the most important component, so this paper classifies the characteristics of all the subject components as the first level feature. As the object of the predicate, the object is the sub-important component, and the characteristics of all the object components are classified as the second level feature. Nominal modifiers are classified as the third level feature. Predicate is the core of a sentence, but it is generally a verb and it is a central word in the dependencies syntax. Verbs have the universal applicability, so they are not as important to text classification as nouns. Therefore, all the predicate component words are classified as the fourth level characteristic. The definite-middle relationship and adverbial-middle relationship are generally produced by adjectives and adverbs. As a sentence component, they may be the three major categories of attributive, complement, and adverbial, which are classified into the fifth, sixth and seventh levels. In addition, words such as Mod (modifier), Pass (passive modification), Tmod (time modification), Amod (adjective modification), and Advmod (adverb modification) are all classified as the eighth level feature.

After classifying the text features in the dataset according to dependencies, this paper proposes the following TFIDF weight calculation method based on dependencies and the synonyms in the WordNet dictionary. The specific steps are as follows:

(1) The synonyms in the text are merged according to the WordNet dictionary, in which the first word of the synonym group in the WordNet dictionary is used as a feature representation for all synonyms.
(2) We calculate the number of times that the feature word t_i appears in the text, which is set to m. Then, according to the result of dependency syntactic analysis implemented by Stanford Parser[1], we get the sentence component to which the feature word t_i belongs to its jth ($1 \leq j \leq m$) occurrence in the text, and classify the jth occurrence of the feature t_i in the text as the $k_{i,j}$ level according to Table 1 and assigns it a weight $w_{i,j}$, which is calculated as follows:

$$w_{i,j} = 2\cos\left[\left(\frac{k_{i,j}}{8}\right)^{\lambda} \times \frac{\pi}{2}\right] \tag{4}$$

where λ is a parameter, which is used to adjust the weight gap between feature grades, and its range is [0, 1];
(3) The improved frequency TF_i with weights for the feature word t_i in the text is calculated as follows:

$$TF_i = \sum_{j=1}^{m} w_{i,j} = \sum_{j=1}^{m} 2\cos\left[\left(\frac{k_{i,j}}{8}\right)^{\lambda} \times \frac{\pi}{2}\right] \tag{5}$$

[1] https://nlp.stanford.edu/software/lex-parser.html.

(4) Finally, we propose the following improved TFIDF weight formula based on dependency and WordNet for feature word t_i:

$$TF\_IDF_i = \frac{\sum_{j=1}^{m} 2\cos\left[\left(\frac{k_{i,j}}{8}\right)^{\lambda} \times \frac{\pi}{2}\right]}{s} \times \log\left(\frac{D}{p_i} + 0.01\right) \quad (6)$$

where s denotes the total number of words in the text where feature t_i is located and D denotes the total number of texts in the dataset, p_i denotes the number of the texts containing the feature t_i.

3.3 Class-Center Vector Clustering Approach Based on WordNet

In the traditional class-centric method, the dimension of a class vector is the union of all the text vectors of the class in the training set, which is very large and sparse. Therefore, the classification accuracy of traditional class-centric methods is not very high. Although, WordNet-based synonym merging can reduce the dimension of the class-center vector to some extent, this is far from enough. To effectively reduce the dimension of the class-center vector, we use the taxonomic hierarchy in WordNet to cluster the feature words of the class-center vector.

WordNet [18] is a large semantic dictionary based on cognitive linguistics and is designed and realized by psychologists, linguisticians and computer engineers in Princeton University. Considering that the average depth of the WordNet taxonomy reaches 10 layers, we use the category nodes in the first to ninth layers of the WordNet taxonomy to perform clustering effect test on the 20Newsgroups corpus, and the experimental results are shown in Fig. 1 below.

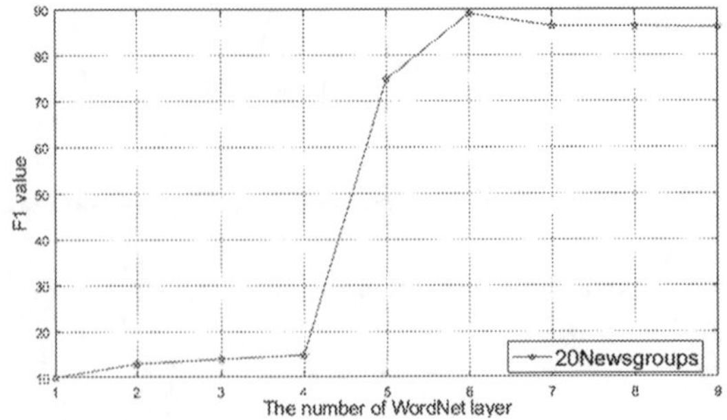

Fig. 1. Influence of the number of WordNet layers on F_1 value

In Fig. 1, when features are clustered to the first to fourth layers in WordNet, because the category nodes in the first to fourth layers of the WordNet are too abstract, all the features are grouped to the top and the abstract hypernym features in WordNet, so the classification effect is very poor. When the feature is clustered to the sixth layer of WordNet, the classification effect achieves the best, in which the F_1 value reaches

88.97%. When features are clustered to the seventh to ninth layers, the classification effect is still good although it has decreased. Therefore, the coding of the synonym sets of largest common subsumes located in the 6–9 layers of WordNet is used as the clustering feature. The specific clustering process is as follows:

Firstly, the initial value of the class-center vector is determined by the arithmetic average of the weight of the feature in all documents of the class. The formula is as follows:

$$V_{C_k^0} = \{(t_{k,j}^0, w_{k,j}^0)|j \in [1, L] \text{ and } w_{k,j}^0 = \frac{1}{S_k}\sum_{i=1}^{S_k} w_{k_{i,j}}\} \tag{7}$$

where $V_{C_k^0}$ represents the initial class-center vector of the kth category; L is the dimension of the initial class-center vector; $t_{k,j}^0$ represents the jth feature in the initial class-center vector of the kth category; $w_{k,j}^0$ is the initial weight value of the jth feature in the initial class-center vector of the kth category; S_k represents the total number of the texts of the category k in the training set, $w_{k_{i,j}}$ represents the weight value of the jth feature in the ith text of category k.

Then, the dataset is clustered through the WordNet dictionary. If the level of the arbitrary initial features $t_{k,j}^0$ in the WordNet is less than or equal to 6, the coding of its synonym group in WordNet is used as its clustering feature. Otherwise, we use the coding of the synonym set of its largest common subsume located in the 6–9 layers of WordNet as its clustering feature. The largest common subsume is the least common subsume that is located in the 6th to 9th layer of WordNet and contains the most characteristic words in the given initial vectors, such as the b node in Fig. 2.

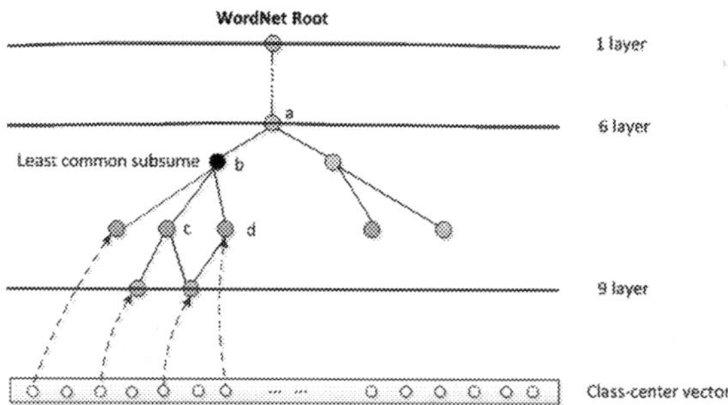

Fig. 2. An instance of the least common subsume in the clustering process

Finally, all the features of the initial class center vector of the kth category are clustered according to the above steps, and then, according to the following formula, the clustered center vector of the kth category is obtained.

$$V_{C_k} = \{(T_{k,j}, W_{k,j}) | j \in [1, n] \text{ and } W_{k,j} = \sum_{t^0_{k,i} \to T_{k,j}} w^0_{k,i}\} \tag{8}$$

where V_{C_k} represents the clustered center vector of the kth class, n is the dimension of the clustered center vector and n is less than or equal to the initial dimension L of the class-center vector. $T_{k,j}$ denotes the jth feature of the kth class after clustering, $W_{k,j}$ is the weight of $T_{k,j}$, $\sum_{t^0_{k,i} \to T_{k,j}} w^0_{k,i}$ represents the sum of weights for all the initial features that participate in the $T_{k,j}$ feature clustering.

3.4 A New Vector Similarity Method for Clustered Class-Center Vectors

Since the dimension of our clustered class-center vector is very different from that of the classified text vector, the similarity between them is not suitable to directly use the traditional cosine similarity method. This paper proposes a new vector similarity method for our clustered class-center vector, in which the similarity between the class-center vector and the classified text vector is expressed as the ratio of the sum of the classified text feature weights that is matched with the class center vector and the sum of all the weights of the class center vectors. The specific calculation processes are as follows:

(1) According to the dependency-based feature selection method and the improved TFIDF calculation method for the feature weight, the clustered class-center vector V_{C_k} for the category C_k and the feature vector V_{d_x} for the classified text d_x are determined;
(2) The V_{C_k}, V_{d_x} are inversely sorted by weights, and the first θ weights are taken. The calculation formula is as follows:

$$V^{\theta}_{C_k} = \{(T_{k,j}, W_{k,j}) | j \in [1, \min(\theta, n)] \text{ and } W_{k,j} \geq W_{k,j+1}\} \tag{9}$$

$$V^{\theta}_{d_x} = \{(t_{x,j}, w_{x,j}) | j \in [1, \min(\theta, q)] \text{ and } w_{x,j} \geq w_{x,j+1}\} \tag{10}$$

where θ represents a range of values from 0 to 3000, that is, selecting the most suitable dimension for the vectors V_{C_k}, V_{d_x} can make the classification effect the best, $V^{\theta}_{C_k}$ represents the class-center vector of the kth class with the θ dimension, $V^{\theta}_{d_x}$ denotes a feature vector of the classified text d_x with the θ dimension, n and q represent the initial dimensions of the vectors V_{C_k}, V_{d_x}, respectively

(3) We propose a new formula to calculate the similarity between the feature vector $V^{\theta}_{d_x}$ of the classified text d_x and the clustered class-center vector $V^{\theta}_{C_k}$ of the kth class as follows:

$$Sim(V^{\theta}_{C_K}, V^{\theta}_{d_x}) = \frac{\sum\limits_{t_i \in Stem(d_x \to C_K)} W_{C_k}(t_i)}{\sum\limits_{t_i \in Stem(C_K)} W_{C_k}(t_i)} \tag{11}$$

where Stem(C_k) denotes the feature set in vector $V^{0}_{C_k}$, Stem $(d_x \to C_k)$ represents a feature set in the class-center vector $V^{0}_{C_k}$ that can be successfully matched by the features in the classified text d_x. For any feature $t_{x,\ i}$ in the classified text d_x, the match rule between it and any $T_{k,j} \in$ Stem(C_k) is as follows: if $t_{x,i}$ and $T_{k,j}$ have the same encoding in WordNet or $t_{x,i}$ belongs to the hyponym of $T_{k,j}$ in the WordNet taxonomy, then $t_{x,i}$ successfully matches with $T_{k,j}$; otherwise, they are mismatch.

4 Experiments and Analysis

In this paper, we used a popular 20Newsgroups[2] dataset as experimental corpus. 20Newsgroups is composed of 20 categories with a total of 19997 texts, in which each text is an article about a certain category. Because the articles in the corpus are moderate in length and grammatical, these articles are very suitable for dependency analysis. In our experiments, 20Newsgroups is randomly separated into a training set and a test set according to the ratio of 9:1. After comparing the optimized experiments on 20Newsgroups, we discovered that the best value of θ in Eqs. (9) and (10) is 3000. The computer configuration used in the experiment is: Intel(R) Core(TM) i7-6700 CPU @ 3.40 GHz Memory 8G.

4.1 Comparison of Improved TFIDF Weight on Different Classification Methods

To verify the universality of our proposed TFIDF weight improvement approach based on dependencies and WordNet synonyms, we combined the improved TFIDF weight with the Bayesian, KNN and class-center classification methods on the 20Newsgroups dataset to evaluate its superiority. The improvements of F_1 values on different classification methods are shown in Table 2:

It can be discovered from Table 2 that dependencies contributes the most to the improvement of the TFIDF weight, in which the dependency-based TFIDF weight improves the F_1 value of Bayesian classification from 83.21% to 86.02% (improvement rate = 3.38%), the F_1 value of KNN classification from 78.28% to 84.15% (improvement rate = 7.50%) and the F_1 value of class-center classification from 78.26% to

2 http://qwone.com/~jason/20Newsgroups.

Table 2. Improvement of F_1 value using improved weight method

Weight approach	Classification method	F_1 improvement (rate %)
Dependencies	Bayesian	83.21 to 86.02 (3.38)
	KNN	78.28 to 84.15 (7.50)
	Class-center	78.26 to 82.72 (5.70)
Dependencies + WordNet synonyms	Bayesian	83.21 to 86.88 (4.41)
	KNN	78.28 to 85.83 (9.64)
	Class-center	78.26 to 83.74 (7.00)

82.72% (improvement rate = 5.70%). After the introduction of WordNet synonyms, our proposed TFIDF weight approach can further improve the effects of various classification methods, which shows that the introduction of WordNet synonyms in the TFIDF weight calculation has a certain degree of contribution to classification accuracy. Overall, our TFIDF weight approach can improve the Bayesian classification by 4.41%, the KNN classification by 9.64% and the class-center classification by 7%, which shows that our TFIDF weight approach is effective for various classification methods.

4.2 Comparison of Three Innovation Points on the Class-Center Method

In this paper, we propose three innovation points: a TFIDF weight improvement approach, a class-center vector clustering approach and a new vector similarity algorithm. To better reveal the role these innovations play in the proposed classification method on the 20Newsgroups dataset, we overlay each innovation point one by one to the original class-centric classification method. The experimental results are shown in Table 3.

Table 3. Comparison of improved class-center method and the original methods

KNN method		Original class-center method		Class-center + improved weight		Improved weight + clustering approach		Improved weight + clustering + new similarity	
Time	F_1	Time	F_1	Time	F_1	Time	F_1	Time	F_1
1 h 55 min	78.26%	20 s	78.26%	20 s	83.74%	18 s	86.01%	15 s	88.97%

Table 3 shows that our improved class-center method significantly improves the F_1 value of the original class-center classification from 78.26% to 88.97% (improvement rate = 13.68%), in which the proposed TFIDF weight approach improves the F_1 value of the original class-center classification from 78.26% to 83.74% (improvement rate = 7%), the proposed class-center vector clustering approach further improves the F_1 value of the class-center classification from 83.74% to 86.01% (improvement rate = 2.9%) and the proposed class-center vector clustering approach further improves the F_1 value of the class-center classification from 86.01% to 88.97% (improvement rate = 3.78%). Moreover, our improved class-center method significantly reduces the classification time of the KNN method from 1 h 55 min to 15 s.

4.3 Comparison of Our Improved Method with Various Classification Methods

To verify the superiority of our improved class-center method in terms of performance, we compared our improved class-center method with various classification methods on the 20Newsgroups dataset, including with the KNN, SVM, Bayesian, 2RM (A method of two-level representation model based on syntactic information and semantic information) and original class-center classification methods. The experimental results are shown in Table 4.

Table 4. Comparison of different classification methods on 20Newsgroups

Classification method	F_1 value (%)	Evaluation in
KNN-based method [19]	78.28	[19]
SVM-based method [19]	84.85	[19]
Bayesian-based method [20]	83.21	[20]
2RM method [21]	83.25	[21]
Original class-center method [22]	78.26	[22]
Our class-center method	88.97	This work

Table 4 shows that our improved class-center method is superior to the current popular classification methods such as KNN, SVM, Bayesian and 2RM in classification accuracy, especially to significantly improve the classification effect of the KNN and class-center vector methods, which benefits from the following three aspects: (1) The dependency-based feature level makes the TFIDF weight calculation more reasonable; (2) The feature word clustering based on WordNet effectively reduces the high dimension and sparsity of the class center vector; and (3) The vector similarity algorithm effectively solves the dimensional inconsistency between the class center vector and the classified text vector.

5 Conclusions

This study reveals: (1) semantic techniques such as dependency level and synonym combination can effectively improve the calculation of text weights based on statistics, and have better performance in various classification methods on the article corpus; (2) WordNet can play an important role in the clustering of text vectors; (3) targeted similarity algorithm can significantly improve the similarity between text vectors with inconsistent dimensions.

In the next step, we will apply our proposed method in this paper and the Chinese semantic dictionary HowNet[3] to Chinese text classifications, thereby further improving the efficiency and accuracy of Chinese text classifications.

Acknowledgements. This work has been supported by the Natural Science Foundation of Guangxi of China under the contract number 2018GXNSFAA138087, the National Natural Science Foundation of China under the contract numbers 61462010 and 61363036, and Guangxi Collaborative Innovation Center of Multi-source Information Integration and Intelligent Processing.

References

1. Li, S.S., Xia, R., Zong, C.Q., Huang, C.R.: A framework of feature selection methods for text categorization. In: Proceedings of the Joint Conference of the 47th Annual Meeting of the ACL and the 4th International Joint Conference on Natural Language Processing of the AFNLP, vol. 2, pp. 692–700 (2009)
2. Deng, X.L., Li, Y.Q., Weng, J., Zhang, J.L.: Feature selection for text classification: a review. Multimedia Tools Appl. **78**(3), 3793–3816 (2018)
3. Abraham, R., Simha, J.B., Iyengar, S.S.: Medical datamining with a new algorithm for feature selection and Naive Bayesian classifier. In: International Conference on Information Technology, pp. 44–49 (2007)
4. Yigit, H.: A weighting approach for KNN classifier. In: International Conference on Electronics, Computer and Computation, vol. 8, pp. 228–131 (2014)
5. Awange, J.L., Paláncz, B., Lewis, R.H., Völgyesi, L.: Support Vector Machines (SVM). Tékhne, Revista de EST udos Politécnicos (2018)
6. Cohen, W.W.: Context-sensitive learning methods for text categorization. In: Conference on Research and Development in Information Retrieval, pp. 307–315 (1996)
7. Chen, J.N., Huang, H.K., Tian, S.F., Qu, Y.L.: Feature selection for text classification with Naive Bayes. Expert Syst. Appl. **36**(3), 5432–5435 (2009)
8. https://blog.csdn.net/amds123/article/details/53696027,last. Accessed 17 May 2019
9. Mao, G.: Research and implementation of text Classification Model Based on Class Center Vector. Dalian University of Technology, Dalian (2010)
10. Salton, G., Yu, C.T.: On the construction of effective vocabularies for information retrieval. In: Proceedings of the 1973 Meeting on Programming Languages and Information Retrieval, pp. 8–60 (1973)
11. Jones, K.S.: A statistical interpretation of term specificity and its application in retrieval. J. Docu. **28**(1), 11–21 (1972)
12. How, B.C., Narayanan, K.: An empirical study of feature selection for text categorization based on term weightage. In: International Conference on Web Intelligence, WI 2004, pp. 599–602. IEEE/WIC/ACM (2004)
13. Qu, S.N. Wang, S.J., Zou, Y.: Improvement of Text Feature Selection Method Based on TFIDF. IEEE Computer Society (2008)
14. Wang, D.X, Gao, X.Y., Andreae, P.: Automatic keyword extraction from single sentence natural language queries. In: PRICAI 2013, pp. 637–648 (2012)

[3] http://www.keenage.com/html/e_index.html.

15. Abdi, H., Williams, L.J.: Principal component analysis. Wiley Interdisc. Rev. Comput. Stat. **2**(4), 433–459 (2010)
16. Tsuge, S., Shishibori, M., Kuroiwa, S., et al.: Dimensionality reduction using non-negative matrix factorization for information retrieval. In: 2001 IEEE International Conference on Systems, Man and Cybernetics. e-Systems and e-Man for Cybernetics in Cyberspace (Cat. No. 01CH37236), vol. 2, pp. 960–965 (2001)
17. Tesiniere, L.: Elements de Syntaxe Structurale. Libairie C, Klincksieck. (1959)
18. Zhu, X., Yang, Y., Huang, Y., Guo, Q., Zhang, B.: Measuring similarity and relatedness using multiple semantic relations in WordNet. Knowledge and Information Systems (2019). https://doi.org/10.1007/s10115-019-01387-6. Accessed 01 August 2019
19. Feng, G.Z., Li, S.T., Sun, T.L., Zhang, B.Z.: A probabilistic model derived term weighting scheme for text classification. Pattern Recogn. Lett. **110**(1), 23–29 (2018)
20. Liu, Y., Huang, R.C.: Research on optimization of maximum discriminant feature selection algorithm in text classification. J. Sichuan Univ. **56**(1), 65–70 (2019). Natural Science Edition
21. Yun, J., Jing, L., Yu, J., et al.: A multi-layer text classification framework based on two-level representation model. Expert Syst. Appl. **39**(2), 2035–2046 (2012)
22. Cao, S.J.: Fuzzy support vector machine of dismissing margin based on the method of class-center. Comput. Eng. Appl. **42**(22), 146–149 (2006)

Dynamic Label Correction for Distant Supervision Relation Extraction via Semantic Similarity

Xinyu Zhu, Gongshen Liu(✉), Bo Su(✉), and Jan Pan Nees

Shanghai Jiao Tong University, Shanghai 200240, China
{jasonzxy,lgshen,subo}@sjtu.edu.cn,
JanPanNees@yahoo.com

Abstract. It was found that relation extraction (RE) suffered from the lack of data. A widely used solution is to use distant supervision, but it brings many wrong labeled sentences. Previous work performed bag-level training to reduce the effect of noisy data. However, these methods are suboptimal because they cannot handle the situation where all the sentences in a bag are wrong labeled. The best way to reduce noise is to recognize the wrong labels and correct them. In this paper, we propose a novel model focusing on dynamically correcting wrong labels, which can train models at sentence level and improve the quality of the dataset without reducing its quantity. A semantic similarity module and a new label correction algorithm are designed. We combined semantic similarity and classification probability to evaluate the original label, and correct it if it is wrong. The proposed method works as an additional module that can be applied to any classification models. Experiments show that the proposed method can accurately correct wrong labels, both false positive and false negative, and greatly improve the performance of relation classification comparing to state-of-the-art systems.

Keywords: Relation extraction · Semantic similarity · Label correction

1 Introduction

Relation extraction (RE) aims to obtain semantic relations between two entities from plain text, such as the following examples: *contains*, *lives in*, *capital of*. It is an important task in natural language processing (NLP), particularly in knowledge graph construction, paragraph understanding and question answering.

Traditional RE suffered from the lack of training data. To solve this problem, distant supervision was proposed [9]. If two entities have a relation in a knowledge base, all the sentences that mention the two entities will be labeled as positive instances. If there is no relation between two entities in the knowledge base, it will be marked as a negative instance (NA).

J. Tang et al. (Eds.): NLPCC 2019, LNAI 11839, pp. 16–27, 2019.
https://doi.org/10.1007/978-3-030-32236-6_2

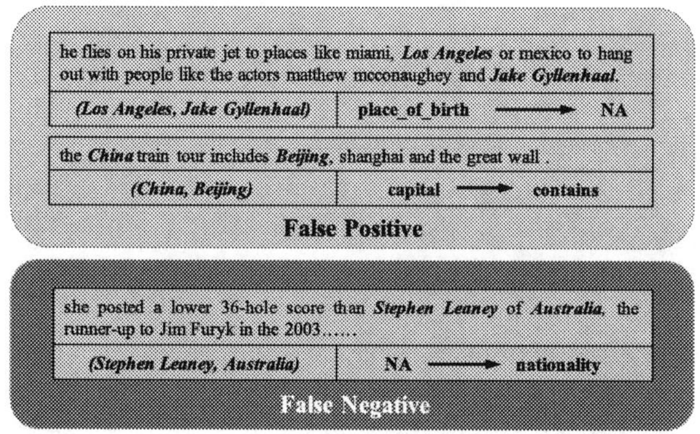

Fig. 1. Some examples of wrong labeled instance in the original training data. False positive instances (above) are caused by the strong assumption of distant supervision. False negative instances (below) are caused by the incomplete knowledge base.

However, the assumption of distant supervision is too strong and it brought lots of wrong instances. Some examples are shown in Fig. 1. *Jake Gyllenhaal* is indeed born in *Los Angeles*, but the sentence in Fig. 1 does not express the relation. We call it a false positive instance. There is no related record of *Stephen Leaney* and *Australia* in the knowledge base, but we can infer from the sentence that the nationality of *Stephen Leaney* is *Australia*. We call it a false negative instance.

Previous studies trained data at bag level based on multi-instance learning (MIL) [3,15,19] to deal with the issue of distant supervision. MIL takes the sentences with same entities and relations as a bag so that we can select some good instances for training. Attention mechanism was also applied to help better select instances [6,18,22]. These studies have three limitations: (1) Cannot select correct instances when all the sentences in a bag is wrong labeled. (2) Cannot deal with the false negative instances. (3) Training on bag level cannot make full use of the dataset.

In this study, we propose a novel dynamic label correction model to address the limitations mentioned above. Our method consists of two modules: semantic similarity module and relation classification module. Specifically, each relation has a vector representation, we calculate the similarity between input sentence and relations based on semantic features. We do not rely on the original label, but consider semantic similarity and classification score together to determine a new label for each sentence. The label correction will be performed dynamically during the training process. Without noisy instances, we can train our model at sentence level instead of bag level. The contributions of this paper include:

- A novel method for relation extraction is proposed, which uses semantic similarity and classification probability to dynamically correct wrong labels for each sentence. This enables us to train the classifier at sentence level with correct instances.

- The methods proposed in this paper is model-independent, which means it can be applied to any relation extraction model.
- Experiments show that our methods can greatly improve the performance compared with the state-of-art models.

2 Related Work

Relation Extraction is an important work in NLP. Early methods proposed various features to identify different relations, particularly with supervised methods [1,4,12,17]. The methods mentioned above all suffered from the lack of labeled training data. To solve this problem, Mintz et al. [9] proposed distant supervision, Riedel et al. [15] and Hoffmann et al. [3] improved this method.

Recent years, neural networks were widely used in NLP. Various models were applied in RE task, including convolutional network [6,10,16,18–20], recurrent neural networks [21] and long short-term memory network [22]. However, the assumption of distant supervision brought many wrong labeled instances, which cannot be solved by previous models.

Some new methods have been proposed to fight against noisy data. Liu et al. [7] infer true labels according to heterogeneous information, such as knowledge base and domain heuristics. Liu et al. [8] set soft labels heuristically to infer the correct labels and train at entity bag level. Lei et al. [5] use extra information expressed in knowledge graph to help improve the performance on noisy data set. Qin et al. [13] use generative adversarial networks to help recognize wrong data. Qin et al. [14] and Feng et al. [2] both try to remove wrong data using reinforcement learning.

Most of the methods above trained models at bag level, which cannot form a mapping at sentence level. [14] and [2] filter wrong data at sentence level. However, they focus on filtering false positive instances but ignore false negative instances, which cannot make full use of the original dataset. To address these issues, we propose a novel framework to dynamically correct wrong labels for each sentence. Our method can deal with both false positive instances and false negative instances, and train at sentence level. What's more, our method do not use extra information from knowledge graph and can be applied easily.

3 Framework

We propose a novel RE framework, which is able to dynamically correct wrong labels during the training process. Without noisy instances, we can train at sentence level instead of bag level, this will make full use of the dataset and achieve better performance.

The proposed framework mainly consists of two parts: semantic similarity calculator and relation classifier. Figure 2 illustrates how the proposed framework works. Features will be extracted from input sentences first by a sentence encoder, such as a convolutional layer in the figure. Afterwards, semantic similarity will be calculated between feature vectors and relation vectors. Classifier

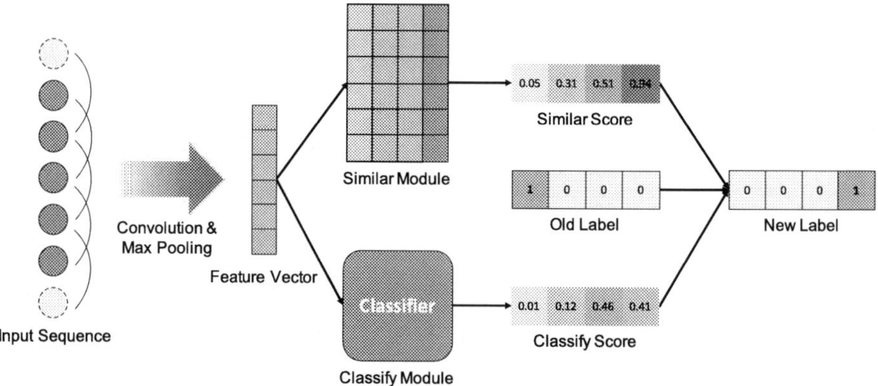

Fig. 2. The architecture of our method for wrong label correction during training process. As an example, according to semantic similarity and original classifier, wrong label is corrected from relation 1 to relation 4.

will also calculate the probability for each relation. Since our method is model-independent, it can be applied to any classifier. Finally, we propose a label correction algorithm that combines the information of both parts to give a new correct label for the sentence. In Fig. 2, relation 4 and relation 3 achieve the highest scores in semantic similarity and classification probability, respectively. The label is finally corrected from relation 1 to relation 4 according to our algorithm. Each part is described in detail below.

3.1 Input Representation

The input of our model is the sequence of words in a sentence. Similar to previous papers, the input representation consists of word embeddings and position embeddings [20].

Given a sentence of N words $s = \{w_1, w_2, \cdots, w_n\}$, each word is converted to a real-value vector by an embedding matrix $W_e \in \mathbb{R}^{d^w \times |V|}$ where d^w is the word embedding dimension and V is a fixed-sized vocabulary. The position embedding is generated by counting the distance between the current word and two entities. Each position embedding dimension is d^p, so the input representation is formed as $R = \{r_1, r_2, \cdots, r_n\}$, where $r_i \in \mathbb{R}^d$, and $d = d^w + 2 \times d^p$.

3.2 Sentence Encoder

Since convolutional neural networks (CNN) is good at dealing with long sentences, we use CNN to extract features from sentences. Given a input representation R, the convolution operation is applied to R with the sliding window of size k. We define the convolution matrix as $W_c \in \mathbb{R}^{d_c \times (k \times d)}$, where d_c is the number of filters. The output of the i-th convolutional layer can be expressed as:

$$p_i = [W_c q + b_c]_i \tag{1}$$

where $q_i = r_{i-k+1:i}(1 \leq i \leq N + k - 1)$ means the concatenation of k word embeddings. As for the boundary of sentences, $\frac{k-1}{2}$ padding tokens are placed at the beginning and the end of the sentence.

Afterwards, we use piecewise max pooling followed PCNN model [19]. The output of convolution layer can be divided into three segments according to the position of two entities. Max pooling operation will be applied to each segment. The final feature vector we obtained can be expressed as:

$$x = [max(p_{i1}), max(p_{i2}), max(p_{i3})] \tag{2}$$

3.3 Semantic Similarity

We believe that each relation has unique semantic features which can be represented by a vector. We define a relation matrix $W_s \in \mathbb{R}^{h \times r}$, where h is the dimension of convolution layer output and r is the number of relations. Each column of W_s can be viewed as the representation of one relation. In our experiments, W_s is initialized by randomly sampling values from a uniform distribution.

Given a feature vector x, the semantic similarity score can be computed by function $S(x, W_s)$. Cosine function is widely used in text semantic similarity, but it only considers the angular difference between vectors. Inspired by Pearson coefficient [11], we propose a improved cosine function in this paper, which consider the average scores of all relations for the same input. The similarity score of vector x is computed as:

$$S_x = \frac{(W_s - \bar{W}_s)(x - \bar{W}_s)}{||W_s - \bar{W}_s|| \cdot ||x - \bar{W}_s||} \tag{3}$$

Semantic similarity is an important part of dynamic label correction. In order to get the best performance, we hope our network can distinguish different relations to the greatest extent. We design a new loss function to help training:

$$J_s = exp(\gamma(m - S_x^+ + S_x^-)) \tag{4}$$

where m is a margin and γ is a scaling factor. The margin gives extra penalization on the difference in scores and the scaling factor helps to magnifies the scores. S_x^+ refers to the similarity between input vector x and the correct relation vector, and S_x^- refers to the highest score among all the wrong relation vectors. By minimizing this loss function, we hope our model can give scores with a difference greater than m between positive label and negative label.

3.4 Label Correction

In previous works, the feature vector is fed into a fully-connected layer and then softmax layer. The output can be seen as the probability score for relations:

$$C_x = softmax(W_r x + b_r) \tag{5}$$

Algorithm 1. Complete Training Process

1. Train similarity model alone in a small clean training set which is labeled manually;
2. Initialize parameters of classification model with random weights;
3. Pre-train the classification model with original labels at bag level.
4. Train the model with dynamic label correction algorithm at sentence level.

where $W_r \in \mathbb{R}^{h \times r}$ and $b_r \in \mathbb{R}^r$. Previous models calculate loss function by comparing relation prediction with the instance label. Due to wrong labels, the model is optimized to the wrong direction.

Our framework introduces the semantic similarity at this stage to correct wrong labels dynamically in each iteration of training. The semantic similarity and classification probability are combined with different weights. The new relation label for input x is computed as:

$$r_{new} = argmax(\lambda C_x + S_x + \beta S_x * L) \tag{6}$$

where $\lambda = max(S_x)$ can be seen as the confidence of classification score. L is a one-hot vector of the original label and β is a constant which control the effect of old label. Afterwards, we can define the cross-entropy loss function of relation prediction based on the new label:

$$J(\theta) = \sum_{i=1}^{n} logp(r_{new}|x;\theta) \tag{7}$$

where $\theta = \{W_{conv}, b_c, W_r, b_r\}$ is the parameter set.

3.5 Model Training

Semantic similarity is the key of our label correction and needs to be trained to a good level in accuracy. The complete training process is described in Algorithm 1. We first randomly choose a few numbers of instances and manually label them. Semantic similarity module is trained with these correct instances. Afterwards, we pre-train the classification model with original labels at bag level. Finally, wrong labels are corrected dynamically with the help of semantic similarity, and the classification model can be trained with new labels at sentence level.

4 Experiments

In this study, a framework is proposed to dynamically correct wrong labels and train model at sentence level. As our framework is model-independent, the experiments focused on the effect of semantic similarity model, the accuracy of label correction and the performance of relation extraction with new labels.

Table 1. Comparison of results between CNN and our model. Distinct is the average difference between positive and negative relations.

Model	Pre	Rec	F1	Distinct
Zeng [20]	-	-	78.9	-
CNN+CE	79.77	80.61	79.91	29.61
CNN+Cos	79.12	81.26	80.18	38.86
CNN+Sim	**79.20**	**84.49**	**81.76**	**59.93**

4.1 Dataset

The proposed method was evaluated on a widely used dataset developed by Riedel [15]. This dataset is generated by aligning relation facts in Freebase with the New York Times (NYT) corpus. Training set contains sentences of 2005–2006, and test set contains sentences of 2007. There are 522611 sentences, 281270 entity pairs and 18252 relational facts in the training data, and 172448 sentences, 96678 entity pairs and 1950 relation facts in the test data. There are 53 relations including a special relation *NA* which indicates no relation between two entities.

The SemEval-2010 Task 8 dataset was also used to evaluate the semantic similarity module, which is also widely used but without noisy data. The dataset contains 8000 training instances and 2717 test instances. There are 9 different relations and a special relation *Other*. Each relation takes into account the directionality between entities, which means that relation *Product-Producer(e1,e2)* is different from the relation *Product-Producer(e2,e1)*.

4.2 Effect of Semantic Similarity

As mentioned before, we design a semantic similarity matrix to better extract the semantic features. To evaluate the effect of our method, we conducted experiments based on the clean data set SemiEval-2010 and compared with the state-of-the-art baseline proposed by [20].

Zeng in Table 1 reports the result in his paper [20], which uses sentence level features and cross entropy loss function. CNN+CE is the model we reproduced using word embedding of size 300. CNN+Cos is the model with cosine functions and CNN+Sim is the model that applies our similarity functions and loss function. Precision, recall and macro-averaged F1 score are calculated. We hope the feature vectors of different relations have a clear distinction, so we added an indicator named Distinct, which calculate the average difference of vector similarity between positive label and negative labels.

We have the following observations from Table 1: (1) CNN+Sim obtains better performance than CNN+CE in both F1 score and Distinct score, indicating that our method has a positive effect on relation classification. (2) The distinction of feature vectors in CNN+Sim has been improved by over 20.

Table 2. Parameter settings

Windows size k	3	Filter number d_c	230	Word dimension d^w	50
Word dimension d^w	50	Position dimension d^p	5	Learning rate	0.001
Dropout Probability	0.5	margin m	1.0	scaling factor γ	2

4.3 Effect of Dynamic Label Correction

The key difference between our model and previous models is that we can dynamically correct both false positive and false negative labels. What's more, without noisy data, our model can perform sentence level classification instead of bag level.

Our analysis indicates that although there are 53 relations in Riedel dataset, most of them are belong to *NA*. Only 10 relations have more than 1000 instances. Considering the negative impact of unbalance in training set, we only performed experiments on these 10 relations.

Baselines. We select the following two state-of-the-art methods for comparison. PCNN+MAX [19] assumes at least one instance in the bag can express the correct relation. It chooses the instance that gets the highest score in each bag. PCNN+ATT [6] adopted selective attention mechanism over instances to reduce the weights of noisy instances. Both PCNN+MAX and CNN+ATT are bag level methods.

Parameter Settings. Our model contains the same parameter settings as the reference papers, in order to present and accurate comparative study. Detailed settings are shown in Table 2. For the dynamic label correction module, we set constant β to 0.7 and the pre-train step to 3300. We set batch size to 50 in PCNN+MAX and 160 in PCNN+ATT.

Precision Recall Curve. In our method, we deal with the false positive and false negative instances, which are not labeled correctly in original test data set. The experiments should be performed on a clean data set without wrong labels. We randomly selected 1500 sentences from the original test data and manually labeled relation for each instance. Precision recall (P-R) curve is used to evaluate the model performance.

In our experiments, we randomly selected 50 instances of each relation and manually labeled them. The semantic similarity module was pre-trained to a high accuracy of 95.64% with this clean dataset. For PCNN+ATT, our semantic similarity is combined using attention weights in original method. In the training process, we first conducted contrast experiments at bag level, followed by the sentence level experiment. In the test process, each sentence is treated as a bag so that each method can conduct a sentence level prediction.

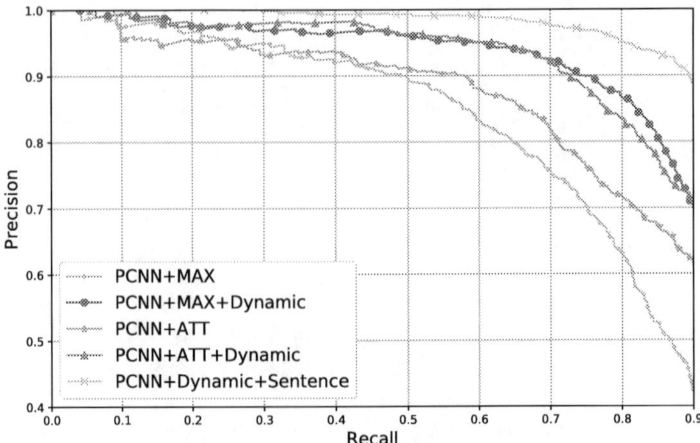

Fig. 3. Precision recall curves of our method and state-of-the-art baselines. PCNN+MAX+Dynamic/PCNN+ATT+Dynamic applied our method to previous models and trained at bag level. PCNN+Dynamic+Sentence used our method and trained at sentence level.

As shown in Fig. 3, both PCNN+MAX and PCNN+ATT achieve much better performance after applying the dynamic label correction. With the help of our method, PCNN+MAX can even outperform the original stronger model PCNN+ATT. When we trained the model at sentence level, it achieves the highest performance. These results indicate that our method can accurately correct the wrong label for each sentence and provide a much cleaner dataset.

NA Evaluation. In Riedel dataset, 166003 test sentences belong to *NA* relation, accounting for the majority of test set. However, many of them are false negative instances, which means there is actually a relation between two entities but it is missing in Freebase. To better illustrate the performance of our method, we performed relation prediction for sentences labeled *NA*. We conducted manual evaluation for the top 100, top 200, and top 300 sentences which were predicted to have a certain relation.

Table 3 shows the Top-N prediction accuracy. We can observe that: (1) Many *NA* sentences are indeed false negative instances, which proves the rationality of our method. (2) After applied our method, the accuracy of relation prediction has been greatly improved, at both bag level and sentence level. (3) The model trained at sentence level with our dynamic label correction achieve the highest accuracy.

4.4 Accuracy of Dynamic Label Correction

To illustrate the effect of dynamic label correction, we recorded sentences of corrected labels during each iteration. Subsequently, we selected top 100, top 200, and top 300 sentences for manual verification.

Table 3. Top-N prediction accuracy for sentences labeled NA. +Dynamic(BL) trained the model at bag level, while +Dynamic(SL) trained at sentence level. Results are ranked in descending order according to predict scores.

Model	100	200	300	Avg
PCNN+MAX	56	53.5	52	53.83
+Dynamic(BL)	72	66.5	61.67	66.72
+Dynamic(SL)	**76**	**71**	**64.33**	**70.44**

Table 4. Top-N accuracy of label correction during training process. Sentences are ranked in descending order according to new label score.

Model	100	200	300	Avg
PCNN+MAX	96	93.5	92.33	93.94
PCNN+ATT	97	95	94	95.33

Results in Table 4 contains the following observations: (1) Both models keep the correction accuracy at high level, which shows that our method can make a stable improvement in the training process. (2) The correction accuracy in PCNN+ATT is 97 compared to 96 with PCNN+MAX. As stated in referenced papers, attention mechanism performs better in sentence features extraction, which is also helpful for our correction algorithm. It's reasonable that PCNN+ATT can get a higher accuracy. (3) Due to the high accuracy in label correction, we can obtain a much cleaner dataset. That is why we can train model at sentence level and achieve the better performance.

4.5 Case Study

Table 5 shows some examples of dynamic label correction. Case 1, Case 2 and Case 3 are examples of false positive instances, false negative instances and similar relation instances, respectively. In each case, we present the classification scores calculated by PCNN+MAX model and the final scores after combining our semantic similarity, respectively.

In case 1, the model trained with noisy labels gives relation *place_of_birth* a higher score. After applying our method, relation *NA* achieves the highest score and the wrong label is corrected accurately. In case 2, our method can give the model higher confidence against the wrong labels. In case 3, although *Armenia* does contain *Yerevan*, the sentence further expresses the relation of capital. The original model gives similar scores for these two relations. Our method allows them to have a much clearer distinction.

These cases clearly indicate that our method can deal with both false positive and false negative instances. Similar relations can also be distinguished accurately by our method, such as *capital* and *contains*, *place lived* and *place of birth*.

Table 5. Some examples of dynamic label correction. *Wrong Rel* refers to the wrong labels in original dataset, and *Correct Rel* refers to the new relation corrected by our method.

	Case study	Wrong Rel	Correct Rel
Case 1	The two pitchers ··· are ***Oakland***'s Barry Zito and Florida's ***Dontrelle Willis***	/person/place_of_birth	NA
Model Score	PCNN+MAX	0.45	0.31
	+Dynamic Label Correction	0.2135	**1.15**
Case 2	··· the unpredictable ***Xavier Malisse*** of ***Belgium*** before coming on strong ···	NA	/location/contains
Model Score	PCNN+MAX	0.08	0.91
	+Dynamic Label Correction	-0.75	**1.74**
Case 3	Mattheson's scores turned up in ***Yerevan***, the capital of ***Armenia***, and were ···	/location/contains	/country/capital
Model Score	PCNN+MAX	0.26	0.38
	+Dynamic Label Correction	0.36	**1.22**

5 Conclusion

In this paper, we propose a novel model to deal with the wrong labels in RE task. Previous work tried to reduce the effect of wrong instances or just remove them. Our method focuses on correcting the wrong labels, which can fundamentally improve the quality of the dataset without reducing its quantity. We introduce the semantic similarity to help dynamically recognize and correct wrong labels during the training process. As a result, we can achieve better performance by training at sentence level instead of bag level. It is worth mentioning that our method is model-independent, which means that our method can work as an additional module and be applied to any classification model. Extensive experiments demonstrate that our method can accurately correct wrong labels and greatly improve the performance of state-of-the-art RE models.

Acknowledgements. This research work has been funded by the National Natural Science Foundation of China (Grant No. 61772337, U1736207), and the National Key Research and Development Program of China NO. 2016QY03D0604.

References

1. Bunescu, R.C., Mooney, R.J.: A shortest path dependency kernel for relation extraction. In: Proceedings of HLT/EMNLP, pp. 724–731. Association for Computational Linguistics (2005)
2. Feng, J., Huang, M., Zhao, L., Yang, Y., Zhu, X.: Reinforcement learning for relation classification from noisy data. In: Proceedings of AAAI (2018)
3. Hoffmann, R., Zhang, C., Ling, X., Zettlemoyer, L., Weld, D.S.: Knowledge-based weak supervision for information extraction of overlapping relations. In: Proceedings of the 49th ACL: Human Language Technologies, vol. 1, pp. 541–550 (2011)
4. Kambhatla, N.: Combining lexical, syntactic, and semantic features with maximum entropy models for extracting relations. In: Proceedings of the ACL 2004 on Interactive Poster and Demonstration Sessions, p. 22 (2004)

5. Lei, K., et al.: Cooperative denoising for distantly supervised relation extraction. In: Proceedings of the 27th International Conference on Computational Linguistics, pp. 426–436 (2018)
6. Lin, Y., Shen, S., Liu, Z., Luan, H., Sun, M.: Neural relation extraction with selective attention over instances. In: Proceedings of the 54th ACL (Volume 1: Long Papers), vol. 1, pp. 2124–2133 (2016)
7. Liu, L., et al.: Heterogeneous supervision for relation extraction: A representation learning approach. arXiv preprint arXiv:1707.00166 (2017)
8. Liu, T., Wang, K., Chang, B., Sui, Z.: A soft-label method for noise-tolerant distantly supervised relation extraction. In: EMNLP, pp. 1790–1795 (2017)
9. Mintz, M., Bills, S., Snow, R., Jurafsky, D.: Distant supervision for relation extraction without labeled data. In: Proceedings of the Joint Conference of the 47th Annual Meeting of the ACL and the 4th International Joint Conference on Natural Language Processing of the AFNLP: Volume 2-Volume 2, pp. 1003–1011. Association for Computational Linguistics (2009)
10. Nguyen, T.H., Grishman, R.: Relation extraction: perspective from convolutional neural networks. In: Proceedings of the 1st Workshop on Vector Space Modeling for Natural Language Processing, pp. 39–48 (2015)
11. Pearson, K.: Note on regression and inheritance in the case of two parents. Proc. Roy. Soc. Lond. **58**, 240–242 (1895)
12. Qian, L., Zhou, G., Kong, F., Zhu, Q., Qian, P.: Exploiting constituent dependencies for tree kernel-based semantic relation extraction. In: Proceedings of the 22nd International Conference on Computational Linguistics, vol. 1, pp. 697–704. Association for Computational Linguistics (2008)
13. Qin, P., Xu, W., Wang, W.Y.: Dsgan: Generative adversarial training for distant supervision relation extraction. arXiv preprint arXiv:1805.09929 (2018)
14. Qin, P., Xu, W., Wang, W.Y.: Robust distant supervision relation extraction via deep reinforcement learning. arXiv preprint arXiv:1805.09927 (2018)
15. Riedel, S., Yao, L., McCallum, A.: Modeling relations and their mentions without labeled text. In: Balcázar, J.L., Bonchi, F., Gionis, A., Sebag, M. (eds.) ECML PKDD 2010. LNCS (LNAI), vol. 6323, pp. 148–163. Springer, Heidelberg (2010). https://doi.org/10.1007/978-3-642-15939-8_10
16. Santos, C.N.d., Xiang, B., Zhou, B.: Classifying relations by ranking with convolutional neural networks. arXiv preprint arXiv:1504.06580 (2015)
17. Suchanek, F.M., Ifrim, G., Weikum, G.: Combining linguistic and statistical analysis to extract relations from web documents. In: the 12th ACM SIGKDD, pp. 712–717. ACM (2006)
18. Wang, L., Cao, Z., De Melo, G., Liu, Z.: Relation classification via multi-level attention CNNs. In: the 54th ACL (long papers), vol. 1, pp. 1298–1307 (2016)
19. Zeng, D., Liu, K., Chen, Y., Zhao, J.: Distant supervision for relation extraction via piecewise convolutional neural networks. In: EMNLP. pp. 1753–1762 (2015)
20. Zeng, D., Liu, K., Lai, S., Zhou, G., Zhao, J.: Relation classification via convolutional deep neural network. In: COLING: Technical Papers, pp. 2335–2344 (2014)
21. Zhang, D., Wang, D.: Relation classification via recurrent neural network. arXiv preprint arXiv:1508.01006 (2015)
22. Zhou, P., et al.: Attention-based bidirectional long short-term memory networks for relation classification. In: Proceedings of the 54th ACL (Volume 2: Short Papers), vol. 2, pp. 207–212 (2016)

Classification over Clustering: Augmenting Text Representation with Clusters Helps!

Xiaoye Tan[1], Rui Yan[1,2(✉)], Chongyang Tao[2], and Mingrui Wu[3]

[1] Center for Data Science, Peking University, Beijing, China
{txye,ruiyan}@pku.edu.cn
[2] Institute of Computer Science and Technology, Peking University, Beijing, China
chongyangtao@pku.edu.cn
[3] Alibaba Group, Seattle, USA
wu.mingrui@yahoo.com

Abstract. Considering that words with different characteristic in the text have different importance for classification, grouping them together separately can strengthen the semantic expression of each part. Thus we propose a new text representation scheme by clustering words according to their latent semantics and composing them together to get a set of cluster vectors, which are then concatenated as the final text representation. Evaluation on five classification benchmarks proves the effectiveness of our method. We further conduct visualization analysis showing statistical clustering results and verifying the validity of our motivation.

Keywords: Classification · Semantic · Clustering · Visualization

1 Introduction

Text classification is an important task in natural language processing with many applications. Suitable text encoding scheme will benefit it a lot. Early studies use discrete and context-insensitive approaches such as TF-IDF [15] and weighted bag-of-words [4]. Along with the prosperity of research on the distributed representation of words [2,10], linear combination of word embeddings in a sentence [14] is widely used for classification. However, this method captures the information from individual words only. Many studies that make use of contextual information commonly adopt neural networks as an encoder to capture the semantic information of the text, including recurrent neural networks (RNN) [16], tree-structure recursive networks [17] and convolutional neural networks (CNN) [3,6,7].

However, the aforementioned methods lack consideration on the semantic segmentation of text. It is intuitive that the words in text play different roles thus contribute to different groups of semantic functionality. Words like "the", "an", "of" act as connection between the syntax structures of the text and contribute little for classification. Other words like "internet", "linux" or "wireless"

J. Tang et al. (Eds.): NLPCC 2019, LNAI 11839, pp. 28–40, 2019.
https://doi.org/10.1007/978-3-030-32236-6_3

indicating a specific domain (science) tend to have a huge impact on the classification performance. Some recent studies attempt to capture different types of word importance via hierarchical attention [21] or multi-head self-attention [8]. However, these attention mechanisms still only consider the relative importance of separate words, which does not group words with similar semantics together to strengthen the semantic expression of the whole text.

As classification is a word sensitive task, people tend to integrate all related words when making decisions about the category of a sentence. Therefore, in this paper, we propose to augment text representation from a higher level: cluster level. Concretely, we divide the words in a text into different latent semantic clusters and get cluster representations by combining contextual embeddings of the words together according to their cluster probability distribution. The cluster representations are then concatenated as the final representation of the text. We further introduce two regularization terms to better guide the clustering process. Considering that not all semantic clusters contain useful information for classification, we design a gating mechanism to dynamically control their contributions for classification.

Experiments are conducted on five standard benchmark datasets of text classification. Quantitative results show that our method outperforms or is at least on a par with the state-of-the-art methods. We also perform visualized and statistical analysis on the intermediate word clustering results which proves the effectiveness of the clustering process.

In summary, the contributions of this paper include:

- We propose an intuitive architecture for text classification with a novel semantic clustering process for better capturing distant topical information in text representation. The semantic clusters in our framework are automatically calculated on-the-fly instead of being fitted in advance.
- Due to the probabilistic nature of soft semantic clustering, we introduce two regularization schemes to better guide the behaviors of our model.
- We conduct extensive experiments to evaluate our proposed method on five text classification benchmarks. Results show that our model could obtain competitive performance compared with state-of-the-art approaches.
- We provide statistical and visualization analysis on cluster distribution captured by our learned model further corroborating our motivation.

2 Model

We propose a latent semantic clustering representation (LSCR) framework as shown in Fig. 1 consisting of four parts: (1) the word representation layer at the bottom converts words into vector representations (embeddings); (2) the encoding layer transforms a series of word embeddings to their corresponding hidden vector representations; (3) the semantics clustering layer attributes all the words into different clusters and composes them together respectively so as

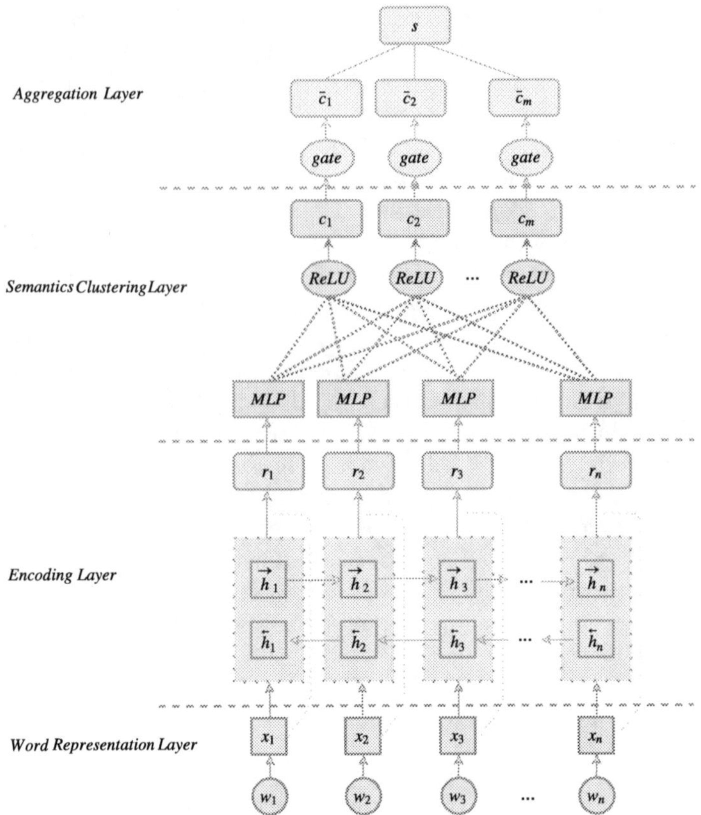

Fig. 1. The framework of our model.

to get a set of cluster representations; (4) the aggregation layer combines those cluster vectors into a single vector as the final representation of the text.

Formally, given a text consisting of n words $(w_1, w_2, \cdots, w_n)$, the word representation layer converts them to their corresponding word embeddings, represented as $\boldsymbol{X} = (\boldsymbol{x}_1, \boldsymbol{x}_2, \cdots, \boldsymbol{x}_n)$. Then in encoding layer, we employ a bidirectional LSTM [13] as the encoder to aggregate information along the word sequence getting final states $\boldsymbol{h}_t = [\overrightarrow{\boldsymbol{h}}_t; \overleftarrow{\boldsymbol{h}}_t]$. We concatenate the hidden state from the encoder with the initial word embedding to enrich the representations. The output of the t-th word from this layer takes the form: $\boldsymbol{r}_t = [\boldsymbol{x}_t; \boldsymbol{h}_t]$.

The final representation of words generated from this layer is defined as $\boldsymbol{R} = (\boldsymbol{r}_1, \boldsymbol{r}_2, \cdots, \boldsymbol{r}_n)$. In the semantics clustering layer, suppose that words from the text could be assigned to m semantic clusters, where m is a tunable hyper-parameter. For each word, we employ a MLP to determine the probabilities of dividing it into every cluster, defined as:

$$\boldsymbol{A} = f_1(\boldsymbol{W}_2 \cdot f_2(\boldsymbol{W}_1 \cdot \boldsymbol{R} + \boldsymbol{b}_1) + \boldsymbol{b}_2) \quad (1)$$

We use the softmax function for f_1, and ReLU for f_2. Concretely, $A_{i,j}$ indicates the probability of the j-th word being clustered into the i-th cluster. For each word w_j of the text, $\sum_{i=1}^{m} A_{i,j} = 1$. After getting the probabilities, the vector representation of the i-th cluster is given by the weighted sum of the contextualized word representations ($\boldsymbol{R}$) in the text, followed by a nonlinear transformation. The process is formulated as:

$$\boldsymbol{C} = \text{ReLU}(\boldsymbol{W}_s(\boldsymbol{A} \cdot \boldsymbol{R}) + \boldsymbol{b}_s) \tag{2}$$

The i-th row of $\boldsymbol{C}$, $\boldsymbol{c}_i$, refers to the vector representation of the i-th cluster. Considering that not all clusters are helpful for text classification. There may exist redundant clusters that contain little or irrelevant information for the tasks. Therefore, in the aggregation layer, we add a gating mechanism on the cluster vector to control the information flow. Concretely, the gate takes a cluster vector $\boldsymbol{c}_i$ as input and output a gate vector $\boldsymbol{g}_i$:

$$\boldsymbol{g}_i = \sigma(\boldsymbol{W}_g \boldsymbol{c}_i + \boldsymbol{b}_g) \tag{3}$$

We do the same operation on other cluster vectors as well, leading to a series of gate vectors $\boldsymbol{G} = (\boldsymbol{g}_1, \boldsymbol{g}_2, \cdots, \boldsymbol{g}_m)$ from the cluster vectors. Then the gated cluster vectors $\bar{\boldsymbol{C}} = (\bar{\boldsymbol{c}}_1, \bar{\boldsymbol{c}}_2, \cdots, \bar{\boldsymbol{c}}_m)$ are calculated as:

$$\bar{\boldsymbol{C}} = \boldsymbol{G} \odot \boldsymbol{C} \tag{4}$$

At last, we concatenate vector representations of all the semantic clusters to form the text representation: $\boldsymbol{s} = [\bar{\boldsymbol{c}}_1, \bar{\boldsymbol{c}}_2, \cdots, \bar{\boldsymbol{c}}_m]$. For classification, the text representation $\boldsymbol{s}$ is followed by a simple classifier which includes a fully connected hidden layer and a softmax output layer to get the predicted class distribution $\boldsymbol{y}$. The basic loss function is the cross-entropy loss $\mathcal{L}$ between the ground truth distribution and the prediction.

2.1 Regularization Terms

Due to the probabilistic nature of our soft semantic clustering scheme, it is natural to integrate probabilistic prior knowledge to control and regularize the model learning process. We consider two regularization terms in word level and class level. In the semantics clustering layer, we get $\boldsymbol{a}_i = (a_{i1}, a_{i2}, \cdots, a_{im})$ indicating the probability distribution of the i-th word to each cluster. The *word-level entropy regularization* term is defined as:

$$\mathcal{L}_{word} = -\sum_{t=1}^{N}\sum_{k=1}^{m} a_{tk} \log(a_{tk}) \tag{5}$$

We expect the probability distribution for a specific word over all the clusters is sparse, which means a word would be attributed to only one or few clusters with greater probability instead of being evenly distributed to all clusters. Thus our optimization goal is to minimize the word-level entropy.

Another class-level regularization term is specifically designed for text classification. Suppose there is a vector $\boldsymbol{v}_{c_i}$ indicating the i-th class' probability distribution over m clusters, which is calculated by averaging the cluster probability distribution of the text belonging to i-th class within a mini-batch during training. We take the average of the word's cluster probability distribution $\boldsymbol{a}$ in the text as the text-level cluster probability distribution $\boldsymbol{v}_s = \frac{1}{N_w}\sum_{i=1}^{N_w}\boldsymbol{a}_i$, where N_w is the number of words in the text. Thus the i-th class' cluster probability distribution is:

$$\boldsymbol{v}_{c_i} = \frac{1}{N_{c_i}}\sum_{k=1}^{N_{c_i}}\boldsymbol{v}_{s_k} \tag{6}$$

where N_{c_i} is the number of samples belonging to i-th class in a mini-batch, $\boldsymbol{v}_{s_k}$ indicates the k-th text-level cluster probability distribution. We hope that different cluster can capture different category related semantics. Thus the distribution between every two classes needs to be different. We take an intuitive and practical method that we expect the peak value of different class-level distribution exists in different cluster. To implement this, we add the maximum value of all the class-level distributions and expect the summation greater. The *class-level regularization* term is defined as:

$$\mathcal{L}_{class} = \sum_{i=1}^{m}\max_{j=1:N_C}(\boldsymbol{v}_{c_j}^{i}) \tag{7}$$

where N_C is the number of category and $\boldsymbol{v}_{c_j}^{i}$ means the i-th dimension (corresponding to i-th cluster) in j-th class probability distribution vector. The larger the summation, the distributions between classes tend to be more different. The final objective function for classification is defined as:

$$\mathcal{L}_{total} = \frac{1}{N}\sum_{i=1}^{N}(\mathcal{L} + \lambda_1\mathcal{L}_{word}) - \lambda_2\mathcal{L}_{class} \tag{8}$$

where N is the number of samples in a mini-batch. The training objective is to minimize $\mathcal{L}_{total}$.

Table 1. Data statistic on the five benchmarks.

Dataset	# Classes	# Training	# Testing	# AvWords	# MaxWords
AGNews	4	120K	7.6K	45	208
Yah.A.	10	1.4M	60K	104	146
Yelp P.	2	560K	38K	153	301
Yelp F.	5	650K	50K	155	501
DBPedia	14	560K	70K	55	151

3 Experiment

3.1 Datasets

To evaluate the effectiveness of our proposed model, we conduct experiments on the text classification task. We test our model on five standard benchmark datasets (**AGNews**, **DBPedia**, **Yahoo! Answers**, **Yelp P.**, **Yelp F.**) including topic classification, sentiment classification and ontology classification as in [23]. **AGNews** is a topic classification dataset that contains 4 categories: world, business, sports and science. **DBPedia** ontology dataset is constructed by choosing 14 non-overlapping classes from DBPedia 2014. The fields used for this dataset contain the title and abstract of each Wikipedia article. **Yahoo! Answers** is a 10-categories topic classification dataset obtained through the Yahoo! Webscope program. The fields include question title, question content and best answer. **Yelp P.** and **Yelp F.** are Yelp reviews obtained from the Yelp Dataset Challenge in 2015. Yelp p. predicts a polarity label by considering stars 1 and 2 as negative, 3 and 4 as positive. Yelp F. predicts the full number of stars from 1 to 5. We use the preprocessed datasets published by [18] and the summary statistics of the data are shown in Table 1.

3.2 Compared Models

We compare our models with different types of baseline models: traditional feature based models i.e. n-gram TF-IDF and bag-of-words (BoW) [23]; word embedding based models such as FastText [5] and SWEM [14]; RNNs like LSTM [23]; reinforcement learning based models including ID-LSTM and HS-LSTM [22]; CNNs consisting of DeepCNN [3], small/large word CNN [23], CNN with dynamic pooling [6] and densely connected CNN with multi-scale feature attention [19]; CNN combined with RNN [20]; self-attentive based model [8]; other models specifically designed for classification [12,18].

3.3 Implementation Details

For word representation, we use the pre-trained 300-dimensional GloVe word embeddings [11]. They are also updated with other parameters during training. We split 10% samples from the training set as the validation set and tuned the hyper parameters on validation set. The input texts are padded to the maximum length appeared in the training set. In the encoding layer, the hidden state of the bi-LSTM is set to 300 dimensions for each direction. The MLP hidden units are 800 for semantic clustering. The dimension of the clustering vectors is set to 600. The cluster number is set to 8 on AGNews and 10 on other datasets. The MLP used for classification has 1000 hidden units. The coefficients of the regularization terms are set to 0.001. We adopt Adam as the optimizer with a learning rate of 0.0005. The batch size is 64. Our models are implemented with Tensorflow [1] and trained on one NVIDIA 1080Ti GPU. For all datasets, training converges within 4 epochs. We will release our codes later.

Table 2. Accuracy of all the models on the five datasets. The result marked with ◇ is re-printed from [19].

Method	AGNews	Yah.A.	DBPedia	Yelp P.	Yelp F.
n-gram TF-IDF [23]	92.4	68.5	98.7	95.4	54.8
BoW [23]	88.8	68.9	96.6	92.2	58.0
FastText [5]	92.5	72.3	98.6	95.7	63.9
SWEM [14]	92.2	73.5	98.4	93.8	61.1
DeepCNN(29 Layer) [3]	91.3	73.4	98.7	95.7	64.3
Small word CNN [23]	89.1	70.0	98.2	94.5	58.6
Large word CNN [23]	91.5	70.9	98.3	95.1	59.5
Dynamic-Pool◇ [6]	91.3	-	98.6	95.7	63.0
Densely Connected CNN [19]	**93.6***	-	**99.2**	96.5	66.0
LSTM [23]	86.1	70.8	98.6	94.7	58.2
char-CRNN [20]	91.4	71.7	98.6	94.5	61.8
ID-LSTM [22]	92.2	-	-	-	-
HS-LSTM [22]	92.5	-	-	-	-
Self-Attentive◇ [8]	91.5	-	98.3	94.9	63.4
LEAM [18]	92.5	77.4	99.0	95.3	64.1
W.C.region.emb [12]	92.8	73.7	98.9	96.4	64.9
LSCR (our work)	**93.6***	**78.2***	99.1	**96.6***	**67.7***

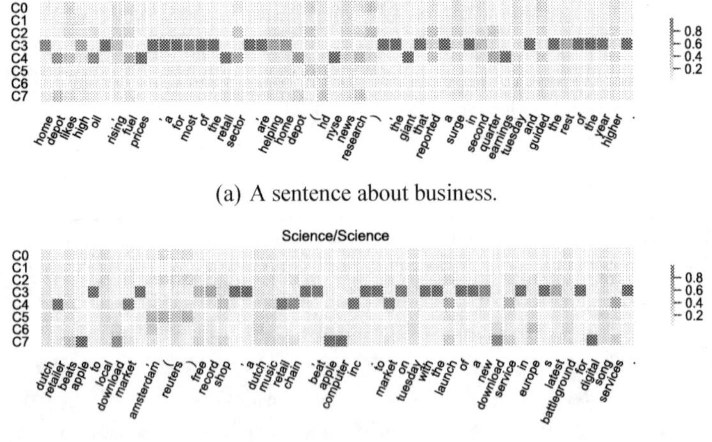

(a) A sentence about business.

(b) A sentence about science.

Fig. 2. The visualization on AGNews about topic classification. The heat map shows the distribution of words among different clusters in the text. The X-axis are words in text. The Y-axis represents the clusters. The title of each figure indicates the predicted class/the ground truth.

3.4 Evaluation Results

We compared our method to several state-of-the-art baselines with respect to accuracy, the same evaluation protocol with [23] who released these datasets. We present the experimental results in Table 2. The overall performance is competitive. It can be seen from the table that our method improves the best performance by 1.0%, 0.1% and 2.5% on Yah A., Yelp P. and Yelp F. respectively and is comparable on AGNews.

Compared with the baselines, our results exceed the traditional feature-based models (n-gram TF-IDF, BoW), the word embedding based representation models (FastText, SWEM) and LEAM by a large margin. Furthermore, we gain great improvement over the LSTM-based models. Though our model and the self-attentive model all aim at getting multiple vectors indicating different semantic information, as our model gather the words into clusters to enrich the representations, we achieve a better performance over theirs. Compared with the deep CNNs, our shallow model with a relatively simpler structure outperforms them as well. The models proposed by [19] and [12] aim at capturing features from different regions. Our results are on par with [19] and win over [12].

3.5 Ablation Study

In this section, we randomly select two datasets (Yelp P. and Yah.A.) and conduct ablation studies on them. We aim at analyzing the effect of gating mechanism and two kinds of regularization terms: word-level and class-level. The results without each part separately are shown in Table 3. "Full Model" denotes the whole model with nothing absent. Models trained with the gating mechanism and the regularization terms outperform their counterpart trained without, which demonstrates the effect of each part.

Table 3. The ablation results on Yelp P. and Yah.A.

Model	Yelp P	Yah.A
Full model	96.6	78.2
w/o Gating mechanism	96.3	77.9
w/o Word level	96.4	78.0
w/o Class level	96.4	78.0

3.6 Discussions

Analysis on Clustering Results. In this section, we take out the intermediate clustering results calculated when we test on AGNews which is a 4-category topic classification dataset including science, business, sports, and world.

Firstly, we visualize the distribution of words in clusters using heat map as shown in Fig. 2. Each column means the probabilities of a word attributed

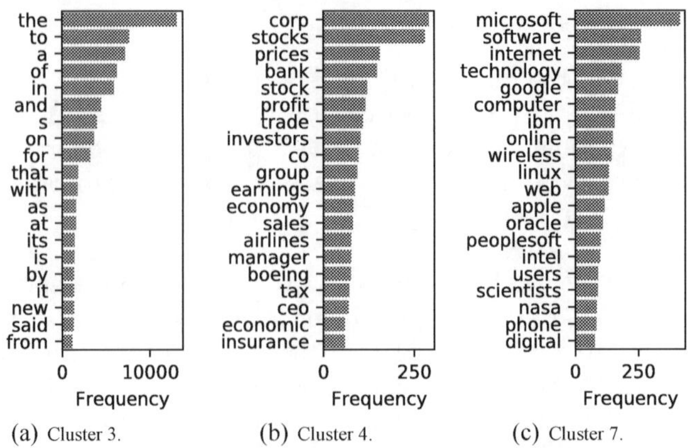

(a) Cluster 3. (b) Cluster 4. (c) Cluster 7.

Fig. 3. The statistical clustering results on AGNews in cluster 3, 4 and 7.

to the clusters which sum up to 1. We can see that most of the meaningless words, high frequency words and punctuation are divided into cluster 3, like *"a"*, *"for"*, *"that"*, etc. The text in Fig. 2(a) belongs to business category and the model predicts it right. We can find that the words about business are in cluster 4 such as *"depot"*, *"oil"*, *"prices"*. Likewise, from Fig. 2(b) we find words about science are assigned to cluster 7 like *"apple"*, *"download"*, *"computer"*. In Fig. 2(b), the text contains words about science and business, which are divided into their corresponding clusters separately. The words like *"beats"*, *"second"*, *"local"*, which are domain independent nouns or adjectives or verbs have a more average probability distribution among all clusters.

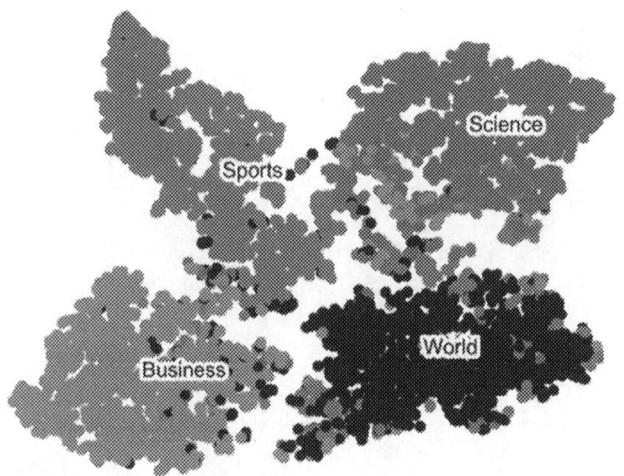

Fig. 4. t-SNE plot of the intermediate clustering probability distribution vector of text on AGNews test set.

We further make statistics about the clustering results over all the words. To be specific, we count the frequency of all the words being assigned to each cluster. A word is assigned to some cluster means that it is attributed to which with maximum probability. For each cluster, we sort the belonged words according to their frequency. We display the top 20 words in cluster 4, cluster 7 and cluster 3 as shown in Fig. 3. We can see that the words in cluster 4 are about business while the words in cluster 7 are science related and in cluster 3, the words are almost meaningless for classification. They are inconsistent with the cluster phenomenon in the heat map.

From the above visualization we have the following observations: first, words that indicate the same topic or with the similar semantics are divided into the same clusters; second, different categories correspond to different clusters; third, representative keywords have much greater probabilities (deeper color in heat map) in the specific cluster. These results exactly correspond to the motivation of the two regularization terms.

To evaluate the relevance between the clustering distribution and the classification results, we utilize t-SNE [9] to visualize the text-level cluster probability distribution on a two-dimensional map as shown in Fig. 4. Each color represents a different class. The point clouds are the text-level cluster probability distribution calculated by averaging the words' cluster probability distribution[1]. The location of the class label is the median of all the points belonging to the class. As can be seen, samples with the same class can be grouped together according to their text-level cluster probability distribution and the boundary between different class is obvious, which again demonstrates the strong relevance between the clustering distribution and the classification results.

Analysis on The Number of Semantic Clusters. As the number of semantic clusters is a tuned hyper parameter, we also analyze how performance is influenced by the number of semantic clusters by conducting experiments on AGNews and Yelp P., varying the cluster number m among $\{2,4,6,8,10,12\}$. From Fig. 5(a) we can find that the accuracy increases as the number of clusters increase and begins to drop after reaching the upper limit. Obviously, the cluster number does not in line with the class number to gain the best performance.

Analysis on Different Text Length. As the text length in datasets varies, we visualize how test accuracy changes with different text length. We perform experiments on AGNews and Yelp F. while the former has shorter text length than the latter. We divide the text length into 6 intervals according to the length scale. As Fig. 5(b) shows, our model performs better on relatively longer texts. With the increase in text length, our model tends to gather more information from the text. This visualization is in line with the overall performance of our model that it performs better on Yah.A., Yelp P. and Yelp F. rather than AGNews and DBPedia as the former three datasets have longer average text length.

[1] The cluster probability distribution is the intermediate result during testing. The initial dimension of the points is the cluster number. Each dimension represents the probability that the text belongs to a cluster.

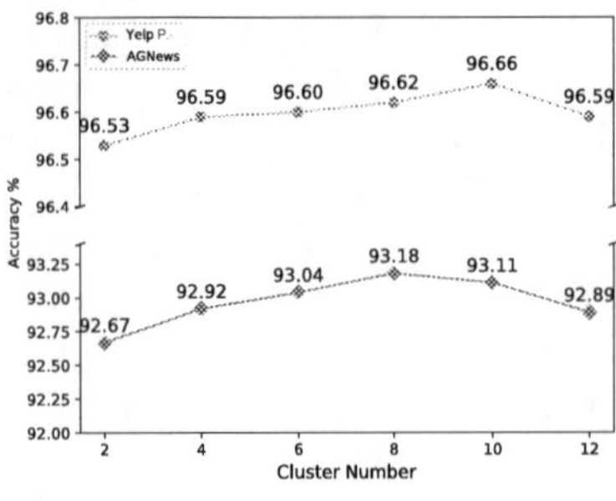

(a) Performance across different cluster numbers.

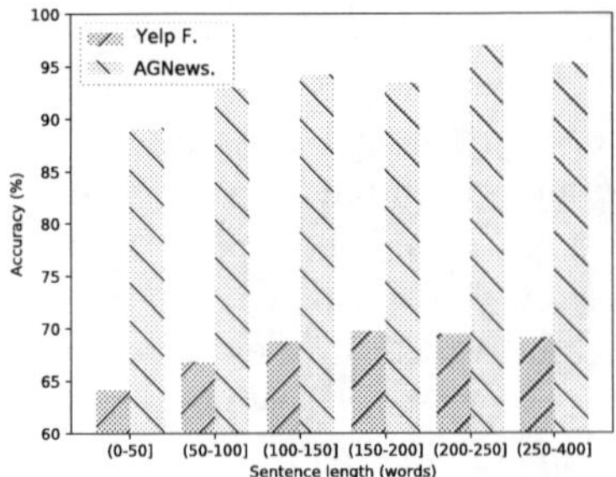

(b) Performance across different sentence length.

Fig. 5. Quantitative analysis on cluster number and sentence length.

4 Related Work

Text representation is an important and fundamental step in modern natural language processing, especially with the current development of approaches based on deep neural networks. Bi-LSTM [13] is a widely-used representation model which conveys information in both directions. Although it alleviates the problem of information vanishment due to the increase of sentence length, our framework can further integrate information by clustering words with similar semantics and give a visual explanation for the results. Another popular representation models are those based on CNN [3,6,23] which can capture the word features locally while our model can break the limitation of distance. A burgeoning and effective model is the structured self-attentive sentence embedding model proposed by [8]. They propose a multi-head self-attention mechanism mapping sentence into different semantic spaces and get sentence representation for each semantic space through attention summation. However, they focus on extracting different aspects of a sentence based on the automatically learned relative importance instead of composing similar aspects together to strengthen the information of each part as our work does.

Except for the above representation models, there are other several models specifically designed for classification. Wang et al. [18] takes the label information into consideration by jointly embedding the word and label in the same latent space. Wang et al. [19] uses a densely connected CNN to capture variable n-gram features and adopts multi-scale feature attention to adaptively select multi-scale features. Qiao et al. [12] utilizes the information of words' relative positions and local context to produce region embeddings for classification.

5 Conclusion and Future Work

In this paper, we propose to transform the flat word level text representation to a higher cluster level text representation for classification. We cluster words due to their semantics contained in their contextualized vectors gotten from the concatenation of the initial word embeddings and the outputs of the bi-LSTM encoder. We further introduce regularization schemes over words and classes to guide the clustering process. Experimental results on five classification benchmarks suggest the effectiveness of our proposed method. Further statistical and visualized analysis also explicitly shows the clustering results and provides interpretability for the classification results. In the future, we will try other encoding basement for capturing the words' semantics and we are interested in considering phrases instead of individual words as the basic elements for clustering. The idea of clustering representation is worth trying on other NLP tasks.

Acknowledgments. We thank the reviewers for their valuable comments. This work was supported by the National Key Research and Development Program of China (No. 2017YFC0804001), the National Science Foundation of China (NSFC No. 61876196, NSFC No. 61828302, and NSFC No. 61672058).

References

1. Abadi, M., et al.: Tensorflow: a system for large-scale machine learning. In: OSDI, vol. 16, pp. 265–283 (2016)
2. Bengio, Y., Ducharme, R., Vincent, P., Jauvin, C.: A neural probabilistic language model. JMLR **3**, 1137–1155 (2003)
3. Conneau, A., Schwenk, H., Barrault, L., Lecun, Y.: Very deep convolutional networks for text classification. In: EACL, pp. 1107–1116. Association for Computational Linguistics, Valencia, Spain, April 2017. http://www.aclweb.org/anthology/E17-1104
4. Joachims, T.: Text categorization with support vector machines: learning with many relevant features. In: Nédellec, C., Rouveirol, C. (eds.) ECML 1998. LNCS, vol. 1398, pp. 137–142. Springer, Heidelberg (1998). https://doi.org/10.1007/BFb0026683
5. Joulin, A., Grave, E., Bojanowski, P., Mikolov, T.: Bag of tricks for efficient text classification. In: EACL, pp. 427–431 (2017)
6. Kalchbrenner, N., Grefenstette, E., Blunsom, P.: A convolutional neural network for modelling sentences. In: ACL, pp. 655–665 (2014)
7. Kim, Y.: Convolutional neural networks for sentence classification. In: EMNLP, pp. 1746–1751 (2014)
8. Lin, Z., et al.: A structured self-attentive sentence embedding. In: ICLR (2017)
9. Maaten, L.V.D., Hinton, G.: Visualizing data using t-SNE. J. Mach. Learn. Res. **9**, 2579–2605 (2008)
10. Mikolov, T., Chen, K., Corrado, G., Dean, J.: Efficient estimation of word representations in vector space. arXiv preprint arXiv:1301.3781 (2013)
11. Pennington, J., Socher, R., Manning, C.: Glove: global vectors for word representation. In: EMNLP, pp. 1532–1543 (2014)
12. Qiao, C., et al.: A new method of region embedding for text classification. In: ICLR (2018)
13. Schuster, M., Paliwal, K.K.: Bidirectional recurrent neural networks. IEEE Trans. Signal Process. **45**(11), 2673–2681 (1997)
14. Shen, D., et al.: Baseline needs more love: on simple word-embedding-based models and associated pooling mechanisms. In: ACL, pp. 440–450 (2018)

15. Sparck Jones, K.: A statistical interpretation of term specificity and its application in retrieval. J. Doc. **28**(1), 11–21 (1972)
16. Sutskever, I., Vinyals, O., Le, Q.V.: Sequence to sequence learning with neural networks. In: NIPS, pp. 3104–3112 (2014)
17. Tai, K.S., Socher, R., Manning, C.D.: Improved semantic representations from tree-structured long short-term memory networks. In: ACL, pp. 1556–1566 (2015)
18. Wang, G., et al.: Joint embedding of words and labels for text classification. In: ACL, pp. 2321–2331 (2018)
19. Wang, S., Huang, M., Deng, Z.: Densely connected CNN with multi-scale feature attention for text classification. In: IJCAI, pp. 4468–4474 (2018)
20. Xiao, Y., Cho, K.: Efficient character-level document classification by combining convolution and recurrent layers. arXiv preprint arXiv:1602.00367 (2016)
21. Yang, Z., Yang, D., Dyer, C., He, X., Smola, A., Hovy, E.: Hierarchical attention networks for document classification. In: NAACL-HLT, pp. 1480–1489 (2016)
22. Zhang, T., Huang, M., Zhao, L.: Learning structured representation for text classification via reinforcement learning. In: AAAI, pp. 6053–6060 (2018)
23. Zhang, X., Zhao, J., LeCun, Y.: Character-level convolutional networks for text classification. In: NIPS, pp. 649–657 (2015)

Document-Based Question Answering Improves Query-Focused Multi-document Summarization

Weikang Li[1], Xingxing Zhang[2], Yunfang Wu[1(✉)], Furu Wei[2], and Ming Zhou[2]

[1] Key Laboratory of Computational Linguistics, MOE, Peking University, Beijing, China
{wavejkd,wuyf}@pku.edu.cn

[2] Microsoft Research Asia, Beijing, China
{xizhang,fuwei,mingzhou}@microsoft.com

Abstract. Due to the lack of large scale datasets, it remains difficult to train neural Query-focused Multi-Document Summarization (QMDS) models. Several large size datasets on the Document-based Question Answering (DQA) have been released and numerous neural network models achieve good performance. These two tasks above are similar in that they all select sentences from a document to answer a given query/question. We therefore propose a novel adaptation method to improve QMDS by using the relatively large datasets from DQA. Specifically, we first design a neural network model to model both tasks. The model, which consists of a sentence encoder, a query filter and a document encoder, can model the sentence salience and query relevance well. Then we train this model on both the QMDS and DQA datasets with several different strategies. Experimental results on three benchmark DUC datasets demonstrate that our approach outperforms a variety of baselines by a wide margin and achieves comparable results with state-of-the-art methods.

Keywords: Document-based Question Answering · Query-focused Multi-document Summarization · Task adaptation

1 Introduction

Automatic document summarization aims to rewrite a document (or documents) into a short piece of text while still retaining the important content from the original. Query-focused Multi-Document Summarization (QMDS) moves one step further, which produces a summary that not only reflects the original documents but also is relevant to the given query. Methods used for QMDS can be grouped into two categories: extractive QMDS and abstractive QMDS. The extractive QMDS copies parts of original documents (usually sentences) as their summaries while its abstractive counterpart can generate new words or phrases, which do not belong to the input documents. Abstractive methods, which is

J. Tang et al. (Eds.): NLPCC 2019, LNAI 11839, pp. 41–52, 2019.
https://doi.org/10.1007/978-3-030-32236-6_4

usually based on the sequence to sequence learning, still cannot guarantee the generated summaries are grammatical and conveys the same meaning as the original documents do. Therefore, we focus on the extractive QMDS method.

In the past years, numerous extractive QMDS methods have been developed. Early attempts mainly focus on feature engineering, where features such as sentence length, sentence position, TF-IDF are utilized [11,13]. Recently, neural network models for extractive summarization attract much attention [2,3,17], which are data-driven and are usually needed to be trained on hundreds or thousands of training examples. Unfortunately, the datasets available for training QMDS models are quite small. For example, the numbers of topic clusters are only 50, 50 and 45 in the DUC 2005, 2006 and 2007 datasets, respectively (see details in Sect. 3.1). The lack of enough training data has become the major obstacle for further improving the performance.

On the other hand, Document-based Question Answering (DQA) datasets have exactly the same format as the QMDS datasets. Given a document, the DQA task (also known as sentence selection) is first to score and then select the high score sentence as the predicted answer of a given question. Especially, there are several large-scale, high-quality datasets for DQA (i.e., SelQA [7]). Moreover, we can easily transform reading comprehension datasets (i.e., SQuAD [16]) to the format of DQA via distant-supervised methods.

With further analysis on the DQA and QMDS datasets, we find that this two kinds of data have similar question length (about 10 words) and document length (about 30 sentences). Considering the similarities of two tasks, we aim to improve the QMDS task with the DQA task.

Specifically, we design a neural network architecture, suitable for both tasks, which mainly consists of a sentence encoder, a query filter and a document encoder. It should be noted that although both tasks share the same network but with different training objectives. Therefore, we propose a novel adaptation method to apply pre-trained DQA models to the QMDS task. We conduct extensive experiments on the benchmark DUC 2005, 2006 and 2007 datasets, and the experimental results demonstrate our approach obtains considerable improvement over a variety of baselines and yields comparable performance with the state-of-the-art results.

Our contributions in this paper can be summarized as follows:

- To the best of our knowledge, we are the first to investigate adapting DQA to the QMDS task.
- We propose a neural network model for both DQA and QMDS tasks and explore a novel adaptation method to improve QMDS with DQA.
- Experimental results validate the efficiency of our proposed approach, which outperforms a variety of baselines.

2 Method

In this section, we first formally define the task, then we introduce the details of our summarization model, and finally, we present the adaptation method to leverage DQA models.

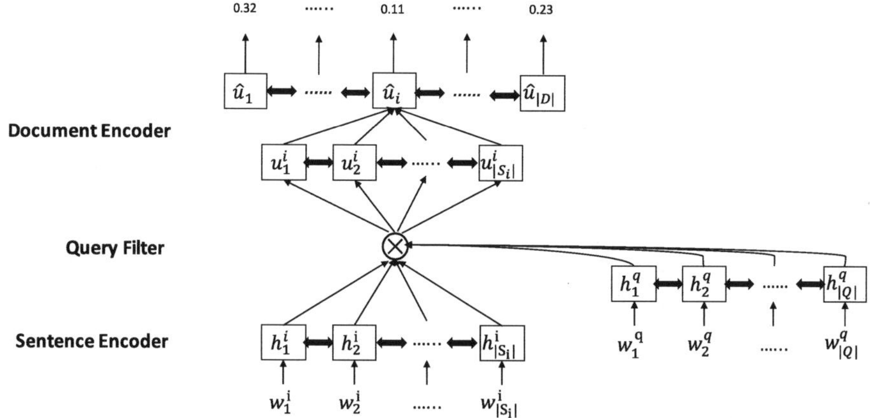

Fig. 1. Framework of our proposed neural network model for QMDS (also suitable for DQA).

2.1 Task Formulation

As mentioned earlier, our model is an extractive model. Given a document cluster (usually contains multiple documents) and a query, our model selects a subset of sentences from the cluster as its summary.

Let $D = (S_1, S_2, \ldots, S_{|D|})$ denote a document in the given document cluster and $S_i = (w_1^i, w_2^i, \ldots, w_{|S_i|}^i)$ a sentence in D. Let $Q = (w_1^q, \ldots, w_{|Q|}^q)$ denote a query for the cluster. Our summarization model is expected to assign a score $\delta(S_i, Q, D)$ for each sentence S_i. Finally a subset of sentences in the document cluster is selected according to $\delta(S_i, Q, D)$ and other constraints as the summary (details of our sentence selection strategies are in Sect. 2.4).

2.2 Model

Since the extractive model aims to select sentences from the document, it is crucial to model the document well firstly. It is well known that a document is hierarchically structured. Especially, a document is composed of sentences, and each sentence is composed of words. To leverage the hierarchical structure, as shown in Fig. 1, we design a hierarchical neural model, where the word level encoders (*Query Filter* and *Sentence Encoder*) aim to learn representations of the query and each sentence in a document and the document level encoder (*Document Encoder*) aims to learn the representation of the document. In the following, we will describe each component of our model in detail.

Sentence Encoder. As mentioned earlier, the sentence-level encoder learns to encode a sentence in a document. We opt for a bidirectional Gated Recurrent Unit (BiGRU) [5] network because it is capable of creating context dependent representations for each word. Given the embeddings of a sequence words $(w_1, w_2, \ldots, w_S)$ (denoted as $(e_1, e_2, \ldots, e_S,)$), a Bi-GRU, which contains two GRUs, processes a sentence in both left-to-right and right-to-left directions and yields two hidden sequences $(h_1^f, h_2^f, \ldots, h_S^f)$ and $(h_1^b, h_2^b, \ldots, h_S^b)$. The final representation of w_j is the concatenation of h_j^f and h_j^b. Now we apply BiGRUs (with different parameters) to a sentence S_i and also to the query Q and obtain $(h_1^i, \ldots, h_{|S_i|}^i)$ and $(h_1^q, \ldots, h_{|Q|}^q)$.

Query Filter. In query-focused summarization, as its name implies, the document cluster must be summarized according to the query. Information selection is crucial in this task. We therefore design a *Query Filter* component to inject such information into document/sentence encoding. Specifically, we apply an attention model [12] upon the *Sentence Encoder*. Let $M \in \mathbb{R}^{|Q| \times |S_i|}$ denote the attention score matrix between the query Q and a sentence S_i in a document and $M_{m,n}$ an element in M. The computation of $M_{m,n}$ is as follows:

$$M_{m,n} = \frac{\exp(h_m^q \; W \; {h_n^i}^{\mathrm{T}})}{\sum_{k=1}^{|Q|} \exp(h_k^q \; W \; {h_n^i}^{\mathrm{T}})} \tag{1}$$

where h_m^q is the representation of the mth word in query Q and h_n^i is the representation of the nth word in sentence S_i.

Once we have obtained the attention matrix M, we are ready to compute the *new* sentence encoding, which includes the query information. We inject the query information into the representation of each word in S_i using attentions from word representations of Q:

$$v_j^i = \sum_{k=1}^{|Q|} M_{k,j} \cdot h_k^q \tag{2}$$

The final representation of a word w_j^i in S_i is a concatenation of h_j^i and v_j^i as well a couple of binary operations between them:

$$f_j^i = \left[v_j^i; h_j^i; v_j^i \odot h_j^i; v_j^i + h_j^i; v_j^i - h_j^i\right] \tag{3}$$

where ; is the concatenation operation and $\odot$ is element-wise multiplication. Now we have finished the sentence level encoding and we will move to the document encoding in the next section.

Document Encoder. The inject of query information has filtered irrelevant information of a sentence, however, it may break the context-dependent information for each word. Besides, a document usually begins with what to talk with and ends with what have talked, which reveals the importance of the sentence order in a document. Thus, we design a hierarchical document encoder, which is composed of a sentence-level encoder and a document-level encoder.

In the sentence level, we again apply one Bi-GRU to encode each word with the input f_j^i and then extract features among words' hidden vectors, $(u_1^i, \ldots, u_{|S_i|}^i)$, to obtain a sentence representation α^i, which is the concatenation of mean and max pooling $[\max_j u_j^i; \frac{1}{|S_i|}\sum_j u_j^i]$. In the document level, we also apply another Bi-GRU to encode each sentence with the input α^i and obtain each sentence's final representation $(\hat{u}_1, \ldots, \hat{u}_{|D|})$. In the end, we apply a feed-forward neural network to compute a salience score p_i for each sentence.

The model is trained to minimize the standard Mean Square Error (MSE) for the QMDS task:

$$L_{sum} = \frac{1}{|D|} \sum_{i \in |D|} (p_i - r(S_i|S_{ref}))^2 \tag{4}$$

where $r(S_i|S_{ref})$ is the ground truth score of S_i in terms of recall ROUGE-2 with respect to human written summaries S_{ref}.

2.3 Adaptation from DQA to QMDS

Since we aim to improve QMDS with DQA, we extend the proposed model to the DQA task by applying a different objective, which is to minimize the cross-entropy between the predicted sentence score p_i and the true sentence score a_i:

$$L_{qa} = -\frac{1}{|D|} \sum_{i \in |D|} [a_i \log p_i + (1 - a_i) \log (1 - p_i)] \tag{5}$$

where a_i is the gold label (either 0 or 1) and 1 means the sentence is able to answer the given question and vice versa.

Considering the model's similarities between these two tasks (the only exception is the objective), we therefore apply the pre-trained DQA model to obtain a good starting point for training the QMDS model. Moreover, the pre-trained DQA model, which is good at capturing the query semantic information, could probably improve the query-sentence matching capability when training the QMDS model. We propose a novel adaptation method which includes two aspects. One is to apply the pre-trained DQA model to initialize the QMDS model. Given the initial parameters θ^0, we firstly learn a DQA model θ^{qa} based on the large DQA datasets D^{qa}. The learning process is formulated as follows:

$$Learn(D^{qa}; \theta^{qa}) = \arg\min_{\theta^0} L_{qa}(\theta^0) \tag{6}$$

Once we have finished the learning of DQA, we use the θ^{qa} as the initialization parameters of the QMDS model. The other is to utilize the pre-trained DQA model to obtain a query relevance score for each sentence in the document, and then use it as a distant supervised signal. Thus, the loss function for QMDS is changed as follows:

$$L_{sum}^{qa} = \frac{1}{|D|} \sum_{i \in |D|} (p_i - q(S_i|Q))^2 + \frac{1}{|D|} \sum_{i \in |D|} (p_i - r(S_i|S_{ref}))^2 \tag{7}$$

where $q(S_i|Q)$ is the query Q relevance score of a sentence S_i predicted by the pre-trained DQA model. Finally, the learning of the QMDS model is formulated as follows:

$$Learn(D^{sum}; \theta^{sum}) = \arg\min_{\theta^{qa}} L_{sum}^{qa}(\theta^{qa}) \tag{8}$$

Table 1. Statistics of the DUC datasets.

Dataset	Clusters	Documents	Data source
DUC 2005	50	1593	TREC
DUC 2006	50	1250	AQUAINT
DUC 2007	45	1125	AQUAINT

Table 2. Statistics of the DQA datasets. With the assumption that the sentence containing the answer span is correct, we convert the span-based SQuAD dataset to the sentence-based SQuAD† dataset.

Dataset	Split	#Documents	#Sentences
SQuAD†	TRAIN	87341	440573
	DEV	5273	26442
SelQA	TRAIN	5529	66438
	DEV	785	9377

2.4 Sentence Selection

The summarization model we have described can estimate the importance of all sentences in the input documents. This section focus on creating a summary with the output of our summarization model.

Once we have assigned each sentence a score via a trained summarization model, we are ready to select a subset of sentences as the final summary. The method we used in our paper is similar to the proposed methods [2,17]. We employ a simple greedy algorithm, similar to the MMR strategy [4]. The algorithm starts with the sentence of the predicted highest score. In each step, a new sentence S_i is added to the summary if it satisfies the following two conditions:

1. It has the highest score in the remaining sentences.
2. It contains significantly new bi-grams compared with the current summary content. We empirically set the cut-off of the new bi-gram ratio to 0.35.

3 Experiments

We describe the experimental setting and report empirical results in this section.

3.1 Datasets

In this paper, we focus on improving the performance on QMDS task with the help of the DQA task. The experiments are conducted on the public Document Understanding Conference (DUC) 2005, 2006 and 2007 datasets. All the documents in the dataset are from news websites and grouped into various thematic clusters. The DUC 2005, DUC 2006 and DUC 2007 datasets consist of 50, 50 and 45 topics respectively, and each topic includes a document set of 25 $\sim$ 50 news articles and a short description of a topical query. The task is to create a summary containing no more than 250 words for each document set to answer the query. There are at least four human written reference summaries provided in each document collection for evaluation. The datasets are briefly described in Table 1. We follow standard practice and train our QMDS models on two years of data and test on the third. It should be noted that 10 clusters are split from the training set to form the dev set.

Two different datasets are used for the DQA task: SelQA [7] and SQuAD [16]. Both datasets contain open-domain questions whose answers are extracted from Wikipedia articles. SelQA is a sentence-based DQA dataset, in which there is at least one correct sentence in the document for a question. The SQuAD is a span-based DQA dataset, and we could derive datasets for answer sentence selection from the original dataset. We assume that the sentences containing correct answer spans are correct, and vice versa. We merge them when training a DQA model. Table 2 shows the statistics of the two datasets above.

3.2 Evaluation Metrics

We employ the widely-adopted automatic evaluation metric ROUGE[1] for evaluation. We reported recall based ROUGE-1 and ROUGE-2 limited to 250 words. It automatically measures the quality of a summary by counting the number of overlapping units such as the n-gram, word sequences and word pairs between the candidate summary and reference summaries created by humans. ROUGE-2 recall is used as the main metric for comparison because it correlates well with human judgments.

3.3 Implementation Details

The proposed model is implemented with TensorFlow. The dimension of word embeddings is set to 300. The word embeddings are initialized with *300D GloVe* vectors [15], and out-of-vocabulary words in the training set are initialized randomly. We fix the embeddings during training. We train the model with Adam

[1] ROUGE-1.5.5 with options: -n 2 -l 250 -m -u -c 95 -x -r 1000 -f A -p 0.5 -t 0.

optimization algorithm [8] with a learning rate of 0.001, $\beta_1 = 0.9$, and $\beta_2 = 0.999$. Our models are trained with a batch size of 5. We set the hidden unit size $d = 80$ for both sentence-level and document-level GRUs and all GRUs have one layer.

3.4 Comparison Systems

To evaluate the overall performance of the proposed method, we compare it with a variety of baseline methods, including some traditional baselines, and several recent extractive query-focused summarization systems, which are typically based on different neural network structures. We don't implement compared models and directly take the reported performance in the original papers. Compared methods includes *LEAD* [19], *QUERY-SIM* [2], *SVR* [14], *MultiMR* [18], *DocEmb* [9], *ISOLATION* [2], *AttSum* [2], *CRSum* [17].

Table 3. Results of different adaptation methods to the DQA on the DUC three datasets using the length of 250 words recall ROUGE-1 (R-1) and ROUGE-2 (R-2).

(a) on the DUC 2005.

Model	R-1	$\Delta/\%$	R-2	$\Delta/\%$
QA-None	33.96	–	6.04	–
QA-Loss	35.78	$1.82^{\uparrow}$	6.47	$0.43^{\uparrow}$
QA-Init	36.45	$2.49^{\uparrow}$	6.92	$0.88^{\uparrow}$
QA-Init&Loss	37.25	$3.29^{\uparrow}$	7.13	$1.09^{\uparrow}$

(b) on the DUC 2006.

Model	R-1	$\Delta/\%$	R-2	$\Delta/\%$
QA-None	36.05	–	6.64	–
QA-Loss	37.40	$1.35^{\uparrow}$	7.46	$0.82^{\uparrow}$
QA-Init	38.74	$2.69^{\uparrow}$	8.44	$1.80^{\uparrow}$
QA-Init&Loss	39.41	$3.36^{\uparrow}$	9.05	$2.41^{\uparrow}$

(c) on the DUC 2007.

Model	R-1	$\Delta/\%$	R-2	$\Delta/\%$
QA-None	37.54	–	8.51	–
QA-Loss	39.22	$1.68^{\uparrow}$	8.85	$0.34^{\uparrow}$
QA-Init	40.44	$2.90^{\uparrow}$	9.69	$1.18^{\uparrow}$
QA-Init&Loss	40.55	$3.01^{\uparrow}$	10.20	$1.69^{\uparrow}$

3.5 Results

Effectiveness of DQA We firstly conduct experiments to verify the effectiveness of pre-trained DQA models. The proposed adaptation method in our paper can be divided into three ways to make use of the pre-trained DQA model. The first one is to pre-train our model on the DQA datasets and then continue to train the model on the QMDS datasets, denoted as *QA-Init* (see Eq. 6). The second one is first to produce a query relevance score for each sentence in the QMDS datasets with a well-trained DQA model and then joint train the model with the supervised query relevance signal and sentence salience signal, denoted as *QA-Loss* (see Eq. 7). The last one is to combine both *QA-Init* and *QA-Loss*, denoted as *QA-Init&Loss* (see Eq. 8). We denote the model trained only with the QMDS datasets as *QA-None*. Table 3 shows the performances of different adaptation methods to use the pre-trained DQA model on three benchmarks.

As shown in Table 3, we can see that the three adaptation methods using DQA are quite effective to improve the QMDS task. Specifically, *QA-Loss* outperforms *QA-None* by 0.43, 0.82 and 0.34 in terms of ROUGE-2 and 1.82, 1.35 and 1.68 in terms of ROUGE-1 on the DUC 2005, 2006 and 2007 datasets, respectively. *QA-Init* achieves a performance gain of 0.88, 1.80 and 1.18 ROUGE-2 points and 2.49, 2.69 and 2.90 ROUGE-1 points over *QA-None*. And *QA-Init&Loss* yields 1.09, 2.41 and 1.69 ROUGE-2 improvements and 3.29, 3.36 and 3.01 improvements. As can be seen, the improvements on the DUC 2005 dataset is smaller than that on the DUC 2006 and 2007 datasets, which may be because of the differences in numbers of documents under a topic cluster. In the DUC 2005 dataset, a topic cluster contains 32 documents on average, while in the other two datasets the number is 25 documents on average. It becomes hard when the number of candidate sentences increases. Among the three adaptations, *QA-Init&Loss* achieves the best performance than the others and *QA-Init* is better than *QA-Loss*.

In the following, we compare our best model *QA-Init&Loss* against several recent models.

Table 4. Experimental results of the QMDS task on three benchmark datasets using the length of 250 words recall ROUGE-1 (R-1) and ROUGE-2 (R-2).

Methods	DUC 2005		DUC 2006		DUC 2007	
	R-1	R-2	R-1	R-2	R-1	R-2
LEAD [2]	29.71	4.69	32.61	5.71	36.14	8.12
QUERY-SIM [2]	32.95	5.91	35.52	7.10	36.32	7.94
SVR [2]	36.91	7.04	39.24	8.87	43.42	11.10
MultiMR [2]	35.58	6.81	38.57	7.75	41.59	9.34
DocEmb [2]	30.59	4.69	32.77	5.61	33.88	6.46
ISOLATION [2]	35.72	6.79	40.58	8.96	42.76	10.79
AttSum [2]	37.01	6.99	**40.90**	**9.40**	**43.92**	**11.55**
CRSum [17]	36.96	7.01	39.51	9.19	41.20	11.17
Our model	**37.25**	**7.13**	39.41	9.05	40.55	10.20

Performance Comparison. For the compared approaches, we list the best results reported in the original literature. The overall performance comparisons on the DUC 2005, DUC 2006 and DUC 2007 datasets are shown in Table 4. Our proposed method obtains the state-of-the-art performance on the DUC 2005 dataset and achieves comparable results on the DUC 2006 and 2007 datasets.

The first block in Table 4 represents non-neural network methods, which apply manual features or well-defined rules. Recent neural network methods are shown in the second block of Table 4. On the DUC 2005 dataset, our model outperforms the previous best method *AttSum* by 0.24 ROUGE-1 points and exceeds the previous best method *SVR* by 0.09 ROUGE-2 points. On the DUC

2006 dataset, our model outperforms the feature-based methods in terms of ROUGE-1 and ROUGE-2 and achieves comparable performances with neural network-based methods. On the DUC 2007 dataset, our model is on par with the public methods except feature-based methods *SVR* and neural network-based methods *AttSum* and *CRSum*. It is noted that *SVR* heavily depends on hand-crafted features, while our model does not use any manual features. Our proposed neural network model is designed to be suitable for both QMDS and DQA tasks, which is different from the QMDS-specific models (e.g., *AttSum* and *CRSum*). Moreover, *CRSum* also extract word-level features via convolutional neural networks. There are two kinds of query type in the DUC (2005–2007) datasets, namely description type query and question type query. As shown in Table 5, we found that the question type queries has a high proportion of clusters on the DUC 2005 dataset (60.0%) and low proportion on the other datasets (only 24.4% on the DUC 2007 dataset), which may explain the a little bit worse performance of our proposed method on the DUC 2007 dataset. QA based initialization and training objective tends to improve question type queries.

Table 5. Statistics of the query with question type in the DUC datasets.

Dataset	Clusters	Question type	Proportion
DUC 2005	50	30	60.0%
DUC 2006	50	24	48.0%
DUC 2007	45	11	24.4%

4 Related Work

As a challenging issue for text understanding, automatic document summarization has been studied for a long period . Except for computing sentence salience, QMDS also needs to concern the query-sentence relevance, which makes it harder than the Generic MDS. Cao et al. [2] propose a neural network model (AttSum) which jointly handles sentence salience ranking and query relevance ranking. It automatically generates distributed representations for sentences as well as the document cluster. Meanwhile, it applies an attention mechanism that tries to simulate human attentive reading behavior when a query is given. Ren et al. [17] find that sentence relations in the document play an essential role, and so propose a Contextual Relation-based Summarization model (CRSum), which firstly uses sentence relations with a word-level attentive pooling convolutional network to construct sentence representations and then use contextual relations with a sentence-level attentive pooling recurrent neural network to construct context representations. Finally, CRSum automatically learns useful contextual features by jointly learning representations of sentences and similarity scores between a sentence and its contexts. Inspired by these two works, we design a hierarchical neural network model, which is not only able to capture sentence relations via a Bi-GRU structure, but also pays attention to the query with the attention mechanism. It should be noted that our proposed model is end-to-end and does not require manual features. So, the proposed model with manual features (CRSum+SF+QF) in the paper [17] is not referred to in our experiment. Meanwhile, our proposed model is also suitable for DQA, which benefits the adaptation from the DQA task to the QMDS task.

Speaking of domain adaptation, works from SDS to MDS is emerging in recent years due to the insufficient labeled data in MDS. Lebanoff et al. [10] describe a novel adaptation method (PG-MMR), which combines an extractive summarization algorithm (MMR) for sentence extraction and an abstractive model (PG) to fuse source sentences. Zhang et al. [20] add a document set encoder to their hierarchical summarization framework and propose three strategies to improve the model performance further. Baumel et al. [1] try to apply the pre-trained abstractive summarization model of SDS to the query-focused summarization task. They sort the input documents and then iteratively apply the SDS model to summarize every single document until the length limit is reached. Different from them, we explore how to apply DQA to improve QMDS. To the best of our knowledge, we are the first to do like this.

5 Conclusion

We propose a novel adaptation of applying DQA to improve the model's performance on the QMDS task. Our proposed network is designed to fit both tasks, which includes a sentence encoder, a query filter and a document encoder. Extensive experiments demonstrate that our proposed method can indeed improve over a variety of baselines and yields comparable results with state-of-the-art methods. The method we have proposed is one of the many possible methods for utilizing DQA datasets (and models). In the future, we plan to explore other adaptation methods, like meta-learning [6] and investigating more tasks related to the QMDS task.

Acknowledgment. This work is supported by the National Natural Science Foundation of China (61773026, 61572245).

References

1. Baumel, T., Eyal, M., Elhadad, M.: Query focused abstractive summarization: Incorporating query relevance, multi-document coverage, and summary length constraints into seq2seq models. arXiv preprint arXiv:1801.07704 (2018)
2. Cao, Z., Li, W., Li, S., Wei, F.: Attsum: Joint learning of focusing and summarization with neural attention. CoRR abs/1604.00125 (2016). http://arxiv.org/abs/1604.00125
3. Cao, Z., Wei, F., Li, S., Li, W., Zhou, M., Houfeng, W.: Learning summary prior representation for extractive summarization. In: Proceedings of the 53rd Annual Meeting of the Association for Computational Linguistics and the 7th International Joint Conference on Natural Language Processing (Volume 2: Short Papers), vol. 2, pp. 829–833 (2015)

4. Carbonell, J., Goldstein, J.: The use of mmr, diversity-based reranking for reordering documents and producing summaries. In: Proceedings of the 21st Annual International ACM SIGIR Conference on Research and Development in Information Retrieval, pp. 335–336. ACM (1998)
5. Cho, K., et al.: Learning phrase representations using rnn encoder-decoder for statistical machine translation. arXiv preprint arXiv:1406.1078 (2014)
6. Gu, J., Wang, Y., Chen, Y., Cho, K., Li, V.O.: Meta-learning for low-resource neural machine translation. arXiv preprint arXiv:1808.08437 (2018)
7. Jurczyk, T., Zhai, M., Choi, J.D.: Selqa: A new benchmark for selection-based question answering. In: 2016 IEEE 28th International Conference on Tools with Artificial Intelligence (ICTAI), pp. 820–827. IEEE (2016)
8. Kingma, D.P., Ba, J.: Adam: A method for stochastic optimization. arXiv preprint arXiv:1412.6980 (2014)
9. Kobayashi, H., Noguchi, M., Yatsuka, T.: Summarization based on embedding distributions. In: Proceedings of the 2015 Conference on Empirical Methods in Natural Language Processing, pp. 1984–1989 (2015)
10. Lebanoff, L., Song, K., Liu, F.: Adapting the neural encoder-decoder framework from single to multi-document summarization. arXiv preprint arXiv:1808.06218 (2018)
11. Li, C., Qian, X., Liu, Y.: Using supervised bigram-based ILP for extractive summarization. In: Proceedings of the 51st Annual Meeting of the Association for Computational Linguistics (Volume 1: Long Papers), vol. 1, pp. 1004–1013 (2013)
12. Luong, M.T., Pham, H., Manning, C.D.: Effective approaches to attention-based neural machine translation. arXiv preprint arXiv:1508.04025 (2015)
13. Ouyang, Y., Li, S., Li, W.: Developing learning strategies for topic-based summarization. In: Proceedings of the Sixteenth ACM Conference on Conference on Information and Knowledge Management, pp. 79–86. ACM (2007)
14. Ouyang, Y., Li, W., Li, S., Lu, Q.: Applying regression models to query-focused multi-document summarization. Inf. Process. Manage. **47**(2), 227–237 (2011)
15. Pennington, J., Socher, R., Manning, C.: Glove: global vectors for word representation. In: Proceedings of the 2014 Conference on Empirical Methods in Natural Language Processing (EMNLP), pp. 1532–1543 (2014)
16. Rajpurkar, P., Zhang, J., Lopyrev, K., Liang, P.: Squad: 100,000+ questions for machine comprehension of text. arXiv preprint arXiv:1606.05250 (2016)
17. Ren, P., Chen, Z., Ren, Z., Wei, F., Ma, J., de Rijke, M.: Leveraging contextual sentence relations for extractive summarization using a neural attention model. In: Proceedings of the 40th International ACM SIGIR Conference on Research and Development in Information Retrieval, SIGIR 2017, pp. 95–104. ACM, New York, NY, USA (2017). https://doi.org/10.1145/3077136.3080792, http://doi.acm.org/10.1145/3077136.3080792
18. Wan, X., Xiao, J.: Graph-based multi-modality learning for topic-focused multi-document summarization. In: IJCAI, pp. 1586–1591 (2009)
19. Wasson, M.: Using leading text for news summaries: evaluation results and implications for commercial summarization applications. In: Proceedings of the 36th Annual Meeting of the Association for Computational Linguistics and 17th International Conference on Computational Linguistics, vol. 2 pp. 1364–1368. Association for Computational Linguistics (1998)
20. Zhang, J., Tan, J., Wan, X.: Towards a neural network approach to abstractive multi-document summarization. arXiv preprint arXiv:1804.09010 (2018)

BSIL: A Brain Storm-Based Framework for Imbalanced Text Classification

Jiachen Tian[1,2], Shizhan Chen[1,2], Xiaowang Zhang[1,2(✉)], and Zhiyong Feng[1,2]

[1] College of Intelligence and Computing, Tianjin University, Tianjin, China
{jiachen6677,shizhan,xiaowangzhang,zyfeng}@tju.edu.cn

[2] Tianjin Key Laboratory of Cognitive Computing and Application, Tianjin, China

Abstract. All neural networks are not always effective in processing imbalanced datasets when dealing with text classification due to most of them designed under a balanced assumption. In this paper, we present a novel framework named BSIL to improve the capability of neural networks in imbalanced text classification built on brain storm optimization (BSO). With our framework BSIL, the simulation of human brainstorming process of BSO can sample imbalanced datasets in a reasonable way. Firstly, we present an approach to generate multiple relatively balanced subsets of an imbalanced dataset by applying scrambling segmentation and global random sampling in BSIL. Secondly, we introduce a parallel method to train a classifier for a subset efficiently. Finally, we propose a decision-making layer to accept "suggestions" of all classifiers in order to achieve the most reliable prediction result. The experimental results show that BSIL associated with CNN, RNN and Self-attention model can performs better than those models in imbalanced text classification.

1 Introduction

A neural networks (NN)-based model often needs a large number of datasets for training when dealing with text classification task with the assumption that the distribution of datasets is balanced and the error cost is equal [10]. However, real-world data is often heavily skewed and, as a result, standard classification algorithms tend to ignore the minority class and overwhelm the majority one [13]. The imbalance of datasets mainly determined as one of essential characteristics of datasets cannot be avoided in our real life such as natural disasters, network intrusion, cancer detection, etc. [7]. Although the sample size of the minority class is much smaller than that of the majority one, they usually carry more important information not be ignored in processing. It becomes interesting and important to improve the capability of existing models to correctly classify samples of the minority class [12].

In this paper, inspired from the idea of brain storm optimization (BSO) algorithm [5], we design a framework for dealing with the imbalanced learning problem, named *brain storm imbalanced learning* (BSIL). This algorithm can simulate our brain well, where the left and right hemispheres collaboratively

J. Tang et al. (Eds.): NLPCC 2019, LNAI 11839, pp. 53–64, 2019.
https://doi.org/10.1007/978-3-030-32236-6_5

work together on a job [4]. The purpose of BSIL is to utilize a distributed extensible framework and within this framework, a deep learning algorithm can improve train models with good performance for an imbalanced dataset. Based on this idea, we first apply "scrambling segmentation" or "global random sampling" to obtain multiple sets of relatively balanced datasets. During the model training process, all classifiers train weight through a parallel ensemble learning method and then iteratively update the optimal weight among them. Finally, all classifiers put all results of their training together for discussion in the decision-making layer for obtaining the best classification scheme.

The novel sampling method in our model can guarantee that all information is retained and each subset has the same distribution as the original dataset. In a parallel training layer, each classifier acts as an agent and is responsible for working within its subset. The built-in weight selection module can ensure that the initial weight of each training epoch is optimal. The efficiency of each classifier is much improved due to the reduced workload. The decision-making layer has a higher robustness for finding the "best available" prediction result of all classifiers.

In a short, we summarize three main contributions as follows:

- We present a brain storm-based framework by applying scrambling segmentation and global random sampling in generating multiple relatively balanced subsets of an imbalanced dataset.
- We develop a distributed and extensible training method to computing relatively balanced subsets efficiently.
- We introduce a decision-making method to generate optimal results for multiple predictions in decision-making layer.

This paper is further organized as follows. In the next section, we discuss related works. Section 3 addresses our method. Section 4 is devoted to experiments and evaluation. We conclude the work in Sect. 5.

2 Related Works

He et al. analyzed the causes regarding the performance degradation of the classifier in detail and summarized the existing research methods [7], which can be divided into data-based level, algorithm-based level, and transfer learning. Kubat et al. raised the problem of imbalanced learning when dealing with the detection of the oil spilled problem in 1998 [9]. Many studies have revealed that imbalanced learning problem is relevant to data complexity. Datta et al. proposed a method for identifying the disjunction problem in a dataset [6].

The research on data level mainly lies in the resampling method. Wang et al. used resampling to cope with online class imbalances. They proposed two resampling techniques (i.e., OOB and UOB), defined class imbalances and verified that data distribution determines the imbalance problem [15]. Charte et al. proposed specializing measures to assess the imbalance level for multilabel classification. Using these measures to test which multilabel datasets are imbalanced, and presented both random undersampling and random oversampling algorithms to reduce the degree of imbalance [3]. Lin et al. proposed two resampling strategies to assist in the data preprocessing [11]. Charte et al. proposed a procedure to hybridize some resampling method with a novel algorithm designed to decouple imbalanced labels [2].

The cost-sensitive model mainly utilizes a cost matrix to impose distinct penalties on different classes. Khan et al. proposed a neural network combined with the cost-sensitive method, which can automatically robust extract feature vectors of the majority and minority class [8].

Transfer learning is to train the model on a related large-scale balanced dataset and then fine-tuning weight according to the target one. Al-Stouhi et al. presented a model combined with the transfer learning mechanism. This method used auxiliary data to make up for the lack of the imbalanced dataset [1]. Wang et al. used the conditional and marginal distribution discrepancies to treat the imbalanced learning problem [14].

3 Our Method

The structure of BSIL adopts the idea of distributed machine learning which is utilized to deal with the problem that large-scale data cannot be processed in a single node. BSIL utilizes a data preprocessing layer to transform the incoming imbalanced datasets into multi-group balanced subsets, then works a distributed ensemble learning framework with optimal weight selection strategy to train multiple agents, and finally uses a brainstorming algorithm to integrate the output of each agent to obtain the final results. This section will focus on the data preprocessing layer (DPL), the parallel training layer (PTL, the distributed ensemble learning framework) and the decision-making layer (DML, the brainstorming algorithm).

3.1 Data Preprocessing Layer (DPL)

To transform an imbalanced dataset into multi-group balanced subsets and ensure that their original distribution characteristics are not broken, we utilize "scrambling segmentation" or "global random sampling" to adjust the dataset (see Fig. 1).

"Scrambling segmentation" randomly scrambles the training dataset, then divides it into the corresponding subset according to the number of classifiers in PTL. This method retains every sample so that the dataset information is not lost. "Global random sampling" randomly samples the data of the entire majority class. It guarantees that the subset and the original training dataset are independently and identically distributed.

Suppose our dataset has only two classes, the majority class $P : \{x_i, y_i\}$ and the minority class $N : \{x_j, y_j\}$. $|P|$ is much large than $|N|$ and $|\cdot|$ is the size of the corresponding class.

We first randomly sample m subsets P_i from P according to the size of the minority class, then we get m training subset $\{P_i, N\}$ which is obtained by combining P_i and N. We use $\{P_i, N\}$ to train the corresponding $agent_i$ and evaluate the performance of each agent and obtain the $F1\_Score$ value F_i related to them. If one of the F_i is greater than the threshold value λ (in our experiment, λ is 60%. This mainly depends on the baseline of the selected model), i.e., one of agents (classifiers) obtains a "good enough" prediction result, $\{P_i, N\}$ can be retained, otherwise, we will sample $m+1$ subsets of P and generate $m+1$ agents.

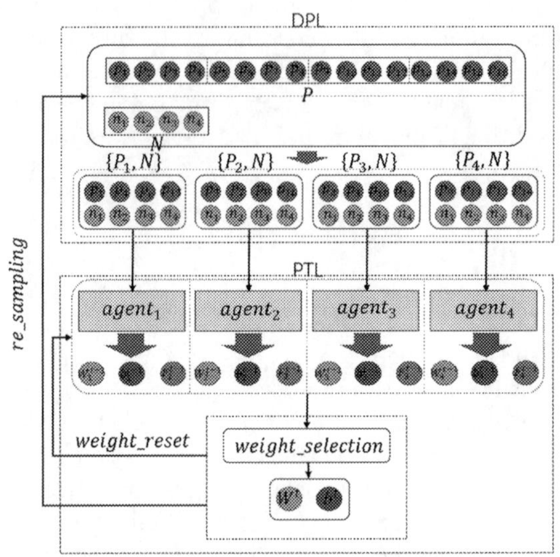

Fig. 1. Training process and internal structure.

3.2 Parallel Training Layer (PTL)

When we have m training subset $\{P_i, N\}$, the number of the agent in the parallel training layer is also fixed to m. In our framework, we used three basic NN-based models as agents (see Fig. 1):

- **Convolutional Neural Networks (CNN)** is the deep neural network with the convolution structure. It has three key operations, including the convolution layer, weight sharing, and pooling layer.
- **Recurrent Neural Network (RNN)** is a type of neural network for processing sequence data. We used the most basic LSTM model which can get long short-term memory information.
- **Self-attention Neural Network (SaNN)** is a very popular NLP neural network which uses a global self-attention mechanism to enable the model to obtain more important feature information.

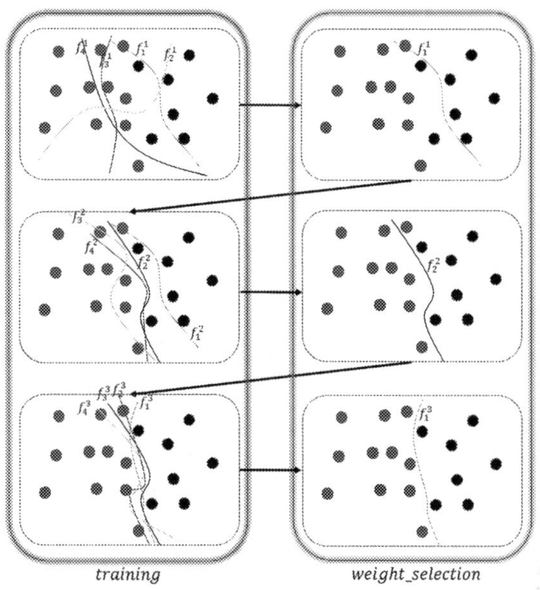

Fig. 2. Weight Selection Process.

Weight Selection Process. Different agents can be considered as any functions f, which map the input samples $\{P_i, N\}$ into a new feature space. In the initial step of model training, since the weight is arbitrarily initialized, the mapping function f obtained by the training does not fit the feature space well. At time $t-1$, the weight selection mechanism selects the best weight $\{W_i^{t-1}, b_i^{t-1}\}$ as the initial weight of the succeeding time t by comparing the accuracy of all agents. Since the model has multiple sets of weights to choose at each time, the feature selection method improves the robustness of the model. Taking Fig. 2 as an example. In the first step, all agents get a set of mapping functions $\{f_1^1, f_2^1, f_3^1, f_4^1\}$ through training. The weight selection method finds that f_1^1 has the highest accuracy and uses $\{W_1^1, b_1^1\}$ as the initial weight of the next step. During time 2, all agents use $\{W_1^1, b_1^1\}$ to train their mapping functions f_i^2. Repeat the above steps, the weight of f_1^3 is finally obtained. We can see that f_1^3 can distinguish the imbalanced dataset very well at this time.

3.3 Decision-Making Layer (DML)

We generally divide the dataset into a training set, a validation set, and a test set. The training set is used to fit the parameters of the classifier. The validation set is used to tune the hyperparameters (i.e., the architecture) of a classifier and can evaluate the performance of each epoch's classifier. The test set is a dataset that is independent of the training dataset, but that follows the same probability distribution as the training dataset and the validation dataset.

Due to the consistency of the above probability distribution, if a classifier has higher accuracy in the validation set, then the classifier will also get higher one in the test set. In our framework, if one agent predict the validation set to obtain a higher $F1\_Score$ in the PTL module, then we believe that it can give us a better result for predicting the test set, so the DML gives it higher confidence. In our experiments, the accuracy of each agent play a role of confidence, which tells us which output of the agent should be trusted.

More formally, each agent train a set of $\{W_i^t, b_i^t\}$ and predict the evaluation dataset to get the $F1\_Score$ value F_i in PTL. F_i participates in the Eq. 1 as a confidence.

$$pred_{final} = \frac{\sum_{n=1}^{N}(F_i \cdot pred_i)}{Z} \tag{1}$$

Here N is the number of agents, F_i is the $F1\_Score$ value, $pred_i$ is the prediction value of each agent. Z is a normalization factor to ensure that each output is 0 or 1. Due to the existence of F_i, the result tends to the outputs of several agents with higher F_i.

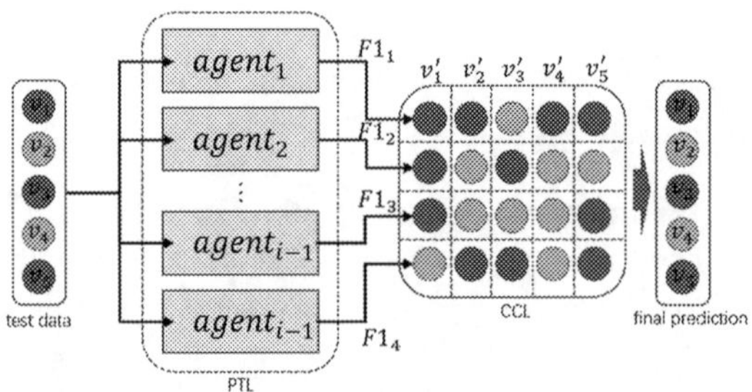

Fig. 3. Decision-making Process in DML.

Taking Fig. 3 as an example, the ground true of the test dataset is [1, 0, 1, 0, 1]. After training, the prediction result of $agent_1$ is [1,1,0,1,1], and F_1 is 40%. The predicted result of $agent_2$ is [1,0,1,0,0], and F_2 is 80%. The predicted result of $agent_3$ is [1,0,0,0,1], and F_3 is 80%. The predicted result of $agent_4$ is [0, 1, 1, 0, 1], and F_4 is 60%. For sample 1, $agent_1$, $agent_2$, $agent_3$ predict it as a positive sample, so the final prediction is 1. For sample 2, although $agent_1$, $agent_4$ predict it as a positive sample, $agent_2$, $agent_3$ predict it as a negative sample, but $agent_2$, $agent_3$ have higher F_i, we should believe them more, so sample 2 is finally predicted to be a negative sample. By analogy, it can be seen that although they did not classify all the samples correctly in their respective task, they finally reached the correct result through discussion.

4 Experiments and Evaluation

In this section, we use the BSIL framework to combine with three different agents(CNN, RNN, and SaNN). We investigate the classification performance of the BSIL framework and compare it with state-of-the-art models for text classification and analyze the robustness of the DML on various datasets.

4.1 Experimental Evaluation Criteria

In imbalanced learning, accuracy has not been a good indicator of the performance of the classifier. The *Precision*, *Recall*, and *F1_Score* values are more reflective of the classification effect of the classifier on the minority class. In our experiments, we used the *F1_Score* value, which is a combination of *Precision* and *Recall*, see Eq. 2.

$$F1\_Score = \frac{2 \cdot Recall \cdot Precision}{Recall + Precision} \tag{2}$$

Precision is referred to as a positive predictive rate. *Recall* is also referred to as the true positive rate or sensitivity (see Eq. 3).

$$Precision = \frac{TP}{TP + FP}, \qquad Recall = \frac{TP}{TP + FN} \tag{3}$$

Where TP is the number of the positive sample which is right predicted. FP is the number of the negative sample which is predicted to be a positive one. FN is the number of the positive sample which is predicted to be a negative one.

4.2 Datasets

We choose five text classification datasets, which include English and Chinese datasets. They can be divided into the sentence and document levels. We used random sampling technology to construct their imbalances. We briefly summarize these datasets as follows:

- **MR**: Movie reviews with one sentence per review. Positive and negative sentiment polarity is included in the classification. Imbalance ratio (IR) is 1250:4250.
- **SST-2**: An extension of MR but with train/dev/test splits provided. IR is 1009:3310.
- **IMDB**: A document-level text classification dataset containing 100,000 movie reviews with binary labels. IR is 12500:50000.
- **SPAM**: A Chinese classification dataset for spam detection. IR is 635:2743.
- **CR**: A car review dataset. IR is 6000:22800.

The first two datasets are for sentence-level classification and the last three datasets are for document-level classification. IMDB is the biggest dataset and SPAM is the Chinese dataset. These five datasets involve as many different as possible (see Table 1).

Table 1. Description of datasets.

Dataset	Average length	Vocabulary size	Train size	Test size
MR	20	18K	1250:4250	CV
SST-2	18	15K	1009:3310	1821
IMDB	294	392K	12500:50000	22500
SPAM	574	22K	635:2743	1034
CR	100	133K	6000:22800	6300

4.3 Model Training and Hyper-parameters

In our experiment, the agents are set to CNN, RNN, and SaNN, respectively. The three agents use different parameter settings:

- **BSIL_LSTM**: Our framework combined with the LSTM model, i.e., all agents utilize the LSTM model. We use a bidirectional RNN, the learning rate is 0.3, the Sequence length is set according to different datasets, the dropout rate is 0.8, the size of the hidden layer is 32, and there are 2 hidden layers.
- **BSIL_CNN**: Our framework combined with the CNN model, i.e., all agents utilize the CNN model. This model uses a total of 100 convolution kernels. The size of the kernel is 1, i.e., each convolution kernel filters a word. The defined length of a sentence is also set according to different datasets.
- **BSIL_SaNN**: Our framework combined with the SaNN model, i.e., all agents utilize the SaNN model. The learning rate is 0.003, the number of scaled dot-product attention module is 8 and the number of encoder is 6.

The word embeddings initialized with the 300-dimensional word vector published by Glove. The objective function uses a cross-entropy loss function. The epochs of training are 10 and the batch size is 32.

4.4 Baselines

Our framework combined with CNN, RNN, and SaNN, so we need to compare with them to prove that they are not suitable for imbalanced dataset. Besides, we have compared many existing state-of-the-art models to illustrate that our models are indeed more suitable for imbalanced dataset than them.

- **LSTM**: The LSTM model mentioned in Sect. 3.2. We use it to compare with BSIL_LSTM.
- **LSTM+attention**: We implement flatten variants of the attention-based LSTM model for different levels of classification.
- **CNN**: The CNN model mentioned in Sect. 3.2. We use it to compare with BSIL_CNN.
- **SaNN**: The SaNN model mentioned in Sect. 3.2. A self-attention mechanism model for classification. We use it to compare with BSIL_SaNN.

- **FastText**: The FastText model is based on RNN.
- **TextCNN**: The TextCNN model is based on CNN.
- **SMOTE_(CNN/RNN/SaNN)**: The SMOTE algorithm is an oversampling method. It generates a new one between two samples, avoiding the problem of repeated sampling.
- **RandomUnderSampler_(CNN/RNN/SaNN)**: RandomUnderSampler is a undersampling method, we use the RandomUnderSampler made by scikit_learn.

4.5 Compared with Baselines

To illustrate the performance improvement of our BSIL model, we compare it with the robust baseline model, which has achieved the best results in their respective tasks.

Table 2. Classification performance of the different approaches.

Model	MR	SST-2	IMDB	SPAM	CR
LSTM	61.4	76.1	78.3	87.6	37.5
CNN	51.5	30.8	73.7	80.6	66.1
SaNN	58.4	54.3	60.2	68.0	24.4
LSTM+attention	64.5	78.7	80.2	89.2	44.4
FastText	60.3	74.1	79.2	88.2	50.5
TextCNN	52.9	49.1	77.0	82.9	60.2
SMOTE_(CNN/RNN/SaNN)	73.3	79.0	81.6	89.6	54.9
RandomUnderSampler_(CNN/RNN/SaNN)	74.5	80.0	81.4	**91.0**	74.8
BSIL_LSTM	**76.1**	**80.4**	**82.1**	90.9	67.7
BSIL_CNN	72.5	67.4	80.8	88.9	**76.4**
BSIL_SaNN	75.4	74.8	80.5	86.9	71.4

Due to our framework combines CNN, RNN, and SaNN, we first compare them with these three models shown in Table 2. We can see that LSTM, CNN, and SaNN have a very low performance on the imbalanced dataset. The *F_Score* of LSTM model on CR dataset only has 37.5% and the SaNN model on CR dataset only has 24.4%. The reason is CR has the more professional vocabulary. Therefore, CR is more suitable for CNN which is better at capturing keywords but lacks the ability of long short-term memory. When the dataset is skewed, the professional vocabulary in the majority class is more than that in the minority one, so the classifier has a serious over-fitting problem. the CNN model on SST-2 only has 30.8%. SST has a high degree of context-dependency, and there are many turning words in the sentence. Therefore, the LSTM model is more suitable for capturing this kind of semantic information. In the imbalanced dataset, the semantic information of minority class is also easily covered by the majority class, resulting in semantic over-fitting. Besides, CR is also a document-level dataset. Each sample is too long, which makes it difficult for SaNN's self-attention mechanism to capture topic information. Therefore, its accuracy rate is only 24.4%.

Compared with the state-of-the-art models in Table 2, our model give the best performance on four datasets. On the SPAM dataset, the undersampling algorithm is only 0.1% higher than ours. In addition to the CR dataset, BSIL combined with LSTM have better performance, BSIL-CNN has the best performance on the CR dataset because its own CNN model is more suitable for extracting local features.

Analysis. The imbalance problem aggravates the skewed distribution of semantic information and keywords in the dataset, and our BSIL model first divides the dataset into multiple balanced data subsets and captures more useful information through the distributed learning model. Unlike the resampling method, our model does not lose useful information or generates virtual information, and ensures the original distribution of the dataset.

4.6 Ablation Experiment for Weight Selection

To illustrate the importance of weight selection in the model, we do ablation experiments on it. We remove the weight selection module from the BSIL model and retain only the distributed model.

Table 3. Ablation experiment for weight selection

Model	MR	SST-2	IMDB	SPAM	CR
Distributed_LSTM	74.5	80.0	81.6	87.6	65.2
Distributed_CNN	71.3	66.3	80.0	88.7	75.1
Distributed_SaNN	75.2	72.9	79.4	86.5	70.3
BSIL_LSTM	**76.1**	**80.4**	**82.1**	**90.9**	**67.7**
BSIL_CNN	**72.5**	**67.4**	**80.8**	**88.9**	**76.4**
BSIL_SaNN	**75.4**	**74.8**	**80.5**	**86.9**	**71.4**

Analysis. The experimental results show that the weight selection module can increase the accuracy of BSIL by 1%-2% (see Table 3). This is because the weight selection module chooses the best initialization scheme for the model. When an agent achieves a poor accuracy in the next step, the weight selection module will improve it and make it get rid of the existing bad situation.

4.7 Comparison Experiment for DML

To demonstrate the robustness of the DML, we compare the $F1\_score$ value of each agent with the final prediction result (see Table 4). The DML uses Eq. 1 to make the final predictions more accurate than the results of each agent. We also find that when BSIL_LSTM trains CR dataset, even though only $agent_3$ achieves 64.3% accuracy, while the other three agents all get very low accuracy, the final result is still 3.4% higher than that of $agent_3$. The same situation occurs when BSIL_SaNN trains CR dataset.

Table 4. BSIL framework combined with different NN-based models

Model (dataset)	$agent_1$	$agent_2$	$agent_3$	$agent_4$	Final result
BSIL_LSTM(MR)	72.4	73.4	72.7	74.5	**76.1**
BSIL_LSTM(SST-2)	78.1	75.4	80.0	–	**80.4**
BSIL_LSTM(IMDB)	77.6	80.4	81.4	80.3	**82.1**
BSIL_LSTM(SPAM)	87.4	90.7	90.9	89.0	**90.9**
BSIL_LSTM(CR)	57.5	54.8	64.3	42.8	**67.7**
BSIL_CNN(MR)	71.3	69.9	69.5	68.0	**72.5**
BSIL_CNN(SST-2)	66.3	57.7	62.8	–	**67.4**
BSIL_CNN(IMDB)	76.5	79.4	78.1	79.9	**80.8**
BSIL_CNN(SPAM)	85.9	87.1	87.7	88.7	**88.9**
BSIL_CNN(CR)	66.1	67.9	74.8	74.2	**76.4**
BSIL_SaNN(MR)	72.4	74.5	73.4	72.7	**75.4**
BSIL_SaNN(SST-2)	70.4	70.8	71.3	–	**74.8**
BSIL_SaNN(IMDB)	77.6	79.2	76.8	79.4	**80.5**
BSIL_SaNN(SPAM)	81.8	83.8	84.6	86.5	**86.9**
BSIL_SaNN(CR)	70.3	41.9	64.2	57.1	**71.4**

Analysis. DML uses the brain storm algorithm to evaluate the final classification result for each sample in the test set. Based on the better results achieved by all agents, the final classification results are improved again. The brain storm algorithm effectively utilizes the principle of the minority obeying the majority and eliminates the result with a high probability of error.

5 Conclusion

In this paper, we propose a brain storm-based framework to improve those neural networks which are not always good at imbalanced text classification by applying brain storm optimization (BSO) in sampling imbalanced datasets. Our proposal is independent of neural networks and thus our approach is more adaptable for neural networks. Besides, our approach is easy to perform better in imbalanced text classification even for those neural networks relying on strict conditions of datasets. In the future work, we are interested to investigate a fine-grained metric to characterize imbalance index in text classification since the judgement of imbalanced datasets in BSIL depends on the ratio of positive samples and negative samples.

Acknowledgments. This work is supported by the National Key Research and Development Program of China (2017YFB1401200, 2017YFC0908401) and the National Natural Science Foundation of China (61672377). Xiaowang Zhang is supported by the Peiyang Young Scholars in Tianjin University (2019XRX-0032).

References

1. Al-Stouhi, S., Reddy, K.: Transfer learning for class imbalance problems with inadequate data. Knowl. Inf. Syst. **48**(1), 201–228 (2016)
2. Charte, F., Rivera, J., del Jesus, J., Herrera, F.: REMEDIAL-HwR: tackling multilabel imbalance through label decoupling and data resampling hybridization. Neurocomputing **326**, 110–122 (2019)
3. Charte, F., Rivera, J., del Jesus, J., Herrera, F.: Addressing imbalance in multilabel classification: measures and random resampling algorithms. Neurocomputing **163**, 3–16 (2015)
4. Chen, W., Cao, Y., Sun, Y., Liu, Q., Li, Y.: Improving brain storm optimization algorithm via simplex search. arXiv, CoRR abs/1712.03166 (2017)
5. Cheng, S., Qin, Q., Chen, J., Shi, Y.: Brain storm optimization algorithm: a review. Artif. Intell. Rev. **46**(4), 445–458 (2016)
6. Datta, S., Nag, S., Mullick, S., Das, S.: Diversifying support vector machines for boosting using kernel perturbation: Applications to class imbalance and small disjuncts. arXiv, CoRR abs/1712.08493 (2017)
7. He, H., Garcia, A.: Learning from imbalanced data. IEEE Trans. Knowl. Data Eng. **9**, 1263–1284 (2008)
8. Khan, H., Hayat, M., Bennamoun, M., Sohel, A., Togneri, R.: Cost-sensitive learning of deep feature representations from imbalanced data. IEEE Trans. Neural Netw. Learn. Syst. **29**(8), 3573–3587 (2018)
9. Kubat, M., Holte, C., Matwin, S.: Machine learning for the detection of oil spills in satellite radar images. Mach. Learn. **30**(2–3), 195–215 (1998)
10. Lai, S., Xu, L., Liu, K., Zhao, J.: Recurrent convolutional neural networks for text classification. In: Proceedings of AAAI 2015, pp. 2267–2273 (2015)
11. Lin, C., Tsai, F., Hu, H., Jhang, S.: Clustering-based undersampling in class-imbalanced data. Inf. Sci. **409**, 17–26 (2017)
12. Moreo A., Esuli A., Sebastiani F.: Distributional random oversampling for imbalanced text classification. In: Proceedings of SIGIR 2016, pp. 805–808 (2016)
13. Sun Y., Kamel M., Wang Y.: Boosting for learning multiple classes with imbalanced class distribution. In: Proceedings of ICDM 2017, pp. 592–602 (2006)
14. Wang, J., Chen, Y., Hao, S., Feng, W., Shen, Z.: Balanced distribution adaptation for transfer learning. In: Proceedings of ICDM 2017, pp. 1129–1134 (2017)
15. Wang, S., Minku, L., Yao, X.: Resampling-based ensemble methods for online class imbalance learning. IEEE Trans. Knowl. Data Eng. **27**(5), 1356–1368 (2015)

A Key-Phrase Aware End2end Neural Response Generation Model

Jun Xu[1], Haifeng Wang[2], Zhengyu Niu[2], Hua Wu[2], and Wanxiang Che[1(✉)]

[1] Research Center for Social Computing and Information Retrieval
Harbin Institute of Technology, Harbin, China
{jxu,car}@ir.hit.edu.cn

[2] Baidu Inc., Beijing, China
{wanghaifeng,niuzhengyu,wu_hua}@baidu.com

Abstract. Previous Seq2Seq models for chitchat assume that each word in the target sequence has direct corresponding relationship with words in the source sequence, and all the target words are equally important. However, it is invalid since sometimes only parts of the response are relevant to the message. For models with the above mentioned assumption, irrelevant response words might have a negative impact on the performance in semantic association modeling that is a core task for open-domain dialogue modeling. In this work, to address the challenge of semantic association modeling, we automatically recognize key-phrases from responses in training data, and then feed this supervision information into an enhanced key-phrase aware seq2seq model for better capability in semantic association modeling. This model consists of an encoder and a two-layer decoder, where the encoder and the first layer sub-decoder is mainly for learning semantic association and the second layer sub-decoder is for responses generation. Experimental results show that this model can effectively utilize the key phrase information for semantic association modeling, and it can significantly outperform baseline models in terms of response appropriateness and informativeness.

Keywords: Key-phrase · End2end · Neural dialog model

1 Introduction

Previous Seq2Seq model for chitchat [10,14] based on the following assumption: each word in the target sequence have direct corresponding relationship with the source sequence, and all the target words are equally important. However, this assumption of seq2seq becomes invalid in the context of chitchat, sometimes only a part of the response has semantic association relationship with the message. Given an utterance, humans may initiate a new topic in response so that the dialogue can continue. We use an example to illustrate this kind of phenomenon in dialogue data, shown as follows:

J. Tang et al. (Eds.): NLPCC 2019, LNAI 11839, pp. 65–77, 2019.
https://doi.org/10.1007/978-3-030-32236-6_6

message: Playing football exhausts me.
response: You can take a rest. By the way, how about going shopping tomorrow?

The phrase "take a rest" responds upon the phrase "exhausts me" in the message. But other content-word parts in the response, such as "going shopping tomorrow", are irrelevant to the message. Therefore, there is semantic association relationship between "exhausts me" and "take a rest", but not between "exhausts me" and "going shopping tomorrow". In this paper, phrases (from the response) being relevant to the message are called **key-phrases**, e.g., "take a rest". This phenomenon is quite common[1]. Therefore, the underlying assumption of previous seq2seq based chitchat models is not valid anymore. For models with the above mentioned assumption, irrelevant response words, or non-key-phrase response words, might deteriorate their performance in semantic association modeling.

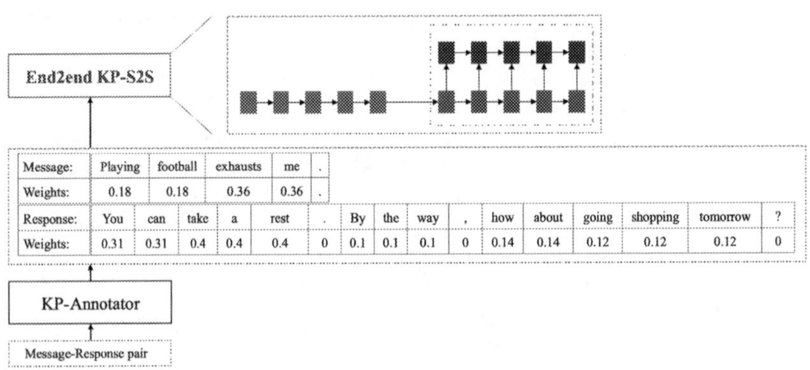

Fig. 1. The architecture of our system which consists of two modules.

In this work, to address the challenge of semantic association modeling, we automatically recognize key-phrases from responses in training data, and then feed these supervision information into an enhanced seq2seq model for better capability in semantic association modeling. For key-phrase recognition in training data, we employ a key-phrase annotator (**KP-Annotator** for short) to calculate weights for each word in responses, where KP-Annotator is built on a manually annotated corpus in a supervised way. Each word weight indicates how much a word in the response is semantically associated with the message. It is expected that response words closely associated with messages have higher weights. Phrases formed by these high-weight words are considered as

[1] We annotated key-phrases for responses from randomly sampled 200 message-response pairs, extracted from Baidu Tieba. We found that there are 78% pairs in which non-key-phrases exist, or only a part of the response is relevant to the message.

key-phrases. Then with message-response pairs and word weights as inputs, we employ a key-phrase aware two-layer-decoder based seq2seq model (**KP-S2S** for short) for semantic association modeling and response generation in a joint way, instead of the pipelined approach in previous works [8,15,18]. During training procedure, we expect that KP-S2S will pay more attention on key-phrases, or important response words, with the use of word-weight information. Then it will significantly reduce the negative impact of non-key-phrase words on semantic association modeling.

KP-S2S consists of an encoder and a two-layer decoder. The first layer sub-decoder (a vanilla LSTM decoding unit) is for semantic association modeling, and the second layer sub-decoder (an enhanced LSTM decoding unit) is for response generation. For semantic association modeling, we employ weighted loss function mechanism and weighted learning rate mechanism in the encoder and the first layer sub-decoder during training procedure. With the two mechanisms, we "mask" non-key-phrase words during gradient calculation and parameter updating in a soft way, and thus it can help semantic association modeling between messages and relevant parts in responses. The first layer sub-decoder is expected to enable KP-S2S to promote informative and appropriate responses, and downgrade generic or inappropriate responses. The second layer sub-decoder is responsible for generation of the whole response. We expect that the use of the second layer sub-decoder can help generate fluent and appropriate responses. In test procedure of KP-S2S, no extra information (e.g., weights of words in a message) is required.

We conduct an empirical study of our model and a set of carefully selected state-of-the-art baseline models on a large Chinese dialogue corpus from Baidu Tieba. Experiment results confirm that in comparison with baselines, our model can produce a much higher ratio of appropriate and informative responses.

In summary, this paper makes the following contributions:

- To the best of our knowledge, this is the first work to explicitly reveal semantic association information in a message-response pair. These annotation results could be applicable for other data-driven conversation models. We demonstrate their effectiveness on HGFU model in our experiment.
- We propose an end2end key-phrase aware hierarchical response generation model with a two-layer decoder. It can effectively learn semantic association between words from message-response pairs, and generate a much higher ratio of informative and appropriate responses in comparison with baselines.

2 The Proposed Approach

2.1 The Architecture

Figure 1 provides the architecture of our system, consisting of (1) Key-phrase annotator (KP-Annotator for short), to annotate key-phrase information in training data and (2) Key-phrase aware seq2seq model (KP-S2S for short), to learn a response generation model.

2.2 Key-Phrase Annotator (KP-Annotator)

Phrase Extraction. We use a Chinese dependency parser [16] to obtain the tree-structure of an utterance, and then extract all grammatical phrases that meet following requirements:

- There is one and only one dependency edge in the phrase, where the edge comes from a word outside of the phrase, to ensure the phrase is "grammatical";
- Words within the phrase are consecutive in the utterance;
- The phrase contains at least two Chinese characters and at most four words;

Scoring Network. We use two one-layer RNNs to encode a phrase Q and an utterance U into s_Q and s_U respectively, and calculate their relevance score as: $s(Q, U) = sigmoid(MLP([s_Q; s_U]))$, where $MLP(.)$ is a multi-layer perceptron. We call this relevance score the weight of the phrase Q.

We train this network with Max-Margin loss such that $s(Q^+, U)$ is larger than $s(Q^-, U)$ with at least Δ threshold, and the objective function is given by

$$L_s = max(\Delta - s(Q^+, U) + s(Q^-, U), 0), \tag{1}$$

where Q^- is a non-key-phrase co-occuring with a key-phrase Q^+ in the same utterance. Q^- and Q^+ are labeled manually. Finally, each word in the response is annotated with the maximum weight of phrases that contain the word (0 if no phrase includes this word). We calculate weights for words in messages similarly.

2.3 Model: KP-S2S

Figure 2 provides the architecture of KP-S2S, which consists of an encoder and a two-layer decoder. The encoder and the first layer sub-decoder are equipped with two weighted mechanism in the training procedure, to effectively capture semantic association between a message and a response. The second layer sub-decoder is designed to balance the generation of key-phrase information and other parts in the response.

The Model. As shown in Fig. 2, architecture of the encoder and the first layer sub-decoder is similar to seq2seq model with attention mechanism. The input to the second layer sub-decoder at time t consists of (1) the t-th output of the first layer sub-decoder m_t, which is calculated by combining the t-th hidden state of the first layer sub-decoder s_t with the t-th attention vector a_t, and (2) the word embedding $e'_{y_{t-1}}$. Note that $e'_{y_{t-1}}$ is independent of the embedding $e_{y_{t-1}}$ used in the first layer sub-decoder, as the first layer sub-decoder embedding e_{y-1} is designed to mainly focus on modeling semantic association between messages and responses, which is different from generating response utterances required by the second layer sub-decoder. The t-th output of response generator is calculated by the t-th hidden state r_t and m_t as follows:

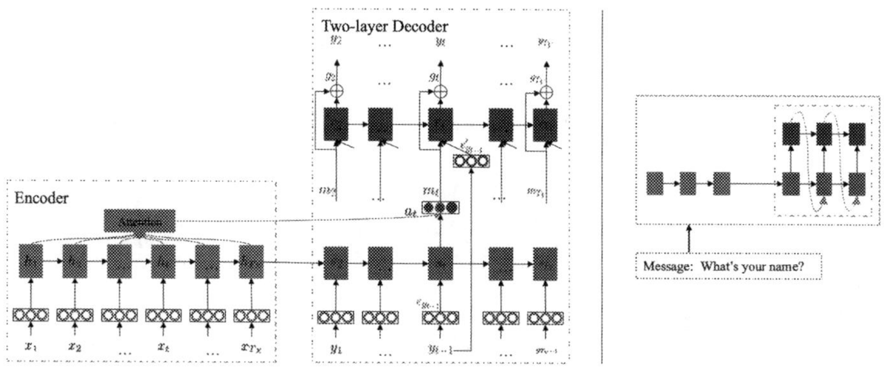

Fig. 2. An overview of the end2end KP-S2S model. The left is the proposed KP-S2S model, and the right is the testing procedure where only message is required for response generation.

$$g_t = W^o[r_t; m_t], \tag{2}$$

$$r_t = F(r_{t-1}, W^i[m_t; e'_{y_{t-1}}]), \tag{3}$$

where F is the LSTM cell, m_t is the output state, W^o and W^i are parameter matrices and $[;]$ denotes a concatenation operation.

With Eq. 3, the i-th output of the second layer sub-decoder is generated based on combination of the input message, predicted key-phrase information (i.e. the output of the first layer sub-decoder) and words ahead of y_i in the response. KP-S2S is expected to generate appropriate and informative responses since (1) the encoder and the first layer sub-decoder focus on modeling key-phrases association, which is helpful to generate informative responses, and (2) the second layer sub-decoder is for the generation procedure of the whole response, beneficial to generate fluent responses.

Two Mechanism. To effectively learn semantic association between a message and a response, two mechanisms, weighted loss function mechanism and weighted learning rate mechanism, are applied to the encoder and the first layer sub-decoder respectively.

- Weighted Loss Function Mechanism We introduce a weighted loss function in which the contribution of each response word to the loss is directly weighted by its weight calculated by the KP-Annotator. We call this weighted loss function as L_{focus} as it focus on words in key-phrases (typically have high weight), it is defined as:

$$L_{focus}(X, Y) = \sum_{t=2}^{T_Y} w_{y_t} L(y_t, m_t; M), \tag{4}$$

where L is the standard loss function in Seq2Seq, $M \in \mathbb{R}^{|V| \times d_h}$ is the output word decoding matrix, m_t is the output of the decoder at time t, y_t is the (t)-th word in response utterance Y. Equation 4 means that response words from key-phrases are more important for the model loss, in comparison with words from non-key-phrases.
$L_{focus}(X, Y)$ is utilized as an auxiliary loss to help capture semantic association with the help of key phrase information (i.e. response words' weight assigned by KP-Annotator).

- Weighted Learning Rate Mechanism
Semantic association relationships captured by the encoder and the first layer decoder are partly stored in the embeddings of words in responses, it is unreasonable to update embeddings of words that not relevant to message. However, Stochastic Gradient Descent (**SGD**) usually keeps a fixed learning rate for all parameters at each optimizing step. In this work, we propose a weighted learning rate mechanism, in which learning rate are adaptive for each word based on its weight. Specifically, embeddings of words in responses are updated at each optimization step as follows:

$$e_{y_t}^{new} = e_{y_t} - (w_{y_t}\lambda)\nabla_{y_t}, \tag{5}$$

where e_{y_t} is the decoder embedding of the t-th word in a response, w_{y_t} is the weight of word y_t and λ is the learning rate kept by SGD.
With Eq. 6, representation learning of words from key-phrases will be guided by the loss more than those from non-key-phrases.
Meantime, as illustrated in [15], humans tend to focus on certain aspects in message to respond, rather than responds on all content in message. It indicates that sometimes not all content in message are semantically associated with response. Taken this into consideration, we utilize weighted learning rate mechanism in the updating of encoder embeddings as follows:

$$e_{x_t}^{new} = e_{x_t} - (w_{x_t}\lambda)\nabla_{x_t}, \tag{6}$$

where e_{x_t} is the encoder embedding of the t-th word in a message, w_{x_t} is the weight of x_t.

With the use of above-mentioned mechanisms, we make our model pay more attention to words from key-phrases. It helps our model to learn semantic association between messages and relevant parts in responses.

2.4 Optimization and Prediction

The loss function is defined as the sum of the standard negative log-likelihood loss utilized in optimizing Se2Seq $L_{generator}(X, Y)$ and $L_{focus}(X, Y)$:

$$L_{KP\_S2S}(X, Y) = L_{generator}(X, Y) + L_{focus}(X, Y).$$

We adopt SGD for model optimization, except that word embeddings the first layer sub-decoder and the encoder are updated with Eqs. 5 and 6.

In the testing procedure, **No extra information** (e.g. weights) besides message itself is needed for response generation as shown in Fig. 2, and there is not internal step of predicting key-phrases.

3 Experiments and Results

3.1 Datasets

For an empirical study of our system, we first collect 20,000,000 message-response (m-r) pairs from Baidu Tieba[2]. Then, we perform Chinese word segmentation for each pair with an open-source lexical analysis tool[3] [1]. We split D into three subsets, D_{train} (3.2m pairs), $D_{validation}$ (9k pairs) and D_{test} (9k pairs). We take the most frequent 50,000 words in D_{train} as the vocabulary and other out-of-vocabulary words as UNKs. We perform word weight calculation on message-response pairs from D_{train} with the use of KP-Annotator.

The training/validation/testing set of KP-Annotator consists of 78k/19k/19k response-phrase (from corresponding message) pairs labeled by human, with equal share of positive pairs and negative pairs.

3.2 Evaluation Metrics

Automatic Metrics. Following previous works, we apply three kinds of embedding-based metrics introduced in [6] and Distinct-i metric was proposed in [3].

Human Evaluation. We randomly sample 300 cases and invite three annotators to evaluate the quality of generated responses from 4 models. For each message-response pair, annotators are asked to rate with a score from {"0", "+1", "+2"}. A response will be rated with "0" if it is inappropriate as an reply to a message. We define inappropriateness from following aspects: (1) disfluenency: a response is not fluent, (2) irrelevance: a response is not semantically relevant to a message, (3) self-contradiction: there is internal semantic conflict within a response. If a response is appropriate but uninformative, it will be rated with "+1". If it is both appropriate and informative, then it will be rated with "+2".

Moreover, we report the appropriate rate (p_{cue_words}) of predicted cue word or coarse words in pipelined models, annotators are invited to label whether predicted words are appropriate to respond given message or not.

[2] https://tieba.baidu.com.
[3] https://github.com/baidu/lac.

3.3 Systems

We conduct empirical comparison of our model with four state-of-the-art models, including (1) **MMI-bidi** [3] which is a seq2seq model using Maximum Mutual Information (MMI) as the objective; (2) **CMHAM** [15] which is Seq2Seq model enhanced with constrained multi-head attention mechanism; (3) **MrRNN** [8] which is a pipelined content-introducing model; and (4) **HGFU** [18] which incorporates auxiliary cue word information into seq2seq.

For fair comparison, decoder in all baseline models are set as a two-layer RNN. The vocab size is 50k, hidden size is 512, embedding size is 512, and model are optimized with adam (lr = 0.001). Embeddings in encoder and decoder are separated.

HGFU^{+}: We utilize a weighted PMI statistic on the same 0.4 billion Tieba message-response pairs, which only influent the prediction of cue word in the testing procedure. Specifically, the concurrency times of word x_i and word y_j is counted as w_{y_j}, the occurrence times of word x_i is still counted as 1 and the occurrence times of word y_j is counted as w_{y_j}. We use the model trained in HGFU for the testing procedure.

KP-S2S: We implement KP-S2S shown in Fig. 2. For training of KP-Annotator, we manually label key-phrases in a message for given response on 100k message-response pairs. Δ is set to 0.1

3.4 Evaluation Results for KP-Annotator

The KP-Annotator can be regarded as a binary classification task. The AUC score of KP-Annotator is 0.864. It indicates that given s message, the weight of key-phrases (i.e. positive) in response will be higher than non-key-phrases (i.e. negative) in 86.4% of cases.

3.5 Evaluation Results for KP-S2S

Table 1 presents human evaluation results of KP-S2S and baseline models. KP-S2S is significantly better (sign test, p-value less than 0,0001) than all the baselines on test set.

We see that in terms of both appropriateness and informativeness, KP-S2S significantly outperforms baseline models. Moreover, KP-S2S tends to generate less inappropriate responses than the baselines, its ratio of responses being rated with "0" is significantly lower than the baselines. It is noticed that with the help of MMI-bidi, S2SAtt still tends to generate inappropriate or generic responses, as shown in Table 1. Moreover, for CMHAM, its multi-head attention mechanism leads to better performance in comparison with MMI-bidi/MrRNN/HGFU, a higher ratio of "+2", and a lower ratio of "0". It indicates CMHAM has a better capability in semantic association modeling. This result is consistent with the conclusion in [15]. But CMHAM still generates more than half of inappropriate responses in test set, and its ratio of responses being rated with "1" (typically safe responses) is even higher than other baselines except MMI-bidi. It indicates

Table 1. Results of human evaluation. p_{cue_words} stands for the appropriate rate of predicted words for given message. The kappa values of models are all higher than 0.5

s	+2	+1	0	Kappa	Avg-score	p_{cue_words}
MMI-bidi	0.16	0.23	0.61	0.79	0.55	-
CMHAM	0.27	0.15	0.58	0.78	0.68	-
MrRNN	0.19	0.08	0.73	0.56	0.46	0.45
HGFU	0.27	0.10	0.63	0.69	0.64	0.53
HGFU$^+$	0.32	0.09	0.57	0.62	0.73	0.69
KP-S2S	**0.47**	**0.07**	**0.46**	0.65	**1.01**	-

that CMHAM cannot effectively deal with irrelevant response words in training data, which interfere with the alignment between message words and relevant response words.

Further, in HGFU$^+$, weighted PMI statistic is utilized to help capturing semantic association between messages and relevant parts in responses, irrelevant parts in responses are largely ignored due to their relatively low weights. In Table 1, we see the appropriate rates of predicted cue word by weighted PMI is increased to 69%, achieving a 16% absolute promotion compared to original PMI. Higher appropriate rates of predicted cue word leads to better generation performance in comparison to original HGFU, the average score increased by 14%. Meantime, we can see that the appropriate rates of predicted cue word or coarse words have a close positive correlation with the average scores of models.

Table 2. Results of automatic evaluation. KP-S2S is significantly better (except p-value of CMHAM vs KP-S2S is 0.0252) than all the baselines.

Models	Emb. Average	Emb. Greedy	Emb. Extrema	Distinct-1	Distinct-2
MMI-bidi	0.74	0.58	0.51	0.07	0.22
CMHAM	0.80	0.61	0.52	0.06	0.22
MrRNN	0.79	0.59	0.52	0.04	0.22
HGFU	0.77	0.59	0.50	0.10	0.36
HGFU$^+$	0.79	0.60	0.52	0.10	0.37
KP-S2S	**0.82**	**0.62**	**0.54**	**0.13**	**0.44**

Table 2 provides the results on automatic evaluation. We see that in terms of embedding based metrics, KP-S2S performs better than the baselines. This results are consistent with human evaluation result in Table 1.

Messages	Generated Responses
去与不去，在于你能不能耐得住寂寞了 (Go or not, depends on whether you can stand loneliness.)	[MMI-bidi] 好的，谢谢，我去看看。(OK, thank you. I'll check it out.) [CMHAM] 我是寂寞了。(I'm lonely.) [MrRNN] 好的，我也寂寞了。(Okay, I'm lonely.) [HGFU] *我耐不住寂寞的寂寞 (I can't bear the loneliness of loneliness.) [**HGFU$^+$**] 我不寂寞啊。(I'm not lonely.) [**KP-S2S**] 单身狗出去交个朋友不行吗? (Can't a single dog go out to make friends?)
多注意，我都是裹的严严实实 (Pay more attention to it. I am wrapped up in my clothes.)	[MMI-bidi] *好的，谢谢，我去试试。(OK, thank you. I'll try.) [CMHAM] *我的是的，你可以试试。(Mine is like this, you can try.) [MrRNN] 好的。(All right.) [HGFU] 嗯，我也裹着严严实实的羽绒服 (Well, I'm also wrapped in a tight down jacket.) [**HGFU$^+$**] 嗯、我裹着被子了。(Well, I'm wrapped in quilts.) [**KP-S2S**] 裹得严严实实，不要感冒 (Wrap up tightly and do not catch cold.)
银行开户慢死了，等了第六天了，还在等 (It is too slowly to open a bank account, I have waited for six days, and still waiting.)	[MMI-bidi] *是啊，我也是这么想的。(Yes, I think so too.) [CMHAM] 好的，我也在等了。(Okay, I'm waiting, too.) [MrRNN] *是什么银行啊，我在哪去了? 还是要用哪个银行。(What bank is it? Where will I go? Which bank to use?) [HGFU] 我也是六天。(I am also six days.) [**HGFU$^+$**] 顺丰么? (Is it expressed by Shun Feng Express?) [**KP-S2S**] 我建议你去工行 (I suggest you to go to the Industrial and Commercial Bank of China.)
这是光驱接口，得用支架 (This is a CD driver interface. It needs a bracket.)	[MMI-bidi] *我的也是光驱。(Mine is also a CD driver.) [CMHAM] 这个是接口么 (Is this interface?) [MrRNN] *谢谢大佬，我还以为是个好光驱啊。(Thank you, big guy. I thought it was a good CD driver.) [HGFU] *这个是什么光驱? 我是这的 (What kind of CD drive is this? I'm this one.) [**HGFU$^+$**] 这个是什么光驱接口? 我是这的 (What kind of CD drive is this? I'm this one.) [**KP-S2S**] 你用的什么支架啊，我在网上买? (What kind of interface do you use? I will buy it online.)

Fig. 3. Examples of generated responses. Inappropriate responses are labeled with *, and underlines indicate semantic association relationships captured by KP-S2S.

3.6 Case Study

For case study, we compared KP-S2S with baselines using some examples, as shown in Fig. 3. In Case 1, the response generated by KP-S2S, "Can't a single dog go out to make friends?", contains a phrase "single dog" which is semantically associated with word "loneliness" in the message. In other Cases, there is also such kind of semantic association between the response generated by KP-S2S and the message, e.g., "catch cold" and "wrapped up in my clothes", "go to the Industrial and Commercial Bank of China" and "open an bank account", "buy it online" and "needs a interface", "search in Baidu" and "how to match the card". It indicates that KP-S2S can successfully learn semantic association from the training data, and such association relations can be seen as knowledge to some extend, as shown in Case 1, 2 and 4. It seems that this kind of knowledge implicitly represented in KP-S2S model bring a significant performance improvement in terms of response appropriateness and informativeness. In contrast, baseline models fail to capture such kind of semantic association.

4 Related Works

Lots of work in chitchat focus on learning response generation models from large scale human-to-human dialogue corpus within a seq2seq framework [3,4,7,9,10,12–14,17,19,20].

Tao et al. [15] tried to extract different semantic aspects from a message and the whole response is expected to focus on only a few words in each semantic aspect. Semantic aspects are calculated by projecting hidden states of the encoder with k different parameter matrices. However, the problem that irrelevant parts interfere with the association modeling between messages and relevant parts in responses still exists. Serban et al. [8] tried to model high-level semantic association between coarse words(e.g. entities) from messages and responses respectively. Coarse words are different from key-phrase as they are restricted to be specific categories of words, including nouns, manually selected verbs and technical entities in utterances. Moreover, as coarse words can come from both relevant and irrelevant part in the response, the problem that irrelevant parts interfere with the association modeling between message and relevant parts still exists. Mou et al. [7] and Yao et al. [18] proposed to introduce cue words to the model, they use PMI scores to model the semantic association between message words and response words. However, irrelevant parts still interfere with the association modeling between message and relevant parts. Only 53% of the predicted cue words based on PMI are appropriate to respond given message.

Many work [5, 11] attempted to calculate quality scores for message-response pairs to promote contribution of high-quality instances to the training. These scores are calculated and utilized at utterance level. Lei et al. [2] using reinforcement learning to put more weights on informative words, however, it is for task-oriented dialogue systems rather than open-domain dialogue.

5 Conclusion

In this paper, we showed that sometimes only a part of response has semantic association relationships with the message. We built a key-phrase annotation model to reveal semantic association in message-response pairs. These annotation results are applicable for other data-driven conversation models. Further, We proposed a key-phrase aware end2end neural response generation model (KP-S2S) that can effectively capture semantic association between messages and relevant parts in responses. Experimental results showed that KP-S2S can generate more appropriate and informative responses than state-of-the-art baseline models. In addition, simple use of key-phrase information in training data can bring performance improvement for a cue-word based response generation model in previous works [18].

References

1. Jiao, Z., Sun, S., Sun, K.: Chinese lexical analysis with deep bi-gru-crf network. arXiv preprint arXiv:1807.01882 (2018)
2. Lei, W., Jin, X., Kan, M.Y., Ren, Z., He, X., Yin, D.: Sequicity: simplifying task-oriented dialogue systems with single sequence-to-sequence architectures. In: Proceedings of the 56th Annual Meeting of the Association for Computational Linguistics (Volume 1: Long Papers), vol. 1, pp. 1437–1447 (2018)

3. Li, J., Galley, M., Brockett, C., Gao, J., Dolan, B.: A diversity-promoting objective function for neural conversation models. In: Proceedings of the 2016 Conference of the North American Chapter of the Association for Computational Linguistics: Human Language Technologies, pp. 110–119 (2016)
4. Li, J., Galley, M., Brockett, C., Spithourakis, G., Gao, J., Dolan, B.: A persona-based neural conversation model. In: Proceedings of the 54th Annual Meeting of the Association for Computational Linguistics (Volume 1: Long Papers), vol. 1, pp. 994–1003 (2016)
5. Lison, P., Bibauw, S.: Not all dialogues are created equal: instance weighting for neural conversational models. In: Proceedings of the 18th Annual SIGdial Meeting on Discourse and Dialogue, pp. 384–394 (2017)
6. Liu, C.W., Lowe, R., Serban, I., Noseworthy, M., Charlin, L., Pineau, J.: How not to evaluate your dialogue system: an empirical study of unsupervised evaluation metrics for dialogue response generation. In: Proceedings of the 2016 Conference on Empirical Methods in Natural Language Processing, pp. 2122–2132 (2016)
7. Mou, L., Song, Y., Yan, R., Li, G., Zhang, L., Jin, Z.: Sequence to backward and forward sequences: a content-introducing approach to generative short-text conversation. In: Proceedings of COLING 2016, The 26th International Conference on Computational Linguistics: Technical Papers, pp. 3349–3358 (2016)
8. Serban, I.V., et al.: Multiresolution recurrent neural networks: an application to dialogue response generation. In: AAAI, pp. 3288–3294 (2017)
9. Serban, I.V., Sordoni, A., Bengio, Y., Courville, A.C., Pineau, J.: Building end-to-end dialogue systems using generative hierarchical neural network models. In: AAAI, vol. 16, pp. 3776–3784 (2016)
10. Shang, L., Lu, Z., Li, H.: Neural responding machine for short-text conversation. In: Proceedings of the 53rd Annual Meeting of the Association for Computational Linguistics and the 7th International Joint Conference on Natural Language Processing (Volume 1: Long Papers), vol. 1, pp. 1577–1586 (2015)
11. Shang, M., Fu, Z., Peng, N., Feng, Y., Zhao, D., Yan, R.: Learning to converse with noisy data: generation with calibration. In: IJCAI, pp. 4338–4344 (2018)
12. Shao, Y., Gouws, S., Britz, D., Goldie, A., Strope, B., Kurzweil, R.: Generating high-quality and informative conversation responses with sequence-to-sequence models. In: Proceedings of the 2017 Conference on Empirical Methods in Natural Language Processing, pp. 2210–2219 (2017)
13. Song, Y., Yan, R., Feng, Y., Zhang, Y., Zhao, D., Zhang, M.: Towards a neural conversation model with diversity net using determinantal point processes. In: AAAI (2018)
14. Sordoni, A., et al.: A neural network approach to context-sensitive generation of conversational responses. In: Proceedings of the 2015 Conference of the North American Chapter of the Association for Computational Linguistics: Human Language Technologies, pp. 196–205 (2015)
15. Tao, C., Gao, S., Shang, M., Wu, W., Zhao, D., Yan, R.: Get the point of my utterance! learning towards effective responses with multi-head attention mechanism. In: IJCAI, pp. 4418–4424 (2018)
16. Wu, X., et al.: Generalization of words for Chinese dependency parsing. In: Proceedings of IWPT 2013, pp. 73–81 (2013)
17. Xing, C., et al.: Topic aware neural response generation. In: AAAI. vol. 17, pp. 3351–3357 (2017)

18. Yao, L., Zhang, Y., Feng, Y., Zhao, D., Yan, R.: Towards implicit content-introducing for generative short-text conversation systems. In: Proceedings of the 2017 Conference on Empirical Methods in Natural Language Processing, pp. 2190–2199 (2017)
19. Zhang, R., Guo, J., Fan, Y., Lan, Y., Xu, J., Cheng, X.: Learning to control the specificity in neural response generation. In: Proceedings of the 56th Annual Meeting of the Association for Computational Linguistics (Volume 1: Long Papers), vol. 1, pp. 1108–1117 (2018)
20. Zhou, G., Luo, P., Cao, R., Lin, F., Chen, B., He, Q.: Mechanism-aware neural machine for dialogue response generation. In: AAAI, pp. 3400–3407 (2017)

A Hierarchical Model with Recurrent Convolutional Neural Networks for Sequential Sentence Classification

Xinyu Jiang[1], Bowen Zhang[2], Yunming Ye[1(✉)], and Zhenhua Liu[3]

[1] School of Computer Science and Technology, Harbin Institute of Technology, Shenzhen, China
yym@hit.edu.cn

[2] School of Computer Science and Technology, Harbin Institute of Technology, Harbin, China

[3] NLP Group, Gridsum, Beijing, China

Abstract. Hierarchical neural networks approaches have achieved outstanding results in the latest sequential sentence classification research work. However, it is challenging for the model to consider both the local invariant features and word dependent information of the sentence. In this work, we concentrate on the sentence representation and context modeling components that influence the effects of the hierarchical architecture. We present a new approach called SR-RCNN to generate more precise sentence encoding which leverage complementary strength of bi-directional recurrent neural network and text convolutional neural network to capture contextual and literal relevance information. Afterwards, statement-level encoding vectors are modeled to capture the intrinsic relations within surrounding sentences. In addition, we explore the applicability of attention mechanisms and conditional random fields to the task. Our model advances sequential sentence classification in medical abstracts to new state-of-the-art performance.

Keywords: Sequential sentence classification · Hierarchical neural networks · Sentence representation

1 Introduction

Text classification is an important task in many areas of natural language processing (NLP) which assigns pre-defined categories to free-text documents [26]. Most traditional high-performance text classification models are linear statistical models, including Naive Bayes [13], Support Vector Machine (SVM) [10,33], Maximum Entropy Models [10], Hidden Markov Models (HMM) [23] and Conditional Random Fields (CRF) [11,12,16], which rely heavily on numerous carefully hand-engineered features. In recent years, non-linear deep neural networks (DNN) which do not require manual features are broadly applied to text classification with excellent result. Many approaches [6,17,21,28,35] are

J. Tang et al. (Eds.): NLPCC 2019, LNAI 11839, pp. 78–89, 2019.
https://doi.org/10.1007/978-3-030-32236-6_7

commonly based on convolutional neural network (CNN) or recurrent neural network (RNN) or a combination of them. However, sentence-level texts are usually sequential (for example, sentences in a document or utterances in a dialog). The above-mentioned works do not take into account sequence order correlation characteristics of natural languages.

In order to distinguish from the general text or sentence classification, the categorization of sentences appearing in sequence is called the sequential sentence classification task [8].Specifically, the classification of each single sentence is related to the element categories of the surrounding sentences, which is different from the general sentence classification that does not involve context. This task is close to the sequence labeling task [14,24,30] which achieves assigning a categorical tag to each member of a series of observations and most approaches for implementing sequence labeling use bi-directional recurrent neural network (bi-RNN) and various extensions to the architecture.

There has been a considerable amount of work in text classification and sequence labeling, but much less work has been reported on the sequential sentence classification task, where categories of surrounding sentences have a great influence on the prediction of the central sentence. To the best of our knowledge, the first approach based on artificial neural network (ANN) to classify sequential short-text (dialog) was proposed by Lee and Dernoncourt [22], but only adding sequential information from preceding utterances. Subsequently, Dernoncourt et al. [9] presented a neural network structure based on both token and character embedding and used a CRF optimization layer to constrain the sequence results. Currently, the most influential approach obtained state-of-the-art results is due to Jin and Szolovits [15], in which the authors make use of the contextual information through adding a long short-term memory (LSTM) layer to processes encoded sentences. These works either introducing an RNN module or a CNN module to separately encode the sentence composition from the token embedding. However, on the one hand, the ability of CNN to extract local n-gram patterns depends on the fixed window size without considering the semantic relations and complicated syntactic of the sentence as a whole. On the other hand, RNN is able to capture tokens dependencies but ignore task-specific features on the feature vector dimension, which perhaps is essential for sentence representation.

In this paper, we present a novel hierarchical neural network architecture to tackle the sequential sentence classification task. Our model is mainly based on two critical components: sentence representation and context modeling. In the sentence representation component, we develop the SR-RCNN approach that is designed to capture both words hiding properties and sequential correlation features for producing the more precise sentences semantic. To benefit from the advantages of CNN and RNN, we first take the bi-directional recurrent structure that introduces appreciably less noise to keep a wider range of word sorting characters when learning the token embedding in a sentence. Second, we combine original word representation and transferred statement information as input to CNN for effectively model higher-level representation of sentences. In the context modeling component, we add the multilayer bi-RNN to enrich the semantic contextual information from preceding and succeeding sentences. In order to verify our ideas, we systematically analyze our model on two benchmarking datasets: NICTA-PIBOSO [16] and PubMed RCT [8]. Our main contributions can be summarized as follows:

1. We introduce a new neural network approach that relies on global and local grammatical patterns to model context relation between sentences for sequential sentence classification. Moreover, we consider two different alternative output strategies to predict the sequential labels.
2. Inspired by the previous best performing research work, we propose the SR-RCNN algorithm based on CNN and RNN which provide complementary linguistic information to optimize the sentence encoding vectors.
3. We report empirical results that the attention mechanism is more suitable for learning weights before the bi-RNN introduces text long-distance sequence features and whether adding a CRF layer to constraint the label sequence results depends on the specific dataset.
4. Our approach effectively improves the performance for sentence level classification in medical scientific abstracts when compared to the previous state-of-the-art methods.

2 Model

The major framework of our approach for sequential sentence classification is displayed in Fig. 1. In this section, we will discuss each component (layer) of our neural network architecture in detail from bottom to top.

2.1 Word Representation

The bottom layer of the model structure is word representation, also known as word embedding [2], which maps tokens from discrete one-hot representations to dense real-valued vectors in a low-dimensional space. All the word vectors are stacked in the embedding matrix $W_{word} \in \mathbb{R}^{d \times |v|}$, where d is the dimension of the word vector and $|v|$ is the vocabulary of the dataset. Given a sentence comprising l words, we denote the sentence as $x = \{x_1, x_2, \ldots, x_l\}$, where x_i is the id of ith word in the vocabulary. Each sentence is converted into corresponding word vectors representation by embedding lookup. The embedding matrix W can be pre-trained from text corpus by embedding learning algorithms [3,25,29].

2.2 Sentence Encoding

CNN is good at extracting position-invariant features and RNN is able to flexibly model sequence dependencies for text classification [34]. We propose an algorithm that combines the capability of text-CNN [18] and bi-RNN [31] called SR-RCNN to enhance feature extraction and get the representation vector of the sentence.

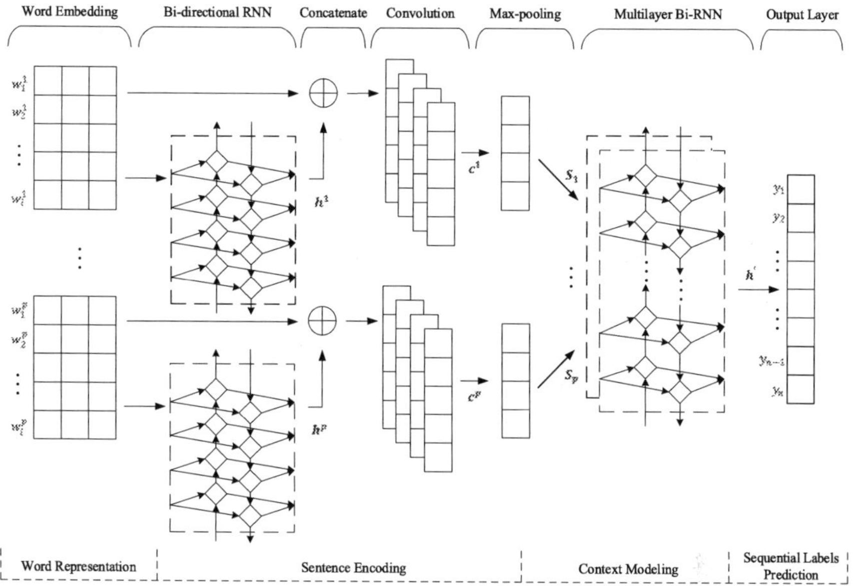

Fig. 1. The proposed neural network model architecture for sequential sentence classification.

We fed the sentence embedding $w = \{w_1, w_2, \ldots, w_l\}$ into bi-RNN to automatically extracts the context-dependent features within a statement. Let $h = \{h_1, h_2, \ldots, h_l\}$ be the hidden representations output from the bi-RNN layer. Then, adding splicing $h_{1:l}$ and original word representation $w_{1:l}$ as the r input to the text-CNN to obtain more local features by one-dimensional convolution in the initial vocabulary information and the processed characteristics that introduces association dependencies . The feature map c_j is generated by:

$$c_j = \sigma(k_j \cdot r_{i:i+t-1} + b_j) \tag{1}$$

where $k_j \in \mathbb{R}^{t \times d}$ denotes a filter that convolutes a window of t words embedding $r_{i:i+t-1}$, and $b_j \in \mathbb{R}$ is a bias term. Here we use four filters with different window size and use ReLU [7] as the activation function σ to incorporate element-wise non-linearity. After that, we employ a max-overtime pooling operation [5] to capture the most important local features over the feature map.

2.3 Context Modeling

After the SR-RCNN component, we add multilayer bi-RNN to the model structure, using its powerful sequence modeling capabilities to capture long-term contextual information between sentences to enrich surrounding statements associated features. The sentence encodes $S = \{S_1, S_2, \ldots, S_p\}$ output by the SR-RCNN is convolved as an input to the multilayer bi-RNN. The bi-RNN takes into account both preceding histories (extracted by forward pass) and following evidence (extracted by backward pass). The output of multilayer bi-RNN is hidden vectors, represented by $h' = \{h'_1, h'_2, \ldots, h'_l\}$, obtained by concatenating its forward and backward context representations. We convolve the output vectors, which can be regarded as the enriching sentence characteristics that take considerations of historical semantics with different granularities. Particularly, we utilize a convolutional layer to convert the context feature vector into a real-valued vector whose length is the number of categories, denoted as C.

2.4 Sequential Labels Prediction

Eventually, there are two output strategies for obtaining the label sequence. One is using the softmax layer to get the output directly, and the other is adding the CRF layer for label sequence optimization instead of modeling tagging decisions independently.

Softmax. Adding a softmax layer for normalization to convert the true value to a relative probability between different categories, calculated as follows.

$$P_i = \frac{\exp(y_i)}{\sum_{i'=1}^{C} \exp(y_{i'})} \tag{2}$$

After the output layer of the neural network is subjected to the softmax function, the next step is to calculate the loss for model training. We use the cross-entropy as the loss function to calculate the error information between the predicted label sequence $P_i(a)$ and gold label sequence $P_i^g(a)$:

$$Loss = -\sum_{a \in D} \sum_{i=1}^{C} P_i^g(a) \cdot \log(P_i(a)) \tag{3}$$

where D is the training data, a represents an abstract, and P_i^g is the one-hot coding scheme of the tag list. When the classification is more correct, the dimension corresponding to the ground truth of P_i will be closer to 1 and the value of $Loss$ will be smaller. During the training phase, the objective is to minimize the cross-entropy loss which guides the network updating parameters through the back propagation.

CRF. In the CRF layer [20], we introduce a labels transition matrix T, where $T_{i,j}$ denotes the transition probabilities of transition from label i to label j in successive sentences. This matrix is the parameter that needs to be trained in the CRF layer of model. It will learn the dependency constraints that may exist between successive tags. The output of the last multilayer bi-RNN is the probability sequence $P_{1:n}$ of n sentences, where $P_{i,j}$ indicates the probability that the jth label assigned to the ith sentence. Then the score of a prediction label sequence $y_{1:n}$ can be defined as:

$$S(y_{1:n}) = \sum_{i=2}^{n} T_{y_{i-1},y_i} + \sum_{i=1}^{n} P_{i,y_i} \tag{4}$$

The conditional probability of a certain sequence is calculated using the softmax function by normalizing the above scores over all possible label sequences. During the training phase, the objective of the model is to maximize the log-probability of the gold label sequence. At inference time, the predicted labels sequence result is chosen as the one that obtains the maximum score. This can be calculated by the Viterbi algorithm [32].

3 Experiments

3.1 Datasets

We verify our proposed approach on two medical abstract datasets: PubMed RCT and NICTA-PIBOSO. Detailed statistics of two datasets are given in Table 1. $|C|$ represents the number of label categories and $|V|$ denotes the vocabulary size. For the train, validation and test datasets, the number of abstracts and the number of statements (in parentheses) are noted.

Table 1. Dataset statistics overview.

Dataset	$\|C\|$	$\|V\|$	Train	Validation	Test
PubMed 20k	5	68k	15k(180k)	2.5k(30k)	2.5k(30k)
PubMed 200k	5	331k	190k(2.2M)	2.5k(29k)	2.5k(29k)
NICTA	6	17k	800(8.6k)	-	200(2.2k)

PubMed RCT[1] is derived from PubMed database and provides two subsets: PubMed 20k and PubMed 200k [8]. It contains five classes: *objectives, background, methods, results* and *conclusions.*
NICTA-PIBOSO[2] released by Kim et al. [16] and was shared from the ALTA 2012 Shared Task [1]. The tag-set is defined as *background, population, intervention, outcome, study design* and *other.*

To offer a fair comparison with the best published results, all corpora have no other pre-processing operations except change to lower-cased. We did not remove any rare words and numbers from the corpora, resulting in a large number of tokens unrelated to the classification are delivered to the model. It is remarkable that our model still functioned well without any additional pre-processing.

[1] The dataset is downloaded from: https://github.com/Franck-Dernoncourt/pubmed-rct.
[2] https://www.kaggle.com/c/alta-nicta-challenge2.

3.2 Experimental Setting

During training, all word embeddings are initialized using the 'PubMed-and-PMC-w2v'[3] which were pre-trained on the corpus combining the publication abstracts from PubMed and the full-text articles from PubMed Central (PMC) open access subset [27] using the word2vec tool with 200 dimensions. The word vectors are fixed during the training phase. In order to get the best performance from the model, we have also tried other word embeddings, but there were no obvious benefits.

The hyperparameter settings of the model on both datasets are described below, all of which are selected by altering one each time while keeping other hyperparameters unchanged. For SR-RCNN module, the hidden layer of bi-RNN has size 128 and the filter windows of text CNN are designed to $c = (1, 2, 3, 4)$ with 256 filters each. For context modeling module, the hidden layer is set to 256 dimensions in multilayer bi-RNN. And the type of the recurrent unit defaults to gated recurrent unit (GRU) in the bi-RNN layer. For optimization, parameters are trained using Adam [19]. In order to accelerate the training process, the model uses batch-wise training of 40 abstracts per batch (for PubMed dataset, 16 for NICTA dataset) and we truncate or zero-pad sentences to ensure that each sentence is 60 tokens in length. Besides, we apply dropout on both the input and output vectors of bi-RNN to mitigate over-fitting. The dropout rate is fixed at 0.8 for all dropout layers through all the experiments.

Previous works relied mainly on F1-score to evaluate system performance, so we also provide F-score as the evaluation indicator for better comparison with existing literature.

4 Results and Discussion

4.1 Comparison with Other Works

We compare our results with several baselines as well as recent state-of-the-art works results on the three datasets. As shown in Table 2, our model performs best on all datasets, promoting previous best published results by 0.5%, 0.5% and 2.5% on the PubMed 20k, PubMed 200k and NICTA-PIBOSO dataset, respectively. It proves that the hierarchical model framework based on SR-RCNN and multilayer bi-RNN is effective in solving the sequential sentence classification task.

Compared to other systems, our approach that automatically learns numerous features from the context does not require careful hand-engineered features. Analyzing the promotion scores for three datasets, NICTA-PIBOSO is the smallest dataset but has the highest improvement. Our approach is applicable to small data without over-fitting. Besides, for the results of PubMed RCT datasets, our model offers better performance with sufficient data to adjust parameters. We

[3] The word vectors are downloaded from: http://evexdb.org/pmresources/vec-space-models/.

Table 2. Experimental comparison results with other seven models.

Model	PubMed 20k	PubMed 200k	NICTA
Logistic Regression	83.1	85.9	71.6
Forward ANN	86.1	88.4	75.1
CRF	89.5	91.5	81.2
Best published [1]	-	-	82.0
bi-ANN [9]	90.0	91.6	82.7
HSLN-CNN [15]	92.2	92.8	84.7
HSLN-RNN [15]	92.6	93.9	84.3
Our Model(LSTM)	92.9	94.1	86.8
Our Model(GRU)	**93.1**	**94.4**	**87.2**

also compare two different types of gated units in bi-RNN. Because more sophisticated recurrent units are indeed better than more traditional recurrent units [4], we focus on LSTM and GRU to implement gating mechanisms. These results indicate that applying GRU in the bi-rnn layers brings better performance on these three abstracts datasets for sequential sentence classification task.

Furthermore, our model is not only effective but also efficient. Experiments are performed on a GeForce GTX 1080 Ti GPU and the entire training procedure (on the PubMed 20k dataset) takes about half an hour with 7 epochs to achieve the best result.

4.2 Model Analysis

We conduct refined experiments to analyze and separate out the contribution of each component of our model. We compared the effectiveness of models variants combination of different sentence representation and context modeling components in the medical scientific abstracts. The overview of the comparison results of all the models is shown in Table 3. '+Att.' indicates that we directly apply the attention mechanism (AM) on the sentence representations. The sentences encoding vectors output from the attention are the weighted sum of all the input. 'n-l' means n layers.

According to the results in Table 3, the performance of the model is consistently improved by using our SR-RCNN method instead of text CNN as sentence representation on all the datasets. It proves that the collaborative component is a good blend of the advantages of the bi-RNN and text CNN for sentence encoding. Moreover, the scores of models with one layer bi-RNN or two layers bi-RNN in PubMed datasets indicate that increasing the number of bi-RNN layers can enhance the capability of the model to enrich contextual features, thereby further improving the classification quality of the model. However, the models with two layers bi-RNN based context modeling are not as good as the models with one layer bi-RNN on the NICTA dataset. This is due to the dataset smallest scale, so

Table 3. Model performance comparison results with different components.

Sentence representation	Context modeling	PubMed 20k	PubMed 200k	NICTA
Text CNN	1-l bi-RNN	92.2	94.1	85.2
Text CNN	1-l bi-RNN + CRF	92.3	94.0	85.6
Text CNN + Att.	1-l bi-RNN	92.3	94.1	85.4
Text CNN + Att.	1-l bi-RNN + CRF	92.4	94.1	85.7
SR-RCNN	1-l bi-RNN	93.0	94.2	**87.2**
SR-RCNN	1-l bi-RNN + CRF	92.8	94.2	86.8
SR-RCNN + Att.	1-l bi-RNN	92.9	94.1	86.1
SR-RCNN + Att.	1-l bi-RNN + CRF	92.7	94.0	86.1
SR-RCNN	2-l bi-RNN	**93.1**	**94.4**	86.7
SR-RCNN	2-l bi-RNN + CRF	92.9	**94.4**	86.6
SR-RCNN + Att.	2-l bi-RNN	93.0	94.2	87.0
SR-RCNN + Att.	2-l bi-RNN + CRF	92.8	94.2	86.7

it is easier to over-fitting in more complex neural network architecture. In addition, we have tried to apply the AM to the pooling layer of text CNN, which contributes to the overall improvements before introducing SR-RCNN architecture. Our intuition is that in abstracts the dependency between the sequential sentences should be weighted before being processed by the bi-RNN.

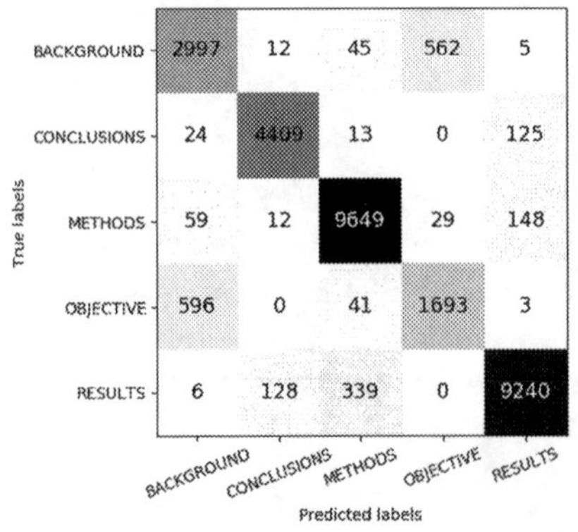

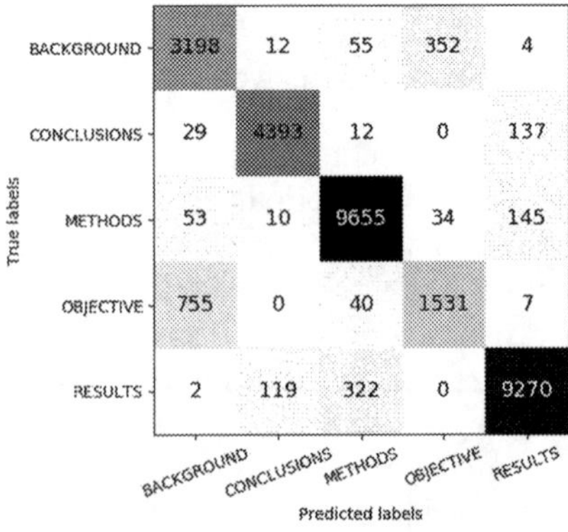

Fig. 2. Confusion matrices on the PubMed 20k test dataset achieved by our model with CRF (matrix on the left) and without CRF (matrix on the right).

Comparing the two structures of the label results directly predicted by the softmax layer and the results of further optimization with the CRF layer, the impact of CRF on the accuracy of the model results is uncertain. For further detailed inspecting of the reasons for the deterioration of the experimental results, taking the model with SR-RCNN and two layers bi-RNN as an example,

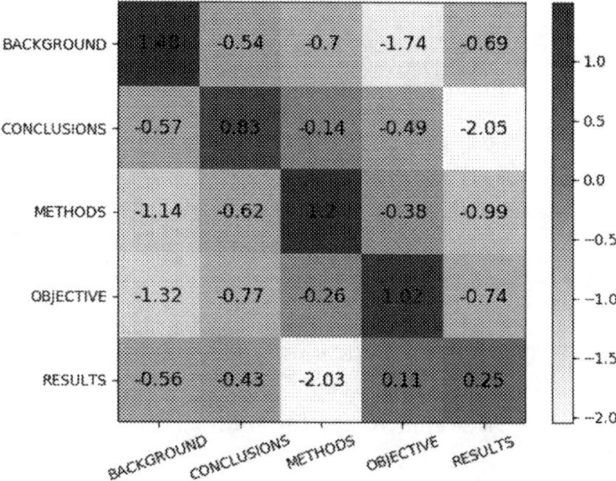

Fig. 3. Transition matrix of CRF layer learned on PubMed 20k dataset.

we list the Fig. 2 which is the confusion matrices of the test results achieved by our model with CRF layer and without CRF layer respectively. Checking every specific value of each matrix, we detect that the biggest gap between two matrices is on the *background* and *objective* labels. For finding the cause of the difference, we examined the transition matrix obtained by the CRF layer which encodes the transition probability between two subsequent labels, as shown in Fig. 3. In the transition matrix, the columns display the current sentence tag and the rows display the previous sentence tag. The *methods* class has the largest percentage of all the sentence classes (9897 of 30135 - 32.84%). We can conclude that a sentence pertaining to *objective* is more likely to be followed by a sentence pertaining to *method* (with a smaller penalty, $-0.7 < -0.26$) than a sentence pertaining to *background* through the transfer matrix. The model with CRF layer is more inclined to predict sentences as *objective* than *background* accordingly. Due to the imbalance of samples (the number of *background* sentences is more than the *objective* sentences), the model without CRF is more inclined to predict the sentence as the *background* (labels with more samples). Not using the CRF layer to add constraints to the final predicted labels on these medical scientific abstracts sets has a better effect, but more experiments are still needed for other specific datasets and related tasks.

5 Conclusion

In this paper, we explore the factors that affect the performance of hierarchical neural networks for sequential sentences classification. Our experiment shows that a stronger sentence level feature extractor (SR-RCNN) and a well sequential feature fusion operator (multilayer bi-RNN) are the key factors that improve the model performance. While the attention mechanism and the CRF optimization layer may shift the results, the overall effect is uncertain. Our results were confirmed on two benchmarking datasets of medical scientific abstracts with state-of-the-art results, which provide a basic guidance for further research and practical application.

Acknowledgment. This research was supported in part by NSFC under Grant No. U1836107 and No. 61572158.

References

1. Amini, I., Martinez, D., Molla, D., et al.: Overview of the ALTA 2012 Shared Task (2012)
2. Bengio, Y., Ducharme, R., Vincent, P., Jauvin, C.: A neural probabilistic language model. J. Mach. Learn. Res. **3**(Feb), 1137–1155 (2003)
3. Bojanowski, P., Grave, E., Joulin, A., Mikolov, T.: Enriching word vectors with subword information. Trans. Assoc. Comput. Linguist. **5**, 135–146 (2017)
4. Chung, J., Gulcehre, C., Cho, K., Bengio, Y.: Empirical evaluation of gated recurrent neural networks on sequence modeling. arXiv preprint arXiv:1412.3555 (2014)
5. Collobert, R., Weston, J., Bottou, L., Karlen, M., Kavukcuoglu, K., Kuksa, P.: Natural language processing (almost) from scratch. J. Mach. Learn. Res. **12**(Aug), 2493–2537 (2011)
6. Conneau, A., Schwenk, H., Barrault, L., Lecun, Y.: Very deep convolutional networks for text classification. arXiv preprint arXiv:1606.01781 (2016)
7. Dahl, G.E., Sainath, T.N., Hinton, G.E.: Improving deep neural networks for LVCSR using rectified linear units and dropout. In: 2013 IEEE International Conference on Acoustics, Speech and Signal Processing, pp. 8609–8613. IEEE (2013)
8. Dernoncourt, F., Lee, J.Y.: Pubmed 200k rct: a dataset for sequential sentence classification in medical abstracts. arXiv preprint arXiv:1710.06071 (2017)
9. Dernoncourt, F., Lee, J.Y., Szolovits, P.: Neural networks for joint sentence classification in medical paper abstracts. arXiv preprint arXiv:1612.05251 (2016)
10. Hachey, B., Grover, C.: Sequence modelling for sentence classification in a legal summarisation system. In: Proceedings of the 2005 ACM Symposium on Applied Computing, pp. 292–296. ACM (2005)
11. Hassanzadeh, H., Groza, T., Hunter, J.: Identifying scientific artefacts in biomedical literature: the evidence based medicine use case. J. Biomed. Inform. **49**, 159–170 (2014)
12. Hirohata, K., Okazaki, N., Ananiadou, S., Ishizuka, M.: Identifying sections in scientific abstracts using conditional random fields. In: Proceedings of the Third International Joint Conference on Natural Language Processing: Volume-I (2008)
13. Huang, K.C., Chiang, I.J., Xiao, F., Liao, C.C., Liu, C.C.H., Wong, J.M.: Pico element detection in medical text without metadata: are first sentences enough? J. Biomed. Inform. **46**(5), 940–946 (2013)
14. Jagannatha, A.N., Yu, H.: Structured prediction models for RNN based sequence labeling in clinical text. In: Proceedings of the Conference on Empirical Methods in Natural Language Processing, Conference on Empirical Methods in Natural Language Processing, vol. 2016, p. 856. NIH Public Access (2016)
15. Jin, D., Szolovits, P.: Hierarchical neural networks for sequential sentence classification in medical scientific abstracts. arXiv preprint arXiv:1808.06161 (2018)
16. Kim, S.N., Martinez, D., Cavedon, L., Yencken, L.: Automatic classification of sentences to support evidence based medicine. In: BMC Bioinformatics, vol. 12, p. S5. BioMed Central (2011)

17. Kim, T., Yang, J.: Abstractive text classification using sequence-to-convolution neural networks. arXiv preprint arXiv:1805.07745 (2018)
18. Kim, Y.: Convolutional neural networks for sentence classification. arXiv preprint arXiv:1408.5882 (2014)
19. Kingma, D.P., Ba, J.: Adam: A method for stochastic optimization. arXiv preprint arXiv:1412.6980 (2014)
20. Lafferty, J., McCallum, A., Pereira, F.: Conditional random fields: probabilistic models for segmenting and labeling sequence data. In: Proceedings of 18th International Conference on Machine Learning, pp. 282–289 (2001)
21. Lai, S., Xu, L., Liu, K., Zhao, J.: Recurrent convolutional neural networks for text classification. In: Twenty-ninth AAAI Conference on Artificial Intelligence (2015)
22. Lee, J.Y., Dernoncourt, F.: Sequential short-text classification with recurrent and convolutional neural networks. arXiv preprint arXiv:1603.03827 (2016)
23. Lin, J., Karakos, D., Demner-Fushman, D., Khudanpur, S.: Generative content models for structural analysis of medical abstracts. In: Proceedings of the HLT-NAACL BioNLP Workshop on Linking Natural Language and Biology, LNL-BioNLP 2006. pp. 65–72. Association for Computational Linguistics, Stroudsburg (2006)
24. Liu, L., et al.: Empower sequence labeling with task-aware neural language model. In: Thirty-Second AAAI Conference on Artificial Intelligence (2018)
25. Mikolov, T., Sutskever, I., Chen, K., Corrado, G.S., Dean, J.: Distributed representations of words and phrases and their compositionality. In: Advances in Neural Information Processing Systems, pp. 3111–3119 (2013)
26. Mirończuk, M.M., Protasiewicz, J.: A recent overview of the state-of-the-art elements of text classification. Expert Syst. Appl. **106**, 36–54 (2018)
27. Moen, S., Ananiadou, T.S.S.: Distributional semantics resources for biomedical text processing. In: Proceedings of LBM, pp. 39–44 (2013)
28. Moriya, S., Shibata, C.: Transfer learning method for very deep CNN for text classification and methods for its evaluation. In: 2018 IEEE 42nd Annual Computer Software and Applications Conference (COMPSAC), vol. 2, pp. 153–158. IEEE (2018)
29. Pennington, J., Socher, R., Manning, C.: Glove: global vectors for word representation. In: Proceedings of the 2014 Conference on Empirical Methods in Natural Language Processing (EMNLP), pp. 1532–1543 (2014)
30. Reimers, N., Gurevych, I.: Optimal hyperparameters for deep lstm-networks for sequence labeling tasks. arXiv preprint arXiv:1707.06799 (2017)
31. Schuster, M., Paliwal, K.K.: Bidirectional recurrent neural networks. IEEE Trans. Signal Process. **45**(11), 2673–2681 (1997)
32. Viterbi, A.: Error bounds for convolutional codes and an asymptotically optimum decoding algorithm. IEEE Trans. Inf. Theory **13**(2), 260–269 (1967)
33. Yamamoto, Y., Takagi, T.: A sentence classification system for multi biomedical literature summarization. In: 21st International Conference on Data Engineering Workshops (ICDEW 2005), pp. 1163–1163, April 2005
34. Yin, W., Kann, K., Yu, M., Schuetze, H.: Comparative study of CNN and RNN for natural language processing (2017). arXiv preprint arXiv:1702.01923 (2017)
35. Zhou, Y., Xu, B., Xu, J., Yang, L., Li, C.: Compositional recurrent neural networks for Chinese short text classification. In: 2016 IEEE/WIC/ACM International Conference on Web Intelligence (WI), pp. 137–144. IEEE (2016)

REKER: Relation Extraction with Knowledge of Entity and Relation

Hongtao Liu[1], Yian Wang[2], Fangzhao Wu[3], Pengfei Jiao[4](✉), Hongyan Xu[1], and Xing Xie[3]

[1] College of Intelligence and Computing, Tianjin University, Tianjin, China
{htliu,hongyanxu}@tju.edu.cn

[2] School of Physics, University of Science and Technology of China, Hefei, China
wya16@mail.ustc.edu.cn

[3] Microsoft Research Asia, Beijing, China
wufangzhao@gmail.com, xingx@microsoft.com

[4] Center for Biosafety Research and Strategy, Tianjin University, Tianjin, China
pjiao@tju.edu.cn

Abstract. Relation Extraction (RE) is an important task to mine knowledge from massive text corpus. Existing relation extraction methods usually purely rely on the textual information of sentences to predict the relations between entities. The useful knowledge of entity and relation is not fully exploited. In fact, off-the-shelf knowledge bases can provide rich information of entities and relations, such as the concepts of entities and the semantic descriptions of relations, which have the potential to enhance the performance of relation extraction. In this paper, we propose a neural relation extraction approach with the knowledge of entity and relation (REKER) which can incorporate the useful knowledge of entity and relation into relation extraction. Specifically, we propose to learn the concept embeddings of entities and use them to enhance the representation of sentences. In addition, instead of treating relation labels as meaningless one-hot vectors, we propose to learn the semantic embeddings of relations from the textual descriptions of relations and apply them to regularize the learning of relation classification model in our neural relation extraction approach. Extensive experiments are conducted and the results validate that our approach can effectively improve the performance of relation extraction and outperform many competitive baseline methods.

Keywords: Relation extraction · Entity concept · Relation description

1 Introduction

Relation extraction (RE) aims to identify semantic relations between known entities from plain text corpus [10]. For example, as shown in Fig. 1, given a sentence "Steve Jobs was the co-founder and CEO of Apple" and two entities "Steve Jobs" and "Apple" in it, the goal of relation extraction is to identify

J. Tang et al. (Eds.): NLPCC 2019, LNAI 11839, pp. 90–102, 2019.
https://doi.org/10.1007/978-3-030-32236-6_8

that there is a Co-Founder relation between the person entity Steve_Jobs and the company entity Apple. Relation extraction is an important task in information extraction field, and is widely used in many real-world applications such as knowledge base completion [13], question answering [17] and so on.

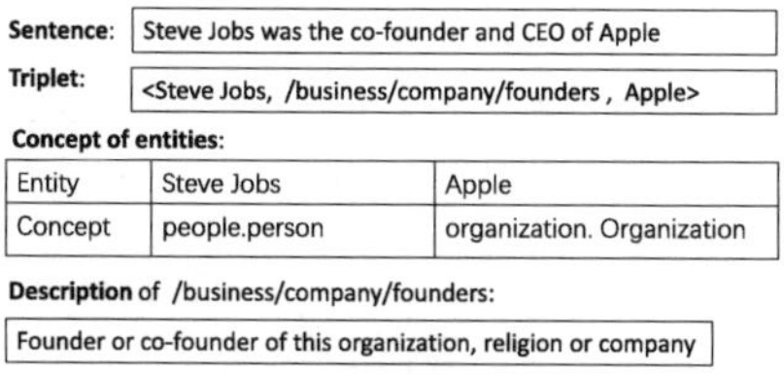

Sentence: Steve Jobs was the co-founder and CEO of Apple

Triplet: <Steve Jobs, /business/company/founders , Apple>

Concept of entities:

Entity	Steve Jobs	Apple
Concept	people.person	organization. Organization

Description of /business/company/founders:

Founder or co-founder of this organization, religion or company

Fig. 1. An illustrative example of relation extraction with the knowledge of both entity (i.e., the concepts of entities) and relation (i.e., the description of relation).

Many methods have been proposed for relation extraction. Early methods for relation extraction mainly depended on human-designed lexical and syntactic features, e.g., POS tags, shortest dependency path and so on [2,3]. Designing these handcrafted features relies on a large number of domain knowledge [19]. In addition, the inevitable errors brought by NLP tools may hurt the performance of relation extraction [8]. In recent years, many neural network based methods have been proposed for relation extraction [8,19,20]. For example, Zeng et al. [19] utilized Piece-Wise Convolutional Neural Network (PCNN) to encode sentences and adopt multi-instance learning to select the most informative sentences for an entity pair. Lin et al. [8] built a sentence-level attention model to make use of the information of all sentences about an entity pair. These methods can automatically extract semantic features of sentences with various neural networks and then feed them into a relation classifier to predict the relation labels of entity pairs in these sentences.

However, most previous works merely consider the relation extraction as a sentence classification task and focus on the text encoder but ignore the off-the-shelf and rich knowledge about entities and relations in knowledge bases. As shown in Fig. 1, entity concepts, also known as the categories of entities, can intuitively provide extra guidance information for the classifier to identify the relation between two entities [11]. For example, the relation between an entity of Person and an entity of Organization would be related with positions (e.g., business.company.founders between "Steve Jobs" and "Apple"). As for knowledge about relations, most existing works merely regard relations as labels in classification, i.e., meaningless one-hot vectors, which would cause a loss of information. In fact, relations contain rich potential semantic information such as their textual descriptions. Considering that human beings can easily understand the meaning of a relation according to its description, we should attach the semantic knowledge from descriptions into relations and integrate it to relation extraction models rather than regarding relations merely as meaningless labels.

To address these issues, in this paper we propose a novel approach that can integrate two additional information (i.e., entity concept and relation description) into the neural relation extraction model named REKER: Relation Extraction with Knowledge of Entity and Relation. First, we encode entity concepts into feature vectors in an embedding way which can capture the context semantic of concepts. Afterwards, we integrate these embedding vectors into the sentence encoder directly to enhance text representation. Second, in order to attach semantics into relation labels, we extract relation textual descriptions from knowledge bases and learn the semantic feature vectors of relations. Then we apply the semantic representation in the relation classification part and regard it as a regular item in loss function. In this way, we can introduce the information of relation descriptions into the relation extraction model.

The major contributions of this paper are summarized as follows:

(1) We propose an effective neural approach to integrate additional knowledge including concepts of entities and textual descriptions of relations to enhance neural relation extraction.
(2) We utilize entity concept embedding to capture the semantic information of entity concepts, and we encode the relation description to attach semantics into relation labels rather than regarding them as meaningless one-hot vectors.
(3) We conduct extensive experiments on two relation extraction benchmark datasets and the results show our approach can outperform the existing competitive methods.

2 Related Work

Relation extraction is one of the most important tasks in NLP and many works have been proposed so far. Traditional approaches depend on the designed features and regard relation extraction as a multi-class classification problem. Kambhatla et al. [7] designed handcrafted features of sentences and then feed them into a classifier (e.g., SVM). The supervised approaches may suffer from the lack of labeled training data. To address this problem, Mintz [10] proposed a distant supervision method which align text corpus to the given knowledge base and automatically label training data. However, distant supervision would result in wrong labeling problem. Hoffmann et al. [4] relaxed the strong assumption of distance supervision and adopted multi-instance learning to reduce noisy data.

Recently with the development of deep learning, many works in RE based on the neural network have achieved a significantly better performance compared with traditional methods. Zeng et al. [20] adopted a Convolutional Neural Network to extract semantic features of sentences automatically. In addition, to reduce the impact of noisy data in distant supervision, Zeng et al. [19] combined the multi-instance learning with a convolutional neural network encoder, Lin et al. [8] adopted a sentence-level attention over multiple instances to pay attention to those important sentences.

Besides, a few works utilize the knowledge about entities or relations in relation extraction. Vashishth et al. [15] employs Graph Convolution Networks for encoding syntactic information of sentences and utilize the side information of entity type and relation alias. However, the information used in [15] may be limited. For example the alias of a relation is always too short to represent the relation semantic. To utilize the rich knowledge of both entity and relation more effectively, we propose a flexible approach that integrates the concepts of entities and descriptions of relations into neural relation extraction models.

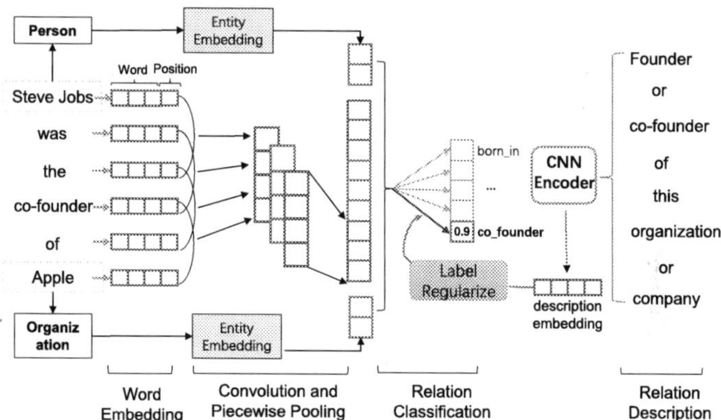

Fig. 2. The architecture of our REKER model.

3 Proposed Method

This section describes our proposed approach. We first give the problem definition and then introduce our approach REKER in detail as shown in Fig. 2. Given a sentence s_i and the mentioned entity pair (e_1, e_2) in s_i, the goal of relation extraction is to predict the relation r_j existing between e_1 and e_2 . Our model estimates the probability $p(r_j|s_i, e_1, e_2)$, $j = 1, 2, 3 \cdots N_r$, where N_r denotes the number of relations.

In this paper, we focus on integrating additional knowledge about entity and relation. As a result, our method can be used both in fully supervised learning and distant supervised learning (i.e., sentence-level and bag-level relation extraction tasks). We will next present our approach in sentence-level relation extraction, which is almost the same as in bag-level tasks.

3.1 Sentence Representation Module

As shown in the overview, we adopt a Convolutional Neural Network (CNN) to encode a sentence into a vector. This module includes three parts: word representation layer, convolution and pooling layer and the entity concept enhancement part.

Word Representation. We transform the words in sentences into distributed representation including word embedding and position embedding which captures the position information.

Word Embedding. Given a sentence $s = \{w_1, w_2, \cdots, w_n\}$, each word w_i in s is represented as a low-dimensional real-valued vector $\mathbf{w_i} \in \mathcal{R}^{d_w}$, where d_w is the dimension.

Position Embedding. Zeng et al. [20] proposed the Position Feature (PF) of words to specify distance from words to entity mentions. The idea is that words closer to the two entity words are more informative. PF is the combination of the relative distance of the current word to `entity1` and `entity2`. The distance is then encoded into low-dimensional vector as position embedding.

Then a word w_i can be represented by concatenating its word embedding and two position embeddings, denoted as $\mathbf{w_i} \in \mathcal{R}^{(d_w+d_p\times 2)}$, where d_p is the dimension of the position embedding vector. Hence, the final word embedding of sentence $s = \{w_1, w_2, \cdots, w_n\}$ can be expressed as a matrix: $\mathbf{X} = [\mathbf{w_1}, \mathbf{w_2}, \cdots, \mathbf{w_n}]$.

Convolution and Pooling. We apply a convolutional layer into the sentence matrix $\mathbf{X}$ to extract senmatic features of sentence. Then a pooling layer is adopted to combine all these features and filter the important features.

Convolution. Given the input matrix $\mathbf{X} = [\mathbf{w_1}, \mathbf{w_2}, \cdots, \mathbf{w_n}]$ and the window size of convolutional filter l, we adopt multiple convolutional filters $\mathbf{F} = \{\mathbf{f_1}, \cdots, \mathbf{f_K}\}$ to capture semantic features of sentences. The convolution operation between the i-th filter and the j-th window is computed as:

$$c_{ij} = \mathbf{f_i} \odot \mathbf{w_{j:j+l-1}}, \tag{1}$$

where $\odot$ is the inner-product operation. The output of the convolution layer is a sequence of vectors $\mathbf{C} = \{\mathbf{c_1}, \mathbf{c_2}, \cdots, \mathbf{c_K}\}$.

Pooling. Traditional max-pooling can only extract the most significant feature from the whole sentence, which would lose some structural information about two entity mentions. As a result, Following Piece-wise Pooling in [19], each $\mathbf{c_i}$ is divided into three segments $\{c_{i1}, c_{i2}, c_{i3}\}$ by the two entities. Then the output of the pooling layer:

$$p_{ij} = \max(\mathbf{c_{ij}}) \quad 1 \leq i \leq K, j = 1, 2, 3. \tag{2}$$

The pooling result of the i-th filter is a 3-dimensional vector $\mathbf{p_i} = [p_{i1}, p_{i2}, p_{i3}]$. We concatenate all K filters vectors $\mathbf{P} \in \mathcal{R}^{3K}$ and feed $\mathbf{P}$ into a nonlinear layer, e.g., tanh to get the output vector for this sentence s_i: $\mathbf{s_i} = \tanh(\mathbf{P})$.

Entity Concept Enhancement. The representation $\mathbf{s_i}$ only considers the feature of sentences and neglects the useful extra knowledge about the entities in the sentence. Here we utilize the concept embedding to enhance representation of the sentence.

Similar to word embedding and position embedding, entity concept embedding is the distributed representation of entity concept and each concept is encoded into a low-dimension and real-value vector. Given a entity pair $\mathtt{e_1}$ and $\mathtt{e_2}$ in sentence s_i, the concepts are denoted as $\mathtt{t_1}, \mathtt{t_2}$ respectively. Then we integrate the concept information into sentence representation via concatenating the concept embedding with the sentence representation $\mathbf{s_i}$. For entities with multiple concepts, we just adopt the average of the concept embeddings.

The final representation of sentence s_i enhanced by entity concepts is:

$$\hat{\mathbf{s_i}} = [\mathbf{t_1}, \mathbf{s_i}, \mathbf{t_2}], \tag{3}$$

where $\mathbf{t_1}, \mathbf{t_2} \in \mathcal{R}^{d_t}$ are the embeddings of t_1, t_2, and d_t is the dimension of the entity concept embedding.

3.2 Relation Classification Module

As illustrated in Fig. 2, we define the final output $\mathbf{o}$ of our model which corresponds to the scores of s_i associated to all relations:

$$\mathbf{o} = \mathbf{R}\hat{\mathbf{s_i}} + \mathbf{b}, \tag{4}$$

where $\mathbf{o} \in \mathcal{R}^{N_r}$ and N_r is the number of relations and $\mathbf{b} \in \mathcal{R}^{N_r}$ is a bias item. Especially $\mathbf{R}$ is the `relation prediction embeddings matrix`. The j-th row vector of $\mathbf{R}$ correspond to the predictive vector of the relation r_i which is used to evaluate the score of s_i associated with relation r_j, denoted as $\mathbf{r_j^P}$.

Afterwards, the conditional probability that the sentence s_i can express the relation r_j is defined with a soft-max layer as:

$$p(r_j|s_i, \theta) = \frac{\exp(\mathbf{o}_{r_j})}{\sum_{j=1}^{N_r}(\mathbf{o}_j)}, \tag{5}$$

where θ is the set of learned parameters in our model. To train our model, we define two kinds of loss function as below:

Cross-Entropy Loss. We use cross entropy to define the loss function and maximize the likelihood of all instances in the training data:

$$\mathcal{L}_b = -\sum_{j=1}^{T} \log p(r_j|s_i, \theta). \tag{6}$$

Mean Squared Error for Relation Embeddings. In order to attach semantics to relation labels rather than meaningless one-hot vector, we introduce relations description embedding to regularize the loss function. We adopt a Convolutional Neural Networks to extract semantic features from the textual descriptions for each relation. The description embedding for relation r_j is denoted as $\mathbf{r_j^d}$.

Hence, we have defined two embedding vectors for each relation: `description embedding` $\mathbf{r_d}$ and `prediction embedding` $\mathbf{r_p}$ which are two views about each relation. They should be, to some extent, closer to each other in the vector space. As a result, we constrain that `description embedding` $\mathbf{r_d}$ is similar with `prediction embedding` $\mathbf{r_p}$. So we define another loss function using mean squared error as a constraint item:

$$\mathcal{L}_r = \sum_{j=1}^{N_r} ||\mathbf{r_j^p} - \mathbf{M}\mathbf{r_j^d}||_2^2, \tag{7}$$

where M is a harmony parameter matrix. In this way, the useful semantic information in relation descriptions can be integrated into relation classification module effectively.

The final loss function is defined:

$$\mathcal{L} = \mathcal{L}_b + \lambda \mathcal{L}_r, \tag{8}$$

where $\lambda > 0$ is a balance weight for the two loss components.

Table 1. Statistics of NYT+Freebase and GDS datasets.

Dataset	# relations	# sentences	# entity-pair	# entity concept
NYT+Freebase Dataset				
Train	53	455,771	233,064	55
Dev	53	114,317	58,635	55
Test	53	172,448	96,678	55
GDS Dataset				
Train	5	11,297	6,498	25
Dev	5	1,864	1,082	25
Test	5	5,663	3,247	25

4 Experiments

4.1 Dataset and Evaluation Metrics

Our experiments are conducted on NYT+Freebase and Google Distant Supervision (GDS) datasets. The details of the two datasets are followed:

NYT+Freebase[1]**:** The dataset is built by [12] and generates by aligning entities and relations in Freebase [1] with the corpus New York Times (NYT). The articles of NYT from year 2005–2006 are used as training data, and articles from 2007 are used as testing data. NYT+Freebase is widely used as a benchmark dataset in relation extraction field [8,15,18,19].

GDS[2]**:** This dataset is recently built in [5] by Google Research. Different from NYT+Freebase, GDS is a human-judged dataset and each entity-pair in the dataset is judged by at least 5 raters.

The statistics of the two datasets is summarized in Table 1.

In addition, we extract off-the-shelf descriptions of the relations from WikiData[3] [16] (a migration project of Freebase).

Evaluation Metrics. Following previous works [8,19], we evaluate our approach with held-out evaluation, which automatically compares the relations extracted in our model against the relation labels in Freebase. Similar to previous works [8,19], we also present the precision-recall curves and P@Top N metrics to conduct the held-out evaluation.

4.2 Experimental Settings

Embedding Initialization. For position embedding and entity concept embedding, we just randomly initialize them from a uniform distribution. For word embedding, we adopt word2vec[4] [9] to train word embeddings on corpus.

Parameter Settings. We tune hyper parameters using the validation datasets in experiments. The best parameter configuration is: the dimension of word embedding $d_w = 50$, the dimension of type embedding $d_t = 20$, the dimension of position embedding $d_p = 5$, the window size of the filter $w = 3$, the number of filters $N_f = 230$, the mini batch size $B = 64$, the weight $\lambda = 1.0$, the dropout probability $p = 0.5$.

4.3 Performance Evaluation

To demonstrate the effect of our approach, in this section, we conduct held-out evaluation and compare with three traditional feature-based methods and five competitive neural network based methods as follows:
Feature-based methods:

Mintz [10] is a traditional method which extracts features from all sentences.

MultiR [4] adopts multi-instance learning which can handle overlapping relations.

MIMLRE [14] is a multi-instance and multi-label method for distant supervision.

[1] http://iesl.cs.umass.edu/riedel/ecml/.
[2] https://ai.googleblog.com/2013/04/50000-lessons-on-how-to-read-relation.html.
[3] https://www.wikidata.org/.
[4] https://code.google.com/p/word2vec/.

Neural network based methods:

PCNN [19] utilizes a convolutional neural network to encode sentences and uses the most-likely sentence for the entity pair during training.

PCNN+ATT [8] adopts a sentence-level attention to reduce the noise data in distant supervision.

BGWA [5] proposes an entity-aware attention model based on Bi-GRU to capture the important information.

RANK+extATT [18] makes joint relation extraction with a general pair-wise ranking framework to learn the class ties between relations, which achieves state-of-art performance.

RESIDE [15] employs graph convolution networks to encode the syntactic dependency tree of sentences and utilizes the side information of entity type and relation alias to enhance relation extraction.

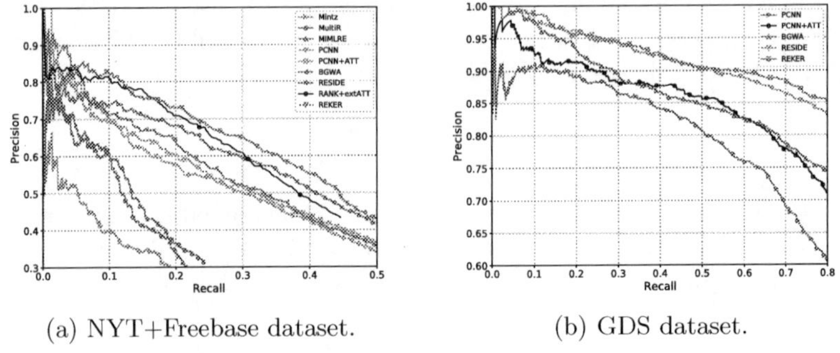

(a) NYT+Freebase dataset.

(b) GDS dataset.

Fig. 3. Precision-recall curves.

Table 2. Precision@Top K of extracted relations in NYT+Freebase dataset.

	Top 100	Top 200	Top 300	Top 500	Top 600	Top 800	Average
Mintz	0.53	0.51	0.49	0.42	0.37	0.34	0.44
MultiR	0.62	0.63	0.63	0.48	0.44	0.40	0.53
MIML	0.68	0.64	0.62	0.51	0.46	0.42	0.56
PCNN	0.78	0.72	0.67	0.60	0.57	0.55	0.65
PCNN+ATT	0.81	0.71	0.69	0.63	0.60	0.57	0.67
BGWA	0.82	0.75	0.72	0.67	0.62	0.54	0.69
RESIDE	0.84	0.79	0.76	0.70	0.65	0.62	0.72
RANK+extATT	0.83	0.82	0.78	0.73	0.68	0.62	0.74
REKER	**0.85**	**0.83**	**0.78**	**0.73**	**0.70**	**0.65**	**0.76**

The Precision-Recall curves of the NYT+Freebase dataset and GDS[5] dataset are shown in Fig. 3. We can see that our method REKER can outperform all other methods in almost the entire range of recall. From the comparison in terms of the Presion Recall curves, we can observe that: (1) all the neural network based methods outperform feature-based methods a lot. This is because that the neural network methods can learn better representation about sentences and then benefit for the relation extraction task. (2) our method REKER outperforms the basic model PCNN, which shows that the two components (i.e., entity and relation knowledge) in our method can indeed improve the performance of relation extraction tasks. (3) our method REKER achieves better performance than RESIDE in the NYT+Freebase dataset, which also incorporates the entity and relation information. This is because the information of relation alias used in RESIDE is limited, and our method REKER adopts the richer relation description to conduct relation label embedding, which can play a direct and global role for the model. (4) since there are only 5 relations in GDS dataset, most methods perform much better than in NYT+Freebase and our method REKER can achieve a slightly better performance than the state-of-art method (i.e., RESIDE). Especially when the recall is beyond 0.5, our model can keep a higher precision.

Table 3. Examples for the effectiveness of Entity Concept.

Sentences	Entity concept	PCNN	PCNN+ENT
... said [e_1]**Kamal_Nath,** the commerce minister of [e_2]**India** ...	[e_1]:**Person** [e_2]:**Country**	**/business/company**	**/people/nationality**
... a former minister of [e_1]**Thailand,** [e_2]**Thaksin_Shinawatra** ...	[e_1]:**Country** [e_2]:**Person**	**/location/contains**	**/people/nationality**

Besides Precision Recall curves, we evaluate models using P@N metric in held-out evaluation under NYT+Freebase dataset following previous works [8, 15, 19], which can provide the precision about the top-ranked relations. According to the P@N result in Table 2, we can see that our model REKER performs best at the entire P@N levels, which further demonstrates that our additional rich knowledge including entity concept and relation description are all useful in the relation extraction task and can extract more true positive relations.

4.4 Effectiveness of Entity and Relation Knowledge

We further conduct extra experiments under NYT+Freebase dataset with each component alone (i.e., PCNN+ENT and PCNN+REL respectively). The Precision Recall Curve is shown in Fig. 4, we have the following conclusions: (1) models with ENT, REL alone all consistently outperform the basic model PCNN, which denotes that the knowledge about entity concepts and relation descriptions are

[5] We compare with recent baselines in GDS since the dataset is newly released in 2018.

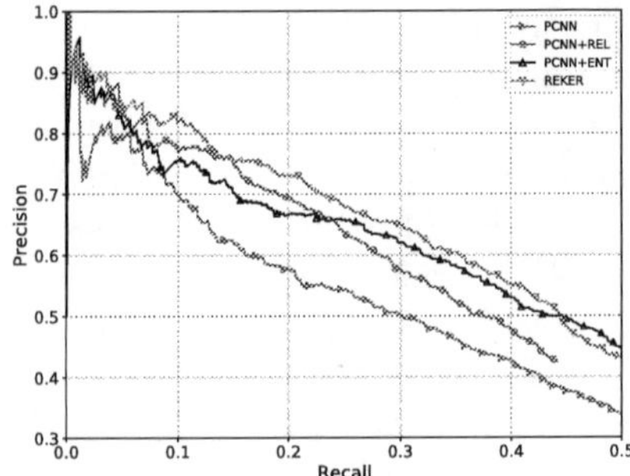

Fig. 4. Comparison of our model variants in terms of Precision-Recall curves.

all beneficial to the relation extraction task. (2) our final model REKER performs best among those methods respectively, which shows that the combination of entity concepts and relation descriptions can bring a further improvement compared with the two components alone.

4.5 Case Study

To indicate the impact of additional knowledge more intuitively, in this section we show some case studies for qualitative analysis.

Entity Concept. In this part, we find out some examples to show the intention of entity concept. As the first sentence in Table 3, the method PCNN extracted `/business/company` from a sentence containing a `Person` entity and a `Country` entity, which didn't make sense. Our method integrating the knowledge of entity concept can effectively avoid these wrong cases and improve the quality of extracted relations.

Relation Description. As introduced above, we believe that relation description can attach semantic information into the relation labels. Hence, we select 25 relations from three largest domains to visualize their feature vectors distribution by projecting them into 2-Dimension space using PCA [6] algorithm. Figure 5(a) shows the visualization result of the 25 relations after training a model without description information. And Fig. 5(b) is the result of the model with relation description. We can find out that relations from the same domains lie closer to each other in Fig. 5(b). In other words, different domains of relations are well separated in the model with the help of relation description information. As a result, incorporating the relation description can capture more semantic correlation between relations, which could benefit the relation classification task.

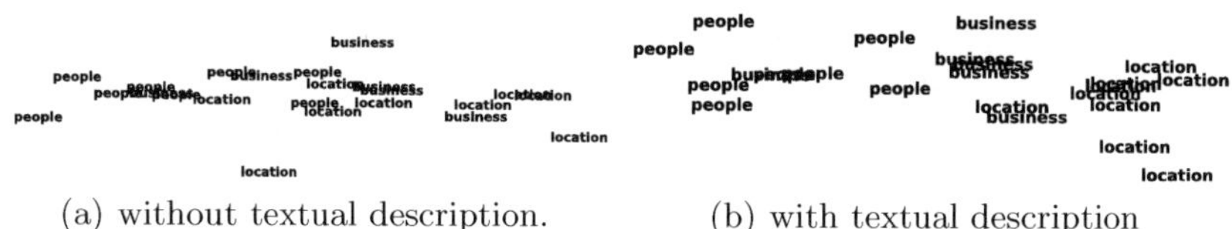

(a) without textual description. (b) with textual description

Fig. 5. Visualization of relation prediction embedding

5 Conclusion

In this paper, we propose a novel approach REKER that integrates the rich knowledge including the relation description and entity concept into a neural relation extraction model. We adopt entity concept embedding to enhance the representation of sentences. Besides, we utilize relation description information to attach semantics into relation labels rather than meaningless one-hot vectors. Experimental results on two benchmark datasets show that our approach REKER can effectively improve the performance of the relation extraction task.

Acknowledgement. This work was supported by the National Key R&D Program of China (2018YFC0831005), the Science and Technology Key R&D Program of Tianjin (18YFZCSF01370) and the National Social Science Fund of China (15BTQ056).

References

1. Bollacker, K., Evans, C., Paritosh, P., Sturge, T., Taylor, J.: Freebase: a collaboratively created graph database for structuring human knowledge. In: SIGMOD, pp. 1247–1250. ACM (2008)
2. Bunescu, R.C., Mooney, R.J.: A shortest path dependency kernel for relation extraction. In: HLT, pp. 724–731. Association for Computational Linguistics (2005)
3. GuoDong, Z., Jian, S., Jie, Z., Min, Z.: Exploring various knowledge in relation extraction. In: ACL, pp. 427–434. Association for Computational Linguistics (2005)
4. Hoffmann, R., Zhang, C., Ling, X., Zettlemoyer, L., Weld, D.S.: Knowledge-based weak supervision for information extraction of overlapping relations. In: ACL, pp. 541–550. Association for Computational Linguistics (2011)
5. Jat, S., Khandelwal, S., Talukdar, P.: Improving distantly supervised relation extraction using word and entity based attention. CoRR abs/1804.06987 (2018)
6. Jolliffe, I.: Principal component analysis. In: International Encyclopedia of Statistical Science, pp. 1094–1096. Springer (2011)
7. Kambhatla, N.: Combining lexical, syntactic, and semantic features with maximum entropy models for extracting relations. In: ACL, p. 22. Association for Computational Linguistics (2004)
8. Lin, Y., Shen, S., Liu, Z., Luan, H., Sun, M.: Neural relation extraction with selective attention over instances. In: ACL, vol. 1, pp. 2124–2133 (2016)
9. Mikolov, T., Sutskever, I., Chen, K., Corrado, G.S., Dean, J.: Distributed representations of words and phrases and their compositionality. In: NIPS, pp. 3111–3119 (2013)

10. Mintz, M., Bills, S., Snow, R., Jurafsky, D.: Distant supervision for relation extraction without labeled data. In: ACL, pp. 1003–1011. Association for Computational Linguistics (2009)
11. Ren, X., et al.: Cotype: joint extraction of typed entities and relations with knowledge bases. In: WWW, pp. 1015–1024 (2017)
12. Riedel, S., Yao, L., McCallum, A.: Modeling relations and their mentions without labeled text. In: Balcázar, J.L., Bonchi, F., Gionis, A., Sebag, M. (eds.) ECML PKDD 2010. LNCS (LNAI), vol. 6323, pp. 148–163. Springer, Heidelberg (2010). https://doi.org/10.1007/978-3-642-15939-8_10
13. Riedel, S., Yao, L., McCallum, A., Marlin, B.M.: Relation extraction with matrix factorization and universal schemas. In: NAACL, pp. 74–84 (2013)
14. Surdeanu, M., Tibshirani, J., Nallapati, R., Manning, C.D.: Multi-instance multi-label learning for relation extraction. In: EMNLP, pp. 455–465. Association for Computational Linguistics (2012)
15. Vashishth, S., Joshi, R., Prayaga, S.S., Bhattacharyya, C., Talukdar, P.: RESIDE: improving distantly-supervised neural relation extraction using side information. In: EMNLP, pp. 1257–1266 (2018)
16. Vrandečić, D., Krötzsch, M.: Wikidata: a free collaborative knowledgebase. Commun. ACM **57**(10), 78–85 (2014)
17. Xu, K., Reddy, S., Feng, Y., Huang, S., Zhao, D.: Question answering on freebase via relation extraction and textual evidence. In: ACL (2016)
18. Ye, H., Chao, W., Luo, Z., Li, Z.: Jointly extracting relations with class ties via effective deep ranking. In: ACL, pp. 1810–1820 (2017)
19. Zeng, D., Liu, K., Chen, Y., Zhao, J.: Distant supervision for relation extraction via piecewise convolutional neural networks. In: EMNLP, pp. 1753–1762 (2015)
20. Zeng, D., Liu, K., Lai, S., Zhou, G., Zhao, J.: Relation classification via convolutional deep neural network. In: COLING, pp. 2335–2344 (2014)

IPRE: A Dataset for Inter-Personal Relationship Extraction

Haitao Wang, Zhengqiu He, Jin Ma, Wenliang Chen(✉), and Min Zhang

School of Computer Science and Technology, Soochow University, Suzhou, China
{htwang2019,zqhe,jma2018}@stu.suda.edu.cn,
{wlchen,minzhang}@suda.edu.cn

Abstract. Inter-personal relationship is the basis of human society. In order to automatically identify the relations between persons from texts, we need annotated data for training systems. However, there is a lack of a massive amount of such data so far. To address this situation, we introduce IPRE, a new dataset for inter-personal relationship extraction which aims to facilitate information extraction and knowledge graph construction research. In total, IPRE has over 41,000 labeled sentences for 34 types of relations, including about 9,000 sentences annotated by workers. Our data is the first dataset for inter-personal relationship extraction. Additionally, we define three evaluation tasks based on IPRE and provide the baseline systems for further comparison in future work.

Keywords: Relation extraction · Dataset · Inter-personal relationships

1 Introduction

Inter-personal relationship, which is the basis of society as a whole, is a strong, deep, or close connection among persons [19]. The types of inter-personal relationship include kinship relations, friendship, work, clubs, neighborhoods, and so on. From billions of web pages, we can explore relations of persons to form as knowledge bases (KBs), such as EntityCube (also named as Renlifang) [24] which is a knowledge base containing attributes of people, locations, and organizations, and allows us to discover a relationship path between two persons. However, inter-personal relationships in the KBs could be incorrect, which caused by supervised relation extractor because of lack of a massive amount of training data. To solve this problem, our task is to build a dataset for training a system to improve the accuracy of inter-personal relationships.

An obvious solution is to label the data by human annotators. However, hiring the annotators is costly and non-scalable, in terms of both time and money. To overcome this challenge, Mintz et al. [13] put forward the idea of distant supervision (DS), which can automatically generate training instances via aligning knowledge bases and texts. The key idea of distant supervision is that given an entity pair $<e_h, e_t>$ and its corresponding relation r_B from KBs such as Freebase [1], we simply label all sentences containing the two entities by relation r_B [7,15,18]. Several benchmark datasets for distant supervision relation extraction have been developed [13,14] and widely used by

J. Tang et al. (Eds.): NLPCC 2019, LNAI 11839, pp. 103–115, 2019.
https://doi.org/10.1007/978-3-030-32236-6_9

many researchers [5,9,11,21]. Through distant supervision, we can easily generate a large scale of annotated data for our task without labor costs. However, the data generated by this way inevitably has wrong labeling problem. While training noise in distant supervision is expected, noise in the test data is troublesome as it may lead to incorrect evaluation. Ideally, we can easily build a large scale of training data by taking the advantage of distant supervision, and hire annotators to label the testing data to overcome the problem of incorrect evaluations.

This paper introduces the Inter-Personal Relationship Extraction (IPRE) dataset in Chinese, in which each entity is a person and each relation is an inter-personal relation, e.g., "姚明" (Yao Ming) and "叶莉" (Ye Li), and their inter-personal relationship is *wife* (妻子), since Ye Li is the wife of Yao Ming. The IPRE dataset includes a set of sentence bags, and each bag is corresponding to two persons and their relation, of which the sentences must contain the two persons. In total, the IPRE dataset has over 41,000 sentences grouped into 4,214 bags related to 5,561 persons and 34 relation types. In the data, there are 1,266 manually-annotated bags used as development and test sets, and 2,948 DS-generated bags used as a training set.

We first define a set of inter-personal relations used in IPRE, which includes 34 types by considering the balance of occurrences in the data. We further present the data collection procedure, a summary of the data structure, as well as a series of analyses of the data statistic. We select some sentences from the collected data into the development and test sets, and annotate them manually. To show the potential and usefulness of the IPRE dataset, benchmark baselines of distantly supervised relation extraction have been conducted and reported. The dataset is available at https://github.com/SUDA-HLT/IPRE.

Our main contributions are:

- To our best knowledge, IPRE is the first dataset for Inter-Personal Relation Extraction. IPRE can be used for building the systems for identifying the relations among persons and then contribute to construct knowledge base such as EntityCube.
- IPRE can serve as a benchmark of relation extraction. We define three different tasks: Bag2Bag, Bag2Sent, and Sent2Sent (described in Sect. 4) for evaluation. We also provide the baseline systems for the three tasks that can be used for the comparison in future work.

2 Related Work

In this section, we make a brief review of distant supervision data and human annotated data for relation extraction.

Riedel2010 [14] has been widely used by many researchers [5,9,11,21,22]. The dataset uses Freebase as a distant supervision knowledge base and New York Times (NYT) corpus as text resource. Sentences in NYT of the years 2005–2006 are used as training set while sentences of 2007 are used as testing set. There are 52 actual relations and a special relation "NA" which indicates there is no relation between given entity pair. The sentences of NA are from the entity pairs that exist in the same sentence of the actual relations but do not appear in the Freebase.

GIDS [8] is a newly developed dataset. To alleviate noise in distant supervision setting, it makes sure that labeled relation is correct and for each instance bag in GIDS, there is at least one sentence in that bag which expresses the relation assigned to that bag. GIDS is constructed from the human-judged Google Relation Extraction corpus, which consists of 5 binary relations: "perGraduatedFromInstitution", "perHasDegree", "perPlaceOfBirth", "perPlaceOfDeath", and "NA".

ACE05 and CONLL04 [16] are the widely used human-annotated datasets for relation extraction. The ACE05 data defines seven coarse-grained entity types and six coarse-grained relation categories, while the CONLL04 data defines four entity types and five relation categories. The test sets of them are about 1,500 sentences, much smaller than ours.

3 IPRE Dataset

In this section, we describe how to construct the IPRE dataset. The premise of distant supervision method is that there is a well-organized knowledge base (e.g., Freebase) to provide entity-relation triples. But for inter-personal relations, there is no such knowledge base publicly available so far. Thus in our approach, we should first extract persons-relation triples by ourselves. Then, we generate sentence bags by aligning the triples to the texts in a large scale of text corpus. Finally, we choose a certain percentage of the sentence bags for human annotation.

3.1 Data Alignment via Distant Supervision

Candidates of Person Entities. There are several sites containing a large amount of wiki-style pages (e.g., Wikipedia and Chinese Baidu Baike), which can provide enough persons-relation triples. We crawl Chinese webpages from the wiki-style sites as our resource to extract persons-relation.

The webpages includes many types of entities besides persons. We need to list the candidates of person entities before extraction. The webpages of an entity usually contains some tags, which are used to describe the category to which the entity belongs. For example, entity "姚明" (Yao Ming) is tagged as "运动员 (athlete), 话题人物 (topic character), 篮球运动员 (basketball player), 篮球 (basketball), 体育人物 (sportsman)". From the tags, we can easily figure out that Yao Ming is a person. We count the number of occurrences of the tags for all entities and manually select the tags with a frequency of more than 100 as the tag set of the category of person. The tag set of person has more than 119 entries, from which top 10 are listed in Table 1. If one of the tags of an entity is included in the tag set, we put the entity into a set of person entities.

Since the webpages might contain some errors involved by the nonprofessional editors, we further clean up the set of person entities. There are three steps: (1) symbol cleanup, all chars should be a Chinese character; (2) multi-source information verification, we check the information in infobox, and the surname should be defined in "Hundred Family Surnames"[1]; (3) length restriction. We limit the length of person entity between 2 and 6 according to relevant regulations about Chinese person name. Finally we obtain a set of 942,344 person entities.

[1] https://en.wikipedia.org/wiki/Hundred_Family_Surnames.

Inter-Personal Relations. The types of inter-personal relationship include kinship relations, friendship, marriage, work, clubs, neighborhoods, and so on. We first define a set of inter-personal relations (IPR), having 34 types.

Table 1. Top 10 tags for persons.

#1	人物 (person)
#2	行业人物 (industry figure)
#3	政治人物 (politician)
#4	教师 (teacher)
#5	学者 (scholar)
#6	体育人物 (sportsman)
#7	官员 (official)
#8	娱乐人物 (entertainment figure)
#9	科研人员 (researcher)
#10	教授 (professor)

Table 2. Relation types in IPR.

ID	Relation Type	# Sentence	# Triple
#1	现夫(husband)	8896	571
#2	生父(father)	7607	986
#3	现妻(wife)	5965	363
#4	老师(teacher)	3174	287
#5	儿子(son)	2936	294
...	...	...	...
#32	公公(father-in-law)	25	7
#33	儿媳(daughter-in-law)	14	8
#34	外公(grandfather)	12	5

From the infobox of the pages, we can obtain more than 1,700 expressions of relations between persons. Some expressions have the same meaning and can be mapped to one entry of IPR. We manually map the expressions to the entries of IPR. Due to the space limitation, we only list some types in Table 2. Based on 34 types and their associated expressions, we can extract persons-relation triples from the infobox.

Text Alignment. We follow the general procedure of distant supervision used for relation extraction [13]. We make a sentence pool from the texts in the webpages. Then we use a name entity tagger to detect the person names in the sentences. If one sentence contains two person names which appear in one relation triple, the sentence is selected. All the sentences that contain an entity pair are grouped into one bag. Finally, we have over 41,000 sentences and 4,214 bags.

3.2 Manually Annotating

After obtaining the data generated by distant supervision, we divide this dataset into training (70%), development (10%) and test (20%) sets, ensuring that there is no overlap between these sets. As we mentioned before, we manually annotate all sentences in the development and test sets for evaluation purpose. Given a sentence and the matched entity pair ($<e_h, e_t>$), there are three steps: (1) the annotators first check whether the sentence is legal; (2) they check if the mentions of e_h and e_t are person names since some Chinese names could be used as common words; (3) they determine the relation of e_h and e_t expressed by the sentence. If one sentence cannot go through the first two steps, it is an illegal sentence. At step (3), the annotators choose one of 34 types if possible, otherwise use NA as the type.

Four workers annotate 9,776 sentences manually and each sentence is marked at least twice. When the annotations are inconsistent, the third annotator will relabel the

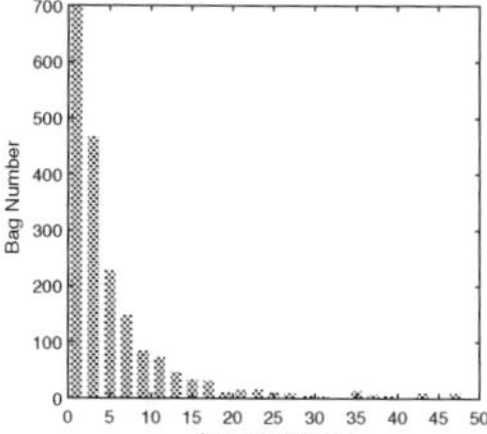

Fig. 1. Sentence number of each bag.

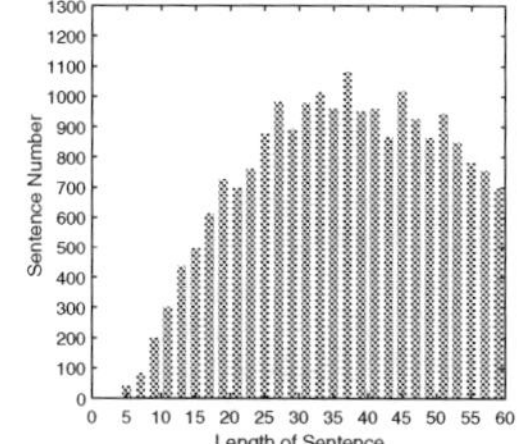

Fig. 2. Sentence length distribution.

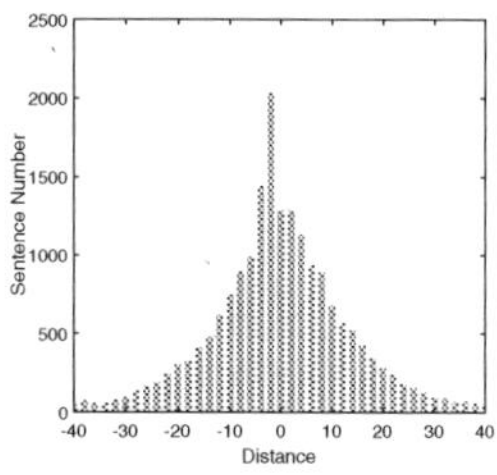

Fig. 3. Distance between entity pair.

data. The Kappa coefficient of annotation results is about 0.87, which is a satisfactory value. In these sentences, there are 899 illegal sentences. In the remaining legal sentences, 3,412 sentences express one relation out of 34 types, while the others are marked as NA. At bag-level, the legal sentences are grouped into 1,266 bags, while 941 bags express at least one relation of 34 types.

3.3 Data Statistics

In order to have a more comprehensive and clear understanding of IPRE, we have statistics on the relevant features of IPRE. Our goal is to construct a dataset with a relatively balanced amount of data among types, so we first count the number of triples for each type and the number of sentences matched. Table 2 shows the statistical results, from which we can see that the majority of the categories have more than 10 triples.

Figure 1 further gives the distribution histogram of the number of sentences contained in each bag. Although there are some bags with only one sentence, the number of sentences in most bags is between 2 and 15, which is a very reasonable distribution.

Figure 2 shows the distribution of sentence length. In order to keep quality of sentences as possible, we limit the length of the sentence to a maximum of 60 in the process of text alignment section. From the figure we can see that the sentence length is mostly more than 15, and it can form a complete semantic unit to a large extent.

Meanwhile, many previous studies have shown that the closer the distance between two entities in the same sentence, the more likely it is that the sentence will reflect the semantic relationship of the entity pair [11,20,21]. From Fig. 3, we can see that in the IPRE dataset, the distance between two entities in most sentences is between 3–20 words, which is a reasonable distance that can reflect the semantic relationship.

4 IPRE as a New Benchmark

Based on IPRE, we design relation extraction tasks from three types of learning strategies. The first one is the most commonly used learning paradigm at bag-level in distant supervision data, namely multi-instance learning (MIL). Here, all sentences corresponding to a relational triple are regarded as a bag, and the relation prediction is at bag-level during both training and testing. The second one is to employ bag-level method as we do in the first one. And since the test set has been labeled manually, it is able to predict the relation at sentence-level when testing. The third one is to treat it as a general task of relation extraction, and to train and predict relation at sentence-level. Figure 4 shows the three tasks.

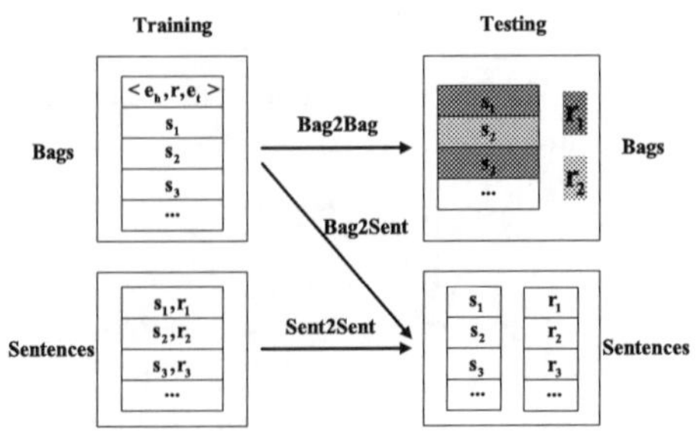

Fig. 4. Three types of task based on IPRE.

4.1 Bag2Bag: Bag-Training and Bag-Testing

In order to mitigate the impact of the wrong labeling problem in distant supervision data, the existing work mainly focuses on MIL [11,21]. However, in the existing corpus constructed by distant supervision, the training set and test set are processed in the same way. That is, the only supervised information is the entity-relation triples existing in KBs, so it is uncertain whether one sentence in a bag is labeled correctly or not. For this reason, what may happen when verify the performance of the relation extraction system at the testing phase is that although an entity-relation is correctly predicted, it is based on sentences that do not actually belong to the relation type.

In real-world scenarios, there is a need for bag-level training and testing. For example, when there is a lot of noise data in the constructed corpus, or we only need to determine the relation type between entities, but do not care about the expression of specific sentences. Based on IPRE, we can make more stringent bag-level relation prediction, as illustrated in Fig. 4. Since we provide the labeling results of all sentences in the development set and test set, we can not only predict the relation types of bags, but also have stricter requirements for the predicted results that the system should output the sentence or sentences in the bag that support the relation prediction. This is more reasonable than the black-box-level bag relation prediction in the existing work.

Here, we give the detail evaluation metrics of Bag2Bag task. In distant supervision data, the number of samples of NA relation is usually very large. Therefore, NA relation is generally not considered in the assessment. Let t_p be the true positive bags, f_p be the false positive bags, f_n be the false negative bags. Thus, we have:

$$P = \frac{I_{t_p}}{I_{t_p} + I_{f_p}}, R = \frac{I_{t_p}}{I_{t_p} + I_{f_n}}, F_1 = \frac{2PR}{P + R} \tag{1}$$

where I is the counting function. It is worth noting that the number of each bag is equal to the number of non-NA relations assigned to this bag when counting the number of bags.

4.2 Bag2Sent: Bag-Training and Sentence-Testing

There is another requirement scenario that we need to train relation extractor at bag-level because there are many noises in the given corpus, or we are looking for more stable model training. However, in the follow-up model application, we need to determine the relation between entities in each specific sentence. Therefore, it is necessary to predict the relation at sentence-level.

Based on IPRE, we can employ bag-level training method in model training process by treating each bag as a semantically enriched sentence, and extract the features of the sentences in the bag that are closely related to the relation prediction of a given entity pair. At the same time, since each sentence is labeled manually in the development set and test set, the relation prediction of a single sentence can be made.

Let t_p be the true positive sentences, f_p be the false positive sentences, f_n be the false negative sentences. NA relation is also not considered like Bag2Bag, and the evaluation metrics of this task is formally the same as Eq. (1).

4.3 Sent2Sent: Sentence-Training and Sentence-Testing

In the research of relation extraction task, more attention is focused on the training and prediction of single sentence. For distant supervision relation extraction, when we construct training data with fewer errors, or the proposed model has better anti-noise ability, or we have the ability to filter the noise in training data, such as the recently proposed method of using reinforcement learning to select sentences [2], it will be a good practice to make sentence-level relation extraction from distant supervision data.

IPRE is a good cornerstone for the research of sentence-level relation extraction task. We can make full use of the characteristics of the training set containing noise data to design more robust and noise-resistant models, and we can also design better strategies to identify noise data. Meanwhile, the fully annotated development set and test set can achieve the purpose of measuring the performance of the model.

The Sent2Sent task shares the same strategy with the Bag2Sent and also uses the Eq. (1) to evaluate the prediction results at sentence-level, as shown in Fig. 4.

5 Baselines

In this section, we present several baseline models for three defined tasks. We first describe three sentence encoders. Then, based on the sentence encoders we build the systems for each task.

5.1 Sentence Encoder

The sentence encoders transform a sentence into its distributed representation. First, the words in the input sentence are embedded into dense real-valued feature vectors. Next, the neural networks are used to construct the distributed representation of the sentence.

Input Representation. Given a sentence $s = \{w_1, ..., w_n\}$, where w_i is the i-th word in the sentence, the input is a matrix composed of n vectors $\boldsymbol{x} = [\boldsymbol{x}_1, ..., \boldsymbol{x}_n]$, where $\boldsymbol{x}_i$ corresponds to w_i and consists of its word embedding and position embedding. Following previous work [11,21], we employ the skip-gram method [12] to the word embedding. Position embeddings are first successfully applied to relation extraction task by Zeng et al. [20], which specifies the relative distances of a word with respect to two target entities. In this way, $\boldsymbol{x}_i \in \mathbb{R}^d$, and $d = d^a + 2 \times d^b$, where d^a and d^b are the dimensions of word embedding and position embedding respectively.

CNN/PCNN Encoder. After encoding the input words, a convolution layer is applied to reconstruct the original input $\boldsymbol{x}$ by learning sentence features from a small window of words at a time while preserving word order information. We use K convolution filters with the same window size l. Then, we combine the K convolution output vectors via a max-pooling operation to obtain a vector of a fixed length K. Formally, the j-th element of the output vector $\boldsymbol{c} \in \mathbb{R}^K$ as follows:

$$\boldsymbol{c}[j] = \max_i(\boldsymbol{W}_j \boldsymbol{x}_{i:i+l-1} + \boldsymbol{b}_j) \tag{2}$$

where $\boldsymbol{W}_j$ and $\boldsymbol{b}_j$ are model parameters.

Further, Zeng et al. [21] adopts piecewise max pooling (PCNN) in relation extraction, which is a variation of CNN. Suppose the positions of the two entities are p_1 and p_2 respectively. Then, each convolution output vector is divided into three segments:

$$[0 : p_1 - 1], [p_1 : p_2], [p_2 + 1 : n - l] \tag{3}$$

The max scalars in each segment are preserved to form a 3-element vector, and all vectors produced by the K filters are concatenated into a vector with length $3K$, which is the output of the pooling layer.

Finally, we apply a non-linear transformation (e.g., tanh) on the output vector to obtain the sentence embedding $\boldsymbol{s}$.

Bi-LSTM Encoder. LSTM units [6] can keep the previous state and memorize the extracted features of the current data input. Following Zhou et al. [23], we adopt a variant introduced by Graves et al. [3], and each unit is computed as:

$$\boldsymbol{h}_t, \boldsymbol{c}_t = LSTM(\boldsymbol{h}_{t-1}, \boldsymbol{c}_{t-1}) \tag{4}$$

In this paper, we use bidirectional LSTM networks (Bi-LSTM) [4] to encode the sentences. Therefore, the forward and backward outputs of the i-th word are concatenated:

$$\boldsymbol{h}_i = [\overrightarrow{\boldsymbol{h}_i}; \overleftarrow{\boldsymbol{h}_i}] \tag{5}$$

Then, an attention layer is exploited to determine which segments in a sentence are most influential. More specifically, for the matrix $\boldsymbol{H} = \{\boldsymbol{h}_1, \boldsymbol{h}_2, ..., \boldsymbol{h}_n\}$, we compute its attention vector as:

$$\boldsymbol{\alpha} = \mathrm{softmax}(\boldsymbol{\omega}^T \tanh(\boldsymbol{H})) \tag{6}$$

where $\boldsymbol{\omega}$ is a trained parameter vector and $\boldsymbol{\omega}^T$ is a transpose. Next, we can obtain the sentence representation as:

$$\boldsymbol{s} = \tanh(\boldsymbol{H}\boldsymbol{\alpha}^T) \tag{7}$$

5.2 Systems for Bag2Bag Task

For the Bag2Bag task, we employ two MIL methods to perform bag-level relation prediction, i.e., expressed at least once (ONE) [21], and attention over instances (ATT) [11]. Suppose that there are T bags $\{B_1, B_2, ..., B_T\}$ and that the i-th bag contains m_i instances $B_i = \{s_i^1, s_i^2, ..., s_i^{m_i}\}$. The objective of MIL is to predict the labels of the unseen bags.

ONE. Given an input instance s_i^j, the network with the parameter θ outputs a vector $\boldsymbol{o}$. To obtain the conditional probability $p(r|s, \theta)$, a softmax operation over all relation types is applied:

$$p(r|s_i^j, \theta) = \frac{\exp(\boldsymbol{o}_r)}{\sum_{k=1}^{N_r} \exp(\boldsymbol{o}_k)} \tag{8}$$

where N_r is number of relation types.

Then, the objective function using cross-entropy at bag-level is defined as follows:

$$\begin{aligned} J(\theta) &= \sum_{i=1}^{T} \log p(r_i|s_i^j, \theta) \\ j^* &= \underset{j}{\text{argmax}}\, p(r_i|s_i^j, \theta) \end{aligned} \tag{9}$$

Here, when predicting, a bag is positively labeled if and only if the output of the model on at least one of its instances is assigned a positive label.

ATT. To exploit the information of all sentences, the ATT model represents the bag B_i with a real-valued vector $\mathbf{emb}_{B_i}$ when predicting relation r. It is straightforward that the representation of the bag B_i depends on the representations of all sentences in it. And a selective attention is defined to de-emphasize the noisy sentences. Thus, we can obtain the representation vector $\mathbf{emb}_{B_i}$ of bag B_i as:

$$\mathbf{emb}_{B_i} = \sum_j \frac{\exp(e_j)}{\sum_k \exp(e_k)} \boldsymbol{s}_i^j \tag{10}$$

where e_j scores how well the input sentence s_i^j and the predict relation r matches. Following Lin et al. [11], we select the bi-linear form:

$$e_j = \boldsymbol{s}_i^j \boldsymbol{A} \boldsymbol{r} \tag{11}$$

where $\boldsymbol{A}$ is a weighted diagonal matrix, and $\boldsymbol{r}$ is the representation of relation r.

After that, the conditional probability $p(r|B_i, \theta)$ through a softmax layer as follows:

$$\begin{aligned} \boldsymbol{o} &= \boldsymbol{M}\mathbf{emb}_{B_i} + \boldsymbol{b} \\ p(r|B_i, \theta) &= \frac{\exp(\boldsymbol{o}_r)}{\sum_{k=1}^{N_r} \exp(\boldsymbol{o}_k)} \end{aligned} \tag{12}$$

Table 3. Results of three tasks

Types		Bag2Bag		Bag2Sent		Sent2Sent	
Method		word	char	word	char	word	char
CNN	ONE	0.352	0.328	0.205	0.200	0.241	0.160
	ATT	0.359	0.328	0.220	0.214		
PCNN	ONE	0.291	0.287	0.149	0.162	0.215	0.156
	ATT	0.305	0.281	0.142	0.147		
Bi-LSTM	ONE	0.280	0.301	0.168	0.174	0.237	0.186
	ATT	0.296	0.334	0.157	0.171		

where $\boldsymbol{M}$ is the representation matrix of relations and $\boldsymbol{b}$ is a bias vector.

Finally, the objective function using cross-entropy at the bag level is defined as:

$$J(\theta) = \sum_{i=1}^{T} \log p(r_i|B_i, \theta) \tag{13}$$

5.3 Systems for Bag2Sent Task

For relation extraction task of bag-training and sentence-testing, we simply treat each sentence in the test set as a bag, and then as a Bag2Bag task. Therefore, we still train the model in the same way as Sect. 5.2. When testing, we separate each sentence into a bag and make relation prediction.

5.4 Systems for Sent2Sent Task

For Sent2Sent task, after we get the representation of sentence s, we apply a MLP to output the confidence vector $\boldsymbol{o}$. Then the conditional probability of i-th relation is:

$$p(r_i|s, \theta) = \frac{\exp(\boldsymbol{o}_i)}{\sum_{k=1}^{N_r} \exp(\boldsymbol{o}_k)} \tag{14}$$

6 Experiments

In this section, we present the experimental results and detailed analyses. To evaluate the effect of Chinese word segmentation, we provide two different inputs: word-level and char-level. For word-level, we use Jieba[2] to perform word segmentation. The evaluation metrics are described in Sect. 4. We report F1 values in the following experiments.

[2] https://github.com/fxsjy/jieba.

6.1 Hyperparameter Settings

In the experiments, we tune the hyperparameters of all the methods on the training dataset and development dataset. The dimension of word embedding d^a is set to 300, the dimension of position embedding d^b is set to 5, the number of filters K and the dimension of hidden state are set to 300, and the window size l of filters is 3. The batch size is fixed to 50, the dropout [17] probability is set to 0.5. When training, we apply Adam [10] to optimize parameters, and the learning rate is set to 0.001.

6.2 Experimental Results

Table 3 shows the F1 values of different models mentioned in Sect. 5. To demonstrate the performance of different sentence representation models in Bag2Bag task, we use F1 value defined in Eq. (1) for the evaluation criterion.

From the table, we have the following observation: (1) Among the models of sentence semantic representation, CNN is still the most outstanding. In the task of inter-personal relation extraction, especially on this dataset, local features are usually sufficient to express the relation between persons, and CNN can capture these local features effectively. (2) For systems based on both PCNN and Bi-LSMT with char-level in the task of Bag2Sent, they perform better than the ones with word-level while the systems of CNN have a different trend. This indicates that for bag-level training, the word information has an uncertain effect. (3) Compared with task of Bag2Bag and Bag2Sent, the char-level models have lower scores than the word-level models for all three methods in the task of Sent2Sent. This indicates that word embedding has better robustness in noisy data, which may be caused by the fact that words are the most basic semantic unit in Chinese.

7 Conclusion

In this paper we introduce the IPRE dataset, a data of over 41,000 labeled sentences (including about 9,000 manually-annotated sentences) for inter-personal relationship. Our data is the first data for extracting relations between persons and much larger than other human-annotated data (such as ACE05 and CONLL04), in terms of both the numbers of sentences and relation types in test sets. Additionally, IPRE can serve as a benchmark of relation extraction. We define three evaluation tasks based on IPRE and provide the baseline systems for further comparison.

Acknowledgements. The research work is supported by the National Natural Science Foundation of China (Grant No. 61572338, 61876115) and Provincial Key Laboratory for Computer Information Processing Technology, Soochow University. Corresponding author is Wenliang Chen. We would also thank the anonymous reviewers for their detailed comments, which have helped us to improve the quality of this work.

References

1. Bollacker, K., Evans, C., Paritosh, P., Sturge, T., Taylor, J.: Freebase: a collaboratively created graph database for structuring human knowledge. In: Proceedings of SIGMOD, pp. 1247–1250 (2008)
2. Feng, J., Huang, M., Zhao, L., Yang, Y., Zhu, X.: Reinforcement learning for relation classification from noisy data. In: Proceedings of AAAI, pp. 5779–5786 (2018)
3. Graves, A., Mohamed, A.r., Hinton, G.: Speech recognition with deep recurrent neural networks. In: Proceedings of ICASSP, pp. 6645–6649. IEEE (2013)
4. Graves, A., Schmidhuber, J.: Framewise phoneme classification with bidirectional LSTM and other neural network architectures. Neural Networks **18**(5–6), 602–610 (2005)
5. He, Z., Chen, W., Li, Z., Zhang, W., Shao, H., Zhang, M.: Syntax-aware entity representations for neural relation extraction. Artif. Intell. **275**, 602–617 (2019)
6. Hochreiter, S., Schmidhuber, J.: Long short-term memory. Neural Comput. **9**(8), 1735–1780 (1997)
7. Hoffmann, R., Zhang, C., Ling, X., Zettlemoyer, L., Weld, D.S.: Knowledge-based weak supervision for information extraction of overlapping relations. In: Proceedings of ACL, pp. 541–550 (2011)
8. Jat, S., Khandelwal, S., Talukdar, P.: Improving distantly supervised relation extraction using word and entity based attention. arXiv preprint arXiv:1804.06987 (2018)
9. Ji, G., Liu, K., He, S., Zhao, J.: Distant supervision for relation extraction with sentence-level attention and entity descriptions. In: Proceedings of AAAI, pp. 3060–3066 (2017)
10. Kingma, D.P., Ba, J.L.: Adam: a method for stochastic optimization. In: Proceedings of ICLR (2014)
11. Lin, Y., Shen, S., Liu, Z., Luan, H., Sun, M.: Neural relation extraction with selective attention over instances. In: Proceedings of ACL, pp. 2124–2133 (2016)
12. Mikolov, T., Sutskever, I., Chen, K., Corrado, G.S., Dean, J.: Distributed representations of words and phrases and their compositionality. In: Proceedings of NIPS, pp. 3111–3119 (2013)
13. Mintz, M., Bills, S., Snow, R., Jurafsky, D.: Distant supervision for relation extraction without labeled data. In: Proceedings of ACL, pp. 1003–1011 (2009)
14. Riedel, S., Yao, L., McCallum, A.: Modeling relations and their mentions without labeled text. In: Machine Learning and Knowledge Discovery in Databases, pp. 148–163 (2010)
15. Riedel, S., Yao, L., McCallum, A., Marlin, B.M.: Relation extraction with matrix factorization and universal schemas. In: Proceedings of HLT-NAACL, pp. 74–84 (2013)
16. Roth, D., Yih, W.T.: A linear programming formulation for global inference in natural language tasks. In: Proceedings of CoNLL, pp. 1–8 (2004)
17. Srivastava, N., Hinton, G.E., Krizhevsky, A., Sutskever, I., Salakhutdinov, R.: Dropout: a simple way to prevent neural networks from overfitting. J. Mach. Learn. Res. **15**(1), 1929–1958 (2014)
18. Surdeanu, M., Tibshirani, J., Nallapati, R., Manning, C.D.: Multi-instance multi-label learning for relation extraction. In: Proceedings of EMNLP, pp. 455–465 (2012)
19. White, L.A.: The Evolution of Culture: The Development of Civilization to the Fall of Rome. Routledge, New York (2016)
20. Zeng, D., Liu, K., Lai, S., Zhou, G., Zhao, J.: Relation classification via convolutional deep neural network. In: Proceedings of COLING, pp. 2335–2344 (2014)
21. Zeng, D., Liu, K., Chen, Y., Zhao, J.: Distant supervision for relation extraction via piecewise convolutional neural networks. In: Proceedings of EMNLP, pp. 1753–1762 (2015)
22. Zhang, N., Deng, S., Sun, Z., Chen, X., Zhang, W., Chen, H.: Attention-based capsule network with dynamic routing for relation extraction. In: Proceedings of EMNLP, pp. 986–992 (2018)

23. Zhou, P., Shi, W., Tian, J., Qi, Z., Li, B., Hao, H., Xu, B.: Attention-based bidirectional long short-term memory networks for relation classification. In: Proceedings of ACL, vol. 2, pp. 207–212 (2016)
24. Zhu, J., Nie, Z., Liu, X., Zhang, B., Wen, J.R.: StatSnowball: a statistical approach to extracting entity relationships. In: Proceedings of WWW, pp. 101–110. ACM (2009)

Shared-Private LSTM for Multi-domain Text Classification

Haiming Wu[1], Yue Zhang[2], Xi Jin[3], Yun Xue[1(✉)], and Ziwen Wang[1]

[1] School of Physics and Telecommunication Engineering, South China Normal University, Guangzhou, China
xueyun@scnu.edu.cn
[2] School of Engineering, Westlake University, Hangzhou, China
[3] Faculty of Mathematics and Statistics, Hubei University, Wuhan, China

Abstract. Shared-private models can significantly improve the performance of cross-domain learning. These methods use a shared encoder for all domains and a private encoder for each domain. One issue is that domain-specific knowledge is separately learned, without interaction with each other. We consider tackling this problem through a shared-private LSTM (SP-LSTM), which allow domain-specific parameters to be updated on a three-dimensional recurrent neural network. The advantage of SP-LSTM is that it allows domain-private information to communicate with each other during the encoding process, and it is faster than LSTM due to the parallel mechanism. Results on text classification across 16 domains indicate that SP-LSTM outperforms state-of-the-art shared-private architecture.

Keywords: Multi-task learning · Shared-private LSTM · Text classification

1 Introduction

When faced with multiple domains datasets, multi-task learning, as an effective approach to transfer knowledge from one text domain to another [1–7], which can improve the performance of a single task [8], has been paid much attention by researchers. In recent years, with the rise of deep learning, the neural-based model for multi-task learning has been widely applied as a common technique in many tasks of natural language processing. Such as, sequence tagging [9,10], syntactic parsing [6,11–13], named entity recognition [7,14], text classification [8,15,16], etc. Compared with discrete representations, the neural-based model can allow efficient knowledge sharing across more than two domains.

It has been shown that, however, the vanilla multi-task learning does not always yield benefit between different NLP tasks [20,21]. And even sometimes, the optimization of one task can reduce the performance of other tasks. There has been an investigation into which tasks are more "compatible" with each other in a multi-task learning environment, therefore, the transfer learning can

J. Tang et al. (Eds.): NLPCC 2019, LNAI 11839, pp. 116–128, 2019.
https://doi.org/10.1007/978-3-030-32236-6_10

only be conducted between selected tasks [22,23]. Another different line of work tries to solve the problem from a modeling perspective, which is to learn common knowledge to share between tasks while keeping task-specific knowledge private [11,24–26].

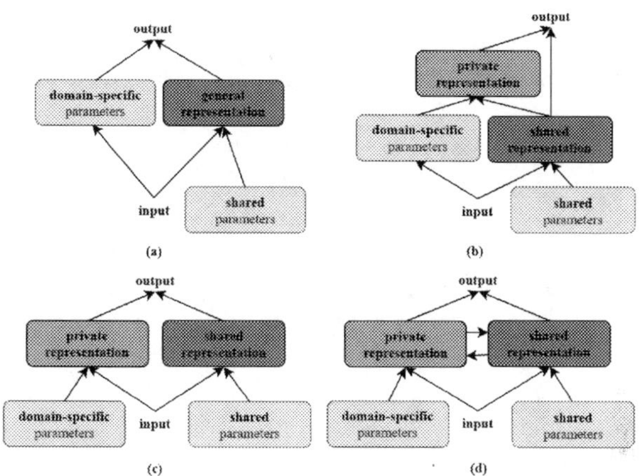

Fig. 1. Shared-private models.

As shown in Fig. 1(a), multi-domains training model [17,18] is introduced. A set of shared parameters are used as a general extractor, followed by an output layer of each domain. Given an input, a shared representation is generated, which is passed a private output layer with domain-specific parameters. And in the work of [19] (Fig. 1(b)), a self-attention of each domain is used to learn domain descriptor vectors based on the general representation. Connecting domain descriptor vectors and the shared representation as the final sentence representation for each sentence. These models take a set of parameters for a general extractor, and a set of parameters of each domain is used to distinguish private information. However, a limitation is that they only use an output layer for each domain, and sentence vectors are from the same domain-agnostic representation, resulting in weak utilization of domain knowledge. Therefore, under the circumstances, it is hard to ensure that the shared extractor can fully extract domain knowledge, the final outputs thus are difficult to complete the task.

One state-of-the-art system for multi-task learning, shown in Fig. 1(c), is a standard shared-private network [8] with common parameters shared across domains, as well as a set of private parameters for each domain. Given an input, both the shared and the private parameters are used for predicting the output. The set of shared parameters are regularized to remove domain-dependent information. To this end, adversarial training is typically used, by maximizing the cross-entropy in predicting the input domain with the shared parameters.

This method separates domain-specific information from domain-common information by adding model parameters. The approach, however, transfers knowledge across domains mainly through shared parameters that represent common knowledge across all domains but do not represent more fine-grained similarities across certain subsets of domains. Furthermore, multiple sets of LSTM are used, which not only has a number of model parameters that scale with the number of domains but also its computation is non-parallel because of the inherent sequential nature endows of LSTM. Accordingly, the method may be less useful when the number of domains is very large. Besides that, these models do not dynamically model domain-specific and domain-common information inside the encoder.

As Fig. 1(d) draws, we consider a new solution for addressing these issues, that is, by using a shared-private LSTM (SP-LSTM) to extract both the domain-specific and the shared representation simultaneously, which allows domain-private and domain-common representations dynamically interact with each other during the encoding process. Given an input, SP-LSTM can internally compute both shared and private representations owing to the shared-private paradigm [8]. The main idea is to model hidden states of all words with the domain knowledge at each recurrent step, and the state is able to get the knowledge from domain-private and domain-common. At each step, each sentence has a single state, which is composed of word-level states and two sentence-level states. And each state is updated recurrently by exchanging information between respective contexts for learning knowledge of local and non-local contexts. Therefore, all states can be computed in parallel as drawn Fig. 2.

The results on a 16-domain classification task show that our method is superior to the standard shared-private model, and gives the best accuracy compared with other methods in the literature. Our code is released at https://github.com/haiming-wu/SP-LSTM.

2 Related Work

Multi-domain Learning. The work of jointly learning multiple domains can improve generalization proposed by [17,18]. A general encoder is used for all domain, and multiple output layers for prediction. Another work [19] adopts a general network with shared sentence representation, and multiple sets of parameters of attention to better capture domain characteristics. Our work is similar to theirs, but we have a set of shared word-level parameters for computing each word-level state, and multiple sets of domain-specific parameters are used to exchange sentence-level states. And domain-specific sentence state is used to update word-level states within a sentence.

Adversarial Training. Adversarial network is first used for generative model [27], and in the work [8], they take adversarial training to separate domain-common features from separate domain-specific features. A task discriminator is used to map the shared representation of sentence to a probability distribution, and estimate the task label of the sentence. Nevertheless, the shared representation from the shared encoder does not want to be identified. Formally, it is transformed into a minimax problem. Finally, the shared domain information is stored in the shared parameters that do not contain any domain-specific knowledge. In similar spirits, we adopt adversarial training to ensure the shared sentence-level parameters do not store domain-specific information.

Sentence-State LSTM. Sentence-state LSTM [30](SLSTM) is an alternative recurrent neural network structure. SLSTM views the whole sentence as a single state, which consists of sub-states for individual words and a whole sentence-level state. And states can be updated recurrently by exchanging information between their contexts. SP-LSTM adopts the same calculation mechanism as SLSTM, and captures the shared and domain-specific information by setting two sentence-level states.

3 Setting

Task. Input a sentence $\boldsymbol{s} = \{w_1, w_2, ..., w_n\}$, where w_i is the i-th word, n is the number of words and all word comes from a vocabulary $\boldsymbol{V}$. The goal is to build a model F, which can predict the sentiment label $y \in \{0, 1\}$ as a binary classification task.

Text Classifier. Firstly, We map word w_i to an embedding x_i by a embedding matrix $\boldsymbol{R}^{|\boldsymbol{V}|\times h}$, where $|\boldsymbol{V}|$ is the size of vocabulary $\boldsymbol{V}$, h is the hidden size, the sentence is thus mapped into $\boldsymbol{x} = \{x_1, x_2, ..., x_n\}$. Then, encoder is used to represent the sequence $\boldsymbol{x}$ as a representation, which can be expressed as follows:

$$\boldsymbol{h} = \text{Encoder}(\boldsymbol{x}, \boldsymbol{\theta}) \tag{1}$$

where $\boldsymbol{h}$ denotes the representation of output, $\boldsymbol{\theta}$ denotes parameters.

Secondly, the representation $\boldsymbol{h}$ is passed into a $softmax$ classification layer:

$$\hat{y} = \text{softmax}(\boldsymbol{W}_c\boldsymbol{h} + \boldsymbol{b}_c) \tag{2}$$

where $\hat{y}$ is the prediction probability distribution, $\boldsymbol{W}_c, \boldsymbol{b}_c$ are weight and bias term, correspondingly.

Training. We train the model on a specified training corpus $\boldsymbol{D}^{tra}$ by minimizing the cross-entropy between the predicted distribution $\hat{y}$ and the true distribution y:

$$L_{loss} = -\sum_{i=1}^{|\boldsymbol{D}^{tra}|} y_i \log(\hat{y}_i) \tag{3}$$

where $|\boldsymbol{D}^{tra}|$ is the size of $\boldsymbol{D}^{tra}$, y_i and $\hat{y}_i$ are distributions about i-th sample.

Multi-domain Learning Setting: Given datasets with multiple domains, multi-tasking learning attempts to investigate the correlation between these related domains to improve the performance of each dataset. Suppose there are m domains $\{\boldsymbol{D}_i\}_{i=1}^{m}$, and each of them comes from a domain i. $\boldsymbol{D}_k$ contains $|\boldsymbol{D}_k|$ data points $(\boldsymbol{s}_j^k, d_k, y_j^k)$, where $j \in \{1, 2, ..., |\boldsymbol{D}_k|\}$, $\boldsymbol{s}_j^k$ is a sequence includes $|\boldsymbol{s}_j^i|$ words $\{w_1, w_2, ..., w_{|\boldsymbol{s}_j^i|}\}$, d_k is a domain label (since we use 1 to m to number each domain, $d_k = k$) and y_j^k indicates the sentiment label (e.g. $y_j^k \in \{0, 1\}$ for binary sentiment classification). The task is to learn a classification function F trained on multiple source domain which will be used for each domain.

4 Method

In this paper, we propose a novel recurrent neural network for multi-task learning, namely, shared-private LSTM (SP-LSTM). As the name suggests that shared parameters are learned through all domains, while private parameters for their own domain. The architecture of our proposed model is illustrated in Fig. 2, which shows that the model mainly has two parts: encoding network of SP-LSTM, regularizer by adversarial training. In the following sections, we will describe each part in detail.

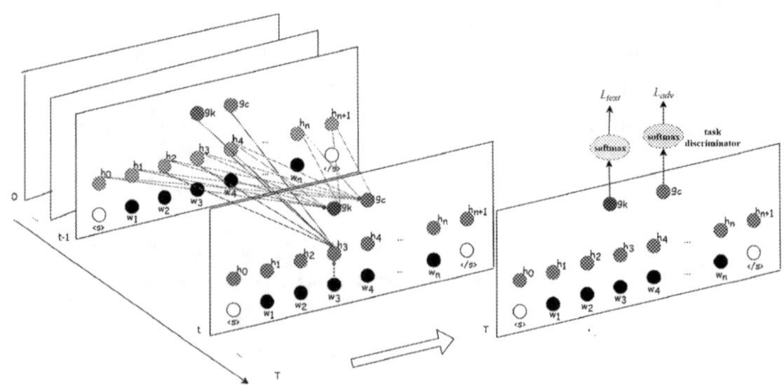

Fig. 2. Shared-private LSTM. (Color figure online)

4.1 Shared-Private LSTM

Shared-private LSTM (SP-LSTM) is designed for multi-task learning, which has three parts at each recurrent step t: hidden vectors of word-level, domain-specific and the shared sentence states. When calculating each state, word hidden state $\boldsymbol{h}_i$ extracts syntactic and semantic information for word w_i under the sentential context, private state $\boldsymbol{g}_k$ extracts knowledge for the whole sentence from domain k and shared state $\boldsymbol{g}_c$ extracts the common knowledge for all the whole sentence. Based on the previous work, we set $< s >, < /s >$ at both ends of each sentence. The hidden state at time step t thus can be denoted by:

$$\boldsymbol{H}^t = \langle \boldsymbol{h}_0^t, \boldsymbol{h}_1^t, ..., \boldsymbol{h}_{n+1}^t, \boldsymbol{g}_k^t, \boldsymbol{g}_c^t \rangle \tag{4}$$

where $\boldsymbol{h}_i^t$ denotes the hidden state for each word w_i and $\boldsymbol{g}_k^t, \boldsymbol{g}_c^t$ are sentence hidden states, the former denotes domain-specific for domain k, the latter is common representation.

SP-LSTM updates all states with a recurrent state transition process, which enriches the state representations incrementally. Then we set $\boldsymbol{h}_i^0 = x_i$, and $\boldsymbol{g}_k^0, \boldsymbol{g}_c^0$ all are the average of $\boldsymbol{h}^0$. At the recurrent step from time $t-1$ to t, the state transitions of word-level from $\boldsymbol{h}_i^{t-1}$ to $\boldsymbol{h}_i^t$, and the exchange of the sentence-level from $\boldsymbol{g}_k^{t-1}$ to $\boldsymbol{g}_k^t$ and $\boldsymbol{g}_c^{t-1}$ to $\boldsymbol{g}_c^t$. Besides that, current cell $\boldsymbol{c}_i^t, \boldsymbol{c}_k^t, \boldsymbol{c}_c^t$ are used to complete this transition of $w_i, \boldsymbol{g}^k, \boldsymbol{g}^c$ respectively as simple as LSTM.

Word-Level Hidden. As shown in Fig. 2, the solid green lines identify that each hidden vector $\boldsymbol{h}_i^t$ is computed based on the vector of x_i, the hidden vectors $\boldsymbol{h}_{i-1}^{t-1}, \boldsymbol{h}_i^{t-1}, \boldsymbol{h}_{i+1}^{t-1}$ under the sentential context and sentence hidden vectors $\boldsymbol{g}_k^{t-1}, \boldsymbol{g}_c^{t-1}$. At the same time, seven gates are utilized to balance the knowledge: $\boldsymbol{i}_i^t$ is a input gate to restrict the original information of w_i, $\boldsymbol{l}_i^t, \boldsymbol{f}_i^t, \boldsymbol{r}_i^t$ are gates that control information flow from hidden vectors $\boldsymbol{h}_{i-1}^{t-1}, \boldsymbol{h}_i^{t-1}, \boldsymbol{h}_{i+1}^{t-1}$. $\boldsymbol{k}_i^t$ is a gate controlling information flow from sentence hidden vector $\boldsymbol{g}_k^{t-1}$ of domain k. $\boldsymbol{s}_i^t$ is a gate that controls information flow from $\boldsymbol{g}_c^{t-1}$, which denotes the influence of common information on $\boldsymbol{h}_i^t$. $\boldsymbol{o}_i^t$ is an output gate from the cell state $\boldsymbol{c}_i^t$ to hidden state $\boldsymbol{h}_i^t$.

The process can be formally expressed as follows:

$$\begin{aligned}
&\boldsymbol{\xi}_i^t = [\boldsymbol{h}_{i-1}^{t-1}, \boldsymbol{h}_i^{t-1}, \boldsymbol{h}_{i+1}^{t-1}] \\
&\begin{bmatrix} \hat{\boldsymbol{i}}_i^t \\ \hat{\boldsymbol{l}}_i^t \\ \hat{\boldsymbol{f}}_i^t \\ \hat{\boldsymbol{r}}_i^t \\ \hat{\boldsymbol{k}}_i^t \\ \hat{\boldsymbol{s}}_i^t \\ \hat{\boldsymbol{o}}_i^t \end{bmatrix} = \sigma\left(\begin{bmatrix} \boldsymbol{W}_i \\ \boldsymbol{W}_l \\ \boldsymbol{W}_f \\ \boldsymbol{W}_r \\ \boldsymbol{W}_k \\ \boldsymbol{W}_s \\ \boldsymbol{W}_o \end{bmatrix} \boldsymbol{\xi}_i^t + \begin{bmatrix} \boldsymbol{O}_i \\ \boldsymbol{O}_l \\ \boldsymbol{O}_f \\ \boldsymbol{O}_r \\ \boldsymbol{O}_k \\ \boldsymbol{O}_s \\ \boldsymbol{O}_o \end{bmatrix} \boldsymbol{x}_i + \begin{bmatrix} \boldsymbol{U}_i \\ \boldsymbol{U}_l \\ \boldsymbol{U}_f \\ \boldsymbol{U}_r \\ \boldsymbol{U}_k \\ \boldsymbol{U}_s \\ \boldsymbol{U}_o \end{bmatrix} \boldsymbol{g}_k^{t-1} + \begin{bmatrix} \boldsymbol{V}_i \\ \boldsymbol{V}_l \\ \boldsymbol{V}_f \\ \boldsymbol{V}_r \\ \boldsymbol{V}_k \\ \boldsymbol{V}_s \\ \boldsymbol{V}_o \end{bmatrix} \boldsymbol{g}_c^{t-1} + \begin{bmatrix} \boldsymbol{b}_i \\ \boldsymbol{b}_l \\ \boldsymbol{b}_f \\ \boldsymbol{b}_r \\ \boldsymbol{b}_k \\ \boldsymbol{b}_s \\ \boldsymbol{b}_o \end{bmatrix} \right) \\
&\boldsymbol{u}_i^t = tanh(\boldsymbol{W}_u \boldsymbol{\xi}_i^t + \boldsymbol{O}_u \boldsymbol{x}_i + \boldsymbol{U}_u \boldsymbol{g}_k^{t-1} + \boldsymbol{V}_u \boldsymbol{g}_c^{t-1} + \boldsymbol{b}_u) \\
&\boldsymbol{i}_i^t, \boldsymbol{l}_i^t, \boldsymbol{f}_i^t, \boldsymbol{r}_i^t, \boldsymbol{k}_i^t, \boldsymbol{s}_i^t = softmax(\hat{\boldsymbol{i}}_i^t, \hat{\boldsymbol{l}}_i^t, \hat{\boldsymbol{f}}_i^t, \hat{\boldsymbol{r}}_i^t, \hat{\boldsymbol{k}}_i^t, \hat{\boldsymbol{s}}_i^t) \\
&\boldsymbol{c}_i^t = \boldsymbol{l}_i^t \odot \boldsymbol{c}_{i-1}^{t-1} + \boldsymbol{f}_i^t \odot \boldsymbol{c}_i^{t-1} + \boldsymbol{r}_i^t \odot \boldsymbol{c}_{i+1}^{t-1} + \boldsymbol{k}_i^t \odot \boldsymbol{c}_k^{t-1} \\
&\qquad + \boldsymbol{s}_i^t \odot \boldsymbol{c}_c^{t-1} + \boldsymbol{i}_i^t \odot \boldsymbol{u}_i^{t-1} \\
&\boldsymbol{h}_i^t = \boldsymbol{o}_i^t \odot tanh(\boldsymbol{c}_i^t)
\end{aligned} \tag{5}$$

where $\boldsymbol{\xi}_i^t$ is the concatenation of hidden vectors of a context window. The values of $\boldsymbol{i}_i^t, \boldsymbol{l}_i^t, \boldsymbol{f}_i^t, \boldsymbol{r}_i^t, \boldsymbol{k}_i^t$ and $\boldsymbol{c}_i^t$ are normalized so that the sum of them is 1. $\boldsymbol{\theta}_w = \{\boldsymbol{W}_x, \boldsymbol{U}_x, \boldsymbol{V}_x, \boldsymbol{b}_x\} (x \in \{i, l, f, r, k, s, u, o\})$ are model parameters that will be shared by all domains. σ is the sigmoid function.

Note that the representation $\boldsymbol{g}_k^{t-1}$ of private is used to update the state of each word, so that domain-specific knowledge is allowed to be captured during encoding. Furthermore, all the parameters $\boldsymbol{\theta}_w$ are shared across all domains.

Domain-Specific Sentence State. Thereafter, $\boldsymbol{g}_k^t, \boldsymbol{g}_c^t$ are domain-private and shared hidden representation. As Fig. 2 draws, blue dashed lines denote the calculation process from $\boldsymbol{g}_k^{t-1}$ to $\boldsymbol{g}_c^{t-1}$. Besides that, the values of $\boldsymbol{g}_k^t, \boldsymbol{g}_c^t$ both are computed based on the values of $\boldsymbol{h}_i^{t-1}$ for all $i \in [0, n+1]$. The formulas are formally presented as follows:

$$\begin{aligned}
\bar{\boldsymbol{h}} &= avg(\boldsymbol{h}_0^{t-1}, \boldsymbol{h}_1^{t-1}, ..., \boldsymbol{h}_{n+1}^{t-1}) \\
\hat{\boldsymbol{f}}_{ki}^t &= \sigma(\boldsymbol{W}_{fk}\boldsymbol{g}_k^{t-1} + \boldsymbol{U}_{fk}\boldsymbol{h}_i^{t-1} + \boldsymbol{b}_{fk}) \\
[\hat{\boldsymbol{i}}_k^t, \hat{\boldsymbol{o}}_k^t]^\mathsf{T} &= \sigma([\boldsymbol{W}_{ik}, \boldsymbol{W}_{ok}]^\mathsf{T} \boldsymbol{g}_k^{t-1} + [\boldsymbol{U}_{ik}, \boldsymbol{U}_{ok}]^\mathsf{T} \bar{\boldsymbol{h}} + [\boldsymbol{b}_{ik}, \boldsymbol{b}_{ok}]^\mathsf{T}) \\
\boldsymbol{f}_{k0}^t, ..., \boldsymbol{f}_{k(n+1)}^t, \boldsymbol{i}_k^t &= \text{softmax}(\hat{\boldsymbol{f}}_{k0}^t, ..., \hat{\boldsymbol{f}}_{k(n+1)}^t, \hat{\boldsymbol{i}}_k^t) \\
\boldsymbol{c}_k^t &= \boldsymbol{i}_k^t \odot \boldsymbol{c}_k^{t-1} + \sum_{i=0}^{n+1} \boldsymbol{f}_{ki}^t \odot \boldsymbol{c}_i^{t-1} \\
\boldsymbol{g}_k^t &= \boldsymbol{o}_k^t \odot \tanh(\boldsymbol{c}_k^t)
\end{aligned} \tag{6}$$

where $\boldsymbol{f}_{k0}^t, \boldsymbol{f}_{k1}^t, ..., \boldsymbol{f}_{k(n+1)}^t$ and $\boldsymbol{i}_k^t$ are gates that control the information from $\boldsymbol{c}_0^{t-1}, \boldsymbol{c}_1^{t-1}, ..., \boldsymbol{c}_{n+1}^{t-1}$ and $\boldsymbol{c}_k^{t-1}$, respectively, and they are normalized. $\boldsymbol{o}_k^t$ is an output gate of $\boldsymbol{g}_k^t$. The parameters $\boldsymbol{\theta}_k = \{W_{xk}, U_{xk}, b_{xk}, x \in \{i, f\}\}$ are private of the domain k.

Shared Sentence State. Subsequent to that, $\boldsymbol{g}_c^t$ is calculated with the calculation process is similar to that of $\boldsymbol{g}_k^t$, which denoted by green dashed lines of Fig. 2.

$$\begin{aligned}
\hat{\boldsymbol{f}}_{ci}^t &= \sigma(\boldsymbol{W}_{fc}\boldsymbol{g}_c^{t-1} + \boldsymbol{U}_{fc}\boldsymbol{h}_i^{t-1} + \boldsymbol{b}_{fc}) \\
[\hat{\boldsymbol{i}}_c^t, \hat{\boldsymbol{o}}_c^t]^\mathsf{T} &= \sigma([\boldsymbol{W}_{ic}, \boldsymbol{W}_{oc}]^\mathsf{T} \boldsymbol{g}_c^{t-1} + [\boldsymbol{U}_{ic}, \boldsymbol{U}_{oc}]^\mathsf{T} \bar{\boldsymbol{h}} + [\boldsymbol{b}_{ic}, \boldsymbol{b}_{oc}]^\mathsf{T}) \\
\boldsymbol{f}_{c0}^t, ..., \boldsymbol{f}_{c(n+1)}^t, \boldsymbol{i}_c^t &= \text{softmax}(\hat{\boldsymbol{f}}_{c0}^t, ..., \hat{\boldsymbol{f}}_{c(n+1)}^t, \hat{\boldsymbol{i}}_c^t) \\
\boldsymbol{c}_c^t &= \boldsymbol{i}_c^t \odot \boldsymbol{c}_c^{t-1} + \sum_{i=0}^{n+1} \boldsymbol{f}_{ci}^t \odot \boldsymbol{c}_i^{t-1} \\
\boldsymbol{g}_c^t &= \boldsymbol{o}_c^t \odot \tanh(\boldsymbol{c}_c^t)
\end{aligned} \tag{7}$$

where $\boldsymbol{f}_{c0}^t, ..., \boldsymbol{f}_{c(n+1)}^t$ and $\boldsymbol{i}_c^t$ are gates, and they are normalized. $\boldsymbol{o}_c^t$ is the output gate for $\boldsymbol{g}_c^t$. $\boldsymbol{\theta}_c = \{W_{xc}, U_{xc}, b_{xc}, x \in \{i, f\}\}$ are model parameters shared with all domains.

At last, we take the tuple $(\boldsymbol{g}_k^T, \boldsymbol{g}_c^T)$ as the output of SP-LSTM at the last time step T. Then, we adopt SP-LSTM to encode a sequence $\boldsymbol{x}_j^k$, which is described as follows:

$$(\boldsymbol{h}_j^k, \boldsymbol{s}_j^k) = (\boldsymbol{g}_k^T, \boldsymbol{g}_c^T)_j = \text{SP-LSTM}(\boldsymbol{x}_j^k, \boldsymbol{\theta}_w, \boldsymbol{\theta}_k, \boldsymbol{\theta}_c) \tag{8}$$

where $\boldsymbol{h}_j^k$ and $\boldsymbol{s}_j^k$ are the final representations of domain-specific and the domain-common.

The difference between SP-LSTM and other RNNs (LSTM, Bi-LSTM, GRU) is due to their different recurrent states. The traditional model RNNs only uses one state to represent the sequence from the beginning to a certain word, While SP-LSTM uses a structural state to represent the full sentence, which consists of two sentence-level states and $n+2$ word-level states, simultaneously. Different from RNNs, $\boldsymbol{h}_i^t$ is used to represent w_i at each step t. As t increases from 0, each word-level and sentence-level states are enriched with increasingly deeper context information.

From the perspective of multi-task learning, RNNs transfers knowledge from one end of the sentence to the other. Accordingly, on the one hand, the number of time steps scales with the size of the input, and on the other hand, RNNs can not capture shared and private knowledge simultaneously. In contrast, SP-LSTM we proposed not only allows bi-directional information flow at each word simultaneously, but also allows it between sentence-level state and every word-level state. At each step, each h_i captures an increasingly larger n-gram context, and they will be used for communication between g_k and g_c. So that SP-LSTM is able to dynamically capture the shared and private knowledge. Then, the number of recurrent steps of SP-LSTM is decided by the end-task performance rather than the sentence size, and it is more suitable for the representation of multi-domain.

4.2 Regularizer: ADV

Adversarial Training. Inspired by the generative adversarial networks (GAN) [27], we incorporate adversarial networks as a regularizer to maintain the common information which is stored by common parameters $\boldsymbol{\theta}_c$.

In theory, GAN is used to simulate a distribution $P_{g(x)}$ that is similar to the real data distribution $P_{data(x)}$, GAN thus builds a generative network G and a discriminative model D that check whether the input is real data, and then, the generative network G will be trained to generate better samples that are similar to the real data, which indicates that the data distribution $P_{g(x)}$ generated by the generative network tends to be consistent with the distribution $P_{data(x)}$ of the real data. It is formally expressed as:

$$L_{Adv} = \min_{\theta_G} \max_{\theta_D} (E_{x \ P_{data}}[\log D(x)] + E_{z \ p(z)}[\log(1 - D(G(z))]) \tag{9}$$

where θ_G, θ_D are parameters of generative network and discriminative model respectively. From the optimization formula, the negative cross-entropy is used as a loss function. And the aim of G is generating a sample that D do not know whether it is real data, so the output from the maximum optimizer is minimized.

Therefore, adversarial training can be applied in our model to optimize parameters $\boldsymbol{\theta}_c$ and $\boldsymbol{\theta}_k$. So a $softmax$ function is used as task discriminator to estimate which domain the input data comes from. Formally:

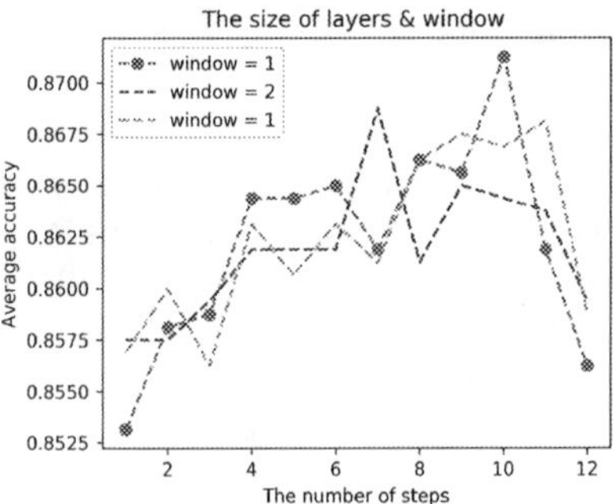

Fig. 3. Average accuracies with various window sizes and steps on four review development datas

$$D(\boldsymbol{s}_j^k, \boldsymbol{\theta}_D) = \text{softmax}(\boldsymbol{W}_D \boldsymbol{s}_j^k + \boldsymbol{b}_D) \tag{10}$$

where $D(\boldsymbol{s}_j^k, \theta_D)$ is the prediction probability distribution of domain label, $\boldsymbol{\theta}_D = \{\boldsymbol{w}_D, \boldsymbol{b}_D\}$ are model parameters.

Then, we define an adversarial loss L_{adv} with minimax optimization function:

$$L_{adv} = -\max_{\theta_c}(\min_{\theta_D} \sum_{k=1}^{m} \sum_{j=1}^{|D_k^{tra}|} d_k \log[D(\boldsymbol{s}_j^k, \theta_D)]) \tag{11}$$

where L_{adv} is minimized the cross-entropy of domain label to fine-tune discriminative model, but maximized for $\boldsymbol{\theta}_c$ of the common model parameters. In our implementation, we use the control gradient method to complete the above calculation.

The Loss Function of Model. Considering that knowledge of each sentence is distributed between the shared and private representations, so the private vectors are joined by the common one as the final representation. Then, we take a *softmax* function to predict the probability distribution $\hat{y}_j^k$ of input $\boldsymbol{s}_j^k$ likes Eq. (2):

$$\hat{y}_j^k = \text{softmax}(\boldsymbol{W}_{tk}[\boldsymbol{h}_j^k, \boldsymbol{s}_j^k] + \boldsymbol{b}_{tk}) \tag{12}$$

The loss L_{text} of text classification can be computed as:

$$L_{text} = -\sum_{k=1}^{m} \sum_{j=1}^{|\boldsymbol{D}_k^{tra}|} y_j^k \log(\hat{y}_j^k) \tag{13}$$

where, y_j^k denotes the real probability distribution.

To sum up, the training of L_{text} is straightforward, its goal is to perform better within its own domain. The adversarial loss L_{adv} has two targets: not only helps the main task achieve higher accuracy, but also keeps the common features away from across private features of each domain. Thus, the total loss function as:

$$L = L_{text} + \lambda L_{adv} \tag{14}$$

where λ is the hyper-parameter of the regularizer L_{adv}.

5 Experiments

5.1 Datasets and Settings

Datasets. In this experiment, we compare the SP-LSTM with state-of-the-art multi-task methods of text classification on FDU-MTL [8]. FDU-MTL is composed of reviews from different domains, in which there are 14 Amazon domains and two movies review domains from the IMDB and the MR datasets. And we use the original split [8]. All experiments are conducted using a GeForce GTX 1080ti GPU with 11 GB memory.

Hyperparameters. Glove 200-dimensional embeddings are adopted to initialize the word embeddings for all of the models, and embeddings are fine-tuned during model training for all tasks. Dropout [28] is applied to embedding hidden states and the output of all encoder model, with a rate of 0.7. The Adam optimizer [29] is selected for all models during the training process, with an initial learning rate of 0.0005. The batch size is set to 4. The hyper-parameters λ and β are 0.05.

5.2 Development Experiments

We choose four development data (MR, books, camera, magazines) to investigate the effect with different configurations of SP-LSTMs on average accuracies. Figure 3 draws average accuracies of SP-LSTMs with three kinds of window sizes against the number of recurrent steps. As can be seen from Fig. 3, when the number of steps increases from 1 to 12, accuracies are subject to certain fluctuations, and generally increase before reaching a maximum value, and then shows a downward trend. It indicates that the effectiveness of recurrent information exchange in SP-LSTM state transition.

Besides, there are no significant differences in the peak accuracies given by different window sizes. Considering efficiency, we choose a window size of 1 and set the number of recurrent steps to 10 according to Fig. 3.

5.3 Results and Analysis

Table 1 shows the final results using different multi-task learning strategies. LSTM+DO denotes the model adopts a general encoder with LSTM, and multiple output layers for prediction. We reproduce it with an average accuracy of 85.28%.

Table 1. Results on the FDU-MTL dataset: the training corpus contains all domains

Model	LSTM +DO	LSTM +ADV	LSTM+ ADV+Diff	DSAM	SP-LSTM+ ADV+Diff	SP-LSTM	SP-SLSTM +ADV
Apparel	83.50	86.00	87.25	85.00	88.00	**89.50**	88.75
Baby	86.75	88.00	87.00	90.00	89.75	89.75	**90.75**
Books	85.75	84.50	86.25	84.50	88.25	88.50	**89.00**
Camera	89.25	89.00	88.25	89.50	91.00	91.00	**91.50**
Electronics	84.75	85.75	85.75	86.25	88.25	87.75	**89.75**
DVD	85.25	85.75	86.00	87.25	87.50	88.50	**88.75**
Health	88.75	88.00	87.50	89.25	87.25	**90.75**	90.00
IMDB	85.25	83.00	86.25	86.75	**87.00**	85.75	85.75
Kitchen	84.25	85.50	87.25	90.00	**90.75**	88.50	88.50
Magazines	90.50	92.25	93.25	93.50	**94.25**	94.00	94.00
MR	74.75	74.75	74.75	**77.25**	76.50	74.00	76.25
Music	82.75	84.25	83.25	82.25	85.25	84.75	**85.25**
Software	86.50	87.50	83.75	86.75	90.00	89.75	**90.75**
Sports	86.50	85.50	86.00	89.25	**90.25**	89.50	90.00
Toys	86.00	85.75	89.75	89.25	89.00	**91.00**	88.75
Video	84.00	85.50	83.75	87.00	**89.50**	88.75	88.75
Avg_Acc.	85.28	85.69	86.00	87.11	88.28	88.23	**88.53**

LSTM+ADV denotes the adversarial shared-private model [8]. They use multiple LSTM to encode sentence from different domains, adversarial training (ADV) is adopted to model parameters. And LSTM-ADV-Diff is their model by adding orthogonality constraints (Diff) that maximizes the difference between shared and private parameters. Our implementation of LSTM-ADV+Diff gives an averaged accuracy of 86.00%, which is comparable to 86.10% reported by themselves.

MSAM denotes the method [19] of learning domain descriptor vectors for multi-domain training. Which learns a general sentence-level vector by Bi-LSTM, and adopts self-attention to learn a domain-specific descriptor vectors. Then, the connecting of the general and domain-specific vectors is passed domain-specific output layers. We rework it with our dataset, and an average accuracy of 87.11% is given.

SP-LSTM+ADV+Diff represents the model of [8], but instead of multiple LSTM, it encodes the sentence only with an SP-LSTM we proposed, which adds orthogonality constraints as regularizer. As can be seen from Table 1, the average accuracy of 88.28% is given, which significantly outperforms LSTM+ADV+Diff, indicating that SP-LSTM is better at encoding in multi-task learning environment. Therefore, We take this method as our baseline.

SP-LSTM denotes our method, which is utilized to represent sentence and give the shared and domain-specific vectors. It gives an average accuracy of

88.23%, which significantly outperforms existing methods. This shows that SP-LSTM is suitable for the encoding of multi-domain.

By further adding the adversarial training regularizer, the performance of SP-LSTM+ADV increases to 88.53%, which shows the effectiveness of adversarial training under our framework. However, the orthogonality constraints are not still useful since the average accuracy of SP-LSTM+ADV+Diff model is 88.28%, which indicates that SP-LSTM and orthogonality constrains are incompatible, and Diff can not help improve the performance of SP-LSTM. Meanwhile, SP-LSTM+ADV gives the best reported results in the literature.

In addition, the advantage of our method is that it runs faster. Under the same model parameters as LSTM+ADV, the test time of our model was 8.30 s, while that of LSTM+ADV was 9.62 s.

6 Conclusion

We investigate SP-LSTM for multi-domain text classification, which separates the domain-specific and domain-common knowledge by using a set of shared word-level parameters to encode word hidden states with domain knowledge, and using a set of shared sentence-level parameters to extract the common information, using a set of domain-specific parameters for storing private knowledge. Results on 16 domains show that our method significantly outperforms traditional shared-private architectures for transfer learning.

Acknowledgments. The work described in this paper was initiated and partly done when Haiming Wu was visiting Westlake University. It is supported by the National Statistical Science Research Project of China under Grant No. 2016LY98, the National Natural Science Foundation of China under Grant No. 61876205, the Science and Technology Department of Guangdong Province in China under Grant Nos. 2016A010101020, 2016A010101021 and 2016A010101022, the Science and Technology Plan Project of Guangzhou under Grant Nos. 201802010033 and 201804010433.

References

1. Daume III, H., Marcu, D.: Domain adaptation for statistical classifiers. J. Artif. Intell. Res. **26**, 101–126 (2006)
2. Daumé III, H.: Frustratingly easy domain adaptation. arXiv preprint arXiv:0907.1815 (2009)
3. Blitzer, J., McDonald, R., Pereira, F.: Domain adaptation with structural correspondence learning. In: Proceedings of EMNLP, pp. 120–128 (2006)
4. Chen, M., Weinberger, K.Q., Blitzer, J.: Co-training for domain adaptation. In: Advances in Neural Information Processing Systems, pp. 2456–2464 (2011)
5. Blitzer, J., Foster, D.P., Kakade, S.M.: Domain adaptation with coupled subspaces (2011)
6. McDonald, R., Petrov, S., Hall, K.: Multi-source transfer of delexicalized dependency parsers. In: Proceedings of EMNLP, pp. 62–72 (2011)
7. Lin, B.Y., Lu, W.: Neural adaptation layers for cross-domain named entity recognition. arXiv preprint arXiv:1810.06368 (2018)

8. Liu, P., Qiu, X., Huang, X.: Adversarial multi-task learning for text classification. arXiv preprint arXiv:1704.05742 (2017)
9. Alonso, H.M., Plank, B.: When is multitask learning effective? Semantic sequence prediction under varying data conditions. arXiv preprint arXiv:1612.02251 (2016)
10. Ruder, S., Bingel, J., Augenstein, I., et al.: Sluice networks: learning what to share between loosely related tasks. stat **23**, 1050 (2017)
11. Braud, C., Plank, B., Søgaard, A.: Multi-view and multi-task training of RST discourse parsers. In: Proceedings of COLING 2016, pp. 1903–1913 (2016)
12. Rasooli, M.S., Tetreault, J.: Yara parser: A fast and accurate dependency parser. arXiv preprint arXiv:1503.06733 (2015)
13. Goodman, J., Vlachos, A., Naradowsky, J.: Noise reduction and targeted exploration in imitation learning for abstract meaning representation parsing. In: Proceedings of ACL, vol. 1, pp. 1–11 (2016)
14. Cao, P., Chen, Y., Liu, K., et al.: Adversarial transfer learning for chinese named entity recognition with self-attention mechanism. In: Proceedings of EMNLP, pp. 182–192 (2018)
15. Li, S., Zong, C.: Multi-domain sentiment classification. In: Proceedings of ACL, pp. 257–260 (2008)
16. Chen, X., Cardie, C.: Multinomial adversarial networks for multi-domain text classification. arXiv preprint arXiv:1802.05694 (2018)
17. Liu, P., Qiu, X., Huang, X.: Recurrent neural network for text classification with multi-task learning. arXiv preprint arXiv:1605.05101 (2016)
18. Nam, H., Han, B.: Learning multi-domain convolutional neural networks for visual tracking. In: Proceedings of CVPR, pp. 4293–4302 (2016)
19. Liu, Q., Zhang, Y., Liu, J.: Learning domain representation for multi-domain sentiment classification. In: Proceedings of ACL, Volume 1 (Long Papers), pp. 541–550 (2018)
20. Mou, L., Meng, Z., Yan, R., et al.: How transferable are neural networks in NLP applications? arXiv preprint arXiv:1603.06111 (2016)
21. Bingel, J., Søgaard, A.: Identifying beneficial task relations for multi-task learning in deep neural networks. arXiv preprint arXiv:1702.08303 (2017)
22. Bollmann, M., Søgaard, A., Bingel, J.: Multi-task learning for historical text normalization: size matters. In: Proceedings of the Workshop on Deep Learning Approaches for Low-Resource NLP, pp. 19–24 (2018)
23. Augenstein, I., Ruder, S., Søgaard, A.: Multi-task learning of pairwise sequence classification tasks over disparate label spaces. arXiv preprint arXiv:1802.09913 (2018)
24. Shi, P., Teng, Z., Zhang, Y.: Exploiting mutual benefits between syntax and semantic roles using neural network. In: Proceedings of EMNLP, pp. 968–974 (2016)
25. Søgaard, A., Goldberg, Y.: Deep multi-task learning with low level tasks supervised at lower layers. In: Proceedings of ACL, vol. 2, pp. 231–235 (2016)
26. Zhang, M., Zhang, Y., Fu, G.: End-to-end neural relation extraction with global optimization. In: Proceedings of EMNLP, pp. 1730–1740 (2017)
27. Goodfellow, I., Pouget-Abadie, J., Mirza, M., et al.: Generative adversarial nets. In: Advances in neural information processing systems, pp. 2672–2680 (2014)
28. Srivastava, N., Hinton, G., Krizhevsky, A., et al.: Dropout: a simple way to prevent neural networks from overfitting. J. Mach. Learn. Res. **15**(1), 1929–1958 (2014)
29. Kingma, D.P., Ba, J.: Adam: A method for stochastic optimization. arXiv preprint arXiv:1412.6980 (2014)
30. Zhang, Y., Liu, Q., Song, L.: Sentence-state LSTM for text representation. arXiv preprint arXiv:1805.02474 (2018)

Co-attention and Aggregation Based Chinese Recognizing Textual Entailment Model

Pengcheng Liu, Lingling Mu(✉), and Hongying Zan

College of Information Engineering, Zhengzhou University, Zhengzhou, China
Liupengcheng2016@163.com, iellmu@zzu.edu.cn

Abstract. Recognizing Textual Entailment is a fundamental task of natural language processing, and its purpose is to recognize the inferential relationship between two sentences. With the development of deep learning and construction of relevant corpus, great progress has been made in English Textual Entailment. However, the progress in Chinese Textual Entailment is relatively rare because of the lack of large-scale annotated corpus. The Seventeenth China National Conference on Computational Linguistics (CCL 2018) first released a Chinese textual entailment dataset that including 100,000 sentence pairs, which provides support for application of deep learning model. Inspired by attention models on English, we proposed a Chinese recognizing textual entailment model based on co-attention and aggregation. This model uses co-attention to calculate the feature of relationship between two sentences, and aggregates this feature with another feature obtained from sentences. Our model achieved 93.5% accuracy on CCL2018 textual entailment dataset, which is higher than the first place in previous evaluations. Experimental results showed that recognition of contradiction relations is difficult, but our model outperforms other benchmark models. What's more, our model can be applied to Chinese document based question answer (DBQA). The accuracy of the experiment results on the dataset of NLPCC2016 is 72.3%.

Keywords: Textual entailment · Co-attention · Aggregation · DBQA

1 Introduction

Recognizing Textual Entailment (RTE), also known as natural language inference (NLI), is one of the important tasks in the field of natural language processing (NLP), and its achievement could be applied to other tasks such as Question Answer (QA), reading comprehension, etc. RTE is a study to determine whether there is a one-way semantic inferential relationship between two sentences. The two sentences are called as premise and hypothesis, respectively. According to whether the hypothesis can be inferred by the corresponding premise, the relationships between two sentences can be divided into three categories: entailment, contradiction and neural (Table 1).

The authors were supported financially by the National Social Science Fund of China (18ZDA315), Programs for Science and Technology Development in Henan province (No. 192102210260) and the Key Scientific Research Program of Higher Education of Henan (No. 20A520038).

J. Tang et al. (Eds.): NLPCC 2019, LNAI 11839, pp. 129–141, 2019.
https://doi.org/10.1007/978-3-030-32236-6_11

Table 1. Textual entailment samples

Premise	Hypothesis	Relationship
长颈鹿的嘴巴闭上了。(The giraffe's mouth closed.)	长颈鹿不吃东西。(The giraffe doesn't eat.)	Entailment
长颈鹿的嘴巴闭上了。(The giraffe's mouth closed.)	长颈鹿的嘴巴张开。(The giraffe's mouth is open.)	Contradiction
长颈鹿的嘴巴闭上了。(The giraffe's mouth closed.)	长颈鹿的脖子长。(The giraffe has a long neck.)	Neutral

In recent years, English textual entailment recognition has been developing rapidly because of the construction of large-scale annotated corpus [1] and the development of deep learning methods [2]. In deep learning neural models, attention based models perform well in English textual entailment recognition, which can effectively extract interactive information between two sentences.

In the field of Chinese recognizing textual entailment, Tan *et al.* [3] proposed the BiLSTM+CNN method and the accuracy achieved 61.9% in RITE2014 Chinese corpus. The hierarchical LSTM method proposed by Chen *et al.* [4] achieved 58.9% accuracy on reading comprehension data M2OCTE. However, the lack of Chinese large-scale corpus makes the use of deep learning model still relatively rare. Table 2 lists the common Chinese RTE datasets. The CCL2018 Chinese RTE task firstly releases a Chinese textual entailment corpus with 100,000 sentences pairs, which provide support for the use of deep neural methods, The current highest accuracy on this corpus is 82.38%. The attention-based models in Chinese textual entailment have a better condition for application due to the improvement of large-scale corpuses.

Table 2. Chinese textual entailment datasets

	Train/Test (number of sentences pairs)	Accuracy (%)
RITE2014	1,976/1,200	61.74 [3]
M2OCTE	8,092/5,117	58.92 [4]
CCL2018	90,000/10,000	82.38[a]

[a]http://www.cips-cl.org/static/CCL2018/call-evaluation.html#task3

Inspired by the models of Decomp-Att [5] and SWEM [6], this paper proposes a textual entailment model based on co-attention and aggregation, which obtains 93.5% on the CCL2018 Chinese textual entailment recognition dataset. The accuracy exceeded the first place in previous evaluations of CCL2018. The model simultaneously calculates a weight matrix of two sentences through co-attention. The weight matrix that denote relationship between two sentences is interacted with encoding features through aggregation. In order to test the cross-task ability of the textual entailment model, this model was applied to QA tasks, and 72.3% accuracy was obtained on the DBQA dataset of NLPCC2016, exceeding the third place in the evaluation of NLPCC2016[1]. The contributions of this model are as follows:

(1) We successfully use co-attention in Chinese textual entailment to recognize the semantic inferential relationship between two sentences.
(2) We use aggregation to get more features of the encoding layer and reduce features loss.
(3) We add a pooling operation to enhance our model's ability of features extraction.

The rest of this paper included: Sect. 2 introduces the related backgrounds of the RTE models. Section 3 describes the model based on co-attention and aggregation in details. Section 4 shows the experimental results and discussions, and Sect. 5 is conclusion and prospect.

2 Related Work

RTE is firstly proposed by Dagan *et al.* [7]. Early studies usually use evaluation datasets such as PASCAL [8], RTE [9] and SICK [10]. Then large-scale annotated corpuses such as SNLI and MultiNLI [11] are published, which facilitate the application of deep learning models on RTE task. The textual entailment methods based on deep learning have two types. The first method, uses the encoder to obtain the features of two sentences respectively, and then uses the aggregation to construct the corresponding feature. The second method uses attention to match words of two sentences, and obtains the feature vector of their relationship.

The first method is characterized by encoding sentences respectively. Bowman *et al.* [1] first use the neural network model to process textual entailment. They use LSTM and RNN to represent the sentence pairs in SNLI, and finally input the connection of these two representations into the multi-layer perceptron. Their experimental results on SNLI achieves 77.6% accuracy. Wang *et al.* [2] first use LSTM to encode and compare two sentences, then use attention to construct a weight matrix for them, and later use LSTM for matching. It is an early work of RTE combining attention and neural network. The SWEM model proposed by Shen *et al.* [6] is based on the max pooling and average pooling of word embedding. It is evaluated on 17 datasets including SNLI and MultiNLI, and most of them achieve the best accuracy. In addition, the InferSent model on the basis of BiLSTM proposed by Conneau *et al.* [12] reaches 84.5% on SNLI.

The second method is proposed based on the first method, which combines attention with sentences encoding and can obtain more interactive information. The attention mechanism that calculates sentences relationship becomes an important part of English RTE models. ESIM proposed by Chen *et al.* [13] consists of two parts: one uses the sequence model to collect the context information of words, and the other uses the tree model to collect the clause information. Both of them use attention to match

[1] http://tcci.ccf.org.cn/conference/2016/pages/page05_evadata.html.

words in sentences. It increases the accuracy of SNLI to above 88% for the first time. Moreover, Decomp-Att proposed by Parikh *et al.* [5] is based on the matching mechanism of sentence pairs. It is characterized by combining the matching mechanism with the attention. It reaches 86.8% on SNLI with a simple structure. Furthermore, The MwAN model proposed by Tan *et al.* [14] combines four attention mechanisms. It achieves 89.4% on SNLI and 91.35% accuracy on sQuAD. The DR-BiLSTM proposed by Ghaeini et al. [15] demonstrates that enhancing the relationship between premise and hypothesis during coding helps to improve the model's effectiveness. Finally, the result of a DRCN model based on the co-attention and RNN proposed by Kim *et al.* [16] is the best on SNLI.

The above models have been widely used in the English textual entailment recognition, but are rarely applied to Chinese textual entailment. Inspired by the models of Decomp-Att, ESIM, SWEM and DR-BiLSTM, this paper proposed a Chinese textual entailment model that merges attention, pooling and aggregation. The model is characterized by combination of the co-attention mechanism and the aggregation mechanism. The structure of it is simpler than the traditional deep neural network models. The experiment results showed that the accuracy on the CCL2018 dataset is 93.5%, which is the best result on this dataset. Our model was also applied to the question and answer task, and achieved an accuracy of 72.3% on the NLPCC2016 document based QA dataset.

3 Model

Our model is called Co-Attention and Aggregation Model (CoAM). It's structure is shown in Fig. 1. It consists of four parts: encoding layer, co-attention layer, aggregation layer and pooling layer. Firstly, we convert the sentences to vector representations and apply multilayer perceptron (MLP) to extract feature further. Then we calculate the corresponding co-attention weights for two sentences. Next, we aggregate the attention weights with the sentence representations. Finally, we use pooling to combine features and use softmax function for the final decision.

3.1 Encoding Layer

The purpose of the encoding layer is to encode the premises and the hypothesizes respectively. Encoding layer uses MLP to make the model simple and fast. After obtaining word embedding sequences $\mathbf{p}$ and $\mathbf{h}$, the features are extracted to obtain $\overline{\mathbf{p}}$ and $\overline{\mathbf{h}}$, as Eqs. (1) to (2).

$$\overline{\boldsymbol{p}} = \delta(W\boldsymbol{p} + b) \tag{1}$$

$$\overline{\boldsymbol{h}} = \delta(W\boldsymbol{h} + \mathrm{b}) \tag{2}$$

Where $\mathbf{p} \in \mathbf{R}^{\mathbf{m} \times \mathbf{d}}, \mathbf{h} \in \mathbf{R}^{\mathbf{n} \times \mathbf{d}}$, $\overline{\boldsymbol{p}} \in \mathbf{R}^{\mathbf{m} \times \mathbf{d}}, \overline{\boldsymbol{h}} \in \mathbf{R}^{\mathbf{n} \times \mathbf{d}}$, and W, b is the network parameter, $\mathbf{d}$ is the dimension of word embedding, and δ is the activation function. The lengths of $\mathbf{p}$ and $\mathbf{h}$ are $\mathbf{m}$ and $\mathbf{n}$ respectively.

3.2 Co-attention Layer

Co-attention layer is to obtain the interactive information of two sentences through the calculation of co-attention between one sentence and another.

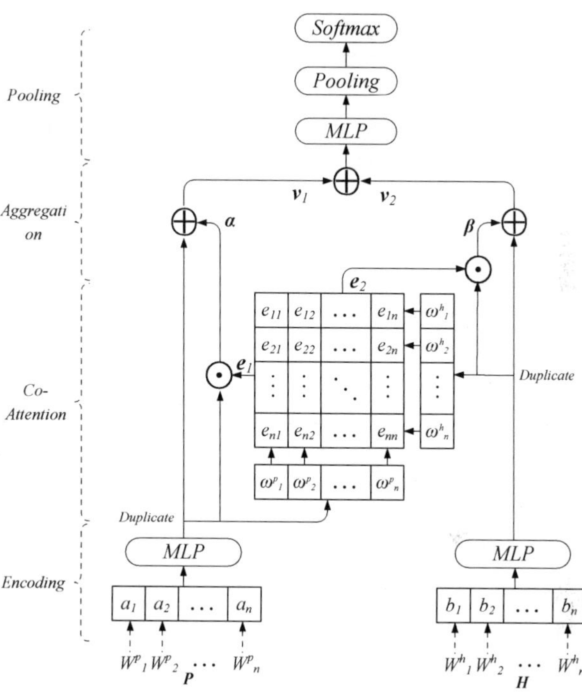

Fig. 1. Co-Attention model's structure chart. From bottom to top, **P** and **H** represent premise and hypothesis sentences of the encoding layer, respectively. MLP stands for multi-layer perceptron, Duplicate stands for copy operation, and ⊕ stands aggregation for multiple vectors, ⊙ represents the dot multiplication operation of two vectors.

Firstly, the words in sentence pairs are aligned. Then the attention weights of each sentence are calculated respectively. The alignment refers to build an m × n matrix $\boldsymbol{E}_{mn}$ with the words in two sequences $\overline{\mathbf{p}}$ and $\overline{\mathbf{h}}$ as the rows and columns respectively. Next, we use attention calculation based on $\boldsymbol{e}_{ij}$ that is the elements of $\boldsymbol{E}_{mn}$ to get the attention weights β_i ($\overline{\mathbf{h}}$ relative to $\overline{\mathbf{p}}$) and the attention weights α_j ($\overline{\mathbf{p}}$ relative to $\overline{\mathbf{h}}$). Finally, we obtain similar parts of the relationships between premises and hypothesizes.

The co-attention mechanism obtains more interactive information than the self-attention, which is helpful for the judgment of the relationship between sentences. The process for calculating the weight matrix are in Eqs. (3) to (5)

$$\mathrm{E_{mn}} = \overline{\mathbf{p}}^T \overline{\mathbf{h}} \tag{3}$$

$$\beta_i = \sum\nolimits_1^n \frac{\exp(\boldsymbol{e}_{ij})}{\sum\nolimits_{k=1}^j \exp(\boldsymbol{e}_{ik})} h_j \tag{4}$$

$$\alpha_j = \sum\nolimits_1^m \frac{\exp(\boldsymbol{e}_{ij})}{\sum\nolimits_{k=1}^j \exp(\boldsymbol{e}_{jk})} p_i \tag{5}$$

Where β_i represents attention weight that $\overline{\mathbf{h}}$ aligned with $\overline{\mathbf{p}}$; α_j attention weight that $\overline{\mathbf{p}}$ aligned with $\overline{\mathbf{h}}$.

3.3 Aggregation Layer

Aggregation layer is to aggregate the features obtained by the co-attention layer with the features of the encoding layer.

The vectors $p_i \in \overline{\mathbf{p}}$ and $h_j \in \overline{\mathbf{h}}$ are aggregated with the attention weights β_i and α_j, respectively. The method of aggregation includes concatenation, subtraction and multiplication, aim to get the results of the comparison between the sentences and their attention weights. A perceptron network layer G forwards the aggregation of each sentence. The outputs of G are the weight vectors $\boldsymbol{v}_{1,i}$ and $\boldsymbol{v}_{2,j}$ corresponding to the words of each sentence, as shown in Eqs. (6) and (7).

$$\boldsymbol{v}_{1,i} = \mathrm{G}([\beta_i; p_i; p_i - \beta_i; p_i \cdot \beta_i]) \tag{6}$$

$$\boldsymbol{v}_{2,j} = \mathrm{G}([\alpha_j; h_j; h_j - \alpha_j; h_j \cdot \alpha_j]) \tag{7}$$

3.4 Pooling Layer

Pooling layer is to further extract the features obtained by aggregation layer. At first, the words' weight vectors $\boldsymbol{v}_{1,i}$ and $\boldsymbol{v}_{2,j}$ are accumulated into sentences' weight vectors $\boldsymbol{v}_1$ and $\boldsymbol{v}_2$, respectively. We use max pooling operation of sentences to get $\boldsymbol{v}_3$, $\boldsymbol{v}_4$ for two sentences. We connect $\boldsymbol{v}_1$, $\boldsymbol{v}_2$, $\boldsymbol{v}_3$ and $\boldsymbol{v}_4$, and feed them to a forward neural network H to obtain a vector $\mathbf{v} \in \boldsymbol{R}^3$. Finally, $\mathbf{v}$ is converted to the final label $\tilde{l}$ by softmax function. The formal representation of the pooling layer is shown as Eqs. (8) to (13).

$$\boldsymbol{v}_1 = \sum\nolimits_1^m \boldsymbol{v}_{1,i} \tag{8}$$

$$\boldsymbol{v}_2 = \sum\nolimits_1^n \boldsymbol{v}_{2,j} \tag{9}$$

$$\boldsymbol{v_3} = Max\text{-pooling}(\mathrm{p_1, p_2, \ldots p_m}) \tag{10}$$

$$\boldsymbol{v_4} = Max\text{-pooling}(\mathrm{h_1, h_2, \ldots h_n}) \tag{11}$$

$$\boldsymbol{v} = \mathrm{H}([\boldsymbol{v_1}; \boldsymbol{v_2}; \boldsymbol{v_3}; \boldsymbol{v_4}]) \tag{12}$$

$$\tilde{l} = \mathrm{softmax}(\mathbf{v}) \tag{13}$$

4 Experiments and Analysis

4.1 Experimental Setup

In the process of data preprocessing, we use the jieba[2] word segmentation tools. Chinese word embedding are trained from the People's Daily and other corpuses by the method proposed by Li *et al.* [17]. Word embedding dimension is 300. Experiment use the PyTorch deep learning framework. The batch size is 64. The MLP hidden layer nodes are set to 300. Learning rate is 0.0004 and dropout rate is 0.3. We use the Adam function as optimization function, and use the cross entropy function as loss function. In addition, early stopping is used to prevent over-fitting. The evaluation uses accuracy which calculated as Eq. (14).

$$Acc = \frac{\tilde{l}_{correct}}{l} \tag{14}$$

Where $\tilde{l}_{correct}$ represents the number of labels that are correctly classified; l is the number of true labels of raw dataset.

4.2 Experiments on Textual Entailment

We used the CCL2018 Chinese Natural Language Inference evaluation dataset. The number of training set is 90,000, development set is 10,000 and test set is 10,000. Three categories are balance in each dataset (Table 3).

Table 3. Category statistics of datasets

	Neutral	Entailment	Contradiction	Total
Train	31,325	29,738	28,937	90,000
Dev	3,098	3,485	3,417	10,000
Test	3,182	3,475	3,343	10,000

[2] https://pypi.org/project/jieba/.

Experimental Results. We use Decomp-Att as the baseline model, and compare the CoAM with other attention models, including ESIM, SWEM, Decomp-Att, MwAtt, Self-Att, BiLSTM, and LSTM+CNN (the best accuracy model in previous evaluation) (Table 4).

The attention models such as CoAM, MwAtt and Self-Att outperformed the models without attention, which indicating that the attention model has good performance in Chinese RTE. Our model CoAM not only reaches the highest micro-average accuracy 93.5%, but it is also effective in the classification of each category. It shows that our model is suitable for Chinese textual entailment recognition tasks than other models. Meanwhile, most attention models have the lowest accuracy rate on contradiction categories, and the highest accuracy rate is the entailment categories. It can be seen that the recognition of contradiction categories is relatively difficult.

Table 4. Model comparison results of CCL2018 dataset. N, E, C represent the accuracy rates in Neural, Entailment and Contradiction categories respectively. The reason that LSTM+CNN without detail categories accuracy is it was the first place in the evaluation.

Models	Acc	N	E	C
Decomp-Att (baseline)	86.5	87.1	88.0	84.4
ESIM	72.8	72.7	75.3	70.2
SWEM	74.2	74.8	75.9	72.0
LSTM+CNN	82.4	–	–	–
BiLSTM	78.3	80.0	79.3	75.6
Self-Att	90.1	90.3	91.7	88.3
MwAtt	91.3	91.8	92.5	89.6
CoAM	**93.5**	**93.8**	**94.9**	**91.7**

Results Analysis. The experimental results of CoAM show that 42.5% of all classification errors is the error of contradiction relationship recognition (Tables 5 and 6). The neutral and entailment error rates are only 30.2% and 27.3%, respectively. The recognition of the entailment relationship is higher than the neutral. Because the entailment relationship has asymmetrical characteristics as a one-way inference relationship.

Table 5. Classification results confusion matrix

		Prediction		
		N	E	C
True	N	2986	107	89
	E	69	3298	108
	C	77	199	3067

Table 6. Error Rate Statistics. Number of errors is incorrect predictions in each category, proportion refers to percentage of each category of error in all errors.

Labels	Number of errors	Proportion
N	196	30.2%
E	177	27.3%
C	276	42.5%

In order to analyze the role of the attention mechanism, we outputs the attention weights between premise and hypothesis in each attention model. The relationship of the example shown in Fig. 2 is contradiction. The recognition result of CoAM is correct, but Decomp-Att and ESIM are wrong.

Figure 2 shows that the attention weights are higher between similar words in models CoAM and ESIM. However, the ESIM is not effective in distinguishing the words with different meaning. The difference of Decomp-Att's attention weights for various words is lower than CoAM. For the sentences "四位芭蕾舞演员正舞台上跳舞 (Four ballet dancers are dancing on the stage)" and "所有的芭蕾舞演员都在舞台上休息 (All the ballet dancers rest on the stage)", the model CoAM and ESIM both can

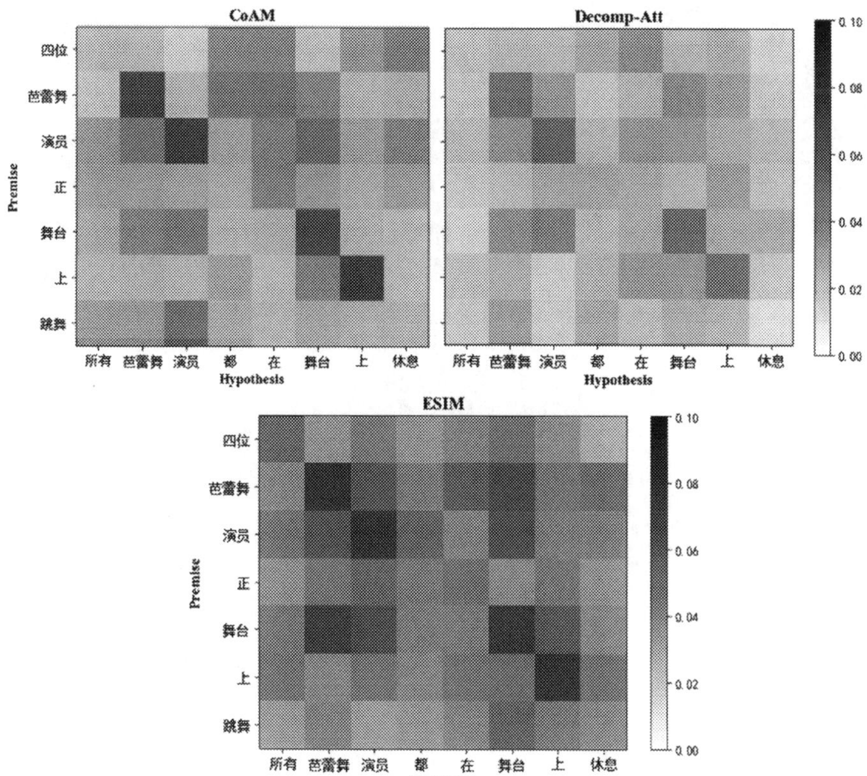

Fig. 2. Attention weight Matrix of models. The darker of the color, the greater of correlation between sentence pair.

recognize the same words, but the ESIM couldn't recognize different words such as "休息 (rest)" and "跳舞 (dancing)". The attention weight of "休息 (rest)" and "跳舞 (dancing)" in ESIM is higher than that in CoAM. The attention weights of the same words in Decomp-Att is lower than that in CoAM. Therefore, the CoAM is more effective in recognizing both the same words and different words than them. The experimental result show the mechanism of co-attention is more effective.

However, the model has two problems (Fig. 3): (1) Limited recognition effect on short text sentence pairs. (2) The recognition of synonyms and antonyms in the model still needs to be improved. For example, in the first example (Fig. 3a), the model failed to obtain the semantic relationship between "皮艇 (kayak)" and "潜水 (diving)". As in the second example (Fig. 3b), the hypothesis sentence is too short to correctly recognize their relationship. In error sample statistics, the length of 45.3% of wrong predicted examples are less than four. The third example (Fig. 3c) shows that the deep semantic relationship is still difficult to be reflected in ordinary attention calculation.

Ablation Study. Ablation analysis shows that attention part and the subtraction operation in aggregation layer are the most important operations (Table 7).

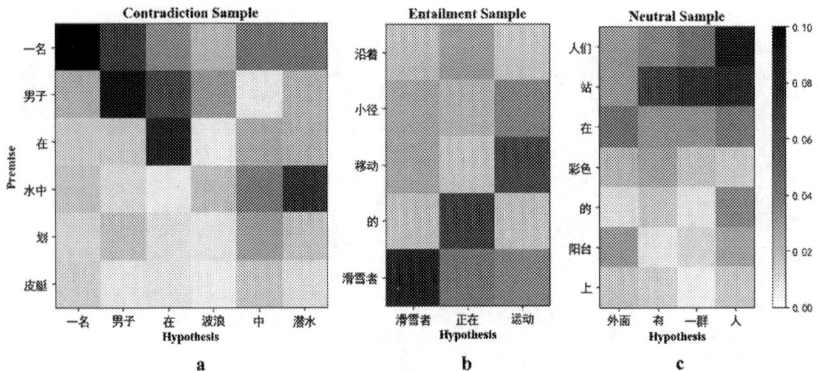

Fig. 3. Attention weight Matrix of Sentence Pairs

Table 7. Model Ablation study results

Model	Acc
CoAM – co-attention	79.2
CoAM – pooling	90.2
$\text{CoAM}^{\text{Aggregation}}$ – dot	91.7
$\text{CoAM}^{\text{Aggregation}}$ – cat	89.3
$\text{CoAM}^{\text{Aggregation}}$ – min	86.3
CoAM	93.5

The co-attention part has the greatest contribution to the whole model, because the correct rate of the whole model drops by 14.28% without it, which is the biggest drop. It is reasonable that the attention operation is helpful to capture the mutual information hypothesis and the premise. After removing the pooling part, the model performance decreased by 3.4%, which was the least, indicating that the pooling mechanism contributed the least to the whole model. In the aggregation layer, the operation of removing the subtraction has the most decline, because textual entailment is to recognize one-way inference relationship, the asymmetric operation is useful. Connection in the aggregation layer is relatively more effective than dot multiplication.

4.3 Experiments on DBQA

Textual entailment recognition has a strong relevance to document-based QA (DBQA) task. The DBQA task is to give a question and an answer and judge whether the answer matches the question. It can be regarded as a binary classification problem of sentences' relationship. In order to verify the adaptability of the model for cross-task, this paper conducted experiments on the DBQA dataset of the NLPCC2016 evaluation task. The NLPCC2016 DBQA dataset has 181,882 QA pairs in training set and 122,531 QA pairs in test set. Every QA pair is divided into two categories: correct and wrong. We use experimental implementation trained on RTE task for fine-turn. The evaluation index uses the Accuracy (ACC), the Macro Average Precision (MAP) and the Mean Reciprocal Rank (MRR).

Table 8. Model comparison result

	ACC	MAP	MRR
1(CNN)	0.7906	0.8586	0.8592
2(CNN+LSTM)	0.7385	0.8263	0.8269
3(Bi-LSTM)	0.7144	0.8111	0.8120
CoAM	0.7233	0.8174	0.7951
Dec-comp(baseline)	0.6954	0.7825	0.7632
ESIM	0.6478	0.6573	0.6733
SWEM	0.6326	0.6623	0.6815

The performance of CoAM on the NLPCC2016 DBQA test set is shown in Table 8. The model 1–3 are the top 3 models in the evaluation. The accuracy rate of our model is 72.3%, which exceeded the accuracy of the third model BiLSTM. The top two models of the evaluation combined external knowledge to improve accuracy. We also outperformed the baseline model and other attention models. Experiments demonstrated the effectiveness of the co-attention model on the QA task, and the ability of the model for cross-tasks.

5 Conclusions and Future Work

We presented a simple co-attention and aggregation based model for Chinese Recognizing Textual Entailment. The main contribution of the model is to combine the attention mechanism and the aggregation mechanism. It uses the encoding part information to improve the extraction ability of the inter-sentence information. Our model achieved the state of the art on the CCL2018 textual entailment dataset with 93.5%, and the model outperformed the other models in the recognition of contradiction categories. At the same time, the model achieved an accuracy of 72.3% on the NLPCC2016 DBQA dataset.

The next step is to improve the recognition of contradiction relationships. On the one hand, to add external knowledge to solve the problem of short sentence recognition. On the other hand, to add semantic information such as synonym or antonyms to increase the performance.

References

1. Bowman, S.R., Angeli, G., Potts, C.: A large annotated corpus for learning natural language inference. In: Proceedings of the 2015 Conference on Empirical Methods in Natural Language Processing, pp. 632–642. ACL, Lisbon (2015)
2. Wang, S., Jiang, J.: Learning natural language inference with LSTM. arXiv preprint arXiv: 1512.08849 (2015)
3. Tan, Y., Liu, Z., Lv, X.: CNN and BiLSTM based Chinese textual entailment recognition. J. Chin. Inf. Proc. **32**(7), 11–19 (2018)
4. Chen, Q., Chen, X., Guo, X.: Multiple-to-One Chinese textual entailment for reading comprehension. J. Chin. Inf. Proc. **32**(4), 87–94 (2018)
5. Parikh, A.P., Täckström, O., Das, D.: A decomposable attention model for natural language inference. In: Proceedings of the 2016 Conference on Empirical Methods in Natural Language Processing, pp. 2249–2255. ACL, Austin (2016)
6. Shen, D., Wang, G., Wang, W.: Baseline needs more love: on simple word-embedding-based models and associated pooling mechanisms. In: Proceedings of the 56th Annual Meeting of the Association for Computational Linguistics (Volume 1: Long Papers), pp. 440–450. ACL, Melbourne (2018)
7. Dagan, I., Glickman, O.: Probabilistic textual entailment: generic applied modeling of language variability. Learning Methods for Text Understanding and Mining, pp. 26–29 (2004)
8. Dagan, I., Glickman, O., Magnini, B.: The PASCAL recognizing textual entailment challenge. In: Quiñonero-Candela, J., Dagan, I., Magnini, B., d'Alché-Buc, F. (eds.) MLCW 2005. LNCS (LNAI), vol. 3944, pp. 177–190. Springer, Heidelberg (2006). https://doi.org/10.1007/11736790_9
9. Dagan, I., Roth, D., Sammons, M.: Recognizing textual entailment: models and applications. Synth. Lect. Hum. Lang. Technol. **6**(4), 1–220 (2013)
10. Burger, J., Ferro, L.: Generating an entailment corpus from news headlines. In: Proceedings of the ACL Workshop on Empirical Modeling of Semantic Equivalence and Entailment, pp. 49–54. ACL, Ann Arbor (2005)

11. Williams, A., Nangia, N., Bowman, S.R.: A broad-coverage challenge corpus for sentence understanding through inference. In: Proceedings of the 2018 Conference of the North American Chapter of the Association for Computational Linguistics: Human Language Technologies, (Volume 1: Long Papers), pp. 1112–1122. ACL, New Orleans (2018)
12. Conneau, A., Kiela, D., Schwenk, H.: Supervised learning of universal sentence representations from natural language inference data. In: Proceedings of the 2017 Conference on Empirical Methods in Natural Language Processing, pp. 670–680. ACL, Copenhagen (2017)
13. Chen, Q., Zhu, X., Ling, Z.: Enhanced LSTM for natural language inference. In: Proceedings of the 55th Annual Meeting of the Association for Computational Linguistics (Volume 1: Long Papers), pp. 1657–1668. ACL, Vancouver (2017)
14. Tan, C., Wei, F., Wang, W.: Multiway attention networks for modeling sentence pairs. In: 27th International Joint Conference on Artificial Intelligence, pp. 4411–4417. Morgan Kaufmann, Sweden (2018)
15. Ghaeini, R., Hasan, S.A., Datla, V., et al.: DR-BiLSTM: dependent reading bidirectional LSTM for natural language inference. In: Proceedings of the 2018 Conference of the North American Chapter of the Association for Computational Linguistics: Human Language Technologies (Volume 1: Long Papers), pp. 1460–1469. ACL, New Orleans (2018)
16. Kim, S., Kang, I., Kwak, N.: Semantic sentence matching with densely-connected recurrent and co-attentive information. In: Proceedings of the AAAI Conference on Artificial Intelligence, pp. 6586–6593. AAAI, Hawaii (2019)
17. Li, S., Zhao, Z., Hu, R., Li, W., Liu, T., Du, X.: analogical reasoning on chinese morphological and semantic relations. In: Proceedings of the 56th Annual Meeting of the Association for Computational Linguistics (Volume 2: Short Papers), pp. 138–143. ACL, Melbourne (2018)

A Knowledge-Gated Mechanism for Utterance Domain Classification

Zefeng Du, Peijie Huang(✉), Yuhong He, Wei Liu, and Jiankai Zhu

College of Mathematics and Informatics,
South China Agricultural University, Guangzhou, China
{seeledu,hyhong,liuliulz09,gabriel}@stu.scau.edu.cn,
pjhuang@scau.edu.cn

Abstract. Utterance domain classification (UDC) is a critical pre-processing step for many speech understanding and dialogue systems. Recently neural models have shown promising results on text classification. Meanwhile, the background information and knowledge beyond the utterance plays crucial roles in utterance comprehension. However, some improper background information and knowledge are easily introduced due to the ambiguity of entities or the noise in knowledge bases (KBs), UDC task remains a great challenge. To address this issue, this paper proposes a knowledge-gated (K-Gated) mechanism that leverages domain knowledge from external sources to control the path through which information flows in the neural network. We employ it with pre-trained token embedding from Bidirectional Encoder Representation from Transformers (BERT) into a wide spectrum of state-of-the-art neural text classification models. Experiments on the SMP-ECDT benchmark corpus show that the proposed method achieves a strong and robust performance regardless of the quality of the encoder models.

Keywords: Utterance domain classification · Gating mechanism · Knowledge-gated · BERT

1 Introduction

Spoken language understanding (SLU), which is the core component of intelligent personal digital assistants (IPDAs) such as Microsoft Cortana, Google Assistant, Amazon Alexa, and Apple Siri [1–3]. The first step of such "targeted" understanding is to convert the recognized user speech into a task-specific semantic representation of the user's intention, and then classify it into a specific domain for further processing, which is called utterance domain classification (UDC) [4–6]. For example, "张学友的一路上有你 (*Jacky Cheung's down the road with you*)" and "打开优酷网 (*Open Youku website*)" in Table 1 should be classified as `music` and `website`, respectively.

Recently neural models have shown promising results on text classification and have been employed to utterance classification [5, 7]. Meanwhile, Bidirectional Encoder Representation from Transformers (BERT) [8] obtains new state-of-the-art results on a wide range of task. What is more, the neural models with pre-trained BERT token embeddings can achieve better performance.

J. Tang et al. (Eds.): NLPCC 2019, LNAI 11839, pp. 142–154, 2019.
https://doi.org/10.1007/978-3-030-32236-6_12

Table 1. Examples of utterances with domain tags from the SMP-ECDT dataset, which is a benchmark corpus for Chinese UDC task. Italics for entity mentions.

Utterance	Domain
*张学友*的*一路上有你* *Jacky Cheung*'s *down the road with you*	音乐 Music
打开*优酷*网 Open *Youku* website	网站 Website

Despite the effectiveness of previous studies, UDC task remains a challenge in real-world applications for two reasons: (1) The background information and knowledge beyond the utterance plays crucial roles in utterance comprehension [9]. (2) The knowledge representation may bring the bias to the downstream model, and the path through which information flows in the network should be controlled [10].

Incorporating knowledge bases (KBs) as prior knowledge into the neural language understanding (NLU) tasks has far been demonstrated to be valuable and effective approaches [9, 11, 12]. And the popular connection mechanism to enrich the utterance representation using knowledge representation is concatenating the knowledge embeddings and the text representations vector directly [9, 12]. However, this approach, that tightly couples the utterance and knowledge representation, lacks an effective mechanism to control the influence of the knowledge information.

To further increase the knowledge representation flexibility, gating mechanisms [10, 13, 14] can be introduced as an integral part of the neural network models. The soft but differentiable gate units are trained to capture the dependencies that make significant contributions to the task. It can thus provide complementary information to the distance-aware dependencies modeled by neural networks [14].

It is therefore desirable to combine the best of both lines of works: the neural network models and the knowledge-based gating mechanism. In this paper, we propose knowledge-gated (K-Gated) mechanism, which leverage domain knowledge from external sources to control the path through which information flows in the neural network for UDC task. The contributions of this paper can be summarized as follows:

- We propose a knowledge-gated (K-Gated) mechanism for UDC task, which leverages domain knowledge from external sources to control the path through which information flows in the neural network.
- In terms of external knowledge, we rely on CN-Probase to provide decent entities and types, and adopt some other reliable knowledge sources to build complement KB for providing richer knowledge representations in special domains in the UDC task.
- We demonstrate consistent improvements across all experiments incorporating the proposed K-Gated mechanism into a wide spectrum of state-of-the-art neural text classification models on the SMP-ECDT benchmark corpus.

2 Related Work

There are many studies on utterance or short text classification to improve efficiency, and a typical example is support vector machine (SVM). After that, deep learning draw attention in natural language processing (NLP) with deep belief networks (DBNs) [16], convolutional neural networks (CNNs) [17], recurrent neural networks (RNNs) [5], and particularly long short-term memory (LSTM) [18–21], the most commonly used RNN.

In recent years, attention mechanisms have been introduced to NLP, showing great capacity for extracting meaning representations for generic text classification tasks, such as intent detection [7], domain classification [2], and document classification [19]. Meanwhile, in terms of pre-trained embedding that are widely used in neural models, BERT [8] obtains new state-of-the-art results on a wide range of task. In this paper, we employ pre-trained BERT token embeddings and incorporate the proposed K-Gated mechanism into a wide spectrum of state-of-the-art neural text classification models for further improvement.

Another line of related research is knowledge-based NLU. In NLU literature, linguistic knowledge [15, 23] or knowledge bases (KBs) [9, 11, 12] can be treated as prior knowledge to benefit language understanding. In this paper, we aim to appropriately incorporate representations obtained from KBs to enhance the neural UDC models, by considering type information of entity mentions inside utterances.

To incorporate knowledge information into neural network models, much of the previous work is based on the idea of generalizing the embedding layer of the encoder to support modeling of external knowledge [9, 12]. The strategy of this method is to concatenate the knowledge embeddings and the text representations vector, aiming at enriching the utterance representations. However, this approach, that tightly couples the utterance and knowledge representation, lacks of an effective mechanism to control the influence of the knowledge information. In contrast to these studies, our approach leverages gating mechanism to control the path through which information flows in the neural network. To our knowledge, our study is the first one to use knowledge-based gating mechanism for neural UDC task.

3 Model

In this section, we present our model for the UDC task. Figure 1 gives an overview of our model.

The first layer maps input utterances $\mathcal{U}$ into vectors by token embeddings (obtained by pre-trained BERT), as well as detects external knowledge inside the utterances using distant supervision and complement KB. Then an encoder layer takes as input the embeddings to produce hidden states F. In the last but one layer, we use a merge layer to exploit the concatenation of the hidden states F and the knowledge representation vectors K to enrich the utterance representation. The gate for knowledge representation vectors is made up of a multi-layer perception (MLP) and a tanh activate function. We apply element-wise dot-product between the gate vector and the knowledge

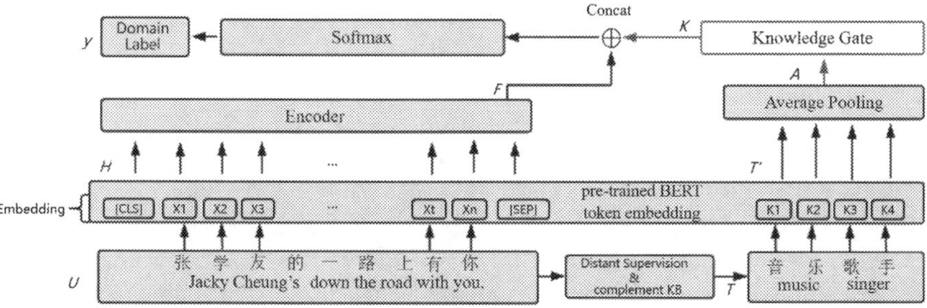

Fig. 1. Overview of the knowledge-gated (K-Gated) model for utterance domain classification.

representation vectors. The final fully connected layer with softmax function uses the concatenation of vector K and F to predict the domain label y^D.

$$y^D = softmax(W(F \oplus K) + b). \tag{1}$$

The design of this structure is motivated by the effectiveness of multiplicative interaction among vectors and by gating mechanism which has been used successfully in a variety of tasks [10, 13, 14]. It also typically corresponds to our finding that the external knowledge is highly correlated with utterances in many cases, so the semantics of external knowledge should be useful for UDC.

3.1 External Knowledge

In terms of external knowledge, we rely on CN-Probase to provide decent entities and types detection for knowledge extraction. CN-Probase is a widely used general Chinese taxonomy for entity type retrieval [24]. However, in a UDC task, general knowledge bases may suffer from absence of some entities and their type information. For instance, in the utterance "横看成岭成峰的下一句 (*The next sentence of mountains is a ridge while seen by the side*)", the entity "横看成岭侧成峰 (*mountain is a ridge while seen by the side*)" in this expression cannot be obtained by distant supervision with CN-Probase. To solve this problem, in our paper, we adopt some other reliable knowledge sources, such as Baidu Baike (extracting knowledge of poetry, lottery, weather and so on), QQ music (extracting knowledge of singer and music), and so on. Our goal is to complement the CN-Probase to provide richer knowledge representations in restricted domains in the UDC task.

To be more specific, given an utterance $\mathcal{U}$, we hope to find a type set $\mathcal{T}$ respected to the entity mention set $\mathcal{M}$ inside it. We achieve it by retrieving relevant knowledge from the KB $\mathcal{K}$ (i.e. distant KB $\mathcal{K}_d$ and compliment KB $\mathcal{K}_c$), including two major steps: *entity linking* and *conceptualization*. Entity linking is an important task in NLP which aims to identify all the mentions in a text and produce a mapping from the set of mentions to the set of knowledge base entities [25]. We acquire $\mathcal{M}$ of an utterance by distant supervise (i.e. CN-Probase[1]) and complement KB $\mathcal{K}_c$, namely we identify $\mathcal{M} = \{m_i\}_{i=1}^{s}$ and map it to *entity-type facts* $\{\mathcal{E}, \mathcal{T}\} = \{e_i, t_i\}_{i=1}^{s}$ in $\mathcal{K}$. Then, we receive the type result t_i for each entity mention $m_i \in \mathcal{M}$ from our abovementioned $\mathcal{K}$ through conceptualization. For instance, given an utterance "*Jacky Cheung*'s *down the road with you*", we obtain the entity mention set $\mathcal{M}$ = {*Jacky Cheung, down the road with you*} by entity linking. Thereafter, we conceptualize the entity mention, namely, the entity mention *Jacky Cheung* acquires its types {*singer, actor*} and *down the road with you* acquires its type {*music*} from $\mathcal{K}$ respectively. Note that we only keep the entity-type facts within domains of our UDC task. Meanwhile, the types represented same domain are redirected to the same domain type (e.g., *poetry-title, poet* and *verse* are redirected to *poetry*). As for the extra knowledge source $\mathcal{K}_c$, we do entity linking and conceptualization through string match. Following that we acquire a sentence-level external knowledge set, and then vectorize it. The external knowledge representation vectors $T_i = [r_1, r_2, \ldots, r_{n_T}] \in \mathbb{R}^{n_T}$ can benefit inferring the domain of utterance, where n_T denotes the dimension size of the external knowledge representation vectors.

3.2 BERT

The model architecture of BERT is a multi-layer bidirectional Transformer encoder based on the original Transformer model [26]. The input representation is a concatenation of WordPiece embeddings, positional embeddings, and the segment embedding. Specially, for single sentence classification, the segment embedding has no discrimination. A special classification embedding ([CLS]) is inserted as the first token and a special token ([SEP]) is added as the final token. Given an input token utterance $\mathcal{U} = (\mathrm{u}_1, \ldots, \mathrm{u}_t)$, the output of BERT is $H = ([\mathrm{CLS}], h_1, \ldots, h_t, [\mathrm{SEP}])$, where t denotes that the utterance has t tokens:

$$H = BERT(\mathcal{U}), \tag{2}$$

where $\mathrm{H} \in \mathbb{R}^{d_m \times t \times n}$ denotes the token embeddings, the d_m is the dimension of these t tokens, n denotes the number of the utterances.

The BERT model is pre-trained with two strategies on large-scale unlabeled text, i.e., masked language model and next sentence prediction. The pre-trained BERT token embedding provides a powerful context-dependent utterances representation and can be used for various target model, e.g., textCNN, BiLSTM [8]. Many NLP tasks are benefit from BERT to get the state-of-the-art and reduce the training time.

3.3 Utterance Encoder

We describe our utterance encoder, which is marked in Fig. 1. The encoder is a stack of several recurrent units or filters where each accepts a single element of the input vector, collects information for that element and propagates it to the next layer. We complete

[1] http://shuyantech.com/api/entitylinking/cutsegment.

utterances representation using BERT[2], published by Google, which is a new way to obtain pre-trained language model token representation [8]. Among numerous neural text classification models proposed for encoding information, we adopt several popular and typical models as encoder to demonstrate the strong applicability and generality of our knowledge-gated method. The selected base models include: textCNN [17], BiLSTM [21], BiRNN with attention mechanism [7], HAN [22] and Transformer [26]. Then the utterance representation vectors H are fed into an encoder to extract contextual feature. For convenience, we define the entire operation as a feature extraction F:

$$F = Encoder(H), \tag{3}$$

where $F \in \mathbb{R}^{d_f \times n}$ denotes utterance representation, d_f denotes the number of hidden states. However, when we use pure BERT for sequence-level classification tasks, BERT fine-tuning is straightforward. We take the final hidden state H' (i.e., the output of the Transformer) for the first token in the input, which by construction corresponds to the special [CLS] token embedding. The only new parameters added during fine-tuning are for a classification layer [8].

$$y^D = softmax(WH' + b). \tag{4}$$

3.4 Gating Mechanisms

As it is described above, external knowledge is useful for UDC task, but it may propagate some redundant information. Gating mechanisms can control the path through which information flows in the network [10]. To automatically capture important external knowledge information, we proposed knowledge-gated mechanism for UDC task performance.

In language modeling, Gated Tanh Units (GTU) [13], Gated Linear Units (GLU) [10] and Gated Tanh-ReLU Units (GTRU) [14] have shown effectiveness of gating mechanisms. GTU is represented by $\tanh(\mathrm{A} * \mathrm{W} + \mathrm{b}) \odot \sigma(\mathrm{A} * \mathrm{V} + \mathrm{c})$, in which the sigmoid gates control features for predicting the next word in a stacked convolutional block. To overcome the gradient vanishing problem of GTU, GLU uses $(\mathrm{A} * \mathrm{W} + \mathrm{b}) \odot \sigma(\mathrm{A} * \mathrm{V} + \mathrm{c})$ instead, so that the gradients would not be downscaled to propagate through many stacked convolutional layers. And the GTRU is represented by $\tanh(\mathrm{A} * \mathrm{W} + \mathrm{b}) \odot \mathrm{relu}(\mathrm{A} * \mathrm{V} + \mathrm{c})$. We named the gated mechanism used in this paper as Gated Tanh-MLP Unit (GTMU) for UDC, shown in Fig. 2.

The GTRU uses relu instead of sigmoid because they believe the sigmoid function in GTU and GLU has the upper bound +1, which may not be able to distill external features effectively [14]. The GTMU uses tanh because we believe the upper bound +1 and the lower bound −1 can keep out improper information by element-wise product,

[2] https://github.com/hanxiao/bert-as-service.

avoid affecting the main track too much as well. Specifically, we compute the features vector g_i as:

$$T_i' = \text{BERT}(T_i), \quad (5)$$

$$A_i = Pooling\left(T_i'\right), \quad (6)$$

$$g_i = \tanh(MLP(A_i)), \quad (7)$$

$$K_i = T_i' \odot g_i, \quad (8)$$

where i denotes the ith utterance, the $T_i \in \mathbb{R}^{n_T}$ is the its external knowledge vector, $T_i' \in \mathbb{R}^{d_m \times t}$ is the knowledge embedding, $A_i \in \mathbb{R}^{d_{mlp}}$ is the knowledge representation, d_{mlp} is the cell-num of the last layer of MLP, $g_i \in \mathbb{R}^{n_T}$ and $\odot$ is the element-wise product between matrices. We using BERT to acquire the knowledge representation. The pooling is average pooling, retaining more information, in comparison to max pooling, which usually believed to lead to better results [27]. The gate vector g_i is calculated by MLP with a tanh activate function. The sentence-level knowledge vectors are provided by correct knowledge vectors during training phase, and by the output from distant supervision and complement KB in the test phase.

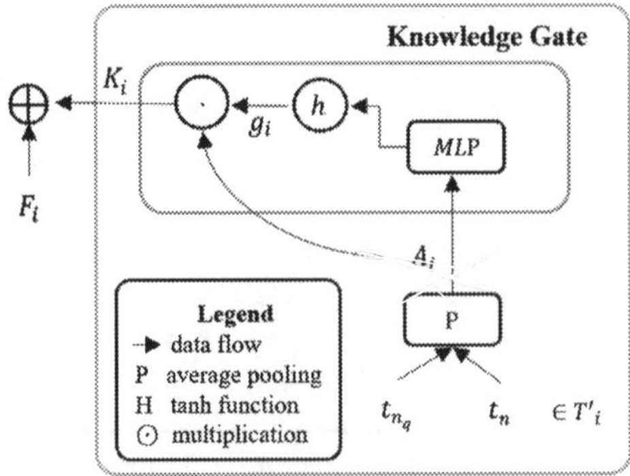

Fig. 2. Our proposed knowledge gate.

The g can be seen as a weighted feature of the knowledge representation. The g keeps the most salient external knowledge features of the whole knowledge representation and the new knowledge representation K is more "reliable" for contributing the prediction results.

4 Experiments

4.1 Dataset

We execute the experiments on the benchmark corpus of SMP-ECDT [28], provided by the iFLYTEK Co. Ltd. SMP-ECDT (**S**ocial **M**edia **P**rocessing - the **E**valuation of **C**hinese Human-Computer **D**ialogue **T**echnology) 2018 is the second evaluation of Chinese human-computer dialogue technology, and subtask 1 is for Chinese utterance domain classification. The benchmark corpus consists of the two top categories *chit-chat* and *task-oriented*. Meanwhile, the *task-oriented* dialogue also includes 30 sub-categories, making this a 31-category classification task. This corpus contains 3736 training data and 4528 test data items, which all are single-turn short utterances that do not include historical turn information.

4.2 Baselines

We incorporate the proposed knowledge-gated mechanism (K-Gated) into a wide spectrum of neural text classification models:

- BERT [8]: This model is BERT for sequence-level classification tasks, and BERT fine-tuning is straightforward. Only new output layer is added during fine-tuning for a classification layer.
- TextCNN [17]: This model is widely used on text classification task. It provides a very strong baseline for domain classification. We set the widths of filters to [3–5] with 100 features each.
- BiLSTM [21]: This model is a basic BiLSTM model for domain classification.
- BiRNN Att [7]: This method uses BiLSTM and attention mechanism for joint intent and slot filling task. Here we use the intent independent training for UDC task.
- HAN [22]: This model usually is used for document classification. Here we use the word part of it because of the short length of utterances.
- Multi-head Att [26]: This model uses Transformer to encode text representation and uses decoder to generate an output sequence. We use the encoder part for UDC.

We also apply the popular connection mechanism to enrich the utterance representation using sentence-level knowledge representation [9, 12], which concatenates the knowledge embeddings A and the text representations vector F. This method, K-Concat, can be treated as the baseline knowledge-based UDC method.

4.3 Training Details

We employ the Jieba tokenize[3] and pre-trained BERT token embeddings to preprocess each utterance, and OOV words are randomly initialized. Then, we utilize every model to performed 10-fold cross validation on the training set of SMP-ECDT corpus and evaluate the proposed model. We explore different sets of hyperparameter settings and determine the Adam optimizer with learning rate 0.001 and batch size as 25, based on

[3] https://github.com/fxsjy/jieba.

the performance on the validation set. The layer-num of the MLP is set as 1–5. The cell-num of each MLP layer is 768. To avoid overfitting, we employ dropout during training, and the dropout rate is set as 0.1–0.5 for validation. The metric utilized to evaluate each model is the accuracy of prediction. All data shown in the following results are the mean of 5 independent experiments. The metric for the experiments is the accuracy metric.

4.4 Results and Analysis

The results are shown in Table 2. As we can see from Table 2, comparing to the pure BERT classifier, all of the state-of-the-art neural text classification models using pre-trained BERT token embedding achieve performance improvement. And K-Gated with "BERT+TextCNN" achieves best result and significantly outperforms the base BERT classifier by 3.06%. Meanwhile, both K-Concat and K-Gated bring consistent improvement across all experiments, regardless of the quality of the encoder model. This finding confirms that the proposed knowledge-based methods are robust: their effectiveness do not depend on the network architecture used to construct the classifier.

Table 2. Accuracies of our models and competing approaches on the test set.

Models	Test acc (%)
BERT [8]	80.60
+K-Concat	81.17
+K-Gated	81.34
BERT+TextCNN [17]	82.68
+K-Concat	82.86
+K-Gated	**83.66**
BERT+BiLSTM [21]	81.67
+K-Concat	82.06
+K-Gated	82.29
BERT+BiRNN Att [7]	81.32
+K-Concat	82.70
+K-Gated	82.81
BERT+HAN [22]	82.57
+K-Concat	82.80
+K-Gated	82.90
BERT+Multi-head Att [26]	80.36
+K-Concat	81.68
+K-Gated	81.90

4.5 Layers in MLP

In this section, we compare the number of the layers in MLP used in the K-Gated and present the results in Table 3.

Table 3. The performance of different number of the layers in MLP.

No. of the layers in MLP	Test acc (%)
1	82.82
2	83.32
3	**83.66**
4	83.15
5	83.24

As we can see from Table 3, if the network has too few free parameters (layers), training could fail to achieve the required error threshold. On the other hand, if the network has too many free parameters, then a large data set is needed. We can see that the MLP with 3 layers achieves the best result.

4.6 Gating Mechanisms

In this section, we compare GLU $(A * W + b) \odot \sigma(A * V + c)$ [13], GTU $\tanh(A * W + b) \odot \sigma(A * V + c)$ [10] and GTRU $\tanh(A * W + b) \odot relu(A * V + c)$ [14] used in UDC task. Table 4 shows that all of four gating mechanisms achieve relatively high accuracy on SMP-ECDT benchmark corpus. The proposed GTMU outperforms the other three gates. It has a three layers MLP generating knowledge features via tanh activation function, which controls the magnitude of the external knowledge according to the given utterances' information.

Table 4. The performance of different gating mechanisms in knowledge gate.

Gating mechanisms	Test acc (%)
GLU	82.88
GTU	83.58
GTRU	83.05
GTMU	**83.66**

4.7 Effect of KB Complement

Finally, we investigate the influence of our complement to CN-Probase in providing a richer knowledge representation in certain restricted domains in the Chinese UDC task. Table 5 shows the performance of the models that employ GTRU gating mechanism on "BERT+TextCNN" without and with our KB complement. As shown in Table 5, compared to the models using only CN-Probase, our complementary approach improved the accuracy by 0.51%.

Table 5. Accuracies of our models on the test set.

Models	Test acc (%)
K-Gated (CN-Probased)	83.15
K-Gated (Full)	**83.66**

5 Conclusion

This paper investigated knowledge dependent UDC and proposed a knowledge-gated mechanism, which leverages domain knowledge from external sources to enrich the representations of utterances and uses knowledge-based gating mechanism to control the path through which information flows in the neural network. Experimental results demonstrated the effectiveness and robustness of the proposed method, K-Gated UDC, on the SMP-ECDT benchmark corpus. In the future, it would be interesting to study how to effectively reduce the type label noises in external knowledge to identify the correct type labels for each mention from a noisy candidate type set.

Acknowledgments. This work was supported by National Natural Science Foundation of China (No. 71472068), National Innovation Training Project for College Students of China (No. 201710564154), and Innovation Training Project for College Students of Guangdong Province (No. 201810564094). We also thank the SCIR Lab of Harbin Institute of Technology and the iFLYTEK Co. Ltd. for providing the SMP-ECDT benchmark corpus.

References

1. Sarikaya, R.: The technology behind personal digital assistants: an overview of the system architecture and key components. IEEE Signal Process. Mag. **34**(1), 67–81 (2017)
2. Yu, K., Chen, R., Chen, B., et al.: Cognitive technology in task-oriented dialogue systems - concepts, advances and future. Chin. J. Comput. **38**(12), 2333–2348 (2015). (in Chinese)
3. Kim, Y., Kim, D., Kumar, A.: Efficient large-scale neural domain classification with personalized attention. In: Proceedings of the 56th Annual Meeting of the Association for Computational Linguistics (ACL 2018), pp. 2214–2224 (2018)
4. Tür, G., Mori, R.: Spoken Language Understanding: Systems for Extracting Semantic Information from Speech. Wiley, Chichester (2011)
5. Xu, P., Sarikaya, R.: Contextual domain classification in spoken language understanding systems using recurrent neural network. In: Proceedings of the 39th International Conference on Acoustics, Speech and Signal Processing (ICASSP 2014), pp. 136–140 (2014)
6. Ke, Z., Huang, P., Zeng, Z.: Domain classification based on undefined utterances detection optimization. J. Chin. Inf. Process. **32**(4), 105–113 (2018). (in Chinese)
7. Liu, B., Lane, I.: Attention-based recurrent neural network models for joint intent detection and slot filling. In: Proceedings of the 17th Annual Conference of the International Speech Communication Association (INTERSPEECH 2016), pp. 685–689 (2016)
8. Devlin, J., Chang, M., Lee, K., et al.: BERT: pre-training of deep bidirectional transformers for language understanding. In: Proceedings of the 2019 Conference of the North American Chapter of the Association for Computational Linguistics: Human Language Technologies (NAACL-HLT 2019), pp. 4171–4186 (2019)

9. Deng, Y., Shen, Y., Yang, M., et al.: Knowledge as a bridge: improving cross-domain answer selection with external knowledge. In: Proceedings of the 27th International Conference on Computational Linguistics (COLING 2018), pp. 3295–3305 (2018)
10. Dauphin, Y.N., Fan, A., Auli, M., et al.: Language modeling with gated convolutional networks. In: Proceedings of the 34th International Conference on Machine Learning (ICML 2017), pp. 933–941 (2017)
11. Shi, C., Liu, S., Ren, S., et al.: Knowledge-based semantic embedding for machine translation. In: Proceedings of the 54th Annual Meeting of the Association for Computational Linguistics (ACL 2016), pp. 2245–2254 (2016)
12. Wang, J., Wang, Z., Zhang, D., Yan, J.: Combining knowledge with deep convolutional neural networks for short text classification. In: Proceedings of the 26th International Joint Conference on Artificial Intelligence (IJCAI 2017), pp. 2915–2921 (2017)
13. Oord, A., Kalchbrenner, N., Espeholt, L., et al.: Conditional image generation with PixelCNN decoders. In: Proceedings of the 30th Annual Conference on Neural Information Processing Systems (NIPS 2016), pp. 4790–4798 (2016)
14. Xue, W., Li, T.: Aspect based sentiment analysis with gated convolutional networks. In: Proceedings of the 56th Annual Meeting of the Association for Computational Linguistics (ACL 2018), pp. 2514–2523 (2018)
15. Heck, L., Tür, D., Tür, G.: Leveraging knowledge graphs for web-scale unsupervised semantic parsing. In: Proceedings of the 14th Annual Conference of the International Speech Communication Association (INTERSPEECH 2013), pp. 1594–1598 (2013)
16. Sarikaya, R., Hinton, G., Ramabhadran, B.: Deep belief nets for natural language call-routing. In: Proceedings of the 36th IEEE International Conference on Acoustics, Speech, and Signal Processing (ICASSP 2011), pp. 5680–5683 (2011)
17. Kim, Y.: Convolutional neural networks for sentence classification. In: Proceedings of the 2014 Conference on Empirical Methods in Natural Language Processing (EMNLP 2014), pp. 1292–1302 (2014)
18. Ravuri, S., Stolcke, S.: A comparative study of recurrent neural network models for lexical domain classification. In: Proceedings of the 41st IEEE International Conference on Acoustics, Speech, and Signal Processing (ICASSP 2016), pp. 6075–6079 (2016)
19. Xiao, Y., Cho, K.: Efficient character-level document classification by combining convolution and recurrent layers. Computing Research Repository, arXiv:1602.00367. Version 1 (2016)
20. Cheng, J., Dong, L., Lapata, M.: Long short-term memory-networks for machine reading. In: Proceedings of the 2016 Conference on Empirical Methods in Natural Language Processing (EMNLP 2016), pp. 551–561 (2016)
21. Vu, N.T., Gupta, P., Adel, H., et al.: Bi-directional recurrent neural network with ranking loss for spoken language understanding. In: Proceedings of the 41st IEEE International Conference on Acoustics, Speech and Signal Processing (ICASSP 2016), pp. 6060–6064 (2016)
22. Yang, Z., Yang, D., Dyer, C., et al.: Hierarchical attention networks for document classification. In: Proceedings of the 2016 Conference of the North American Chapter of the Association for Computational Linguistics: Human Language Technologies (NAACL-HLT 2016), pp. 1480–1489 (2016)
23. Chen, Y., Tur, D., Tür, G., et al.: Syntax or semantics? Knowledge-guided joint semantic frame parsing. In: Proceedings of 2016 IEEE Spoken Language Technology Workshop (SLT 2016), pp. 348–355 (2016)
24. Chen, J., Wang, A., Chen, J., et al.: CN-Probase: a data-driven approach for large-scale Chinese taxonomy construction. In: Proceedings of the 35th IEEE International Conference on Data Engineering (ICDE 2019) (2019)

25. Moro, A., Raganato, A., Navigli, R.: Entity linking meets word sense disambiguation: a unified approach. Trans. Assoc. Comput. Linguist. **2**, 231–244 (2013)
26. Vaswani, A., Shazeer, N., Parmar, N., et al.: Attention is all you need. In: Proceedings of the 41st Annual Conference on Neural Information Processing Systems (NIPS 2017), pp. 6000–6010 (2017)
27. Boureau, Y., Ponce, J., LeCun, Y.: A theoretical analysis of feature pooling in visual recognition. In: Proceedings of the 27th International Conference on Machine Learning (ICML 2010), pp. 111–118 (2010)
28. Zhang, W., Chen, Z., Che, W., et al.: The first evaluation of Chinese human-computer dialogue technology. Computing Research Repository, arXiv:1709.10217. Version 1 (2017)

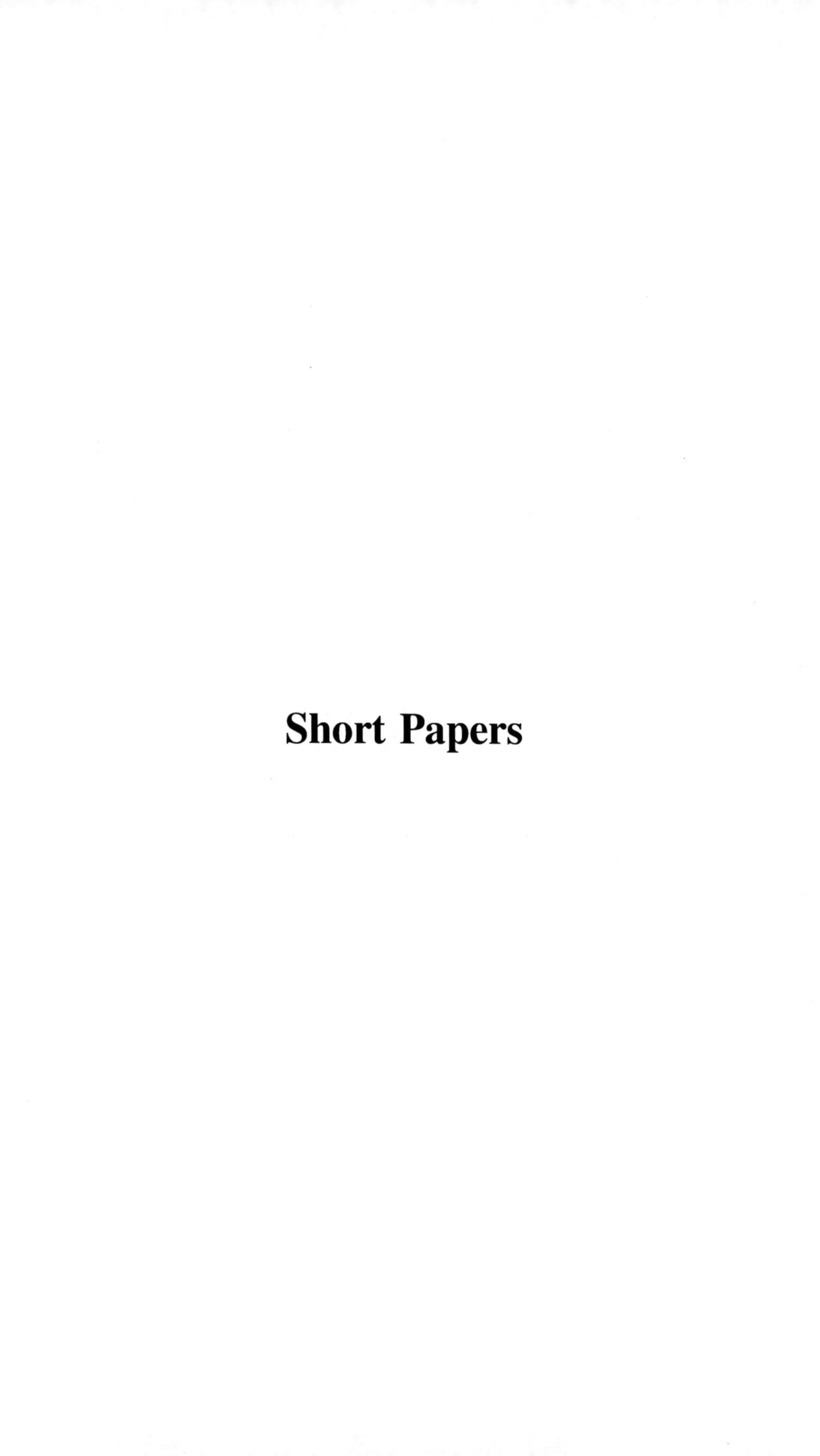

Short Papers

Automatic Translating Between Ancient Chinese and Contemporary Chinese with Limited Aligned Corpora

Zhiyuan Zhang[1], Wei Li[1], and Qi Su[2(✉)]

[1] MOE Key Lab of Computational Linguistics, School of EECS, Peking University, Beijing, China
{zzy1210,liweitj47}@pku.edu.cn

[2] School of Foreign Languages, Peking University, Beijing, China
sukia@pku.edu.cn

Abstract. The Chinese language has evolved a lot during the long-term development. Therefore, native speakers now have trouble in reading sentences written in ancient Chinese. In this paper, we propose to build an end-to-end neural model to automatically translate between ancient and contemporary Chinese. However, the existing ancient-contemporary Chinese parallel corpora are not aligned at the sentence level and sentence-aligned corpora are limited, which makes it difficult to train the model. To build the sentence level parallel training data for the model, we propose an unsupervised algorithm that constructs sentence-aligned ancient-contemporary pairs by using the fact that the aligned sentence pair shares many of the tokens. Based on the aligned corpus, we propose an end-to-end neural model with copying mechanism and local attention to translate between ancient and contemporary Chinese. Experiments show that the proposed unsupervised algorithm achieves 99.4% F1 score for sentence alignment, and the translation model achieves 26.95 BLEU from ancient to contemporary, and 36.34 BLEU from contemporary to ancient.

Keywords: Sentence alignment · Neural machine translation

1 Introduction

The ancient Chinese was used for thousands of years. There is a huge amount of books and articles written in ancient Chinese. However, both the form and grammar of the ancient Chinese have been changed. Chinese historians and littérateurs have made great efforts in translating such literature into contemporary Chinese, a big part of which is publicly available on the Internet. However, there is still a big gap between these literatures and parallel corpora, because most of the corpora are coarsely passage-aligned, the orders of sentences are different. To train an automatic translating model, we need to build a sentence-aligned corpus first.

Translation alignment is an important pre-step for machine translation. Most of the previous work focuses on how to apply supervised algorithms on this task using features extracted from texts. The Gale Church algorithm [5, 7] uses statistical or dictionary

J. Tang et al. (Eds.): NLPCC 2019, LNAI 11839, pp. 157–167, 2019.
https://doi.org/10.1007/978-3-030-32236-6_13

information to build alignment corpus. Strands [17,18] extracts parallel corpus from the Internet. A logarithmic linear model [25] is also used for Chinese-Japanese clause alignment. Besides, features such as sentence lengths, matching patterns, Chinese character co-occurrence in Japanese and Chinese are also taken into consideration. The observation that Chinese character co-occurrence also exists in ancient-contemporary Chinese is also used to ancient-contemporary Chinese translation alignment [11,12].

The method above works well, however, these supervised algorithms require a large parallel corpus to train, which is not available in our circumstance. These previous algorithms did not make good use of the characteristics of ancient-contemporary Chinese pair. To overcome these shortcomings, we design an unsupervised algorithm for sentence alignment based on the observation that differently from a bilingual corpus, ancient-contemporary sentence pairs share many common characters in order. We evaluate our alignment algorithm on an aligned parallel corpus with small size. The experimental results show that our simple algorithm works very well (F1 score 99.4), which is even better than the supervised algorithms.

Deep learning has achieved great success in tasks like machine translation. The sequence to sequence (seq-to-seq) model [21] is proposed to generate good translation results on machine translation. The attention mechanism [1] is proposed to allow the decoder to extract phrase alignment information from the hidden states of the encoder. Most of the existing NMT systems are based on the seq-to-seq model [3,9,22] and the attention mechanism. Some of them have variant architectures to capture more information from the inputs [20,24], and some improve the attention mechanism [2,4,8,13,15,16], which also enhanced the performance of the NMT model. Inspired by the work of pointer generator [19], we use a copying mechanism named pointer-generator model to deal with the task of ancient-contemporary translation task because ancient and contemporary Chinese share common characters and some same proper nouns.

Experimental results show that a copying mechanism can improve the performance of seq-to-seq model remarkably on this task. We show some experimental results in the experiment section. Other mechanisms are also implied to improve the performance of machine translation [10,14].

Our contributions lie in the following two aspects:

- We propose a simple yet effective unsupervised algorithm to build the sentence-aligned parallel corpora, which make it possible to train an automatic translating model between ancient Chinese and contemporary Chinese even with limited sentence-aligned corpora.
- We propose to apply the sequence to sequence model with copying mechanism and local attention to deal with the translating task. Experimental results show that our method can achieve the BLEU score of 26.41 (ancient to contemporary) and 35.66 (contemporary to ancient).

2 Proposed Method

2.1 Unsupervised Algorithm for Sentence Alignment

We review the definition of sentence alignment first.

Given a pair of aligned passages, the source language sentences S and target language sentences T, which are defined as

$$S := \{s_1, s_2, \cdots, s_n\}, \quad T := \{t_1, t_2, \cdots, t_m\} \tag{1}$$

The objective of sentence alignment is to extract a set of matching sentence pairs out of the two passages. Each matching pair consists of several sentence pairs like (s_i, t_j), which implies that s_i and t_j form a parallel pair.

For instance, if $S = \{s_1, s_2, s_3, s_4, s_5\}, T = \{t_1, t_2, t_3, t_4, t_5\}$ and the alignment result is $\{(s_1, t_1), (s_3, t_2), (s_3, t_3), (s_4, t_4), (s_5, t_4)\}$. It means source sentence s_1 is translated to target sentence t_1, s_3 is translated to t_2 and t_3, s_4 and s_5 are translated to t_4 while s_2 is not translated to any sentence in target sentences. Here we may assume that source sentences are translated to target sentences in order. For instance (s_1, t_2) and (s_2, t_1) can not exist at the same time in the alignment result.

Translating ancient Chinese into contemporary Chinese has the characteristic that every word of ancient Chinese tends to be translated into contemporary Chinese in order, which usually includes the same original character. Therefore, correct aligned pairs usually have the maximum sum of lengths of the longest common subsequence (LCS) for each matching pair.

Let $\mathbf{lcs}(s[i_1, i_2], t[j_1, j_2])$ be the length of the **longest common subsequence** of a matching pair of aligned sentences consisting of source language sentences $s[i_1, i_2]$ and target language sentences $t[j_1, j_2]$, which are defined as

$$s[i_1, i_2] = \begin{cases} s_{i_1} s_{i_1+1} \cdots s_{i_2} (i_1 \leq i_2) \\ [empty\_str] \ (i_1 > i_2) \end{cases}, \quad t[j_1, j_2] = \begin{cases} t_{j_1} t_{j_1+1} \cdots t_{j_2} (j_1 \leq j_2) \\ [empty\_str] \ (j_1 > j_2) \end{cases} \tag{2}$$

where $[empty\_str]$ denotes an empty string. The longest common subsequence of an empty string and any string is 0.

We use the dynamic programming algorithm to find the maximum score and its corresponding alignment result. Let $f(i, j)$ be the maximum score that can be achieved with partly aligned sentence pairs until s_i, t_j. To reduce the calculation cost, we only consider cases where one sentence is matched with no more than 5 sentences:

$$f(i, j) = \max_{\{i-i', j-j'\}=\{1,M\}, 0 \leq M \leq 5} \{f(i', j') + \mathbf{lcs}(s[i'+1, i], t[j'+1, j])\} \tag{3}$$

The condition $\{i - i', j - j'\} = \{1, M\}, 0 \leq M \leq 5$ ensures that one sentence is matched with no more than 5 sentences and $M = 0$ holds if and only if one sentence is not matched with any of the sentences. We can preprocess all $\mathbf{lcs}(s[i'+1, i], t[j'+1, j])(\{i - i', j - j'\} = \{1, M\}, 0 \leq M \leq 5)$ scores and store them for using in algorithm, which has a time complexity of $O(mn)$. The pseudo code is shown in Algorithm 1. Then for every $f(i, j)$, we only need to enumerate i', j' for $O(1)$ times and the time complexity of proposal dynamic programming algorithm is $O(mn)$.

When the size of corpus grows, this algorithm will be time-consuming, which means our algorithm is more suitable for passage-aligned corpora instead of a huge text. In reality, we find that when translating a text written in ancient Chinese into contemporary

Algorithm 1. Dynamic Programming Algorithm to Find the Alignment Result.

```
Preprocess lcs scores and store them in memory. Initialize f[i, j] ← 0.
for i ∈ [1, n]
  for j ∈ [1, m]
    for i', j' ∈ {(i', j') : {i − i', j − j'} = {1, M}, 0 ≤ M ≤ 5, i' > 0, j' > 0}
      Get now_lcs ← lcs(s[i' + 1, i], t[j' + 1, j]) from memory.
      if f[i', j'] + now_lcs > f[i, j]
        f[i, j] = f[i', j'] + now_lcs
        Update the corresponding alignment result.
      endif
    endfor
  endfor
endfor
```

Chinese. Translators tend not to change the structure of the text, namely, a book written in ancient Chinese and its contemporary Chinese version are a passage-aligned corpus naturally. Therefore, we can get abundant passage-aligned corpora form Internet.

2.2 Neural Machine Translation Model

Sequence-to-sequence model was first proposed to solve machine translation problem. The model consists of two parts, an encoder and a decoder. The encoder is bound to take in the source sequence and compress the sequence into hidden states. The decoder is used to produce a sequence of target tokens based on the information embodied in the hidden states given by the encoder. Both encoder and decoder are implemented with Recurrent Neural Networks (RNN).

To deal with the ancient-contemporary translating task, we use the encoder to convert the variable-length character sequence into h_t, the hidden representations of position t, with an Bidirectional RNN:

$$\overrightarrow{h_t} = f(x_t, \overrightarrow{h_{t-1}}), \quad \overleftarrow{h_t} = f(x_t, \overleftarrow{h_{t+1}}), \quad h_t = [\overrightarrow{h_t}; \overleftarrow{h_t}] \tag{4}$$

Where f is a function of RNN family, x_t is the input at time step t. The decoder is another RNN, which generates a variable-length sequence token by token, through a conditional language model,

$$s_t = f(c_t, s_{t-1}, Ey_{t-1}), \quad c_t = g(\boldsymbol{h}, s_{t-1}) \tag{5}$$

Where E is the embedding matrix of target tokens, y_{t-1} is the last predicted token. We also implement a beam search mechanism, a heuristic search algorithm that expands the most promising node in a limited set, for generating a better target sentence.

In the decoder, suppose l is the length of the source sentence, then the context vector c_t is calculated based on the hidden states s_t of the decoder at time step t and all the hidden states $\boldsymbol{h} = \{h_i\}_{i=1}^{l}$ in the encoder, which is also known as the attention mechanism,

$$\beta_{t,i} = v_a^{\mathrm{T}} \tanh(W_a s_t + U_a h_i + b_a), \quad a_{t,i} = \frac{\exp(\beta_{t,i})}{\sum_{j=1}^{l} \exp(\beta_{t,j})} \tag{6}$$

We adopt the global attention mechanism in the baseline seq-to-seq model,

$$c_t = \sum_{i=1}^{l} a_{t,i} h_i \tag{7}$$

where $a_{t,i}$ is the attention probability of the word in position i of the source sentence in the decoder time step t and h_i is the hidden state of position i of the source sentence.

Because in most cases ancient and contemporary Chinese have similar word order, instead of the normal global attention in the baseline seq-to-seq model, we apply *local attention* [13,23] in our proposal. When calculating the context vector c_t, we calculate a pivot position in the hidden states $\boldsymbol{h}$ of the encoder, and calculate the attention probability in the window around the pivot instead of the whole sentence,

$$c_t = \sum_{i=1}^{l} p_{t,i} a_{t,i} h_i \tag{8}$$

where $p_{t,i}$ is the mask score based on the pivot position in the hidden states $\boldsymbol{h}$ of the encoder.

Machine translation model treats ancient and contemporary Chinese as two languages, however, in this task, contemporary and ancient Chines share many common characters. Therefore, we treat ancient and contemporary Chinese as one language and share the character embedding between the source language and target language.

2.3 Copying Mechanism

As is stated above, ancient and contemporary Chinese share many common characters and most of the name entities use the same representation. Copying mechanism [6] is very suitable in this situation, where the source and target sequence share some of the words. We apply pointer-generator framework in our model, which follows the same intuition as the copying mechanism. $p_t(w)$, the output probability of token w is calculated as,

$$p_t(w) = p_t^G p_t^V(w) + (1 - p_t^G) \sum_{\mathrm{src}_i = w} a_{t,i}, \quad p_t^G = \sigma(W_g s_t + U_g c_t + b_g) \tag{9}$$

where p_t^G is dynamically calculated based on the hidden state s_t and the context vector c_t, $P_t^V(w)$ is the probability for token w in traditional seq-to-seq model. $a_{t,i}$ is the attention probability at the time step t in decoder and position i in source sentence which satisfies $\mathrm{src}_i = w$, namely the token in position i in source sentence is w. σ is the sigmoid function.

The encoder and decoder networks are trained jointly to maximize the conditional probability of the target sequence. We use cross-entropy as the loss function. We use characters instead of words because characters have independent meaning in ancient Chinese and the number of characters is much lower than the number of words, which makes the data less sparse and greatly reduces the number of OOV. We also can implement the pointer-generator mechanism in summarization on our AT-seq-to-seq model to copy some proper nouns directly from the source language.

Table 1. Vocabulary statistics. We include all the characters in the training set in the vocabulary.

Language	Vocabulary	OOV rate
Ancient	5,870	1.37%
Contemporary	4,993	1.03%

3 Experiments

3.1 Datasets

Sentence Alignment. We crawl passages and their corresponding contemporary Chinese version from the Internet. To guarantee the quality of the contemporary Chinese translation, we choose the corpus from two genres, classical articles and Chinese historical documents. After proofreading a sample of these passages, we think the quality of the **passage-aligned** corpus is satisfactory. To evaluate the algorithm, we crawl a relatively small **sentence-aligned** corpus consisting of 90 aligned passages with 4,544 aligned sentence pairs. We proofread them and correct some mistakes to guarantee the correctness of this corpus.

Translating. We conduct experiments on the data set built by our proposed unsupervised algorithm. The data set consists of 57,391 ancient-contemporary Chinese sentence pairs in total. We split sentence pairs randomly into train/dev/test dataset with sizes of 53,140/2,125/2,126 respectively. The vocabulary statistics information is in Table 1.

3.2 Experimental Settings

Sentence Alignment. We implement a log-linear model on contemporary-ancient Chinese sentence alignment as a baseline. Following the previous work, we implement this model with a combination of three features, sentence lengths, matching patterns and Chinese character co-occurrence [11, 12, 25]. We split the data into training set (2,999) and test set (1,545) to train the log-linear model. Our unsupervised method does not need training data. Both these two methods are evaluated on the test set.

Translating. We conduct experiments on both translating directions and use BLEU score to evaluate our model. We implement a one-layer Bidirectional LSTM with a 256-dim embedding size, 256-dim hidden size as encoder and a one-layer LSTM with attention mechanism as decoder. We also implement local attention or pointer generator mechanism on the decoder in our proposed model. We adopt Adam optimizer to optimize our loss functions with a learning rate of 0.0001. The training batch size of our model is 64 and the generating batch size is 32. The source language and target language share the vocabulary.

Table 2. Evaluation of logarithmic linear models and our method.

Features	Precision	Recall	F1-score
Length	0.821	0.855	0.837
Pattern	0.331	0.320	0.325
Length and Pattern	0.924	0.912	0.918
Co-occurrence	0.982	0.984	0.983
Length and Co-occurrence	0.987	0.989	0.988
Pattern and Co-occurrence	0.984	0.980	0.982
All features	0.992	0.991	0.992
our method	**0.994**	**0.994**	**0.994**

Table 3. Evaluation result (BLEU) of translating between **An** (ancient) and **Con** (contemporary) Chinese in test dataset

Method	An-Con	Con-An
Seq-to-Seq	23.10	31.20
+ copying	26.41	35.66
+ Local Attention	**26.95**	**36.34**

3.3 Experimental Results

Sentence Alignment. Our unsupervised algorithm gets an F1-score of 99.4%, which is better than the supervised baseline with all features, 99.2% (shown in Table 2). Our proposal algorithm does not use the features of sentence lengths and matching pattern. If we only adopt the feature of Co-occurrence, the performance of our proposal is 1.1% higher on F1-score than that of the supervised baseline (98.3%). To conclude, our proposal algorithm uses fewer features and use no training data but perform better than the supervised baseline.

Translating. Experimental results show our model works well on this task (Table 3). Compared with the basic seq-to-seq model, copying mechanism gives a large improvement, because the source sentences and target sentence share some common representations, we will also give an example in the case study section. Local attention gives a small improvement over the traditional global attention, this can be attributed to shrinking the attention range, because most of the time, the mapping between ancient and contemporary Chinese is clear. A more sophisticated attention mechanism which makes full use of the characteristics of ancient and contemporary Chinese may further improve the performance.

4 Discussion

4.1 Sentence Alignment

We find that the small fraction of data (0.6%) that our method makes mistakes are mainly because of the change of punctuation. For example, in ancient Chinese, there is a comma "," after "异哉," (How strange!), while in contemporary Chinese, "怪啊!" (How strange!), an exclamation mark "!" is used, which makes the sentence to be an independent sentence. Since the sentence is short and there is no common character, our method fails to align the sentences correctly. However, such problems also exist in supervised models.

4.2 Necessity of Building a Large Sentence-Aligned Corpus

From Table 4, we can see that the results are very sensitive to the scale of the training data size. Therefore, our unsupervised method of building a large sentence-aligned corpus is necessary. If we do not build a large sentence-aligned corpus by our sentence alignment algorithm, we will only have limited sentence-aligned corpora and the performance of translating will be worse.

Table 4. Evaluation result (BLEU) of translating between **An** (ancient) and **Con** (contemporary) Chinese with different number of training samples.

Language	5,000	10,000	20,000	53,140
An-Con	3.00	9.69	16.31	26.95
Con-An	2.40	10.14	18.47	36.34

4.3 Translating Result

Under most circumstances, our models can translate sentences between ancient Chinese and contemporary Chinese properly. For instance in Table 5, our models can translate "薨 (pass away)" into "去世 (pass away)" or "逝世 (pass away)", which are the correct forms of expression in contemporary Chinese. And our models can even complete

Table 5. Example of translating from **An** (ancient) to **Con** (contemporary) Chinese.

Source	六月辛卯，中山王焉薨。
(Translation in English)	(On Xinmao Day of the sixth lunar month, Yan, King of Zhongshan, passed away.)
Target	六月十二日，中山王刘焉逝世。
(Translation in English)	(On twelfth of the sixth lunar month, Liu Yan, King of Zhongshan, passed away.)
Seq2Seq	六月十六日，中山王刘裕去世。
(Translation in English)	(On sixteenth of the sixth lunar month, Liu Yu, King of Zhongshan, died.)
Our model	六月二十二日，中山王刘焉逝世。
(Translation in English)	(On twenty-second of the sixth lunar month, Liu Yan, King of Zhongshan, passed away.)

some omitted characters. For instance, the family name "刘 (Liu)" in "中山王刘焉 (Liu Yan, King of Zhongshan)" was omitted in ancient Chinese because "中山王 (King of Zhongshan)" was a hereditary peerage offered to "刘 (Liu)" family. And our model completes the family name "刘 (Liu)" when translating. For proper nouns, the seq-to-2seq baseline model can fail sometimes while the copying model can correctly copy them from the source language. For instance, the seq-to-seq baseline model translates "焉 (Yan)" into "刘裕 (Liu Yu, a famous figure in the history)" because "焉 (Yan)" is relatively low-frequent words in ancient Chinese. However, the copying model learns to copy these low-frequency proper nouns from source sentences directly.

Translating dates between ancient and contemporary Chinese calendar requires background knowledge of the ancient Chinese lunar calendar, and involves non-trivial calculation that even native speakers cannot translate correctly without training. In the example, "辛卯 (The Xinmao Day)" is the date presented in the ancient form, our model fails to translate it. Our model fails to transform between the Gregorian calendar and the ancient Chinese lunar calendar and choose to generate a random date, which is expected because of the difficulty of such problems.

5 Conclusion

In this paper, we propose an unsupervised algorithm to construct sentence-aligned sentence pairs out of a passage-aligned corpus to build a large sentence-aligned corpus. We propose to apply the sequence to sequence model with attention and copying mechanism to automatically translate between two styles of Chinese sentences. The experimental results show that our method can yield good translating results.

References

1. Bahdanau, D., Cho, K., Bengio, Y.: Neural machine translation by jointly learning to align and translate. In: Bengio, Y., LeCun, Y. (eds.) 3rd International Conference on Learning Representations, ICLR 2015, San Diego, 7–9 May 2015, Conference Track Proceedings (2015)

2. Calixto, I., Liu, Q., Campbell, N.: Doubly-attentive decoder for multi-modal neural machine translation. In: Proceedings of the 55th Annual Meeting of the Association for Computational Linguistics, ACL 2017, Vancouver, 30 July–4 August, Volume 1: Long Papers, pp. 1913–1924 (2017)
3. Cho, K., et al.: Learning phrase representations using RNN encoder-decoder for statistical machine translation. In: EMNLP 2014, pp. 1724–1734 (2014)
4. Feng, S., Liu, S., Yang, N., Li, M., Zhou, M., Zhu, K.Q.: Improving attention modeling with implicit distortion and fertility for machine translation. In: COLING 2016, pp. 3082–3092 (2016)
5. Gale, W.A., Church, K.W.: A program for aligning sentences in bilingual corpora. Comput. Linguist. **19**, 75–102 (1993)
6. Gu, J., Lu, Z., Li, H., Li, V.O.K.: Incorporating copying mechanism in sequence-to-sequence learning. In: Proceedings of the 54th Annual Meeting of the Association for Computational Linguistics, ACL 2016, 7–12 August 2016, Berlin, Volume 1: Long Papers (2016)
7. Haruno, M., Yamazaki, T.: High-performance bilingual text alignment using statistical and dictionary information. Nat. Lang. Eng. **3**(1), 1–14 (1997)
8. Jean, S., Cho, K., Memisevic, R., Bengio, Y.: On using very large target vocabulary for neural machine translation. In: ACL 2015, pp. 1–10 (2015)
9. Kalchbrenner, N., Blunsom, P.: Recurrent continuous translation models. In: EMNLP 2013, pp. 1700–1709 (2013)
10. Lin, J., Sun, X., Ma, S., Su, Q.: Global encoding for abstractive summarization. In: Proceedings of the 56th Annual Meeting of the Association for Computational Linguistics, ACL 2018, Melbourne, 15–20 July 2018, Volume 2: Short Papers, pp. 163–169 (2018)
11. Lin, Z., Wang, X.: Chinese ancient-modern sentence alignment. In: Shi, Y., van Albada, G.D., Dongarra, J., Sloot, P.M.A. (eds.) ICCS 2007, Part II. LNCS, vol. 4488, pp. 1178–1185. Springer, Heidelberg (2007). https://doi.org/10.1007/978-3-540-72586-2_164
12. Liu, Y., Wang, N.: Sentence alignment for ancient and modern Chinese parallel corpus. In: Lei, J., Wang, F.L., Deng, H., Miao, D. (eds.) AICI 2012. CCIS, vol. 315, pp. 408–415. Springer, Heidelberg (2012). https://doi.org/10.1007/978-3-642-34240-0_54
13. Luong, T., Pham, H., Manning, C.D.: Effective approaches to attention-based neural machine translation. In: Proceedings of the 2015 Conference on Empirical Methods in Natural Language Processing, EMNLP 2015, Lisbon, 17–21 September 2015, pp. 1412–1421 (2015)
14. Ma, S., Sun, X., Wang, Y., Lin, J.: Bag-of-words as target for neural machine translation. In: Proceedings of the 56th Annual Meeting of the Association for Computational Linguistics, ACL 2018, Melbourne, 15–20 July 2018, Volume 2: Short Papers, pp. 332–338 (2018)
15. Meng, F., Lu, Z., Li, H., Liu, Q.: Interactive attention for neural machine translation. In: COLING 2016, pp. 2174–2185 (2016)
16. Mi, H., Wang, Z., Ittycheriah, A.: Supervised attentions for neural machine translation. In: EMNLP 2016, pp. 2283–2288 (2016)
17. Resnik, P.: Parallel strands: a preliminary investigation into mining the web for bilingual text. In: Farwell, D., Gerber, L., Hovy, E. (eds.) AMTA 1998. LNCS (LNAI), vol. 1529, pp. 72–82. Springer, Heidelberg (1998). https://doi.org/10.1007/3-540-49478-2_7
18. Resnik, P.: Mining the web for bilingual text. In: Dale, R., Church, K.W. (eds.) ACL. ACL (1999)
19. See, A., Liu, P.J., Manning, C.D.: Get to the point: summarization with pointer-generator networks. In: Barzilay, R., Kan, M. (eds.) Proceedings of the 55th Annual Meeting of the Association for Computational Linguistics, ACL 2017, Vancouver, 30 July–4 August, Volume 1: Long Papers, pp. 1073–1083. Association for Computational Linguistics (2017). https://doi.org/10.18653/v1/P17-1099

20. Su, J., Tan, Z., Xiong, D., Ji, R., Shi, X., Liu, Y.: Lattice-based recurrent neural network encoders for neural machine translation. In: Singh, S.P., Markovitch, S. (eds.) Proceedings of the Thirty-First AAAI Conference on Artificial Intelligence, 4–9 February 2017, San Francisco, pp. 3302–3308. AAAI Press (2017)
21. Sutskever, I., Vinyals, O., Le, Q.V.: Sequence to sequence learning with neural networks. In: Advances in Neural Information Processing Systems, pp. 3104–3112 (2014)
22. Sutskever, I., Vinyals, O., Le, Q.V.: Sequence to sequence learning with neural networks. In: NIPS 2014, pp. 3104–3112 (2014)
23. Tjandra, A., Sakti, S., Nakamura, S.: Local monotonic attention mechanism for end-to-end speech recognition. CoRR abs/1705.08091 (2017)
24. Tu, Z., Lu, Z., Liu, Y., Liu, X., Li, H.: Modeling coverage for neural machine translation. In: ACL 2016 (2016)
25. Wang, X., Ren, F.: Chinese-Japanese clause alignment. In: Gelbukh, A. (ed.) CICLing 2005. LNCS, vol. 3406, pp. 400–412. Springer, Heidelberg (2005). https://doi.org/10.1007/978-3-540-30586-6_43

FlexNER: A Flexible LSTM-CNN Stack Framework for Named Entity Recognition

Hongyin Zhu[1,2], Wenpeng Hu[3], and Yi Zeng[1,2,4,5](✉)

[1] Institute of Automation, Chinese Academy of Sciences, Beijing, China
{zhuhongyin2014,yi.zeng}@ia.ac.cn
[2] University of Chinese Academy of Sciences, Beijing, China
[3] School of Mathematical Sciences, Peking University, Beijing, China
wenpeng.hu@pku.edu.cn
[4] Center for Excellence in Brain Science and Intelligence Technology, Chinese Academy of Sciences, Shanghai, China
[5] National Laboratory of Pattern Recognition, Institute of Automation, Chinese Academy of Science, Beijing, China

Abstract. Named entity recognition (NER) is a foundational technology for information extraction. This paper presents a flexible NER framework (https://github.com/bke-casia/FLEXNER) compatible with different languages and domains. Inspired by the idea of distant supervision (DS), this paper enhances the representation by increasing the entity-context diversity without relying on external resources. We choose different layer stacks and sub-network combinations to construct the bilateral networks. This strategy can generally improve model performance on different datasets. We conduct experiments on five languages, such as English, German, Spanish, Dutch and Chinese, and biomedical fields, such as identifying the chemicals and gene/protein terms from scientific works. Experimental results demonstrate the good performance of this framework.

Keywords: Named entity recognition · Data augmentation · LSTM-CNN

1 Introduction

The NER task aims to automatically identify the atomic entity mentions in textual inputs. This technology is widely used in many natural language processing pipelines, such as entity linking, relation extraction, question answering, etc. This paper describes a portable framework that can use different layer stacks and sub-network combinations to form different models. This framework does not rely on language/domain-specific external resources so it can reduce coupling.

Electronic supplementary material The online version of this chapter (https://doi.org/10.1007/978-3-030-32236-6_14) contains supplementary material, which is available to authorized users.

J. Tang et al. (Eds.): NLPCC 2019, LNAI 11839, pp. 168–178, 2019.
https://doi.org/10.1007/978-3-030-32236-6_14

While state-of-the-art deep learning models [3,14,15] resolve this problem in the sequence labeling manner, their models are usually trained on a fixed training set where the combination of entity and context is invariant, so the relationship between entity and context information is not fully exploited. Intuitively, adding diverse training samples [11,28] is helpful to train a better model, but expanding the existing training data is expensive. The Wikipedia entity type mappings [17] or the distant supervision [16] provide a way to augment the data, but these methods rely heavily on outside knowledge resources. The DS-based entity set expansion might introduce noisy instances, which potentially leads to the semantic drift problem [23]. Ideally, we would wish to overcome these two problems, increasing the diversity of training data without external resources, and adapting our approach to any datasets. We solve the first problem by data transformation operations inside the dataset. Our method only uses the ground truth entities in the training set, which naturally reduces the influence of noisy instances. For the second problem, we use a bilateral network to enhance the learning representation, which can achieve better results on different datasets.

The context pattern provides semantics for inferring the entity slot, i.e., from "*Germany imported 47000 sheep from Britain*" we got a context pattern "A imported 47000 sheep from B" which implies that A and B are locations. If this sentence becomes "*America imported 47000 sheep from Britain*", the appearance of *America* is also reasonable, but a person cannot appear in these placeholders. We refer to these rules as context pattern entailment, which can be emphasized and generalized by increasing entity-context diversity during model training. The data augmentation technique [5] aims to apply a wide array of transformations to synthetically expand a training set. This paper proposes two innovative data augmentation methods on the input stage. Compared with the distant supervision, our approach does not rely on additional knowledge bases since our approach can inherently and proactively enhance low resource datasets.

We conduct experiments on five languages, including the English, German, Spanish, Dutch and Chinese, and biomedical domain. Our bilateral network achieves good performance. The main contributions of this paper can be summarized below.

(i) We augment the learning representation by increasing entity-context diversity. Our method can be applied to any datasets almost without any domain-specific modification.
(ii) To improve the versatility of our approach, we present the bilateral network to integrate the baseline and augmented representations of two subnetworks.

2 Related Work

The CNN based [3], LSTM based [14] and hybrid (i.e., LSTM-CNNs [1,15]) models resolve this task in the sequence labeling manner. Yang et al. [26] build a neural sequence labeling framework[1] to reproduce the state-of-the-art models,

[1] https://github.com/jiesutd/NCRFpp.

while we build a portable framework and also conduct experiments in different languages and domains. Yang et al. [27] use cross-domain data and transfer learning to improve model performance.

ELMo [18] and BERT [4] enhance the representations by pre-training language models. BERT randomly masks some words to train a masked language model, while our data augmentation is a constrained entity-context expansion. Our approach aims to retain more entity type information in the context representation. CVT [2] proposes a semi-supervised learning algorithm that uses the labeled and unlabeled data to improve the representation of the Bi-LSTM encoder.

The data augmentation method can be carried out on two stages, the raw input stage [21] and the feature space [5]. Data augmentation paradigm has been well addressed in computer vision research, but receives less attention in NLP. Shi et al. [23] propose a probabilistic Co-Bootstrapping method to better define the expansion boundary for the web-based entity set expansion. Our approach is designed to enhance the entity-context diversity of the training data without changing the entity boundary, which naturally reduces the impact of noisy instances.

The proposed framework is flexible and easy to expand. We can further consider the structural information [7] and build the model in a paradigm of continual learning [8].

3 Methods

3.1 Model Overview

An NER pipeline usually contains two stages, predicting label sequence and extracting entities. Firstly, this model converts the textual input into the most likely label sequence $y^* = \arg\max_{y \in Y(z)} p(y|z)$, where z and $Y(z)$ denote the textual sequence and all possible label sequences. Secondly, the post-processing module converts the label sequence into human-readable entities. The sequence labeling neural network usually contains three components for word representations, contextual representations and sequence labeling respectively.

Word Representations. This component projects each token to a d-dimensional vector which is composed of the word embedding and character level representation. The word embedding can be a pre-trained [9] or randomly initialized fixed-length vector. The character level representation can be calculated by a CNN or RNN [26], and the character embeddings are randomly initialized and jointly trained.

Contextual Representations. This component can generate contextual representations using CNN or RNN. Besides, our model can use different stack components to extract features, as shown in the left part of Fig. 2. The major difference between these stack components is the way they extract local features. In the LSTM-CNN stack, the CNN extracts the local contextual features from the hidden state of Bi-LSTM, while in the CNN-LSTM stack the CNN extracts the local features from the word vectors and the Bi-LSTM uses the context of local features.

Sequence Labeling. This component outputs the probability of each token and selects the most likely label sequence as the final result. This paper adopts the conditional random field (CRF) [13] to consider the transition probability between labels.

$$p(y|z;W,b) = \frac{\prod_{i=1}^{n} \exp(W_{y_{i-1}y_i}^{T} z_i + b_{y_{i-1}y_i})}{\sum_{y' \in Y(z)} \prod_{i=1}^{n} \exp(W_{y'_{i-1}y'_i}^{T} z_i + b_{y'_{i-1}y'_i})} \tag{1}$$

where $\{[z_i, y_i]\}, i = 1, 2...n$ represents the i-th word z_i and the i-th label y_i in the input sequence respectively. $Y(z)$ denotes all the possible label sequences for the input sequence z. W and b are weight matrix and bias vector, in which W_{y_{i-1},y_i} and b_{y_{i-1},y_i} are the weight vector and bias corresponding to the successive labels (y_{i-1}, y_i). $p(y|z;W,b)$ is the probability of generating this tag sequence over all possible tag sequences.

During the training process, the model parameters are updated to maximize the log-likelihood $L(W,b)$. For prediction, the decoder will find the optimal label sequence that can maximize the log-likelihood $L(W,b)$ through the Viterbi algorithm.

$$L(W,b) = \sum_{j} \log p(y^j|z^j;W,b) \tag{2}$$

$$y^* = \arg \max_{y \in Y(z)} p(y|z;W,b) \tag{3}$$

3.2 Data Augmentation

Sentence-Centric Augmentation (SCA). As shown in Fig. 1(a), this method enhances the context representation by increasing entity diversity. This operation augments the entity distribution of any sample. We generate augmented sentences as follows:

1. Extract the categorical entity glossary $E = \{E_1, E_2, ..., E_c\}$ based on the original corpus S, where c is class number. An entity may be composed of multiple words, so we needs to convert label sequence into complete entities.
2. Resample the sentence $s_i \sim \text{Uniform}(S)$ and light up each entity slot $a_{(i,j)} \sim \text{Bernoulli}(p)$. p (0.5 to 0.9) is chosen according to different datasets.
3. Replace the lighted entities $a_{(i,k)} \in E_j$ with $\hat{a}_{(i,k)} \sim \text{Binomial}(E_j \backslash \{a_{(i,k)}\})$. This is a crossover operation.

Entity-Centric Augmentation (ECA). In SCA, we can control the augmentation for context, but the entity control is not easy. As shown in Fig. 1(b), ECA

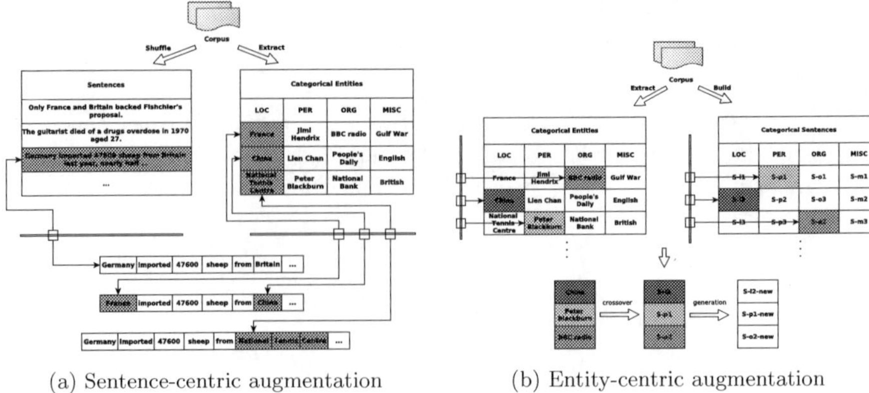

(a) Sentence-centric augmentation (b) Entity-centric augmentation

Fig. 1. The schematic diagram of data augmentation operations where the black arrows represent the random selectors

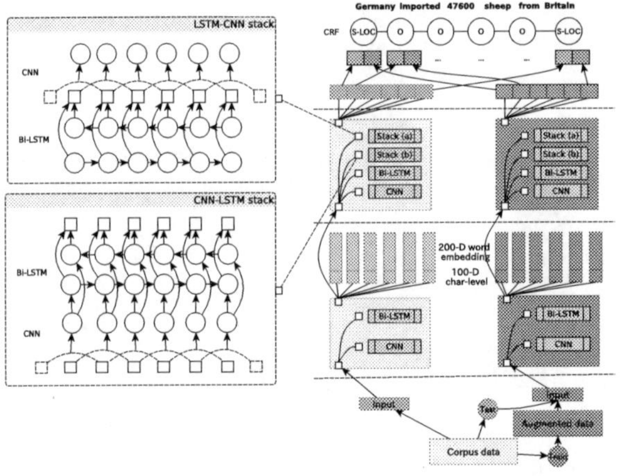

Fig. 2. An overview of bilateral architecture

enhances the entity representation by increasing context diversity. This operation augments the sentence distribution of an entity. We can better control the augmentation for entities.

1. Extract the categorical entity glossary $E = \{E_1, E_2, ..., E_c\}$ from the training data.
2. Build the categorical sentence set $S = \{S_1, S_2, ..., S_c\}$. The main idea is to classify the training samples according to the type mention of entities. Let $e_{(i,1)} \in E_i$ and $e_{i,1} \in s_j$, then $s_j \in S_i$. In Fig. 1(b), the S-li denotes the i-th sentence containing at least one l (**LOC**) entity.
3. Sample an entity $e_{(i,1)}$ with a probability of $p = F(e_{(i,1)})/F(E_i)$ where $F(\cdot)$ is the frequency. Sample a sentence $s_i \sim \text{Uniform}(S_i)$, and then perform the crossover operation.

If we iteratively substitute entities once a time in SCA, it behaves like ECA to some extent, but the distribution of entity and context is different. The basis of the two augmentation methods is different, because ECA can be extended to augment the vertex representation of a knowledge graph, while SCA focuses on text-level expansion. Here we use a random selector to simplify the augmentation process and make this work widely available. But this may lead to some noisy samples, e.g., "Germany imported 47600 sheep from national tennis centre". Quality control is critical when faced with data in a specific domain and is reserved for future work. Our approach actively extracts entities from within the dataset, thus not relying on the external resources. Our approach can be generally applied to augment the entity-context diversity for any datasets.

3.3 Bilateral Architecture

As shown in Fig. 2, the bilateral architecture is composed of a baseline network on the left side and an augmented network on the right side. In the word and contextual representation layers, each sub-network can optionally use the Bi-LSTM, CNN and mixed stack layers to form flexible network combinations. This strategy can generate at least 64 ($(2 \times 4)^n, n \geq 2$, where n is the number of sub-networks) types of bilateral networks. We compare different layer stack networks and their combinations in experiments. The data augmentation operations are only activated during the model training.

The inputs to the left and right sub-networks are different, so they form the function that adapts to different patterns. The right sub-network is more generalized, but the weakness is that it may generate noisy samples. This bilateral network also supports the joint training, but the inputs to both sides are the same. The bilateral network is a case of the multi-lateral network which also can be easily extended by adding more sub-networks. This paper adopts the IOBES scheme [19]. The outputs of bilateral sub-networks are concatenated as the input to the final CRF layer.

3.4 Training Procedure

We introduce two training methods, the separate training and the joint training. The separate training contains three steps.

(1) We train the left sub-network of Fig. 2 (freezing the right sub-network) using the human-annotated data. The left and the right sides represent the baseline and augmented models respectively. The outputs of the two sub-networks share the same CRF layer. In this step, the CRF layer only accepts the output of the baseline network. The output and the gradient of the augmented network are masked so the parameters of the augmented network are not updated. The baseline network learns the original features of the training data.
(2) Then, we train the right sub-network (freezing the left sub-network) with the human-annotated and the augmented data. The augmented data is generated dynamically based on the algorithm in subsection Data Augmentation.

Contrary to step (1), the CRF layer only accepts the output of the augmented network. This step also updates the weights of the full connection layer before the CRF layer. The augmented network enhances representations by increasing entity-context diversity.

(3) We retrain the last CRF layer (freezing all the components before the CRF layer) with the human-annotated data to fuse the representation. In this step, the functions of two sub-networks are kept, so the outputs of them are concatenated to form the rich representation from different perspectives.

We refer to the step (1) and (2) as the pre-training and step (3) as the fine-tuning. The separate training method can form two functional sub-networks, each of which retains its own characteristics.

For the joint training, we input the same sample into two sub-networks. Although the joint training can update the parameters simultaneously, the separate training achieved better results. This is because the separate training accepts different sentences in different sub-networks. The separate training retains the functionality of each sub-network, and features can be extracted independently from different perspectives, while the joint training processes the same task and focuses on extending layer width, so it did not fully extract diverse features.

4 Experiments

4.1 Dataset and Evaluation

Different Languages. For different languages, we adopt the CoNLL-2002 [22] and CoNLL-2003 [24] datasets which are annotated with four types of entity, location (LOC), organization (ORG), person (PER), miscellaneous (MISC) in English, German, Dutch, Spanish. The Chinese dataset [25] is a discourse-level dataset from hundreds of Chinese literature articles where seven types of entities (Thing, Person, Location, Time, Metric, Organization, Abstract) are annotated.

Biomedical Field. For the biomedical NER, we use the SCAI corpus which is provided by the Fraunhofer Institute for Algorithms and Scientific Computing. We focused on the International Union of Pure and Applied Chemistry (IUPAC) names (e.g., adenosine 3', 5'-(hydrogen phosphate)) like the ChemSpot [20]. The second dataset is the GELLUS corpus [12] which annotates cell line names in 1,212 documents drawn from the biomedical literature in the PubMed and PMC archives.

4.2 Results on NER for Different Languages

We use (C) and (W) to represent the **c**haracter level input and **w**ord level input respectively, i.e., the (C)CNN and (W)LSTM denote this model use the CNN to accept the input of character embeddings and the Bi-LSTM to accept the input of word embeddings respectively.

Table 1. Results of different network combinations on the CoNLL-2003 English dataset

Layers	Models					
Character input	LSTM			CNN		
Word input	LSTM	CNN	Stack (a)	LSTM	CNN	Stack (b)
Baseline	91.00 ± 0.04[a]	89.89 ± 0.06	90.99 ± 0.06	90.95 ± 0.06[b]	90.13 ± 0.04	90.15 ± 0.04
Augment	90.87 ± 0.11	90.01 ± 0.08	91.10 ± 0.05	91.06 ± 0.06	90.32 ± 0.06	89.67 ± 0.07
Baseline+ Baseline	91.02 ± 0.05	89.85 ± 0.03	90.99 ± 0.05	90.98 ± 0.04	90.09 ± 0.03	90.19 ± 0.04
Baseline+ Augment	**91.36 ± 0.08**	90.24 ± 0.09	**91.47 ± 0.06**	91.14 ± 0.07	90.52 ± 0.06	90.54 ± 0.05

English. Table 1 shows the results of 24 models on the English NER. This paper reproduces the baseline models and tests the stack models. To eliminate the influence of random factors we ran the experiments three times. [a] and [b] denote the models of (C)LSTM-(W)LSTM-CRF [14] and (C)CNN-(W)LSTM-CRF [15] models respectively. In some cases, our baseline models slightly underperform (0.1–0.2% F1) than the corresponding prototypes, but the bilateral models (Baseline+Augment) achieve better performances than the prototypes of [1,3,14]. Concatenating two separate baseline models (Baseline+Baseline) almost did not change results, while the Baseline+Augment model produces better results. This demonstrates data augmentation is helpful to enhance the representations to generate better results. The entity-based data transformation paradigm has great potential to improve the performance of other tasks. More details could be found in the supplementary material[2].

4.3 Results on Biomedical NER

In biomedical domain, one of the challenges is the limited size of training data. However, expanding biomedical datasets is more challenging because annotators need to design and understand domain-specific criteria, which complicates the process. There are many feature-based systems, but they cannot be used in different areas. Automatically expanding datasets is a promising way to enhance the use of deep learning models. Our method achieves good performance in the following two corpora. In the GELLUS corpus, the augmented and the bilateral models improve 5.11% and 6.08% F1 sore than our baseline model. This means that our approach will be a good choice in the biomedical field (Table 2).

Due to space constraints, extensive discussions and case studies will be introduced in the supplementary material (see Footnote 2).

[2] https://github.com/bke-casia/FLEXNER/blob/master/pic/appendix.pdf.

Table 2. Results of IUPAC Chemical terms and Cell lines on the SCAI chemicals corpus and the GELLUS corpus respectively

Algorithm	SCAI	GELLUS
OSCAR4 [10]	57.3	–
ChemSpot [20]	68.1	–
CRF [6]	–	72.14
LSTM-CRF [6]	–	73.51
This work (Baseline)	69.08	78.78
This work (Baseline × 2)	69.06	78.80
This work (Augment)	**69.98**	83.89
This work (Bilateral)	69.79	**84.86**

5 Conclusion

This paper introduces a portable NER framework FlexNER which can recognize entities from textual input. We propose a data augmentation paradigm which does not need external data and is straightforward. We augment the learning representation by enhancing entity-context diversity. The layer stacks and sub-network combinations can be commonly used in different datasets to provide better representations from different perspectives.

It seems effortless to extend this framework to the multilingual NER research since we can use different sub-networks to learn different languages and then explore the interaction among them. Data quality control is an important task that seems to improve the learning process. Besides, this method is potential to be used in low-resource languages and may benefit in other entity related tasks. In the future, we also plan to apply this system to biomedical research, i.e., extracting the functional brain connectome [29] or exploring the relations between drugs and diseases.

Acknowledgement. This study is supported by the Strategic Priority Research Program of Chinese Academy of Sciences (Grant No. XDB32070100).

References

1. Chiu, J.P., Nichols, E.: Named entity recognition with bidirectional LSTM-CNNs. arXiv preprint arXiv:1511.08308 (2015)
2. Clark, K., Luong, M.T., Manning, C.D., Le, Q.V.: Semi-supervised sequence modeling with cross-view training. arXiv preprint arXiv:1809.08370 (2018)
3. Collobert, R., Weston, J., Bottou, L., Karlen, M., Kavukcuoglu, K., Kuksa, P.: Natural language processing (almost) from scratch. J. Mach. Learn. Res. **12**, 2493–2537 (2011)
4. Devlin, J., Chang, M.W., Lee, K., Toutanova, K.: Bert: pre-training of deep bidirectional transformers for language understanding. arXiv preprint arXiv:1810.04805 (2018)

5. DeVries, T., Taylor, G.W.: Dataset augmentation in feature space. arXiv preprint arXiv:1702.05538 (2017)
6. Habibi, M., Weber, L., Neves, M., Wiegandt, D.L., Leser, U.: Deep learning with word embeddings improves biomedical named entity recognition. Bioinformatics **33**(14), i37–i48 (2017)
7. Hu, W., Chan, Z., Liu, B., Zhao, D., Ma, J., Yan, R.: GSN: a graph-structured network for multi-party dialogues. In: Proceedings of IJCAI 2019 (2019)
8. Hu, W., et al.: Overcoming catastrophic forgetting for continual learning via model adaptation. In: Proceedings of ICLR 2019 (2019)
9. Hu, W., Zhang, J., Zheng, N.: Different contexts lead to different word embeddings. In: Proceedings of COLING 2016 (2016)
10. Jessop, D.M., Adams, S.E., Willighagen, E.L., Hawizy, L., Murray-Rust, P.: OSCAR4: a flexible architecture for chemical text-mining. J. Cheminformatics **3**(1), 41 (2011)
11. Jiang, L., Meng, D., Yu, S.I., Lan, Z., Shan, S., Hauptmann, A.: Self-paced learning with diversity. In: Proceedings of NeuIPS 2014 (2014)
12. Kaewphan, S., Van Landeghem, S., Ohta, T., Van de Peer, Y., Ginter, F., Pyysalo, S.: Cell line name recognition in support of the identification of synthetic lethality in cancer from text. Bioinformatics **32**(2), 276–282 (2015)
13. Lafferty, J., McCallum, A., Pereira, F.C.: Conditional random fields: Probabilistic models for segmenting and labeling sequence data (2001)
14. Lample, G., Ballesteros, M., Subramanian, S., Kawakami, K., Dyer, C.: Neural architectures for named entity recognition. arXiv preprint arXiv:1603.01360 (2016)
15. Ma, X., Hovy, E.: End-to-end sequence labeling via bi-directional LSTM-CNNs-CRF. arXiv preprint arXiv:1603.01354 (2016)
16. Mintz, M., Bills, S., Snow, R., Jurafsky, D.: Distant supervision for relation extraction without labeled data. In: Proceedings of ACL 2009 (2009)
17. Ni, J., Florian, R.: Improving multilingual named entity recognition with Wikipedia entity type mapping. arXiv preprint arXiv:1707.02459 (2017)
18. Peters, M.E., Neumann, M., Iyyer, M., Gardner, M., Clark, C., Lee, K., Zettlemoyer, L.: Deep contextualized word representations. arXiv preprint arXiv:1802.05365 (2018)
19. Ratinov, L., Roth, D.: Design challenges and misconceptions in named entity recognition. In: Proceedings of CoNLL 2009, pp. 147–155 (2009)
20. Rocktäschel, T., Weidlich, M., Leser, U.: ChemSpot: a hybrid system for chemical named entity recognition. Bioinformatics **28**(12), 1633–1640 (2012)
21. Saito, I., et al.: Improving neural text normalization with data augmentation at character-and morphological levels. In: Proceedings of IJCNLP 2017 (2017)
22. Sang, E.F.T.K.: Introduction to the CoNLL-2002 shared task: language-independent named entity recognition. In: Proceedings of CoNLL 2002 (2002)
23. Shi, B., Zhang, Z., Sun, L., Han, X.: A probabilistic co-bootstrapping method for entity set expansion. In: Proceedings of COLING 2014, pp. 2280–2290 (2014)
24. Tjong Kim Sang, E.F., De Meulder, F.: Introduction to the CoNLL-2003 shared task: language-independent named entity recognition. In: Proceedings of HLT-NAACL 2003, pp. 142–147 (2003)
25. Xu, J., Wen, J., Sun, X., Su, Q.: A discourse-level named entity recognition and relation extraction dataset for Chinese literature text. arXiv preprint arXiv:1711.07010 (2017)
26. Yang, J., Liang, S., Zhang, Y.: Design challenges and misconceptions in neural sequence labeling. In: Proceedings COLING 2018 (2018)

27. Yang, Z., Salakhutdinov, R., Cohen, W.W.: Transfer learning for sequence tagging with hierarchical recurrent networks. arXiv preprint arXiv:1703.06345 (2017)
28. Zhou, L., Hu, W., Zhang, J., Zong, C.: Neural system combination for machine translation. arXiv preprint arXiv:1704.06393 (2017)
29. Zhu, H., Zeng, Y., Wang, D., Xu, B.: Brain knowledge graph analysis based on complex network theory. In: Ascoli, G.A., Hawrylycz, M., Ali, H., Khazanchi, D., Shi, Y. (eds.) BIH 2016. LNCS (LNAI), vol. 9919, pp. 211–220. Springer, Cham (2016). https://doi.org/10.1007/978-3-319-47103-7_21

Domain Adaptive Question Answering over Knowledge Base

Yulai Yang[1,2,3], Lei Hou[1,2,3(✉)], Hailong Jin[1,2,3], Peng Zhang[1,2,3], Juanzi Li[1,2,3], Yi Huang[4], and Min Hu[4]

[1] DCST, Tsinghua University, Beijing 100084, China
yyl277078178@163.com, greener2009@gmail.com, tsinghua_phd@163.com, zpjumper@gmail.com, lijuanzi@tsinghua.edu.cn
[2] KIRC, Institute for Artificial Intelligence, Tsinghua University, Beijing, China
[3] Beijing National Research Center for Information Science and Technology, Beijing, China
[4] China Mobile Research Institute, Beijing, China
{huangyi,humin}@chinamobile.com

Abstract. Domain-specific question answering over knowledge base generates an answer for a natural language question based on a domain-specific knowledge base. But it often faces a lack of domain training resources such as question answer pairs or even questions. To address this issue, we propose a domain adaptive method to construct a domain-specific question answering system using easily accessible open domain questions. Specifically, generalization features are proposed to represent questions, which can categorize questions according to their syntactic forms. The features are adaptive from open domain into domain by terminology transfer. And a fuzzy matching method based on character vector are used to do knowledge base retrieving. Extensive experiments on real datasets demonstrate the effectiveness of the proposed method.

Keywords: Natural language question answering · Knowledge base · Domain adaptation

1 Introduction

Domain-specific question answering over knowledge base (KBQA) is an important way of using domain knowledge, which takes natural language questions as input and returns professional and accurate answers. Many previous approaches rely on hand-crafted patterns or rules, which are time-consuming and inevitably incomplete. To avoid the complex hand-crafted patterns construction, some methods try to generate patterns automatically. Abujabal et al. [1] propose a distant supervision method to learn question patterns and align them with the knowledge base by question and answer (QA) pairs. Besides, end-to-end methods based on neural networks are widely used in KBQA task. They represent both questions and answers as semantic vectors by neural networks, and calculate the similarities between vectors to select the final answers. These methods

J. Tang et al. (Eds.): NLPCC 2019, LNAI 11839, pp. 179–188, 2019.
https://doi.org/10.1007/978-3-030-32236-6_15

need the QA pairs for supervised training, which are not easy to obtain in a specific domain compared with open domain. Therefore, how to utilize existing open domain resources for domain adaptation poses a critical challenge.

To address the above issues, we propose a method which can construct a domain adaptive KBQA system with open domain questions. We define a new pattern to represent questions with the Parsing and POS results which can be easily obtained through existing NLP tools, and then train a key entity and property phrases detection model with open domain questions based on the learned representations. In order to adapt the key phrase detection model to specific domains, we utilize a terminology transfer method to make the distributions of domain questions and general questions consistent in feature space as far as possible. Finally, we retrieve the knowledge base via a character vector-based fuzzy matching to get the final answer. The key phrase detection model is evaluated on an open domain and two domain-specific datasets, one is insurance and the other is China Mobile products. For each specific domain, we construct a KBQA dataset to evaluate the performance of the entire model.

In summary, the main contributions of this paper can be described as follows:

- We propose a general method to construct a domain adaptive KBQA system using open domain questions without any hand-crafted template and QA pair.
- We define a new and simple question representation pattern which is effective for key phrase detection and domain adaptation.
- Experiments show that our domain adaptive method can achieve good performance in both real-world insurance and China Mobile products domain datasets.

The rest of this paper is organized as follows. Section 2 formulates the problem. Section 3 presents the framework and method details. Section 4 describes the method evaluations, Sect. 5 discusses the related work, and finally Sect. 6 concludes this work with some future research directions.

2 Problem Formulation

Definition 1 (Knowledge Base). *A knowledge base/graph $\mathcal{K}$ is a collection of subject-predicate-object triples $(\mathbf{s}, \mathbf{p}, \mathbf{o})$, which also form a graph (hence the name). $\mathbf{s}$ is an entity $e \in \mathcal{E}$ or a concept/class $c \in \mathcal{C}$, $\mathbf{p} \in \mathcal{P}$ is a property and $\mathbf{o}$ could also be literals $l \in \mathcal{L}$ besides entities and concepts.*

Domain knowledge base is often a collection of the domain facts, and Fig. 1 presents a fragment of the insurance knowledge base. Nodes are the subjects such as “com_abrs” or the objects such as “安邦人寿 (AnBang)”. Directed edges are the predicates which describe the relations or properties between subjects and objects such as “company”.

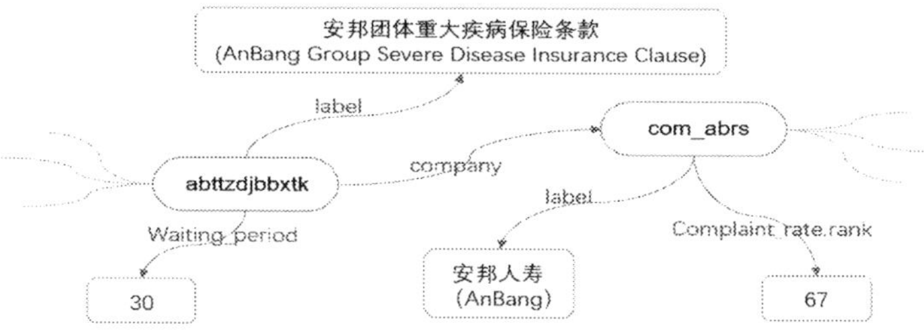

Fig. 1. Example knowledge base fragment.

Definition 2 (Question). *A question*[1] *is a linguistic expression used to make a request for information. We only consider the factual question in this paper. A factual question contains an entity mention and its potential answer is directly connected to the entity in knowledge base* $\mathcal{K}$.

We further divide questions into open domain questions $\mathbf{Q}_{open}$ and domain-specific questions $\mathbf{Q}_{domain}$. $\mathbf{Q}_{open}$ does not focus on any domain and can be easily acquired on the Internet, while $\mathbf{Q}_{domain}$ is closely related to a particular field (e.g., *insurance*), which is difficult to be acquired in large scale.

Definition 3 (Domain Adaptive Question Answering over Knowledge Base, DKBQA). *Given a set of open domain questions* $\mathbf{Q}_{open}$, *a domain specific question* $\mathbf{Q}_{domain}$ *and a domain knowledge base* $\mathcal{K}$, *DKBQA aims to detect the key entity and property phrases of the question by analyzing the open domain questions* $\mathbf{Q}_{open}$, *and get answer directly by knowledge base retrieving with a structured query which has mapped the key phrases into* $\mathcal{K}$.

Since the limited number of domain questions affects the performance of DKBQA, we apparently expect to utilize the large amount of open domain questions. Then how to make the domain adaption becomes the critical issue.

3 Method

The architecture of DKBQA system is a pipeline paradigm, involving the following five steps as shown in Fig. 2: (1) representing the question as a pattern sequence by the existing POS and Parsing tools; (2) recognizing the key entity phrase $\mathbf{p}_e$ and property phrase $\mathbf{p}_p$ in $\mathbf{Q}_{domain}$ by a key phrase detection model trained on the open domain questions $\mathbf{Q}_{open}$; (3) generating candidate properties through knowledge base retrieving; (4) matching one property by calculating the similarity between $\mathbf{p}_p$ and the candidates; (5) retrieving $\mathcal{K}$ to get answer.

[1] https://en.wikipedia.org/wiki/Question.

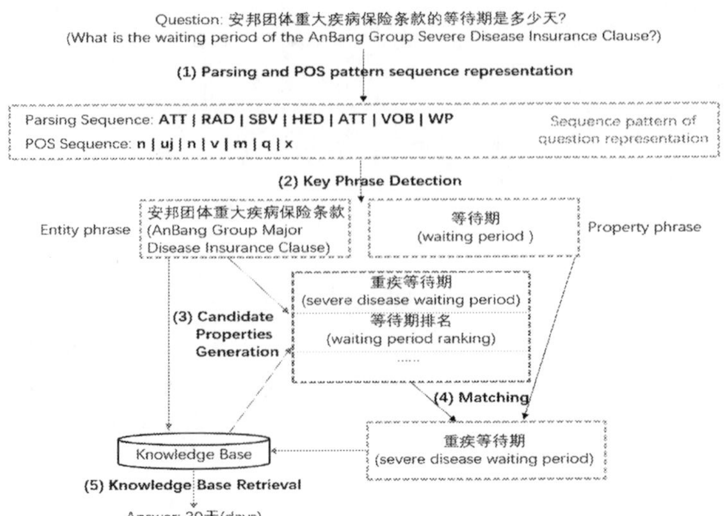

Fig. 2. Architecture of DKBQA system

3.1 Question Pattern

We try to find a representation method to catch the key semantic information and merge questions into some patterns. Dependency parsing is a good feature because it is a strong abstract expression of sentence and dependency grammar can describe the relationship between a head and its dependents which can be naturally mapped into a semantic expression. For convenience, we only use the sequence of syntactic tags as the pattern ignoring the dependency information. To enhance the ability of sentence representation, we add the POS tag feature into sequence pattern. Through observation and preliminary statistics, the Parsing and POS tags patterns can effectively classify questions with the same keyword position so that we can transform different questions with the same Parsing and POS tags into one sequence pattern. As question pattern aims to classify questions with token sequence ignoring the token meaning, the representation is insensitive to the accuracy of the Parsing and POS.

3.2 Key Phrase Detection

By observing questions in various domains, we find that no matter which domain the questions belong to, they almost share the same syntactic form with different domain terminologies. Based on this observation, the domain phrase detection can be divided into two sub-problems: detect the key phrases in the open domain questions by the Parsing and POS sequence pattern, and adapt the common pattern forms from open domain to the specific domain via terminology transfer.

Key Phrase Detection in Open Domain. Phrase detection can be treated as a sequence labeling problem. As shown in Fig. 3, our goal is to build a tagging system which accepts a question pattern sequence as input and outputs the key phrases positions. Specifically, we employ a dependency parser tool (LTP) [4] to represent a question into the Parsing and POS pattern, and a Bi-RNN model to predict the entity and property phrases. The model is learned from pairs of question pattern and its corresponding golden phrase locations from the manually annotated training data. As using the question pattern instead of the natural language form, the annotation work becomes easy and simple. Given an input question pattern $\mathbf{X}$ with annotated phrase locations, we first transform $\mathbf{X}$ into a one-hot vector. In this step, we divide the question pattern $\mathbf{X}$ into two forms which are the Parsing Sequence $\mathbf{X}_{par}$, and the POS Sequence $\mathbf{X}_{pos}$. After question representation, we use two Bi-RNN models to encode the pattern sequences into hidden vectors $\mathbf{V}_{par}$ and $\mathbf{V}_{pos}$ separately. Then we concatenate the two vectors as $\mathbf{V}_e$, and decode $\mathbf{V}_e$ via a linear layer. At last, the network outputs a probability of each position being entity and property with a $softmax$ layer.

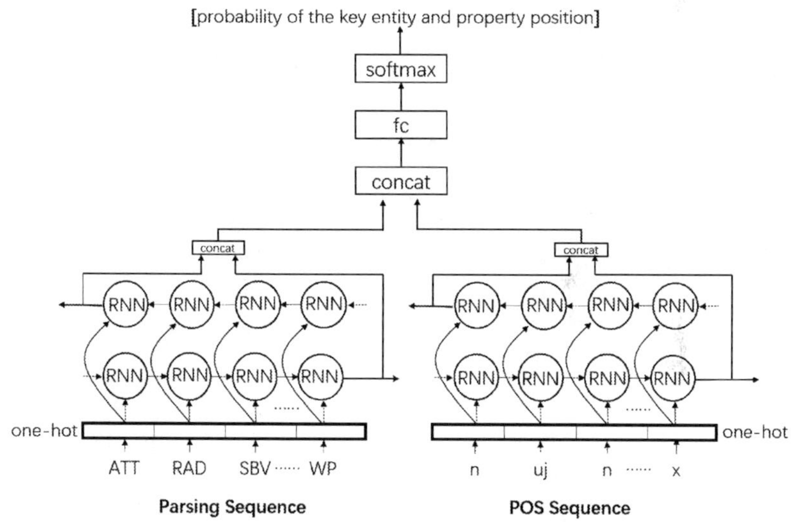

Fig. 3. The architecture of the key phrase detection model

Terminology Transfer. In this subsection, we expect to adapt the above model into a specific domain by constructing a terminology lexicon, making the specific domain questions have similar sequence patterns and characteristic distributions in the Parsing and POS feature space. Intuitively, we can directly employ the labels of the entities in domain knowledge base $\mathcal{K}$ as the terminology lexicon items by adding the POS tags and high frequencies. For the universality consideration, we do not attempt to build an additional synonym list for entities.

Instead, we add some domain-specific terms obtained from domain related documents in order to increase the dictionary coverage, based on the assumption that these terms may become the unit of query phrases. We obtain domain-specific terms through a term extraction method proposed by Pan [9]. Through terminology transfer, we can make the POS and Parsing results close to the open domain ones especially for some long or low-frequency phrases, and improve the availability of the prediction model in the specific domain. An example is shown as Fig. 4.

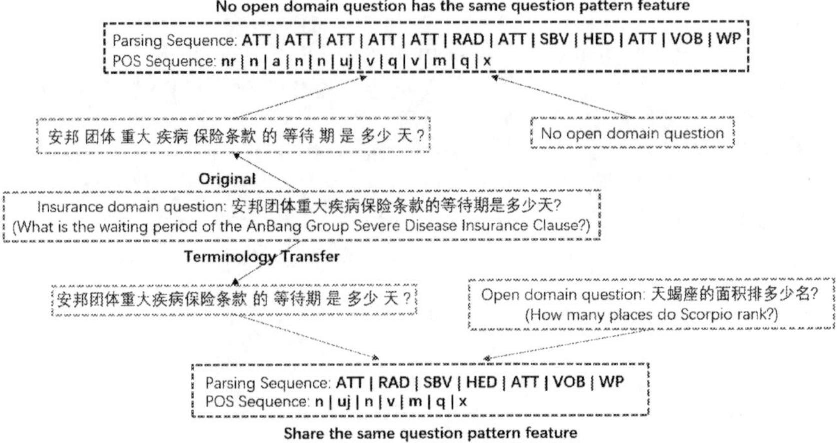

Fig. 4. An example of terminology transfer

3.3 Knowledge Base Search

Key phrase detection recognizes the KB-independent key phrases of the query which reflects the user intention. To connect the query vocabulary to semantic items in knowledge base $\mathcal{K}$, we construct a lexicon $\mathbf{L}$ which consists of an entity lexicon $\mathbf{L}_E$ and a property lexicon $\mathbf{L}_P$. Then we utilize a character-vector based fuzzy query method to retrieve the lexicon.

Character Vector Lexicon. The lexicon $\mathbf{L}$ is consist of two parts: (1) the labels and IDs of the entities or properties in $\mathcal{K}$ just like the terminology lexicon, and (2) the character vector presentation for each label. As our domain knowledge base is in Chinese, we utilize Chinese Wiki corpus to train the character vector via the CBOW [8] model. The difference from conventional word2vec is that the training is conducted on single characters instead of words. We add all the character vectors together to represent a phrase. The properties in a domain-specific knowledge base are always better distinguished than the open domain one as its small size and obvious domain boundaries.

Matching. We retrieve the knowledge base by a fuzzy matching method. Firstly, get an ID of the most related entity with the query subject phrase. Secondly, generate a set of candidate properties from all the properties directly connected with the entity. And then we can select a property by the same fuzzy matching method as entity retrieval. Once the entity and property are obtained, we can form a structured query to get the result directly by knowledge base retrieval. Fuzzy matching is implemented with the cosine similarity between query vocabulary and semantic items.

4 Experiment

4.1 Dataset

Open Domain Dataset. Open domain questions are chosen from the training set of the NLPCC 2016 KBQA task[2], which contains 14,609 Chinese questions. Specifically, we select 2,646 questions as training set and 500 questions as test set for manual annotation. In order to provide a good generalization ability, we make some statistics of the whole questions to preserve the Parsing and POS features distribution. We find that the Parsing pattern has a strong generalization ability, i.e., 36 parsing patterns can present 4,127 questions. The generalization ability of the POS pattern is weak, but it can provide a good recognition ability.

Specific Domain Datasets. Specific domain datasets include two parts. One is the insurance domain dataset, the other is the China Mobile products dataset. Each of them contains 100 manually generated questions, and all answers can be found in the domain knowledge bases. For each query intention, there are some diverse forms of natural language representation.

4.2 Experiment Settings

Baseline Approaches. For key phrase detection, we utilize a traditional method based on TF-IDF and templates as the baseline (TPL+TFIDF) which first divides the questions into entity and property parts by manually constructed templates, extracts the keywords by TF-IDF separately, and merges the high-scoring and adjacent ones to a phrase as the result.

For domain KBQA, we construct a system based on templates and n-gram as the baseline (TPL+NGram). In TPL+NGram, several templates is constructed to recognize the candidate entities and properties. Then we retrieve the knowledge base with a variety of combining forms of the entity and property generated by 3-gram method. To make the comparison fair, the NLP tools and dictionaries are same among all methods.

Evaluation Metrics. We use the Accuracy to evaluate the key phrase detection, and Precision, Recall and F1-score to evaluate the overall performance.

[2] http://tcci.ccf.org.cn/conference/2016/pages/page05_evadata.html.

Settings. For each question, we use jieba[3] to get the POS sequence because of its flexible user dictionary and LTP[4] to get the Parsing sequence. Then we represent pattern sequences in one-hot forms. The parameters in key phrase detection model are: learning rate = 0.05, dropout rate = 0.1, RNN layers = 2, activation is ReLU, the loss function is cross entropy and the optimizer is SGD. The models are implemented by mxnet[5].

4.3 Results

Key Phrase Detection. We utilize both open and specific domain datasets to evaluate the performance of key phrase detection model respectively. The result is shown in Table 1. "CMCC" represents China Mobile products domain. "Ent_Acc" and "Pro_Acc" represent the accuracy of key entity and property phrases detection respectively. "Dict" represents domain dictionary. "TT" is short for the terminology transfer method. The results verify that our model works well in both open and specific fields.

Table 1. Key phrase detection results

	Open domain		Insurance domain		CMCC domain	
	Ent_Acc	Pro_Acc	Ent_Acc	Pro_Acc	Ent_Acc	Pro_Acc
$TPL + TFIDF$	47.0	58.8	–	–	–	–
$TPL + TFIDF + Dict$	–	–	49.0	31.0	74.0	39.0
$Ours - POS - TT$	77.8	67.4	43.0	29.0	44.0	36.0
$Ours - TT$	**80.4**	**70.4**	43.0	30.0	45.0	39.0
$Ours - POS$	–	–	52.0	37.0	**77.0**	62.0
$Ours$	–	–	**54.0**	**48.0**	**77.0**	**63.0**

Domain KBQA Results. We utilize insurance and CMCC domain questions to evaluate the performance of DKBQA system over the pre-constructed domain knowledge bases. The results are shown in Table 2. Compared with TPL+NGram, DKBQA achieves better Recall and F1 score. Although the outputs of the key phrase detection model still have some errors, the errors are not completely invalid and can still contain some words of the key phrases. Through the character-based fuzzy matching method, we can correct the previous errors with a high probability, and achieve a better result finally.

[3] https://pypi.org/project/jieba.
[4] https://www.ltp-cloud.com.
[5] https://mxnet.incubator.apache.org.

Table 2. Domain KBQA results

	Insurance domain			CMCC domain		
	Precision	Recall	F1 Score	Precision	Recall	F1 Score
TPL + NGram	**95.7**	47.0	63.0	**92.8**	52.0	66.7
DKBQA	90.5	**74.0**	**81.4**	90.8	**79.0**	**84.5**

5 Related Work

The approaches of KBQA can be divided into two categories according to different question representations: symbol representation based and distributed representation based approaches.

Symbol representation based approach aims to parse natural language questions into structured queries such as Sparql or Sql. One kind of approach uses a domain-independent meaning representation derived from the combinatory categorical grammar (CCG) parse. Another kind of approach tries to get standard query by the matching between questions and templates which are manually constructed based on knowledge base [2,6]. These methods all have these two deficiencies: (1) the construction of CCG dictionary or templates is a very complex and time-consuming job; (2) Dictionaries and templates are difficult to cover the diversity of natural languages. Yih et al. [11] present a semantic parsing method via staged query graph generation which leverages the knowledge base in an early stage to prune the search space. This method is widely used because it simplifies the semantic matching issue.

Distributed representation based approach utilizes the distributed vectors to represent the question and knowledge base, then learns a rank model with existing QA pairs to score each candidate answer. Bordes et al. [3] attempt to embed questions and answers in a shared vector space. With the development of neural network technology, the distributed representation based approach is becoming more and more widely used [12].

Domain adaptation describes the task of learning a predictor in a target domain while labeled training data only exits in a different source domain [10]. A common method first learns an input representation with both domain corpus by autoencoder, then trains the predictor with the representation of the labeled source domain dataset [5,7].

6 Conclusion and Future Work

In this paper, we present a domain adaptive approach to construct a domain KBQA system with the open domain questions. Our system achieves good performance on both insurance and CMCC domain datasets. In the future, we would like to extend our method to deal with complex questions and improve the domain adaptability.

Acknowledgements. The work is supported by NSFC key projects (U1736204, 61533018, 61661146007), Ministry of Education and China Mobile Joint Fund (MCM20170301), a research fund supported by Alibaba Group, and THUNUS NExT Co-Lab.

References

1. Abujabal, A., Yahya, M., Riedewald, M., Weikum, G.: Automated template generation for question answering over knowledge graphs. In: Proceedings of the 26th International Conference on World Wide Web, pp. 1191–1200 (2017)
2. Adolphs, P., Theobald, M., Schäfer, U., Uszkoreit, H., Weikum, G.: YAGO-QA: answering questions by structured knowledge queries. In: Proceedings of the 5th IEEE International Conference on Semantic Computing, pp. 158–161 (2011)
3. Bordes, A., Chopra, S., Weston, J.: Question answering with subgraph embeddings. In: Proceedings of the 2014 Conference on Empirical Methods in Natural Language Processing, pp. 615–620 (2014)
4. Che, W., Li, Z., Liu, T.: LTP: a Chinese language technology platform. In: 23rd International Conference on Computational Linguistics, Demonstrations Volume, COLING 2010, pp. 13–16 (2010)
5. Chen, M., Xu, Z.E., Weinberger, K.Q., Sha, F.: Marginalized denoising autoencoders for domain adaptation. In: Proceedings of the 29th International Conference on Machine Learning (2012)
6. Fader, A., Zettlemoyer, L.S., Etzioni, O.: Paraphrase-driven learning for open question answering. In: Proceedings of the 51st Annual Meeting of the Association for Computational Linguistics, pp. 1608–1618 (2013)
7. Glorot, X., Bordes, A., Bengio, Y.: Domain adaptation for large-scale sentiment classification: a deep learning approach. In: Proceedings of the 28th International Conference on Machine Learning, pp. 513–520 (2011)
8. Mikolov, T., Sutskever, I., Chen, K., Corrado, G.S., Dean, J.: Distributed representations of words and phrases and their compositionality. In: Advances in Neural Information Processing Systems, pp. 3111–3119 (2013)
9. Pan, L., Wang, X., Li, C., Li, J., Tang, J.: Course concept extraction in MOOCs via embedding-based graph propagation. In: IJCNLP, no. 1, pp. 875–884. Asian Federation of Natural Language Processing (2017)
10. Wiese, G., Weissenborn, D., Neves, M.L.: Neural domain adaptation for biomedical question answering. In: Proceedings of the 21st Conference on Computational Natural Language Learning, pp. 281–289 (2017)
11. Yih, W.T., Chang, M.W., He, X., Gao, J.: Semantic parsing via staged query graph generation: question answering with knowledge base. In: Meeting of the Association for Computational Linguistics and the International Joint Conference on Natural Language Processing (2015)
12. Zhang, Y., et al.: Question answering over knowledge base with neural attention combining global knowledge information. CoRR abs/1606.00979 (2016)

Extending the Transformer with Context and Multi-dimensional Mechanism for Dialogue Response Generation

Ruxin Tan, Jiahui Sun, Bo Su(✉), and Gongshen Liu(✉)

School of Electronic Information and Electrical Engineering,
Shanghai Jiao Tong University, Shanghai, China
{tanruxin,sjh_717,subo,lgshen}@sjtu.edu.cn

Abstract. The existing work of using generative model in multi-turn dialogue system is often based on RNN (Recurrent neural network) even though the Transformer structure has achieved great success in other fields of NLP. In the multi-turn conversation task, a response is produced according to both the source utterance and the utterances in the previous turn which are regarded as context utterances. However, vanilla Transformer processes utterances in isolation and hence cannot explicitly handle the differences between context utterances and source utterance. In addition, even the same word could have different meanings in different contexts as there are rich information within context utterance and source utterance in multi-turn conversation. Based on context and multi-dimensional attention mechanism, an end-to-end model, which is extended from vanilla Transformer, is proposed for response generation. With the context mechanism, information from the context utterance can flow to the source and hence jointly control response generation. Multi-dimensional attention mechanism enables our model to capture more context and source utterance information by 2D vectoring the attention weights. Experiments show that the proposed model outperforms other state-of-the-art models (+**35.8**% better than the best baseline).

Keywords: Multi-turn conversation · Response generation · Context and multi-dimensional mechanism

1 Introduction

Generally, dialogue system is divided into two forms. One is task-oriented which is used to solve some specific problems [16], such as restaurant reservations, etc. The other is non-task-oriented, also called chatbot which is mainly used to chat with people [7]. Yan et al. reveal that non-task-oriented dialogue system on open domains is more common [18]. There are also two methods for non-task-oriented system: (1) Retrieval-based model, which learns to select the best response from the candidate repositories. (2) Generative model, which regards dialogue system problems as translation problems. As generative model can produce diverse responses, it is more challenging and attracts more attention.

J. Tang et al. (Eds.): NLPCC 2019, LNAI 11839, pp. 189–199, 2019.
https://doi.org/10.1007/978-3-030-32236-6_16

Various generative models have been proposed to apply in dialogue system, such as sequence-to-sequence [10], hierarchical recurrent attention network [17]. Unfortunately, these models are all based on recurrent neural network (RNN) which needs to maintain chronological order. Therefore, the inherently sequential nature precludes parallelization. Recently, the Tranformer structure [15] has shown excellent performance especially in machine translation. But unlike the strong one-to-one correspondence between parallel language pairs, in dialogue system, there is often some dependency between adjacent utterances [12]. Zhou et al. have used the Transformer structure to solve the dialogue system problems but this structure is simply used in the retrieval-based model and only as an input layer to encode the input utterances [20]. More importantly, all those models mentioned above ignore the fact that different contexts and source utterance often have different effects on even the same word, and original attention cannot fully capture this difference [11].

In this work, we propose an end-to-end Transformer with context structure and multi-dimensional attention mechanism to solve the problems mentioned above. At the encoder side of the proposed model, an extra context encoder is added to handle context utterances. In the last layer of the encoder, we integrate the information of the context encoder into the source through the context-source attention mechanism and context gating sub-layer, which jointly affects the response generation of the decoder. By sharing the parameters with source encoder, the introduction of the context encoder does not add too many model parameters. At the same time, we introduce the multi-dimensional attention mechanism. Specifically, on the encoder side, the self-attention of the first layer in the Transformer is replaced by the multi-dimensional attention which calculates different attention weights for each feature of the word token, thus making full use of the alignment between each feature of the token and different utterances.

We have compared our proposed model with some state-of-the-art models using both automatic evaluation and side-by-side human comparison. The results show that the model significantly outperforms existing models on both metrics.

The key contributions of this paper can be summarized as follows:

(1) The proposed model is an end-to-end Transformer model for solving response generation in multi-turn conversation. It reveals that the Transformer model is effective in dialogue system field.
(2) Multi-dimensional attention mechanism is applied in dialogue system to better capture information within utterances.

2 Related Work

Shang et al. apply the basic recurrent neural network (RNN) encoder-decoder framework to handle the dialogue context and source [10]. Based on that, Serban et al. use hierarchical models (HRED) [8] and its variant (VHRED) [9] to capture the different impacts of utterances. Attention mechanism (HRAN) is then applied on these models [17]. They extend RNN to various hierarchical models to improve model performance at the expense of model complexity. The Transformer is first used for machine translation [15], and Zhou et al. have applied it to dialogue but not an end-to-end training way [20].

Attention mechanism is widely used in NLP [1,15]. As the calculated attention score is a *scalar*, it does not take the effects of different contexts on each dimension of the word vector into account. To avoid it, Shen et al. propose multi-dimensional attention [11], the attention score is a 2D vector but so far there is no literature to prove whether the mechanism is applicable in dialogue system.

3 Approach

3.1 Problem Statement

Our goal is based on scenarios that generate responses in multi-turn conversation. Following Serban et al. [8], the data sets are triples $D = \{(U_{i,1}, U_{i,2}, U_{i,3})\}_{i=1}^{N}$, which represent *context utterance, source utterance, response utterance*, respectively. N is corpus size. $\forall i$, $U_{i,1} = (u_{i,1,1}, ..., u_{i,1,T_{i,1}})$, $U_{i,2} = (u_{i,2,1}, ..., u_{i,2,T_{i,2}})$, $U_{i,3} = (u_{i,3,1}, ..., u_{i,3,T_{i,3}})$ with their utterance length are $T_{i,1}, T_{i,2}, T_{i,3}$ respectively. Specifically, $u_{i,j,k}$ is the k-th word of the j-th utterance in one triple where the triple is the i-th within whole N size corpus. Similarly, $T_{i,j}$ is the length of the j-th utterance in one triple where the triple is i-th, that is, $U_{i,j}$.

We aim to estimate a generation probability $p(U_3|U_1, U_2)$ and the proposed model is able to produce a totally new response $U_3 = (u_{3,1}, ..., u_{3,T_3})$ according to the generation probability. In the next part, we will explain how to integrate context information into source and how to combine multi-dimensional attention.

3.2 RNN-Based Model and Transformer

In this part, RNN-Based Model used in dialogue system are introduced briefly.

RNN-Based Model. Generally, on the encoder side, the RNN reads one word at one time step and stops until the utterance end flag is read. Then, the decoder starts decoding according to the state of the encoder and each time step decodes a word until the end flag. Details are as follows.

Given a context utterance $U_1 = (u_{1,1}, ..., u_{1,T_1})$[1], and source utterance $U_2 = (u_{2,1}, ..., u_{2,T_2})$, the encoder first calculates the hidden state of U_1:

$$h_{1,t} = f(u_{1,t}, h_{1,t-1}) \tag{1}$$

[1] The subscript i is omitted for clarity.

where f is an RNN function unit such as LSTM [3] or GRU [2]. The last hidden state of the context utterance side h_{1,T_1} is used as the initial state of the source utterance side [10]:

$$h_{1,T_1} = h_{2,0} \tag{2}$$

Similarly,

$$h_{2,t} = f(u_{2,t}, h_{2,t-1}) \tag{3}$$

Then the last hidden state of the source utterance h_{2,T_2} is used as the context vector c to produce response $U_3 = (u_{3,1}, ..., u_{3,T_3})$ word by word:

$$c = h_{2,T_2} \tag{4}$$

$$s_t = f(u_{3,t-1}, s_{t-1}, c) \tag{5}$$

$$p_t = softmax(s_t, u_{3,t-1}) \tag{6}$$

where s_t is the hidden state of the decoder and p_t is the probability distribution of candidate words at time t. The context vector c can be calculated at different times for decoding. Specifically, each $u_{3,t}$ corresponds to a context vector c_t:

$$c_t = \sum_{j=1}^{T_1+T_2} \alpha_{t,j} h_j \tag{7}$$

$$h_j = \begin{cases} h_{1,j}, j < T_1 \\ h_{2,j-T_1}, j \geq T_1 \end{cases} \tag{8}$$

where $\alpha_{t,j}$ is given by:

$$\alpha_{t,j} = \frac{exp(e_{t,j})}{\sum_{k=1}^{T_1+T_2} exp(e_{t,k})} \tag{9}$$

$$e_{t,j} = g(s_{t-1}, h_j) \tag{10}$$

where g is a multilayer perceptron. Notice that $e_{t,j}$ and $\alpha_{t,j}$ are both *scalar*.

3.3 Our Model

Figure 1(b) shows our proposed model architecture. Compared with vanilla Transformer (see in Fig. 1(a)), we keep the original decoder part unchanged and extend the encoder part with a context encoder to handle context utterance. In addition, we replace the attention mechanism used in the Transformer with the multi-dimensional attention mechanism.

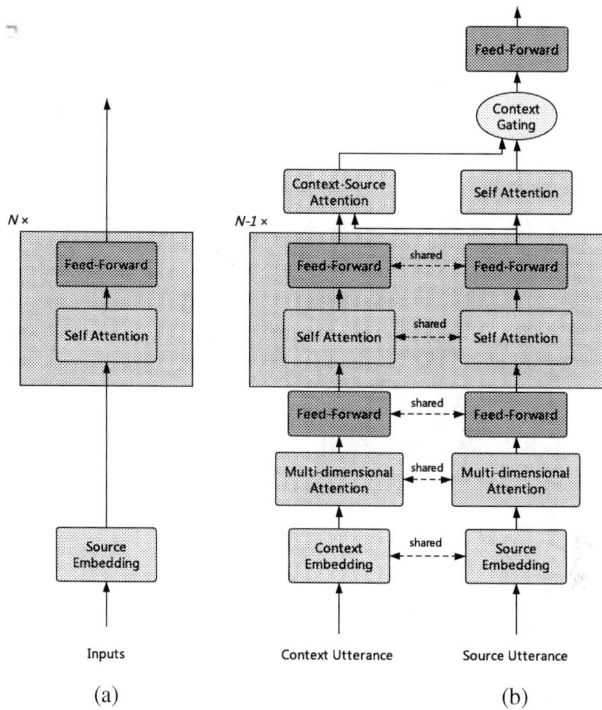

Fig. 1. (a) Vanilla Transformer encoder and (b) Our Transformer encoder with context and multi-dimensional mechanism

Multi-dimensional Attention. The attention weights $e_{t,j}$ and $\alpha_{t,j}$ calculated by both RNN and the Transformer models are *scalar*, but multi-dimensional mechanism will calculate an attention value for each dimension of the word vector, thus producing a 2D vector attention weights [11]. For the original attention method as shown in Eq. 10, the multilayer perceptron function of **g** is given by:

$$g(s_{t-1}, h_j) = w^T \sigma(W_1 h_j + W_2 s_{t-1}) \tag{11}$$

where we assume $h_j, s_{t-1} \in \mathbb{R}^d$, $w^T \in \mathbb{R}^d$ and d is the dimension of model. $W_1, W_2 \in \mathbb{R}^{d\times d}$ are parameters to learn. So the output of **g**, i.e. attention weights are *scalar*. In multi-dimensional attention, the Eq. 11 is replaced with:

$$g(s_{t-1}, h_j) = W^T \sigma(W_1 h_j + W_2 s_{t-1}) \tag{12}$$

$W^T \in \mathbb{R}^{d\times d}$ is a matrix. In this way, the attention weights distributed in each dimension of word vector can be obtained. The process is shown in Fig. 2.

Transformer with Context Mechanism. Context Encoder: At the bottom of our model, multi-dimensional attention is used to directly handle the word embedding of context utterance and then we stack $N-1$ layers where each single layer contains two same sublayers: self-attention layer and feed-forward layer.

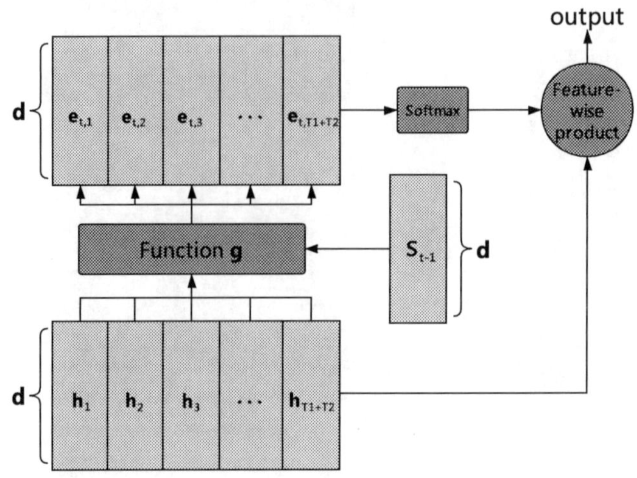

Fig. 2. Multi-Dimensional attention mechanism

Source Encoder: The first N layers of the encoder are the same as the context encoder. In order to avoid excessive increase of model parameters, shared parameters source encoder is used. The key issue is how to integrate the context utterance information into the source. Inspired by the idea of the encoder-decoder attention on the decoder side and the residual gating layer [5], in the last layer of the source encoder, we first use context-source attention to integrate context into source, then a *gate* is used to control the two attention mechanism information ratio between the output of self-attention on source and the output of context-source attention, which is

$$G = \sigma(W_G[C^{s-att}, C^{c-att}] + b_G) \tag{13}$$

$$C = G \odot C^{s-att} + (1 - G) \odot C^{c-att} \tag{14}$$

where C^{s-att} is the output of source self-attention, C^{c-att} is the output of context-source attention with W_G, b_G being learning parameters. G is a function about the concatenation of C^{c-att} and C^{s-att}, C is their gated sum.

4 Experiments

4.1 Data Sets

The data set of dialogue system is a big challenge but not the issue of interest in this paper, so we use Douban [17,20], a commonly used data set, for evaluation.

To preprocess, we ensure that the length of each utterance is no more than 50 words. Following Serban et al. [8] and Tian et al. [14], we take the same way to divide the corpus into the triples $\{U1, U2, U3\}$. $U1$ stands for context, $U2$ stands for source and $U3$ stands for response. Thus, for Douban, there are 214,786 training data, 1,682 valid data, 13,796 test data. We use context and source utterance to jointly generate source vocabulary and response utterance to generate target vocabulary, with each vocabulary size is 40,000, covering 98.70% of words in context and source utterance, 99.06% of words in response utterance.

Table 1. BLEU scores, response length and entropy on different models

Model	BLEU-1	BLEU-2	BLEU-3	BLEU-4	Length	Entropy
S2S	3.1673	1.3067	0.9547	0.6935	5.2573	6.8027
HRED	4.5128	2.1032	0.6604	0.2215	6.6455	6.2849
VHRED	4.4365	1.8764	0.5314	0.1616	6.3933	6.3915
HRAN	4.6247	1.0947	0.7194	0.4529	5.2308	6.0189
Our Model	3.9658	1.4360	1.1581	**0.9419**	5.4480	**7.6751**

4.2 Baselines and Evaluation Metric

We use the following models as the baselines: (1) S2S (seq2seq) [10]. (2) HRED [8]. (3) VHRED [9]. (4) HRAN [17].

The parameters of all baseline models are subject to the settings in the original paper unless otherwise specified. All models are trained on a single GTX 1080 Ti GPU and implemented by the open source framework THUMT [19].

How to evaluate the performance of the generative model in dialogue system is also an open problem at present. Following Tian et al. [14], BLEU scores are selected as the evaluation metric which can measure the performance of generative model to some extent [13].

In addition, We use side-by-side human evaluation to verify performance between models and three volunteers are recruited[2] to manually score responses (see the paper [17] for more detail about how to conduct human evaluation).

4.3 Results and Analysis

For the proposed model, the number of encoder and decoder layers is $N = 6$, word embedding size is 512, model hidden size is 2,048 and the number of head in self-attention is 8. During training, Adam [4] is used for optimization. In decoding, the beam size is set to 4.

[2] They are all native speakers and have graduate degrees or above.

Comparison with Baselines. BLEU scores on different models are shown in Table 1. We can observe that our proposed model outperforms other models by a large margin under the more commonly used n-garm=4, that is, BLEU-4 with approximately **35%** higher than the second best model seq2seq (S2S). A similar situation exists in BLEU-3 as well.

Surprisingly, the performance improvement of the HRED and VHRED models is significant in BLEU-1 and BLEU-2. We further analyze the true output of different models and observe that HRED and VHRED are more inclined to output abundant repetitions of words like *the* or *you*, such responses are longer but universal and meaningless. Thus, the two models perform better when the n-gram value is smaller. We compute their response length and entropy [6]. The results are shown in Table 1. Our model has the highest entropy which means that the output diversity is higher. Even though the HRED and VHRED models output longer response, their entropy is much lower, it means that they are inclined to produce *safe* response.

Table 2. Human judgment results, *Win* means our model is better than the other model. We average the results of the three volunteers

Model	Win	Loss	Tie
Our Model v.s. S2S	**32.6%**	18.2%	49.2%
Our Model v.s. HRED	**38.9%**	13.8%	47.3%
Our Model v.s. VHRED	**38.2%**	13.5%	48.3%
Our Model v.s. HRAN	**33.7%**	15.6%	50.7%

Table 2 shows human judgment results compared with different models. Our model surpasses (win-loss) other models by 25.1% (HRED), 24.7% (VHRED), 18.1% (HRAN) and 14.4% (S2S), respectively.

Table 3. Ablation study results. CM and MDM denote the *context mechanism* and *multi-dimensional mechanism*. For vanilla Transformer, the input is a concatenation of context utterance and source utterance. Here BLEU means BLEU-4

Model	BLEU
Our Model	**0.9419**
No MDM	0.7999
No CM (vanilla Transformer)	0.6534

Effect of Context Mechanism. The experiment is conducted on the model without such mechanism, that is, vanilla Transformer. The results are shown in Table 3. Surprisingly, the result of vanilla Transformer is even slightly worse than seq2seq.

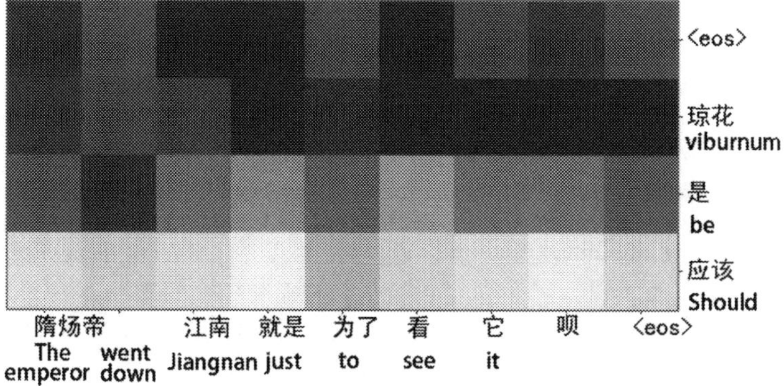

Fig. 3. A visual example of context-source attention. On the y-axis are the context tokens, on the x-axis are the source tokens.

Further, we visually analyze the attention matrix in the context-source attention. Figure 3 is an example where context utterance is *Should (应该) be (是)viburnum (琼花)* and source utterance is *The emperor (隋炀帝) went down (下) Jiangnan (江南) just (就是) to (为了) see (看) it (它)*. As we expected, the most informative word of context utterance should be *viburnum* so it gets relatively larger attention than other words in context utterance. Also note the word *it* in source utterance, which correctly focuses more attention on the word *viburnum*.

Effect of Multi-Dimensional Mechanism. The effect of multi-dimensional mechanism is shown in Table 3. By adding the multi-dimensional attention mechanism, our model performance is further improved by approximately **17%**.

We visualize the multi-dimensional mechanism. Figure 4 is the word "算账" multi-dimensional attention distribution heatmaps in two different utterances. One utterance is "我 算账 很好 谢谢" (*I am good at accounting, thanks.*), where "算账" here means *accounting*. The other "这 喝酒 喝 得 好 难受 没 找 你 算账 不错 了 哈哈" (*This wine tastes terrible, you should be grateful that I did not find fault with you*), where "算账" means *find fault*. Within different utterances, nearly each dimension of multi-dimensional attention vector in the same word has totally different values. It indicates that the multi-dimensional attention mechanism is not redundant and even more important in a multi-turn conversation which needs more context-focused.

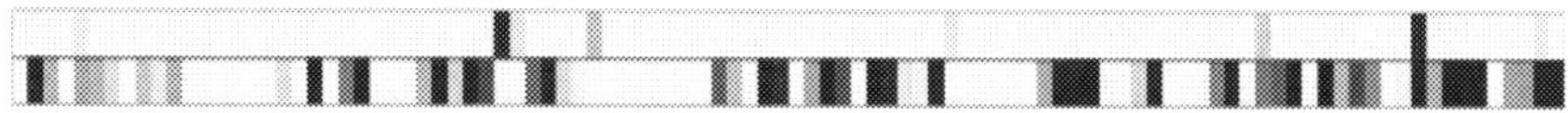

Fig. 4. Multi-dimensional attention distribution comparison of the same word in different utterances. For the sake of illustration, we only show the first 100 dimensions in a 512D attention vector.

5 Conclusion

We extend the Transformer with context and multi-dimensional mechanism for multi-turn conversation. With our proposed mechanism, our model can better capture information from both context utterance and source utterance.

Acknowledgement. This research work has been funded by the National Natural Science Foundation of China (Grant No. 61772337, U1736207), and the National Key Research and Development Program of China NO. 2016QY03D0604.

References

1. Bahdanau, D., Cho, K., Bengio, Y.: Neural machine translation by jointly learning to align and translate. arXiv preprint arXiv:1409.0473 (2014)
2. Cho, K., et al.: Learning phrase representations using RNN encoder-decoder for statistical machine translation. In: EMNLP, pp. 1724–1734 (2014)
3. Hochreiter, S., Schmidhuber, J.: Long short-term memory. Neural Comput. **9**(8), 1735–1780 (1997)
4. Kingma, D.P., Ba, J.: Adam: A method for stochastic optimization. arXiv preprint arXiv:1412.6980 (2014)
5. Kuang, S., Xiong, D.: Fusing recency into neural machine translation with an inter-sentence gate model. arXiv preprint arXiv:1806.04466 (2018)
6. Mou, L., Song, Y., Yan, R., Li, G., Zhang, L., Jin, Z.: Sequence to backward and forward sequences: a content-introducing approach to generative short-text conversation. In: COLING 2016: Technical Papers, pp. 3349–3358 (2016)
7. Ritter, A., Cherry, C., Dolan, W.B.: Data-driven response generation in social media. In: EMNLP, pp. 583–593. Association for Computational Linguistics (2011)
8. Serban, I.V., Sordoni, A., Bengio, Y., Courville, A.C., Pineau, J.: Building end-to-end dialogue systems using generative hierarchical neural network models. In: AAAI, vol. 16, pp. 3776–3784 (2016)
9. Serban, I.V., et al.: A hierarchical latent variable encoder-decoder model for generating dialogues. In: AAAI, pp. 3295–3301 (2017)
10. Shang, L., Lu, Z., Li, H.: Neural responding machine for short-text conversation. In: ACL (Volume 1: Long Papers), vol. 1, pp. 1577–1586 (2015)
11. Shen, T., Zhou, T., Long, G., Jiang, J., Pan, S., Zhang, C.: Disan: directional self-attention network for RNN/CNN-free language understanding. In: AAAI (2018)
12. Sordoni, A., et al.: A neural network approach to context-sensitive generation of conversational responses. In: NAACL: Human Language Technologies, pp. 196–205 (2015)
13. Tao, C., Mou, L., Zhao, D., Yan, R.: Ruber: an unsupervised method for automatic evaluation of open-domain dialog systems. In: AAAI (2018)
14. Tian, Z., Yan, R., Mou, L., Song, Y., Feng, Y., Zhao, D.: How to make context more useful? an empirical study on context-aware neural conversational models. In: ACL (Volume 2: Short Papers), vol. 2, pp. 231–236 (2017)
15. Vaswani, A., et al.: Attention is all you need. In: Advances in Neural Information Processing Systems, pp. 5998–6008 (2017)
16. Williams, J.D., Asadi, K., Zweig, G.: Hybrid code networks: practical and efficient end-to-end dialog control with supervised and reinforcement learning. In: ACL (Volume 1: Long Papers), vol. 1, pp. 665–677 (2017)

17. Xing, C., Wu, Y., Wu, W., Huang, Y., Zhou, M.: Hierarchical recurrent attention network for response generation. In: AAAI (2018)
18. Yan, Z., Duan, N., Chen, P., Zhou, M., Zhou, J., Li, Z.: Building task-oriented dialogue systems for online shopping. In: AAAI, pp. 4618–4626 (2017)
19. Zhang, J., et al.: Thumt: an open source toolkit for neural machine translation. arXiv preprint arXiv:1706.06415 (2017)
20. Zhou, X., et al.: Multi-turn response selection for chatbots with deep attention matching network. In: ACL (Volume 1: Long Papers), vol. 1, pp. 1118–1127 (2018)

Co-attention Networks for Aspect-Level Sentiment Analysis

Haihui Li[1,2], Yun Xue[1(✉)], Hongya Zhao[2], Xiaohui Hu[1], and Sancheng Peng[3]

[1] School of Physics and Telecommunication Engineering, South China Normal University, Guangzhou 510006, China
xueyun@scnu.edu.cn

[2] Industrial Central, Shenzhen Polytechnic, Shenzhen 518055, China

[3] Laboratory of Language Engineering and Computing, Guangdong University of Foreign Studies, Guangzhou 510006, China

Abstract. Aspect-level sentiment analysis has identified its significance in sentiment polarity classification of consumer review. For the purpose of specific target sentiment analysis, we put forward a co-attentive deep learning method in the manner of human processing. To start with, the GRUs are taken to extract the hidden states of the different word embeddings. Further, via the interactive learning of the co-attention network, the representations of the target and the context can be obtained. In addition, the attention weights are determined based on the self-attention mechanism to update the final representations. The experimental results evaluated on the SemEval 2014 and Twitter establish a strong evidence of the high accuracy.

Keywords: Aspect-level sentiment analysis · Co-attention · GRU

1 Introduction

Natural language processing (NLP) concerns the interactions between computers and human natural languages, which provides morphologic, syntactic and semantic tools to transform stored text from raw data into useful information [1]. As one major interest of NLP, sentiment analysis refers to the ability to identify both the terms and the positive or negative tone of the text. An increasing amount of available text data, such as opinions, critics and recommendations on the Internet, adopts sentiment analysis approaches for opinion mining and product recommendation. Instead of classifying the overall contextual polarity of a document, recent studies focus on finding the attitudes on certain topics within the texts. For instance, in the sentence *Average to good Thai food, but terrible delivery*, the sentiment polarity is positive when target is *Thai food* while the sentiment polarity becomes negative for the target *delivery*. For this reason, aspect-level sentiment analysis paves a way for greater depth of analysis, which is more fine-grained and more sophisticated due to its distinguishing the specific

J. Tang et al. (Eds.): NLPCC 2019, LNAI 11839, pp. 200–209, 2019.
https://doi.org/10.1007/978-3-030-32236-6_17

target together with the corresponding contexts. As such, research is ongoing to design and deploy new algorithms for aspect-level sentiment analysis.

More recently, the progresses in NLP tasks are, however, largely driven by the flourish of deep learning algorithms in line with the increased computational resources. The deep learning models can learn the semantic representations from high dimensional original data automatically without carefully designed features, that is, it can use end-to-end training without any prior knowledge [2]. On this occasion, the recurrent neural networks (RNNs) show their superiority in sentiment analysis because it is capable of tackling variable length of input data. Notably, two of the most commonly used RNNs, namely long short-term memory (LSTM) and gated recurrent unit (GRU), are currently widespread in aspect-level sentiment.

Whereas, according to the complexity of human natural language, issues of sentiment analysis are far from solved. Aiming at teaching a computer to handle the texts that is distinctly human, the attention mechanism is introduced. Attention mechanism is initially inspired by human visual attention, which is both creative and practical in image recognition [3]. There are some research using attention mechanism to resolve aspect-level sentiment analysis tasks as well [4]. Further, aiming to carry out the working flow in a manner of human processing, the deployment of the model is taken as the key point. Above all, the online users pay attention to specific words out of interest instead of reading word by word in most cases. By considering the information delivered by the target word and its contexts, the sentiment of this review is updated in the mind. Since humans consistently outperform computers in the semantic interpretation, researchers tend to revise current algorithms to optimize the procedures [5].

In order to carry out the human analyzing practice, a co-attention based neural network is established to facilitate the aspect-level sentiment analysis in this work, whose major significance is its attending target and context information simultaneously. The attentive representation of each part is established while the interaction between the target and the context is studied, and thus to determine the contribution of different words in the target aspect. The utilization of the co-attention based deep learning model, targets at optimizing the model efficiency and improving the working accuracy.

2 Related Work

2.1 Aspect-Level Sentiment Analysis

Previous work has proved that the RNNs have achieved impressive performance in representation learning. Concerning the sentiment analyzing approaches, the LSTM model integrates the RNN with a memory unit and a set of gate units to transmit long-term information, aiming to extract the representations from input data and store it for long or short time durations [6]. As such, specific models, such as Target-Dependent LSTM (TD-LSTM), are developed for target dependent sentiment analysis. Likewise, GRU, which is very similar to the LSTM unit, is applied to aspect-level sentiment analysis as well. GRU can be considered as a lighter version of RNN with lower computation cost and simpler model structure. In comparison to LSTM, the GRU shows its strong capability of modeling long-term sequences of texts as well.

In addition, the integration of attention mechanisms with deep learning models is devised for settling specific tasks. For the purpose of sentiment analysis of specific target, [7] propose attention-based LSTM with target embedding (ATAE-LSTM). [2] design the Interactive attention networks (IAN) model for well representing a target and its collocative context to facilitate the sentiment classification. [8] establish the attention-over-attention (AOA) based network to model target and context in a joint way and explicitly capture the interaction between them. For describing the relation between target and its left/right contexts, [9] apply a rotatory attention mechanism to the model of three Bi-LSTMs. [10] present GRU has a better working performance than LSTM while integrating with attention mechanism.

2.2 Co-attention Network

The main purpose of employing the attention mechanism is that both targets and contexts deserve special treatment. The representations of each part can be learned via self and interactive learning. For example, the phrase *picture quality* will definitely be associated to the expression of *clear-cut* within one text, where the effects on each other are established. On the other hand, there can be more than one word in the target. For example, in the sentence *customer service is terrible*, the word *service* is of more importance than *customer* in delivering the negative sentiment. For this reason, the co-attention network can be carried out to ensure the detection of within and cross-domain interactions [7].

Originally, the co-attention is developed to intimate the eye movements for decision-making, in the same way of human focusing on a series of identical attention regions through repeatedly looking back and forth [11]. Currently, the co-attention network is applied to the image detection tasks, which refers to the mechanism that jointly reasons about the visual attention of different part within one image [12]. Thereby, remarkable evolution is made in the fusion of visual and language representations in images [13]. In aspect-level sentiment analysis, the co-attention mechanism can be used to remove unrelated information and obtain the essential representations. In [14], Zhang et al. preliminary verify co-attention mechanism in capturing the correlation between aspect and contexts. To this end, methods can be applied to update the co-attentive representation of both parts in further steps.

3 Methodology

3.1 Model Establishing

We propose a model that aims to get the discriminative representations of both the target and the contexts in aspect-level sentiment analysis tasks. The algorithm is devised by using the GRU together with the co-attention network, as shown in Fig. 1.

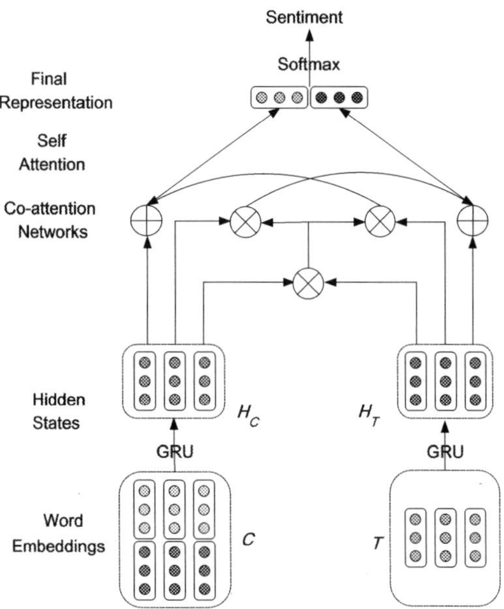

Fig. 1. Overall architecture of model

For a given sequence of n words $[w_{\tilde{c}}^1, w_{\tilde{c}}^2, \ldots, w_{\tilde{c}}^n] \in \mathbb{R}^n$, we call it the context. Within the context, a target with m words $[w_t^1, w_t^2, \ldots, w_t^m] \in \mathbb{R}^m$ contains one or more consecutive words.

We take the word embeddings to represent words from the vocabulary, from which the target and the context can be transformed into $\tilde{C} = [v_{\tilde{c}}^1, v_{\tilde{c}}^2, \ldots, v_{\tilde{c}}^n] \in \mathbb{R}^{(d_w \times n)}$ and $T = [v_t^1, v_t^2, \ldots, v_t^m] \in \mathbb{R}^{(d_w \times m)}$ respectively where d_w represents the dimension of the word embeddings. Thus, the target word embeddings are sent to mean-pooling for getting the average value according to Fig. 1.

$$t = \sum_{j=1}^{m} v_t^j / m \tag{1}$$

Hereafter, the outcome t is concatenated into the contexts and a revised word embedding $C = [v_c^1, v_c^2, \ldots, v_c^n] \in \mathbb{R}^{(2d_w \times n)}$ is therefore obtained.

To extract the internal feature of the word embeddings, the GRU is employed to learn the hidden semantics where $H_C \in \mathbb{R}^{(d_h \times n)}$ and $H_T \in \mathbb{R}^{(d_h \times m)}$ are the hidden representations of the context and the target, separately and d_h is the dimension of the hidden layer. The context representation is based on the importance of different words in it and the effect of word sequence in the target. So does the target. The attention weight matrix is computed via the interactive learning of the co-attention network, which is

$$H = relu(H_C^T W H_T) \tag{2}$$

where $W \in \mathbb{R}^{(d_h \times d_h)}$ stands for the parameter matrix and H_C^T is the transposed matrix of H_C.

Apparently, there is a natural symmetry between the contexts and target, based on which the co-attention mechanism is performed. Besides, the word sequences within a fixed part are also taken to express the significances. In this way, the target representation R_T and the context representation R_C are given in Eqs. 3 and 4.

$$R_C = relu(W_C H_C + W_T H_T H^T) \tag{3}$$

$$R_T = relu(W_T H_T + W_C H_C H) \tag{4}$$

where W_C and W_T are the parameter matrices while H^T is the transposed matrix of H.

At this stage, we employed the self-attention to convey the importance of each word in the sequence thoroughly. The self-attention weights of the context and the target are expressed as α and β:

$$\alpha = softmax(w_C R_C) \tag{5}$$

$$\beta = softmax(w_T R_T) \tag{6}$$

where w_C and w_T refer to the parameter vectors and softmax represents the normalization function. The vector representation of the target and the context are determined by using the weighted summation:

$$r_C = \sum_{j=1}^{n} \alpha^i R_C^i \tag{7}$$

$$r_T = \sum_{j=1}^{m} \beta^j R_T^j \tag{8}$$

The final representation $r \in \mathbb{R}^{2d_h}$ for sentiment classification is obtained via concatenating the two parts. By sending r to the softmax classifier, the sentiment distribution of the given target can be identified as

$$x = W_r r + b_r \tag{9}$$

$$y_i = \frac{exp(x_i)}{\sum_{j=1}^{C} exp(x_j)} \tag{10}$$

where W_r is the parametric matrix, b_r is the bias and C is the number of sentiment polarities.

3.2 Model Training

The training process is carried out by using the cross entropy with L_2 regularization as the loss function, which is expressed as:

$$J = -\sum_{i=1}^{C} g_i log y_i + \lambda_r (\sum_{\theta \in \Theta} \theta^2) \tag{11}$$

where g_i is the real distribution of sentiment and y_i is the predicted one. Besides, λ_r is the weight of L_2 regularization. The gradients, as well as other parameters are updated through back propagation with the learning rate λ_l:

$$\Theta = \Theta - \lambda_l \frac{\partial J(\Theta)}{\partial \Theta} \tag{12}$$

4 Experiments

4.1 Experimental Setting

We carry out our experiments on three public datasets as shown in Table 1. The customer reviews of the laptop and the restaurant are available on SemEval 2014 Task4[1] and the last one is provided in [15]. All the reviews in the experiment are labeled as three different polarities: positive, neutral and negative. In this work we adopt the accuracy as the evaluation metric to demonstrate the working performance. The initialization of all word embeddings is conducted using Glove[2]. All the parameter matrices involved are generated within the distribution $U(-0.1, 0.1)$ randomly and the bias set as 0. The hidden states dimension of GRU is set as 200 with the learning rate of 0.001. In addition the L_2 regularization weight is set as 0.0001. The dropout rate is 0.5 to prevent overfitting.

Table 1. Statistics of dataset

Dataset	Positive	Neutral	Negative
Laptop-Training	994	464	870
Laptop-Testing	341	169	128
Restaurant-Training	2164	637	807
Restaurant-Testing	728	196	196
Twitter-Training	1561	1560	3127
Twitter-Testing	173	173	346

4.2 Results

Comparative models are presented as follows:

LSTM: The LSTM network is taken to detect the hidden states of the both the target and the context.

[1] The detail introduction of this task can be seen at: http://alt.qcri.org/semeval2014/task4/.

[2] Pre-trained word vectors of Glove can be obtained from http://nlp.stanford.edu/projects/glove/.

TD-LSTM: The contexts information is detected via two LSTM on both left and right contexts of target [16].

ATAE-LSTM: The LSTM, together with the concatenating process, is applied to get the representation of the target and the context. The attention network aims to select the word of sentiment significance [7].

MemNet: This model develops a multiple-attention-layer deep learning approach instead of using sequential neural networks [17].

IAN: The representations are modeled on the foundation of the LSTM based interactive attention networks. Hidden states are taken to compute the attention scores by the pooling process [2].

RAM: The integration of LSTM and Recurrent Attention is established, targeting at solving the multiple words attention issue [18].

AOA-LSTM: The bidirectional LSTMs are used for getting the hidden states of the target and the context, which are sent to attention-over-attention networks for calculating the final representations [8].

LCR-Rot: LCR-Rot performs the left context, target phrase and right context with 3 separated LSTMs. A rotatory attention network is used to model the relation between target and left/right contexts [9].

Specifically, the proposed model with merely self-attention is considered for comparison. The testing accuracy of each dataset is shown in Table 2.

Table 2. Experimental outcomes

	Methods	Restaurant (%)	Laptop (%)	Twitter (%)
Baselines	LSTM	74.30	66.50	66.50
	TD-LSTM [16]	75.60	68.10	70.80
	ATAE-LSTM [7]	77.20	68.70	–
	MemNet [17]	78.16	70.33	68.50
	IAN [2]	78.60	72.10	–
	RAM [18]	80.23	74.49	69.36
	AOA-LSTM [8]	81.20	74.50	–
	LCR-Rot [9]	81.34	75.24	72.69
Proposed model	self-attention	81.51	73.82	72.10
	co-attention+self-attention	**81.61**	**75.86**	**73.85**

Among all the baseline models, LSTM shows the lowest accuracy than any other methods, since the representations are computed of each word equally. The TD-LSTM shows a better working performance due to its introducing the target. More reasonable representations are generated by assigning the attentions to weight different parts in the sentence. The ATAE-LSTM concentrates on identifying the significance of different words, which gets a 77.2% and a 68.7% on the restaurant and laptop reviews, respectively. Similarly, the Memnet model obtains a comparative result. Further, the IAN model, by using the interactive attention mechanism, strengthens the representations and better the working performance. With multiple attention networks applied, RAM improves the accuracy by 1.63% and 2.39% of restaurant and laptop compared to those of IAN. As for AOA-LSTM and LCR-Rot, the interaction between the target and the context is highlighted and the even higher accuracy can be obtained.

Our model takes advantages of the importance of different parts within the sentence. With only self-attention applied, the proposed model is less competitive than LCR-Rot in the average accuracy. Notably, the application of co-attention network updates the representation of the target and the context. As such, the effects on both the target and the context from each other are considered to further determine the word representations via the interactive learning. By combing with the self-attention mechanism, the final representations are addresses precisely. We can observe that the proposed model outperforms other methods in all datasets to prove its capability.

4.3 Visualization of Attention

Our model is further evaluated by visualizing the attention vectors in the sentence. According to the review *Granted the space is smaller than most, it is the best service you will find in even the largest of restaurants*, two targets can be identified, which are *space* and *service*. The sentiment polarity for *space* is negative while that for *service* is positive. In Fig. 2, the contribution of different words are listed for aspect-level sentiment analysis. The former illustrates the attention weight for target *space* and the latter for *service*. Words in the darker color are of greater weight, and vice versa.

Fig. 2. Attention weights assignment

Our model assigns the importance to *the* and *is small* to carry out the negative sentiment of *space*. However, the word *the* has no direct sentiment towards the target, which can be taken as an error by separating the idiom *the space*. For the target *service*, the word *find* is paid the most attention with *it is* and *best* following. Hence, the model can identify the sentiment polarity towards *service* as positive. In this case, the compositional expression *it is* deliver affirmation of the sentence while the comma before it does not have the same function. In this way, the proposed model misunderstands the meaning of the comma and identifies its significance. Yet we cannot have a 100% accurate rate exactly in a human processing way. In spite of the aforementioned errors, our model is still able to analyze the sentiment of different target aspects in one sentence properly.

5 Conclusion

In this work, the GRU based co-attention network, in line with human analyzing practice, was developed for aspect-level sentiment analysis task. Aiming to obtain the representations of the word embeddings, the co-attention mechanism was performed to effectively detect the interaction between the target and the context and further identify the words with greater importance. Further, the self-attention was employed to facilitate the determination of the attention weight. As a manner of human processing, the proposed model benefits from the precise and essential presentations of the target and the context. Experiments are conducted on open data sets of review to validate that our model stably outperforms other widely-used models. As such, a better working performance was achieved in aspect-level sentiment analysis.

Further work should be addressed to the relation among different word embeddings to explore the effects on the attentive representation. Although it seems clear that the proposed model can accurately classify the sentiment polarity, it is still an open question whether it is distinctively in accordance with human focusing.

Acknowledgments. This work was supported by the National Natural Science Foundation of China under Grant No. 61876205, and the Science and Technology Plan Project of Guangzhou under Grant Nos. 201802010033 and 201804010433.

References

1. Goldstein, I.: Automated classification of the narrative of medical reports using natural language processing. Citeseer (2011)
2. Ma, D., Li, S., Zhang, X., Wang, H.: Interactive attention networks for aspect-level sentiment classification. In: Proceedings of the 26th International Joint Conference on Artificial Intelligence, pp. 4068–4074. AAAI Press (2017)
3. Zeng, J., Ma, X., Zhou, K.: Enhancing attention-based LSTM with position context for aspect-level sentiment classification. IEEE Access **7**, 20462–20471 (2019)
4. Du, J., Gui, L., He, Y., Xu, R., Wang, X.: Convolution-based neural attention with applications to sentiment classification. IEEE Access **7**, 27983–27992 (2019)
5. Hu, X., Li, K., Han, J., Hua, X., Guo, L., Liu, T.: Bridging the semantic gap via functional brain imaging. IEEE Trans. Multimedia **14**(2), 314–325 (2012)
6. Wang, J., Zhang, J., Wang, X.: Bilateral LSTM: a two-dimensional long short-term memory model with multiply memory units for short-term cycle time forecasting in re-entrant manufacturing systems. IEEE Trans. Industr. Inf. **14**(2), 748–758 (2018)
7. Wang, Y., Huang, M., Zhao, L., et al.: Attention-based LSTM for aspect-level sentiment classification. In: Proceedings of the 2016 Conference on Empirical Methods in Natural Language Processing, pp. 606–615 (2016)
8. Huang, B., Ou, Y., Carley, K.M.: Aspect level sentiment classification with attention-over-attention neural networks. In: Thomson, R., Dancy, C., Hyder, A., Bisgin, H. (eds.) SBP-BRiMS 2018. LNCS, vol. 10899, pp. 197–206. Springer, Cham (2018). https://doi.org/10.1007/978-3-319-93372-6_22

9. Zheng, S., Xia, R.: Left-center-right separated neural network for aspect-based sentiment analysis with rotatory attention. arXiv preprint arXiv:1802.00892 (2018)
10. Li, L., Liu, Y., Zhou, A.: Hierarchical attention based position-aware network for aspect-level sentiment analysis. In: Proceedings of the 22nd Conference on Computational Natural Language Learning, pp. 181–189 (2018)
11. Lin, L., Luo, H., Huang, R., Ye, M.: Recurrent models of visual co-attention for person re-identification. IEEE Access **7**, 8865–8875 (2019)
12. Lu, J., Yang, J., Batra, D., Parikh, D.: Hierarchical question-image co-attention for visual question answering. In: Advances in Neural Information Processing Systems, pp. 289–297 (2016)
13. Nguyen, D.-K., Okatani, T.: Improved fusion of visual and language representations by dense symmetric co-attention for visual question answering. In: Proceedings of the IEEE Conference on Computer Vision and Pattern Recognition, pp. 6087–6096 (2018)
14. Zhang, P., Zhu, H., Xiong, T., Yang, Y.: Co-attention network and low-rank bilinear pooling for aspect based sentiment analysis. In: IEEE International Conference on Acoustics, Speech and Signal Processing (ICASSP 2019), pp. 6725–6729. IEEE (2019)
15. Dong, L., Wei, F., Tan, C., Tang, D., Zhou, M., Xu, K.: Adaptive recursive neural network for target-dependent Twitter sentiment classification. In: Proceedings of the 52nd Annual Meeting of the Association for Computational Linguistics (Volume 2: Short Papers), pp. 49–54 (2014)
16. Tang, D., Qin, B., Feng, X., Liu, T.: Effective LSTMs for target-dependent sentiment classification. In: Proceedings of COLING 2016, the 26th International Conference on Computational Linguistics: Technical Papers, pp. 3298–3307 (2016)
17. Tang, D., Qin, B., Liu, T.: Aspect level sentiment classification with deep memory network. In: Proceedings of the 2016 Conference on Empirical Methods in Natural Language Processing, pp. 214–224 (2016)
18. Chen, P., Sun, Z., Bing, L., Yang, W.: Recurrent attention network on memory for aspect sentiment analysis. In: Proceedings of the 2017 Conference on Empirical Methods in Natural Language Processing, pp. 452–461 (2017)

Hierarchical-Gate Multimodal Network for Human Communication Comprehension

Qiyuan Liu, Liangqing Wu, Yang Xu, Dong Zhang(✉), Shoushan Li, and Guodong Zhou

School of Computer Science and Technology, Soochow University, Suzhou, China
{qyliu,lqwu,yxu2017,dzhang17}@stu.suda.edu.cn,
{lishoushan,gdzhou}@suda.edu.cn

Abstract. Computational modeling of human multimodal language is an emerging research area in natural language processing spanning the language, visual and acoustic modalities. Comprehending multimodal language requires modeling not only the interactions within each modality (intra-modal interactions) but more importantly the interactions between modalities (cross-modal interactions). In this paper, we present a novel neural architecture for understanding human communication called the Hierarchical-gate Multimodal Network (HGMN). Specifically, each modality is first encoded by Bi-LSTM which aims to capture the intra-modal interactions within single modality. Subsequently, we merge the independent information of multi-modality using two gated layers. The first gate which is named as modality-gate will calculate the weight of each modality. And the other gate called temporal-gate will control each time-step contribution for final prediction. Finally, the max-pooling strategy is used to reduce the dimension of the multimodal representation, which will be fed to the prediction layer. We perform extensive comparisons on five publicly available datasets for multimodal sentiment analysis, emotion recognition and speaker trait recognition. HGMN shows state-of-the-art performance on all the datasets.

Keywords: Multimodal · Human communication · Hierarchical-gate

1 Introduction

Computational modeling of human multimodal language is an upcoming research area in natural language processing. This research area focuses on modeling tasks such as multimodal sentiment analysis, emotion recognition, and personality traits recognition. We utilize three modalities to Communicate our intentions: language modality (words, phrases and sentences), vision modality (gestures and expressions), and acoustic modality (paralinguistics and changes in vocal tones). These multimodal signals are highly structured with two prime forms of interactions: intra-modal and cross-modal interactions [11]. Intra-modal interactions

J. Tang et al. (Eds.): NLPCC 2019, LNAI 11839, pp. 210–219, 2019.
https://doi.org/10.1007/978-3-030-32236-6_18

represent information within a specific modality, independent of other modalities. Cross-modal interactions represent interactions between modalities. Modeling these interactions lies at the heart of human multimodal language analysis processing [2].

Intra-modal interactions are usually captured by Convolutional Neural Networks or Long Short-Term Memory Networks. The methods of getting cross-modal interactions are different. Traditional methods like TFN [14] use outer product to fuse different modalities which is a coarse-grained fusion method that can not capture the complex interactions between modalities. MARN (Multi-attention Recurrent Network) [16] utilizes attention mechanism to capture the importance between modalities, but ignores the temporal information. The existing methods do not take into account both modality and temporal information importances.

In order to overcome the challenges of the above methods, we propose a novel model called the Hierarchical-gate Multimodal Network (HGMN). Each modality is first encoded by Bi-LSTM which aims to capture the intra-modal interactions within single modality. Subsequently, we merge the independent information of multi-modality using two gated layers. The first gate which is named as modality-gate will calculate the weight of each modality. And the other gate called temporal-gate will capture the importances of temporal information. Finally, the max-pooling strategy is used to reduce the dimension of the multimodal representation, which will be fed to the prediction layer. We perform extensive comparisons on five publicly available datasets for multimodal sentiment, emotion analysis and speaker trait recognition. HGMN shows state-of-the-art performance on all the datasets.

2 Related Work

Researchers dealing with multimodal human communication have largely focused on three major types of models.

The first category is Early Fusion models which rely on concatenation of all modalities into a single view to simplify the learning setting. These approaches then use this concatenated view as input to a learning model. Hidden Markov Models (HMM) [1], Support Vector Machines (SVM) and Hidden Conditional Random Fields (HCRF) [10] have been successfully used for structured prediction.

The second category is Late Fusion models which learn different models for each modality and combine the outputs using decision voting [5,12]. While these methods are generally strong in modeling intra-modal interactions, they have shortcomings for cross-modal interactions since these inter-modality interactions are normally more complex than a decision vote.

The third category of models rely on collapsing the time dimension from sequences by learning a temporal representation for each of the different modalities. Such methods have used average feature values over time [8]. Essentially these models apply conventional multi-modality learning approaches, such as

Multiple Kernel Learning, subspace learning or co-training to the Multimodal representations. Other approaches have trained different models for each view and combined the models using decision voting, tensor products or deep neural networks [9].

Different from the first category models, our proposed approach in this paper models both intra-modal and cross-modal interactions. In addition, different from the second and third categories, we simultaneously handle the modality contribution and sequence contribution in time-dependent interactions by two kinds of gated mechanisms.

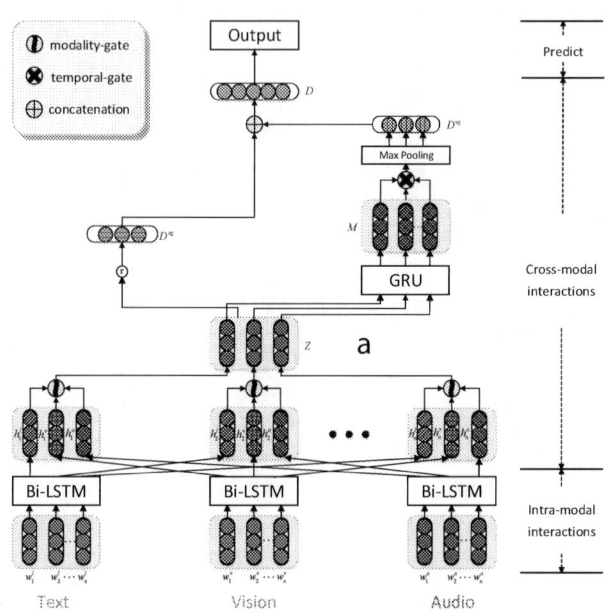

Fig. 1. Overview figure of Hierarchical-gate Multimodal Network (HGMN) pipeline.

3 HGMN Model

In this section we outline our pipeline for human communication comprehension: the Hierarchical-gate Multimodal Network (HGMN). Specifically, HGMN consists of three main components: (1) Intra-modal Interactions Calculation. (2) Cross-modal Interactions Identification which includes the Hierarchical-gate network. (3) Prediction layer. Figure 1 shows the overview of HGMN model.

3.1 Intra-modal Interactions Calculation

The input to HGMN is a multi-modality sequence consisting of language, video, and audio for $M = \{l; v; a\}$. At first, in terms of language modality, we assume

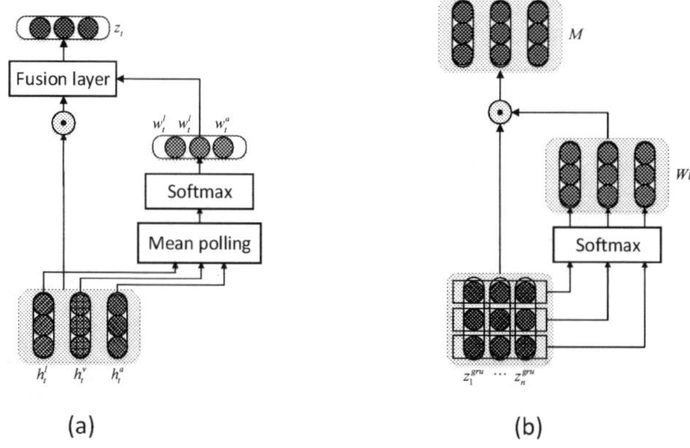

Fig. 2. Modality-Gate (a) and Temporal-Gate (b).

that an utterance contains n words. $w_t^l \in \mathbb{R}^{d^l}$ represents the t-th word in the utterance. Then, we use a bidirectional LSTM (namely, Bi-LSTM) to encode the forward and backward contexts. The Bi-LSTM contains the forward $\overrightarrow{\text{LSTM}}$ which reads the utterance from w_1^l to w_n^l and a backward $\overleftarrow{\text{LSTM}}$ which reads from w_n^l to w_1^l:

$$\overrightarrow{h_t^l} = \overrightarrow{\text{LSTM}}(w_t^l, \overrightarrow{h_{t-1}^l}); t \in [1, n] \tag{1}$$

$$\overleftarrow{h_t^l} = \overleftarrow{\text{LSTM}}(w_t^l, \overleftarrow{h_{t+1}^l}); t \in [n, 1] \tag{2}$$

We obtain an annotation for a given word by concatenating the forward hidden state $\overrightarrow{h_t^l} \in \mathbb{R}^d$ and backward hidden state $\overleftarrow{h_t^l} \in \mathbb{R}^d$ as h_t^l, which summarizes the contextual information of whole utterance centered around the word w_t^l. The sequence output of the language modality is $H^l = [h_1^l; h_2^l; \cdots; h_n^l]; H^l \in \mathbb{R}^{n \times 2d}$. Similarly, the vision modality and audio modality is represented as $H^v \in \mathbb{R}^{n \times 2d}$ and $H^a \in \mathbb{R}^{n \times 2d}$ after the individual Bi-LSTM over all time-steps.

3.2 Cross-Modal Interactions Identification

In this subsection, we will introduce the cross-modal interactions identification. We have got the hidden state of each modality in last subsection. Let $h_t = [h_t^l; h_t^v; h_t^a]$ represent the modalities concatenated hidden state of the t-th word in the utterance, $h_t \in \mathbb{R}^{3 \times 2d}$.

Modality-Gate. As the first gated layer, modality-gate will fuse different modalities according to the weight of each modality. Figure 2(a) shows the construction of the modality-gate. Modality-gate calculate the weight of each modality through two steps: (1) Calculate the mean of each modalitys hidden state. (2) Feed the concatenated mean of three modalities to a softmax layer.

$$a_t^m = \text{Meanpooling}(h_t^m); m \in \{l, v, a\} \tag{3}$$

$$[\mathrm{s}_t^l, s_t^v, s_t^a] = \mathrm{softmax}([a_t^l, a_t^v, a_t^a]) \tag{4}$$

$$z_t = h_t^l \cdot s_t^l + h_t^v \cdot s_t^v + h_t^a \cdot s_t^a; z_t \in \mathbb{R}^{2d} \tag{5}$$

s_t^m is the weight of modality m at time tth. Firstly, we multiply the features of each modality with corresponding weight. Then, summing the weighted modalities features together will get the fusion representation z_t. $Z = [z_1; z_2; \cdots; z_n]$ is the fusion representation of a sentence.

Temporal-Gate. We have got the weighted modalities fusion representation by utilizing modality-gate. Then, temporal-gate will compute the weights of every time-steps. Figure 2(b) shows the construction of the temporal-gate. However, there is still a problem that there is no connection between the fusion representation previously obtained. So we use a GRU layer to solve this problem.

$$z_t^{gru} = \mathrm{GRU}(z_t); z_t^{gru} \in \mathbb{R}^d \tag{6}$$

z_t^{gru} in the above equation is the hidden state of GRU. We set its length to be d which is the same as the Bi-LSTM layer. The sequence output of the sentence is $Z^{gru} = [z_1^{gru}; z_2^{gru}; \cdots; z_n^{gru}]$; $Z^{gru} \in \mathbb{R}^{n \times d}$.

$$S = \mathrm{softmax}(\mathrm{Z}^{gru\mathrm{T}}); S \in \mathbb{R}^{d \times n} \tag{7}$$

$$M = \mathrm{Multiply}(Z^{gru}, S^{\mathrm{T}}); M \in \mathbb{R}^{n \times d} \tag{8}$$

We feed Z^{gru} to a softmax layer to calculate the importance of each time-step information which is shown in Eq. (7). At last, we multiply S with Z^{gru} to get the weighted feature M.

3.3 Prediction

In order to ensure that no information is missed, we use two parts to predict: (1) The output of the temporal-gate. (2) The output of modality-gate. We utilize a max-pooling layer to filter and reduce the temporal-gate features. We use D^{mg} and D^{tg} to represent the outputs of modality and temporal gate, respectively:

$$D^{tg} = \mathrm{MaxPooling}(M); D^{tg} \in \mathbb{R}^d \tag{9}$$

For the second part, we use a fully connected layer to filter features,

$$D^{mg} = \tanh(W_m \cdot Z + b_m); D^{mg} \in \mathbb{R}^{2d} \tag{10}$$

Where W_m and b_m are the parameters of the fully connected layer. We concatenate D^{tg} and D^{mg} for the final prediction:

$$D = D^{tg} \oplus D^{mg} \tag{11}$$

$$p_\theta(i) = \mathrm{softmax}(\mathrm{W}_p \cdot D + b_p) \tag{12}$$

4 Experimentation

4.1 Dateset

We benchmark HGMN's understanding of human communication on three tasks: (1) multimodal speaker traits recognition, (2) multimodal sentiment analysis and (3) multimodal emotion recognition. We perform experimentations on five publicly available datasets and compare the performance of HGMN with the performance of competitive approaches on the same datasets.

Trait Recognition: POM (Persuasion Opinion Multimodal) dataset [6] contains movie review videos annotated for the following speaker traits: confidence, passion, dominance, credibility, entertaining, reserved, trusting, relaxed, nervous and humorous. 903 videos were split into 600 for training, 100 for validation and 203 for testing.

Sentiment Analysis: YouTube dataset [4] contains videos from the social media web site YouTube that span a wide range of product reviews and opinion videos. Out of 46 videos, 30 are used for training, 5 for validation and 11 for testing.

MOUD: To show that HGMN is generalizable to other languages, we perform experimentation on the MOUD dataset [8] which consists of product review videos in Spanish. Each video consists of multiple segments labeled to display positive, negative or neutral sentiment. Out of 79 videos in the dataset, 49 are used for training, 10 for validation and 20 for testing. **ICT-MMMO** dataset consists of online social review videos that encompass a strong diversity in how people express opinions, annotated at the video level for sentiment. The dataset contains 340 multimodal review videos, of which 220 are used for training, 40 for validation and 80 for testing.

Emotion Analysis: CMU-MOSEI [4] is a collection of 22634 opinion video clips. Each opinion video is annotated with sentiment in the range $[-3, 3]$. There are 16188 segments in the train set, 1832 in the validation set and 4614 in the test set.

4.2 Modality Features

Text Modality: All the datasets provide manual transcriptions. We use glove [7] to convert the transcripts of videos into a sequence of word vectors. The dimension of the word vectors is 300.

Vision Modality: Facet is used to extract a set of features including per-frame basic, advanced emotions and facial action units as indicators of facial muscle movement.

Audio Modality: We use COVAREP [3] to extract low level acoustic features including 12 Melfrequency cepstral coefficients (MFCCs), pitch tracking and voiced/unvoiced segmenting features, glottal source parameters, peak slope parameters and maxima dispersion quotients.

Modality Alignment: To reach the same time alignment between different modalities we choose the granularity of the input to be at the level of words. The words are aligned with audio using P2FA [13] to get their exact utterance times. Time-step t represents the t-th spoken word in the transcript. We treat speech pause as a word with vector values of all zero across dimensions. The visual and acoustic modalities follow the same granularity. We use expected feature values across the entire word for vision and acoustic since they are extracted at a higher frequency (30 Hz for vision and 100 Hz for acoustic).

Table 1. Results for sentiment analysis on the ICT-MMMO, YouTube and MOUD dataset

Dataset task metric	ICT-MMMO		YouTube		MOUD	
	A^2	F1	A^3	F1	A^2	F1
SOTA2	$73.8^{\ddagger}$	$73.1^{\ddagger}$	$51.7^{\ddagger}$	$51.6^{\ddagger}$	$81.1^{\triangle}$	$80.9^{\flat}$
SOTA1	$76.3^{\flat}$	$76.2^{\flat}$	$55.0^{\flat}$	$53.5^{\flat}$	$81.1^{\flat}$	$81.2^{\triangle}$
HGMN	**79.6**	**79.4**	**56.3**	**54.2**	**81.6**	**81.6**
ΔSOTA	↑ 3.3	↑ 3.2	↑ 1.3	↑ 0.7	↑ 0.5	↑ 0.4

4.3 Baseline

SVM (§) a SVM is trained on the concatenated multimodal features for classification or regression [17].

EF-LSTM (♯) concatenates the inputs from different modalities at each time-step and uses that as the input to a single LSTM.

SAL-CNN (∘) is a model that attempts to prevent identity-dependent information from being learned by using Gaussian corruption introduced to the neuron outputs.

TFN (•) explicitly models view-specific and cross-view dynamics by creating a multi-dimensional tensor that captures unimodal, bimodal and trimodal interactions across three modalities. It is the current state of the art for CMU-MOSI dataset.

BC-LSTM (†) [9] is a model for context-dependent sentiment analysis and emotion recognition.

DF (♮) [5] is a model that trains one deep model for each modality and performs decision voting on the output of each modality network.

MARN (△) [16] is a model which can discover interactions between modalities through time using a neural component called the Multi-attention Block (MAB) and storing them in the hybrid memory of a recurrent component called the Long-short Term Hybrid Memory (LSTHM).

Table 2. Results for trait recognition on the POM dataset. Human traits use shorthand, for example, Con. represent Confident.

Dataset task metric	POM									
	Con. A^7	Pas. A^7	Dom. A^7	Cre. A^7	Ent. A^7	Res. A^5	Tru. A^5	Rel. A^5	Ner. A^5	Hum. A^5
SOTA2	30.0$^\flat$	33.0$^\triangle$	38.4$^\triangle$	31.6$^\flat$	33.5$^\triangle$	36.9$^\triangle$	55.7$^\triangle$	52.2$^\triangle$	47.3$^\triangle$	45.6$^\bullet$
SOTA1	34.5‡	35.7‡	41.9‡	34.5‡	37.9‡	38.4‡	57.1‡	53.2‡	47.8‡	47.3‡
HGMN	**36.4**	**35.9**	**43.9**	**34.7**	**38.7**	**39.4**	**57.6**	**55.7**	**49.8**	**47.8**
ΔSOTA	↑ 1.9	↑ 0.2	↑ 2.0	↑ 0.2	↑ 0.8	↑ 1.0	↑ 0.5	↑ 2.5	↑ 2.0	↑ 0.5
	MAE									
SOTA2	1.016†	0.993‡	0.589†	0.942†	0.927†	0.879°	0.533°	0.597$^\natural$	0.697°	0.767†
SOTA1	0.952‡	0.983†	0.835‡	0.903‡	0.913‡	0.821‡	0.521‡	0.566‡	0.654‡	0.727‡
HGMN	**0.947**	**0.978**	**0.831**	**0.901**	**0.906**	**0.813**	**0.517**	**0.565**	**0.650**	**0.721**
ΔSOTA	↑ 0.005	↑ 0.005	↑ 0.004	↑ 0.002	↑ 0.007	↑ 0.008	↑ 0.004	↑ 0.001	↑ 0.004	↑ 0.006
	r									
SOTA2	0.395‡	0.428‡	0.313‡	0.367‡	0.395‡	0.333‡	0.212$^\flat$	0.255‡	0.318‡	0.386‡
SOTA1	0.431$^\flat$	**0.450**$^\flat$	0.411$^\flat$	0.380$^\flat$	0.452$^\flat$	0.368$^\flat$	0.296‡	**0.309**$^\flat$	0.333$^\flat$	0.408$^\flat$
HGMN	**0.433**	0.444	**0.426**	**0.387**	**0.462**	**0.389**	**0.302**	**0.309**	**0.337**	**0.419**
ΔSOTA	↑ 0.002	↓ 0.006	↑ 0.015	↑ 0.007	↑ 0.010	↑ 0.021	↑ 0.006	-	↑ 0.004	↑ 0.011

MFN (‡) [15] is a modal that explicitly accounts for both interactions in a neural architecture and continuously models them through time.

GMFN (♭) [18] is a novel multimodal fusion technique called the Graph Memory Fusion Network that dynamically fuses modalities in a hierarchical manner.

4.4 Results and Discussion

Tables 1, 2 and 3 summarizes the comparison between HGMN and proposed baselines for multimodal traits recognition, sentiment analysis and emotion analysis.

The results of our experiments can be summarized as follows: HGMN achieves the best performance for multimodal human communication comprehension. Table 1 shows the sentiment analysis experiment results of HGMN and other

Table 3. Results for emotion analysis on the CMU-MOSEI dataset

Dataset task metric	CMU-MOSEI Emotion											
	Anger		Disgust		Fear		Happy		Sad		Surprise	
	WA	F1	WA	F1	WA	F1	WA	F1	WA	F1	WA	F1
SOTA2	60.5$^\bullet$	72.0$^\triangle$	67.0$^\natural$	73.2$^\triangle$	60.0$^\triangle$	**89.9**$^\triangle$	66.3$^\flat$	66.6$^\bullet$	59.2$^\sharp$	61.8$^\triangle$	53.3‡	85.4‡
SOTA1	62.6$^\flat$	72.8$^\flat$	69.1$^\flat$	76.6$^\flat$	64.2§	**89.9**$^\flat$	66.5$^\bullet$	71.0$^\triangle$	60.4$^\flat$	66.9$^\flat$	53.7$^\flat$	85.5$^\flat$
HGMN	**63.1**	**73.0**	**69.9**	**77.4**	**64.6**	**89.9**	**67.2**	**71.5**	**61.1**	**67.2**	**54.4**	**86.5**
ΔSOTA	↑ 0.5	↑ 0.2	↑ 0.8	↑ 0.8	↑ 0.4	-	↑ 0.7	↑ 0.5	↑ 0.7	↑ 0.3	↑ 0.7	↑ 1.0

baselines on the three datasets. Our approach has achieved the highest accuracies and F1 in all cases. Table 2 shows the performance of the HGMN on POM dataset, where it achieves the best performance on all 10 speaker trait classification tasks. Table 3 shows the emotion analysis experiment results on the CMU-MOSEI dataset. Our approach has achieved the best WA and F1 in most cases.

5 Conclusion

This paper introduced a novel approach for multi-modality sequential learning called Hierarchical-gate Multimodal Network (HGMN). Each modality is first encoded by Bi-LSTM which aims to capture the intra-modal interactions within single modality. Subsequently, we merge the independent information of multimodality using two gate layers. The first gate which is named as modality-gate will calculate the weight of each modality. And the other gate called temporal-gate will capture the importances of every time-step. We also use a GRU layer to capture cross-modal interactions between two gates. We systematically investigate three typical multimodal tasks, i.e., multimodal sentiment analysis, multimodal emotion recognition and speaker traits recognition, to justify the effectiveness of our proposed approach. Detailed evaluation on multiple multimodal benchmark datasets, such as CMU-MOSEI and POM, shows that our proposed approach significantly improves the state-of-the-art.

Acknowledgments. The research work is partially supported by the Key Project of NSFC No. 61702149 and two NSFC grants No. 61672366, No. 61673290.

References

1. Baum, L.E., Petrie, T.: Statistical inference for probabilistic functions of finite state Markov chains. Ann. Math. Stat. **37**(6), 1554–1563 (1966)
2. Chen, M., Wang, S., Liang, P.P., Baltrušaitis, T., Zadeh, A., Morency, L.P.: Multimodal sentiment analysis with word-level fusion and reinforcement learning. In: Proceedings of the 19th ACM International Conference on Multimodal Interaction, pp. 163–171. ACM (2017)
3. Degottex, G., Kane, J., Drugman, T., Raitio, T., Scherer, S.: COVAREPA collaborative voice analysis repository for speech technologies. In: IEEE International Conference on Acoustics, Speech and Signal Processing (ICASSP), pp. 960–964. IEEE (2014)
4. Morency, L.P., Mihalcea, R., Doshi, P.: Towards multimodal sentiment analysis: harvesting opinions from the web. In: Proceedings of the 13th International Conference on Multimodal Interfaces, pp. 169–176. ACM (2011)
5. Nojavanasghari, B., Gopinath, D., Koushik, J., Baltrušaitis, T., Morency, L.P.: Deep multimodal fusion for persuasiveness prediction. In: Proceedings of the 18th ACM International Conference on Multimodal Interaction, pp. 284–288. ACM (2016)

6. Park, S., Shim, H.S., Chatterjee, M., Sagae, K., Morency, L.P.: Computational analysis of persuasiveness in social multimedia: a novel dataset and multimodal prediction approach. In: Proceedings of the 16th International Conference on Multimodal Interaction, pp. 50–57. ACM (2014)
7. Pennington, J., Socher, R., Manning, C.: GloVe: global vectors for word representation. In: Proceedings of the 2014 Conference on Empirical Methods in Natural Language Processing (EMNLP), pp. 1532–1543 (2014)
8. Poria, S., Cambria, E., Gelbukh, A.: Deep convolutional neural network textual features and multiple kernel learning for utterance-level multimodal sentiment analysis. In: Proceedings of the 2015 Conference on Empirical Methods in Natural Language Processing, pp. 2539–2544 (2015)
9. Poria, S., Cambria, E., Hazarika, D., Majumder, N., Zadeh, A., Morency, L.P.: Context-dependent sentiment analysis in user-generated videos. In: Proceedings of the 55th Annual Meeting of the Association for Computational Linguistics (Volume 1: Long Papers), pp. 873–883 (2017)
10. Quattoni, A., Wang, S., Morency, L.P., Collins, M., Darrell, T.: Hidden conditional random fields. IEEE Trans. Pattern Anal. Mach. Intell. **10**, 1848–1852 (2007)
11. Rajagopalan, S.S., Morency, L.-P., Baltrušaitis, T., Goecke, R.: Extending long short-term memory for multi-view structured learning. In: Leibe, B., Matas, J., Sebe, N., Welling, M. (eds.) ECCV 2016. LNCS, vol. 9911, pp. 338–353. Springer, Cham (2016). https://doi.org/10.1007/978-3-319-46478-7_21
12. Wörtwein, T., Scherer, S.: What really matters—an information gain analysis of questions and reactions in automated PTSD screenings. In: Seventh International Conference on Affective Computing and Intelligent Interaction (ACII), pp. 15–20. IEEE (2017)
13. Yuan, J., Liberman, M.: Speaker identification on the SCOTUS corpus. J. Acoust. Soc. Am. **123**(5), 3878 (2008)
14. Zadeh, A., Chen, M., Poria, S., Cambria, E., Morency, L.P.: Tensor fusion network for multimodal sentiment analysis. arXiv preprint arXiv:1707.07250 (2017)
15. Zadeh, A., Liang, P.P., Mazumder, N., Poria, S., Cambria, E., Morency, L.P.: Memory fusion network for multi-view sequential learning. In: Thirty-Second AAAI Conference on Artificial Intelligence (2018)
16. Zadeh, A., Liang, P.P., Poria, S., Vij, P., Cambria, E., Morency, L.P.: Multi-attention recurrent network for human communication comprehension. In: Thirty-Second AAAI Conference on Artificial Intelligence (2018)
17. Zadeh, A., Zellers, R., Pincus, E., Morency, L.P.: Multimodal sentiment intensity analysis in videos: facial gestures and verbal messages. IEEE Intell. Syst. **31**(6), 82–88 (2016)
18. Zadeh, A.B., Liang, P.P., Poria, S., Cambria, E., Morency, L.P.: Multimodal language analysis in the wild: CMU-MOSEI dataset and interpretable dynamic fusion graph. In: Proceedings of the 56th Annual Meeting of the Association for Computational Linguistics (Volume 1: Long Papers), pp. 2236–2246 (2018)

End-to-End Model for Offline Handwritten Mongolian Word Recognition

Hongxi Wei[1,2(✉)], Cong Liu[1,2], Hui Zhang[1,2], Feilong Bao[1,2], and Guanglai Gao[1,2]

[1] School of Computer Science, Inner Mongolia University, Hohhot 010021, China
cswhx@imu.edu.cn
[2] Provincial Key Laboratory of Mongolian Information Processing Technology, Hohhot, China

Abstract. This paper proposed an end-to-end model for recognizing offline handwritten Mongolian words. To be specific, a sequence to sequence architecture with attention mechanism is used to perform the task of generating a target sequence from a source sequence. The proposed model consists of two LSTMs and one attention network. The first LSTM is an encoder which consumes a frame sequence of one word image. The second LSTM is a decoder which can generate a sequence of letters. The attention network is added between encoder and decoder, which allow the decoder to focus on different positions in a sequence of frames during the procedure of decoding. In this study, we have attempted two schemes for generating frames from word images. In the first scheme, frames are generated with overlapping. Each adjacent two frames overlap half a frame. In the second scheme, frames are generated without overlapping. In addition, the height of the frame is also taken into consideration in our study. By comparison, the better scheme for generating frames has been determined. Experimental results demonstrate that the proposed end-to-end model outperforms the state-of-the-art method.

Keywords: Offline handwritten recognition · Traditional Mongolian · Segmentation-free · Sequence to sequence · Attention

1 Introduction

Mongolian language is mainly used in China (e.g. Inner Mongolia Autonomous Region), Republic of Mongolia, Russia and their neighboring areas. The Mongolian language used in China is called *traditional Mongolian*. Correspondingly, the Mongolian language used in Republic of Mongolia and Russia is called *Cyrillic Mongolian*, in which its letters are the same as alphabets of Russian. In this study, we focused on the problem of offline handwritten word recognition for the traditional Mongolian. In the rest of this paper, the traditional Mongolian is called Mongolian without particularly emphasizing.

In recent years, a large number of Mongolian documents in handwriting format have been scanned into images. In general, these scanned handwriting documents can

J. Tang et al. (Eds.): NLPCC 2019, LNAI 11839, pp. 220–230, 2019.
https://doi.org/10.1007/978-3-030-32236-6_19

be converted into texts by utilizing the technology of offline handwritten recognition. However, offline handwritten Mongolian word recognition (HMWR) is a challenging task due to the huge number of vocabularies, special word formations, and various handwriting styles.

Mongolian is an alphabetic language. All letters of one Mongolian word are conglutinated together in the vertical direction to form a backbone, and letters have initial, medial or final visual forms according to their positions within a word [1]. A blank space is used to separate two words. The Mongolian language is also a kind of agglutinative language. Its word formation and inflection are built by connecting different suffixes to the roots or stems. Hence, the number of vocabularies of the Mongolian is huge, and frequently used vocabulary is about one million. Moreover, the Mongolian language has a very special writing system, which is quite different from Arabic, English and other Latin languages. Its writing order is vertical from top to bottom and the column order is from left to right. A fragment of one handwritten Mongolian document and an example of one Mongolian word are illustrated in Fig. 1.

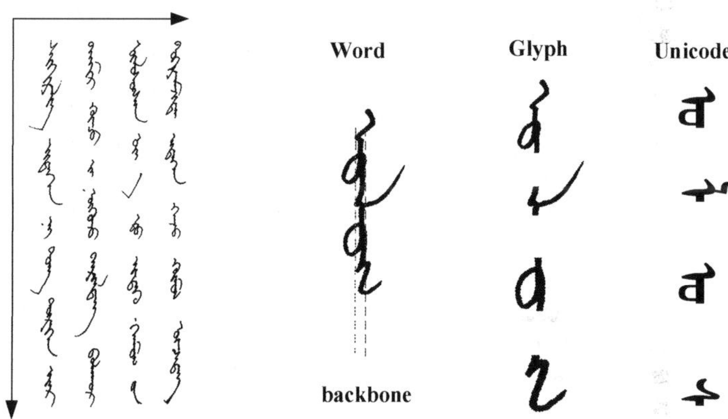

Fig. 1. A sample of handwritten Mongolian text.

In Fig. 1, we can see that it is so difficult to segment handwritten Mongolian words into individual glyphs. Therefore, the conventional character segmentation based schemes [2–6] are infeasible to HMWR. Holistic word recognition is an alternative solution. With the success of deep learning, convolutional neural network (CNN) has been applied successfully in offline handwritten word recognition by the manner of segmentation-free [7–11]. However, CNN based methods classify its input into a certain class among the vocabularies. So, they often suffer from the problem of out-of-vocabulary (OOV), especially for Mongolian language with large vocabularies. More recently, sequence to sequence model becomes popular for the task of offline handwritten recognition [12–14]. Therein, word or text images are fed into the encoder of a sequence to sequence model, and then sequences of letters are generated by a decoder as recognition results. As long as the decoder is able to generate the whole alphabets, sequence to sequence model can solve the problem of OOV.

As far as we know, there is little literature about offline handwritten Mongolian word recognition. In [15, 16], Fan et al. proposed a DNN-HMM hybrid model for realizing HMWR. Specifically, each Mongolian word image is divided into a number of sub-characters, and then every sub-character was modeled by an HMM. The observing sequences in HMMs are obtained by using a DNN. Through evaluating on an offline handwritten Mongolian (MHW) dataset, experimental result demonstrates that this model is the state-of-the-art so far.

In this paper, we proposed a novel end-to-end model for recognizing offline handwritten Mongolian words. To be specific, a sequence to sequence architecture with attention mechanism is used to perform the task of generating a target sequence (i.e. a sequence of letters) from a source sequence (i.e. a frame-sequence of one word image). The proposed model consists of two LSTMs and one attention network. The first LSTM is considered as an *encoder* which consumes frame-sequences of one word image. The second LSTM is taken as a *decoder* which can generate a sequence of letters. The attention network is added between encoder and decoder, which can not only improve the effect of parallelism but also decrease training time. This kind of model has been extensively employed for neural machine translation. In this study, our model incorporates a set of improvements for accomplishing the aim of offline handwritten Mongolian word recognition.

The rest of the paper is organized as follows. The proposed model is given in Sect. 2. Experimental results are shown in Sect. 3. Section 4 provides the conclusions.

2 The Proposed Model

The proposed model is designed as a sequence to sequence architecture with attention mechanism, which is composed of a BiLSTM based encoder, a LSTM based decoder, and a DNN based attention network is adopted to connect between the encoder and the decoder. Frames of each word image should be inputted into a DNN based feature extractor before being fed into the BiLSTM based encoder. The detailed architecture is shown in Fig. 2.

2.1 Details of the Proposed Model

In this model, the original inputs are handwritten Mongolian word images. So, all word images should be transformed into a certain kind of sequences in advance. In order to attain this aim, each word image is normalized, and then divided into multiple frames with equal size. After that, the sequence of frames is passed to the encoder and converted into hidden states of the corresponding encoder. Then, the hidden states are fed into the attention network, in which a part of the hidden states are enhanced and the rest are faded. Next, the processed hidden states are put into the decoder. Finally, the decoder is able to generate a sequence of letters as the output of the model.

The decoder of the proposed model is also an LSTM which requires the attention network to choose the most relevant states for the current output letter and filter out irrelevant states. The attention network allows the decoder to focus on different

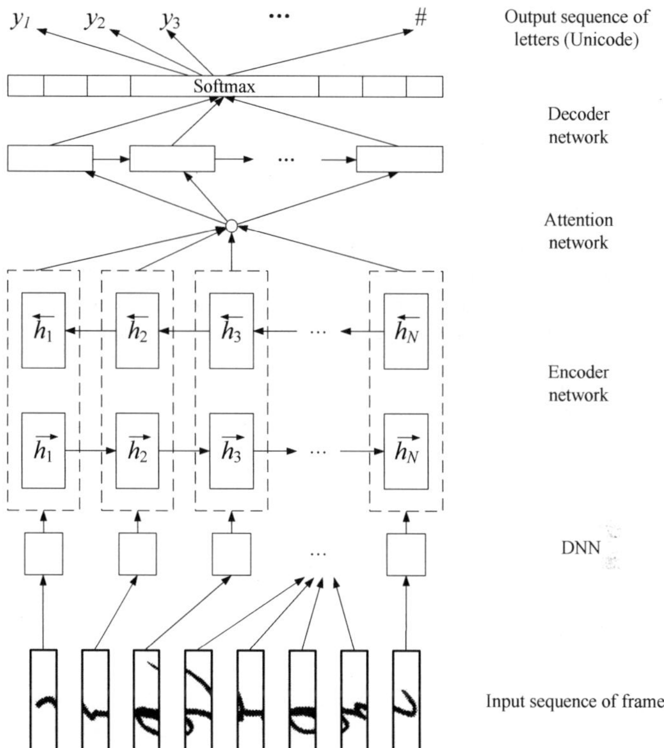

Fig. 2. The architecture of the proposed model.

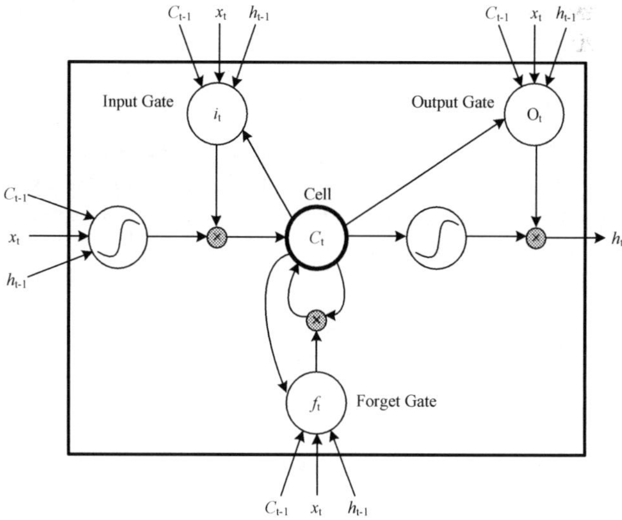

Fig. 3. The structure of a memory cell.

positions in a sequence of frames during the procedure of decoding. The attention network plays an important part in the proposed model.

LSTM network is able to learn long-term dependencies, which includes a set of memory cells [17]. The structure of a single memory cell is presented in Fig. 3. A LSTM network transmits the previous information in two ways [18]: the output (or hidden) vector (denoted by h) and the state vector (denoted by c), that combined using three gates, are explicitly designed to store and propagate long-term dependencies.

The gate i is named the input gate. Its value will be updated in the state vector. The gate f is named the forget gate, which can learn the information from the previous state that can be thrown away. With the output of these two gates, the memory cell creates a new state vector. Finally, the gate o is named the output gate, which can generate the output vector of the memory cell. The following equations are used in each memory cell to produce the output vector and the state vector of the moment t, severally.

$$i_t = \sigma(W_{xi} \cdot x_t + W_{hi} \cdot h_{t-1} + W_{ci} \cdot c_{t-1} + b_i) \tag{1}$$

$$f_t = \sigma\left(W_{xf} \cdot x_t + W_{hf} \cdot h_{t-1} + W_{cf} \cdot c_{t-1} + b_f\right) \tag{2}$$

$$c_t = f_t \cdot c_{t-1} + i_t \cdot tanh(W_{xc} \cdot x_t + W_{hc} \cdot h_{t-1} + b_c) \tag{3}$$

$$o_t = \sigma(W_{xo} \cdot x_t + W_{ho} \cdot h_{t-1} + W_{co} \cdot c_t + b_o) \tag{4}$$

$$h_t = o_t \cdot tanh(c_t) \tag{5}$$

Where W (e.g. W_{xi}) and b (e.g. b_i) are trainable parameters, σ is the sigmoid function, and i, f, o, c and h are the input gate, the forget gate, the output gate, the state vector and the output vector, respectively. The BiLSTM of our proposed model contains a forward LSTM and a backward LSTM, and each LSTM consists of 64 memory cells.

2.2 Generating Input Sequence of Frames

The scheme which transforms a word image into a sequence of frames may influence the recognition performance. In this study, we have attempted two schemes for obtaining frames. In the first scheme, frames are generated with overlapping. Each adjacent two frames overlap half a frame, as illustrated in Fig. 4(a). In the second scheme, frames are generated without overlapping, as illustrated in Fig. 4(b). The height of the frame is also taken into consideration. Its effect has been tested in our experiment (see Sect. 3).

2.3 Data Augmentation

In various machine learning tasks, data augmentation schemes can improve performance by generating new data derived from the original data. Here, new samples of

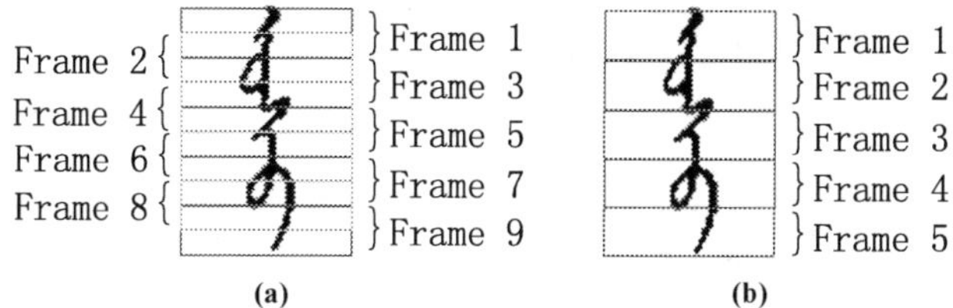

Fig. 4. Two schemes for obtaining frames. (a) Two adjacent frames overlap half a frame. (b) Two adjacent frames without overlapping.

word images can be synthesized through a series of simple operations including rotation and scale in horizontal and vertical directions, respectively. The detailed operations are introduced as below.

The word images are scaled in the horizontal direction and the scaling factor is sampled from a uniform distribution $U(0.8,\ 1.2)$. The vertical direction is the writing direction of the Mongolian, in which letters are conglutinated together in this direction. We scale the image in the vertical direction to simulate the height variation. To further simulating the variation of each letter, we first segment the image into random number of slices, and then scale each slice with a different scaling factor. The number of slices is random selected based on the whole image height. A taller image is segmented into more slices with high probability. The scaling factor of each slice is sampled from a uniform distribution $U(0.8,\ 1.2)$.

Fig. 5. Samples generated by data augmentation. (a) The original word image; (b)– (d) The generated samples using data augmentation scheme.

Furthermore, we rotate the image in a small angle to simulate the slanted written Mongolian words. The rotating angle is sampled from the Gaussian distribution N(0, 3). These three operations are applied to the original image in a pipeline: (1) Image is scaled in the horizontal direction, randomly. (2) The scaled image is scaled in the vertical direction, randomly. (3) The scaled image is rotated, randomly. In theory, this method can generate a large number of samples to improve the generalization ability of the trained model. Several generated word images are provided in Fig. 5.

3 Experimental Results

3.1 Dataset

In this study, an offline handwritten Mongolian words (MHW) dataset [16] is used to evaluate our proposed model. The training set covers 5,000 vocabularies and each one has 20 samples. The MHW contains two testing sets. The first one (denoted by Testing Set I) has 1,000 words randomly selected from the training set and each word has 5 samples. The writers are the same as the training set. The second one (denoted by **Testing Set II**) has 939 words different from the training set. Each word has 15 samples and the writers are different from the training set. In the dataset, each word image has been placed into the center of a bounding box with 48 pixels width.

3.2 Baseline

To evaluate the performance of the proposed model, a state-of-the-art method (i.e. a DNN-HMM hybrid model with Unicode labels) presented in [15, 16] is taken as a baseline. The DNN consists of 4 hidden layers and each hidden layer has 1024 nodes. The output of DNN is a triple of Unicode labels, which is formed by the current label concatenated with the previous one and the following one. The HMM is used to model the sequence property. We did not re-implement this model, and just list the original results (**82.16%** and **73.16%**) reported in [16].

3.3 The Performance of the Proposed Model

The height of the frame is an important factor affecting the recognition accuracy. In [16], the authors only used a certain scheme to form the frame sequence, in which the frame height is 11 pixels and the overlap is 10 pixels. In this experiment, we tested various frame heights and overlap sizes.

In Fig. 6, when the frame height is decreased from 8 pixels to 2 pixels with an interval of 2 pixels, the accuracy is increasing. The best accuracies on the two testing sets are **87.68%** and **81.12%**, respectively. It demonstrates that the smaller of the frame height the higher accuracy is obtained. The attention mechanism can determine the most relevant frames associated with a certain output label. In ideal, the relevant frames should only contain the corresponding glyph of the output label. When the frame is taller, a frame may contain more than one glyph, which results in decreasing the accuracy. Therefore, the shorter frame is better.

In Fig. 7, when the frame height is set to 2 pixels, the overlapping scheme is better. To improve the accuracy of the non-overlapping scheme, the frame height is set to one pixel. But, the improvement is not enough to beat the overlapping scheme. We can conclude that the overlapping scheme is better than the non-overlapping scheme. Because that the overlapping scheme can provide extra context information of frames to LSTM so as to obtain better performance.

The effect of data augmentation has been tested in our experiment. The results are presented in Fig. 8. We can see that the accuracy is improved by increasing the number of samples. Here, the number of samples for the training set augments twice as much

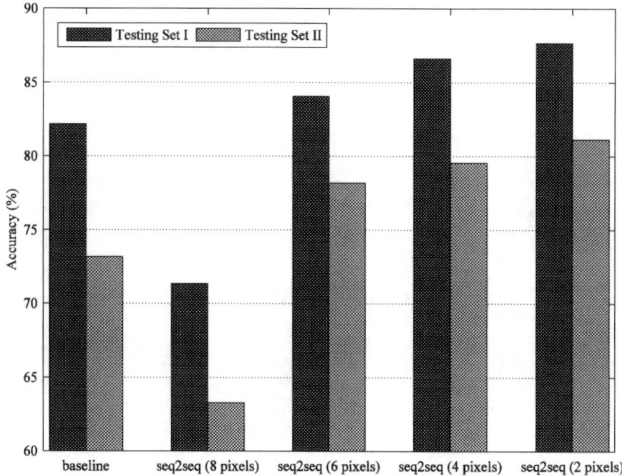

Fig. 6. The performance of the proposed model.

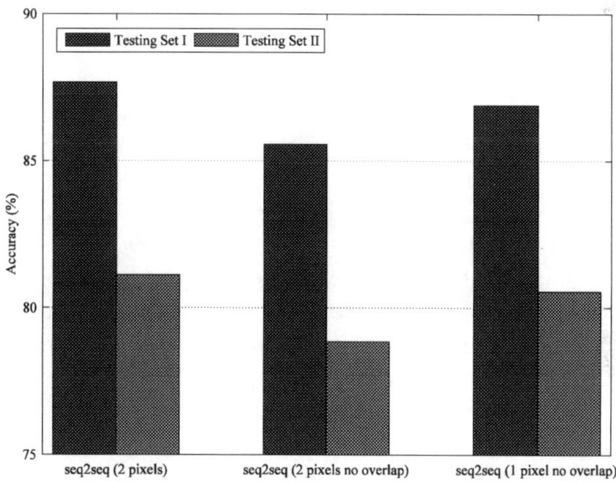

Fig. 7. The comparative results between generated frames with overlapping and non-overlapping.

(denoted by **augment1**) and triple as much (denoted by **augment2**), separately. For testing set I, the corresponding accuracies are increased to **90.30%** and **90.68%**, severally. For testing set II, the accuracies are also increased to **84.10%** and **84.16%**, respectively. Therefore, we can conclude that data augmentation scheme can improve the performance.

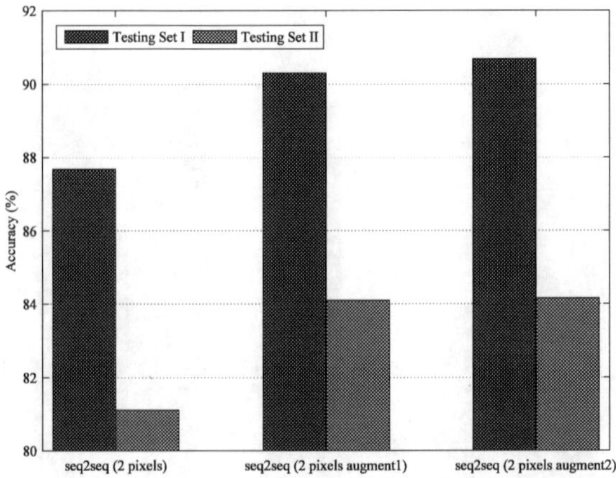

Fig. 8. The performance of data augmentation.

4 Conclusions

In this paper, we proposed an end-to-end model for recognizing offline handwritten Mongolian words. Specifically, a sequence to sequence structure with attention mechanism is used to perform the task of generating a target sequence from a source sequence. The proposed model consists of two LSTMs and one attention network. The first LSTM is an encoder which processes a sequence of frames. The second LSTM is a decoder which can generate a sequence of letters as recognition results. The attention network is added between encoder and decoder, which allow the decoder to focus on different positions in a sequence of frames during the procedure of decoding.

In this work, we have attempted two schemes for generating frames from handwritten Mongolian word images. In the first scheme, frames are generated with overlapping that each adjacent two frames overlap half a frame. In the second scheme, frames are generated without overlapping. In addition, the height of the frame is also taken into consideration. By comparison, our proposed model is superior to the state-of-the-art DNN-HMM hybrid model on a dataset of offline handwritten Mongolian words. Moreover, we have compared several heights of frames. The frame heights are set to 8 pixels, 6 pixels, 4 pixels and 2 pixels, separately. When the frame height is set to 2 pixels, the best performance can be attained. It demonstrates that the smaller of the frame height the higher accuracy can be obtained. It is in line with the working mechanism of attention. The architecture of sequence to sequence can handle the problem of OOV. Therefore, the proposed model is especially suited for realizing large vocabulary HMWR.

Acknowledgement. This paper is supported by the National Natural Science Foundation of China under Grant 61463038.

References

1. Wei, H., Gao, G.: A keyword retrieval system for historical Mongolian document images. Int. J. Doc. Anal. Recogn. (IJDAR) **17**(1), 33–45 (2014)
2. Wei, H., Gao, G.: Machine-printed traditional Mongolian characters recognition using BP neural networks. In: Proceeding of 2009 International Conference on Computational Intelligence and Software Engineering (CiSE 2009), pp. 1–7. IEEE (2009)
3. Hu, H., Wei, H., Liu, Z.: The CNN based machine-printed traditional Mongolian characters recognition. In: Proceedings of the 36th Chinese Control Conference (CCC 2017), pp. 3937–3941. IEEE (2017)
4. Gao, G., Su, X., Wei, H., Gong, Y.: Classical Mongolian words recognition in historical document. In: Proceedings of the 11th International Conference on Document Analysis and Recognition (ICDAR 2011), pp. 692–697. IEEE (2011)
5. Su, X., Gao, G., Wang, W., Bao, F., Wei, H.: Character segmentation for classical Mongolian words in historical documents. In: Li, S., Liu, C., Wang, Y. (eds.) CCPR 2014, Part II. CCIS, vol. 484, pp. 464–473. Springer, Heidelberg (2014). https://doi.org/10.1007/978-3-662-45643-9_49
6. Su, X., Gao, G., Wei, H., Bao, F.: A knowledge-based recognition system for historical Mongolian documents. Int. J. Doc. Anal. Recogn. (IJDAR) **19**(4), 221–235 (2016)
7. Yuan, A., Bai, G., Yang, P., Guo, Y., Zhao, X.: Handwritten English word recognition based on convolutional neural networks. In: Proceedings of the 13th International Conference on Frontiers in Handwriting Recognition (ICFHR 2012), pp. 207–212. IEEE (2012)
8. Yang, W., Jin, L., Tao, D., Xie, Z., Feng, Z.: DropSample: a new training method to enhance deep convolutional neural networks for large-scale unconstrained handwritten Chinese character recognition. Pattern Recogn. **58**, 190–203 (2016)
9. Elleuch, M., Tagougui, N., Kherallah, M.: Towards unsupervised learning for Arabic handwritten recognition using deep architectures. In: Arik, S., Huang, T., Lai, W.K., Liu, Q. (eds.) ICONIP 2015, Part I. LNCS, vol. 9489, pp. 363–372. Springer, Cham (2015). https://doi.org/10.1007/978-3-319-26532-2_40
10. Kim, I., Xie, X.: Handwritten Hangul recognition using deep convolutional neural networks. Int. J. Doc. Anal. Recogn. (IJDAR) **18**(1), 1–13 (2015)
11. Adak, C., Chaudhuri, B.B., Blumenstein, M.: Offline cursive Bengali word recognition using CNNs with a recurrent model. In: Proceedings of the 15th International Conference on Frontiers in Handwriting Recognition (ICFHR 2016), pp. 429–434. IEEE (2016)
12. Zhang, X., Tan, C.L.: Unconstrained handwritten word recognition based on trigrams using BLSTM. In: Proceedings of the 22nd International Conference on Pattern Recognition (ICPR 2014), pp. 2914–2919. IEEE (2014)
13. Messina, R., Louradour, J.: Segmentation-free handwritten Chinese text recognition with LSTM-RNN. In: Proceedings of 13th International Conference on Document Analysis and Recognition (ICDAR 2015), pp. 171–175. IEEE (2015)
14. Voigtlaender, P., Doetsch, P., Ney, H.: Handwriting recognition with large multidimensional long short-term memory recurrent neural networks. In: Proceedings of the 15th International Conference on Frontiers in Handwriting Recognition (ICFHR 2016), pp. 228–233. IEEE (2016)

15. Fan, D., Gao, G.: DNN-HMM for large vocabulary Mongolian offline handwriting recognition. In: Proceedings of the 15th International Conference on Frontiers in Handwriting Recognition (ICFHR 2016), pp. 72–77. IEEE (2016)
16. Fan, D., Gao, G., Wu, H.: MHW Mongolian offline handwritten dataset and its application. J. Chin. Inf. Process. **32**(1), 89–95 (2018)
17. Hochreiter, S., Schmidhuber, J.: Long short-term memory. Neural Comput. **9**(8), 1735–1780 (1997)
18. Graves, A., Mohamed, A., Hinton, G.E.: Speech recognition with deep recurrent neural networks. In: Proceedings of the 38th International Conference on Acoustics, Speech and Signal Processing (ICASSP 2013), pp. 6645–6649 (2013)

A Recursive Information Flow Gated Model for RST-Style Text-Level Discourse Parsing

Longyin Zhang, Xin Tan, Fang Kong(✉), and Guodong Zhou

School of Computer Science and Technology, Soochow University, Suzhou, China
{lyzhang7,xtan}@stu.suda.edu.cn,
{kongfang,gdzhou}@suda.edu.cn

Abstract. Text-level discourse parsing is notoriously difficult due to the long-distance dependency over the document and the deep hierarchical structure of the discourse. In this paper, we attempt to model the representation of a document recursively via shift-reduce operations. Intuitively, humans tend to understand macro and micro texts from different perspectives, so we propose a recursive model to fuse multiple information flows and strengthen the representation of text spans. During parsing, the proposed model can synthetically grade each information flow according to the granularity of the text. Experimentation on the RST-DT corpus shows that our parser can outperform the state-of-the-art in nuclearity detection under stringent discourse parsing evaluations.

Keywords: RST · Discourse parsing · Tree-LSTM

1 Introduction

A document usually consists of many related text units organized in the form of constituency and dependency. As a representative linguistic theory about discourse structures, Rhetorical Structure Theory (RST) [11] describes a document as a discourse constituency tree. As shown in Fig. 1, each leaf node of the tree corresponds to an Element Discourse Unit (EDU) and relevant leaf nodes are connected by rhetorical relations to form bigger text spans recursively until the final tree is built. In particular, a label (either *nucleus* or *satellite*) is assigned according to the nuclearity of two neighboring document units, where the *nucleus* is considered more important.

In this paper, we address the task of RST-style discourse parsing, which aims to identify the overall rhetorical structure of the entire document. With the release of RST Discourse Treebank (RST-DT), text-level discourse parsing has been attracting more and more attention. However, the RST-DT corpus is limited in size since corpus annotation is time consuming and labor extensive. In this condition, most of previous studies heavily rely on manual feature engineering [5,8]. With the increasing popularity of deep learning in NLP, some

J. Tang et al. (Eds.): NLPCC 2019, LNAI 11839, pp. 231–241, 2019.
https://doi.org/10.1007/978-3-030-32236-6_20

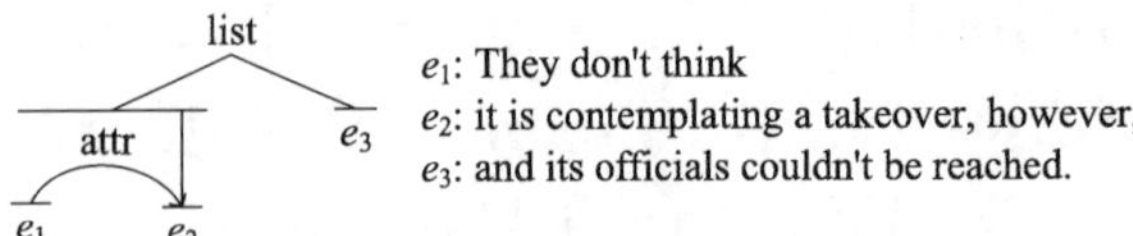

Fig. 1. An example of RST discourse tree, where e_1, e_2, e_3 and e_4 are EDUs, *list* and *attr* are discourse relation labels, and arrows indicate the nucleuses of relations.

researchers turn to DNNs [3,9,10]. For example, Li *et al.* [9] propose a recursive deep model to compute the representation for each text span based on its subtrees. However, recursive deep models usually suffer from gradient vanishing.

In addition, humans tend to understand macro and micro texts from different perspectives. Li *et al.* [10] propose a hierarchical Bi-LSTM model to learn representations of text spans, which can store document-level information for a long period of time. However, text spans in RST-DT are formed recursively in nature, it is hard for sequence LSTMs to capture discourse structure information.

To address above challenges, we propose the recursive information flow gated model (R-IFGM) to learn representations of text spans. The proposed model can well store information for a long time and thus avoid gradient vanishing. In particular, we introduce two additional information flows, i.e., the state transition information for long distance dependency and the principal component of the text span for low-latitude representation of the text. Specially, the R-IFGM model can grade these information flows according to the granularity of each text span automatically. Compared with the state-of-the-art, the resulting parser obtains competitive performance under stringent discourse parsing evaluations and can strongly outperform the corresponding best parser in nuclearity detection with an absolute gain of 3.2% in F1-measure due to the modeling of multiple information flows in a recursive way.

2 Parsing Model

A shift-reduce discourse parser maintains two data structures: a stack of partially completed subtrees and a buffer of EDUs yet to be parsed. The parser is initialized with the stack empty and the buffer contains all EDUs (e_1, e_2, ..., e_N) of the document in order. When the action *reduce* is performed, the parser will choose both the type of nuclearity and relation between the two popped elements. The shift-reduce system transforms the structure building problem into a labeling decision problem. During parsing, the parser consumes transitions (a_1, a_2, ..., a_k, ..., a^{2N-1}) constantly according to the state of buffer and stack, where $a_k \in \{shift, reduce\}$. Mutually, the state of buffer and stack will change according to the predicted action label. When the buffer becomes empty and the stack has only one element, the shift-reduce process is ended. The last element in the stack is the target discourse constituency tree.

2.1 EDU Representation

The LSTM model is meant to maintain a rough summary of the portion of the sentence has been processed so far. Since an EDU is a sequence of words, we employ a Bi-LSTM to encode each sequence constituted by the concatenation of word embeddings and POS embeddings, obtaining $H = (H_1, H_2, \ldots, H_n)$. Then we use the unweighted average to get a summarization of the hidden states, obtaining $\bar{H}$. Previous studies on discourse parsing have proved that words at the beginning and end of EDUs provide quite useful information [5,7,9]. Following their works, we formulate the representation of an EDU as:

$$x_e = [\bar{H}; w_1; w_n; p_1] \tag{1}$$

$$[h_0; c_0] = W_e x_e + b_e \tag{2}$$

where $[h_0; c_0]$ is a transformed representation of the EDU (leaf node) for LSTM-style computation.

2.2 Composition Function for Text Span Representation

The representations for non-leaf nodes serve as structure and relation classification. When the action *reduce* is performed, the top two elements in the stack are entered into a *composition function* to form the representation for a bigger text span. The proposed R-IFGM is also a recursive *composition function* that can generate the representation for each text span in a bottom-up fashion. Figure 2 shows the architecture of R-IFGM, which is also a variant of the Tree-LSTM [14]. The architecture illustrates the input (x), cell (c) and hidden (h) nodes at the time t. It extends the sequence LSTM by splitting the previous hidden state vector h_{t-1} into a left child's state vector h_{t-1}^L and a right child's state vector h_{t-1}^R, splitting the previous cell vector c_{t-1} into c_{t-1}^L and c_{t-1}^R.

Different from other tree-structured LSTMs, we bring two additional information flows as external inputs. For the state transition information, we employ a state tracker here to track the changing states of the stack and buffer to capture the long distance dependency. For the text span's principal component, we introduce the *smooth inverse frequency* (SIF) [1] into this paper to supply a low dimension representation of the text span to form. Additionally, the hidden states of the left and right child nodes supply the structure information

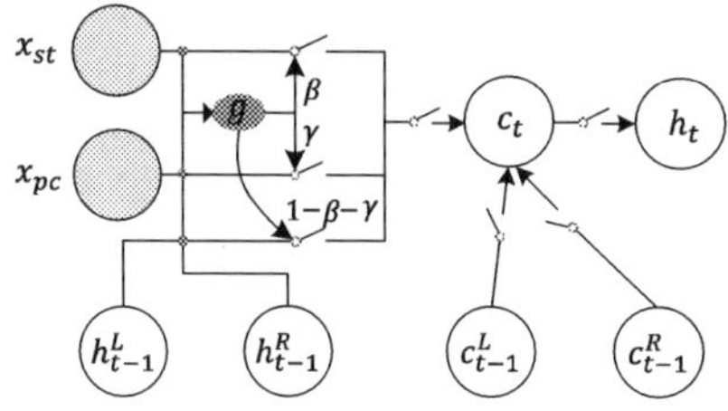

Fig. 2. Topology of the proposed recursive information flow gated model (R-IFGM).

in nature. Generally, we expect the model to have the ability to automatically assign weights on the three gates to choose which information is more important in representing the parent node. Therefore, we use a mutually-exclusive gating mechanism to balance the three information flows.

When the action *reduce* is performed, the representations of two text spans are popped from the stack and fed into the *composition function* to compute the representation for the new parent node at the time t. The *composition function* calculates the parent node's cell vector c_t and the hidden state h_t as follows:

$$I_h = W_h h_{t-1} + b_h \tag{3}$$

$$I_s = W_s x_{st} + b_s, I_{pc} = W_{pc} x_{pc} + b_{pc} \tag{4}$$

$$\beta = \frac{e^{I_s}}{\sum_{I \in D} e^{I}}, \gamma = \frac{e^{I_{pc}}}{\sum_{I \in D} e^{I}} \tag{5}$$

$$g_t = W_g(\beta x_{st} \oplus \gamma x_{pc} \oplus (1 - \beta - \gamma) h_{t-1}) + b_g \tag{6}$$

$$c_t = \sum_{N \in \{L,R\}} f_{t-1}^N \odot c_{t-1}^N + i_t \odot g_t \tag{7}$$

$$h_t = o_t \odot \tanh(c_t) \tag{8}$$

where h_{t-1} refers to the concatenation of the top two hidden states popped from the stack, $D = \{I_h, I_{pc}, I_s\}$, f_{t-1}^N is the forget gate, i_t is the input gate, o_t is the output gate, $\oplus$ is the concatenation, and $\odot$ is the element-wise product. The new pair (h_t, c_t) that represents a new text span is then pushed onto the stack. The external inputs x_{pc} and x_{st} are detailedly described in Sect. 2.3.

2.3 The Principal Component of Text Span and State Transition

Getting a precise representation of the text span is difficult as many documents are quite long sequences, so auxiliary information is urgently needed. In this section, we give an explanation about the two external inputs, i.e., the text span's principal component and the state transition information.

The Principal Component of Text Span. Usually, it is difficult to capture semantic information recursively when the document tree is extremely deep. So, a method to abstract the most principal component of each text span is necessary. In a discourse tree, each inner node can uniquely identify a text area, which contains a set of EDUs that provide complete semantic information for the text area. We aim to translate each text span into a lower latitude representation. The SIF proposed by Arora *et al.* [1] is an unsupervised sentence embedding method. It achieves significantly better performance than certain supervised methods including LSTMs on most of textual similarity tasks. For a start, we borrow the SIF [1] to get unsupervised representation of each EDU in the text span. Then, we get a summarization of this text span by the unweighted average on the representations of EDUs. When the action *reduce* is performed, the top two text spans in the stack are popped to form a bigger text span and we formulate the principal component of the text span as:

$$s = [s_1, \ldots, s_m] = \mathrm{SIF}(E, p(w), a) \tag{9}$$

$$x_{pc} = average(s) \tag{10}$$

where E is the set of EDUs in the text span, $p(w)$ denotes the estimated probabilities of words in the Wall Street Journal articles used in Treebank-2, and a is the weighting parameter mentioned in the paper [1].

State Transition. Our proposed discourse parser is a shift-reduce discourse parser, which maintains a stack and a buffer. During parsing time, the stack and buffer generate a series of changing states according to the transition actions. We aim to use a state tracker to capture the long distance dependency. The state tracker is a sequence tracking LSTM [2] and it is meant to maintain a low-resolution summary of the portion of the discourse has been processed so far. We choose the first element in the buffer and the top two elements in the stack to represent the state at the tth step, obtaining $state_t = [h^0_{t\_b}; h^{-1}_{t\_s}; h^{-2}_{t\_s}]$. Then, we take those changing states as a series of inputs to the state tracker. The output at the time t will supply state transition information for the *composition function* (see Sect. 2.2) and it also supplies features for the transition classifier to predict the next transition action at the time t.

$$x_{st}, c_t = \mathrm{LSTM}(c_{t-1}, state_t) \tag{11}$$

3 Classification and Training

In this work, we combine the nuclearity and relation together, obtaining a set of NR labels. We build two classifiers in this paper for transition and NR classification. For the first classifier, we use the hidden state $i = x_{st}$ of the state tracker as its input at the time t. For the second, we use the hidden states of the two text spans encoded by R-IFGM as additional inputs for the NR tags are assigned directly between them. And the overall input is defined as $i' = [x_{st}; h_{span_l}; h_{span_r}]$. For each classifier, we feed these vectors into respective output layers:

$$y_s = \tanh(W_s i + b_s) \tag{12}$$

$$y_{nr} = \tanh(W_{nr} i' + b_{nr}) \tag{13}$$

where $W_s \in \mathbb{R}^l$, $W_{nr} \in \mathbb{R}^{m \times l'}$, $b_s \in \mathbb{R}$, $b_{nr} \in \mathbb{R}^m$ are model parameters, $m = 41$ is the number of combinations of nuclear and relation tags in RST-DT.

For transition classification, we expect the output score of the correct label to be much larger than the wrong one. And, we set a max-margin value as a threshold for this difference. For the NR classifier, we train it to maximize the conditional log-likelihood of gold labels. During training, the two classifiers are trained according to their respective goals and update the shared parameters alternatively. We add an additional max-margin objective to strengthen the nuclearity classification. And the general training objective is defined as:

$$\mathcal{L}(\Theta) = -\log(p_{nr_g}) + \frac{\lambda}{2}\|\Theta\|^2 + \frac{\Sigma_{i=0}^{l_{y_s}}\max(0, M - y_{s_g} + y_{s_i})}{l_{y_s}} + \zeta\frac{\Sigma_{i=0}^{l_{y_n}}\max(0, M - y_{n_g} + y_{n_i})}{l_{y_n}} \quad (14)$$

where p_{nr_g} is the softmax probability of the gold relation label, $l_{y_s} = 2$, $l_{y_n} = 3$ are the sizes of transition and nuclearity prediction, and M is the margin value.

4 Experimentation

The RST-DT corpus annotates 385 documents from the WSJ which is mainly divided into two data sets (347 for training and 38 for testing). Following previous works, we binarize those non-binary subtrees with right-branching and use the 18 coarse-grained relations to evaluate our parser with gold-standard EDUs.

4.1 Experimental Settings

The metrics of RST discourse parsing evaluation include span, nuclearity and relation indication. Moery *et al.* [12] prove that most gains reported in recent publications are an artefact of implicit difference in evaluation procedures, and the original RST-Parseval overestimates the performance of discourse parsing. In this work, we randomly select 34 documents from the training set as the development set and employ a more stringent metric [12] to evaluate our parser. For fair comparison, scores we report are micro-averaged F_1 scores in default.

We optimized following parameters during training: the learning rate is 0.001, the dropout rate is 0.2, the dimension of POS tags is 50, the hidden size of R-IFGM is 640. The l_2 regularization parameter and the parameter ζ in the loss function are set by 10^{-5} and 0.6 respectively. We use word representation based on the 1024D vectors provided by ELMo [13] and we do not update the vectors during training. The model is trained with Adam to minimize the loss objective. We trained the model iteratively on the training set by 10 rounds. The development corpus was used to choose the best model and the final model was evaluated on the test set after parameter tuning.

4.2 Experimental Results

We show three groups of comparisons here to illustrate the results of our experiments with respect to span (S), nuclearity (N), relation (R) and full (F).

Table 1. Performance comparison for different settings of our system.

System setting	S	N	R	F
Baseline	67.9	55.3	43.5	43.2
R-IFGM	68.2	57.7	46.1	45.7

Table 2. Performance comparison for different approaches (borrowed from [12]).

Parser	S	N	R	F
Feng and Hirst [5]	**68.6**	55.9	45.8	44.6
Ji and Eisenstein [7]	64.1	54.2	**46.8**	**46.3**
Joty *et al.* [8]	65.1	55.5	45.1	44.3
Hayashi *et al.* [6]	65.1	54.6	44.7	44.1
Braud *et al.* [4]	59.5	47.2	34.7	34.3
Li *et al.* [10]	64.5	54.0	38.1	36.6
Braud *et al.* [3]	62.7	54.5	45.5	45.1
Ours	68.2	**57.7**	46.1	45.7

Comparison with the Baseline Model. Inspired by Li *et al.* [9] and Li *et al.* [10], we select the Tree-LSTM as our baseline model. This is done by manually setting λ and γ equal to zero, and other settings are consistent with R-IFGM. Then, we let the model to decide the value of λ and γ automatically. From the comparison in Table 1, the information flows of us is useful and the performance on nuclearity and relation indication is greatly improved by using R-IFGM to compute the representation of each text span. In particular, we analyze how the model assigns weights for these information flows in Sect. 4.3.

Comparison with Other Systems. We compare our parser with seven parsers mentioned in [12] using the same evaluation metrics, and one can refer to the paper for more details. As shown in Table 2, we divide these systems into systems based on traditional methods and neural networks. From the results, systems in the first group are competitive with systems in the second group. Our parser is also based on neural network methods and it can strongly outperform other systems in nuclearity detection. The scores of ours in span and relation are relatively lower than the corresponding best results but better than most parsers. It is worth emphasizing that we exclude these complicated features others use in the aim to show the effect of the deep learning model itself.

In this work, we propose the R-IFGM model aiming to improve the model of Li *et al.* [9] and Li *et al.* [10]. Therefore, we compare with their works to further evaluate the performance of our method. Unfortunately, Moery *et al.* [12] replicate nine parsers in their paper except the parser of Li *et al.* [9]. Therefore, we use the same evaluation metrics used in [9] and [10] to examine the effect of our model, and the performance of their parsers is borrowed from

Table 3. Performance comparison with models of Li *et al.* [9] and Li *et al.* [10].

Parser	S	N	R
Li *et al.* [9]	82.4	69.2	56.8
Li *et al.* [10]	84.2	70.0	56.3
Ours	85.1	71.4	58.1

published results. For fair comparison, we employ the same word embeddings as Li *et al.* [10], and the overall performance is reported in Table 3. From the results, our proposed model can outperform the two parsers in span, nuclearity and relation detection, which further proves the effectiveness of our model.

4.3 Analysis

Why the R-IFGM can help improve RST discourse parsing? To answer this question, we count the distribution of text spans' EDU numbers and find that about a quarter of text spans contain more than 7 EDUs. In addition, the longest document in RST-DT contains 304 EDUs and each document contains about 56 EDUs on average. In this condition, we give another statistic about the averaged proportion of each information flow with respect to the EDU number, as shown in Fig. 3. We assume that the more EDUs a text span has, the higher level of granularity the text span has. The figure shows that when the EDU number becomes larger, the proportion of structure information gets lower and the model will pay more attention to the state transition information and the text span's principal component.

General recursive deep models usually suffer from gradient vanishing. The baseline model of us works like a traditional Tree-LSTM model. It itself can store long distance information and thus effectively avoid gradient vanishing. To show the difference between the proposed R-IFGM and the baseline model, we give another statistic about the precision of span, nuclearity and relation

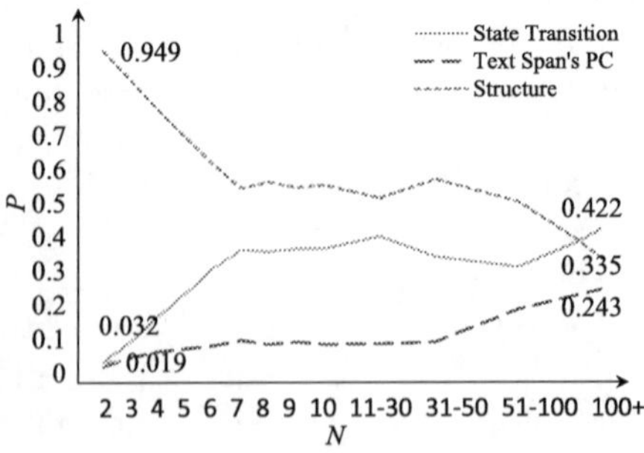

Fig. 3. The averaged proportion (P) of each information flow with respect to the EDU number (N) of each text span.

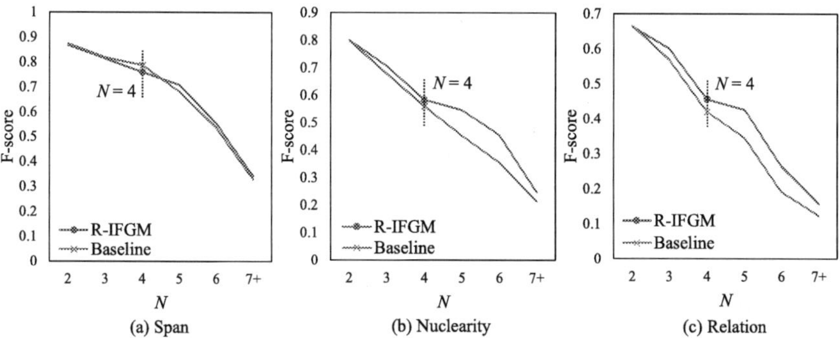

Fig. 4. The performance of our parser over text spans with different EDU numbers.

detection for text spans with respect to the number of EDUs, as shown in Fig. 4. In the prediction of text spans with less than 5 EDUs, the superiority of the proposed R-IFGM is not obvious and it is even worse than the baseline model in span detection. The statistic shows that when the number of EDUs becomes larger, the proposed R-IFGM performs relatively better. This superiority is evident in nuclearity and relation detection. From the statistic, we can draw an experimental conclusion that the proposed model has the ability to grade the information flows according to the granularity of each text span, and thus enable it to understand a document from different perspectives.

5 Related Work

Discourse parsing has largely concentrated on the RST-DT, which is the largest corpus of documents annotated with discourse structures. Early works on discourse parsing rely mainly on hand-crafted features [5,7,8]. Among these studies, SVM and variants of CRF models are mostly employed, and lexical, syntactic and semantic features are heavily used. With the increasing popularity of DNNs, there exist some neural network-based discourse parsers. Li *et al.* [9] firstly propose to build a recursive deep model in discourse parsing. Braud *et al.* [4] use a heuristic method to constrain their proposed seq2seq parser to build trees. Li *et al.* [10] build a CKY chart parser with the attention-based hierarchical Bi-LSTM. The parser proposed by Braud *et al.* [3] is a variant of the transition-based parser with a number of sophisticated features.

Inspired by Li *et al.* [9], we build a recursive deep model to generate representations for text spans. This recursive framework computes the representation for each parent based on its children recursively in a bottom-up fashion. However, recursive deep models are known to suffer from gradient vanishing. Li *et al.* [10] propose to employ an attention-based hierarchical Bi-LSTM to alleviate this problem. Nevertheless, it is hard for sequence LSTMs to provide discourse structure information. In this work, we absorb the advantages of both Li *et al.* [9] and Li *et al.* [10], and propose a TreeLSTM-style discourse parser.

In particular, humans tend to understand macro and micro texts from different perspectives and the documents in RST-DT are known to have quite deep structures. Therefore, we introduce the R-IFGM to synthetically grade the information flows of us automatically according to the granularity of each text span.

6 Conclusion

We propose a transition-based discourse parser based on a recursive deep model. The R-IFGM of us can fuse multiple information flows according to the granularity of each text span to enrich the representation for text spans. Compared with previous works, our parser obtains competitive performance under stringent discourse parsing evaluations. Our future work will focus on extending text-level discourse parsing to related tasks like macro-sentiment analysis.

Acknowledgements. This work is supported by Artificial Intelligence Emergency Project 61751206 under the National Natural Science Foundation of China, and Project 61876118 under the National Natural Science Foundation of China.

References

1. Arora, S., Liang, Y., Ma, T.: A simple but tough-to-beat baseline for sentence embeddings. In: Proceedings of ICLR (2016)
2. Bowman, S.R., Gauthier, J., Rastogi, A., Gupta, R., Manning, C.D., Potts, C.: A fast unified model for parsing and sentence understanding. arXiv preprint: arXiv:1603.06021 (2016)
3. Braud, C., Coavoux, M., Søgaard, A.: Cross-lingual RST discourse parsing. arXiv preprint: arXiv:1701.02946 (2017)
4. Braud, C., Plank, B., Søgaard, A.: Multi-view and multi-task training of RST discourse parsers. In: Proceedings of COLING 2016, pp. 1903–1913 (2016)
5. Feng, V.W., Hirst, G.: A linear-time bottom-up discourse parser with constraints and post-editing. In: Proceedings of the 52nd ACL, vol. 1, pp. 511–521 (2014)
6. Hayashi, K., Hirao, T., Nagata, M.: Empirical comparison of dependency conversions for RST discourse trees. In: Proceedings of the 17th SIGDIAL, pp. 128–136 (2016)
7. Ji, Y., Eisenstein, J.: Representation learning for text-level discourse parsing. In: Proceedings of the 52nd ACL, vol. 1, pp. 13–24 (2014)
8. Joty, S., Carenini, G., Ng, R.T.: Codra: a novel discriminative framework for rhetorical analysis. Comput. Linguist. **41**(3), 385–435 (2015)
9. Li, J., Li, R., Hovy, E.: Recursive deep models for discourse parsing. In: Proceedings of EMNLP 2014, pp. 2061–2069 (2014)
10. Li, Q., Li, T., Chang, B.: Discourse parsing with attention-based hierarchical neural networks. In: Proceedings of EMNLP 2016, pp. 362–371 (2016)
11. Mann, W.C., Thompson, S.A.: Rhetorical structure theory: toward a functional theory of text organization. Text Interdiscip. J. Study Discourse **8**(3), 243–281 (1988)
12. Morey, M., Muller, P., Asher, N.: A dependency perspective on RST discourse parsing and evaluation. Comput. Linguist. **44**, 198–235 (2018)

13. Peters, M.E., et al.: Deep contextualized word representations. arXiv preprint: arXiv:1802.05365 (2018)
14. Zhu, X., Sobihani, P., Guo, H.: Long short-term memory over recursive structures. In: ICML 2015, pp. 1604–1612 (2015)

Relation Classification in Scientific Papers Based on Convolutional Neural Network

Zhongbo Yin[1], Shuai Wu[1], Yi Yin[2], Wei Luo[1(✉)], Zhunchen Luo[1], Yushani Tan[1], Xiangyu Jiao[3], and Dong Wang[4]

[1] Academy of Military Science, Beijing 100142, China
lwowen79@gmail.com
[2] Haiyan County Xiangyang Primary School, Jiaxing 314300, China
[3] JiLin University, Changchun 130012, China
[4] Information Engineering University, Zhengzhou 450000, China

Abstract. Scientific papers are important for scholars to track trends in specific research areas. With the increase in the number of scientific papers, it is difficult for scholars to read all the papers to extract emerging or noteworthy knowledge. Paper modeling can help scholars master the key information in scientific papers, and relation classification (RC) between entity pairs is a major approach to paper modeling. To the best of our knowledge, most of the state-of-the-art RC methods are using entire sentence's context information as input. However, long sentences have too much noise information, which is useless for classification. In this paper, a flexible context is selected as the input information for convolution neural network (CNN), which greatly reduces the noise. Moreover, we find that entity type is another important feature for RC. Based on these findings, we construct a typical CNN architecture to learn features from raw texts automatically, and use a softmax function to classify the entity pairs. Our experiment on SemEval-2018 task 7 dataset yields a macro-F1 value of 83.91%, ranking first among all participants.

Keywords: Relation classification · Convolution neural network · Scientific paper modeling · Entity type · Context scope

1 Introduction

As the main source of recording new technology, mining scientific papers is a common method to track the progress of research. In most cases, scholars cannot read all of papers to extract noteworthy aspects in their research field. Information extraction (IE), including named entity recognition (NER) and relation extraction (RE), is a primary NLP method for analyzing scientific papers. This paper focuses on relation classification (RC, sub-method of RE) between entities in scientific papers. Relation classification can be used to predict the relations

Z. Yin, S. Wu and Y. Yin have equal contribution to this paper.

J. Tang et al. (Eds.): NLPCC 2019, LNAI 11839, pp. 242–253, 2019.
https://doi.org/10.1007/978-3-030-32236-6_21

between entity pairs [16]. For example, the following sentence contains an example of the **Part-Whole** relation between entity pairs: **corpus-sentences**.

The <e1>corpus</e1> consists of seven hundred semantically neural <e2> sentences</e2>.

Most traditional RC methods rely on handcrafted features or additional NLP tools to extract lexical features [6,12,15]. However, this is time consuming and leads to error propagation. In addition, the traditional RC approaches use a large number of pairwise similarity features (eg, matching characters, word n-grams or co-occurrence subsequences) to measure textual semantic similarity. But these features may be difficult to represent syntactic information, which is more important for analyzing relations between entities.

In order to represent the syntactic information between entities, some DNN-based methods have been proposed and achieved remarkable results [3,8,14]. Since SemEval-2010 task 8 provides a benchmark for classifying relations between target nominals in a given sentences set, quite a number of DNN-based RC methods have been optimized and developed. Daojian's work [16] is the most representative progress, it builds a new CNN architecture for RC. They use convolution networks to extract lexical and sentence level features, then feed them into softmax classifier. Furthermore, Qin's work [8] proposes a stacked neural network model in which CNN is used for sentence modeling, and a feature extraction collaborative gated neural network (CGNN) is proposed.

This paper is based on the work of Pengda [9] which deals RC with a CNN architecture to automatically control feature learning from raw sentences and minimize the application of external toolkits and resources. As Daojian [16] proposes an entity position feature to highlight the entity's function in RC, it uses several additional dimensions following each word's embedding to represent the relative distances from the current word to the first and second entity. Since the position feature's dimension (e.g. 5 or 10) is much smaller than word embedding's (e.g. 100 or 300), it will disappear during the excessive training times.

Thus, we use Pengda's Entity Tag Feature [9] to emphasize the entity pair information, which uses the tagged words (*<e1s>*, *<e1e>*, *<e2s>*, *<e2e>*) to indicate start and end position features of entities. Unlike Daojian's work, these tag words are represented as independent word embedding to avoid the disappeared problem.

To the best of our knowledge, most previous DNN-based methods used entire sentence's information as the context for extracting features for RC [13], [?]. However, our goal is RC rather than sentence classification. Even if using position or entity tag feature to highlight the entity function, it still exists a lot of noise for long sentences. In previous works, many researchers just used the context between two entities, which got a remarkable performance promotion [9]. However, sometimes, when there are few context words between two entities, semantic information cannot be detected. Therefore, we propose a flexible context scope selection algorithm that has achieved significant improvements in experiment.

What's more, inspired by Schwartz's work [10], we consider the entity type to be a useful feature for RC. For example, the **Compare** relation may mean that ***X is compared to Y***, where X or Y have the same entity type, such as two technologies or two models. Therefore, we attempt to include the type feature into feature set and achieve better RC performance.

2 Methodology

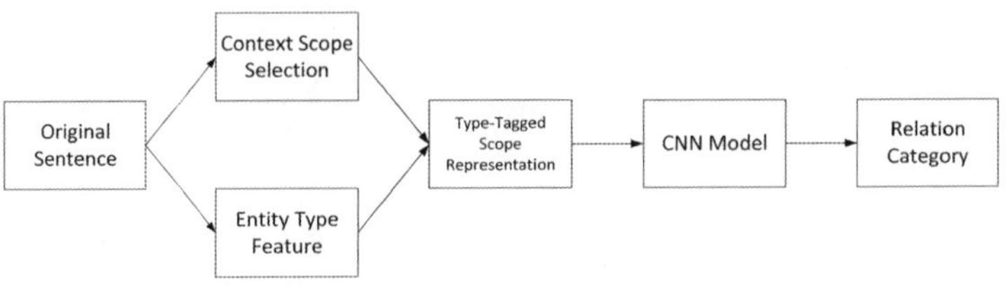

Fig. 1. Relation classification framework

Our RC framework is shown in Fig. 1. First, we select the scope of context words and construct an entity type dictionary to map the entity into a specific type item. To represent the tagged type and scope information, we convert all of them into word embeddings. Then, all the embeddings will be transmitted to three convolution networks with kernel sizes are 3, 4 and 5 respectively. Finally, the three convolution outputs are pooled into the same dimensional vector, which will be concatenated as an input to the softmax relation classifier.

2.1 Context Scope Selection

Most of the existing DNN-based methods use entire sentence context words embedding as input. As the following sentence, there is a **Compare** relation between ***bag-of-words method*** and ***segment order-sensitive methods***. However, the sub sentences before <*e1s*> and after <*e2e*> have little relevance to the target relation category. Notwithstanding, the sub sentence between <*e1s*> and <*e2e*> has more relevance information to the target relation.

Further, in their optimum configuration, < e1s > *bag − of − wordsmethod* < e1e > *areequivalentto* < e2s > *segmentorder − sensitivemethods* < e2e > *in terms of retrieval accuracy, but much faster.*

As a result, we propose a flexible and suitable context scope selection algorithm. Firstly, we select the words of entity pair's names and the intermediate words as the major context. Then, we notice that the major context feature is too weak when there are few intermediate words between entity pair. Actually, we got the worst classification performance while the intermediate words number smaller than 2 in experiment. In such a case, we extend context scope before the first entity and after the second entity while the number of words in the

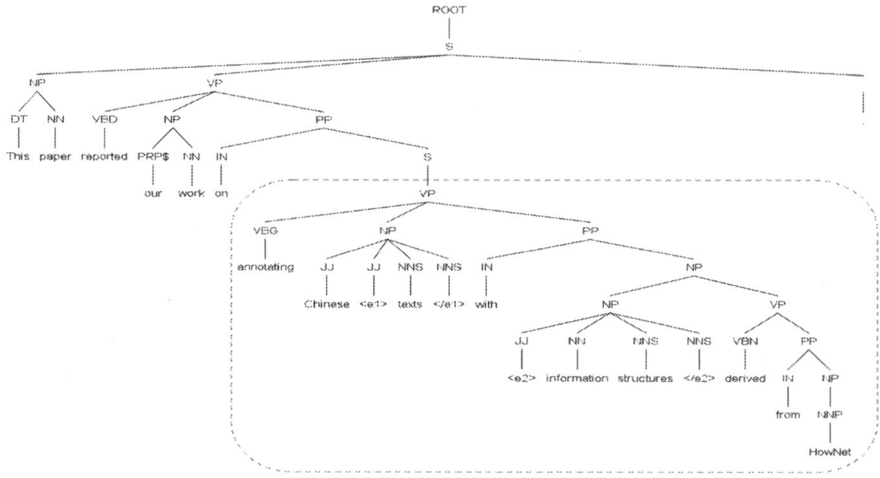

Fig. 2. Context selection procedure

middle is smaller than 2. The specific **Context Selection** section's procedure in Fig. 1 is depicted in Fig. 2. We use the Stanford NLP group's parser[1] to parse the sentence with compositional vector Grammar and select the minimal sub tree (sentence) containing the major context as the extend context [5].

2.2 Entity Type Feature

Some relation categories are closely related to entity types. For instance, the **Compare** relation is usually used to describe the similarity between two entities which have the same type, such as two ***models*** or two ***technologies***. Moreover, at least one entity of the **Result** relation is ***Measurement*** type such as *accuracy*, *precision* and *recall*. Therefore, the RC performance will be improved if we include the entity type into feature set.

To determine the entity type, we build an entity type vocabulary in computational linguistic domain. This vocabulary is based on the ACL Anthology Reference Corpus [2] which contains lots of scholarly publications about computational linguistics. Furthermore, Behrang [7] manually annotated thousands of term's type in this ACL Corpus. In the Behrang's work, terms are annotated with one of the 7 types: **technology, system, language resources, language resources (specific product), model, measurement and other**. We use these term-type pairs to build the original entity type vocabulary. Then, the original vocabulary is filtered and expanded by some prior language knowledge.

[1] https://nlp.stanford.edu/software/lex-parser.html.

Table 1. Samples of entity type vocabulary

Entity	Type	Entity	Type
human-computer interaction	technology	WordNet	language resources product
bayesian network	technology	Reuters-21578	language resources product
NLTK	tool	n-gram model	model
Stanford Core NLP	tool	maximum entropy model	model
dictionary	language resources	BLEU	measurement
syntactic rule	language resources	F-score	measurement

The original vocabulary contains 2583 manual annotated entity-type pairs. It contains 762 overlap pairs and 770 **Other** pairs. After filtering out these pairs, we receive a vocabulary containing 1024 entity-type pairs. Then we use SemEval-2018 task 7.1.1 training set [11] to expand the vocabulary. We have two rules. First, we believe that the entity pair for **Compare** relation have the same entity type. Second, there are at least one entity's type is *Measurement* in **Result** relation's entity pair. After expanding by these rules, we receive a vocabulary containing 1654 entity-type pairs. Some instances in the vocabulary are listed in Table 1.

2.3 CNN Architecture

As depicted in Fig. 3, our relation classification convolutional neural network (RCNN) structure contains four steps: vector representation, convolution, pooling and classifying. In the vector representation step, all of the words selected in context scope selection and entity type setting parts are mapped into 300-dimensions vector. At the same time, we keep only the last 50 words of the sentence if the sentence contains more than 50 words. We add additional padding vector while the sentence's words smaller than 50. In the convolution step, the selected vector are delivered into three CNNs whose kernel size are 3, 4 and 5 respectively. It means that all the 3-grams, 4-grams and 5-grams features will be

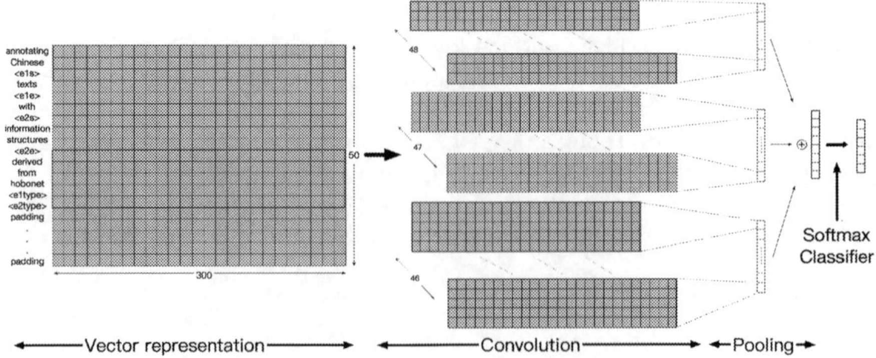

Fig. 3. Convolutional neural network for relation classification

considered. To normalize different length of each input sentence, the convolution output will be pooled into the same dimensional vector space. Finally, we use the multi-class classifier softmax to classify the instance into a specific relation category.

Table 2. Hyper-parameters used in our experiment

Embedding-dim	Batch-size	Dropout	Learning-rate	Classifier	Max-sentence	Kernel-size
300	30	0.5	1e-4	Softmax	50	3,4,5

The experiment settings are listed in Table 2, we use the Wikipedia general English 300-dimensional embedding which contains 408 million words[2] to represent the words in the context. The experiments results show that the hyper-parameters in the Table 2 gains the most good performance.

3 Experiment

3.1 Dataset

We use SemEval-2018 task7.1.1 dataset [11] which contains titles and abstracts of scientific papers in computational linguistic domain. Six predefined semantic relations are manually annotated in this dataset. It contains 1248 training and 355 testing examples. As in Table 3, in the training set, every instance is classified into one of the following relations: Usage, Result, Model-Feature, Part-Whole, Topic, Compare.

Table 3. Samples of semantic relations

Relation	Explanation
Part-Whole	X is a part or component of Y
Model-Feature	X is a model, feature or characteristic of Y
Result	X yields Y (e.g. improvement or decrease)
Usage	X (e.g. method, tool) is used for Y (e.g. task, data, system)
Compare	X is compared to Y (e.g. two systems, feature sets or results)
Topic	X (e.g. author, paper) puts forward Y (e.g. san idea, an approach)

[2] https://www.cs.york.ac.uk/nlp/extvec/wiki_extvec.gz.

3.2 Effect of New Context Scope

The results in Table 4 are acquired in different context scopes and whether using type feature. The precision is higher than recall in each experiment. Additionally, major context scope's classification performance is better than entire sentence scope. It shows that the major context (entity pair names and words between them) contains more accurate and cleaner semantic information than entire sentence context as for RC. Further more, our flexible context achieve a better performance than major context which scores the best macro-F1: 83.27. By analyzing the specific instances of these experiments, we find that many wrong predicted long sentence instances in entire sentence context (context1) have been corrected in major context (context2) and our flexible context (context3) experiment as in Table 5. Additionally, some wrong predicted instances in context2 which are few words between entity pairs have been corrected in context3.

Table 4. Results for changing scope and adding type feature

Feature	Precision	Recall	macro-F1
entire sentence scope	64.56	57.24	60.68
+type feature	65.78	59.24	62.34
major context scope	76.50	63.58	69.44
+type feature	77.06	66.32	71.29
flexible context scope	87.10	77.39	81.96
+type feature	**89.01**	**78.23**	**83.27**

Table 5. Context scope selection experiment result examples

Sentence	Scope	Prediction	True/False
We present an implementation of the model based on finite-state models, demonstrate the <e1s> model's <e1e> ability to significantly reduce <e2s> character and word error rate <e2e>, and provide evaluation results involving automatic extraction of translation.	context1	Compare	False
	context2	Result	True
	context3	Result	True
With its higher-order <e1> representations </e1> of <e2> contexts </e2> , TDL analyzes and describes the inher- ently inter-sentential nature of quantification and anaphora in a strictly lexicalized and compositional manner .	context1	Part-Whole	False
	context2	Part-Whole	False
	context3	Model-Feature	True

3.3 Effect of Entity Type Information

As in Table 4, all of the comparison experiments get promotion when we add entity type embedding to the original feature set. As in Table 6, the wrong prediction is corrected when the entity type feature has been included into feature set. The experiment performance promotion prove that the type feature we proposed is helpful for identifying the semantic relation between two entities in RC.

Table 6. Type feature experiment result examples

Sentence	Type	Prediction	True/False
Experiments with the TREC2003 and TREC- 2004 QA tracks indicate that <e1s> rankings <e1e> produced by our metric correlate highly with <e2s>official rankings<e2e>, and that POURPRE outperforms direct application of existing metrics.	None	Model-Feature	False
	Yes	Compare	True

As depicted in Fig. 4, every word in the selected input sentence is mapped into embedding before deliver to CNN.As in word representation step, except the general word embedding, the entity tag (*<e1s>*, *<e1e>*, *<e2s>*, *<e2e>*) also mapped into embeddings. Additionally, the last two green embeddings are used to encode entity type features. For a bit more promotion, we use entity tag feature to substitute entity position feature (*<e1s>*, *<e1e>*, *<e2s>*, *<e2e>*) to explore the representation improvements. RCNN-ST means relation classification CNN in Sect. 3.1 with flexible context scope and type feature. As Fig. 4, we develop three schemes to distribute the type feature on the sentence side(RCNN-STa), double around entity(RCNN-STb) and single around entity(RCNN-STc). For these adjustments, we get the classification performance as Table 7. To our surprise, we get much promotion while the type position adjust to both side and single side around entity.

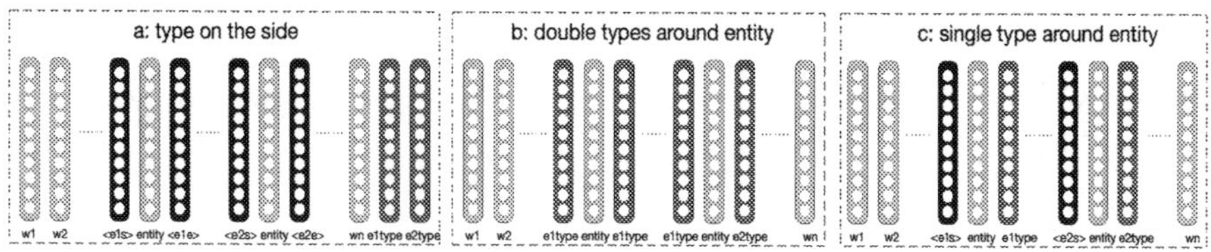

Fig. 4. Type feature position setting

Table 7. Results for testing type position feature

RCNN-STa	RCNN-STb	RCNN-STc
83.27	83.51	83.91

3.4 Comparison Experiment

This experiment compares our RCNN-STc approach with three state-of-art neural models (Dongxu (2015) [17], Daojian (2014) [16], Pengda (2016) [9]). The feature set they used is listed in Table 8. The results are shown in Fig. 5. As we can see, our RCNN-STc approach gets the best results in every training samples proportion.

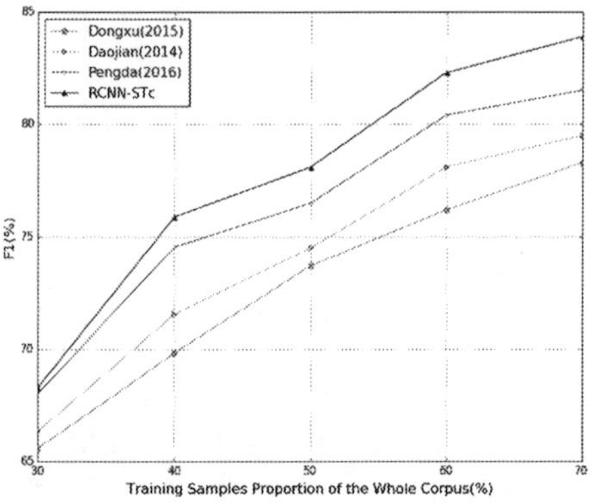

Fig. 5. Results for compare with other methods

3.5 Generalization on Different Datasets

We use two more different datasets to test our method. One is the dataset provided by SemEval-2010 Task 8. There are 9 directional relations and an additional **other** relation, resulting in 19 relation classes in total [4]. The second dataset is a revision of MIML-RE annotation dataset, provided by Gabor [1]. They use both the 2010 and 2013 KBP official document collections, as well as a July 2013 dump of Wikipedia as the text corpus for annotation. We test our RCNN and RCNN-STc on these datasets. The relation classification results is depicted in Fig. 6.

Table 8. Feature sets of comparison method

Classifier	Feature sets
Daojian(2014)	word embedding(dim=50), position feature, Wordnet
Dongxu(2015)	word embedding(dim=300), position feature, position indicators
Pengda(2016)	word embedding(dim=300), entity tag
RCNN-STc	word embedding(dim=300), entity tag, context selection, entity type

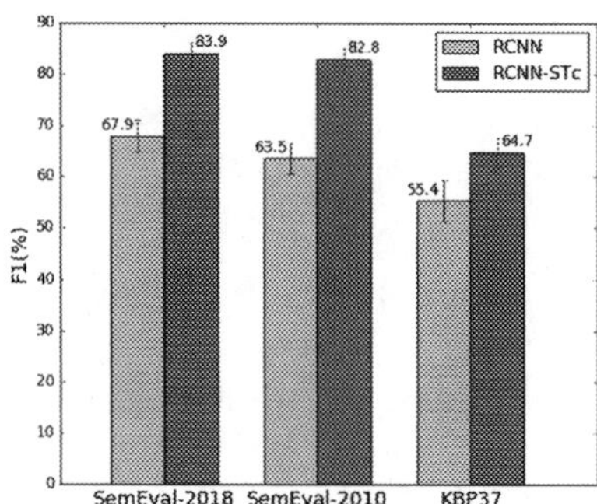

Fig. 6. Results for comparison in different datasets

4 Conclusion

The contributions of this paper can be summarized as follows: Firstly, we construct a typical CNN architecture for RC without sophisticated NLP preprocessing. Secondly, we explore a flexible scope context input for CNN, which extremely reduce the useless context's noise influence. Thirdly, we build an entity type vocabulary and add the type embedding into feature set, which enhance the entity's semantic representation consequently. At last, we discuss the way to feed CNN with type feature position embedding, which transmitting more original sequence information. Finally, our proposed method gets 83.91% macro-F1 value and ranks first in SemEval-2018 task 7.

Acknowledgements. Firstly, we would like to thank Bin Mao, Changhai Tian and Yuming Ye for their valuable suggestions on the initial version of this paper, which have helped a lot to improve the paper. Secondly, we want to express gratitudes to the anonymous reviewers for their hard work and kind comments, which will further improve our work in the future. Additionally, this work was supported by the National Natural Science Foundation of China (No. 61602490).

References

1. Angeli, G., Tibshirani, J., Wu, J., Manning, C.D.: Combining distant and partial supervision for relation extraction. In: Proceedings of the 2014 Conference on Empirical Methods in Natural Language Processing (EMNLP), pp. 1556–1567 (2014)
2. Bird, S., et al.: The ACL anthology reference corpus: a reference dataset for bibliographic research in computational linguistics (2008)
3. Guo, J., Che, W., Wang, H., Liu, T., Xu, J.: A unified architecture for semantic role labeling and relation classification. In: Proceedings of COLING 2016, the 26th International Conference on Computational Linguistics: Technical Papers, pp. 1264–1274 (2016)
4. Hendrickx, I., et al.: Semeval-2010 task 8: multi-way classification of semantic relations between pairs of nominals. In: Proceedings of the Workshop on Semantic Evaluations: Recent Achievements and Future Directions, pp. 94–99. Association for Computational Linguistics (2009)
5. Klein, D., Manning, C.D.: Accurate unlexicalized parsing. In: Proceedings of the 41st Annual Meeting of the Association For Computational Linguistics (2003)
6. Kozareva, Z.: Cause-effect relation learning. In: Workshop Proceedings of TextGraphs-7 on Graph-Based Methods for Natural Language Processing, pp. 39–43. Association for Computational Linguistics (2012)
7. QasemiZadeh, B., Schumann, A.K.: The ACL RD-TEC 2.0: a language resource for evaluating term extraction and entity recognition methods. In: LREC (2016)
8. Qin, L., Zhang, Z., Zhao, H.: A stacking gated neural architecture for implicit discourse relation classification. In: Proceedings of the 2016 Conference on Empirical Methods in Natural Language Processing, pp. 2263–2270 (2016)
9. Qin, P., Xu, W., Guo, J.: An empirical convolutional neural network approach for semantic relation classification. Neurocomputing **190**, 1–9 (2016)
10. Schwartz, R., Reichart, R., Rappoport, A.: Minimally supervised classification to semantic categories using automatically acquired symmetric patterns. In: Proceedings of COLING 2014, the 25th International Conference on Computational Linguistics: Technical Papers, pp. 1612–1623 (2014)
11. SemEval2018: Semeval (2018). https://competitions.codalab.org/competitions/17422
12. Surdeanu, M., Tibshirani, J., Nallapati, R., Manning, C.D.: Multi-instance multi-label learning for relation extraction. In: Proceedings of the 2012 Joint Conference on Empirical Methods in Natural Language Processing and Computational Natural Language Learning, pp. 455–465. Association for Computational Linguistics (2012)
13. Xu, K., Feng, Y., Huang, S., Zhao, D.: Semantic relation classification via convolutional neural networks with simple negative sampling. arXiv preprint: arXiv:1506.07650 (2015)
14. Yin, Z., et al.: IRCMS at SemEval-2018 task 7: evaluating a basic CNN method and traditional pipeline method for relation classification. In: Proceedings of the 12th International Workshop on Semantic Evaluation, New Orleans, Louisiana, pp. 811–815. Association for Computational Linguistics, June 2018. https://doi.org/10.18653/v1/S18-1129, https://www.aclweb.org/anthology/S18-1129
15. Yin, Z., Tang, J., Ru, C., Wei, L., Luo, Z., Ma, X.: A semantic representation enhancement method for Chinese news headline classification (2017)

16. Zeng, D., Liu, K., Lai, S., Zhou, G., Zhao, J.: Relation classification via convolutional deep neural network. In: Proceedings of COLING 2014, the 25th International Conference on Computational Linguistics: Technical Papers, pp. 2335–2344 (2014)
17. Zhang, D., Wang, D.: Relation classification via recurrent neural network. arXiv preprint: arXiv:1508.01006 (2015)

Effective Soft-Adaptation for Neural Machine Translation

Shuangzhi Wu[1(✉)], Dongdong Zhang[2], and Ming Zhou[2]

[1] Harbin Institute of Technology, Harbin, China
wushuangzhi2010@163.com
[2] Microsoft Research Asia, Beijing, China
{dozhang,mingzhou}@microsoft.com

Abstract. Domain mismatch between training data and test data often degrades translation quality. It is necessary to make domain adaptation for machine translation tasks. In this paper, we propose a novel method to tackle Neural Machine Translation (NMT) domain adaptation issue, where a soft-domain adapter (SDA) is added in the encoder-decoder NMT framework. Our SDA automatically learns domain representations from the training corpus, and dynamically compute domain-aware context for inputs which can guide the decoder to generate domain-aware translations. Our method can softly leverage domain information to translate source sentences, which can not only improve the translation quality on specific domain but also be robust and scalable on different domains. Experiments on Chinese-English and English-French tasks show that our proposed method can significantly improve the translation quality of in-domain test sets, without performance sacrifice of out-of-domain/general-domain data sets.

Keywords: Domain adaptation · Machine translation

1 Introduction

Neural machine translation (NMT) have been proved to be the current most effective approach to the machine translation task, which basically works in an attention-based encoder-decoder framework. Similar with the situation in statistical machine translation (SMT), NMT approach still suffers from the domain adaptation problem. Its performance degrades when domain mismatches between training data and test data. Motivated by previous work on domain adaptation for SMT, most existing work on NMT domain adaptation mainly focuses on either the data adaptation or the model adaptation.

Data adaptation can be performed either by data selection or instance weighting. For example, [18] revisited the instance weighting method in SMT and adapted it to NMT by assigning more weights on in-domain data and less weights on out-of-domain data in the objective function. This resulted in translation quality improvement on in-domain data but drop on out-of-domain data.

J. Tang et al. (Eds.): NLPCC 2019, LNAI 11839, pp. 254–264, 2019.
https://doi.org/10.1007/978-3-030-32236-6_22

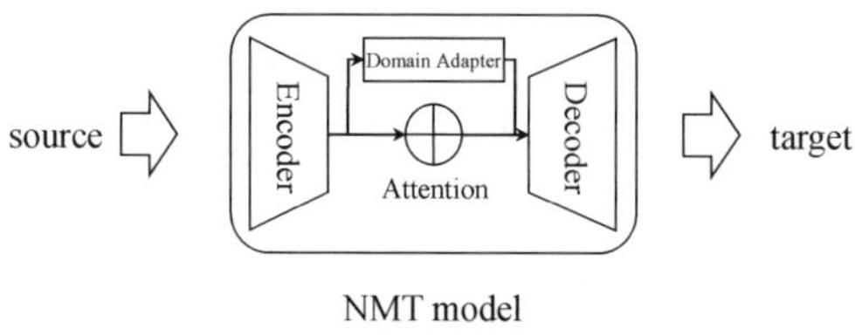

Fig. 1. Global overview of our model architecture.

Model adaptation tries to transfer the model parameters to in-domain. In the work by [6,9,15], NMT models were pre-trained over out-of-domain or general-domain data sets, followed by continuous training over in-domain corpus so that the model parameters can be fine-tuned towards in-domain test sets. To avoid the overfitting in the in-domain training stage, [5] proposed to train NMT models with the mixture of pre-tagged training corpus where domain-specified tags were associated with source instances. They used oversampling to balance the proportion of in-domain and out-of-domain data. In the evaluation, the inputs also needed to be tagged into correct domains before performing translation.

These NMT domain adaptation approaches mostly concentrate on improving the effect of the small scale in-domain corpus when training NMT models. The more the in-domain training corpus affects the NMT model, the better performance could be achieved on in-domain testsets. They are a kind of static domain adaptation strategy, where prior domain types of inputs are needed before translating. In many practical translation tasks, the inputs always come from different domains and the domain information of each input may be not clearly described or hard to be captured. Previous methods are not robust and scalable enough to tackle cases like this. In addition, previous methods mostly focus on training models with translation quality improvement on in-domain test sets.

In this paper, we propose a dynamic domain adaptation approach for NMT, in which a novel soft-domain adapter (SDA) is introduced. Our SDA can learn domain representations from the training corpus. In decoding, SDA can dynamically generate domain context for each input sentences based on the encoder states and domain representations. As shown in Fig. 1, on the basis of normal encoder-decoder NMT framework, there is an SDA consuming the encoder outputs to compute domain context of source inputs. Then, the decoder is fed with both the domain context and attention information to generate target translations. With SDA, our NMT decoder can softly leverage domain information to guide domain-aware translations. Therefore, our method belongs to a dynamic domain adaptation strategy, which not only can improve the translation quality of specific domain, but also can be scalable to multiple domains even without prior domain knowledge. We conducted the experiments on benchmark data sets of IWSLT2014 English-French and IWSLT2015 Chinese-English translation tasks. Experimental results show that our model significantly improves translation qualities on the in-domain test sets compared with NMT baselines and outperforms most of state-of-the-art methods.

2 NMT Background

NMT is an end-to-end framework [1,16] which directly models the conditional probability $P(Y|X)$ of target translation $Y = y_1, y_2, \ldots, y_n$ given source sentence $X = x_1, x_2, \ldots, x_m$, where m and n are source and target length respectively. An NMT model consists of two parts: an encoder and a decoder. Both of them utilize recurrent neural networks (RNN) which can be a Long Short-Term Memory (LSTM) [7] or a Gated Recurrent Unit (GRU) [4] in practice. In this paper, we use GRU for all RNNs.

The RNN encoder bidirectionally encodes the source sentence into a sequence of context vectors $H = \boldsymbol{h}_1, \boldsymbol{h}_2, \boldsymbol{h}_3, \ldots, \boldsymbol{h}_m$, where $\boldsymbol{h}_i = [\overrightarrow{\boldsymbol{h}}_i, \overleftarrow{\boldsymbol{h}}_i]$, $\overrightarrow{\boldsymbol{h}}_i$ and $\overleftarrow{\boldsymbol{h}}_i$ are calculated by two RNNs from left-to-right and right-to-left respectively. Then the decoder predicts target words one by one with probability

$$P(Y|X) = \prod_{j=1}^{n} P(y_j|y_{<j}, H) \tag{1}$$

Typically, for the jth target word, the probability $P(y_j|y_{<j}, H)$ is computed as

$$P(y_j|y_{<j}, H) = g(\boldsymbol{s}_j, y_{j-1}, \boldsymbol{c}_j) \tag{2}$$

where g is a nonlinear function that calculates the probability of y_j, and $\boldsymbol{s}_j$ is the RNN hidden state. The context $\boldsymbol{c}_j$ is calculated at each timestamp j based on H by the attention network [1].

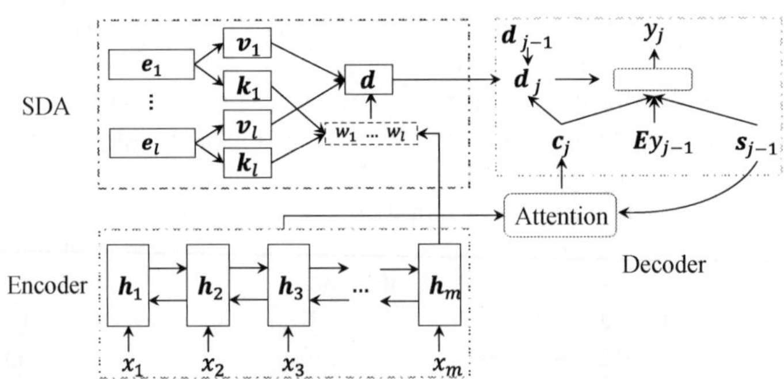

Fig. 2. Overview of our NMT model with soft-domain adapter (SDA-NMT). All characters in bold refers to vectors and Ey_i refers to embedding of y_i.

3 Our Method

In this paper, we propose to model domain distribution in the conventional NMT model. Given a source sentence $X = x_1, x_2, \ldots, x_m$, its target translation $Y = y_1, y_2, \ldots, y_n$, where m and n is source and target sentence length respectively, we define $D = D_1, D_2, \ldots, D_l$ of l dimensions as the latent domain distribution of the source sentence where l is the number of different domains. D_i specifies the i-th dimension in D. We then introduce this latent variable D into NMT. The original translation procedure of Eq. 1 can be reformulated as

$$\begin{aligned} P(Y|X) &= \sum_{D_i \in D} P(Y, D|X) \\ &= \sum_{D_i \in D} P(Y|D, X) \cdot P(D|X) \\ &= \sum_{D_i \in D} P(y_1, y_2, \ldots, y_n|D, X) \cdot P(D|X) \end{aligned} \tag{3}$$

For translation Y, it is generated as $y_1, y_2, \ldots, y_n$ following the way in a conventional sequence-to-sequence model. For domain distribution D, we design a novel **S**oft-**d**omain **A**dapter (**SDA**) for NMT to model domains of source sentences. Figure 2 sketches the high-level overview of our SDA-based NMT model where the SDA is added between the NMT encoder and decoder. The goal of SDA module is to learn domain representations from training data in the training phase. Then during decoding, SDA will generate a specialized domain context for the input sentence. The decoder will take the domain context as an extra input, further update it at each timestep and utilize it to generate domain-aware translation. Next we will describe the SDA module in detail.

3.1 Soft-Domain Adapter (SDA) Module

For each domain D_i in D, we denote $\boldsymbol{e}_i$, $i \in [1, l]$, as its corresponding domain representation.[1] These representations are randomly initialized and trained during training as latent variables. Based on these representations, the SDA first maps $\boldsymbol{e}_i$ into two vectors by a linear transformation, denoted as $\boldsymbol{k}_i$ and $\boldsymbol{v}_i$,

$$\boldsymbol{k}_i = W_k \boldsymbol{e}_i + b_k \tag{4}$$

$$\boldsymbol{v}_i = W_v \boldsymbol{e}_i + b_v \tag{5}$$

where W_k, W_v are weight matrices and b_k and b_v are bias vectors. The $\boldsymbol{k}_i$ is used for indexing the corresponding domain D_i and $\boldsymbol{v}_i$ is used as value of D_i. Similar to the attention mechanism [1], we then calculate normalized similarity scores between the source sentence and each D_i by

$$w_i = \frac{\exp(\boldsymbol{h}_m^T \boldsymbol{k}_i)}{\sum_{j=1}^{l} \exp(\boldsymbol{h}_m^T \boldsymbol{k}_j)} \tag{6}$$

where $\boldsymbol{h}_m$ is the last concatenated hidden vector from the RNN encoder. In this way, we can get a normalized score vector, $\boldsymbol{W} = w_1, w_2, \ldots, w_l$. With this score

[1] In the rest of this paper, the characters in bold refer to vectors.

vector, a specific domain context $\boldsymbol{d}$ for the current input can be generated by the following equations,

$$\widetilde{\boldsymbol{d}} = \sum_{i=1}^{l} w_i \boldsymbol{v}_i \tag{7}$$

$$\begin{aligned} \boldsymbol{d} &= \mathrm{FFN}(\widetilde{\boldsymbol{d}}) \\ &= \max(0, \widetilde{\boldsymbol{d}} W_1 + b_1) W_2 + b_2 \end{aligned} \tag{8}$$

where W_1, W_2 are weight matrices and b_1, b_2 are biases. Equation 7 is a weighted sum operation. FFN (feed forward network) is a non-linear layer [17] which can be described as two convolutions with kernel size 1. We use FFN to extract more important features in $\widetilde{\boldsymbol{d}}$. $\boldsymbol{d}$ is then used in the decoder. The top-left part of Fig. 2 gives a brief description of SDA module. Due to space limitation, the detailed decoding procedure is only illustrated at timestamp j. Our SDA is added between the NMT encoder and decoder. The encoder part and attention mechanism are the same with a conventional NMT model as described in Sect. 2. Next we will introduce our domain-aware decoder.

3.2 Domain-Aware Decoder

We incorporate the domain context into decoder, the Eq. 2 is rewritten as below,

$$P(y_j | y_{<j}, D, H) = g(\boldsymbol{s}_j, y_{j-1}, \boldsymbol{c}_j, \boldsymbol{d}_j) \tag{9}$$

$\boldsymbol{d}_j$ is updated at each decoding step j based on $\boldsymbol{d}$, $\boldsymbol{c}_j$ and $\boldsymbol{d}_{j-1}$.

The reason we update the domain context $\boldsymbol{d}$ at each timestep is motivated by the observation that: mostly, some parts of the source sentence may be domain sensitive, while other parts may be domain in-sensitive such as some function words, common words. In decoder, we update $\boldsymbol{d}_j$ by the following equation,

$$\boldsymbol{d}_j = \boldsymbol{r}_j \otimes \boldsymbol{d} \tag{10}$$

where $\boldsymbol{r}_j$ is an update gate formulated by

$$\boldsymbol{r}_j = \sigma(W_r \boldsymbol{c}_j + U_r \boldsymbol{d}_{j-1}) \tag{11}$$

where W_r, U_r are weight matrices, $\boldsymbol{c}_j$ is the source context calculated by the attention mechanism, σ is the sigmoid activation function and $\otimes$ is the element-wise multiplication. The right part of Fig. 2 gives a brief description of our DA-based decoder. The attention mechanism follows the standard structure as described in [1].

3.3 Model Training

Our NMT model is trained on the mixture of multi-domain corpus. To ensure our SDA module can accurately learn domain representations, we propose an extra domain-related objective function to guide the model training. In our translation task, we can acquire the domain tag of each training instance (i.e. which sentence belongs to in-domain and which is from out-of-domain) in advance. For each training instance, we define a golden one-hot domain vector $\boldsymbol{G}$ with l dimension, l is the number of domains. We calculate another cross-entropy loss between the domain weights $\boldsymbol{W}$ described in Sect. 3.1 and the golden vector $\boldsymbol{G}$,

$$J^D(\theta) = \sum_{(X,D)\in S} \log P(D|X) \tag{12}$$

where S is the training set, θ is the model parameters. Then we add this function to the original cross-entropy loss to form the final objective function,

$$J(\theta) = \sum_{(X,Y,D)\in S} \log P(Y|X,D) + \log P(D|X) \tag{13}$$

With this function, our SDA module is trained in a supervised way. We can also train our model without log $P(D|X)$. Thus the SDA module is implicitly trained and the objective function is the same with the conventional NMT model. We will further discuss the effect of term log $P(D|X)$ in experiments. In the following parts of this paper, we use **SDA-NMT-DG** to represent the domain guided SDA model and **SDA-NMT** to represent the SDA-NMT-DG without the domain objective function log $P(D|X)$.

4 Experiments

4.1 DataSet

In the Chinese-English task, we leverage the high quality bilingual data from IWSLT 2015 workshop [2] which contains about 200 K sentence pairs as in-domain corpus. We use the dev 2010 set for development and test 2010–2015 (tst2010-tst2015) are used as in-domain testsets. For out-of-domain corpus, we

Table 1. Evaluation results of Chinese-English in-domain test sets with BLEU% metric. "NMT-IWSLT" refers to a conventional NMT model trained on in-domain corpus and "NMT-LDC" denotes an NMT model trained on out-of-domain data.

	tst2010	tst2011	tst2012	tst2013	tst2014	tst2015	Average
NMT-IWSLT (in-domain)	12.29	16.18	14.30	15.05	12.15	14.91	14.15
NMT-LDC (out-of-domain)	10.54	13.51	12.09	13.91	12.13	14.77	12.83
Fine-tuning	14.27	17.96	15.11	16.39	14.64	16.56	15.83
[5] (Mixed fine-tuning)	14.73	18.83	16.21	17.50	15.62	17.82	16.80
[13] (+Discriminator)	14.89	19.18	16.38	18.09	15.43	19.10	17.18
SDA-NMT	14.78	19.35	16.40	18.26	15.73	19.04	17.26
SDA-NMT-DG	**15.42**	**20.04**	**17.28**	**19.50**	**16.32**	**19.95**	**18.09**

use a subset from LDC corpus[2] which has around 2.6 M sentence pairs from News domain. NIST 2003, NIST 2005, NIST 2006, NIST 2008 and NIST 2012 are used as out-of-domain testsets. All English words are lowercased.

In the English-French translation task, the IWSLT 2014 English-French training corpus [3] is used as in-domain training data and the out-of-domain corpus is from WMT 2015 English-French translation task. The development data is TED dev2010 and we use test 2010 (tst2010) as testset. Both are with single reference per source sentence.

4.2 Implementation Details

As we have just an in-domain and an out-of-domain, the hyper parameter l is set to 2. In the neural network training, the vocabulary size is limited to 35 K high frequent words for both source and target languages in the Chinese-English translation task. All low frequent words are normalized into a special token unk and post-processed by following the work in [11]. For English-French task, we further split the words into sub-words using byte pair encoding (BPE)[3] [14] which has been shown to be effective for rare word problem in NMT. For all the NMT models, the size of word embedding is set to 512. The dimensions of the hidden states for all RNNs are set to 1024. The dimension of $\boldsymbol{k}_i$ and $\boldsymbol{v}_i$ are set to 512. The inner layer of FNN is set to 1024.

4.3 Baselines

We compare our proposed method with original NMT baselines and several state-of-the-art domain adaptation methods.

- NMT: An in-house reimplementation of [1]. In the following of this paper, we use NMT-IWSLT to represent the NMT model trained on in-domain corpus, NMT-WMT and NMT-LDC refers to NMT model trained on out-of-domain data.
- Fine-tuning: Fine-tune the out-of-domain model on the in-domain corpus.
- Mixed fine-tuning: [5] proposed a new training procedure named mixed fine-tuning.
- Instance weighting: [18] proposed to assign different weights to in-domain and out-of-domain instances.
- +Discriminator: [13] proposed a multi-task learning framework for NMT domain adaptation.

All the evaluation results are reported with the case-insensitive IBM BLEU-4 [12].

[2] LDC2002E17, LDC2002E18, LDC2003E07, LDC2003E14, LDC2005E83, LDC2005T06, LDC2005T10, LDC2006E17, LDC2006E26, LDC2006E34, LDC2006E85, LDC2006E92, LDC2006T06, LDC2004T08, LDC2005T10.

[3] https://github.com/rsennrich/subword-nmt.

4.4 Evaluation on IWSLT In-Domain Chinese-English Task

We first evaluate our method on IWSLT In-domain Chinese-English translation task. The evaluation results of in-domain testsets against baselines are listed in Table 1. We can see that NMT-IWSLT, which is trained on small scale corpus, is much better than NMT-LDC on the in-domain testsets in terms of average BLEU score. That is mainly because the domain of IWSLT corpus (spoken domain) is different from LDC corpus (news domain) and NMT models are sensitive to the training domain.

Though simple, "Fine-tuning" is an effective method which can improve the performance a lot compared with both NMT-IWSLT and NMT-LDC. "Mixed fine-tuning [5]" and "+Discriminator [13]" can achieve further improvements compared with "Fine-tuning". Overall, our SDA-NMT-DG achieves the highest BLEU scores on all the testsets. Compared with NMT-IWSLT baseline, our SDA-NMT-DG gains 3.94 more BLEU points on average. This is mainly because our method can generate dynamically domain-aware context for each instance where proper domain knowledge can be taken into account during decoding. We also investigate the effect of domain objective function. Even without this objective function, the SDA-NMT can still outperform other methods on most of the testsets, which shows that our method can implicitly learn domain knowledge. However, the SDA-NMT is not as good as SDA-NMT-DG, this demonstrates that the golden domain tags can benefit the SDA module in training.

4.5 Evaluation on In-Domain IWSLT English-French Task

In this section, we further evaluate our method on IWSLT English-French translation task. Table 2 shows the comparison results from 7 systems with the evaluation metrics of BLEU. A state-of-the-art result taken from [18] on this testset is also listed which proposed a "Instance weighting" strategy for NMT.

Table 2. Evaluation results of English-French IWSLT dev and test sets with BLEU% metric.

	dev2010	tst2010
NMT-IWSLT (in-domain)	25.25	30.57
NMT-WMT (out-of-domain)	25.42	29.73
[18] (Instance weighting)	30.40	36.50
[5] (Mixed fine-tuning)	30.88	36.66
[13] (+Discriminator)	31.18	36.87
SDA-NMT	31.59	36.96
SDA-NMT-DG	**31.86**	**37.54**

According to Table 2, our SDA-NMT-DG still outperforms the other models, where about 7 more BLEU points are gained compared to NMT-IWSLT baseline.

Compared with the [18], SDA-NMT-DG achieves 1 more BLEU score. This shows that our proposed approach to modeling domain-aware context benefits NMT systems on in-domain testsets. In addition, the SDA-NMT-DG is still better than SDA-NMT.

4.6 Evaluation on Out-of-Domain NIST Chinese-English Task

In this section, we investigate the performance of SDA-NMT-DG on the NIST out-of-domain Chinese-English translation task. Table 3 shows all the evaluation results. From the table, we can see that "Fine-tuning" performs the worst with more than 11 BLEU scores decrease compared with NMT-LDC in terms of average BLEU. This shows that even though "Fine-tuning" can improve the in-domain performance, it dramatically deteriorates the out-of-domain translation quality.

Overall, our SDA-NMT-DG achieves comparable BLEU scores compared with NMT-LDC baseline and is better than all the other domain adaptation systems. This is because our SDA can dynamically generate domain-aware representations and guide the decoder to generate out-of-domain translations. We can also find that, for some tests such as NIST2006, SDA-NMT-DG is even better than NMT-LDC baseline. Actually, these testsets are multilingual sets where Web data is contained. These web data may be drawn from user forums, discussion groups, and blogs. They are more likely to the TED data. For these multiple domain testsets, our model can perform even better than NMT-LDC.

Table 3. Evaluation results of Chinese-English out-of-domain test sets with BLEU% metric.

	NIST2003	NIST2005	NIST2006	NIST2008	NIST2012	Average
NMT-LDC (out-of-domain)	**41.85**	**39.58**	39.96	30.49	29.80	36.34
Fine-tuning	29.17	28.11	26.09	21.31	20.60	25.06
[5] (Mixed fine-tuning)	39.23	37.94	36.98	28.38	27.10	33.97
[13] (+Discriminator)	39.36	37.38	38.59	28.81	28.36	34.50
SDA-NMT	41.03	38.97	38.81	30.50	29.00	35.66
SDA-NMT-DG	41.10	39.20	**40.64**	**31.14**	**30.08**	**36.43**

5 Related Work

Recently, neural machine translation (NMT) has achieved better performance than SMT in many language pairs [10,19]. Our work builds on the recent literature on domain adaptation strategies in NMT. The NMT model is trained in an end-to-end way which is very sensitive to the training domain. Some effort has been done to improve the NMT model on the in-domain testsets. [9] proposed to transfer out-of-domain knowledge to in-domain by fine-tuning out-of-domain models on in-domain corpus. [8] involved appending a domain indicator token to each source sequence. Based on these work, [5] further refined the model by integrating source-tokenization into the domain fine-tuning paradigm. While it requires no changes to the NMT architecture, these approaches are inherently limited because they stipulate that domain information for unseen test examples be known. For example, if using a trained model to translate user-generated sentences, we do not know the domain a-prior, and this approach cannot be used. There is another line of work. Inspired by the instance weighting methods in SMT, [18] applied this method to NMT models by assign different weights for each instance during training. More weights are assigned to in-domain instances in the NMT loss function.

Different from the work above, [13] proposed a multi-task learning framework for domain adaptation. They added a discriminator on the top of the NMT encoder which is used to classify which domain the source sentence belongs to. However, this is not effective enough to leverage domain information for NMT model. In this paper, we introduce SDA into the conventional NMT model. This module can learn domain distribution of training data and generate domain-aware representation for each source instances.

6 Conclusion and Future Work

In this paper, we propose a novel soft-domain adapter based neural machine translation model. Our model can learn domain representations from the training data and generate domain-aware context for input sentences. Then the decoder can generate domain-aware translations with the help of domain contexts. Experimental results show that our method can boost the translation quality on the in-domain testsets without deteriorating the out-of-domain performance.

In future work, along this research direction, we will conduct multiple domain translation experiments (more than two), such as a mixture domain of spoken, news and travel, to verify the effectiveness.

References

1. Bahdanau, D., Cho, K., Bengio, Y.: Neural machine translation by jointly learning to align and translate. In: ICLR 2015 (2015)
2. Cettolo, M., Niehues, J., Stüker, S., Bentivogli, L., Cattoni, R., Federico, M.: The IWSLT 2015 evaluation campaign. In: Proceedings of IWSLT, Da Nang, Vietnam (2015)
3. Cettolo, M., Niehues, J., Stüker, S., Bentivogli, L., Federico, M.: Report on the 11th IWSLT evaluation campaign. In: Proceedings of the International Workshop on Spoken Language Translation, IWSLT 2014, Hanoi, Vietnam (2014)
4. Cho, K., et al.: Learning phrase representations using RNN encoder-decoder for statistical machine translation. In: Proceedings of ENMLP 2014 (2014)
5. Chu, C., Dabre, R., Kurohashi, S.: An empirical comparison of simple domain adaptation methods for neural machine translation. arXiv preprint arXiv:1701.03214 (2017)

6. Freitag, M., Al-Onaizan, Y.: Fast domain adaptation for neural machine translation. arXiv preprint arXiv:1612.06897 (2016)
7. Hochreiter, S., Schmidhuber, J.: Long short-term memory. Neural Comput. **9**(8), 1735–1780 (1997)
8. Kobus, C., Crego, J., Senellart, J.: Domain control for neural machine translation. arXiv preprint arXiv:1612.06140
9. Luong, M.T., Manning, C.D.: Stanford neural machine translation systems for spoken language domains. In: Proceedings of IWSLT 2015 (2015)
10. Luong, T., Pham, H., Manning, C.D.: Effective approaches to attention-based neural machine translation. In: Proceedings of EMNLP 2015 (2015)
11. Luong, T., Sutskever, I., Le, Q., Vinyals, O., Zaremba, W.: Addressing the rare word problem in neural machine translation. In: Proceedings of ACL 2015 (2015)
12. Papineni, K., Roukos, S., Ward, T., Zhu, W.J.: BLEU: a method for automatic evaluation of machine translation. In: Proceedings of ACL 2002 (2002)
13. Pryzant, R., Britz, D., Le, Q.: Effective domain mixing for neural machine translation. In: Second Conference on Machine Translation (WMT) (2017)
14. Sennrich, R., Haddow, B., Birch, A.: Neural machine translation of rare words with subword units. arXiv preprint arXiv:1508.07909 (2015)
15. Servan, C., Crego, J., Senellart, J.: Domain specialization: a post-training domain adaptation for neural machine translation. arXiv preprint arXiv:1612.06141 (2016)
16. Sutskever, I., Vinyals, O., Le, Q.V.: Sequence to sequence learning with neural networks. In: Advances in Neural Information Processing Systems (2014)
17. Vaswani, A., et al.: Attention is all you need. Curran Associates, Inc. (2017)
18. Wang, R., Utiyama, M., Liu, L., Chen, K., Sumita, E.: Instance weighting for neural machine translation domain adaptation. In: Proceedings of EMNLP 2017 (2017)
19. Wu, Y., et al.: Google's neural machine translation system: Bridging the gap between human and machine translation. arXiv preprint arXiv:1609.08144 (2016)

Neural Machine Translation with Bilingual History Involved Attention

Haiyang Xue[1], Yang Feng[1(✉)], Di You[2], Wen Zhang[1], and Jingyu Li[1]

[1] Key Laboratory of Intelligent Information Processing Institute of Computing Technology, Chinese Academy of Sciences (ICT/CAS), Beijing, China
{xuehaiyang,fengyang,zhangwen,lijingyu}@ict.ac.cn
[2] Worcester Polytechnic Institute, Worcester, MA, USA
dyou@wpi.edu

Abstract. The using of attention in neural machine translation (NMT) has greatly improved translation performance, but NMT models usually calculate attention vectors independently at different time steps and consequently suffer from over-translation and under-translation. To mitigate the problem, in this paper we propose a method to consider the translated source and target information up to now related to each source word when calculating attentions. The main idea is to keep track of the translated source and target information assigned to each source word at each time step and then accumulate these information to get the completion degree for each source word. In this way, in the later calculation of the attention, the model can adjust the attention weights to give a reasonable final completion degree for each source word. Experimental results show that our method can outperform the strong baseline systems significantly both on the Chinese-English and English-German translation tasks and produce better alignment on the human aligned data set.

Keywords: Neural machine translation · Bilingual history information · Attention mechanism

1 Introduction

Neural machine translation (NMT) [1–3,12,15] has made great progress and drawn much attention recently. NMT models mainly fit in the attention-based encoder-decoder framework where the encoder encodes the source sentence into representations in a common semantic space and at each time step the decoder first collects source information over all the source words via an attention function and then generates a target word based on the collected source information.

Although there may exist different attention functions, including additive attention and dot-product attention [15], the main mechanism is almost the same which first gets the weight for each source representation according to its

J. Tang et al. (Eds.): NLPCC 2019, LNAI 11839, pp. 265–275, 2019.
https://doi.org/10.1007/978-3-030-32236-6_23

relevance to the current target-side information and then outputs the weighted sum of source representations as the source information for each time step to translate. From this process, we can see that the calculation of the attention at each time step is only related to the current target-side information and the keys (usually the representations of source words). It does not involve the previous attention directly and hence is independent to each other at different time steps. As a result, the attention component cannot get to know the completion degree of each source word which leads to *over-translation* or *under-translation* [13]. Table 1 gives examples of over-translation and under-translation. Example (1) shows the case of over-translation where "23" has been translated twice. If the model can get the translation derived from "23", it may not attend too much on it when calculating attention. Example (2) indicates the case of under-translation where the source words "5 zhōunián" have not been translated. Once the model can get the translated part of "5 zhōunián", it will adjust to give more attention to it. As a conclusion, if the model can maintain the translated source and target translation up to now related to each source word, it can work out more reasonable attention. On these grounds, in order to address the problem of over-translation and under-translation, we propose a method to involve the bilingual history information into the calculation of attention. The main idea is to gather the translated source and target information for each source word at each time step, and then accumulate the translated bilingual history up to now related to each source word with GRUs. In this way, we can evaluate the completion degree for each source word and give reasonable suggestion for the calculation of attention. Experiments on the Chinese-to-English and English-to-German translation tasks show that our method can achieve significantly improvements over strong baselines and can also produce better alignment.

Table 1. Two examples of Chinese-to-English NMT.

(1)	**Src**	rénlèi gòngyǒu 23 duì rǎnsètǐ
	Trans	There were 23 23 pairs of chromosomes in human beings
(2)	**Src**	qìng xiānggǎng huíguī **5 zhōunián** gōngwùyuán shūhuà dàsài jiāng jǔxíng
	Trans	Chinese civil service calligraphy competition to be held on Hong Kong's return

2 Background

Our work is initially based on the representative attention-based NMT model [1]. The basic framework is a mature end-to-end system following the encoder-decoder framework whose encoder consists of a RNN or bi-directional RNN to generate the representations of the source sentence as a sequence of vectors. The framework employed another RNN network as decoder to learn to align and translate by reading the vectors at the same time. In particular, the framework above possesses an extra attention module which is a mechanism for improving alignment. We'll explain the model and its sub-components in detail in the following section.

Encoder. The encoder employs two GRUs to run through the source words bi-directionally and obtain two sequences of hidden states as follows:

$$\overrightarrow{\mathbf{h}}_j = \overrightarrow{\mathbf{GRU}}\left(x_j, \overrightarrow{\mathbf{h}}_{j-1}\right) \tag{1}$$

$$\overleftarrow{\mathbf{h}}_j = \overleftarrow{\mathbf{GRU}}\left(x_j, \overleftarrow{\mathbf{h}}_{j+1}\right) \tag{2}$$

The formal representation of each word in the source sequence is the given by concatenating the corresponding hidden states in both direction, which is shown by Eq. 3:

$$\mathbf{h}_j = \left[\overrightarrow{\mathbf{h}}_j; \overleftarrow{\mathbf{h}}_j\right] \tag{3}$$

Attention. The design of attention section is inspired by the intuition that corresponding pair of source-end word and target-end word can be highly connected when generating a new word. Thus, the module aims at building direct connections between those highly related source and target words.

Above all, we need to compute the relevance between target word $\mathbf{y}_j$ and $\mathbf{h}_i$, which can be evaluated as

$$e_{ji} = \mathbf{v}_a^T \tanh\left(\mathbf{W}_a \mathbf{s}_{i-1} + \mathbf{U}_a \mathbf{h}_j\right) \tag{4}$$

For computational convenience, we will use following formula to normalize the relevance of $\mathbf{h}_i$ in the source hidden state sequence in j-th decoding step:

$$\alpha_{ji} = \frac{\exp\left(e_{ji}\right)}{\sum_{j'=1}^{l_s} \exp\left(e_{j'i}\right)} \tag{5}$$

Finally, the attention can be compute as weighted summation of all source hidden states by their normalized relevance obtained in the previous step

$$\mathbf{a}_i = \sum_{l=1}^{l_s} \alpha_{ji} \mathbf{h}_j \tag{6}$$

where l_s is the length of source inputs. **Decoder:** The decoder works by predicting a probability distribution over all the words within the vocabulary and output the target word with the greatest probability. It also use a variant of GRU network to roll the target information, the details of which are described in [1]. Then the current target hidden state s_i is given by

$$\mathbf{s}_i = f(\mathbf{y}_{i-1}, \mathbf{s}_{i-1}, \mathbf{a}_i) \tag{7}$$

The probability distribution $\mathcal{D}_i$ over the target vocabulary at the i-th step depends on the combinational effect of previous ground truth word, the attention $\mathbf{a}_i$ and the rolled target information $\mathbf{s}_i$, the relationship can be described mathematically as

$$\mathbf{t}_i = g(\mathbf{y}_{i-1}, \mathbf{a}_i, \mathbf{s}_i) \tag{8}$$

$$\mathbf{o}_i = \mathbf{W}_o \mathbf{t}_i \tag{9}$$

$$\mathcal{D}_i = \text{softmax}\,(\mathbf{o}_i) \tag{10}$$

where g represents a linear transformation, $\mathbf{t}_i$ can be mapped to $\mathbf{o}_i$ by $\mathbf{W}_o$ so that each target word has only one corresponding dimension in $\mathbf{o}_i$.

Intuitively, the probability α_{ji} and the variable e_{ji} jointly reflect the influence of $\mathbf{h}_j$ in deciding next hidden state and even generating next target word.

3 The Proposed Method

The attention component collects source information at each time step by weightedly summing the semantic of all the source words and then the decoder produces a target word according to the generated attention. In this process, there is a semantic projection between the source attention and the target information. It implies that the semantics held by the source attention and the generated target word is equivalent. Thus we can derive the consumed source semantic and the generated target semantic related to each source word at each step. With this, we can get the accumulated consumed source semantic and generated target semantic up to each time step. The bilingual history semantic can well indicate completion degree of each source word and hence help to generate more reasonable attention.

Figure 1 gives the architecture of our method. After the target word y is generated y_i, the source information related to the source word x_j is accumulated via a GRU to be $\tilde{\mathbf{h}}_j^i$, and similarly the target information related to the source word x_j is accumulated to $\tilde{\mathbf{s}}_j^i$. Then to generate the next target word y_{i+1}, the accumulated bilingual information is involved to calculated the attention weight of x_j and the weighted sum over the source hidden states is treated as the attention and fed to the decoder.

In this paper, we attempt to add different part of information as

* **SA-NMT:** Only involve the source information up to now in the calculation of attention;
* **TA-NMT:** Only involve the target information up to now in the calculation of attention;
* **BA-NMT:** Involve both the source and target information up to now in the calculation of attention.

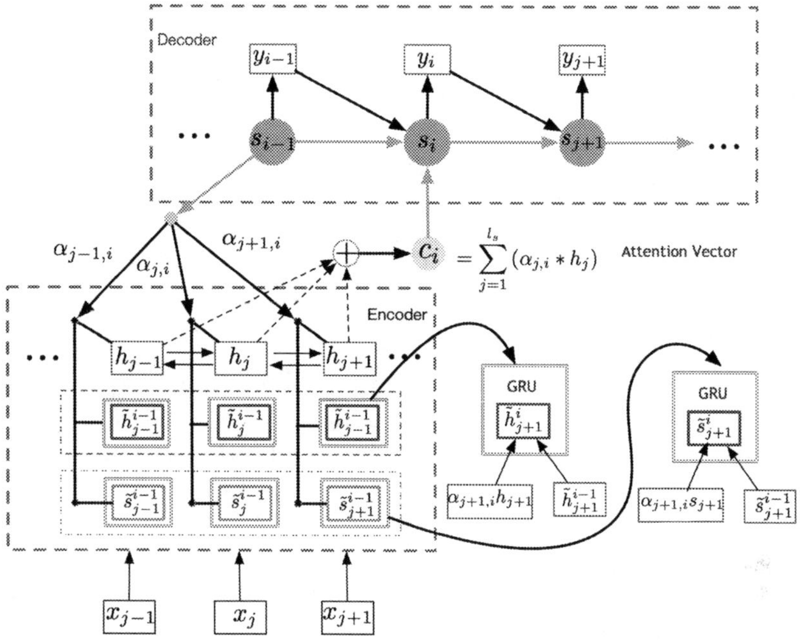

Fig. 1. The architecture of our method with bilingual history involved attention.

3.1 Source History Involved Attention

At the i-th time step, assume the source information related to the source word x_j is $\tilde{\mathbf{h}}_j^{i-1}$. To generate the target word y_i, we calculate the attention with source history information involved and get

$$e_{ji} = \mathbf{v}_a^T \tanh\left(\mathbf{W}_a \mathbf{s}_{i-1} + \mathbf{U}_a \mathbf{h}_j + \mathbf{V}_h \tilde{\mathbf{h}}_j^{i-1}\right) \tag{11}$$

Then we can get the attention following Eqs. 5 and 6.

According to the attention wight α_{ji} to the source word x_j, we can think at the i-th time step, the quantity of the translated source information related to x_j is

$$\mathbf{I}_{ji}^S = \alpha_{ji} * \mathbf{h}_j \tag{12}$$

But we cannot accumulate the source information related to the source word directly by adding them, as at each time step the translated information is not normalized against the source word. Here we employ a GRU to accumulate it, hoping the learnable update gate and reset gate can perform normalization dynamically. Based on the source information up to the $i-1$-th time step, we can update to get the source information up to the i-th time step related to the word x_j as

$$\tilde{\mathbf{h}}_j^i = \mathbf{GRU}(\mathbf{I}_{ji}^S, \tilde{\mathbf{h}}_j^{i-1}) \tag{13}$$

We initialize $\tilde{\mathbf{h}}_j^0$ with 0, which means that no source words have been translated yet. Besides, the accumulated source information also attention the calculation of logit shown in Eq. 8. Before fed to logit, a weighted sum with the attention weights is performed over the history source information related to each source word as

$$\begin{aligned} \tilde{\mathbf{h}}^{i-1} &= \sum_j \alpha_{ji} * \tilde{\mathbf{h}}_j^{i-1} \\ \mathbf{t}_i &= g(\mathbf{y}_{i-1}, \mathbf{a}_i, \mathbf{s}_i, \tilde{\mathbf{h}}^{i-1}) \end{aligned} \tag{14}$$

3.2 Target History Involved Attention

When calculating the attention, it can be considered that the source-side information contained in the current attention is equal to the information of the current generated target word. So each source word corresponds to the current target information:

$$\mathbf{I}_{ji}^T = \alpha_{ji} * \mathbf{s}_{i-1} \tag{15}$$

Then again, $\mathbf{I}_{ji}^T$ is not normalized for the source words, and we still need GRU to accumulate it:

$$\tilde{\mathbf{s}}_j^i = \mathbf{GRU}(\mathbf{I}_{ji}^T, \tilde{\mathbf{s}}_j^{i-1}) \tag{16}$$

where $\tilde{\mathbf{s}}_j^i$ denotes historical information accumulated by the target end. We also take these historical target information into account when calculating attention, so we rewrite the attention model Eq.(4) as follows:

$$e_{ji} = \mathbf{v}_a^T \tanh\left(\mathbf{W}_a \mathbf{s}_{i-1} + \mathbf{U}_a \mathbf{h}_j + \mathbf{V}_s \tilde{\mathbf{s}}_j^{i-1}\right) \tag{17}$$

Note that $\tilde{\mathbf{s}}_j^i$ measures the relevance between the translated historical information of target-end and the corresponding j-th source hidden state. Then, we rewrite the $\mathbf{t}_i$ in Eq.(8) as follows:

$$\begin{aligned} \tilde{\mathbf{s}}^{i-1} &= \sum_j \alpha_{ji} * \tilde{\mathbf{s}}_j^{i-1} \\ \mathbf{t}_i &= g(\mathbf{y}_{i-1}, \mathbf{a}_i, \mathbf{s}_i, \tilde{\mathbf{s}}^{i-1}) \end{aligned} \tag{18}$$

3.3 Bilingual History Involved Attention

Figure 1 illustrates concatenation pattern of the bilingual history involved attention mechanism. The bilingual historical information is the amount of information that has been translated for each source word and the amount of information that has been translated for the target when calculating attention. Intuitively, we combine the bilingual history together by rewriting the attention model. Thus we have

$$\begin{aligned} e_{ji} &= \mathbf{v}_a^T \tanh(\mathbf{W}_a \mathbf{s}_{i-1} + \mathbf{U}_a \mathbf{h}_j \\ &\quad + \mathbf{V}_h \tilde{\mathbf{h}}_j^{i-1} + \mathbf{V}_s \tilde{\mathbf{s}}_j^{i-1}) \end{aligned} \tag{19}$$

4 Related Work

Attention in neural machine translation [1,7] is an imperative mechanism to improve the effect of an Encoder + Decoder model based on RNN, which is designed to assign weights to different inputs. Now some new models [13]are proposed to improve the performance of attention mechanism. Some of them [13] integrate the previous attention history into the current attention for better alignment.

Self-attention is another popular mechanism in recent studies. Look-ahead attention proposed by [17] are able to model dependency relationship between distant target words. The model extends the mechanism by referring to previous generated target words, while by and large, previous works focus on learning to align with source words. [5] further presented a variational self-attention mechanism extracts different aspects of the sentence and partition them into multiple vector representations.

Exploiting historical information to improve the performance of Attention is also a novel mechanism. [8] proposed to introduce source-end historical information onto attention, which use interactive attention to rewrite the source information during translation. Interactive attention to keep tracking the source history by reading and writing operations. [16] proposed to introduce target-end historical information onto attention, which focuses on integrating the decoding history. However, the utilization of historical information basically limited to either source-end or target-end by then, our work managed to combine bilingual history together.

5 Experiments

5.1 Data Preparation

We mainly evaluated our approach on the widely used NIST Chinese-English translation task. In addition, to show the usefulness of our approach, we also provided the results of the English-German translation task. So we carried out experiments on two datasets:

NIST Zh→En: Our training data for the Chinese-English training task consists of 1.25M sentence pairs[1]. We chose the NIST 2002 test set as our development set, and the NIST 2003, 2004, 2005, 2006 datasets as the test sets.

WMT14 En→De: Our training data for the English-German training task consists of 4.45M sentence pairs. We use newstest2013 as the valid set, and newstest2014 as the test set.

In our experiments, we used the case-insensitive 4-gram BLEU [10] for **Zh→En** and case-sensitive for **En→De** to evaluate the translation performance.

[1] These sentence pairs are mainly extracted from LDC2002E18, LDC2003E07, LDC2003E14, Hansards portion of LDC2004T07, LDC2004T08 and LDC2005T06.

Table 2. Performance comparison on Zh→En translation. The "‡" indicates statistically significant improvement over RNNsearch*. "⋆" means statistically significant improvement over NN-Coverage and IA-Model. Here $\rho < 0.05$ [14].

Systems	MT03	MT04	MT05	MT06	Average
RNNsearch	35.75	38.68	34.69	37.61	*36.68*
RNNsearch*	42.03	44.58	42.33	42.40	*42.84*
NN-Coverage	42.69	44.92	42.74	42.79	*43.29*
IA-Model	42.83	45.14	42.94	43.12	*43.51*
Transformer-base	44.56	45.81	44.12	43.31	*44.45*
BA-NMT	**43.73**‡	**45.77**‡⋆	**43.58**‡⋆	**43.91**‡⋆	***44.25 +1.41***

5.2 Systems

We involved following systems as below:

RNNsearch: We implemented the conventional attention-based Neural Machine Translation of [1] with PyTorch[2].

RNNsearch*: This is an improved system of RNNsearch, the detail we can see in this link[3].

NN-Coverage: A variants of attention-based NMT model [13] which maintain a soft coverage on each source representation to keep track of the history to improve the attention mechanism.

IA-Model: An improved NMT model which can capture translation status with an interactive attention to track attention history.

5.3 Configuration

For the NIST Zh→En data set, we adopted 16 k byte pair encoding (BPE) merging operations [11] in the source and target end, respectively. The length of the sentences was limited up to 128 tokens on both ends. For WMT En→De, the number of merge operations in BPE is set to 32 K for both source and target languages, and the maximum length of sentences in the En→De task is also set to 128.

We deployed shared configuration for all the systems. All the embedding sizes were both set to 512, the size of all hidden units in encoder and decoder RNNs was also set to 512, and all parameters were initialized by using uniform distribution over $[-0.1, 0.1]$. The mini-batch stochastic gradient descent (SGD) algorithm was employed. We batch sentence pairs according to the approximate length, and limit input and output tokens to 4096. In addition, the learning rate was adjusted by adam optimizer [4] ($\beta_1 = 0.9$, $\beta_2 = 0.999$, and $\epsilon = 1e^{-6}$). Dropout was applied on the output layer with dropout rate of 0.2. The beam size was set to 10.

[2] http://pytorch.org.
[3] https://github.com/nyu-dl/dl4mt-tutorial.

5.4 Ablation Study

We employed several methods to improve the performance of our model. For instance, we keep track of source history and put it into attention model, which settles the problem of missing translation to a certain extent. Furthermore, we model the dependency relationship between the previous generated target words and the source words where each pair of source word and generated target word is one-to-one correspondence.

Table 3. Ablation study with average BLEU scores.

Systems	Zh→En
RNNsearch	36.68
RNNsearch*	42.84
+ SA-NMT	43.52
+ TA-NMT	43.83
+ BA-NMT	**44.25**

Table 4. Performance comparison on En→De translation.

Systems	En→De
RNNsearch*	25.76
+ SA-NMT	26.11
+ TA-NMT	26.32
+ BA-NMT	**26.58**

The translation performance is listed in Table 3 measuring in BLEU score. It is obvious that in all the cases, our proposed history involved attention model outperforms RNNsearch* system. Specifically, we obtained a BLEU score of 43.52 when only employing the Source History Involved Attention, which indicated that feeding predicted words as context can sufficiently mitigate exposure bias. In comparison, we improved RNNsearch* by 0.68 BLEU points, which also proves its effectiveness. Likewise, we are also gratified by the result of only applying Target History Involved Attention, which achieved a comparable BLEU score as Source History Involved Attention, we improved RNNsearch* by 0.99 BLEU points. Eventually, we managed to combine the above two attention mechanism together and expect to get a more remarkable improvement.

On the En-De dataset, as shown in Table 4, BA-NMT shows superiority on test dataset, and achieves the gains of 0.8 BLEU points over RNNsearch* system. Given the above results, we can conclude that BA-NMT can indeed better utilize the historical information and bring improvement on the translation performance.

5.5 Alignment Quality

As the results of BLEU scores have proved that our method can achieve more accurate translation, we then try to verify this conclusion from another perspective. Since there is a common belief that the better translation should have better alignment with the source sentence, intuitively, we try to evaluated the quality of the alignments derived from the attention module of NMT using AER [9]. As for dataset, we consider the human aligned dataset from [6], containing 900 Chinese-English sentence pairs, to evaluate alignment quality in our experiment.

In practice, we adopted the method that retain the alignment link with the highest probability in Eq.(5). As a comparison, we report the results of both the baseline system and our system. Measured by BLEU score, the results shown in Table 5 illustrate that our system BA-NMT is able to produce more accurate translation than the RNNsearch*. Meanwhile, our corresponding AER score is lower, suggesting better alignments.

Table 5. Comparison of alignment quality on Zh→En translation task, the BLEU and AER scores are evaluated on different test sets.

Systems	BLEU	AER
RNNsearch*	42.84	44.03
BA-NMT	**44.25**	**42.16**

6 Conclusion

In this work, we demonstrate a novel Bilingual History Involved Attention for the attention-based NMT. Our core innovation is that our model allows to maintain track of both the target history and the source history, which is beneficial for our model to better utilize the historical information and generate more accurate translation. We further explore the application of our model on NMT tasks and conduct experiments by using three strategies to integrate the historical information into NMT. Results of empirical studies are consistent with our expectation, which proves that our Bilingual History Involved Attention model is capable of achieving better alignment quality than baseline model, especially in the complicated cases. Besides, the proposed model could effectively alleviated the problem of over-translation and under-translation.

References

1. Bahdanau, D., Cho, K., Bengio, Y.: Neural machine translation by jointly learning to align and translate. In: ICLR 2015 (2015)
2. Cho, K., et al.: Learning phrase representations using rnn encoder-decoder for statistical machine translation. arXiv preprint arXiv:1406.1078 (2014)

3. Kalchbrenner, N., Blunsom, P.: Recurrent continuous translation models. In: Proceedings of the 2013 Conference on Empirical Methods in Natural Language Processing, pp. 1700–1709 (2013)
4. Kingma, D.P., Ba, J.: Adam: a method for stochastic optimization. arXiv preprint arXiv:1412.6980 2014
5. Lin, Z., et al.: A structured self-attentive sentence embedding. arXiv preprint arXiv:1703.03130 (2017)
6. Liu, Y., Sun, M.: Contrastive unsupervised word alignment with non-local features. In: Proceedings of the Twenty-Ninth AAAI Conference on Artificial Intelligence, AAAI 2015, pp. 2295–2301. AAAI Press (2015)
7. Luong, M.-T., Pham, H., Manning, C.D.: Effective approaches to attention-based neural machine translation. arXiv preprint arXiv:1508.04025 (2015)
8. Meng, F., Lu, Z., Li, H., Liu, Q.: Interactive attention for neural machine translation. arXiv preprint arXiv:1610.05011 (2016)
9. Och, F.J.: Minimum error rate training in statistical machine translation. In: Proceedings of the 41st Annual Meeting of the Association for Computational Linguistics, Sapporo, Japan, pp. 160–167. Association for Computational Linguistics (2003)
10. Papineni, K., Roukos, S., Ward, T., Zhu, W.-J.: Bleu: a method for automatic evaluation of machine translation. In: Proceedings of the 40th Annual Meeting on Association for Computational Linguistics, pp. 311–318. Association for Computational Linguistics (2002)
11. Sennrich, R., Haddow, B., Birch, A.: Neural machine translation of rare words with subword units. In: Proceedings of the 54th Annual Meeting of the Association for Computational Linguistics (Volume 1: Long Papers), Berlin, Germany, pp. 1715–1725. Association for Computational Linguistics (2016)
12. Sutskever, I., Vinyals, O., Le, Q.V.: Sequence to sequence learning with neural networks. In: Ghahramani, Z., Welling, M., Cortes, C., Lawrence, N.D., Weinberger, K.Q. (eds.) Advances in Neural Information Processing Systems 27, pp. 3104–3112. Curran Associates Inc. (2014)
13. Tu, Z., Lu, Z., Liu, Y., Liu, X., Li, H.: Modeling coverage for neural machine translation. arXiv preprint arXiv:1601.04811 (2016)
14. Collins, M., Koehn, P., Kučerová, I.: Clause restructuring for statistical machine translation. In: Proceedings of the 43rd Annual Meeting on Association for Computational Linguistics, pp. 531–540. Association for Computational Linguistics (2005)
15. Vaswani, A., et al.: Attention is all you need. In: Advances in Neural Information Processing Systems, pp. 5998–6008 (2017)
16. Wang, M., Xie, J., Tan, Z., Su, J., Xiong, D., Bian, C.: Neural machine translation with decoding history enhanced attention. In: Proceedings of the 27th International Conference on Computational Linguistics, pp. 464–1473 (2018)
17. Zhou, L., Zhang, J., Zong, C.: Look-ahead attention for generation in neural machine translation. In: Huang, X., Jiang, J., Zhao, D., Feng, Y., Hong, Y. (eds.) NLPCC 2017. LNCS (LNAI), vol. 10619, pp. 211–223. Springer, Cham (2018). https://doi.org/10.1007/978-3-319-73618-1_18

Joint Modeling of Recognizing Macro Chinese Discourse Nuclearity and Relation Based on Structure and Topic Gated Semantic Network

Feng Jiang, Peifeng Li(✉), and Qiaoming Zhu

School of Computer Science and Technology,
Soochow University, Suzhou, China
fjiang@stu.suda.edu.cn, {pfli,qmzhu}@suda.edu.cn

Abstract. Nowadays, in the Natural Language Processing field, with the object of research gradually shifting from the word to sentence, paragraph and higher semantic units, discourse analysis is one crucial step toward a better understanding of how these articles are structured. Compared with micro-level, this has rarely been investigated in macro Chinese discourse analysis and faces tremendous challenges. First, it is harder to grasp the topic and recognize the relationship between macro discourse units due to their longer length and looser relation between them. Second, how to mine the relationship between nuclearity and relation recognition effectively is another challenge. To address these challenges, we propose a joint model of recognizing macro Chinese discourse nuclearity and relation based on Structure and Topic Gated Semantic Network (STGSN). It makes the semantic representation of a discourse unit can change with its position and the topic by Gated Linear Unit (GLU). Moreover, we analyze the results of our models in nuclearity and relation recognition and explore the potential relationship between them. Conducted experiments show the effectiveness of the proposed approach.

Keywords: Macro Chinese discourse · Structure and Topic Gated Semantic Network · Gated Linear Unit · Nuclearity recognition · Relation recognition

1 Introduction

In the field of Natural Language Processing (NLP), discourse analysis is becoming increasingly important as the object of research gradually shifts from the word to sentence, paragraph, and higher semantic units. Discourse analysis primarily examines the text coherence and cohesion, including the analysis on structure, nuclearity, and relation. There are two hierarchical levels of discourse analysis: micro level and macro level. The micro level takes a clause or a sentence as an Elementary Discourse Unit (EDU) and researches on intra-sentence or inter-sentence discourse relations. While the macro level takes a paragraph as a discourse unit, and researches on discourse relations between paragraphs and chapters [19] to revealing and insightful a higher level of text coherence above the sentence.

J. Tang et al. (Eds.): NLPCC 2019, LNAI 11839, pp. 276–286, 2019.
https://doi.org/10.1007/978-3-030-32236-6_24

In this work, we focus on recognizing macro Chinese discourse nuclearity and relation, which helps to understand the central topic of the text better. To the best of our knowledge, Macro Chinese Discourse Treebank (MCDTB) [9] is only available macro Chinese discourse corpus, which annotated with macro discourse structure. Its annotation style is consistent with that of Rhetorical Structure Theory Discourse Treebank (RST-DT) [1], including the structure, nuclearity, and relation of macro discourse structure. In RST-DT, many existing studies associate structure recognition with nuclearity recognition, while fewer studies associate nuclearity recognition with relation recognition due to the explicit dependence of nuclearity and relation in RST-DT. However, in MCDTB, the nuclearity of a discourse unit is decided by whether it can better represent the theme of a document in a global view [3].

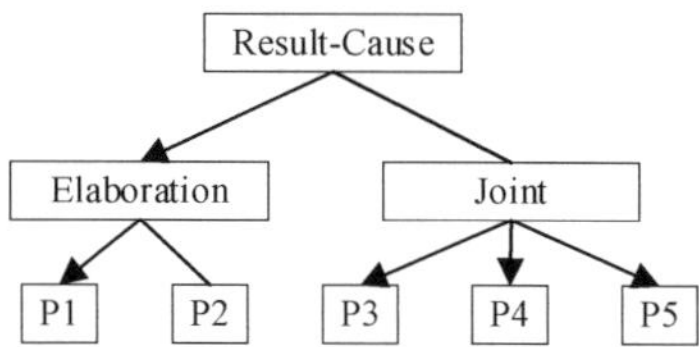

Fig. 1. The macro discourse tree of chtb0056 in MCDTB.

As shown in Fig. 1, to make a clearer explanation of the macro discourse structure, we take the chtb0056 in MCDTB as an example. There are five paragraphs (P1, P2, P3, P4, and P5) as DUs and three bigger discourse units with relations (Elaboration, Joint, and Result-Cause) in the article. The directed edge indicates that the child node is the primary discourse unit (Nucleus), and the undirected edge indicates that the child node is secondary (Satellite). Researching discourse nuclearity and relation recognition can benefit a variety of downstream applications including question answering, machine translation, text summarizing, and so forth. In the task of text summarizing, after constructing a macro discourse tree, we can follow the arrow from the top down to the leaf node to get a more natural summary. For example, according to Fig. 1, chtb0056's abstract is the topic sentence of P1.

On the other hand, macro Chinese discourse nuclearity and relation recognition faces tremendous challenges. First, different from micro-level, macro-level discourse unit has a larger granularity and longer length, and its topic should be grasped from a higher level. Therefore, it is crucial for macro discourse nuclearity and relation recognition that how to effectively combine semantic information and structure and topic information to represent discourse units. Second, previous works [8, 21] show there is a big gap between nuclearity and relation recognition. Therefore, how to join these two tasks suitably is another challenge.

In this study, we propose a joint model based on Structure and Topic Gated Semantic Network (STGSN) to recognize macro Chinese discourse nuclearity and relation. To obtain the macro semantic representation of a discourse unit, STGSN uses macro structure information of a discourse unit and the topic of the whole document to control the flow of information by Gated Linear Unit (GLU) [4]. Therefore, the semantic representation of a discourse unit can change with its position and the topic. In addition, we propose a joint model of nuclearity and relation recognition that reduces a single model's recognition errors by exploring the potential relation between the nuclearity of discourse units and relations among them.

Our key contributions are summarized as follows. First, to the best of our knowledge, we are the first to use neural network model on nuclearity recognition and relation recognition in macro Chinese discourse and propose a joint model to associate these two tasks. Second, we propose a Structure and Topic Gated Semantic Network (STGSN) for achieving the macro semantic representation of discourse unit changed with its position and the topic, which improves the performance by recognizing the type of fewer samples better. Third, we propose joint learning of nuclearity and relation recognition that reduces a single model's recognition errors and explore the potential relationship between the nuclearity of discourse units and relations among them.

The rest of the paper is organized as follows. Section 2 overviews the related work. Section 3 describes the proposed model in detail. Section 4 presents experiments and discussions. We conclude the paper in Sect. 5 and shed light on future directions.

2 Related Work

In English, previous studies of nuclearity and relation recognition mainly focus on full discourse parsing, with RST-DT [1] being one of the most popular discourse corpora. RST-DT is based on Rhetorical Structure Theory (RST) [14] and contains 385 documents from the Wall Street Journal. It is annotated with the discourse structure, nuclearity, and relation to representing the relationship between two or more discourse units. Since both micro and macro discourse structures with a document annotated as a tree, it does not explicitly distinguish between micro-level and macro-level discourse structure. In RST-DT, most existing approaches [5, 6, 20] either model discourse structure, nuclearity and relation recognition separately, while other studies regard nuclearity as subsidiary attributes of structure [7] or relation [10, 11], ignoring the importance of nuclearity recognition and the implicit relationship among nuclearity and relation. However, a few studies focus on the macro level. Sporleder and Lascarides [17] used a maximum entropy model to identify the macro discourse structure, after pruning and revising the original discourse trees on RST-DT corpus, but they did not recognize nuclearity and relation on the macro level.

In Chinese, Li et al. [13] proposed Chinese discourse treebank (CDTB) on the micro level and there are some successful attempts [12, 18] for discourse analysis tasks on this corpus. On the macro level, MCDTB [9] is the only available macro Chinese discourse corpus. Its annotation style is consistent with that of RST-DT, including the structure, nuclearity, and relation, but only annotated on the macro level. Currently, MCDTB contains 720 news documents annotated with 3 categories and 15 relations. Jiang et al. [8] proposed two topic similarity features as supplements to structural features and tried to use the maximum entropy model to identify the discourse nuclearity on MCDTB. Chu et al. [2] used Conditional Random Field (CRF) to build a local model, and then proposed a joint model of structure identification and nuclearity recognition by Integer Linear Programming (ILP) to reduce the error transmission between the associated tasks. Zhou et al. [21] proposed a distributed representation of macro discourse semantics on word vectors in a global view. Besides, he used some original features to improve the performance of relation recognition.

3 Overview of the Framework

In this section, we propose a joint model of nuclearity recognition and relation recognition based on Structure and Topic Gated Semantic Network (STGSN), and its high-level illustration is shown in Fig. 2. It includes three modules: (1) Text Encoding, (2) Structure and Topic Gated Semantic Network, and (3) Joint Learning with Non-linear Transformation Layer.

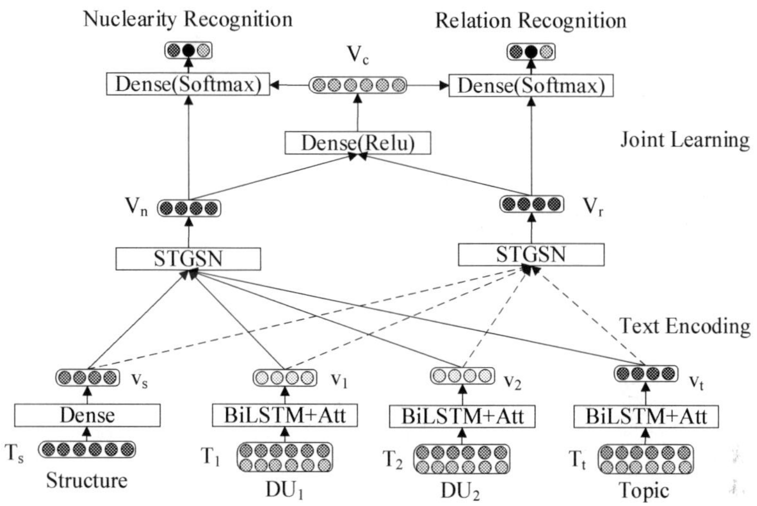

Fig. 2. The Joint model based on STGSN.

To recognize the nuclearity and recognition of two discourse units DU_1 and DU_2, we put their words with part-of-speech sequences as semantic information. What's more, we use DU_1 and DU_2's position features used in Jiang et al. [8] as structure information and the title of the document as topic information. All of them make up the input of our model. Then the Text Encoding module first encodes DU_1, DU_2, and topic into the semantic vectors V_1, V_2, and V_t by the BiLSTM and Attention layer. Besides, it encodes the position information (the number of the start and end of a discourse unit, the distance from the start and end of the document and so on) of DU_1 and DU_2 into the structure vector V_s. Then, these semantic and structure representations are separately fed into two STGSNs for nuclearity recognition and relation recognition. Finally, we feed V_n and V_r into a nonlinear transformation layer for capturing the relationship between nuclearity recognition and relation recognition and get a combined vector V_c which will be concentrated with V_n and V_r into each task in the joint learning module.

3.1 Text Encoding

In the Text Encoding module, DU_1, DU_2, and topic are represented as the sequence $X = (w_1, w_2, \ldots, w_n)$, where n is the number of words in a discourse unit or the title of a document. We first use Word2Vec [15] to initialize the word embedding e_i of the word w_i and its part-of-speech embedding p_i. Then we merge all of the word embedding and part-of-speech embedding in a discourse unit to a sequence $T = (t_1, t_2, \ldots, t_n)$ to represent this discourse unit and t_i is showed as Eq. 1.

$$t_i = [e_i, p_i] \quad 1 \leq i \leq n \tag{1}$$

We use BiLSTM to obtain the semantic representation of a discourse unit and use the attention mechanism (weighted summation of each time step) [16] to capture the more important parts of the discourse unit as Eq. 2.

$$V_j = \mathrm{Attention}\left(\mathrm{BiLSTM}\left(T_j\right)\right) \tag{2}$$

Following Jiang et al. [8]'s structural features, we use randomly initialized hard-coded embedding s_k to represent the structural features (where k is the number of features), and use a concatenation layer to connect them and feed them into a dense layer for getting structure vector (V_s) as Eq. 3.

$$V_s = W_s[s_1, s_2, \ldots, s_k] + b_s \tag{3}$$

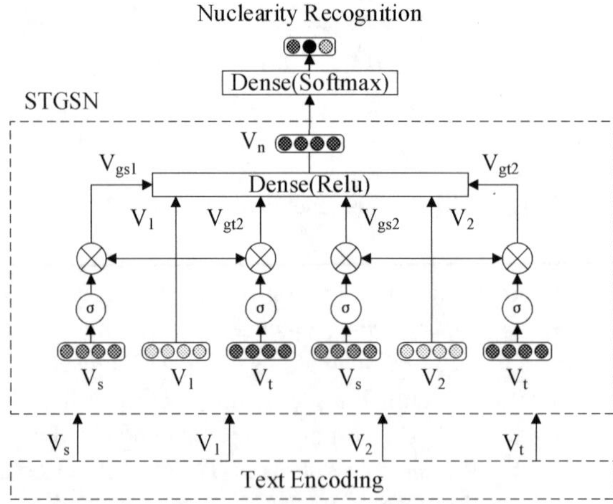

Fig. 3. The Structure and Topic Gated Semantic Network for nuclearity recognition.

3.2 Local Model

As shown in Fig. 3, we illustrate STGSN with a local model for nuclearity recognition and there is the same model for relation recognition. After text encoding, we propose a Structure and Topic Gated Semantic Network. First, we use a discourse unit's structure information (V_s) and the topic of the document (V_t) to control the flow of semantic information (V_1 or V_2) by Gated Linear Unit (GLU) [4], to make the discourse unit's semantic representation can change with its position and the topic, which are formulated as Eqs. 4 and 5.

$$V_{gsi} = V_i \otimes \sigma\left(W_{gs} V_s + b_{gs}\right) \quad i \in 1,2 \tag{4}$$

$$V_{gti} = V_i \otimes \sigma\left(W_{gt} V_t + b_{gt}\right) \quad i \in 1,2 \tag{5}$$

Then we concentrate them and feed them into a dense layer with ReLU active function to get the final representation V_n as Eq. 6. Finally, we feed the final vector V_n into a standard softmax layer for nuclearity recognition as Eq. 7. During training, we use Adam optimizer to optimize the network parameters by maximizing the log-likelihood loss function between the predicted label $\hat{y}$ and the real label y.

$$V_n = W_n\left[V_1, V_{gs1}, V_{gt1}, V_2, V_{gs2}, V_{gt2}\right] + b_n \tag{6}$$

$$\hat{y} = softmax\left(W_{soft} V_n + b_{soft}\right) \tag{7}$$

3.3 Joint Learning with Nonlinear Transformation Layer

To make the information in the nuclearity and relation recognition interact and help each other, we use a dense layer with ReLU active function to capture the implicit relationship between V_n and V_r. Then, we concentrate the output vector V_c with V_n and V_r in their own task and feed them to a standard softmax layer for recognition like in the local model. Besides, for paying more attention to relation recognition with lower performance, we joint learn for nuclearity recognition and relation recognition with weighting the sum of their losses, as Eq. 8, where $\lambda = 0.8$.

$$Loss = \lambda Loss_r + (1 - \lambda) Loss_n \tag{8}$$

4 Experimentation

To verify the performance of the proposed model, we conduct a set of experiments. We seek to answer the following research questions: (1) How does the STGSN perform on macro Chinese discourse nuclearity recognition and relation recognition? (2) How do nuclearity recognition and relation recognition interact with each other on macro Chinese discourse?

4.1 Experimental Setup

We evaluate our model on MCDTB [9], a Chinese macro discourse corpus. It contains 720 news from CTB 8.0 and annotated RST style discourse tree in each news. Following RST-DT and CDTB, MCDTB divides nuclearity into Nucleus-Satellite (NS), Satellite-Nucleus (SN), and Nucleus-Nucleus (NN), and it removes *Transition* and has three categories (*Elaboration, Causality, and Coordination*) and 15 types of relations.

To ensure the objectivity, we use five-fold cross-validation to experiment. In the processing of each article, we transform the non-binary trees of the original data into the left-binary trees and then extract their nuclearity and relation. To solve the problem of too few samples, we use topic sentences of discourse units as their semantic representation for re-sampling and get 6530 samples finally.

The distribution of nuclearity and relation is shown in Table 1. We use micro-averaged F1-score (Mic-F1) and include the macro-averaged F1-score (Mac-F1) to emphasize the performance of infrequent types. Considering the fewer samples, we use smaller hyper parameters to adjust parameters on the verification set. The key hyper parameters are as follows: lstmsize: 32, densesize: 64, batchsize: 64, epoch: 10, embeddingdim: 300, maxlength: 300, dropout: 0.2.

Table 1. The distribution of nuclearity and relation.

Nuclearity			Relation		
NS	SN	NN	Elaboration	Causality	Coordination
4060	160	2130	2406	828	3296

4.2 Experimental Results

To answer the research question (1), we compare the performance of our models with the following representative baselines. **BiLSTM [T]:** In this baseline, just like in local model based on STGSN, we apply an attention layer following a BiLSTM network on a sequence of word embeddings belonging to a discourse unit or a title. Then we concentrate three parts (two discourse units and a title) and feed them into a Multi-Layer Perceptron (MLP) for classification. **BiLSTM [S+T]:** This method is similar to **BiLSTM [T]** except that we add a discourse unit's structure information as a feature.

We additionally use two traditional machine learning models: Jiang et al. [8]'s Topic Similarity Model (**TSM**) for nuclearity recognition and Zhou et al. [21]'s Macro Semantics Representation Model (**MSRM**) for relation recognition as other baselines. In MSRM, we exclude some features (the depth of a discourse unit and the number of child node a discourse unit containing before binary processing) because these features cannot be extracted if we want to build a discourse tree from raw data.

Table 2 shows the comparison results on the test set about nuclearity recognition and relation recognition separately. From Table 2, we make the following observations:

Table 2. The performance of each model in nuclearity and relation recognition.

Models	Nuclearity		Relation	
	Mic-F1	Mac-F1	Mic-F1	Mac-F1
BiLSTM [T]	66.25	43.22	54.52	48.38
BiLSTM [S+T]	82.09	55.41	65.15	51.49
STGSN (Local)	**82.90**	**56.08**	66.45	56.81
Joint Model	81.95	55.23	**67.63**	**57.87**
TSM	82.41	55.73	–	–
MSRM	–	–	66.29	51.51

There is a great gap between the performance of BiLSTM [S+T] with structure information and BiLSTM [T] without it. It indicates that structural features are very important for nuclearity and relation recognition.

STGSN (Local) that we proposed outperforms all other single models including neural network and traditional machine learning model. This observation shows that STGSN is effectively rich for nuclearity and relation recognition with changing the representation of a discourse unit by its position and the topic. Compared with concentrating varieties of features simply, STGSN can grasp the meaning of each discourse unit more accurately, thus improving the accuracy of fewer samples type (Causality) recognition (See in Table 4).

The Joint Model recognizes relation better while has a slight degradation in nuclearity recognition. This is related to the joint distribution of the nuclearity and relation in the corpus. (Discussed in Sect. 4.3).

Table 3. The performance of each model in various nuclearity.

Models	NS			NN		
	P	R	F1	P	R	F1
BiLSTM [T]	72.65	79.94	76.06	57.08	50.80	53.60
BiLSTM [S+T]	90.42	83.20	86.66	72.57	87.77	79.45
STGSN (Local)	91.98	82.95	**87.23**	73.14	90.80	**81.02**
Joint Model	87.59	**86.67**	87.06	**75.47**	82.20	78.64
TSM	**92.41**	81.79	86.78	71.90	**91.28**	80.43

Table 4. The performance of each model in various relations.

Models	Elaboration			Causality			Coordination		
	P	R	F1	P	R	F1	P	R	F1
BiLSTM [T]	56.82	49.68	52.79	49.09	3.05	5.23	59.92	79.27	68.17
BiLSTM [S+T]	64.63	**68.81**	66.53	14.04	1.86	3.25	73.45	87.29	79.70
STGSN(Local)	66.12	65.41	65.59	37.95	12.79	18.72	73.22	85.86	78.99
Joint Model	**67.65**	62.41	64.72	37.89	**25.55**	**29.55**	**74.79**	84.50	79.32
MSRM	66.45	68.16	**67.30**	**62.50**	3.62	6.85	73.29	**89.26**	**80.49**

4.3 Analysis and Discuss

In particular, STGSN (Local) significantly improves 5.32% Mac-F1 for relation recognition while only gets an improvement of 0.67% Mac-F1 for nuclearity recognition. To explore why it comes further, we make the statistic of each model's performance in different nuclearity and relation recognition as shown in Tables 3 and 4. In relation recognition, the improvement of STGSN (Local) is mainly originated from recognizing the type that has fewer samples better. However, in nuclearity recognition, the STGSN (Local) does not significantly improve due to the number of SN (as shown in Table 1) is too small.

To figure out the research question (2), we have calculated the matrix of nuclearity and relation in the corpus, STGSN (Local)'s and Joint Model's predictions respectively, as shown in Table 5. We make two key observations based on Table 5. On the one hand, the NS-Elaboration (Ela.), NN-Coordination (Coo.) and NS-Coordination (Coo.) are the most types and our model recognized well as we expected. On the other hand, for STGSN (Local), there are many mistakes mainly suffer from two sides: recognizing more samples as NN-Elaboration (Ela.), and too many samples belong to NS-Causality (Cau.) are not recognized very well. While the Joint Model can handle them better, which reduces the errors from recognizing NN-Elaboration (Ela.) and recognizes more samples belong to NS-Causality (Cau.) correctly with making good use of the potential relationship between nuclearity recognition and relation recognition.

Table 5. The matrix of nuclearity and relation in corpus and our models' predictions.

	Corpus			STGSN (Local)			Joint Model		
	Ela.	Cau.	Coo.	Ela.	Cau.	Coo.	Ela.	Cau.	Coo.
NS	2316	730	1014	2133	321	1208	2167	523	1293
SN	72	58	30	0	0	0	0	0	0
NN	18	40	2252	242	10	2616	54	3	2490

5 Conclusions

In this work, we propose a joint model of macro Chinese discourse nuclearity and relation recognition based on the Structure and Topic Gated Semantic Network. On the one hand, we propose a Structure and Topic Gated Semantic Network (STGSN) instead of simply connecting semantic features with structure and topic features. On the other hand, we build a joint model of nuclearity recognition with relation recognition and explore the implicit relationship between them to improve recognition performance. Experimental results on the MCDTB corpus show that our model achieves the best performance. Our future work will focus on how to build an end-to-end macro discourse analysis system for helping other NLP tasks.

Acknowledgments. The authors would like to thank three anonymous reviewers for their comments on this paper. This research was supported by the National Natural Science Foundation of China under Grant Nos. 61836007, 61773276 and 61472354.

References

1. Carlson, L., Marcu, D., Okurowski, M.E.: Building a discourse-tagged corpus in the framework of rhetorical structure theory. In: van Kuppevelt, J., Smith, R.W. (eds.) Current and New Directions in Discourse and Dialogue. Text, Speech and Language Technology, vol. 22, pp. 85–112. Springer, Dordrecht (2003). https://doi.org/10.1007/978-94-010-0019-2_5
2. Chu, X., Jiang, F., Zhou, Y., Zhou, G., Zhu, Q.: Joint modeling of structure identification and nuclearity recognition in macro Chinese discourse treebank. In: Proceedings of the 27th International Conference on Computational Linguistics, pp. 536–546 (2018)
3. Chu, X., Zhu, Q., Zhou, G.: Discourse primary-secondary relationships in natural language processing. Jisuanji Xuebao/Chin. J. Comput. **40**, 842–860 (2017). https://doi.org/10.11897/SP.J.1016.2017.00842
4. Dauphin, Y.N., Fan, A., Auli, M., Grangier, D.: Language modeling with gated convolutional networks. In: Proceedings of the 34th International Conference on Machine Learning, vol. 70, pp. 933–941. JMLR. org (2017)
5. Feng, V.W., Hirst, G.: A linear-time bottom-up discourse parser with constraints and post-editing. In: Proceedings of the 52nd Annual Meeting of the Association for Computational Linguistics. Long Papers, vol. 1, pp. 511–521 (2014)
6. Hernault, H., Prendinger, H., Ishizuka, M., et al.: HILDA: a discourse parser using support vector machine classification. Dialogue Discourse **1**(3), 1–33 (2010)
7. Jia, Y., Ye, Y., Feng, Y., Lai, Y., Yan, R., Zhao, D.: Modeling discourse cohesion for discourse parsing via memory network. In: Proceedings of the 56th Annual Meeting of the Association for Computational Linguistics. Short Papers, vol. 2, pp. 438–443 (2018)
8. Jiang, F., Chu, X., Xu, S., Li, P., Zhu, Q.: A macro discourse primary and secondary relation recognition method based on topic similarity. J. Chin. Inf. Process. **32**(1), 43–50 (2018)
9. Jiang, F., Xu, S., Chu, X., Li, P., Zhu, Q., Zhou, G.: MCDTB: a macro-level Chinese discourse treebank. In: Proceedings of the 27th International Conference on Computational Linguistics, pp. 3493–3504 (2018)
10. Joty, S., Carenini, G., Ng, R.: A novel discriminative framework for sentence-level discourse analysis. In: Proceedings of the 2012 Joint Conference on Empirical Methods in Natural Language Processing and Computational Natural Language Learning, pp. 904–915 (2012)

11. Joty, S., Carenini, G., Ng, R., Mehdad, Y.: Combining intra-and multi-sentential rhetorical parsing for document-level discourse analysis. In: Proceedings of the 51st Annual Meeting of the Association for Computational Linguistics. Long Papers, vol. 1, pp. 486–496 (2013)
12. Kong, F., Zhou, G.: A cdt-styled end-to-end Chinese discourse parser. ACM Trans. Asian Low Resour. Lang. Inf. Process. (TALLIP) **16**(4), 26 (2017)
13. Li, Y., Kong, F., Zhou, G., et al.: Building Chinese discourse corpus with connective-driven dependency tree structure. In: Proceedings of the 2014 Conference on Empirical Methods in Natural Language Processing (EMNLP), pp. 2105–2114 (2014)
14. Mann, W.C., Thompson, S.A.: Rhetorical structure theory: a theory of text organization. University of Southern California, Information Sciences Institute (1987)
15. Mikolov, T., Sutskever, I., Chen, K., Corrado, G.S., Dean, J.: Distributed representations of words and phrases and their compositionality. In: Advances in Neural Information Processing Systems, pp. 3111–3119 (2013)
16. Rocktäschel, T., Grefenstette, E., Hermann, K.M., Kočiskỳ, T., Blunsom, P.: Reasoning about entailment with neural attention. arXiv preprint: arXiv:1509.06664 (2015)
17. Sporleder, C., Lascarides, A.: Combining hierarchical clustering and machine learning to predict high-level discourse structure. In: Proceedings of the 20th International Conference on Computational Linguistics, p. 43. Association for Computational Linguistics (2004)
18. Sun, C., Kong, F.: A transition-based framework for Chinese discourse structure parsing. J. Chin. Inf. Process. **32**(12), 48 (2018)
19. Van Dijk, T.A.: Narrative macro-structures. PTL J. Descr. Poet. Theory Lit. **1**, 547–568 (1976)
20. Wang, Y., Li, S., Wang, H.: A two-stage parsing method for text-level discourse analysis. In: Proceedings of the 55th Annual Meeting of the Association for Computational Linguistics. Short Papers, vol. 2, pp. 184–188 (2017)
21. Zhou, Y., Chu, X., Zhu, Q., Jiang, F., Li, P.: Macro discourse relation classification based on macro semantics representation. J. Chin. Inf. Process. **33**(3), 1–7 (2019)

Attentional Neural Network for Emotion Detection in Conversations with Speaker Influence Awareness

Jia Wei, Shi Feng(✉), Daling Wang, Yifei Zhang, and Xiangju Li

School of Computer Science and Engineering, Northeastern University, Shenyang, China
weijia_neu@163.com, lixiangju100@163.com,
{fengshi,wangdaling,zhangyifei}@cse.neu.edu.cn

Abstract. Emotion detection in conversations has become a very important and challenging task. Most of previous studies do not distinguish different speakers in a dialogue and fail to characterize inter-speaker dependencies. In this paper, we propose **S**peaker **I**nfluence-aware **N**eural **N**etwork model (SINN) to predict the emotion of the last utterance in a conversation, which explicitly models the self and inter-speaker influences of historical utterances with GRUs and hierarchical attention matching network. Moreover, the empathy phenomenon is also considered by an emotion state tracking component in SINN. Finally, the target utterance representation is enhanced by speaker influence aware context modeling, where the attention mechanism is used to extract the most relevant features for emotion classification. Experiment results on DailyDialog dataset confirm that our model consistently outperforms the state-of-the-art methods.

Keywords: Emotion detection · Conversation · Speaker influence · Attention

1 Introduction

Since the explosive growth of social media, massive conversations are produced through platforms (e.g., WeChat, Twitter and Weibo) on the Internet every day. Conversational emotion recognition plays a critical role in many applications such as cyber-crime investigation, human-robot interaction, customer service and so on. Thus, how to effectively detect emotions in conversations has attracted increasing attention from both academic and commercial communities.

A conversation consists of a sequence of utterances (2 at least) and each utterance is produced by a participant (the speaker). In this paper, we focus on the dyadic conversation between two speakers. It is generally known that the emotional dynamics in conversations are driven by two factors: self and inter-speaker emotional influence [1]. Self-influence reflects the speakers' own willingness to keep or change their emotions during dialogue. That means the emotion of the current utterance is closely related to the emotions of the speaker's past utterances. On the other hand, inter-speaker influence relates to emotional dynamics induced by the counterparts in the dialogue.

J. Tang et al. (Eds.): NLPCC 2019, LNAI 11839, pp. 287–297, 2019.
https://doi.org/10.1007/978-3-030-32236-6_25

Despite the complex interactive emotional states of speakers in dialogue, most of the previous literature does not distinguish different speakers in a conversation and treat the context utterances only as a textual sequence. Recently, Hazarika et al. proposed CMN model to feed speakers' historical utterances into memory network [2], where each speaker is associated with a separate memory cell. Following this idea, Hazarika et al. further utilized GRU to model the influence between speakers [3]. Although these methods have achieved promising results, the inter-speaker influences are modeled by linear GRU utterance sequence or memory network, which could not fully capture the dependencies between the speakers during the dialogue.

To tackle these challenges, we propose a **S**peaker **I**nfluence-aware **N**eural **N**etwork model (dubbed as SINN) for emotion detection in conversations, which models the self and inter-speaker emotional influences explicitly and comprehensively. Specifically, SINN first adopts GRUs to deal with historical utterances of the target utterance based on each speaker. Furthermore, to incorporate inter-speaker influences, these histories are fed into two separate sections, which will extract speakers' interactive emotional features and track empathic states simultaneously. After that, the interactions between self as well as inter-speaker influence features with the target utterance are calculated by the attention mechanism to synthesize important contextual features. Eventually, the target utterance and the weighted contextual features are concatenated as a final representation which is used to predict the emotion category on the target.

To sum up, the main contributions of this paper are as follows:

- We propose a novel framework called **S**peaker **I**nfluence-aware **N**eural **N**etwork (SINN) to detect emotions in conversations. SINN leverages a hierarchical matching network to explicitly model self and inter-speaker influence and utilizes integrated components to comprehensively model the inter-speaker influence.
- We propose an attention mechanism to dynamically weight the speaker influence features, and learned an enhanced contextual representation.
- Extensive experimental results on benchmark dataset confirm that our SINN model outperforms state-of-the-art comparative methods for the emotion detection task.

2 Related Work

Most of the contextual sentiment analysis studies utilize some kinds of contextual information in the conversation. Huang et al. proposed a hierarchical LSTM model with two levels of LSTM networks to model the retweeting/replying process and capture the long-range dependencies between a tweet and its contextual tweets [4]. Ren et al. utilized two sub-modules to study features from conversation-based context, author-based context and topic-based context about a target tweet, respectively [5]. Andrea et al. employed a model named SVM^{hmm} using Markovian formulation of the SVM to predict the sentiment polarity of entire sequences of tweets [6].

A large section of researches tends to regard a tweet/microblog as a conversation with sequential characteristics. However, conversations in the real world contain quite different contextual information. Zhang et al. built a large-scale human-computer conversation data and adopted a single-level architecture by using Convolutional

Neural Networks (CNNs) for sentiment classification [7]. Gupta et al. proposed a model consisting of two LSTM layers using two different word embedding matrices, Glove and SSWE, for detecting emotions in textual conversations [8]. Luo et al. proposed a self-attentive bidirectional long short-term memory network, which used self-attention to extract the dependence of all the utterances in the conversation [9].

However, the main shortage of these methods is that they do not treat the speakers in a conversation individually. Hazarika et al. utilized a Conversational Memory Network (CMN) to amend this shortcoming [2]. CMN considers utterance histories of each speaker to model emotional memories and uses memory network to capture inter-speaker dependencies. Then, Hazarika et al. proposed another improved model named as Interactive COnversational memory Network (ICON) [3]. Different from CMN, ICON adopts an interactive scheme that incorporates self and inter-speaker influences simultaneously and adopts a multiple hop scheme on them. Our model is inspired by ICON partially while quite different with ICON, where we adopt a more comprehensive approach to model the inter-speaker influences from two aspects, namely interactive dependency as well as empathy.

3 Proposed Model

Suppose there are n utterances in a dyadic two-person conversation, where the communication between two speakers P_A and P_B goes on alternately. Here, a conversation $\mathcal{C}=(u_A^1, u_B^2, u_A^3, u_B^4, \ldots, u_\lambda^n)$ is ordered temporally, where u_λ^n is the nth utterance spoken by person P_λ, $\lambda \in \{A, B\}$. Our goal is to predict the emotion (Anger, Happiness, Sadness, Surprise and Neutral) of the last utterance in the conversation. The schematic overview of our proposed model SINN is shown in Fig. 1.

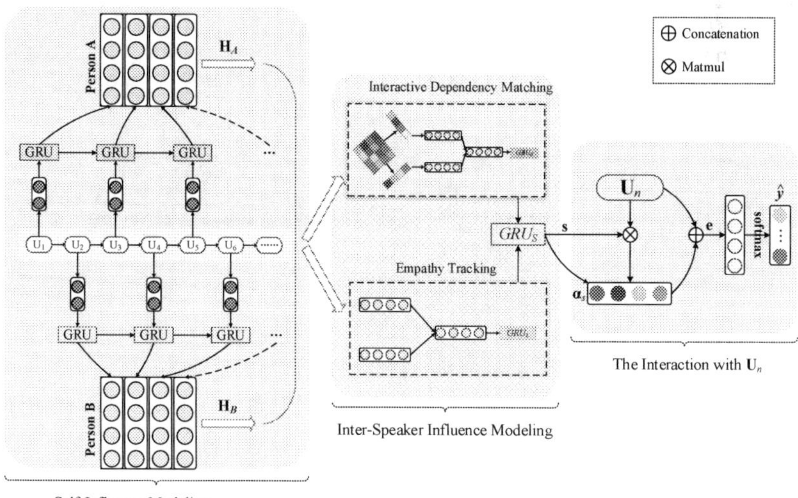

Fig. 1. The architecture of Speaker Influence-aware Neural Network (SINN)

As illustrated in Fig. 1, our SINN network can be divided into three main parts: (1) self-influence modeling, (2) inter-speaker influence modeling, and (3) the interaction with the utterance to be predicted. The second part can be further broken down into two components: (a) interactive dependency matching and (b) empathy tracking.

3.1 Self-Influence Modeling

In this part, the first thing to do is to encode an utterance with distributed representation. For the nth utterance in the conversation C, pre-trained d-dimensional ELMo embeddings are adopted to represent each word of it. An utterance with m words is then represented as $\mathbf{U}_n = (\omega_1, \omega_2, \ldots, \omega_m)$, where ω_i is d-dimensional word embedding for the ith word in the utterance, and we can get a $m \times d$ embedding matrix $\mathbf{W}$. Then we use CNNs and GRUs to extract features of matrix $\mathbf{W}$.

CNNs are effective in extracting representations of a sentence based on its constituting words. In this paper, we use a simple CNN with a single convolutional layer to deal with $\mathbf{W}$. The outputs are then fed into a max-pooling layer followed by a concatenation operation. In addition, we also employ GRU to extract sequential characteristics of an utterance. Each GRU cell computes a hidden state $h_t = GRU(h_{t-1}, x_t)$, where x_t is the current input and h_{t-1} is the previous GRU state. We will explain the detail of GRU in the subsequent modules. The input of GRU here is individual words, and the hidden state of the last word is taken as the features of the entire utterance via GRU.

Eventually, the representation of an utterance $\mathbf{U}_n$ is a concatenation of the features from CNN and GRU, which enriches the representation of the utterance.

After the single utterance representation, we need to capture the self-influence on all historical utterances separately. The dialogue in C goes on alternately between two interlocutors. Here, for a $C = (u_A^1, u_B^2, u_A^3, u_B^4, \ldots, u_\lambda^n)$, we split it into two series according to each speaker, getting $C_A = (u_A^1, u_A^3, \ldots, u_A^i)$ and $C_B = (u_B^2, u_B^4, \ldots, u_B^j)$ defined as new sequence $C_\lambda = (u_{\lambda,1}, u_{\lambda,2}, \ldots, u_{\lambda,T})$, where $\lambda \in \{A, B\}$, $i<n$, $j<n$, $T \in \{i,j\}$. For each $C_\lambda \in \{C_A, C_B\}$, we feed it into the GRU_λ to grasp the temporal history respectively. Specifically, at each timestep t, we get hidden state h_t as follows:

$$r_t = \text{sigmod}(\mathbf{W}^r h_{t-1} + \mathbf{V}^r x_t + \mathbf{b}^r) \tag{1}$$

$$z_t = \text{sigmod}(\mathbf{W}^z h_{t-1} + \mathbf{V}^z x_t + \mathbf{b}^z) \tag{2}$$

$$c_t = \tanh(\mathbf{W}^c (h_{t-1} \odot r_t) + \mathbf{V}^c x_t + \mathbf{b}^c) \tag{3}$$

$$h_t = z_t \odot h_{t-1} + (1 - z_t) \odot c_t \tag{4}$$

where $\mathbf{W}$, $\mathbf{V}$ and $\mathbf{b}$ are parameter matrices and vector, and $\odot$ is dot product operation. x_t is the current input, which is the current utterance's representation $\mathbf{U}_t$ $(t \in [1, T])$ obtained from the approach mentioned above.

These hidden states of all timesteps can be concatenated together to form self-influence matrix $\mathbf{H}_\lambda = [h_{\lambda,1}, h_{\lambda,2}, \ldots, h_{\lambda,T}]$, $\mathbf{H}_\lambda \in \{\mathbf{H}_A, \mathbf{H}_B\}$. $\mathbf{H}_A$ or $\mathbf{H}_B$ represents the historical information of a speaker with his own previous utterances. After that, we encode two matrices $\mathbf{H}_A$ and $\mathbf{H}_B$ to further explore correlations between utterances.

3.2 Inter-Speaker Influence Modeling

It is a remarkable fact that each speaker or even an utterance in C will affect the progress of a conversation. In this part, we will introduce a novel approach to distill these influential factors through two components, interactive dependency matching component and empathy tracking component synchronously.

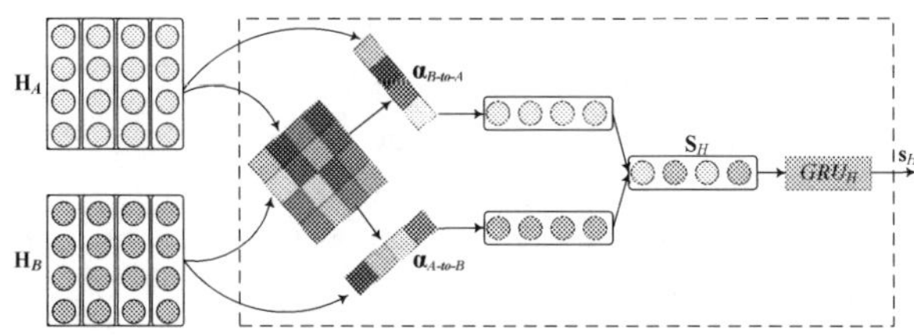

Fig. 2. Schematic overview of Interactive Dependency Matching

Interactive Dependency Matching: Since utterances constantly interfere with each other, we introduce an interactive mechanism to condense the hidden interplays between them. Figure 2 depicts the detail architecture of it. In order to compute features that are interdependent, we first calculate the confusion matrix $\mathbf{H} = \mathbf{H}_A \times \mathbf{H}_B^{\mathrm{T}}$. Given the confusion matrix $\mathbf{H}$, we apply it with attention mechanism [10] from two directions, which could be seen as a B-to-A attention and an A-to-B attention. Therefore, attention mechanism can help us to mine the significant interactive information between $\mathbf{H}_A$ and $\mathbf{H}_B$. Particularly, we need to calculate the attention scores of both sides involved, $\boldsymbol{\alpha}_{B\text{-to-}A}$ (the effect of person P_B on P_A) as well as $\boldsymbol{\alpha}_{B\text{-to-}A}$ (the effect of person P_A on P_B) which is inspired by [11]. Explicitly, the computations are as follows:

$$u_{\mathrm{A}} = \tanh(\mathbf{W}_{w_1}\mathbf{H}^{\mathrm{T}} + \mathbf{b}_{w_1}) \tag{5}$$

$$\boldsymbol{\alpha}_{B\text{-to-}A} = \mathrm{softmax}(u_A^{\mathrm{T}}\mathbf{u}_{w_1}) \tag{6}$$

$$\mathbf{H}_A^{'} = \mathbf{H}_A \boldsymbol{\alpha}_{B\text{-to-}A} \tag{7}$$

where $\mathbf{W}_{w_1}, \mathbf{b}_{w_1}, \mathbf{u}_{w_1}$ are weight matrices and vector, and $\boldsymbol{\alpha}_{B\text{-to-}A} \in \mathbb{R}^{l_A}$ (l_A is the length of preceding utterances of P_A) is the attention weight vector implying the influence of person P_B's utterances on P_A. More precisely, each element in $\boldsymbol{\alpha}_{B\text{-to-}A}$ is the score that represents the importance of each utterance among P_A's previous utterances. More than that, due to the joining of $\mathbf{H}_B$, which represents the history of P_B, $\boldsymbol{\alpha}_{B\text{-to-}A}$ can also indicates the hidden trails of how P_B acts on P_A interactively. After this attention, we get a weighted matrix $\mathbf{H}_A^{'}$ of P_A's history based on the attention scores $\boldsymbol{\alpha}_{B\text{-to-}A}$.

We can get $\mathbf{H}_B^{'}$ by using the following formulas with different parameters:

$$u_B = \tanh(\mathbf{W}_{w_2}\mathbf{H} + \mathbf{b}_{w_2}) \tag{8}$$

$$\boldsymbol{\alpha}_{A\text{-to-}B} = \text{softmax}(u_B^{\mathrm{T}}\mathbf{u}_{w_2}) \tag{9}$$

$$\mathbf{H}_B^{'} = \mathbf{H}_B\boldsymbol{\alpha}_{A\text{-to-}B} \tag{10}$$

Then, we use Eq. 11 to integrate $\mathbf{H}_A^{'}$ and $\mathbf{H}_B^{'}$ into a complete interactive distribution of all previous utterances. Intuitively, we recover the original sequences of C ignoring speakers. $\mathbf{S}_H$ temporally denotes the interdependent abstract of each utterance and evaluates its importance at the same time. However, for extracting features more effectively, we adopt GRU_H to refine $\mathbf{S}_H$ and the output is viewed as a portion of our inter-speaker influence, which is expressed by $\mathbf{s}_H$.

$$\mathbf{S}_H = [\mathbf{H}_{A,1}^{'}, \mathbf{H}_{B,1}^{'}, \mathbf{H}_{A,2}^{'}, \mathbf{H}_{B,2}^{'}, \ldots\ldots, \mathbf{H}_{\lambda,\mathrm{n}-1}^{'}] \tag{11}$$

Empathy Tracking: In this component, we model the emotional tracking of those historical utterances. The main purpose of this module is to ensure that we can maintain the empathic trend of C, which will play a great role in inferring the final emotion. Since the emotion is extremely straightforward, we don't need to achieve it with such complicated process as component introduced above. For the sake of simplicity, $\mathbf{H}_A$ and $\mathbf{H}_B$ are first aggregated by Eq. 12 along the temporal dimension, which incorporates with respective emotional labels at the same time.

$$S_L = [\mathbf{H}_{A,1}L_{A,1}, \mathbf{H}_{B,1}L_{B,1}, \mathbf{H}_{A,2}L_{A,2}, \mathbf{H}_{B,2}L_{B,2}, \ldots\ldots, \mathbf{H}_{\lambda,\mathrm{n}-1}L_{\lambda,\mathrm{n}-1}] \tag{12}$$

Similarly, we adopt another GRU_L to refine $\mathbf{S}_L$ to $\mathbf{s}_L$ denoting empathic features as another portion of our inter-speaker influence.

From the above two components, we can get a comprehensive historical features of $\mathbf{U}_n$. Eventually, we combine both the s_H and s_L through a GRU_S to merge them forming the inter-speaker influence features for further progress.

$$\mathbf{s} = GRU_S(\mathbf{s}_H \oplus \mathbf{s}_L) \tag{13}$$

3.3 The Interaction with U_n

After accumulating the speaker influences of entire history, this step calculates the attentional weight of $\mathbf{s}$ with respect to target utterance $\mathbf{U}_n$. In Eqs. 5, 6, 8, 9, attention scores are got by considering the inner relevance of one input only. While quite different with aforementioned attentions, here we adopt an interactive mechanism to yield attention vector. In order to capture the attentive dependence of **s** relevant to $\mathbf{U}_n$, we perform a mutual calculation between them, which can be expressed as follows:

$$\boldsymbol{\alpha}_s = \text{softmax}\left(\mathbf{s}^{\mathrm{T}}\mathbf{U}_n\right) \tag{14}$$

$$\mathbf{e} = (\boldsymbol{\alpha}_s \odot \mathbf{s}) \oplus \mathbf{U}_n \tag{15}$$

From Eq. 14, we get the attention scores $\boldsymbol{\alpha}_s$ based on the $\mathbf{U}_n$, which assigns higher attention to the information relevant to $\mathbf{U}_n$. We update the **s** according to $\boldsymbol{\alpha}_s$ and concatenate it with $\mathbf{U}_n$ to be our final emotional representation **e**. The **e** contains the information about the $\mathbf{U}_n$ along with its context from entire previous utterances. To generate the final prediction of $\mathbf{U}_n$, **e** is fed into a fully-connected layer followed by a softmax layer to predict the target emotion.

The model is trained by minimizing the cross-entropy along with a L_2 regularization term. We also adopt dropout and early stopping to ease overfitting.

4 Experiments

4.1 Dataset

We conduct experiments on the DailyDialog dataset [12], which is a high-quality multi-turn dialog dataset reflecting our daily communication way. As far as we know, DailyDialog dataset is rarely used in the field of conversation sentiment analysis. On the original dataset, each utterance in a dialogue is annotated with one of seven emotion labels, which are Anger, Disgust, Fear, Happiness, Sadness, Surprise, and Neutral. Moreover, we find that Disgust and Fear emotions account for only a small proportion, with merely 353 (0.34%) and 174 (0.17%) utterances. In order to relieve the severe imbalance of data, we remove the dialogue that contains Disgust or Fear. Moreover, we split a dialogue with *n* utterances into *n*-1 sub dialogues that each sub dialogue includes at least two utterances, namely one historical utterance. After that, we get a modified dataset with 5 emotion labels, the distribution is shown in Table 1.

From Table 1 we can see that Neutral and Happiness appear more frequently, which is truly in accordance with our daily life. Other details can be counted that the speaker turns are roughly 8, and the average words per utterance is about 15.

Table 1. The statistics of the modified DailyDialog dataset

Emotion	Train	Dev	Test	Proportion
Neutral	61028	6140	5248	72416 (82.7%)
Anger	645	58	92	795 (0.9%)
Happiness	10113	642	914	11669 (13.3%)
Sadness	861	65	93	1019 (1.2%)
Surprise	1458	96	100	1654 (1.9%)
Total	74105	7001	6447	87553 (100%)

4.2 Experimental Setup

To initialize the word embedding matrix, we use the pre-trained 1024-dimension ELMo embedding of the output of second LSTM layer in ELMo model. All weight parameters are initialized using the default Tensorflow initializer and we use Adam optimization algorithm to train them with learning rate of 0.001. The number of convolutional filters is set 128 and the filter sizes are set as 2, 3 and 4. The number of GRU cells is 128 for all GRU modules except GRU_S, which contains 256 GRU cells. The weight of L_2 regularization term λ is set 0.001. Dropout rate of 0.5 is set to obtain better performance. Batch size is 128 finally.

We evaluate our experiments in terms of accuracy, and F1-score of the 5 emotion labels individually. Macro-averaged accuracy (Acc for short) and F1-score (F1 for short) are also reported on the whole data. Because the dataset has unbalanced classes as shown in Table 1, weighted averaged accuracy and F1-score are displayed for better contrast, as did in CMN [2] as well as ICON [3].

4.3 Baselines

In our experiments, we compare our proposed SINN network with the following baseline methods with the same word embeddings for fair comparison:

- **Hierarchical GRU-GRU (HGG** for short**):** This baseline contains two-level GRU networks. The first level is a word-level GRU, which can generate a representation of a single utterance. And the second level is an utterance-level GRU, which can model all the utterances in conversation temporally.
- **Hierarchical CNN-GRU (HCG** for short**):** Similar with HGG, HCG is also a two-level network, while we replace the first level GRU with CNN to model the word-level representation of an utterance.
- **CMN** [2]**:** This model uses GRUs to extract both speakers' utterances as historical memories. Then the current utterance is sent to two memory networks as a query with historical memories and employs attention mechanism on them. This step is performed R hops on these memories. In the original experiment, CMN gets its best performance when the number of hops is 3. Thus for a better comparison, we also set hops as 3 to apply CMN model to our dataset.
- **ICON** [3]**:** ICON is built based on CMN by the same authors. It also utilizes separate memory networks for both speakers' historical utterances. The difference with the CMN is that ICON incorporates self and inter-speaker influences in a dialogue with fewer trainable parameters. The hops are also set 3 on the memories.

4.4 Results and Discussion

The experimental results are shown in Table 2. As expected, our proposed model SINN, with novel approach to grasp speaker influence features, outperforms other baseline models obviously.

From Table 2, we can find that as a multi-level network, HGG performs relatively poorly compared with HCG. The reason may be due to the fact that CNNs is more efficient in extracting the features of a sentence than GRUs. That supports the way that we adopt CNN to extract the features of an utterance in our model. However, we still can not ignore the sequential characteristics of an utterance, so we use GRU to deal with it too. Both HGG and HCG perform worse than other baselines, the main reason can be that a simple two-layer architecture fails to excavate the deep dependencies between speakers which is extraordinary important in conversations.

ICON is the state-of-the-art model in [3], while on DailyDialog dataset CMN gets much advantage over ICON but is still not as good as our model. Both the ICON and CMN consider the interactions between speakers in conversation, and ICON incorporates self and inter-speaker influences in a conversation with fewer trainable parameters which may be the reason why ICON is inferior to CMN. That is to say, ICON is not guaranteed to work well in all situations.

Our final SINN model outperforms all the baseline models significantly by merging the self-influence with the inter-speak influence jointly to improve the representations of historical utterances and interacting with the target utterance by attention mechanism. We can see that the improvement is more than 20% on the macro averaged accuracy and F1-score, which confirms our initial assumption that utilizing the self and inter-speaker emotional influences is helpful for emotion prediction.

For each category in Table 2, we notice that SINN outperforms all the compared models except for Anger emotion on Acc and F1, and Sadness emotion on Acc. This situation may be caused by the fact that the number of training data of these two categories is not enough due to data imbalance, so that predicting emotion of Anger or Sadness is harder than the other emotions. However, in terms of weighted averaged accuracy and F1-score, our SINN acquires great improvement (more than 20%) compared with all other baselines, which can still support our view in the weighted condition. As CMN and ICON did in their experiments, we also use weighted averaged accuracy and F1-score to demonstrate the performance of our model.

Table 2. Comparison with the baseline models. Acc means accuracy, F1 means F1-score.

Model	Neutral		Anger		Happiness		Sadness		Surprise		Macro Avg		Weighted Avg	
	Acc	F1	Acc	F1	Acc	F1	Acc	F1	Acc	F1	Acc	F1	Acc	F1
HGG	0.887	0.900	0.383	0.259	0.570	0.535	0.198	0.184	0.269	0.279	0.461	0.431	0.816	0.819
HCG	0.882	0.903	0.343	0.289	0.584	0.521	0.203	0.173	0.467	0.350	0.496	0.447	0.816	0.821
CMN	0.883	0.908	0.518	**0.392**	0.628	0.525	**0.349**	0.282	0.398	0.423	0.555	0.506	0.826	0.830
ICON	0.879	0.902	**0.533**	0.350	0.578	0.509	0.276	0.249	0.420	0.394	0.537	0.481	0.816	0.821
SINN-$_{IDM}$	0.882	0.913	**0.649**	**0.372**	0.662	0.540	**0.356**	0.313	**0.506**	**0.453**	**0.611**	0.518	0.834	0.836
SINN-$_{ET}$	0.899	0.915	0.295	0.315	**0.728**	0.562	0.289	0.327	0.481	0.425	0.536	0.509	0.842	0.840
SINN	**0.899**	**0.919**	0.490	0.350	**0.691**	**0.611**	0.327	**0.345**	**0.470**	**0.426**	**0.575**	**0.530**	**0.849**	**0.851**

4.5 Ablation Experiments

In this section, we implement several model variants for ablation experiments to verify how our model operates in various parts. The results are also shown in Table 2.

- **SINN-$_{\text{IDM}}$:** Due to the fact that baselines above don't consider the previous emotion labels of the target utterance, here we eliminate the empathy tracking component of our model for a better comparison.
- **SINN-$_{\text{ET}}$:** It is SINN without interactive dependency matching component.

As shown in Table 2, we can observe that both SINN-$_{\text{IDM}}$ and SINN-$_{\text{ET}}$ outperform baseline models on average, indicating that either SINN-$_{\text{IDM}}$ or SINN-$_{\text{ET}}$ can provide important inter-speaker clues to enhance the representations of historical utterances. And SINN-$_{\text{IDM}}$ outperforms SINN-$_{\text{ET}}$ on several categories, which are Anger, Sadness and Surprise with less samples, and some even better than final SINN. This situation is caused by the data imbalance since any negligible difference may arouse great margin on these categories. However, both SINN-$_{\text{IDM}}$ and SINN-$_{\text{ET}}$'s performance are still lower than SINN in terms of weighted averaged accuracy and F1-score, which means that the integrated entirety owns more ability than separate parts and each part plays an indispensable role on the whole SINN model.

5 Conclusion

In this paper, we propose a novel SINN modeling the self and inter-speaker influences to identify the emotions in the conversations. Our proposed SINN can extract the deep inter-speaker influences from two effective components and merge them with the target utterance in an intricate way. Moreover, we adopt multiple attention mechanism to help our model to pick up important information for predicting the final emotion. We demonstrated the effectiveness of our model on the high-quality conversational data DailyDialog and the results show that our model is superior to the state-of-the-art methods largely. This work can also be extended to multi-participant conversation which is left to our future work.

Acknowledgements. The work was supported by the National Key R&D Program of China under grant 2018YFB1004700, and National Natural Science Foundation of China (61872074, 61772122).

References

1. Morris, M., Keltner, D.: How emotions work: The social functions of emotional expression in negotiations. Res. Organ. Behav. **22**, 1–50 (2000)
2. Hazarika, D., Poria, S., Zadeh, A., Cambria, E., Morency, L., Zimmermann, R.: Conversational memory network for emotion recognition in dyadic dialogue videos. In: NAACL-HLT, pp. 2122–2132 (2018)
3. Hazarika, D., Poria, S., Mihalcea, R., et al.: ICON: interactive conversational memory network for multimodal emotion detection. In: EMNLP, pp. 2594–2604 (2018)
4. Huang, M., Cao, Y., Dong, C.: Modeling Rich Contexts for Sentiment Classification with LSTM. arXiv preprint arXiv:1605.01478 (2016)
5. Ren, Y., Zhang, Y., Zhang, M., Ji, D.: Context-sensitive twitter sentiment classification using neural network. In: AAAI, pp. 215–221 (2016)

6. Vanzo, A., Croce, D., Basili, R.: A context-based model for sentiment analysis in twitter. In: COLING, pp. 2345–2354 (2014)
7. Zhang, L., Chen, C.: Sentiment classification with convolutional neural networks: an experimental study on a large-scale chinese conversation corpus. In: CIS, pp. 165–169 (2016)
8. Gupta, U., Chatterjee, A., et al.: A Sentiment-and-Semantics-Based Approach for Emotion Detection in Textual Conversations. arXiv preprint arXiv:1707.06996 (2017)
9. Luo, L., Yang, H., Chin, Y. L.F.: EmotionX-DLC: self-attentive BiLSTM for detecting sequential emotions in dialogues. In: SocialNLP@ACL, pp. 32–36 (2018)
10. Yang, Z., Yang, D., Dyer, C., et al.: Hierarchical attention networks for document classification. In: HLT-NAACL, pp. 1480–1489 (2016)
11. Shen, C., Sun, C., Wang, J., et al.: Sentiment classification towards question-answering with hierarchical matching network. In: EMNLP, pp. 3654–3663 (2018)
12. Li, Y., Su, H., Shen, X., Li, W., Cao, Z., Niu, S.: DailyDialog: A Manually Labelled Multi-turn Dialogue Dataset. arXiv preprint arXiv:1710.03957 (2017)

Triple-Joint Modeling for Question Generation Using Cross-Task Autoencoder

Hongling Wang[1], Renshou Wu[1], Zhixu Li[1,2(✉)], Zhongqing Wang[1], Zhigang Chen[3], and Guodong Zhou[1]

[1] School of Computer Science and Technology, Soochow University, Suzhou, China
{hlwang,zhixulim,gdzhou}@suda.edu.cn, rswu@stu.suda.edu.cn, wangzq.antony@gmail.com

[2] IFLYTEK Research, Suzhou, China

[3] State Key Laboratory of Cognitive Intelligence, iFLYTEK, Hefei, People's Republic of China
zgchen@iflytek.com

Abstract. Question Generation (QG) aims to generate a question based on the context. Given the intrinsic connections between QG and QA (Question Answering), we focus on training a joint model for both QG and QA, and take one step further to integrate one more context self-encoding (CSE) task into the joint model, as a junction auxiliary task to better integrate QG and QA. In particular, our model employs a cross-task autoencoder to incorporate QG, QA and CSE into a joint learning process, which could better utilize the correlation between the contexts of different tasks in learning representations and provide more task-specific information. Experimental results show the effectiveness of our triple-task training model for QG, and the importance of learning interaction among QA and CSE for QG.

Keywords: Question Generation · Autoencoder · Joint learning

1 Introduction

Question Generation (QG) is an important task in machine comprehension and perception of knowledge, which has also aroused a lot of attention in cognitive science and artificial intelligence during the last decade. Recently, some studies [15,17] consider the interaction between QG and QA, leveraging their probabilistic correlation to guide the learning process. Among them, [15] uses the "duality" between QA and QG as a regularization term to influence the learning of QA and QG models. Both [15,17] report that the co-training models could improve both QA and QG performance. But in most cases, existing work on joint learning for QG and QA which learns the correlation between two uni-task models with a shared encoding layer [17]. However, a shared encoding layer tends to learn common information between tasks, but might ignore those information that is only useful for one task, which we call as task-specific information.

J. Tang et al. (Eds.): NLPCC 2019, LNAI 11839, pp. 298–307, 2019.
https://doi.org/10.1007/978-3-030-32236-6_26

In this paper, we take one step further to integrate one more context self-encoding (CSE) task into the joint model, as a junction auxiliary task to better integrate QG and QA. CSE is an autoencoder, which could provide more complete information (i.e., both common information and task-specific information) for QA and QG. In particular, our model incorporates QG, QA and CSE into a single learning process with a so-called cross-task autoencoder. The proposed cross-task autoencoder reconstructs one input from the middle representations of other different tasks. For example, it reconstructs context from the intermediate representations of QG and QA task, that could better utilize the correlation between the context of different tasks in representation learning and provide more task-specific information. Experimental results show that our Triple-Joint Model yields much better performance over several state-of-the-art models.

2 Related Work

Typically, QG could be processed by transforming input text into symbolic representation, which then will be transformed into a question. The traditional methods for QG are either based on rules [1], or slot-filling with question templates [7], which often involve pipelines of independent components that are difficult to be tuned for final performance measures. To address the weaknesses above, some end-to-end neural models are proposed. For example, [4] use a sequence-to-sequence model with an attention mechanism derived from the encoder states.

Given the intrinsic connections between QA and QG, some recent efforts propose to train a joint model for both QA and QG. [17] take both QA and QG as generation tasks and adopt an attention-based sequence-to-sequence architecture. Alternatively, [15] use the "duality" between QA and QG as a regularization term to influence the learning of QA and QG models. They implemented simple yet effective QA and QG models, both of which are neural network based approaches.

As stated by [12], the objective and its importance are the two core aspects of a question. We could hardly judge the quality of a question without knowing the context of the question. Thus, people tend to introduce context information into a QG system to guide the generation of questions, instead of using the input answer only. To the best of our knowledge, we are the first to do triple-joint learning for QA and QG models by introducing one more task, that is, context self-encoding (CSE).

3 Basic Uni-task Model

In this section, we first give a general definition of the QG task, then introduce our uni-task model that could be applied for QG task alone.

3.1 Tasks Definition

The primary task in this paper is QG, which can be formally defined as follows:

Given an answer $A = (w_1^a, w_2^a, ...w_{T_A}^a)$, and relevant sequential sentences $C = (w_1^c, w_2^c, ..., w_{T_C}^c)$ as input context, the task is to generate a sequential text, say question $Q = (w_1^q, w_2^q, ..., w_{T_Q}^q)$, that could be answered by the answer A according to C, where T_x denotes the length of x ($x \in \{C, Q, A\}$).

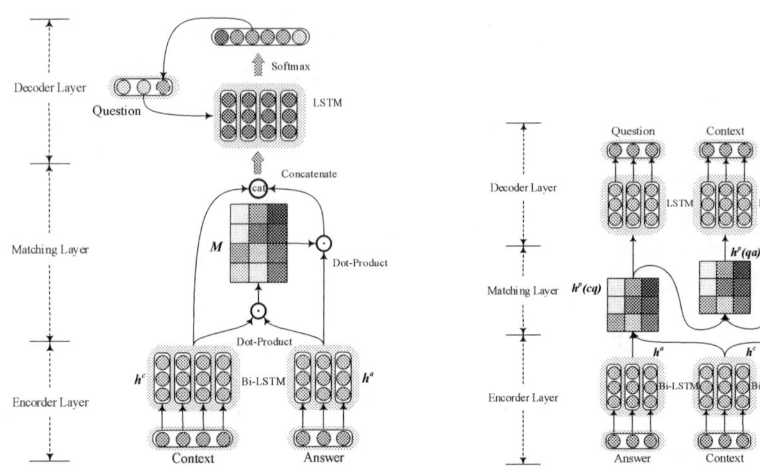

Fig. 1. Uni-Task model overview

Fig. 2. Triple-Joint model overview

3.2 Overview of Uni-task Model

Figure 1 depicts the overview of our uni-task model for QG task, which can be separated into three parts: encoder layer, dot-product matching layer and decoder layer.

3.3 Encoder Layer

We first convert the words x_t into continuous representations with an embedding matrix W_e. After that, the input sequence is processed by a bidirectional recurrent network [8].

$$\overrightarrow{h_t} = \overrightarrow{f}(x_t, h_{t-1}), \tag{1}$$

$$\overleftarrow{h_t} = \overleftarrow{f}(x_t, h_{t+1}) \tag{2}$$

$$h_t = [\overrightarrow{h_t}; \overleftarrow{h_t}] \tag{3}$$

where $h_t \in \mathbb{R}^n$ is a hidden state at time t. $f(\cdot)$ is LSTM.

3.4 Dot-Product Matching Layer

In order to incorporate answer information into context representation, We introduce a match mechanism to decide the importance of each individual representation automatically, using Dot-Product to calculate a pair-wise matching matrix M which indicates the pair-wise matching degree of one context word and one answer word.

Formally, when given context and answer representation h^c and h^a, we can compute a context and answer pair representation h^p as follows:

$$h_t^p = f(h_{t-1}^p, [h_t^c, c_t]) \tag{4}$$

where c_t is an attention-pooling vector of the whole answer, which can be computed as a weighted sum of the sequence of annotations $(h_1^a, \cdots, h_{T_a}^a)$ to which an encoder maps the answer, that is,

$$c_t = \frac{\sum_{i=1}^{T_a} exp(M(t,i))h_i^a}{\sum_{k=1}^{T_a} exp(M(t,k))} \tag{5}$$

where $M(t,i)$ is the weight of annotation h_i^a in time step t, which is the pair-wise matching degree of one context word and one answer word, i.e.,

$$M(t,i) = \frac{h_t^c (h_i^a)^T}{\sqrt{d_k}} \tag{6}$$

where d_k is the dimension of h^c.

3.5 Decoder Layer

We implement a attention-based LSTM decoder to read the context-answer pair representation h^p and generate question word by word. At each time step, the decoder generates a question word y_i by sampling from a distribution of the target vocabulary until sampling the token representing the end of sentence. The hidden state of the decoder s_i and the pair representation h_i^p at each time step i of the encoding process are computed with a weight matrix W_α to obtain the global attention $\alpha_{i.j}$ and the context vector c_i. It is described below:

$$p_{gen}(y_i|y_1, ..., y_{i-1}, \mathbf{x}) = g(y_{i-1}, s_i, c_i) \tag{7}$$

$$s_i = f(s_{i-1}, y_{i-1}, c_i) \tag{8}$$

$$c_i = \sum_{j=1}^{T_x} \alpha_{ij} h_j^p \tag{9}$$

$$\alpha_{ij} = \frac{exp(e_{ij})}{\sum_{k=1}^{T_x} exp(e_{ik})} \tag{10}$$

$$e_{ij} = a(s_{i-1}, h_j^p) \tag{11}$$

where $f(\cdot)$ is LSTM, $g(\cdot)$ is a nonlinear, potentially multi-layered function that outputs the probability of y_t, and $a(\cdot)$ is a feedforward neural network.

3.6 Training and Inference

Given the context c and answer a, our uni-task model for QG can be trained end-to-end using stochastic gradient descent by minimizing the negative conditional log likelihood of the reference y with respect to θ:

$$\mathcal{L}_{single} = -\sum_{t=1}^{T} \log p(y_t | y_{<t}, c, a; \theta) \tag{12}$$

where θ represents the trainable model parameters.

4 Triple-Joint Modeling Using Cross-Task Autoencoder

There are some existing work on joint learning for QG and QA which learns the correlation between two uni-task models through a shared encoding layer [16,17]. However, a shared encoding layer tends to learn common information between tasks, but might ignore the task-specific information. To address above limitations, we propose a Triple-Joint model for QG by integrating with QA and CSE. In particular, our joint model incorporates QG, QA and CSE into a single training process with a cross-task autoencoder.

4.1 Cross-Task Autoencoder

Autoencoder is able to encode texts in a way to better preserve syntactic, semantic, and discourse coherence [5]. However, the basic autoencoder model is not suitable for exploiting the complex correlations of representations from different tasks, given that it will learn different level representation for inputs with different reconstruction losses.

Meanwhile, considering that the context is the core junction to connect QG and QA task, while QG and QA tasks are good choices to guide the autoencoder to learn the context representation, we integrate a context self-encoding task(CSE) into QA&QG joint model and propose a cross-task autoencoder to learn complete context information (i.e., both common information and task-specific information) for different task in order to alleviate the weak point of shared layer in traditional joint learning. Unlike the basic autoencoder which reconstructs the input itself, this cross-task autoencoder reconstructs input from the intermediate representations of different tasks. It incorporates representation learning and correlation learning into a single process, thus some correlations of QG, QA and CES could be captured in the reconstruction loss.

As illustrated in Fig. 2, our triple-joint model with cross-task autoencoder can be viewed as a combination of three sub-networks, each of which is a basic uni-task model. Among them, CSE task is the core junction to connect QG task and QA task. These sub-networks are connected by the intermediate representation of context. Each sub-network in the triple-joint model is responsible for a task. In the learning process, the three sub-networks are coupled at their intermediate representation of matching layer. After learning, the three sub-networks could exhibit the corresponding complete representation.

For our triple-joint cross-task autoencoder, both the input x_1, x_2, x_3 and output y_1, y_2, y_3 are the same context, question and answer. The model first encoding context, question and answer into vector representation h^c, h^q and h^a, then reconstructs question based on the match representation $h^p(c, a)$ of h^c and h^a, as well as the answer based on match representation $h^p(c, q)$ of h^c and h^q. Meanwhile, the match representation $h^p(a, q)$ of $h^p(c, a)$ and $h^p(c, q)$ is used to reconstruct context, different from $h^p(c, a)$ and $h^p(c, q)$, $h^p(a, q)$ is computed as follows:

$$\tilde{h^p}(a, q) = tanh([h^p(c, a); h^p(c, q)]W_r) \tag{13}$$

$$gate = \sigma([h^p(c, a); h^p(c, q)]W_g) \tag{14}$$

$$h^p(a, q) = gate \cdot \tilde{h^p}(a, q) + (1 - gate) \cdot h^c \tag{15}$$

where the projections are parameter matrices $W_r \in \mathbb{R}^{2d_{model} \times d_{model}}$, $W_g \in \mathbb{R}^{2d_{model} \times d_{model}}$, $\sigma(\cdot)$ denotes the sigmoid activation function, the output vector $h^p(a, q)$ is a linear interpolation of the input h^c and the intermediate vector $\tilde{h^p}(a, q)$. A *gate* is used to control the composition degree to which the intermediate vector is exposed.

4.2 Training and Inference

Given a training corpus include context c, question q and answer a, the Cross-Task Autoencoder can also be trained end-to-end. The loss function consists three parts: the loss computed by QG task, QA task and CES task respectively. To simplify the notations, the network parameters are grouped as θ.

$$\begin{aligned} \mathcal{L}_{Joint} = \lambda_1 \mathcal{L}_{single}(q'; c, a; \theta_q) + \lambda_2 \mathcal{L}_{single}(a'; c, q; \theta_a) \\ + (1 - \lambda_1 - \lambda_2)\mathcal{L}_{single}(c'; c, a, q; \theta_c) \end{aligned} \tag{16}$$

where λ_1 and λ_2 are hyper-parameters to tune the impacts of the QG and QA tasks. Meanwhile, it is trade off between two groups of objectives: correlation losses and reconstruction losses. An appropriate value for λ_1 and λ_2 are crucial.

5 Experiments

5.1 Experimental Settings

The experimental settings include dataset, hyper-parameters and evaluation metrics.

Dataset. We mainly focus on the Stanford Question Answering Dataset (SQuAD) [11] processed by [4] to train and evaluate our model. Since the dataset processed by [4] lacks the answer corresponding to the question, we seek the corresponding document of question from document-list provided by [4], which is used to find the corresponding answer to expand the dataset.

Table 1. Automatic evaluation results of different models

Model	BLEU 1	BLEU 2	BLEU 3	BLEU 4	METEOR	ROUGE-L
Seq2seq	31.34	13.79	7.36	4.26	9.88	29.75
Att-Seq2seq	43.09	25.96	17.50	12.28	16.62	39.75
MPQG	-	-	-	12.84	18.02	41.39
MPQG+R	-	-	-	13.98	18.77	42.72
JointQA	44.72	27.21	18.43	13.05	17.94	42.76
Triple-Joint CAE	**46.72**	**29.34**	**20.40**	**14.76**	**19.12**	**44.05**

Hyper-paramters. We implement our experiments in PyTorch on an NVIDIA Tesla V100 GPU. For word embedding, we use pre-trained case-sensitive GloVe embeddings [10] for both contexts, questions and answers. The number of LSTM hidden units (h_{model}) is 600 and we set the number of LSTMs layers to 2 in both the encoder and the decoder. $\lambda_1 = \lambda_2 = 0.4$.

Evaluation Metrics. Following the previous studies [4], we choose the evaluation package released by [2] to evaluate the performance of our model, which was originally used to score image captions. The package includes BLEU 1, BLEU 2, BLEU 3, BLEU 4 [9], METEOR [3] and ROUGE-L [6] evaluation scripts.

5.2 Comparison with Baselines

To evaluate the performance of our model, we compare our model with several state-of-the-art QG methods as listed below, where we directly adopt the experimental settings and results reported by [4] for the first 5 baselines in the list.

- Seq2seq [14] is a basic encoder-decoder sequence learning system.
- Att-Seq2Seq [4] using a conditional neural language model with a global attention mechanism, they entirely ignored the answer.
- MPQG [13] follows the classic encoder-decoder framework. The encoder takes a passage and an answer as input then performs answer understanding by matching the answer with the passage from multiple perspectives.
- MPQG+R [13] is the model developed from MPQG. Here the model is fine-tuned with the policy gradient reinforcement learning algorithm after pre-training.
- JointQA [17] is a QG and QA joint model, which encodes the document and generates a question (answer) given an answer (question).

Table 1 shows automatic metric evaluation results for our models and baselines. As can be observed, our triple-joint model with cross-task autoencoder (**Triple-Joint CAE** for short in the tables) reaches better performances on QG tasks than the baseline models. In particular, compared with the JointQA model, our model has 1.71, 1.18 and 1.29 relative gain in BLEU4, METEOR and ROUGE-L respectively, which proves that our auxiliary task CSE makes some contributions to our primary tasks, and the effectiveness of the employed cross-task autoencoder in joint learning.

Table 2. Influence of different auxiliary tasks

Model	BLEU 1	BLEU 2	BLEU 3	BLEU 4	METEOR	ROUGE-L
Uni-Task Model	45.11	27.89	19.21	13.76	18.41	43.61
QG&CES-Joint Model	45.32	28.14	19.32	13.88	18.51	43.72
QG&QA-Joint Model	45.78	28.62	19.71	14.18	18.73	43.85
Triple-Joint CAE	**46.72**	**29.34**	**20.40**	**14.76**	**19.12**	**44.05**

Table 3. Examples of generated questions, where the golden answers are underlined, and the text copied from context are in Italian style in the generated questions.

Context	In the First World War, Devonport was the headquarters of Western Approaches Command until 1941 and *Sunderland flying boats* were operated by the Royal Australian Air Force
Golden	What force used Sunderland flying boats out of Devonport?
Uni-Task	Who operated the *Sunderland boats*?
Triple-Joint	Who operated the *Sunderland flying boats*?

5.3 Influence of Different Auxiliary Tasks

We compared the performance of our proposed model with Uni-Task Model and Joint model to further illustrate the influence of the QA task and CSE task for QG task.

The experimental results are shown in Table 2. We can observe that: (1) Our Uni-Task model could outperform the state-of-the-art MPQG model and the JoinQA model, which demonstrates that our dot-product matching strategy, although simple, works effectively in the model. (2) Both the QG&CES-Joint model and QG&QA-joint model outperform the Uni-Task model, which proves that joint models can utilize the intrinsic connections between the two tasks, and learn more useful information. (3) Compared with the Uni-Task model and the Joint models, our Triple-Joint CAE model performs better. This indicates that cross-task autoencoder could better utilize the correlation between the context of different tasks in representation learning, so this CSE task could provide more complete information for QG.

5.4 Discussion and Analysis

In this subsection, we provide an examples and analyze the performance of different question types.

Case Study. Table 3 lists an example for case study. Basically, our model could generate questions that are semantically similar to the golden questions. For example, it can be observed that our model tends to use the text related to the answer from the context to generate questions, which are more semantically consistent with the context and the target answers.

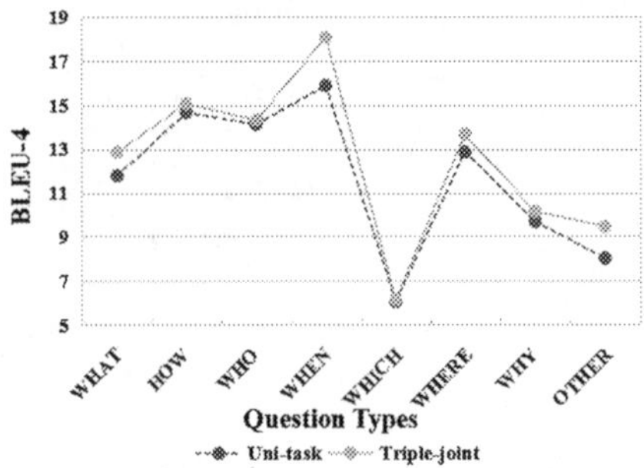

Fig. 3. Comparison by question types.

Analysis on Type of Generated Questions. We classify the questions into different types, i.e., WHAT, HOW, WHO, WHEN, WHICH, WHERE, WHY and OTHER, and evaluate the generated questions and answers for each question type. Figure 3 shows the automatic metric evaluation results of different question types. As can be seen, the Triple-Joint CAE model always performs better than the Uni-Task model, while the best performance can be observed on the WHEN problems. For the majority question types, WHAT, HOW, WHO and WHEN, our model performs well. For type WHICH, it can be observed that neither precision nor recall are acceptable. The reason may cause this: WHICH-type questions account for about 7.2% in training data, which may not be sufficient to learn to generate this type of questions.

6 Conclusion

This work incorporates QG, QA and CSE into a single training process with cross-task autoencoder for joint representation learning. Experiments conducted on processed SQuAD dataset show that our triple-joint model outperforms several state-of-the-art QG models we compare with in this paper. As a future work, we will consider using Variational Autoencoder (VAE) to generate more semantically reasonable questions, which has been shown successful on several areas such as image generation.

Acknowledgments. This research is partially supported by National Natural Science Foundation of China (Grant No. 61632016, 61572336, 61572335, 61772356), and the Natural Science Research Project of Jiangsu Higher Education Institution (No. 17KJA520003, 18KJA520010).

References

1. Ali, H., Chali, Y., Hasan, S.A.: Automation of question generation from sentences. In: Proceedings of QG2010: The Third Workshop on Question Generation, pp. 58–67 (2010)

2. Chen, X., et al.: Microsoft COCO captions: data collection and evaluation server. arXiv preprint arXiv:1504.00325 (2015)
3. Denkowski, M., Lavie, A.: Meteor universal: language specific translation evaluation for any target language. In: Proceedings of the Ninth Workshop on Statistical Machine Translation, pp. 376–380 (2014)
4. Du, X., Shao, J., Cardie, C.: Learning to ask: neural question generation for reading comprehension. In: Proceedings of the 55th Annual Meeting of the Association for Computational Linguistics (Volume 1: Long Papers). vol. 1, pp. 1342–1352 (2017)
5. Li, J., Luong, M.T., Jurafsky, D.: A hierarchical neural autoencoder for paragraphs and documents. arXiv preprint arXiv:1506.01057 (2015)
6. Lin, C.Y.: ROUGE: a package for automatic evaluation of summaries. Text Summarization Branches Out (2004)
7. Lindberg, D., Popowich, F., Nesbit, J., Winne, P.: Generating natural language questions to support learning on-line. In: Proceedings of the 14th European Workshop on Natural Language Generation, pp. 105–114 (2013)
8. Mikolov, T., Karafiát, M., Burget, L., Černockỳ, J., Khudanpur, S.: Recurrent neural network based language model. In: Eleventh Annual Conference of the International Speech Communication Association (2010)
9. Papineni, K., Roukos, S., Ward, T., Zhu, W.J.: Bleu: a method for automatic evaluation of machine translation. In: Proceedings of the 40th Annual Meeting on Association for Computational Linguistics, pp. 311–318. Association for Computational Linguistics (2002)
10. Pennington, J., Socher, R., Manning, C.: GloVe: global vectors for word representation. In: Proceedings of the 2014 Conference on Empirical Methods in Natural Language Processing (EMNLP), pp. 1532–1543 (2014)
11. Rajpurkar, P., Zhang, J., Lopyrev, K., Liang, P.: SQuAD: 100,000+ questions for machine comprehension of text. arXiv preprint arXiv:1606.05250 (2016)
12. Rus, V., Arthur, C.G.: The question generation shared task and evaluation challenge. The University of Memphis. National Science Foundation. Citeseer (2009)
13. Song, L., Wang, Z., Hamza, W.: A unified query-based generative model for question generation and question answering. arXiv preprint arXiv:1709.01058 (2017)
14. Sutskever, I., Vinyals, O., Le, Q.V.: Sequence to sequence learning with neural networks. In: Advances in Neural Information Processing Systems, pp. 3104–3112 (2014)
15. Tang, D., Duan, N., Qin, T., Yan, Z., Zhou, M.: Question answering and question generation as dual tasks. arXiv preprint arXiv:1706.02027 (2017)
16. Wang, J., et al.: A multi-task learning approach for improving product title compression with user search log data. arXiv preprint arXiv:1801.01725 (2018)
17. Wang, T., Yuan, X., Trischler, A.: A joint model for question answering and question generation. arXiv preprint arXiv:1706.01450 (2017)

Deep Multi-task Learning with Cross Connected Layer for Slot Filling

Junsheng Kong[1], Yi Cai[1(✉)], Da Ren[1], and Zilu Li[2]

[1] South China University of Technology, Guangzhou, China
ycai@scut.edu.cn
[2] Guangzhou Tianhe Foreign Language School, Guangzhou, China

Abstract. Slot filling is a critical subtask of Spoken language understanding (SLU) in task-oriented dialogue systems. This is a common scenario that different slot filling tasks from different but similar domains have overlapped sets of slots (shared slots). In this paper, we propose an effective deep multi-task learning with Cross Connected Layer (CCL) to capture this information. The experiments show that our proposed model outperforms some mainstream baselines on the Chinese E-commerce datasets. The significant improvement in the F1 socre of the shared slots proves that CCL can capture more information about shared slots.

Keywords: Multi-task learning · Slot filling · Shared slots · CCL

1 Introduction

Spoken Language Understanding, which aims to interpret the semantic meanings conveyed by input utterances, is an important component in task-oriented dialog systems. Slot filling, a sub-problem of SLU, extracts semantic constituents by using the words of input utterance to fill in predefined slots in a semantic frame [1].

Slot filling problem can be regarded as a sequence labeling task, which assigns an appropriate semantic label to each word with a given input utterance. State-of-the-art sequence labeling models are typically based on BiLSTM-CRF [2,3]. There are a variety of task-oriented dialog systems of different domains such as air travel [4], computer shopping guide and phone shopping guide.

It is common that there is semantic correspondence between slots defined in different domains. Consider these two sentences:

1. I want to buy a computer which is about $\{_{price\_middle}$ four thousand yuan$\}$ and has a ram of $\{_{ram\_size}$ 8 G$\}$.
2. I plan to get a new mobile phone of $\{_{brand}$ Huawei$\}$, which costs about $\{_{price\_middle}$ 3000 yuan$\}$.

These two sentences respectively come from the domain of computer shopping guide and the domain of phone shopping guide. We can find out that these

J. Tang et al. (Eds.): NLPCC 2019, LNAI 11839, pp. 308–317, 2019.
https://doi.org/10.1007/978-3-030-32236-6_27

two sentences have the same slot "price_middle" which means the median of psychological price. We denote the same slot between the slot filling tasks of different domains as shared slot.

Multi-task Learning (MTL) has been applied to various models and problems. But most of the current multitasking learning methods [5] only share parameters at the bottom layer. We believe that this model structure can't make good use of the information of shared slots. To achieve this goal, we propose the CCL to encourage all tasks to learn a common label representation. We combine the multi-task BiLSTM-CRF model and this layer to address for slot filling problem with shared slots.

The main contribution of this work lies on:

1. We propose an original MTL architecture with CCL to capture the information of shared slots. The experiment results show the effectiveness of the CCL.
2. We build three datasets for slot filling tasks on three domains: computer, mobile phone, and camera. These datasets enrich the experimental data in Chinese slot filling field.

The rest of the paper is organized as follows: Sect. 2 introduces related work. Section 3 describes the details of our method. In Sect. 4, we illustrate our experiments. Finally, we draw our conclusions in Sect. 5.

2 Related Work

Our work is in line with existing methods using neural network for slot filling. Slot filling can be treated as a sequence labeling problem. Here, we use the IOB [6] scheme for representing segmentation. In recent years, deep learning approaches have been explored due to its successful application in many NLP tasks. For slot filling problem, deep learning search has started as extensions of DNNs and DBNs [7] and is sometimes merged with CRFs [8]. Especially with the rediscovery of LSTM cells [9] for RNNs, this architecture has started to emerge [10]. Many neural network architectures have been used such as simple RNNs [11, 12], convolutional neural networks (CNNs) [13], LSTMs [14] and variations like encoder-decoder [15] and external memory [16]. In general, these works adopt a BiLSTM as the major labeling architecture to extract various features, then use a CRF layer [2] to model the label dependency.

MTL has attracted increasing attention in both academia and industry recently. By jointly learning across multiple tasks [17], we can improve performance on each task and reduce the need for labeled data. There has been several attempts of using multi-task learning on sequence labeling task [18–21]. Hakkani-Tur et al. [5] proposed a multi-domain SLU model using BiLSTM. They train the multi-domain model by using data from all the domains and let the data from each domain to reinforce each other. Kim et al. proposed neural generalization of the feature augmentation domain adaptation methods [22]. Their model uses an LSTM to captures global patterns by training on data.

3 Model

To better utilize the shared slots' information between multiple tasks, we propose a novel multi-task architecture with CCL (MT-BiLSTM-CRF-CCL). As shown in Fig. 1, the architecture contains four layers: (1) Embedding Layer, (2) Shared BiLSTM Layer, (3) Cross Connected Layer, (4) Task-oriented CRF Output Layer.

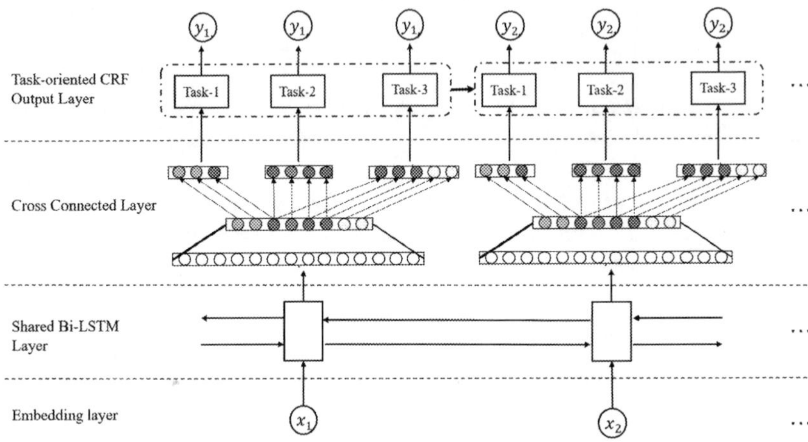

Fig. 1. The architecture of our proposed model

When learning multiple task $t = \{1, 2, \ldots, T\}$, we denote the task-specific label set as L_t. Each task shares the same BiLSTM layer to get the representations, partially share the last fully connected layer, and has their own CRF output layer. In the training procedure, each task updates the whole model's parameters one by one in each training epoch. Different from previous multi-task work, we propose a novel CCL for multi-task learning to capture the information of shared slots. We will introduce the details of these four layers as follows.

3.1 Embedding Layer

In this layer, we take the characters as the input of our model. It has been shown that character-based methods outperform word-based methods for Chinese sequence tagging problem [23,24]. In the character sentence $S = \{c_1, c_2, \ldots, c_n\}$, each character c_i is represented using

$$x_i^c = e^c(c_i) \tag{1}$$

where e^c denotes a character embedding looking table.

3.2 Shared BiLSTM Layer

Long short-term memory (LSTM) [9] is a recurrent neural network (RNN) that models interactions between input vectors and hidden layers. Since most sequence tagging tasks benefit from both historical and future context information of the words when deciding on the label for a given token, most LSTM sequence taggers use the bi-directional model. The BiLSTM uses two LSTMs to enables the hidden states to capture both historical and future context information of the words.

We build a shared BiLSTM layer for several tasks to get the representation of the input sentences. The shared BiLSTM layer is trained with the feedback by all the tasks. Mathematically, the input of this BiLSTM layer is the output of the embedding layer $X = \{x_1^c, x_2^c, \ldots, x_n^c\}$. The output of BiLSTM layer is a sequence of the hidden states for each input word, denoted as $H = (h_1, h_2, \ldots, h_n)$. Each final hidden state is the concatenation of the forward $\overrightarrow{h}$ and backward $\overleftarrow{h}$ hidden states. We view BiLSTM as a function $BiLSTM(x_i)$:

$$\overrightarrow{h}_i = LSTM(x_i, \overrightarrow{h}_{i-1}), \overleftarrow{h}_i = LSTM(x_i, \overleftarrow{h}_{i-1}) \tag{2}$$

$$BiLSTM(x_i) = h_i = \overrightarrow{h}_i(x_i) \oplus \overleftarrow{h}_i(x_i) \tag{3}$$

In addition, we stack multiple BiLSTMs to make the model deeper, in which the output h_i^l of layer l becomes the input of layer $l+1$, e.g. $h_i^{l+1} = BiLSTM^{l+1}(h_i^l)$.

3.3 Cross Connected Layer

In previous multi-task work on multi-domain, each task makes a task-oriented fully connected layer or a task-oriented CRF as the output layer. The information between multiple tasks is shared at the BiLSTM layer. But this multi-task model only shares parameters at the bottom layer, it is difficult for multi-task model to obtain information between slot labels. Therefore, in order to better extract the information of shared slots, we propose a novel CCL to encourage the multi-task model to learn a shared label representation between different tasks. CCL has two processes: union process and separate process.

Union Process: This process transforms the hidden states h_i into the union label representation D_i on the union slots L_u.
The union slots L_u is

$$L_u = \bigcup_t L_t. \tag{4}$$

The shared label representation D_i is

$$D_i = h_i \, W_{fc}. \tag{5}$$

Here, the dimensionality of W_{fc} is $s \times l$ where s is the hidden size and l is the size of union slots L_u.

The parameters will be updated by all of shared slots' training data of all tasks, and this make our model get better use of the information of shared slots.

Separate Process: This process convert the shared label representation D_i to the task-oriented label representation $D_{(i,t)}$ for task t. For each task-oriented label representation $D_{(i,t)}$, it only use the label representation of corresponding slots. This process avoids the problem caused by that we mix all slots into one label representation. The procedure of the separate algorithm is summarized as Algorithm 1.

Algorithm 1: Separate slots

```
for t in 1, 2, ..., T do
    for (index, slot) in L_u do
        if slot in L_t then
            D_(i,t).append(D_i[index])
        end
    end
end
```

Among the algorithm, the "index" and "slot" here represent the subscript and label value of the L_u respectively.

3.4 Task-Oriented CRF Output Layer

Label dependencies are crucial for sequence labeling tasks. For example, in the task with IOB annotation, it is not only meaningless but illegal to annotate I-price_middle after B-brand (i.e., mixing the price and the brand). Therefore, jointly decoding a chain of labels can ensure the resulting label sequence to be meaningful. CRF has been included in most state-of-the-art models to capture such information and further avoid generating illegal annotations [25]. Consequently, we build a task-oriented standard CRF layer upon the CCL layer for all tasks.

The CRF layer takes the output of the CCL $D_{(1,t)}, D_{(2,t)}, \ldots, D_{(n,t)}$ as input. For task t, the probability of a label sequence $y_t = l_1, l_2, \ldots, l_n$ is

$$P(y_t|s) = \frac{exp(\sum_i (W^{l_i}_{CRF-t} h_{(i,t)} + b^{(l_{(i-1,t)}, l_{(i,t)})}_{CRF-t}))}{\sum_{y'} (exp(\sum_i (W^{l_i}_{CRF-t} h_{(i,t)} + b^{(l_{(i-1,t)}, l_{(i,t)})}_{CRF-t})))} \tag{6}$$

where y' represents an arbitary label sequence, $W^{l_i}_{CRF-t}$ is a model parameter specific to l_i of task t, and $b^{(l_{(i-1,t)}, l_{(i,t)})}_{CRF-t}$ is a bias specific to $l_{(i-1,t)}$ and $l_{(i,t)}$.

We predict the output sequence by using the Viterbi algorithm [26] to find the highest scored label sentence. Given a set of training data $\{(s_i, y_i)|_{i=1}^{N}\}$, the loss function is

$$L = -\sum_{l=1}^{N} log(P(y_i|s_i)). \tag{7}$$

4 Experiments

4.1 Datasets

We evaluate the proposed model on the datasets across multiple domains: E-commerce Computer, E-commerce Camera, E-commerce Phone. These datasets are obtained from the websites of the camera, computer and mobile phone. Then, we manually filter and tag the data to get the final datasets. These datasets are divided into three parts: train set, development set and test set. The vocabulary size of the dataset is 1189. The Table 1 shows the statistics of these datasets. These datasets are available online[1].

Table 1. The statistics of the datasets

Dataset	Train	Dev	Test	Label num	Avg. length
E-commerce Computer	6145	1087	1113	47	17.20
E-commerce Camera	3408	522	521	25	21.84
E-commerce Phone	3455	626	616	37	19.00

4.2 Experimental Setting

We use the 100-dimensional character embedding from Wikimedia documents trained by word2vec. For the shared BiLSTM Layer, we use a 2-layers BiLSTM. The hidden size of BiLSTM is set to be 100. The training procedure consists of two stages: joint training and fine-tuning. We use the Adam optimizer to train our architecture. The batch size 2 and 32 are applied in joint training stage and fine-tuning stage, respectively. The dropout rate is set to be 0.25.

In this experiment, we use several mainstream models including BiLSTM, BiLSTM-CRF, MT-BiLSTM, MT-BiLSTM-CRF. For the single task, we use a BiLSTM and a fully connected layer to form BiLSTM model and apply a CRF layer upon the BiLSTM layer to get BiLSTM-CRF model. For multi-task model (MT-BiLSTM, MT-BiLSTM-CRF), we share the embedding layer and the first LSTM layer.

[1] https://github.com/JansonKong/Deep-Multi-task-Learning-with-Cross-Connected-Layer-for-Slot-Filling.

4.3 Experimental Results

We compare the performance of our models to all four baselines. The comparison is conducted on three datasets: E-commerce camera dataset, E-commerce computer dataset, E-commerce phone dataset. The evaluation measures are widely-used Precision, Recall and F1-Measure in information retrieval area. The results are shown on Table 2.

From the results, on the E-commerce camera dataset, single-task BiLSTM model obtains a F1-score of 89.08% and the single-task BiLSTM-CRF model obtains a F1-score of 90.71%. Compared with single-task models, the multi-task models (MT-BiLSTM, MT-BiLSTM-CRF, MT-BiLSTM-CCL, MT-BiLSTM-CRF-CCL) get better results which prove that multi-task models work better on these tasks. The results present that our MT-BiLSTM-CRF-CCL model outperform all the neural network baselines (p-value < 0.005). Compared with the strong baseline MT-BiLSTM-CRF model (p-value < 0.005), MT-BiLSTM-CRF-CCL model increases respectively by 3.66%, 2.93% and 1.21% in the F1 scores on these datasets.

In order to verify the effectiveness of CCL, We also combine MT-BiLSTM model with CCL to get MT-BiLSTM-CCL model. The results show that the MT-BiLSTM-CCL model has made a huge improvement in the F1 score compared with MT-BiLSTM model. This result proves the effectiveness of the CCL.

To verify that CCL layer can effectively utilize the information of shared slots, we calculate the F1 values of shared slots and non-shared slot respectively. The results are showed on Fig. 2. Compared with the other two models(BiLSTM-CRF, MT-BiLSTM-CRF), we identify that our models with CCL have a similar F1 score on non-shared slots. However, with CCL, both MT-BiLSTM-CRF-CCL and MT-BiLSTM-CCL achieves a significant improvement of F1 score on non-shared slots. This strongly demonstrates that CCL can effectively utilize the information of shared slots from multiple datasets.

Table 2. Experiment results on three datasets

Model	Camera			Computer			Phone		
	P	R	F1	P	R	F1	P	R	F1
BiLSTM	0.878	0.904	0.8908	0.837	0.823	0.8295	0.812	0.797	0.8045
BiLSTM-CRF	0.904	0.910	0.9071	0.896	0.864	0.8800	0.863	0.863	0.8677
MT-BiLSTM	0.909	0.910	0.9092	0.870	0.837	0.8534	0.892	0.902	0.8969
MT-BiLSTM-CRF	0.916	0.919	0.9175	0.905	0.891	0.8981	0.907	0.910	0.9086
MT-BiLSTM-CCL	0.944	**0.952**	0.9480	0.908	0.908	0.9078	0.893	0.914	0.9033
MT-BiLSTM-CRF-CCL	**0.957**	0.951	**0.9541**	**0.931**	**0.924**	**0.9274**	**0.916**	**0.926**	**0.9207**

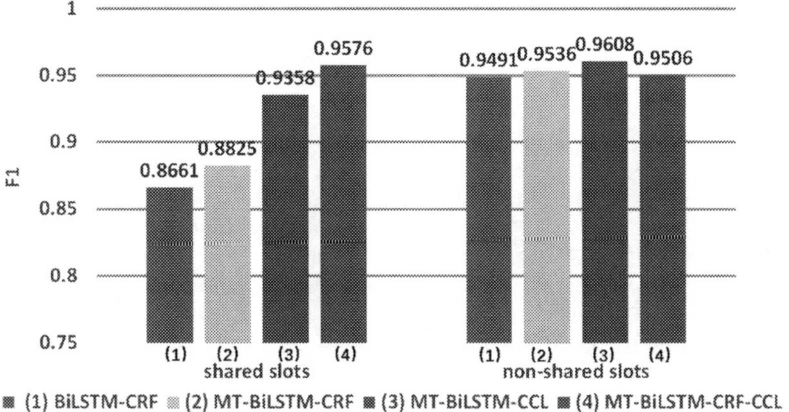

Fig. 2. F1 scores for shared slots and non-shared slots on the E-commerce camera dataset

5 Conclusion

In this paper, we focus on the phenomenon of shared slots between multiple slot filling tasks. In response to this phenomenon, we have proposed a deep multi-task architecture with CCL to capture the information of shared slots. To verify the validity of our approach, we build datasets in three domains. The experimental results show that our model can improve the performance of different slot filling tasks with shared slots. In addition, the proposed method is directly effective and can be easily applied to a similar multi-task model. In the future, we will try to use the CCL to solve other similar problems like text classification tasks with same labels.

Acknowledgment. This work presented in this paper is partially supported by the Fundamental Research Funds for the Central Universities, SCUT (Nos. 2017ZD048, D2182480), the Tiptop Scientific and Technical Innovative Youth Talents of Guangdong special support program (No.2015TQ01X633), the Science and Technology Planning Project of Guangdong Province (No.2017B050506004), the Science and Technology Program of Guangzhou (Nos. 201704030076, 201802010027).

References

1. Mesnil, G., et al.: Using recurrent neural networks for slot filling in spoken language understanding. IEEE/ACM Trans. Audio Speech Lang. Process. **23**(3), 530–539 (2015). https://doi.org/10.1109/TASLP.2014.2383614, https://doi.org/10.1109/TASLP.2014.2383614
2. Huang, Z., Xu, W., Yu, K.: Bidirectional LSTM-CRF models for sequence tagging. CoRR abs/1508.01991 (2015). http://arxiv.org/abs/1508.01991
3. Reimers, N., Gurevych, I.: Optimal hyperparameters for deep LSTM-networks for sequence labeling tasks. CoRR abs/1707.06799 (2017). http://arxiv.org/abs/1707.06799

4. Price, P.J.: Evaluation of spoken language systems: the ATIS domain. In: Speech and Natural Language: Proceedings of a Workshop Held at Hidden Valley, Pennsylvania, USA, 24–27 June 1990 (1990). https://aclanthology.info/papers/H90-1020/h90-1020
5. Hakkani-Tür, D., et al.: Multi-domain joint semantic frame parsing using bi-directional RNN-LSTM. In: 17th Annual Conference of the International Speech Communication Association, Interspeech 2016, San Francisco, CA, USA, 8–12 September 2016, pp. 715–719 (2016). https://doi.org/10.21437/Interspeech.2016-402, https://doi.org/10.21437/Interspeech.2016-402
6. Ramshaw, L.A., Marcus, M.: Text chunking using transformation-based learning. In: Third Workshop on Very Large Corpora, VLC@ACL 1995, Cambridge, Massachusetts, USA, 30 June 1995 (1995). https://aclanthology.info/papers/W95-0107/w95-0107
7. Deoras, A., Sarikaya, R.: Deep belief network based semantic taggers for spoken language understanding. In: 14th Annual Conference of the International Speech Communication Association, INTERSPEECH 2013, Lyon, France, 25–29 August 2013, pp. 2713–2717 (2013). http://www.isca-speech.org/archive/interspeech_2013/i13_2713.html
8. Xu, P., Sarikaya, R.: Convolutional neural network based triangular CRF for joint intent detection and slot filling. In: 2013 IEEE Workshop on Automatic Speech Recognition and Understanding, Olomouc, Czech Republic, 8–12 December 2013, pp. 78–83 (2013). https://doi.org/10.1109/ASRU.2013.6707709, https://doi.org/10.1109/ASRU.2013.6707709
9. Hochreiter, S., Schmidhuber, J.: Long short-term memory. Neural Comput. **9**(8), 1735–1780 (1997). https://doi.org/10.1162/neco.1997.9.8.1735
10. Yao, K., Peng, B., Zhang, Y., Yu, D., Zweig, G., Shi, Y.: Spoken language understanding using long short-term memory neural networks. In: 2014 IEEE Spoken Language Technology Workshop, SLT 2014, South Lake Tahoe, NV, USA, 7–10 December 2014, pp. 189–194 (2014). https://doi.org/10.1109/SLT.2014.7078572, https://doi.org/10.1109/SLT.2014.7078572
11. Yao, K., Zweig, G., Hwang, M.Y., Shi, Y., Yu, D.: Recurrent neural networks for language understanding. In: Interspeech, pp. 2524–2528 (2013)
12. Mesnil, G., et al.: Using recurrent neural networks for slot filling in spoken language understanding. IEEE/ACM Trans. Audio Speech Lang. Process. **23**(3), 530–539 (2014)
13. Xu, P., Sarikaya, R.: Convolutional neural network based triangular CRF for joint intent detection and slot filling. In: 2013 IEEE Workshop on Automatic Speech Recognition and Understanding, pp. 78–83. IEEE (2013)
14. Yao, K., Peng, B., Zhang, Y., Yu, D., Zweig, G., Shi, Y.: Spoken language understanding using long short-term memory neural networks. In: 2014 IEEE Spoken Language Technology Workshop (SLT), pp. 189–194. IEEE (2014)
15. Zhai, F., Potdar, S., Xiang, B., Zhou, B.: Neural models for sequence chunking. In: Proceedings of the Thirty-First AAAI Conference on Artificial Intelligence, San Francisco, California, USA, 4–9 February 2017, pp. 3365–3371 (2017). http://aaai.org/ocs/index.php/AAAI/AAAI17/paper/view/14776
16. Peng, B., Yao, K., Jing, L., Wong, K.: Recurrent neural networks with external memory for spoken language understanding. In: Natural Language Processing and Chinese Computing - 4th CCF Conference, NLPCC 2015, Proceedings, Nanchang, China, 9–13 October 2015, pp. 25–35 (2015). https://doi.org/10.1007/978-3-319-25207-0_3, https://doi.org/10.1007/978-3-319-25207-0_3

17. Caruana, R.: Multitask learning. Mach. Learn. **28**(1), 41–75 (1997). https://doi.org/10.1023/A:1007379606734
18. Peng, N., Dredze, M.: Improving named entity recognition for Chinese social media with word segmentation representation learning. In: Proceedings of the 54th Annual Meeting of the Association for Computational Linguistics, ACL 2016, Volume 2: Short Papers, 7–12 August 2016, Berlin, Germany (2016). http://aclweb.org/anthology/P/P16/P16-2025.pdf
19. Peng, N., Dredze, M.: Multi-task domain adaptation for sequence tagging. In: Proceedings of the 2nd Workshop on Representation Learning for NLP, Rep4NLP@ACL 2017, Vancouver, Canada, 3 August 2017, pp. 91–100 (2017). https://aclanthology.info/papers/W17-2612/w17-2612
20. Yang, Z., Salakhutdinov, R., Cohen, W.W.: Transfer learning for sequence tagging with hierarchical recurrent networks. In: 5th International Conference on Learning Representations, ICLR 2017, Conference Track Proceedings, Toulon, France, 24–26 April 2017 (2017). https://openreview.net/forum?id=ByxpMd9lx
21. Zhao, X., Haihong, E., Song, M.: A joint model based on CNN-LSTMs in dialogue understanding. In: 2018 International Conference on Information Systems and Computer Aided Education (ICISCAE), pp. 471–475. IEEE (2018)
22. Kim, Y., Stratos, K., Sarikaya, R.: Frustratingly easy neural domain adaptation. In: 26th International Conference on Computational Linguistics, Proceedings of the Conference: Technical Papers, COLING 2016, Osaka, Japan, 11–16 December 2016, pp. 387–396 (2016). http://aclweb.org/anthology/C/C16/C16-1038.pdf
23. Liu, Z., Zhu, C., Zhao, T.: Chinese named entity recognition with a sequence labeling approach: based on characters, or based on words? In: Huang, D.-S., Zhang, X., Reyes García, C.A., Zhang, L. (eds.) ICIC 2010. LNCS (LNAI), vol. 6216, pp. 634–640. Springer, Heidelberg (2010). https://doi.org/10.1007/978-3-642-14932-0_78
24. Li, H., Hagiwara, M., Li, Q., Ji, H.: Comparison of the impact of word segmentation on name tagging for Chinese and Japanese. In: Proceedings of the Ninth International Conference on Language Resources and Evaluation, LREC 2014, Reykjavik, Iceland, 26–31 May 2014, pp. 2532–2536 (2014). http://www.lrec-conf.org/proceedings/lrec2014/summaries/358.html
25. Lafferty, J.D., McCallum, A., Pereira, F.C.N.: Conditional random fields: probabilistic models for segmenting and labeling sequence data. In: Proceedings of the Eighteenth International Conference on Machine Learning (ICML 2001), Williams College, Williamstown, MA, USA, June 28–July 1, 2001, pp. 282–289 (2001)
26. Forney, G.D.: The viterbi algorithm. Proc. IEEE **61**(3), 268–278 (1973)

A Sequence-to-Action Architecture for Character-Based Chinese Dependency Parsing with Status History

Hang Liu[1,2], Yujie Zhang[1(✉)], Meng Chen[2], Jinan Xu[1], and Yufeng Chen[1]

[1] School of Computer and Information Technology, Beijing Jiaotong University, Beijing, China
{yjzhang,jaxu,chenyf}@bjtu.edu.cn

[2] JD AI, Beijing, China
{liuhang55,chenmeng20}@jd.com

Abstract. Character-based Chinese dependency parsing jointly learns Chinese word segmentation, POS tagging and dependency parsing to avoid the error propagation problem of pipeline models. Recent works on this task only rely on a local status for prediction at each step, which is insufficient for guiding global better decisions. In this paper, we first present a sequence-to-action model for character-based dependency parsing. In order to exploit decision history for prediction, our model tracks the status of parser particularly including decision history in the decoding procedure by employing a sequential LSTM. Additionally, for resolving the problem of high ambiguities in Chinese characters, we add position-based character embeddings to exploit character information with specific contexts accurately. We conduct experiments on Penn Chinese Treebank 5.1 (CTB-5) dataset, and the results show that our proposed model outperforms existing neural network system in dependency parsing, and performs preferable accuracy in Chinese word segmentation and POS tagging.

Keywords: Character-based Chinese dependency parsing · Decision history · Character information

1 Introduction

Character-based Chinese dependency parsing is a joint model for Chinese word segmentation, POS tagging and dependency parsing, which aims to prevent the error propagation problem of pipeline models [1]. The model is usually implemented using transition-based framework and is viewed as a transition sequence decision task [2]. Existing approaches for joint model are categorized into two types: conventional discrete feature-based approaches [1,3,4] and neural network-based models [5,6]. Feature-based models tackle the effort in hand-crafting effective feature combination and define large feature templates to capture features, and maintain state-of-the-art performance. Neural network-based

J. Tang et al. (Eds.): NLPCC 2019, LNAI 11839, pp. 318–326, 2019.
https://doi.org/10.1007/978-3-030-32236-6_28

models uses dense vectors and LSTM to reduce the cost of feature engineering, and achieves competitive performance in all three tasks when using very few features. Despite of existing approaches success, there are still two problems.

The first problem is insufficient history information. In transition-based framework, these transition actions modify the current parser state after each decision, and the previous parser state is discarded. Recent evidence on word-level dependency parsing [7] and natural language inference [8] reveals that history information of actions taken and parser state is of crucial important. However, feature-based joint models and neural network-based joint models rely on local parser state for the action prediction at that point in transition sequence. This prevents model from exploring sufficient context information of parser state for making better decisions.

The second problem is the ambiguity of Chinese character. A Chinese simplified character may be derived from two traditional characters and therefore becomes more ambiguous. For example, the character "发" in the "头发" (hair) and " 发财" (make a fortune) has different meanings that are the " 髮" (hair) and "發" (make) respectively. It is worth noting that when representing the meaning of "髮" (hair), the character "发" is located at the end of the word as an object, while when representing the meaning of "發" (make), the character "发" is located at the beginning of the word as a verb. Most previous models rely on single one-hot representation [1,3,4] or distributed representation [5,6] of character. However, existing character embedding did not catch such position information for disambiguation.

In order to address these two problems, we take advantage of the seq2seq [9] to capture history information and propose a sequence-to-action joint model. In the encoder of the model, we use attention mechanism and position-based character embeddings to capture character information with specific contexts. In the decoder, a sequential LSTM is used to track history information, including previous transition actions taken by the parser and all other previous parser state in the decoding procedure. We evaluate our model on CTB-5 dataset, and find that it significantly outperforms the bi-LSTM [5] joint model in each task and compares favorably with the state-of-the-art feature engineering joint models.

Our contributions are summarized as follows:

- We first conduct encoder-decoder architecture for Character-based Chinese dependency parsing, which allows the model to track the history of decision taken by parser.
- The sequence-to-action joint model incorporates position-based character embedding to capture more exact meanings of a character within specific contexts.
- We evaluate our model on CTB-5 dataset and the results show that our model outperforms existing bi-LSTM joint model.

2 Sequence-to-Action Joint Model

This section describes our proposed model. Transition-based parsing is a task of predicting a series of transition actions $y \in Y$ for a given sentence, where

$Y = \{\text{SH, AP, RR, RL}\}$. Following the arc-standard algorithm [10], our model consists of one buffer and one stack. The buffer contains character in the input sentence, and the stack contains partially-built dependency subtrees.

The subtrees in the stack are formed by the following transition actions:

- SH(pos): Shift the first character of the buffer to the top of the stack as a new word, and the POS tag (pos) is attached to the word.
- AP: Append the first character of the buffer to the end of the top word of the stack.
- RR: Reduce the right word of the top two words of the stack, and make the right child node of the left word.
- RL: Reduce the left word of the top two words of the stack, and make the left child node of the right word.

Given one sentence $S = (c_1, ..., c_i, ..., c_n)$, the aim of the model is to predict the groundtruth of actions:

$$y^* = \arg\max \Pi_{t=1}^{|y|} P(y_t | parser_t) \tag{1}$$

where $P(.)$ is the sequence-to-action joint model here. y_t and $parser_t$ are the action and parser state at time step t respectively. $|y|$ is the action number.

The sequence-to-action architecture we proposed for Chinese parsing is illustrated as in Fig. 1, which consists of two components: **an encoder layer** converts the input sentence into distributed representation; **a decoder layer** captures parser state and tracks history information to make decisions.

2.1 Encoder Layer

Given input sentence $S = (c_1, ..., c_i, ..., c_n)$, the encoder layer first converts them into vectors $(v_1, ..., v_i, ..., v_n)$ by looking up M and the corresponding position-based character vectors $(v_i^s, v_i^b, v_i^m, v_i^e)$ are retrieved by looking up *PM*, where M and *PM* are the embedding tables. b, m, e and s are the position of character within a word, representing *begin*, *middle*, *end* and *single* respectively.

In the work of Chen et al. [11], one of position-based character vectors is selected according to the position of character in word. However, in our work the position of character is unknown before parsing. Different from their work, we calculate the character vector from all of the position-based character vectors by using the attention mechanism and taking a context of K length window as attention. Formally, the contextual character vectors could be computed as:

$$w_i = \frac{1}{2K+1} \sum_{k=i-K}^{k=i+K} v_k \tag{2}$$

$$u_i^p = w_i^T W v_i^p + \langle U^T, w_i \rangle + \langle V^T, v_i^p \rangle \tag{3}$$

$$a_i^p = softmax(u_i^p) \tag{4}$$

$$v_i' = \sum_{p \in \{b,m,e,s\}} a_i^p \cdot v_i^p \tag{5}$$

where w_i is the context embedding, considering a local window of character embeddings. We adopt the biaffine attention mechanism for attention score function [12]. Here, W, U, V are trainable parameters, and p is the position of character.

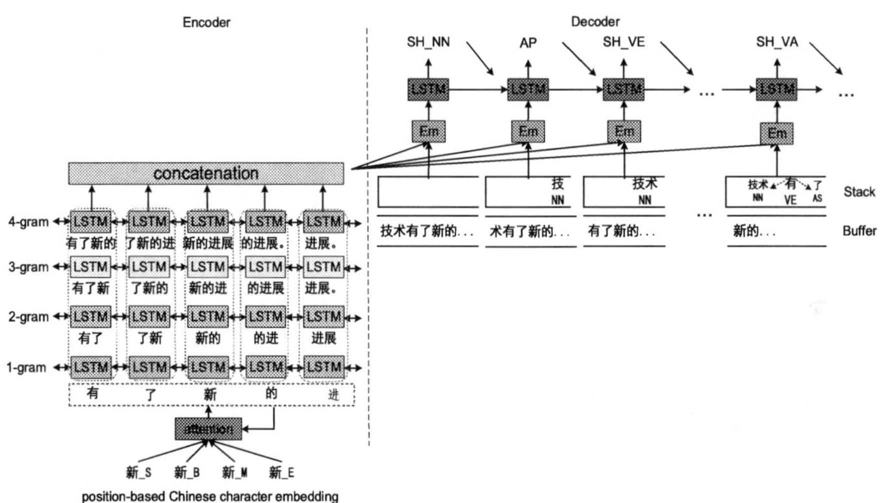

Fig. 1. Our sequence-to-Action Architecture for character-based Chinese dependency parsing. The dashed box is the feature extractor, capturing parser state. The encoder uses position-based embedding and bidirectional LSTM to produce the semantic representation. After that, the decoder captures parser state and tracks history information to predict transition actions.

Then four bidirectional LSTMs are used to capture uni-gram, bi-gram, tri-gram and four-gram character strings in the input sentence respectively. All n-gram inputs to bidirectional LSTM are given by looking up M or character string embeddings [5] by contextual character vectors. The hidden outputs of four bidirectional LSTMs are concatenated to produce the semantic representation for each character in S.

2.2 Decoder Layer

In order to capture all of the state information and all previous decisions taken by the parser, we employ a sequential LSTM to maintain a history of the portion of the sentence that has been processed so far. In this layer, a feature function is used to extract the feature representations of characters from the encoder and built subtrees, including n-gram features, POS features and dependency structure features (encoded by using Tree-LSTM [13]) of the top three items of the stack, and n-gram feature of first item of the buffer. The feature representations extracted by feature function is a local state. The sequential LSTM takes inputs from the local state and previous decision at each time step. It can be formulated as:

$$h_t = LSTM(parser_t, y_{t-1}, h_{t-1}) \tag{6}$$

$$P(y_t|parser_t) = softmax(W_1 h_t + b_1) \tag{7}$$

where W_1, b_1 are trainable parameters, y_{t-1} is the transition action at the last time step.

2.3 Training

We train the sequence-to-action joint model with the objective function for greedy training, which can be formulated as:

$$J(\theta) = -\frac{1}{N}\sum_{t=1}^{t=N} \log P(y_t|parser_t) + \frac{\lambda}{2} \parallel \theta \parallel^2 \tag{8}$$

where N is the number of actions in one sentence, θ denotes all the trainable parameters of our model. Adam [14] is adopted as optimizer.

3 Experiments

3.1 Experiment Settings

In this section, we evaluate our parsing model on the Penn Chinese Treebank 5.1 (CTB-5), following the splitting of Jiang et al. [15]. The dataset statistic is shown in Table 1. All word and character embeddings are initialized with 200-dimension word2vec vectors [16]. The POS and action embeddings are initialized to random values with 200 dimensions. The bidirectional LSTMs' hidden states is 200 dimensions and LSTM's hidden state is 400 dimensions. We set the window size $K = 2$ and the initial learning rate is 0.001. We also employ a dropout strategy [17] to avoid over-fitting and the dropout rate is set to 0.33. The batch size is set to 32.

Table 1. Statistics of dataset.

	sentence	word	oov
Training	18 k	494 k	*
Development	350	6.8 k	553
Test	348	8.0 k	278

3.2 Results

We use word-level F1 score to evaluate word segmentation, POS tagging and dependency parsing, following previous works [1,3–6]. Dependency parsing task is evaluated with the unlabeled attachment scores excluding punctuation. The output of POS tags and dependencies cannot be correct unless the corresponding words are segmented correctly.

Table 2 lists the comparison results of our joint model compared with other state-of-the-art joint models. We can see that out proposed model can significantly outperform the basic bi-LSTM joint model with 0.1% (word segmentation), 0.7% (POS) and 1.44% (dependency) respectively for improvements. This demonstrates the effectiveness of our proposed sequence-to-action architecture for neural character-based Chinese dependency parsing. Besides, our model achieves better F1 score than the neural joint models of Kurita17 and Li18 on dependency parsing. Although the performance is slightly lower than those of feature engineering-based models, like Hatori12, Zhen14 and Zhang14, our model achieves competitive performance. The performance improvement of our model is due to make full use of context features and parser state by employing encoder and decoder. It also suggests that our model can combines with feature engineering for better performance.

Table 2. Comparison with previous models on the CTB dataset.

Models	Method	Representation	Seg	POS	Dep
Hatori12 [1]	beam	large feature set(66, sparse)	97.75	94.33	81.56
Zhang14 [3]	beam	large feature set(101, sparse)	97.67	94.28	**81.63**
Zhen14 [4]	beam	large feature set(53, sparse)	97.52	93.93	79.55
Kurita17 [5]	greedy	large feature set(50, dense)	**98.24**	**94.49**	80.15
Li18 [6]	greedy	3LSTM vectors	96.64	92.88	79.44
bi-LSTM [5]	greedy	4LSTM vectors	97.72	93.12	79.03
Our	greedy	(4LSTM, 3POS, 3subtree) vectors	**97.88**	**93.82**	**80.47**

3.3 Effect of Components

We perform some ablation experiments to analyze the effect of the different components on our models. As illustrated in Table 3, the first row is the baseline bi-LSTM joint model [5]. Compared to the baseline model, we use sequential LSTM as decoder instead of MLP for prediction, and F1 score increases by 0.41% and 0.59% on POS and dependency parsing respectively. It proves the decoder with LSTM can capture the helpful information from previous state and decisions, which is more effective for POS and dependency parsing. By adding the position-based character embedding, the word segmentation and dependency parsing performances are increased to 97.82% and 80.02% respectively. It is

Table 3. Effects of the different components.

Models	Seg	POS	Dep
bi-LSTM joint model	97.72	93.12	79.03
+decoder LSTM	97.51	93.53	79.62
+position embedding	97.82	93.42	80.02
+POS,subtree	**97.88**	**93.82**	**80.47**

because the character representation is more accurate by capture meanings of character within specific local contexts. Elmo [18] and Bert [19] have been well known as pre-trained language model for acquiring contextual character vectors. However, our current condition of computing power could not support such complicated training task. We will conduct the comparison with them in the future. In this paper, we evaluated the contribution of position embedding to our model. Besides, our model achieves further improvement in each task by additionally adopting POS features and subtree features.

4 Related Work

Transition-based joint model for Chinese word segmentation, POS tagging and dependency parsing was proposed by Hatori et al. [1]. Zhang et al. [3] and Zhen et al. [4] extended this work by adding word-structure features to extract intra-word dependencies. Kurita et al. [5] proposed the first embedding-based joint parsing model and used the character string embeddings to replace incomplete or unknown words embeddings. All above mentioned works relied heavily on handcrafted features and it was a hard and time consuming task to define a good feature-set. In contrast to these, the neural parsing model we presented in this work only used a little feature and achieves comparable performance. Besides, Kurita et al. [5] also explored bi-LSTM models to avoid the detailed feature engineering, but they only extracted local state to make decisions and neglected parser history information. Li et al. [6] provided rich character-level POS and dependency annotations to better understanding deeper structure of Chinese words.

5 Conclusion

In this paper, we propose a novel sequence-to-action joint model for character-based dependency parsing to track history information of parser in the decoding procedure. Besides, we use position-based character embeddings to capture exact character meanings within specific contexts. Experimental results demonstrate that our proposed model significantly outperforms the existing neural models for joint paring, and achieves comparable performance with the state-of-the-art joint models.

In the future, we will expand the scale of the experiment and further verify the effectiveness of the proposed method. In addition, we further explore better way to learning character representations, such as Elmo and Bert.

Acknowledgments. The authors are supported by the National Nature Science Foundation of China (61876198, 61370130 and 61473294).

References

1. Hatori, J., Matsuzaki, T., Miyao, Y., Tsujii, J.I.: Incremental joint approach to word segmentation, POS tagging, and dependency parsing in Chinese. In: Proceedings of the 50th Annual Meeting of the Association for Computational Linguistics: Long Papers-Volume 1, pp. 1045–1053. Association for Computational Linguistics (2012)
2. Nivre, J. An efficient algorithm for projective dependency parsing. In: Proceedings of the Eighth International Conference on Parsing Technologies, pp. 149–160 (2003)
3. Zhang, M., Zhang, Y., Che, W., Liu, T.: Character-level Chinese dependency parsing. In: Proceedings of the 52nd Annual Meeting of the Association for Computational Linguistics, Volume 1: Long Papers, vol. 1, pp. 1326–1336 (2014)
4. Guo, Z., Zhang, Y., Su, C., Xu, J., Isahara, H.: Character-level dependency model for joint word segmentation, POS tagging, and dependency parsing in Chinese. IEICE Trans. Inf. Syst. **99**(1), 257–264 (2016)
5. Kurita, S., Kawahara, D., Kurohashi, S.: Neural joint model for transition-based Chinese syntactic analysis. In: Proceedings of the 55th Annual Meeting of the Association for Computational Linguistics, Volume 1: Long Papers, pp. 1204–1214 (2017)
6. Li, H., Zhang, Z., Ju, Y., Zhao, H.: Neural character-level dependency parsing for Chinese. In: Thirty-Second AAAI Conference on Artificial Intelligence (2018)
7. Dyer, C., Ballesteros, M., Ling, W., Matthews, A., Smith, N.A.: Transition-based dependency parsing with stack long short-term memory. In: Proceedings of the 53rd Annual Meeting of the Association for Computational Linguistics and the 7th International Joint Conference on Natural Language Processing, Volume 1: Long Papers, vol. 1, pp. 334–343 (2015)
8. Bowman, S.R., Gauthier, J., Rastogi, A., Gupta, R., Manning, C.D., Potts, C.: A fast unified model for parsing and sentence understanding. In: Proceedings of the 54th Annual Meeting of the Association for Computational Linguistics, Volume 1: Long Papers, vol. 1, pp. 1466–1477 (2016)
9. Sutskever, I., Vinyals, O., Le, Q.V.: Sequence to sequence learning with neural networks. In: Proceedings of the 27th International Conference on Neural Information Processing Systems, vol. 2, pp. 3104–3112. MIT Press (2014)
10. Nivre, J.: Incrementality in deterministic dependency parsing. In: Proceedings of the Workshop on Incremental Parsing: Bringing Engineering and Cognition Together, pp. 50–57. Association for Computational Linguistics (2004)
11. Chen, X., Xu, L., Liu, Z., Sun, M., Luan, H.: Joint learning of character and word embeddings. In: Proceedings of the 24th International Conference on Artificial Intelligence, pp. 1236–1242. AAAI Press (2015)
12. Dozat, T., Manning, C.D.: Deep biaffine attention for neural dependency parsing. arXiv preprint arXiv:1611.01734 (2016)

13. Tai, K.S., Socher, R., Manning, C.D.: Improved semantic representations from tree-structured long short-term memory networks. In: Proceedings of the 53rd Annual Meeting of the Association for Computational Linguistics and the 7th International Joint Conference on Natural Language Processing, Volume 1: Long Papers, vol. 1, pp. 1556–1566 (2015)
14. Kingma, D.P., Ba, J.: Adam: a method for stochastic optimization. arXiv preprint arXiv:1412.6980 (2014)
15. Jiang, W., Huang, L., Liu, Q., Lv, Y.: A cascaded linear model for joint Chinese word segmentation and part-of-speech tagging. In: Proceedings of the 46th Annual Meeting of the Association for Computational Linguistics (2008)
16. Mikolov, T., Chen, K., Corrado, G., Dean, J.: Efficient estimation of word representations in vector space. arXiv preprint arXiv:1301.3781 (2013)
17. Srivastava, N., Hinton, G., Krizhevsky, A., Sutskever, I., Salakhutdinov, R.: Dropout: a simple way to prevent neural networks from overfitting. J. Mach. Learn. Res. **15**(1), 1929–1958 (2014)
18. Peters, M., et al.: Deep contextualized word representations. In: Proceedings of the 2018 Conference of the North American Chapter of the Association for Computational Linguistics: Human Language Technologies, Volume 1: Long Papers, pp. 2227–2237 (2018)
19. Devlin, J., Chang, M.W., Lee, K., Toutanova, K.: Bert: pre-training of deep bidirectional transformers for language understanding. arXiv preprint arXiv:1810.04805 (2018)

A New Fine-Tuning Architecture Based on Bert for Word Relation Extraction

Fanyu Meng(✉), Junlan Feng, Danping Yin, and Min Hu

China Mobile Research Institute, Beijing, China
{mengfanyu,fengjunlan,yindanping,humin}@chinamobile.com

Abstract. We introduce a new attention-based neural architecture to fine-tune Bidirectional Encoder Representations from Transformers (BERT) for semantic and grammatical relationship classificaiton at word level. BERT has been widely accepted as a base to create the state-of-the-art models for sentence-level and token-level natural language processing tasks via a fine tuning process, which typically takes the final hidden states as input for a classification layer. Inspired by the Residual Net, we propose in this paper a new architecture that augments the final hidden states with multi-head attention weights from all Transformer layers for fine-tuning. We explain the rationality of this proposal in theory and compare it with recent models for word-level relation tasks such as dependency tree parsing. The resulting model shows evident improvement comparing to the standard BERT fine-tuning model on the dependency parsing task with the English TreeBank data and the semantic relation extraction task of SemEval-2010Task-8.

Keywords: Relation extraction · Dependency parsing · Attention

1 Introduction

Recently a series of great works on language model pre-training have shown to be effective for improving a large suite of downstream NLP tasks spanning from sentence-level tasks to token-level tasks [2,8,12,13]. Particularly, the recent release of the BERT models have become the latest milestone in NLP. It is seen as an inflection point for the NLP field. BERT uses masked language models to obtain pre-trained deep bidirectional representations of characters, words and sentences. The state-of-the-art of a wide range of NLP tasks have been advanced via a standard BERT fine-tuning process. In sequence-level and token-level classification tasks, it takes the final hidden states (the last layer output of the multi-head transformer) of the first [CLS] sequence token or each individual token as input for a classification layer over a label set.

In this paper, we are motivated to extend BERT including the BERT architecture and the model itself to a category of NLP tasks: word-level relation classification. It focuses on classifying relationship between two words in a sentence

J. Tang et al. (Eds.): NLPCC 2019, LNAI 11839, pp. 327–337, 2019.
https://doi.org/10.1007/978-3-030-32236-6_29

such as syntactic dependency relationship in dependency parsing and semantic relationship between nominal words.

Dependency parsing is defined as a task to provide a simple description of the grammatical structure of a sentence. Dependency parsers are often evaluated on the Penn Treebank (PTB) and the Chinese Treebank (CTB 5.1) with the unlabeled attachment score (UAS) and the labeled attachment score (LAS) metrics (excluding punctuation) [10]. UAS measures the accuracy that a model can predict if there is a head-modifier relationship between any given pair of tokens in a sentence. LAS measures the accuracy that a model can predict the specific relationship between any given pair of tokens in a sentence. We follow these evaluation metrics in our experiments.

The classification of semantic relationship between pairs of words is defined to classify various semantic relations between words, such as Cause-Effect (CE) ,Component-Whole (CW) relationship between nominal words [7].

In this paper, we focus on improving BERT fine-tuning process for the above tasks. For dependency parsing, we follow the general framework of Graph-based dependency parsers. For semantic relationship extraction, we treat it as a straight forward classification task. The contributions of our paper are summarized follows:

- We propose a new architecture to fine-tune BERT for word-level relation classification tasks. Rather than taking only the final hidden states as input for a feed-forward classifier, we propose to augment the hidden states with Transformer multi-head attention weights for classification. In experiments, this approach evidently improves the accuracy of the dependency tree parsing and the semantic relation extraction comparing to the standard BERT fine-tuning process.
- We construct a probing task to test and visualize the extent to which BERT representations preserve the word relationship as BERT primarily built on Self-Attention Transformer mechanism.

2 Related Work

2.1 Deep Neural Network for Dependency Parsing

Since the earlier work in [11], Graph-based dependency parsing has been typically formulated with the common structure prediction framework.

Given an input sentence, the parsing task is to select the dependency tree with the highest scores, which is decomposed to the sum of local arc scores for each head to dependent arc.

[1] made the first successful attempt to employ modern neural network into dependency parsing. The input to this network is the concatenation of three embedding vectors of involved words including word embedding, POS tag embedding and arc-tag embedding. Embedding vectors in this work are fed into a non-linear multiple layer perceptron (MLP) classifier. Since then, many other

researchers have proposed various deep learning architectures to advance the state-of-the-art.

[9] employed a biLSTM (Bidirectional Long Short-Term Memory) network for both transition-based parsing and graph-based parsing. For the graph-based parsing, the biLSTM is considered as the feature function ϕ for a given arc (w_h, w_m) from the head word w_h and the modifier w_m, where LSTM encodes each word separately and then concatenate them as the arc feature.

$$\phi(s, w_h, w_m) = h(s, w_h) \circ h(s, w_m) \tag{1}$$

These features are used as input for a MLP classifier, which is similar to [1] work.

[5] included a graph-based dependency parser in their multitask neural model architecture. For dependency parsing, similarly it relies on LSTM to embed higher level attention features from low-level word embedding features. Instead of concatenating two LSTM encoded word embeddings as the input for the classifier, Hashimoto et al. (2016) applied a linear attention mechanism to combine them as:

$$\phi(s, w_h, w_m) = h(s, w_h) \cdot (W_d h(s, w_m)) \tag{2}$$

[4] proposed a biaffine network for dependency parsing. It follows the previous work to encode words via a BiLSTM network by taking word embeddings and POS tag embeddings as input. The hidden BiLSTM state for each word is fed to two MLP classifiers to respectively classify the word as a head or a modifier. The MLP output vectors are multiplied to derive arc scores for UAS and LAS. This approach obtains 95.7% UAS and 94.2% LAS. CVT + Multi-Task (Clark et al., 2018) advanced the latest state-of-the-art to 96.61% UAS and 95.02% LAS with a multi-task approach.

2.2 Semantic Relation Extraction

Semantic relation classification is a crucial component in numerous real-life NLP tasks. Multilevel convolutional neural network (CNN) and BiLSTM are the most popular model architectures applied in recent years. On top of that, various entity-aware attentions are proposed in recent research to advance the state-of-the-art performance [15].

The fundamental differences between above approaches are the attention mechanisms, MLP attention, bilinear attention, deep biaffine attention, and entity-aware attention on top of a base LSTM/CNN model. The BERT architecture is purely built on self-attention transformers. Hence, we believe it is natural to extend BERT for word-relation tasks. In the next section, we describe our proposal in detail.

3 Our Approach

Fundamentally, BERT's model architecture is a multi-layer bidirectional Transformer encoder [14]. Transformer entirely relies on self-attention to draw global dependencies among tokens within a given sequence. Intuitively, it is natural to believe the learnt attention weights between words are good candidate features for word relation extraction. In this Section, we first explain pair-wise attention, which is a key concept in our approach. Second, we propose our new architecture to fine-tune BERT explicitly using pair-wise attention weights for the classification layer. Third, we employ this procedure to dependency parsing and semantic relation tasks.

3.1 Pair-Wise Attention

A given input sequence $s = t_1, ..., t_N$ is represented as an embedding matrix X with each row corresponding to a word embedding vector x_i for the token t_i. For each x_i, Transformer creates a Query vector q_i, a Key vector k_i by linearly projecting x_i with different, learnt weight matrices W^Q, W^K. We denote the dimensions of q_i,k_i respectively as d_q, d_k. These vectors are packed into matrices Q, K. For a given layer l and a given head h, attention weights are computed as:

$$\begin{aligned} z^{l,h} &= Attention(Q, K) \\ &= softmax(\frac{QK^T}{\sqrt(d_k)}) \end{aligned} \tag{3}$$

Each element $z^{lh}_{i,j}$ in $z^{l,h}$ represents the attention of the ith token to the jth token.

Instead of performing a single attention function, [14] found it is beneficial to have multiple attention heads H. Hence, for a BERT model with L layers and H attention heads, there are $L * H$ attention weights $z^{l,h}_{i,j}$ for a token pair (t_i, t_j). We pack these weights in a vector $a^{i,j}$:

$$\begin{aligned} a^{i,j} = (z^{1,1}_{i,j}, ..., z^{l,h}_{i,j}, ..., z^{L,H}_{i,j}) \\ i, j \in (1, ..., N) \end{aligned} \tag{4}$$

In Fig. 1, each cell corresponds to an attention weight $z^{l,h}_{i,j}$. The color density represents how much attention they give to each other. It needs to be noted that these weights are not symmetric, $a^{i,j} \neq a^{j,i}$.

We refer to this vector $a^{i,j}$ as the pair-wise attention vector. Figure 1 illustrates the procedure how pair-wise attention is formed. In experiments, we conducted a probing study to analyze and visualize the association between pair-wise attention and dependency relationship.

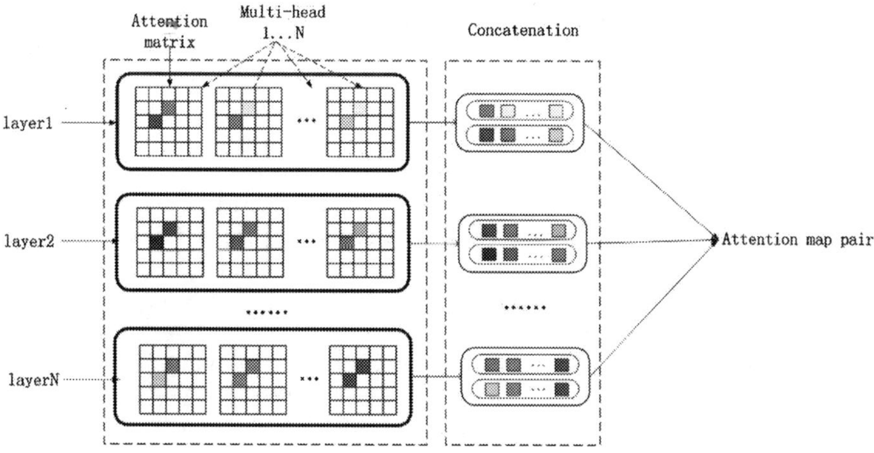

Fig. 1. The process of attention map pair extraction

3.2 Fine-Tuning with Pair-Wise Attention

For word relation extraction tasks, we propose to augment the basic BERT fine tuning architecture with pair-wise attention weights. Figure 2 illustrates our procedure. Inspired by the residual net [6], we add a connection from attention layers to the classifier layer as direct input. Our argument is that these weights directly represent the rich relationship between words and they are not fully represented by the hidden vectors in the output layer. To infer the relationship between a pair of tokens t_i, t_j, we feed the last layer hidden representations $T_i, T_j \in \Re^H$ as well as the pair-wise weight vector $a_{i,j}$. into a classification layer over the relation label set. We denote this input vector as $C \in \Re^{2M+L*H*2}$, where M is the hidden size of BERT, H is the number of self-attention heads, and L is the number of layers.

$$C = T_i \circ T_j \circ a^{i,j} \circ a^{j,i} \tag{5}$$

There are various ways to integrate the four parts. Here we use the simplest concatenation without further complicating the classifier architecture and adding more parameters. The only new parameters added during fine-tuning are for the classification layer $W \in \Re^{K*(2M+L*H*2)}$. K is the number of classifier labels. For a sentence with N tokens, each pair of words is processed independently. During training , the classifier label is given. Pairs with no labels are associated with a label *NONE*. During testing, each pair of words is classified into one of the labels.

As Fig. 2 illustrates, this fine-tuning procedure is similar to the standard BERT fine-tuning procedure with exceptions that input to the classifier is beyond simple hidden vectors from the final layer of BERT. In our experiment we use the $BERT_{BASE}$ model with $L = 12, H = 768, A = 12$ as the hyper parameters.

3.3 Fine-Tuning for Dependency Paring

We experiment two existing strategies to apply BERT: feature-based and fine-tuning. The feature-based approach uses the BERT pre-trained model to extract features for the classifier. Only the parameters of the classifier are updated during training. The fine-tuning approach tunes the pre-trained BERT model parameters along with the classifier weights during training. Features in our case include BERT embeddings of the involved two words from the final layer as well as our proposed pair-wise attention vectors. For dependency parsing, we use the PTB corpus as our training and testing data. Accuracies are measured using UAS and LAS as we explained in the Introduction Section.

As with other graph-based models, the predicted dependency tree at training time is the one where each word is a dependent of its highest scoring head. At test time, we employ the Minimum Spanning Tree (MST) to construct a well-formed tree from local classification scores.

Comparing to the previous work, we didn't use other widely used features like POS tag embeddings to tune the performance. To focus on our motivation, we only use BERT pair-wise attention weights and embeddings for the classifier.

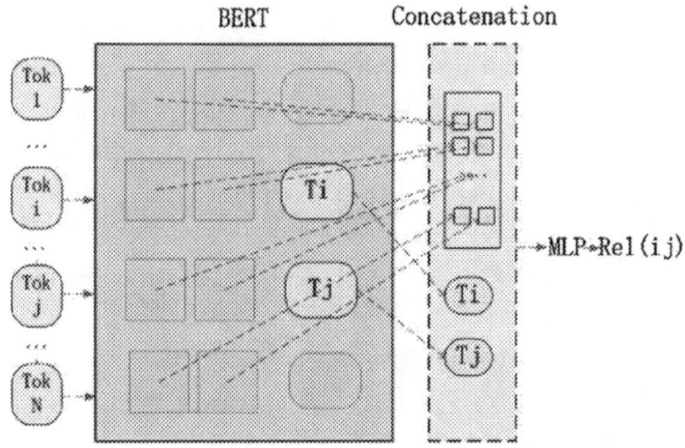

Fig. 2. The process of relation extraction based on Bert

3.4 Fine-Tuning for Semantic Relation Extraction

It is straightforward to apply our proposed model to semantic relation extraction between words. More specifically, we run our experiments on the SemEval-2010 Task 8: Multi-way classification of semantic relations between pairs of nominals, one of the most popular relation classification tasks.

Most previous models for relation classification rely on the high-level lexical and syntactic features obtained by NLP tools such as WordNet, dependency parser, POS tagger, and named entity recognizers. We follow the same spirit as the above. We limit ourselves to only BERT features. Experimental results will be given in the Experiments Section.

4 Experiments

We perform three sets of experiments in our study. One is for dependency parsing with different models including our proposed one. Second is our experiments for the semantic relation task. Third, we conduct a probing study to measure and directly visualize the contribution of pair-wise attention weights to dependency tree parsing as well as semantic relation extraction.

4.1 Dependency Parsing

For dependency parsing, we use the English Penn Treebank (PTB) data with 42067 sentences for training, 3370 sentences for evaluation and 3761 sentences for testing. We parse all sentences in the dataset with the Stanford parser (v3.6.0) and split the data into training, development and testing in the standard way as [1] configured.

With this default setup, we experiment five different models for dependency parsing.

- Feature-based, pre-trained contextual embeddings (fea:emb): Use BERT to extract fixed contextual word embeddings as features
- Feature-based, pre-trained contextual embeddings, Pair-wise attention (fea:emb+att): Use BERT to extract fixed contextual embeddings and pair-wise attention weights as features
- Feature-based, pre-trained contextual embeddings, Pair-wise attention (fea:ptb:emb+att): The baseline BERT model is further trained with the PTB raw data as a language model. The obtained model is then used to extract fixed contextual embeddings and pair-wise attention weights.
- Fine-tuning, contextual embeddings (fine-tune:emb): Fine-tune BERT along with training the classifier. Use contextual embeddings as the only feature
- Fine-tuning,
  contextual embeddings, Pair-wise attention (fine-tune:emb+att): Fine-tune BERT along with training the classifier using contextual embeddings as well as pair-wise attention weights

Table 1. Accuary of UAS and LAS of on PTB

TASK	PTB		SemiEval-2010
MODEL	UAS	LAS	F1
fea:emb	62.1	55.5	50.8
fea:emb+att	77.2	68.3	61.1
fea:ptb:emb+att	76.9	67.4	61.1
fine-tune:emb	87.8	86.0	76.5
fine-tune:emb+att	89.3	87.8	**78.4**
fine-tune:emb+att(mst)	**90.9**	**88.9**	*

Table 1 presents the dependency classification accuacy with different models. The fine-tuned model with contextual embeddings and pair wise attentions achieve the best accuracy by a large margin. The contribution of pair-wise attention without fine-tuning is 15.1% absolute improvement UAS above the baseline 62.1% and 12.8% improvement on LAS. Fine-tuning dramatically pushes up the performance to 90.9% UAS and 88.9% , which is close to the state-of-the-art performance without additional features [4]. We can conclude that BERT is able to densely represent syntactic information into contextual embeddings as well as transformer attentions. The pair-wise attentions we proposed made a significant contribution. The third model $fea : ptb : emb + att$ tunes the BERT model parameters as a masked language model with the PTB dataset and then use it to extract features. The obtained model leads to accuracy drop nearly 1 point. It is not a successful practice given that the size of PTB dataset is not comparable to BERT original training corpus.

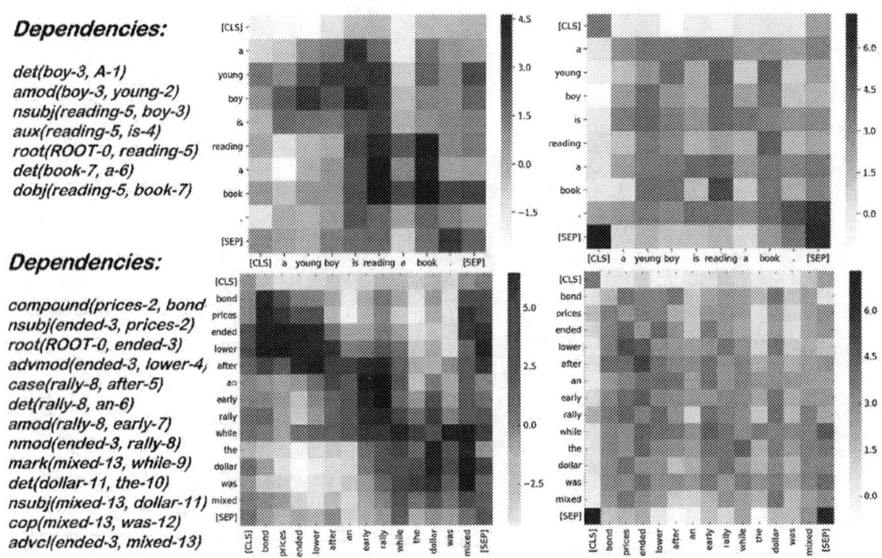

Fig. 3. Attention map of top2 important features of different sentences for dependency relationship extraction

One practical problem we have to face in our experiments is the incompatibility between the WordPiece tokenization BERT uses and PTB tokenization. Such way of tokenization makes the sentence non-grammatical and bings further challenge to dependency parsing. To ease this dilemma, we ignore those words which are not in BERT vocabulary. Here in our experiments, we choose to use our simple approach to ignore the so-called unknown words.

Limited by the BERT vocabulary, the tokenization problem becomes an obstacle for us to take full advantage of the BERT pre-trained model. The best performance we achieve with current experiments is 90.9% UAS with MST, which is nearly 5.7% lower than the latest state-of-the-art(with additional features). In the Discussion section, we share our ongoing work to solve these problems.

4.2 Semantic Realtion Classification

We keep the same setup to perform fine-tuning for the task 8 of SemEval-2010. Table 1 provides the results. The fine-tuned model with contextual word embeddings and attention weights achieves the best performance. However, it's still far behind the state-of-the-art model for this task, 9.0% lower. Much richer information including WordNet, Pos Tagging, Entity recognition, etc. is integrated into previous approaches. Without these features, state-of-the-art result has a 6% decrease. Here we limit ourselves to explore a general BERT fine-tuning architecture.

4.3 Probing Study

To further investigate the contribution of pair-wise attention weights, we conduct a probing study. We use a tree-based method to analyze the feature importance. According to our result, the most important 100 features for classification are all pair-wise weights, which support our hypothesis. We visualize several attention matrix to gain direct insights what attention weights represents in terms of word relationship.

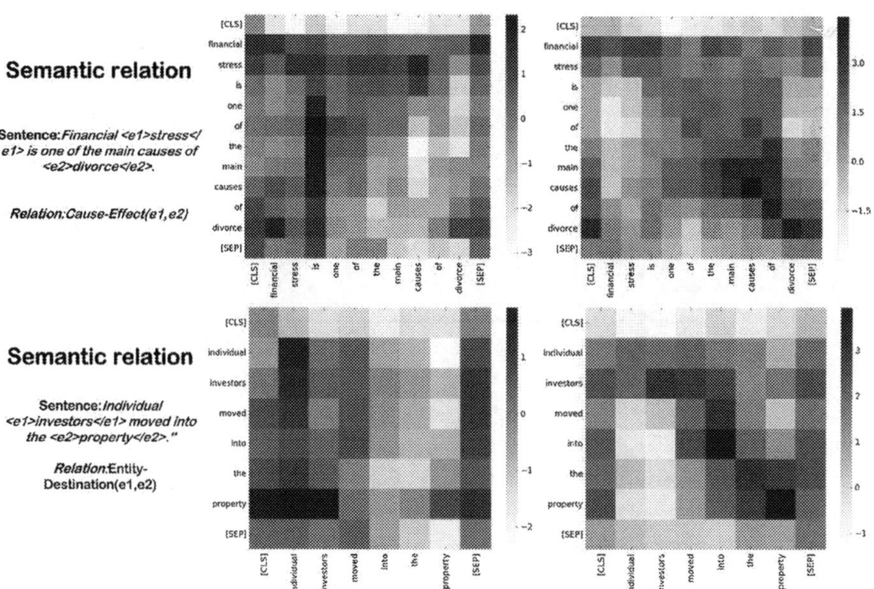

Fig. 4. Attention map of top2 important features of different sentences for nonimal relationship extraction

Figure 3 illustrates the top 2 attention matrices, which are selected for the given sentence according to their contribution to dependency parsing. For instance, the dependency *det(book-7, a-6)* is highlighted with *book* in the x axis and a in the y axis in the first graph. Similar patterns can be observed for difference sentences.

Figure 4 illustrates the top 2 important attention matrices according for the semantic relation task. For both examples, we can observe the first weight matrix graph highlights the connection between entities and the second highlights the type of relation.

5 Conclusion

In this paper, we present a new fine-tuning architecture for word-level relationship extraction. We introduce the pair-wise attention to augment BERT embeddings for dependency parsing and semantic relation extraction. Experimental results prove the effectiveness of our proposal. We also conduct a probing study to visualize how attention weight directly associates with word relation. Work presented in this paper will be open-sources on Github soon once we clean our code.

6 Discussion

In near future, we will strengthen our experiments in this paper in a few aspects. One is to solve the incompatibility between the tokenization the BERT model uses and the dependency-parsing task, where tokenization causes significant problems. Our way handling it in this paper is coarse. Second, we are in the middle to integrate the biaffine attention mechanisms proposed in [4], which is the state-of-the-art. We believe with these efforts we can possibly advance the state-of-the-art on relation extraction tasks.

In long run, we are interested to combine many tasks into one learning process. The recent success of Transfer Learning [3,12,13], evidently helps advance many down-stream NLP tasks. In this paper, we extend BERT to fine-tune for relation extraction tasks. While conducting our experiments, we observe the strong reliance among many tasks. Traditional methods traditionally rely on a rich set of features, which often come from other NLP processing tools. The linguistic levels of morphology, syntax, and semantics would benefit each other. Along the past decades, there are many datasets accumulated for various tasks in different contexts. It is ideal if we could jointly learn these tasks and have them benefit each other during training in a mathematically optimal way instead of connecting them as a pipeline.

References

1. Chen, D., Manning, C.: A fast and accurate dependency parser using neural networks. In: EMNLP, pp. 740–750, January 2014
2. Dai, A.M., Le, Q.V.: Semi-supervised sequence learning. CoRR abs/1511.01432 (2015)
3. Devlin, J., Chang, M., Lee, K., Toutanova, K.: BERT: pre-training of deep bidirectional transformers for language understanding. CoRR abs/1810.04805 (2018)
4. Dozat, T., Manning, C.D.: Deep biaffine attention for neural dependency parsing. CoRR abs/1611.01734 (2016)
5. Hashimoto, K., Xiong, C., Tsuruoka, Y., Socher, R.: A joint many-task model: Growing a neural network for multiple NLP tasks. CoRR abs/1611.01587 (2016)
6. He, K., Zhang, X., Ren, S., Sun, J.: Deep residual learning for image recognition. CoRR abs/1512.03385 (2015)
7. Hendrickx, I., Kim, S., Kozareva, Z., Nakov, P., Padó, S., Pennacchiotti, M., Romano, L., Szpakowicz, S.: Semeval-2010 task 8: Multi-way classification of semantic relations between pairs of nominals, pp. 33–38, January 01 2010
8. Howard, J., Ruder, S.: Fine-tuned language models for text classification. CoRR abs/1801.06146 (2018)
9. Kiperwasser, E., Goldberg, Y.: Simple and accurate dependency parsing using bidirectional LSTM feature representations. CoRR abs/1603.04351 (2016)
10. de Marnee, M.C., Manning, C.: Stanford typed dependencies manual, January 2008
11. McDonald, R., Pereira, F., Ribarov, K., Hajič, J.: Non-projective dependency parsing using spanning tree algorithms. In: Proceedings of the Conference on Human Language Technology and Empirical Methods in Natural Language Processing, HLT 2005, pp. 523–530. Association for Computational Linguistics, Stroudsburg, PA, USA (2005). https://doi.org/10.3115/1220575.1220641
12. Peters, M.E., Neumann, M., Iyyer, M., Gardner, M., Clark, C., Lee, K., Zettlemoyer, L.: Deep contextualized word representations. CoRR abs/1802.05365 (2018)
13. Radford, A., Narasimhan, K., Salimans, T., Sutskever, I.: Improving language understanding by generative pre-training (2018)
14. Vaswani, A., Shazeer, N., Parmar, N., Uszkoreit, J., Jones, L., Gomez, A.N., Kaiser, L., Polosukhin, I.: Attention is all you need. CoRR abs/1706.03762 (2017)
15. Wang, L., Cao, Z., de Melo, G., Liu, Z.: Relation classification via multi-level attention CNNs. pp. 1298–1307 (01 2016). 10.18653/v1/P16-1123

Rumor Detection with Hierarchical Recurrent Convolutional Neural Network

Xiang Lin[1], Xiangwen Liao[1(✉)], Tong Xu[2], Wenjing Pian[1], and Kam-Fai Wong[3]

[1] College of Mathematics and Computer Science, Fuzhou University, Fuzhou, China
742734768@qq.com, {liaoxw,wenjingpian}@fzu.edu.cn

[2] Anhui Province Key Laboratory of Big Data Analysis and Application, School of Computer Science and Technology, University of Science and Technology of China, Hefei, China
tongxu@ustc.edu.cn

[3] The Chinese University of Hong Kong, Sha Tin, Hong Kong
kfwong@se.cuhk.edu.hk

Abstract. Automatic rumor detection for events on online social media has attracted considerable attention in recent years. Usually, the events on social media are divided into several time segments, and for each segment, corresponding text will be converted as vectors for various neural network models to detect rumors. During this process, however, only sentence-level embedding has been considered, while the contextual information at the word level has been largely ignored. To address that issue, in this paper, we propose a novel rumor detection method based on a hierarchical recurrent convolutional neural network, which integrates contextual information for rumor detection. Specifically, with dividing events on social media into time segments, recurrent convolution neural network is adapted to learn the contextual representation information. Along this line, a bidirectional GRU network with attention mechanism is integrated to learn the time period information via combining event feature vectors. Experiments on real-world data sets validate that our solution could outperform several state-of-the-art methods..

Keywords: Rumor detection · Recurrent convolutional neural network

1 Introduction

A rumor is commonly defined as a statement whose truth value is unverifiable or deliberately false [1]. As the fast development of social media, the exponentially increasing rumors have caused a huge amount of loss in people's lives and properties. For instance, in 2015, a rumor about "shootouts and kidnappings by drug gangs happening near schools in Veracruz" spread through Twitter and Facebook, which caused severe chaos [9]. Therefore, automatic rumor detection techniques are urgently required to quickly identify rumor messages and dynamically monitor the propagation.

Traditionally, most of the literature regarded rumor detection as a two categories classification problem. To that end, large efforts have been made on rumor detection via

J. Tang et al. (Eds.): NLPCC 2019, LNAI 11839, pp. 338–348, 2019.
https://doi.org/10.1007/978-3-030-32236-6_30

machine learning methods, in which a wide variety of features manually crafted from the content are incorporated. Usually, these features included geographic location information, verification questions and corrections [2, 3], emotional polarity [4, 5], and propagation tree features [6]. Along this line, support vector machine [4], decision tree [3, 5, 8] and other classifiers were used to classify rumors. However, these methods require manual extraction of features, which takes a considerable amount of time and manpower. Moreover, the robustness of obtained features is questionable, especially for thc imbalanced data set. At the same time, some other researchers attempt to detect rumors via feature representation learning methods. These methods processed the text at the sentence level, and used deep neural networks like bidirectional GRU network [9] and convolutional neural network [10], to mine key features in complicated social media sceneries. An obvious limitation of these models is that they used sentence embeddings on the text of each time period, but ignored contextual information at the word level, resulting in lower prediction performance.

To address that issue, in this paper, we proposed a novel rumor detection method based on a hierarchical recurrent convolutional neural network, which integrates contextual information for rumor detection. Specifically, with dividing events on social media into time segments, recurrent convolution neural network is adapted to learn the contextual representation information. Along this line, a bidirectional GRU network with attention mechanism is integrated to learn the time period information via combining event feature vectors. Extensive validations on real-world data sets have verified the effectiveness of our method with significant improvements compared with several state-of-the-art methods.

2 Related Work

In general, two categories of methods were widely studied for rumors detection, i.e., rumor detection based on traditional machine learning techniques, and rumor detection based on feature representation learning methods.

For the first category, usually, the prior arts manually design features for rumor detection with extracting these features from the textual content. Then, they used various classifiers to detect rumors. For instance, Castillo et al. [5] proposed four classification features (user features, message features, topic features, and propagation features) to detect rumors. Also, Qazvinian et al. [12] extracted content-based features, network-based features and Weibo-specific features to identify rumors. In 2015, Zhao et al. [2] used terms such as "unconfirmed", "rumor" or "debunked" to find enquiries and corrections tweets. At the same time, Ma et al. [7] used dynamic time series to capture changes in a set of social environment features over time. Later, Ma et al. [6] proposed a tree-based method in 2017, which captured high-order propagation patterns on Twitter. Due to the deepening of feature design, the detection performance of rumors based on traditional machine learning has been significantly improved, but the manual design features require a lot of manpower and material resources, while the features are not robust enough. The above problems are still unresolved.

For the second category, recently, LSTM [13], RNN [14], CNN [15] and some other related techniques have been applied to text feature representation learning. These methods were also applied to feature representation learning in rumor detection problems. In 2016, Ma et al. [9] used neural network models to detect rumors for the first time. They applied RNN models to learning information changes at different time intervals associated with each event. In 2017, Yu et al. [10] converted the Weibo text to doc2vec and then applied CNN to learning the event representation. Ruchansky et al. [16] proposed a hybrid model CSI, which used singular value decomposition to obtain the user's feature vector and then applied the LSTM network to learning text features to detect rumors. In 2018, Ma et al. [18] proposed a top-down RvNN model and a bottom-up RvNN model for rumor detection. Guo et al. [19] proposed a novel hierarchical neural network combining with social information to detect rumors. Liao et al. [11] proposed a hierarchical attention network to obtain the hidden layer representations to detect rumors. Ma et al. [17] used the framework of multi-task learning to conduct rumor detection and stance classification.

In summary, the methods based on feature representation learning have achieved significant results, but these methods mainly focused the text representation of each time period at the sentence level, which ignored the contextual information at the word level. Thus, this defect may severely impact the accuracy of rumor detection.

3 Proposed Method

3.1 Problem Definition

In general, rumor detection in social media could be formulated as a binary classification problem, which will be defined as follow: Given a set of Weibo (or Twitter) events $E = \{e_1, e_2, e_3, \ldots\}$, where e_i represents an event containing a number of microblogs (or tweets). For computational efficiency, we follow previous work [19] and divide the posts in e_i into different time intervals; a set of categories $L = \{l_1, l_2\}$, where l_1, l_2 represent rumor and non-rumor, respectively. Using the model algorithm, each event E is mapped to a category, i.e., $E \rightarrow L$. The input to the question is the relevant microblog (or tweet) information for an event e_i to output the label of event: Rumor or Non-rumor.

3.2 Recurrent Convolutional Neural Networks with Feature Attention Network

As shown in Fig. 1, we first use a recurrent convolution neural network [20] to learn contextual representation information, and then utilize a bidirectional GRU network, as well as an attention mechanism which contains the event feature vector to learn the time period information.

For each social media event, our model has two inputs:

(1) A textual representation w_{ijk} of the social media event in each time period, where i represents the social media event, and j is the jth time period and k indicates the kth word of the social media text.

(2) The feature vector F_e of each event, including user-based features, content-based features, signal features, and so on.

Corresponding, the output of this model is the judgement whether target social media event is a rumor.

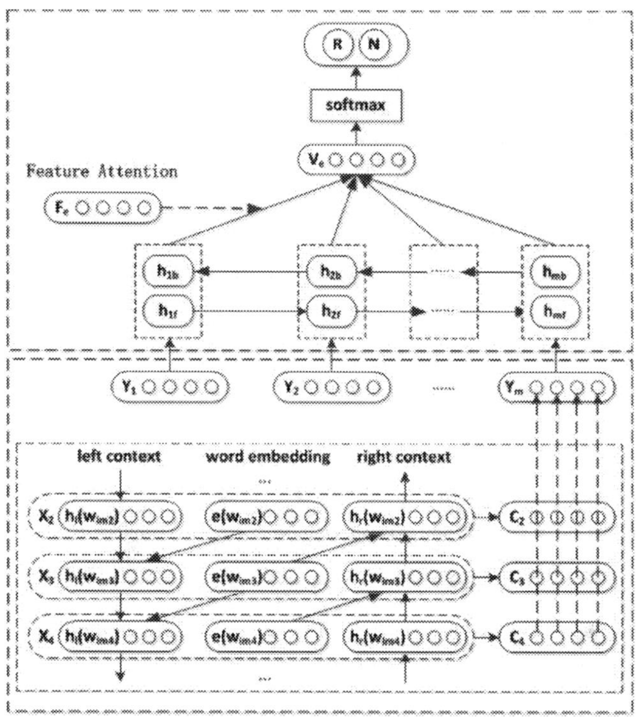

Fig. 1. Our RCNN-FAN framework for rumor detection.

To deal with this problem, our model mainly consists of two modules below:

(1) **Social media text representation based on a recurrent CNN.** This module captures contextual information with the recurrent structure and constructs the representation of text using a convolutional neural network. The module outputs the textual representation Y_t of the contextual information.
(2) **Time period representation based on BiGRU-FeatureAttention network.** This module regards the text representation Y_t learned by the previous module as the input, obtains the time hidden layer representation V_e via the BiGRU-FeatureAttention network, and then uses the fully-connected layer for event classification.

Social Media Text Representation Based on a Recurrent CNN. This module mainly includes a bidirectional recurrent neural network (bidirectional LSTM) and a convolutional neural network. Here $h_l(w_{ijk})$ is the hidden state of the previous word of word w_{ijk}, and $h_r(w_{ijk})$ is the hidden state of the next word of word w_{ijk}. $h_l(w_{ijk})$ and $h_r(w_{ijk})$ can be obtained by the following formula:

$$h_l(w_{ijk}) = f(W_l h_l(w_{ijk-1}) + W_{el} e(w_{ijk-1})) \tag{1}$$

$$h_r(w_{ijk}) = f(W_r h_r(w_{ijk+1}) + W_{er} e(w_{ijk+1})) \tag{2}$$

Where $e(w_{ijk-1})$ and $e(w_{ijk+1})$ are word embedding representations of the word w_{ijk-1} and the word w_{ijk+1}, respectively. Also, $h_l(w_{ijk-1})$ and $h_r(w_{ijk+1})$ represent the hidden states of the word w_{ijk-1} and the word w_{ijk+1}, respectively. W_l, W_{el}, W_r, and W_{er} are their respective weight matrices, and f is a nonlinear activation function tanh.

After calculating the two context hidden states $h_l(w_{ijk})$ and $h_r(w_{ijk})$ of current word w_{ijk}, two states are merged with the word embedding representation of current word as

$$X_k = (h_l(w_{ijk}), e(w_{ijk}), h_r(w_{ijk})) \tag{3}$$

We use a convolutional layer to learn its text representation to get the result X_k, and then use a maximum pooled layer to convert text representation vectors into fixed lengths. Where C_k is the result of X_k processed by the convolutional layer Conv1D, Y_t represents the text representation vector of the tth time period, and the ath element of Y_t is the maximum value of the ath element of $C_k(k \in [1, n])$

$$C_k = Conv1D(X_k) \tag{4}$$

$$Y_t = \max_{k \in [1,n]} C_k \tag{5}$$

Time Period Representation Based on BiGRU-FeatureAttention Network. This module contains a bidirectional GRU and a feature attention layer. The input of the bidirectional GRU is a text representation vector for each time period, and the bidirectional GRU layer can use information of the previous and subsequent time segments to learn the hidden layer representation of current time period.

$$h_{tf} = \overrightarrow{GRU}(Y_t), t \in [1, m] \tag{6}$$

$$h_{tb} = \overleftarrow{GRU}(Y_t), t \in [m, 1] \tag{7}$$

$$h_t = (h_{tf}, h_{tb}) \tag{8}$$

Where h_{tf} is the hidden layer representation of the forward GRU in time period t, h_{tb} is the hidden layer representation of the backward GRU in time period t, and m is the length of time segment, i.e., the number of time segments. Besides, h_t is the output of the bidirectional GRU in the tth time period, obtained by the connection of h_{tf} and h_{tb}.

We add a feature attention layer after the bidirectional GRU, so that the model can learn key information in this time period. The input of feature attention layer is the output h_t of bidirectional GRU at each time period, and hidden layer representation vector V_e of event is generated. Formula for the feature attention layer is as follows:

$$u_t = \tanh\left(W_h h_t + W_f F_e + b_h\right) \tag{9}$$

$$\beta_t = \frac{exp\left(u_t^T u_d\right)}{\sum_m exp\left(u_m^T u_d\right)} \tag{10}$$

$$V_e = \sum_t \beta_t h_t \tag{11}$$

Where h_t is the hidden layer representation of the bidirectional GRU, F_e is the event feature vector and we obtain u_t. The content-based features and the user-based features are used in the feature vector F_e. Description of features are summarized in Table 1. The SIGNAL TEXT feature in Table 1 is a signal text that determines whether there is an enquiry or correction in the text, such as “really?”, “rumor”, and so on. In 2015, Zhao et al. [2] used regular expressions to match signal texts. Similarly, we also use regular expressions to match the signal text, such as “*is\s(?:that|this|it)\s true*”, “*real?|really?|unconfirmed*”, and so on.

Table 1. The features of the social media event.

	Feature	Description
Content-based features	AVERAGE LENGTH	The average length of twitter
	SIGNAL TEXT	The fraction of twitter with enquiries and corrections
User-based features	VERIFIED USERS	The fraction of verified users
	AUTHOR DESCRIPTION	The fraction of users that provide a personal description
	AVERAGE COUNT FOLLOWERS	The average of user count followers
	AVERAGE COUNT FRIENDS	The average of user count friends

Also, we have β_t as the result obtained by normalization of u_t via the softmax function and we obtain the hidden layer representation V_e of the event. Then, the event hidden layer representation V_e is fed into a fully connected layer, and we use the softmax function to get the label $\widehat{L_e}$ of social media event for classification.

$$\widehat{L_e} = \text{softmax}(W_e V_e + b_e) \tag{12}$$

3.3 Model Training

In the proposed model, the cross-entropy error between probability distribution of prediction and ground truth is defined as the loss function. Correspondingly, the formula for cross-entropy loss function is as follows, where y^e represents the true label of the event (1 for rumor, and 0 for non-rumor), $\widehat{L_e}$ denotes a predicted event category label, and E represents the event dataset for training.

$$\text{Loss} = -\sum\nolimits_{e \in E} \left[y^e \log\left(\widehat{L_e}\right) + (1 - y^e) \log\left(1 - \widehat{L_e}\right) \right] \tag{13}$$

In order to minimize the occurrence of over-fitting, we use the L2 regularization for GRU layer weights, and use the dropout probability for GRU layer. We also use the Adam optimization algorithm [21] to improve the convergence speed. In each iterative process of the algorithm, the model regards the event dataset as input, which is trained via RCNN-FAN to obtain the label of the event for calculating the loss.

4 Experiments and Results

4.1 Datasets

We evaluate our proposed model on a public dataset used by Ma et al. [9] in 2016. This dataset includes two parts: Twitter and Sina Weibo. This dataset is used in the literature [6, 9–11, 16, 19] and is a classic dataset for rumor detection problems.

The Sina Weibo dataset contains 4664 events, in which each contains multiple Weibo texts. The content of each Weibo text is completely provided by the original dataset. Meanwhile, the Twitter dataset contains 992 events, each with multiple tweets. However, since the dataset only gives the id of the tweet in each event, the content of the tweet needs to be downloaded via the Twitter API interface. Considering that many tweets might be unavailable as time goes by, the same for some tweets for certain events, e.g., event with ID "E354". Therefore, we removed some data to ensure the quality of experiments (Table 2).

Table 2. Statistics of the datasets.

Statistic	Sina Weibo	Twitter
Events #	4664	992
Rumors #	2313	498
Non-rumors #	2351	494
Microblogs #	3805656	1101985
Users #	2746818	491229
Avg. time length/event (hours)	2460.7	1582.6
Avg. # of posts/event	816	1111
Max # of posts/event	59318	62827
Min # of posts/event	10	10

4.2 Experimental Setup

The running environment used in this experiment is as follows: Intel(R) Xeon(R) CPU E5-2620 v4 2.10 GHz, with the operating system as Ubuntu 14.04.5 LTS, the memory as 32 GB RAM, and the GPU as Tesla K40m. Besides, we used the development platform Python 3.6.2. The learning rate is set to 0.001, the regularization coefficient λ is set to 0.01, the dropout probability is set to 0.2. The word vector of Twitter is trained using the public 100-dimensional glove word vector. Since there is no public word vector suitable for this experiment in the Sina Weibo, word vector is trained by the model. The time period segmentation method of this experiment uses the method that splits social media text of an event into parts of equal size to ensure that the number of social media texts is equal in each time period [19].

We compared our model with the following state-of-the-arts baselines:

(1) **DTC model** [5]. This model extracts four categories of features from the collected tweet data and then uses the J48 decision tree to detect rumors.
(2) **SVM-TS model** [7]. This model proposes a dynamic series time structure (DSTS) to capture the temporal characteristics, then use the SVM classifier for identifying rumors.
(3) **DT-Rank model** [2]. This model first uses some regular expressions to identify tweets with enquiry and correction signals, then clusters these tweets, and matches tweets from non-signal tweets according to the summary statement after clustering. Finally, the tweets are sorted using statistical features.
(4) **GRU-2 model** [9]. This model uses tf-idf to calculate the text representation of each time period, then uses the double-layer GRU model for training.
(5) **CAMI model** [10]. This model learns the text representation via the paragraph vector, and then uses the CNN model to train.
(6) **CSI model** [16]. This model uses the RNN model to process microblog events, then performs the singular value decomposition of the user-user association matrix to get the user score of event.
(7) **HSA-BLSTM model** [19]. This model uses the bidirectional LSTM and the attention mechanism with the social feature vector to identify rumors.
(8) **HAN-FC model** [11]. This model uses doc2vec on the text of each time period and then utilizes a hierarchical attention network to detect rumors.

4.3 Performance Comparison

In order to verify the validity of the experiment, we compared our model with several state-of-the-arts baselines. The results of these experiments are shown in Table 3, in which RCNN-FAN (Recurrent Convolutional Neural Networks with Feature Attention Network) presents our technical framework. There are two categories, i.e., R stands for rumor and N stands for non-rumor. Also, four evaluation metrics were utilized to measure the performance, namely Accuracy, Precision, Recall and F1.

Table 3. Results of comparison with different methods (R: Rumor; N: Non-rumor).

Method	C	Sina Weibo				Twitter			
		Acc.	Pre.	Rec.	F1	Acc.	Pre.	Rec.	F1
DT-Rank	R	0.755	0.711	0.832	0.767	0.614	0.618	0.584	0.601
	N		0.812	0.682	0.741		0.610	0.643	0.626
DTC	R	0.831	0.847	0.815	0.831	0.709	0.690	0.772	0.729
	N		0.815	0.847	0.830		0.733	0.643	0.685
SVM-TS	R	0.857	0.839	0.885	0.861	0.716	0.689	0.793	0.738
	N		0.878	0.830	0.857		0.754	0.639	0.692
GRU-2	R	0.910	0.876	0.956	0.914	0.723	0.712	0.743	0.727
	N		0.952	0.864	0.906		0.735	0.704	0.719
HSA-BLSTM	R	0.934	0.943	0.933	0.938	0.765	0.729	**0.838**	0.780
	N		0.924	0.936	0.930		**0.813**	0.693	0.748
CAMI	R	0.937	0.937	0.940	0.938	0.753	0.727	0.823	0.772
	N		0.938	0.934	0.936		0.789	0.682	0.732
CSI	R	0.951	0.939	0.962	0.950	0.773	0.806	0.714	0.758
	N		0.963	0.942	0.952		0.746	**0.831**	0.787
HAN-FC	R	0.964	0.955	**0.977**	0.966	0.787	0.778	0.800	0.789
	N		**0.974**	0.949	0.962		0.797	0.775	0.786
RCNN-FAN	R	**0.970**	**0.966**	**0.977**	**0.971**	**0.799**	**0.814**	0.770	**0.792**
	N		**0.974**	**0.962**	**0.968**		0.785	0.827	**0.805**

In traditional machine learning experiments, the SVM-TS model achieved the accuracy of 85.7% and 71.6% in the two datasets, respectively, and obtained the best effect in traditional machine learning. For experiments based on feature representation, the HAN-FC model achieves the accuracy of 96.4% and 78.7% in the two datasets, and the best results are obtained for all baselines. It can also be seen that the method based on feature representation learning is better than the method based on traditional machine learning. Our RCNN-FAN model achieved 97% accuracy in the Sina Weibo dataset and achieves 79.9% accuracy in the Twitter dataset, which outperformed the HAN-FC model by 0.6% and 1.2%, respectively. Moreover, it outperformed the SVM-TS model by 11.3% in the Sina Weibo dataset and 8.3% in the Twitter dataset, and it performed much better than the baselines. In addition, the Weibo dataset and Twitter datasets expressed different effects. This may because there is more noise information on the Twitter dataset [9], and some data is not available, it has a certain impact on the final experimental results.

In addition, on the Sina Weibo dataset, the accuracy, recall, and F1 values of our model reaches the highest value of the baselines, and most of the values exceed the highest values of the baselines. On the Twitter dataset, the F1 value of our model also exceeds the highest value in the baselines.

5 Conclusion

In this paper, we proposed a novel method to automatically identify rumors on social media. To be specific, RCNN-FeatureAttention network was adapted to learn the contextual representation information, as well as the bidirectional GRU network with a feature attention layer to learn the time period information. Extensive validations on real-world data sets have verified the effectiveness of our proposed solution, which significantly outperformed several state-of-the-art methods.

Acknowledgement. This research project was supported by the National Natural Science Foundation of China (No. 61772135 and No. U1605251), the Open Project of Key Laboratory of Network Data Science & Technology of Chinese Academy of Sciences (No. CASNDST201708 and No. CASNDST201606), the Open Project of National Laboratory of Pattern Recognition at the Institute of Automation of the Chinese Academy of Sciences (201900041), Fujian Provincial Natural Science Foundation Project (2017J01755), CERNET Innovation Project (NGII20160501).

References

1. DiFonzo, N., Bordia, P.: Rumor Psychology: Social and Organizational Approaches. American Psychological Association, Washington, D.C. (2007)
2. Zhao, Z., Resnick, P., Mei, Q.: Enquiring minds: early detection of rumors in social media from enquiry posts. In: 24th International Conference on World Wide Web, Florence, pp. 1395–1405 (2015)
3. Liang, G., He, W., Xu, C., et al.: Rumor identification in microblogging systems based on users' behavior. IEEE Trans. Comput. Soc. Syst. **2**, 99–108 (2015)
4. Zhang, Q., Zhang, S., Dong, J., et al.: Automatic detection of rumor on social network. In: 4th CCF Conference on Natural Language Processing and Chinese Computing, Nanchang, pp. 113–122 (2015)
5. Castillo, C., Mendoza, M., Poblete, B.: Information credibility on twitter. In: International Conference on World Wide Web, Hyderabad, pp. 675–684 (2011)
6. Ma, J., Gao, W., Wong, K.F.: Detect rumors in microblog posts using propagation structure via kernel learning. In: 55th Annual Meeting of the Association for Computational Linguistics, Vancouver, pp. 708–717 (2017)
7. Ma, J., Gao, W., Wei, Z., et al.: Detect rumors using time series of social context information on microblogging websites. In: 24th ACM International Conference on Information and Knowledge Management, Melbourne, pp. 1751–1754 (2015)
8. Sun, S., Liu, H., He, J., et al.: Detecting event rumors on Sina Weibo automatically. In: The Web Technologies and Applications - 15th Asia-Pacific Web Conference, Sydney, pp. 120–131 (2013)
9. Ma, J., Gao, W., Mitra, P., et al.: Detecting rumors from microblogs with recurrent neural networks. In: 25th International Joint Conference on Artificial Intelligence, New York, pp. 3818–3824 (2016)
10. Yu, F., Liu, Q., Wu, S., et al.: A convolutional approach for misinformation identification. In: 26th International Joint Conference on Artificial Intelligence, Melbourne, pp. 3901–3907 (2017)
11. Liao, X.W., Huang, Z., Yang, D.D., et al.: Rumor detection in social media based on hierarchical attention network. Sci Sin Inform **48**(11), 1558–1574 (2018). (in Chinese)

12. Qazvinian, V., Rosengren, E., Radev, D.R., et al.: Rumor has it: identifying misinformation in microblogs. In: The Conference on Empirical Methods in Natural Language Processing, Edinburgh, pp. 1589–1599 (2011)
13. Hochreiter, S., Schmidhuber, J.: Long short-term memory. Neural Comput. **9**, 1735–1780 (1997)
14. Elman, J.L.: Finding structure in time. Cogn. Sci. **14**, 179–211 (1990)
15. Lecun, Y., Boser, B., Denker, J.S., et al.: Backpropagation applied to handwritten zip code recognition. Neural Comput. **1**, 541–551 (1989)
16. Ruchansky, N., Seo, S., Liu, Y.: CSI: a hybrid deep model for fake news detection. In: the 2017 ACM on Conference on Information and Knowledge Management, Singapore, pp. 797–806 (2017)
17. Ma, J., Gao, W., Wong, K.F.: Detect rumor and stance jointly by neural multi-task learning. In: The Web Conference Companion, Lyon, pp. 585–593 (2018)
18. Ma, J., Gao, W., Wong, K.-F.: Rumor detection on twitter with tree-structured recursive neural networks. In: The Meeting of the Association for Computational Linguistics, Australia, pp. 1980–1989 (2018)
19. Guo, H., Cao, J., Zhang, Y., et al.: Rumor detection with hierarchical social attention network. In: The ACM International Conference on Information and Knowledge Management, Italy, pp. 943–951 (2018)
20. Lai, S., Xu, L., Liu, K., et al.: Recurrent convolutional neural networks for text classification. In: 29th AAAI Conference on Artificial Intelligence, USA, pp. 2267–2273 (2015)
21. Kingma, D.P., Ba, J.: Adam: a method for stochastic optimization. arXiv:1412.6980 (2014)

Automatic Proofreading in Chinese: Detect and Correct Spelling Errors in Character-Level with Deep Neural Networks

Qiufeng Wang(✉), Minghuan Liu, Weijia Zhang, Yuhang Guo, and Tianrui Li

School of Information Science and Technology, Southwest Jiaotong University, 999 Xi'an Road, Chengdu, China
{qfwang,ericliu,wjzhang,guoyuhang,trli}@my.swjtu.edu.cn

Abstract. Rapid increase of the scale of text carries huge costs for manual proofreading. In comparison, automatic proofreading shows great advantages on time and human resource, drawing more researchers into it. In this paper, we propose two attention based deep neural network models combined with confusion sets to detect and correct possible Chinese spelling errors in character-level. Our proposed approaches first model the context of Chinese character embedding using Long Short-Term Memory (LSTM) networks, then score the probabilities of candidates from its confusion set through attention mechanism, choosing the highest one as the prediction answer. Also, we define a new methodology for obtaining (preceding text, following text, candidates, target) quads and provides a supervised dataset for training and testing (Our data has been released to the public in https://github.com/ccit-proofread.). Performance evaluation indicates that our models achieve the state-of-the-art performance and outperform a set of baselines.

Keywords: Error detection of Chinese text · Error correction of Chinese text · LSTM model · Attention mechanism

1 Introduction

The increasing scale of text carries a huge cost for manual proofreading, calling for necessary and meaningful automatic text proofreading, which is to automatically detect and correct the errors in pieces of text with machine. Text proofreading contains spelling check, grammar check, punctuation check, digit check, and others. Most of current works including ours focus on spelling check, which is an important preprocessing task since spelling errors appear in every written language. For instance, given one sentence of text:

Electronic supplementary material The online version of this chapter (https://doi.org/10.1007/978-3-030-32236-6_31) contains supplementary material, which is available to authorized users.

J. Tang et al. (Eds.): NLPCC 2019, LNAI 11839, pp. 349–359, 2019.
https://doi.org/10.1007/978-3-030-32236-6_31

Ex.1-right 今天的天气很好。
Ex.1-right *The weather is good today.*

However, due to some reasons, OCR identification error, for example, misrecognize "今(jin) " as "令(ling)", then it becomes:
Ex.1-wrong 令天的天气很好。

The sentence above shows a spelling error, in which "令(make, order, pinyin:*ling*)" is a wrongly written character. Our task aims to detect it and correct it properly into "今(this, now, pinyin:*jin*)" while taking no action on the other characters. Therefore, spelling check generally contains two steps, e.g. detection and correction [14]. Detection identifies errors and correction corrects them.

Many challenges are required to be solved for proofreading Chinese spelling errors. (i) Chinese words have no obvious boundary. So many works [14] take it as a prerequisite to introduce automatic word segmentation although segmentation itself may give rise to errors, and ultimately affects the whole performance. (ii) The number of Chinese characters is large and they own similarities. *Grand Chinese Characters Dictionary* collects more than 56,000 Chinese characters. Besides, these Chinese characters have a lot of similarities like similar pronunciation, similar shape and similar meaning [3]. (iii) A single model always behaves variously in different error ratio text.

In this work, we propose two novel attention based deep neural network models to address the above problems. We frame spelling check as a prediction problem, and introduce confusion sets which provides sets of possible candidate characters that are potential to be confused. To train the model, we introduce a new method to build a spelling check dataset. Simplified Chinese text collected from Wiki and Baidu containing no error are converted to (preceding text, following text, candidates, target) quads. Since the error rate of a qualified publishing book must be lower than 0.01%, we set four different proportions of errors like 0.1%, 0.5%, 1% and 2% to evaluate the proofreading performance in different situations. In the appendix, we elaborate on the production process of the dataset.

Our work includes three solutions to meet the above three challenges. (i) We avoid automatic segmentation errors by handling in character-level, which means we detect and correct character errors rather than words. (ii) We collect character-level confusion sets as priori knowledge to reduce the suggested correction candidates, which cover errors due to character similarities. (iii) We extract more global information using encoders to reduce the impact of local errors. Moreover, we introduce confidence threshold to make our model adjustable for different error ratio text.

2 Related Work

Automatic detection and correction in text is a significant task in NLP. Researches for English launch earlier and have developed maturely; however, study on Chinese begins late and still on exploration. In this section, we introduce related work for automatic text proofreading on spelling check in English and Chinese.

For English, Golding et al. [15] proposed Bayesian and Winnow algorithm based on machine learning methods, took spelling errors correction as words disambiguation by learning the features of words in confusion sets and comparing them with specific contextual feature to choose the most suitable word. Hirst et al. [16] used semantic information to detect real word errors by computing semantic distances between words and contexts with WordNet. If the distance is close, the word is right; otherwise is wrong. A weakness of this method is that there is no consideration of the relation between easily confused words.

For Chinese, Tseng et al. [11] proposed a bake-off for Chinese spelling check, leading a lot of works on this task. Many current works used word segmentation and language models based on large-scale corpus statistics to detect spelling errors in text. Zhang et al. [14] proposed an approximate Chinese word matching algorithm. With a Tri-gram language model, detection and correction were achieved at the same time. Zhuang et al. [18] extracted both syntax and semantic features from confusion sets of similar characters using N-gram and LSA language model. Liu et al. [4] scored words from provided confusion sets in specific context by N-gram model and found the highest one as results. Some researchers [17] applied hybrid approaches for detection and correction and achieved good results.

In our work, we incorporate attention mechanisms with confusion sets for spelling errors detection and correction. Attention mechanisms have been applied in various works, which allow models to draw deep dependencies between two parts. They were first raised in [7], then adopted by MT works [1], resolving alignment between the source and the corresponding target. Vaswani et al. [12] raised multi-head attention and self-attention, making attention mechanisms even more prevalent.

3 Models

In this section, a normal definition of our task and embedding of Chinese character is firstly given. Afterwards, brief introductions and modeling of LSTM networks are given. Lastly, our proposed deep neural network models based on attention mechanism for spelling errors detection and correction are presented.

3.1 Task Definition and Embedding

In this paper, we adopt deep neural networks to mine deep information of a sequence, modeling the preceding and following contexts of one specific character. Given a sequence $x = \{x_1, x_2, \cdots, x_{k-1}, x_k, x_{k+1}, \cdots, x_{n-1}, x_n\}$, where x_k the k-th character in one given sequence, n is the sequence length. We want to identify if x_k is wrong, then the confusion set $\mathcal{D}(x_k)$ of x_k is introduced. Our task is to estimate the probability of candidate d_k from the preceding context xp_k

and the following context sequence xf_k as $P(d_k \mid xp_k, xf_k, \theta)$, where $d_k \in \mathcal{D}(x_k)$, $xp_k = \{x_1, x_2, \cdots, x_{k-1}\}$, $xf_k = \{x_{k+1}, x_{k+2}, \cdots, x_n\}$, θ is hyperparameter of Deep Neural Network. For data representation, we map all characters into vector representations using embedding function $\mathcal{E}$ with all vectors stacked in a embedding matrix $L \in \mathbb{R}^{h \times \|V\|}$, where h the dimension of vectors and V the vocabulary size.

3.2 Modeling with Long Short-Term Memory (LSTM)

LSTM has recently made considerable success in several NLP tasks, showing a remarkable ability to represent long sequences in vectors. LSTM is a great improvement of Recurrent Neural Network (RNN) [2], aiming to solve problems of gradient vanishing and exploding over long sequences for RNN.

For deep neural network models in NLP, an RNN Encoder architecture is always adopted for modeling text [5,9]. We believe RNN encoders are enough to extract information needed for our task. Inspired by Tang et al. [10], for one specific character to be checked, we utilize two standard LSTM networks, namely, LSTM_p and LSTM_f to model its preceding and following contexts, encoding which into fixed length vectors. For x_k, LSTM_p encodes preceding context $\{x_1, x_2, \cdots, x_{k-1}\}$ into $\overrightarrow{h_{k-1}}$ while LSTM_f encodes following context $\{x_{k+1}, x_{k+2}, \cdots, x_l\}$ reversely into $\overleftarrow{h_{k+1}}$. For the whole context the composite output vector h_k is obtained by concatenation:

$$h_k = \left[\overrightarrow{h_{k-1}}; \overleftarrow{h_{k+1}}\right] \tag{1}$$

In the next subsection we use the attention mechanism to further extract important information from h_k. The goal is to calculate the importance of the preceding and following context for predicting correct candidates.

3.3 Attention Based Neural Network Models

Attention mechanisms allow models to mine deep relation between two parts. A general attention function proposed by Luong et al. [5] computes context vectors c_t as follows:

$$r(h_t, h_s) = h_t^T W_a h_s \tag{2}$$

$$a_t(s) = softmax(r(h_t, h_s)) \tag{3}$$

$$c_t = \sum_s a_t(s) h_s \tag{4}$$

where $W_a \in \mathbb{R}^{\|h_t^T\| \times \|h_s\|}$, h_t the target hidden state, h_s the source hidden state, $r(h_t, h_s)$ the relation score and $a_t(s)$ the normalization score of h_t and h_s. Next we propose two models based on the attention mechanism:

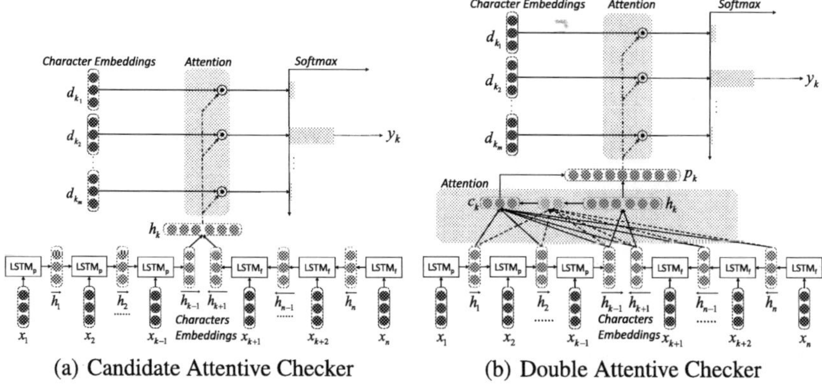

Fig. 1. Attention based neural network models

The Candidate Attentive Checker

We try to adopt an attention function to mark each candidate in specific context. A normal thought computes candidate scores through c_t. Note that Eq. 4 computes every c_t as a weighted average, and each h_s is computed from the same context, which is relevant with each other. However, candidates in confusion sets are independent, which means the sum operation in Eq. 4 will instead impair the information. Hence we decide to directly calculate the score α_{k_i} of hidden state h_k obtained by concatenation and i-th candidate d_{k_i} without computing weighted average context vectors as:

$$\alpha_{k_i} = softmax(h_k^T W_s d_{k_i}) \tag{5}$$

where $W_s \in \mathbb{R}^{\|h_k^T\| \times \|d_{k_i}\|}$. In this type, α_k is a variable-length vector, whose size equals the number of candidates.

As shown in Fig. 1(a), candidate attentive checker employs the above attention mechanism beyond the context vector and candidates. The model computes an attention score α_{k_i} of each i-th candidate d_{k_i} with respect to character x_k followed by 5. The model marks y_k with the highest score as the answer prediction.

$$y_k = argmax(\alpha_k) \tag{6}$$

The Double Attentive Checker

The candidate attentive checker is able to focus on candidates that are most likely to fit for contextual features. Such context vectors concatenated only by the last hidden states of LSTM_p and LSTM_f are impacted more by closer characters, tending to cause long-distance dependencies loss. If these characters are wrong in the given sequence, it will result in bad effects on current prediction. Hence we go further by applying an general attention mechanism as Eqs. (2, 3 and 4), illustrated in Fig. 1(b), to extract dependencies between each hidden state h_s

of input sequence x and the context vector h_k. By doing such, double attentive checker pays more attention on correctly relevant characters without losing long-distance information. We compute the dependency representation vector p_k as follows:

$$r_{k_s} = h_k^T W_a h_s \tag{7}$$

$$\alpha_{k_s} = softmax(r_{k_s}) \tag{8}$$

$$c_k = \sum_s \alpha_{k_s} h_s \tag{9}$$

$$p_k = [c_k; h_k] \tag{10}$$

Ultimately, double attentive checker computes scores through attention similar as candidate attentive checker. y_k with the highest score is the prediction.

$$\alpha_{k_i} = softmax(p_k^T W_s d_{k_i}) \tag{11}$$

$$y_k = argmax\,(\alpha_k) \tag{12}$$

where $W_s \in \mathbb{R}^{3h \times h}$.

3.4 Model Training

Our models use the cross entropy as the objective function, and plus an L2 regularization term to prevent overfitting as follows:

$$loss = -\sum_{i=1}^{N} \sum_{d \in \mathcal{D}(x_i)} \delta_d(x_i) log(P_d(x_i;\theta)) + \lambda \|\theta\|^2 \tag{13}$$

where N the samples of training data, $\mathcal{D}(x_i)$ the confusion set of x_i, $\delta_d(x_i)$ indicates whether candidate d is the right answer of x_i, whose value is 1 or 0, θ is the parameter set, and λ is the regularization weight. And $P_d(x_i)$ is the probability predicting x_i as d given by the attention score after the softmax layer.

3.5 Confidence Modification

Both Candidate Attentive Proofreader and Double Attentive Proofreader take the candidate with the highest score as the prediction answer. In order to adapt to text of different error scales and prevent these models from choosing an unreasonable answer, we propose to employ a confidence modification on our models. Given character x_k and the answer prediction y_k, we apply the following modification function to acquire the final answer z_k,

$$z_k = \begin{cases} y_k & \alpha_{k_{arg\,y_k}} \cdot t > \alpha_{k_{arg\,x_k}} \\ x_k & others \end{cases} \tag{14}$$

where t is the confidence threshold parameter of recognizing the prediction answer. When a model scores y_k lower than the threshold, then it is not very confident about its choice and will keep the original character x_k. Through confidence modification, we keep these non-errors as much as possible and only choose answers with high confidence.

4 Experiments

We first describe our experimental setup, then evaluate our models by comparing with some baselines and report the empirical results in this section.

4.1 Experimental Setup

Training Details. We first set vocabulary size $\|V\|$ as 10 K, which contains the top 10 K characters ordered by frequency in Wiki, and map all Out of Vocabulary (OOV) characters to '<UNK>' tokens. We select embedding size h $[\underline{128}, 256, 512]$, and mini-batch size $[64, \underline{128}, 256]$. Embeddings are trained with the model. We consider adam update rule [8] with initial learning rate $[0.0005, \underline{0.001}, 0.01]$. We apply dropout with probability $[0.1, \underline{0.2}, 0.3, 0.4]$ to LSTM cells and embedding layer. We assign the threshold parameter t in Eq. 14 as 0.001. All experiments are run on single GPU, GeForce GTX TITAN Xp with 12 GB VRAM. We use our dataset for training and testing. Each training set and test set extract 200 K sentences from the dataset. Note that test set is mixed with errors and we set four different ratios to test model performances, which include 0.1%, 0.5%, 1% and 2%.

Comparision Settings. Since there is no such available benchmark approaches for this task, we compare with the following baseline methods:

MDMM (Mays, Damerau and Mercer Model): This statistical model was proposed by Mays et al. [6] which is based on Bayes theorem to tackle the English real-word correction. They regard this task as a noisy channel problem in which an intended statement undergoes introduction of typos and then the most likely statement are predicted by their system.

DAM (Dynamic Alpha Model): This is a method proposed by Hearn et al. [13] to address the problem in MDMM that there is no probability mass left to be distributed among the confusion set sometimes. They introduce a prior belief of parameters and modify the prior belief using fluctuation factors.

CSNG (Confusion sets based N-gram/language model): This method was previously proposed by Liu et al. [4] to detect and correct real-word errors in Chinese. It extracted adjacent bigrams and trigrams feature to compute the probability with the confusion words in the aim word's confusion set, then scores those words with multi-features. We test this model on characters.

CAC (Candidate Attentive Checker), **DAC** (Double Attentive Checker): Our proposed attention based deep model as discussed at Sect. 3.3.

Evaluation Metrics. To evaluate the proofreading performance of our models, followed by Tseng et al. [11], we select the widely-used measurements of Precision, Recall, F1 Score computed by characters both on detection-level and correction-level as our metrics.

4.2 Empirical Results

Tables 1 and 2 show the results of our models compared with baseline methods on test data of four different error ratios. It is clearly that our proposed models outperform all previous baseline methods on both detection-level and correction-level, which indicates that our models utilize more context information with sets of candidates than those who only focus on local features. In addition, on detection-level, DAM tends to emphasize the recall much more than precision, leading to bad effects on F1 scores; on the opposite, CAC and DAC both get better precisions and F1 scores. It should be noted that in this task, with the same F1 score, precision is usually more important than recall because the number of non-errors is always much larger than errors.

Furthermore, as the error ratio increases, recalls drop while precisions elevate, showing that these two models perform better on data containing more errors. Moreover, DAC performs better than CAC overall, but their differences are less evident with error ratio grows due to DAC extracting more useful global information using attention mechanism in less errors sentences, which is less possibly influenced by nearby errors. In experiments on our dataset, these baselines get quietly worse performances especially precisions than results shown in their paper, but with the error ratio increasing, we get closer empirical results to theirs. So we guess that their experiments are conducted on data of relatively

Table 1. Detection-level performance comparison

	0.001			0.005			0.01			0.02			Overall		
	P	R	F	P	R	F	P	R	F	P	R	F	P	R	F
MDMM	0.064	0.409	0.110	0.254	0.403	0.312	0.399	0.392	0.396	0.567	0.385	0.459	0.321	0.398	0.319
DAM	0.027	**0.781**	0.052	0.125	**0.783**	0.216	0.221	**0.767**	0.343	0.363	**0.750**	0.489	0.184	**0.770**	0.275
CSNG	0.065	0.689	0.118	0.246	0.655	0.358	0.382	0.635	0.477	0.534	0.598	0.565	0.307	0.573	0.380
CAC	0.267	0.753	0.394	0.619	0.693	0.654	0.747	0.647	0.693	0.839	0.586	0.690	0.618	0.670	0.608
DAC	**0.296**	0.766	**0.427**	**0.651**	0.702	**0.676**	**0.771**	0.654	**0.708**	**0.856**	0.587	**0.696**	**0.644**	0.677	**0.627**

Table 2. Correction-level performance comparison

	0.001			0.005			0.01			0.02			Overall		
	P	R	F	P	R	F	P	R	F	P	R	F	P	R	F
MDMM	0.050	0.322	0.087	0.194	0.308	0.238	0.317	0.312	0.315	0.447	0.303	0.361	0.252	0.311	0.250
DAM	0.020	0.572	0.038	0.089	0.557	0.153	0.160	0.555	0.248	0.259	**0.534**	0.349	0.132	0.554	0.197
CSNG	0.062	0.656	0.113	0.229	0.610	0.333	0.346	**0.576**	0.432	0.464	0.519	0.490	0.275	0.590	0.342
CAC	0.252	0.711	0.372	0.563	0.631	0.595	0.657	0.569	0.610	0.700	0.488	0.575	0.543	0.600	0.538
DAC	**0.279**	**0.721**	**0.402**	**0.594**	**0.640**	**0.616**	**0.678**	0.575	**0.622**	**0.719**	0.493	**0.585**	**0.568**	**0.607**	**0.556**

high error ratio, and their methods may be powerless on data with a low error ratio. In the appendix, we present some example answers from CAC and DAC.

4.3 Error Ratio Analysis

A good spelling checker should correct more errors than it introduces, hence we denote Error Difference = (#errors before checking − #errors after checking)/#errors before checking, and compare baselines with our models. In Table 3, we show the comparision results. We can observe that on a very low error ratio as 0.001, all compared models detect more non-errors and lead to more errors than before. But it is obvious that ours take less errors in. On bigger ratios, both CAC and DAC reduce the number of errors while almost all baselines still not. Our proposed methods can be helpful in real-case applications.

Table 3. Error difference performance comparison

	0.001	0.005	0.01	0.02
MDMM	−5.677	−0.874	−0.280	0.010
DAM	−27.543	−4.910	−2.153	−0.780
CSNG	−9.241	−1.399	−0.452	−0.002
CAC	−1.35	0.203	0.349	0.376
DAC	**−1.10**	**0.265**	**0.381**	**0.394**

4.4 Confidence Threshold Analysis

To understand the pattern of our models' confidence, we have an ablation study of confidence threshold parameter t. Figure 2 illustrates the F1 performance of CAC and DAC against different numbers of t on test sets. We can observe that the trend of detection F1 and correction F1 are almost the same and we can modify the threshold to effectively meet the need of different estimated error ratios. For data of 0.1%, the empirical optimal confidence threshold is 0.00005 and for data of 0.5% it is 0.0006; for data of 1%, it is good to apply 0.0018 and for data of 2%, performances around 0.005 are similar. A lower confidence threshold means more errors are not going to be detected and corrected; on the other hand, a larger threshold gives our model more confidence to detect and correct a spelling error. With the t growing larger than some value, the F1 begins to decrease, which indicates that we can decide an appropriate threshold for our models to gain better performances. By doing such we can also avoid the bad error difference on data of 0.001.

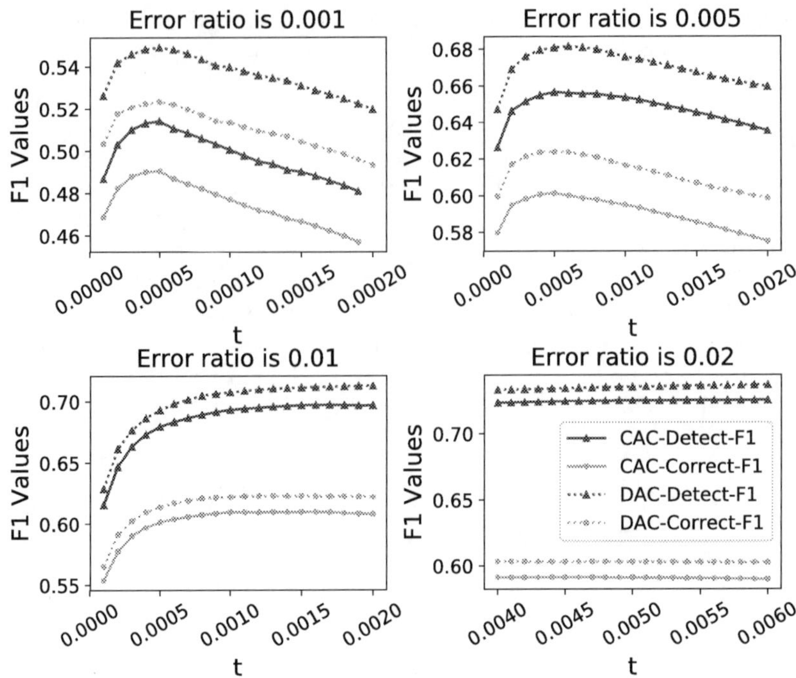

Fig. 2. F1 against different threshold t

5 Conclusion

In this paper, we proposed two attention based deep models combined with confusion sets used for proofreading spelling errors in character-level. We regarded spelling check as a prediction task, and through attention mechanism we computed the relation score between every candidate characters and the context encoded by LSTMs. For the lack of supervised dataset we define a new methodology for obtaining (preceding text, following text, candidates, target) quads. We evaluate our methods on test sets of four different error ratios and report the state-of-the-art performance.

References

1. Bahdanau, D., Cho, K., Bengio, Y.: Neural machine translation by jointly learning to align and translate. arXiv preprint arXiv:1409.0473 (2014)
2. Elman, J.L.: Distributed representations, simple recurrent networks, and grammatical structure. Machine Learning **7**(2–3), 195–225 (1991)
3. Liu, C., Lai, M., Chuang, Y., Lee, C.: Visually and phonologically similar characters in incorrect simplified chinese words. In Proceedings of the 23rd International Conference on Computational Linguistics: Posters, pages 739–747. Association for Computational Linguistics, 2010

4. Liu, L., Cao, C.: Chinese real-word error automatic proofreading ßased on combining of local context features. Computer Science **43**(12), 30–35 (2016)
5. Luong, T., Pham, H., Manning, C.D.: Effective approaches to attention-based neural machine translation. In Proceedings of the 2015 Conference on Empirical Methods in Natural Language Processing, pages 1412–1421, 2015
6. Mays, E., Damerau, F.J., Mercer, R.L.: Context based spelling correction. Information Processing & Management **27**(5), 517–522 (1991)
7. Mnih, V., Heess, N., Graves, A., et al.: Recurrent models of visual attention. In Advances in neural information processing systems, pages 2204–2212, 2014
8. Kinga, D., Adam, J.: A method for stochastic optimization. In: International Conference on Learning Representations (ICLR) (2015)
9. Hermann, K., Grefenstette, E., Espeholt, L., Will Kay, et al.: Teaching machines to read and comprehend. arxiv.org/abs/1506.03340, 2015
10. Tang, D., Qin, B., Feng, X., Ting L.: Effective lstms for target-dependent sentiment classification. In Proceedings of COLING 2016, the 26th International Conference on Computational Linguistics: Technical Papers, pages 3298–3307, 2016
11. Tseng, Y.H., Lee, L.H., Chang, L.P., Chen, H.H.: Introduction to sighan 2015 bake-off for chinese spelling check. In Proceedings of the Eighth SIGHAN Workshop on Chinese Language Processing, pages 32–37, 2015
12. Vaswani, A., Shazeer, N., Parmar, N., Uszkoreit, J., Jones L., et al.: Attention is all you need. In Advances in Neural Information Processing Systems, pages 6000–6010, 2017
13. Hearn, A.W., Hirst, G., Budanitsky, A.: Real-word spelling correction with trigrams: A reconsideration of the mays, damerau, and mercer model. In International Conference on Intelligent Text Processing and Computational Linguistics, pages 605–616. Springer, 2008
14. Zhang, L., Huang, C., Zhou, M., Pan, H.: Automatic detecting/correcting errors in chinese text by an approximate word-matching algorithm. In Proceedings of the 38th Annual Meeting on Association for Computational Linguistics, pages 248–254. Association for Computational Linguistics, 2000
15. Golding, A.R., Roth, D.: A winnow-based approach to context-sensitive spelling correction. Machine learning **34**(1–3), 107–130 (1999)
16. Hirst, G., Budanitsky, A.: Correcting real-word spelling errors by restoring lexical cohesion. Natural Language Engineering **11**(1), 87–111 (2005)
17. Zhao, H., Cai, D., Xin, Y., Wang, Y., Jia, Z.: A hybrid model for chinese spelling check. ACM Transactions on Asian and Low-Resource Language Information Processing (TALLIP) **16**(3), 21 (2017)
18. Zhuang, L., Bao, T., Zhu, X., Wang, C., Naoi, S.: A chinese ocr spelling check approach based on statistical language models. In Systems, Man and Cybernetics, 2004 IEEE International Conference on, volume 5, pages 4727–4732. IEEE, 2004

Linguistic Feature Representation with Statistical Relational Learning for Readability Assessment

Xinying Qiu[1], Dawei Lu[2], Yuming Shen[1(✉)], and Yi Cai[3]

[1] School of Information Science and Technology, Guangdong University of Foreign Studies, Guangzhou, China
ymshen2002@163.com

[2] School of Liberal Arts, Renmin University of China, Beijing, China

[3] School of Software Engineering, South China University of Technology, Guangzhou, China

Abstract. Traditional NLP model for readability assessment represents document as vector of words or vector of linguistic features that may be sparse, discrete, and ignoring the latent relations among features. We observe from data and linguistics theory that a document's linguistic features are not necessarily conditionally independent. To capture the latent relations among linguistic features, we propose to build feature graphs and learn distributed representation with Statistical Relational Learning. We then project the document vectors onto the linguistic feature embedding space to produce linguistic feature knowledge-enriched document representation. We showcase this idea with Chinese L1 readability classification experiments and achieve positive results. Our proposed model performs better than traditional vector space models and other embedding based models for current data set and deserves further exploration.

Keywords: Linguistic feature embedding · Statistical Relational Learning · Readability assessment

1 Introduction

Document-level readability assessment is an important research aspect in linguistic complexity for many different languages. It could be defined as measuring the comprehension difficulty perceived by humans when processing linguistic input at document level. The majority of machine-learning assessment methods are based on the framework of supervised learning with human-designed linguistic features [1]. Although such feature-driven classification models achieved some of the top performances that are hard to be transcended, their sparse and discrete characteristics did not take into consideration the latent relations among linguistic features. Recent development in readability assessment model learns word representation by encoding knowledge on word-level difficulty into word-embedding [2]. However, readability level does not reflect only at word-level complexity, but also at syntactic, structural, and discourse sophistication.

J. Tang et al. (Eds.): NLPCC 2019, LNAI 11839, pp. 360–369, 2019.
https://doi.org/10.1007/978-3-030-32236-6_32

We propose, therefore, to learn linguistic feature embedding models that cover four categories (i.e. shallow features, syntactic features, POS features, and discourse features) from their relation graphs to construct an enriched, dense, and low dimensional document representation for automatic readability assessment.

In particular, based on our observation on the linguistic feature data, we hypothesize that the linguistic features that demonstrate high impact on readability differences contain, among themselves, multiple types of correlation connected with latent linguistic factors. We illustrate our observation with the following examples:

Table 1. Examples of linguistic feature relations and their latent factors.

	Linguistic feature 1	Linguistic feature 2	Correlation	Latent factors
1	Percentage of conjunctions	Average height of parse tree	Positive	Complex parse tree contains more conjunctions
2	Average number of characters per word	Percentage of unique functional words	Negative	Length of Chinese functional word is short
3	Number of punctuation clauses per sentence	Average number of unique idioms per sentence	Neutral	Unrelated

In the above Table 1, the two linguistic features and their relation form a triplet that could be explained with the latent factors of linguistic implications. For example, documents of low readability may have more complex discourse structures such that the percentage of conjunctions and the average height of parse tree are both large because complex parse trees may contain more conjunctions. In the second example, since Chinese functional word is mostly composed of one or two characters, the higher the percentage of unique functional words within a document, probably the lower the average number of characters per word for that document. Both features may affect document readability but in different directions. We propose to automatically infer these latent factors and the existence of relationships among linguistic features by applying the latent feature model of Statistical Relational Learning (SRL) [3–5].

We showcase this linguistic feature embedding (LFE) model in the area of Chinese L1 readability assessment. By projecting the document representation vectors onto the space of linguistic feature embedding representation, we provide a linguistic knowledge-enriched and low-dimensional model that achieves better performance in readability prediction.

2 Related Research

In applying NLP technology for readability assessment, Sung (2015) evaluated 30 linguistic features and classification model using primary school text books in traditional Chinese used in Taiwan [6]. Jiang et al. (2014) proposed classification model and feature sets for readability prediction using L1 primary school text books in simplified Chinese. However, the features developed for Chinese are far from enough [7]. In their following work, Jiang et al. (2015) model word representation with their difficulty distribution in sentences and proposed a graph-based classification framework with coupled bag-of-word model [8]. Recently, Jiang et al. (2018) incorporated word-level difficulty from three knowledge source into a knowledge graph and trained an enriched word embedding representation [2]. However, the word-level difficulty knowledge did not distinguish source knowledge for L1 and L2 instruction. Besides, differences in document-level readability is not reflected solely on word-level complexity, but also contain discrepancy in syntactic, discourse, and structural sophistication.

3 Methodology

In this work, we propose a new linguistic feature embedding model to construct document representation for readability assessment. Our overall research structure as illustrated in Fig. 1 consists of four stages: feature design, feature relation graph and embedding learning, document representation, and readability classification. We discuss technology detail in this section.

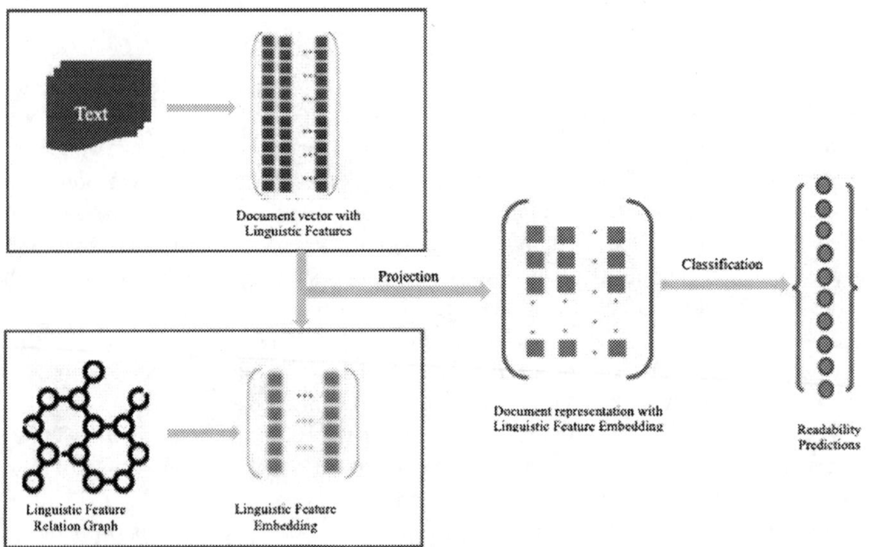

Fig. 1. Research structure

3.1 Linguistic Features

We designed 102 linguistic features of 4 categories: Shallow features, POS features, Syntactic features, and Discourse features. We cover the features used in Flesch index [9], Feng (2010) [10], Vajjala and Meurers (2012) [11], Todirascu (2016) [12],

Qiu et al. (2017) [13] among many others as discussed in the Related Research section and adapted them for Chinese language. Please refer to Table 2 for feature descriptions.

For pre-processing, we use NLPIR[1] for word segmentation, LTP[2] platform for POS tagging, and named entity recognition, and NiuParser[3] for syntactic parsing, grammatical labeling, and clause annotation.

Table 2. Summary of linguistic metrics

Feature category	Sub-category	Features used in metrics
Shallow features	Character	Common characters, stroke-counts
	Words	Words of different character length
	Sentence	Sentence length by word count, n-gram count, and character count
	Document	Document length by character count and symbol count
POS features		Adjective, functional words, verbs, nouns, content words, idioms, adverbs
Syntactic features	Phrases	Noun phrases, verbal phrases, prepositional phrases
	Clauses	Independent clause, punctuation clause, dependency distance, word-count by punctuation clause
	Sentences	Sentence count, parse tree height, sentence dependency distance
Discourse features	Entity density	Entities, named entities, entity nouns, named entity nouns
	Coherence	Conjunctions, pronouns

3.2 Features Graph and Translation-Based Method

In Statistical Relational Learning (SRL), the representation of an object can contain its relationships to other objects. Thus, the data is in the form of a graph, consisting of nodes (entities) and labelled edges (relationships between entities).

A feature graph is a multi-relational graph, composed of the linguistic features as nodes and three types of relations as edges: the positive, negative and irrelevant correlations. An instance of edge is a triplet of fact (*head feature*, *relation*, *tail feature*). For example, the triplet of fact (*percentage of conjunctions, positive correlation*, *average height of parse tree*), represents a relation type of positive correlation between two linguistic features as head and tail features respectively. While the triplet of fact (*average number of characters per word, negative correlation, percentage of unique functional words*) represents a negative relation with the two linguistic features as head and tail connected by relation edge. We speculate that we could infer such a multi-relational graph for the linguistic features that impact document-level readability differences.

[1] http://ictclas.nlpir.org/.

[2] http://www.ltp-cloud.com/.

[3] http://www.niuparser.com/.

The translation-based approach has been proposed to model multi-relational data, which attempts to embed a multi-relational graph into a continuous vector space while preserving certain properties of the original graph. Generally, each entity h (or t) is represented as a k-dimensional vector $\mathbf{h}$ (or $\mathbf{t}$) and relation r is characterized by the translating vector $\mathbf{r}$. For example, in **Trans E** [3], given two entity vectors $\mathbf{h}$, $\mathbf{t}$ and a translation vector $\mathbf{r}$ between them, the model requires $\mathbf{h} + \mathbf{r} \approx \mathbf{t}$ for the observed triple (h, r, t). Hence, **Trans E** assumes the score function

$$f_r(h, t) = \|\mathbf{h} + \mathbf{r} - \mathbf{t}\|_2$$

is low if (h, r, t) holds, and high otherwise. To differentiate between correct and incorrect triples, **Trans E** score difference is minimized using margin based pairwise ranking loss. Formally, we optimize the following function:

$$\sum_{x \in S^+} \sum_{y \in S^-} \max(0, f(x) - f(y) + \gamma),$$

with respect to the entity and relation vectors. The γ is a margin separating correct and incorrect triples. S+ is the set of all positive triples, i.e., observed triples in the graph. The negative set S− are randomly corrupting the correct triples, that is, for a given correct triplet (h, r, t), a negative triplet $(\mathrm{h}', \mathrm{r}, \mathrm{t}')$ is obtained by randomly sampling a pair of entities $(\mathrm{h}', \mathrm{t}')$ from S+. Then we get the set:

$$S^- = \{(h', r, t) | (h', r, t) \notin S^+\} \cup \{(h, r, t') | (h, r, t') \notin S^+\}$$

In this paper, we use **Trans E** to learn the linguistic feature embeddings on feature graphs.

3.3 Document Representation with Linguistic Embedding

With our hand-crafted linguistic features, we first design document representation model as vectors of discrete linguistic feature value. We also learn the embedding representation for each feature from their relation graph. Therefore, we project the document vectors onto the linguistic feature embedding space to obtain an enriched representation with linguistic feature embedding. Specifically, given a document vector $d = (x_{1,}x_{2,} \ldots x_n)$ where n is the number of linguistic features, x_i is the value of the ith feature for document d, and a linguistic feature embedding matrix $\mathrm{L} \in R^{n \times m}$ where m is the embedding dimension, we project the document vector d onto the linguistic feature embedding space by taking a vector-matrix multiplication to form a new representation as: $d_t = (l_1, l_2, \ldots l_m)$. where l_i is the projected value of linguistic features at dimension i.

4 Experiment

We evaluate our proposed Linguistic Feature Embedding (LFE) model from the following perspectives. **RQ1**: Whether LFE is effective for readability assessment, compared with using hand-crafted feature (HCF)? **RQ2**: Whether LFE can improve the performance of traditional readability assessment model with Bag of Word document representation? **RQ3**: Whether LFE is effective compared with other embedding-based representation model? We showcase our evaluation of LFE in the area of Chinese L1 readability assessment.

4.1 Data

We provide a corpus for L1 readability assessment using textbooks from most widely used for primary school (Grades 1 through 6), secondary school (Grade 7 and 8), and high-school (Grade 10) education from three publishers, (i.e., People's Press, Jiangsu Education Press, and Beijing Normal University Press). We excluded playwrights, poetry, and classical literature to keep the genre of the text more simplistic and monotonous (Table 3).

Table 3. Data statistics

Grade	1	2	3	4	5	6	7	8	9	10	Total
# of Docs	93	147	164	157	148	163	96	138	94	32	1232
Percentage	7.6%	12.01%	13.4%	12.83%	12.09%	13.32%	7.84%	11.27%	7.68%	2.61%	100%

4.2 Learning Linguistic Feature Embedding

We use two types of feature graphs in the paper. The first type of feature graph is obtained by learning the positive, negative and irrelevant correlations among linguistic features of 4 categories. We set the positive correlation between two linguistic features if the Pearson correlation coefficient is above 0.7, the negative correlation if the coefficient is below −0.7 and the irrelevant correlation if the coefficient is between 0.7 and −0.7. The second type of feature graph is obtained by using human annotation for 4 categories linguistic features. In our experiments, we use 25 and 102 features of L1 for constructing the above two type of feature graphs. In training Trans E, the optimal parameters are determined by the validation set. After parameter tuning, we use the learning rate α for stochastic gradient descent at 0.01, the margin γ of 1, the embedding dimension k of 300, and batch size of 50.

4.3 Models and Experiment Setting

We have a total of 102 linguistic metrics for L1. We identify the features that are correlated with readability levels at 90%, 95%, and 99% confidence interval with linear regression. The 90% confidence interval gives us 25 out of 102. Our model comparisons with 95% and 99% confidence interval metrics produces similar results. We only present experimentation with the complete set of 102 features and the 90% interval set of 25 features. We use SVM and Logistic Regression as our multi-class classifiers to build predictive models for document-level readability.

To represent documents, we use the following approaches:

25HCF and 102HCF: We use only the scores of 25 linguistic features at 90% confidence interval to construct document vector representation. For 102HCF, we use the complete set of features.

25LFE and 102LFE: This is to represent documents by projecting 25-feature vectors onto the 25 linguistic feature embedding space learned with Trans-E. For 102LFE, we use the complete set of features.

25LFE-Anno: We have one of our coauthors, a linguistics Ph.D and professor, to manually annotate the pair-wise relations among the 25 linguistic features. We then use the annotated feature graph to learn feature embedding and then infer document representation by taking a vector-matrix multiplication.

BOW: This is the default baseline representation where each document is a vector of terms weighted with *ltc* variant of TF*IDF.

W2V_Emb: We use the word embedding [14] of 300-dimension trained with Wikipedia to represent each word. We use the word vector average to represent each document.

CNNF: We trained a CNN model [15] for predicting readability with epoch of 100, batch size of 50, and learning rate of 0.1. We use the hidden layer output as features to represent document. For each document we have a 400-dimension vector representation.

For evaluating multi-class classification, we use Accuracy and Distance-1 Adjacent Accuracy. Adjacent-level Accuracy is often used in computational linguistics where predicting a text to be within one level of the true level label is still considered accurate [9]. According to our data distribution as shown in Table 4, the Majority Vote accuracies is 13.4%, and adjacent accuracy is 38.24%. With Uniform Random evaluation, we have a baseline of 10% accuracy and 30% adjacent accuracy. We perform 10-fold training-test cross-validation and paired two-tailed T-test for significance test.

4.4 Results and Analysis

To address RQ1, we compare hand-crafted feature representation and linguistic feature embedding as presented in Tables 4 and 5. We can see that compared with 25HCF, the LFE model performs significantly better with Logistic Regression (LR) in both accuracy and adjacent accuracy, and with SVM in adjacent accuracy. LFE performs similarly as 25HCF in accuracy with SVM classifier. Embedding learned with human annotation (25LFE-anno) performs significantly better than both hand-crafted model of 25HCF and 25LFE which is inferred with machine-learning. When experimenting with the complete set of 102 features, the LFE model performs significantly better HCF with both classifiers and for both accuracy and adjacent accuracy.

To address RQ2, we present results in Tables 6 and 7. Significant results are bolded. We can see that appending HCF features to the BOW vector achieves better results than BOW model alone. But, BOW+25LFE and BOW+102LFE performs even better than augmenting with HCF. Furthermore, BOW+25LFE_Anno, which is embedding learned with human annotated relation provides us with the best performance in adjacent accuracy, and best accuracy when combined with 25HCF and BOW. We observe similar performance of LFE with 102-feature experiments.

Overall, LFE model alone achieves significantly better performance for readability assessment. When combined with other HCF and BOW representation, it also contributes to the improvement in predictive performance.

Table 4. Comparing linguistic feature embedding (25LFE, 25LFE-Anno) with Hand-Crafted Feature (25HCF)

Representation model	25 HCF		25 LFE		25 LFE-Anno	
Classifiers	Accuracy	Adj. Accu.	Accuracy	Adj. Accu.	Accuracy	Adj. Accu.
SVM	0.2637	0.6106	0.2638	**0.6127**	0.2627	0.6032
LR	0.2394	0.5815	**0.3259**	**0.7003**	**0.3381**	**0.71**

Table 5. Comparing Linguistic Feature Embedding (102LFE) with Hand-Crafted Feature (102HCF)

Representation model	102 HCF		102 LFE	
Classifiers	Accuracy	Adj. Accu.	Accuracy	Adj. Accu.
SVM	0.2529	0.5398	**0.2538**	**0.6466**
LR	0.2818	0.6223	**0.3221**	**0.7063**

Table 6. Compare 25-feature LFE model with traditional models with BOW representation

Representation model	Classifiers	Accuracy	Adjacent accuracy
BOW (baseline)	SVM	0.377	0.7812
	LR	0.377	0.7546
BOW+25HCF	SVM	**0.385**	0.7764
	LR	**0.378**	**0.7569**
BOW+25LFE	SVM	**0.4055**	**0.8067**
	LR	**0.3983**	**0.7788**
BOW+25LFE_Anno	SVM	**0.409**	**0.8091**
	LR	**0.4004**	**0.7821**
BOW+25HCF+25LFE	SVM	**0.4021**	**0.8058**
	LR	**0.3998**	**0.7775**
BOW+25HCF+25LFE_Anno	SVM	**0.4104**	**0.8084**
	LR	**0.399**	**0.7774**

Figure 2 presents experiment results for RQ3, where we compare LFE with two popular word-embedding based representation with LR as the classifier. We can see that 25-LFE, 25LFE-Anno, and 102LFE all perform significantly better than other models based on CNN feature or word embedding feature.

Table 7. Compare 102-feature LFE model with traditional models with BOW representation

Representation model	BOW (baseline)		BOW + 102HCF		BOW + 102LFE		BOW + 102HCF + 102LFE	
Classifiers	SVM	LR	SVM	LR	SVM	LR	SVM	LR
Accuracy	0.377	0.377	**0.389**	**0.3817**	**0.4006**	**0.3908**	**0.3931**	**0.396**
Adjacent accuracy	0.7812	0.7546	**0.7836**	0.7501	**0.8012**	**0.7768**	**0.7917**	**0.7659**

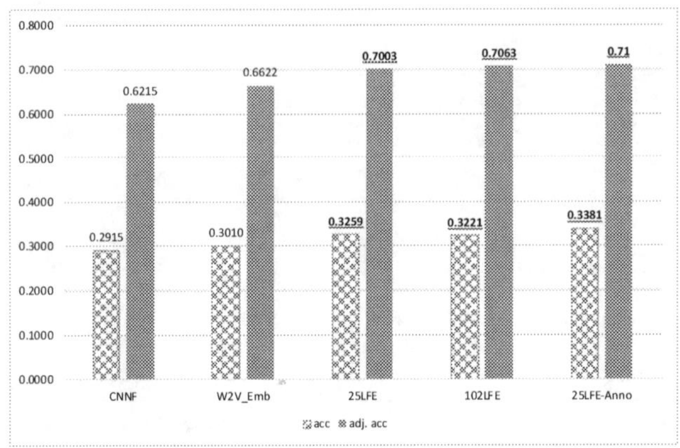

Fig. 2. Compare LFE model with other word-embedding models for readability assessment. Significant performance is bolded and underlined.

5 Conclusions

We present in this paper a model to learn distributed representation of linguistic features for readability assessment. Our assumptions include the following: (1) Distributed model could be extended to features beyond word-level differences for knowledge-enriched representation; (2) There may exist latent factors that connects linguistic features to form certain types of relationship; and (3) The similarities and inter-relations among the linguistic features and their membership to different feature categories demonstrate that the linguistic features possess the statistical properties of feature graphs of "homophily", "block structure" and "global and long-range statistical dependencies".

We propose to automatically infer the multi-relations among linguistic features and project the document representations onto the linguistic feature embedding space. We showcase the model implementation in the area of Chinese L1 readability assessment with positive results. We hope to extend the current research on extra datasets and other types of latent factor models to refine and strengthen the linguistic knowledge informed representation models.

Acknowledgements. This work was supported by National Social Science Fund (Grant No. 17BGL068). We thank Prof. Jianyun Nie and anonymous reviewers for their valuable suggestions and thoughtful feedback. We thank undergraduate students Zhiwei Wu, Yuansheng Wang, Xu Zhang, Yuan Chen, Hanwu Chen, Licong Tan, and Hao Zhang for their helpful assistance and support.

References

1. Collins-Thompson, K., Callan, J.: A language-modelling approach to predicting reading difficulty. In: Proceedings of HLT-NAACL, Boston (2004)
2. Jiang, Z., et al.: Enriching word embeddings with domain knowledge for readability assessment. In: Proceedings of COLING 2018, pp. 366–378 (2018)
3. Bordes, A., Usunier, N., Garcia-Duran, A., Weston, J., Yakhnenko, O.: Translating embeddings for modeling multi-relational data. In: Advances in Neural Information Processing Systems, pp. 2787–2795 (2013)
4. Getoor, L., Taskar, B.: Introduction to Statistical Relational Learning (Adaptive Computation and Machine Learning). The MIT Press, Cambridge (2007)
5. Pearl, J.: Probabilistic Reasoning in Intelligent Systems: Networks of Plausible Inference. Morgan Kaufmann Publishers Inc., San Francisco (1988)
6. Sung, Y.T., et al.: Leveling L2 texts through readability: combining multilevel linguistic features with the CEFR. Mod. Lang. J. **99**(2), 371–391 (2015)
7. Jiang, Z., Sun, G., Gu, Q., Chen, D.: An ordinal multi-class classification method for readability assessment of Chinese documents. In: Buchmann, R., Kifor, C.V., Yu, J. (eds.) KSEM 2014. LNCS (LNAI), vol. 8793, pp. 61–72. Springer, Cham (2014). https://doi.org/10.1007/978-3-319-12096-6_6
8. Jiang, Z., et al.: A graph-based readability assessment method using word coupling. In: Proceedings of EMNLP 2015, pp. 411–420 (2015)
9. Flesch, R.: A new readability yardstick. J. Appl. Psychol. **32**(3), 221 (1948)
10. Feng, L.: Automatic readability assessment. Ph.D Thesis. The City University of New York (2010)
11. Vajjala, S., Meurers, D.: On improving the accuracy of readability classification using insights from second language acquisition. In: Proceedings of the ACL 2012 BEA 7th Workshop, pp. 163–173 (2012)
12. Todirascu, A., et al.: Are cohesive features relevant for text readability evaluation? In: Proceedings of COLING 2016, pp. 987–997 (2016)
13. Qiu, X., Deng, K., Qiu, L., Wang, X.: Exploring the impact of linguistic features for Chinese readability assessment. In: Huang, X., Jiang, J., Zhao, D., Feng, Y., Hong, Yu. (eds.) NLPCC 2017. LNCS (LNAI), vol. 10619, pp. 771–783. Springer, Cham (2018). https://doi.org/10.1007/978-3-319-73618-1_67
14. Mikolov, T., et al.: Distributed representations of words and phrases and their compositionality. In Advances in Neural Information Processing Systems, pp. 3111–3119 (2013)
15. Kim, Y.: Convolutional neural networks for sentence classification. arXiv preprint arXiv:1408.5882 (2014)

Neural Classifier with Statistic Information of User and Product for Sentiment Analysis

Changliang Li[1(✉)], Jiayu Xie[2], and Yaoguang Xing[3]

[1] Kingsoft AI Lab, Beijing, China
lichangliang@kingsoft.com
[2] University College London, London, England
ucakjxi@ucl.ac.uk
[3] Tsinghua University, Beijing, China
xyg17@mails.tsinghua.edu.cn

Abstract. Sentiment analysis models based on neural network architecture have achieved promising results. Some works bring improvement to these neural models via taking user and product into account. However, the way of utilizing significant role user and product by now is limited to embed them into vectors on word or semantic level, and ignore statistic information carried by them such as all the marks given by one user. In this paper, we propose a novel neural classifier, which extracts and feeds statistic information carried by user and product to neural networks. Our proposed method can utilize user preference and product characteristics so as to yield excellent performance on sentiment analysis. To fully evaluate the efficiency of our model, we conduct experiment on three popular sentiment datasets: IMDB, Yelp13 and Yelp14. And the experiment results show that our model achieves state-of-the-art on all three datasets.

Keywords: Sentiment analysis · Neural classifier · Natural language processing

1 Introduction

Sentiment analysis, also called opinion mining, is the field of study that analyzes people's opinion and sentiments towards entities such as products, events and topics and so on [1]. In general, sentiment analysis has been investigated mainly at three levels: document level, sentence level and entity and aspect level [1]. Our work focuses on document level. Sentiment analysis at document level is to distinguish humans' opinion and sentiment that a document expresses.

To involve statistic information into sentiment analysis, we firstly feed the statistic representation of the user and product to two independent neural networks with same architecture. Meanwhile, we use Long Short-Term Memory network to generate semantic representation of document of pure text. And then we

J. Tang et al. (Eds.): NLPCC 2019, LNAI 11839, pp. 370–380, 2019.
https://doi.org/10.1007/978-3-030-32236-6_33

merge the representation of statistic and text information in vector space and predict the sentiment label depend on it. The experiment results show that our model achieves state-of-the-art on all three datasets.

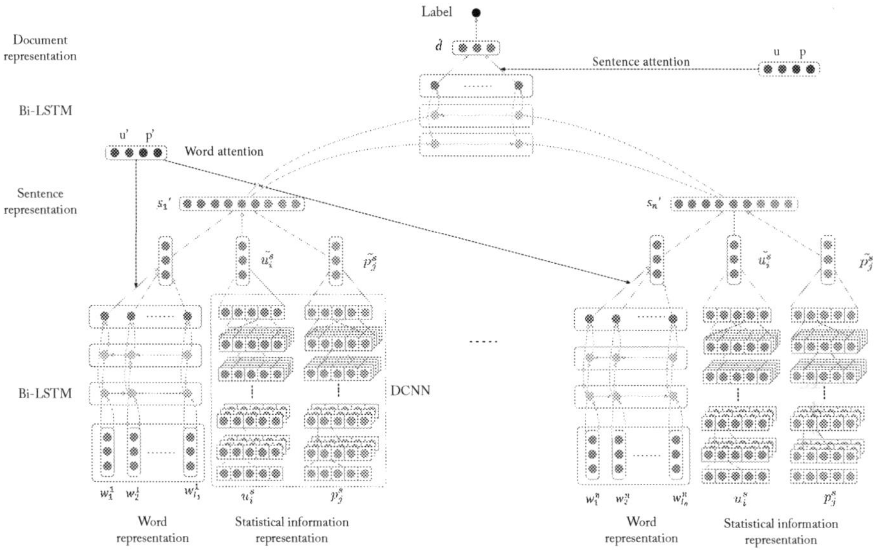

Fig. 1. Neural Classifier with Statistic Information

2 Related Work

In recent years, models based on CNN for sentiment classification have achieved great success [2]. [2] utilized CNN to classify sentence class with word level embedding, which constructs words with their embedding as a matrix and applied with convolution and max pooling. Recurrent neural network is another main approach for sentiment classification because it can capture the sequential information. [3,4] involve global user and product information into Long Short-term Memory network. Besides, a series of recursive neural network models such as Recursive Neural Tensor Network (RNTN) [6] were proposed for sentiment analysis and gave good performance. Moreover, attention has become an effective mechanism to obtain superior results [7].

Despite the progress of those methods have achieved, it is still a challenging and open task for sentiment analysis. Therefore, we are motivated to design a powerful model, which can fully employ statistic information for sentiment classification.

3 Neural Classifier with Statistic Information

In this section, we give the description of our neural classifier with statistic information in detail. Figure 1 gives the overall architecture of our model. We employ deep convolutional neural networks (DCNN) for representing statistic information of user and product, and bidirectional long short-term memory (Bi-LSTM) network for pure text. Attention on word and sentence level is involved to compute sentence and document representation in vector space. Document representation in vector space is used as features for sentiment classification.

3.1 Statistic Information of User and Product

In our work, we build a user-product score matrix $M_{UP} \in \mathbb{R}^{n_u \times n_p}$, where n_u represents the number of users and n_p represents the number of products. The element m_{ij} in matrix represents the score of the j-th product marked by the i-th user. If the i-th user did not rate the j-th product, we set $m_{ij} = -1$. Because each user rates only a small amount of product in the corpus, the user-product score matrix M_{UP} is very sparse given big data.

To address this problem, we extract the principle component features of M_{UP} via principal component analysis (PCA) algorithm. We obtain a new matrix $M_U \in \mathbb{R}^{n_u \times d_p}$ via applying PCA over user rows, where d_p means the reduced dimension. Each row of this matrix u_r^s represents the statistic information of the r-th user.

In the similar way, we obtain another matrix $M_P \in \mathbb{R}^{n_p \times d_u}$ via applying PCA over the product rows of M_{UP}^T where T means transpose, and d_u means the reduced dimension. Each row of this matrix p_r^s represents the statistic information of the r-th product.

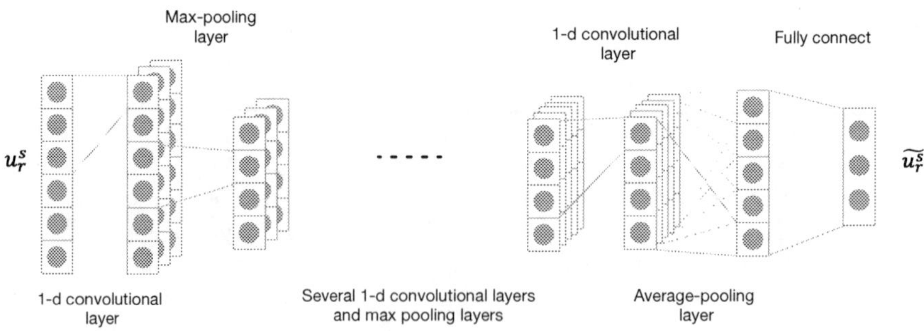

Fig. 2. DCNN architecture for statistic information

3.2 Hidden Representation for Statistic Information

Based on representations u_r^s and p_r^s, we utilize DCNN architecture to capture hidden representation $\widetilde{u_r^s}$ and $\widetilde{p_r^s}$ of statistic information respectively. The details are given as follow.

Because the user and product shares the same computation process, we take user as illustration in this section. Figure 2 shows the DCNN architecture employed to extract statistic information of user.

The DCNN architecture consists of multiple 1-dimensional convolutional layers, max-pooling layers and a global average-pooling layer.

Given an input vector u_r^s, there is a discrete input function $g(x, u_r^s) : \{1, 2, ..., l\} \rightarrow \mathbb{R}$, which extracts the x-th value of the vector u_r^s, and a discrete kernel function $f(x) : \{1, 2, ..., k\} \rightarrow \mathbb{R}$, where l represents the vector length of statistic vector u_r^s, and k represents the kernel size. The employed 1-dimensional convolution operation $h(t, u_r^s)$ with stride d_c and kernel function $f(x)$ is defined as the following equation:

$$h(t, u_r^s) = b + \sum_{a=1}^{k} f(a) \cdot g(t \cdot d_c + a, u_r^s) \tag{1}$$

Where a and $t \cdot d_c + a$ are the indices of the kernel and input respectively, b is a bias term and $d_c = 1$. The feature map u_r^c obtained by activation function ReLU [8] and above convolution operation is defined as:

$$u_r^c = [ReLU(h(1, u_r^s)), ..., ReLU(h(l - k + 1, u_r^s))] \tag{2}$$

Afterwards, we utilize max-pooling layer to extract features. The max-pooling operation $m(t, u_r^c)$ with stride d_m is defined as:

$$m(t, u_r^c) = \max_{a=1}^{k} g(t \cdot d_m + a, u_r^c) \tag{3}$$

Then we obtain the output vector of this layer as follow:

$$u_r^m = [m(0, u_r^c), m(1, u_r^c), ..., m(l_m, u_r^c)] \tag{4}$$

Where $l_m = \left\lfloor \frac{(l-k+1)-k}{d_m} \right\rfloor$. Then the output of max-pooling layer u_r^m is followed by another 1-dimensional convolutional layer and max-pooling layer. The rest processes are made in the same manner until the last layer. The last convolutional layer is followed by a global average-pooling layer rather than max-pooling layer. The global average pooling avg with the output $\hat{u_r^c}$ of the last convolutional layer is defined as:

$$\overline{u_r^c} = avg(\hat{u_r^c}) = \frac{\sum_{a=1}^{L} g(a, \hat{u_r^c})}{L} \tag{5}$$

Where L is the length of vector $\hat{u_r^c}$. In our description above, one feature $\overline{u_r^c}$ is obtained by one kernel. And the DCNN uses multiple kernels, so we obtain multiple features which are concatenated together to obtain vector v. The vector v is followed by a fully connected layer:

$$\widetilde{u_r^s} = tanh(W \cdot v + b) \tag{6}$$

We regard the output of the fully connected layer $\widetilde{u_r^s}$ as the representation of the user statistic information. Similarly, the representation of product statistic information $\widetilde{p_r^s}$ is obtained in the same way.

3.3 Representation for Pure Text

Given a sentence of pure text, which consists of a sequence of words $\{w_1^i, w_2^i, ..., w_{l_i}^i\}$, we firstly represent all words using their corresponding embeddings $\{e_1^i, e_2^i, ..., e_{l_i}^i\}$, where e_j^i means word embeddings of the j-th word. We then employ Bi-LSTM network to obtain sentence representation in vector space.

Firstly, we compute the forward output $\overrightarrow{h_t^i}$ and backward output $\overleftarrow{h_t^i}$ by the following equations.

$$\overrightarrow{h_t^i} = \mathcal{H}(e_j^i, \overrightarrow{h_{t-1}^i}),\ \overleftarrow{h_t^i} = \mathcal{H}(e_j^i, \overleftarrow{h_{t-1}^i}) \tag{7}$$

Where $\mathcal{H}$ denotes the recurrent unit of Bi-LSTM ; $\overrightarrow{h_{t-1}^i}$ means previous hidden state;

As a result, we can obtain the final h_t^i as follow:

$$h_t^i = \overrightarrow{h_t^i} + \overleftarrow{h_t^i} \tag{8}$$

Moreover, in sentiment analysis task, every word from different users and products contributes differently. So we use attention mechanism to capture this information. Since we have a series of hidden state sequence $\{h_1^i, h_2^i, ..., h_n^i\}$ for a sentence, then we compute its hidden state s_i by the following equation:

$$s_i = \sum_{j=1}^{l_i} \alpha_j^i h_j^i \tag{9}$$

α_j^i means word level attention weight and is obtained by:

$$\alpha_j^i = \frac{\exp(\tau(h_j^i, \mathrm{u}, \mathrm{p}))}{\sum_{k=1}^{l_i} \exp(\tau(h_k^i, \mathrm{u}, \mathrm{p}))} \tag{10}$$

We embed each user and each product into vectors u and p. where τ is a function to calculate the importance of the word. τ is defined as:

$$\tau(h_k^i, \mathrm{u}, \mathrm{p}) = v^{\mathrm{T}} \tanh\left(W_H h_k^i + W_U \mathrm{u} + W_P \mathrm{p} + b\right) \tag{11}$$

Where v^{T}, b, W_H, W_U and W_P are parameters which need to be trained.

3.4 Document Representation

Since we have obtained the i-th sentence representation s_i based on pure text, we concatenate s_i with the corresponding user statistic vector $\widetilde{u_r^s}$ and product statistic vector $\widetilde{p_r^s}$ as the full representation for i-th sentence:

$$s_i' = [s_i, \widetilde{u_r^s}, \widetilde{p_r^s}] \tag{12}$$

As the similar computation process on word level, all sentences of a document $\{s_1', s_2', ..., s_n'\}$ are fed to hierarchical Bi-LSTM network with attention mechanism on sentence level to obtain document representation $\hat{d}$.

$$\hat{d} = \sum_{i=1}^{n} \beta_i s_i' \tag{13}$$

Where β_i means sentence level attention weight. Sentence level attention shares the same mechanism with word level attention but with different parameters.

3.5 Sentiment Classification

Since $\hat{d}$ is a high level representation of the document semantic representation. Hence, we regard it as features for sentiment classification. We use a non-linear layer to project document semantic representation $\hat{d}$ into the target space of C classes:

$$h_k = \tanh(W_c\hat{d} + b_c) \tag{14}$$

Softmax function is followed to obtain the sentiment distribution:

$$p_c = \frac{\exp(h_c)}{\sum_{k=1}^{C} \exp(h_k)} \tag{15}$$

Where C is the number of sentiment classes; p_c is the predicted probability of sentiment class c. In our model, cross-entropy error between gold sentiment distribution and predicted sentiment distribution is defined as loss function for optimization while training:

$$cost = -\sum_{d \in D} \sum_{c=1}^{C} t_c(d) \log(p_c(d)) \tag{16}$$

Where $t_c(d)$ is the gold probability of sentiment class c with ground truth being 1 and others being 0 and D is the training documents set.

4 Experiment

4.1 Dataset

We evaluate the validity of our model with three popular movie review datasets: IMDB, yelp13 and yelp14, which have been widely used for sentiment analysis research. The sentiment label of IMDB dataset ranges from 1 to10. The sentiment labels of Yelp 2014 and Yelp 2013 datasets range from 1 to 5. The higher label value is, the more positive it represents. Yelp datasets are collected form Yelp site, which is the largest review websites in America including larger number of movie reviews. IMDB dataset is collected from Internet Movie Database, which is the world's most popular and authoritative source for movie including rich reviews.

The statistical information of the three datasets is shown in Table 1.

Table 1. Statistical information of the three datasets

Dataset	#classes	#users	#products	#reviews	#docs/ user	#docs/ product	#sents/ doc	#words/ sen	#words/ doc
IMDB	10	1,310	1,635	84,919	64.82	51.94	16.08	24.54	394.6
Yelp 2014	5	4,818	4,194	231,163	47.97	55.11	11.41	17.26	196.9
Yelp 2013	5	1,631	1,633	78,966	48.42	48.36	10.89	17.38	189.3

We use the dataset setting as the same with [1] which split training, validation and test sets in the proportion of 8:1:1 (80% for training, 10% for test, 10% for validation). Validation set is used to find the optimal parameters for model.

4.2 Metrics

We employ standard accuracy rate to measure the overall sentiment classification performance. And we also employ Root-Mean-Square Error (RMSE) to measure the divergences between predicted sentiment label and ground truth label. The higher accuracy and the smaller RMSE is, the better performance is.

4.3 Baselines

In order to fully assess the efficiency of our model, we compare with the following methods, which are widely used as baselines in other sentiment analysis works [5,9,10].

- Majority Method [7].
  Refer to the [7], the widely used in the method of sentiment classification.
- Supported Vector Machine (SVM) classifiers
  This class of methods employs different features to train a SVM classifier.
- UPNN [3]
  Embeds user and product into high dimensions vectors and utilizing CNN to predict the sentiment label.

- RNTN+RNN [6]
  This model takes phrases of any length as input, using RNN to obtain document representation for sentiment classification
- NSC [4]
  NSC is a hierarchical LSTM model for classify sentiment level of a document.
- NSC+UPA [4]
  NSC+UPA gives excellent performance on document level sentiment classification task.

4.4 Experiment Result

Table 2 gives the experiment results of all the models. Acc.(Accuracy) and RMSE are the evaluation metrics mentioned above. The best performances are in bold.

Table 2. Experiment results of all the models

Models	IMDB		Yelp2013		Yelp2014	
	Acc.	RMSE	Acc.	RMSE	Acc.	RMSE
Majority	0.196	2.495	0.411	1.060	0.392	1.097
RNTN+RNN	0.400	1.764	0.582	0.821	0.574	0.804
SVM-ngram	0.399	1.783	0.569	0.814	0.577	0.804
SVM-TextFeature	0.402	1.793	0.556	0.845	0.572	0.800
SVM-AvgWordvec	0.304	1.985	0.526	0.898	0.530	0.893
SVM-SSWE	0.312	1.973	0.549	0.849	0.557	0.851
UPNN (CNN and no UP)	0.405	1.629	0.577	0.812	0.585	0.808
UPNN (Full)	0.435	1.602	0.596	0.784	0.608	0.764
NSC	0.443	1.465	0.627	0.701	0.637	0.686
NSC+LA	0.487	1.381	0.631	0.706	0.630	0.715
NSC+UPA	0.533	1.281	0.650	0.692	0.667	0.654
NCSI	**0.553**	**1.174**	**0.661**	**0.672**	**0.670**	**0.643**

Table 3. Effect of Statistical Information

Models	IMDB		Yelp2013		Yelp2014	
	Acc.	RMSE	Acc.	RMSE	Acc.	RMSE
W/O up_sta	0.512	1.299	0.632	0.713	0.656	0.666
W/O pro_sta	0.541	1.291	0.657	0.668	0.665	0.657
W/O user_sta	0.520	1.230	0.637	0.687	0.670	0.647
Full model	**0.553**	**1.174**	**0.661**	**0.672**	**0.670**	**0.643**

From Table 2, we can see that our model outperforms all other methods on all datasets in term of both metrics.

It is easy to understand that Majority has a poor performance because it only uses rough statistics and ignores any semantic information.

We can see that the performance of SVM based methods is not good as methods based on neural networks. RNTN+RNN is effective in modelling document representation with semantic composition. It achieves comparable performance with the best result of SVM series. UPNN uses convolution neural network to capture text information and performs slightly better than SVM series and RNTN+RNN. UPNN(full) takes user and product information and improves the performance of UPNN.

NSC model gets excellent performance because it captures the sequence text information via using LSTM architecture, which is good at remembering information for long periods. NSC+LA brings improvement via introducing local attention mechanism. NSC+UPA introduces user and product information to NSC via attention mechanism and significantly boosts the performance.

The results of UPNN series and NSC series have proven that the use of user and product information can improve the performance.

In term of accuracy rate, we can see that our model outperforms previous best model NSC+UPA 2%, 1.1% and 0.3% on three datasets respectively.

In term of RMSE, our model outperforms previous best model NSC+UPA 0.107, 0.02 and 0.011 over three datasets respectively.

The improvement can be interpreted that user and product information is employed as their words' embeddings in other works. But our approach is more focused on using their statistic information. As a result, our model is effective to capture more information including both semantic and statistic, which is crucial for sentiment classification.

In sum, we can make a safe conclusion that our model improves robustness and performance of neural classifier on sentiment analysis task via taking user and product statistic information into account.

4.5 Ablation Study: Effect of Statistic Information

The ablation study is performed to evaluate whether and how each component of our model contributes to our full model.

We ablate two important components and conduct different approaches in this experiment.

W/O user_sta, refers to no user statistic information is employed.

W/O pro_sta, refers to no product statistic information is employed.

W/O up_sta, refers to neither of user and product statistic information is employed.

Table 3 gives the results that explain the effect brought by statistic information proposed in our work.

From Table 3, we can see that statistic information employed brings improvement on sentiment classification. Each statistic information can improve the result with different degrees in terms of two metrics. Model without using any statistic information performs worst.

Between two components, user statistic information brings a little bigger improvement. This is probably due to the fact that the sentiment is expressed by the user who directly determines the final sentiment. Product is objective entity while user's review is subjective analysis. So the user information may play more important role. Using both statistic information (full model) achieves the best performance.

5 Conclusion

In this work, we propose a novel neural classifier with statistic information for sentiment analysis on document level. Our model extracts and feeds statistic information carried by user and product to neural networks. It can utilize user preference and product characteristics and yield better semantic representation. Experiment results on three popular datasets have shown that our model achieves state-of-the-art. This paper gives a new way for sentiment analysis. Our future work will explore more statistic information which can be used to boost the performance on sentiment analysis. And another interesting future work is to extend this model to aspect level sentiment analysis.

References

1. Tagging, Domain-Sensitive Temporal.: Synthesis Lectures on Human Language Technologies
2. Kim, Y.: Convolutional neural networks for sentence classification. arXiv preprint arXiv:1408.5882 (2014)
3. Tang, D., Qin, B., Liu, T.: Learning semantic representations of users and products for document level sentiment classification. In: Proceedings of the 53rd Annual Meeting of the Association for Computational Linguistics and the 7th International Joint Conference on Natural Language Processing (Volume 1: Long Papers), vol. 1 (2015)
4. Chen, H., et al.: Neural sentiment classification with user and product attention. In: Proceedings of the 2016 Conference on Empirical Methods in Natural Language Processing (2016)
5. Li, C., Xu, B., Wu, G., He, S., Tian, G., Zhou, Y.: Parallel recursive deep model for sentiment analysis. In: Cao, T., Lim, E.-P., Zhou, Z.-H., Ho, T.-B., Cheung, D., Motoda, H. (eds.) PAKDD 2015. LNCS (LNAI), vol. 9078, pp. 15–26. Springer, Cham (2015). https://doi.org/10.1007/978-3-319-18032-8_2
6. Socher, R., et al.: Recursive deep models for semantic compositionality over a sentiment treebank. In: Proceedings of the 2013 Conference on Empirical Methods in Natural Language Processing (2013)

7. Tang, D., Qin, B., Liu, T.: Aspect level sentiment classification with deep memory network. arXiv preprint arXiv:1605.08900 (2016)
8. Maas, A.L., Hannun, A.Y., Ng, A.Y.: Rectifier nonlinearities improve neural network acoustic models. In: Proceedings of icml, vol. 30, no. 1 (2013)
9. Tang, D., et al.: Target-dependent sentiment classification with long short term memory. CoRR, abs/1512.01100 (2015)
10. Wang, Y., Huang, M., Zhao, L.: Attention-based LSTM for aspect-level sentiment classification. In: Proceedings of the 2016 Conference on Empirical Methods in Natural Language Processing (2016)

A New Algorithm for Component Decomposition and Type Recognition of Tibetan Syllable

Jie Zhu[1,2(✉)], Shugen Wang[3,4], Yanru Wu[1,2], Meijing Guan[1,2], and Yang Feng[3,4]

[1] Department of Computer Science, Tibetan University, Lhasa, China
rocky_tibet@qq.com, 1106539970@qq.com, zimogmj@qq.com
[2] National-Local Joint Engineering Research Center for Tibetan Information Technology, Lhasa, China
[3] Key Laboratory of Intelligent Information Processing, Institute of Computing Technology, Chinese Academy of Sciences (ICT/CAS), Beijing, China
{wangshugen,fengyang}@ict.ac.cn
[4] University of Chinese Academy of Sciences, Beijing, China

Abstract. In this paper, aiming at the problems including but not limited to Tibetan sorting, Tibetan syllable component attribute statistics, Tibetan speech recognition in the application field of component recognition of Tibetan syllable, we propose a new algorithm for component decomposition and type recognition of Tibetan syllable based on TSRM (Tibetan Syllable Rule Model). Experimental results on mixed-arranged complex Tibetan texts show that our newly proposed algorithm can achieve a score around 90% both accuracy rate and recall rate for Component Decomposition and Type Recognition of Tibetan Syllable.

Keywords: Tibetan syllable · Component decomposition · Type recognition

1 Introduction

Tibetan Information Processing (TIP) has yielded heartening fruits in both character and word level with endeavor of experts in the past three or four decades. International and National Standard for Tibetan Coding for Information Exchange, National Standard for keyboard layout and font style of Tibetan encoding character set have been promulgated successively one after another. In 2018, National Standards for Information Processing of Tibetan Word Segmentation and Character Sorting have been promulgated. The publication of

Supported by National Science Foundation of China (No. 61751216), Key Projects of National Key Research and Develop Plan (No. 2017YFB140220), National Team and Key Laboratory Construction Project for Computer and Tibetan Information (TEF[2018[81).

J. Tang et al. (Eds.): NLPCC 2019, LNAI 11839, pp. 381–392, 2019.
https://doi.org/10.1007/978-3-030-32236-6_34

these standards indicates that certain research areas of TIP have achieved recognized results and are extending to the application field gradually. Although great achievement has been made in TIP in character and word processing aspect, appropriate algorithms and models for different application scenarios and fields still need to be designed and developed to carry out meticulous research, e.g., the granularity of Tibetan word segmentation in the search engine field can be different from speech synthesis, Tibetan syllables should be separated while attributes and categories of each character should be recognized in fields of sorting and spelling, and so on.

The reason why it is important to research in component decomposition and type recognition of Tibetan Syllable is listed as below:

Firstly, as sorting is one of the basic problems that computer must deal with, which widely exists in spreadsheets and database table of computers, the analogous problem, i.e. sorting of Tibetan character, without doubt, plays an important role in TIP. The sorting of Tibetan syllable is the core in sorting of Tibetan characters, in which the identification of the category of each component is of vital importance, after which, Tibetan strings are sorted according to the sorting rules.

Secondly, Tibetan syllables are spelled automatically in the order of Prefix Character (PC), Super Character (SC), Base Character (BC), Under Character (UC), Vowel (V), First Postfix (FP) and Second Postfix (SP) after the category of each component identified.

Finally, statistics in various attributes need to be gathered on large scale amount of Tibetan texts, e.g., word frequency, syllable frequency, attribute of components in syllables, and so on. In particular, the statistics of attribute and the entropy calculation in Tibetan syllables are fundamental and have reference value for Tibetan coding and design of keyboard layout.

This paper mainly studies the algorithm for component decomposition and type recognition of Tibetan syllable. In this paper, we propose a new algorithm improving the efficiency and execution speed of the algorithm for component decomposition and type recognition of Tibetan syllable with Tibetan Syllable Rule Model (TSRM). The rest of the paper is organized as follows.

In the second part, we introduce the research basis of this topic. In the third part, we study and design the algorithm for component decomposition and type recognition of Tibetan syllable. In the fourth part, we carry out relevant experiments on the new algorithm proposed. The fifth part is the conclusion and prospect of this paper.

2 Related Work

The research on algorithm for component decomposition and type recognition of Tibetan syllable arises with the sorting of Tibetan in computer. As early as the 1990s, Zhaxi Ciren [1] studied the algorithm for sorting of Tibetan syllable and proposed decomposition and sorting of Tibetan syllable according to Unicode Tibetan characters. Jiang Di et al. [2] proposed the concepts of structural order and character order, and discussed the structure of Tibetan syllable in detail. Huang Heming et al. [3] discussed the method of Tibetan sorting based on DUCET, the basic idea is that other six position of Tibetan syllables except the BC are replaced with spaces if there are no Tibetan characters in them.

Based on a definition of Tibetan component priority, Bianba Wangdui et al. [4] proposed a sorting algorithm for cotemporary Tibetan syllable by Cartesian product. Zhu Jie et al. [5] studied the sorting algorithm of Tibetan and proposed the algorithm of location for BC based on GB for Tibetan Coded. In these articles, Tibetan syllable are all sorted by splitting the syllable and getting BC from the string coding sequence by Tibetan grammar rules, and then determining each component of them gradually.

People found that the key of the sorting algorithm for Tibetan is component recognition of Tibetan syllable during research on sorting algorithm. Bianba Wangdui et al. [6] studied and proposed an algorithm for components recognition of Tibetan syllable to recognize BC with Tibetan grammar rules, the number of syllable and position of component according to Tibetan structure, writing rules and grammatical rules. In general, this algorithm of recognition is a step-by-step process from left to right. Cai Hua [7] studied component recognition automatically of Tibetan syllable and proposed 7 types of structures, while each structure was divided into several different sub-categories and then components of Tibetan syllables were determined according to structures of sub-categories. Renqing Zhuome et al. [8] studied the structure of Tibetan syllables and put forward 7 types of structures, while each structure was divided into different sub-categories and 5-tuple structure were divided into 11 sub-categories.

Another method for component recognition of Tibetan syllables was proposed by Huang Heming et al. [9]. According to the feature of Tibetan encoding, the concepts of placeholder and non-placeholder were proposed, then Tibetan syllables were divided into syllables of placeholder and non-placeholder. For the case of syllables of placeholder, every component of the syllable was judged by the restrictions of the PC, but leave over misjudgment of syllable components like གངས་ , and others alike. For the case of syllables of non-placeholder, every component of the syllable was judged by the combination rule between SC and BC, appending with UC and BC, and rule between PC and Superposition Character (SPC), and positions among non-placeholder codes, and so on.

In the literature mentioned above, the general method of component recognition of Tibetan syllable is by judgment of the syllable structure from left to right as writing order with the number of character elements. With category structure obtained of component of Tibetan syllable, the sub-category structure of it was judged according to rules of Tibetan grammar, especially rules of syllable composition. The category of component of each character is determined with order of positions of elements in the sub-category structure in the end. The feature of this kind of method is that not only the judgment of number of elements is contained, but also the judgment of structures of both category and sub-category are contained. As every coin has two sides, with various judgments of grammatical rules, complex structures of both branch and cycle structure lead to a high time complexity.

In this paper, we propose a novel algorithm for component decomposition and type recognition of Tibetan syllable with TSRM [10] from another aspect. For each Tibetan syllable, without Sanskrit translated Tibetan, it can be divided into three parts of prefix, vowel and suffix. Then, PC, SC, BC and UC can be recognized from the part of prefix, while FP and SP can be recognized from the part of suffix. The characteristic of the algorithm is, with complex grammatical judgment process placed in TSRM, only category recognition of the part of prefix need to be considered in component recognition, so the time complexity can be reduced greatly.

3 Algorithm for Component Recognition of Tibetan Syllable

3.1 Problem Analysis

A complete modern Tibetan syllable consists of 7 parts, as shown in Fig. 1. Among them, 1 represents PC, 2 represents SC, 3 represents BC, 4 represents UC, 5 represents V, 6 represents FP, 7 represents SP. In practice, except BC in position 3, other 6 positions can be empty. Therefore, a Tibetan syllable is composed of at least 1 character and at most 7 characters. Tibetan syllable is a sequence of Tibetan character codes stored in computer, as shown in Table 1. A Tibetan syllable is composed of at least 1 code and at most 7 codes while the coding position of BC is uncertain in such sequence and can appear in the first, second or third position. The complexity of component recognition increases greatly due to the uncertainty of BC's position, which directly affects the other codes' position in a coding sequence. In the previous literature, BC is determined firstly in component recognition of Tibetan syllable, according to the constitute rule of Tibetan syllable and the grammar theory of Tibetan. Therefore, the category of each component can be recognized with the aid of structural types and grammatical rules, but the time complexity of this cluster of algorithms is very high due to the algorithm complexity. In this paper, a Tibetan syllable is divided into three parts of prefix, vowel and suffix with TSRM, and then PC, SC, BC and UC are recognized from the part of prefix while FP and SP are

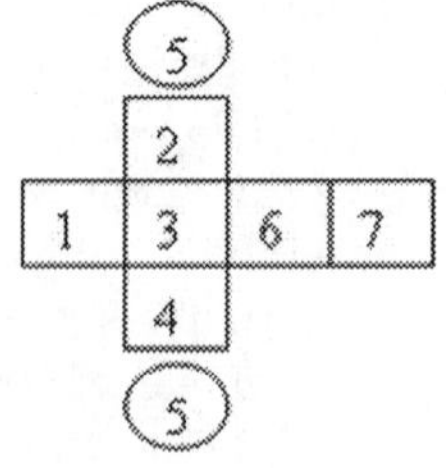

Fig. 1. Tibetan syllable.

Table 1. Relationships among Tibetan syllables, the position of base character and its coding.

Syllable	Coding	BC/NUM	Syllable	Coding	BC/NUM
ག	0F42	1/1	བརྒྱ	0F56 0F62 0F92 0FB1	3/4
གད	0F42 0F51	1/2	གྱུར	0F42 0FB1 0F74 0F62	2/4
སྒ	0F66 0F92	2/2	གྱུརད	0F42 0FB1 0F74 0F62 0F51	2/5
གངས	0F42 0F44 0F66	1/3	རྒྱུག	0F62 0F92 0FB1 0F74 0F42	2/5
འགོ	0F60 0F42 0F7C	2/3	བརྒྱལ	0F56 0F62 0F92 0FB1 0F63	3/5
བརྒ	0F56 0F62 0F92	3/3	རྒྱུགས	0F62 0F92 0FB1 0F74 0F42 0F66	2/6
རྒན	0F62 0F92 0F53	2/3	བསྒྲགས	0F56 0F66 0F92 0FB2 0F42 0F66	3/6
འགངས	0F60 0F42 0F44 0F66	2/4	བསྒྲིགས	0F56 0F66 0F92 0FB2 0F72 0F42 0F66	3/7

recognized from the part of suffix. Finally, the category of each component is determined after the component decomposition of Tibetan syllable.

3.2 Algorithm for Syllable Decomposition of Tibetan Syllable

According to TSRM, the set of pre-combination charter of Tibetan syllable is established with Tibetan grammar. The set will consist of three parts of prefix set Trule, vowel set Tvowel, and suffix set Tpostfix. The content of Trule, Tvowel and Tpostfix are shown as below:

Trule={ཀ , ཁ , ག , ང , ཅ , ཆ , ཇ , ཉ , ཏ , ཐ , ད , ན ,
པ , ཕ , བ , མ , ཙ , ཚ , ཛ , ཝ , ཞ , ཟ , འ , ཡ , ར , ལ , ཤ ,
ས , ཧ , ཨ , རྐ , རྒ , རྔ , རྗ , རྙ , རྟ , རྡ , རྣ , རྦ , རྨ , རྩ , རྫ ,
ལྐ , ལྒ , ལྔ , ལྕ , ལྗ , ལྟ , ལྡ , ལྤ , ལྦ , ལྷ , སྐ , སྒ , སྔ , སྙ , སྟ ,
སྡ , སྣ , སྤ , སྦ , སྨ , སྩ , ཀྱ , ཁྱ , གྱ , པྱ , ཕྱ , བྱ , མྱ , ཀྲ , ཁྲ ,
གྲ , ཏྲ , ཐྲ , དྲ , ནྲ , པྲ , ཕྲ , བྲ , མྲ , ཤྲ , སྲ , ཧྲ , ཀླ , གླ , བླ ,
རླ , ཟླ , སླ , ཀྭ , ཁྭ , གྭ , ཉྭ , དྭ , ཚྭ , ཞྭ , ཟྭ , རྭ , ལྭ , ཤྭ , ཧྭ ,
གྲྭ , ཕྱྭ , རྩྭ , གཅ , གཉ , གཏ , གད , གན , གཙ , གཞ , གཟ , གཡ , གཤ , གས , དཀ ,
དཀྱ , དཀྲ , དག , དགྲ , དགྱ , དང , དཔ , དཔྱ , དཔྲ , དབ , དབྱ , དབྲ , དམ , དམྱ , བཀ ,
བཀྱ , བཀྲ , བཀླ , བརྐ , བསྐ , བརྐྱ , བསྐྱ , བསྐྲ , བག , བགྱ , བགྲ , བརྒ , བསྒ , བརྒྱ , བསྒྱ ,
བསྒྲ , བརྔ , བསྔ , བཅ , བརྗ , བརྙ , བསྙ , བཏ , བརྟ , བལྟ , བསྟ , བད , བརྡ , བལྡ , བསྡ ,
བརྣ , བསྣ , བཙ , བརྩ , བསྩ , བརྫ , བཞ , བཟ , བཟླ , བརླ , བཤ , བས , བསྲ , བསླ , འག ,
འགྱ , འགྲ , འཁ , འཁྱ , འཁྲ , འཆ , འཇ , འཐ , འད , འདྲ , འཕ , འཕྱ , འཕྲ , འབ , འབྱ ,
འབྲ , འཚ , འཛ , མཁ , མཁྱ , མཁྲ , མག , མགྱ , མགྲ , མང , མཆ , མཇ , མཉ , མཐ , མད ,
མན , མཚ , མཛ , རྐྱ , སྐྱ , སྐྲ , རྒྱ , སྒྱ , སྒྲ , རྨྱ , སྤྱ , སྤྲ , སྦྱ , སྦྲ , སྨྱ , སྨྲ }

Tvowel= {ϕ, ◌ི , ◌ེ , ◌ོ , ◌ུ } where ϕ denotes an implied vowel character.

Tpostfix={ϕ,ག ,ང , ད ,ན , བ ,མ , འ ,ར , ལ ,ས , གས ,ངས , བས ,མས , ནད ,རད , ལད },

where ϕ denotes space without FP or SP.

As per TRSM, our algorithm splits a Tibetan syllable into three parts: prefix, vowel and suffix. The algorithm for syllable decomposition of Tibetan syllable is shown in Algorithm 1.

Algorithm 1. Algorithm for syllable decomposition of Tibetan syllable.

```
Input:
    Tibetan syllable;
Output:
    prefix, vowel and suffix;
Creating object fr to read Tibetan syllables;
Creating variables of output string: Tv, Tr, Tp;
Creating string: syllable;
syllable=fr.read();
while syllable ≠ null do
    if Tv ∈ syllable in Tvowel then
        Tv ⇐ the vowel;
        Tr ⇐ the string before the vowel;
        Tp ⇐ the string after the vowel;
    else
        Tr ⇐ syllable;
        if Tr is not in Trule then
            Tp ⇐ the last character of syllable;
            Tr ⇐ the surplus string of syllable;
        end if
        if Tr is not in Trule then
            Tp ⇐ the last two characters of syllable;
            Tr ⇐ the surplus string of syllable;
        end if
    end if
end while
```

3.3 Algorithm for Component Recognition of Tibetan Syllable

The algorithm for component recognition of Tibetan syllable can be carried out into three steps of component recognition of prefix, vowel and suffix. The second step and the third step are simple while the first step as component recognition of prefix is difficult. The part of prefix in TARM consists of at least 1 character and at most 4 characters. The relationship between the number of syllable prefix and the position of BC is shown in Table 2. The prefix is recognized and divided into four different categories by number of characters in the first step of component recognition of prefix while the component recognition of prefix with character number of 1 and 4 is simple and the algorithm focuses on prefix with character number of 2 and 3.

As can be seen from Table 2, the syllable prefix can be judged as BC directly when there is only 1 character in it, while the syllable prefix can be judged as

Table 2. The relationship between the number of syllable prefix and the position of BC.

BC	BC in prefix/NUM	BC	BC in prefix/NUM
ག	1/1	བསྒ	3/3
གཙ	2/2	གྲྭ	1/3
སྒ	2/2	དགྱ	2/3
གྱ	1/2	སྒྲ	2/3
གྲ	1/2	བསྒྱ	3/4

the PC, SC, BC and UC when there are 4 characters.

It is difficult to judge the position of BC for it can be in the positions of 1 and 2 of the encoding sequence when the character number of prefix is 2, while it can be in the positions of 1, 2 and 3 of the encoding sequence when the character number of prefix is 3.

For the case of prefix with character number of 2, the first character should be judged whether in set {ར་མགོ, ལ་མགོ, ས་མགོ}, if the first character is in this set, then the first character is determined as SC and the second character is determined as BC. Next, the second character should be judged whether in set UC {◌ྱ, ◌ྲ, ◌ླ, ◌ྭ}, if the second character is in set UC, then the first character is determined as BC and the second character is determined as UC. However, the second character is not in set UC, then the first character is determined as PC and the second character is determined as BC.

For the case of prefix with character number of 3, the third character should be judged whether in set UC {◌ྱ, ◌ྲ, ◌ླ, ◌ྭ}, if the third character is in set UC, then the second character should be judged whether in set UC {◌ྱ, ◌ྲ, ◌ླ, ◌ྭ} as well, if the second character is also in set UC, then the first character is determined as BC and the second and third characters are determined as UC. However, if the second character is not in the set UC, then the first character should be judged whether in set SC {ར་མགོ, ལ་མགོ, ས་མགོ}, if the first character is in set SC, then the first character is determined as SC, the second character is determined as BC and third characters is determined as UC. But, if the third character is not in the set UC, then the first character is determined as PC, the second character is determined as SC and third characters is determined as BC.

The algorithm for component recognition of Tibetan syllable is shown in Algorithm 2.

4 Experiment

The experiment is divided into two groups: one is the experiment on item, and the other one is the experiment on original corpus. In the experiment on item, the original corpus was classified into three categories of mixing with other languages, non-vowel syllable and vowel syllable. The first experimental file of category of mixing with other languages, named TEST1, is established from the

Algorithm 2. Algorithm for component recognition of Tibetan syllable.

```
Input:
   Tv, Tr, Tp, syllable;
Output:
   Type of each component for syllable;
Creating output string variables TrP, TrU, TrB, TrD, Ap, they are PC, SC, BC, UC and second
   UC respectively;
Tv is V, TpF and TpS are FP and SP respectively;
Creating string: syllable;
while Tr ≠ null do
   if Tr.lenth=1 then
      TrP ⇐ ϕ, TrU ⇐ ϕ, TrB ⇐ Tr, TrU ⇐ ϕ;
   else
      if Tr.lenth=2 then
         if the first character ∈ SC then
            TrP ⇐ ϕ, TrU ⇐ the first character, TrB ⇐ the second character, TrD ⇐ ϕ;
         else
            if the second character ∈ UC then
               TrP ⇐ ϕ, TrU ⇐ ϕ, TrB ⇐ the first character, TrD1 ⇐ the second character;
            else
               TrP ⇐ the first character, TrU ⇐ ϕ, TrB ⇐ the second character, TrD ⇐ ϕ;
            end if
         end if
      else
         if Tr.lenth=3 then
            if the third character ∈ D AND the second character ∈ D then
               TrP ⇐ ϕ, TrU ⇐ ϕ, TrB ⇐ the first character, TrD ⇐ the second character, Ap
               ⇐ the third character;
            else
               if the third character ∈ D AND the first character ∈ U then
                  TrP ⇐ ϕ, TrU ⇐ the first character, TrB ⇐ the second character, TrD ⇐ the
                  third character; Ap ⇐ ϕ;
               else
                  TrP ⇐ the first character, TrU ⇐ the second character, TrB ⇐ the third
                  character, TrD ⇐ ϕ; Ap ⇐ ϕ;
               end if
            end if
         else
            if Tr.lenth=4 then
               TrP ⇐ the first character, TrU ⇐ the second character, TrB ⇐ the third char-
               acter, TrD ⇐ the fourth character;
            else
               print err
            end if
            Tv ⇐ Vowel;
            if Tp!=ϕ then
               if Tp.lenth=1 then
                  TpF ⇐ Tp, TpS ⇐ ϕ;
               end if
               if Tp.lenth=2 then
                  TpF ⇐ the first character, TpS ⇐ the second character;
               end if
            end if
         end if
      end if
   end if
end while
```

Tibetan original corpus with other linguistic symbols. The second experimental file of category of non-vowel syllable, named TEST2, is established from the Tibetan original corpus with consisting of vowel syllables. The third experimental file of category of vowel syllable, named TEST3, is established from the Tibetan original corpus with consisting of vowel syllables. What's more, the fourth experimental file, named TEST4, is established by download Tibetan corpus from Internet, which contains all the features of three experimental files TEST1, TEST2 and TEST3 above.

4.1 Experimental Corpus

The experimental corpus consists of 100 articles download from China Tibetan Net (www.tibet3.com), which contains news, culture, writing, education, economy, law, pilgrimage, general knowledge and folkways, and so on. The size of TEST1, TEST2, TEST3 and TEST4 are 120 KB, 790 KB, 1.65 MB and 1.71 MB, respectively. TEST1 consists of four articles with mixing of many linguistic symbols. The content of TEST4 is complex for it consists of 100 original articles with not only all kinds of Tibetan coding, e.g., Tibetan symbols, Tibetan characters, Sanskrit translated Tibetan and mistaken Tibetan syllables, but also characters and symbols in Chinese coding and symbols and characters in English.

4.2 Evaluation Criteria and Evaluation

Documents can be divided into two categories of related and unrelated, while the retrieval results can be divided into retrieved and non-retrieved according to the definition of Accuracy Rate (A), Recall Rate (R), and Precision Rate (P) in Information Retrieval (IR). The confusion matrix can be shown in Table 3 by evaluation criteria in IR. The Tibetan syllables that consist of correct Tibetan syllable, mistaken Tibetan syllable and Sanskrit translated Tibetan can be divided into two categories of modern Tibetan syllable and non-modern Tibetan syllable. The modern Tibetan syllable are syllables conformed to Tibetan grammar, while the non-modern Tibetan syllable are syllables not conformed to Tibetan grammar including Sanskrit translated Tibetan, special Tibetan syllables in ancient articles corpus, and mistaken Tibetan syllable as well, for convenience. The modern Tibetan syllables correspond to relevant documents, while the non-modern Tibetan syllables correspond to non-related documents. The Tibetan syllable with component recognized correctly corresponds to retrieved documents, while the Tibetan syllable with component recognized incorrectly corresponds to non-retrieved documents.

Let TP represent the number of modern Tibetan syllable components that recognized correctly. Let FP represent the number of non-modern Tibetan syllable components that recognized correctly. FP can be considered as recognized correctly accidentally. Let FN represent the number of modern Tibetan syllable

Table 3. The incidence table of Tibetan syllable decomposition.

	Modern Tibetan syllable	Non-modern Tibetan syllable
Identified correctly	TP	FP
Identified incorrectly	FN	TN

components that recognized incorrectly. Let FN represent the number of non-modern Tibetan syllable components that recognized incorrectly. A, R, and P are used to evaluate the experimental result of component recognition.

A is defined as:

$$A = \frac{TP + TN}{TP + FP + FN + TN} \tag{1}$$

R is defined as:

$$R = \frac{TP}{TP + FN} \tag{2}$$

P is defined as:

$$P = \frac{TP}{TP + FP} \tag{3}$$

We check the experimental result manually, numbers of syllable decomposition and component recognition TP, FP, FN, TN, and evaluation criteria of A, R, P are shown in Table 4.

Table 4. Experimental results of syllable decomposition and component recognition.

File	TP	FP	FN	TN	A/%	R/%	P/%
TEST1	8823	0	769	5	91.98	91.98	100
TEST2	75126	0	8673	165	89.67	89.65	100
TEST3	121612	0	10879	458	91.81	91.78	100
TEST4	196738	0	19552	623	90.98	90.96	100

Several screenshots of experimental result selected randomly are shown in Fig. 2. Screenshots of four experimental files TEST1, TEST2, TEST3 and TEST4 are shown from left to right and from top to bottom respectively.

Through the analysis of the experimental result, the reason for syllable decomposed incorrectly can be summarized as following:

(1) The Tibetan syllable is split incorrectly. Because there are many compact cases and stick to other syllables in Tibetan words, e.g., ས་ ར་ འ་ འི་ འུ་ འོ་ འང་ འམ་, that cannot restore to two syllables and result in syllable decomposed incorrectly. The occupancy of compact cases as འི་ འུ་ འོ་ འང་ འམ་ among them is more than 90% in experimental result of FN.

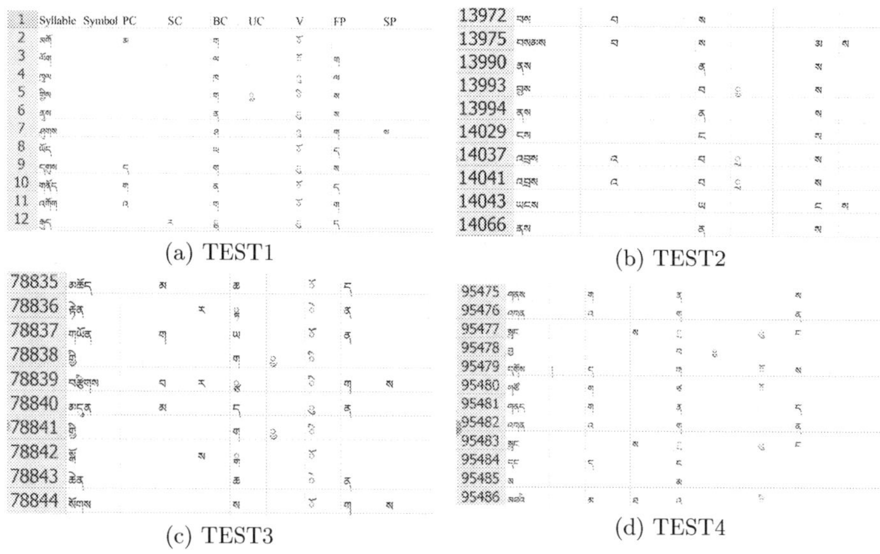

(a) TEST1

(b) TEST2

(c) TEST3

(d) TEST4

Fig. 2. Screenshots of experimental result.

(2) The ambiguity rule characters are judged incorrectly. Rule characters from {གད ,གན , གས ,དག , དང ,དབ , དམ ,བག , བད ,བས , མག ,མད , མང ,མན } as ambiguity rule characters can either be prefix part of a syllable or be a syllable separately and lead to syllable decomposed incorrectly. The occupancy of experimental file TEST2 is around 70% in experimental result of FN.

(3) The non-modern Tibetan syllable is decomposed incorrectly. For non-modern Tibetan syllable of Sanskrit translated Tibetan, special Tibetan syllables in ancient article, and mistaken Tibetan syllable are not conformed to TSRM lead to syllable decomposed incorrectly, e.g., པཊྟེ is decomposed to པ as PC, ཊ as SC, ྟ as BC, and ེ as V. FP is 0 for it is a non-Tibetan syllable and not conformed to modern Tibetan grammar, either in the same grammatical system generally.

5 Conclusion and Prospect

In this paper, we propose a new algorithm for component decomposition and type recognition of Tibetan syllable which can decompose each Tibetan syllable very well and recognize the type of each component correctly by application of TSRM respectively. The algorithm for spelling of Tibetan syllables automatically which can spell most Tibetan syllables that conformed to Tibetan grammar is proposed ahead based on TSRM in another article ever before, while the algorithm for spelling checking of Tibetan syllable which can detect mistaken Tibetan syllables very well is proposed before is also on basis of TSRM in another former article. Compared with other algorithms alike, the algorithm proposed in this work can improve efficiency of component decomposition and type recognition greatly with implemented simply. Both TSRM previously and the algorithm for component decomposition and type recognition of Tibetan syllable proposed in this paper are in accordance with grammar rule. In the future, machine learning algorithm maybe used in TIP for further research.

References

1. Zhaxi, F.: Tibetan sorting rules and come true automatic sorting in computer. China Tibetology **4**, 128–135 (1999)
2. Jiang, D., Zhou, J.W.: On the sequence of Tibetan words and the method of making sequence. J. Chin. Inf. Process. **14**(1), 56–62 (2000)
3. Huang, H.M., Zhao, C.X.: A DUCET-based Tibetan sorting algorithm. J. Chin. Inf. Process. **22**(4), 109–113 (2008)
4. Banba, W., Drolkar, Dong, Z.C., et al.: Study on the sorting algorithm of Tibetan dictionary. J. Chin .Inf. Process. **19**(1), 191–196 (2015)
5. Druggye, N.: A method for ordering Tibetan text based on Tibetan coded GB. J. Tibetan Univ. **23**(1), 33–35 (2008). Natural Science Edition
6. Banba, W., Zhuo, G., Chen, Y.L., et al.: Study on recognition algorithms for Tibetan construction elements. J. Chin. Inf. Process. **28**(3), 104–111 (2014)
7. Tshedpa. Research on the automatic recognition and sorting of Tibetan word components on the unicode. J. Tibetan Univ. **29**(2), 80–86 (2014). Natural Science Edition
8. Renqing, Z., Qi, K.Y., Gongbao, Z.: Research the types of seven-tuple syllables in Tibetan. J. Northwest Univ. Natl. **36**(97) 32–36 (2015). (Natural Science)
9. Huang, H.M., Da, F.P.: Collation-based judgment of modern Tibetan syllable. J. Comput. Appl. **9**(7), 2003–2005 (2009)
10. Zhu, J., Li, T.R., Ge, S., et al.: Tibetan syllable rule model and applications. Acta Scientiarum Naturalium Universitatis Pekinensis **49**(1), 68–74 (2013)

Event Temporal Relation Classification Based on Graph Convolutional Networks

Qianwen Dai, Fang Kong(✉), and Qianying Dai

Natural Language Processing Laboratory, School of Computer Science and Technology, Soochow University, Suzhou 215006, Jiangsu, China
kongfang@suda.edu.cn

Abstract. Classifying temporal relations between events is an important step of understanding natural language, and a significant subsequent study of event extraction. With the development of deep learning, various neural network frameworks have been applied to the task of event temporal relation classification. However, current studies only consider semantic information in local contexts of two events and ignore the syntactic structure information. To solve this problem, this paper proposes a neural architecture combining LSTM and GCN. This method can automatically extract features from word sequences and dependency syntax. A series of experiments on the Timebank-Dense corpus also show the superiority of the model presented in this paper.

Keywords: Temporal relation · Graph convolutional networks · Syntactic dependency

1 Introduction

An event is a description of a certain behavior or state in a specific time and environment [1]. From the perspective of time, events may occur in a time interval or last for a period of time. Therefore, these events usually follow a sequential order. Event temporal relation classification is to identify the order of events according to the characteristics of time clues. Classifying temporal relations between events is a basic task of natural language processing. It has direct application in tasks such as question answering, event timeline generation and document summarization.

Temporal relations between events are various, such as "BEFORE", "AFTER", etc. Temporal relation classification aims to classify these relations correctly. Figure 1 shows some examples of event temporal relations. S1 is an intra-sentence event pair (***boom***, ***layoffs***) with 'BEFORE' relation. S2 is a cross-sentence event pair (***break***, ***visit***) with 'AFTER' relation.

Previous works studied this task as the classification problem based on pattern matching and statistical machine learning. However, these methods need external resources to obtain semantic information, and depend on a large number of annotated

This work is supported by Project 61876118 under the National Natural Science Foundation of China, and Key Project 61836007 under the National Natural Science Foundation of China.

J. Tang et al. (Eds.): NLPCC 2019, LNAI 11839, pp. 393–403, 2019.
https://doi.org/10.1007/978-3-030-32236-6_35

entity attributes, which are difficult to be obtained in the practical scenarios. With the development of deep learning, temporal relation classification no longer depends on manual features and external resources. However, existing studies only consider semantic information in local contexts of two events and ignore syntactic information. How to make better use of syntactic structure information becomes the key.

S1: And at the big brokerage houses, after ten years of ***boom***, they're talking about ***layoffs***.

S2: a. The main negative is the risk that the pope's visit will persuade a great many more cubans to ***break*** loose of the cuban government.
b. If so, then the pope's ***visit*** would really open up a new chapter in the government's relations with its own society.

Fig. 1. Examples of event temporal relation

In this paper, we proposes a neural architecture combining LSTMs and GCNs to better compute the representation for each word based on the syntactic dependency tree. Compared with existing studies, our model can achieve competitive results.

2 Related Work

Previous works of temporal relation classification are based on pattern matching and statistical machine learning. Mani et al. [1] built MaxEnt classifier on hand-tagged features for classifying temporal relations. Later Chambers et al. [2] used a two-stage classifier which first learned imperfect event attributes and then combined them with other linguistic features obtained from WordNet [3] and VerbOcean [4] in the second stage to perform the classification. The following works mostly expanded the feature sets (Cheng et al. [5]; Bethard and Martin [6]; Kolomiyets et al. [7]).

In recent years, neural networks has been widely applied in the temporal relation classification. Xu et al. [8] perform LSTM with max pooling separately on each feature channel along dependency path. Cheng et al. [9] extracted the shortest dependency path from the dependency syntax tree, obtained good results through Bi-LSTMs. Choubey et al. [10] introduced more event context information based on the shortest dependency path and used Bi-LSTMs for Classifying Temporal Relations between Intra-Sentence Events.

In addition, Ning et al. [11] developed a probabilistic knowledge base acquired from the news domain, existing temporal extraction systems can be improved via this resource. Then Ning et al. [12] presented a joint inference framework using constrained conditional models (CCMs) for temporal and causal relations.

Compared with feature-based methods, neural networks based on dependency path achieves more advanced performance. But it causes lack of information and doesn't take the syntactic structure into consideration. In this paper, we present a sequential model with LSTMs and GCNs that can better compute the representation for each word by combining semantic and syntactic information. Thus, the overall performance of event temporal relation classification is improved.

3 Graph Convolutional Networks

3.1 Graph Convolutional Networks

GCNs (Kipf and Welling (2017) [13]) are neural networks that operate directly on graph structures. It convolves the features of neighboring nodes and also propagates the information of a node to its nearest neighbors. Let $G = (V, E)$ be a undirected graph where V is the set of nodes ($|V| = n$), E indicates the edge set. We can define a matrix $X \in \mathbf{R}^{d \times n}$ denoting d-dimensional input node features. GCNs retrieve new node features at layer k + 1 by encoding neighboring nodes' features with the following equation:

$$\boldsymbol{h}_v^{(k+1)} = RELU\left(\frac{\sum_{u \in N_{(v)}} \boldsymbol{W}\boldsymbol{h}_u^{(k)} + \boldsymbol{b}}{|N_{(v)}|}\right) \tag{1}$$

Here, $W \in \mathbf{R}^{d \times d}$ and $b \in \mathbf{R}^d$ are a weight matrix and a bias, respectively; *RELU* is the rectifier linear unit activation function. v is the target node and N_v represents the neighborhood of v, including v itself. h_v^k is hidden representation of node u at layer k and $h_v^1 = x_v$.

3.2 Syntactic Graph Convolutional Networks

The above GCNs can only be used for the topological structure of undirected graph, while syntactic dependency trees are directed and there are various types of edges. This paper refers to the Syntactic GCNs proposed by Marcheggiani [14] and modifies the computation in order to incorporate label information.

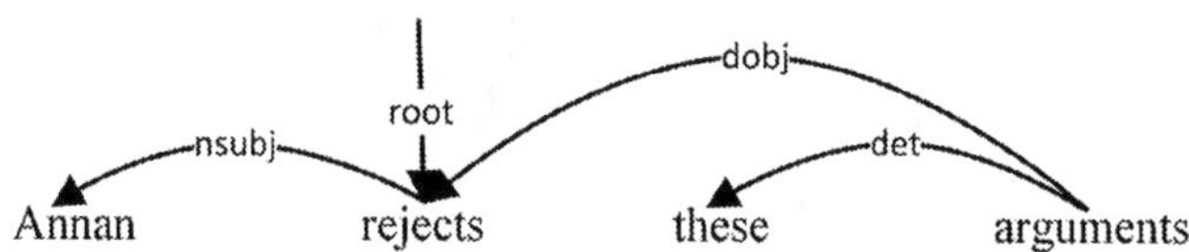

Fig. 2. An example sentence annotated with syntactic dependencies

We add an arc in the opposite direction for each arc in the syntactic dependency tree. The syntactic dependency tree can be viewed as a graph whose edges are labeled. The label $L(u, v)$ for edge $(u, v) \in E$ contains two pieces of information. It describes the syntactic dependency type and indicates whether the edge is in the same or opposite direction as the syntactic dependency arc. For example, Fig. 2 shows the dependency graph of sentence “Annan rejects these arguments”. After adding arcs in the opposite direction, both (rejects, Annan) whose label is nsubj and (Annan, rejects) whose label is nsubj’ belong to the edge set. We correspond label types to different weight matrices and bias terms to represent different combinations of directions and dependency types. In other words, the syntatic GCN parameters are label-specific. The computation can be written as shown below. The specific model is shown in Fig. 3 (the bias terms are omitted in the figure).

$$\boldsymbol{h}_v^{(k+1)} = \mathbf{ReLU}\left(\frac{\sum_{u \in N_{(v)}} \boldsymbol{W}_{L_{(u,v)}} \boldsymbol{h}_u^{(k)} + \boldsymbol{b}_{L_{(u,v)}}}{|N_{(v)}|}\right) \tag{2}$$

Due to various dependency types and the arcs added, there are too many parameters in the model. To avoid over-fitting, we only keep the direction of each label and do not care about specific categories. So the label $L(u, v)$ can be reduced to three types: (1) the same direction as the syntactic dependency arc, (2) the opposite direction to the syntactic dependency arc, or (3) point to itself.

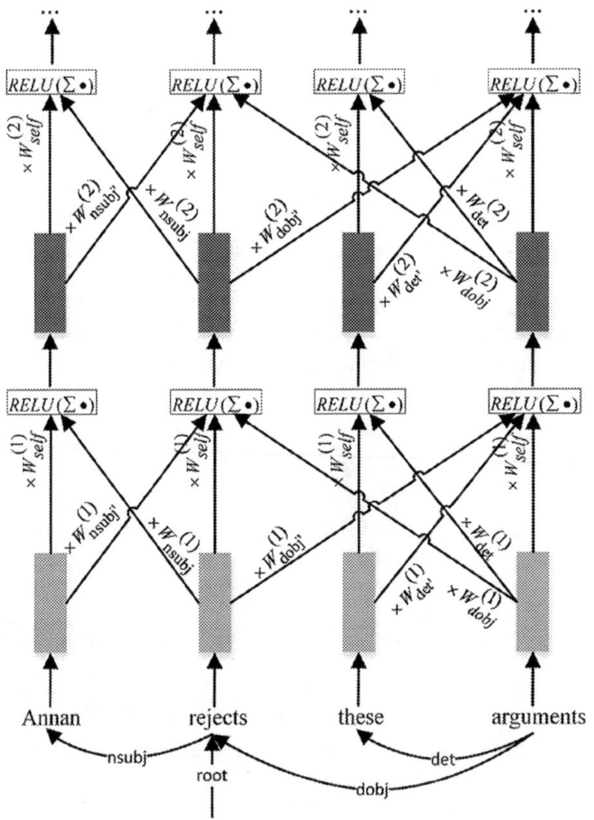

Fig. 3. Syntactic GCN

4 Event Temporal Relation Model Based on GCNs

The overall architecture of the proposed event temporal relation system is illustrated in Fig. 4. The system contains two identical network modules, corresponding to the processing process of two event sentence sequences. Each moudle is composed of four components: word embedding layer, Bi-LSTM layer, Syntactic GCN layer and max pooling layer. At the top of the model, there is the hidden layer, followed by the softmax layer for classification. The model is described in detail below.

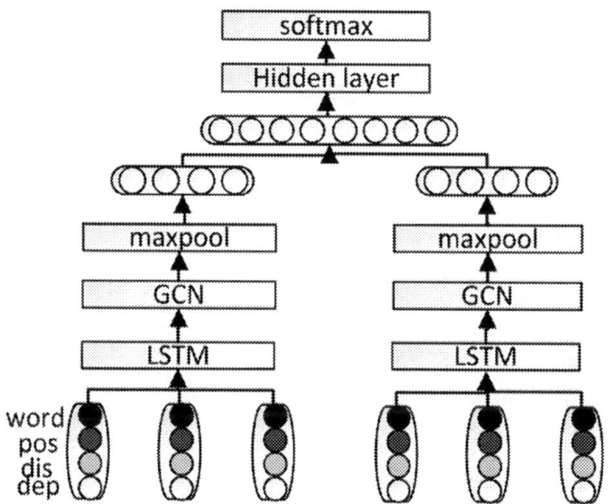

Fig. 4. Event temporal relation classification model based on GCN

4.1 Word Representations

Given the sentences of an event pair, for each word in the sentences, we create a word representation X_t. The word representation is the concatenation of four vectors: (i) a pre-trained word embedding x_{word} (ii) a randomly initialized part-of-speech tag embedding x_{pos} (iii) a randomly initialized embedding x_{dis} which represents the distance between the word and the event word (iv) a randomly initialized dependency relation type embedding x_{dep}. It is noteworthy that x_{dep} cover the shortage of syntactic GCNs that ignoring dependency relation types to some extent. The final word representation as follows:

$$\boldsymbol{X}_t = \boldsymbol{x}_{word} \oplus \boldsymbol{x}_{pos} \oplus \boldsymbol{x}_{dis} \oplus x_{dep} \tag{3}$$

4.2 Bidirectional LSTM Layer

Recurrent neural network is one of the most effective ways to represent sentences. In order to further improve the representation ability of our model, we use Bi-LSTM to transform the underlying input. At the same time, Bi-LSTM can make up the inability of GCNs to capture dependencies between nodes far away from each other in the graph. For each word representation X_t, Bi-LSTM layer encodes it in two directions respectively. By concatenating outputs of two directions, we create a complete context-aware representation of a word:

$$\overrightarrow{\boldsymbol{h}_t} = LSTM(\boldsymbol{X}_t, \overrightarrow{\boldsymbol{h}_{t-1}}), \tag{4}$$

$$\overleftarrow{\boldsymbol{h}_t} = LSTM(\boldsymbol{X}_t, \overleftarrow{\boldsymbol{h}_{t+1}}), \tag{5}$$

$$\boldsymbol{h}_t = \overrightarrow{\boldsymbol{h}_t} \oplus \overleftarrow{\boldsymbol{h}_t} \tag{6}$$

4.3 Syntactic GCN Layer

GCN is used to solve the problem of general neural networks that not easy to deal with topological structure. We use GCN to extract syntactic features from dependency trees. The representation calculated by Bi-LSTM layer is fed to a GCN defined in Eq. (2). The output h_t^k of GCN is obtained. So the vector representation of event sentences are $H_1^k = \left\{h_{1_1}^k, h_{1_2}^k, \ldots h_{1_n}^k\right\}$ and $H_2^k = \left\{h_{2_1}^k, h_{2_2}^k, \ldots h_{2_n}^k\right\}$.

4.4 Max Pooling Layer

Max pooling layer is added to select the maximum value of each column of the GCN outputs and the most informative data to form the final representation of event sentences.

$$\boldsymbol{l} = \max_{\mathrm{dim}=1}(\boldsymbol{H}^k) \tag{7}$$

4.5 Hidden Layer

Finally, the representation of two event sentences produced by max pooling layer are concatenated and fed into the hidden layer.

$$\boldsymbol{L} = \mathrm{concat}(\boldsymbol{l}_1 + \boldsymbol{l}_2), \tag{8}$$

$$\boldsymbol{Y} = \tanh(\boldsymbol{L}\boldsymbol{W}_h + \boldsymbol{b}_h) \tag{9}$$

Where l_1, l_2 are the representations of two event sentences, respectively. W_h is the weight matrix and b_h is bias of tanh function.

4.6 Temporal Relation Classifier

After the hidden layer, a softmax classififier predicts probabilites for each of the six classes:

$$o = \text{softmax}(\boldsymbol{YW}_o + \boldsymbol{b}_o) \tag{10}$$

Where Y represents the output of the event sentences vector through the hidden layer, and W_o is the weight matrix and b_o is bias of softmax function.

In this paper, stochastic gradient descent algorithm is used to minimize the negative logarithmic likelihood function for model training. The objective function is defined as follows:

$$j(\theta) = -\sum\nolimits_{i=1}^{n} \log p(y_i|x_i, \theta) \tag{11}$$

Where θ is the trainable parameter set of the model; n Represents the number of training samples; x_i Represents the ith sample of the training sample and y_i is the corresponding label.

5 Experiments

5.1 Datasets

We tested the proposed model on the TimeBank-Dense (TB-D) dataset to certify its validity and correctness.

TimeBank-Dense contains 36 documents annotated with 6 temporal relation types, including "AFTER", "BEFORE", "SIMULTANEOUS", "INCLUDES", "IS_INCLUDED", "VAGUE". "VAGUE" indicates event pairs whose temporal relations are unclear or missing. TB-D annotates 6088 event pairs and their specific distribution is shown in Table 1.

Table 1. Event pairs distribution of TB-D corpus

Relation	Inter-sentence	Cross-sentence
AFTER	436	684
BEFORE	542	806
SIMULTANEOUS	49	44
INCLUDE	94	182
IS_INCLUDED	174	173
VAGUE	793	2111
Overall	2088	4000

5.2 Cross-Validation and Hyper-parameters

We use a sentence-level 5-fold cross validation on the TB-D corpus and take the micro-average overall F1-score as the final result. We randomly sampled 15% of the training set acted as validation set. Early stopping is used to save the best model based on the validation data. The patience is set as 10. We use 200-dimensions pre-trained word embeddings from GloVe (Pennington et al., 2014) [15]. For POS and relative distance, we adopt the 50-dimensions look up table initialized randomly. For dependency relation, we adopt the 30-dimensions.

The batch size is 64. Adam optimization algorithm is adopted and the initial learning rate is 0.001. In order to prevent neural networks from over-fitting, we adopt dropout separately after embedding, Bi-LSTM, and hidden layer. The dropout ratio is 0.5. We set each single LSTM output with 128 dimensions, layer number is 3. GCN output is 256 dimensions, layer number is 2. The hidden layer is set as 200-dimensions.

5.3 Results and Discussion

Comparison with Previous Studies. We compare the proposed system with two best performing feature-based systems and the best system in the neural network architecture.

- **CAEVO:** Chambers et al. [16] (2014) proposed a hybrid system based on filter architecture. The system combines hand-crafted rules and hand-tagged features.
- **MIRZA:** Mirza and Tonelli [17] (2016) mined the value of low dimensions word embeddings by concatenating them with sparse traditional features. Their traditional features includes entity attributes, temporal signals, semantic information of WordNet, etc.
- **Cheng:** Cheng et al. [9] (2017) built a LSTM classifier based on dependency path. They extracted the shortest dependency path and take the word, part of speech and dependency relation as input features.

Table 2 shows the detail results. Compared with MIRZA, F1 increased by 4.5%, proving that neural networks has a significant effect on mining deep information of sentences. The comparison with Cheng also shows the superiority of our work.

Table 2. Comparison with the existing methods

Relation	CAEVO	MIRZA	Cheng	Ours
AFTER	–	43.0	44.0	57.4
BEFORE	–	47.1	46.0	54.2
SIMULTANEOUS	–	–	–	–
INCLUDE	–	4.9	2.5	27.8
IS_INCLUDED	–	25.0	17.0	32.3
VAGUE	–	61.3	62.4	62.5
Overall	49.4	51.9	52.9	**56.8**

Effect of GCNs. In order to confirm the impact of GCN, we compare our model against its version which lacks GCN layers and which lacks LSTM layers. Table 3 lists the detail comparisions. The last two columns represent our model, and k represents the layer number of GCN.

Experimental results show the efficiency of our model in temporal relation classification. GCN performs better than LSTM, no matter its layer number is 1 or 2. The classifier with LSTM and one GCN layers (K = 1) performs the best, which proves the complementarity of GCNs and LSTMs. Compared with the LSTM, F1 increased by 3.0%. The reason why the improvements is clear. Bidirectional LSTM only encodes semantic information while GCN takes the features of neighboring nodes into consideration and models syntactic information. The experimental results prove the necessity of syntactic structure for temporal relation classification.

2 GCN layers performs better than 1 GCN layer when LSTM layers are dropped altogether. But when combined with the LSTM, F1 of 1 GCN layer increased by 2.8% while F1 of 2 GCN layers decreased by 1.4%. This suggests that extra GCN layers are effective but when there are too many layers it is largely redundant with respect to what LSTMs already capture.

In addition, to measure the influence of ignoring dependency relation types, we delete x_{dep} from the word vector X_t. Removing dependency types leads to a drop of 0.4% F1. It shows that the loss of syntactic dependency types has an effect on the results. We still can't throw out the type information completely.

Table 3. The effect of GCN on experimental performance

Relation	LSTM	GCN (k = 1)	GCN (k = 2)	LSTM +GCN $-x_{dep}$(k = 1)	LSTM +GCN (k = 1)	LSTM +GCN (k = 2)
AFTER	53.6	54.3	58.6	59.1	57.4	55.0
BEFORE	48.4	48.4	51.0	53.7	54.2	49.1
SIMULTANEOUS	–	–	–	–	–	–
INCLUDE	12.9	16.3	16.4	29.6	27.8	18.6
IS_INCLUDED	28.5	28.7	31.3	26.9	32.3	29.1
VAGUE	60.9	61.2	62.1	61.6	62.5	61.7
Overall	53.8	54.0	56.0	56.4	**56.8**	54.6

6 Conclusion

In this paper, we propose an event temporal relation model based on graph convolutional networks (GCN). We combine LSTM and GCN to extract not only sequential features but also regional dependency features for each word. It overcomes the inability of traditional neural network model to process syntactic structure information of text. Compared with most previously proposed methods, our model is competitive.

However, there is room for improvement. For example, the current researches mainly focus on event pairs, which may lead to inconsistent situations when constructing time chains later. In future studies, we can introduce linear programming to improve the overall performance of the model.

References

1. Zheng, X., Li, P.F., Zhu, Q.M., et al.: Annotation and classification of temporal relation between chinese events. Comput. Sci. **42**(7), 276–279 (2015)
2. Mani, I., Verhagen, M., Wellner, B., et al.: Machine learning of temporal relations. In: Proceedings of the 21st International Conference on Computational Linguistics and the 44th Annual Meeting of the Association for Computational Linguistics. Association for Computational Linguistics, pp. 753–760 (2006)
3. Chambers, N., Wang, S., Jurafsky, D.: Classifying temporal relations between events. In: Meeting of the ACL on Interactive Poster and Demonstration Sessions. Association for Computational Linguistics, pp. 173–176 (2007)
4. Miller, G.A.: WordNet: a lexical database for English. Commun. ACM **38**(11), 39–41 (1995)
5. Chklovski, T., PVerbocean, P.: Mining the Web for fine-grained semantic verb relations. In: Conference on Empirical Methods in Natural Language Processing (2004)
6. Cheng, Y., Asahara, M., Matsumoto, Y.: NAIST. Japan: temporal relation identification using dependency parsed tree. In: Proceedings of the 4th International Workshop on Semantic Evaluations. Association for Computational Linguistics, pp. 245–248 (2007)
7. Bethard, S., Martin, J.H.: CU-TMP: temporal relation classification using syntactic and semantic features. In: Proceedings of the 4th International Workshop on Semantic Evaluations. Association for Computational Linguistics, pp. 129–132 (2007)
8. Kolomiyets, O., Bethard, S., Moens, M.F.: Extracting narrative timelines as temporal dependency structures. In: Proceedings of the 50th Annual Meeting of the Association for Computational Linguistics: Long Papers-Volume 1. Association for Computational Linguistics, pp. 88–97 (2012)
9. Xu, Y., Mou, L., Li, G., et al.: Classifying relations via long short term memory networks along shortest dependency paths. In: Proceedings of the 2015 Conference on Empirical Methods in Natural Language Processing, pp. 1785–1794 (2015)
10. Cheng, F., Miyao, Y.: Classifying temporal relations by bidirectional LSTM over dependency paths. In: Proceedings of the 55th Annual Meeting of the Association for Computational Linguistics (Volume 2: Short Papers), pp. 1–6 (2017)
11. Choubey, P.K., Huang, R.A.: Sequential model for classifying temporal relations between intra-sentence events. arXiv preprint arXiv:1707.07343 (2017)
12. Ning, Q., Wu, H., Peng, H., et al.: Improving temporal relation extraction with a globally acquired statistical resource. arXiv preprint arXiv:1804.06020 (2018)
13. Ning, Q., Feng, Z., Wu, H., et al.: Joint reasoning for temporal and causal relations. In: Proceedings of the 56th Annual Meeting of the Association for Computational Linguistics (Volume 1: Long Papers), pp. 2278–2288 (2018)
14. Kipf, T.N., Welling, M.: Semi-supervised classification with graph convolutional networks. arXiv preprint arXiv:1609.02907 (2016)
15. Marcheggiani, D., Titov, I.: Encoding sentences with graph convolutional networks for semantic role labeling. arXiv preprint arXiv:1703.04826 (2017)

16. Pennington, J., Socher, R., Manning, C.D.: Glove: global vectors for word representation. In: Proceedings of EMNLP (2014)
17. Chambers, N., Cassidy, T., McDowell, B., et al.: Dense event ordering with a multi-pass architecture. Trans. Assoc. Comput. Linguist. **2**, 273–284 (2014)
18. Paramita, M., Tonelli, S.: On the contribution of word embeddings to temporal relation classification. In: 26th International Conference on Computational Linguistics (Coling 2016): Technical Papers, pp. 2818–2828 (2016)

Event Factuality Detection in Discourse

Rongtao Huang[1], Bowei Zou[1,2(✉)], Hongling Wang[1], Peifeng Li[1], and Guodong Zhou[1]

[1] Natural Language Processing Lab, Soochow University, Suzhou, China
rthuang.suda@gmail.com,
{zoubowei,hlwang,pfli,gdzhou}@suda.edu.cn
[2] Institute for Infocomm Research, Singapore, Singapore

Abstract. Event factuality indicates whether an event occurs or the degree of certainty described by authors in context. Correctly identifying event factuality in texts can contribute to a deep understanding of natural language. In addition, event factuality detection is of great significance to many natural language processing applications, such as opinion detection, emotional reasoning, and public opinion analysis. Existing studies mainly focus on identifying event factuality by the features in the current sentence (e.g. negation or modality). However, there might be many different descriptions of factuality in a document, corresponding to the same event. It leads to conflict when identifying event factuality only on sentence level. To address such issues, we come up with a document-level approach on event factuality detection, which employs Bi-directional Long Short-Term Memory (BiLSTM) neural networks to learn contextual information of the event in sentences. Moreover, we utilize a double-layer attention mechanism to capture the latent correlation features among event sequences in the discourse, and identify event factuality according to the whole document. The experimental results on both English and Chinese event factuality detection datasets demonstrate the effectiveness of our approach. The performances of the proposed system achieved 86.67% and 86.97% of F1 scores, yielding improvements of 3.24% and 4.78% over the state-of-the-art on English and Chinese datasets, respectively.

Keywords: Event factuality · Discourse information · BiLSTM · Attention mechanism

1 Introduction

Text-oriented event factuality measures whether an event has occurred or the degree of certainty described by authors in context. Event factuality detection in texts can contribute to a deep understanding of natural language. In addition, it is of great significance for many natural language processing applications, such as question answering [1], opinion detection [2], emotion analysis [3] and rumor monitoring [4].

Event factuality is generally measured and represented by its polarity and modality. Polarity indicates whether an event has occurred in context, while modality conveys the degree of certainty. The intersection of the two dimensions produces four types of event factuality, that is, *CerTain Positive* (CT+), *CerTain Negative* (CT−),

J. Tang et al. (Eds.): NLPCC 2019, LNAI 11839, pp. 404–414, 2019.
https://doi.org/10.1007/978-3-030-32236-6_36

PoSsible Positive (PS+), *PoSsible Negative* (PS−). Besides, if an event's factuality cannot be identified, we usually label it as *Underspecified* (Un).

新浪体育讯 这个夏天AC米兰的股权交易成为一场大戏，此前中央电视台财经频道的《环球财经连线》节目援引路透社的报道称：百度集团将以4.37亿美元收购（PS+）AC米兰。

Sina Sports News This summer AC Milan's equity transaction became a big show. Previously, the CCTV's "Global Finance Connection" program quoted Reuters as reporting that Baidu Group will ***acquire (PS+)*** *AC Milan for $437 million.*

在15日的《环球财经连线》节目中，央视称："目前，百度总裁李彦宏与意大利AC米兰的谈判已经有了进展，预计将以4亿3700万美元收购（PS+）AC米兰。"

In the "Global Finance Connection" program on the 15th, CCTV said: "At present, the negotiation between Baidu President Li Yanhong and Italy's AC Milan has progressed, and it is expected to ***acquire (PS+)*** *AC Milan for $437 million."*

这消息一出，就引来一片质疑之声，因为AC米兰80%股份估值5亿欧元，如果接盘，还需要考虑2亿欧元的债务，那么4.37亿美元，约3.93亿欧元收购（PS-）AC**米兰的消息看起来有些禁不起推敲。**

When this news came out, it led to a voice of doubt because AC Milan's 80% stake was valued at 500 million euros. If it took over, Baidu still needs to consider 200 million euros of debt. Thus the news of ***acquiring (PS-)*** *AC Milan for 437 million dollars, about 393 million euros does not seem to work.*

据新浪消息，19日早间，百度方面否定其参与收购（CT-）**意甲俱乐部AC米兰。此前央视报道称，百度已完成了这一4.37亿美元的收购**（CT+）**计划。**

Fig. 1. An example of event factuality (Bold: Event).

In a document, there might be different descriptions of factuality in different sentences, corresponding to the same event. As shown in Fig. 1, the acquisition event appears five times in a document, ignoring the contextual information and judging event factuality only based on individual sentence in which each event is located. Among them, the first and second times are CCTV's speculation on the occurrence of this event, with factuality PS+. At the third time, the author questioned the occurrence of the acquisition event by "看起来有些禁不起推敲 (*does not seem to work*)", thus its factuality is PS−. Obviously, at the fourth time, Baidu, the participant in the acquisition event, explicitly denied the occurrence of the event via a negative cue "否定 (*denied*)", so its factuality is CT−. Finally, for the last mention, it is judged from the sentence perspective with factuality CT+. However, for the same event, whether it has occurred or not can only be one situation (positive/negative). Furthermore, in the same document, the degree of certainty of the event ultimately comes down to one attitude (certainty/possible). Based on the analysis in Fig. 1, as a direct participant in the acquisition event, Baidu clearly denied the occurrence of the event (the fourth mention), thus CT− is inferred as the document-level factuality of the event.

Existing studies on event factuality detection usually focus on the sentence level. Cao et al. proposed a three-dimensional representation system, expressing event factuality as a triple of <polarity, level, tense> [5]. Qian et al. extracted event triggers, event sources, negative and speculative cues from raw texts [6]. However, compared to document-level event factuality in Fig. 1, sentence-level event factuality easily leads to conflicts between different mentions of the same event, which makes it difficult to apply to NLP tasks such as information extraction and knowledge base construction. In addition, according to statistics on the English and Chinese event factuality datasets, 25.4% (English) and 37.8% (Chinese) of instances are inconsistent between sentence-level factuality and document-level factuality for the same event mention.

To address the above issue, we propose a document-level event factuality detection approach. Specifically, we employs BiLSTM networks to learn the contextual information of the event in sentences. Such BiLSTM feature encoder can effectively model the forward and backward information around the event. Then, we come up with a double-layer attention mechanism to capture the latent correlation features among event sequences in discourse. In particular, first, the intra-sequence attention mechanism can capture the dependence between cues and event in the sentence. Second, the inter-sequence attention mechanism can extract the document-level feature representation of the event from the event sequence. Finally, the probability of the event factuality is decoded by a softmax layer.

The experimental results on both English and Chinese event factuality detection datasets [7] demonstrate the effectiveness of our approach. The performances of the proposed system achieve 86.67% and 86.97% of F1 scores, yielding improvements of 3.24% and 4.78% over the state-of-the-art on English and Chinese datasets, respectively. In addition, the related experiments also verify the effectiveness of event triggers, negative and speculative cues on document-level event identification.

2 Related Work

Early studies on event factuality detection concentrated on the sentence level. Minard et al. released the MEANTIME corpus [8] and analyzed that the event factuality is characterized by certainty, tense and polarity. According to their theory, certainty includes three subcategories of "certainty", "uncertainty", and "unspecified"; Tense distinguishes among "past", "future", and "unspecified"; And polarity is divided into "positive", "negative", and "unspecified". Besides, Minard proposed an event factuality detection system, FactPro [9, 10]. Saurí et al. released the FactBank corpus [11] and divided factuality values into seven categories according to the modality and polarity of the event, i.e. Fact (CT+), Counterfact (CT−), Probable (PR+), Not probable (PR−), Possible (PS+), Not possible (PS−) and underspecified (Uu). Moreover, Saurí proposed the De Faco system [12], which traverses the dependency syntax tree of the event from top to bottom, and calculates the factuality of the event layer by layer. Recently, neural networks are effectively applied to various NLP tasks. Qian et al. [6] extracted event factuality information from raw text and proposed a generative adversarial network with auxiliary classification for event factuality detection.

In Chinese, Cao [13] annotated the Chinese event factuality based on the ACE 2005 corpus and proposed a 3D representation system, regarding the event factuality as a <polarity, level, tense> triplet. On the basis, He et al. [14] proposed a Convolutional Neural Network (CNN) based Chinese event factuality detection model.

However, all of the above studies focus on identifying event factuality by relevant features (e.g. negative and speculative cues) in sentence level. Qian annotated an event factuality data set for Chinese and English news texts in his PhD thesis [7], which marked the event factuality on both document level and sentence level, and proposed a document-level event factuality detection method based on adversarial networks.

3 Document-Level Event Factuality Detection

In this paper, we propose a document-level event factuality detection approach that comprehensively considers effective information related to the target event in a document. First, a BiLSTM neural network is employed to learn contextual information of the target event. Then, we utilize a double-layer attention mechanism to capture latent correlation features among the event sequence in discourse. Figure 2 illustrates the framework for our event factuality detection approach.

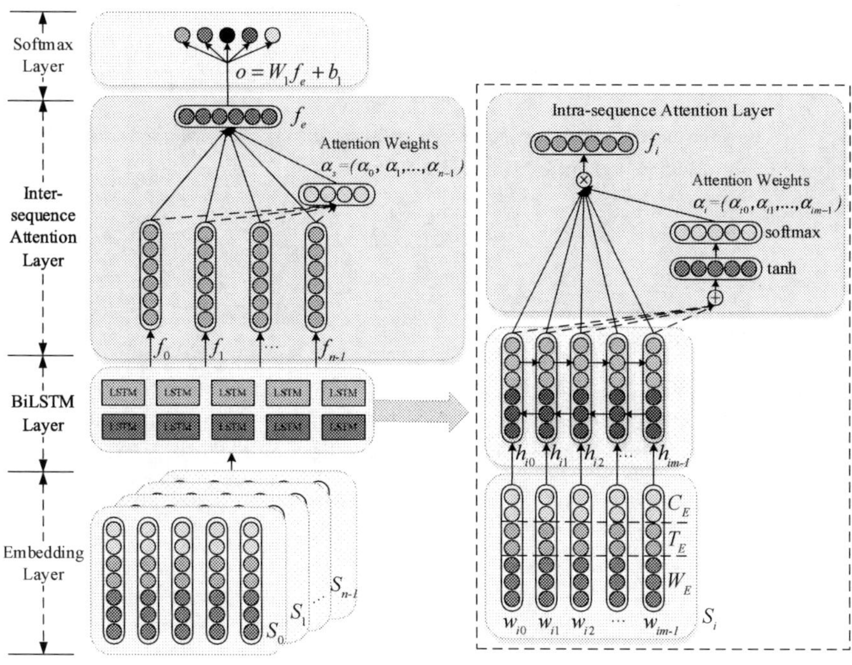

Fig. 2. Framework of event factuality detection model in discourse.

3.1 Embedding Layer

First, we encode the sentence sequence that contains the target event and corresponding features in discourse. Specifically, given the target event E, assume that the sentence sequence containing E is $(S_0, S_1, \ldots, S_{n-1})$, where $S_i = (w_{i0}, w_{i1}, \ldots, w_{im-1})$, m is the length of S_i. We transform each word w_{ij} into a real-valued vector with dimension d_w by using a word embedding matrix $W_E \in \mathbb{R}^{d_w \times |V|}$, where V is the input vocabulary.

Event Trigger: We transform each trigger tag into a vector with the dimension d_t by a matrix $T_E \in \mathbb{R}^{d_t \times |V_t|}$, where V_t is the set of trigger tags, $V_t = \{0, 1\}$, 1 denotes an event trigger, while 0 indicates a non-trigger.

Negative and Speculative Cue: Similarly, we transform each cue tag into a vector with the dimension d_c by a matrix $C_E \in \mathbb{R}^{d_c \times |V_c|}$, where V_c is the set of cue tags, $V_c = \{0, 1, 2\}$, 1 denotes a negative cue, and 2 indicates a speculative cue, while 0 represents a non-cue.

Finally, we represent the sentence sequence as a matrix $\mathrm{X} \in \mathbb{R}^{d_0 \times m}$, where $d_0 = d_w + d_t + d_c$, m is the length of the sequence.

3.2 BiLSTM Layer

To capture the contextual information of the target event in a sentence, we employ BiLSTM [15] networks to learn the forward representation $\vec{H}$ and the backward representation $\overleftarrow{H}$ of the sentence. Then, the characteristic representation of the target event $H \in \mathbb{R}^{m \times n_h}$ is obtained by splicing $\vec{H}$ and $\overleftarrow{H}$, where $n_h = 2 \times n_h^*$, and n_h^* indicates the number of the hidden layer units in the BiLSTM.

$$H = \vec{H} \oplus \overleftarrow{H} \tag{1}$$

3.3 Intra-sequence Attention Layer

We employ an intra-sequence attention mechanism [16] to learn the weight distribution of each element in the sentence, and combine the information according to the weight distribution to acquire the characteristic representation of the event $f \in \mathbb{R}^{n_h}$ in the sequence:

$$H_m = \tanh(H) \tag{2}$$

$$\alpha = \mathrm{softmax}\left(v \cdot H_m^T\right) \tag{3}$$

$$f = \tanh(\alpha \cdot H) \tag{4}$$

where tanh is the hyperbolic tangent function, "·" denotes the point multiplication operation, and $v \in \mathbb{R}^{n_h}$ are model parameters.

3.4 Inter-sequence Attention Layer

Given a target event, suppose that there are n sentences including the target event in the document, the sentence sequence can be represented as $X = (X_0, X_1, \ldots, X_{n-1})$, and the corresponding features are $F_s = (f_0, f_1, \ldots, f_{n-1})$, where $f_i = f$. To acquire the importance of different sentences on the document-level event factuality, we similarly utilize the attention mechanism to assign different weights to different sentences, and combine the sentence-level features according to the weight distribution to acquire the document-level characteristic representation of the target event $f_e \in \mathbb{R}^{n_h}$:

$$H_{ms} = \tanh(F_s) \tag{5}$$

$$\alpha_s = \mathrm{softmax}\left(v_s \cdot H_{ms}^T\right) \tag{6}$$

$$f_e = \tanh(\alpha_s \cdot F_s) \tag{7}$$

3.5 Softmax Layer

Event factuality detection is essentially a classification task, so we utilize a softmax layer as the classifier. The input of softmax layer is the document-level event characteristic representation f_e, and the output is the probability of the factuality values, as follows:

$$o = \mathrm{softmax}(W_1 f_e + b_1) \tag{8}$$

where $W_1 \in \mathbb{R}^{c \times n_h}$, $b_1 \in \mathbb{R}^c$ are model parameters, and c is the number of event factuality values. We also employ the cross-entropy cost to measure the error between the predicted value and the true value.

4 Experimentation

This section introduces experimental datasets, evaluation metrics, experimental tools and parameter settings. Then we show experimental results and demonstrate the effectiveness of the proposed approach and features.

4.1 Experimental Settings

In this paper, we adopt the English and Chinese event factuality datasets [7], which annotated the event factuality on both document-level and sentence-level. The number of English and Chinese documents are 1,730 and 4,650, respectively, which is from China Daily, Sina Bilingual News, and Sina News. Table 1 lists the distribution of event factuality categories. From lines 1–2, we can see that the *certain positive* (CT+) category includes the largest number of instances, accounting for 66.5% (English) and 51.7% (Chinese), while *possible negative* (PS−) and *underspecified* (Un) are only about 1%. Therefore, we mainly evaluate and compare the performances of the system in the CT+, CT− and PS+.

In addition, to find the difference of event factuality between sentence-level and document-level, we statistic the number of documents that meet the following conditions: for the same event, there are n sentences in the document whose factuality is different from the document-level (lines 3–7 in Table 1). We can see that (1) in 25.4% (English) and 37.8% (Chinese) of documents, the annotations of the sentence-level factuality of the same event are inconsistent with the document-level, which indicates that identifying event factuality only on sentence-level may lead to conflict; and (2) in such documents, there are more CT− and PS+ categories (document-level) and fewer CT+ categories.

Table 1. Statistics of dataset (#document).

Items	Chinese						English					
	CT+	CT−	PS+	PS−	Un	Total	CT+	CT−	PS+	PS−	Un	Total
Discourse	2,403	1,342	848	36	21	4,650	1,150	279	274	12	15	1,730
Sentence	11,487	3,924	2,879	123	593	19,006	4,401	662	574	37	81	5,575
n = 0	2,066	487	319	9	9	2,890	1,026	164	93	2	5	1,290
n = 1	231	390	269	10	5	905	108	56	91	5	4	264
n = 2	68	217	159	9	4	457	12	28	54	2	2	100
n = 3	17	126	54	2	1	200	1	15	22	1	1	40
n ≥ 4	21	122	47	6	2	198	8	17	15	2	0	36

We use a fixed 80%/10%/10% split for training, developing, and testing, respectively. For measurement, traditional Precision, Recall, and F1-score are used to evaluate the performance in event factuality detection. In addition, the Macro-Averaging and Micro-Averaging is also adopted to evaluate the average performance over three factuality categories from different aspects.

The Chinese negative and speculative cues adopt in this paper are annotated in the CNeSp[1] corpus [17], and the English are from the BioScope[2] corpus [18]. We employ ELMo[3] as the pre-trained word embeddings with the dimension 1,024. In our experiment, the dependency syntax paths of the Chinese are generated by the Chinese language processing toolkit[4], and the part-of-speech and dependency syntax paths of English are generated by the Stanford CoreNLP[5]. Besides, we set the hidden units in LSTM $n_h^* = 100$ and the dimension of the event triggers, negative and speculative cues as 100 and 200, respectively. Other parameters are initialized randomly, and all the models are optimized using the stochastic gradient descent (SGD) with momentum.

To verify the effectiveness of our approach, we compare several baselines on event factuality detection, which are briefly introduced as follows.

1 http://nlp.suda.edu.cn/corpus/CNeSp/.

2 http://www.inf.u-szeged.hu/rgai/bioscope.

3 https://github.com/HIT-SCIR/ELMoForManyLangs.

4 http://hlt-la.suda.edu.cn.

5 https://stanfordnlp.github.io/CoreNLP/index.html.

BiLSTM: The BiLSTM model with word embeddings.
BiLSTM+Att: The attention-based BiLSTM model with word embeddings.
BiLSTM+Att_E: The attention-based BiLSTM model with word embeddings and event trigger embeddings.
BiLSTM+Att_C: The attention-based BiLSTM model with word embeddings and negative and speculative cues embeddings.
BiLSTM+Att_E_C: The attention-based BiLSTM model with word embeddings, event trigger embeddings, negative and speculative cues embeddings.
Att+Adv: The document-level approach [7] based on adversarial networks with the dependency syntax path of the cues in adjacent sentences to the target event.
BiLSTM+Att+J: The joint learning model, which adds an identical network structure (sentence-level channel) to the framework shown in Fig. 2 (document-level channel). In the sentence-level channel, only the current sentence including the target event is considered, and features are the same as the document-level channel.

4.2 Results and Analysis

Effect of Various Models. Tables 2 and 3 show the performances of systems on event factuality detection. We can see that, our approach (BiLSTM+Att_E_C) achieved 86.67% and 86.97% of F1 scores (Micro-Average), yielding improvements of 3.24% and 4.78% over the state-of-the-art on English and Chinese datasets, respectively, which indicates that comparing with the Att-Adv, our approach is simpler and more effective. It does not need to use syntactic structure information to avoid introducing feature-level noise and enhance generalization.

In addition, the comparative tests show that: (1) On all models, the CT+ category has the highest performance, followed by CT−, and PS+ has the lowest. The main reason is that there are more authentic, less rigorous or false reports in news texts; (2) the BiLSTM+Att model outperforms the BiLSTM model, with 2.86% gain in Macro-Average, which indicates that attention mechanism can capture the latent correlations among the event sequence and demonstrates the effectiveness of attention mechanism for this task; (3) the performances of the joint learning model are slightly lower than the best. The reason may be that sentences in the document have different factuality descriptions of the same event, and there is no inevitable connection with the document-level event factuality.

Table 2. Performances on English event factuality detection (P%/R%/F1%).

Models	CT+	CT−	PS+	Macro-Average	Micro-Average
BiLSTM	76.51/93.18/84.00	64.93/58.06/60.49	58.17/22.23/31.78	66.54/57.82/61.87	73.12/75.30/74.19
BiLSTM+Att	81.11/93.64/86.91	71.13/59.68/64.81	74.48/53.71/62.40	75.57/69.01/72.13	78.84/80.95/79.88
BiLSTM+Att_E_C	90.45/90.08/90.26	**78.68/88.21/83.14**	**78.88/77.41/78.06**	**82.67/85.23/83.93**	**85.77/87.59/86.67**
Att+Adv (Qian)	87.28/91.18/83.25	80.57/76.26/77.82	66.81/60.98/62.61	78.22/76.14/76.49	82.77/83.75/83.25
BiLSTM+Att +J	**86.17/95.91/90.74**	80.99/77.42/78.82	87.74/66.66/75.75	84.97/79.99/82.38	85.26/87.80/86.51

Table 3. Performances on Chinese event factuality detection (P%/R%/F1%).

Models	CT+	CT−	PS+	Macro-Average	Micro-Average
BiLSTM	76.58/88.03/81.91	80.73/72.43/76.33	71.57/57.22/63.59	76.29/72.56/74.38	76.89/77.39/77.14
BiLSTM+Att	80.07/89.10/84.33	85.26/76.47/80.59	72.96/63.89/68.10	79.43/76.49/77.92	80.17/80.43/80.30
BiLSTM+Att_E_C	**89.00/91.71/90.28**	84.64/86.34/85.42	82.09/75.18/78.35	85.24/84.41/84.81	**86.45/87.49/86.97**
Att+Adv (Qian)	83.89/89.33/86.49	80.96/79.79/80.30	77.08/67.12/71.44	80.64/78.75/79.41	81.94/82.45/82.19
BiLSTM+Att +J	87.12/92.52/89.74	**84.76/87.50/86.09**	**86.26/72.23/78.52**	**86.05/84.08/85.05**	86.22/87.07/86.64

Effect of Different Features. We discover that the event triggers in English datasets are mostly verbs and the corresponding part-of-speech can represent the tense to a certain degree. Therefore, we added the part-of-speech of the trigger as the tense feature to the model.

BiLSTM+Att_E_C_P: The attention-based BiLSTM model with word embed-dings, event trigger embeddings, cue embeddings, and part-of-speech of the trigger.

Dual_Path: The two-channel learning model based on the model proposed in this paper. The characteristics of channel one are the same as the BiLSTM-Att_E_C model, and the characteristics of channel two are the dependent syntax path of the negative or speculative cues in adjacent sentences to the target event.

Table 4 shows the comparison of the BiLSTM+Att models with different feature embeddings. We can see that (1) the performances are significantly improved when adding the characteristics of event triggers, negative and speculative cues. It indicates that such features provide the obvious help for event factuality identification; (2) when adding the part-of-speech features, the performances are slightly reduced in English datasets, the reason may be that the part-of-speech can not effectively represent the tense of events; (3) when adding the Dependent syntax path, the performances are reduced, which may be that there is no semantic connection between the cues in adjacent sentences and the target event.

Table 4. Effect of features on event factuality detection (P%/R%/F1%).

Features	English		Chinese	
	Macro-Average	Micro-Average	Macro-Average	Micro-Average
BiLSTM+Att	75.57/69.01/72.13	78.84/80.95/79.88	79.43/76.49/77.92	80.17/80.43/80.30
BiLSTM+Att_E	76.07/75.12/75.59	81.31/83.73/82.50	79.87/76.64/78.21	80.44/81.09/80.76
BiLSTM+Att _C	81.89/79.92/80.88	83.59/85.91/84.73	82.46/82.94/82.70	83.60/84.20/83.90
BiLSTM+Att _E_C	**82.67/85.23/83.93**	**85.77/87.59/86.67**	**85.24/84.41/84.81**	**86.45/87.49/86.97**
BiLSTM+Att _E_C_P	84.10/78.87/81.39	84.75/87.10/85.91	N/A	N/A
Dual_Path	81.94/74.46/77.97	82.37/84.82/83.57	81.28/79.38/80.30	81.93/82.28/82.11

5 Conclusion

In this paper, we propose a document-level approach on event factuality detection, which employs BiLSTM neural networks to learn contextual information of event in sentences. Moreover, we utilize a double-layer attention mechanism to capture the latent correlation features among the event sequence in the discourse and identify event factuality according to the whole document. Experiments on both English and Chinese event factuality detection datasets demonstrate the effectiveness of our approach. In the future, we will explore how to better extract and represent the tense and the source of events. On the other hand, self-attention mechanisms can effectively learn the internal structure information in sequence. Thus how to transfer the self-attention mechanism to the document-level event factuality detection is also needs to be explored.

Acknowledgments. This research was supported by National Natural Science Foundation of China (Grants No. 61703293, No. 61672368, No. 61751206). The authors would like to thank the anonymous reviewers for their insightful comments and suggestions.

References

1. Saurí, R., Verhagen, M., Pustejovsky, J.: Annotating and recognizing event modality in text. In: Proceedings of 19th International FLAIRS Conference (2006)
2. Wiebe, J., Wilson, T., Cardie, C.: Annotating expressions of opinions and emotions in language. Lang. Resour. Eval. **39**(2–3), 165–210 (2005)
3. Klenner, M., Clematide, S.: How factuality determines sentiment inferences. In: Proceedings of the Fifth Joint Conference on Lexical and Computational Semantics, pp. 75–84 (2016)
4. Qazvinian, V., Rosengren, E., Radev, D.R., et al.: Rumor has it: identifying misinformation in microblogs. In: Proceedings of the Conference on Empirical Methods in Natural Language Processing, pp. 1589–1599. Association for Computational Linguistics (2011)
5. Cao, Y., Zhu, Q., Li, P.: 3D Representation of Chinese event factuality. In: Proceedings of the 15th Chinese Lexical Semantic Workshop, pp. 7–13 (2014)
6. Qian, Z., Li, P., Zhang, Y., et al.: Event factuality identification via generative adversarial networks with auxiliary classification. In: IJCAI, pp. 4293–4300 (2018)
7. Qian, Z.: Research on Methods of Event Factuality Identification. Soochow University, Jiangsu (2018). (in Chinese)
8. Minard, A.L., Speranza, M., Urizar, R., et al.: MEANTIME, the NewsReader multilingual event and time corpus (2016)
9. Minard, A.L., Speranza, M., Caselli, T., et al.: The EVALITA 2016 event factuality annotation task (FactA). In: Final Workshop 7 December 2016, Naples, vol. 32 (2016)
10. Minard, A.L., Speranza, M., Sprugnoli, R., et al.: FacTA: evaluation of event factuality and temporal anchoring. In: Proceedings of the 2nd Italian Conference on Computational Linguistics, pp. 187–192 (2015)
11. Saurí, R., Pustejovsky, J.: FactBank: a corpus annotated with event factuality. Lang. Resour. Eval. **43**(3), 227 (2009)

12. Saurí, R.: A factuality profiler for eventualities in text. Unveröffentlichte Dissertation, Brandeis University. Zugriff auf, vol. 1 (2008). http://www.cs.brandeis.edu/~roser/pubs/sauriDiss
13. Cao, Y., Zhu, Q., Li, P.: The construction of Chinese event factuality corpus. J. Chin. Inf. Process. **27**(6), 38–44 (2012). (in Chinese)
14. He, T., Li, P., Zhu, Q.: Approach to identify Chinese event factuality. J. Chin. Inf. Process. **44**(5), 241–244+256 (2017). (in Chinese)
15. Graves, A., Schmidhuber, J.: Framewise phoneme classification with bidirectional LSTM and other neural network architectures. Neural Netw. **18**(5), 602–610 (2005)
16. Bahdanau, D., Cho, K., Bengio, Y.: Neural machine translation by jointly learning to align and translate. In: ICLR (2015)
17. Zou, B., Zhu, Q., Zhou, G.: Negation and speculation identification in Chinese language. In: Proceedings of the 53rd Annual Meeting of the Association for Computational Linguistics and the 7th International Joint Conference on Natural Language Processing (Volume 1: Long Papers), vol. 1, pp. 656–665 (2015)
18. Vincze, V., Szarvas, G., Farkas, R., et al.: The BioScope corpus: biomedical texts annotated for uncertainty, negation and their scopes. BMC Bioinform. **9**(11), S9 (2008)

A Multi-pattern Matching Algorithm for Chinese-Hmong Mixed Strings

Shun-Ping He, Li-Ping Mo(✉), and Di-Wen Kang

College of Information Science & Engineering,
Jishou University, Jishou 416000, Hunan, China
zmx89@jsu.edu.cn

Abstract. To solve the problem of rapid retrieval of Chinese-Hmong mixed text, a multi-pattern matching algorithm in double-bytes unit combined with the idea of AC algorithm and the mismatch processing strategy of Horspool algorithm is proposed for the Chinese-Hmong mixed strings. In this algorithm, a deterministic finite automaton is constructed based on the pattern-set according to the idea of AC algorithm, and the moving distance of the pattern is calculated by the bad-character rule of the Horspool algorithm, and the text is only traversed once to complete the quick search task of all patterns by using the finite automata. The experimental results show that the proposed algorithm has a good performance in multi-pattern matching for Chinese-Hmong mixed texts in different scale, even for the mixed texts containing more than 100,000 characters, the matching efficiency is also significantly higher than the AC algorithm.

Keywords: Natural language processing · Multi-pattern matching · AC algorithm · Horspool algorithm

1 Introduction

Square Hmong characters were created in the late Qing Dynasty of China and have been mainly used in the Hmong settlements such as Wuling Mountain District. Hmong informatization is one of great significances to promote the development of the local national cultural tourism industry and the digital protection of the intangible heritage of the Hmong culture. Information retrieval is a bottleneck to hinder the further research of the Hmong informatization. A high-performance pattern matching algorithm for strings is crucial to realize the fast retrieval of the square Hmong information.

According to the word formation, a square Hmong character represents a morpheme or word [1]. The square Hmong words in practical applications mainly containing single character or two characters, and few words containing 3 characters or more. Moreover, the square Hmong characters are usually mixed with Chinese characters, appear in the Chinese-Hmong songbook and script. The information retrieval mainly searches for a meaningful square Hmong string or Chinese-Hmong string from the mixed text. Obviously, compared to English, the mixed character set of the square Hmong characters and Chinese characters is a large character set, and the probability that the Chinese-Hmong string is repeated in the text is very low, so mismatches are common. In previous research, Zeng et al. proposed a Horspool extension algorithm for

J. Tang et al. (Eds.): NLPCC 2019, LNAI 11839, pp. 415–425, 2019.
https://doi.org/10.1007/978-3-030-32236-6_37

matching the square Hmong string [2]. This algorithm directly extend a byte unit to a word unit, and treats the double-bytes of square Hmong character as a whole. Only when the double bytes are completely equal, it is regarded as a square Hmong character matched. The experimental results show that the mentioned algorithm can solve the string search problem of square Hmong text. However, the algorithm is a single-pattern matching algorithm, which cannot search for multiple Chinese-Hmong mixed strings in text at one time. This paper presents an AC-EH algorithm, which combines the above Horspool extension algorithm with the AC algorithm, and can used to solve the multi-pattern matching problem of Chinese-Hmong mixed strings.

The rest of this paper is organized as follows. Section 2 introduces the basic principles of AC algorithm and Horspool algorithm. Section 3 depicts the proposed AC-EH algorithm. Section 4 verifies the feasibility of proposed algorithm by using the case study and experiment analysis. Section 5 concludes the paper.

2 Principles of AC Algorithm and Horspool Algorithm

2.1 AC Algorithm

Aho-Corasick automata algorithm (AC algorithm) is one of the most famous multi-pattern matching algorithms, and it utilizes the common prefix relationship among patterns to achieve efficient jumps in pattern mismatch. To some extent, AC algorithm can be regarded as an extension of the KMP algorithm in a multi-pattern context, but it has far better performance than the KMP algorithm [3, 4]. Similar to the contribution of the KMP algorithm to the field of single pattern matching, AC algorithm has had a profound impact on the development of multi-pattern matching algorithms, it and its improved algorithms are still widely applied in various fields of pattern matching.

AC algorithm is based on the Deterministic Finite Automata (DFA) constructed according to the pattern-set, and converts the comparison of characters into the transition of the states of the DFA. The AC automata is represented as a six-tuple $M = (K, A, g, f, S, Z)$, where the following hold.

(1) K is a finite set, and each element of it is called a state.
(2) A is a finite alphabet set, and each element of it is called an input symbol.
(3) g is a state transition function, which is a map on $K \times A \rightarrow K$, corresponding to the function *goto*.
(4) f is a failure function, which is also a map on $K \times A \rightarrow K$, indicating a state transition when a pattern mismatch occurs, corresponding to the function *failure*.
(5) $S \in K$, is the only initial state.
(6) $Z \subset K$, is the final state set. The final state marked as double circles is also called an acceptable state or an ending state, corresponding to the function *output*.

The AC algorithm first preprocesses the pattern-set, establishes a function table corresponding to the functions *goto*, *failure* and *output*, and constructs a DFA used for pattern matching with a mismatch pointer accordingly. Then, with the DFA, the three functions described above are used to scan the text to be matched to find all occurrence positions of each pattern in the text. If the current state fails to match, it goes to the state indicated by the mismatch pointer of the current state, and the matching is continued.

AC algorithm eliminates the influence of the pattern-set size on the matching speed by preprocessing. For the text T to be matched with length n and the pattern-set $P = \{p_1, p_2, p_3, \ldots, p_q\}$ with q patterns, AC algorithm only needs to scan T once to complete the searching for each pattern in P without backtracking, and can find all the patterns that have been successfully matched. Obviously, the time complexity of the AC algorithm is only related to the length n of T, is $O(n)$.

2.2 Horspool Algorithm

The Horspool algorithm is derived from the BM algorithm. The BM algorithm with a time complexity of $O(n)$ is one of the most famous single pattern matching algorithms, which calculates the maximum value of pattern shift distance using bad-character rule and good-suffix rule at the same time [5]. Due to skipping a lot of characters that don't need to match, the performance of the BM algorithm is 3–5 times better than that of the KMP algorithm in practical applications [6, 7]. There are many improved versions of the BM algorithm [8–12], and the Horspool algorithm is one of them, which fixes the last character of the current matching-window as a bad-character, and only uses the bad-character rule to calculate the moving distance of the pattern [12]. Because the calculation of the distance based on good-suffix rule and the selection of the maximum value in BM algorithm are all avoided, its efficiency is significantly higher than that of the BM algorithm in practical applications.

For simplicity, the substring currently matched in T to be matched is denoted as $T[i]\ldots T[i+m-1]$. Where, i is the starting position of the substring, and $0 \leq i \leq n-m$. $T[i]\ldots T[i+m-1]$ is also called a matching-window. Suppose $T[i+j]$ and $P[j]$ represent the currently processed character in T and P, respectively. Where, j is the matching position of the substring, and $0 \leq j \leq m-1$. The algorithm takes the last character $T[i+m-1]$ in window as a bad-character, and compares it with the last character $P[m-1]$ of the pattern. If the matching successes, the algorithm continues to compare the remaining characters in T and P one by one from right to left until they are completely equal or there is a mismatch at a certain character position. If the matching fails, $T[i+m-1]$ acts as a bad-character, and the algorithm tries to find the last position $k(-1 \leq k \leq m-2)$ where the bad-character $T[i+m-1]$ appears in P, and then moves P to the position where $T[i+m-1]$ and $P[k]$ are aligned, and the next match will be continued.

To get the moving distance the pattern, for each character in T, the rightmost k of the positions it appears in P, and the distance of position k from $P[m-1]$ must be stored in advance. This distance is denoted as $shift[P[k]]$, which indicates the moving distance of P when $T[i+m-1]$ is a bad-character, and is calculated by the following Eq. (1).

$$shif[P[k]] = m-1-k \quad (-1 \leq k \leq m-2) \tag{1}$$

In Eq. (1), $k = -1$ means that the current character does not appear in P, and the moving distance P is m.

Horspool algorithm performs character comparison from right to left, shifts the pattern from left to right, and fixes the last character of the current matching-window as a bad-character, and only needs to scan the text T to be matched once to find all the substrings that match the pattern, so the time complexity is $O(n)$. Obviously, the more common the character mismatch, the better the performance of the Horspool algorithm.

3 Proposed AC-EH Algorithm

3.1 Basic Principle of AC-EH Algorithm

The proposed AC-EH algorithm takes double-bytes as a matching-unit to execute matching for Chinese-Hmong mixed strings by combining the basic idea of AC algorithm with the mismatch processing strategy of Horspool algorithm. Similar to the AC algorithm, the AC-EH algorithm preprocesses the pattern-set before performing matching, that is, constructs three lookup tables corresponding to functions *goto*, *output*, and *shift* based on the pattern-set. The values of the three tables will be filled in during the calculation of the three functions. And then, the algorithm includes three stages. Firstly, the DFA is constructed and the corresponding functions *goto* and *output* are calculated according to the basic AC algorithm. Secondly, the function *shift* of the pattern is generated by using the bad-character heuristic rule of Horspool algorithm. Finally, the pattern matching is operated on the DFA. In the matching process, the functions *goto*, *output* and *shift* are used to scan the text to be matched and search for the patterns by moving DFA. When a mismatch occurs, the last character in the matching-window is fixed as a bad-character according to the mismatch processing strategy of the Horspool algorithm and the bad-character-based heuristic rule, and the pattern is moved based on the *shift* value of the current bad-character, and the matching is continued.

3.2 Construction of DFA and Calculation of Function *goto*

Construction of DFA and calculation of function *goto* are crossed. AC-EH algorithm creates an initial state 0 of the DFA, and starts from the initial state 0, for each pattern $p_i[1...Len]$ of the pattern-set P $(1 \le i \le q)$, generates the value of the function *goto* and other states of DFA. Suppose that the length of the text T to be matched is n, the pattern-set with q patterns is $P = \{p_1, p_2, p_3, ..., p_q\}$, and the maximum and minimum lengths of each pattern in P are *MaxLen* and *MinLen*, respectively. Let's denote the current state as D_k, the steps for generating DFA and function *goto* are as follows.

Step1: Take the initial state 0 as D_k.
Step2: When D_k faces the input character $p_i[j]$ $(1 \le j \le Len)$, it is checked whether there is such a state D_t in the direct successors of D_k (i.e. $goto(D_k, p_i[j]) = D_t$). If it does, goto Step3, otherwise, goto Step4.
Step3: $D_k = D_t$, take the next character $p_i[j+1]$ as the current input character, and goto Step2.
Step4: Construct $goto(D_k, p_i[j]) = D_t$ and check if the current input character is the last character $p_i[Len]$ of the pattern p_i. If yes, goto Step5; otherwise, goto Step3.
Step5: D_t is denoted as the final state.

3.3 Calculation of Function *Output* and Function *Shift*

Assume that the current state D_k is a final state, and there is a path from the initial state 0 to the state D_k. If all characters on the path are sequentially connected to obtain the string t_1, then $output(D_k) = t_1$.

In the process of pattern matching with DFA, if the input character a is faced in the current state D_k, and a state D_t that makes $goto(D_k, a) = D_t$ is not found, the *shift* value is calculated by the following Eq. (2).

$$shift(a) = \begin{cases} Min\{j|P_k[j] = a, 1 < j \leq MinLen, 1 \leq k \leq q)\} & a \text{ is as a non-first character of string in the pattern} \\ MinLen & \text{others} \end{cases} \quad (2)$$

3.4 Description of AC-EH Algorithm

The AC-EH algorithm steps of multi-pattern matching using DFA for Chinese-Hmong mixed strings are as follows:

Step1: Preprocess pattern-set, generate functions *goto* and *output*, and construct DFA.

Step2: Traverse DFA, calculate the *shift* value of each character in T according to Eq. (2), and record it in the *shift* table.

Step3: Align the last character of the pattern p_{MinLen} with a length of *MinLen* in DFA with the last character of T, take the character a in the position where T is aligned with the first character of p_{MinLen} as the current character, and let the matching pointer point to a.

Step4: Take the initial state 0 as the current state D_k, record the position *Pos* of the character a in T, and move the matching pointer from a, then match characters one by one from left to right.

Step5: If match fails, move both pointer and DFA to the left based on the *shift* value at the position of character a, and then goto Step4. Otherwise, $D_k = goto(D_k, a)$, that is, take the next state $goto(D_k, a)$ as the current state.

Step6: Check if state D_k is a final state. If yes, call the function *output*, store the value of $output(D_k)$ and *Pos* value in the *output* table, then move the pointer and DFA to the left to *MinLen* characters, and then goto Step4. Otherwise, take the next character in T as the current character a, start the next comparison.

Step7: End the matching process. At this time, if the *output* table is empty, it means that T does not contain any pattern in P. Otherwise, the contents of the *output* table are just those patterns in P that appear in T.

4 Case Study and Related Experiment Analysis

4.1 Case Study

Given the Chinese-Hmong mixed text T to be matched and the pattern-set $P = \{p_1, p_2, p_3, p_4, p_5\}$ as shown in Fig. 1. The *MinLen* value of the pattern in P is 5. The *shift* value of each character in T is calculated according to Eq. (2) as shown in Fig. 2.

T = "东方居毬飞生肖打癞房星尾东方算在哪堂东方打毬飞"
$P = \{p_1, p_2, p_3, p_4, p_5\}$
p_1 = "东方居毬飞", p_2 = "东方打毬飞", p_3 = "东方打生肖",
p_4 = "东方算星尾", p_5 = "东方算在哪堂"

Fig. 1. The content of the text T and the pattern-set P

Character	东	方	居	毬	飞	生	肖	打	癞	房	星	尾	算	在	哪	堂
Shift Value	5	1	2	3	4	3	4	2	5	5	3	4	2	3	4	5

Fig. 2. The *shift* value of each character in T

The following Figs. 3, 4, 5, 6 and 7 show the execution of the AC-EH algorithm.

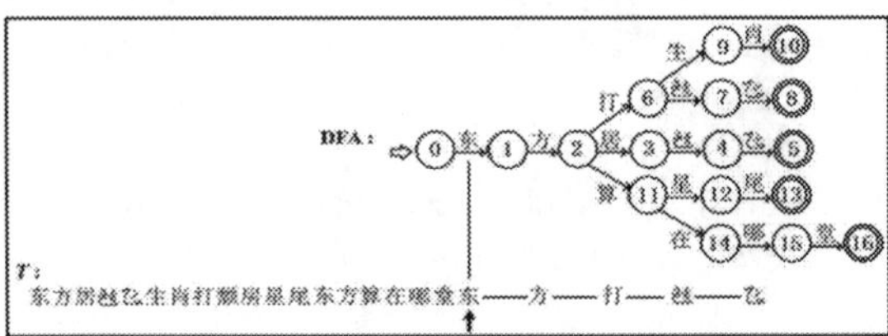

Fig. 3. The 1st diagram of algorithm execution case

In Fig. 3, since the *MinLen* value is 5, the last 5 characters of T are aligned with the characters of the shortest pattern in the DFA. Starting from the initial state 0 in DFA and the current character '东' in T, the pointer is moved from left to right. The comparison in a character-by-character manner is done. When the final state 8 is reached, the pattern p_2 matches successfully. At this time, the *output* value of the final state 8 is p_2, and the position where p_2 appears in T is 19. Then, values p_2 and 19 are stored in the output table. And then, according to *MinLen* value, the pointer and the DFA are both moved 5 character-positions to the left as shown in Fig. 4.

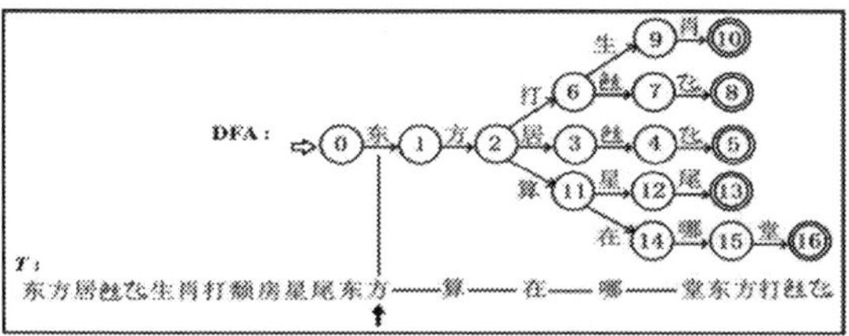

Fig. 4. The 2nd diagram of algorithm execution case

In Fig. 4, matching is performed from the initial state 0. At this time, the current character '方' in T does not match the character '东' in the aligned position of DFA. Since the *shift* value of the character '方' is 1, the pointer and the DFA are both moved 1 character-position to the left as shown in Fig. 5.

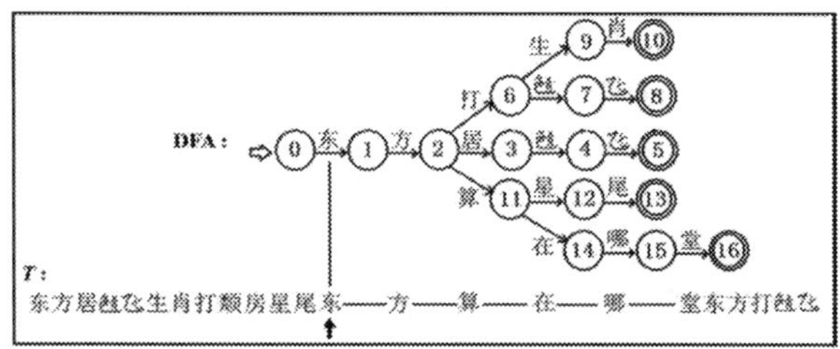

Fig. 5. The 3rd diagram of algorithm execution case

In Fig. 5, matching is performed from the initial state 0. At this time, the current character '东' in T matches the character '东' of the aligned position in the DFA. Starting from the character '东'', the pointer is moved from left to right, and the comparison in a character-by-character manner is done again. When the final state 16 is reached, the pattern p_5 matches successfully. At this time, the *output* value of the final state 16 is p_5, and the position where p_5 appears in T is 13. Then values p_5 and 13 are stored in the *output* table. According to *MinLen* value, the pointer and the DFA are both moved 5 character-positions to the left as shown in Fig. 6.

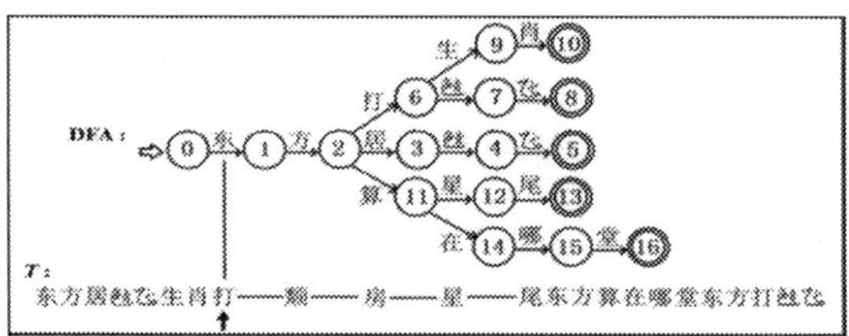

Fig. 6. The 4th diagram of algorithm execution case

In Fig. 6, similar to the method described above, the pointer and the DFA are both moved to the left by 2, 3, and 2 character-positions in sequence until the current character '东' in T matches the character '东' of the aligned position in the DFA (as shown in Fig. 7). Starting from the character '东', the matching pointer is moved from left to right, the comparison in a character-by-character manner is done again. When the final state 5 is reached, the pattern p_1 matches successfully. At this time, the *output* value of the final state 5 is p_1, and the position where p_1 appears in T is 1. Then, values p_1 and 1 are also stored in the output table. Finally, the matching is completed and the result is obtained by *output* table, that is, $\{(p_2,19), (p_5, 13), (p_1,1)\}$.

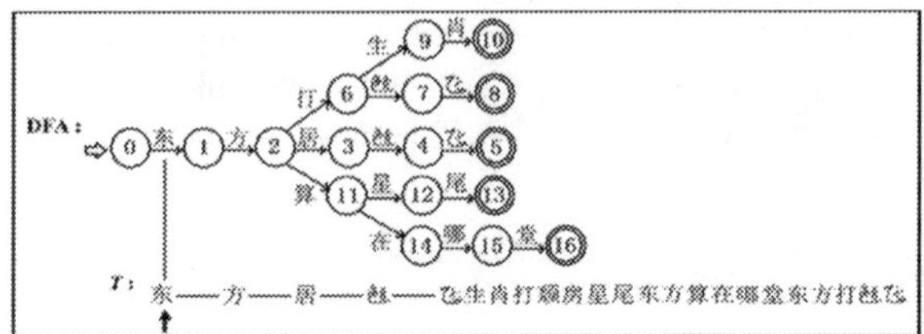

Fig. 7. The 5th diagram of algorithm execution case

4.2 Experiment Analysis

AC-EH algorithm was implemented in Java, all multi-pattern matching experiments were carried out under the conditions of Intel(R) Core(TM) i5-3470 CPU @ 3.20 GHz, 4G memory and Win7 operating system. For the pattern-set composed of 5 patterns of length 1–10 and 3 mixed texts T_1, T_2 and T_3 to be matched with lengths of 5185, 37770 and 147645 words, both AC-EH algorithm and AC algorithm had an accuracy of 100%. Time-consuming data of two algorithms in experiments are shown in Table 1. The *TNo*, *TLen*, *PLen*$_1$-*PLen*$_5$, *AC-EH_Time*(ms), and *AC_Time*(ms) in the table respectively represent the number and length of the text to be matched, length of the five patterns, and time-consuming data of the AC-EH algorithm and the AC algorithm.

Table 1. Time-consuming comparison of two algorithms

TNo	*TLen*	*PLen*$_1$	*PLen*$_2$	*PLen*$_3$	*PLen*$_4$	*PLen*$_5$	*AC-EH_Time*	*AC_Time*
T_1	5185	1	1	1	1	1	6.770030	6.825193
		2	2	2	2	2	5.965028	6.885809
		3	3	3	3	3	5.200117	6.930709
		4	4	4	4	4	5.007366	6.795045
		5	5	5	5	5	5.067660	6.975610
		6	6	6	6	6	4.819424	6.507041
		7	7	7	7	7	4.885172	7.446423
		8	8	8	8	8	4.778373	7.305949
		9	9	9	9	9	5.080809	7.562844
		10	10	10	10	10	5.071509	7.551619

(*continued*)

Table 1. (*continued*)

TNo	*TLen*	$PLen_1$	$PLen_2$	$PLen_3$	$PLen_4$	$PLen_5$	*AC-EH_Time*	*AC_Time*
T_2	37770	1	1	1	1	1	13.082075	10.677013
		2	2	2	2	2	9.653281	10.356616
		3	3	3	3	3	8.607421	11.226723
		4	4	4	4	4	7.597803	10.621849
		5	5	5	5	5	8.734105	11.134998
		6	6	6	6	6	7.187924	10.582401
		7	7	7	7	7	7.051941	11.020822
		8	8	8	8	8	6.687605	10.877140
		9	9	9	9	9	7.169965	11.508313
		10	10	10	10	10	6.850209	11.037500
T_3	147645	1	1	1	1	1	31.151309	19.064743
		2	2	2	2	2	26.267099	16.522093
		3	3	3	3	3	21.268714	16.583350
		4	4	4	4	4	19.912399	17.339282
		5	5	5	5	5	17.442873	16.643965
		6	6	6	6	6	16.167058	16.615101
		7	7	7	7	7	16.362695	17.449288
		8	8	8	8	8	15.448009	17.432931
		9	9	9	9	9	15.641402	19.183729
		10	10	10	10	10	14.888356	17.025298

According to Table 1, the time-consuming line chart of the two algorithms for matching different length patterns is shown in Fig. 8.

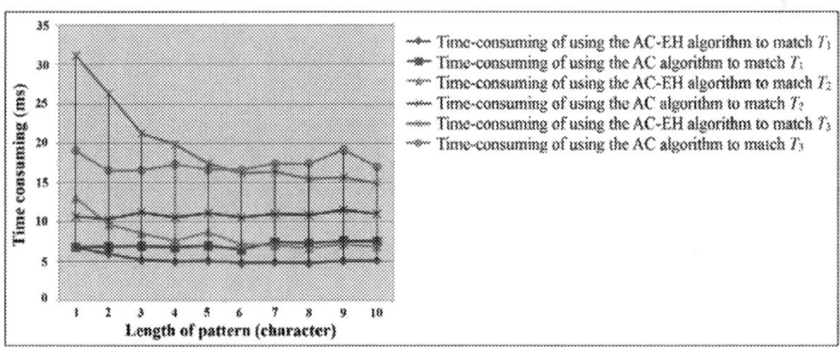

Fig. 8. Time-consuming of two algorithms for patterns with different length

From Table 1 and Fig. 8, it is easy to find that: (1) When the text such as T_1 to be matched is very short, the time performance of the AC-EH algorithm is significantly better than that of the AC algorithm regardless of the pattern length. (2) When the text to be matched is longer but the pattern is relatively shorter (for case, T_2 matches the pattern with length 1, T_3 matches the pattern of length 1–5), the time performance of the AC-EH algorithm is slightly inferior to the AC algorithm. (3) When the length of the pattern is gradually increased (for case, T_2 matches the pattern with the length 2 to 10, T_3 matches the pattern with the length 6 to 10), the time performance of the AC algorithm remains basically stable, and that of the AC-EH algorithm is gradually improved, which is significantly better than that of the AC algorithm.

In summary, the matching speed of the AC-EH algorithm is significantly faster than that of the AC algorithm when the length of Chinese-Hmong mixed text and pattern is increased to a certain extent. Even for the Chinese-Hmong mixed text containing more than 100,000 words, the performance of the AC-EH algorithm can be better. Considering that the length of Chinese-Hmong mixed texts in the actual application are rarely more than 100,000 words, and the patterns that need to be searched (such as a lyrics) is usually longer, the AC-EH algorithm is suitable for solving the problem of multi-pattern matching for Chinese-Hmong mixed strings.

5 Conclusions and Future Work

This paper proposes a multi-pattern matching algorithm for Chinese-Hmong mixed strings by combining AC algorithm with Horspool extension algorithm. This algorithm is simple, easy to implement, has high matching efficiency, and suitable for realizing the rapid retrieval technology of Chinese-Hmong mixed text. In the future, we intend to study the parallel fuzzy search algorithm for Chinese-Hmong mixed strings with fuzzy Petri net.

Acknowledgments. This work was supported by the National Natural Science Foundation of Hunan Province (No. 2019JJ40234), the Natural Science Foundation of China (No. 61462029), the Research Study and Innovative Experimental Project for College Students in Hunan Province (No. 20180599) and the Research Study and Innovative Experimental Project for College Students in Jishou University (No. JDCX20180122).

References

1. Yang, Z.B., Luo, H.Y.: On the folk coinage of characters of the Miao people in Xiangxi area. J. Jishou Univ. (Soc. Sci. Edn.) **29**(6), 130–134 (2008)
2. Zeng, L., Mo, L.P., Liu, B.Y., et al.: Extended Horspool algorithm and its application in square Hmong string pattern matching. J. Jishou Univ. (Nat. Sci. Edn.) **39**(4), 150–156 (2018)
3. Aho, A.V., Corasick, M.J.: Efficient string matching: an aid to bibliographic search. Commun. ACM **18**(6), 333–340 (1975)
4. Han, G.H., Zeng, C.: Theoretical research of KMP algorithm. Microelectron. Comput. **30**(4), 30–33 (2013)
5. Boyer, R.S., Moore, J.S.: A fast string searching algorithm. Commun. ACM **20**(10), 762–772 (1977)

6. Cole, R., Hariharan, R., Paterson, M., Zwick, U.: Tighter lower bounds on the exact complexity of string matching. SIAM J. Comput. **24**(6), 30–45 (1995)
7. Cole, R., Hariharan, R.: Tighter upper bounds on the exact complexity of string matching. SIAM J. Comput. **26**(3), 803–856 (1997)
8. Zhao, X., He, L.F., Wang, X., et al.: An efficient pattern matching algorithm for string searching. J. Shanxi Univ. Sci. Technol. (Nat. Sci. Edn.) **35**(1), 183–187 (2017)
9. Guibas, L.J., Odlyzko, A.M.: A new proof of the linearity of the Boyer-Moore string searching algorithm. SIAM J. Comput. **9**(4), 672–682 (1980)
10. Sunday, D.M.: A very fast substring search algorithm. Commun. ACM **33**(8), 132–142 (1990)
11. Wang, W.X.: Research and improvement of the BM pattern matching algorithm. J. Shanxi Normal Univ. (Nat. Sci. Edn.) **32**(1), 37–39 (2017)
12. Horspool, R.N.: Practical fast searching in strings. Softw.-Pract. Exper. **10**(6), 501–506 (1980)

Constructing the Image Graph of Tang Poetry

Bihua Wang[1,2(✉)], Renfen Hu[1,2], and Lijiao Yang[1,2]

[1] Institute of Chinese Information Processing,
Beijing Normal University, Beijing, China
282843696@qq.com, irishere@mail.bnu.edu.cn,
yanglijiao@bnu.edu.cn

[2] Ultra Power-BNU Joint Laboratory for Artificial Intelligence, Beijing, China

Abstract. Images are the soul of poetry. The usage of images enables poetry to express its deepest emotions in very concise expression. While the structured language of poetry bring convenience to computer processing, the accumulation of a large number of images also brings difficulty to deep semantic understanding. Starting from the definition of object imagery, this paper selects 304 Tang poems as experimental samples, extracts the object images from poems. Then it calculates the emotional tendency of object images according to the emotion system. Finally, it calculates the similarity between images to achieve the relevancy between the images and establishes the map of image relationship. This paper presents the relationship between images using visualization methods, which would help poetry learners understand the images intuitively, and provide reference for correlation study of Tang poetry.

Keywords: Image · Tang poetry · Poem graph

1 Introduction

The application of computer technology in literary research not only overcomes the shortcomings of traditional literary research like time-consuming and high cost, but also makes the research results more objective. As a result, computer assisted Chinese traditional literary research has been paid more and more attention as the natural language processing technology develops rapidly.

Compared with novels, dramas and other literary forms, poetry have a more stable structure. After over 20 years of development, computer-aided poetry research has made remarkable achievements in fields of resource base establishment, text classification, etc. Hu and Yu developed a computer-aided research system for Tang and Song poems based on the corpus of Tang and Song poems consisted of more than 6 million words [1]. The system improved the poems retrieval and realized automatic phonetic notation of Tang poems. Hu and Zhu took the text, title, authorship and style of poetry into account, classified the topics of Tang poetry automatically and achieved optimal classification results [2]. Yi proposed the model that distinguished the poems with graceful style from the bold poems. The work could be seen as a variation on the poetic topic classification [3].

J. Tang et al. (Eds.): NLPCC 2019, LNAI 11839, pp. 426–434, 2019.
https://doi.org/10.1007/978-3-030-32236-6_38

Knowledge graph aims to simplify information access, reveal knowledge structure and help knowledge development through data mining, analysis, classification and mapping [4]. In recent years, some institutions and researchers have made attempts to construct the knowledge map of poetry. The poetry portal Souyun has established a chronological map of Tang and Song literature and a map of the geographical distribution of poets in successive dynasties [5]. Zhou put forward a series of conceptions for constructing the Tang poetry knowledge map [6]. As we can see, these work focus more on the visualizing the external knowledge rather than the internal knowledge of Tang Poetry. In other words, the present visualization of Tang poetry lacks fine-grained knowledge relations, such as the relationship between themes and images.

Some researchers also attempt to explore the knowledge of Tang Poetry in deep level: Hu used the context-based vector space model (VSM) to describe the semantics of words approximately, so that to calculate the semantic similarity between words of poetry [7]. Li clustered the poetry images, then took images of poetry as classification features [8]. Inspired by the previous work, this paper attempts to use VSM to express the affective disposition of each image, calculate the similarity between images and establish the image map of Tang poetry.

2 Our Method

To construct the image graph of Tang poetry, we have to define the image firstly. Considering different scholars have different opinions on the definition of image, the image in this paper is consistent with Yuan Xingpei's point of view [9]. That is to say image is an object image which integrates subjective feelings, or a subjective emotion expressed by objective objects. Strict and regular style of Tang poetry makes it use words concisely. Authors of poems often chooses the most appropriate "object image" ("象") to express his "meaning" ("意") in short five-character or seven-character sentences. For example, the sentence "Straight smoke above desert, sunset above long river" ("大漠孤烟直，长河落日圆") combine four object images: "desert", "smoke", "long river" and "sunset" to create a desolate and lonely mood. In this sentence, four object images are contaminated with lonely feelings of the whole poem and tend to be images of loneliness. This chapter describes the image map construction through four parts: classification system of poetry emotion, pretreatment, image representation and image similarity calculation.

2.1 Classification System of Poetry Emotion and Data Source

As mentioned above, an object image with the author's subjective emotion is the image. Therefore, we can regard the classification of images as the classification of poetry emotion, the object images in the poems with same emotion will be contaminated with the same emotion and tend to fall into the same category. However, because the emotion is complex and hard to measure, the classification of emotion will inevitably have confusing and overlapping problems. Zhu [10] thought that the classification of poetry emotion or style is inseparable from the classification of human emotion, it drew on the three-dimensional theory put forward by Wundt [11], took pleasure-unhappiness, calmness-excitement, tension-relaxation as dimensions and the emotion of poetry were divided into 12 categories: depression, ease, sadness, cheerfulness, excitement and so on. Considering that the difference between tension and excitement, relaxation and calmness in poetry is relatively minor, this paper defines 4 emotions of poetry by taking pleasure-unhappiness as the main yardstick, then thinks about the dimension of calmness-excitement. The classification of poetry is shown in Table 1.

Table 1. Emotion system of Tang poetry

	Pleasure	Unhappiness
Calmness	tranquil	passionate
Excitement	melancholy	grief

According to the emotion classification in Table 1, we select poems from Three Hundred Tang Poems for artificial emotion annotation [12]. We got 304 Tang poems as experimental samples and the distribution of categories are as follows: 67 tranquil poems, 47 passionate poems, 143 melancholy poems, and 47 grief poems.

2.2 Pretreatment of Experimental Samples

According to the definition of images, we must select the object images from poems to acquire images. And in order to get the object images in poetry, we should first pretreat the samples of poetry, including word segmentation and object image extraction. There are some differences of the word definition between ancient poetry and modern Chinese. For example, in modern Chinese, "Chang he" (长河), "Xian yun" (闲云), "Bai yun" (白云) and others like these are regarded as phrases, but to be regarded as words in Tang poetry which makes the word vocabulary of modern Chinese is not suitable for Tang poetry segmentation. Most Tang poems are modern-style poems (referring to innovations in classical poetry during the Tang Dynasty), and their rigorous and regular rhythmic structure brings us a new approach for Tang poetry segmentation. Firstly, we divide each five-character clause into "two-two-one-character" clause, and the seven-character clause into "two-two-three-character" clause, for instance, dividing "白日依山尽" into "白日/依山/尽", dividing "芳草萋萋鹦鹉洲" into "芳草/萋萋/鹦鹉洲". Then, we reserve the bigrams with frequency higher than 5 and the trigrams are segmented by these bigrams to get a new one-character and two-character word vocabulary. Finally, we reserve three-character words with frequency higher than 3, combine the one-character, two-character and three-character word list to get the final Tang poetry vocabulary. In view of the fact that the final word list will retain phrases such as "Yuan Ti" (猿啼) and "Yan Fei" (雁飞), which will introduce noise during the extraction of object images, we combine the pyhanlp word segmentation tool and Tang poetry word vocabulary to segment the Tang poems.

To the step of extracting the object images, we need to further refine the definition of object image. The object of object images in this paper refers to the name or descriptions of things, nouns such as "Xian yun" (闲云), "Ming yue" (明月) can be regarded as images, while verbs such as "Chou chu" (踌躇), "Du zuo" (独坐) as well as time nouns such as "Xi nian" (昔年), "Jin ri" (今日) will not be regarded as images. After removing the noise artificially, samples of the object image are shown in Table 2.

Table 2. Object images extracted from Tang poems

Authorship	Title	Object images
张九龄	感遇	兰叶 春 桂华 秋 生意 自尔 佳节 林 栖者 风 草木 本心 何求 美人
王维	渭川田家	斜光 牛羊 野老 牧童 荆扉 雉雊 麦苗 蚕 眠 桑叶 田夫 荷锄 语依依
孟浩然	夏日南亭怀辛大	山光 池月 东 荷风 香气 清响 知音 感此 故人 中宵 梦
陈子昂	登幽州台歌	古人 来者 天地 涕
王湾	次北固山下	客路 青山 行舟 绿水 潮 两岸 风 海日 残 夜 江春 旧年 乡书 何处 洛阳 边

2.3 Image Representation

Just as the relationship of character symbols and meanings are multi-directional, the relationship between object images and emotions in poetry is not one-to-one correspondence. That is, the same emotion can be expressed with different object images, the same object image can also represent different emotions. For example, "美人" (beauty) represents people as an object image, in sentence "美人卷珠帘, 深坐蹙蛾眉", the "Beauty" is a woman image full of loneliness, but in "战士军前半死生，美人帐下犹歌舞" the "Beauty" is a Lost warf-Kingdoms image to express the sadness and grief of the author. It can be seen that the same objective object image of "美人" in poems with different emotions represents different images and the more categories an object image appears in, the more complex the image it represents.

Vector Space Model (VSM) is one of the most widely used text representation models. It can transform text content into vectors and express the similarity between texts according to the distance between vectors. For example, the text d is represented in vector space model as Eq. (1).

$$V(d) = (W_1, W_2, \cdots, W_n) \tag{1}$$

Where $W_i(1 < i < n)$ is the weight of the feature i, and its value represents the ability to represent the text d. Work [8] used VSM model to describe poetry object images, but the proportion of a certain emotion category in the total experimental samples was not considered during the calculation of emotion propensity. For the image with complex emotion, it is easier to incline to the emotion category with larger samples. This paper also uses VSM to represent images approximately, as in Eq. (2), each object image is represented as a vector, and each dimension of the vector represents the tendency of the image to a certain emotional category.

$$Im = (t_1, t_2, \cdots, t_n) \tag{2}$$

Where n represents the number of emotional categories, $t_i(1 < i < n)$ is the tendency of image Im to this emotional category, which is calculated by Eq. (3).

$$t_i = \frac{F_i}{\sum_{k=1}^{n} F_k} \times \frac{1}{n_t} (\log \frac{N}{d_{t_i}}) \tag{3}$$

In Eq. (3), F_i denotes the occurrence frequency of image Im in the emotional category i in the samples of experiment. $\sum_{k=1}^{n} F_k$ denotes the total occurrence frequency of image Im appears in the samples of experiment. N is the total number of poems and d_{t_i} is the poem number of the emotion represented by dimension t_i. n_t is the number of emotion category.

According to the method mentioned above, the extracted object images can be transformed into vector forms. Some examples are shown in Table 3.

Table 3. Samples of image emotional tendency

Image	Affective Disposition			
	tranquil	passionate	melancholy	grief
美人	0.095	0.117	0.071	0.060
白云	0.142	0.058	0.095	0
杨柳	0.095	0	0.142	0
梦	0	0.052	0.148	0.027
雨	0.087	0.108	0.058	0.074

As we can see, the more non-zero dimensions an image has, the more complex its emotion will be. For example, images “美人” (beauty), “雨” (rain) has all emotion labels, the two object images are both inclined to passionate and tranquil emotions. On the contrary, the image “杨柳” (willow) only appears in the poems with melancholy and tranquil labels, and its emotional tendency is relatively pure.

2.4 Similarity Computation of Image

In Sect. 2.3, we use the vector space model to represent the image as a vector in the vector space. Based on the two vectors, we can calculate the similarity by Euclidean Distance, Pearson Correlation Coefficient, Cosine Similarity, etc. In this paper, cosine similarity is used to calculate the similarity between images. The calculation equation is shown in (4).

$$\cos(Im_1, Im_2) = \frac{\sum_{i=1}^{n} Im_{1i} \times Im_{2i}}{\sqrt{\left(\sum_{i=1}^{n} (Im_{1i})^2\right)\left(\sum_{i=1}^{n} (Im_{2i})^2\right)}} \tag{4}$$

where Im_1 and Im_2 represent the affective disposition of two images, n is the dimension of vectors, Im_{1i} and Im_{2i} are tendencies of dimension i in Im_1 and Im_2 respectively. The larger the cosine value between two images, the more similar the two vectors are.

By calculating the cosine similarity, we can get the similar relationship between the images. Some image samples and ten of their most similar images are listed in Table 4.

Table 4. Similar images TOP10 calculated according to emotion tendency

Image	Similar images（TOP10）
明月	春 心 烟 月明 芳草 杜鹃 杨柳 两岸 南山 游子
雁	水 树 鬌 月 羽 园 波澜 淮 宫 路
美人	雨 后 落日 草 衣裳 声 春风 风 钟 舟
将军	征人 大漠 青冢 古来 去时 国 胡儿 病 汉将 歌声
泪	雁 洛阳 少妇 故乡 孤城 长江 音书 尘 殿 消息

Of course, we can also obtain similar images of one certain image by other methods. Word2vec is a tool for natural language processing released by Google in 2013 [13], it vectorizes all words to quantify the relationships between words. In this paper, word vectors are trained on the basis of extracted object images and the similarity between images is also calculated by cosine similarity. The results corresponding to Table 4 are shown in Table 5.

Table 5. Similar images TOP10 calculated according to word2vec

Image	Similar images（TOP10）
明月	风 月 君 万里 下 山 心 泪 中 梦
雁	上 秋 春风 城中 霜雪 长安 闲暇 山石 琵琶 省中
美人	家 春 客 声 上 水 琵琶 马 心 将军
将军	声 人 月 客 时 风 心 泪 何处 中
泪	人 客 水 君 上 声 时 夜 何 明月

As we can see in Table 4, the more emotion categories an image involves in, the more complex emotion its similar images will be. For instance, the image "将军" (general) appears in the poems of passionate, melancholy and grief emotion, and its similar image "征人" (a traveler on a long journey), "大漠" (desert), "男儿" (man) also contains passionate, melancholy and grief emotion. It can also be said in this paper what the emotion tendency calculates is the similarity of emotion complexity between images.

The affective disposition of similar images obtained by word2vec method is simpler. As Table 5 shows, the images similar to the "将军" (general) is more inclined to the emotional color of melancholy and grief but lacks images related to the passionate emotion. This is because the emotion of Tang poetry is often complex and changeable, sometimes the first couplet depicts a tranquil scene while the tail couplet can not hide melancholy of the author. Compared with the method proposed in this paper, word2vec focuses more on the context information of target image, which can better capture the changes of internal emotion of poetry, but fail to grasp the overall emotional tone of poetry. The two image representations both have their own advantages and disadvantages and they can be applied to researches according to different tasks.

3 Visualization

With image representation, we can cluster the images of Tang poems and construct an image Graph. We use the Embedding Projector to map images firstly. Embedding Projector is a tool included in TensorBoard for visualizing embedding [14]. PCA algorithm is used for image dimensionality reduction, the intuitive distances of points close to high-dimensional distances. Figure 1 takes the image "将军" as an example and selects 100 nearest neighbors to visually show the distribution of images.

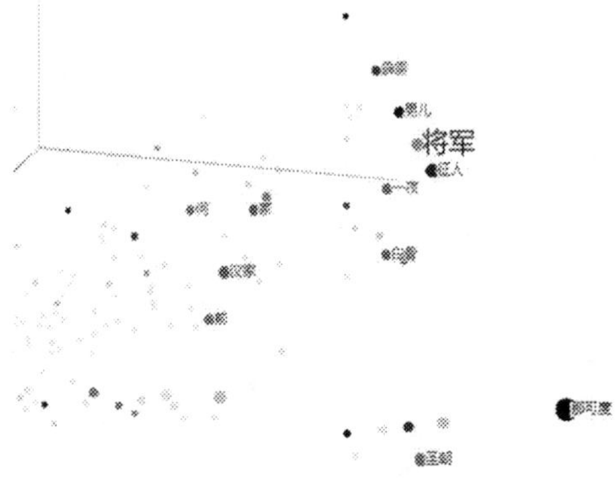

Fig. 1. Image distribution (takes the image "将军" as an example).

In order to inspect the emotional transition between images, we use networkx [15] to construct an object image network graph by assuming the first 500 images and their most 10 similar images are nodes, and adding edges between similar images. Figure 2 is a partial intercepted graph.

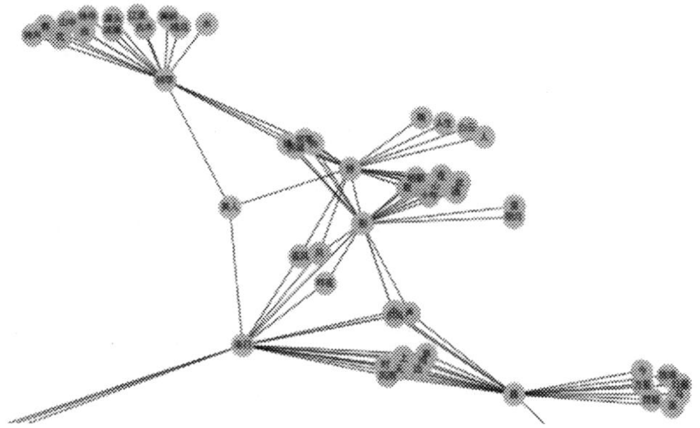

Fig. 2. Partial network of Tang poetry images.

The images with complex emotions often assume the role of the transients. For example, in Fig. 2, "桃李" (peaches and plums), "钟" (bell), "影" (shadow), "落日" (setting sun) and "路" (road) are central nodes, each emits 10 similar images. "桃李" (peaches and plums) is a pure tranquil image, but its similar images "洞庭" (Dongting), "舟" (boat) expand the network to an images more inclined to melancholy emotions because they contain melancholy emotions. Image "美人" (beauty) connects three image nodes whose emotion are more complex than other images in the Fig. 2.

4 Conclusion and Future Work

Image is the key to interpret poetry texts and emotions of authors. Using the definition of image as a clue, this paper selects poems from Three Hundred Tang Poems as experimental objects to extract object images. Since the definition of image is the object image with the author's subjective emotion, we calculate the affective disposition of the object image, then calculate similarity between the images according to the affective disposition. Finally, we cluster images and construct the image graph based on image similarity to visualize the similar relationship between images.

Of course, we still have a lot of work to do:

- Firstly, image and poetry quantity involved in Three Hundred Tang Poems is limited, which will affect the accuracy of calculating the image emotion tendency. We have also used text classification method to extend the experimental data, but the poetry sentiment classification task is difficult to obtain convincing accuracy, which limits the scalability of the data.
- Secondly, some noise will be introduced during the extraction of object images.
- last but not least, happiness is alike in happy family, while different in those unhappy. In the actual annotation, we can feel that the poetry emotion of the unhappiness is more complicated than the pleasure dimension, it is also worth considering whether the emotion classification system should be further refined.

All these problems need to be solved in our future research, we also expect there will be more scholars focusing on the research of Tang poetry's deep-seated semantic computing.

Acknowledgments. This work is supported by the Fundamental Research Funds for the Central Universities, National Language Committee Research Program of China (No. ZDI135-42), National Social Science Fund of China (No. 18CYY029) and The Ministry of Education Humanities and Social Science Project (No. 18YJAZH112).

References

1. Junfeng, H., Shiwen, Y.: The Computer aided research work of Chinese ancient poems. Acta Sci. Nat. Univ. Pekin. **05**, 727–733 (2001)
2. Renfen, H., Yuchen, Z.: Automatic classification of Tang poetry themes. Acta Sci. Nat. Univ. Pekin. **51**(02), 262–268 (2015)
3. Yong, Y.: A study on style identification and Chinese couplet responses oriented computer aided poetry composing. Ph.D. Dissertation of Chongqing University (2005)
4. Shiffrin, R.M., Börner, K.: Mapping knowledge domains. Proc. Natl. Acad. Sci. **101**(1), 5183–5185 (2004)
5. Souyun Homepage. https://sou-yun.cn/
6. Lina, Z., Liang, H., Ziyang, G.: Construction of knowledge graph of Chinese Tang poetry and design of intelligent knowledge services. Libr. Inf. Serv. **63**(2), 24–33 (2019)
7. Junfeng, H., Shiwen, Y.: Word meaning similarity analysis in Chinese ancient poetry and its applications. J. Chin. Inf. Process. **04**, 39–44 (2002)
8. Qi, L.: Research and Implement of Classical Poetry Artistic Conception Classification. Donghua University (2014)
9. Xingpei, Y.: Images in Chinese classical poetry. China Acad. J. Electron. Publ. House **2**, 9–15 (2007)
10. Yuchen, Z.: A Study on Poety Form by LuYou's Poem. Beijing Normal University (2014)
11. Wundt, W.: Outlines of Psychology, 2nd edn. Wilhelm Engelmann, Leipzig (1897)
12. Hengtang, T.: Three Hundred Tang Poems. Xiyuan Publishing House, Beijing (2003)
13. Tomas, M.: Word2vec Project. https://code.google.com/archive/p/word2vec/
14. Embedding Projector Homepage. https://projector.tensorflow.org/
15. Networkx Package. https://networkx.github.io/

Research on Fine-Grained Sentiment Classification

Zhihui Wang(✉), Xiaodong Wang, Tao Chang, Shaohe Lv, and Xiaoting Guo

National Key Laboratory of Parallel and Distributed Processing, College of Computer Science and Technology, National University of Defence Technology, Changsha 410073, China

{wangzhihui13,xdwang,changtao15,shaohelv,guoxiaoting18}@nudt.edu.cm

Abstract. Aiming at the fine-grained sentiment classification that distinguishes the emotional intensity, the commonly used dataset SST-1 is analyzed in depth. Through the analysis, it is found that the dataset has serious problems such as data imbalance and small overall scale, which seriously restricts the classification effect. In order to solve the related problems, data augmentation method is adopted to realize the optimization of the dataset. The IMDB and other data which are relatively homologous to the original dataset are annotated, and the focus is to expand the categories with fewer numbers. By this way, the problem of data imbalance is effectively alleviated and the original data scale is expanded. Then, based on the Bidirectional Encoder Representations from Transformers (BERT) model, which has good overall performance on natural language processing, the benchmark classification model is built. Through multiple comparison experiments on the original dataset and the enhanced data, the influence of the deficiency of the original dataset on the classification effect is verified. And, it is fully demonstrated that the enhanced data can effectively improve the test results and solve the problem of large differences in performance between different categories well.

Keywords: Fine-grained · Sentiment classification · Data imbalance · Data augmentation · BERT

1 Introduction

Text classification is a quite important module in text processing. And its application is also very extensive, including: spam filtering, news classification, part-of-speech tagging, sentiment classification and so on [1]. For the sentiment classification, the coarse-grained classification without distinguishing the emotional intensity can already have good effects, and the accuracy can basically reach more than 80%. However, for the more fine-grained multi-category sentiment

Supported by National Key Laboratory of Parallel and Distributed Processing, College of Computer Science and Technology, National University of Defence Technology.

J. Tang et al. (Eds.): NLPCC 2019, LNAI 11839, pp. 435–444, 2019.
https://doi.org/10.1007/978-3-030-32236-6_39

classification, there are two problems. First, the number of related datasets is small, and the overall size is small. Second, the research on this problem is relatively scarce, making the effect of fine-grained sentiment classification much worse. And it is difficult to meet the needs of practical applications. When expressing emotions, people's emotional attitudes are not simply happy, annoying or neutral. Even in the same emotional polarity, there is a big difference in intensity. In the aspects of public opinion control, hot spot analysis, and object evaluation, the effects of different intensity emotional texts are not uniform. Therefore, the research on fine-grained sentiment classification that distinguishes emotional intensity has important practical significance.

With the vigorous development of deep learning technology, there have been scholars introduced it into the sentiment classification. It has been proved that the deep learning models can achieve excellent results and become the mainstream trend to solve this problem. In related researches, the commonly used datasets are mainly about the data of movie reviews, and they are basically coarse-grained sentiment classification. For the fine-grained sentiment classification, the lack of data makes the performance of the classification model limited. At the same time, subjectivity has a great influence on the division of emotional intensity. Especially for ambiguous texts, it is difficult to give a label that is satisfactory to all parties. And it also has a great impact on classification performance.

In this paper, the fine-grained sentiment classification that distinguish emotional intensity is analyzed and studied. By the data enhancement method, the classification effect is improved. And the problem of uneven effect of different categories is effectively improved. In this paper, the existing fine-grained sentiment classification dataset is analyzed in depth, and the problems of unbalanced data and small data size are found. In order to solve related problems, the data enhancement method is adopted. The original dataset is expanded and optimized by using data that is relatively homologous to the original dataset. By this method, the problem of data imbalance is effectively alleviated. Finally, the benchmark classification model is constructed by using BERT [2]. Through multiple comparison experiments, it is fully demonstrated that the enhanced data can effectively improve the classification results, and solve the problem of large performance difference between different categories. And the validity of our method is verified.

2 Related Work

2.1 Fine-Grained Sentiment Classification

The term "fine-grained" in the fine-grained sentiment classification can have multiple meanings. It can refer to different attributes or aspects of the object being judged, such as performance, appearance, quality in the comments of the goods. And it can also refer to the fine-grained intensity of emotion and the finer division of emotional tendencies. The fine-grained sentiment classification studied in this paper refers to the latter, the fine-grained intensity of emotion.

Generally, it can be divided into five categories: very positive, positive, neutral, negative, and very negative.

Fine-Grained Sentiment Classification Dataset. In sentiment classification, there are many datasets available, but these datasets usually only contain two categories, positive and negative or subjective and objective. The public dataset of fine-grained sentiment classification is very rare. Currently, only the SST-1 dataset of Stanford Sentiment Treebank has been widely used. This situation has caused great difficulties in the research of fine-grained sentiment classification. The Stanford Sentiment Treebank is an extension of the movie review dataset constructed by Pang et al. [3]. The original dataset includes a total of 10662 movie review data and each movie review is a short sentence. The source of the data is the ROTTEN TOMATOES website. It provides film-related reviews, information and news. For the original dataset, half of the data is annotated positive and the other half is negative. Each piece of data is extracted from a long movie review and reflects the overall view of the reviewer. Then, the data is re-processed using the Stanford Parser and annotated by the Amazon Mechanical Turk. The processed data contains two datasets. One is fine-grained SST-1 datasets, it is composed of five categories: very positive, positive, neutral, negative, very negative. The other is the SST-2 dataset, it only contains two categories: positive and negative. In the study of sentiment classification problems, these two datasets are widely used as criteria for testing model classification ability.

Research on Fine-Grained Sentiment Classification. Most classification models have a classification accuracy of 80% or higher on the two-category dataset. Compared with the sentiment classification datasets with only two categories, the fine-grained sentiment classification effect studied in this paper is much worse. After the SST-1 data set is proposed, Socher et al. experiment with two traditional machine learning methods, Support Vector Machine and Naive Bayes [4], with accuracy of 40.7% and 41.0%, respectively. Then, the recurrent neural network is used, the standard recursive neural network [5] achieved a accuracy of 43.2%. Meanwhile, they propose the Recursive Neural Tensor Network (RNTN) and achieved a accuracy of 45.7%. Hadji et al. [6] propose the Deep Recursive Neural Network (DRNN). This model refreshes the best effect on this dataset, and the accuracy reached 49.8%. Convolutional neural network [7] and recurrent neural network are commonly used in the field of natural language processing, and have achieved good results in this dataset. The accuracy of the Convolutional Neural Network (CNN) model proposed by Kim et al. [8] reaches 47.4%. And the Dynamic Convolutional Neural Network (DCNN) proposed by Kalchbrenner et al. [9] achieves a accuracy of 48.5%. Yin et al. [10] propose a Multichannel Variable-size Convolutional Neural Network (MVCNN), and it achieves the accuracy of 49.6%. Tai et al. [11] conduct experiments with Long Short-Term Memory (LSTM), Bidirectional LSTM and Tree-LSTM, and obtained accuracy of 46.4%, 49.1%, and 51.0%, respectively. The Linguistically

Bidirectional LSTM (LR-Bi-LSTM) model proposed by Qian et al. [12] achieve the accuracy of 50.6%. In addition, Zhou et al. [13] combine convolutional neural network and recurrent neural network to solve classification problems. The Bidirectional LSTM with Two-Dimensional Convolutional Neural Network (BLSTM-2DCNN) model achieved the best performance on this dataset, and the accuracy reaches 52.4%.

2.2 Pre-training Model - BERT

BERT is a pre-training model released by Google in 2018. It has made breakthroughs in 11 natural language processing (NLP) tasks, including text classification tasks. And it is known as Google's strongest NLP model. For a specific task, it is only necessary to fine tune the BERT. It is a multi-layer, bidirectional Transformer [14] encoder based on fine-tuning. And it is trained using two unsupervised predictive tasks, Mask LM [15] and Next Sentence Prediction. Currently, the BERT model has been open sourced and released a variety of models of 12 and 24 layers for researchers to apply and further improve.

3 Research on Fine-Grained Sentiment Classification Based on SST-1 Dataset

This paper first analyzes the SST-1 dataset in depth. Through analysis, it is found that the data is not balanced and the overall scale is small. In order to solve the problem of the original dataset, the data enhancement method is proposed to expand and optimize the dataset. By this way, the problems of data imbalance and small overall size are effectively alleviated. Then, the benchmark classification model is constructed by using BERT, and the effectiveness of the method is verified by comparison experiments.

3.1 Dataset Analysis

The SST-1 dataset is divided into three parts: training set, dev set and test set. The training set contains 8854 data, the dev set contains 1101 data, and the test set contains 2210 data. The specific composition of each part is shown in Fig. 1.

The average length of the data is roughly the same, and the number of words per data is about 19. However, as can be seen from Fig. 1, there is a large difference in the number of different categories, and there is a serious imbalance in the data. For the training set, the negative and positive categories account for the largest proportion of more than 25%. While the number of very positive and very negative categories is small, and the proportion of neural category is relatively small. The distribution of data in the dev set and the test set is basically consistent with the training set. In the process of data annotation by the relevant personnel of our research group, according to the quantitative statistics, the ratio of the strong emotional review data and the weak emotional review data and the neural is about 10:2:1. Therefore, the distribution of data

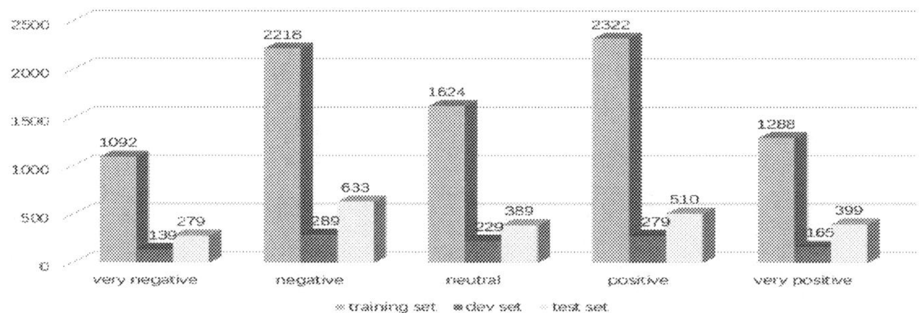

Fig. 1. Composition of SST-1 dataset.

in each category in the dataset is different from the actual distribution. When judging a movie, the audience usually publishes reviews to express their emotions when there is a clear emotional attitude. Therefore, the actual distribution is that the proportion of the data of the strong emotional attitude is more, while the data of the weak emotional attitude is less.

3.2 Optimization Method Based on Data Enhancement

Problem Analysis and Method Establishment. Data imbalance is a common problem in machine learning, and it will affect the effect of the model. Usually, the category with more data can achieve better results. At the same time, the data of its adjacent category will also be affected and the classification effect will be reduced. Therefore, whether the data is balanced or not plays an important role.

It can be seen from the analysis in Sect. 3.1 that there is a serious imbalance problem in the SST-1 dataset. And it will inevitably affect the classification effect. For this problem, common solutions include oversampling, undersampling, changing classification algorithms, and cost-sensitive learning. Meanwhile, we can see that the SST-1 dataset not only has the problem of data imbalance, but also the overall size is small. Take the SST-2 dataset as an example, the total amount is about 10000, and there are nearly 5000 data in each category. However, the SST-1 dataset has five categories, but the total amount is only about 10000. For fine-grained sentiment classification, the difference between emotions of the same polarity and different intensity is much smaller than the coarse-grained. During the annotation process, the group members also have different opinions on the labels of some data, and the classification is more difficult. Therefore, we think that we can use data enhancement methods, use more data to train classification models and improve the model's ability to classify fine-grained sentiment. Referring to the situation of other multi-class datasets, and taking into account the difficulty of the classification, the current goal is to expand the amount of data to 100000. Meanwhile, the expansion target will be dynamically changed according to the change of classification effect during the expansion process. In order to maintain consistency, other attributes of the original data set should be as unchanged as possible, and the data is expanded on this basis. The categories with small number are the key of the data expansion. This method not only solves the problem of data imbalance, but also increases the scale of the dataset and provides data support for subsequent research.

Expansion Method. In order to maintain data consistency, the movie review dataset is used when expanding the data. There are two selected data sources. One is the English IMDB dataset, and the other is the Chinese Douban movie review dataset. For raw data, each piece of data is a piece of text that expresses the emotions of the reviewer. In this paper, the same processing method as the original data set is adopted. A short sentence that reflects the overall opinion of the reviewer is selected from each review. Then, the short sentence is annotated to become new data. The specific process is shown in Fig. 2.

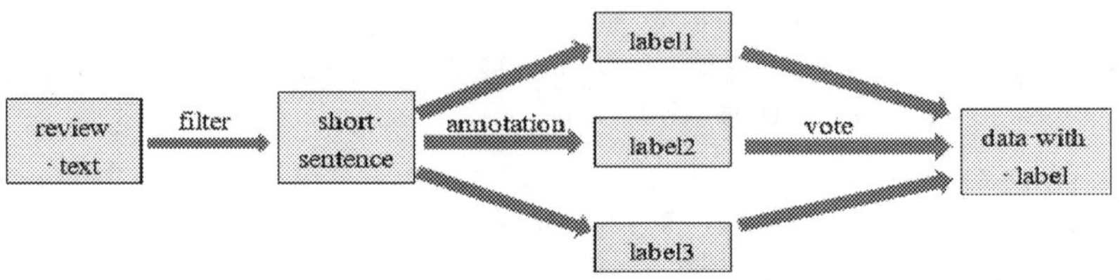

Fig. 2. Process of annotation.

3.3 Benchmark Classification Model Construction

As a powerful pre-training model, BERT has achieved good results in many NLP tasks. To verify the effectiveness of the proposed method, this paper uses this model to fine-tune and build a benchmark classification model. For the processing of data, it is usually necessary to convert the text into a vector. Then the text features are extracted through various types of network structures to obtain higher-level vectors. Finally other structure is added to obtain the final result according to specific tasks.

Text Features Extraction. Based on the above process, this paper first uses the BERT to extract features from the original text. In the selection of the model, the pre-training model of 24-layer scales are used for its better effect. With this model, we can obtain high-level sentence vectors that can better represent the semantics of text. In the process of generating sentence vector, this paper uses the tool - bert-as-service. The output of the penultimate layer is selected to prevent the model from being too close to the two pre-training tasks of the BERT. Finally, fine-tuning is performed on this basis. For the 24-layer model, the output corresponds to a 1024-dimensional vector for each text.

Construction of Classification Model. After completing the extraction of the text features and obtaining the higher level sentence vector, the next step is the construction of the classification model. Since the obtained sentence vector can represent the semantics of the text well, so three fully connected layers are selected for the specific classification model. For the first fully connected layer, the 1024-dimensional sentence vector is compressed to 256 dimensions. Then the 256-dimensional vector is further compressed to 12 dimensions. At the same time, to prevent over-fitting of the model, dropout is added in the process. For the last layer, the 12-dimensional vector is reduced to 5 dimensions. Finally, the specific category to which the text belongs is obtained according to the largest component of the 5-dimensional vector.

4 Experiment Results and Analysis

In order to verify the effectiveness of the data enhancement method, we performed experiments on the original dataset using 24-layer BERT model and corresponding classification model according to the method in Sect. 3.3. By analyzing the experiment results, it is verified that the imbalance of the dataset does have an impact on the classification results. In this paper, we adopt the data enhancement method to solve the problem of data imbalance, and uses the same classification model and the same test set to perform experiment. Through experiments, better classification results are obtained on the optimized dataset. And the problem of uneven effect in each category is effectively improved.

4.1 Classification Effect on SST-1 Dataset

Firstly, the classification model based on 24-layer BERT is used to solve the classification problem of SST-1 dataset. The training set contains a total of 8544 training data and five categories. Through training, the model achieved the accuracy of 48.8% on the dev set. The accuracy of each category and the confusion matrix is shown in Table 1.

In the dev set, from the overall point of view, the negative and positive categories have the most number of data, and the accuracy reaches more than 60%. The accuracy of these two categories far exceeds the accuracy of other categories and the whole. Although the neutral category is not the least, the effect is the worst of all categories.

Then, the two categories with the highest accuracy are analyzed. In the training set, both negative and positive categories have the largest number of data, and they are more fully trained, and the model is biased towards these two categories. Therefore, these two categories have the highest accuracy and also affect the effect of adjacent categories.

Although the number of neutral category is more, the effect is the worst. There are three main reasons. First, during the training process, the category data is relatively small, the model is not fully trained on this category of data. Second, the discrimination of the neutral category itself is difficult. The third

Table 1. Confusion matrix of dev set.

Predicted value	Real value				
	Very negative	Negative	Neural	Positive	Very positive
Very negative	35.5%	10.1%	4.1%	0.6%	1.2%
Negative	**52.2%**	**64.4%**	38.5%	11.3%	6.5%
Neural	6.5%	9.7%	14.9%	7.0%	2.4%
Positive	5.1%	15.1%	**39.5%**	**66.5%**	**49.4%**
Very positive	0.7%	0.7%	3.1%	14.6%	40.4%

and most important reason is that the two adjacent categories are the most. The model is biased towards the two adjacent categories during the training process, and more data is judged as two adjacent categories.

4.2 Effect Comparison After Data Enhancement

To compare the effects on the original dataset, we train the model on the original dataset, the accuracy on the test set is 50.6%, and the specific results of the model is shown in Table 2.

Table 2. Confusion matrix of test set (24-layers BERT).

Predicted value	Real value				
	Very negative	Negative	Neural	Positive	Very positive
Very negative	30.1%	9.3%	3.3%	0.2%	0.3%
Negative	**59.5%**	**66.8%**	**42.2%**	8.4%	3.3%
Neural	6.5%	14.1%	22.4%	6.9%	2.5%
Positive	3.2%	9.5%	30.6%	**69.4%**	**51.4%**
Very positive	0.7%	0.3%	1.5%	15.1%	42.6%

Classification Effect on Big-Scale Equilibrium Data. Then, the classification model is used to train on the large equilibrium training set, and the classification effect is tested on the original test set. Through training, the model achieved the accuracy of 52.3% on the test set. And the effect has basically reached the current optimal performance. The problem of large difference between different categories is effectively improved and the effectiveness of the proposed method is confirmed. The specific classification effect is shown in Table 3.

Compared with the original data set, the difference between the different categories of effects is reduced, and the overall accuracy is also improved. Meanwhile, the effect of the neutral is still the worst, below 40%. For a review, it is

Table 3. Confusion matrix (data size: 10000).

Predicted value	Real value				
	Very negative	Negative	Neural	Positive	Very positive
Very negative	**54.8%**	17.9%	8.5%	1.2%	1.3%
Negative	30.5%	**51.2%**	27.5%	4.3%	2.8%
Neural	9.0%	24.0%	**39.6%**	13.7%	3.0%
Positive	3.9%	5.1%	20.8%	**59.8%**	37.8%
Very positive	1.1%	1.9%	3.6%	21.0%	**55.1%**

usually biased towards some emotion, which makes it more difficult to judge this category. And this is one of the research points to further improve the classification effect.

While the overall effect and the differences between the different categories have improved, the classification effects of the positive and negative have declined. The reason for this phenomenon is mainly the data with blurred boundaries. After training on the unbalanced data set, the model is more biased towards these two categories. However, after the training data is balanced, the model's bias towards these two categories is significantly reduced. Because the training data is not enough, the model can not classify data well enough. When the data with blurred boundary is encountered, it can only be judged as two adjacent categories in an average but less accurate manner. Therefore, the classification results of data with fuzzy classification boundaries are different from before and the effect of these two categories is reduced.

5 Conclusion

According to the fact that the effect of fine-grained sentiment classification problem is relatively poor compared with coarse-grained sentiment classification, this paper finds out the problem of unbalanced data and small data size by analyzing the commonly used dataset SST-1. In order to solve related problems, this paper uses data enhancement method to optimize the dataset. A more balanced and larger dataset is constructed and the problem of data imbalance is effectively alleviated. This paper builds a benchmark classification model based on BERT. And the effectiveness of the method is verified by comparison experiments, the classification effect is improved, and the problem of large difference between different classification effects is effectively improved. However, the current data size is still not large enough, and there is still a big gap between the overall classification effect and the effect of coarse-grained sentiment classification. In the future, other data sources will be utilized to further expand the data. At the same time, practical applications will be combined and more detailed evaluation indicators will be developed to explore the fine-grained sentiment classification problem in more depth.

References

1. Huang, Z., Tang, X., Xie, B., et al.: Sentiment classification using machine learning techniques with syntax features. In: International Conference on Computational Science & Computational Intelligence (2015)
2. Devlin, J., Chang, M.W., Lee, K., et al.: BERT: pre-training of deep bidirectional transformers for language understanding. https://arxiv.org/abs/1810.04805. Accessed 14 May 2019
3. Pang, B., Lee, L.: Seeing stars: exploiting class relationships for sentiment categorization with respect to rating scales. In: Proceedings of the ACL, Ann Arbor, pp. 115–124 (2005)
4. Ding, Z., Xia, R., Yu, J., et al.: Densely connected bidirectional LSTM with applications to sentence classification. https://arxiv.org/abs/1802.00889. Accessed 14 May 2019
5. Socher, R., Pennington, J., Huang, E.H., et al.: Semi-supervised recursive autoencoders for predicting sentiment distributions. In: Proceedings of the 2011 Conference on Empirical Methods in Natural Language Processing, EMNLP 2011, Edinburgh, pp. 151–161 (2011)
6. Hadji, I., Wildes, R.P.: What do we understand about convolutional networks? https://arxiv.org/abs/1803.08834. Accessed 14 May 2019
7. Cardie, C.: Deep recursive neural networks for compositionality in language. In: International Conference on Neural Information Processing Systems, pp. 2096–2104. MIT Press, Montreal (2014)
8. Kim, Y.: Convolutional neural networks for sentence classification. In: Proceedings of the 2014 Conference on Empirical Methods in Natural Language Processing, EMNLP 2014, Doha, pp. 1746–1751 (2014)
9. Kalchbrenner, N., Grefenstette, E., Blunsom, P.: A convolutional neural network for modelling sentences. In: Annual Meeting of the Association for Computational Linguistics, ACL 2014, Baltimore, pp. 655–665 (2014)
10. Yin, W., Schütze, H.: Multichannel variable-size convolution for sentence classification. In: Proceedings of the Nineteenth Conference on Computational Natural Language Learning, CoNLL 2015, Beijing, pp. 204–214 (2015)
11. Tai, K.S., Socher, R., Manning, C.D.: Improved semantic representations from tree-structured long short-term memory networks. In: Annual Meeting of the Association for Computational Linguistics, ACL 2015, Beijing, pp. 1556–1566 (2015)
12. Qian, Q., Huang, M., Lei, J., Zhu, X.: Linguistically regularized LSTMs for sentiment classification. https://arxiv.org/abs/1611.03949. Accessed 14 May 2019
13. Zhou, P., Qi, Z., Zheng, S., et al.: Text classification improved by integrating bidirectional LSTM with two-dimensional max pooling. In: Computational Linguistics, COLING 2016, Osaka, pp. 3485–3495 (2016)
14. Vaswani, A., et al.: Attention is all you need. In: Annual Conference on Neural Information Processing Systems, NIPS 2017, Long Beach (2017)
15. Taylor, W.L.: "Cloze Procedure": a new tool for measuring readability. J. Q. **30**(4), 415–433 (1953)

Question Generation Based Product Information

Kang Xiao, Xiabing Zhou[(✉)], Zhongqing Wang, Xiangyu Duan, and Min Zhang

Natural Language Processing Lab, School of Computer Science and Technology, Soochow University, Suzhou, China
20184227061@stu.suda.edu.cn, {zhouxiabing,wangzq, xiangyuduan,minzhang}@suda.edu.cn

Abstract. With the continuous development of the Internet, the field of e-commerce generates many comments on products. It is of great significance for both merchants and customers to generate product-related questions by utilizing a large amount of review information of products. In order to get rid of the traditional constraints of generating models based on artificial rules and make the question generation more accurate, this paper proposes a question generation model based on product information. Compared with the existing approaches, this model can generate questions more relevant to the products, and more fluent. In particular, the model can not only avoid the problem that the vocabulary exceeds the dictionary, but also extract the vocabulary needed for question generation from the original text and the dictionary. The experimental results show that in the task of generating short text based on comments, compared with the existing neural network model, the effectiveness has been greatly improved.

Keywords: Product information · Neural network · Attention replication mechanism · Entity recognition · Question generation model

1 Introduction

With the development of the Internet era, e-commerce has become one of the most dynamic economic activities in the country. China has the world's largest e-commerce market, with about 533 million shopping users [1]. Through the analysis of commodity review information, it is helpful for more customers to understand commodity information in detail and merchants to improve product quality.

Faced with a large number of comments, it is difficult for merchants and customers to catch the key product information. Through some product Q&A information, merchants can more intuitively understand the aspects that customers concern about, and customers can more directly find what they need. However, the amount of Q&A information in reality is often much smaller than that in comments. As shown in Table 1, the amount of comment information and Q&A information of 5 products is counted from an e-commerce platform. Therefore, it is a challenging task how to automatically generate commodity questions from a large amount of comment information.

J. Tang et al. (Eds.): NLPCC 2019, LNAI 11839, pp. 445–455, 2019.
https://doi.org/10.1007/978-3-030-32236-6_40

Table 1. Product reviews and Q&A quantity

Item	TV	Oven	Cellphone	Electric kettle	Microwave oven
Comment number	43837	18050	33448	97843	18743
Question number	506	112	274	419	104

Automatic question generation is a research hotspot in the field of natural language processing. The traditional method which is mainly through manually set relevant rules or templates to generate questions. For example, Labutov et al. [2] put forward the question of manual text-based template construction. However, such method required lots of manpower and generated question patterns that were relatively fixed and inflexible, especially when applied to new areas, the new rules and templates still need to be defined. Recently, more and more scholars are trying to use neural network model to generate questions. For example, Serban et al. [3] proposed a sequence-to-sequence neural network based on structured data.

However, the current research mainly focuses on generating a natural question related to the text content, which is mostly based on the known dictionary, and cannot well solve the world out of vocabulary (OOV) problem. The main content of this paper is to generate questions related to product information based on comments. The characters of comments are shorter and more colloquial, and they are more prone to the new and unrecorded words. Also, generating questions must be relevant to the product. Therefore, the previous question generation model cannot well solve the above challenges, and it is extremely easy to generate inaccurate words and unsmooth sentences, as shown in the following example:

[E1] *评论信息：反应速度快，外观漂亮，屏幕也大，显示很鲜艳。*
(comment: Quick response, beautiful appearance, the screen is also large, the display is very bright)
生成问题：效果怎么样？
(generated question: what is the effect)

[E2] *评论信息：一次失败的购物体验首先手机宽度，完全处于一只手拿大，两只手拿小，没有外边框，极其容易误触。*
(comment: A failed shopping experience first of all, the width of the phone, completely in one hand to hold large, two hands to hold small, no outer border, extremely easy to miscontact.)
生成问题：手机宽外面好吗？
(generated question: the phone wide out ok?)

As can be seen from E1, when there is no word matching the product information in the given dictionary, the generated question will be inconsistent with the product content. In E2, the model based on neural network is unable to accurately divide the boundary of entities, and it is extremely easy to make mistakes in selecting words.

In order to solve the above challenges, in this paper, we propose a Question Generation based on Product Information (QGPI). In this model, the information entities related to the products are first marked, which makes the generated question more related to products. Secondly, this model uses the sequence-to-sequence model [4] based on replication mechanism. When the word is not included in the vocabulary, the original words in comment are selected, which avoids the OOV problem and makes the generated questions more smooth and flexible. The experimental results show that, the ROUGE value and BLEU value of our model both better than other models.

2 Related Works

In the past two decades, question generation methods are mainly divided into two categories: rule-based methods and neural network-based methods.

Traditional question generation is primarily rule-based or template-based. They convert the input sentence into a syntactic representation, which is then used to generate questions. Mostow et al. [5] generated self-questioning strategies for reading comprehension, which define three templates (how, what, why) to generate question. Mannem et al. [6] introduced a semantic-based system that uses syntax to help generate question. Lindberg et al. [7] created the question by using the main semantic information to build the system template. Chali and Hasan [8] used the topic model to identify the topic of sentences as heuristic rules and generate question through the entity and predicate parameter structure of sentences. Mazidi and Tarau [9] considered the frequency of sentence patterns and the consistency of semantic information transmitted by sentence patterns to produce question. However, this class of methods has some common disadvantages: dependencies and non-portability. Systems are often difficult to maintain because the rules may vary from person to person. At the same time, most systems are not easily migrated to other domains because they only have relevant rules set by proprietary domains.

In order to break through the shackle of the traditional method based on the custom rules, many scholars begin to use the neural network model to solve the question generation task. Serban et al. [3] proposed a sequence-to-sequence neural network model based on structured data (subject, relation, object) to generate simple factual question. Du et al. [10] proposed a sequence-to-sequence model of attention mechanism based on the state of encoder, and added some characteristics of words in the encoder layer to generate question. Zheng et al. [11] used a template-based method to construct the questions in key sentences, and sorted all the questions by using the multi-feature neural network model to select the top1 question. Bao et al. [12] proposed a dual antagonism network to generate cross-domain question. Different from previous research on question generation, this paper is based on product review data, which is often illogical and colloquial. People with different meanings have different expressions, and OOV problems are more likely to occur in this question generation. At the same time, question generation based on product reviews requires that the question is closely related to the product. Therefore, the previous question generation model cannot well solve the above challenges.

3 Question Generation Based on Product Information

3.1 The Framework of QGPI

In this section, we introduce the QGPI, and the general framework is shown in Fig. 1. Firstly, the model annotates some entities related to product information to strengthen the correlation between generated question and products. Secondly, long short-term memory (LSTM) is used to learn the text information of comments. Thirdly, the attention mechanism is used to retain important content and identify relevant entities. Finally, the important words retained in the text are combined with the existing vocabulary by replication mechanism to make the words more accurate and the generated question statements smoother.

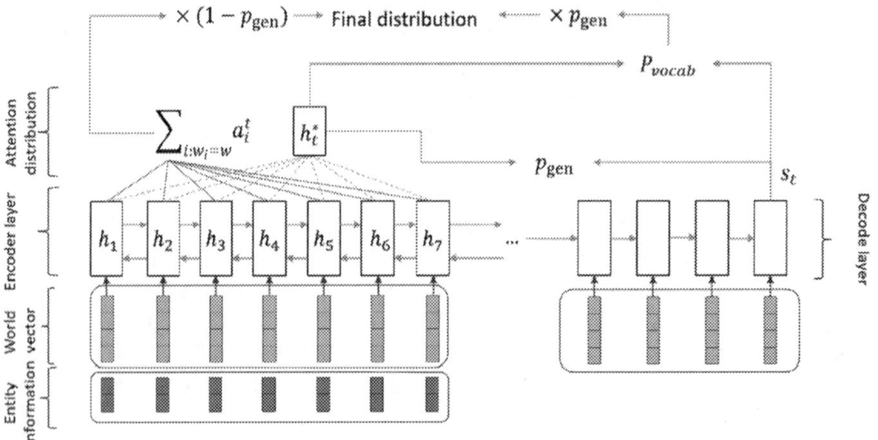

Fig. 1. Overview of the QGPI framework

3.2 Document Representation

We represent each comment d as n words $\{w_1, w_2, w_3, \ldots.., w_n\}$. We transform each token w_i into its corresponding word vector x_i. For comment d, the relevant content of the comment is learned by using LSTM model [13]. On the basis of forward LSTM, backward LSTM is introduced. Each time step t in a bi-directional LSTM model produces the document representation of vector h_t by forward sequence $\overrightarrow{h_t}$ hidden layer and hidden layer of backward sequence $\overleftarrow{h_t}$:

$$\overrightarrow{h_t} = \mathrm{LSTM}(h_{t-1}, x_t) \tag{1}$$

$$\overleftarrow{h_t} = \mathrm{LSTM}(h_{t+1}, x_t) \tag{2}$$

$$h_t = W_{\vec{h}} \overrightarrow{h_t} + W_{\overleftarrow{h}} \overleftarrow{h_t} + b_t \tag{3}$$

The decode layer is a unidirectional LSTM network structure. In training, the text representation of the corresponding question is received; In testing, the state emitted by the previous layer is captured. Finally, after passing through the decoding layer, a decoding state s_t will be generated.

3.3 Product Information Labeling

In order to better generate product-related questions, the model proposed in this paper especially imparts product-related entity information into the text learning process. By labeling the entities related to product information, the generated questions are more inclined to develop questions around these entities. Experimental results show that this method is effective.

Therefore, in the process of learning comment information, it is necessary to judge whether the word is an entity and mark it. $[1, 0]$ label after the word vector when the word is an entity:

$$x_i^{'} = contact(x_i, [1, 0]) \tag{4}$$

when the word is not an entity, we add the label [0,1] after the word vector:

$$x_i^{'} = contact(x_i, [0, 1]) \tag{5}$$

where *contact* is a connection function, whose main function is to connect two vectors head to tail. The newly generated word vector $x_i^{'}$ is then input into the network.

After adding the label, the spatial distance between entity and non-entity vectors will increase, which is conducive to network differentiation.

3.4 Attention Mechanism

In order to learn more accurate questions and enhance the influence of product-related content, the attention mechanism is introduced [14]. Attention mechanism combines comment information and question information to extract the important words generated by the final question. Attention mechanism uses comment information to represent h_i and question information to represent s_t to construct the weight of words in text comments:

$$e_i^t = v^T \tanh(W_h h_i + W_s s_t + b_{attn}) \tag{6}$$

$$a^t = \mathrm{softmax}(e^t) \tag{7}$$

where v,W_h,W_s,b_{attn} are learnable parameters.

The dictionary information is added at the end of the model to fully account for the fact that the words in the generation question com e not only from the comments themselves, but also from words not included in the comments. Through the weighted sum of hidden layer state generated based on the attention mechanism h_t^*, and the decode layer state s_t, the probability distribution of the generation of related question of vocabulary learning in the dictionary can be written:

$$h_t^* = \sum\nolimits_i a_i^t h_i \tag{8}$$

$$P_{vocab} = \text{softmax}\left(V'\left(V\left[s_t, h_t^*\right] + b\right) + b'\right) \tag{9}$$

where V,V',b and b' are learnable parameters. P_{vocab} is the probability distribution of all the words in the vocabulary.

3.5 Replication Mechanism

In this model, in order to better balance the vocabulary from the dictionary or the comment itself and avoid OOV phenomenon, for each time step t, a generation probability $p_{gen} \in [0, 1]$ is added, which is obtained by the calculated h_t^*, decoding the state s_t and the input x_t of the decode layer:

$$p_{gen} = \sigma\left(w_{h^*}^T h_t^* + w_s^T s_t + w_x^T x_t + b_{ptr}\right) \tag{10}$$

where vectors $w_{h^*}^T$,w_s^T,w_x^T and scalar b_{ptr} are learnable parameters. σ is the sigmoid function.

p_{gen} is equivalent to a probability sampling, can from P_{vocab} likely to get the dictionary words, can also copy the word in the original comment. So you get a probability distribution of all words:

$$P(w) = p_{gen} P_{vocab}(w) + \left(1 - p_{gen}\right) \sum\nolimits_{i:w_i = w} a_i^t \tag{11}$$

It can be noted from Eq. (11) that if w is not in the vocabulary, then $P_{vocab}(w) = 0$, then the words generated in the question come from the content associated with the product from the comments, avoiding the OOV problem. In contrast, many sequence-to-sequence models are limited by predefined vocabulary, resulting in inaccurate or incorrect terms.

The final loss function of the model is shown in Eq. (12)–(13). At each time step t, the loss function is the negative logarithmic likelihood expression of the target vocabulary w_t^*:

$$loss_t = -\log\left(P\left(w_t^*\right)\right) \tag{12}$$

$$\text{loss} = \frac{1}{T} \sum\nolimits_{t=0}^{T} loss_t \tag{13}$$

4 Experiment

4.1 Experimental Data

The data of this experiment are mainly from the comments of related products on JD, a Chinese e-commerce platform, and a series of questions about the products raised by consumers. The amount of data obtained is shown in Table 2:

Table 2. Experiment data

Item	Camera	Cellphone	Oven	Pad	TV	Microwave oven	Juicer	Pot
Comment number	62973	90983	36271	77644	58115	25433	27843	28743
Question number	1091	2834	1418	1448	1334	1120	1019	1136

For accessing to the data of this paper, we made the following treatment: World2vec was used for similarity calculation. First of all, we remove comments or questions with calculated similarity greater than 70% and then for each question, pick comments that have a similarity above 60%, at last we select the top 3 comments from similarity ranking, and splicing them together as a short text, thus forming a question with a pair of matching short text. The data form is shown in Table 3.

Table 3. The data sample

Sample	Content
Short text (top 3 comments splicing)	看了评论,抱着侥幸心理,结果还是卡烫卡烫的,看网页烫,打电话三分钟就烫烫,发烫的吓人就是感觉有点烫耐用,打游戏发烫,不过有很多高科技。 (Read the comment, holding the fluke psychology, the result is still card very hot card very hot, look at the web page very hot, make a phone call three minutes very hot, very hot scary is to feel a little hot durable, play games very hot, but there are a lot of high-tech)
Question	玩游戏烫不烫? (Is it hot to play games?)

In this paper, in order to label product-related entity information more accurately, two students marked the entity at the same time, and the third student checked the difference.

4.2 Experimental Settings

- **Data Setting**: In this paper, 80% is used as training set and 20% as test data.
- **Hyper-parameters**: The size of hidden layer is 256. The dimension of word embed-ding is 128. The maximum time step of the encoder is 400. The maximum time step size of decoder is 100. Batch size is 16 and learning rate is 0.15.
- **Evaluation Metric**: The results were evaluated with ROUGE and BLEU values. ROUGE is usually used to measure the "similarity" between the automatically generated text and the reference text. This experiment used ROUGE to evaluate the difference between the generated question and the original question, which more reflected the semantic level. BLEU is mainly used in the field of machine translation, which requires high accuracy of translated words. This experiment is used to measure the accuracy of generating question words.

4.3 Results and Analysis

Baselines: This experiment mainly carried out five groups of comparative experiments, and the comparative experimental model is as follows

- **Seq2seq**: Sequence to sequence model based on LSTM.
- **Seq2seq+attn**: Sequential to sequential model of LSTM based on attention mechanism.
- **NQG_NER**: Du et al. [10] proposed a sequence to sequence model based on attention mechanism, adding some characteristics of words in the encode layer. This experiment is mainly to add the entity characteristics.
- **Pointer-generator**: See et al. [4] proposed a sequence-to-sequence model based on replication coverage mechanism, which can avoid OOV problems. This model has been proved feasible in the field of abstract generation.

From ROUGE values of different models in Table 4, it can be seen that the pointer-generator model and GQPI have significantly better effects than the other three sequence-based models. The main reason is that the data based on product reviews tend to be illogical and colloquial, so OOV problem can easily occur in the generation of question, which cannot be well solved by previous models based on neural network. Since both GQPI and the pointer-generator are based on replication coverage mechanism, it can select not only the corresponding words from the dictionary, but also the relevant words from the original text, thus making the sentence smoother. At the same time, the addition of product-related information in GQPI makes the generated questions revolve around the product, and performs better than pointer-generator model.

From BLEU values, it can be seen that our model is obviously superior to other model, and in the comparison with the Pointer-generator model, the BLEU value is 5 percentage points higher, which further indicates that the model in this paper is more accurate in generating.

For product questions often revolve around the entity information related to product, in addressing the review data, due to the increased the term entity information in the network, which makes the model for the division of physical boundaries and draw

Table 4. Automatic evaluation results of different systems by ROUGE and BLEU

Model	ROUGE			BLEU		
	1-gram	2-gram	L	value	1-gram	2-gram
Seq2seq	0.14	0.03	0.13	3.70	21.1	6.1
Seq2seq +attn	0.14	0.03	0.14	2.47	24.8	8.1.
NQG_NER	0.16	0.04	0.15	5.26	32.8	9.7
Pointer-generator	0.24	0.09	0.23	5.88	49.2	20.2.
Our model	**0.26**	**0.10**	**0.25**	**11.02**	**50.2.**	**22.2**

more accurate, raised the questions generated by the accuracy, also let the generated questions more in line with the actual situation of the product.

4.4 Result Sample Analysis

In order to better understand the effect of network, Table 5 shows three examples of network generation question, from which relevant reasons can be analyzed.

From the first question of network model generation, it can be seen that when OOV problem occurs, that is, "屏幕" is not in the vocabulary, the general neural network will choose the word with the highest probability from the vocabulary, and even cannot generate related words. The resulting question is very different from the standard question.

Table 5. Sample of questions generated by seq2seq+attn, pointer-generator and our model.

Item	Content
Short text	屏幕除了处理器电池,其余都不错,屏幕比7p阴阳屏好多了还行,屏幕反应有延迟屏幕解锁比后置慢,后盖仔细看有很多凹点,处理得不好,其余有很多高科技。 (The screen is good except for the processor battery. The screen is much better than the 7p Yin and Yang screen. The back cover has a lot of concave points carefully, the treatment is not good, the rest has a lot of high-tech.)
Question	屏幕怎么样,有阴阳屏吗? (What about the screen? Is there a Yin and Yang screen?)
Seq2seq+attn	处理怎么样? (How about treatment?)
Pointer-generator	你们屏幕开吗? (Is your screen on?)
Our model	屏幕怎么样? (What about the screen?)

From the question generated by the pointer-generator model, it can be found that the model can select the words of the original text, but the sentence may not be smooth, mainly because the network cannot accurately identify the entities, and fail to accurately divide the boundaries of the entities.

Through comparison, it can be found that although the question generated by the model proposed in this paper cannot completely reproduce the content of the standard question, it reflects the focus of the question. It also uses the entity vocabulary accurately, and forms a smoother sentence.

5 Conclusion

This paper proposes a comment question generation model based on product information, which uses the replication mechanism of attention. When the word is not included in the vocabulary, the original words are selected to solve the OOV problem. The model is based on the short text of the comment data and the more colloquial character. In addition, the entity information of the text is added, so that the generated question is more concerned with the product itself, and the sentences are smoother. The experimental results show that our model has a better effect compared with other neural network models.

Acknowledgements. This research work has been partially supported by two NSFC grants, NO. 61702518 and NO. 61806137.

References

1. Analysis of the current market situation and forecast of the development trend of China's e-commerce industry in 2018. http://www.chyxx.com/industry/201808/666932.html. Accessed 28 April 2019
2. Labutov, I., Basu, S., Vanderwende, L.: Deep questions without deep understanding. In: ACL, pp. 889–898 (2015)
3. Serban, I.V., et al.: Generating factoid questions with recurrent neural networks: the 30 m factoid question-answer corpus. arXiv preprint arXiv:1603.06807 (2016)
4. See, A., Liu, P.J., Manning, C.D.: Get to the point: Summarization with pointer-generator networks. In: ACL, pp. 1073–1083 (2017)
5. Mostow, J., Chen, W.: Generating instruction automatically for the reading strategy of self-questioning. In: AIED, pp. 465–472 (2009)
6. Mannem, P., Prasad, R., Joshi, A.: Question generation from paragraphs at UPenn: QGSTEC system description. In: QG2010, pp. 84–91 (2010)
7. Lindberg, D., Popowich, F., Nesbit, J., Winne, P.: Generating natural language questions to support learning on-line. In: EWNLG, pp. 105–114 (2013)
8. Chali, Y., Hasan, S.A.: Towards topic-to-question generation. Comput. Linguist. **41**(1), 1–20 (2015)
9. Mazidi, K., Tarau, P.: Infusing nlu into automatic question generation. In: INLG, pp. 51–60 (2016)
10. Du, X., Shao, J., Cardie, C.: Learning to ask: neural question generation for reading comprehension. In: ACL, pp. 1342–1352 (2017)

11. Zheng, H.T., Han, J., Chen, J.Y., Sangaiah, A.K.: A novel framework for automatic Chinese question generation based on multi-feature neural network model. Comput. Sci. Inf. Syst. **15**(3), 487–499 (2018)
12. Bao, J., Gong, Y., Duan, N., Zhou, M., Zhao, T.: Question generation with doubly adversarial nets. IEEE/ACM Trans Audio Speech Lang. Process. **26**(11), 2230–2239 (2018)
13. Graves, A., Schmidhuber, J.: Framewise phoneme classification with bidirectional LSTM and other neural network architectures. Neural Networks **18**(5–6), 602–610 (2015)
14. Bahdanau, D., Cho, K., Bengio, Y.: Neural machine translation by jointly learning to align and translate. arXiv preprint arXiv:1409.0473 (2014)

Conversion and Exploitation of Dependency Treebanks with Full-Tree LSTM

Bo Zhang, Zhenghua Li(✉), and Min Zhang

School of Computer Science and Technology, Soochow University, Suzhou, China
bzhang17@stu.suda.edu.cn, {zhli13,minzhang}@suda.edu.cn

Abstract. As a method for exploiting multiple heterogeneous data, supervised treebank conversion can straightforwardly and effectively utilize linguistic knowledge contained in heterogeneous treebank. In order to efficiently and deeply encode the source-side tree, we for the first time investigate and propose to use Full-tree LSTM as a tree encoder for treebank conversion. Furthermore, the corpus weighting strategy and the concatenation with fine-tuning approach are introduced to weaken the noise contained in the converted treebank. Experimental results on two benchmark datasets with bi-tree aligned trees show that (1) the proposed Full-Tree LSTM approach is more effective than previous treebank conversion methods, (2) the corpus weighting strategy and the concatenation with fine-tuning approach are both useful for the exploitation of the noisy converted treebank, and (3) supervised treebank conversion methods can achieve higher final parsing accuracy than multi-task learning approach.

Keywords: Supervised treebank conversion · Full-tree LSTM · Treebank exploitation · Corpus weighting · Concatenation with fine-tuning · Multi-task learning

1 Introduction

In recent years, neural network based dependency parsing has made great progress and outperforms the traditional discrete-feature based approaches [1,3–5,17]. In particular, Dozat and Manning (2017) [4] propose a simple yet effective deep biaffine parser, which achieves the state-of-the-art performance in many languages and datasets.

Meanwhile, exploiting various heterogeneous treebanks for boosting parsing performance is always the focus in the research community [6–10,12–14,18]. However, due to the lack of manually labeled data where each sentence has two

---

Supported by National Natural Science Foundation of China (Grant No. 61525205, 61876116). Zhenghua Li is the corresponding author. We thank the anonymous reviewers for the helpful comments and Qingrong Xia and Houquan Zhou for their help on preparing this English version.

J. Tang et al. (Eds.): NLPCC 2019, LNAI 11839, pp. 456–465, 2019.
https://doi.org/10.1007/978-3-030-32236-6_41

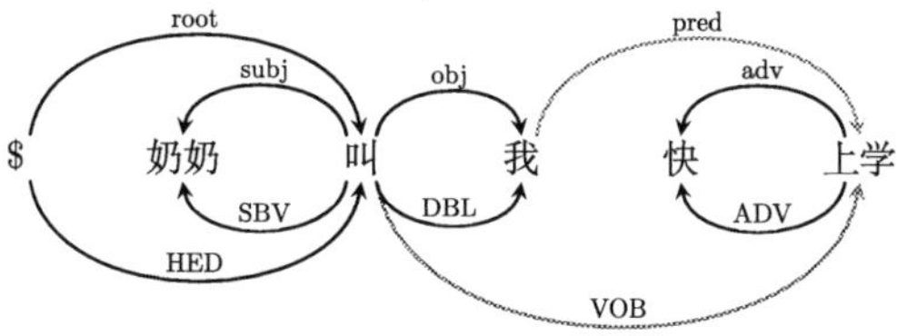

Fig. 1. Example of treebank conversion from the source-side HIT (under) to the target-side SU (upper).

syntactic trees complying with two different annotation guidelines, called bi-tree aligned data, as shown in Fig. 1, previous works mainly focus on the unsupervised treebank conversion methods [8,10,12,13,18] and indirect treebank exploitation methods [6,9,14].

Jiang et al. (2018) [7] first propose the task of supervised treebank conversion by manually constructing a bi-tree aligned dataset. As shown in Fig. 1, given an input sentence x, treebank conversion aims to convert the source-side tree $\mathbf{d}^{src}$ to the target-side tree $\mathbf{d}^{tgt}$.

There are two main challenges for treebank exploitation via treebank conversion. One is how to convert $\mathbf{d}^{src}$ to $\mathbf{d}^{tgt}$ with high quality (*treebank conversion*), and the other is how to effectively exploit the converted treebank for higher parsing accuracy of target side (*treebank exploitation*).

Jiang et al. (2018) [7] then propose the pattern embedding (PE) and the shortest path TreeLSTM (SP-Tree) approach for treebank conversion. The PE approach uses a custom pattern to encode $\mathbf{d}^{src}$, which captures the syntactic structure correspondence between the target-side and source-side. Given a dependency $i \leftarrow j$ in $\mathbf{d}^{tgt}$, they define nine patterns in accordance with the structure and the distance of w_i and w_j in $\mathbf{d}^{src}$. And then these patterns are mapped into embedded vectors as the representation of $\mathbf{d}^{src}$. The SP-Tree approach uses the bidirectional shortest path TreeLSTM to deeply encode $\mathbf{d}^{src}$. For scoring a dependency $i \leftarrow j$ in $\mathbf{d}^{tgt}$, they use the concatenation of the TreeLSTM hidden vectors of w_i, w_j and w_a as the representation of $\mathbf{d}^{src}$, where a is the lowest common ancestor node of w_i and w_j in $\mathbf{d}^{src}$.

Following Jiang et al. (2018) [7], our preliminary experiments show that (1) the performance of the PE approach is unstable since it only encodes $\mathbf{d}^{src}$ quite locally, especially when the two treebanks are very divergent, and (2) the SP-Tree approach is very inefficient. for a sentence with n words, the SP-Tree approach requires running TreeLSTM n^2 times. In order to solve these problems, we propose to use Full-tree LSTM as a tree encoder for treebank conversion, called Full-Tree approach. We find that with proper dropping-out of the outputs of the Full-Tree LSTM hidden cells, the Full-Tree approach can achieve slightly higher conversion performance than the SP-Tree approach and is much more efficient.

In terms of treebank exploitation, since the target-side treebank and converted treebank comply with same guideline, Jiang et al. (2018) [7] simply concatenate them to train a parser, called the concatenation approach, which cannot handle the noise contained in the converted treebank. We propose two ways to better exploit the converted treebank, i.e., the corpus weighting strategy and the concatenation with fine-tuning approach.

We conduct experiments on two benchmarks of bi-tree aligned data, and the results show that (1) compared with the treebank conversion approaches of Jiang et al. (2018) [7], the Full-Tree LSTM approach can stably and efficiently achieve higher accuracy, (2) the corpus weighting strategy and the concatenation with fine-tuning approach can both effectively exploit the converted treebank and further improve the performance of the target-side parsing, and (3) our approaches are significantly better than Jiang et al. (2018) [7] both on treebank conversion and exploitation and can significantly outperform the multi-task learning baseline.

2 Related Works

At present, major languages in the world often possess multiple large-scale heterogeneous treebanks, e.g., Tiger and Tüba-D/Z for German, Talbanken and Syntag for Swedish, ISST and TUT for Italian, etc. We focus on exploitation of Chinese heterogeneous treebanks, and select HIT-CDT [2], PCTB7 [16], and SU-CDT [7] for case study.

Unsupervised Treebank Conversion. Niu et al. (2009) [12], Zhu et al. (2011) [18], and Li et al. (2013) [8] propose to convert source-guideline treebank into the target guideline with a statistical model, and use the converted treebank as extra training data for boosting parsing performance. Without bi-tree aligned data, these methods rely on heuristic rules or use automatically generated target-side trees as pseudo gold-standard reference during training.

Indirect Treebank Exploitation. Li et al. (2012) [9], Guo et al. (2016) [6], and Stymne et al. (2018) [14] propose to indirectly exploit heterogeneous treebanks without explicit conversion based on guide features, multi-task learning (MTL), or treebank embedding.

Supervised Treebank Conversion. Jiang et al. (2018) [7] first propose supervised treebank conversion task based on a newly constructed bi-tree (SU^{HIT}) aligned dataset. They also propose two treebank conversion approaches (PE and SP-Tree) and use the concatenation approach to exploit the converted treebank.

In this work, we follow Jiang et al. (2018) [7] and focus on the supervised treebank conversion task. We propose to use the Full-Tree LSTM to encode the source-side tree to deal with the disadvantages of their PE and SP-Tree approaches in efficiency and efficacy. For treebank exploitation, we propose to use the corpus weighting strategy and the concatenation with fine-tuning approach, in order to increase the impact of manually labeled data and weaken the noise contained in converted treebank.

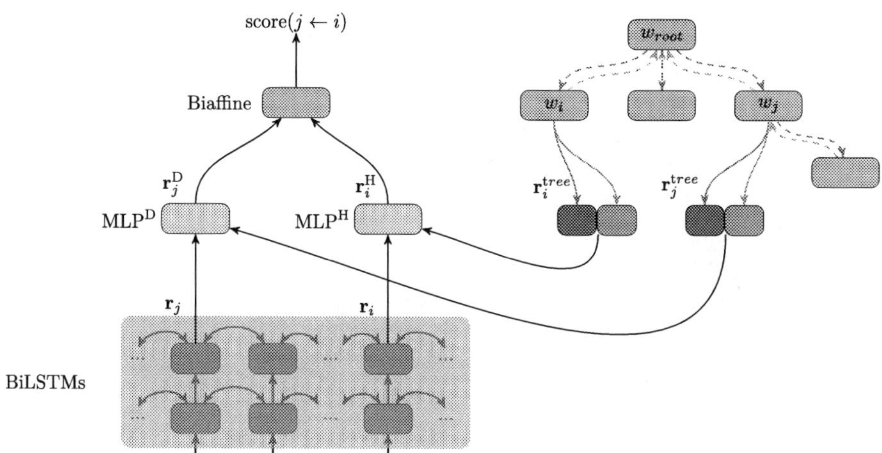

Fig. 2. Computation of score($j \leftarrow i$) by conversion model. The left part is the biaffine parser and the right part is the Full-Tree LSTM structure.

3 Treebank Conversion Based on Full-Tree LSTM

Basic Parser. We build all our models based on the state-of-the-art biaffine parser. As a graph-based dependency parser, it applies multi-layer bidirectional LSTMs (BiLSTM) to encode the input sentence, and employs a deep biaffine transformation to compute the scores of all possible dependencies and uses viterbi decoding to find the highest-scoring tree. The left part of Fig. 2 shows how to score a dependency $j \leftarrow i$. Due to space limitation, please refer to Dozat and Manning (2017) [4] and Jiang et al. (2018) [7] for more details.

Full-Tree LSTM is proposed by Tai et al. (2015) [15] to use the information of the whole syntactic tree, whereas SP-Tree LSTM is proposed by Miwa and Bansal (2016) [11] as an extension of Full-Tree LSTM in task of relation extraction, which only encodes the information of nodes on the shortest path of two focused words. In this work, we use Full-Tree LSTM as the encoder of the source-side tree to treebank conversion. Compared with the shallow PE approach, the Full-Tree approach uses bidirectional TreeLSTM to deeply encode $\mathbf{d}^{src}$ with strong stability. Compared with the SP-Tree approach, the Full-Tree approach requires less calculation to obtain word-level representation incorporating $\mathbf{d}^{src}$ for all words in sentence.

As shown in the right part of Fig. 2, we use the bidirectional Full-Tree (BiFull-Tree) LSTM to encode the $\mathbf{d}^{src}$ (bottom-up and top-down). Given a $\mathbf{d}^{src}$, the bottom-up Full-Tree LSTM starts from the leaves node and accumulates information until the root node (the inner red dashed line), whereas the top-down Full-Tree LSTM propagates information in opposite direction (the outer blue dashed line).

Following Jiang et al. (2018), we stack Full-Tree LSTM on the top of the BiLSTM layer of the basic biaffine parser. Moreover, we also consider the dependency label of the $\mathbf{d}^{src}$, and embed a label into a dense vector as the extra input of Full-tree LSTM. For example, the input vector for w_k in the Full-tree LSTM is $\mathbf{x}_k = \mathbf{h}_k \oplus \mathbf{e}^{l_k}$, where $\mathbf{h}_k$ is the top-level BiLSTM output vector at w_k, and l_k is the label between w_k and its head word in $\mathbf{d}^{src}$, and $\mathbf{e}^{l_k}$ is the label embedding.

In the bottom-up Full-tree LSTM, an LSTM node computes a hidden vector based on the combination of the input vector and the hidden vectors of its children in $\mathbf{d}^{src}$. The right part of Fig. 2 and Eq. 1 illustrate the computation of the Full-Tree LSTM output vector at w_k.

$$
\begin{aligned}
\tilde{\mathbf{h}}_k &= \sum_{m \in \mathcal{C}(k)} \mathbf{h}_m \\
\mathbf{i}_k &= \sigma\left(\mathbf{W}^{(i)}\mathbf{x}_k + \mathbf{U}^{(i)}\tilde{\mathbf{h}}_k + \mathbf{b}^{(i)}\right) \\
\mathbf{f}_{k,m} &= \sigma\left(\mathbf{W}^{(f)}\mathbf{x}_k + \mathbf{U}^{(f)}\mathbf{h}_m + \mathbf{b}^{(f)}\right) \\
\mathbf{o}_k &= \sigma\left(\mathbf{W}^{(o)}\mathbf{x}_k + \mathbf{U}^{(o)}\tilde{\mathbf{h}}_k + \mathbf{b}^{(o)}\right) \\
\mathbf{u}_k &= \tanh\left(\mathbf{W}^{(u)}\mathbf{x}_k + \mathbf{U}^{(u)}\tilde{\mathbf{h}}_k + \mathbf{b}^{(u)}\right) \\
\mathbf{c}_k &= \mathbf{i}_k \odot \mathbf{u}_k + \sum_{m \in \mathcal{C}(k)} \mathbf{f}_{k,m} \odot \mathbf{c}_m \\
\mathbf{h}_k &= \mathbf{o}_k \odot \tanh\left(\mathbf{c}_k\right)
\end{aligned}
\tag{1}
$$

where $\mathcal{C}(k)$ means the children of w_k in the $\mathbf{d}^{src}$, and $\mathbf{f}_{k,m}$ is the forget vector for w_k's child w_m.

In the top-down Full-tree LSTM, an LSTM node computes a hidden vector based on the combination of the input vector and the hidden vector of its single father node in the $\mathbf{d}^{src}$. The calculation process is consistent with Eq. (1).

At each time step, the hidden vector of the BiFull-Tree LSTM is the concatenation of the bottom-up and top-down Full-Tree LSTM hidden vectors, denoted as $\mathbf{r}^{tree}$. For example, the output vector of the BiFull-Tree LSTM at w_k is $\mathbf{r}_k^{tree} = \mathbf{h}_k^{\uparrow} \oplus \mathbf{h}_k^{\downarrow}$, where $\mathbf{h}_k^{\uparrow}$ is the hidden vector of the bottom-up Full-Tree LSTM at w_k, and $\mathbf{h}_k^{\downarrow}$ is the hidden vector of the top-down Full-Tree LSTM.

Taking scoring a dependency $j \leftarrow i$ as an example, we integrate information of $\mathbf{d}^{src}$ encoded by the BiFull-Tree LSTM into target-side parser by the Eq. (2).

$$
\begin{aligned}
\mathbf{r}_j^{\mathrm{D}} &= \mathrm{MLP}^{\mathrm{D}}\left(\mathbf{h}_j \oplus \mathbf{r}_j^{tree}\right) \\
\mathbf{r}_i^{\mathrm{H}} &= \mathrm{MLP}^{\mathrm{H}}\left(\mathbf{h}_i \oplus \mathbf{r}_i^{tree}\right)
\end{aligned}
\tag{2}
$$

Finally, the $\mathbf{r}_j^{\mathrm{D}}$ and $\mathbf{r}_i^{\mathrm{H}}$ are fed into the biaffine layer to compute a more reliable score of the dependency $i \leftarrow j$, with the help of the guidance of $\mathbf{d}^{src}$.

4 Treebank Exploitation

Treebank exploitation is how to make full use of the converted source-side treebank to improve the performance of the target-side parsing in our scenario. Considering the noise contained in the converted data and the big gap between the

Table 1. Data statistics.

Data	Sent num	Dependency num	Consistency	
			Dependency	Label
SU^{HIT}	10,761	50,866	81.68%	73.73%
HIT train	52,450	980,791		
SU^{PCTB}	11,579	49,979	66.37%	55.14%
PCTB train	43,114	961,654		

size of the converted and manually labeled data (SU^{HIT} has 980,791 converted dependencies, and only 50,866 manually labeled dependencies), the concatenation approach is too simple to effectively exploit converted data. In this work, we use the corpus weighting strategy and the concatenation with fine-tuning approach to strengthen the impact of manually labeled data on the parser, which brings significant improvement over the concatenation approach.

The corpus weighting strategy is an effective method of using multiple corpus training models. We apply it as a method to rationally use data containing noise. Specifically, before each iteration, we randomly sample training sentences separately from the target-side and converted data in the proportion of $1 : M$. Then we merge and randomly shuffle the sampled data for one-iteration training. We treat $M \geq 1$ as a hyper-parameter tuned on the dev data. The concatenation with fine-tuning approach first train on the concatenation of the target-side and converted data and follow by fine-tuning for the target-side data.

Multi-task learning, as a strong baseline for treebank exploitation, aims to incorporate labeled data of multiple related tasks for improving performance. Following Jiang et al. (2018) [7], we treat the source-side and target-side parsing as two individual tasks, which share parameters of word/tag embeddings and multi-layer BiLSTM and separate parameters of the MLP and biaffine layers. Due to space limitation, please refer to Jiang et al. (2018) [7] for the details.

5 Experimental Results and Analysis

5.1 Data

We employ the $SU^{\mathrm{HIT|PCTB}}$ conversion datasets to conduct our experiments. Table 1 shows the number of sentences and annotated dependencies, respectively. For SU^{HIT} dataset, we directly employ the data settings of Jiang et al. (2018) [7]. For SU^{PCTB}, we randomly choose 1k and 2k sentences as the dev and test datasets, and use the remaining 8k sentences for training.

In order to measure the similarity (or homogeneity) between the source-side and target-side guidelines, we list the ratios of consistent dependencies and relations following the practice in Jiang et al. (2018) [7]. We can see that the PCTB is much more divergent from SU than HIT, and thus it is more difficult to convert PCTB into the SU guideline.

Table 2. Dropping-out the outputs of the Full-Tree LSTM hidden cells on conversion accuracy on the dev data.

Dropout ratio	SU^{HIT}		SU^{PCTB}	
	UAS	LAS	UAS	LAS
0	86.00	81.13	80.49	75.92
0.3	86.20	81.46	81.50	77.05
0.5	86.32	81.66	81.69	77.54
0.7	**86.42**	**81.69**	81.92	77.68
0.8	85.93	81.21	**82.31**	**78.02**
0.9	85.78	81.18	81.64	77.31

5.2 Settings and Evaluation Metrics

We implement all the models with Pytorch 0.4.1, and release the codes at https://github.com/sdzhangbo/Supervised-Treebank-Conversion.

In order to fairly compare with our Full-Tree method with the PE and SP-Tree methods, we strictly follow the experimental settings of Jiang et al. (2018) [7]: two-layer BiLSTMs with 300 output dimension; The MLP output dimension is 200 for the biaffine parser and MTL; embedding dimension of the source-side dependency labels is 50, the output dimension of TreeLSTM is 100, and the output dimension of MLP is 300 for the conversion model.

For evaluation, we employ the unlabeled attachment score (UAS) and labeled attachment score (LAS) for both conversion and exploitation.

5.3 Results of Treebank Conversion on the Dev Data

We count the time of encoding 1k sentences of the three approaches, and find that the Full-Tree approach is little slower than the PE approach (2 vs. 1) and is much more efficient than the SP-Tree approach (2 vs. 229).

We carefully tune the dropout ratio of the Full-Tree LSTM output, as shown in Table 2. Specifically, 0 means that dropout is unused. We omit the results of 0.1/0.2/0.4/0.6 due to space limitation. On SU^{HIT}, the model achieves best LAS performance of 81.69% when we use the dropout ratio of 0.7, which outperforms the dropout ratio of 0 by 0.56% (81.69–81.13). The model achieves the highest LAS of 78.02% when the dropout ratio is 0.8 on SU^{PCTB}, which outperforms the model without Full-Tree LSTM output dropout by 2.1% (78.02–75.92). We can conclude that dropout of Full-Tree LSTM output has a positive impact on the conversion performance, i.e., the lower the data consistency, the more obvious of the performance improvement.

5.4 Results of Treebank Exploitation on the Dev Data

Table 3 shows the results comparison of the three treebank exploitation methods on the dev data. The results of concatenation approach of Jiang et al. (2018)

Table 3. Effect of corpus weighting strategy and concatenation with fine-tuning approach on dev data.

Methods		Exploit converted HIT		Exploit converted PCTB	
		UAS	LAS	UAS	LAS
Concatenation		81.50	76.30	79.73	75.09
Corpus weighting	$M = 1$	81.37	76.14	79.80	75.25
	$M = 2$	82.10	**76.97**	79.89	**75.46**
	$M = 3$	81.85	76.61	**80.01**	75.30
	$M = 4$	81.66	76.55	79.50	75.31
	$M = 5$	**82.14**	76.84	79.34	74.77
	$M = 6$	81.37	76.26	79.84	75.23
Concatenation with fine-tuning		**82.24**	**77.17**	**80.56**	**76.11**

[7] is shown in the third row, The results of corpus weighting strategy is shown from row 4 to row 9. The tenth row shows the results of concatenation with fine-tuning approach. We can see the best model of corpus weighting outperforms the concatenation model by 0.67% (76.97–76.30) and 0.37% (75.46–75.09) on the two datasets, respectively. And the concatenation with fine-tuning approach outperforms the concatenation model by 0.87% (77.17–76.30) and 1.02% (76.11–75.09) on the two datasets, respectively.

Table 4. Conversion accuracy of PE, SP-Tree and Full-Tree approaches on test data.

Methods	SU^{HIT}		SU^{PCTB}	
	UAS	LAS	UAS	LAS
PE	86.66	82.03	74.71	67.11
SP-Tree	**86.69**	**82.09**	81.94	77.95
Full-Tree	86.28	82.04	**82.45**	**78.45**

We can see that the corpus weighting strategy and the concatenation with fine-tuning approach can effectively exploit converted treebank that contains noise, which can further improve the target-side parser performance.

5.5 Results of Conversion and Exploitation on the Test Data

Table 4 shows the results comparison of the three treebank conversion methods. The Full-Tree method achieves almost the same performance compared with PE and SP-Tree on SU^{HIT}, which has high data consistency. However, on the SU^{PCTB} data with lower data consistency, the Full-Tree method outperforms the

Table 5. Parsing accuracy of different parsers on test data.

Methods	SU^{HIT}		SU^{PCTB}	
	UAS	LAS	UAS	LAS
Single parser	75.57	70.81	76.78	72.48
MTL and HIT	80.08	75.46	78.80	74.61
Jiang et al. (2018)	81.33	76.73	80.09	76.03
Ours	**81.86**	**77.27**	**80.90**	**76.77**

SP-Tree by 0.5% (78.45–77.95), and advances the PE by large margin (11.34%, 78.45–67.11) in LAS, which indicates that the PE method heavily relies on the conversion data and cannot exploit the source-side data stably. The Full-Tree and SP-Tree method can both stably encode the source-side tree information, which can achieve better convert performance over data with low consistency. Considering the speed, the Full-Tree is a superior encoding method.

Finally, Table 5 lists the performance of the target-side parser with the help of the source-side treebank by different exploitation methods. The third row shows the results of our basic model that only use the target-side data. The experimental results of using MTL to exploit the source-side data is shown in row 4. The fifth and sixth row show the results of applying the concatenation approach and the concatenation with fine-tuning approach to exploit the target-side and converted source-side data, respectively.

On the two datasets, we find that the MTL method respectively outperforms the baseline by 4.65% (75.46–70.81) and 2.13% (74.61–72.48) and our method respectively outperforms the baseline by 6.46% (77.27–70.81) and 4.29% (76.77–72.48), which indicate that heterogeneous data with common information can effectively improve the performance of the target-side parsing. Additionally, our method also outperforms the concatenation approach of Jiang et al. (2018) [7] by 0.54% (77.27–76.73) and 0.74% (76.77–76.03).

Moreover, the treebank conversion method can further improve the performance of target side parser, which outperforms the MTL method by 1.81% (77.27–75.46) and 2.16% (76.77–74.61) on the two datasets, which indicates the treebank conversion method is a more straightforward and effective way to utilize heterogeneous data.

6 Conclusions

To exploit multiple heterogeneous Chinese dependency treebanks, we propose a supervised treebank conversion method based on Full-Tree LSTM. Experimental results on two conversion datasets show that (1) our Full-Tree LSTM approach can efficiently and deeply encode the source-side tree, and is superior to the PE and SP-Tree approaches of Jiang et al. (2018) [7]; (2) the corpus weighting strategy and the concatenation with fine-tuning approach are both helpful in exploiting noisy converted data for further improving the target-side parsing performance; (3) compared with the MTL method, supervised treebank conversion is a more effective way to exploit heterogeneous treebanks and can achieve higher final parsing accuracy. Moreover, we also find that proper dropping-out of the outputs of TreeLSTM hidden cells significantly affects the performance of the Full-Tree LSTM approach.

References

1. Andor, D., et al.: Globally normalized transition-based neural networks. In: Proceedings of ACL, pp. 2442–2452 (2016)
2. Che, W., Li, Z., Liu, T.: Chinese dependency treebank 1.0 (LDC2012T05). In: Philadelphia: Linguistic Data Consortium (2012)
3. Chen, D., Manning, C.: A fast and accurate dependency parser using neural networks. In: Proceedings of EMNLP, pp. 740–750 (2014)
4. Dozat, T., Manning, C.D.: Deep biaffine attention for neural dependency parsing. In: Proceedings of ICLR (2017)
5. Dyer, C., Ballesteros, M., Ling, W., Matthews, A., Smith, N.A.: Transition-based dependency parsing with stack long short-term memory. In: Proceedings of ACL, pp. 334–343 (2015)
6. Guo, J., Che, W., Wang, H., Liu, T.: A universal framework for inductive transfer parsing across multi-typed treebanks. In: Proceedings of COLING, pp. 12–22 (2016)
7. Jiang, X., Li, Z., Zhang, B., Zhang, M., Li, S., Si, L.: Supervised treebank conversion: data and approaches. In: Proceedings of ACL, pp. 2706–2716 (2018)
8. Li, X., Jiang, W., Lü, Y., Liu, Q.: Iterative transformation of annotation guidelines for constituency parsing. In: Proceedings of ACL, pp. 591–596 (2013)
9. Li, Z., Che, W., Liu, T.: Exploiting multiple treebanks for parsing with quasi-synchronous grammar. In: Proceedings of ACL, pp. 675–684 (2012)
10. Magerman, D.M.: Natural language parsing as statistical pattern recognition. arXiv preprint cmp-lg/9405009 (1994)
11. Miwa, M., Bansal, M.: End-to-end relation extraction using LSTMs on sequences and tree structures. In: Proceedings of ACL, pp. 1105–1116 (2016)
12. Niu, Z.Y., Wang, H., Wu, H.: Exploiting heterogeneous treebanks for parsing. In: Proceedings of ACL, pp. 46–54 (2009)
13. Nivre, J., Scholz, M.: Deterministic dependency parsing of English text. In: Proceedings of COLING 2004, pp. 64–70 (2004)
14. Stymne, S., de Lhoneux, M., Smith, A., Nivre, J.: Parser training with heterogeneous treebanks. arXiv preprint arXiv:1805.05089 (2018)
15. Tai, K.S., Socher, R., Manning, C.D.: Improved semantic representations from tree-structured long short-term memory networks. In: Proceedings of ACL, pp. 1556–1566 (2015)
16. Xue, N., Xia, F., Chiou, F.D., Palmer, M.: The penn Chinese treebank: phrase structure annotation of a large corpus. Nat. Lang. Eng. **11**(2), 207–238 (2005)
17. Zhou, H., Zhang, Y., Huang, S., Chen, J.: A neural probabilistic structured-prediction model for transition-based dependency parsing. In: Proceedings of ACL, pp. 1213–1222 (2015)
18. Zhu, M., Zhu, J., Hu, M.: Exploitating multiple treebanks using a feature-based approach. In: Proceedings of ACL, pp. 715–719 (2011)

Analysis of Back-Translation Methods for Low-Resource Neural Machine Translation

Nuo Xu[1], Yinqiao Li[1], Chen Xu[1], Yanyang Li[1], Bei Li[1], Tong Xiao[1,2(✉)], and Jingbo Zhu[1,2]

[1] Northeastern University, Shenyang, China
{xunuo0629, xuchen}@stumail.neu.edu.cn, li.yin.qiao.2012@hotmail.com, blamedrlee@outlook.com, libei_neu@outlook.com, {xiaotong, zhujingbo}@mail.neu.edu.cn
[2] NiuTrans Research, Shenyang, China

Abstract. Back translation refers to the method of using machine translation to automatically translate target language monolingual data into source language data, which is a commonly used data augmentation method in machine translation tasks. Previous researchers' works on back translation only focus on rich resource languages, while ignoring the low resource language with different quality. In this paper, we compare various monolingual selection methods, different model performance, pseudo-data and parallel corpus ratios, and different data generation methods for the validity of pseudo-data in machine translation tasks. Experiments on Lithuanian and Gujarati, two low-resource languages have shown that increasing the distribution of low-frequency words and increasing data diversity are more effective for models with sufficient training, while the results of insufficient models are opposite. In this paper, different back-translation strategies are used for different languages, and compared with common back-translation methods in WMT news tasks of two languages, and the effectiveness of the strategies is verified by experiments. At the same time, we find that combined back-translation strategies are more effective than simply increasing the amount of pseudo-data.

Keywords: Low-resource · Back-translation · Machine translation

1 Introduction

Neural machine translation model based on large volume dataset [1] to learn the mapping between the source and the target has advanced the state-of-the-art on various language pairs [2]. The availability of massively parallel corpus is critical to train strong systems. But the resource of massive bitext is limited and there are abundant of monolingual sentences which can be furthermore leveraged to increase the amount of bilingual corpus [3]. Back-translation is a common and effective data augmentation method without modification to the training strategy, which we translate the target monolingual data into the source by reverse translation models. Surprisingly, researchers find the pseudo-data ratio and the improvement of translation quality is non-linear related [4]. There are several research on selecting the appreciate monolingual data from the mass data, such as

J. Tang et al. (Eds.): NLPCC 2019, LNAI 11839, pp. 466–475, 2019.
https://doi.org/10.1007/978-3-030-32236-6_42

extracting the monolingual data according to the word frequency or the words with high loss [4], or scoring by language models to pick in-domain corpus [5]. For the data generation method, it is not limited to the beam search manner, but based on sampling method [6] or noisy beam search to generate the synthetic data.

In the translation tasks of low resource language pair, the quantity and quality of parallel corpora are more unsatisfactory than the rich-source language, which makes the translation model obtained by using bilingual data less robust and accurate. For example, some methods that can effectively improve the translation performance in rich resource translation tasks may not achieve the desired improvement on condition of low resource languages. Therefore, the research on the back-translation strategy for low-resource language has not been widely investigated. In this paper we verify the effectiveness of various back-translation strategies on low-resource translation tasks through experimenting and analyzing.

We focus on BT strategies from four aspects as the following: how to select the monolingual data, the methods to generate pseudo corpus, the translation performance of target-to-source translation model, and the ratio of synthetic data in the bilingual corpus. We investigate the data selection method according to the frequency of rare words and high predictive loss words, or scoring by in-domain language model. For the performance of pseudo-data generation models, we explore the effect of different convergence states and hyper-parameter settings. Additionally, we furthermore analyze several synthetic source sentence generation methods, including random or restricted sampling from the model distribution or conventional beam search. We experimented different strategies on two low-resource language tasks, including Lithuania to English and Gujarat to English. Our analysis shows that on condition of 1:1 between the synthetic data and real bitext, we achieved 1.5/0.5 BLEU improvements on the validation set and the test set respectively. Similarly, 0.4/0.7 BLEU improvements were obtained on Gujarat to English language pair. Meanwhile, we found that the appropriate back translation strategy improves the translation performance effectively than simply increasing the synthetic data volume.

2 Related Work

2.1 Back Translation

Neural machine translation model solely based on parallel corpus has achieved promising performance. Due to the limitation of bitext resource, researchers often prefer leveraging the abundant monolingual data to furthermore enhance the translation quality. BT is one of the data augmentation methods which is simple and effective and wildly used among the researchers. Experiment results show that even if the parallel corpus is rich enough, using the back-translation method can also effectively improve the translation quality.

2.2 Data Generation Strategy

Beam Search. Beam search retains several candidates in each decoding step, and finally obtains the approximate global optimal translation. This method is more accurate than the ordinary greedy search algorithm, which only retains the word with the highest probability in each decoding step, but for the entire target sentence, it may be not the global optimal choice. The beam search alleviates this problem by collecting several high-probability words into the consideration to participate in the next prediction, so as to obtain the target hypothesis with the highest overall probability [8]. Equation 1 represents the decoding algorithm where is the length of the target sentence and is the length of the source sentence:

$$y = \underset{y}{\operatorname{argmax}} P(y^{<1>}, y^{<2>}, y^{<3>}, \ldots y^{<T_y>} | x^{<1>}, x^{<2>}, \ldots x^{<T_x>}) \quad (1)$$

TopK Probability Search. The TopK-based decoding method is a translation-based probability decoding method. The decoding process is divided into two steps. Firstly, the method selects words with the highest probability according to the distribution of the target vocabulary. The second step is to sample the words restricted from the highest-N candidates among the vocabulary [6]. This method slightly increases the diversity of the prediction distribution compared with beam search. However, the pseudo data generated by this method is not much different from beam search due to the constrained sampling space.

Sampling Probability Search. Sampling is a more flexible probabilistic decoding method. This method removes the restriction on the candidate set in the TopK search mode, and randomly selects words from the whole vocabulary distribution [6]. In this way, we can gain more diverse and noisy synthetic data than beam search or restricted sampling, which can improve the robustness of the model by the source side inaccurate samples. Nevertheless, lots of noise brought into the model may damage the model precision.

Compared with the beam search, TopK and Sampling as Fig. 1:

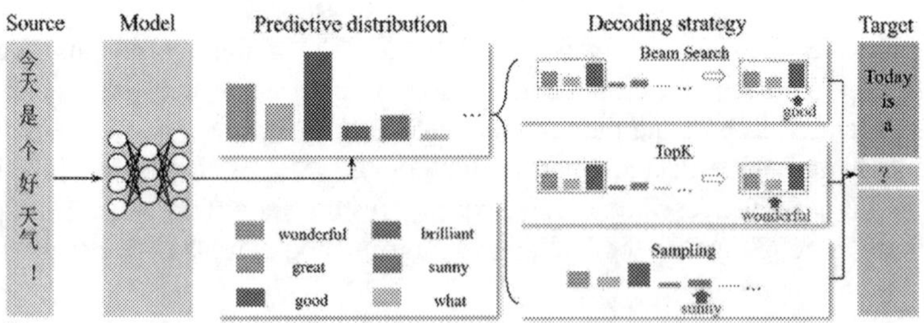

Fig. 1. Contrast diagram of beam search, TopK and Sampling

3 Experiments

3.1 Data Processing

This paper experiments various back-translation strategies in the Lithuanian-English (Lt-En), Gujarat-English (Gu-En) news translation tasks from the 2019 WMT (Workshop on Machine Translation). The parallel corpus in the Lt-En task comes from Europarl v9, ParaCrawl v3, and Rapid corpus of EU press releases. In the Gu-En task, it comes from Bible Corpus, crawled corpus, Localisation extracted from OPUS and parallel corpus extracted from Wikipedia. The English monolingual data is from News Crawl 2015–2018. We filter the parallel corpus and monolingual data by garbled filtering, length ratio filtering, word alignment, language model scoring [7], deduplication and etc.

After the above filtering steps, we retain nearly 1.9M parallel corpus in the Lt-En task, 79K parallel corpus in the Gu-En task and 10M English monolingual data. We use the sacrebleu.perl [8] script to calculate the BLEU as the evaluation metric of translation quality. We perform BPE on the training data [9], and the number of merge operations is 32k.

There are only a few test sets available for low resource language pairs, i.e., the validation set and test sets issued by WMT19. According to our preliminary analysis, the small number of test set sentences, the huge distinction between the construction of the validation set and training data together with the diverse domains involved in the content, will have a great impact on the evaluation of the models. So we randomly cut out 2000 bilingual sentence pairs from the parallel corpus as our test set, which shares the same distribution as the training data, for reverse translation model experiments (4.2) and data generation method experiments (4.3).

For simplicity, Train denotes the test set extracted from the training data, Dev denotes the official validation set, and Test denotes the official test set.

3.2 Baselines

This paper employs the Transformer [10] model for the experiments. We use Tensor2Tensor and Fairseq open source system for model training and decoding. There are 6 layers in both encoder and decoder. The hidden layer dimension is 512 and 1024 and the attention number is 8 and 16 for the Transformer_base and the Transformer_big setting respectively. The batch size is 4096, and the maximum sentence length is 250. The residual dropout is 0.1, the initial learning rate is set to 0.001, and the optimizer is Adam. We train 15 epochs for Transformer_base, 30 epochs for Transformer_big, and average the last 5 checkpoints. During the experiment, 8 GPU devices is used for model training. The length penalty used to generate Lithuanian pseudo data is 0.7 and 1.0 for Gujarat. The Transformer_base baseline scores are shown in Table 1:

Table 1. Bidirectional baselines performance

Language direction	Corpus size	BLEU	
		Dev	Test
Lt-En	1.9 M	27.1	29.2
Gu-En	79 K	3.2	3.5

4 Analysis

4.1 Pseudo Dataset Size

This part of the experiment is based on the Transformer_base setting. To investigate the impact of the pseudo data size on the scarce resources scenario, we experiment with the Gujarati language, as it has much less parallel data. By varying the ratio of parallel corpus to pseudo data, we observe the influence of different pseudo corpus scales on the model performances. The experimental results are shown in Fig. 2:

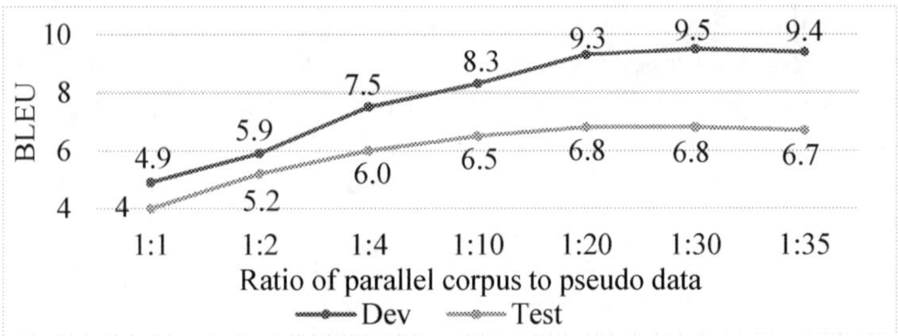

Fig. 2. The effect of pseudo data ratio on model performance

According to the experimental results, we find that the model performance does not grow linearly with the pseudo dataset size. The positive effect of the pseudo dataset size becomes marginalized when more pseudo data are added. We believe that this is due to the quality of the pseudo data. The pseudo data is generated by the translation model trained on the parallel corpus, so its quality is impossible to beat the parallel corpus. Adding excessive pseudo data reduces their effectiveness.

4.2 Reverse Translation Models

This part of the experiment makes use of the larger Lt-En corpus. It compares how pseudo data generated from the reverse translation models with different convergence states affect the performance. The performances of the reverse translation models are shown in Table 2:

The pseudo data generated by these four models are mixed with the parallel corpus in turn. The experimental results are shown in Table 3. During the convergence, the neural network fits the training data progressively. If the pseudo data from the insufficiently trained model are directly used, then the mismatch between the data distribution and the pseudo data distribution will have a negative effect on the final performance. In addition, we also find from Tables 2 and 3 that the convergence state of the model affects the accuracy of the model prediction more even the performance gap among the converged models of different scales is similarly remarkable.

Table 2. Reverse translation models performance

Parameter	Epoch	Convergence state	BLEU	
			Dev	Test
Transformer_base	3epochs	Not converged	15.1	9.5
Transformer_base	8epochs	Not fully converged	19.9	11.3
Transformer_base	15epochs	Fully converged	20.2	11.5
Transformer_big	30epochs	Fully converged	21.0	12.7

For different scaled reverse translation models, the better the performance, the more the performance boost from the corresponded pseudo dataset are observed. However, high reverse translation model performance does not result in significant performance distinction on the models trained with the corresponding pseudo data.

Table 3. The effect of different models performance on pseudo data

Pseudo data generation model	Corpus size	BLEU		
		Dev	Test	Train
–	1.9 M	27.1	29.2	45.1
Transformer_base in unconverged state	3.9 M	28.6	29.2	45.4
Transformer_base in not fully converged	3.9 M	29.5	29.4	46.2
Transformer_base in fully converged	3.9 M	30.2	29.8	46.4
Transformer_big in fully converged	3.9 M	30.6	29.1	46.3

4.3 Pseudo Data Generation Methods

This part of the experiment is based on the Transformer_base model. English monolingual data are randomly selected and the generation methods are beam search, TopK, and Sampling. The experimental results are shown in Table 4:

We can see that the Sampling method obtains the best performance over the others in Lt-En tasks. It is possibly due to the fact that Sampling introduces noisy data while in one way enriches the linguistic phenomenon within the training data, making the model more robust. For a translation task with sufficient parallel sentence pairs, the considerable amount of parallel data prevents the model from performance degradation led by the sampling noise. In contrast, Sampling method became the worst one in the Gu-En task, which has much less training data than Lt-En. We hypothesize that it is the result of which the reverse translation model trained on the small parallel corpus is unable to generate high quality translation for back-translation. Moreover, insufficient parallel data could be easily overwhelmed by the huge amount of noise within the pseudo corpus and thus cannot serve as a good training signal. Model will therefore be misled by the noise and degrade severely.

Table 4. The effect of different data generation methods on pseudo data

Language direction	Generation method	Corpus size	BLEU		
			Dev	Test	Train
Lt-En	–	1.9M	27.1	29.2	45.1
	Beam search	3.9M	30.2	29.8	46.4
	TopK	3.9M	30.3	29.5	45.9
	Sampling	3.9M	31.6	30.1	45.5
Gu-En	–	79K	3.2	3.5	27.1
	Beam search	160K	4.8	4.0	22.3
	TopK	160K	4.6	3.9	22.1
	Sampling	160K	3.4	3.1	20.6

On the Train test set, since the Sampling method diversifies the pseudo corpus hence be inconsistent with the training data, its results were the worst on the Train test set. This gap is even large in Gu-En task, where the monolingual data are out of the parallel data domain.

To investigate the reason why the Sampling method is more effective in the Lt-En task than the Beam Search, we analyze their pseudo data as well as the parallel corpus. We first construct the vocabulary from the parallel corpus and collect word statistics of the parallel corpus, the pseudo corpus generated by both Beam Search and Sampling. We then group every 2 K words as a whole and present the frequency results of the last seven groups in Fig. 3:

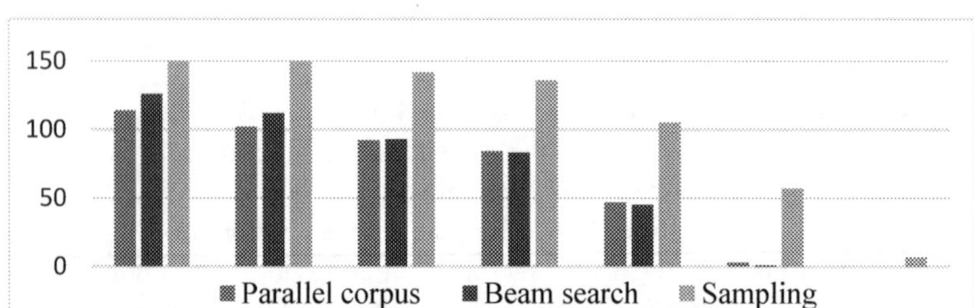

Fig. 3. Data distribution

As can be discovered in Fig. 3, the word frequency distribution of the Beam Search is very similar to the one of the parallel corpus, and the pseudo data generated by Sampling contains more low frequency words. This is because the Sampling method randomly selects words during generation, which is equivalent to assigning non-zero probability to low-frequency words compared to all zero in Beam Search, making the data distribution of pseudo data more diverse. Therefore, we suspect that one of the key reasons for the effectiveness of the Sampling method is encouraging the occurrence of low frequency words in the source language. We conduct several experiments to verify our hypothesis, and the results of which are shown in Table 5:

Table 5. Results of the comparison experiment related to the Sampling method

Language direction	Generation method	Corpus size	BLEU	
			Dev	Test
Lt-En	Beam search	3.9M	30.2	29.8
	Sampling	3.9M	31.6	30.1
	Beam search + Sampling	3.9M	31.4	29.8
	Low frequency words + Beam search	3.9M	30.8	29.6

We extract the sentence pairs (1.1 M) from the pseudo data generated by Sampling method, which contains the source-side low-frequency words in the parallel corpus, and deduplicate it with the previous extracted 2 M English monolingual data. Then we extract sentence pairs that share the same English part from the pseudo data generated by Beam Search. It can be seen from the Table 5 that mixing these two kinds of pseudo data has 1.2 BLEU performance improvement over only Beam Search method, and is only inferior to the result of Sampling method about 0.2 BLEU. We further select samples with Lithuanian low-frequency words aligned and find the result of the Dev set is improved by 0.6 BLEU. Therefore, we believe that the effectiveness of Sampling method comes in two ways, where it increases the occurrences of low-frequency words for the source-side and the diversity of pseudo data through randomness. However, we believe that the pseudo data generated by Sampling requires good performance of the baseline model to against the noise introduced in Sampling pseudo data.

4.4 Monolingual Data Selection Strategies

This section describes the impact of various monolingual selection strategies on the back-translation method. Previous studies have shown that in the training process, words that are difficult to be predicted on the target language side tend to be more accurate after adding pseudo data [4]. Therefore, we select sentences containing these difficult words as the monolingual data for generating the pseudo corpus. These difficult words include the low-frequency words of both the source and target languages and the target language words with high prediction loss. For the source-side low-frequency words, we use the GIZA++ [11] word alignment tool to find their corresponding target-side words in order to select the target-side monolingual sentences. Based on the above definitions of difficult words, three monolingual corpuses containing these three types of difficult words are selected for experiments. At the same time, we also use the language model to select the monolingual data. The language model architecture is Transformer_base, and the data generation method is beam Search. The experimental results are shown in Table 6:

According to Table 6, it is found that in the Lt-En task, the target-side low-frequency words and the ones with high target-side prediction loss are not as good as the random selection baseline. Compared with the random selection baseline, using the data selected by the source-side low-frequency words and the language model improve 0.6 and 0.7 BLEU on the Dev set, and 0.4 and 0.6 BLEU on the Test set respectively. In the Gu-En task, all four methods outperform the random selection baseline. The best experimental results are achieved by using the source-side low-frequency words and the language model. We believe that target-side data quality plays a crucial role in model training as it ensures the target correctness. The higher the quality, the better the model fits then the better the performance. Increasing low-frequency words in the source-side forces the model to fit them better and thus more robust to their appearance. However, the use of the target-side low-frequency words for monolingual data selection may result in a large number of low-frequency words in the generated translations and potentially degrade the performance.

Table 6. The effect of different monolingual selection methods on pseudo data

Selection method	Language direction	BLEU		Language direction	BLEU	
		Dev	Test		Dev	Test
Random	Lt-En	30.2	29.8	Gu-En	4.8	4.0
Freq(target)		30.0	29.8		5.0	4.3
Freq(source)		30.8	29.6		5.2	4.6
Loss		29.9	28.6		5.3	4.7
Language model		30.9	29.8		5.2	4.8

4.5 General Results

Based on our previous observations, this section combines the most effective pseudo data generation methods with the monolingual selection strategies. Under the Transformer_base model setting, the experimental results are shown in Table 7. We find that selecting only 880 K samples that contain the high prediction loss word have even more significant improvement than the 1.6 M counterpart on the Test set.

Table 7. Combined experimental results

Experimental description	Language direction	Coupus size	BLEU	
			Dev	Test
Language model + Sampling	Lt-En	3.9 M	31.7	30.3
Freq(source) + Sampling	Lt-En	3.9 M	31.5	30.3
Language model + Beam search	Gu-En	160 K	5.2	4.8
Loss + Beam search	Gu-En	160 K	5.3	4.7
Synthetic(1:10) + Loss + Beam search	Gu-En	880 K	9.1	6.9

5 Conclusion

We investigate the effect of several strategies on back-translation, including synthetic-data ratio, reverse translation model performance and different synthetic generation methods. Experiment results show that enlarge the synthetic volume can significant improve the translation quality on low resource languages. We find convergence state impacts more on the quality of synthetic data than the performance of target-to-source translation model. For the generation method, sampling is more helpful when the translation model is strong enough, while beam search shows more benefits when the model converges insufficiently.

Acknowledgments. This work was supported in part by the National Science Foundation of China (Nos. 61876035, 61732005 and 61432013) and the National Key R&D Program of China (No. 2019QY1801).

References

1. Bahdanau, D., Cho, K., Bengio, Y., et al.: Neural machine translation by jointly learning to align and translate. In: International Conference on Learning Representations (2015)
2. Luong, T., Pham, H., Manning, C.D., et al.: Effective approaches to attention-based neural machine translation. In: Empirical Methods in Natural Language Processing, pp. 1412–1421 (2015)
3. Sennrich, R., Haddow, B., Birch, A., et al.: Improving neural machine translation models with monolingual data. In: Meeting of the Association for Computational Linguistics, pp. 86–96 (2016)
4. Fadaee, M., Monz, C.: Back-translation sampling by targeting difficult words in neural machine translation. In: Empirical Methods in Natural Language Processing, pp. 436–446 (2018)
5. Axelrod, A., Vyas, Y., Martindale, M., Carpuat, M., Hopkins, J.: Classbased n-gram language difference models for data selection. In: IWSLT (International Workshop on Spoken Language Translation), pp. 180–187 (2015)
6. Edunov, S., Ott, M., Auli, M., et al.: Understanding back-translation at scale. In: Empirical Methods in Natural Language Processing, pp. 489–500 (2018)
7. Moore, R.C., Lewis, W.D.: Intelligent selection of language model training data. In: Meeting of the Association for Computational Linguistics, pp. 220–224 (2010)
8. Post, M.: A Call for Clarity in Reporting BLEU Scores. arXiv: Computation and Language, pp. 186–191 (2018)
9. Sennrich, R., Haddow, B., Birch, A., et al.: Neural machine translation of rare words with subword units. In: Meeting of the Association for Computational Linguistics, pp. 1715–1725 (2016)
10. Vaswani, A., Shazeer, N., Parmar, N., et al.: Attention is all you need. In: Neural Information Processing Systems, pp. 5998–6008 (2017)
11. Brown, P.F., Pietra, V.J., Pietra, S.D., et al.: The mathematics of statistical machine translation: parameter estimation. Computat. Linguist. **19**(2), 263–311 (1993)

Multi-classification of Theses to Disciplines Based on Metadata

Jianling Li, Shiwen Yu, Shasha Li(✉), and Jie Yu

School of Computer Science, National University of Defense Technology, Changsha 410073, China
jianlingl@mail.nwpu.edu.cn,
{yushiwen14, shashali, yj}@nudt.edu.cn

Abstract. Thesis classification is fundamental to a wide range of efficient research management. Current thesis classification is limited to major, research direction and classification number manually labeled by students themselves, which lacks standard and accuracy. Furthermore, previous auto-classification studies do not take account of interdisciplinary. This study intends to make a major contribution to Chinese thesis classification by taking advantage of the metadata such as title, keywords in the thesis. We propose a novel hierarchical classification model based on methods in metadata semantic representation and the corresponding similarity calculation. Experiments on 4K+ Theses show our methods have significant effect.

Keywords: Thesis metadata semantic representation · Similarity calculation · Multi-classification

1 Introduction

The classification of academic papers has been existing for ages. Depending on the classification, people hope to store, search, manage and study academic papers more efficiently. Currently, theses in China are labeled in various granularities, such as “major”, “research direction” and “Chinese Library Classification Number”. However, these labels have at least three problems unsolved:

- Research institutions often disagree on the domain and the naming of a major. For example, School of Computer Science in Northwestern Polytechnical University has four departments, named “Computer Systems and Microelectronics”, “Computer Science and Software”, “Computer Information Engineering” and “Information Security and Electronic Commerce Technology”. However, School of CS in National University of Defense Technology has “Computer Science and Technology”, “Software Engineering”, “Electronic Science and Technology” and “Cyberspace Security”.
- There is no strict rule for students to fill in those labels. For example, during the preprocessing of metadata, we find it is not rare for students to write the wrong “Chinese Library Classification Number” in their theses.

J. Tang et al. (Eds.): NLPCC 2019, LNAI 11839, pp. 476–485, 2019.
https://doi.org/10.1007/978-3-030-32236-6_43

- Current theses classifications have not considered interdisciplinary. According to the ***Classification and Code of Disciplines***[1], the thesis showed in Fig. 1 involves at least three disciplines—"Radar Engineering", "Wireless Communication Technology" and "Military Information Engineering and Information Countermeasure Technology", any of which is reasonable, but no one can replace another.

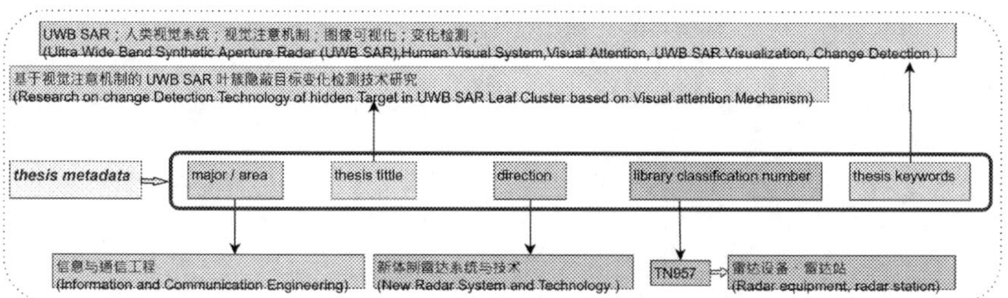

Fig. 1. Example of metadata of a thesis

The 2018 theses statistical report by ***WanFang Data***[2] shows that about 97.8% of the theses included by it are written in Chinese. Therefore, we focus on Chinese theses classification. In China, two taxonomies are the most popular and commonly used—***Chinese Library Classification*** and ***Classification and Code of Disciplines.*** After investigation, we believe the ***Classification and Code of Disciplines*** are more suitable for theses classification [1]. The reasons are: 1, it has a clearer structure and is easier to use; 2, it is internationally accepted; 3, it is designed for academic purpose while the other is designed for general books. An example of ***Classification and Code of Disciplines*** is shown in Fig. 2—the second and third level disciplines under "Computer Science" (which itself is a first-level discipline).

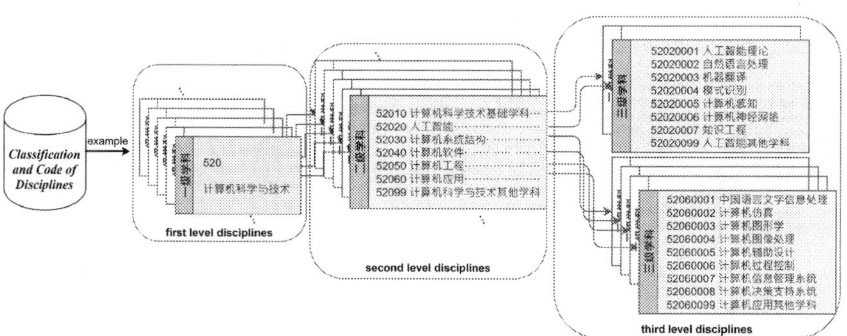

Fig. 2. Example of Classification and code of disciplines

1 The version we are using is GB/T13745-2009. This taxonomic hierarchy is divided into three levels: first-level disciplines, second-level disciplines, and third-level disciplines.

2 Wanfang Data is one of the most popular knowledge service platforms in China.

Previous studies were focused on journal papers [1]. Researches on multi-classification of theses to disciplines are certainly inadequate considering the importance of this field.

Although current labels in theses metadata are not the direct goal we desire, they can be of great use to the multi-classification task. Our multi-classification system is based on the semantic representation of metadata of theses. The main contributions are:

(a) We proposed several methods for high-level semantic representation by weighted splicing low-level semantic representations. The weights are determined by the relevance between the characters (, words or phrases) of the metadata term and the central words[3].
(b) We proposed a novel method for similarity measure of vectors with different lengths. This method is based on cosine similarity and especially aimed at the weighted spliced semantic vectors.
(c) An open-source multi-classification software system of theses to disciplines, available at http://git.trustie.net/jianlingl/thesis_muti-classification.git.

2 Related Work

In natural language processing, semantic representation is crucial for tasks such as word disambiguation, similarity calculation, and analogy reasoning. Popular representation methods include one-hot representation based on bag of words, distribution-based representation based on counting, and word embedding representation by expressing words as dense low-dimensional real-value vectors [2]. But in Chinese, things are more complicated. Characters in Chinese may have multiple meanings. As a result, centralized models for ambiguity of words is proposed, such as semantic modeling that considers the position information of characters together with their multiple meanings [3], modeling that focus on multi-meaning words [4], modeling that is powered by HowNet [5], modeling that considers Chinese character component (radical) [6], etc. these methods are dependent on semantic dictionary, which makes them time-consuming, laborious and difficult to scale.

As mentioned above, the metadata of theses are useful to the multi-classification task. But theses metadata are usually phrases. For English, A phrase semantic representation is composed of the semantic representations of words, where the traditional compositional model is faced with low accuracy and data sparsity. Consequently, the model which learns the representations of words and phrase simultaneously [2, 7] and model which extends the semantic are proposed. Inspired by previous works and focused on our task and language, we proposed several methods for high-level semantic representation by weighted splicing low-level semantic representations.

The similarity in natural language can be divided into semantic similarity and distribution similarity. The former is based on the similarity of cognitive taxonomy, and the latter is based on the similarity of the topic [9]. We focus on semantic

[3] We define the title and keywords of a thesis as its central words.

similarity. The existing similarity calculation methods include edit distance, Jaccard similarity coefficient, cosine similarity, TF-IDF coefficient, similarity measure method of vectors with different lengths—Distance correlation, etc. Chinese phrase text similarity measure methods consider the position of the same word in the phrase text [10]. Inspired by previous works, we proposed a novel method for similarity measure of vectors with different lengths, which is especially aimed at our weighted spliced semantic vectors.

Multi-classification of text can be of great use in scientific research and application. The earliest text multi-classification system appeared in 1999 as an automatic classification system for e-mail. It mainly uses information entropy theory and Bayes algorithm to realize multi-classification of text. While the researches of multi-classification of Chinese text started rather late, the methods of which are mainly based on the similarity comparison in semantic vector space.

The framework of our multi-classification system is shown in Fig. 3, where the semantic representations of the metadata are weighted spliced with low-level representations (words or characters) and the representations of the discipline phrases are directly spliced with low level representations. By calculating the similarity between the paper metadata and the discipline phrases, we can obtain all three level discipline classifications.

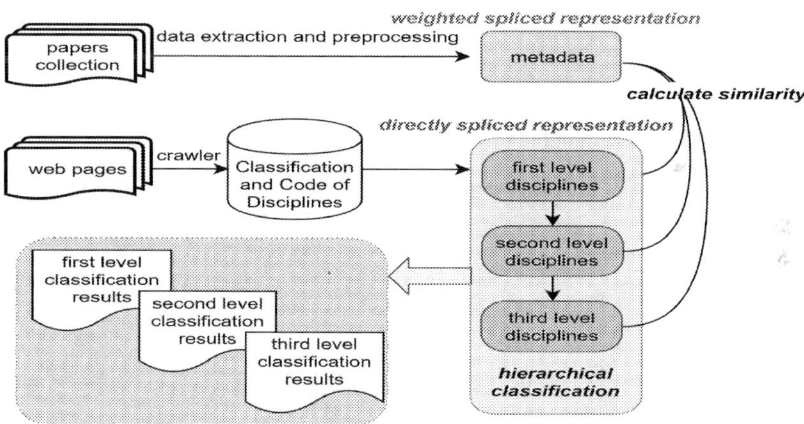

Fig. 3. Model framework.

3 Model

There are four parts in our multi-classification model: semantic representation of theses metadata, semantic representation of discipline phrase, similarity measure method and hierarchical classification algorithm of theses.

3.1 Semantic Representation of Theses Metadata

We represent theses metadata as vectors, which splice the weighted semantic vectors of the character (, words or phrases) of the metadata term. The weights are determined by the relevance between the characters (, words or phrases) and the central words because the influences of every character (, word or phrase) for the meaning of metadata term are usually not the same. We quantize influences of the characters (, words or phrases) by the similarity between them and the central words. In our work, the central words are defined as the title and keywords of the thesis.

For example, In thesis "具有深度信息的视频图像中的人物步态识别技术研究" ("Research on Character Gait Recognition Technology in Video Images with Depth Information"), the research direction of the thesis "图形与图像处理技 术" ("graphics and image processing technology") contains very obvious features for classification. In our model, we give character "图" ("image") a higher weight than character "形" ("shape") since "图" is more relevant to the central word of this thesis—the title. The same story happens between words "图像" ('image and picture') and "图形" ("graphics"), in which the former is more relevant.

After given the weights, the semantic vectors of characters (or words) are spliced into one vector representing the metadata term. Algorithm details are shown in pseudocode below.

algorithm 1 weighed low-level representation splice for metadata

```
input: metadata, central_words
output: metadata representation
function METADATA_REP(metadata, central_words)
    MetadataEm ← []
    for low_level_structure in metadata and not in StopWords do
        weigh ← GET_WEIGH(low_level_structure, central_words)
        Em ← weigh * W2Vmodel[low_level_structure]
        MetadataEm.append(Em)
    end for
    return MetadataEm
end function

function GET_WEIGH(low_level_structure, central_words)
    Weigh ← 0.00001
    try :
        Weigh ← Similarity(low_level_structure, central_words)
    return Weigh
end function
```

Semantic vectors of characters and words are obtained by word embedding model which is already implemented in gensim (a python library). We also build a list of stop-words to ignore noisy characters and words. The parameter *central_words* is the key to weights determination. We chose the titles and keywords of the theses as *central_words*.

The proposed algorithm can not only be used to represent metadata but also be used to represent any hierarchical compositional semantic representation. For instance, the semantic representation of a paragraph can be weighted spliced with the semantic vectors of sentences. The only thing needs making efforts is to determine the weights of the low-level terms according to the task.

3.2 Semantic Representation of Discipline Phrase

This algorithm is slightly different from that in the representation of theses metadata. Instead of weighting characters and words and splicing their semantic vectors, we simply splice these vectors. For example, we splice vectors of "图像" ("image") and "处理" ("processing") to represent the third-level discipline "图像 处理" ("image processing").

During experiments, we realize that second-level disciplines often have abundant semantic information. It is not easy for us to represent them only by splicing their characters or words. So, we splice together all the third-level disciplines under this second-level discipline into a long-phrase and use the same splicing method to obtain the semantic representation of the long-phrase.

3.3 Similarity Measure Method

Previous phrase similarity measure methods are not suitable for multi-classification of theses to disciplines. Therefore, we proposed a novel method for similarity measure of vectors with different lengths based on cosine similarity and specially aimed at the weighted spliced semantic vectors. The similarity measure method can be described by the equation below:

$$Sim\_(mdEmb, dpEmb) = \frac{\sum_{i=0}^{lm-1} \left(\max_{0 \le j \le ld-1} sim(mdEmb[i], dpEmb[j]) \right)}{lm} \tag{1}$$

In the equation, $mdEmb$ is the semantic vector of the metadata; $dpEmb$ is the semantic vector of the discipline; $mdEmb[i]$ is the i-th low-level semantic vector (the vector of a character or word) of the metadata; $dpEmb[j]$ is the j-th low-level semantic vector of the discipline; lm is the number of low-level semantic vectors, which together compose into the metadata; ld is the number of discipline's low-level semantic vectors; $sim()$ in the right part is the cosine similarity function. If the vector embeddings of the metadata and discipline are the same, the similarity value calculated by this equation will be 1. This equation calculates two high-level semantic representations by taking the average of the maximum of the similarity values of their low-level semantic vectors.

3.4 Hierarchical Classification Algorithm of Thesis

Because ***Classification and Code of Disciplines*** has obvious hierarchical characteristics, we use Hierarchical classification in our system. We first sort all first-level disciplines by the similarity between them and metadata of the thesis. Since the metadata are multiple, we accumulate all similarities between the discipline and all metadata as the similarity. Then, instead of traversing all the second-level disciplines, we only consider those whose parent disciplines are among the top-N first-level disciplines sorted before, where N is defined by user interests. We define N as 3 in our experiments. The top-N second-level disciplines are obtained in the same way as the first-level, and so do the third-level disciplines. Hierarchical classification is timesaving and very helpful in noise filtering; it can also give us a systematic classification result details are shown below:

```
algorithm 2 Hierarchical Classification of theses
input: theses, 1st_level_disciplines_all , TopN
output: 1st_level_disciplines, 2nd_level_disciplines, 3rd_level_disciplines
function HIERARCH_CLASSIFY(theses, 1st_level_disciplines_all, TopN)
        1st_level_disciplines ← get_disciplines(theses, grade1disciplines, TopN)

        2nd_level_disciplines_subsets ← get_2nd_level_disciplines_subset(1st_level_disciplines)
        2nd_level_disciplines ← get_disciplines(theses, 2nd_level_disciplines_subsets, TopN)

        3rd_level_disciplines_subsets ← get_3rd_level_disciplines_subset(2nd_level_disciplines)
        3rd_level_disciplines ← get_disciplines(theses, 3rd_level_disciplines_subsets, TopN)
    return 1st_level_disciplines, 2nd_level_disciplines, 3rd_level_disciplines
end function
```

4 Experiment

We extracted all metadata from the theses corpus and all discipline phrases in the ***Classification and Code of Disciplines***, together with their hierarchical structures, into a database. The metadata we concern are the title, the keywords, the area, the major, the research direction, the Chinese Library Classification Number and the degree type.

4.1 Dataset

The dataset is built with 4146 theses published between 2013 and 2017 in National University of Defense Technology. These theses cover a wide range of topics, such as Aerospace, Computer Science, Electronic Information, Control Science, and Management Science.

Training Set

All 4146 master theses are in the training set. The preprocessing of theses is simple: first split the text of the thesis into characters and words separately, then ignore special characters and those in the list of stop-words (or characters). We use ***jieba*** (a python library) to help us split text into words. This data set is used to train the word2vec models.

Test Set

We randomly selected 190 theses from the training set and manually labeled them by 2 volunteers independently. Each thesis is labeled with multiple first-level, second-level and third-level disciplines. After the labeling, another volunteer decided the final labels of the theses on which the 2 volunteers disagreed. We evaluated the consistency between the 2 volunteers and found they agreed on 89.01% first-level disciplines, 86.54% second-level disciplines and 88.89% third-level disciplines. At last, we got 307 first-level, 457 second-level and 497 third-level manually labeled disciplines in the 190 theses.

4.2 Evaluation

The results of multi-classification of theses to disciplines are shown in Table 1, where the R is the recall rate and MAP (mean average precision) is used to deal with limitations of point estimation. The MAP algorithm is shown below:

```
algorithm 3 MAP for TopN results
input: labeledDisciplines, classifiedDisciplines_TopN
output: MAP
function MAP_TopN(labeledDisciplines, classifiedDisciplines_TopN)
    for labeleldata in labeledDisciplines do
        score_ ← 0
        if labeleldata in classifiedDisciplines_TopN then
            score_ ← 1.0/(classifiedDisciplines_TopN.index(labeleldata) + 1)
            hitCount ← hitCount + 1
        end if
        Score ← Score + score_
    end for
    if hitCount bigger than 0 then
        return Score/hitCount
    else
        return 0
    end if
end function
```

labeledDisciplines are manually labeled disciplines, *classifiedDisciplines* are the predicted disciplines from our system. *classifiedDisciplines_TopN.index(x)* will return the ranked place number of x in the predicted disciplines. For each manually labeled discipline, if it is near the top of the disciplines given by our system, then we will give it a high score; If it is near the bottom, we give it a low score; If it is not in the classification results, we ignore it. In the end, we take the average of all scored disciplines as the final score. For example, if a manually labeled discipline is in the second place of the predicted disciplines, it will be scored as 0.5.

For the recall calculation, if one of the top-N predicted disciplines is the same as one of the manually labeled disciplines, we say the prediction is true positive. In this paper, we did several controlled experiments and listed the results in Table 1.

The MAP value can reflect the ranking accuracy of the correct disciplines in the prediction results, which means that the higher MAP the more accurate the prediction is. As shown in the table, the semantic representation of metadata we proposed has brought a significant improvement. ***Character based weighted splicing method*** is better than ***words based weighted splicing method. Phrase based weighted splicing method*** gets the best R and MAP score in the first-level classification, which we believe is because the metadata terms of the theses are often in phrase form.

Phrase based weighted splicing method* is composed with two steps: represent phrase semantic by weighted splicing characters, and then represent metadata by weighted splicing phrases. This method gets the best scores in the second-level and the third-level classifications. In practice, we can use ***Phrase based weighted splicing method*** in the first-level classification and use ***Phrase based weighted splicing method**** in the rest. A prediction instance is shown in Fig. 4.

Table 1. Multi-calssification results of theses based on different methods(xxx_R means recall of xxx-level disciplines classification, xxx_MAP means MAP of xxx-level disciplines classification)

Metadata_rep+ similarty	Racall and MAP					
	1st_R	1st_MAP	2nd_R	2nd_MAP	3rd_R	3rd_MAP
Character based accumulating+W2V. n_Similarity	75.79%	53.38%	-	-	-	-
*Character based splicing +Sim_*	84.21%	68.07%	-	-	-	-
Word based accumulating +W2V.n_Similarity	69.51%	50.24%	-	-	-	-
*Word based splicing+Sim_*	73.68%	55.66%	-	-	-	-
Character based weighted splicing+Sim_	92.11%	67.81%	85.78%	59.74%	81.14%	54.14%
Word based weighted splicing +Sim_	89.77%	57.42%	80.10%	50.30%	73.25%	46.90%
Phrase based weighted splicing+Sim_	**94.21%**	***72.85%***	88.01%	68.71%	78.63%	***56.81%***
Phrase based weighted splicing*+Sim_	92.63%	67.46%	***89.54%***	***68.84%***	***80.41%***	56.01%

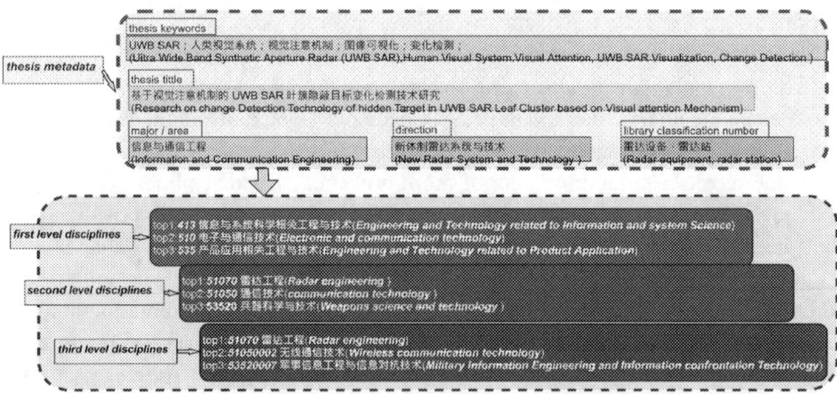

Fig. 4. Thesis multi-classification example

5 Conclusion

Multi-classification of theses to disciplines is of great use in scientific research and application. Following the ***Classification and Code of Disciplines***, we proposed a multi-classification system based on metadata and semantic embedding. A significant improvement in this task has been brought by our weighted splicing algorithms, of which the extensibility is also promising. Considerably more work will need to be done to this field.

Acknowledgements. The research is supported by the National Key Research and Development Program of China (2018YFB1004502) and the National Natural Science Foundation of China (61532001, 61303190).

References

1. 邱均平, 赵岩杰, 罗力 科学评价中的论文分类方法研究[J] 情报学报 **30**(5) (2011)
2. Mikolov, T., Sutskever, I., Chen, K., et al.: Distributed representations of words and phrases and their compositionality. In: Advances in Neural Information Processing Systems (2013)
3. Chen, X., Xu, L., Liu, Z., et al.: Joint learning of character and word embeddings. In: International Conference on Artificial Intelligence. AAAI Press (2015)
4. Chen, X., Liu, Z., Sun, M.: A unified model for word sense representation and disambiguation. In: Conference on Empirical Methods in Natural Language Processing (EMNLP 2014), Doha, Qatar, 25–29 October 2014, vol. 2, pp. 1025–1035 (2014)
5. Xie, R., Yuan, X., Liu, Z., et al.: Lexical sememe prediction via word embeddings and matrix factorization. In: Twenty-Sixth International Joint Conference on Artificial Intelligence. AAAI Press (2017)
6. Sun, Y., Lin, L., Yang, N., Ji, Z., Wang, X.: Radical-enhanced Chinese character embedding. In: Loo, C.K., Yap, K.S., Wong, K.W., Teoh, A., Huang, K. (eds.) ICONIP 2014, Part II. LNCS, vol. 8835, pp. 279–286. Springer, Cham (2014). https://doi.org/10.1007/978-3-319-12640-1_34
7. Hashimoto, K., Tsuruoka, Y.: Adaptive joint learning of compositional and non-compositional phrase embeddings (2016)
8. Passos, A., Kumar, V., Mccallum, A.: Lexicon infused phrase embeddings for named entity resolution. Computer Science (2014)
9. Utsumi, A., Suzuki, D.: Word vectors and two kinds of similarity. In: International Conference on ACL. DBLP (2006)
10. 王莹莹, 任贤, 龙鹏飞. 中文短语文本相似度计算新方法[J]. 软件导刊 **10**(1), 79–81 (2011)
11. 王莹莹. 中文短语相似度计算方法研究及应用 长沙理工大学

Chinese Event Factuality Detection

Jiaxuan Sheng[1], Bowei Zou[1,2(✉)], Zhengxian Gong[1], Yu Hong[1], and Guodong Zhou[1]

[1] Natural Language Processing Lab, Soochow University, Suzhou, China
shengjiaxuan1996@gmail.com, tianxianer@gmail.com, {zoubowei,zhxgong,gdzhou}@suda.edu.cn
[2] Institute for Infocomm Research, Singapore, Singapore

Abstract. There are a large number of expression forms and semantic information in natural language, which contain fake, speculative, and fuzzy statements. Identifying event factuality is vital to various natural language applications, such as information extraction and knowledge base population. Most of existing methods for Chinese event factuality detection adopt shallow lexical and syntactic features to determine the factuality of target event via end-to-end classification models. Although such methods are easy to implement, they ignore the linguistic features related to event factuality, which limits the performances on this task. On this basis, we introduce three kinds of linguistic features to represent event factuality, including factuality cue, event polarity, and tense. Then, we employ a CNN-based feature encoder to capture their latent feature representations automatically. Finally, we integrate three kinds of features with word embeddings to identify the factuality label of target event. The experimental results show that our method achieves 94.15% of accuracy, with 12.34% of improvement on the state-of-the-art. In addition, we also demonstrate and analyze the effectiveness of three linguistic features for Chinese event factuality detection.

Keywords: Event factuality detection · Linguistic features · Convolutional Neural Network

1 Introduction

Event factuality in text refers to the author's description of the degree of certainty about whether events actually occur or not in the real world [1]. There are a large number of semantic expressions and descriptions in natural language texts, such as false, speculative, vague, and so on. These information often involves the factuality of events, distinguishing them from real events is of great significance to the downstream natural language processing applications related to events, such as event detection and event relation extraction. Generally, existing studies classify events factuality into the following four categories[1]:

- Certainty (CT+): events has occurred;
- Impossible (CT–): events will never happen;

[1] FactBank annotation guideline [1] to classify and define the categories of event factuality.

J. Tang et al. (Eds.): NLPCC 2019, LNAI 11839, pp. 486–496, 2019.
https://doi.org/10.1007/978-3-030-32236-6_44

- Possible (PS+): events may occur;
- MayNot (PS–): events may not occur.

Note that the event factuality studied in this paper is only rely on the attitudes and perceptions reflected from the textual expression, rather than the original factuality of the event in the real world. For example, given a sentence, "特朗普**叛国**罪名可能不会被确认 (*Trump's **treason** may not be confirmed in the end)*", we are concerned about the description of the event itself in sentence rather than whether the event "***treason***" really happened. Thus the event "***treason***" is MayNot (PS–) in the above instance.

Existing studies on event factuality detection mainly focus on the coarse-grained level such as judging whether an event actually occurs or not, or only identifying the linguistic coverage of a cue of negation or speculation in sentence. For example, Schuetze et al. (2017) employed a CNN model to detect the unspecified event on a biomedical domain corpus [2]. Qian et al. (2015) utilized event factuality reporting structures (i.e., *someone guesses/claims/doubts*) and syntactic structures with negative words to identify whether the target event is within the scope of the reporting structure or the negative syntactic structure, so as to obtain the corresponding categories of event factuality [3]. These approaches only rely on a single linguistic feature to judge the value of event factuality which are limited. However, they ignore the other syntactic information, such as tense and the interaction of various features on the value of event factuality. In this paper, we propose an event factuality detection approach based on linguistic features, which includes (1) factuality cue, which aims to determine the degree of certainty about whether the event actually happened, such as reporting predicates (e.g., "推测" (*Speculate*), "证实" (*Confirm*)) and adverbs/adjectives expressing degree of certainty (e.g., "必须" (*must*), "可能" (*possible*)); (2) event polarity, which aims to determine about whether an event occurred or existed, such as negative cue; and (3) tense, which aims to detect the time of event took place, such as past tense, future tense.

(E1) 他证实新院的校长黄茂树现在没有正式**就职**，就遭人检举有双重国籍.
(*He has confirmed that Huang Maoshu, the president of the New College, has not yet officially **taken office** and has been accused of having dual nationality.*)

(E2) 信息部要求美国移民局执行法院判决，**释放**张宏宝以保障他的人权.
(*He Information Ministry asked the U.S.Immigration Service to enforce the court's ruling and **realease** Zhang Hongbao to guarantee his human rights.*)

For example, (E1) and (E2) both include the factuality cue, the event polarity and the tense. In sentence E1, the target event "就职 (*take office*)" is certainty (CT+) according to the reporting predicate "证实 (*confirmed*)" which has a deterministic tendency towards the clause, However, the tense word "现在 (*yet*)" and the negative cue "没有 (*not*)" indicate that the factuality type of target event is CT–. Based on the above analyses, the final factuality type of target event "就职 (*take office*)" is CT–. It can be seen that the event factuality is often determined by several clues in sentence, and there may be contradictions among them, which pose the challenge for the task. For example, in E2, the word related to the event "释放 (*release*)" are the modal word "要求 (*asked*)" (we regard modal word as the first type of feature, i.e. factuality cues). Thus the factuality type of the target event is PS+.

In this paper, we propose a feature encoder based on Convolutional Neural Network (CNN) to automatically extract and learn the three types of linguistic features. Then we utilize the latent feature representations to fused with pre-trained word embeddings to detect event factuality. Experimental results on Chinese Event Factuality Datasets[i] show that our approach achieves 94.15% (F1), with 12.34% of improvement on the state-of-the-art system. In addition, we also demonstrate the effectiveness of the proposed three types of linguistic features in practical application scenarios.

2 Related Work

Early event factuality detection in text processing mainly focused on biomedical domain. For instance, Kilicoglu et al. (2003) employed a heuristic rule-based method on the biomedical corpus, GENIA [4], which identified the degree of certainty and polarity of events according to the association between event predicates and modal or negative words [5]. Sauri et al. (2003) constructed the FactBank corpus [1] based on the TimeML corpus [6]. They show that factuality can be characterized by the combination of the degree of certainty (*Certain/Probable/Possible*) and polarity (*Positive/Negative),* while it classified the value of event factuality into six categories in a more fine-grained way above two dimensions. In addition, events whose factuality cannot be judged means *underspecified.* Qian et al. (2017) employed a maximum entropy classifier to identify "*underspecified*" event category in FactBank corpus, and then developed a series of heuristic rules to classify other events [3].

For event factuality detection in Chinese, Cao et al. (2016) constructed a Chinese dataset [7] based on ACE 2005 event extraction dataset [8]. They classified event factuality into 5 categories and annotated basic factors related to event factuality (i.e., reporting predicates, negative cues, sources, clauses). In addition, He et al. (2017) developed a CNN-based model to identify event factuality, where they utilized Word2Vec [9] and Chinese synonym word forest [10] to detect the similarity between words in Chinese synonym word forest and reporting predicates in sentence so as to extracted more cues related to event factuality in sentence. Finally, the linguistic rules are applied to detect event factuality with the cues which are described above [11]. These approaches are not only rely on domain knowledge, such as rule-based methods, but also failed to consider the interaction of linguistic features related to event factuality, which limited the performance and can be costly to obtain.

3 Chinese Event Factuality Detection Model

This section describes our approach for Chinese event detection, which is recast as a classification task to determine the value of target event factuality in sentence. It can be categories into five below: *"Certainly", "Impossible", "Possible", "May not" and "Unspecified"*. For the probability $\mathrm{P}(e) = \max\{\mathrm{P}_i(e|S)\}, 1 \leq \mathrm{i} \leq 5$, is the probability of target event e conditioned on sentence S containing the target event, which aims to select the maximum probability value of target event factuality in 5 categories.

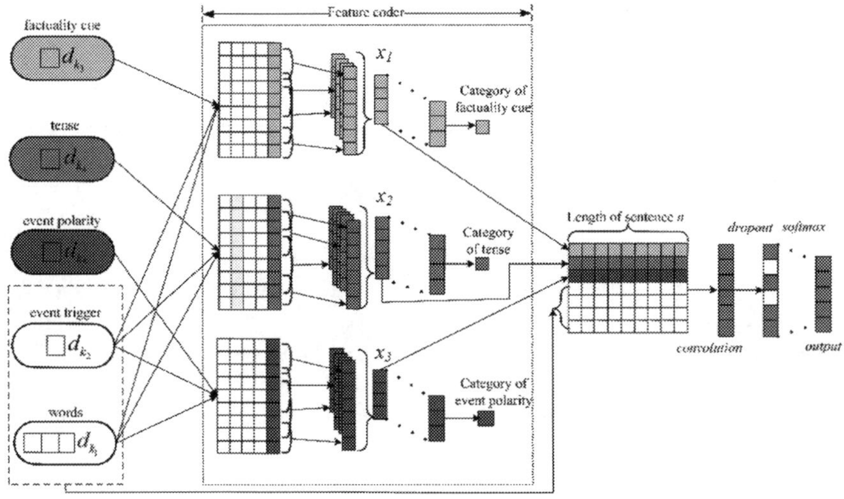

Fig. 1. Architecture of Chinese event factuality detection model

Figure 1 shows the framework of our model based on CNN, which consists of the two parts: (1) feature encoding layer, which aims to extract three types of linguistic features (factuality cue, event polarity, tense) in sentence and encode them as feature vectors on CNN-based encoder; (2) chinese event factuality classification model, which aims to utilize three types of linguistic features vectors to fused with pre-trained word vectors and event trigger vectors that fed into CNN model to obtain event factuality.

3.1 Feature Encoding Layer

3.1.1 Factuality Cue

In this paper, factuality cues are defined as a special type of vocabulary that reveal the degree of certainty whether the event actually occurs, including the reporting predicate (i.e., "*speculate*", "*confirm*"), the adverb or adjective expressing degree of certainty (i.e., "*must*", "*possibility*"). Factuality cues are categorized into three categories according to their attributes, such as "报道 (*report*)" and "证明 (*prove*)" as definite, "估计 (*estimate*)" and "怀疑 (*doubt*)" as possible, "打听 (*inquiry*)" and "咨询 (*consult*)" as uncertain. Factuality cues are represented by vector matrix C_E. In addition, in order to capture the semantic information of event trigger in sentence, we utilize a sentence to segmentation (given sentence S with length N, $S = (w_1, w_2, \ldots, w_i, \ldots, w_n)$, where w_i denotes the i_{th} word in sentence S), the event trigger labels matrix T_E, which is represented as follows: (1) A token is labeled as "Trigger" if w_i is the event trigger in sentence; (2) A token is labeled as "NTrigger" if w_i is not the event trigger in sentence. The reminder of this section is organized as follows:

(1) Embedding layer

As the input of our model, it is consist of three matrix as follows: (1) word embedding matrix $M_E \in \mathbb{R}^{d_{k1} \times |v_n|}$, where d_{k1} is the dimension of each word in sentence and V_n is the number of words in sentence; (2) event trigger labels matrix $T_E \in \mathbb{R}^{d_{k2} \times |v_{k2}|}$, where d_{k2} is the dimension of event trigger labels, V_{k2} = {Trigger, NTrigger}, and indicate a set of event trigger labels; (3) $C_E \in \mathbb{R}^{d_{k3} \times |v_{k3}|}$, the factuality cue matrix, where d_{k3} is the dimension of factuality cue and V_{k3} is a set of factuality cues in sentence.

(2) Convolutional layer

In this paper, we employ CNN-based model to classify factuality cues. Given a sentence S with the length N, the dimension is transferred into $d_{w1} = d_{k1} + d_{k2} + d_{k3}$ according to embedding table. We utilize $X_{cue} \in \mathbb{R}^{d_{w1} \times |v_n|}$ as the input, while we consider a fixed size window W_1 to capture its local features in the current layer. Here, the window size is set as l to capture a new feature.

After fed into the convolutional layer, the input matrix X_{cue} is processed with a convolutional operation:

$$c_i = tanh(W_1 \cdot X_{cue} + b_1) \tag{1}$$

where $b_1 \in \mathbb{R}^{|v_n|}$ is the bias term, *tanh* is nonlinear activation function. These new features are consists of a new feature matrix:

$$c_{cue} = [c_1, c_2, \ldots, c_{n-l+1}] \tag{2}$$

(3) Maxpooling layer

To extract the most active convolutional features from c_{cue}, we consider to select the max value ($\hat{c} = \max\{c_{cue}\}$), which is taken as input to maxpooling layer. This operation can effectively reduce the number of features of input matrix and filter out the features with weak representativeness [12].

We utilize m filters of three different window sizes h_1, h_2, h_3 with convolutional operation to obtain various new feature matrices, and then the maxpooling layer is applied to select the max value from each new feature matrix. Finally, they are concatenated into the matrix X_1:

$$X_1 = [\hat{c}_{cue1}, \hat{c}_{cue2}, \hat{c}_{cue3}, \ldots, \hat{c}_{cuem}]^T \tag{3}$$

(4) Sofxmax layer

X_1 is fed into the softmax layer:

$$o = softmax(W_2 \cdot X_1 + b_2) \tag{4}$$

where $W_2 \in \mathbb{R}^{d_{n2} \times n_m}$ is the parameter matrix, and $b_2 \in \mathbb{R}^{n_2}$ is the bias term. The dimension of o is n_2 = 3, which is the probability of three types of factuality cues, we select the maximum probability as factuality cue category *Vcue*.

3.1.2 Tense

Tense is the time when an event occurs. event factuality will be different because of the different tenses, such as "他已经去了美国(*he has* **gone** *to America*)" and "他将前往美国(*he will* **go** *to America*)", The factuality cues of "*gone*" and "*go*" both are certainty, but the tense of "*gone*" is past and "*go*" is future, which makes the event factuality of "*gone*" to be CT+ and "*go*" to be PS+. Thus, tense is of significance to identify the event factuality in NLP tasks. Tense usually appear in the form of tense words (i.e., "现在 (*now*)", "将 (*will*)") or adverbs (i.e., "要求 (*demand*)" denote the tense as future, "已经 (*already*)" denote the tense as past). Tense will be classified into four categories: "过去 (past)", "现在 (now)", "将来 (future)" and "未指明 (unspecified)".

The matrices M_E, T_E and S_E (the tense words matrix where $S_E \in \mathbb{R}^{d_{k4} \times |v_{k4}|}$, d_{k4} is the dimension of tense words, and V_{k4} is a set of tense words in sentence) are concatenated into a matrix $X_{ten} \in \mathbb{R}^{d_{w2} \times |v_n|}$, where $d_{w2} = d_{k1} + d_{k2} + d_{k4}$. Similarly, Matrix X_{ten} is encoded according to the factuality cue encoding method. Finally, we obtain the tense category V_{ten}.

3.1.3 Event Polarity

Event polarity describes whether the event itself occurs or exists, such as "他现在还没有去美国 (*He hasn't* **gone** *to America yet*)", and the negative cue "没有 (*hasn't*)" reverses the target event polarity (CT+ → CT–). And it plays an important role in identifying the negative events (CT–, PS–). We classify event polarity into three categories: positive, negative and unspecified.

In this paper, the negative cues vocabulary are extracted on CNeSp Corpus[2], we utilize the sentence S to match with the vocabulary, and then vectorized them to a matrix P_E, where $P_E \in \mathbb{R}^{d_{k5} \times |v_{k5}|}$, d_{k5} is the dimension of negative cues in sentence, and V_{k5} is a set of negative cues in sentence.

The matrices M_E, T_E and P_E are concatenated into a matrix $X_{pol} \in \mathbb{R}^{d_{w3} \times |v_n|}$, where $d_{w3} = d_{k1} + d_{k2} + d_{k5}$. Similarly, Matrix X_{pol} is encoded according to the factuality cue encoding method and we obtain the event polarity category V_{pol}.

3.2 Chinese Event Factuality Detection Model

Currently, CNN have been proven effective in extracting sentence-level features [13]. For example, Kim et al. (2014) utilized a CNN-based model to extract sentence-level features for sentence classification [14].

Event factuality will produces different values at the interaction of the three types of linguistic features. Thus, three types of linguistic feature vectors X_1, X_2 and X_3 obtained by feature encoding layer are concatenated into X_{fea}, where $X_{fea} = X_1 + X_2 + X_3$. And then we utilized X_{fea} to fused with M_E and T_E to obtain the matrix X_4, where $X_4 = X_{fea} + M_E + T_E$ and $X_4 \in \mathbb{R}^{d_w \times |v_n|}$.

2 http://nlp.suda.edu.cn/corpus/CNeSp.

To learn the parameters of the network, we supervise the labels which are adopted from CNN-based model with the gold labels in the training set, and utilize the following training objection function:

$$J(\theta) = -\frac{1}{m}\sum\nolimits_{i=1}^{m} logP(e_i|s_i,\theta) + \frac{\lambda}{2}\|\theta\|^2 \quad (5)$$

where $\theta = \{W_1, W_2, b_1, b_2\}$ is the set of parameters, λ is the regularization coefficient, $p(e_i|s_i,\theta)$ is the confidence score of the golden label e_i of the training instance $s_{i,}$ m is the number of the training instances. To train the CNN-based model, the Adam algorithm is applied to convergence.

4 Experimentation

4.1 Settings

We evaluate our model on Chinese event factuality datasets [8], which annotated 4,852 instances with factuality cue, event polarity, and tense of event. The dataset only considers five types of event factuality, including CT+, CT–, PS+, PS–, and U. We divide the dataset into training set, development set, and test set, according to the proportion of 65%, 15%, 20%. Table 1 shows the statistics of five types of event factuality. We can see that the number of CT+ is far more than that of CT–, PS– and U. The main reason is that this dataset mainly comes from news texts, thus the certain information is more common.

Table 1. The statistics of Chinese event factuality dataset.

	CT+	CT−	PS+	PS−	U
Training	2,392	69	568	40	28
Dev	597	17	141	9	7
Test	810	20	156	14	48

For the hyper-parameters, we adopt windows size in the set {3, 4, 5} to generate feature maps, and utilize 100 feature maps for each window size in this set. We set the learning rate as 0.001, the dropout as 0.5, the mini-batch size as 50. The word embeddings are initialized by Word2Vec[3] with 300 dimensions from Mikolov et al. (2013). Finally, Adam algorithm is applied to optimize our model. The performance is measured by Precision (P), Recall (R), F1-score (F1).

[3] https://github.com/Embedding/Chinese-Word-Vectors.

4.2 Experimental Results

To verify the effectiveness of the proposed three linguistic features, we add each feature into the Baseline, respectively, which are described as follows:

- Baseline: A CNN-based system, which contains only word embeddings and the target event embedding with the dimension 100 initialized randomly.
- Baseline+Cue: Baseline system adds the factuality cue embedding with the dimension 100 initialized randomly.
- Baseline+Polarity: Baseline system adds the event polarity embedding with the dimension 200 initialized randomly.
- Baseline+Tense: Baseline system adds the tense embedding with the dimension 100 initialized randomly.
- ALL-Features: Baseline system adds the above three kind of embeddings.

Table 2. Effects of three types of linguistic features

System	Marco-Ave			Micro-Ave		
	P (%)	R (%)	F (%)	P (%)	R (%)	F (%)
Baseline	46.14	33.48	38.81	81.33	81.33	81.33
Baseline+Cue	67.54	46.68	55.02	84.02	84.02	84.02
Baseline+Polarity	75.98	71.38	73.61	82.28	82.28	82.28
Baseline+Tense	68.44	49.66	57.56	91.64	91.64	91.64
ALL-Features	**87.86**	**81.64**	**84.64**	**94.15**	**94.15**	**94.15**

Table 2 lists the performances of three types of linguistic features on Chinese event factuality detection. The results show that when adding all of the three types of features, our proposed model achieves the best performance, which significantly better than Baseline (Micro-Ave[4]: 94.15% vs 81.33%, Macro-Ave: 84.64% vs 38.81%). It demonstrates the effectiveness of these features on Chinese event factuality detection. Besides, the results show the different effectiveness among features: (1) the Baseline +Polarity system achieves better performances than the others in Macro-Ave. It might be due to the better ability of Baseline+Polarity models in identifying the negative events (CT– and PS–), with fewer instances by adding the event polarity features; (2) The performance of Baseline+Tense is higher than the others on Micro-Ave. It is mainly attributed to that tense features play an important role in identifying the possible type of events. For example, two sentences are given as follows:

[4] In this paper, five types of event factuality are positive samples, so the value of P, R, F1 are equal when calculated on Micro-Ave.

(E3) 他们扯下了旗帜，并**逮捕**了向他们投掷石头的人.
(*They have torn down the flag and* ***arrested*** *people who threw stones at them.*)
(E4) 他总统将于本月底**前往**平壤访朝.
(*The president will* ***go*** *to Pyongyang at the end of this month for visit.*)

the tense of the target event in E3 is past and in E4 is future. Thus, the event factuality is CT+ in E3 and PS+ in E4. Both of them are completely determined by tense.

4.3 Comparison with the State-of-the-Art

Table 3 compares our model with the state-of-the-art system. He et al. (2017) developed a CNN-based model to identify event factuality, where they utilized Word2Vec [9] and Chinese synonym word forest [10] to detect the similarity between words in Chinese synonym word forest and reporting predicates in sentence so as to extracted more cues related to event factuality in sentence. Finally, the linguistic rules are applied to detect event factuality with the cues which are described above [11].

Compared to He's model, our model improves the F1 of Macro-Ave and Micro-Ave by 22.82% and 12.34%, respectively. All the improvements are due to the three types of linguistic features that enhance the model's understanding of different events factualities through semantic relations. Our model can effectively identify uncertain events (PS+, PS–, U) (+31.84% for PS+, +48.80% for PS–, +44.86% for U). It can contribute to the outstanding result of our model mining uncertain semantic information. In addition, our model have lower performance than He's on CT–, due to heuristic linguistic rules which are designed to identify the negative events, such as when an odd number of negative cues appear in sentence. The event polarity of the target event is judged to be negative and vice versa, the model mine deeper negative semantic information.

Table 3. Comparison with the state-of-the-art system

	He [10] (2017)			ALL-Features (ours)		
	P (%)	R (%)	F (%)	P (%)	R (%)	F (%)
CT+	87.38	90.37	89.00	**95.20**	**97.94**	**96.55**
CT–	**65.73**	**81.88**	**72.83**	60.00	75.00	66.67
PS+	62.11	51.70	56.24	**94.12**	**82.76**	**88.08**
PS–	56.24	33.33	41.20	**90.00**	**90.00**	**90.00**
U	58.67	23.78	32.24	**100**	**62.50**	**76.92**
Macro-Ave	70.52	59.14	61.82	**87.86**	**81.64**	**84.64**
Micro-Ave	81.81	81.81	81.81	**94.15**	**94.15**	**94.15**

4.4 Chinese Event Factuality Detection

In this paper, the factuality cue, event polarity and tense all depend on the annotated samples just described as Subsect. 3.2, therefore, this subsection employ our model on raw texts.

Table 4. Performances of Chinese event factuality detection systems on raw text

System	Macro-Ave			Micro-Ave		
	P (%)	R (%)	F (%)	P (%)	R (%)	F (%)
Auto+Cue	51.80	36.79	43.03	80.18	80.18	80.18
Auto+Polarity	57.60	32.28	41.37	81.50	81.50	81.50
Auto+Tense	54.35	34.60	42.28	80.79	80.79	80.79
Auto+All-Features	68.38	39.76	50.55	82.42	82.42	82.42
Manual ALL-Features	**87.86**	**81.64**	**84.64**	**94.15**	**94.15**	**94.15**

Table 4 compares the performances of detecting event factuality with automatically identifying three types of linguistic features, respectively (line 1–3) and automatically identifying three types of linguistic features as the same time (line 4). Finally, we identify event factuality with annotating three types of linguistic features (line 5). Among the models (line 1–4), the F1 scores of Macro-Ave are far below the F1 scores of Micro-Ave. The performance gaps among these models are due to three features have data imbalance in its own classification, such as the proportion of past tense and present tense is 78.63% and 1.46% respectively. It is challenging to identifying feature classes with fewer instances.

5 Conclusion

We presented a Chinese event factuality detection method, which introduced factuality cue, event polarity and tense to describe event factuality and then employed CNN feature encoder to extract these linguistic features respectively. Finally, we identify the event factuality based on CNN model. In addition, we will optimize the model to solve the problems mentioned in Subsect. 4.4 and it is the direction of future work.

Acknowledgments. This research was supported by National Natural Science Foundation of China (Grants No. 61703293, No. 61672368, No. 61673290). The authors would like to thank the anonymous reviewers for their insightful comments and suggestions.

References

1. Sauri, R., Verhagen, M., Pustejovsky, J.: Annotating and recognizing event modality in text. In: Proceedings of 19th International FLAIRS Conference (2006)
2. Schütze, H., Adel, H.: Exploring different dimensions of attention for uncertainty detection. In: Lapata, M., Blunsom, P., Koller, A. (eds.) Proceedings of the 15th Conference of the European Chapter of the Association for Computational Linguistics (EACL 2017), Stroudsburg, pp. 22–34. Association for Computational Linguistics (2017)
3. Qian, Z., Li, P., Zhu, Q.: A two-step approach for event factuality identification. In: Proceedings of 19th International Conference on Asian Language Processing (IALP 2015), pp. 10–16 (2015)
4. Kim, J.D., Ohta, T., Tateisi, Y., Tsujii, J.: GENIA corpus—a semantically annotated corpus for bio-textmining. Bioinformatics **19**(suppl 1), i180–i182 (2003)
5. Kilicoglu, H., Rosemblat, G., Cairelli, M.J., et al.: A compositional interpretation of biomedical event factuality. In: Proceedings of the 2nd Workshop on Extra-Propositional Aspects of Meaning in Computational Semantics (ExProM 2015), pp. 22–31 (2015)
6. Pustejovsky, J., Castano, J.M., Ingria, R., et al.: TimeML: robust specification of event and temporal expressions in text. In: Proceedings of the 5th International Workshop on Computational Semantics (IWCS, 2003) (2003)
7. Linguistic Data Consortium. ACE (Automatic Concept Extraction) Chinese Event Guidelines V5.5.1. [EB/OL], 7 Jan 2005
8. Cao, Y., Zhu, Q., Li, P.: The construction of Chinese event factuality corpus. J. Chin. Inf. Process. **27**(6), 38–44 (2012). (in Chinese)
9. Mikolov, T., Chen, K., Corrado, G., Dean, J.: Efficient estimation of word representations in vector space. In: Proceedings of Workshop at ICLR (ICLR 2013) (2013)
10. Tian, J., Zhao, W.: Word similarity calculating method based on synonym word forest. J. Jilin Univ. **28**(06), 602–608 (2010). (in Chinese)
11. He, T., Li, P., Zhu, Q.: Approach to identify Chinese event factuality. J. Chin. Inf. Process. **44**(5), 241–244+256 (2017). (in Chinese)
12. Neubauer, C.: Shape, position and size invariant visual pattern recognition based on principles of neocognitron and perceptron. [EB/OL] (1992)
13. Liu, Y., Wei, F., Li, S., et al.: A dependency based neural network for relation classification. Compare Science, pp. 285–290 (2015)
14. Kim, Y.: Convolutional Neural Networks for Sentence Classification. arXiv preprint arXiv: 1408.5882 (2014)t

Research of Uyghur-Chinese Machine Translation System Combination Based on Semantic Information

YaJuan Wang[1,2,3,4], Xiao Li[1,3(✉)], YaTing Yang[1,3(✉)], Azmat Anwar[1,2,3], and Rui Dong[1,3]

[1] Xinjiang Technical Institute of Physics & Chemistry, Chinese Academy of Sciences, Urumqi, China
{wangyajuan,xiaoli,yangyt,azmat,dongrui}@ms.xjb.ac.cn

[2] University of Chinese Academy of Sciences, Beijing, China

[3] Xinjiang Laboratory of Minority Speech and Language Information Processing, Urumqi, China

[4] Department of Information Security Engineering, Xinjiang Police College, Urumqi, China

Abstract. Uyghur-Chinese Machine Translation System Combination bears some drawbacks of not considering semantic information when doing the combination and the individual systems which participated in system combination lacking diversity. This paper tackles these problems by proposing a system combination method which was generated multiple new systems from a single Statistical Machine Translation (SMT) engine and combined together. These new systems are generated based on a bilingual phrase semantic representation model. Specifically, the Uyghur-Chinese bilingual phrase bilinear semantic similarity score and cosine semantic similarity score were firstly computed by a bilingual phrase semantic representation model and then several new systems were generated by adding features to the original feature set of the phrase-based translation model by static features and dynamic features. Finally, the newly generated system is combined with the baseline system to obtain the final combination results. Experimental results on the Uyghur-Chinese CWMT2013 test sets show that our approach significantly outperforms the baseline by 0.63 BLEU points respectively.

Keywords: Bilingual phrase semantic representation · Statistical machine translation · System combination · Static feature · Dynamic feature

1 Introduction

Although NMT systems have been shown to outperform statistical machine translation (SMT) systems in many rich-resource language pairs translation tasks and for low-resource language pairs translation tasks such as Uyghur-Chinese, the advantage of NMT systems are not obvious due to the limitation of the training data [1, 2]. SMT is still one of the most popular methods in Uygur-Chinese machine translation [3]. In recent years, in order to improve the quality of Uyghur-Chinese machine translation,

J. Tang et al. (Eds.): NLPCC 2019, LNAI 11839, pp. 497–507, 2019.
https://doi.org/10.1007/978-3-030-32236-6_45

the system combination technology has been applied in Uyghur-Chinese machine translation [4, 5]. Although previous work has improved the performance of Uyghur-Chinese machine translation to some extent, many problems remain to be studied. Semantic information has been shown to improve the performance of a single statistical machine translation system [6, 7], but whether it will improve the performance of system combination remains to be proven.

The diversity of translation systems is one of the key factors of system combination, so that each combination method cannot be separated from the participation of multiple SMT systems. For Uyghur-Chinese machine translation task, the development of multiple SMT systems requires a considerable cost. From the perspective of effective utilization of resources, it is of great practical significance to derive new systems from a single system and integrate them. So, this paper proposes the method on the Uyghur-Chinese Machine Translation System Combination Based on Semantic Information. It extends the application of semantic information from a single translation system to system combination scenario and uses the extracted semantic similarity as a new feature to generate multiple new systems from a single SMT system and to combine multiple systems together.

2 Related Work

With the rapid development of the deep neural network model, more and more researchers have been focused on the semantic representation of bilingual phrases [6–11]. Zhang et al. [6] learned the bilingual phrases representation by using recursive automatic encoder (RAE), and extracted the root node of a binary tree as the semantic representation of bilingual phrases, and proposed a max-margin objective function. Zhang et al. [7] also applied RAE to learn bilingual phrase representation, however they aimed to extract nodes of all levels of binary tree to represent semantic information of different granularity levels (whole phrase, sub-phrase and word) of the whole phrase and propose a two-dimensional attention network to explore the semantic interaction between different levels of granularity.

The most common method of system combination are sentence-level combination and word-level combination [12–17]. However, no matter which combination method is adopted, multiple translation systems are indispensable. A large number of translation systems based on different translation models are not easy to implement for Uyghur-Chinese translation. Therefore, how to achieve system combination without abundantly available systems has attracted much attention. Xiao et al. [18] used bagging and boosting methods to change the distribution of training data and generate a set of "weak translation systems" from the baseline system, and finally used the system combination method to combine these "weak translation systems" to produce a powerful translation system.

Different from their work, we generate new systems by adding semantic features, which are better than the baseline systems due to the introduction of semantic information. Combining these systems with the baseline system can achieve in a more powerful translation result. To make full use of semantic information, a sentence-level fusion method based on N-Best List Reranking is exploited to select a unique hypothesis from multiple translation hypotheses as the final translation result output.

3 System Combination Based on Semantic Information

When implementing the Uyghur-Chinese machine translation system combination, the deep neural network model is firstly used to extract the semantic information of Uyghur-Chinese bilingual phrases, and this information is used as a semantic feature to generate a new set of translation systems from a single phrase-based SMT system. Finally, the combination results of the Uyghur-Chinese machine translation system are obtained by combining the generated systems.

3.1 Preparing Training Data

A key issue in the extraction of bilingual phrase semantic information is how to learn a phrase representation that truly represents the underlying semantics of a bilingual phrase. In order to obtain a large number of translation equivalents (positive phrase pairs) and non-translation pairs (negative phrase pairs) for Uygur-Chinese bilingual phrase, we used forced decoding method [19] method to obtain the positive phrase pair required for the training model. The basic idea of forced decoding is to use the trained decoder to translate the source language data, forcing the decoder to generate the same translation as the reference translation. An example of a positive phrase pairs is shown in Fig. 1.

بارىسىغان يول قاردا توسۇلۇپ قېلىپ . ||| 路段 因 暴风雪 阻路 ，
قىزچاق يازغان ماقالە ||| 女孩 写 的 作文
ئاخىرقى 500 مىڭ ||| 最后 五十万
تەشكىللەش رولى ۋە ئاساسى ||| 组织 作用 和 基础
يېڭى يىللىق ئاتكىرتكىنى ||| 新年 贺卡
دەرس مەزمۇنىنى ||| 授课 内容

Fig. 1. Examples of positive phrase pairs

Existing completely random substitution method to generate negative phrase pars is not sufficient for the learning of bilingual semantic representation, two different sampling methods are used to generate the negative phrase pairs to enhance the learning ability of the model.

1. Negative phrase pairs are generated by completely random substitute all the words of the Uyghur source phrase and Chinese target phrases.
2. Randomly replace any word in the Uyghur source phrase to generate a Uyghur negative phrase. The Chinese target phrase negative phrase is generated by the same method.

Thus, two negative phrase pairs are generated for each positive phrase pair. Moreover, a positive phrase pair and a negative pair constitutes a training sample of the model. Note that the length of negative phrase pairs should be consistent with that of positive phrase pairs.

3.2 Building Bilingual Phrase Semantic Representation Model

The goal of learning the semantic representation of bilingual phrases is to measure the semantic similarity between bilingual phrases. However, due to the large difference between Uyghur and Chinese, the clues of the phrase itself are not enough to measure the potential semantic similarity of bilingual phrases. So, the two-dimensional attention-based recursive automatic encoder (RAE) shown in Fig. 2 is used as the bilingual phrase semantic representation model.

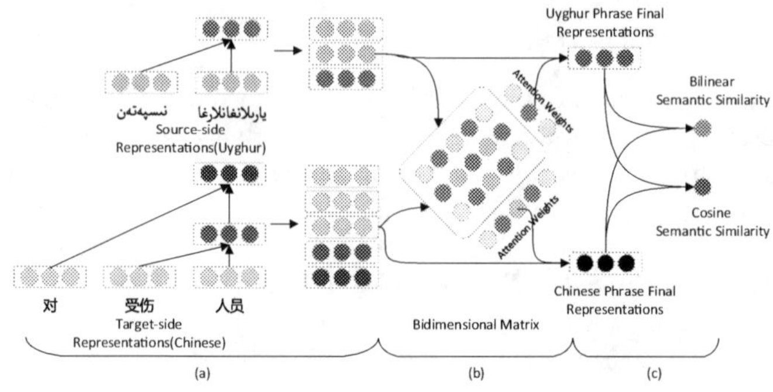

Fig. 2. Uyghur-Chinese bilingual phrase semantic representation model

Firstly, the RAE is used to generate the hierarchical structure of the Uyghur source phrase and the Chinese target phrase respectively. At the same time, multi-level granularity representation is obtained from the generated hierarchical structure.

Secondly, a two-dimensional attention network is constructed here. Based on the learned attention weights, the final representation of the Uyghur source phrase and Chinese target phrase are obtained by integrating the multi-level representation generated from the RAE through Eqs. (1) and (2):

$$p_s = \sum\nolimits_i a_{s,i} M_{s,i} \quad (1)$$

$$p_t = \sum\nolimits_j a_{t,j} M_{t,j} \quad (2)$$

Where, $a_{s,i}$ and $a_{t,j}$ are attention weights, $M_{s,i}$ and $M_{t,j}$ indicate the multi-level representation learned by RAE. Finally, after obtaining the semantic representation of the bilingual phrase, the semantic similarity between the Uyghur phrases and Chinese phrases can be calculated. The learned Uyghur phrase representation and Chinese phrase representation need to be mapped to a shared semantic space through the nonlinear mapping shown as Eqs. (3) and (4) before calculating semantic similarity.

$$S_s = f\left(W^{(5)}p_s + b^s\right) \tag{3}$$

$$S_t = f\left(W^{(6)}p_s + b^s\right) \tag{4}$$

We evaluate the semantic equivalence between S_s and S_t using bilinear model and cosine model.

1. Bilinear model
   Bilinear model compares the source and target phrase representations using a function that is independently linear in both representations. The semantic similarity score is computed as Eq. (5):

$$s(f, e) = s_s^T S s_t \tag{5}$$

2. Cosine model
   Cosine model calculates the cosine value of the angle between S_s and S_t. The semantic similarity score is computed as Eq. (6):

$$s(f, e) = \frac{s_s^T s_t}{\|s_s\|\|s_t\|} \tag{6}$$

3.3 System Combination

Generating New System

We employ the semantic information to extend the original feature space and generate several new systems based on the extension feature space. At present, most of the state-of-art SMT systems are based on linear models. Let $h_m(f, e)$ be a feature function, and λ_m be its weight, a standard SMT model D can be formally written as in Eq. (7):

$$e^* = \text{argmax}_e \sum\nolimits_m \lambda_m h_m(f, e) \tag{7}$$

Firstly, we specify Ω to denote the feature space defined by the original set of features used in D. N denotes a new feature space after adding semantic features and $\Omega \subset$ N. According to research by Passban et al. [20], new features can be added in both static and dynamic ways. In this paper, we follow the principle of adding a new semantic feature in the feature space at a time. A new derived system can be generated by the following two methods:

1. Adding static feature
   The bilinear similarity score and the cosine similarity score are added behind the original translation model feature h_i to supplement the translation model, to obtain

the new features $h_i^{'}$ of the translation model, and to generate new systems in the new feature space N.

2. Dynamic features
   The bilinear similarity score and the cosine similarity score are taken as new independent features h_n^b and h_n^c and are added into the linear model to generate new systems in the new feature space N.

After the new generations systems is constructed, each system tunes its feature weights independently to optimize the evaluation metrics on the development set. Let $\mathrm{D} = \{d_1, \cdots, d_n\}$ be the set of new systems obtained by adding semantic features. H_i be the n-best list produced by d_i. Then H(D) is the translation candidate list to the system combination model shown in Eq. (8).

$$\mathrm{H(D)} = \bigcup_i H_i \tag{8}$$

Constructing of the Combination Framework

This paper uses the sentence-level combination method to select the best translation hypothesis from the translation candidate list. This method can also be seen as the translation hypothesis reranking. The method selects the final translation hypothesis according to the scoring function of the Eq. (9).

$$e^* = \mathrm{argmax}_{e \in H(D)} \sum\nolimits_{t=1}^{T} \beta_t \cdot \phi_t(e) + \Psi(e, H_D) \tag{9}$$

where $\phi_t(e)$ is the system score for the t-th single system, β_t is the system weight for the t-th single system that used to represent the preference of the t-th single system. $\Psi(e, H_D)$ is a set of linear combinations based on n-gram features. The framework of the system combination is shown in Fig. 3.

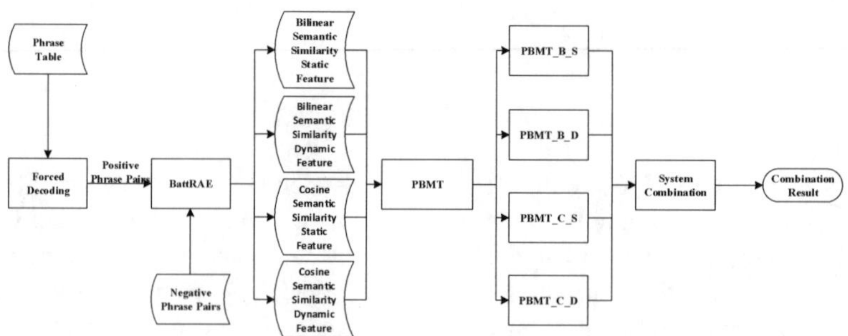

Fig. 3. Uyghur-Chinese machine translation system combination framework

4 Experiments

4.1 Setup

The training corpus used in the experiments is divided into two groups. The first group is the training corpus of CWMT2013, which has about 0.1 M parallel sentence pairs. It is used to extract the training data needed for the bilingual phrase semantic representation model. We used forced decoding on the above parallel corpus and collected 1.4 M phrase pairs. Each positive phrase pair corresponds to two negative phrase pairs to form two training samples and finally generates about 2.8 M training data for the bilingual phrase semantic representation model. The second group is the training corpus of CWMT2017. After filtering out the sentence pairs repeated with CWMT2013, there are about 0.33 M parallel sentence pairs remained, which are used to build a baseline translation system and perform system combination experiments.

For system combination, we building a standard phrase-based Uyghur-Chinese statistical machine translation system on 3.3 M parallel corpus of CWMT 2017 using Moses platform as the baseline system. We employ the CWMT2013 development set as the validation data and use the CWMT2013 test set as the test set. We utilized minimum error rate training to optimize the weights of our all translation systems and evaluate the translation quality through the case-insensitive BLEU-4 metric [21]. In order to verify the impact of semantic information on system combination, we set up two experiments for comparison:

1. Semantic information on single system experiment: Add the bilinear similarity score and the cosine similarity score to the baseline system by static features and dynamic features, respectively.
2. Semantic information on system combination experiment: Four new systems are derived based on the added features, and the derived systems are combined with the baseline system.

4.2 Experimental Results and Analysis

The Influence of Semantic Information on a Single System

We firstly perform an experiment to observe whether the introduction of bilingual phrase semantic information will affect the quality of a single SMT system. By modifying the similarity calculation function of the model, the bilinear similarity score and cosine similarity score are obtained. These two scores are treated as features added to SMT system.

Therefore, according to different similarity scores and different feature application methods, the introduction of semantic features can be divided into bilinear similarity static features (BS), bilinear similarity dynamic features (BD), cosine similarity static features (CS) and cosine similarity dynamics (CD). And when adding two new dynamic features, in order to observe the influence of the initial weight on the translation effect, we set the initial weights from 0.0 to 0.9(interval 0.1), and perform 18 experiments in total. The experimental results on the test set are shown in Figs. 4 and 5.

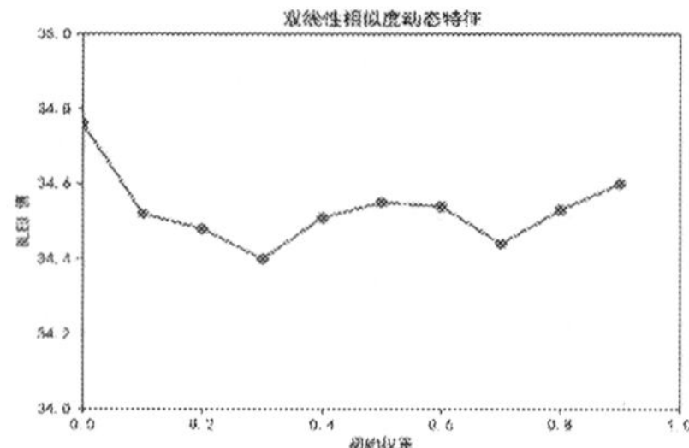

Fig. 4. BLEU value on different weights of bilinear similarity dynamic feature

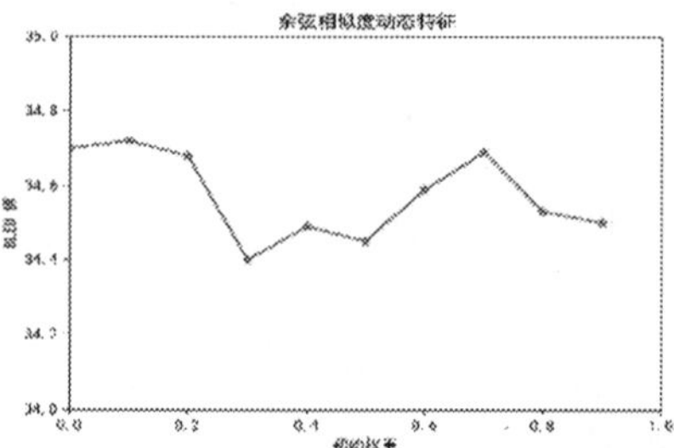

Fig. 5. BLEU value on different weights of cosine similarity dynamic feature

Experimental results show that the initial weight has a direct impact on the translation effect. When adding the bilinear similarity dynamic feature, a good BLEU value is obtained when the initial weight of 0.0; when the cosine similarity dynamic feature is added, the highest BLEU value is obtained when the initial weight is set to 0.1. The experimental results after adding semantic features are shown in Table 1. As shown in Table 1, the introduction of the semantic information of the Uyghur-Chinese bilingual phrases can indeed improve the effect of a single system. The bilinear static feature with the highest score has increased the BLEU value by 0.43 compared with the baseline system. From the similarity method, the bilinear similarity score performs better than the cosine similarity score. From the feature type, the dynamic feature performs better than the static feature, but the introduction of dynamic features requires additional feature functions and different weights need to be set to find the optimal value, so it is more complicated to implement.

The Influence of Semantic Information on System Combination

According to the experimental setup, the system generated from the bilinear similarity static feature is called PBSMT-BS (SYS1) and the system generated from the bilinear similarity dynamic feature is called PBSMT-BD (SYS2). The system generated from the cosine similarity static feature is called PBSMT-CS (SYS3) and the system generated after adding the cosine similarity dynamic feature is called PBSMT-CD (SYS4).

Table 1. Experimental results of semantic features influence on a single system

System	Test	Gains on Test
PBSMT(baseline)	34.38	N/A
PBSMT+B-S(SYS1)	34.81	0.43
PBSMT+B-D(SYS2)	34.76	0.38
PBSMT+C-S(SYS3)	34.55	0.17
PBSMT+C-D(SYS4)	34.72	0.34

In order to observe the impact of the new system on the baseline system, we gradually combined each new system with the baseline system. The results of the system combination are shown in Table 2.

Table 2. The effect of semantic features on system combination

System	Test	Gains on Test
PBSMT(baseline)	34.38	N/A
+SYS1	34.78	0.4
+SYS2	34.83	0.45
+SYS3	34.86	0.48
+SYS4	35.01	0.63

As shown in Table 2, we get the best results of the 35.01 BLEU value after combining the newly generated four systems with the baseline system. Although the BLEU value is decreased after joining the SYS1 system, when with the combination of SYS2 and subsequent SYS3 and SYS4 systems, the effect of system combination is steadily improved compared with the baseline system. The total improvement of the BLEU value is 0.63, which is 0.2 higher than the best single system SYS1. Experimental results show that the semantic information of bilingual phrases can further enhance the effect of system combination on the basis of improving a single translation system.

5 Conclusion

We present a system combination method of Uyghur-Chinese machine translation system based on semantic information, which can introduce semantic information into the process of system combination. Experimental results show that for Uyghur-Chinese translation task, the introduction of bilingual phrase semantic information can not only improve the performance of the single statistical machine translation but also further improve the performance of system combination.

However, the current system combination method is mainly based on statistical methods and due to the fact that the neural machine translation are quite different from statistical machine translation, the existing system combination methods cannot suitable for them. For the future work, we plan to find a new method for system combination which is more suitable for the neural machine translation.

Acknowledgements. This research is supported by the Xinjiang Uygur Autonomous Region Level talent introduction project (Y839031201), National Natural Science Foundation of China (U1703133), Subsidy of the Youth Innovation Promotion Association of the Chinese Academy of Sciences (2017472), the Xinjiang Key Laboratory Fund under Grant (2018D04018).

References

1. Bentivogli, L., Bisazza, A., Cettolo, M., Federico, M.: Neural versus phrase-based machine translation quality: a case study. arXiv preprint arXiv:1608.04631 (2016)
2. Koehn, P., Knowles, R.: Six challenges for neural machine translation. arXiv preprint arXiv: 1706.03872 (2017)
3. Li, X., Jiang, T., Zhou, X., Wang, L., Yang, Y.: Uyghur-Chinese machine translation key technology research overview. J. Netw. New Media **5**(1), 19–25 (2016)
4. Su, J., Zhang, X., Turghun, O., Li, X.: Joint multiple engines Uyghur-Chinese machine translation system. Comput. Eng. **37**(16), 179–181 (2011)
5. Wang, Y., Li, X., Yang, Y., Mi, C.: Research of Uyghur-Chinese machine translation system combination based on paraphrase information. Comput. Eng. **45**(4), 288–295+301 (2019)
6. Zhang, J., Liu, S., Li, M., Zhou, M., Zong, C.: Bilingually-constrained Phrase Embeddings for Machine Translation, pp. 111–121. Association for Computational Linguistics, Baltimore (2014)
7. Zhang, B., Xiong, D., Su, J., Qin, Y.: Alignment-supervised bidimensional attention-based recursive autoencoders for bilingual phrase representation. IEEE Trans. Cybern., 1–11 (2018)
8. Gao, J., He, X., Yih, W., Li, D.: Learning Semantic Representations for the Phrase Translation Model. Computer Science (2013)
9. Su, J., Xiong, D., Zhang, B., Liu, Y., Yao, J., Zhang, M.: Bilingual Correspondence Recursive Autoencoder for Statistical Machine Translation, pp. 1248–1258. Association for Computational Linguistics, Lisbon (2015)
10. Zhang, B., Xiong, D., Su, J.: BattRAE: Bidimensional Attention-Based Recursive Autoencoders for Learning Bilingual Phrase Embeddings (2017)
11. Abend, O., Rappoport, A.: The State of the Art in Semantic Representation, pp. 77–89. Association for Computational Linguistics, Vancouver, Canada (2017)
12. Banik, D., Ekbal, A., Bhattacharyya, P., Bhattacharyya, S.: Assembling translations from multi-engine machine translation outputs. Appl. Soft Comput. **78**, 230–239 (2019)
13. Freitag, M., Peter, J.-T., Peitz, S., Feng, M., Ney, H.: Local System Voting Feature for Machine Translation System Combination, pp. 467–476. Association for Computational Linguistics, Lisbon (2015)
14. Ma, W.-Y., McKeown, K.: System combination for machine translation through paraphrasing. In: Proceedings of the 2015 Conference on Empirical Methods in Natural Language Processing, pp. 1053–1058 (2015)

15. Marie, B., Fujita, A.: A smorgasbord of features to combine phrase-based and neural machine translation. In: Proceedings of the 13th Conference of the Association for Machine Translation in the Americas (Volume 1: Research Papers), pp. 111–124. (2018)
16. Zhu, J., Yang, M., Li, S., Zhao, T.: Sentence-level paraphrasing for machine translation system combination. In: Che, W., et al. (eds.) ICYCSEE 2016. CCIS, vol. 623, pp. 612–620. Springer, Singapore (2016). https://doi.org/10.1007/978-981-10-2053-7_54
17. Freitag, M., Huck, M., Ney, H.: Jane: open source machine translation system combination. In: Proceedings of the Demonstrations at the 14th Conference of the European Chapter of the Association for Computational Linguistics, pp. 29–32 (2014)
18. Xiao, T., Zhu, J., Liu, T.: Bagging and boosting statistical machine translation systems. Artif. Intell. **195**, 496–527 (2013)
19. Wuebker, J., Mauser, A., Ney, H.: Training phrase translation models with leaving-one-out. In: Proceedings of the 48th Annual Meeting of the Association for Computational Linguistics, pp. 475–484. Association for Computational Linguistics (2010)
20. Passban, P., Hokamp, C., Liu, Q.: Bilingual distributed phrase representation for statistical machine translation. In: Proceedings of MT Summit XV, pp. 310–318 (2015)
21. Papineni, K., Roukos, S., Ward, T., Zhu, W.-J.: BLEU: a method for automatic evaluation of machine translation. In: Proceedings of the 40th Annual Meeting on Association for Computational Linguistics, pp. 311–318. Association for Computational Linguistics (2002)

Subject Recognition in Chinese Sentences for Chatbots

Fangyuan Li[1], Huanhuan Wei[1], Qiangda Hao[1], Ruihong Zeng[1], Hao Shao[1(✉)], and Wenliang Chen[2]

[1] Gowild Robotics Co., Ltd., Shenzhen, China
fyli.winnie@gmail.com, weihuanhuan5@163.com, haoqiangda3@gmail.com, petertsengruihon@gmail.com, shaohao820@gmail.com

[2] School of Computer Science and Technology, Soochow University, Suzhou, China
wlchen@suda.edu.cn

Abstract. Subject (In this paper, subject means "主体/zhu ti" in Chinese, while we use "grammatical subject" to denote traditional "主语/zhu yu" in Chinese.) recognition plays a significant role in the conversation with a Chatbot. The misclassification of the subject of a sentence leads to the misjudgment of the intention recognition. In this paper, we build a new dataset for subject recognition and propose several systems based on pre-trained language models. We first design annotation guidelines for human-chatbot conversational data, and hire annotators to build a new dataset according to the guidelines. Then, classification methods based on deep neural network are proposed. Finally, extensive experiments are conducted to testify the performance of different algorithms. The results show that our method achieves 88.5% F_1 in the task of subject recognition. We also compare our systems with three other Chatbot systems and find ours perform the best.

Keywords: Chatbot · Subject recognition · Deep neural network

1 Introduction

As an entry-level product in the era of artificial intelligence, chatbots have attracted wide attention from both academic and industry. In a chatbot framework, intention recognition significantly influence the conversational performance. Nevertheless, a large number of chatbots performs worse in intention recognition, especially in the recognition of the subject of a sentence. As shown in Fig. 1, although the chatbot successfully identifies specific topics including "singing" and "constellation", it fails to distinguish characters such as "you" and "me" around them. The underlying reason is that, situations such as missing subject, unknown reference and sentence ambiguity often occur in spoken Chinese. Consequently, it is more difficult to perform semantic analysis than in written Chinese.

To our best knowledge, there exists no effective resolution to the problem of character recognition in chatbots. A number of research works has been devoted

J. Tang et al. (Eds.): NLPCC 2019, LNAI 11839, pp. 508–518, 2019.
https://doi.org/10.1007/978-3-030-32236-6_46

User: So boring. Can you sing a song for me?
Chatbot: OK. Twinkle twinkle little star, how I wonder what you are...
User: Great, let me sing a song for you.
Chatbot: OK. Twinkle twinkle little star, how I wonder what you are...
User: ......
User: By the way, my constellation is Libra.
Chatbot: You don't care much about me. I'm Aries.

Fig. 1. Example of subject error in chatbot

to identifying the grammatical subjects [7,11,13], the agents [1,10], the emotion or opinion holders [4,16] and targets extraction [12,15]. However, none of these achievements can be directly used to identify core characters in a conversational context. In this paper, the term "subject" (主体/zhu ti) is defined as the characters around events, opinions and descriptions. It is different from the traditional "grammatical subject" (主语/zhu yu) in three aspects:

(1) **The domains and scopes are different.** The grammatical subject of a sentence can be composed of nouns, pronouns, noun phrases, adjectives, verbs, predicate phrases and subject-predicate phrases. The subject in this paper pays attention to a specific person around the core content in a sentence. For example, in the sentence "learning to drive is difficult", the grammatical subject is the verb-object phrase "learning to drive". However, there is no specific character which can be denoted as a subject.
(2) **The designations are different.** The grammatical subject is usually the declarative object of a sentence, while the subject is the specific person to whom the declarative object belongs. For example, in the sentence "my dream is beautiful", the grammatical subject is "dream", while the subject is "I".
(3) **The numbers are different.** There may be multiple grammatical subjects in a sentence, but generally there is only one subject. In simple sentences, the grammatical subject is unique, but there may or may not exist a subject. In complex sentences, grammatical subjects may appear in both main clauses and subordinate clauses, however, only one character can be regarded as the subject. E.g., "I" and "you" are both grammatical subjects of "I think you are beautiful", while the subject is "you" around the core contents "beautiful".

In real applications, subject recognition is difficult due to incomplete semantics and unclear references, especially without context information. For example, "Cheer up mom loves you" (加油妈妈爱你), it is difficult to distinguish the real subject between "user's mom" or "user". At present, there is no widely acknowledged definition and annotation guidelines of subject recognition. To our best knowledge, there is not an annotated dataset available for this task. There are three main contributions of this paper:

- The first annotation guidelines of subject recognition are proposed.
- A dataset is constructed manually according to the annotation guidelines which can be downloaded publicly.
- Neural network based subject recognition methods are constructed, extensive experiments are conducted to verify the effectiveness from both the model evaluation aspect and the manual evaluation aspect.

2 Related Work

Subject recognition in the field of chatbots has certain relevance to many tasks in Natural Language Processing (NLP), such as Summarization, Sentiment Analysis and Semantic Role Labeling (SRL). Sentence-level summarization aims at extracting the Subject-Verb-Object (SVO) tuple in a sentence. Most of them focus on extracting the SVO based on syntactic analysis [7,11,13]. Sentiment analysis is the field of analyzing people's opinions, sentiments and emotions. Previous studies have been mainly dedicated to opinion mining and sentiment classification [12,17], while less attention is paid to the extraction of opinion holders and targets. Opinion holders extraction is usually based on linguistic rules which are constructed by named entity recognition and syntactic analysis features [4,16]. Opinion targets are related to opinion words. Plenty of researchers extract them after recognizing the opinion words [12,15]. Semantic Role Labeling studies the relationship between predicates and other components in sentences. The conventional approach to SRL [1,10] is to construct a syntax tree and prune it with heuristic rules. Then classifiers are used to identify and classify potential arguments. Finally, global semantic roles are obtained by inference.

Subject recognition has certain relevance to the tasks above, but there are still some differences. The grammatical subject of a sentence in text summarization can only be regarded as a candidate for the subject of a sentence in this paper. In sentiment analysis, both the opinion holder and the opinion target can be the subject. The extraction of agents and patients in SRL is similar to subject recognition. The subject of a sentence can be either the agent or the patient. For example, the subject of the sentence "I'm mad at you" (我快要被你气死了) is the patient, while the subject of the sentence "I like you" (我喜欢你) is the agent. Therefore, all previous solutions can not handle the task of subject recognition issue directly.

3 Dataset Construction for Subject Recognition

As far as we know there is no open high-quality subject annotation dataset in the field of chatbots. Due to the diversity of Chinese expression, irregularity of spoken Chinese, reference ambiguous or omitted of dialogue context and error propagation of speech recognition, it is difficult to form a common annotation guidelines for subject recognition. Based on a large number of real industrial chatbots interaction data annotated by human, this paper provides a relatively general subject annotation guidelines and constructs a dataset according to it. The annotation guidelines only for single sentences. All the data is derived from conversational corpus of users and chatbots in industrial products.

3.1 Subject Data Annotation Guidelines

Categories of Subject Classification. The range of subjects discussed in this paper are all *limited*[1]. A subject can be one of the follows: personal pronouns, name, properties, body parts of people, people belongings, some relationship of people and anthropomorphic animals. This paper defines five kinds of subject labels: "I", "You", "I & You", "Others" and "None".

(1) **"I"** is the speaker of the sentence, including first person words (我/咱 (I/my/ me), 我们 (our/us)), my properties, my body parts, my belongings and those sentences which omit "I" but is the sentence subject evidently.
(2) **"You"** is the target of the speaker. It contains second person words (你/你们 (you/ your)), the chatbot's name, your properties, your body parts, your belongings and those sentences which obviously omit "You" as subject.
(3) **"I & You"** means the core topics or events of the sentence are done by both sides of the speaker and target. E.g. "I am as beautiful as you".
(4) **"Others"** refers to someone else, neither the speaker nor the target of the speaker. Third person, person name (except chatbot's or user's name) or a particular person or group can regards as "Others".
(5) **"None"** mainly contains: (1) The following components as subjects, such as objects, time words, place words, state words, abstract nouns and proper nouns, etc. (2) There is no subject in a sentence. (3) Sentence omits the subject and the omitted subject cannot be determined.

General Annotation Rules. Based on a large number of manual annotation experiences, we abstract five general annotation rules which can be suitable for most scenarios. Rules are built on grammatical structures of sentences, as described in Table 1. It should be noted that not all sentences which satisfy the five structures above can be labeled. The key point is to first identify the core content of the sentence, and then label the core content's role as the subject.

Default Supplement of Subject Omission. In the specific scenario of human-chatbot dialogue, we can supply a default subject to the sentences which omit the subject in some cases.

(1) **Situations of adding "I" as the default subject**
   - A VO structure sentence omits the subject and the object is a second person word. E.g. "Love you", "Thank you".
   - A sentence omits the subject and describes the inner emotions and mental state of users. E.g., "I feel sad because I was hurt" (受伤了难受).

[1] The term *limited* refers to specific reference and definite quantity, while *non-limited* means those generic reference and non-definite quantity. The subject discussed in this paper belongs to the limited, so the non-limited people are usually not regarded as subjects, such as the "men" in "All men must die".

Table 1. General rules for subject annotation

No.	Rule details	Example	Subject
1	A sentence startswith subject, has no object. Labeling grammatical subject.	*I am happy(我很开心).*	I
2	An SVO sentence, object is not a clause. Labeling grammatical subject.	*I like you(我喜欢你).*	I
3	An SVO sentence, object is a clause. Labeling grammatical subject of object clause.	*I think you are a fool(我觉得你很傻).*	You
4	A Verb-Object(VO) structure sentence, object is not a clause, the omitted subject can be determined, Labeling omitted subject.	*(I) was beaten by someone this morning(被人打了).*	I
5	A VO structure sentence, object is a clause, subject is the grammatical subject of the clause in most cases.	*(I) hope you are getting smarter(希望你越来越聪明)*	You

(2) **Situations of adding "You" as the default subject**
   - An imperative sentence which has a intention of chatbot function, such as setting alarms, playing music, etc. E.g. "Set a 10 o'clock alarm clock for me."
   - A VO structure sentence omits the subject and the object is a first person. , such as "Give me a smile" (给我笑一个).

(3) **Adding subject according to verb directionality**
Some verbs have obvious directionality, such as "把/ba", "被/bei", "给/gei", "帮/bang", "替/ti, "让/rang", "告诉/gao su", etc. In most cases, the subject of a sentence exists before these verbs. If the subject is omitted, it can be restored according to the verb direction and the personal pronouns of the object. E.g., "You amused me (被你逗乐了)" in Chinese omits the subject "I".

Subject Choice in Sentence with Multiple Predicates. When a sentence contains juxtaposed components or is complex with clauses, there is usually more than one predicate. The following rules can be used to choose the most important one: (1) Prioritize the parts which contain chatbots function intents. (2) Give preference to the sub-sentence which describes the user's emotions. (3) Other juxtaposed situations such as causal relationship, and transition relationship, the subject of the highlighted part of the whole sentence can be chosen as the subject.

Another solution is to split each juxtaposed component into multiple sentences and label subject for each sub-sentence. The rules above are all heuristic, readers should adjust in real practice.

3.2 Methods for Subject Dataset Construction

Data Filtering. Due to the limitations of the accuracy in Speech Recognition, there exist a large number of mistakes in chatbot corpus that should be filtered. In general, the *Perplexity* calculated by language models can be a metric to evaluate the fluency of sentences. The formula of sentence *Perplexity* value is: $Perplexity(s) = \sqrt[N]{\frac{1}{P(w_1,w_2,...,w_n)}} = \sqrt[N]{\frac{1}{\prod p(w_i)}}$, where s represents a sentence, N is the number of words in s, $p(w_i)$ means the probability of the i-th word. The smaller the *Perplexity* value is, the more fluent the sentence is. We use a traditional n-gram language model kenLM[2], and use large-scale news corpora and chatbot dialogue corpus which contain approximately 100 million sentences as the training data. In this paper, we use 500 *Perplexity* as the threshold to judge whether a sentence is fluent. The accuracy is 84.3% through manual sampling evaluation. After that, in order to ensure data diversity, we improve the Longest Common Subsequence (LCS) algorithm to filter similar data by ignoring punctuation, modal particles and other meaningless words in the sentence.

Semi-automatic Labeling. Annotation is an iterative process. We summarize and generalize some labeling rules based on a small part data of pre-labeling. Then, we tag data with different feature labels by these rules. After that, we put the data with similar labels together to annotate. It can greatly improve the efficiency and the consistency. We use the following features: number of subject words, the category of the subject word, whether the sentence starts with subject words, whether the sentence ends with subject words, the dependency relation "SBV"[3] in sentence, etc. We re-train the model on the annotate data and find out the underperformed sentences. Then, annotators reviewed them manually. Finally, a new model is trained on the checked data to predict unlabeled data.

3.3 Data Labeling Consistency Detection

Each data is annotated by two different annotators, the disagreement is judged by an auditor. We calculate a *Kappa* value for the two annotators to get the label consistency. The formula is: $Kappa = \frac{p_o - p_e}{1 - p_e}$, where p_o means the relative observed agreement among annotators, p_e is the hypothetical probability of chance agreement. In general, the $Kappa > 0.75$ indicates a satisfying labeling consistency, while the $Kappa < 0.4$ indicates unsatisfied labeling consistency. Our dataset's *Kappa* is 0.875. The result shows that the annotation guidelines in this paper is relatively uniform and less divergent. Labeling consistency and the quality of the data is high.

4 Subject Recognition of Chatbots

In this section, we first introduce a variety of baseline classification models based on deep neural networks. Then, according to the characteristics of the subject

[2] https://github.com/kpu/kenlm.
[3] A subject-verb relation in LTP. https://github.com/HIT-SCIR/ltp.

recognition task, the subject recognition models based on the pre-trained language models are constructed.

4.1 Subject Recognition Models Based on Deep Neural Network

In resent years, significant achievements have been made in text classification based on deep neural network models. In such models, words are usually embedded into fixed-length vectors. In this paper, a number of text classification models are introduced to verify the effectiveness of subject recognition based on the manual annotated data sets.

Kim [5] proposes a text classification model named TextCNN, based on features obtained from convolution kernels in a CNN network. Bi-LSTM model improves the traditional RNN network by incorporating context and temporal information Zhou [18] adds Attention mechanism to Bi-LSTM network to capture the core information in sentences by calculating temporal weights. Lai [6] combines the advantages of Bi-LSTM and CNN, and proposes RCNN (Recurrent Convolutional Neural Networks) model. The Adversarial LSTM model proposed by Miyato [8] generates a common training model for adversarial samples by randomly adding noise to word vectors to prevent over-fitting. Transformer [14] model abandons CNN and RNN, and uses only self-Attention mechanism, which greatly improves the computing speed while better captures the global information. FastText [3] is a classification model based on n-gram features. It has fast training speed and can maintain quite good performance.

4.2 Subject Recognition Based on ELMo

Contextual lexical information and word sequence have great influence on subject recognition. For example, “I like you” and “You like me” contain exactly the same vocabulary information, but the subjects are completely opposite because of the different word order. The word vectors obtained from traditional word vector models, such as Word2vec and GloVe, are static and unable to represent the differences between sentences. ELMo (Embedding from Language Models) [9] is a word vector model proposed by Allen NLP. It is essentially a bidirectional language model, in which words can be represented with context information. In real applications, word embeddings from ELMo can be dynamically adjusted in order to suit the subject recognition tasks.

To make full use of the context information and make better semantic representations, the ELMo word vectors are trained based on all data sets using Bi-LSTM with Attention. While fully mining the sequential information in text, the model can automatically capture the key information of words. Based on ELMo, three main subject recognition frameworks are constructed: (1) ELMo+Bi-LSTM; (2) ELMo+Bi-LSTM+Attention; (3) ELMo+TextCNN.

4.3 Subject Recognition Based on BERT

BERT (Bidirectional Encoder Representations from Transformers) [2] is a language representation model trained on large-scale text. It adopts Transformer as the main framework of the algorithm, which can better capture the bidirectional relationship in the corpus. The main feature of BERT is that it abandons the traditional RNN and CNN, and converts the distance between two words in any position to 1 through attention mechanism. It can effectively solve the long-term dependence problem in NLP tasks, and refreshes the highest record of 11 NLP tasks in GLUE benchmark at that time. Similar to ELMo, BERT can generate current word representation according to the semantics of the context words, which is very suitable for the subject recognition task in this paper.

5 Experiments

5.1 Dataset and Evaluation Metrics

We filtered duplicate conversational corpora with methods in Sect. 3.2. Totally 49,924 sentences are obtained and labeled with the guidelines in Sect. 3.1. Readers can download the dataset on Github[4]. We divided the dataset into three parts: training set (70%, 31,446), validation set (10%, 4,448) and test set (20%, 9,030). Additional 1,000 sentences as manual evaluation data set, which has no intersection with the above data sets.

We used the models listed in Sect. 4, and utilized Python3 as coding language. A pre-trained word embedding model is used in BERT, while in ELMo and fastText, word embeddings are trained on all data. For the others models, word embeddings were trained by Word2vec[5] with all data. We used the skip-gram architecture of Word2vec and the dimension is set to be 300.

We utilized Precision (P), Recall (R) and F_1 score as evaluation metrics. Particularly, due to the imbalance of the data with different labels, we used weighted P, R and F_1 score as final evaluation metrics. In order to verify the improvement of conversational dialogue in chatbots by subject identification, we did manual evaluation on three popular chatbots. Firstly, we got the replies through chatting with three chatbots on 1,000 test sentences. Secondly, we invited two language experts to annotate the subjects of these replies. The annotation methods are as follows:

- The subject of the reply is able to correspond the query. Labeling "correct".
- The subject of the reply is unable to correspond the query. Labeling "error".
- There is no subject in the reply but is still an appropriate answer. Labeling "notbad".
- The reply is not related to the query or a safe response. Labeling "unknown".

The higher ratio of "correct+notbad" indicates the better performance of chatbots, while the higher ratio of "error" reveals the worse performance on subject recognition. We assumed that if the subject recognition in the query is right, the subject of the reply will be correct. Therefore, we used subject recognition model to predict the subjects for the sentences, and then counted

[4] https://github.com/winnie0/ChineseSubjectRecognition.

[5] https://radimrehurek.com/gensim/models/word2vec.html.

the number of "Error to Correct" (E2C), which denotes the number of sentences in which wrong subjects are transformed to be correct using subjects predicted by the model. We also defined a *Transformation Ratio* (TR), as the ratio of the number of E2C, divided by the number of sentences with errors in subjects. This metric can reflect the improvement of conversational dialogue in chatbots by subject recognition task.

5.2 Experimental Results

Models Results. We carried out experiments on seven baseline models, three ELMo models and the BERT model, experimental results are shown in Table 2. The results show that TextCNN performed best (84.5% F_1) in models with Word2vec word embedding, and Transformer was slightly worse (81.9% F_1). The possible explanation is that the amount of data is not large enough. The results of other models were not much different. ELMo+Bi-LSTM was optimal among the three models which used the ELMo word embedding (85.5% F_1). It was useless to add Attention on ELMo+Bi-LSTM as shown by the results. We could see that all basic models increased F_1 by using the ELMo word embedding, which was improved by 2.2% on Bi-LSTM, 1.7% on Bi-LSTM+Attention and

Table 2. Experimental results of subject recognition

Model	Val_P	Val_R	Val_F_1	Test_P	Test_R	Test_F_1
TextCNN	85.2	84.6	84.9	84.8	84.4	84.5
RCNN	84.3	84.1	84.1	83.8	83.7	83.6
Bi-LSTM	84.6	83.6	84.0	83.8	82.9	83.3
Bi-LSTM+Attention	84.2	83.6	83.8	83.9	83.5	83.6
AdversarialLSTM	86.8	80.9	82.8	84.9	81.5	82.6
Transformer	82.3	81.5	81.9	82.3	81.7	81.9
fastText	83.0	83.4	83.0	83.0	83.4	83.1
ELMo+Bi-LSTM	85.0	85.4	85.1	85.6	85.4	**85.5**
ELMo+Bi-LSTM+Attention	84.7	85.1	84.8	85.3	85.5	85.3
ELMo+TextCNN	85.3	85.7	85.3	84.9	85.2	85.0
BERT	88.4	88.6	88.5	88.5	88.6	**88.5**

Table 3. Manual evaluation results of subject recognition

chatbots	correct	error	notbad	unknown	correct R	error R	E2C	error dec R	TR
Bot A	457	116	131	311	45.0%	11.4%	66	6.5%	56.9%
Bot B	418	88	222	287	41.2%	8.7%	63	6.2%	71.6%
Bot C	521	74	226	194	51.3%	7.3%	45	4.4%	60.8%

0.5% on TextCNN. These results illustrated that the ELMo word embedding can capture the semantic information of sentences better and enhance the effect of subject recognition. However, the fine-tuning mode of the BERT model achieved excellent classification performance, which was superior to all other classification models, and reached 88.5% F_1 score.

Manual Evaluation. The manual evaluation results on 1,000 sentences of three popular chatbots are shown in Table 3. The model reduced the subject error rate by 6.5%, 6.2% and 4.4% in three chatbots respectively, and the transformation ratios were 56.9%, 71.6% and 60.8%, which were improved significantly.

6 Conclusion

In this paper, we present a newly built dataset for subject recognition in chatbots and propose a novel model for the task. Based on the data in real applications, we propose an annotation guidelines, and the manually annotated dataset contains 44,924 sentences. According to the characteristics of the subject recognition task, a number of classification models are proposed based on the pre-trained language models. Finally, we conduct experiments to verify the effectiveness of proposed models. In the future, we plan to expand the number of annotated data sets. Chatbots in real applications will also be improved based on the achievements to enhance the interaction experience with human.

Acknowledgements. The authors are supported by the National Natural Science Foundation of China (Grant No. 61603240). Corresponding author is Hao Shao. We also thank the anonymous reviewers for their insightful comments.

References

1. Christensen, J., Soderland, S., Etzioni, O., et al.: An analysis of open information extraction based on semantic role labeling. In: K-CAP, pp. 113–120. ACM (2011)
2. Devlin, J., Chang, M.W., Lee, K., Toutanova, K.: Bert: pre-training of deep bidirectional transformers for language understanding. arXiv preprint arXiv:1810.04805 (2018)
3. Joulin, A., Grave, E., Bojanowski, P., Mikolov, T.: Bag of tricks for efficient text classification. arXiv preprint arXiv:1607.01759 (2016)
4. Kim, S.M., Hovy, E.: Identifying opinion holders for question answering in opinion texts. In: AAAI 2005 Workshop, pp. 1367–1373 (2005)
5. Kim, Y.: Convolutional neural networks for sentence classification. arXiv preprint arXiv:1408.5882 (2014)
6. Lai, S., Xu, L., Liu, K., Zhao, J.: Recurrent convolutional neural networks for text classification. In: AAAI (2015)
7. Li, F., et al.: Structure-aware review mining and summarization. In: COLING, pp. 653–661 (2010)
8. Miyato, T., Dai, A.M., Goodfellow, I.: Adversarial training methods for semi-supervised text classification. arXiv preprint arXiv:1605.07725 (2016)

9. Peters, M.E., et al.: Deep contextualized word representations. arXiv preprint arXiv:1802.05365 (2018)
10. Punyakanok, V., Roth, D., Yih, W.t.: The importance of syntactic parsing and inference in semantic role labeling. Comput. Linguist. **34**(2), 257–287 (2008)
11. Qi, H., Yang, M., Meng, Y., Han, X., Zhao, T.: Skeleton parsing for specific domain Chinese text. J. Chin. Inf. Process. **18**(1), 1–5 (2004). (in Chinese)
12. Qiu, G., Liu, B., Bu, J., Chen, C.: Opinion word expansion and target extraction through double propagation. Comput. Linguist. **37**(1), 9–27 (2011)
13. Rusu, D., Dali, L., Fortuna, B., Grobelnik, M., Mladenic, D.: Triplet extraction from sentences. In: IMSCI, pp. 8–12 (2007)
14. Vaswani, A., et al.: Attention is all you need. In: Advances in Neural Information Processing Systems, pp. 5998–6008 (2017)
15. Wang, R., Ju, J., Li, S., Zhou, G.: Feature engineering for CRFs based opinion target extraction. J. Chin. Inf. Process. **26**(2), 56–61 (2012). (in Chinese)
16. Wiegand, M., Klakow, D.: Convolution kernels for opinion holder extraction. In: NAACL-HLT, pp. 795–803 (2010)
17. Zhou, H., Huang, M., Zhang, T., Zhu, X., Liu, B.: Emotional chatting machine: emotional conversation generation with internal and external memory. In: AAAI (2018)
18. Zhou, P., et al.: Attention-based bidirectional long short-term memory networks for relation classification. In: ACL (2016)

Research on Khalkha Dialect Mongolian Speech Recognition Acoustic Model Based on Weight Transfer

Linyan Shi, Feilong Bao(✉), Yonghe Wang, and Guanglai Gao

Inner Mongolian Key Laboratory of Mongolian Information Processing Technology, College of Computer Science, Inner Mongolia University, Hohhot 010021, China
shilinyan_2016@163.com, cswyh92@163.com, {csfeilong, csggl}@imu.edu.cn

Abstract. Due to the lack of labeled training data, the performance of acoustic models in low-resource speech recognition systems such as Khalkha dialect Mongolian is poor. Transfer Learning can solve the data-sparse problem by learning the source domain (high resource) knowledge to guides the training of the target domain (low resource) model. In this paper, we investigate the modeling method of using different transfer learning ways in the Khalkha dialect Mongolian ASR system. First, the English and Chahar dialect are used as the source domains, and the trained acoustic model on the above source domains are conducted to initialize the Khalkha acoustic model parameter. Furthermore, the different training strategies, the portability of different hidden layers, and the impact of the pre-training model on the transfer model were applied to validate their effectiveness in the Khalkha dialect ASR task. The experimental results show that the optimal acoustic model is chain TDNN based on weight transfer method with Chahar dialect as the source domain. The final WER is 15.67%, which is relatively reduced by 38% compared to the random initialization model.

Keywords: Speech recognition · Khalkha Mongolian dialect · Weight transfer · Time delay neural network · Chain model

1 Introduction

Currently, Automatic speech recognition (ASR) system has a large dependence on the amount of the annotated data. How to improve the performance of the low-resource Khalkha dialect Mongolian acoustic model is the main content of this paper.

Mongolian is a kind of cross-border language and has many dialects, such as Chahar dialect and Khalkha dialect. It is used in Mongolia, Inner Mongolia of China and some regions of Russia. The Mongolian in China is mainly Chahar dialect, which is the official Mongolian. It is usually written in traditional Mongolian letters, we call it Traditional Mongolian. Meanwhile, in Mongolia, Khalkha dialect is the standard Mongolian and usually written in Cyrillic Mongolian letters, we call it Cyrillic Mongolian. The ASR system based on Chahar dialect started at 2003 in China and was established in [1]. Then some methods were proposed in [2–4] to optimize the acoustic

J. Tang et al. (Eds.): NLPCC 2019, LNAI 11839, pp. 519–528, 2019.
https://doi.org/10.1007/978-3-030-32236-6_47

model. In Literature [5, 6], NN-based acoustic models were widely used in Chahar dialect ASR and achieved remarkable promotion. Recently, Hybrid Frame Neural Network in [7, 8] achieved remarkable promotion with the WER score of the best system reaching 6.99%. However, because of the difficulty in collecting and labeling the data, the study of Khalkha dialect ASR is still in its infancy.

Transfer learning is a relatively abstract concept with different manifestations in different fields. In 2010, Pan showed that transfer learning can apply the knowledge learned from one model to another model [9], which can effectively solve the problem of data sparseness. With the development of machine learning and deep learning, deep neural network models have been applied to various classification fields. Professor Bengio [10] suggested that the features learned from the hidden layer near the input (lower) are more general, and near the output (higher) are more specific. This has played a key guiding role in the development of transfer learning. The application of transfer learning in the field of ASR system is mainly embodied in pre-training. In [11] the English ASR acoustic model based on DNN achieved better results in the target domain French than the baseline system.

In this paper, we first apply the random initialization chain TDNN structure to the acoustic model of the Khalkha dialect Mongolian ASR system and investigate the TDNN architectures using of different hidden layers splicing structure. Finally, in the weight transfer experiments, we compared the single-stage and two-stage training strategy, analyzed the portability of different hidden layers in TDNN, and verified influence of parameters and epochs on model performance.

2 Model Description

2.1 Baseline Model

Time delay neural network (TDNN), a multi-layer feed forward network model, is applied to the acoustic model modeling of this paper. A TDNN model is shown in Fig. 1.

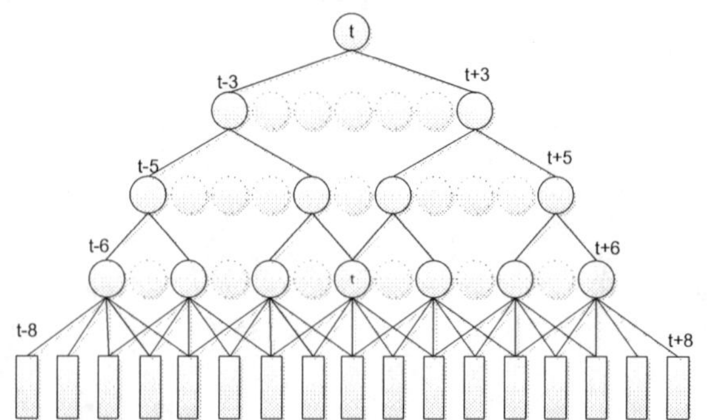

Fig. 1. Structure of sub-sampling Time Delay Neural Network

The initial layer learns the affine transforms from the narrow temporal context and the deeper layers learn the hidden affine transforms from increasingly wider contexts [8]. Therefore, the longer temporal relationships information from the input context can be learned at the higher layers and TDNN has the much more powerful ability to learn longer temporal relationships than the conventional feed forward neural network. The network formed by all the dotted lines and solid lines in the Fig. 1 is the traditional fully connected TDNN, and the solid line separately connected is the sub-sampling TDNN. The TDNN with sub-sampling only calculates units at certain time intervals in each hidden layer (solid lines). It can reduce the complexity of the model and obtain rich context information.

In order to further improve the performance, this paper adopts a chain training method to train the TDNN acoustic model. The chain model applies the discriminative training criterion based on Maximum Mutual Information (MMI) at the sequence level instead of the traditional frame-level cross-entropy (Cross-Entropy, CE) training criterion. The objective function of the CE criterion assumes that frames are independent of each other when updating parameters. The MMI training criterion calculates and updates all the parameters of the eigenvectors of all input speech frames to optimize the model parameters. Therefore, the MMI criterion can obtain better timing information than CE. The MMI criterion is shown in Eq. 1. Where o^m is the observation sequence, w^m is the corresponding word sequence, and $S = \{(o^m, w^m)\}$ is the input training set. s^m is a sequence of states corresponding to the observed sequence. θ is the model parameter and k is the acoustic scale factor.

$$J_{MMI}(\theta; S) = \sum_{m=1}^{M} log P(w^m|o^m, \theta) = \sum_{m=1}^{M} log \frac{P(o^m|s^m, \theta)^k P(w^m)}{\sum_w P(o^m|s^m; \theta)^k P(w)} \tag{1}$$

Essentially, the MMI criterion is to calculate the ratio of the probability value of the word sequence corresponding to the correct recognition result to the sum all word sequences in Lattice. In this paper, the MMI criterion is to maximize the mutual information between the Khalkha dialect observation sequence and the Cyrillic Mongolian word sequence.

2.2 Weight Transfer Model

This paper first constructs the khalkha dialect Mongolian ASR system based on weight transfer. The posterior probability distribution knowledge in Chahar dialect and English acoustic model is transferred to the Khalkha dialect Mongolian acoustic model separately. In fact, different knowledge is represented by the weights (parameters) of hidden layer. Therefore, the model based on weight transfer is implemented by transferring hidden layers. There is a principle for the selection of transferable layers: the hidden layer near the input in the neural network usually learns general features, which have low correlation with the training set. Meanwhile, the hidden layer near the output learns more specialized features, which are not suitable for transferring.

The main steps of the weight transfer method are as follows: Train an acoustic model using the source domain data with a larger data set, and retain the n hidden layers. Then add m randomly initialized hidden layers and a soft-max layer above the n layers. Finally, the transferred model is retrained using the target domain data with the small data set. The model structure based on weight transfer is shown in Fig. 2. The left side of Fig. 2 shows the pre-training model, and the right side is the model based on weight transfer, which includes both transferred layers and randomly initialized hidden layers.

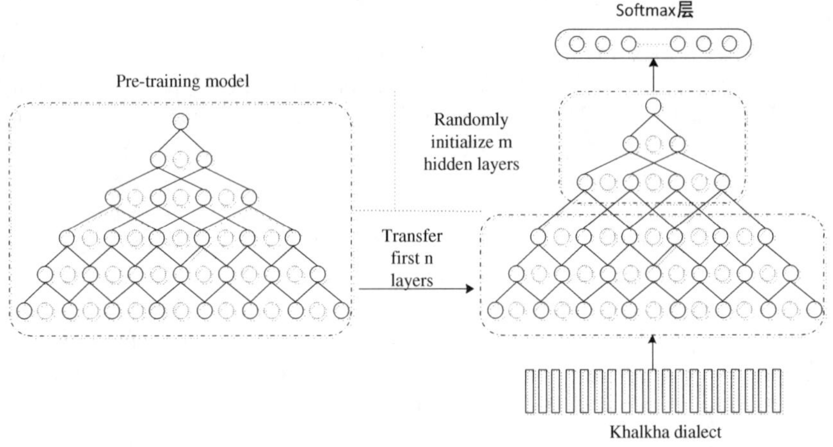

Fig. 2. The model structure based on weight transfer

The model has two different training strategies, we called them single-stage training and two-stage training strategy. The two-stage strategy is to train the model with different learning rate in two full training sessions. We freeze the transferred layers and only train new added layers in the first step, then fine-tune the whole network in the second step. In addition, the single-stage strategy is to train the transferred layers and new added layers with different learning rate in one full training session. Universally, the new added layers need a lager learning rate than the transferred layers.

3 Experiments Setup

3.1 Dataset

We carry out experiments on Khalkha dialect Mongolian corpus to verify the performance of the proposed method. The Khalkha dialect Mongolian corpus contains of about 10 h of speech data, a total of 6,987 Khalkha dialect audio, with a sampling frequency of 16 kHz, including 10 speakers from different parts of Mongolia. In our experiments, the data set is divided into two parts, the training set and the test set, and is not duplicated. The training set is about 80% of the whole corpus and the test set is about 20% of the whole corpus.

In decoding, we collected about 72 million Mongolian texts from the Cyrillic Mongolian web sites to training a standard unpruned 3-gram language model. The pronunciation dictionary selects the high-frequency vocabulary in the Cyrillic text library, which contains a total of 29,625 words.

For training the Chahar dialect Mongolian models, we used the Chahar dialect Mongolian corpus. The data set consists of about 78 h and 300 h of spoken speech, respectively. We use the original 16 kHz sampling rate.

The English models were trained on two corpora taken from the LibriSpeech. This dataset consists of about 1000 h of read speech, sampled at 16 kHz, from the domain of audio books. In our experiments, we used 100 h of Clean training set and 460 h of mixed data sets for training respectively.

3.2 Setup

Our system is trained with Kaldi speech recognition toolkit [12]. The GMM is trained to estimate state likelihoods which are then used in a standard hybrid HMM/TDNN setup. Input features for the GMMs are 13-dimensional MFCCs with a context of 7 frames (i.e., ± 3). Per-speaker CMVN is applied and speaker adaptation is done using fMLLR. The features are also globally normalized prior to training the TDNN.

In the experiment, the word error rate was used as the evaluation criterion. The mathematical formula is as Eq. 2,

$$WER = \frac{S + D + I}{T} \times 100\% \tag{2}$$

where S represents the number of substitution, D represents the number of deletion, I represents the number of insertion, and T is the total number of words in the sentence. The smaller the WER result, the better the recognition performance.

4 Experiments and Analysis

Table 1 shows the results of pre-training models for Chahar dialect Mongolian and English. In these experiments, all of the models are constructed a TDNN model with 6 hidden layers and an objective criterion with lattice-free maximum mutual information (LF-MMI). The global learning rate is the same in all stages and the learning rate for each layer is the global learning rate scaled by its learning rate factor.

Table 1. The pre-training model.

No.	Model	Train set	WER(%)
1	Pre_CM	CM78	14.57
2	Pre_CM_big	CM300	9.24
3	Pre_EN	LibriSpeech100	8.46
4	Pre_EN_big	LibriSpeech400	7.58

In the Table 1, "Pre_CM" stands for the Chahar dialect Mongolian pre-training model with 78 h of Chahar dialect training set. We also use the 300-h Chahar dialect Mongolian corpus training big model, and denoted as "Pre_CM_big". For the English models, we use the 100-h and 460-h LibriSpeech corpus for training, and verify them on "test_clean" data set. We refer to these models as "Pre_EN" and "Pre_EN_big", respectively. Further, the language model is 3-gram.

4.1 Experiment Results of Baseline System

In this section, we experiment with the baseline model of the Khalkha dialect Mongolian. And investigate the influence of forward information and backward information on the performance of the model in the frame splicing structure of the hidden layer. The specific splicing structure is shown in Table 2.

Table 2. The configuration information of the TDNN hidden layer.

No.	TDNN_1	TDNN_2	TDNN_3	TDNN_4	TDNN_5
1	[−2,2]	[−2,2]	[−2,2]	[−2,2]	[−2,2]
2	{−1,0,1}	{−1,0,1}	{−1,0,1}	{−1,0,1}	{−1,0,1}
3	{−1,0,1}	{−1,0,1}	{−1,0,1}	{−3,0,3}	{−1,0,1}
4	{−1,0,3}	{−3,0,1}	{−3,0,−3}	{−1,0,1}	{−3,0,3}
5	{−6,−3,0}	{−6,−3,0}	{−6,−3,0}	{−6,−3,0}	{−3,0,3}
6	{0}	{0}	{0}	{0}	{−6,−3,0}

The experimental results of the five different splicing structures are shown in Table 3. Compared with the "TDNN_1", the "TDNN_5" reduced the WER by 6.9%. The results show that both the forward information and the backward information in the hidden layers can improve the performance of the model, and the forward information is more important than the backward information.

Table 3. The results of Chain model

No.	Model	Training	WER(%)
1	TDNN_1	LF-MMI	27.18
2	TDNN_2	LF-MMI	26.61
3	TDNN_3	LF-MMI	25.79
4	TDNN_4	LF-MMI	26.13
5	TDNN_5	LF-MMI	25.28

4.2 Experiment Results of Weight Transfer

Experiments of Single-Stage and Two-Stage. In the section, we applied "Pre_CM" and "Pre_EN" as the pre-training models for the weight transfer. The splicing frames information of the model is same as "TDNN_5". We transferred the first four hidden layers of the pre-training model, added two layers of randomly initialized hidden layers and a soft-max layer at the top of the network. The newly added hidden layer receives the same context information as the original hidden layer, that is, the frame splicing structure is $\{-3, 0, 3\}$ and $\{-6, -3, 0\}$. The experimental results of two different training strategies are shown in Table 4.

Table 4. The results of single-stage and two-stage

No.	Source domain	Model	Training strategy		WER(%)
1	–	TDNN_5	–		25.28
2	CM_78h	Pre_CM-WT	Two-stage	S_1	20.34
				S_2	19.52
3		Pre_CM-WT	Single-stage		19.15
4	EN_100h	Pre_EN-WT	Two-stage	S_1	22.95
				S_2	21.27
5		Pre_EN-WT	Single-stage		21.19

In the two-stage training, the transferred layers were fixed and the newly added layers were trained with the global learning rate In the first step. In the second step, the network was fine-tuned at a lower learning rate. The learning factor for the "Pre_EN-WT" model is 0.25, and the "Pre_CM-WT" model is 0.1. In the single-stage training, the learning factor of the transferred layers were 0.1 (Chahar dialect) and 0.25 (English). Meanwhile, the added layers used the global learning rate.

We can find from Table 4, the model 3 has a relative error rate reduction of 24% compared to the randomly initialized Model 1. The model 5 has a 16% reduction compared to Model 1. The experimental results show that the weight transfer method can improve the performance of the Khalkha dialect Mongolian acoustic model. At the same time, Chahar dialect as the source domain can achieve better results. This result indicates that there are still many language-related features in the first four hidden layers. In addition, we found that the single-stage training strategy is better than the two-stage training strategy. This is evidence that the features of each layer in the neural network are not isolated, and there is some connection between the features of adjacent layers, and such co-adapted features cannot be learned by the upper layers alone.

Experiments of Transfer Different Layers. In the chain TDNN acoustic model, the closer to the output layer, the more specialized the features are learned. Therefore, there should be one or several boundary layers from generalization to specialization. This section of the experiment verified the effect of different transferred layers on the performance of the Khalkha dialect Mongolian acoustic model. The experimental results are shown in Fig. 3.

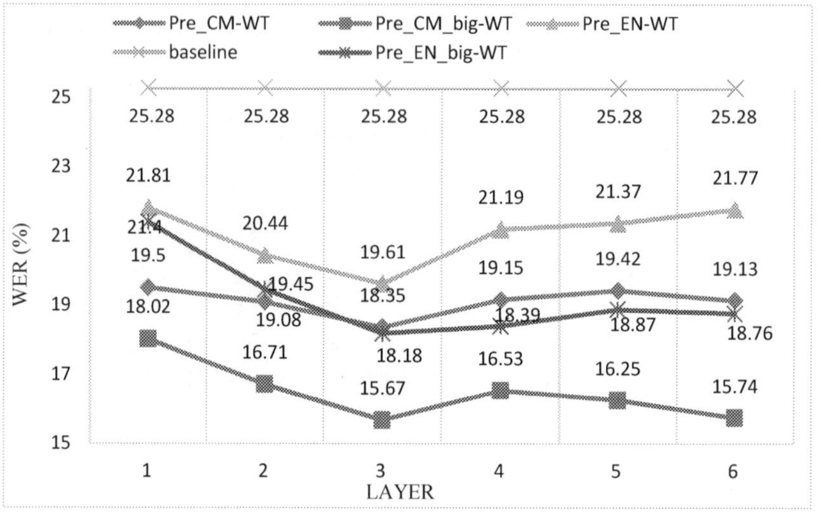

Fig. 3. The results of different transferring layers

In this section, we did four sets of weight transfer experiments. The weight transfer models are "Pre_CM-WT"(we called it A), "Pre_CM_big-WT"(B), "Pre_EN-WT"(C) and "Pre_EN_big-WT"(D). The experimental results show that the features of the first three layers of the model are general and have low correlation with the source domain training set. The WER of A, B, C, D is 18.18%, 15.67%, 19.61% and 18.35%, drops by 27%, 38%, 22% and 28% compared to baseline system. Further, the WER increased from the fourth layer, because these features tend to be specialized and have a high correlation with the training set. When transferring the first five layers, only one randomly initialized layer needs to be trained, and the optimal solution can be easier found by the method of random gradient descent. When transferring the whole hidden layers, the WER is reduced. There are two reasons for this phenomenon. First, transferring whole hidden layers can better represent the co-adapted features of the adjacent layers. Second, fine-tuning can improve the performance of the acoustic model, proved in previous experiments.

Experiments of Pre-training Model. In this section, we verified the effects of the number of parameters and epochs in the pre-training model. The experiment results are shown in Table 5.

In the experiment, this paper reduces the number of pre-training model parameters and epochs. The WER of the model 5/6 increases by 0.11 and 1.27, respectively, in the source domain. While in the target domain, the WER is basically the same as the fully trained model 1. We found that small epochs can achieve the same performance in the target domain (Khalkha dialect). This shows that in the initial stage of training, neural networks usually learn more language-independent features, and these features have better transfer effects. We also found the number of parameters will affect the performance of the model no matter in source domain and target domain.

Table 5. The results of different pre-training model.

No.	Source domain (CM78)			Target domain	
	Model	Epoch	WER(%)	Model	WER(%)
1	Pre_CM	4	14.57	Pre_CM_WT	18.35
2	Pre_CM (80%)	4	14.81	Pre_CM (30%)_WT	18.76
3	Pre_CM (50%)	4	15.17	Pre_CM (50%)_WT	19.41
4	Pre_CM (30%)	4	15.36	Pre_CM (80%)_WT	19.73
5	Pre_CM	2	14.68	Pre_CM_WT	18.36
6	Pre_CM	1	15.84	Pre_CM_WT	18.41

5 Conclusion

In this paper, we have investigated weight transfer learning approaches in Khalkha dialect Mongolian ASR using TDNN neural network based on Lattice-free MMI in different acoustic conditions, the experimental results show that the weight transfer learning approaches can obtain better performance in low-resource ASR systems. Compared among different training strategies, single-stage training is better than two-stage. In the single-stage training, the WER is reduced by 24% and 16% with Chahar dialect and English as the source domain, respectively. Further, transferring the top three layers can obtain the greatest performance improvement. With 300 h Chahar dialect as source domain, we can achieve 38% relative WER reduction over the baseline system. We also found that reducing the number of epochs in the pre-training model has little effect on the performance of the model based on weight transfer. Therefore, pre-training models that are not fully trained can also be transferred. Finally, by using the single-stage training Strategy, the weight transfer model transferred 3 layers can get the best performance. The WER of the Khalkha dialect Mongolian speech recognition system is 15.67%, which is relatively reduced by 38% comparing to the baseline system.

Acknowledgment. This work was supported by the National Natural Science Foundation of China (Nos. 61563040, 61773224); Natural Science Foundation of Inner Mongolia (Nos. 2018MS06006, 2016ZD06).

References

1. Gao, G.L., Zhang, S.: A Mongolian speech recognition system based on HMM. In: Proceedings of the International Conference on Intelligent Computing, pp. 667–676 (2006)
2. Bao, F., Gao, G.: Improving of acoustic model for the Mongolian speech recognition system. In: Chinese Conference on 2nd Pattern Recognition, CCPR 2009, pp. 1–5 (2009)
3. Bao, F., Gao, G., Wang, H.: Mongolian speech keyword spotting method based on stem. J. Chin. Inf. Process. **30**(1), 124–128 (2016)
4. Bao, F., Gao, G., Yan, X., et al.: Segmentation-based Mongolian LVCSR approach. In: Proceedings of the 38th ICASSP, pp. 1–5 (2013)
5. Zhang, H., Bao, F., Gao, G.L.: Mongolian speech recognition based on deep neural networks. In: Proceedings of the 15th Chinese Computational Linguistics and Natural Language Processing Based on Naturally Annotated Big Data, pp. 180–188 (2015)
6. Zhang, H., Bao, F., Gao, G.L., et al.: Comparison on neural network based acoustic model in Mongolian speech recognition. In: Proceedings of the 2016 International Conference on 20th Asian Language Processing (IALP), pp. 1–5 (2016)
7. Wang, Y., Bao, F., Zhang, H., et al.: Research on Mongolian speech recognition based on FSMN. In: Natural Language Processing and Chinese Computing, pp. 243–254 (2017)
8. Wang, Y., Bao, F.L., Gao, G.L.: Research on Mongolian speech recognition based on TDNN-LSTM. In: Natural Language Processing and Chinese Computing, pp. 221–226 (2018)
9. Pan, S., Yang, Q.: A survey on transfer learning. IEEE Trans. Knowl. Data Eng. **22**(10), 1345–1359 (2010)
10. Bengio, Y., et al.: Deep learning of representations for unsupervised and transfer learning. In: ICML Unsupervised and Transfer Learning, pp. 17–36 (2012)
11. Swietojanski, P., Ghoshal, A., Renals, S.: Unsupervised cross-lingual knowledge transfer in DNN-based LVCSR. In: 2012 IEEE Spoken Language Technology Workshop (SLT). IEEE (2013)
12. Povey, D., Ghoshal, A., Boulianne, G., et al.: The Kaldi speech recognition toolkit. In: Workshop on Automatic Speech Recognition and Understanding (No. EPFL-CONF-192584). IEEE Signal Processing Society (2011)

GANCoder: An Automatic Natural Language-to-Programming Language Translation Approach Based on GAN

Yabing Zhu, Yanfeng Zhang(✉), Huili Yang, and Fangjing Wang

Northeastern University, Shenyang, China
zhangyf@mail.neu.edu.cn

Abstract. We propose GANCoder, an automatic programming approach based on Generative Adversarial Networks (GAN), which can generate the same functional and logical programming language codes conditioned on the given natural language utterances. The adversarial training between generator and discriminator helps generator learn distribution of dataset and improve code generation quality. Our experimental results show that GANCoder can achieve comparable accuracy with the state-of-the-art methods and is more stable when programming languages.

Keywords: GAN · Semantic parsing · Automatic programming · NLP

1 Introduction

With the development of deep learning and natural language processing (NLP), translation tasks and techniques have been significantly enhanced. The problem of cross-language communication has been well solved. In this digital age, we are no longer a passive receiver of information but also a producer and analyst of data. We need to have data management, query, and analysis skills. Especially, programming is an essential skill in the era of AI. However, it requires strong professional knowledge and practical experience to learn programming languages and write codes to process data efficiently. Although programming languages, such as SQL and Python, are relatively simple, due to education and professional limitations, it is still difficult for many people to learn. How to lower the access threshold of learning programming languages and make coding easier is worth studying.

In this paper, we explore how to automatically generate programming codes from natural language utterances. The inexperienced users only need to describe what they want to implement in natural language, then the programming codes with the same functionality can be generated via a generator [1], so that can simply complete complex tasks, such as database management, programming, and data processing.

Automatic programming is a difficult task in the field of artificial intelligence. It is also a significant symbol of strong artificial intelligence. Many researchers

J. Tang et al. (Eds.): NLPCC 2019, LNAI 11839, pp. 529–539, 2019.
https://doi.org/10.1007/978-3-030-32236-6_48

have been studying how to convert natural language utterances into program code for a long time. Before deep learning is applied, pattern matching was the most popular method. But due to the need for a large number of artificial design templates and the diversity and fuzziness of natural language expressions, matching-based methods are not flexible and hard to meet the needs. With the development of machine translation, some researchers try to use statistical machine learning to solve the problem of automatic programming, but due to the difference between the two language models, the results are not satisfactory.

In recent years, GANs have been proposed to deal with the problem of data generation. The game training between GAN's discriminator and generator make the generator learn data distribution better. In this paper, we propose an automatic program generator GANCoder, a GAN-based encoder-decoder framework which realizes the translation between natural language and programming language. In the training phase, we adopt GAN to improve the accuracy of automatic programming generator [2]. The main contributions of this model are summarized as follows. (1) Introducing GAN into automatic programming tasks, the antagonistic game between GAN's Generator and Discriminator can make Generator learn better distribution characteristics of data; (2) Using Encoder-Decoder framework to achieve the end-to-end conversion between two languages; (3) Using grammatical information of programming language when generating program codes, which provides prior knowledge and template for decoding, and also solves the problem of inconsistency between natural language model and programming language model. Our results show that GANCoder can achieve comparable accuracy with the state-of-the-art methods and is more stable when working on different programming languages.

2 Related Work

2.1 Semantic Parsing and Code Generation

Semantic parsing is the task of converting a natural language utterance to a logical form: a machine-understandable representation of its meaning, such as first-order logical representation, lambda calculus, semantic graph, and etc. Semantic parsing can thus be understood as extracting the precise meaning of an utterance [3]. Applications of semantic parsing include machine translation, question answering and code generation. We focus on code generation in this paper.

The early semantic analysis systems for code generation are rule-based and limited to specific areas, such as the SAVVY system [4]. It relies on pattern matching to extract words and sentences from natural language utterances according to pre-defined semantic rules. The LUNAR system [22] works based on grammatical features, which converts the natural language into a grammar tree with a self-defined parser, and then transforms the grammar tree into an SQL expression. Feature extraction by handcraft not only relies on a large amount of manual work but also impacts the performance of such semantic analysis systems which is relatively fragile. Because the pre-specified rules and semantic templates cannot match the characteristics of natural language expression with ambiguity and expression diversity, the early system functionalities are relatively simple. Only simple semantic analysis tasks are supported. Later, researchers have proposed WASP [17] and KRISP [18], combined with the grammar information of the logical forms, using statistical machine learning and SVM (Support Vector Machine) to convert natural utterances' grammar tree to the grammar tree of the logical forms. Chris Quirk et al. propose a translation approach from natural language utterances to the If-this-then-that program using the KRISP algorithm [5].

Encoder-Decoder frameworks based on RNNs (Recurrent Neural Networks) have been introduced into the code generation tasks. These frameworks have shown state-of-the-art performance in some fields, such as machine translation, syntax parsing, and image caption generation. The use of neural networks can reduce the need for custom lexical, templates, and manual features, and also do not need to produce intermediate representations. Li Dong et al. use the Encoder-Decoder model to study the code generation task and propose a general neural network semantic parser [3]. Xi Victoria Lin et al. propose an encoder-decoder-based model that converts natural language utterances into Linux shell scripts [6]. As shown in Fig. 1, as an end-to-end learning framework, encoder encodes natural language utterances into intermediate semantic vectors, and decoder decodes intermediate vectors into logical forms. Generally speaking, encoder and decoder can be any neural networks, but LSTM and RNN are mostly used.

Although programming languages are sequential strings in form, they have a hierarchical structure. A number of works utilize the hierarchical structure property of programs to generate codes. For example, the selective clause and the where clause in SQL belong to different logical levels. Based on this observation, researchers propose tree-based LSTM and tree-based CNN [7,8]. Besides, EgoCoder, a hierarchical neural network based on Python program's AST (Abstract Syntax Tree), achieves code auto-completion and code synthesis [9]. Yin and Neubig propose an Encoder-Decoder model that uses syntax information as the prior knowledge to help decoder reduce search space [10].

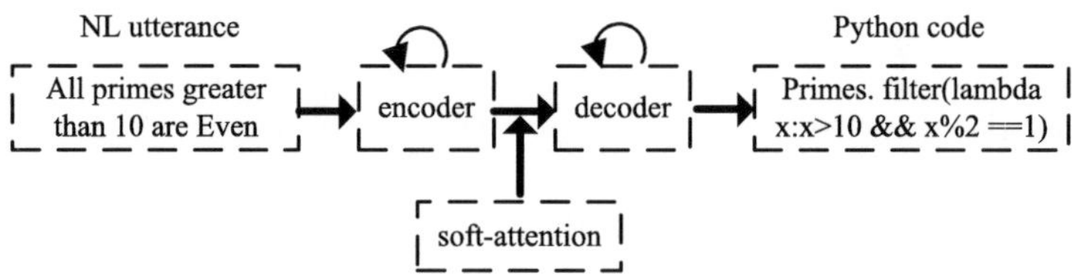

Fig. 1. Encoder-Decoder model for code generation

2.2 Generative Adversarial Network (GAN)

GAN [2], proposed by Ian Goodfellow in 2014, is a method of unsupervised learning. GAN consists of a generator network and a discriminator network.

The generator produces what we want, and the discriminator judges whether the output of the generator is fake or subject to the real distribution. Generator and discriminator improve themselves and adjust parameters via their adversarial training. Since GAN was proposed, it has attracted a lot of attention, and more GANs have been used in image generation, speech synthesis, etc. and achieved much success. CDGAN [19], WGAN [20], VAEGAN [21] are typical models of GANs. Since the object processed in NLP is discrete characters, the gradient of discriminator cannot be passed to the generator, so the application of GAN in NLP is not very successful. Lantao Yu et al. proposed SeqGAN [12] to optimize the GAN network by using the strategy gradient in reinforcement learning to improve the quality of text generation. This is also a successful attempt of GAN in NLP tasks.

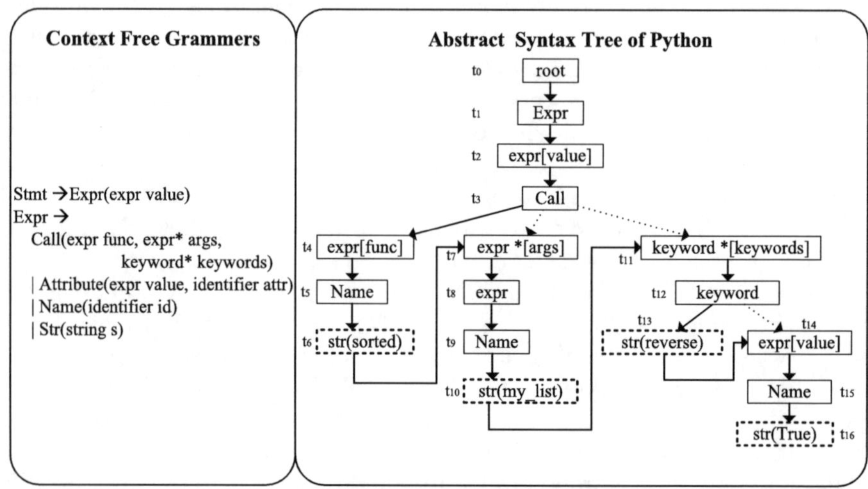

Fig. 2. Python context free grammar (left) and abstract syntax tree structure (right)

3 Model

3.1 GAN-Based Semantic Parsing

We aim to design an automatic programming model which can generate a program code sequence $Y = \{y_1, y_2, \cdots, y_m\}$ based on a natural language utterance $X = \{x_1, x_2, \cdots, x_n\}$. We introduce GAN into the Encoder-Decoder framework, and propose a new model GANCoder, as shown in Fig. 3. In GANCoder, the generator G_θ uses an encoder-decoder framework, which converts the natural language utterances into program codes, where θ represents parameters. The encoder encodes the natural language utterances as intermediate semantic vectors, and the decoder decodes the semantic vectors into ASTs with the guidance of the programming language grammar information. At last, we parse the

ASTs into program codes. The discriminator is responsible for judging whether the ASTs generated by the generator are consistent with the natural language utterance semantics. We use GAN to improve the generative model G_θ, the optimization equation of the GAN network is as follows [13]:

$$min_{G_\theta} max_{D_\emptyset} \mathcal{L}(\theta, \emptyset) = \mathbf{E}_{X \sim p_x} \log D_\emptyset(X) + \mathbf{E}_{Y \sim G_\theta} \log(1 - D_\emptyset(Y)) \quad (1)$$

$$G_\theta = p(Y|X) = \prod_{t=1}^{|Y|} p(y_t | Y_{<t}, X, Grammar_{CFG}) \quad (2)$$

where $Y_{<t} = y_1, y_2, \cdots, y_{t-1}$ represents the sequence of the first $t-1$ characters of the program fragment, and $Grammar_{CFG}$ represents the CFG (Context-Free Grammars) of the programming language, which provides guidance in the code generation process. $X \sim p_x$ indicates that the data sample X is subject to the distribution of real data, and $Y \sim G_\theta$ means that the generator generates the data sample Y. Generator and discriminator play two-player minimax game. Discriminator can differentiates between the tow distributions. In practice, Eq. 1 may not provide sufficient gradient for generator when generating discrete data in NLP. Inspired by the optimization strategy of strategy gradient proposed by SeqGAN, combined with the characteristics of automatic programming tasks, we optimize GANCoder as follows:

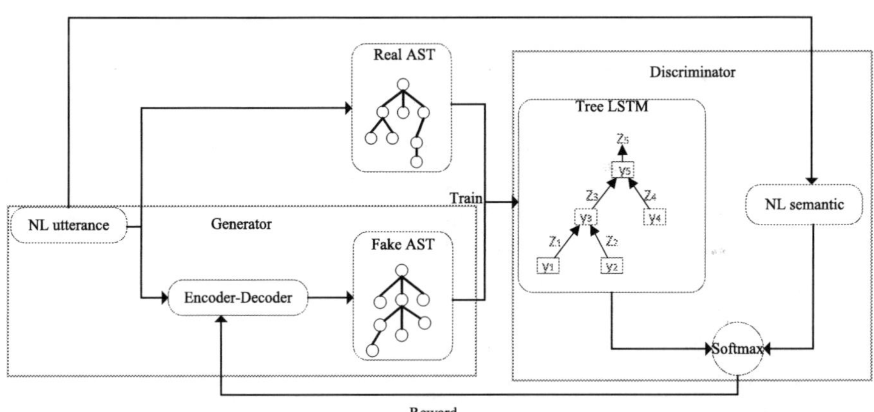

Fig. 3. GAN-based automatic program generator

$$\mathcal{J}(\theta) = \mathbf{E}_{Y \sim G_\theta} \log(G_\theta(y_1|s_0) \prod_{t=2}^{T} G_\theta(y_t|Y_{1:t-1}))\mathcal{R}(Y_{1:t}) \quad (3)$$

$$\mathcal{R}(Y_{1:t}) = D_\emptyset(Y_{1:T}) \quad (4)$$

where $\mathcal{R}(Y_{1:t})$ represents the generator reward function, which quantifies the quality of the generated program fragments. In the other words, it is the probability of semantic between the natural language utterances and the generated program fragments.

3.2 CFG-Based GAN Generator

The main task of the GAN generator is to encode the semantics of natural language utterances and then to decode the semantics into AST based on CFG of the programming language. The conversion from one language to another uses the Encoder-Decoder model to reduce the interaction between different languages. The two ends are independently responsible for the processing of their data, simplifying the complexity of the problem. This end-to-end learning framework is more general, and both ends can select their own deep learning models according to the characteristics of the data. Figure 4 shows the framework diagram of the Generator.

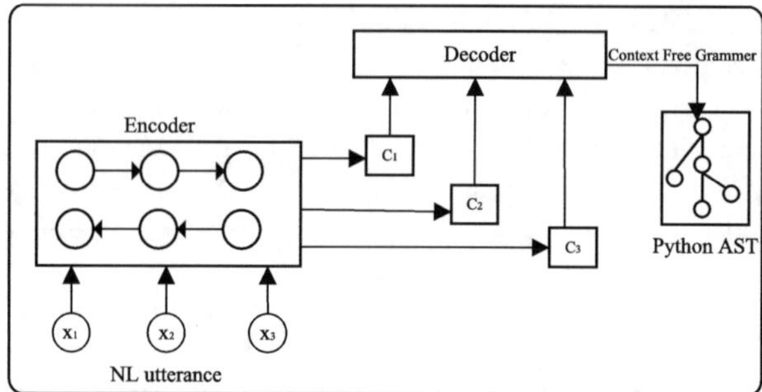

Fig. 4. Encoder-Decoder-based generator in GANCoder

The encoder is responsible for encoding the semantics of the natural language utterances, as shown in Fig. 4. We use a bidirectional LSTM to encode the text sequence of natural language description. $\overleftarrow{h_t}$, and $\overrightarrow{h_t}$ respectively represent the hidden state of the t-th unit of the natural language description sequence from left to right and from right to left, let $h_t = [\overleftarrow{h_t} : \overrightarrow{h_t}]$ be the intermediate hidden vector of the character. The last character's intermediate vector is the semantic presentation of the whole natural utterance.

The decoder decodes the intermediate semantic vector generated by Encoder. Inspired by the model proposed in [10], we first decode the intermediate semantic vector into an abstract syntax tree based on the CFG of the programming language. According to the characteristics of CFG and AST, we define two kinds of actions, corresponding to the generation of non-leaf nodes and leaf nodes in the abstract syntax tree in Fig. 2 (right). Logically, we use LSTM to recursively build AST top-down and left-right, as shown in Fig. 2 (right). We convert the task into predicting the grammatic action sequence. Based on the CFG, not only can the template be generated for the decoding process, but also the prediction range can be constrained, so that the search space can be reduced to improve the calculation efficiency.

Unlike encoder, decoder uses a normal LSTM to maintain state variables to form an AST,

$$s_t = f_{LSTM}([a_{t-1} : c_t : p_t], s_{t-1}) \tag{5}$$

$$p_{action} = Softmax(s_t) \tag{6}$$

where "[:]" represents the concatenation operation between multiple vectors, s_t represents the state vector at time t in the decoder. The probability of different grammatical actions can be calculated using the $Softmax(s_t)$ function. a_{t-1} represents the vector of the previous action, and c_t represents the state based on the input $h_X = \{h_{x_1}, h_{x_2}, \cdots, h_{x_{|X|}}\}$. We use the soft-attention mechanism to calculate the attention, as shown in Fig. 4. Then the decoder predicts the probability of each action by the state at time t. When a character is generated during a predicted action, we use PointNet to copy the character from the natural language description to AST [11]. In the process of constructing an AST, the Beam Search algorithm is used to avoid over-fitting. As shown in Fig. 2 (right), t_i represents the step of decoding. The order in which nodes are generated is also clearly marked in Fig. 2 (right).

3.3 Tree-Based Semantic GAN Discriminator

The Generator can generate an AST of the program fragments, and the discriminator quantifies the similarity of the semantic relationship between the generated ASTs and the natural language utterances. How to quantify the semantic similarity between two different languages is very difficult. In the discriminator, the encoding of natural language utterances still uses the same encoder method in the generator, which uses a bidirectional LSTM to encode the entire sequence into intermediate semantic vectors. When encoding the semantics of a program, there are two different ways. The first is to treat the program code sequence as a string, and still use the same method as the generator processint it in a bidirectional LSTM. The processing is simple, but the logic and syntax information of the program cannot be captured. The second method is to use the structure of the AST generated by the generator to encode the semantics of the program. However, the semantics of the encoding program is somewhat different from the generation of the AST. In the generator, the structure of the AST is generated recursively top-down and left-right, but in the discriminator, the entire AST is encoded bottom-up from leaf node to root nodes of AST, and the final vector is used as the semantic vector of the program fragment. In this way, the syntax and logic of the program fragment can be learned in a bottom-up manner [13,14].

Let h_r be the final encoding vector for the entire abstract syntax tree. Then the h_r and the semantic vector h_{NL} of the natural language description are classified into two categories:

$$out = h_r W^{dis} h_{NL} + b^{dis} \tag{7}$$

$$P_{sim} = softmax(out) = \frac{e^{sim}}{\sum_{e \in out} e^i} \tag{8}$$

where $P_{sim} \in [0, 1]$ represents the probability that the AST is consistent with the semantics of the natural language description. Since the AST is generated based on the CFG of the programming language, the AST is grammatically standardized. The semantics of the generated program fragments need to be consistent with the natural language semantics.

4 Experiments

The experiment and evaluation are carried out in a single machine environment. The specific hardware configuration is: processor Intel-i7-8700, memory 32 GB, NVIDIA GTX1080 graphics card, memory 8 GB. The software environment is: Ubuntu16.04, Python2.7, pytorch3, cuda9. Natural language, Python program characters, and context-free grammar characters embedding are initialized by the xavier_uniform method [23]. The optimization function of the model is Adam.

4.1 Datasets

1. Django is a web framework for Python, where each line of code is manually labeled with the corresponding natural language description text. In this paper, there are 16,000 training data sets and 1805 verification data sets.
2. Atis is the flight booking system dataset, where the natural language utterances are the user booking inquiries, and the codes are expressed in the form of λ calculus. There are 4434 training data sets and 140 test data sets.
3. Jobs is a job query dataset, where the user queries are natural language utterance, and the program codes are expressed in the form of Prolog. There are 500 training data sets and 140 test data sets.

4.2 Experimental Results and Analysis

If the sequence of the generated program is the same as the program sequence of the training data, it means that the generated data is correct, and the correctness of the test set indicates the generation effect of the model. As can be seen from Table 1, regarding the Django and Jobs datasets, the pre-trained GANCoder model improves 2.4% and 0.72% over the normal generator, respectively, and improves 2.6% and 2.93% over that without pre-training. This demonstrates that when training GANCoder, the pre-training has dramatically improved the model. On the ATIS training set, the normal generator is the best. In this model, GAN crashes, which is related to the training data and the grammar rule details of different logical forms. The natural language description sequence of the Jobs data set is relatively simple, so the accuracy of the model is high. The Python language of the Django dataset has relatively good syntax information, but the logic of the program is also more difficult. The game training of GAN also has a good effect. The ATIS dataset is logically difficult, but the grammar information is simple, which cannot provide more details when generating ASTs.

Table 2 compares the state-of-the-art code generation models with our GANCoder model presented in this paper. Compared to the traditional Encoder-Decoder models, such as SEQ2SEQ and SEQ2TREE, GANCoder increases the accuracy by 24.6% and 30.3% on the Django dataset. These two models work better on the Jobs dataset, but the results on the other two datasets are not satisfactory. The ASN model achieves the best performance on the ATIS dataset but cannot obtain results on the other two datasets. The LPN+COPY model and the SNM+COPY model show good results on the Django dataset, but they also do not have results on the other two datasets. Although the GANCoder proposed in this paper is not always the best compared with the other models, GANCoder can achieve relatively stable and satisfactory results on various datasets and is a promising code generation method worth improving.

Table 1. Model accuracy based of three training methods

Dataset	Generator_normal	GAN_without_pretraining	GAN_with_pretraining
Django	67.3	67.1	69.7
Jobs	85.71	83.5	86.43
ATIS	82.6	81.5	79.23

Table 2. Accuracy comparison of different models

Models	ATIS	Django	Jobs
SEQ2SEQ [3]	84.2	45.1	87.1
SEQ2TREE [3]	84.6	39.4	90.0
ASN [15]	85.3	–	–
LPN+COPY [16]	–	62.3	–
SNM+COPY [10]	–	72.1	–
GANCoder (Our model)	81.5	69.7	86.43

5 Conclusion

This paper proposes a semantic programming-based automatic programming method GANCoder. Through the game confrontation training of GAN generator and discriminator, it can effectively learn the distribution characteristics of data and improve the quality of code generation. The experimental results show that the proposed GANCoder can achieve comparable accuracy with the state-of-the art code generation model, and the stability is better. The method proposed in this paper can only realize the conversion between single-line natural language description and single-line code. Future work will study how to convert long natural language description text and multi-line code.

Acknowledgements. This work was partially supported by National Key R&D Program of China (2018YFB1003404), National Natural Science Foundation of China (61672141), and Fundamental Research Funds for the Central Universities (N181605017).

References

1. Kamath, A., Das, R.: A survey on semantic parsing. CoRR abs/1812.00978 (2018)
2. Goodfellow, I., Pouget-Abadie, J., Mirza, M., et al.: Generative adversarial nets. In: Proceedings of the 28th Advances in Neural Information Processing Systems (NIPS 2014), pp. 2672–2680 (2014)
3. Dong, L., Lapata, M.: Language to logical form with neural attention. In: Proceedings of the 54th Annual Meeting of the Association for Computational Linguistics, Berlin, Germany, pp. 33–43 (2016)
4. Woods, W.A.: Progress in natural language understanding: an application to lunar geology. In: Proceedings of the 54th Annual Meeting of the Association for Computational Linguistics of the June 4–8, 1973: National Computer Conference and Exposition, pp. 441–450. ACM (1973)
5. Quirk, C., Mooney, R.J., Galley, M.: Language to code: learning semantic parsers for if-this-then-that recipes. In: ACL (1), pp. 878–888 (2015)
6. Lin, X.V., Wang, C., Zettlemoyer, L., et al.: NL2Bash: a corpus and semantic parser for natural language interface to the linux operating system. In: LREC 2018 (2018)
7. Tai, K.S., Socher, R., Manning, C.D.: Improved semantic representations from tree-structured long short-term memory networks. In: ACL (1), pp. 1556–1566 (2015)
8. Mou, L., Li, G., Zhang, L., et al.: Convolutional neural networks over tree structures for programming language processing. In: AAAI 2016, pp. 1287–1293 (2016)
9. Zhang, J., Cui, L., Gouza, F.B.: EgoCoder: intelligent program synthesis with hierarchical sequential neural network model. CoRR abs/1805.08747 (2018)
10. Yin, P., Neubig, G.: A syntactic neural model for general-purpose code generation. In: ACL (1), pp. 440–450 (2017)
11. Vinyals, O., Fortunato, M., Jaitly, N.: Pointer networks. In: NIPS 2015, pp. 2692–2700 (2015)
12. Yu, L., Zhang, W., Wang, J., et al.: SeqGAN: sequence generative adversarial nets with policy gradient. In: AAAI 2017, pp. 2852–2858 (2017)
13. Liu, X., Kong, X., Liu, L., et al.: TreeGAN: syntax-aware sequence generation with generative adversarial networks. In: ICDM 2018, pp. 1140–1145 (2018)
14. Chen, L., Zeng, G., Zhang, Q., Chen, X.: Tree-LSTM Guided attention pooling of DCNN for semantic sentence modeling. In: Long, K., Leung, V.C.M., Zhang, H., Feng, Z., Li, Y., Zhang, Z. (eds.) 5GWN 2017. LNICST, vol. 211, pp. 52–59. Springer, Cham (2018). https://doi.org/10.1007/978-3-319-72823-0_6
15. Rabinovich, M., Stern, M., Klein, D.: Abstract syntax networks for code generation and semantic parsing. In: Proceedings of the 55th Annual Meeting of the Association for Computational Linguistics, Vancouver, Canada, pp. 1139–1149 (2017)
16. Ling, W., Blunsom, P., Grefenstette, E., et al.: Latent predictor networks for code generation. In: Proceedings of the 54th Annual Meeting of the Association for Computational Linguistics, Berlin, Germany, pp. 599–609 (2016)
17. Wong, Y.W., Mooney, R.J.: Learning for semantic parsing with statistical machine translation. In: HLT-NAACL 2006 (2006)
18. Kate, R.J., Mooney, R.J.: Using string-kernels for learning semantic parsers. In: ACL 2006 (2006)

19. Radford, A., Metz, L., Chintala, S.: Unsupervised representation learning with deep convolutional generative adversarial networks. ICLR (Poster) (2016)
20. Arjovsky, M., Chintala, S., Bottou, L.: Wasserstein generative adversarial networks. In: ICML 2017, pp. 214–223 (2017)
21. Larsen, A.B.L., Snderby, S.K., Larochelle, H., Winther, O.: Autoencoding beyond pixels using a learned similarity metric. In: ICML 2016, pp. 1558–1566 (2016)
22. Woods, W.A.: Progress in natural language understanding: an application to lunar geology. In: Proceedings of the June 4–8, 1973, National Computer Conference and Exposition, pp. 441–450. ACM (1973)
23. Pennec, X., Ayache, N.: Uniform distribution, distance and expectation problems for geometric features processing. J. Math. Imaging Vis. **9**(1), 49–67 (1998)

Automatic Chinese Spelling Checking and Correction Based on Character-Based Pre-trained Contextual Representations

Haihua Xie[1(✉)], Aolin Li[1], Yabo Li[1], Jing Cheng[1], Zhiyou Chen[1], Xiaoqing Lyu[2], and Zhi Tang[2]

[1] State Key Laboratory of Digital Publishing Technology (Peking University Founder Group Co. LTD.), Beijing, China
{xiehh,lial,liyabo,cheng.jing,czy}@founder.com.cn
[2] Institute of Computer Science and Technology of Peking University, Peking University, Beijing, China
{lvxiaoqing,tangzhi}@pku.edu.cn

Abstract. Automatic Chinese spelling checking and correction (CSC) is currently a challenging task especially when the sentence is complex in semantics and expressions. Meanwhile, a CSC model normally requires a huge amount of training corpus which is usually unavailable. To capture the semantic information of sentences, this paper proposes an approach (named as DPL-Corr) based on character-based pre-trained contextual representations, which helps to significantly improve the performance of CSC. In DPL-Corr, the module of spelling checking is a sequence-labeling model enhanced by deep contextual semantics analysis, and the module of spelling correction is a masked language model integrated with multilayer filtering to obtain the final corrections. Based on experiments on SIGHAN 2015 dataset, DPL-Corr achieves a significantly better performance of CSC than conventional models.

Keywords: Chinese spelling checking and correction · Character-based model · Pre-trained contextual representations · Language model

1 Introduction

The target of Chinese spelling checking and correction (CSC) is to detect and correct the misuse of characters or words in Chinese sentences. Similar to spelling checking in English, there are two types of spelling errors in Chinese, real-word spelling errors and non-word spelling errors. Real-word spelling errors refer to the misuse of two real words (i.e., words in the lexicon), such as 'word' and 'world', '中止' and '终止'. Non-word spelling errors refer to misspelling a real word to be one not in the lexicon, e.g., 'word' is misspelled to be 'wrod', '偶尔' is misspelled to be '偶而'.

J. Tang et al. (Eds.): NLPCC 2019, LNAI 11839, pp. 540–549, 2019.
https://doi.org/10.1007/978-3-030-32236-6_49

CSC can be normally divided into two phases. The first phase is spelling errors detection, which is to detect and locate the spelling errors in a sentence. The second phase is spelling errors correction, which is to give correction suggestions for the detected errors. The candidate corrections are normally selected from a large-size confusion set of similar-pronunciation and similar-shape characters. The final correction result is determined based on the confidence of each candidate correction which is evaluated based on language modeling [1].

Due to the variability and complexity of Chinese semantic expressions, automatic CSC is currently a challenging task. Firstly, spelling errors often occur among single-character words, of which the use is flexible and complicated. Secondly, non-words in a sentence are not necessarily errors. For instance, '偶而' is usually a non-word misspelled for '偶尔', whereas it is correct in the sentence '人生应该随偶而安'. On the other hand, non-words produced by spelling errors usually cannot be correctly segmented by word segmentation, thus word-based matching cannot be applied to detect them. Furthermore, the target of CSC is to detect misused characters instead of words. All in all, word-based models that take words as the basic processing objects are not suitable for the CSC task.

In the current research community of CSC, correction of non-word spelling errors is the main problem, whereas the SOTA performance is about 70% [2]. The accuracy of real-word spelling correction is even lower, because such errors are usually occur among words with similar meanings. Deep semantic analysis of the context is required for correcting real-word spelling errors. Besides the low accuracy of correction, CSC also encounters a problem of high false positive rates. Words that appear rarely in the training data or the lexicon, such as technical terms and people names, are often mistakenly considered spelling errors.

This paper proposes a model for the CSC task, named as DPL-Corr, which aims to handle the problems mentioned above. Instead of building a set of spelling error instances that are infinite, DPL-Corr is mainly designed based on pre-trained contextual representations, so that the knowledge of grammars and concepts learned from a large-size corpus can be readily utilized to reduce the size of training data. Due to the inherent shortcomings of word-based CSC, DPL-Corr is designed based on character-based pre-trained contextual representations. A masked language model is designed to give candidate corrections of detected spelling errors, and select the final correction. According to our experiments conducted on the dataset of SIGHAN 2015, DPL-Corr achieves a F1 score of 0.6528 which beats the previous SOTA models on this task by a wide margin.

2 Background and Related Works

In the existing approaches for the CSC task, language modeling, word segmentation, confusion sets, and spelling errors set are widely used resources and techniques. The procedure of CSC normally consists of two steps, spelling errors detection and spelling errors correction. The target of spelling errors detection is to detect and locate the spelling errors in a sentence, and spelling errors correction is to give correction suggestions for those errors.

Spelling errors detection is the primary part in CSC. Heish et al. [3] recognizes spelling errors based on language model verification and the set of spelling errors generated from a confusion set, which is a dictionary containing frequently used characters as keys and corresponding characters of similar shapes or pronunciations as values. Zhao et al. [4] constructs a directed acyclic graph for each sentence and adopts the single-source shortest path algorithm to recognize common spelling errors. Wang et al. [5] constructs a mass of corpus with automatically generated spelling errors, and then implements a supervised sequence tagging model for spelling error detection.

For spelling error correction, Heish et al. [3] employs a confusion set to replace all suspect spelling errors and applies a n-gram model to choose the optimal correction. Such mechanism is efficient, whereas the false negative rate is high. Yang et al. [6] applies the ePMI matrix to count the co-occurrences of words and characters, and selects the candidate corrections based on the ePMI matrix. Li et al. [7] translates sentences with spelling errors into grammatically correct sentences, and selects the corrections from the translation results. Wang et al. [8] utilizes a seq2seq model to copy correct characters through a pointer network or generate characters from the confusion set to correct spelling errors.

Most of the above methods are low in efficiency or performance, because they normally require construction of a large-size confusion set and a spelling errors set, and training of a classifier based on a large-scale corpus. Besides, the errors in word segmentation can strongly affect the performance of the CSC task.

3 Workflow of DPL-Corr for CSC

As shown in Fig. 1, the input of DPL-Corr is a Chinese passage consists of several sentences, and the output is the passage after spelling checking and correction. Below is a brief introduction of the middle three steps in the workflow.

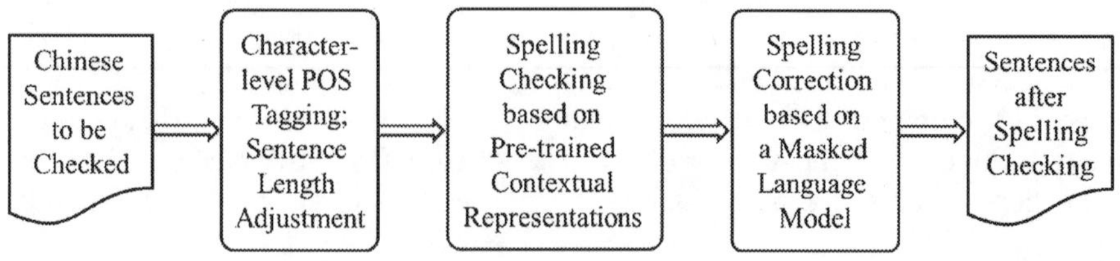

Fig. 1. The workflow of Chinese spelling checking and correction in DPL-Corr.

1. Character-level POS Tagging and Sentence Length Adjustment
   During training and inference, the following preprocessing operations are performed on the raw input Chinese sentences.

(a) Character-level POS Tagging
POS tags are helpful for detecting certain spelling errors. For instance, if the word after '的' in a sentence is a verb, '的' is very likely to be misused (because '的' is usually followed by a noun). To give a POS tag for each character, character-level POS tagging is performed as follows.
   i. Segmenting words for the input sentences and assigning a POS tag for each word.
   ii. Based on the POS tags of words, each character is given a character-level POS tag using the labeling schema 'BIES'. For instance, the POS tag of '乌鲁木齐' is 'ns', and the POS tag of each character is: 'ns-B' for '乌', 'ns-I' for '鲁', 'ns-I' for '木', 'ns-E' for '齐'.

(b) Sentence length adjustment
The length of sentences may affect the performance of CSC. Lengthy sentences increase difficulty of computing contextual embeddings, and they might contain multiple spelling errors which break the semantic integrity of the sentence. On the other hand, sentences being too short are disadvantageous in spelling checking because language models are less keen on capturing contextual meaning of short texts. Thus, DPL-Corr has a limit of 15 to 30 characters for the input sentences. Lengthy sentences will be truncated to the first 30 characters, and short sentences will be concatenated with sentences before or after the sentence.

2. Spelling checking based on pre-trained contextual representations
The module of spelling checking in DPL-Corr is designed based on character-based pre-trained contextual representations. Character-based models, such as BERT and XLNet, take characters as the basic processing objects. Because the pre-trained contextual representations are normally trained based on a large-scale corpus, the module of spelling checking in DPL-Corr requires only a small amount of training data to fine-tune the model.
3. Spelling correction based on a masked language model
The module of spelling correction is designed based on a masked language model to give the candidate corrections. In the input of the correction module, the detected errors are masked, and the model gives suggested characters to fill in each vacancy (i.e., a masked character) in the sentence. To reduce false positives, DPL-Corr adopts several means including confidence filtering, ranking filtering, and confusion set filtering to eliminate the inappropriate corrections and select the final optimal result.

4 Detailed Steps of DPL-Corr for CSC

4.1 Pre-trained Context Representations Based Spelling Checking

The module of spelling checking in DPL-Corr is illustrated in Fig. 2. The input to the module is a sequence of Chinese characters and their POS tags. Let x denote a character, c_pos(x) denote its character-level POS tag, PCRMod represent a pre-trained contextual representations model, and POSMat represent a POS encoding matrix. The output of encoding x by PCRMod is shown below.

$$r(x) = PCRMod(x) \tag{1}$$

r(x) is the contextual embedding of x which is dynamically computed given both past and future textual information of the entire input sequence, and its dimension is 1*768.

c_pos(x) is the POS tag of x represented by a one-hot vector, with a dimension of 1*144. 144 is the total number of character-level POS tags, because there are 36 POS tags and 4 character-level labels ('B', 'I', 'E', 'S'). After being encoded by POSMat, the POS of x is projected into a lower dimensional space.

$$e\_pos(x) = POSMat(c\_pos(x)) \tag{2}$$

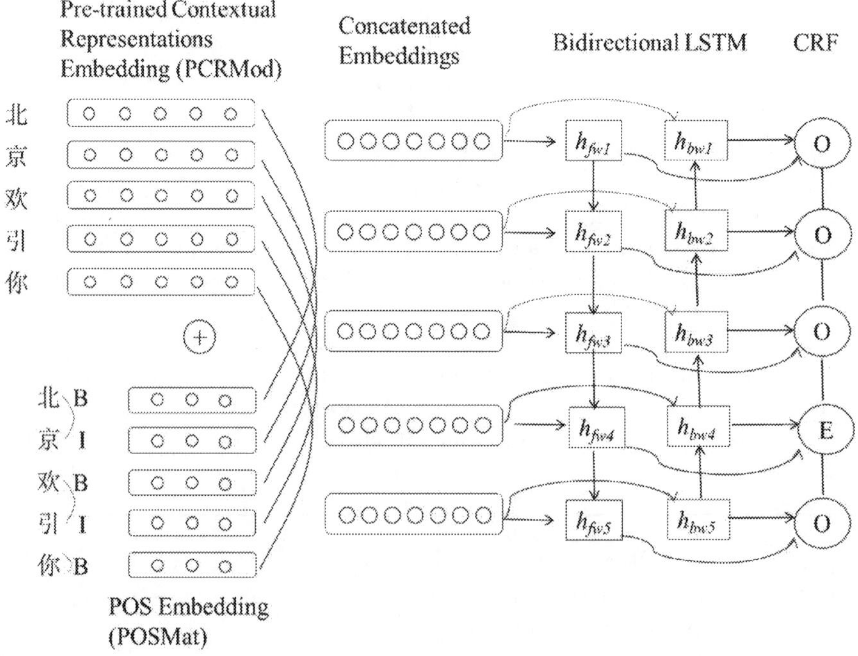

Fig. 2. The framework of Chinese spelling checking in DPL-Corr.

POSMat is a matrix of dimension 144*72. POSMat is randomly initialized and updated during training. e_pos(x) is a vector of dimension 1*72. The character embedding and the POS embedding are concatenated and fed into the Bi-LSTM network.

$$w(x) = catenation(r(x), e\_pos(x)) \tag{3}$$

w(x) is a vector of dimension 1*840, which is input to the Bi-LSTM network that produces u(x) as illustrated in formula (4).

$$u(x) = Bi\_LSTM(w(x)) \tag{4}$$

u(x) is a vector of dimension 1*256, which is input to the CRF layer which outputs the most likely label for x. Label 'E' indicates that x is a spelling error and label 'O' otherwise. Let $X^i = \{x_1^i,...,x_K^i\}$ denote the ith input character sequence to DPL-Corr, and K is the length of X^i. $U^i = \{u_1^i,...,u_K^i\}$ is the input to the CRF layer and $u_k^i = \text{u}(x)$. $L^i = \{l_1^i,...,l_K^i\}$ is the labeling sequence, and l_k^i is the label of x_k^i. The confidence of labeling U^i with L^i is shown in formula (5).

$$P(L^i, U^i) = \sum_{k=1}^{K} (H_{(l_{k-1}^i, l_k^i)} + \varphi(l_k^i, u_k^i)) \tag{5}$$

H is the probability transition matrix of labels. H is 2*2 matrix because there are only two labels ('E' and 'O'). $H_{(l_{k-1}^i, l_k^i)}$ is the transition probability from label l_{k-1}^i to label l_k^i. Additionally, $\varphi(l_k^i, u_k^i)$ is the score given to u_k^i being labeled as l_k^i. φ is a $2{*}V$ matrix where V is the size of the vocabulary and 2 is the size of the label set. Both H and φ are randomly initialized and updated during the training process.

The characters labeled as 'E' are supposed to be suspect spelling errors, and they will be masked and given correction suggestions in the following step.

4.2 Spelling Correction Based on Masked Language Modeling

DPL-Corr adopts a masked language modeling (MLM) approach for spelling correction. The correction module is shown in Fig. 3.

As introduced in the previous section, characters labeled as 'E' are replaced with a special token '[MASK]'. Then the partially masked sequence of characters is fed into the MLM layer to produce a $1{*}V$ vector $\{C_1, C_2, ..., C_{V-1}, C_V\}$ at each position with token '[MASK]'. C_i is the confidence value of fitting the ith character in the vocabulary to the targeted position. To enhance the accuracy of selecting the correction result, the following three steps (called as multilayer filtering) are proposed.

1. Ranking threshold filtering
   If the masked suspect character (e.g., '引' in Fig. 3) is ranked within, for instance, top 100 candidate corrections given by the MLM layer, the suspect is very likely to be a correct use in the sentence. As a result, the suspect will be removed from the list of spelling errors.
2. Confusion set filtering
   Most spelling errors are similar to the correct characters either morphologically or phonetically. Based on a publicly available Chinese confusion set, the candidates that are dissimilar in shape or pronunciation to the suspect are filtered out. Such confusion set filtering is performed to candidates in descending order of the confidence values until a qualified character appears.

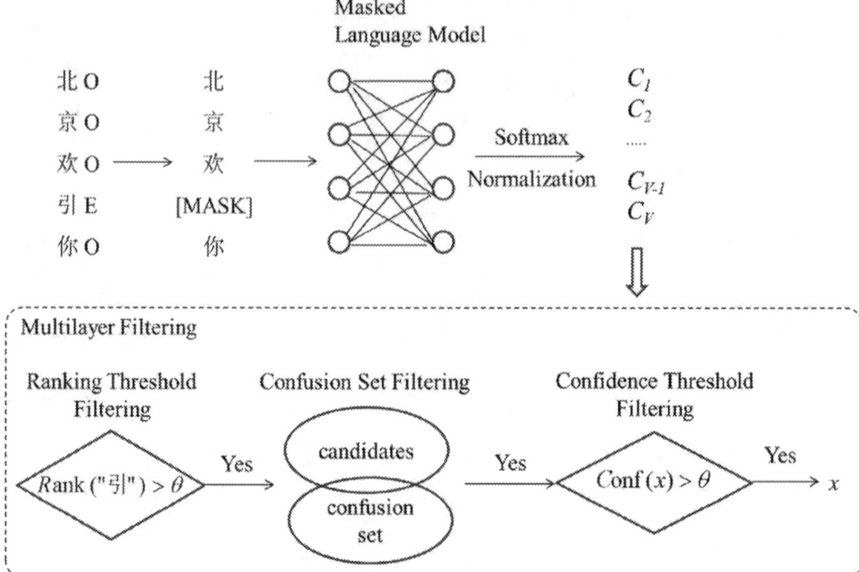

Fig. 3. The framework of Chinese spelling correction in DPL-Corr.

3. Confidence threshold filtering
   After the above steps, the candidate with the highest confidence value will be checked to see if its confidence is higher than a certain threshold so it is a credible choice as a correction. Otherwise the suspect at the current position will not be treated as an error.

There is no parameter to be updated in the correction module during training. The MLM model is pre-trained and directly used in this module. The values of the confidence threshold and ranking threshold are manually selected and adjusted according to the correction performance.

5 Experiments and Analysis

5.1 Experimental Datasets

SIGHAN 2015 dataset [2] is used in our experiments. The dataset contains spelling errors made by people learning Chinese and annotations made by Chinese native speakers. Real-word spelling errors and non-word spelling errors are both contained in the dataset. The size of our experimental data is shown below.

- Training set: 970 passages, 3143 spelling errors.
- Test set: 1100 passages, half of which contain at least one spelling errors, and the other half contain no errors.

SIGHAN competitions allow participants to use extra textual and computing resources. Most participants in the SIGHAN 2015 bake-off used datasets from previous SIGHAN competitions for model training. To guarantee fairness, our experiment incorporated both SIGHAN 2013 and 2014 datasets into our training set. The performance of a CSC model is evaluated from the following two aspects.

- Error detection: whether a spelling error is correctly detected.
- Error correction: whether a spelling error is correctly detected and corrected.

Accuracy (Acc.), precision (Pre.), false positive rate (FPR) and recall (Rec.) are used as the evaluation metrics. Besides adding SIGHAN datasets of previous years to our training corpus, we conducted data augmentation targeting at certain types of spelling errors, mostly misuse of single-character words. For instance, we obtained some amount of published articles and randomly replaced the correct character with its erroneous counterparts and vice versa, such as '地' and '的', '在' and '再', etc.

5.2 Performance Analysis

Table 1 shows the performance of DPL-Corr and its comparisons with SOTA models of SIGHAN 2015 bake-off. DPL-Corr adopts BERT as its pre-trained contextual representations with ranking threshold set to 150 and confidence threshold set to 0.5. In Table 1, CAS-Run1 and CAS-Run2 are the two models with the best overall performances in SIGHAN 2015 bake-off. Additionally, in order to thoroughly analyze the results, we evaluated DPL-Corr under various configurations and thresholds as detailed in Table 1.

Table 1. Performance of various models for Chinese spelling checking and correction.

Model	FPR	Error detection				Error correction			
		Acc.	Pre.	Rec.	F1	Acc.	Pre.	Rec.	F1
CAS-Run1	**0.1164**	0.6891	**0.8095**	0.4945	0.614	0.68	**0.8037**	0.4764	0.5982
CAS-Run2	0.1309	0.7009	0.8027	0.5327	0.6404	0.6918	0.7972	0.5145	0.6254
DPL-Corr	0.1818	**0.7091**	0.7674	**0.6**	**0.6735**	**0.6955**	0.759	**0.5727**	**0.6528**
w/o PCR	0.2182	0.6636	0.7143	0.5455	0.6186	0.6482	0.7022	0.5145	0.5939
w/o POS	0.2091	0.6727	0.7262	0.5545	0.6289	0.6573	0.7146	0.5236	0.6044
w/o filters[a]	0.1818	0.7091	0.7674	0.6	0.6735	0.6645	0.7375	0.5109	0.6037

[a] Because the multilayer filters are performed during error correction, the performance of error detection of the last model is same to that of the final model.

We conducted in-depth analysis on the experimental results. The performance of error detection and error correction for various types of spelling errors is calculated. Regarding a certain type of errors, we first counted the number of passages that contain such type of errors, and then we applied the metrics introduced in Sect. 5.1 to evaluate the performance of CSC on these passages. It is worth noticing that some passages contain multiple types of errors, therefore repeated calculations were inevitable during evaluation on different types of errors. The results are shown in Table 2.

Table 2. Performance of DPL-Corr for different spelling error types.

Error type	FPR	Error detection				Error correction			
		Acc.	Pre.	Rec.	F1	Acc.	Pre.	Rec.	F1
Non-word spelling errors	0.1594	0.7789	0.8182	0.7171	0.7643	0.7669	0.8131	0.6932	0.7484
Real-word spelling errors	0.2007	0.6505	0.7143	0.5017	0.5894	0.6355	0.7015	0.4716	0.564
Misuse of single-char words[a]	0.1741	0.699	0.7667	0.5721	0.6553	0.6617	0.7407	0.4975	0.4975
Misuse of '的地得'	0.1485	0.7723	0.8235	0.6931	0.7527	0.7525	0.8148	0.6535	0.7253

[a] Misuse of single-character words is a type of real-word spelling errors, and misuse of '的地得' is a type of misuse of single-character words.

By observing Table 2, DPL-Corr is better at correcting non-word spelling errors than real-word spelling errors. Furthermore, data augmentation is verified to be effective because the correction performance of misuse of '的地得', in which data augmentation is performed, is superior to that of misuse of single-character words. In summary, the experimental results indicate that: (1) correction of real-word spelling errors remains challenging; (2) the quality of the training data has a significant impact on spelling errors correction.

6 Conclusions

The framework proposed in this paper for the CSC task is able to utilize the semantic and grammatical knowledge learned from a large-scale corpus, which helps to improve the performance of CSC. Meanwhile, because of the application of character-based models, the impact of incorrect word segmentation on CSC can be avoided. Besides, a novel structure of error correction is designed based on a masked language model, which utilizes the contextual information to give correction suggestions. According to our experiments conducted on the dataset of SIGHAN 2015, the proposed model achieves a CSC performance of F1 value 0.6528, which is better than the previous SOTA model.

Our model performs well in correcting non-word spelling errors and misuse of single-character words. However, our model has an unsatisfactory performance in corrections of real-word spelling errors, which are also the main difficulty of CSC. Besides, the rates of false negatives and false positives are still high, especially for those sentences with many technical terms in specific domains.

Several suggestions to improve our model are presented below.

1. For real-word spelling errors, especially the misuse of words with similar meanings, deep semantic analysis of the sentence is necessary for determining which word is more appropriate. A model with the ability of long-distance context representations is helpful for providing such deep semantic analysis.
2. Selection of candidate corrections based on a confusion set is inefficient, because characters with similar shapes or pronunciations contained in the confusion set are artificially collected and limited. An algorithm of evaluating the similarity of the shapes and pronunciations of two characters can be helpful for improving the effect of selecting candidate corrections.
3. Spelling errors are varied. For each specific type of spelling errors, using a corresponding specific set of training set and even designing a single model for it can significantly enhance the performance of CSC.
4. There are fixed grammatical rules for the use of certain words. Linguistic knowledge is helpful for determining if such words are used correctly. Thus, linguistic knowledge based automatic CSC is a promising direction.

Acknowledgement. This work is supported by the projects of National Natural Science Foundation of China (No. 61472014, No. 61573028 and No. 61432020), the Natural Science Foundation of Beijing (No. 4142023) and the Beijing Nova Program (XX2015B010). We also thank all the anonymous reviewers for their valuable comments.

References

1. Chen, K.-Y., Lee, H.-S., Lee, C.-H., et al.: A study of language modeling for Chinese spelling check. In: Proceedings of the Seventh SIGHAN Workshop on Chinese Language Processing, pp. 79–83 (2013)
2. Tseng, Y.-H., Lee, L.-H., Chang, L.-P., et al.: Introduction to SIGHAN 2015 bakeoff for Chinese spelling check. In: Proceedings of the Eighth SIGHAN Workshop on Chinese Language Processing, pp. 32–37 (2015)
3. Hsieh, Y.-M., Bai, M.-H., Chen, K.-J.: Introduction to CKIP Chinese spelling check system for SIGHAN bakeoff 2013 evaluation. In: Proceedings of the Seventh SIGHAN Workshop on Chinese Language Processing, pp. 59–63 (2013)
4. Zhao, H., Cai, D., Xin, Y., et al.: A hybrid model for Chinese spelling check. ACM Trans. Asian Low Resour. Lang. Inf. Process. **16**(3), 1–22 (2017)
5. Wang, D.-M., Yan, S., Li, J., et al.: A hybrid approach to automatic corpus generation for Chinese spelling check. In: Proceedings of the 2018 Conference on Empirical Methods in Natural Language Processing, pp. 2517–2527 (2018)
6. Yang, Y., Xie, P.-J., Tao, J., et al.: Embedding grammatical features into LSTMs for Chinese grammatical error diagnosis task. In: Proceedings of the Eighth International Joint Conference on Natural Language Processing, Shared Tasks, pp. 41–46 (2017)
7. Li, C.-W., Chen, J.-J., Chang, J.-S.: Chinese spelling check based on neural machine translation. In: Proceedings of the 32nd Pacific Asia Conference on Language, Information and Computation (2018)
8. Wang D.-M., Tay, Y., Zhong L.: Confusionset-guided pointer networks for Chinese spelling check. In: Proceedings of the 57th Conference of the Association for Computational Linguistics, pp. 5780–5785 (2019)

A Context-Free Spelling Correction Method for Classical Mongolian

Min Lu, Feilong Bao(✉), and Guanglai Gao

College of Computer Science, Inner Mongolia University, Hohhot, China
csfeilong@imu.edu.cn

Abstract. Spelling errors in the classical Mongolian text are mainly caused by misuse of polyphonic letters which present the same shape in the certain position of the word. About half to three-quarters of the classical Mongolian words are misspellings which have the correct appearances but wrong codes. In this paper, we code the Mongolian words by glyph codes to map the words to their shapes one-to-one. In addition, we also proposed the correction of out-of-vocabulary words (OOV) based on the Evolved Transformer by formalizing the correction task as a translation from misspellings to target spellings. The experimental results show that this approach achieves the new state-of-the-art performance.

Keywords: Classical Mongolian · Spelling errors · Glyph codes · OOV correction

1 Introduction

Spelling correction is the very first step of a natural language processing (NLP) system to ensure that all of the input text is spelled correctly before they were fed into subsequent steps. Most traditional systems in this field were built on Levenshtein Distance and statistical methods [6,16,19]. Recently, Recurrent Neural Networks (RNNs) have been found to be effective in natural language correction [20]. Chollampatt and Ng [2] proposed character-level statistical machine translation to "translate" unknown words into correct words. The nested RNN [7] were used to handle spelling correction in English which consists of a character-level RNN (CharRNN) and a word-level one (WordRNN). In addition, attention was further extended by Vaswani et al. [18], where the self-attentional Transformer architecture achieved state-of-the-art results in Machine Translation. Aiming to automate the laborious process of designing neural networks architectures, Evolved Transformer [14] was proposed then and achieved the more outstanding performance in Machine Translation. Transformers have not been applied to the spelling correction yet.

The existing methods, however, cannot be directly applied to classical Mongolian words. Classical Mongolian is an alphabetic writing language that uses [3] as the standard code. It is designed to encode every speech sound (vowel and

J. Tang et al. (Eds.): NLPCC 2019, LNAI 11839, pp. 550–559, 2019.
https://doi.org/10.1007/978-3-030-32236-6_50

consonant) with a Unicode code point. In classical Mongolian, a single encoded letter may map to many different glyphs, and a single glyph may map to many different encoded letters, too. For example, a letter "U+1820" maps to ᠠ, ᠠ, ᠠ, ᠠ and ᠠ according to its contexts. On the other hand, a glyph ᠲ maps to letter "U+1832" and letter "U+1833". The mismatch between encoded letters and glyphs makes classical Mongolian very easy to be misspelled. Numerous words present correct appearance but are typed with incorrect codes in the text since all the text editors care about is the appearance of the input words and nothing else. Those misspellings with correct shapes are formally known as pronunciation errors which we devote ourself to solve in this paper. They make up more than 90% in Mongolian spelling errors.

To solve the Mongolian spelling errors, an efficient mapping strategy between the word and shape is crucial before correction. [13] and [21] proposed a presentation character to represent the word based on morphology. However, it is a knowledge-dependent and labor-intensive work. In this paper, we propose the direct mapping between words and shapes by representing the words with glyph codes instead of Unicode codes. Then utilizing the vocabulary which is also coded in glyph code to find out the correct spelling. In addition, the Evolved Transformer [14] is applied to correct the out-of-vocabulary words (OOV). The glyph-code representation proposal successfully avoids complex mapping algorithm [13,21]. It is also served for the generation of the training data for OOV correction module, which can be seen as the translation from glyph codes to their correct spellings. The main contributions are as follows:

- Glyph code is presented to convert the Mongolian text encoded with the standard code into its corresponding glyph representation. It not only avoids the costly resource collection process such as error patterns but makes words matched the dictionary efficiently.
- We apply the Evolved Transformer to correct OOV words. It yields significant improvements over the overall correction performance.

In the following sections, we introduce the related work firstly, then propose our solution, describe the experiments, and close the paper with a conclusion at last.

2 Related Work

Neural network models have not drawn much attention in spelling correction for classical Mongolian yet. The most successful spelling correction system is the dictionary-based system [13] which was the first work to use presentation character to represent the word. It mapped the Unicode code to presentation character by rules. Most works operated on Mongolian standard codes directly. The earliest rule-based MHAHP system [4] was just designed to detect Mongolian spelling errors. [5] extended the rules and summarized the common errors. However, the performance was limited by the complex error types. [15] proposed statistical translation framework, which regarded spelling proofreading as the translation from the wrong words to the correct ones.

Dictionary-based approaches typically perform poorly in the absence of complete vocabularies. More recent work in other languages has applied character-level models to machine translation and speech recognition as well, suggesting that it may be applicable to many other tasks that involve the problem of OOVs [1,8,10]. [20] present the character-based RNN model with an attention mechanism for performing language correction which allows for orthographic errors to be captured and avoids the OOV problem suffered by word-based neural machine translation methods. [12] demonstrate the use of LSTM with a delay, for jointly learning error patterns and language models for detection and correction in Indic OCR. [11] proposed semi-character RNN based on psycholinguistics experiments. More recently, the QANet [22] and Evolved Transformer [14] architectures alternate between self-attention layers and convolution layers for Question Answering applications and Machine Translation respectively.

The research on the correction of Mongolian out-of-vocabulary words (OOV) has not been sufficiently discussed yet. In this work, we utilize both the lexicon which maps the glyph codes of the words to their correct spellings and novel Evolved Transformer architecture to correct the pronunciation errors in Mongolian text.

3 Method

Figure 1 shows the general framework of Mongolian spelling correction. Firstly, input strings are encoded into shape codes, then undergo dictionary matching to restore the words from shape representation. The dictionary is built manually with a vocabulary of 172,456, of which about 20,000 items are loan words. The key of each item is the Mongolian glyph codes, and the value is the correct spelling. We add the OOV correction module to the general architecture by applying novel seq2seq model – Evolved Transformer [14]. The polyphone error won't be discussed in this work for it belongs to context-sensitive real-word error. For convenience, words are presented with their national Latin transliteration (keyboard correspondence).

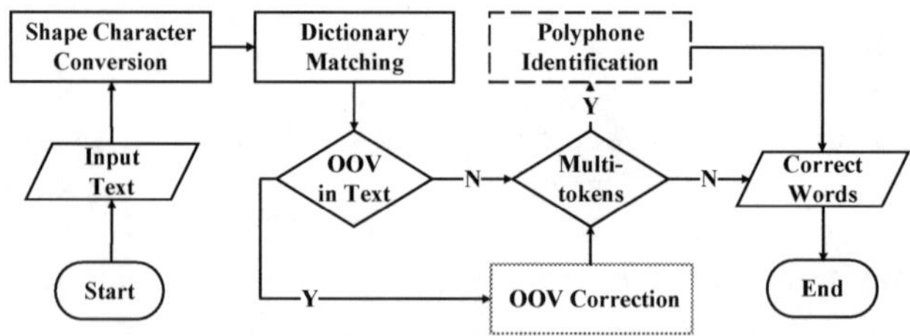

Fig. 1. General framework of Mongolian spelling correction.

3.1 Glyph Code Conversion

Glyph Segmentation Process. Glyph code encoding is to code the words in their glyph sequence in order after segmentation by the cutting line from top to bottom. As seen in Fig. 2, the word ᠬᠣᠨᠢ (meaning: sheep, Latin: hqni) were segmented into 4 glyphs.

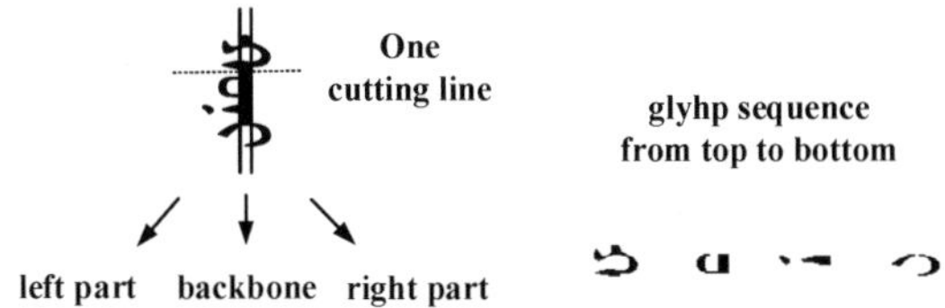

Fig. 2. The Mongolian word and its glyph code sequence.

In this work, we adopt the simple and efficient segmentation algorithm inspired by the characteristic of the backbone. Classical Mongolian is written vertically. Each letter in a word is linked from top to bottom by a vertical line which is called the backbone of the word. The backbones are mostly placed in the middle of the words, consisting of dense black pixels with blank space on one or both sides. The projection line of the backbone on the horizontal x-axis serves as the cutting line. There is at most one or two consecutive white-pixel (255 in value) regions and one consecutive black-pixel (0 in value) region. The algorithm for determining the cutting line is as follows: First, being scanned from top to bottom, lines with only one continuous black pixels are chosen as the candidate cutting lines. Then the frequency of each candidate and its numbers of the dependent lines[1] are recorded. After that, each candidate is scored by the summation of its own frequency and its number of the dependent line. Finally, the one with the highest score is identified as the cutting line.

100 glyphs are defined in total after segmentation of about 200,000 distinct words (See Fig. 3). The images were all generated as binary images in Portable Network Graphic Format (.png). A glyph can be composed of multiple letters, and a letter can be composed of several glyphs as well. The glyphs with higher labels such as glyph 93, can be further segmented by multi-level segmentation. In this work, only one-level segmentation is considered which can perform well enough.

Glyph Segmentation Reasoning. Why not use the entire word image directly to represent the words instead of their glyph sequence? It's because some typeface differences are hard to distinguish with the naked eye. Taking the words

[1] If the black-pixel area of the line and other ones between them can completely cover the black pixels of the current candidate, the line is considered as the dependent line of the current candidate.

1		14		27		40		53		66		79		92	
2		15		28		41		54		67		80		93	
3		16		29		42		55		68		81		94	
4		17		30		43		56		69		82		95	
5		18		31		44		57		70		83		96	
6		19		32		45		58		71		84		97	
7		20		33		46		59		72		85		98	
8		21		34		47		60		73		86		99	
9		22		35		48		61		74		87		100	
10		23		36		49		62		75		88			
11		24		37		50		63		76		89			
12		25		38		51		64		77		90			
13		26		39		52		65		78		91			

Fig. 3. Glyphs and its labels.

(Latin: aNharvn) and (Latin: aegharvn) for instance, the shape of the second letter is slightly different. The former is correctly coded by "U+1829" (Latin: N) and the latter is coded by two codes "U+1821" (Latin: e), "U+182D" (Latin: g) wrongly. These seemingly identical words mislead the user's incorrect input. When we generate the entire word image for those words and match the dictionary (matching the pixel value), the matching will fail. In order to avoid the failure of in-vocabulary words correction caused by inappropriate matching algorithm, glyph sequence is adopted to represent the words. The most similar glyphs were categorized into the same groups. The words with a tiny difference in shape can match the same code sequences with the target words so that they can be matched successfully.

3.2 OOV Correction

We choose to use the Evolved Transformer architecture [14] to "translate" OOV misspellings into correct words. The input of the model is the corresponding labels of glyphs as seen in Fig. 3. The output is the correct Unicode spelling. It produces a ranked list of candidate words, in which the top one is the most likely result. As for the word (See Fig. 2), the input sequence should be the array of [69, 2, 83, 6], and the output is the letters of correct spelling ["U+182C", "U+1823", "U+1828", "U+1822"] (Latin: [h, q, n, i]).

The goal of the Evolved Transformer is to examine the use of neural architecture search methods to design better feed-forward architectures for seq2seq tasks. It applies tournament selection architecture search and warm start it with the Transformer to evolve the better and more efficient architecture. The encoding search space is inspired by the NASNet search space [9], but is altered to allow it to express architecture characteristics found in recent state-of-the-art feed-forward seq2seq networks. The search space was designed as one that can represent the Transformer with which the initial population was seeded. It consists of two stackable cells, one for the model encoder and one for the decoder

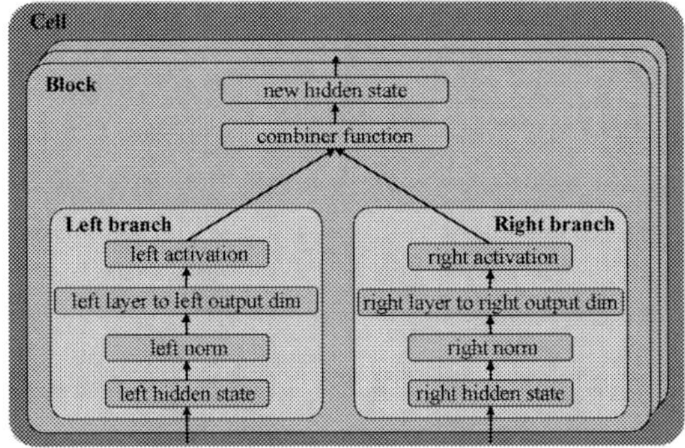

Fig. 4. Architecture composition from encoding.

(see Fig. 4). Each cell contains NASNet-style blocks, which receive two hidden state inputs and produce new hidden states as outputs. The encoder contains six blocks and the decoder contains eight blocks, so that the Transformer can be represented exactly. The blocks perform separate transformations to each input and then combine the transformation outputs together to produce a single block output; The transformations applied to each input is referred to as a branch. The search space contains five branch-level search fields (input, normalization, layer, output dimension and activation), one block-level search field (combiner function) and one cell level search field (number of cells).

To perform the search directly on the computationally demanding task, Progressive Dynamic Hurdles (PDH) was developed to dynamically allocate more resources to more promising candidate models. The model can learn morphological knowledge well to find and organize the proper letters corresponding to the glyph codes. In the absence of a dictionary as a reference, it is adapted to apply for solving spelling errors.

4 Experiment

In this section, we will first evaluate the performance of OOV correction by comparing the Evolved Transformer to the Transformer model. All the comparative experiments were conducted in the Tensor2Tensor [17] training regime on a single GPU. OOV correction is intended to generate words which conform to Mongolian morphological rules according to input word shapes. We evaluate it by shape accuracy and spelling accuracy. Shape accuracy measures the performance of generating words which can present the same shape with the input words without caring about the spellings. The latter one, as it implies, evaluates the performance of generating the correct spellings. They were all tested on common words and loan words. We will then benchmark the performance of our overall performance against the evolutionary method [13]. It is evaluated by the standard binary classification evaluation metrics of *precision*, *recall* and *f*-measure.

4.1 Experimental Data

The datasets for the Evolved Transformer is the aligned sets of glyph sequences and correct spellings extracted from the dictionary. The training set consisted of 140,000 items including loan words of about 15,000 items and 125,000 items of commonly used words. 6,000 items from the remaining entries of the dictionary were extracted as test data for OOV correction. Loan words and commonly used words were accounted for half of the set respectively. For testing the overall performance, we firstly crawled texts of 35 MB from the Mongolian news website. The words whose frequencies were not too high or too low were selected Then. After filtering shape errors among them, we selected the 8,000 tokens at last to correct them manually by several native Mongolian people. The aligned set of with and without correction is used to test the overall performance.

4.2 Result and Analysis

OOV Words Correction. As we can see in Tables 1 and 2, we compared the Evolved Transformer (ET) to the Transformer on variant model scales and embedding sizes. Seeing from the results, ET demonstrates stronger performance than the Transformer almost at all sizes, with the largest difference of 6.00% in spelling accuracy and 1.57% in shape accuracy. By the "Tiny" ET, we get the comfortable results that the highest spelling accuracy of commonly-used words reaches 96.40% and that of loan words reaches 82.16%. The shape accuracy is generally higher and more stable than spelling accuracy with the highest accuracy of 99.83%.

Table 1. Comparison between the transformer and ET on different models.

Model	Model size	Common set		Loan set	
		Spelling Acc	Shape Acc	Spelling Acc	Shape Acc
ET	Tiny	96.40%	99.83%	82.16%	96.70%
Transformer	Tiny	93.70%	99.56%	76.16%	95.67%
ET	Base	84.03%	98.53%	67.90%	90.80%
Transformer	Base	81.96%	97.16%	66.10%	89.23%

As demonstrated in Table 1, we choose the smaller models as "Tiny" and "Base" size models for our character-level task of which the vocabulary is only 100. The result indicates that the "Tiny" model fits our task better. "Tiny" model yields the better results both in the correction of commonly used words and loan words than the "Base" model. It's mainly because of the degeneracy. Beyond that, for both the Transformer and ET, we tried three additional embedding sizes [64, 256, 384] under the better architecture – "Tiny" size model to explore the best embedding size for our task. As can be seen in Table 2, the embedding size larger than 128 did not make any improvement for ET. While the performance of the Transformer continued to grow until the size 384. The gap between the two models becomes smaller with the increasing of embedding size. With the consideration of both model size and effectiveness, the "Tiny" model at its default setting is identified as our method for correcting OOV words.

Table 2. Comparison between the Transformer and ET in different embedding size.

Model	Embedding size	Common set		Loan set	
		Spelling Acc	Shape Acc	Spelling Acc	Shape Acc
ET	64	96.10%	99.60%	80.06%	96.50%
Transformer	64	92.16%	99.60%	74.53%	95.10%
ET	128	96.40%	99.83%	82.16%	96.70%
Transformer	128	93.70%	99.56%	76.16%	95.67%
ET	256	96.30%	99.60%	80.06%	96.43%
Transformer	256	95.80%	99.36%	79.06%	96.50%
ET	384	83.80%	98.36%	67.46%	89.93%
Transformer	384	95.60%	99.50%	79.46%	96.33%

It should be noted that the correction performance of loan words is far lower than commonly-used words. It's mainly for inadequate loan words in the training data. The model failed to learn the specific word-formation rules of loan words and usage of control character[2], which is written frequently in loan words but hardly in common words.

Overall Performance. We conduct three experiments to show respectively the quality of the construction of our dictionary and the correction effect of OOV words as shown in Table 3. The baseline model [13] is the superior work based on rules and dictionaries. From the experiment, we can see that the proposed methods with and without OOV correction module are all outperforms the baseline systems in each criteria. The f-measure of the proposed method is respectively 3.30% and 6.39% higher than the baseline model. It can also be seen that the recall rate is relatively lower in both single dictionary matching methods. It is a common shortcoming in every dictionary-based system because the dictionary cannot cover all the human words, especially for languages with rich inflection. After joining the OOV correction module, the recall is improved further by 5.99% against the single glyph match method. It leads to a 3.00% increase in the f-measure finally.

The experiment shows the excellent results, which confirms that our dictionaries, as well as the OOV correction module, were built pretty well.

[2] Control characters are used in conjunction with Mongolian letters to control the word shapes. They mainly refer to three Mongolian Free Variation Selector: "U+180B", "U+180C", "U+180D".

Table 3. Evaluation for the overall performance. G_Match refers to the performance after the glyph-based dictionary matching only. G_Match+ET refers to the experimental effect of adding OOV correction by the Evolved Transformer.

Criteria	Baseline	G_Match	G_Match+ET
P	95.13%	99.03%	99.04%
R	91.00%	93.31%	98.90%
F	93.02%	96.09%	98.97%

5 Conclusion

To address the serious pronunciation errors in classical Mongolian text, this paper proposed the glyph codes to represent the words. It is an efficient representation method which avoids designing and building enormous and complicated mapping rules. In addition, we proposed the first OOV correction module and add it to the general correction framework. It is handled by the Evolved Transformer model with great performance. Experimental results demonstrate that our method can meet the practical demands well. In future work, we will expand the training data further for loan words and will also explore a uniform architecture to correct both OOV words and polyphones.

Acknowledgments. This work was supported by the National Natural Science Foundation of China (Nos. 61563040, 61773224); Natural Science Foundation of Inner Mongolia (Nos. 2018MS06006, 2016ZD06).

References

1. Chan, W., Jaitly, N., Le, Q., Vinyals, O.: Listen, attend and spell: a neural network for large vocabulary conversational speech recognition. In: 2016 IEEE International Conference on Acoustics, Speech and Signal Processing (ICASSP), pp. 4960–4964. IEEE (2016)
2. Chollampatt, S., Ng, H.T.: Connecting the dots: towards human-level grammatical error correction. In: Proceedings of the 12th Workshop on Innovative Use of NLP for Building Educational Applications, pp. 327–333 (2017)
3. GB25914-2010: Information technology of traditional Mongolian nominal characters, presentation characters and control characters using the rules. China National Standardization Technical Committee, Beijing (2010)
4. Hua, S.: Modern Mongolian automatic proofreading system–MHAHP. J. Inner Mongolia Univ. Philos. Soc. Sci. Ed. **4**, 49–53 (1997)
5. Jiang, B.: Research on rule-based method of Mongolian automatic correction. Ph.D. thesis (2014)
6. Kernighan, M.D., Church, K.W., Gale, W.A.: A spelling correction program based on a noisy channel model. In: Proceedings of the 13th Conference on Computational Linguistics, vol. 2, pp. 205–210. Association for Computational Linguistics (1990)
7. Li, H., Wang, Y., Liu, X., Sheng, Z., Wei, S.: Spelling error correction using a nested RNN model and pseudo training data. arXiv preprint arXiv:1811.00238 (2018)

8. Ling, W., Trancoso, I., Dyer, C., Black, A.W.: Character-based neural machine translation. arXiv preprint arXiv:1511.04586 (2015)
9. Liu, C., et al.: Progressive neural architecture search. In: Ferrari, V., Hebert, M., Sminchisescu, C., Weiss, Y. (eds.) ECCV 2018. LNCS, vol. 11205, pp. 19–35. Springer, Cham (2018). https://doi.org/10.1007/978-3-030-01246-5_2
10. Maas, A., Xie, Z., Jurafsky, D., Ng, A.: Lexicon-free conversational speech recognition with neural networks. In: Proceedings of the 2015 Conference of the North American Chapter of the Association for Computational Linguistics: Human Language Technologies, pp. 345–354 (2015)
11. Sakaguchi, K., Duh, K., Post, M., Van Durme, B.: Robsut wrod reocginiton via semi-character recurrent neural network. In: Thirty-First AAAI Conference on Artificial Intelligence (2017)
12. Saluja, R., Adiga, D., Chaudhuri, P., Ramakrishnan, G., Carman, M.: Error detection and corrections in indic OCR using LSTMs. In: 2017 14th IAPR International Conference on Document Analysis and Recognition (ICDAR), vol. 1, pp. 17–22. IEEE (2017)
13. Si, L.: Mongolian proofreading algorithm based on non-deterministic finite automata. J. Chin. Inf. Process. **23**(6), 110–116 (2009)
14. So, D.R., Liang, C., Le, Q.V.: The evolved transformer. arXiv preprint arXiv:1901.11117 (2019)
15. Su, C., Hou, H., Yang, P., Yuan, H.: Based on the statistical translation framework of the Mongolian automatic spelling correction method. J. Chin. Inf. Process. 175–179 (2013)
16. Toutanova, K., Moore, R.C.: Pronunciation Modeling for Improved Spelling Correction (2002)
17. Vaswani, A., et al.: Tensor2tensor for neural machine translation. CoRR abs/1803.07416 (2018). http://arxiv.org/abs/1803.07416
18. Vaswani, A., et al.: Attention is all you need. In: Advances in Neural Information Processing Systems, pp. 5998–6008 (2017)
19. Wilcox-O'Hearn, A., Hirst, G., Budanitsky, A.: Real-word spelling correction with trigrams: a reconsideration of the Mays, Damerau, and Mercer model. In: Gelbukh, A. (ed.) CICLing 2008. LNCS, vol. 4919, pp. 605–616. Springer, Heidelberg (2008). https://doi.org/10.1007/978-3-540-78135-6_52
20. Xie, Z., Avati, A., Arivazhagan, N., Jurafsky, D., Ng, A.Y.: Neural language correction with character-based attention. arXiv preprint arXiv:1603.09727 (2016)
21. Yan, X., Bao, F., Wei, H., Su, X.: A novel approach to improve the Mongolian language model using intermediate characters. In: Sun, M., Huang, X., Lin, H., Liu, Z., Liu, Y. (eds.) CCL/NLP-NABD -2016. LNCS (LNAI), vol. 10035, pp. 103–113. Springer, Cham (2016). https://doi.org/10.1007/978-3-319-47674-2_9
22. Yu, A.W., Dohan, D., Luong, M.T., Zhao, R., Chen, K., Norouzi, M., Le, Q.V.: QANet: combining local convolution with global self-attention for reading comprehension. arXiv preprint arXiv:1804.09541 (2018)

Explainable AI Workshop

Explainable AI: A Brief Survey on History, Research Areas, Approaches and Challenges

Feiyu Xu[1(✉)], Hans Uszkoreit[2], Yangzhou Du[1], Wei Fan[1], Dongyan Zhao[3], and Jun Zhu[4]

[1] AI Lab, Lenovo Research, Lenovo Group, Beijing, China
{fxu,duyz1,fanwei2}@lenovo.com
[2] DFKI GmbH, Germany and Giance Technologies, Saarbrucken, Germany
uszkoreit@dfki.de
[3] Institute of Computer Science and Technology, Peking University, Beijing, China
zhaody@pku.edu.cn
[4] Department of Computer Science and Technology, Tsinghua University, Beijing, China
dcszj@mail.tsinghua.edu.cn

Abstract. Deep learning has made significant contribution to the recent progress in artificial intelligence. In comparison to traditional machine learning methods such as decision trees and support vector machines, deep learning methods have achieved substantial improvement in various prediction tasks. However, deep neural networks (DNNs) are comparably weak in explaining their inference processes and final results, and they are typically treated as a black-box by both developers and users. Some people even consider DNNs (deep neural networks) in the current stage rather as *alchemy*, than as real science. In many real-world applications such as business decision, process optimization, medical diagnosis and investment recommendation, explainability and transparency of our AI systems become particularly essential for their users, for the people who are affected by AI decisions, and furthermore, for the researchers and developers who create the AI solutions. In recent years, the explainability and explainable AI have received increasing attention by both research community and industry. This paper first introduces the history of Explainable AI, starting from expert systems and traditional machine learning approaches to the latest progress in the context of modern deep learning, and then describes the major research areas and the state-of-art approaches in recent years. The paper ends with a discussion on the challenges and future directions.

Keywords: Explainable artificial intelligence · Intelligible machine learning · Explainable interfaces · XAI · Interpretability

J. Tang et al. (Eds.): NLPCC 2019, LNAI 11839, pp. 563–574, 2019.
https://doi.org/10.1007/978-3-030-32236-6_51

1 A Brief History of Explainable AI

In wiktionary, the word "explain" means for humans "to make plain, manifest, or intelligible; to clear of obscurity; to illustrate the meaning of" [22]. In scientific research, a scientific explanation is supposed to cover at least two parts: (1) the object to be explained (the "Explanandum" in Latin), and (2) the content of explanation (the "Explanans" in Latin).

Explainable AI is not a new topic. The earliest work on Explainable AI could be found in the literature published forty years ago [15,18], where some expert systems explained their results via the applied rules. Since AI research began, scientists have argued that intelligent systems should explain the AI results, mostly when it comes to decisions. If a rule-based expert system rejects a credit card payment, it should explain the reasons for the negative decision. Since the rules and the knowledge in the expert systems are defined and formulated by human experts, these rules and knowledge are easy for humans to understand and interpret. Decision tree is a typical method designed with explainable structure. As illustrated in Fig. 1, starting at the top and going down, the solution path in the decision tree presents the reasoning of a final decision.

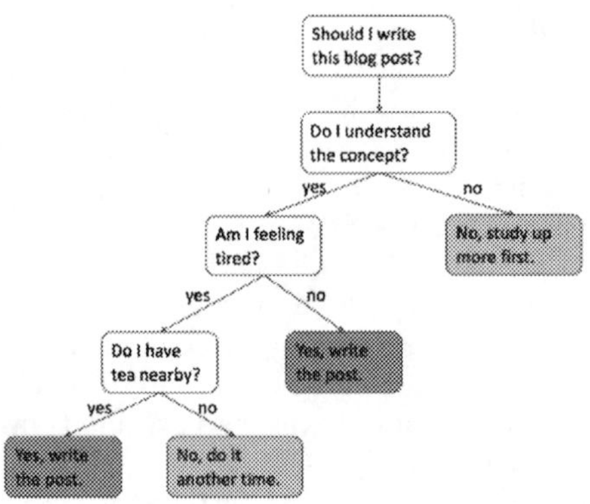

Fig. 1. An example of decision tree, used by starting at the top and going down, level by level, according to the defined logic. (Image courtesy of Jordan [9])

However, Explainable AI has become a new research topic in the context of modern deep learning. Without completely new explanatory mechanisms, the output of today's Deep Neural Networks (DNNs) cannot be explained, neither by the neural network itself, nor by an external explanatory component, and not even by the developer of the system. We know that there are different architectures of DNNs designed for different problem classes and input data, such as CNN, RNN, LSTM, shown in Fig. 2. All of them have to be considered as black boxes - whose internal inference processes are neither known to the observer nor interpretable by humans [7].

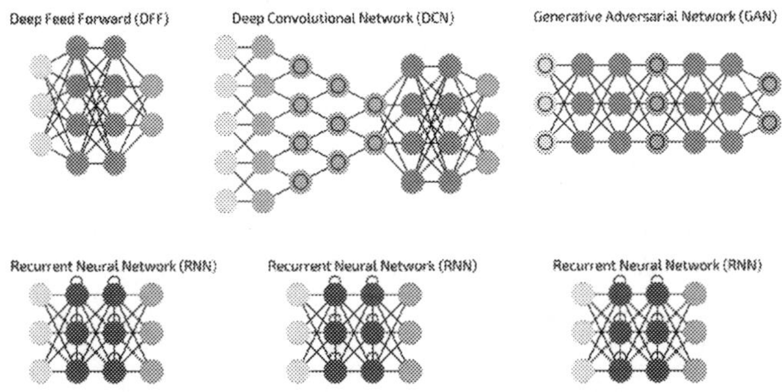

Fig. 2. A chart of several typical Deep Neural Networks (DNNs). (Image courtesy of Van Veen [21])

Explainability of a machine learning model is usually inverse to its prediction accuracy - the higher the prediction accuracy, the lower the model explainability. The DARPA Explainable AI (XAI) program presents a nice chart to illustrate this interesting phenomena, as shown in Fig. 3, where decision trees have an excellent degree of explainability but exhibit worst prediction accuracy among the listed learning techniques. In the other extreme, Deep Learning methods are better in predictive capacity than any other learning methods but they are least likely to be explicable.

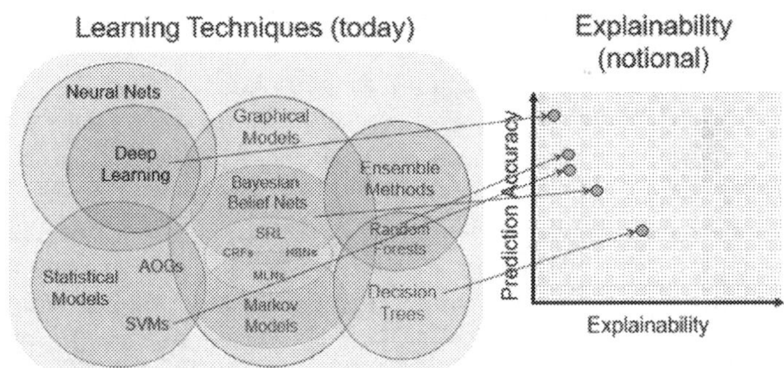

Fig. 3. Explainability of machine learning models appear inverse to their prediction accuracy. (Image courtesy of DARPA [20])

In recent years, AI researchers aim to open the black-box of neural networks and turn it into a transparent system. As shown in Fig. 4, there are two main strands of work in Explainable AI - transparency design and post-hoc explanation. The transparency design reveals how a model functions, in the view of developers. It tries to (a) understand model structure, e.g., the construction of a decision tree; (b) understand single components, e.g., a parameter in logistic regression; (c) understand training algorithms, e.g., solution seeking in a convex optimization. The post-hoc explanation explains why a result is inferred, in the view of users. It tries to (d) give analytic statements, e.g. why a goods is recommended in a shopping website; (e) give visualizations, e.g. saliency map is used to show pixel importance in a result of object classification; (f) give explanations by example, e.g. K-nearest-neighbors in historical dataset are used to support current results. A thorough description of the categorization of explanation methods is found in Lipton et al. [12]. A comprehensive survey on recent development of Explainable AI is provided in [5].

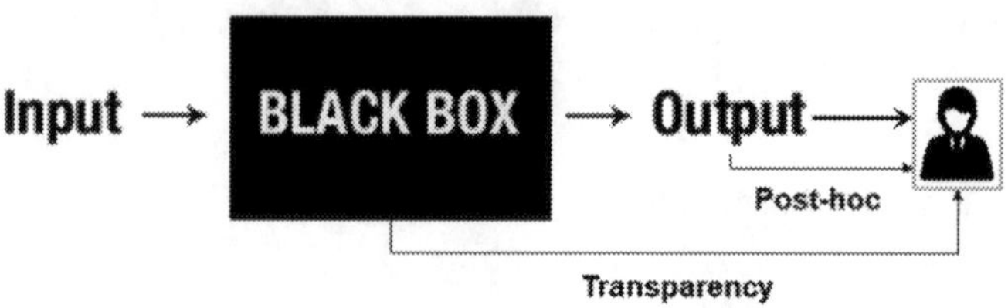

Fig. 4. Two categories of Explainable AI work: transparency design and post-hoc explanation.

2 Relevance of Explainable AI

Increasing attention has recently been paid to Explainable AI across the world both in research and in industry. In April 2017, DARPA funded the "Explainable AI (XAI) program", aimed at improving explainability of AI decision [20]. In July 2017, the Chinese government released "The Development Plan for New Generation of Artificial Intelligence" to encourage high-explainability AI and strong-extensibility AI [17]. In May 2018, the "General Data Protection Regulation" (GDPR) was published, in which the European Union grants their citizens a "right to explanation" if they are affected by algorithmic decision-making [6]. Explainable AI will become increasingly important to all groups of stakeholders, including the users, the affected people, and the developers of AI systems.

Explainable AI is important to the users who utilize the AI system. When the AI recommends a decision, the decision makers would need to understand the underlying reason. For example, medical doctor needs to understand what pathological features in the input data were guiding the algorithm before accepting auto-generated diagnosis reports. A maintenance engineer needs to understand which abnormal phenomena were captured by the inference algorithm before following the repair recommendations. A financial investor wants to understand what influencing factors were regarded as the critical ones by the system algorithm before making the final investment decision. We have to verify that the AI inference works as expected, because wrong decisions can be costly and dangerous. Caruana et al. [3] presented a famous example "Pneumonia - Asthma" to illustrate this point. An AI system which had been trained to predict the pneumonia risk of a person arrived at totally wrong conclusions. From real data the model had learned that asthmatic patients with heart problems have a much lower risk of dying of pneumonia than healthy persons. This cannot be true since asthma is a factor that negatively affects the recovery. The training data were systematically biased, because in contrast to healthy persons, the majority of these asthma patients were under strict medical supervision. Hence this group had a significant lower risk of dying of pneumonia. It should be noted, though, that both the learning and the inference algorithms probably worked correctly and also that the training data represented real cases. The insight that the selection of the training data was not appropriate for predictions affecting other populations may remain undiscovered if we have a black-box AI system.

Explainable AI is important to the people who are affected by AI decision. If the AI makes its own decisions, e.g., braking of the car, shutting down a plant, selling shares, assessing a job, issuing a traffic punishment order, the affected people must be able to understand the reason. There are already legal regulations that codify this demand [6]. Houston schools were using an AI algorithm, called Educational Value-Added Assessment System (EVAAS), to evaluate the performance of teachers. However, this AI system was successfully contested by teachers in court, because negative reviews of teachers could not be explained by the AI system [2].

Explainable AI could help developers to improve AI algorithm, by detecting data bias, discovering mistakes in the models, and remedying the weakness. Lapuschkin et al. [10] presented an impressive example. As shown in Fig. 5, they observed that the Fisher Vector method usually shows lower accuracy than Deep Neural Networks in the task of object recognition. However, two methods reach almost equal accuracy of recognition rate in the category "horse", which is unexpected. A saliency map method called "Layer-wise Relevance Propagation" [11]

	aeroplane	bicycle	bird	boat	bottle	bus	car
Fisher	79.08%	66.44%	45.90%	70.88%	27.64%	69.67%	80.96%
DeepNet	88.08%	79.69%	80.77%	77.20%	35.48%	72.21%	86.30%
	cat	**chair**	**cow**	**diningtable**	**dog**	**horse**	**motorbike**
Fisher	59.92%	51.92%	47.60%	58.06%	42.28%	80.45%	69.34%
DeepNet	81.10%	51.04%	61.10%	64.62%	76.17%	81.60%	79.33%
	person	**pottedplant**	**sheep**	**sofa**	**train**	**tvmonitor**	**mAP**
Fisher	85.10%	28.62%	49.58%	49.31%	82.71%	54.33%	59.99%
DeepNet	92.43%	49.99%	74.04%	49.48%	87.07%	67.08%	72.12%

Fig. 5. Upper: the prediction accuracy of Fisher Vector and Deep Neural Network in tasks of object recognition; Lower: model diagnosis using saliency map method. (Image courtesy of Lapuschkin et al. [10])

was then employed to analyze which pixel areas exactly make the models arrive at their predictions. The authors observed that the two models use different strategies to classify images of that category. The Deep Neural Network looked at the contour of the actual horse, whereas the Fisher Vector model mostly relied on a certain copyright tag, that happens to be present on many horse images. Removing the copyright tag in the test images would consequently significantly decrease the accuracy of the Fisher Vector model.

3 Relevant Explainable AI Problems and Current Approaches

As shown in Fig. 6, there are three typical approaches to understand the behavior of a Deep Neural Network: (a) making the parts of the network transparent - the color of the neuron indicates its activation status; (b) learning semantics of the network components - a neuron could have a meaning if it is often activated by a certain part of the object; (c) generation of explanations - a human-readable textual explanation tells the underlying reason to support current decision.

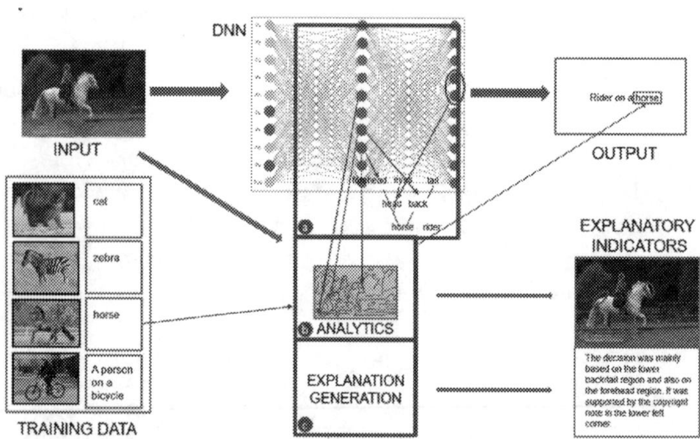

Fig. 6. Three approaches for understanding a neural network, indicated by red-boxes (a), (b) and (c) (Color figure online)

3.1 Making the Parts in DNN Transparency

This section introduces two popular techniques, namely sensitivity analysis (SA) [1,14] and layer-wise relevance propagation (LRP) [16], for explaining prediction of deep learning models.

SA explains a prediction based on the model's locally evaluated gradient.

$$R_i = \|\frac{\partial}{\partial x_i} f(x)\|. \tag{1}$$

It assumes that the most relevant input features are the most sensitive for the output. SA doesn't explain the function value $f(x)$, but rather quantifies the importance of each input variable x_i.

In contrast to SA, LRP explains predictions relative to the state of maximum uncertainty. It redistributes the prediction $f(x)$ backwards using local redistribution rules until it assigns a relevance score R_i to each input variable. The relevance score R_i of each input variable determines the variable's importance to the prediction.

$$\sum_i R_i = \sum_j R_j = ... = \sum_k R_k = ... = f(x). \tag{2}$$

The Relevance conservation is the key property of the redistribution process. This property ensures that no relevance is artificially added or removed during redistribution. Thus, LRP truly decomposes the function values $f(x)$ in contrast to SA.

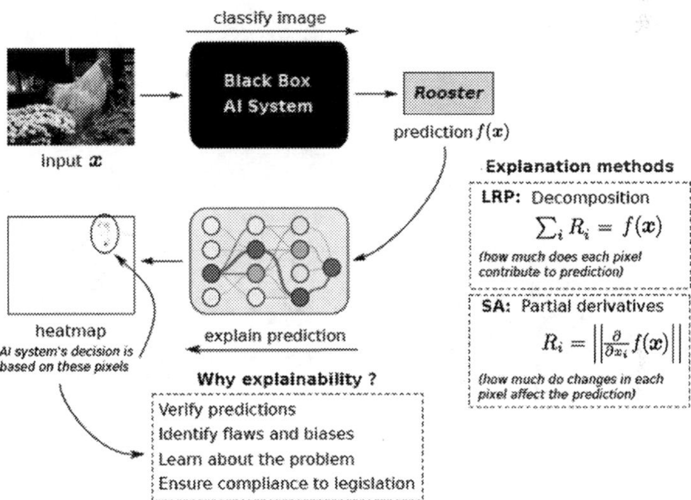

Fig. 7. Explaining predictions of an AI system using SA and LRP. (Image courtesy of Samek [14] (Color figure online)

Figure 7 summarizes the process of explanation. The AI system correctly classifies the input image as "rooster". SA indicates yellow flowers which occlude part of the rooster need to be changed to make the image look more like the predicted. However, such result would not indicate which pixels are actually pivotal for the prediction "rooster". In contrast to SA, the heatmap computed with LRP identifies pixels which are pivotal for the prediction "rooster".

Additionally, SA and LRP are evaluated on three different classification tasks, namely the annotation of images, the classification of text documents and the recognition of human actions in videos. Figure 8(A) shows two images from the ILSVRC2012 [4] dataset, which have been correctly classified as "volcano" and "coffee cup", respectively. From the figure, we can see that SA heatmaps are much noisier than the ones computed with LRP. SA doesn't indicate how much every pixel contributes to the prediction. LRP produces better explanations than SA. Figure 8(B) shows SA and LRP heatmaps overlaid on top of a document from the 20Newsgroup dataset. In contrast to LPR, SA methods don't distinguish between positive and negative evidence. Similarly, Fig. 8(C) shows LRP heatmaps not only visualizes the relevant locations of the action within a video frame, but also identifies the most relevant time points within a video sequence.

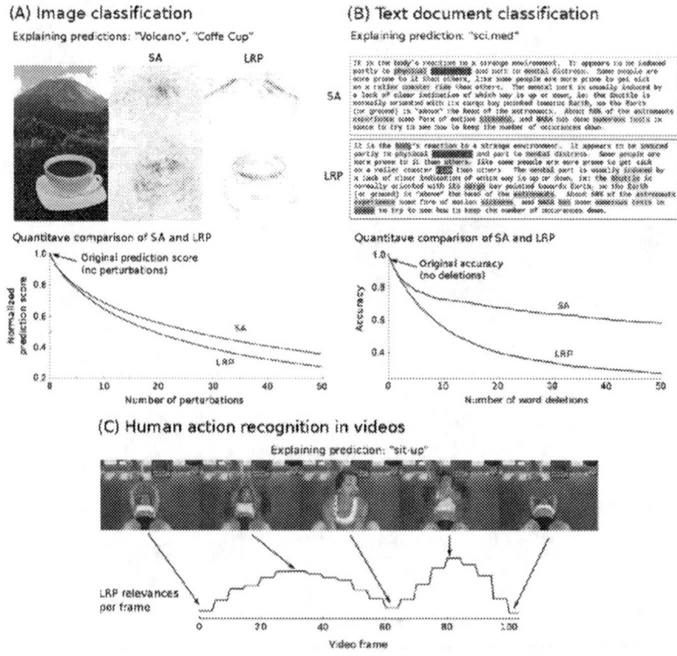

Fig. 8. Explaining prediction of three different problems using SA and LRP. (Image courtesy of Samek [14])

3.2 Learning Semantic Graphs from Existing DNNs

Zhang et al. [23] proposes a method that learns a graphical model, called "explanatory graph", which reveals the knowledge hierarchy hidden inside a pre-trained Convolutional Neural Network (CNN), as shown in Fig. 9. The graph consists of multiple layers, each of them corresponds to a convolutional layer in the CNN. Each node in the graph represents a specific part of the detected object, as shown in the right side of the figure. These nodes are derived from responses of CNN filters with a disentangle algorithm. The edge connecting nodes indicates their co-activation relationship in filter response and the spatial relationship in parts location. The layer shows different granularity of the part of objects - larger parts appear in higher layers while smaller parts appear in lower layers. This work, however, adopts an explanatory graph as a bridge to understand the ordinary CNN. In later work [24], the authors introduce additional losses to force each convolutional filter in CNN to represent a specific object part directly, and produce an interpretable CNN.

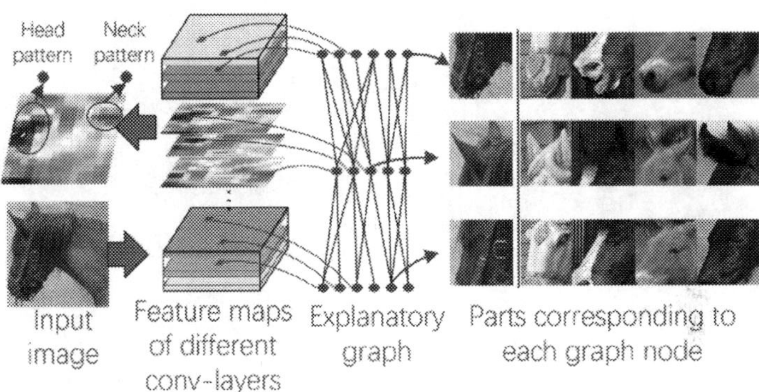

Fig. 9. An explanatory graph represents the knowledge hierarchy hidden in convolutional layers of a CNN. (Image courtesy of Zhang et al. [23])

3.3 Generation of Explanations

This section introduces a novel framework which provides visual explanations of a visual classifier [8]. Visual explanations are both image relevant and class relevant. From Fig. 10 we can find image descriptions provides a sentence based on visual information but not necessarily class relevant, while class definitions are class relevant but not necessarily image relevant. In contrast, Visual explanation such as "This is a western grebe because this bird has a long white neck, pointy

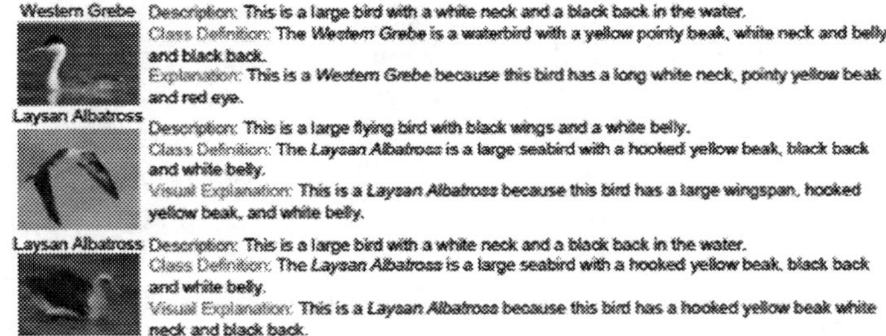

Fig. 10. Visual explanations are both image relevant and class relevant. (Image courtesy of Hendricks [8]) (Color figure online)

yellow beak, and a red eye." includes the "red eye" property which is important to distinguish between "western grebe" and "laysan albatross". Therefore, Visual explanations are both image relevant and class relevant. It explains why the predicted category is the most appropriate for the image.

Figure 11 shows the generation of explanatory text on both an image and a predicted class label. The input is run through a deep fine-grained recognition pipeline to pick out nuanced details of the image and classifying it. The features and the label are then forwarded to the LSTM stack to produce a sequence of words.

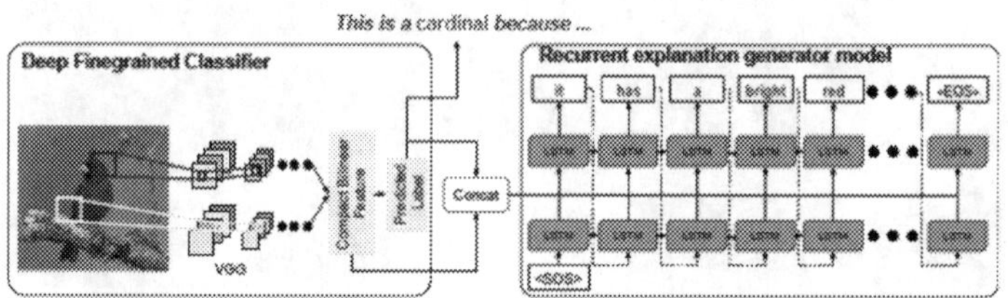

Fig. 11. Generation of explanatory text with joint classification and language model. (Image courtesy of Hendricks [8])

4 Challenges and Future Directions

The development of Explainable AI is facing both scientific and social demands. We expect AI systems could help humans make decisions in mission-critical tasks. Therefore, We need a more trustworthy and transparent AI, instead of alchemy AI [19]. Ali Rahimi, the winner of the test-of-time award in NeurIPS 2017, expressed his expectations concerning AI solutions as follows: "We are building systems that govern healthcare and mediate our civic dialogue. We would influence elections. I would like to live in a society whose systems are built on top of verifiable, rigorous, thorough knowledge, and not on alchemy. Let's take machine learning from alchemy to electricity" [13]. The term "electricity" in his speech could be replaced by "chemistry" from our perspective, meaning that AI Deep Learning AI should become part of science.

DARPA has invested 50 Million USD and launched a 5-year research program on Explainable AI (XAI) [20], aiming to produce "glass-box" models that are explainable to a "human-in-the-loop", without greatly sacrificing AI performance, as shown in Fig. 12. Human users should be able to understand the AI's cognition both in real-time and after the results achieved, and furthermore might be able to determine when to trust the AI and when the AI should be distrusted. In Phase 1, it is planned to achieve initial implementations of their explainable learning systems. In Phase 2, it is to build a toolkit library consisting of machine learning and human-computer interface software modules that could be utilized for developing future explainable AI systems.

It is known that humans can acquire and use both explicit knowledge and implicit knowledge. Moreover, humans can combine the two forms of knowledge

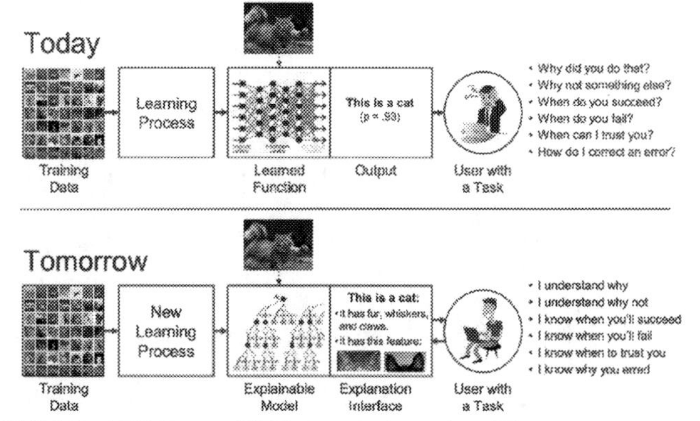

Fig. 12. Explainable AI (XAI) Concept presented by DARPA. (Image courtesy of DARPA XAI Program [20])

to a certain degree. For humans, understanding and explaining require explicit knowledge. However, DNNs acquire and use implicit knowledge in the form of probabilistic models. As they stand, they cannot understand anything. Other AI methods model explicit knowledge, such as Knowledge Graphs. Today the two worlds in AI technology are still largely separated. Researchers are now strengthening their efforts to bring the two worlds together. The need-driven research on Explainable AI is a source and a catalyst for the work dedicated to this grand challenge.

References

1. Baehrens, D., Schroeter, T., Harmeling, S., Kawanabe, M., Hansen, K., Müller, K.: How to explain individual classification decisions. J. Mach. Learn. Res. **11**, 1803–1831 (2010). http://portal.acm.org/citation.cfm?id=1859912
2. Cameron, L.: Houston Schools Must Face Teacher Evaluation Lawsuit (2017). https://www.courthousenews.com/houston-schools-must-face-teacher-evaluation-lawsuit/
3. Caruana, R., Lou, Y., Gehrke, J., Koch, P., Sturm, M., Elhadad, N.: Intelligible models for healthcare: predicting pneumonia risk and hospital 30-day readmission. In: Proceedings of the 21st ACM SIGKDD International Conference on Knowledge Discovery and Data Mining, pp. 1721–1730. ACM (2015)
4. Deng, J., Dong, W., Socher, R., Li, L., Li, K., Li, F.: ImageNet: a large-scale hierarchical image database. In: 2009 IEEE Computer Society Conference on Computer Vision and Pattern Recognition (CVPR 2009), Miami, Florida, USA, 20–25 June 2009, pp. 248–255 (2009). https://doi.org/10.1109/CVPRW.2009.5206848
5. Došilović, F.K., Brčić, M., Hlupić, N.: Explainable artificial intelligence: a survey. In: 2018 41st International Convention on Information and Communication Technology, Electronics and Microelectronics (MIPRO), pp. 0210–0215, May 2018. https://doi.org/10.23919/MIPRO.2018.8400040

6. Goodman, B., Flaxman, S.: European union regulations on algorithmic decision-making and a "right to explanation". AI Mag. **38**(3), 50–57 (2017)
7. Guidotti, R., Monreale, A., Ruggieri, S., Turini, F., Giannotti, F., Pedreschi, D.: A survey of methods for explaining black box models. ACM Comput. Surv. (CSUR) **51** (2019)
8. Hendricks, L.A., Akata, Z., Rohrbach, M., Donahue, J., Schiele, B., Darrell, T.: Generating visual explanations. In: Leibe, B., Matas, J., Sebe, N., Welling, M. (eds.) ECCV 2016. LNCS, vol. 9908, pp. 3–19. Springer, Cham (2016). https://doi.org/10.1007/978-3-319-46493-0_1
9. Jeremy, J.: Decision trees (2017). https://www.jeremyjordan.me/decision-trees/
10. Lapuschkin, S., Binder, A., Montavon, G., Muller, K.R., Samek, W.: Analyzing classifiers: Fisher vectors and deep neural networks. In: Proceedings of the IEEE Conference on Computer Vision and Pattern Recognition, pp. 2912–2920 (2016)
11. Lapuschkin, S., Binder, A., Montavon, G., Müller, K.R., Samek, W.: The LRP toolbox for artificial neural networks. J. Mach. Learn. Res. **17**(114), 1–5 (2016). http://jmlr.org/papers/v17/15-618.html
12. Lipton, Z.C.: The mythos of model interpretability. ACM Queue Mach. Learn. **16**, 30 (2018)
13. Rahimi, A.: NIPS 2017 Test-of-Time Award presentation (2017). https://www.youtube.com/watch?v=ORHFOnaEzPc
14. Samek, W., Wiegand, T., Müller, K.R.: Explainable artificial intelligence: understanding, visualizing and interpreting deep learning models. arXiv preprint arXiv:1708.08296 (2017)
15. Scott, A.C., Clancey, W.J., Davis, R., Shortliffe, E.H.: Explanation capabilities of production-based consultation systems. Am. J. Comput. Linguist. **62** (1977)
16. Simonyan, K., Vedaldi, A., Zisserman, A.: Deep inside convolutional networks: visualising image classification models and saliency maps. In: 2nd International Conference on Learning Representations, ICLR 2014, Workshop Track Proceedings, Banff, AB, Canada, 14–16 April 2014 (2014). http://arxiv.org/abs/1312.6034
17. State Council Chinese Government: Development Plan for New Generation Artificial Intelligence (2017). http://www.gov.cn/zhengce/content/2017-07/20/content_5211996.htm
18. Swartout, W.R.: Explaining and justifying expert consulting programs. In: Proceedings of the 7th International Joint Conference on Artificial Intelligence (1981)
19. Tony, P.: LeCun vs Rahimi: Has Machine Learning Become Alchemy? (2017). https://medium.com/@Synced/lecun-vs-rahimi-has-machine-learning-become-alchemy-21cb1557920d
20. Turek, M.: DARPA - Explainable Artificial Intelligence (XAI) Program (2017). https://www.darpa.mil/program/explainable-artificial-intelligence
21. Van Veen, F.: The Neural Network Zoo (2016). http://www.asimovinstitute.org/neural-network-zoo/
22. Wiktionary: Explain (2019). https://en.wiktionary.org/wiki/explain
23. Zhang, Q., Cao, R., Shi, F., Wu, Y.N., Zhu, S.C.: Interpreting CNN knowledge via an explanatory graph. In: Thirty-Second AAAI Conference on Artificial Intelligence (2018)
24. Zhang, Q., Wu, Y.N., Zhu, S.C.: Interpretable convolutional neural networks. In: Proceedings of the IEEE Conference on Computer Vision and Pattern Recognition, pp. 8827–8836 (2018)

Interpretable Spatial-Temporal Attention Graph Convolution Network for Service Part Hierarchical Demand Forecast

Wenli Ouyang(✉), Yahong Zhang, Mingda Zhu, Xiuling Zhang, Hongye Chen, Yinghao Ren, and Wei Fan

Artificial Intelligence Lab, Lenovo Research, Beijing, China
{ouyangwl1, zhangyh33, zhumd4, zhangxl35, chenhy17, renyh6, fanwei2}@lenovo.com

Abstract. Accurate service part demand forecast plays a key role in service supply chain management. It enables better decision making in the planning of service part procurement and distribution. To achieve high responsiveness, the service supply chain network exhibits a hierarchical structure: forward stocking locations (FSL) close to the end customer, distribution centers (DC) in the middle and center hub (CH) at the top. Hierarchical forecasts require not only good prediction accuracy at each level of the service supply chain network, but also the consistency between different levels. The accuracy and consistency of hierarchical forecasts are important to be interpretable to the decision-makers (DM). Moreover, service part demand data is the spatial-temporal time series that the observations made at neighboring regions and adjacent timestamps are not independent but dynamically correlated with each other. Recent advances in deep learning enable promising results in modeling the complex spatial-temporal relationship. Researchers use convolutional neural networks (CNN) to model spatial correlations and recurrent neural networks (RNN) to model temporal correlations. However, these deep learning models are non-transparent to the DMs who broadly require justifications in the decision-making processes. Here an interpretable solution is in the urgent demand. In this paper, we present an interpretable general framework **STAH** (**S**patial-**T**emporal **A**ttention Graph Convolution network for **H**ierarchical demand forecast). We evaluate our approach on Lenovo Group Ltd.'s service part demand data in India. Experimental results demonstrate the efficacy of our approach, showing superior accuracy while increasing model interpretability.

1 Introduction

Service parts for products like notebooks, cellphones, household appliances, and automobiles have grown into a business worth more than $200 billion worldwide [1]. Service parts need to be managed at an appropriate level within the service supply chain to provide after-sales services to customers. Considering the high number of parts managed, the high responsiveness required due to downtime cost for customers and the risk of stock obsolescence, the service supply chain management is a difficult task for decision-makers (DM). The most difficult one in the decision processes is how to

J. Tang et al. (Eds.): NLPCC 2019, LNAI 11839, pp. 575–586, 2019.
https://doi.org/10.1007/978-3-030-32236-6_52

estimate service part demand accurately. Generally, the service supply chain network is multiple hierarchical structures: forward stocking locations (FSL) close to the end customer, distribution centers (DC) in the middle and center hub (CH) at the top. A good service part management needs an accurate demand forecast at each level and the consistent demand forecast between different levels. For instance, service part demand in the CH can be disaggregated into one of DCs, which are further disaggregated into one of FSLs. The aggregation consistency is a critical point for decision-maker (DM) to interpret and accept the forecast results, which means the disaggregated demands should add up equally to the aggregated ones. Moreover, service part demand data is spatial-temporal time series that the observations made at neighboring regions and timestamps are not independent but dynamically correlated with each other. The key challenge to providing accurate service part demand forecast is how to discover inherent spatial-temporal patterns and extract the spatial-temporal correlation of data effectively. In recent years, many researchers use deep learning methods to deal with spatial-temporal data, i.e., convolutional neural network (CNN) to extract spatial features of grid-based data and recurrent neural network (RNN) to extract temporal features of time-series data. Compared with the time series analysis model and traditional machine learning method, the deep learning method achieves great results and shows its advantages in modeling end-to-end nonlinear interactions, incorporating exogenous variable and extract features automatically [2]. However, these deep learning models are described as “black-box” and non-transparent to DMs who broadly require justifications in the decision-making processes.

To tackle the above challenges, we propose an interpretable general framework **STAH** (**S**patial-**T**emporal **A**ttention Graph Convolution network for **H**ierarchical demand forecast) to predict service part demand hierarchically. Instead of using CNNs, this model uses interpretable hierarchical graph convolution networks (GCN). It is capable to handle non-Euclidean hierarchical data structure such as the service supply chain network structure. To increase interpretability even further, attention mechanism is used in both hierarchical GCNs and RNN encoder-decoder to localize discriminative regions and timestamps both spatially and temporally. The main contributions of this paper are summarized as follows:

- We develop a neural network structure for the hierarchical forecast that met the aggregation consistency inherently. The neural network has multiple levels of outputs, each of which is corresponding to each level of the service supply chain network. The high-level output is the sum of the connected low-level ones. The objective function of this model is the combination of the objective function of each output at each level.
- We propose a spatial hierarchical attention module that captures multilevel spatial correlations from the graph-based hierarchical service supply chain network and a temporal alignment attention module that identify the most relevant historical observations and align forecast results with them.
- We apply inter-temporal regularization to restrict the difference of the learned spatial attention maps among different timestamps. This can help to avoid the case in which the learned attention maps of each spatial region focus on one specific temporal state and largely ignore the other temporal ones.

2 Related Review

2.1 Hierarchical Forecast

Some time series analysis models such as ARIMA (Autoregressive Integrated Moving Average model), ETS (Smoothing State Space model), etc. are applied in hierarchical forecast [3–6]. This forecasting method estimates time series at all levels independently. This approach doesn't guarantee aggregation consistency in the hierarchical structure and the separate predictive models don't take account of spatial correlations between each region. The "bottom-up" approach is adopted to meet the aggregation consistency constraint [5]. It forecasts all of the bottom-level disaggregated series and then adds the results of the forecast to form the higher-level series until it reaches the top-level one. However, this approach still doesn't consider spatial correlations and the disaggregated data tends to have a low signal-to-noise ratio, the overall prediction accuracy will be poor [7]. The optimal combined forecasting is the mainstream [4, 5, 8]. It estimates the initial forecast at bottom-levels and reconciles these forecasts based on aggregation consistency. Ordinary Least Square (OLS) and Weight Least Square (WLS) are used to estimate the covariance matrix based on historical observations.

2.2 Convolutions on Graphs

CNNs can effectively extract the local patterns of the standard grid data. To generalize CNNs to data of graph structures, two basic approaches are proposed. One is to perform convolutional filtering on graph's nodes and their neighbors directly [9], the other is to manipulate in the spectral domain with graph Fourier transforms [10]. However, this method requires explicitly computing the Laplacian eigenvectors, which is impractical for real large graphs. [11] find a model to circumvent this problem by using Chebyshev polynomial approximation to realize eigenvalue decomposition. [12] simply this model by limiting the application of each filter to the 1-neighbor of each node, approximating the largest eigenvalue and applying a normalization trick to the convolution matrix. In this way, they reduce the computational complexity to linear. This simplified model is called GCN, which is used in this paper.

2.3 Attention Mechanism

Since the attention mechanism is propose by [13], it has been applied in various tasks such as natural language processing, image caption and speech recognition. The attention mechanism can select the information that is relatively critical to the current task from all inputs. Together with RNNs and CNNs, attention mechanism has proven to be useful to learn representation and improve performances in applied tasks [14, 15]. Recently, [16] extend the attention mechanism to process graph-structured data and achieved state-of-art results. In the time series forecast task, [17] proposed a multi-level attention network to adjust the correlations among multiple time series generated from different locations. [18] proposed a spatial-temporal forecast model that applies the attention mechanism in both spatial and temporal dimensions.

3 STAH: The Model

In this section, we first mathematically formulate the definition of hierarchical service part demand forecast and then we present the technical details of the proposed model STAH. The system architecture of the proposed model STAH is shown in Fig. 1. We represent the output layer in a hierarchical structure that has multiple levels of outputs, each of which is corresponding to each level of the service supply chain network. The high-level output is the sum of the connected low-level ones. The aggregation consistency is met inherently in the hierarchical output layer. The proposed neural network STAH is composed of spatial hierarchical attention module and temporal alignment attention module. The values of all features at each timestamp are firstly processed by spatial hierarchical attention module and then feed into temporal alignment attention module to generate hierarchical forecast.

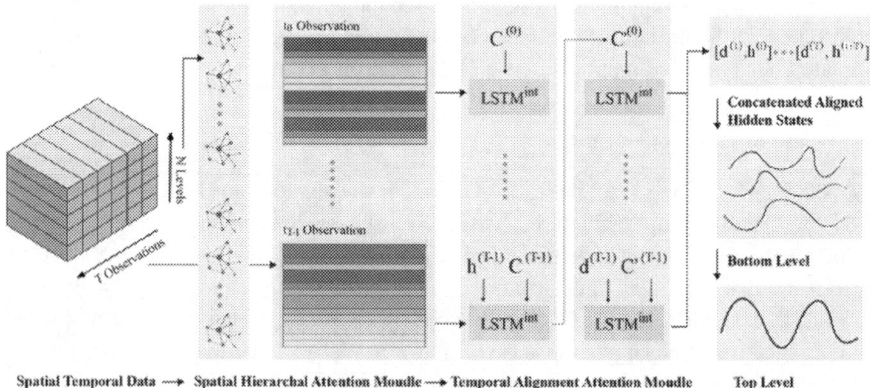

Fig. 1. The system architecture of the proposed **S**patial-**T**emporal **A**ttention Graph Convolution network for **H**ierarchical demand forecast (STAH).

3.1 Hierarchical Service Part Demand Forecast

The service supply chain network is a hierarchical structure that have multiple levels, as shown in Fig. 2. Suppose service part demand and exogenous variables are recorded as time series on each region at each level as $\boldsymbol{x}_{i,j}^{(t)} = (y_{i,j}^{(t)}, a_{i,j}^{(t)}, b_{i,j}^{(t)}, \ldots, c_{i,j}^{(t)}) \in \mathbb{R}^{F+1}$, where y is service part demand. $a, b, \ldots, c$ are exogenous variables. i, j and t represent level i, region j and timestamp t. F is the number of exogenous variables. $\boldsymbol{X}_i^{(t)} = \left(\boldsymbol{x}_{i,1}^{(t)}, \boldsymbol{x}_{i,2}^{(t)}, \ldots, \boldsymbol{x}_{i,n_i}^{(t)}\right) \in \mathbb{R}^{n_i \times (F+1)}$ denotes the values of all the features of all regions at level i and time t. We define the number of the regions at all levels as $n = \sum_1^N n_i$. $\boldsymbol{X}^{(t)} = \left(\boldsymbol{X}_1^{(t)}, \boldsymbol{X}_2^{(t)}, \ldots, \boldsymbol{X}_N^{(t)}\right) \in \mathbb{R}^{n \times (F+1)}$ denotes the value of all the features of all the regions at all the level at time t. The same processes apply to y and $\boldsymbol{Y}_i^{(t)} \in \mathbb{R}^{n_i}$ denotes the service part demand of all regions at level i and time t. $\boldsymbol{Y}^{(t)} \in \mathbb{R}^n$ denotes the service part demand of all the regions at all the level at time t. Then the hierarchical service part demand forecast problem is formulated as a multi-step prediction given input with a fixed temporal length, i.e., learning a function $f : \mathbb{R}^{n \times (F+1) \times T} \rightarrow \mathbb{R}^{n \times \Delta}$ that maps the historical values of all the features to the demand in the following interval Δ.

$$\left[\boldsymbol{X}^{(1)}, \ldots, \boldsymbol{X}^{(T)}\right] \overset{f(\cdot)}{\rightarrow} \left[\boldsymbol{Y}^{(T+1)}, \ldots, \boldsymbol{Y}^{(T+\Delta)}\right] \tag{1}$$

The aggregation consistency can be formulated as $\boldsymbol{Y}^{(t)} = T_c \boldsymbol{Y}_1^{(t)}$, where index 1 represents the bottom level and T_c denotes an $n \times n_1$ summing matrix derived from the hierarchical structure. It consists of an $(n - n_1) \times n_1$ submatrix $T_{c,a}$ and an $n_1 \times n_1$ identity matrix.

$$T_c = \begin{bmatrix} T_{c,a} \\ I_{n_1} \end{bmatrix} \tag{2}$$

3.2 Spatial Hierarchical Attention Module

The service supply chain network generally organizes as a hierarchical graph structure. In order to process this multilevel non-Euclidian data structure, multiple GCNs are used, each of which is applied to process the data of each level in the hierarchical graph structure, as shown in Fig. 2. We introduce the notion of graph convolution operator "$* \mathcal{g}$" based on the conception of spectral graph convolution, as the multiplication of $\boldsymbol{X}_i^{(t)}$ at level i and time t with a kernel Θ,

$$\Theta * \mathcal{g}\, \boldsymbol{X}_i^{(t)} = \Theta(L)\boldsymbol{X}_i^{(t)} = \Theta(U\Lambda U^T)\boldsymbol{X}_i^{(t)} = U\Theta(\Lambda)U^T\boldsymbol{X}_i^{(t)} \tag{3}$$

where graph Fourier basis $U \in \mathbb{R}^{n_i \times n_i}$ is the matrix of eigenvectors of the normalized graph Laplacian $L = I_{n_i} - D^{-\frac{1}{2}}WD^{-\frac{1}{2}} = U\Lambda U^T \in \mathbb{R}^{n_i \times n_i}$. $D \in \mathbb{R}^{n_i \times n_i}$ is the diagonal degree matrix with $D_{ii} = \sum_j W_{ij}$. $\Lambda \in \mathbb{R}^{n_i \times n_i}$ is the diagonal matrix of eigenvalues of L. Two approximation strategies are applied to simplify Eq. (1). One approximation is Chebyshev Polynomial Approximation. The kernel Θ can be restricted to a polynomial of Λ as $\Theta(\Lambda) = \sum_{k=0}^{K-1} \theta_k \Lambda^k$, where $\theta \in \mathbb{R}^K$ is a vector of polynomial coefficients. K is the kernel size of graph convolution. Chebyshev polynomial $T_k(x)$ is used to approximate kernels as a truncated expansion of order $K - 1$ as $\Theta(L) \approx \sum_{k=0}^{K-1} \theta_k T_k(\tilde{L})$ with rescaled $\tilde{\Lambda} = 2\Lambda/\lambda_{max} - I_n$, where λ_{max} denotes the largest eigenvalue of L [19]. The graph convolution can then be rewritten as,

$$\Theta * g\, \boldsymbol{X}_i^{(t)} = \Theta(L)\boldsymbol{X}_i^{(t)} \approx \sum_{k=0}^{K-1} \theta_k T_k(\tilde{L})\boldsymbol{X}_i^{(t)} \quad (4)$$

where $T_k(\tilde{L}) \in \mathbb{R}^{n_i \times n_i}$. Another approximation is 1st-order Approximation. Set $K = 1$ and assume $\lambda_{max} \approx 2$. Thus, the Eq. (4) can be simplified to,

$$\Theta * g\, \boldsymbol{X}_i^{(t)} \approx \theta_0 \boldsymbol{X}_i^{(t)} - \theta_1 (D^{-\frac{1}{2}} W D^{-\frac{1}{2}}) \boldsymbol{X}_i^{(t)} \quad (5)$$

where θ_0 and θ_1 are two shared parameters of the kernel. Set $\theta = \theta_0 = -\theta_1$ and renormalize W and D by $\tilde{W} = W + I_{n_i}$ and $\tilde{D}_{ii} = \sum_j \tilde{W}_{ij}$. Then, the graph convolution can be expressed as,

$$\Theta * g\, \boldsymbol{X}_i^{(t)} = \theta(\tilde{D}^{-\frac{1}{2}} \tilde{W} \tilde{D}^{-\frac{1}{2}}) \boldsymbol{X}_i^{(t)} \quad (6)$$

Applying a stack of graph convolutions with the 1st-order approximation vertically can achieves the similar effect as K-localized convolutions do horizontally. In the spatial dimension, the service parts demand of different regions has highly dynamic influence among each other. Here, we propose a hierarchical attention model to capture the spatial correlations at the same level in the hierarchical graph structure. The spatial attention at level i and time t is defined as,

$$\boldsymbol{S}_i^{(t)} = \boldsymbol{V} \cdot \sigma\left(\boldsymbol{X}_i^{(t)} \boldsymbol{W} (\boldsymbol{X}_i^{(t)})^T + \boldsymbol{b}\right) \quad (7)$$

$$\tilde{S}_{i,j,k}^{(t)} = \frac{\exp\left(S_{i,j,k}^{(t)}\right)}{\sum_{k=1}^{N} \exp\left(S_{i,j,k}^{(t)}\right)} \quad (8)$$

where $\boldsymbol{S}_i^{(t)} \in \mathbb{R}^{n_i \times n_i}$ represents attention matrix at level i and time t and $S_{i,j,k}^{(t)}$ is an element in $\boldsymbol{S}_i^{(t)}$ representing the correlation strength between region j and region k. $\boldsymbol{W} \in \mathbb{R}^{(F+1) \times (F+1)}$, $\boldsymbol{V}, \boldsymbol{b} \in \mathbb{R}^{n_i \times n_i}$ are learnable parameters and sigmoid σ is used as the activation function. When performing the graph convolution, the spatial attention matrix $\tilde{\boldsymbol{S}}_i^{(t)} \in \mathbb{R}^{n_i \times n_i}$ is accompanied with the $T_k(\tilde{L})$. The graph convolution formula (4) changes to

$$\Theta * g\, \boldsymbol{X}_i^{(t)} = \Theta(L)\boldsymbol{X}_i^{(t)} \approx \sum_{k=0}^{K-1} \theta_k (T_k(\tilde{L}) \odot \tilde{\boldsymbol{S}}_i^{(t)}) \boldsymbol{X}_i^{(t)} \quad (9)$$

And the formula (6) changes to

$$\Theta * g\, \boldsymbol{X}_i^{(t)} = \theta((\tilde{D}^{-\frac{1}{2}} \tilde{W} \tilde{D}^{-\frac{1}{2}}) \odot \tilde{\boldsymbol{S}}_i^{(t)}) \boldsymbol{X}_i^{(t)} \quad (10)$$

where $\odot$ is the Hadamard product. In order to encourage the spatial attention model to preserve the similarity and meanwhile avoid focusing on one timestamp, we design the inter-temporal regularization that measures the difference among spatial attention matrix. We employ the square Frobenius Norm of the difference between $\boldsymbol{S}_i^{(t_1)}$ and $\boldsymbol{S}_i^{(t_2)}$, defined as

$$Reg = \left\| \boldsymbol{S}_i^{(t_1)} - \boldsymbol{S}_i^{(t_2)} \right\|_F = \sqrt{\sum\nolimits_{j=1}^{n_i} \sum\nolimits_{k=1}^{n_i} \left(S_{i,j,k}^{(t_1)} - S_{i,j,k}^{(t_2)} \right)^2} \tag{11}$$

We randomly choose m pairs of spatial attention matrixes from each training sample for this regularization term and add this term *Reg* to the original objective function for the model training.

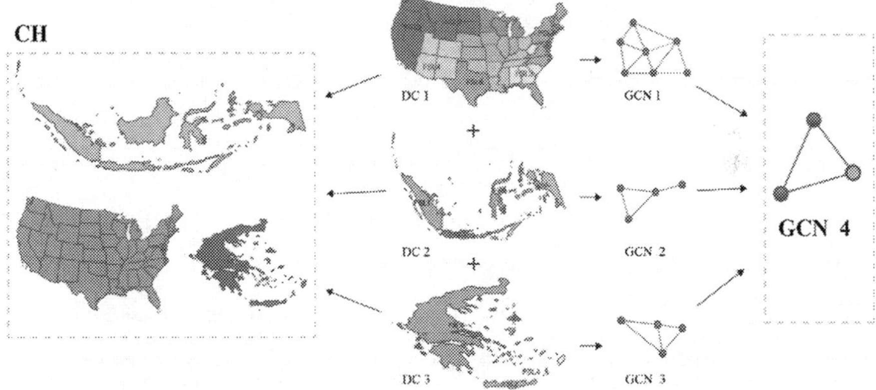

Fig. 2. The hierarchical structure of a typical service supply chain network that consists one CH, three DCs and many FSLs. Four GCNs are used to model spatial correlation within one CH and three DCs.

3.3 Temporal Alignment Attention Module

We denote $\widetilde{\boldsymbol{X}}_i^{(t)} = \Theta * g\, \boldsymbol{X}_i^{(t)} \in \mathbb{R}^{n_i \times D}$ and $\tilde{\boldsymbol{X}}^{(t)} = \left(\tilde{\boldsymbol{X}}_1^{(t)}, \tilde{\boldsymbol{X}}_2^{(t)}, .., \tilde{\boldsymbol{X}}_N^{(t)} \right) \in \mathbb{R}^{n \times D}$. D is feature dimension after the graph convolution. Take $\{\tilde{\boldsymbol{X}}^{(t)}\}_{t=1}^{T}$ as input, RNN encodes $\{\tilde{\boldsymbol{X}}^{(t)}\}_{t=1}^{T}$ into hidden states $\left\{\boldsymbol{h}^{(t)}\right\}_{t=1}^{T}$ via:

$$\boldsymbol{h}^{(t)} = LSTM^{int}\left(\tilde{\boldsymbol{X}}^{(t)}, \boldsymbol{h}^{(t-1)}\right) \tag{12}$$

where $LSTM^{int}$ is a long short memory architecture (LSTM) encoder to capture the long-range dependency proposed by [20]. To predict the desired service part demands $\{\boldsymbol{Y}^{(t)}\}_{t=T+1}^{T+\Delta}$, we adopt a LSTM decoder defined as

$$\boldsymbol{d}^{(t)} = LSTM^{dec}\left(\tilde{\boldsymbol{X}}^{(t)}, \boldsymbol{d}^{(t-1)}\right) \tag{13}$$

where $\boldsymbol{d}^{(t)} \in \left\{\boldsymbol{d}^{(t)}\right\}_{t=T+1}^{T+\Delta}$ is the hidden state to learn in the decoding process. Ideally, the learned hidden states $\left\{\boldsymbol{h}^{(t)}\right\}_{t=1}^{T}$ and $\left\{\boldsymbol{d}^{(t)}\right\}_{t=T+1}^{T+\Delta}$ carries contextual information in current and previous timestamps. However, the performance of the encoder-decoder networks decreases significantly when the length of time series increases. To alleviate this problem, we propose a temporal alignment attention model. At first, we concatenate Δ successive encoder hidden states as:

$$\boldsymbol{P}_i = \left[\boldsymbol{h}^{(i)}; \boldsymbol{h}^{(i+1)}; \ldots; \boldsymbol{h}^{(i+\Delta-1)}\right], 1 \leq i \leq T - \Delta + 1 \tag{14}$$

Similarly, we concatenate all the decoder hidden states as:

$$\tilde{\boldsymbol{P}} = \left[\boldsymbol{d}^{(T+1)}; \boldsymbol{d}^{(T+2)}; \ldots; \boldsymbol{d}^{(T+\Delta)}\right] \tag{15}$$

Then, we compute the relevance score between $\boldsymbol{P}_i \in \{\boldsymbol{P}_i\}_{i=1}^{T-\Delta+1}$ and $\tilde{\boldsymbol{P}}$ as $e_i = \tilde{\boldsymbol{P}}\boldsymbol{P}_i^T$ and find the maximum one, with $i_{max} = \text{argmax}\{e_i\}_{i=1}^{T-\Delta+1}$. Finally, we merge each pair in $\left\{\boldsymbol{h}^{(t)}\right\}_{t=i_{max}}^{i_{max}+\Delta-1}$ and $\left\{\boldsymbol{d}^{(t)}\right\}_{t=T+1}^{T+\Delta}$ into $\left\{\tilde{\boldsymbol{d}}^{(t)}\right\}_{t=T+1}^{T+\Delta}$ that contains the aligned long-distance encoder hidden states. We approximate the future service part demands with regression:

$$\hat{\boldsymbol{Y}}_1^{(t)} = \boldsymbol{A}\tilde{\boldsymbol{d}}^{(t)} + \boldsymbol{B} \tag{16}$$

$$\hat{\boldsymbol{Y}}^{(t)} = T_c \boldsymbol{Y}_1^{(t)} \tag{17}$$

where $\hat{\boldsymbol{Y}}_1^{(t)}$ denotes the predicted service part demand at bottom level and $\hat{\boldsymbol{Y}}^{(t)}$ denotes the predicted service part demands at all levels of the hierarchical structure. $\boldsymbol{A}$ and $\boldsymbol{B}$ are parameters to learn. For model learning, we apply mean squared error coupled with regularization term Reg multiplied by a coefficient λ:

$$\mathcal{L}_{loss} = \frac{1}{N}\left(\sum\nolimits_{n=1}^{N}\left(\sum\nolimits_{t=T+1}^{T+\Delta}\left(\hat{\boldsymbol{Y}}^{(t)} - \boldsymbol{Y}^{(t)}\right) + \lambda Reg\right)\right) \tag{18}$$

where N is the number of the batch size. In the training procedure, we leverage mini-batch Stochastic Gradient Decent (SGD) based algorithm, named Adam. We set the batch size as 128 and the starting learning rate as 0.001 which is reduced by 10% after 10,000 iterations.

4 Experiments

4.1 Experimental Datasets

We use one real-life dataset: Lenovo Group Ltd.'s service part demand data in India that has one DC and 17 FSLs. The dataset contains 17,467 stock keeping units (SKU) of service parts demand over five years. Except service parts demand data, other internal data like installed base, service parts category, etc., and external data like weather condition and holiday are collected. All the data is aggregated by week. We reduce the original dimensionality of categorical data by taking the 4th root of the number of categories. We use four years of data as the training set, the following six months as the validation set, and the final six months as the testing set.

4.2 Experimental Setup

In the experiments, we compute 26 weeks ahead rolling forecasts with 52 weeks historical demand observations and other features, i.e. $\Delta = 26$ and $T = 52$. The Adjacency matrix of the DC graph in India is computed based on the distances among FSLs in the service supply chain network. The weighted adjacency matrix $\boldsymbol{W}$ can be formed as,

$$w_{i,j} = \begin{cases} \exp\left(-\frac{d_{i,j}^2}{\sigma^2}\right), i \neq j \text{ and } \exp\left(-\frac{d_{i,j}^2}{\sigma^2}\right) \geq \varepsilon \\ 0, \text{otherwise.} \end{cases}$$

where $w_{i,j}$ is the weight of edge which is decided by $d_{i,j}$ (the distance between FSL i and j). σ^2 and ε are thresholds to control the matrix $\boldsymbol{W}$, assigned to 500 km and 10 km, respectively. Considering the computing efficiency, 1st-order approximation is used in this paper. Two stacks of the 1st-order approximation GCNs are applied vertically and convolution kernel of the first and the second GCN layers are $D_1 = 64$ and $D_2 = 32$, respectively. The LSTM encoder-decoder network is also two-layer LSTM, with 512 and 128 hidden states, respectively. The number of pairs of spatial attention matrixes $m = 10$ in the term *Reg*. To measure and evaluate the performance of different methods, Mean Absolute Percentage Errors (MAPE), and Root Mean Squared Errors (RMSE) are adopted. We compare our framework STAH with the following baselines: (1) Bottom-up Moving Average (MA); (2) Bottom-up Auto-Regressive Integrated Moving Average (ARIMA); (3) LSTM encoder-decoder (STAH without the spatial hierarchical attention module), (4) STAH model without temporal alignment attention.

4.3 Experiment Results

The prediction accuracy at each level and the average statistical results for the dataset are shown in Table 1, respectively. From the tables, we can see in general that the DC level prediction has less errors than the FSL level forecasts and our proposed model achieves the best performance in both levels. As we can see, Deep learning approaches generally achieved better prediction results than tradition models. Compared with baseline 3) that did not incorporate spatial topology, our model STAH has achieved a significant improvement. This demonstrates our model can effectively utilize spatial structure to make more accurate predictions.

Table 1. The comparison of MAPE and RMSE obtained by different methods.

Method	MAPE		RMSE	
	FSL	DC	FSL	DC
Bottom-up MA	8.97	5.92	1.32	16.85
Bottom-up ARIMA	10.12	6.37	1.53	18.76
Baseline 3)	7.32	5.71	1.21	13.64
Baseline 4)	6.84	4.98	1.13	12.19
STAH	**6.63**	**4.79**	**1.04**	**10.86**

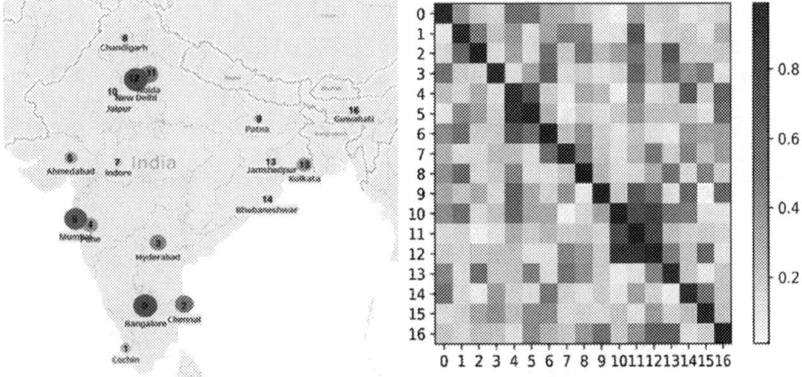

Fig. 3. The spatial attention matrix obtained from spatial hierarchical attention module.

In order to investigate the role of spatial attention mechanism in our model intuitively, we perform a case study: picking out ten service parts belonging to the same category and showing the average spatial attention matrix of the DC graph structure in the training set. As shown on the right side of Fig. 3, each element represents the correlation strength between the i-th FSL and the j-th FSL in India. The service part demand on the 10th FSL is closely related to the ones on the 11th and 12th FSLs. This is because they are close in space and customers in that regions who have service parts replacement requirements can go to one of them with no difference. This certainly explains why the spatial hierarchical attention module improves forecast accuracy and shows an interpretability advantage.

Compared with baseline 4), when removing the temporal alignment attention mechanism, the performance drops. So, we can conclude the temporal alignment attention contribute positively. Furthermore, we visualize one service part historical demand at the DC level together with the prediction results, as shown in Fig. 4. It highlights the aligned segment of service part historical demand and predicted service part demand. We find that two highlighted parts have similar trend and seasonality.

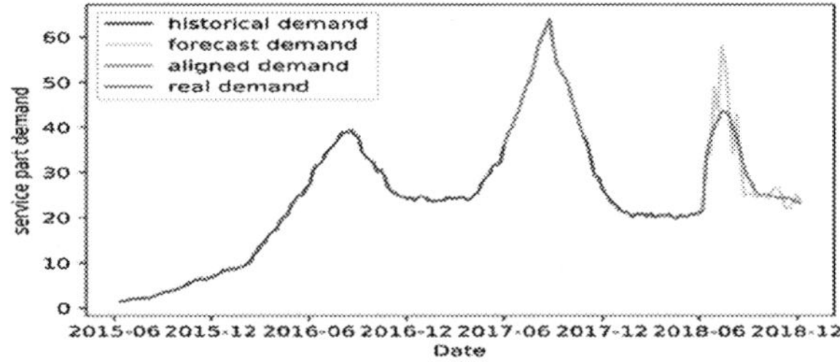

Fig. 4. Demonstration of the temporal alignment attention mechanism in the model STAH by visualizing one service part demand at the DC level.

Table 2. Demonstration the influence of the number of pairs of spatial attention matrixes in the *REG* term.

m	MAPE		RMSE	
	FSL	DC	FSL	DC
0	6.82	4.98	1.17	11.14
2	6.76	4.92	1.13	11.06
5	6.69	4.83	1.08	10.92
10	**6.63**	**4.79**	**1.04**	**10.86**
100	6.73	4.87	1.12	11.36

To study the effects of the hyperparameter m, we test 5 different values $m = 0, 2, 5, 10, 100$, as shown in Table 2. We observe the increase of the number of pairs of spatial attention matrixes m, the performance of the model first increases and then decreases. Larger m can decrease the flexibility and increase the generalization of the model at the cost of decrease model complexity and more prune to underfitting.

5 Conclusion and Future Work

In this paper, we propose a novel deep learning framework STAH for hierarchical service part demand forecast. Experiments show that our model not only achieves better performances but also increase the interpretability. In the future, we will further apply this model on more complicated service supply chain networks that have more levels to test the model's potential capability. Moreover, our proposed model can be applied into more general spatial-temporal structured sequence forecasting scenarios, such as electricity demand, preference prediction in recommendation system, etc.

References

1. Bacchetti, A., Saccani, N.: Spare parts classification and demand forecasting for stock control: investigating the gap between research and practice. Omega **40**, 722–737 (2012)

2. Assaad, M., Boné, R., Cardot, H.: A new boosting algorithm for improved time-series forecasting with recurrent neural networks. Inf. Fusion **9**, 41–55 (2008)
3. Box, G.E.P., Jenkins, G.M., Reinsel, G.C., Ljung, G.M.: Time series analysis: forecasting & control (2015)
4. Hyndman, R.J., Ahmed, R.A., Athanasopoulos, G., Shang, H.L.: Optimal combination forecasts for hierarchical time series. Comput. Stat. Data Anal. **55**, 2579–2589 (2011)
5. Athanasopoulos, G., Ahmed, R.A., Hyndman, R.J.: Hierarchical forecasts for Australian domestic tourism. Int. J. Forecast. **25**, 146–166 (2009)
6. de Livera, A.M., Hyndman, R.J., Snyder, R.D.: Forecasting time series with complex seasonal patterns using exponential smoothing. J. Am. Stat. Assoc. **106**, 1513–1527 (2011)
7. Ben Taieb, S., Rajagopal, R., Yu, J., Neves Barreto, M.: Regularization in hierarchical time series forecasting with application to electricity smart meter data. In: Conference on Artificial Intelligence (2017)
8. Wickramasuriya, S.L., Athanasopoulos, G., Hyndman, R.J.: Optimal forecast reconciliation for hierarchical and grouped time series through trace minimization. J. Am. Stat. Assoc. **114**, 804–819 (2018)
9. Niepert, M., Ahmed, M., Kutzkov, K.: Learning convolution neural networks for graphs. In: International Conference on Machine Learning, pp. 2014–2023 (2016)
10. Bruna, J., Zaremba, W., Szlam, A., LeCun, Y.: Spectral networks and locally connected networks on graphs. In: International Conference on Learning Representations (2014)
11. Defferrard, M., Bresson, X., Vandergheynst, P.: Convolutional neural networks on graphs with fast localized spectral filtering. In: Advances in Neural Information Processing Systems, pp. 3844–3852 (2016)
12. Kipf, T.N., Welling, M.: Semi-supervised classification with graph convolutional networks. In: International Conference on Learning Representations (2017)
13. Xu, K., et al.: Show, attend and tell: neural image caption generation with visual attention. In: International Conference on Machine Learning (2015)
14. Cheng, J., Dong, L., Lapata, M.: Long short-term memory-networks for machine reading. In: Conference on Empirical Methods on Natural Language Processing (2016)
15. Lin, Z., et al.: A structured self-attentive sentence embedding. In: International Conference on Learning Representations (2017)
16. Veličković, P., Cucurull, G., Casanova, A., Romero, A., Liò, P., Bengio, Y.: Graph attention networks. In: International Conference on Learning Representations (2018)
17. Liang, Y., Ke, S., Zhang, J., Yi, X., Zheng, Y.: Geoman: multi-level attention networks for geo-sensory time series prediction. In: International Joint Conference on Artificial Intelligence, pp. 3428–3434 (2018)
18. Guo, S., Lin, Y., Feng, N., Song, C., Wan, H.: Attention based spatial-temporal graph convolutional networks for traffic flow forecasting. In: Conference on Artificial Intelligence (2019)
19. Hammond, D.K., Vandergheynst, P., Gribonval, R.: Wavelets on graphs via spectral graph theory. Appl. Comput. Harmon. Anal. **30**, 129–150 (2011)
20. Hochreiter, S., Schmidhuber, J.: Long short-term memory. Neural Comput. **9**, 1735–1780 (1997)

Disentangling Latent Emotions of Word Embeddings on Complex Emotional Narratives

Zhengxuan Wu[1(✉)] and Yueyi Jiang[2]

[1] Stanford University, Stanford, CA 94085, USA
wuzhengx@stanford.edu
[2] University of California San Diego, La Jolla, CA 92093, USA
yujiang@ucsd.edu

Abstract. Word embedding models such as GloVe are widely used in natural language processing (NLP) research to convert words into vectors. Here, we provide a preliminary guide to probe latent emotions in text through GloVe word vectors. First, we trained a neural network model to predict continuous emotion valence ratings by taking linguistic inputs from Stanford Emotional Narratives Dataset (SEND). After interpreting the weights in the model, we found that only a few dimensions of the word vectors contributed to expressing emotions in text, and words were clustered on the basis of their emotional polarities. Furthermore, we performed a linear transformation that projected high dimensional embedded vectors into an *emotion space*. Based on NRC Emotion Lexicon (EmoLex), we visualized the entanglement of emotions in the lexicon by using both projected and raw GloVe word vectors. We showed that, in the proposed *emotion space*, we were able to better disentangle emotions than using raw GloVe vectors alone. In addition, we found that the sum vectors of different pairs of emotion words successfully captured expressed human feelings in the EmoLex. For example, the sum of two embedded word vectors expressing *Joy* and *Trust* which express *Love* shared high similarity (similarity score .62) with the embedded vector expressing *Optimism*. On the contrary, this sum vector was dissimilar (similarity score −.19) with the embedded vector expressing *Remorse*. In this paper, we argue that through the proposed *emotion space*, arithmetic of emotions is preserved in the word vectors. The affective representation uncovered in emotion vector space could shed some light on how to help machines to disentangle emotion expressed in word embeddings.

Keywords: Word embeddings · Emotional semantics · Affective computing

1 Introduction

Constructing human-friendly Artificial Intelligence (AI) is essential for humans as it will help us get the most benefits from AI systems [13]. Being able to detect emotions through language is the building block of such AI agents [11,17]. One such way is through word embeddings - encoding words in vectors. Researchers have proposed various word embedding methods such as GloVe and Word2Vec [10,15]. However, to date, understanding the expressed human emotions in text from word embeddings by an

J. Tang et al. (Eds.): NLPCC 2019, LNAI 11839, pp. 587–595, 2019.
https://doi.org/10.1007/978-3-030-32236-6_53

agent remains a challenging problem, as word embedding based models are generally missing the direct interpretations of the word vectors [1,5].

In this study, we provide different strategies for interpreting the emotional semantics of words through word embeddings. We visualize word clusters by projecting word vectors into 2-dimensional space where embedding vectors are clustered by their emotional polarities. Additionally, based on the weights of a pretrained neural network model, we are able to project words into an *emotion space*. We show that the arithmetic of emotions holds, which is consistent with the principle introduced by Plutchik [16]. An example is as follows:

$$v_{\text{Love}} = v_{\text{Joy}} + v_{\text{Trust}} \tag{1}$$

We also show that words with opposite emotion valence separated in the *emotion space*. Rather than relying on dictionaries or hidden layers of neural networks, we provide a preliminary method of probing emotion entanglements in word vectors, making one initial step in exploring the latent emotions in word embeddings from modeling emotions in complex narratives.

2 Related Works

Word embeddings are widely applied in sentiment analysis with neural network models [2,3,19]. However, these models often lack clear interpretations of word vectors [7]. To date, only few studies have probed the semantics of emotions from word embeddings [8,18]. These studies attempted to interpret natural language models through visualization of word vectors and hidden layers of the models. For example, researchers have visualized the hidden layers' representation of word vectors in 2-dimensional space in which words with similar meanings are clustered together [4,6]. Additionally, other methods have focused on visualizing the hidden layers of neural network models using gradients and weights inferred from the models [7,8,18].

In this study, we aim to provide a systematic way of identifying emotions directly from text. Using embedded vectors, our method is different from the existing research that has focused on deriving latent semantic information from hidden layers of the neural network models [7,8]. Throughout the paper, we provide preliminary evidence for detecting emotions in word vectors through word embeddings specifically in emotional expressions.

3 Dataset

In this paper, we used Stanford Emotional Narratives Dataset (SEND) as our dataset. SEND is comprised of transcripts of video recordings in which participants shared emotional stories, and it has been well explored in computational models of emotion [12,19]. In each transcript, timestamps were generated for every word based on force-alignments[1] of audio inputs, and continuous emotional valence ratings were collected by annotators[2]. These ratings serve as the target variable in our model, which were scaled between $[-1,1]$ and sampled every 0.5 s.

The dataset includes 193 transcripts that last on average 2 mins 15 s, for a total duration of 7 hrs and 15 mins. We divided these transcripts into a **Train set** (60% of the dataset, 117 videos, 38 targets, 4 hrs 26 mins long), a **Validation set** (20%, 38 videos, 27 targets, 1 hr 23 mins long) and a **Test set** (20%, 38 videos, 27 targets, 1 hr 26 mins long).

4 Autoregressive Model

To interpret the word vectors, we trained an autoregressive linear model to predict emotional valence ratings. We first used 300-dimensional GloVe word vectors which were pre-trained on wikipages [15]. Then, we used `interp` function in `numpy` package to assign each word a valence rating by linearly interpolating the original ratings using the timestamps for each word.

By concatenating the word vector $v_t \in \mathbb{R}^{e\times 1}$ where e is 300 for GloVe from the current time point (at time t) with the hidden state vector $h_{t-\tau} \in \mathbb{R}^{300\times 1}$ where h is 300 from last time point (at time $t-\tau$), we produced a hidden vector $h_t \in \mathbb{R}^{600\times 1}$ for the current time point. The hidden vector was then passed into a linear layer with bias to produce a output vector $o_t \in \mathbb{R}^{300\times 1}$. Subsequently, the output vector was passed into a linear layer which produced a single pseudo-rating prediction u_t for the current time point. The final rating prediction r_t was produced by a self-learned linear filter by taking $r_{t-\tau}$ into account:

$$h_t = \text{Concat}(h_{t-\tau}, v_t) \tag{2}$$

$$o_t = [\mathbf{W}_\text{h}, \mathbf{W}_\text{v}]h_t + \mathbf{b}_\text{h} \tag{3}$$

$$u_t = \mathbf{W}_\text{o} o_t + \mathbf{b}_\text{o} \tag{4}$$

$$r_t = \sigma r_{t-\tau} + (1-\sigma)u_t \tag{5}$$

with weight matrices $\mathbf{W}_\text{h}, \mathbf{W}_\text{v} \in \mathbb{R}^{300\times 300}$, $\mathbf{W}_\text{o} \in \mathbb{R}^{300\times 1}$ and bias vectors $\mathbf{b}_\text{h} \in \mathbb{R}^{600\times 300}$, $\mathbf{b}_\text{o} \in \mathbb{R}^{300\times 1}$. We used σ to denote the weight on previous rating prediction.

5 Model Evaluation

Before interpreting the model results, we ensured that the optimal performance was achieved. Similar to the evaluation metric used in a previous study on SEND [19], Concordance Correlation Coefficient (CCC, as defined by [9]) was evaluated. Specifically, we compared model performance on the **Validation set** and **Test set** with the human

---

[1] https://github.com/ucbvislab/p2fa-vislab.

[2] We have 25 ratings per transcript from annotators. The target variable is the average collected ratings.

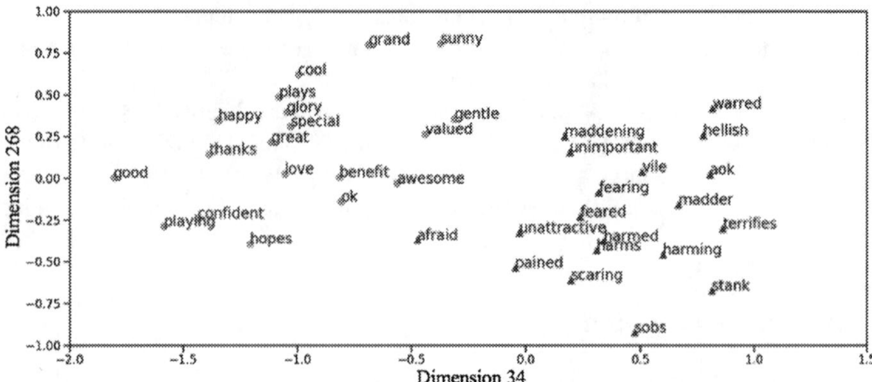

Fig. 1. Visualization of word clusters by their emotional polarities (i.e., positive or negative). Positive words are represented as red circles, while negative words are shown in blue triangles. (Color figure online)

benchmark provided by SEND. Our model achieved a CCC of $.37 \pm .11$ on the **Validation set** and $.35 \pm .15$ on the **Test set**, comparing to human's performance of a CCC of $.47 \pm .12$ on the **Validation set** and $.46 \pm .14$ on the **Test set**. In our final model, the learnable parameter σ is 0.84, indicating that the current prediction at time t is primarily dependent on the previous state at time $t-1$.

6 Experiment and Results

6.1 Pure on Weights

By using the weights from two linear layers, each dimension was assigned a score to quantify its contribution to emotion valence in words (Algorithm 1). Higher absolute weights are associated with larger gradient changes in outputs, indicating higher importance in emotion expression in a given dimension.

Algorithm 1: Scoring algorithm for ranking important dimensions of GloVe vectors in emotion expression

Result: Scores for each dimension

```
dim_scores = {};
for i ∈ {1, ..., 300} do
    _score = 0.0;
    for w_j ∈ W_{v_i} do
        _score += w_j · W_{o_i};
    end
    dim_scores[i] = abs(_score);
end
```

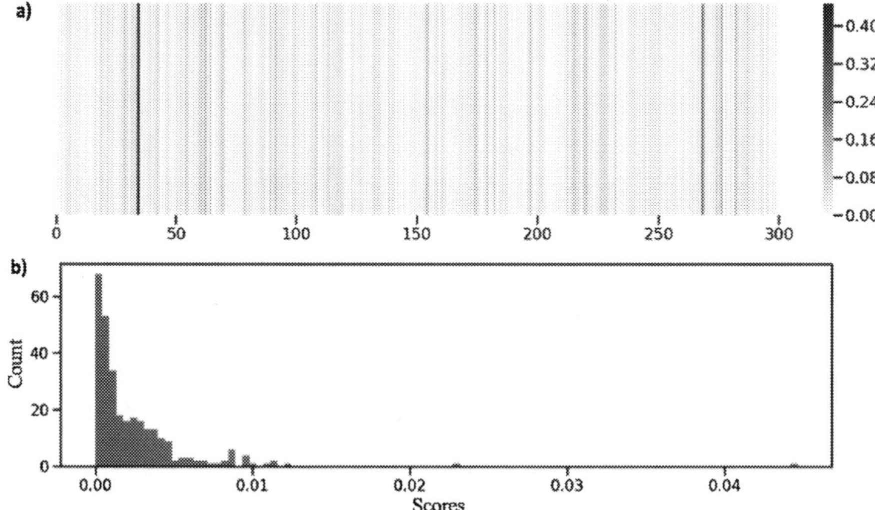

Fig. 2. Illustration of calculated scores on each dimension of the 300-dimensional GloVe vectors. (a) Heatmap of scores for each dimension in GloVe vectors. (b) Distribution of scores across all dimensions.

Based on the scores, we first produced a heatmap (Fig. 2a) for all 300 dimensions in GloVe vectors to visualize the importance of each dimension. In addition, we plotted the distribution of scores (Fig. 2b). We found that a large portion of dimensions were non-expressive in emotion valence. Specifically, we discovered that the 34th dimension of the GloVe vectors is the most important dimension in expressing emotions in word vectors.

6.2 2-D Emotion Visualization

Based on the scores for all dimensions, we picked out the top 2 dimensions and visualized the clustering effect of words. We used out-of-sample words from LIWC 2007 [14] from which we selected top 19 words ranked by their gradients of forward propagation for positive and negative polarities, respectively. Figure 1 shows that words with positive meaning are well separated from words with negative meaning in this space. Subsequently, we showed that the dimensions picked by our scoring algorithm (Algorithm 1) could be used to separate words into clusters that represent two emotion polarities, positive and negative emotions.

6.3 Entanglement of Emotions

EmoLex has eight categories of word groups by emotions: *Joy*, *Trust*, *Anticipation*, *Surprise*, *Fear*, *Anger*, *Disgust* and *Sadness*. To show the entanglements of emotions in GloVe word vectors, we first randomly selected word pairs from any two distinct emotions of the eight emotion categories. We then exhaustively calculated the average

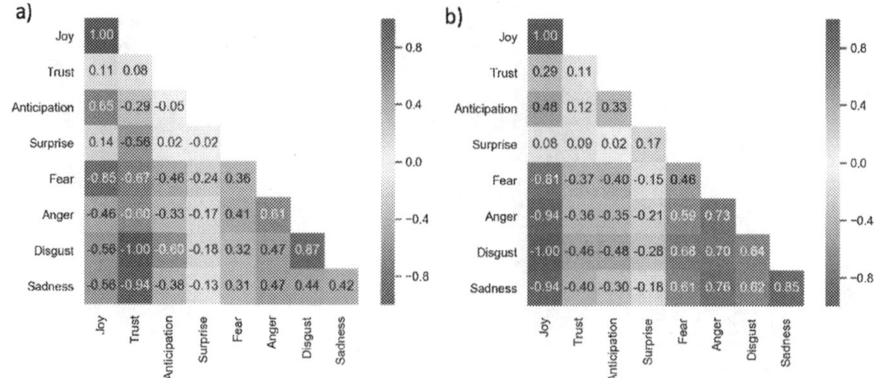

Fig. 3. Heatmaps of cosine similarities scores between words with paired emotions. (a) is produced by using the raw GloVe vector. (b) is produced by using the projected GloVe vectors.

cosine similarity scores between these word pairs and produced heatmaps with 8×8 similarity scores by

$$\text{similarity} = \cos(\theta) = \frac{\mathbf{A} \cdot \mathbf{B}}{\|\mathbf{A}\|\|\mathbf{B}\|} = \frac{\sum_{i=1}^{n} A_i B_i}{\sqrt{\sum_{i=1}^{n} A_i^2}\sqrt{\sum_{i=1}^{n} B_i^2}} \tag{6}$$

To investigate if words are better clustered by emotional polarity in the proposed *emotion space*, we projected word vectors to this space by calculating element-wise multiplication of the weight $\mathbf{W}_v$ from our model and raw word vectors. Based on the heatmap (Fig. 3), we found that word vectors in the *emotion space* were better clustered by emotional polarity than raw GloVe vectors. For example, using the raw GloVe vectors, words expressing *Anticipation* had a low similarity score ($-.29$) with *Trust*, even though both words are associated with positive valence. However, after we projected the words into the *emotion space*, the similarity scores drastically increased. Thus, the results suggest that the projected GloVe vectors may provide better interpretations of emotion expressions in words.

6.4 Arithmetic of Emotions

In this section, we demonstrate that with the linear projection matrix $\mathbf{W}_v$ from the pre-trained model, word vectors is transformed into a *emotion space* where the arithmetic of emotions (Table 1) is better represented compared to using raw GloVe vectors. According to Plutchiks wheel of emotions [16], feelings are combinations of two emotions. For example, *Love* is a combination of *Joy* and *Trust*. We want to examine if this arithmetic of emotions is preserved with word embeddings, which means whether the sum of word vectors expressing *Joy* and *Trust* has a high similarity score with the word vector of *Love*. First, we formulated vectors representing the feeling that EmoLex is

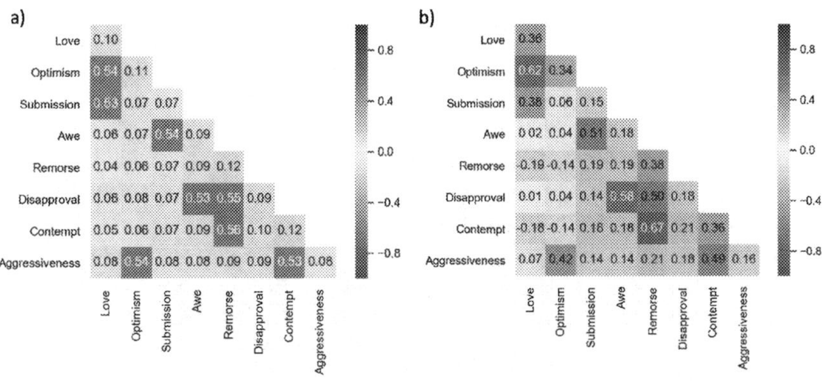

Fig. 4. Heatmaps of cosine similarities scores between words with paired feelings. (a) is produced by using the raw GloVe vector. (b) is produced by using the projected GloVe vectors.

Table 1. Taxonomy of feelings and arithmetic of emotions. The **Opposite** column represents a list of opposite feelings of the first column which is based on Plutchiks wheel of emotions [16].

Feelings	Emotions	Opposite	Emotions
Love	Joy + Trust	Remorse	Sadness + Disgust
Optimism	Anticipation + Joy	Disapproval	Surprise + Sadness
Submission	Trust + Fear	Contempt	Disgust + Anger
Awe	Fear + Surprise	Aggressiveness	Anger + Anticipation

missing. For instance, we randomly paired words expressing *Joy* and *Trust* and added up word vectors from each pair to formulate a groups of vectors representing the feeling *Love*. Then, similar to the previous analysis, we calculated the average similarity scores between any two pairs of feelings using the generated word vectors. Ideally, the similarity score between two opposite feelings should be low whereas the score between two similar feelings should be high.

Based on our heatmap (Fig. 4), we found that arithmetic of emotions was not well preserved with raw GloVe vectors given the fact that the vectors of feelings had extremely low similarity scores with themselves. For example, the similarity scores between *Love* and itself is only .10. Meanwhile, opposite feelings had higher similarity scores than expected. In the *emotion space*, the distribution of similarity scores were more systematic. For example, the similarity scores between *Love* and itself increased to .36 whereas the similarity scores between two opposite feelings *Love* and *Remorse* decreased to −.19.

7 Conclusion

In the present study, we demonstrate that word embeddings with GloVe preserve latent emotions in text. By ranking weights across dimensions of the GloVe vectors, we show that majorities of dimensions are not associated with emotion representations in words. Additionally, from the top two dimensions ranked by importance, we demonstrate that words can be clustered by emotional polarity (Fig. 1).

Using a projection matrix to transform the original GloVe vectors, we find that in the proposed *emotion space*, arithmetic of emotions is better represented compared to using the raw vectors alone. By comparing the similarities across vectors, we demonstrate that words with opposite emotional meanings are well separated in the *emotion space*. Meanwhile, we show that arithmetic of emotions is a good proxy of human feelings in the proposed space, consistent with the Plutchik's theory of emotions. Our preliminary exploration shed some lights on modeling the inter-relations in different emotion categories through word embeddings, and encourages more refined research in probing emotion expressions in other types of word embeddings.

References

1. Bordes, A., Weston, J., Usunier, N.: Open question answering with weakly supervised embedding models. In: Calders, T., Esposito, F., Hüllermeier, E., Meo, R. (eds.) ECML PKDD 2014. LNCS (LNAI), vol. 8724, pp. 165–180. Springer, Heidelberg (2014). https://doi.org/10.1007/978-3-662-44848-9_11
2. Donahue, J., et al.: Long-term recurrent convolutional networks for visual recognition and description. In: Proceedings of the IEEE Conference on Computer Vision and Pattern Recognition, pp. 2625–2634 (2015)
3. Ebrahimi Kahou, S., Michalski, V., Konda, K., Memisevic, R., Pal, C.: Recurrent neural networks for emotion recognition in video. In: Proceedings of the 2015 ACM on International Conference on Multimodal Interaction, pp. 467–474. ACM (2015)
4. Faruqui, M., Dyer, C.: Improving vector space word representations using multilingual correlation. In: Proceedings of the 14th Conference of the European Chapter of the Association for Computational Linguistics, pp. 462–471 (2014)
5. Gu, J., Bradbury, J., Xiong, C., Li, V.O., Socher, R.: Non-autoregressive neural machine translation. arXiv preprint arXiv:1711.02281 (2017)
6. Ji, Y., Eisenstein, J.: Representation learning for text-level discourse parsing. In: Proceedings of the 52nd Annual Meeting of the Association for Computational Linguistics (Volume 1: Long Papers), vol. 1, pp. 13–24 (2014)
7. Li, J., Chen, X., Hovy, E., Jurafsky, D.: Visualizing and understanding neural models in nlp. arXiv preprint arXiv:1506.01066 (2015)
8. Li, M., Lu, Q., Long, Y., Gui, L.: Inferring affective meanings of words from word embedding. IEEE Trans. Affect. Comput. **8**(4), 443–456 (2017)
9. Lin, L.I.K.: A concordance correlation coefficient to evaluate reproducibility. Biometrics **45**(1), 255–268 (1989)
10. Mikolov, T., Chen, K., Corrado, G., Dean, J.: Efficient estimation of word representations in vector space. arXiv preprint arXiv:1301.3781 (2013)
11. Morelli, S.A., Ong, D.C., Makati, R., Jackson, M.O., Zaki, J.: Empathy and well-being correlate with centrality in different social networks. Proc. Nat. Acad. Sci. USA **114**(37), 9843–9847 (2017)

12. Ong, D.C., Wu, Z., Zhi-Xuan, T., Reddan, M., Kahhale, I., Mattek, A., Zaki, J.: Modeling emotion in complex stories: the Stanford Emotional Narratives Dataset (Invited Revision to Journal)
13. Ong, D.C., Zaki, J., Goodman, N.D.: Affective cognition: exploring lay theories of emotion. Cognition **143**, 141–162 (2015)
14. Pennebaker, J.W., Francis, M.E., Booth, R.J.: Linguistic inquiry and word count: Liwc 2001. Mahway: Lawrence Erlbaum Associates **71**(2001), 2001 (2001)
15. Pennington, J., Socher, R., Manning, C.: Glove: global vectors for word representation. In: Proceedings of the 2014 Conference on Empirical Methods in Natural Language Processing (EMNLP), pp. 1532–1543 (2014)
16. Plutchik, R.: A general psychoevolutionary theory of emotion. In: Theories of Emotion, pp. 3–33. Elsevier, Amsterdam (1980)
17. Preston, S.D., De Waal, F.B.: Empathy: its ultimate and proximate bases. Behav. Brain Sci. **25**(1), 1–20 (2002)
18. Seyeditabari, A., Zadrozny, W.: Can word embeddings help find latent emotions in text? preliminary results. In: The Thirtieth International Flairs Conference (2017)
19. Wu, Z., Zhang, X., Zhi-Xuan, T., Zaki, J., Ong, D.C.: Attending to emotional narratives. IEEE Affective Computing and Intelligent Interaction (ACII) (2019)

Modeling Human Intelligence in Customer-Agent Conversation Using Fine-Grained Dialogue Acts

Qicheng Ding[1(✉)], Guoguang Zhao[2], Penghui Xu[1], Yucheng Jin[1], Yu Zhang[1], Changjian Hu[2], Qianying Wang[1], and Feiyu Xu[2]

[1] Lenovo Research, Technical Strategy and Innovation Platform, Beijing, China
dingqc1@lenovo.com

[2] Lenovo Research, AI Lab, Beijing, China
zhaogg1@lenovo.com

Abstract. Smart service chatbot, aiming to provide efficient, reliable and natural customer service, has grown rapidly in recent years. The understanding of human-agent conversation, especially modeling the conversational behavior, is essential to enhance the machine intelligence during the customer-chatbot interaction. However, there is a gap between qualitative behavior description and the corresponding technical application. In this paper, we developed a novel fine-grained dialogue act framework specific to smartphone customer service to tackle this problem. First of all, following a data-driven process, we defined a two-level classification to capture the most common conversational behavior during smartphone customer service such as affirm, deny, gratitude etc., and verified it by tagging chatlog generated by human agent. Then, using this framework, we designed a series of technically feasible dialogue policies to output human-like response. As an example, we realized a smart service chatbot for a smartphone customer using the dialogue-act-based policy. Finally, a user study was conducted to verify its efficiency and naturalness. Since the dialogue acts are meaningful abstraction of conversational behavior, the dialogue-act-based chatbot could be more explainable and flexible than the end-to-end solution.

Keywords: Dialogue act · Dialogue policy · Customer service · Chatbot

1 Introduction

With the proliferation of artificial intelligence (AI), many companies have built a service bot to increase customer engagement and save the cost [1]. Chatbots have been largely used as digital assistants on messaging platforms such as Messenger and WeChat. Messenger announced they had more than 300,000 chatbots until May, 2018.

Q. Ding and G. Zhao—Both authors contributed equally to this research.

J. Tang et al. (Eds.): NLPCC 2019, LNAI 11839, pp. 596–606, 2019.
https://doi.org/10.1007/978-3-030-32236-6_54

Moreover, according to a Business Intelligence research[1], chatbots allow companies to have a significant yearly cost saving up to 46%.

Unlike an open-ended dialogue chatbot such as XiaoIce, service chatbot is a task-focused agent that aims to make customers satisfied by solving their issues in focused scope effectively such as after-sale service for their products [2]. Compared to live chat, chatbot has many advantages in customer service such as quick response, 24/7 availability, multitasking. However, as a service provider, we may worry about if putting customer conversations in the hand of machines will degrade the service quality and damage customer experience. Therefore, we need to learn from human agent by extracting their conversational behavior and applying them to chatbots.

Therefore, to bridge the qualitive human conversational strategies with automated chatbot interaction, a technical-feasible approach that quantitatively describe the conversational behavior is necessary. Dialogue acts represent the intention behind an utterance in conversation to achieve a conversational goal [3], and they can be technically recognized like [4, 5]. Analyzing the human conversation in terms of dialogue acts such as statements or requests, can give essential meta-information about conversation flow and content [6], and can be used as a first step to develop automated chatbots [7]. For example, one basic descriptive strategy is "Checking if the customer has any other question when he/she expresses that his/her issue has been solved". This can be codified into a technical solution using dialogue acts, such as "After the agent outputs Proposing Solution act, if the user inputs dialogue acts that relate to problem has been solved, such as Accept, Thank or Will Try, then the agent should output acts combination such as Thank + Offer Help to check if the user has any other question".

Researchers have established various of dialogue framework such as [6, 8, 9], however, in terms of smartphone customer service, a specific dialogue act framework is needed. There is more domain-specific behavior such as "I will try the solution" that need extra act to capture. Besides, we observed that customer and agent demonstrate different conversational behavior, therefore, these two roles need different act frameworks for better description, recognition and prediction. Additionally, one sentence can have multiple intents [5]. Dialogue act framework needs to consider using multiple acts to extract major intentions. However, this paper intends to utilize dialogue acts to construct technically feasible dialogue policies. The multiple acts will increase the complexity of framework dramatically. As a preliminary exploration, we focus on depicting the major act in each user input and representing agent output with multiple acts.

In this work, following a data-driven process, we developed a novel fine-grained dialogue act framework to describe quantitatively conversational behavior in the field of smartphone customer service. Then, to transfer the human intelligence to machine intelligence, we designed a series of technically feasible dialogue policies using dialogue acts to generate human-like response automatically. On top of these, we realized a smartphone customer service chatbot as an example and conduct a user study to verify its efficiency and experience. The major contributions here include (1) a novel two-level fine-grained dialogue act framework specific to smartphone customer service;

[1] https://chatbotsmagazine.com/chatbot-report-2018-global-trends-and-analysis-4d8bbe4d924b?gi=3dd7bc9b669c.

(2) a technically-feasible process to transfer human intelligence into machine intelligence by dialogue-act-based policy which makes the technical realization more flexible and explainable; (3) a smartphone customer service chatbot to verify the feasibility and experience of our dialogue act framework.

2 Related Work

Many researchers with different backgrounds studying human conversations and developing computational speech and dialogue act models [3, 10]. [8, 11, 12] used more generic labels in order to cover the majority of dialogue acts in a conversation. In 1997, Core and Allen [11] presented the Dialogue Act Marking in Several Layers (DAMSL) as a standard for conversation annotation. The framework contains 220 tags, divided into four main categories: communicative status, information level, forward-looking function, and backward-looking function. [8, 12] established less fine-grained framework for general conversation. However, the generic framework falls short in understanding and analyzing customer service conversations.

Specific to task-oriented dialogue such as customer service, Ivanovic modeled Instant Messaging dialogue using 12 act labels, e.g., Statement, Open-Questions, then proposed a method to predict utterances in task-oriented dialogue using their labels [13]. Following Ivanovic's work, Kim et al. [9] classified dialogue acts in both one-on-one and multi-party Instant Messaging chats. More recent works of dialogue acts modeling for customer service conversations on Twitter can be seen [5] etc.

Considering that our research aims to code conversational behavior in smartphone customer service, we need to expand aforementioned acts and develop a more fine-grained framework. The most similar work to ours is that Oraby et al. on developing a taxonomy of dialogue acts frequently observed in customer service on Twitter [6]. They proposed a two-level framework, the first level is more generic including Greeting, Statement etc. The second level contains over twenty specific acts such as Opening, Yes-No Question etc. Rather than focusing on Twitter, we seek to model the dialogue behavior occurring in smartphone customer service domain.

3 Dialogue Act Framework

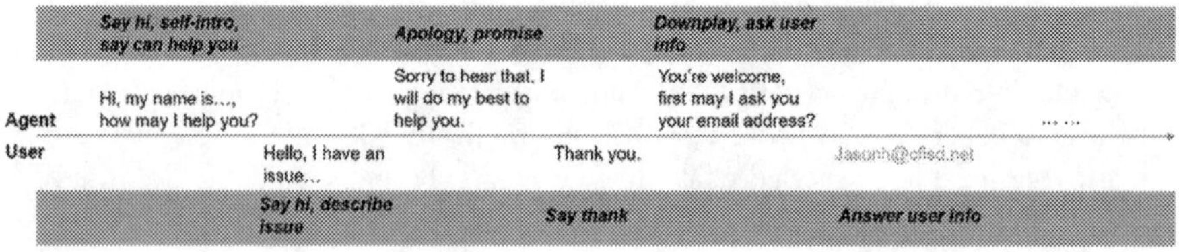

Fig. 1. An example of human agent chatlog abstraction

This section describes how we built a dialogue act framework for smartphone customer service. We selected randomly twenty human conversation chatlog from customer service center, then tagged each sentence using keywords to represent the main meanings (abstraction) as shown in Fig. 1. Then we captured major conversational behavior such as asking issue, affirm/deny a feedback etc. Due to the different roles of customer and agent, they exhibited different keyword sets, therefore, we established two frameworks to classify customer and agent act respectively: dialogue act/user and dialogue act bot (We use "user act" and "bot act" due to the usage in human-bot interaction).

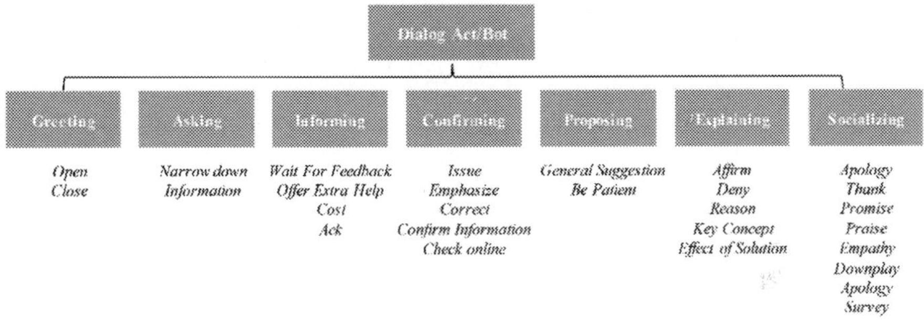

Fig. 2. The dialogue act framework for bot act part

We established the dialogue act framework using iterative reconstruction. At first, we compared each keyword with acts from previous work, then selected the most suitable one as our dialogue act and gave it an operative definition. If there is a keyword that cannot be classified by existing acts, we will define a new one and recheck all tagged core meaning to see if there is any one belong to this new act. We continued this iteration until there is no new act appeared, this procedure could assure that our framework covers the major conversational behavior. Finally, we re-organized all the acts into a two-level hierarchical framework.

Figures 2 and 3 demonstrate the dialogue act/user and dialogue act/bot respectively. Dialogue act/user contains six first-level acts: Greeting, Asking, Informing, Feedback, Explaining and Socializing. Dialogue act/bot has two more first level acts: Confirming and Proposing, and no Feedback category. As for the second level, there are quite different acts because of the different purposes of customer and agent.

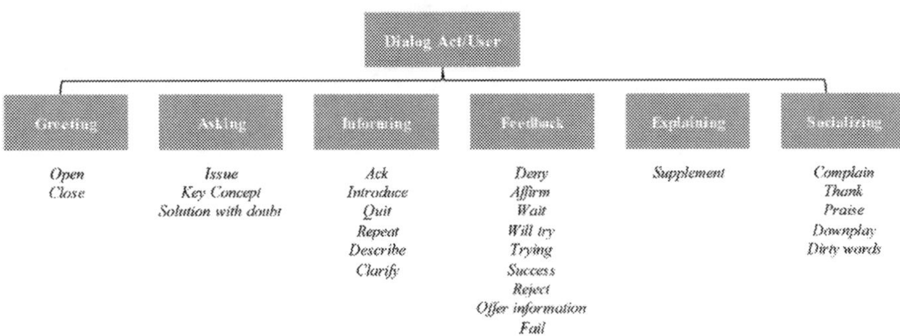

Fig. 3. The dialogue act framework for user act part

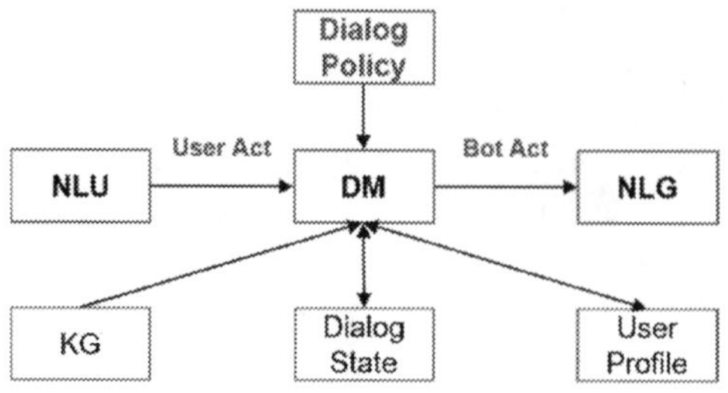

Fig. 4. A service chatbot framework using dialogue act as information carrier.

4 Dialogue-Act-Based Policy

After establishing the dialogue act framework, the next step is to construct technically feasible policies so that human intelligence can be transferred into chatbot. Additionally, since we used dialogue acts as information carrier, the whole process such as what kind of user behavior, what kind of bot response etc., is clear to us, then we could modify the bot strategy by simply changing the output bot acts. Therefore, the chatbot can be more explainable and flexible.

Figure 4 illustrates our service chatbot framework using dialogue act as information carrier. The NLU module (natural language understanding) extracts user input such as intents, user behavior and passes to DM (dialogue management) module by dialogue act. The DM combines user act, KG (knowledge graph), dialogue state and user profile together to generate policies, and passes to NLG (natural language generation) through bot act. The NLG is responsible to output human-like sentence based on bot act.

To better handle user response, we divided the conversation into four phases: Opening, Targeting, Solving and Ending. Opening contains conversation at the beginning to the user states phone issues, following is Targeting phase which refers to varied questions (e.g., phone model) leading to final solutions. Solving phase starts with proposing final solutions, and ends with the user accepts the solution or transfers to live agent. Ending phase includes questions before closing the conversation.

With the conversation phased, bot could customize its next step. Figure 5 demonstrates dialogue policies examples. For each policy, dialogue act/user describes user's input (e.g., Open). Then bot combines user act, dialogue state (Opening phase) together to plan next bot intent (e.g., Waiting for Issue), and use dialogue act/bot to express its strategy (e.g., Greeting-Open + Informing-Introduce + Asking-Offer Help). After that, the NLG generates human-like response based on the dialogue-act-based policy (e.g., "Hi, my name is XX. How may I help you?").

User Act	Sub-act	Bot Next Intent	Bot Act	Example	Case Phase	Context
Greeting	Open	**Waiting for issue**	Greeting-Open + Informing-Introduce + Asking - Offer Help	Hi, my name is Moli. How may I help you?	Opening	No question left for last visit
		Check the question left on last visit	Greeting-Open + Asking-Before Issue	Hi, how about the XX question you mentioned last time?	Opening	Have question left for last visit
		Treat as Digress			Targeting/Solving/Ending	
	Close	**Close Case by offering extra help**	Greeting-Close + Informing-Offer Extra Help	Bye, if you need other help, please contact ...	Ending	Closing case for the first time
		Close Case directly	Greeting-Close	Bye	Ending	Closing case again

Fig. 5. Examples of dialogue act-based dialogue policy

5 Technical Realization

The main DM tasks include status-tracking, decision-making and topic-management. Therefore, the DM architecture (Fig. 6) is roughly divided into three parts: Hypothesis Rank and Select (HRS) and Carry Over, Task Processing Layer, and Making Plans.

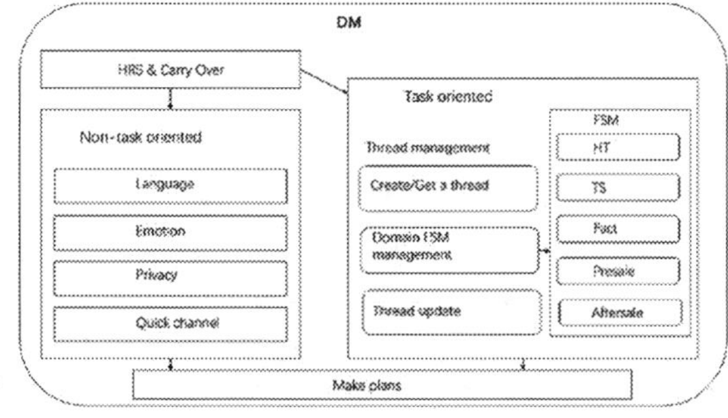

Fig. 6. Dialogue Management architecture, include task-oriented module and non-task-oriented module

Hypothesis Rank and Select and Carry Over

The main purpose of this layer is to determine the user intent. There are two ways to determine the user's intent. One is that the NLU can directly and undoubtedly present the user's intent. The other is that the NLU can present the user vague intent or only some hints. At this moment, the system needs to use context to infer the user's real intent and confirm with users by dialogue acts. Since the first way is self-explanatory, this section will focus less on the first way but more on the second way.

The arbitrariness and incompleteness of the user expression brings a challenge for the dialogue system to understand user intent. In a real conversation, the user does not speak a complete sentence, which often lacks a subject or a predicate. At the same time, users are very resistant to repeating previously given information, such as addresses, models, and emails etc. According to the analysis of online logs, the main problems solved by contextual inference are shown in Table 1 below. If the user's intentions are uncertain, we can confirm with the user through the interaction of dialogue acts.

Table 1. The task of module is slot inference and intention inference

Question type	Description
Slot inference	Get the current required slots from User Profile, such as mailbox, SN code, IMEI
Intention inference	When the user's intention is unclear, the system can use context reasoning to confirm its real intention

Task Processing Layer

Task processing layer has two major parts. One is the non-task-oriented processing, which includes unsupported languages, emotions, privacy etc. The process in this part is mainly for prompting users with specific words. The second is task-oriented task domain processing. The so-called "task domain" refers to the question asked by the user, which is closely related to specific business problem provided by the current system. A specific task is the user's specific problem, also known as the user intent.

We use a two-tier structure to fully process user intents. We name the first level as "conversation thread", meaning that the current user intent is managed as a session thread that continues until the user solves the problem. On the second level, we use different finite state machines to follow up the processing state of the user intent and adopt different strategies to interact with the user in different states, so as to complete solving the user questions.

Conversation Thread Management

According to specific scenarios, and for the convenience of managing individual conversations, we defined three states: Active, Pause, and Finish. For example, a new intent is started before the user finishes an intent. The original intent is paused, and the new intent is activated. When the new intent completes (Finish), the user can arbitrarily choose whether to continue (Active) or abandon (Finish) the original intent.

Slot Based Finite State Machine

For multiple states in a conversation, it is better to use a state machine for maintenance. This system adopts the hierarchical structure. The first layer state machine is responsible for switching process between the five task domains (how to; trouble shooting; after sale; presale; facts). The state machine design for each task domain is slightly different. This study takes "How to" domain as an example to explain the design process.

Table 2. The state's meaning of HowTo finite state machine and corresponding dialogue acts

FSM state	Description	Dialogue act
init	Original state	Opening
slotNotFull	Insufficient slot information	Asking information
waitUserInput	Wait for information from the user	Waiting feedback
slotClarify	Verify the information provided by the user	Confirm information
slotFull	Verify user intent	General suggestion
deliverAnswer	Push answers to users	Implementable suggestion
errorHandling	Error handling	None

Table 2 shows the specific meaning of discrete states in "How to" domain. In addition, a task-driven dialogue system requires information from users. For example, in the booking system, users are required to provide their location of departure and destination, etc., known collectively as slots. Here, we define states based on slots and use finite state machines to maintain transitions between states (Fig. 7).

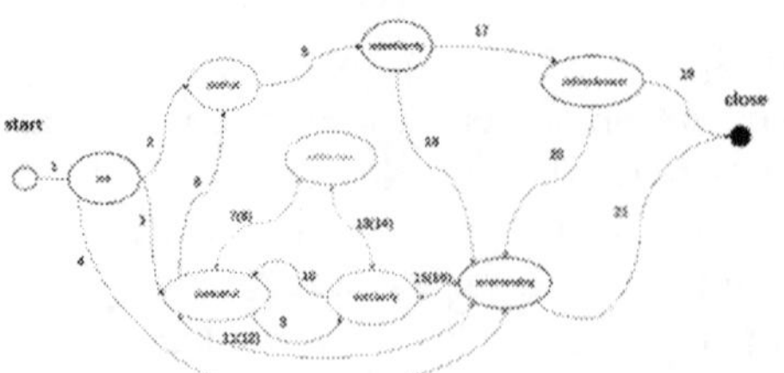

Fig. 7. HowTo state transition example

Make Plans

This part will generate dialogue acts of bot, then pass the acts to NLG module. We will not elaborate this part since it is not the main topic of this paper.

6 User Study

In this section, we conducted a preliminary user study to verify our customer service chatbot's efficiency and experience. We pre-defined typical smartphone customer issues such as cannot power on, cannot charge etc., and asked participants to solve these issues using our chatbot. We then recorded their subjective evaluation and comments about their feeling with our chatbot.

Participant
Considering that our chatbot's target smartphone users mainly speak English, therefore, we recruited 12 native English smartphone users (6 males, 6 females, age range 18–30) to eliminate the extra influence from language and gender.

Task Design
We selected randomly 25 typical smartphone issues such as order issue, cannot turn on, and each participant was asked to solve 15 issues randomly. The purpose of a task is to give the participant a scenario that his/her phone has something wrong and need to solve with our chatbot. Therefore, for each task we designed a brief background to provide basic information such as who, where, when and what.

Questionnaire
Refer to [14], we constructed our questionnaire to record their demographics and evaluation of their experience with chatbot. The questionnaires include: demographics (name, age, gender, nationality etc.), post-task (Table 3) and post-test (Table 4).

Table 3. The post-task questionnaire

Dimension	Sample item	Question type
Dialogue efficiency	It took me too much time to complete the task	5 Likert scale
Dialogue control	I always knew what to say next	5 Likert scale
Reliability	The chatbot did what I expected	5 Likert scale

Table 4. The post-test questionnaire

Dimension	Sample item	Question type
Dialogue control	I felt the conversation being under my control	5 Likert scale
Dialogue control	I always knew what to say next	5 Likert scale
Satisfaction	Overall, I feel satisfied about the chatbot's performance	5 Likert scale
Satisfaction	I would like to visit the chatbot again	5 Likert scale
Naturalness	The chatbot behaved naturally	5 Likert scale
Efficiency	Conversation with the chatbot was efficient	5 Likert scale

(*continued*)

Table 4. (*continued*)

Dimension	Sample item	Question type
Efficiency	Talking to the chatbot was confusing	5 Likert scale-reverse
Usefulness	The chatbot makes issue solving more efficient	5 Likert scale
Understanding	I had the feeling the chatbot understood me well	5 Likert scale
Naturalness	What the chatbot said made sense to me	5 Likert scale
Naturalness	The chatbot's reactions are appropriate	5 Likert scale

Procedure

Figure 8 illustrates the user study procedure: set up testing environment, then asked the participant to fill the demographics and let the participant be familiar with this testing. After that, the participant completed 15 tasks with rand sequence. After each task, the participant completes post-task questions, after all tasks, the participant completed post-test questions and answered several open questions such as comments to our chatbot. Each participant received 20 USD as incentives.

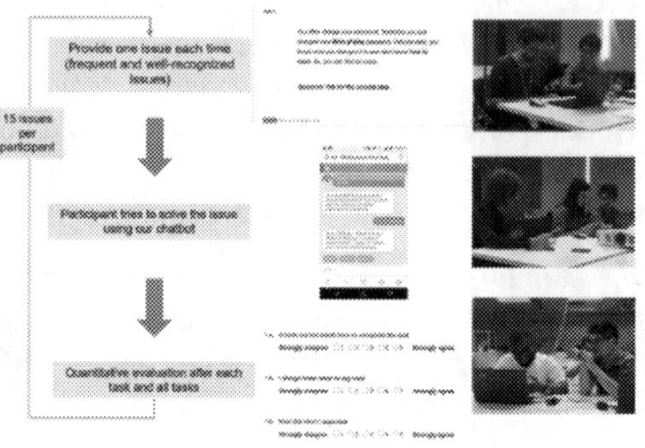

Fig. 8. User study experiment setup and procedure

Result

Figure 9 shows the statistics of post-task questions. Both dialogue control and reliability achieved acceptable performance. The dialogue efficiency was slightly lower than 3, which might because that participants expected more direct solution rather than an external link. For example, participant thought that they could get the order status directly through our chatbot rather than a website link that need extra interaction to get the answer. Figure 10 demonstrates the average scores of post-test questions. As we can see, all the scores are higher than 3, which means that our chatbot acquired promising efficiency and experience, especially the perceived conversation naturalness and satisfaction, dialogue control and understanding. Additionally, we collected participants' comments about our chatbot, e.g., "this chatbot solved my issue quickly", "The best part is it responds instantly, unlike the human agent that needs a long-time waiting", "The conversation is not robotic" etc. All these positive feedback support that our chatbot can handle customer service issue properly by using dialogue act framework. However, we also got some negative feedback such as "the chatbot cannot respond properly when it cannot understand my question", "it seems that cannot support multiple-turn conversation". In the future, we will expand this preliminary user study to be more systematic experiment, so that we can draw more solid conclusions.

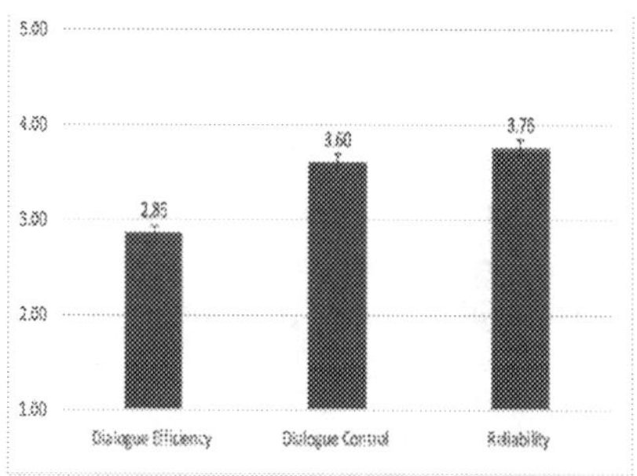

Fig. 9. The post-task results

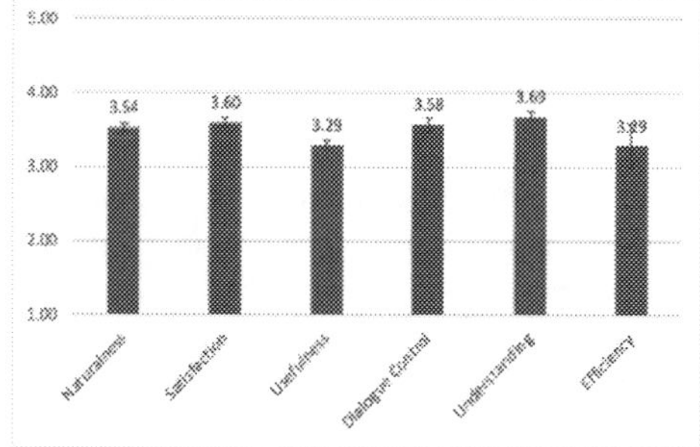

Fig. 10. The post-test results

7 Conclusion and Future Work

This paper established a fine-grained dialogue act framework specific to smartphone customer service. Compared with previous work, this framework contains more domain-related conversational behavior. Besides, two separated frameworks capture customer and agent acts respectively. Then, we designed a series of dialogue-act-based policies to transfer human strategies to automatic human-bot interaction. After that, we realized a customer service chatbot using the established acts and policies. Finally, a user study demonstrated the efficiency and naturalness. Compared with end-to-end chatbots, this dialogue-act-based realization can be more explainable since we know exactly what kind of user behavior the chatbot is dealing with and how. In addition, our dialogue policies are also represented by dialogue acts, we could modify the chatbot's strategy flexibly by changing the bot act combination.

In the future, we would continue to refine the dialogue act framework so that it could cover conversational behavior as more and as accurately as possible. The dialogue act framework is not only an information carrier between qualitative human strategy and technical application, it could also be used in human-bot interaction analysis, i.e., using this act framework to analyze the interactive patterns when the user is talking with our chatbot, and then proposing proper strategies to tackle unraveled problems.

References

1. Jacobs, I., et al.: The top 10 Chatbots for enterprise customer service. Forrester Report (2017)
2. Xu, A., et al.: A new chatbot for customer service on social media. In: Proceedings of the 2017 CHI Conference on Human Factors in Computing Systems. ACM (2017)
3. Austin, J.L.: How To Do Things with Words. Oxford University Press, Oxford (1975)
4. Klüwer, T., Uszkoreit, H., Xu, F.: Using syntactic and semantic based relations for dialogue act recognition. In: Proceedings of the 23rd International Conference on Computational Linguistics: Posters. Association for Computational Linguistics (2010)

5. Zhao, T., Kawahara, T.: Joint dialog act segmentation and recognition in human conversations using attention to dialog context. Comput. Speech Lang. **57**, 108–127 (2019)
6. Oraby, S., et al.: Modeling and computational characterization of Twitter customer service conversations. ACM Trans. Interact. Intell. Syst. (TiiS) **9**(2–3), 18 (2019)
7. Jo, Y., et al.: Modeling dialogue acts with content word filtering and speak preferences. In: Proceedings of the Conference on Empirical Methods in Natural Language Processing. Conference on Empirical Methods in Natural Language Processing. NIH Public Access (2017)
8. Stolcke, A., et al.: Dialogue act modeling for automatic tagging and recognition of conversational speech. Comput. Linguist. **26**(3), 339–373 (2000)
9. Kim, S.N., Cavedon, L., Baldwin, T.: Classifying dialogue acts in multi-party live chats. In: Proceedings of the 26th Pacific Asia Conference on Language, Information, and Computation (2012)
10. Bigelow, J.C.: Language, mind, and knowledge (minnesota studies in the philosophy of Science, Vol. VII). Linguist. Philos. **1**(2), 301–304 (1977)
11. Core, M.G., Allen, J.: Coding dialogs with the DAMSL annotation scheme. In: AAAI Fall Symposium on Communicative Action in Humans and Machines, Boston, MA (1997)
12. Jurafsky, D., Shriberg, E., Biasca, D.: Switchboard-DAMSL labeling project coder's manual. Technická Zpráva 97–02 (1997)
13. Ivanovic, E.: Using dialogue acts to suggest responses in support services via instant messaging. In: Proceedings of the Australasian Language Technology Workshop 2006 (2006)
14. Klüwer, T., et al.: Evaluation of the KomParse conversational non-player characters in a commercial virtual world. In: LREC (2012)

Feature-Less End-to-End Nested Term Extraction

Yuze Gao[1(✉)] and Yu Yuan[2]

[1] The Institute for Infocomm Research of A*STAR, Singapore, Singapore
yuze.gao@outlook.com
[2] School of Languages and Cultures,
Nanjing University of Information Science and Technology, Nanjing, China
hittle.yuan@gmail.com

Abstract. In this paper, we proposed a deep learning-based end-to-end method on domain specified automatic term extraction (ATE), it considers possible term spans within a fixed length in the sentence and predicts them whether they can be conceptual terms. In comparison with current ATE methods, the model supports nested term extraction and does not crucially need extra (extracted) features. Results show that it can achieve a high recall and a comparable precision on term extraction task with inputting segmented raw text.

Keywords: Term extraction · Span extraction · Term span

1 Introduction

Automatic Term Extraction (ATE) or terminology extraction, which is to automatically extract domain specified phrases from a given corpus of a certain academic or technical domain, is widely used in text analytic like topic modelling, data mining and information retrieval from unstructured text. To specify, Table 1 shows a simple example of the tasks, the numbers in the brackets (for example [0, 4]) indicate the start and end index of the term in the sentence separately. Given a sentence, the task is to extract the [0, 4], [0, 5], [1, 1] terms which are specific terms in a domain.

Table 1. Terms example in sentence

Sentence	"Mouse interleukin-2 receptor alpha gene expression"
Terms to extract	1. [0, 4] –> "#DNA domain or region"
	2. [0, 5] –> "#other_name"
	3. [1, 1] –> "#protein_molecule"

Typically, ACE approaches make use of linguistic information (part of speech tagging, phrase chunking and constituent parsing), extracted features or defined

J. Tang et al. (Eds.): NLPCC 2019, LNAI 11839, pp. 607–616, 2019.
https://doi.org/10.1007/978-3-030-32236-6_55

rules to extract terminological candidates, i.e. syntactically plausible terminological noun phrases (NPs). Furthermore, in some approaches, potential terminological entries are then filtered from the candidate list using statistical, machine learning or deep learning methods. Once filtered, with low ambiguity and high specificity, these terms are particularly useful for conceptualizing a knowledge domain or for supporting the creation of a domain ontology or a terminology base.

2 Related Works

Current methods can mainly be divided into five kinds: rule-based method, statistical method, predominant hybrid-based, machine learning-based and deep learning-based.

Rule-based approaches [1,2] heavily rely on the syntax information. The portability and extensibility is also low. Error propagation from the syntax information would hamper the accuracy of models. For example, the POS-tag rule-based system [3] suffer from low recall due to erroneous POS-tagging. Moreover, complex structure using modifier always pose parsing challenges for most simple POS-tag rule-based algorithms. *Statistical ATE system* [4] calls for large quality and quantity dataset to make a reasonable statistic of frequency, distribution and etc. When predicting, the low frequency or new-occur term may be easily neglected. *Predominant hybrid ATE* tries to combine the advantages of both rule-based and statistical approach. Generally, statistical methods are employed to trim the search space of candidates terms that identified by various linguistic heuristic and rules. However, combining the linguistic filters and statistical distribution ranking would lead to a degenerated precision with the increase of recall. *Machine-learning based ATE* [5–8] is to design and learn different features in the raw text or from syntax information, and then integrate these features into a machine learning method (such as conditional random field, supporting vector classifier). However, different domain, especially language shares different feature patterns, making this method specified to one language or domain. *Deep learning-based ATE* like sequence labelling methods [9] are also proposed recent years, but they do not support nested term extraction. [10] also proposed a co-training method using CNN and LSTM, and expand its training data by adding high confidence predicted results, but this method easily leads to error propagation [11].

To overcome some disadvantages of current ATE methods, we proposed another end-to-end method that based on deep learning, it supports nested term extraction and can achieve comparable experiment results without using extra features and syntax information. The **code** and **data** is shared on github[1].

3 Model

In our model, we formulate the term extraction task as a progress of classifications and filtering, which consider all possible spans or segmentation in the

[1] https://github.com/CooDL/NestedTermExtraction.

sentence and distinguish them whether they can be domain specified terms in the sentence (see Fig. 1 for more details about our model architecture). In the following sections, we will illustrate our classification and ranking-based term extraction system in details.

3.1 Term Spans

First, we would introduce the span or token segment ([12] also used in coreference resolution) used in our model. To specify, given a sentence $\boldsymbol{S} = w_1, w_2, ..., w_i, ..., w_n$ with $\boldsymbol{n}$ words, supposing every token sequence fragment $[w_i, w_j](1 \leq i \leq j \leq n)$ is a span candidate, then there will be $\boldsymbol{T} = \frac{n(n+1)}{2}$ term span candidates in a sentence with n words. Refer to Table 2 for more details about term span.

Table 2. Term span example

Sentence ($\boldsymbol{n} = 6$)	"Mouse interleukin-2 receptor alpha gene expression"
True term spans	[0, 4], [0, 5], [1, 1]
Model processed spans ($\boldsymbol{k} = 5$)	[0, 0], [0, 1], [0, 2], [0, 3], [0, 4], [1, 1], [1, 2], [1, 3], [1, 4], [1, 5], [2, 2], [2, 3], [2, 4], [2, 5], [3, 3], [3, 4], [3, 5], [4, 4], [4, 5], [5, 5]

3.2 Model Architecture

Briefly, our model can be divided into three parts (see Fig. 1 for more details): First is the feature preparation part (in red rectangle) that builds span representation vectors. Second is the classification part that classifies the span candidates to collect 'true positive spans' (TPS, that are potential to be terms). Finally is the ranking part that ranks the collected TPS based on ranking scores and sift the n-best span candidates. We will elaborate in next two parts (**Sentence Features** and **Span Representation**) for how to build the span representation in details.

Sentence Features. This part describes how the sentence sequence features are built from the raw segmented sentence (Refer to the red rectangle part in Fig. 1 for more details). In this step, both char level and word level information are used to build the sequence features, we use the framework of [13] to build the hidden features. Especially, we use the Conventional Neural Network (CNN) [14] on character level feature building, and Long Short Term Memory Neural Network (LSTM) [15] on word level feature building, which is the best combination described in the [13].

Moreover, before using the hidden features, we apply an attention mechanism layer over the sequence features to refine and condense the sequence hidden

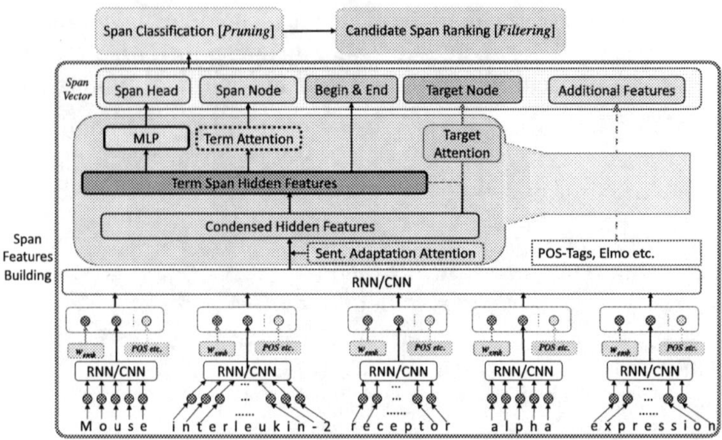

Fig. 1. Model architecture (Color figure online)

features. To specify, we use a pre-defined vector $\mathbf{v_s}$ as target vector over the sequence hidden features $H = [h_1, h_2, \ldots, h_n]$ with dot products. Then, we make a reduce sum operation on the hidden dimension axis and compute a soft-max contribution weight on every token in the sentence. Here, p_i is the probability (contribution weight) to the pre-defined vector $\mathbf{v_s}$.

$$p_i = \frac{h_i \cdot \mathbf{v_s}}{\sum_{k=1}^{n} h_k \cdot \mathbf{v_s}} \quad (1 \le i \le n) \tag{1}$$

The probability (contribution weight) of each token in the sentence is applied on its corresponding token.

$$h_{si} = h_i * p_i \quad (1 \le i \le n) \tag{2}$$

Here the h_{si} can be seen as the refined feature on terminology. We use the $H_s = [h_{s1}, h_{s2}, \ldots, h_{si} \ldots, h_{sn}]$ as the sentence sequence features for span representation.

Span Representation. Once we get the initial candidate spans in Sect. 3.1 and the hidden features of the sentences in Eq. 2, we can design feature patterns and build the span representations from H_s (Eq. 2).

To specify, given a sentence $S = w_1, w_2, \ldots, w_i, \ldots, w_n$, its final feature layer is $H_s = [h_{s1}, h_{s2}, \ldots, h_{si} \ldots, h_{sn}]$. Suppose a candidate span $Span_m = [i, j], (0 \le i \le j \le n \; and \; j - i \le \boldsymbol{k})$, $\boldsymbol{k}$ is the maximum length of the terms in the term candidate set $\boldsymbol{T}$. For ***Each Span***, we construct four kind features from H_s:

(I). ***Span Node*** is designed to contain the continuous information of the candidate term span for our model. For example the POS-tag sequence of the candidate. For a ***Span***, suppose its continuous hidden feature vectors in H_s are

$H_m = [h_i, h_{i+1}, \ldots, h_j]$, we first flatted hidden vectors and concatenate them, then we use a Multi-Layer Perceptron (MLP) to refine the flatten vector to a vector V_n with the same dimension on hidden features. We use the V_n as the span node vector.

$$V_n = MLP([h_i : h_{i+1} : \ldots : h_j]) \tag{3}$$

(II). ***Span Head*** is designed to contain the head word information if any and whether all the words in span can form a complete Noun Phrase. We use a pre-defined vector $\mathbf{v_t}$ which has the same dimension with hidden features as term target vector, and apply a term attention over its hidden feature sequence H_m to get its head feature vector V_h of the span. First the vector $\mathbf{v_t}$ is applied on H_m with multiply products to reduce the hidden feature of each word to a logit.

$$P_h^{[x]} = \frac{h_x * \mathbf{v_t^T}}{\sum_{x=i}^{j} h_k * \mathbf{v_t^T}} \qquad (h_x, h_k \in H_m) \tag{4}$$

Then the soft-max score from the logits is applied on their corresponding tokens.

$$V_h = \sum_{x=i}^{j} h_x * P_h^{[x]} \qquad (h_x \in H_m) \tag{5}$$

Here the x means the token in the span token sequence.

(III). ***Start and End Words*** V_{be} is designed to contain the feature information of begin and end word to the model. For example, generally, the term cannot start with a **PREP** word.

$$V_{be} = [h_i : h_j] \tag{6}$$

(IV). ***Sentence Targeted Attention Node*** is designed to embed some feature information like whether the candidate span can express a concept to the complete sentence and leverage the information from the sentence level into term spans. We use the mean vector of a span hidden features as a target vector and apply dot-wise attention over the sentence hidden features. This kind of attention mechanism is widely used in targeted sentiment analysis [16,17]. To specify, given a span with hidden feature sequence H_m, suppose its mean vector is $\hat{h_m}$. Here $\hat{\sum}$ means 'average sum' on token axis.

$$\hat{h_m} = \hat{\sum_{x=i}^{j}} h_x \quad (h_x \in H_m) \tag{7}$$

We use $\hat{h_m}$ as a target vector and apply its transposed on sentence level hidden feature sequence H_s with multiply products to reduce the hidden feature of each token to a logit $\hat{h_s}$. The logits will be softmaxed on the token axis in the sentence.

$$P_s^{[x]} = \frac{h_s[x] * \hat{h_m}^T}{\sum_{k=1}^{n} h_s[k] * \hat{h_m}^T} \quad (h_s[x], h_s[k] \in H_s) \tag{8}$$

The computed probability above is applied to its corresponding token in the sentence hiddens H_s, and the weighted sum product V_s is the span targeted attention node.

$$V_s = \sum_{i=1}^{n} h_s[x] * P_s^{[x]} \tag{9}$$

Apart from these four features, we also give each span a length feature vector V_l to indicate the length of the span. So, given a candidate span $Span^M$, it has a span representation S_M, which has a five times dimension with the hidden feature. Here the concatenate operation over the feature dimension axis.

$$S_M = [V_n, V_h, V_{be}, V_s, V_l] \tag{10}$$

Additional Features*. Other kind source features such as ELMO [18][2], Part-Of-Speech will also be refined via all the procedures (I, II, III, IV).

3.3 Classification and Ranking

After obtaining the span representations, we use these representations do the classification and ranking steps. First, based on the span representations S_M, we do a binary classification (CLF_{FC}) to classify these span candidates into true and false groups (TF_G).

$$TF_G = CLF_{FC}(S_M) \tag{11}$$

After classification, a scoring step will be applied over the 'true' span group (T_G, $T_G \in TF_G$). Here, we obtain the scores (R_{scores}) from a regression function (REG) which use the span representation S_M as inputs. $S_M^{T_G}$ is the span representation of true group T_G. The regression function (REG) is designed to give each span candidate a score between 0 and 1.

$$R_{scores} = \{REG(S_M^{T_i}), \quad S_M^{T_i} \in S_M^{T_G}\} \tag{12}$$

The scores of the T_G span group are then handed to a ranker as ranking (or confidence) scores. The top-K span results from the ranking step would be thought as the final output (TM_S) of our SCR model, which are with higher ranking scores (or confidence).

$$TM_S = RANKER|_{n=1}^{K}(R_{scores}) \tag{13}$$

Here K is a threshold value, we compute K $= \alpha \cdot |TotalWords|$. $|TotalWords|$ is the total words currently processed. α is a ratio indicate that how much terms are in a certain number of words. In our model, there are two loss source: one is the classification loss and one is the ranking step loss. We use a two-stage optimization strategy to minimizing the model loss.

$$Loss_{(classifier)} = -(y * log(p) + (1 - y) * log(1 - p)) \tag{14}$$

$$Loss_{(ranker)} = \sum_{y \in Y_{\{gold\}}} (1 - Sigmoid(y)) + \sum_{y' \in Y_{\{K-gold\}}} Sigmoid(y') \tag{15}$$

[2] For ELMO feature, we use the pre-trained model presented by the nlp toklit allennlp: https://github.com/allenai/allennlp/blob/master/tutorials/how_to/elmo.md.

4 Experiments and Analysis

Data. In our experiments, we use the GENIA3.02 [19][3], a human annotated, and biology corpus for information extraction and text mining systems. There are total 99,111 terms (distribution indicated in the red line) in 18,539 sentences (total 490,766 words). In these terms, 22675 terms are nested in or overlapped with other terms. 76436 terms are independent. We split the total corpus by sentence into Train/Dev/Test parts with a ratio 0.9: 0.05: 0.05 and shuffle the Train when training model.

(Hyper) Parameters. We used for our experiments are listed in the Table 3 below. The dropout [20] is only applied in the training progress to avoid over-fitting. We would stop the training processing after the evaluating loss has no increasing for a threshold times in *EarlyStop*.

4.1 Results and Analysis

Baselines. Currently, most ATE system are not designed to support nested term extraction. As there exists few systems supporting nested term extraction, resulting the weakness in lateral contrast. Here, we list some state-of-the-art ATE systems and their performance on the GENIA corpus.

1. Wang et al. [10], a co-training method that uses minimal training data and achieve a comparable results with the state-of-the-art on GENIA corpus.
2. Yuan et al. [5], a feature-based machine learning method using n-grams as term candidates and 10 kinds features is pre-processed for each candidate.Our best models for testing are chosen with the loss of development dataset and their performance is list in Table 4. In the table, [5] achieves a satisfying result with Random Forest method in their paper, but the feature preparation is complex and time-consuming. The training data is also re-balanced on the positive and negative instances.

For our classifier model, it has a high recall on the extracting terms, however the precision is not satisfying. The pre-trained word embedding [+GloVe] has little contribution, one reason is that there exists nearly 40% of the words in dataset is out of vocabulary. With extra features like POS-tags [+POS-tag], both precision and recall increase, which indirectly gives some evidences that span representations are not precise and concrete as the external POS-tags features on the POS-tag aspect. However, the ELMO features [+ELMO], which we thought should work better than the POS-tag features, do not bring much improvement as it raises pretty little in precision and falls in recall. When we utilize the POS-tag, ELMO feature and GloVe pre-trained embedding together [+ALL], we get a further improvement on recall of the classifier. But also cause a sharp increase in the resource consuming. The effect of ELMO feature weakens when we decrease the dimension of ELMO feature.

[3] http://www.geniaproject.org/genia-corpus.

Table 3. Hyper-parameters

$DIM_{Word\ Embedding}$	150
$DIM_{POS-tag\ Embedding}$	30
$DIM_{Word\ LSTM}$	150
$DIM_{Span\ Length}$	30
Word LSTM Layers	2
POS-tag LSTM Layers	1 (optional)
Learning Rate	0.01
Batch Size	100
Random Seed	626
Dropout	0.6
Term Ratio	0.23
Early Stop	26

Noted that: Decreasing the term ratio α will increase the precision but degenerate the recall. All the results in Table 4 are under the settings in Table 3

Table 4. Results on Test Set

		Precision	Recall	F1
Wang et al. [10]		0.647	0.780	0.707
Yuan et al. [5]		**0.7466**	0.6847	0.7143
Our model (Classifier)	Random embedding	0.5044	**0.9639**	0.6622
	GloVe	0.5093	**0.9557**	0.6575
	+POS-tag	0.5198	**0.9632**	0.6753
	+ELMo	0.5220	**0.9541**	0.6748
	+ALL	0.5163	**0.9698**	0.6738
Our model (Ranker)	Random embedding	0.7237	0.8343	0.7751
	GloVe	0.7244	0.8356	0.7760
	+POS-tag	**0.7265**	**0.8375**	**0.7780**
	+ELMo	0.7252	**0.8386**	0.7778
	+ALL	**0.7316**	0.8327	**0.7789**

For the ranker model, it is expected to filter the pruned span candidates, and it gains a better precision score than the classifier, but a low recall score problem due to some loss of true positive terms. The POS-tag features [+POS-tag] bring improvement in both precision and recall but not significant than the classifier. The effect of pre-trained embedding vector [+GloVe] also vanishes, which can be seen as a fluctuation in error margin. The ELMO features [+ELMO] do increase the recall, but not obviously. Compared with using all the features [+ALL], the ranker model uses POS-tag [+POS-tag] is slight poor in precision. The ELMO feature does not help much to improve both our classifier and ranker model. It makes us doubt that if the 'hard' features work better than the 'soft' features in the ATE task.

4.2 Other Experiments

Span Length: We compare the model performance under different maximum span length (from 1 to 15), and list them on Test set in the Figures (Figs. 2 and 3) on our classifier model and ranker model below.

For the classifier, as we increase the maximum term length, the recall increase to a stable value (approximate 0.96) without dropping, which means the saturation of its recall ability. It is reasonable that the precision decreases to a fluctuated point as the candidates space increases several times when increasing the maximum term length.

For the ranker, the precision and recall increase to a stable state. However, when the length is less than 2, the ranker model has low precision. But, shorter maximum length means lower span candidates space, which means the model should obtain a higher precision. We will explain why in the next part.

Overall, it can be noticed that the final result (from the ranker) has not been influenced too much when increasing max-length, which indicating that the model will maintain stable and can distinguish the true positive instances.

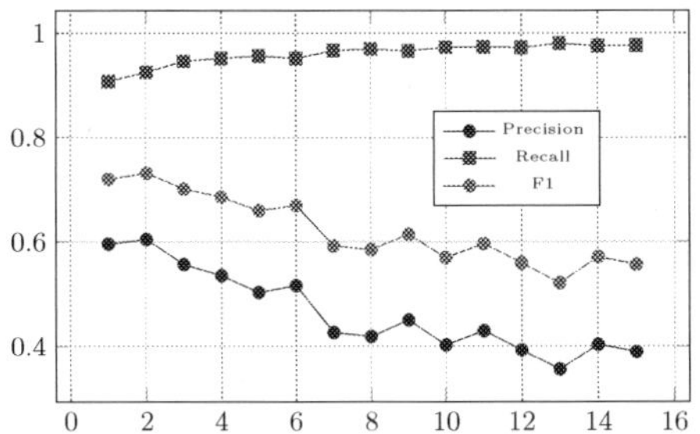

Fig. 2. Classifier on lengths (Testset)

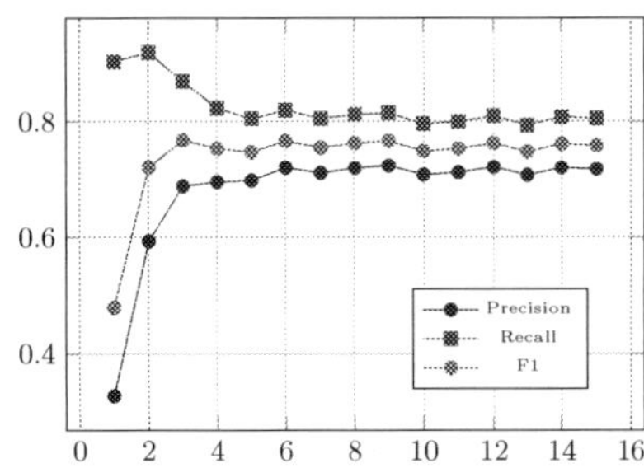

Fig. 3. Ranker on lengths (Testset)

5 Conclusion and Future Work

We proposed a deep learning-based end-to-end term extraction method in this paper. It employs classification and ranking on the span (n-grams) candidates in the sentences. Compared with current methods, it supports the nested term extraction and can achieve a comparable result with merely the segmented raw text as input. Based on the sentence and term span hidden features, four kinds reasonable feature patterns are designed to convey different information. Experimental results show that these features indeed can embed some information. Though the model achieve a satisfying results, the ranker still loss many true positive instances, which decrease the recall score from 0.95 to 0.83. Moreover, threshold-based output is not so applicable on unknown or unfamiliar domain or data as we do not know the term distribution and ratio.

Future works may focus on is to immigrate the architecture on a better feature extracting model (such as BERT [21] or GPT2.0 [22]). The ranking step should be designed more reasonable to pick up the outputs. More reasonable feature patterns can be designed to convey useful information.

References

1. Ranka, S., Cvetana, K., Ivan, O., Biljana, L., Aleksandra, T.: Rule-based automatic multi-word term extraction and lemmatization. In: Proceedings of LREC 2016 (2016)
2. Frantzi, K., Ananiadou, S., Mima, H.: Automatic recognition of multi-word terms: the C-value/NC-value method. IJDL **3**(2), 115130 (2000)
3. Zhang, Z., Gao, J., Ciravegna, F.: Jate 2.0: Java automatic term extraction with apache solr. In: Proceedings of the 10th LREC (2016)

4. Li, L., Dang, Y., Zhang, J., Li, D.: Domain term extraction based on conditional random fields combined with active learning strategy. In: JICS (2012)
5. Yuan, Y., Gao, J., Zhang, Y.: Supervised learning for robust term extraction. In: 2017 International Conference on Asian Language Processing (IALP). IEEE (2017)
6. GuoDong, Z., Jian, S.: Exploring deep knowledge resources in biomedical name recognition. In: Proceedings of the IJWNLP (2004)
7. Nazar, R., Cabre, M.T.: Supervised learning algorithms applied to terminology extraction. In: Proceedings of the 10th TKEC (2012)
8. da Silva Conrado, M., Salgueiro Pardo, T.A., Rezende, S.O.: A machine learning approach to automatic term extraction using a rich feature set. In: Proceedings of the NAACL HLT 2013 Student Research Workshop (2013)
9. Kucza, M., Niehues, J., Stker, S.: Term extraction via neural sequence labeling a comparative evaluation of strategies using recurrent neural networks. In: Proceedings of Interspeech (2018)
10. Wang, R., Liu, W., McDonald, C.: Featureless domain-specific term extraction with minimal labelled data In: Proceedings of the Australasian Language Technology Association Workshop 2016 (2016)
11. Kamal, N., Ghani, R.: Analyzing the effectiveness and applicability of co-training. In: CIKM, vol. 5 (2000)
12. Lee, K., He, L., Lewis, M., Zettlemoyer, L.: End-to-end neural coreference resolution. arXiv preprint arXiv:1707.07045 (2017)
13. Yang, J., Zhang, Y.: NCRF++: an open-source neural sequence labeling toolkit. In: Proceedings of ACL 2018 (2018)
14. Alex, K., Sutskever, Ilya., Hinton, G.E.: Imagenet classification with deep convolutional neural networks. In: ANIPS (2012)
15. Sepp, H., Schmidhuber, J.: Long short-term memory. Neural Comput. **9**(8), 1735–1780 (1997)
16. Liu, J., Zhang, Y.: Attention modeling for targeted sentiment. In: Proceedings of the 15th Conference of the EACL, Short Papers (2017)
17. Gao, Y., Zhang, Y., Xiao, T.: Implicit syntactic features for targeted sentiment analysis. In: Proceedings of IJCNLP 2017 (2017)
18. Peters, M.E., et al.: Deep contextualized word representations. arXiv preprint arXiv:1802.05365 (2018)
19. Kim, J.-D., Ohta, T., Teteisi, Y., Tsujii, J.: Genia corpusa semantically annotated corpus for bio-textmining. Bioinformatics **19**, i180–i182 (2003). (Oxford)
20. Srivastava, N., Hinton, G., Krizhevsky, A., Sutskever, I., Salakhutdinov, R.: Dropout: a simple way to prevent neural networks from overfitting. JMLR **15**(1), 1929–1958 (2014)
21. Devlin, J., Chang, M.-W., Lee, K., Toutanova, K.: BERT: pre-training of deep bidirectional transformers for language understanding. arXiv preprint arXiv:1810.04805 (2018)
22. Radford, A., Wu, J., Child, R., Luan, D., Amodei, D., Sutskever, I.: Language models are unsupervised multitask learners. OpenAI Blog **1**(8), 9 (2019)

Using Aspect-Based Analysis for Explainable Sentiment Predictions

Thiago De Sousa Silveira(✉), Hans Uszkoreit, and Renlong Ai

Giance Technologies, Beijing, China
{Thiago.Silveira,hans.uszkoreit,renlong.ai}@giance.ai
https://giance.ai

Abstract. Sentiment Analysis is the study of opinions produced from human written textual sources and it has become popular in recent years. The area is commonly divided into two main tasks: Document-level Sentiment Analysis and Aspect-based Sentiment Analysis. Recent advancements in Deep Learning have led to a breakthrough, reaching state-of-the-art accuracy scores for both tasks, however, little is known about their internal processing of these neural models when making predictions. Aiming for the development of more explanatory systems, we argue that Aspect-based Analysis can help deriving deep interpretation of the sentiment predicted by a Document-level Analysis, working as a proxy method. We propose a framework to verify if predictions produced by a trained Aspect-based model can be used to explain Document-level Sentiment classifications, by calculating an agreement metric between the two models. In our case study with two benchmark datasets, we achieve 90% of agreement between the models, thus showing the an Aspect-based Analysis should be favoured for the sake of explainability.

Keywords: Sentiment Analysis · Aspect-based Sentiment Analysis · Explainable Artificial Intelligence

1 Introduction

With the advent of the Web 3.0, social media have become a rich source of subjective and opinionated data produced by real users, which is crucial for many areas of study. Sentiment Analysis is one of these areas, defined by the study of opinions, emotions, sentiments that people have towards products, services, organizations or topics [17]. Analyzing emotions is a way to understand human behaviour, making Sentiment Analysis useful in many real-world applications, such as in healthcare, finance, market and product analysis.

Research on Sentiment Analysis contains many tasks, we highlight two of them: Document-level Sentiment Analysis and Aspect-based Sentiment Analysis. Document-level Sentiment Analysis (DLSA) refers to sentiment classification models aimed at predicting a score or a polarity class for a given document [17]. Aspect-based Sentiment Analysis (ABSA) focuses on predicting sentiments

J. Tang et al. (Eds.): NLPCC 2019, LNAI 11839, pp. 617–627, 2019.
https://doi.org/10.1007/978-3-030-32236-6_56

towards targeted aspects in the document [13]. In this context, aspects refers to attributes, components and entities mentioned in the text that are targets of opinions written by the user. For both Document-level and Aspect-based tasks, Deep Neural Networks are the current state-of-the-art [12,15,16].

Deep Neural Networks are famous for their learning capabilities and are able to obtain high accuracy scores in text classification tasks, however they lack explainability. The learned weights within the architecture of a neural network is often used as a black-box in making predictions. The decision-making process for individual classifications are deficient of transparency and can be subject to bias and generalization. Consequently, calls for explainable systems have been made by the academia and government agencies [6], conceiving a new area of research called Explainable Artificial Intelligence (XAI).

There has been many attempts to make AI more explanatory and those can be grouped along several dimensions. One dimension concerns the relation between the explanatory machinery to the original AI models and algorithms. We witness approaches that add explainable functionalities into the existing AI systems; for instance, generative models attempt to add human-readable explanations to classifications [7]. Another class of XAI focuses on designing a separate system that interprets the decisions of a learned model by analyzing the relationship between contents of the input, inference activation patterns and output. As an example, LIME [10] analyzes the impact of the input perturbations in the predicted output of a model. A third class of approaches attempts to investigate alternatives to existing techniques that are more explanatory by the redefinition of the task and thus also by the form of the output.

The approach presented in this work falls in the third category and thus must not be judged as an attempt to merely improve and extend the existing technology for DLSA. We observe ABSA task as a more *explanatory alternative* to DLSA. We argue on the reasons to view the detection of pairs of aspects and opinions as explanatory and we then investigate the relation between the two in their learning and inference performance. We also discuss the advantages and disadvantages of the more demanding ABSA technology, especially the additional modelling and annotation effort.

2 Related Work

Early work on Sentiment Analysis studied sentiment of reviews using supervised learning methods via extracting features from textual data [8]. The largest limitation of these early work is that they solely focused on predicting a sentiment polarity for entire textual document (review, social media post). Aiming for a more fine-grained analysis, *Aspect-based Sentiment Analysis* was coined as a separate task than *Document-level Sentiment Analysis* [13]. In this context, ABSA focuses on predicting sentiments for each aspect (entity, attributes) within a review.

For ABSA and DLSA tasks, deep neural networks have proven to be very useful in handling sentiment classification. As of the date of publication of this work, the state of the art for DLSA and ABSA involve fine-tuning contextual word representations. Models such as XLNET [16] and BERT [4] create context-dependent bidirectional representations of words learned from real world unlabelled data; these vector representations can be easily fine-tuned into other tasks, such as document classification. The state of the art results for the DLSA task was found by fine-tuning XLNET for polarity classification [16] on movie reviews from IMDB (Accuracy 96.21%) and Yelp (Accuracy 72.2%). For ABSA task, fine-tuning BERT using double input (text and aspect) can achieve state-of-the-art results on SemEval datasets (F1 77.97% on restaurants dataset) and Sentihood datasets (Accuracy 93.6%) [12,15].

Although deep neural networks are able to achieve high accuracy in sentiment classification tasks, these models have low levels of explainability. To a human observer, the neural network acts like a black-box and little is known about how it makes predictions [14]. The lack of transparency is a problem, because the classifications may be subject to harmful bias, generalizations or spurious correlations. For example, in the United States, a criminal risk estimation system (COMPAS) was found to make unknowingly racially biased predictions [1]. Moreover, AI systems can implicitly learn moral-sensitive bias from human texts [2]. Such problems have triggered government institutions to impose regulations on AI, such as the European Union Right to Explanation [6].

Those problems have also led the community to search for ways to create AI systems that are explainable, so-called XAI. In [5], the authors define explainability of a system as explaining data processing and representation of data within the black box model. As for explanation on data processing, LIME [10] proposes a technique to construct a local interpretable model by performing alterations in the input and checking the outputs, finding the most important features that impact the result. In addition, DeepLIFT [11] proposed a method to calculate importance scores of input features to a predicted output, a backprogation algorithm is used to compare the activation of neurons to input features. Lastly, generative methods have been proposed, such as [7], in which the authors training a model to not only predict a class, but also provide a visualization of learned weights and generate a human-readable text containing a justification.

Regarding Sentiment Analysis, few studies focus on explaining sentiment predictions. While lexicon-based and rule-based Sentiment Analysis methods are explainable by themselves, XAI methods for supervised models can generally be used in Sentiment Classification, both ABSA and DLSA tasks [18]. Although there has been few mentions about explainable sentiment analysis, such as in [3]; to our knowledge, explainability is under-researched in the area, mainly when considering the relationship between ABSA and DLSA tasks.

3 Aspect-Based Sentiment Analysis as an Explanation for Document-Level Sentiment Analysis

Aspect-based Sentiment Analysis and Document-level Sentiment Analysis have different levels of explainability. Models for DLSA have low explainability. As

DLSA only predicts a sentiment score or sentiment class for a document, it is unclear what the predicted single value represents to the end user. For instance, long documents contain multiple sentences with many, sometimes diverse, arguments and the opinions are spread around many points of discussion in the text, which we call aspects. By just predicting a unique score, DLSA neglects these multiple opinionated data and a single value prediction loses meaning and interpretability.

On a different direction, Aspect-based Sentiment Analysis has a higher level of explainability. In fact, ABSA identifies aspects in the text and their associated sentiment; thus, predicting a vector of aspect-opinion tuple for each document. In this case, an opinion can be a sentiment polarity or continuous score, or even opinion words contained from the text. Although the decision process is not transparent, ABSA models produce richer opinionated details from documents in comparison with unique valued predictions performed by DLSA models.

To exemplify, consider the user review about a restaurant: "*Although I disliked the service, the food was very delicious and the decoration is awesome!*". A document-level sentiment analysis would predict the polarity class *positive* for the review. However, an ABSA model would state that "service" is *negative*, "food" is *positive* and the "decoration" is *positive*. In this example, the classification made by the DLSA model is a general summarization and lacks the complete picture. By adding an aspect-based analysis, human understanding of the DLSA model's classification is benefited and explanation is enhanced.

It is important to state the difference regarding explainability of using ABSA in comparison with other proposed XAI methods. Many of previous proposed methods range from highlighting input features to generating a true explanation, i.e., stating in natural language why a decision was made. Actually, a sentiment analysis model that was trained on a sentiment lexicon could highlight the positive and negative sentiment words that affect the DLSA decision. However, the user would still have to read the remainder of the text to understand why, for instance, a review is classified as positive or negative. By using ABSA, on the other hand, the output contains the aspects of the object that have been associated with positive or negative sentiment. In this way, the ABSA system is explanatory by design, a human observer can understand the multiple targets of sentiment in the text, as well as their associated opinions and thus rationalize the decision made by DLSA models.

Additionally, ABSA does not only provide an output that enables the end user to understand the reasons for the overall sentiment of a document, the prediction process considers the sentiment dimensions provided by the aspects. An ABSA system does not calculate a document-level sentiment from the learned weights of positive and negative polarity indicators but makes separate decisions for every dimension of sentiment in the document. In this way, unrelated sentiment features to an aspect are disregarded, which can be helpful when the review also includes non-targeted sentiments. Further, it also helps avoiding bias that DLSA commonly suffer, such as in cases when the opinions of one aspect, maybe not even an important one, are associated to several sentiment-carrying words but another central aspect, maybe a central part or function of a product, is associated with a single sentiment word. Thus, the ABSA approach is more explanatory by design as it bring more semantic meaning into interpretation of the neural inference.

4 Framework

Given the argument that ABSA can be used for providing a deep level of detail for explicability in Sentiment Analysis, we propose a framework with the goal of identifying if an Aspect-based Sentiment Analysis model can be used as a explainable model for a DLSA model.

The proposed framework applies an evaluation methodology reviewed by [5]: the completeness of a model can be evaluated by how closely an alternative model approximates to the model under scrutiny. In our framework, ABSA can be seen as an alternative model, while the DLSA is the original model with aimed to be explained. Given a dataset of sentiment reviews, we perform predictions with DLSA models (original) and ABSA (alternative model) and we average each individual aspect-based sentiment predictions for each document of the dataset. Then, with the original predictions and the averaged alternative predictions, we calculate the agreement level between the models. If the agreement is high enough, we can say that ABSA can be used to explain DLSA.

Algorithm 1. Averaging of Aspects' sentiments

```
procedure AverageSentiment(S)
    if type == "classification" then
        countPolarity = {}
        for all s ∈ S do
            countPolarity[s]+ = 1
        if countPolarity["pos"] > countPolarity["neg"] then return "pos"
        if countPolarity["neg"] > countPolarity["pos"] then return "neg"
        if countPolarity["pos"] == countPolarity["neg"] then return "neu"
        return "neu"
    else if type == "score" then
        return 1/|S| Σ_{i=1}^{|S|} S_i
```

Formally, Let C be a collection of textual documents for which we desire to have sentiment predictions, each document $d \in C$ contains many aspects $d = \{a_1, a_2, \ldots, a_n\}$. Also, let ρ_{dlsa} and ρ_{absa} be two trained models for DLSA and ABSA, respectively. In this framework, $\forall d \in C$, we use the models ρ_{dlsa} and ρ_{absa} to produce sentiment predictions P_{dlsa} and P_{absa}, respectively. A given prediction $p_i \in P_{dlsa}$ represents a polarity class (positive, negative, or neutral) for $d_i \in C$, but the same prediction $p_i \in P_{absa}$ consists on a list of sentiments for each aspect in d_i ($p_i = \{s_1, s_2, \ldots, s_n\}$). To make the two prediction sets comparable, each $p_i \in P_{absa}$ must be averaged. Algorithm 1 is the proposed method to average the sentiment of the data, either by majority voting on the polarity of the aspects or by taking the mean of the scores.

Then, given P_{dlsa} and the averaged predictions for P_{absa}, both models can be compared by an agreement metric. Accuracy can be used as an agreement metric to calculate the percentage of documents that were classified with the same polarity by both methods. This framework shows that ABSA can be used to explain DLSA sentiment classifications if two conditions are obeyed: (1) if agreement is high enough (>85%); otherwise, the two models are not equivalent; (2) if models used for ABSA and DLSA have similar architecture and training data; elseways, the agreement could be merely by chance or by other means. To illustrate, Fig. 1 shows the workflow of the framework.

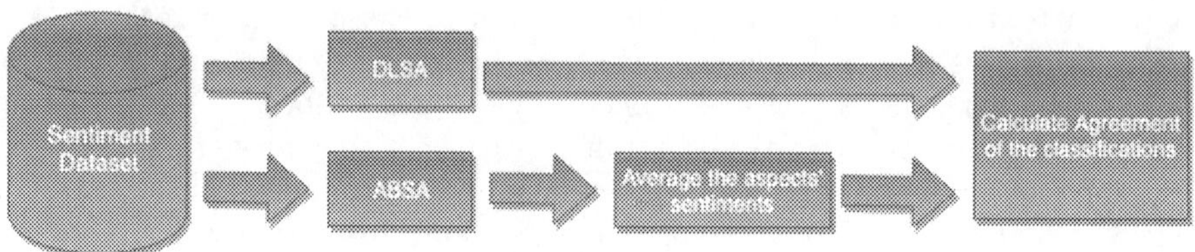

Fig. 1. A framework for agreement calculation between Aspect-based Sentiment Analysis and Document-level Sentiment Analysis

5 Case Study

To show the applicability of the framework for explainability in sentiment analysis, we make a case study applying the framework to show how ABSA predictions can be used to interpret Sentiment Analysis.

For this case study, we used two datasets from SemEval2016 Task 5, widely used for Aspect-based Sentiment Analysis [9]: (1) **Restaurants** dataset contains 2276 reviews about restaurants and 12 aspects annotated for their sentiment polarity. (2) **Laptops** dataset contains 2500 user reviews about laptops and 81 aspects that describe parts and functionality of the laptops. As for data treatment, the text was converted to lower case and grammatical errors were corrected. For the laptops dataset, we removed some of the aspects as these aspects rarely occur in the dataset. Both datasets contain three polarity classes: positive, negative and neutral.

The two datasets do not contain document-level sentiment annotations. We derived their gold standard sentiment via majority voting of the given annotated aspect sentiment for each document. Aspect-less documents or conflicted sentiments are removed. To avoid bias, a human annotator checked the document-level annotations for wrong summarizations.

The two datasets were used to train supervised models for DLSA and ABSA. We fine-tuned pre-trained BERT models [4]. We used the uncased BERT-base model with 12-layer, 12-heads, 110 million parameters for 3 epochs. For DLSA the inputs is only the document text and for the ABSA, the network receives two inputs: the document text and an aspect textual representation (either term or an aspect class), divided by a separator. To accommodate the contextual representations, we defined the input size as 128 words.

As for the experiment, we used the provided train and test from SemEval dataset. In our experiments we calculate the Accuracy and Macro-F1 for each model and the agreement between the DLSA and averaged ABSA.

5.1 Results and Discussion

The following shows the results of this case study and a further discussion. First, Table 1 shows the accuracy and F1 metrics for BERT models on both datasets, as well as the agreement level between BERT DLSA and the averaging of BERT ABSA predictions. The same table also contains the results for the version of the datasets reviewed by the annotation regarding the document-level sentiment polarity. The results show that BERT reaches state of the art accuracy scores. Whatsmore, the agreement between DLSA and ABSA is around 90%. Such high level of agreeement show that averaging aspect's sentiment of a document correlates with the overall sentiment of the document. In this case, we are basing the comparison of our predictions with the same pre-trained model, BERT, thus the agreement would not happen by chance.

Table 1. Agreement results for DLSA and ABSA using BERT.

Dataset	BERT DLSA		BERT ABSA		Agreement
	Accuracy	F1	Accuracy	F1	
Restaurant 2016 (Majority Vote)	85.34	72.36	87.89	73.05	90.11%
Restaurant 2016 (Reviewed)	85.68	73.57	87.89	73.05	90.63%
Laptops 2016 (Majority Vote)	81.5	65.18	81.27	65.16	89.70%
Laptops 2016 (Reviewed)	82.02	65.96	81.27	65.16	90.30%

It is also worth to analyze the results obtained by the datasets reviewed by the annotator in comparison with the version automatically made by majority voting. In this case, the datasets made by majority voting approximates to the version annotated by the user in Accuracy and F1 for the DLSA and the agreement keeps statistically the similar. Such findings have two implications: (1) DLSA and ABSA are indeed interrelated, such that using an dataset for DLSA by averaging ABSA is able to approximate the result of using datasets annotated by humans; (2) Majority voting can be used for automatically producing document-level sentiment datasets from aspects' sentiment annotations, instead of manually annotating them.

Additionally, we analyze and discuss the 10% of disagreement between the models. Table 2 shows the disagreement between the classes of DLSA and ABSA averaging through the framework for the Restaurants (left) and Laptops (right) dataset. Interesting, we see that the disagreement often happens regarding neutral class. Some documents classified as neutral by the DLSA method is often predicted to be positive or negative by averaging ABSA predictions. Such behaviour is reasonable as neutral classes often contains conflicted polarity information and the ABSA averaging is an approximation of the overall sentiment. Naturally, it is expected for neutral and the remaining polarity classes to be conflicted. Nevertheless, both DLSA and ABSA models have somewhat between 80%–87% of the time, thus some mistakes will certainly happen, showing that it is important to have accurate, yet consistent models.

Table 2. Comparison between DLSA classification and ABSA averaging for the restaurant and laptops dataset.

		ABSA averaging					
		Restaurant dataset			Laptop dataset		
		Pos	Neg	Neu	Pos	Neg	Neu
DLSA	Pos	0	10	5	0	5	10
	Neg	7	0	1	7	0	12
	Neu	20	15	0	8	16	0

To clarify on the disagreement made by the involvement of neutral classes, Table 3 present some examples of classified documents by DLSA and ABSA. The examples chosen for this case study can show us two characteristics: (1) contradicting aspect sentiment for the disagreement sentences; and (2) detailed opinionated data makes a difference in understanding the sentiment classification. As for the former, besides cases in which the classification commits mistakes, the disagreement between DLSA and ABSA average often occurs because there are multiple contrasting sentiment within a document. However, the second characteristic is more compelling: DLSA predictions are not self explanatory. The examples given Table 3 exemplify the argument of this work. When presented individually, predictions made by DLSA methods do not contains explanations to why it was sentiment was assigned. In fact, a human observer can only understand the DLSA sentiment predictions by analyzing the opinions associated to the aspects, thus providing explainability to the whole system.

6 Conclusion

This work has discussed that Aspect-based Sentiment Analysis is a more explanatory method than the commonly used Document-level Sentiment Analysis. ABSA provides detailed opinionated analysis of aspects and their sentiment

Table 3. Classification examples for DLSA and ABSA. The sentences with red background have disagreement between DLSA and the average of ABSA's sentiments. In green, there are examples of sentences in which both methods agree.

Dataset	Sentence	DLSA	ABSA	ABSA AVG
Restaurants	It is not the cheapest sushi but has been worth it every time.	pos	Food Prices=neg Food Quality=pos	neu
	Great pizza, poor service	neu	Food Quality=pos Service=neg	neu
	It is a great little place with tons of potential to be a neighbourhood joint if the service were not so impersonal and corporate-like.	pos	Restaurant=pos Service=pos	pos
Laptops	This, added with the fact that the speed of the hard drive is very slow for the money, detracts from the computer is value.	neg	Hard Disc=neg Price=neu Laptop=pos	neu
	For the price ($800!), you get a nice fast laptop, but if you ask me, it is missing some things that i feel should be automatically included.	neu	Price=neu Laptop=pos Operation Perf.=neg Design Features=neu	neu
	It is a steal when considering the specs and performance as well.	neg	Price=neg Design Features=neg Operation Perf.=neg	neg

polarity, and by design it eases interpretation by the end user, in contrast with a DLSA architectures that just predicts single sentiment class for a document, lacking details and explanations. Using ABSA is a big step in the direction of more explanatory system designs in Sentiment Analysis. To show an example of how ABSA can be used to enhance explainability, we proposed a framework to compare ABSA and DLSA models. The framework was applied in a case study in two user reviews scenarios and showing that generalizing ABSA predictions can lead to high agreement levels with DLSA models.

We can extend the discussion about the level of explanatory AI systems are required to achieve. The explanations developed in this article are shallow in comparison with research that aims to shed light onto the contents of a black-box model, however, no system can produce a complete explanation, due to its complexity. In the current state of XAI, we should opt for explanations that allow the user to understand the decision made by a neural network, therefore being dependent on the user. For example, for a medical diagnosis system, the explanatory output may differ depending on whether the user is a patient or a physician. Additionally, we may want to derive deeper ABSA explanations by assigning different user-adapated weights to different aspects. These two topics are worthy to be investigated in the future.

References

1. Angwin, J., Larson, J., Kirchner, L., Mattu, S.: Machine bias, March 2019. https://www.propublica.org/article/machine-bias-risk-assessments-in-criminal-sentencing
2. Caliskan, A., Bryson, J., Narayanan, A.: Semantics derived automatically from language corpora contain human-like biases. Science **356**, 183–186 (2017)
3. Clos, J., Wiratunga, N., Massie, S.: Towards explainable text classification by jointly learning lexicon and modifier terms (2017)
4. Devlin, J., Chang, M., Lee, K., Toutanova, K.: BERT: pre-training of deep bidirectional transformers for language understanding. CoRR abs/1810.04805 (2018). http://arxiv.org/abs/1810.04805
5. Gilpin, L.H., Bau, D., Yuan, B.Z., Bajwa, A., Specter, M., Kagal, L.: Explaining explanations: an overview of interpretability of machine learning. In: 2018 IEEE 5th International Conference on Data Science and Advanced Analytics (DSAA), October 2018. https://doi.org/10.1109/dsaa.2018.00018
6. Goodman, B., Flaxman, S.: European union regulations on algorithmic decision-making and a "right to explanation". AI Mag. **38**, 50–57 (2017)
7. Huk Park, D., et al.: Multimodal explanations: Justifying decisions and pointing to the evidence. In: Proceedings of the IEEE Conference on Computer Vision and Pattern Recognition, pp. 8779–8788 (2018)
8. Pang, B., Lee, L., Vaithyanathan, S.: Thumbs up?: sentiment classification using machine learning techniques. In: Proceedings of the ACL-02 Conference on Empirical Methods in Natural Language Processing, EMNLP 2002, vol. 10, pp. 79–86. Association for Computational Linguistics, Stroudsburg, PA, USA (2002). https://doi.org/10.3115/1118693.1118704
9. Pontiki, M., et al.: Semeval-2016 task 5: aspect based sentiment analysis. In: Proceedings of the 10th International Workshop on Semantic Evaluation (SemEval-2016), pp. 19–30 (2016)
10. Ribeiro, M.T., Singh, S., Guestrin, C.: Why should i trust you?. In: Proceedings of the 22nd ACM SIGKDD International Conference on Knowledge Discovery and Data Mining - KDD 2016 (2016). https://doi.org/10.1145/2939672.2939778
11. Shrikumar, A., Greenside, P., Kundaje, A.: Learning important features through propagating activation differences (2017)
12. Sun, C., Huang, L., Qiu, X.: Utilizing BERT for aspect-based sentiment analysis via constructing auxiliary sentence. CoRR abs/1903.09588 (2019). http://arxiv.org/abs/1903.09588
13. Thet, T.T., Na, J.C., Khoo, C.S.: Aspect-based sentiment analysis of movie reviews on discussion boards. J. Inf. Sci. **36**(6), 823–848 (2010). https://doi.org/10.1177/0165551510388123
14. Xu, F., Uszkoreit, H., Du, Y., Fan, W., Zhao, D., Zhu, J.: Explainable AI: a brief survey on history, research areas, approaches and challenges. In: International Conference on Natural Language Processing and Chinese Computing, Explainable Artificial Intelligence Workshop (2019)
15. Xu, H., Liu, B., Shu, L., Yu, P.S.: BERT post-training for review reading comprehension and aspect-based sentiment analysis. CoRR abs/1904.02232 (2019). http://arxiv.org/abs/1904.02232
16. Yang, Z., Dai, Z., Yang, Y., Carbonell, J.G., Salakhutdinov, R., Le, Q.V.: XLNet: generalized autoregressive pretraining for language understanding. CoRR abs/1906.08237 (2019). http://arxiv.org/abs/1906.08237

17. Zhang, L., Wang, S., Liu, B.: Deep learning for sentiment analysis: a survey. CoRR abs/1801.07883 (2018). http://arxiv.org/abs/1801.07883
18. Zucco, C., Liang, H., Di Fatta, G., Cannataro, M.: Explainable sentiment analysis with applications in medicine. In: 2018 IEEE International Conference on Bioinformatics and Biomedicine (BIBM), pp. 1740–1747. IEEE (2018)

Discrimination Assessment for Saliency Maps

Ruiyi Li[1,2(✉)], Yangzhou Du[2], Zhongchao Shi[2], Yang Zhang[2], and Zhiqiang He[2]

[1] Institute of Computing Technology, Chinese Academy of Sciences, Beijing, China
liruiyi18g@ict.ac.cn

[2] Lenovo Group, Beijing 100094, China
{liry8,duyz1,shizc2,zhangyang20,hezq}@lenovo.com

Abstract. Saliency methods can effectively mark which patterns in the input have higher impacts in model decision, and highlight the relationship between the features and inference results. However, different saliency maps have different performance in classification tasks. Through experiments, we find that some saliency maps show more discriminative ability, while others do not. Saliency methods with higher discrimination ability will be more helpful to human while making final decision, for example, the dominant features of malignant area are expected to be identified in medical diagnosis. In this work, a method is proposed to evaluate whether the saliency methods can provide effective discriminant information. In addition to giving intuitive judgment, we will also introduce a quantitative measurement method. We regard the saliency map as a weighting vector in class discrimination, which is analogue to the projection direction of Linear Discriminant Analysis (LDA) [12], and measure the discriminant ability of saliency map by comparing the difference between the vector direction of saliency map and the projection direction of LDA. Through this metric, our experiments will present the ranking of popular saliency map methods, in terms of discriminative ability.

Keywords: Saliency methods · Discriminant analysis · Interpretability

1 Introduction

With the development of machine learning, the neural network model has shown unparalleled performance in more and more tasks, and even reached and exceeded the human level in some fields. However, compared to classical machine learning methods, such as linear model, decision tree, support vector machine, it is difficult to understand how neural networks make decisions. In mission-critical tasks, if the inference result generated by the algorithm cannot be explained, people will have a big concern to use it. Therefore, in mission-critical scenarios, such as autonomous driving and medical diagnosis, the application of neural networks is strictly limited.

J. Tang et al. (Eds.): NLPCC 2019, LNAI 11839, pp. 628–636, 2019.
https://doi.org/10.1007/978-3-030-32236-6_57

In the existing work, a large number of researchers have gradually begun to pay attention to the interpretability of models. People often call algorithmically transparent models interpretable, while opaque models are considered as "black boxes". What is transparency? It is difficult to assess comprehensively the interpretability of a model by the definition of each parameter in the model or the complexity of the model.

In Lipton's article [5], interpretability is the way to trust models. The interpretable definition of the model can be divided into the following aspects. The first is simulation, that is, whether human can manually simulate machine learning model. The second is decomposability, that is, whether each part has an intuitive explanation. The third is security, that is, whether the model can prevent deception and whether decision-making does not depend on the wrong information. We believe that the saliency map can get the decision basis of the model, that is, the ability to explain whether the model is safe or not is the most important.

In the neural network model, we can see that many researchers successfully deceive the model by adding noise, which leads to the wrong results of the model. Just as Yuan et al. did in the adversarial examples [13]. Although the accuracy of models and other indicators sometimes exceed human standards, it is still difficult for people to trust the results of models, especially in some areas related to human security. This is also one reason why some people call the neural network model as alchemy.

It is hoped that an explanation-based tool can be used to clarify the basis for the model to make decisions and to help model designers to improve their models, eliminating biased information and other unintended effects learned by the model. In tasks such as image recognition, the saliency method becomes a popular tool that highlights the feature information of the input that is highly correlated with the model and obtains the underlying semantic patterns within the model.

However, because interpretability itself is difficult to define, there are few suitable indicators to evaluate these saliency methods. Sanity Checks [1] argues that some explanatory methods are so biased towards human intuition that they are misguided that the results are independent of data and machine learning models. In this work, we analyze it from another angle. We focus on a class of discriminant saliency methods. How do we distinguish two or more different classes in our daily life? If professionals tell you all the characteristics of each class, it may be difficult for laymen to remember and understand. However, just tell you the main difference between the two classes, it's easy to get an intuitive impression and trust that explanation.

Therefore, we hope that we can evaluate whether saliency maps contain enough discriminant information to make it easy for people to determine whether a neural network model is trustworthy. The most intuitive understanding of discriminant information is, how do we decide that a number is 1 instead of 7?

It's the short horizontal line in the top area of the digit. However, different neural network models have different decision-making bases, and saliency maps are not necessarily intuitive. We want to know a way to quantify this discriminant information, so we measure quantitatively by comparing it with LDA.

In the projection direction of LDA, the inter-class distance can be maximized and the intra-class divergence can be minimized, and the optimal projection vectors for distinguishing different classes can be obtained. We use saliency maps generated by interpretive methods as projection vectors to distinguish categories, at the same time, the projection vector of LDA is used as ground-truth to compare the discriminating ability of different saliency maps. However, such methods have certain limitations, that is, we assume that the samples are largely linearly separable.

At the same time, we visualize the samples, saliency maps and LDA projection vectors, and more intuitively observe the difference of discriminant information produced by different saliency methods.

Our Contributions

1. We figure out different saliency map methods have different performance in terms of discrimination. In discriminant tasks, in order to help users better, we should choose a saliency method with strong discriminant ability.
2. In order to quantify the discrimination ability of saliency map, we consider it as a projection vector to distinguish different categories, analogous to the projection vector of LDA. At the same time, we use the projection direction of LDA as the ground-truth, and measure the difference between the two vector directions to obtain the discriminant ability of saliency map.
3. Through our metric, We find that some saliency maps can only provide little discriminant information, while others have stronger discriminant ability. The experimental results on data sets such as MNIST [4] show that Grad-CAM [11] is superior to other saliency map methods.
4. At the same time, the experimental results in different neural network structures show unique explanatory information. AlexNet can be based on more different information when making decisions.

2 Related Work

In the research of the interpretability of the neural network model, a large number of researchers have done excellent work, hoping to open the black box of the neural network, and promote the progress of human society with the powerful computational performance and predictive ability of the model.

2.1 Saliency Method

In the neural network model, we put the data into the model to get the results, how to know which information is the most important in the input data, and has the greatest impact on the judgment of the model? The saliency map method is to find an effective way of this part of the information. Among the saliency map methods, some directly start from the data and use different input data combination methods to determine which data is sensitive to the model. SHAP [6] uses the direct method to find the most important information in the input, which originates from the classical game theory method. LIME [8] pays attention to the explanation of local models. It believes that no matter how complex the models are, there is always a linear function that can approximate the model in a certain local area. LIME seeks for a reasonable linear explanation of this part.

Others use the flow of data in the model to determine which inputs the model is sensitive to. LRP [10] pushes the results back to the input data layer by layer, so as to get an effective saliency map. CAM [15] and GradCAM [11] believe that the parameters of the neural network model contain explanatory intuitive information, so the feature of the neural network model is combined with the parameters to get the interpretation of the model in judgment.

2.2 Visualization of Features

Other methods do not focus on explaining a single input sample, but rather on seeing intuitively what patterns the model learns and stores for judgment. Interpreting CNN Knowledge Via An Explanatory Graph [14] wants to know what models each neuron in the model represents.

Some cognitive neurological experiments have now demonstrated that artificially constructed neural network models are very similar to real animal brains, and that images can be used to stimulate specific groups of neurons in James' experiments [2]. And in another highly enlightening experiment, Ponce et al. [7] constructed a framework that combines depth-generated neural networks and genetic algorithms to synthesize images that maximize the activation of animal neurons, in which animal memories can even be seen.

2.3 Evaluation Method

There are now some models for evaluating saliency map methods. AOPC [9] examines the impact on the results by evaluating whether the weight ranking of all points in the saliency map is correct and eliminating the highest weight points in turn. Sanity Checks [1] evaluates whether interpretation is independent of data and model. Some saliency map methods are not sensitive to data, some are similar to edge detection, but they are not helpful to interpret models.

3 Methodology

Some existing saliency map methods can already provide some intuitive information: the neural network model depends on which part of the input to judge. However, such explanatory information can sometimes be very vague, and it is difficult to present enough information in some categories and similar tasks. For example, the difference between plastic buckets and bags in automatic driving tasks can lead to serious consequences. So clear information is needed to distinguish between these two categories, especially when such differences can have serious consequences.

Therefore, it is very important to measure whether a saliency assessment method can provide enough discriminatory information. How to determine the difference between the two categories? LDA can provide a projection vector in the binary classification problem. This projection vector can point out which input information is more helpful to distinguish the two categories, which provides us with a simple ground-truth.

Mapping the input information to a vector that maximizes the distance between classes and minimize divergence within class can give us enough discriminant information, especially when two simple classes are discriminated. Then the projection vector of LDA is taken as the basic method of measurement.

To formalize the problem, the *input* information is a vector $x \in \mathbb{R}^d$, a *classification model* describes a function $S : \mathbb{R}^d \rightarrow \mathbb{R}^C$, where C is the number of classes in the classification work. An explanation method that can generate saliency maps is described as a function $Out_{maps} : E(S(x), x)$, where Out_{maps} is the saliency maps showing weights of input information and E is the explanation method.

Next, the projection vector of LDA is taken as ground-truth, and the discriminant information of the explanation method is measured by Pearson correlation coefficient [3] and Cosine similarity.

In order to better describe discriminant information in saliency maps, all samples need to be counted and analyzed. At the same time, in order to avoid training errors, all the pre-processing and model training parameters are unified to obtain more accurate discriminant assessment.

4 Experiments

In the experiment, the saliency map methods and the neural network model are evaluated respectively. In the first part, we mainly show whether different saliency map methods can mine discriminant information in the model. Although some saliency map methods can clearly mark out which information in the input plays a decisive role in the model determination, it is difficult to distinguish such information from other categories of saliency maps. We may know that this part is really useful, but if this part of the information of all samples is useful, it is difficult to obtain enlightening knowledge.

In the second part, we mainly evaluate whether different models can provide enough discriminant information. When carrying out discriminatory tasks, we can choose a model with more discriminatory information or construct a Neural Network with sufficient discriminatory information to complete the corresponding tasks.

In order to observe the information of saliency maps more intuitively, we only focus on the impact of the information on the output, regardless of whether it is positive or negative. Therefore, it is a very straightforward and simple way to take absolute values of all the weight information in the saliency map in the experiment. At the same time, all figures are displayed in pseudo-color, with blue as the minimum and yellow as the maximum.

4.1 Saliency Method Assessment

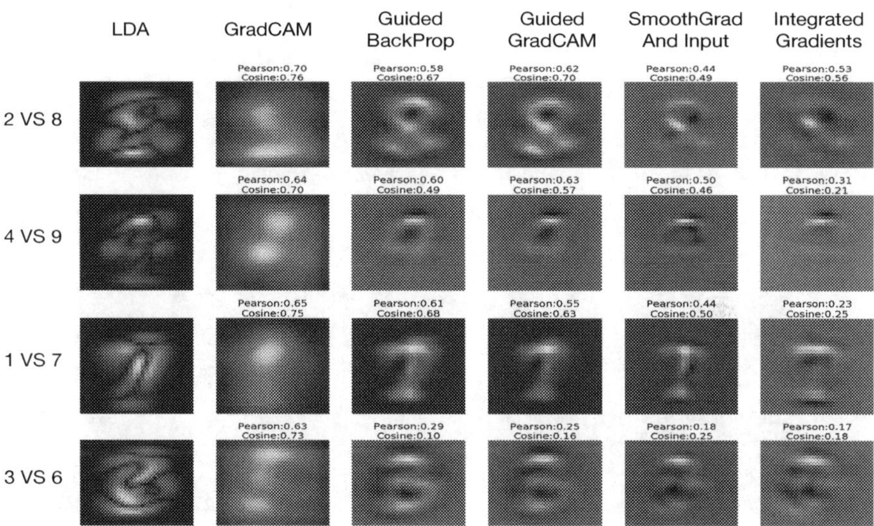

Fig. 1. *Evaluation of different saliency map methods.* Four pairs of digits were used to compare the results. GradCAM performed well in all tests, but the other saliency map methods were not effective. Especially when the category difference is small, such as 3 and 6, it is difficult to provide enough discriminant information.

Different saliency map methods provide completely different saliency information, among which GradCAM can provide more discriminant information. At the same time, the other saliency map methods focus on the generality of categories, and it is difficult to reflect the difference information between categories, so they have a low score in the evaluation. When the difference between categories is small, GradCAM can provide the discriminant information steadily, while the other methods are difficult to distinguish the difference. Category information is displayed in Fig. 1.

The Fig. 2 shows the statistical results of all samples, the yellow line is the median and the green triangle is the mean of the data. It can be seen that there is a big difference between GradCAM method and other saliency map methods, GradCAM displays more discriminatory information, while Integrated Gradients was the worst performers.

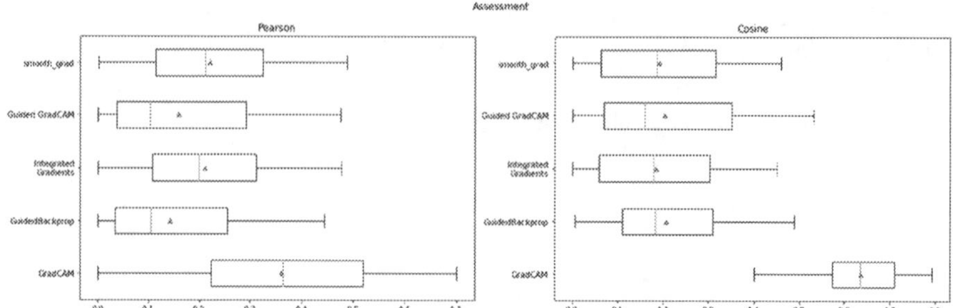

Fig. 2. *The evaluation values of different saliency map methods.* Each saliency map in the sample is evaluated separately, and the results are taken as absolute values to get the above illustrations. The rectangle in the box-plot marks the range of the first quartile and the third quartile, and the line segment in the rectangle is the median of the data.

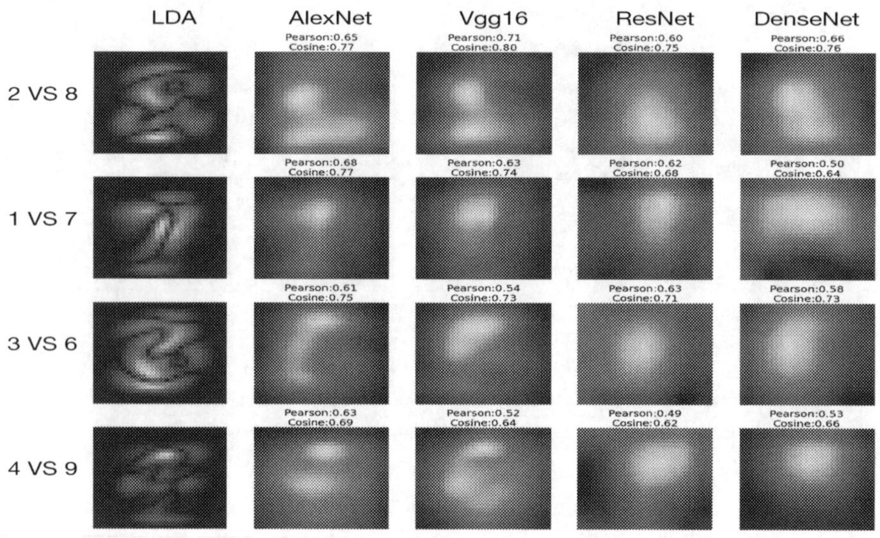

Fig. 3. *Evaluate different neural network models.* Four different neural network models were compared in the experiment, and the best gradCAM method in 4.1 assessments was used to explain the model. The same four different categories were used for the experiment.

4.2 Neural NetWork Assessment

Four different Neural Network models, AlexNet, ResNet, Vgg16 and DenseNet, are used in the experiment. We hope to find out whether there are enough discriminant information in different network models.

In the Fig. 3, it is showed that different network models show completely different discriminant information although they have similar measurements. AlexNet and Vgg16 are similar, while ResNet and DenseNet fully show the interpretation information of another style. Although their scores are similar, they make decisions based on different regions.

5 Conclusions and Futrue Work

In this paper, we have quantitatively evaluated the discriminant information provided by different saliency map methods. We can see that some saliency map methods can provide some more intuitive explanations, but such explanations lack sufficient discriminant information and it is hard to believe that the models have found the differences between different categories.

At the same time, experiments on various neural network models show that they predict based on different information. We have reason to believe that such information reflects the difference of model structure to some extent. (The exact same parameters and data were used in the experiment, the only difference is that the model structure is different.)

However, due to the difficulty of multi-classification tasks and the huge amount of computation, only a part of the MNIST data set is used in this experiment. In future experiments, we need to validate our ideas in more data sets and large tasks. We hope to find a saliency method, which can provide clear discriminant information and improve the interpretation ability of the model. Let the excellent performance of the neural network model be applied to more valuable tasks.

References

1. Adebayo, J., Gilmer, J., Muelly, M., Goodfellow, I., Hardt, M., Kim, B.: Sanity checks for saliency maps. In: Bengio, S., Wallach, H., Larochelle, H., Grauman, K., Cesa-Bianchi, N., Garnett, R. (eds.) Advances in Neural Information Processing Systems 31, pp. 9505–9515. Curran Associates, Inc., Red Hook (2018). http://papers.nips.cc/paper/8160-sanity-checks-for-saliency-maps.pdf
2. Bashivan, P., Kar, K., DiCarlo, J.J.: Neural population control via deep image synthesis. Science **364**(6439), eaav9436 (2019)
3. Benesty, J., Chen, J., Huang, Y., Cohen, I.: Pearson correlation coefficient. Noise Reduction in Speech Processing. STSP, vol. 2, pp. 1–4. Springer, Berlin (2009). https://doi.org/10.1007/978-3-642-00296-0_5
4. LeCun, Y., Cortes, C., Burges, C.: Mnist handwritten digit database. AT&T Labs. http://yann.lecun.com/exdb/mnist2, 18 (2010)
5. Lipton, Z.C.: The mythos of model interpretability, 61, 10 (2016)
6. Lundberg, S.M., Lee, S.I.: A unified approach to interpreting model predictions. In: Guyon, I., et al. (eds.) Advances in Neural Information Processing Systems, vol. 30, pp. 4765–4774. Curran Associates, Inc., Red Hook (2017). http://papers.nips.cc/paper/7062-a-unified-approach-to-interpreting-model-predictions.pdf
7. Ponce, C.R., Xiao, W., Schade, P.F., Hartmann, T.S., Kreiman, G., Livingstone, M.S.: Evolving images for visual neurons using a deep generative network reveals coding principles and neuronal preferences. Cell **177**(4), 999–1009 (2019)
8. Ribeiro, M.T., Singh, S., Guestrin, C.: "Why should i trust you?": Explaining the predictions of any classifier (2016)

9. Samek, W., Binder, A., Montavon, G., Bach, S., Müller, K.R.: Evaluating the visualization of what a deep neural network has learned. IEEE Trans. Neural Networks Learn. Syst. **28**(11), 2660–2673 (2016)
10. Samek, W., Wiegand, T., Müller, K.R.: Explainable artificial intelligence: understanding, visualizing and interpreting deep learning models (2017)
11. Selvaraju, R.R., Cogswell, M., Das, A., Vedantam, R., Parikh, D., Batra, D.: Grad-cam: visual explanations from deep networks via gradient-based localization (2016)
12. Webb, A.R.: Linear Discriminant Analysis (2003)
13. Yuan, X., He, P., Zhu, Q., Li, X.: Adversarial examples: attacks and defenses for deep learning. IEEE Trans. Neural Networks Learn. Syst. **30**(9), 2805–2824 (2019)
14. Zhang, Q., Cao, R., Feng, S., Ying, N.W., Zhu, S.C.: Interpreting cnn knowledge via an explanatory graph (2017)
15. Zhou, B., Khosla, A., Lapedriza, A., Oliva, A., Torralba, A.: Learning deep features for discriminative localization. In: Computer Vision and Pattern Recognition (2016)

A Modified LIME and Its Application to Explain Service Supply Chain Forecasting

Haisheng Li(✉), Wei Fan, Sheng Shi, and Qiang Chou

Lenovo Research, Beijing, China
{lihs6, fanwei2, shisheng2, chouqiang1}@lenovo.com

Abstract. Recently, researchers are focusing more on the study of explainable artificial intelligence due to its usefulness on various scenarios that request trust, such as deciding if one should trust a prediction, choosing between models, improving an untrustworthy model and identifying why a model should be trusted. One main research issues is how to improve the interpretability, while preventing any deterioration of accuracy of the model. For this issues the model-agnostic explanation method is a kind of solution. In the paper we propose a modified LIME algorithm based on locally fitted by decision tree regression called tree-LIME which is a model-agnostic method. Further, we clarify the fidelity measure definition in regression explanation problem by using mean absolute error (MAE). The experiments on real service supply chain forecasting application show that (1) our proposed approach can improve the fidelity of the explainer which lead to a more accurate explanations for individual instances and (2) our approach gives a more intuitive and visualized tree expression for explanation. (3) The approach also works well when applied to service supply chain forecasting.

Keywords: Explainable artificial intelligence · Model-agnostic · Local explanation · Decision tree

1 Introduction

Explainable artificial intelligence, the objective of which is to explain the black-box machine learning models, is an important topic in machine learning research and its applications. The interpretation of black-box model not only corresponds to assessing trust, but also relates to deploying a new model. Many sophisticated methods, especially deep neural networks and ensemble methods, are very complicated and even for human experts are struggle to interpret them. So interpretable machine learning has been a resurgence in recent years.

There are a number of methods to perform model explanation. In general these approaches can be categorized into two types: model-agnostic methods [1–5] and model-specific methods [6–9]. (i) Considering the explanation problem, model-agnostic methods firstly learn an interpretable model that locally or globally [10] approximates the given model. Then, using the learned interpretable model to explain given model. (ii) Considering the explanation problem, model-specific method is to judiciously design representation form of the algorithm and make the algorithm explainable in itself. In fact, frequently used linear model and decision tree essentially

J. Tang et al. (Eds.): NLPCC 2019, LNAI 11839, pp. 637–644, 2019.
https://doi.org/10.1007/978-3-030-32236-6_58

belong to this types. Whether model-agnostic method or model-specific method have their advantages and drawbacks. The model-agnostic method faced the fidelity problem, e.g. the explainable model cannot effectively approximate original model. While for the model-specific method a tradeoff often must be made between accuracy and interpretability [11]. Besides, except these two typical category approaches there are still other explainable methods. In [12], depending on the natural language processing method, the author train a deep neural network with picture-text pair to explain the content of the picture. In [13], author interpret deep neural network GANs by identifying a group of interpretable units and visualize to interpret.

In this paper, we focus on the model-agnostic method and we think that for model-agnostic method the fidelity should be measured. If an explainable model cannot effectively approximate original model, then explanation is imprecise. Specifically, we explore a new kind of LIME (local interpretable model-agnostic explanation) based approach called tree-LIME to perform explanations. LIME is a local interpretable model-agnostic explanation method proposed in [14–16]. It explains the complicated machine learning model by locally approximate the model being explained in explainable feature space. The LIME is local linear and it can explain the predictions of any classifier and regressor.

In our approach, we modify the locally linear model of LIME to decision tree regression and by clarify the fidelity definition for regression we apply our approach to service supply chain forecasting which is a time series forecasting problem and is modeled to regression problem. So the main contributions are as follows.

- Tree-LIME, a modified method base on LIME, which can effectively locally approximate the original model to be explained with the tree interpretable representation.
- Clarify the fidelity definition for regression between explainable model and original model by computing mean absolute error (MAE).
- Applying the propose method to explain the service supply chain forecasting and show its advantage in fidelity and representation.

2 Tree-LIME and Regression Fidelity

2.1 Locally Fitting by Decision Tree Regression

Model-agnostic explainable method LIME is a method that locally approximate the original model in explainable feature space. In the local region of feature space, LIME use a linear model to explain the samples needed to be explained. In our method, we use decision tree regression to approximate and explain samples. Specifically, define model g ∈ G as an explanation, where G is a class of potentially interpretable models. Let the model being explained be denoted f $: R^d \rightarrow R$. In regression, f(x) is the response variable. LIME produces explanation as following:

$$\xi(\mathrm{x}) = \frac{argmin}{g \in G} L(f, g, \pi_x) + \Omega(g) \tag{1}$$

where, $L(f, g, \pi_x)$ is fidelity component and π_x is a proximity measure between an instance to x which defined the local region to be fitted. $\Omega(g)$ is interpretability component.

For original LIME, the author select a sparse linear model K-LASSO as the explainable model g. In our method we use decision tree regression model CART as the g. The changes for the local explainable model will lead two kind of effects. Firstly using a nonlinear tree model replace liner model will increase local fidelity. Secondly instead of using a linear model as an interpretable representation, the replacement leads to tree formation representation. As we will show in experiment later, locally nonlinear fitting can improve the fidelity and tree representation for explanation is transparent and concise. Before that, we will define fidelity measure for regression.

2.2 MAE as the Fidelity Measure

For the Model-agnostic explainable method, approximation to original model is important. The fidelity is to measure this kind of property. However for classification and regression, the fidelity will be varied. In classification it have been defined in several researches. While for regression, there is still no definition.

In [10], the author define the fidelity for classification as the percentage of test-set examples on which the classification made by an explainable model agrees with its original counterpart model. It can be formally defined as:

$$Fidelity_{classification} = \frac{N_{f=g}}{N} \tag{2}$$

Where, f represents original model and g is explainable model. N is the size of test dataset of the original model f and $N_{f=g}$ represents the number that explainable model agrees with original model on test dataset.

For regression problem, the mean absolute error (MAE) is a usually used evaluation metrics and in this paper we compute the MAE between the explainable model's result and original model's result as the fidelity measure. So it can be formally defined as:

$$Fidelity_{regression} = MAE_{g,f} = \frac{1}{n}\sum\nolimits_{i=1}^{n} |g_i - f_i| \tag{3}$$

Where, g_i is the explainable model's approximate result and f_i is original model's forecasting result. In experiment chapter, we will use this definition to comparing two explainable model's fidelity for regression problem.

3 Experiment

In our experiment, we compare our proposed approach with original LIME on service supply chain forecasting data which is to forecast the usages of each week for computer repairing parts, such as mainboard, hard-drive and LCD panels. We purified this data from real-world application of service supply chain and preprocess this time series data to the form of tabular data, so we can model this time series forecasting problem to a regression problem. After the extraction, the dataset contains 271242 train samples and 25068 test samples. Then, we train an ensemble model on this dataset which is the ensemble with two varied XGBoost models. For this ensemble it is hard to explain even for machine learning practitioners. We use the proposed tree-LIME and original LIME to explain this ensemble, then compare the Fidelity measure and show the interpretable representations.

3.1 About Service Supply Chain Data

In details, service supply chain forecasting data are for predicting the usage quantities of computer's repairing parts, which is prepared for customer's repairing. For large computer manufacturers the service supply chain usually maintain thousands of repairing parts for their customers. The supply chain's planner are tasked with predicting their weekly usages for up to one quarter (13 weeks) or half a year (26 weeks) in advance. The usage quantities of repairing parts are influenced by many factors, including the parts commodity, the product segmentation and the machine types. With hundreds of individual planners predicting usages based on their unique circumstances, accuracy of results can be quite varied. In our extracted dataset, historical usages for 5414 parts are provided, so we have history usages of 5415 parts to form train dataset. In test dataset we need to forecast the usages of 2136 parts for up to one quarter (13 weeks). Because in every week we can extract one sample for training and testing dataset, the train dataset contain 271242 instances and test dataset have 25068 instances to be forecasted. According to the problem, 10 attributes are extracted so far and details are as follows:

1. TopmostPN: parts number, e.g. ID
2. IB: install base which means the quantity of computers in warranty
3. Commodity: the commodity types of the parts
4. BU: the business unit that the part belongs to
5. Segment: the segmentation of product, which allocate the correspond parts
6. IB_duration: the IB's duration weeks from first the first part in warranty
7. Usage_duration: the duration weeks that first usage occurred
8. Year: which year that the usages occurred
9. Month: which month that the usages occurred
10. WeekofYear: which week of the year that the usages occurred

3.2 Fidelity on Service Supply Chain Forecasting

In this chapter, we compare proposed tree-LIME with the original LIME using Fidelity measures. We randomly pick up 50 instances out of 25068 instances from test dataset. Firstly we forecast these 50 instances by original XGBoost ensemble. Then we explain these instances separately by tree-LIME and LIME. At last, computing the Fidelity measure of tree-LIME and LIME based on XGBoost ensemble result. To conquer randomness, we repeat this experiment 3 times. In experiment, the parameter of tree depth is set 4. The reason we do not do this experiment on whole 25068 test dataset is that the explanation process is time consuming. Table 1 shows the fidelity values for three times experiments. It can be seen from Table 1 that for all three time experiments on pickup samples, fidelity values of tree-LIME is lower than original LIME. We can come to a conclusion that the fidelity performance of tree-LIME is better than original LIME which it is benefitted from nonlinearly fitting in local feature space. In fact for a complicated dataset from real life application, the boundary of feature space are usually nonlinear.

Table 1. Comparition of fidelity

Fidelity	Experiment-1	Experiment-2	Experiment-3
LIME	9.64	6.43	11.28
Tree-LIME	6.22	3.66	3.63

3.3 Analysis About the Depth of the Tree

In our approach, one of the important parameters is the depth of the tree. The tree depth is the important parameter because it can adjust the tradeoff of the explainer's fidelity and its interpretability. When the depth is too deep for a tree, it becomes hard to interpret. However, we think when the depth of the tree is shallow, tree model will degenerated to liner model and will reduce fidelity. In the following experiment, we validate that the depth of the tree will effect fidelity. We design two groups experiment. For each group we randomly picked 50 instances and set tree depth as 3, 4 and 5 separately to compute fidelity value. As shown in Table 2 when the tree depth is 5, the fidelity value of both groups achieved the best fidelity performance. The experiments validate our conjecture about the effect of tree depth. In real application considering the user's limitation, some users may accept the tree of 4 layers while the others may accept that up to 10 layers. we recommend this parameter is set to 4 or 5.

Table 2. Comparition of the tree depth's effect

Fidelity	Depth = 3	Depth = 4	Depth = 5
Group-1	7.33	6.22	4.89
Group-2	3.93	3.66	3.02

3.4 Interpretability and the Tree Representation

Considering interpret representation in various applications and for different users, a linear model [17], a decision tree, a decision rule list may or may not be interpretable. In the following we show the difference of the interpretable representation between our approach and original LIME. When we change the linear fitting method to the non-linear tree fitting method in the local explainable space, the interpretable representation is changed correspondingly. We perform further study on representation cases between LIME and tree-LIME. Figures 1 and 2 show the explanation result of an instance in service supply chain forecasting which is forecasted by our XGBoost ensemble either. For this instance, the forecasting result of our ensemble is 4 pieces of usage, the approximation result of LIME is $0.236 \approx 0$ pieces and our tree-LIME is $4.824 \approx 5$ pieces. The parameter of tree depth for tree-LIME is set to 4. Again from the view of fidelity, tree-LIME's fidelity is 1, LIME is 4 and tree-LIME is better than LIME. In the following we concentrate on the explanation representations of two methods. The explanation representation result is shown in Figs. 1 and 2.

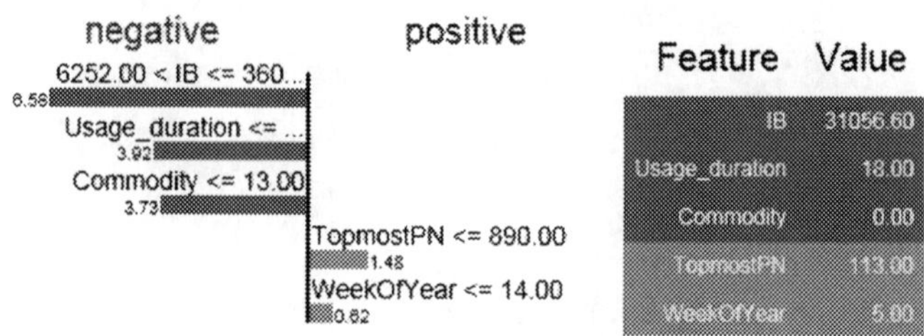

Fig. 1. LIME representation

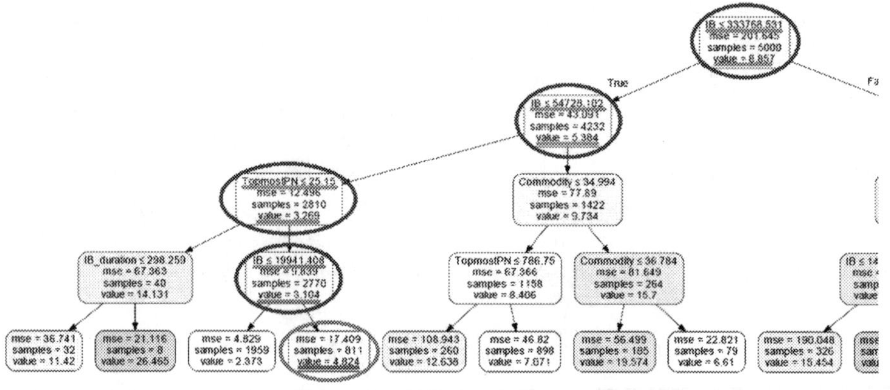

Fig. 2. Tree-LIME representation

In Fig. 1, LIME uses the weight of the linear model as the interpretable representation output. The positive weight means the corresponding feature have the positive effect for the regression result and vice versa. As shown in Fig. 1, LIME's explanation result can be translated that if 6252.00 < IB <= 36063.00, Usage_duration < 38.00, Commodity <= 13.00, TopmostPN <= 890.00 and WeekOfYear <= 14.00, then forecasting result is 4 pieces. In Fig. 2, tree-LIME leads to a tree interpretable representation. Decision tree is inherently explainable and it is the decision rule in essence too. From Fig. 2 we can find that the forecasting result is 4 pieces because 19941.408 < IB <= 54728.102 and TopmostPN > 25.15.

So the problem is which kind of representation is better? As shown in Figs. 1 and 2, The interpretable representations obtained by LIME and tree-LIME are indistinguishable, so it is hard to say which is better. For representation problem, there have not been adequate study in different representations and it is likely that different representations are appropriate for different kinds of users and domains [18]. From the view of transparent and concise interpretation, the translated decision rules of tree-LIME is less than LIME, meanwhile tree-LIME is more fidelity than LIME. We think LIME and tree-LIME can both explain the service supply chain forecasting result well and the explanation of LIME and tree-LIME are both reasonable for real service supply chain planers. The advantage of our proposed approach is that the approach obtained more concisely explanations at the same time that the fidelity is higher.

The appropriation problem of explanation representation is really hard to evaluate. Considering decision rule is a kind of general thinking mode, we think in practice the explanation should be sample, concise and easy to translate to decision rules.

One not mentioned problem is categorical features problem for regression. In Figs. 1 and 2, the 'Commodity' feature is an example. For regression the general way to cope with categorical feature is the integer encoding, but it is troublesome when explaining the model for tree representation in our approach. It is meaningless that a categorical feature is greater than some values or less than some values. For this problem, selecting other tree representation may be a good choice and this will be for future works.

4 Conclusion and Future Work

This paper investigates the fidelity and interpretability representation of local model-agnostic explainer LIME. Although LIME can explain any classifier and regressor, its fidelity and interpretability representation for regression can be improved. Our major contribution is a modified approach called tree-LIME, which uses the tree representation and increases the capability of local approximation, e.g. fidelity. Further, for regression problem we clarify the fidelity definition by using mean absolute error (MAE) between explainable model and original model. Our experiments on service supply chain application demonstrate that the proposed approach can increase fidelity and explain the forecasting result well. In the future, we will cope with how to better explain categorical features, experiment on multiple datasets and evaluate interpretability representation with human subjects.

References

1. Lundberg, S.M., Lee, S.-I.: A unified approach to interpreting model predictions. In: Advances in Neural Information Processing Systems, pp. 4765–4774 (2017)
2. Lundberg, S.M., Erion, G.G., Lee, S.-I.: Consistent individualized feature attribution for tree ensembles. arXiv preprint arXiv:03888 (2018)
3. Mittelstadt, B., Russell, C., Wachter, S.: Explaining explanations in AI. In: Proceedings of the Conference on Fairness, Accountability, and Transparency, pp. 279–288. ACM (2019)

4. Ribeiro, M.T., Singh, S., Guestrin, C.: Nothing else matters: model-agnostic explanations by identifying prediction invariance. In: 30th Conference on Neural Information Processing Systems, Barcelona, Spain (2016)
5. Štrumbelj, E., Kononenko, I.: Explaining prediction models and individual predictions with feature contributions. Knowl. Inf. Syst. **41**(3), 647–665 (2014)
6. Chang, Y.-Y., Sun, F.-Y., Wu, Y.-H., Lin, S.-D.: A memory-network based solution for multivariate time-series forecasting. arXiv preprint arXiv:02105 (2018)
7. Lakkaraju, H., Bach, S.H., Leskovec, J.: Interpretable decision sets: a joint framework for description and prediction. In: Proceedings of the 22nd ACM SIGKDD International Conference on Knowledge Discovery and Data Mining, pp. 1675–1684. ACM (2016)
8. Wang, F., Rudin, C.: Falling rule lists. In: Artificial Intelligence and Statistics, pp. 1013–1022 (2015)
9. Letham, B., Rudin, C., McCormick, T.H., Madigan, D.: Interpretable classifiers using rules and bayesian analysis: building a better stroke prediction model. Annal. Appl. Stat. **9**(3), 1350–1371 (2015)
10. Craven, M., Shavlik, J.W.: Extracting tree-structured representations of trained networks. In: Advances in Neural Information Processing Systems, pp. 24–30 (1996)
11. Caruana, R., Lou, Y., Gehrke, J., Koch, P., Sturm, M., Elhadad, N.: Intelligible models for healthcare: predicting pneumonia risk and hospital 30-day readmission. In: Proceedings of the 21st ACM SIGKDD International Conference on Knowledge Discovery and Data Mining, pp. 1721–1730. ACM (2015)
12. Hendricks, L.A., Akata, Z., Rohrbach, M., Donahue, J., Schiele, B., Darrell, T.: Generating visual explanations. In: Leibe, B., Matas, J., Sebe, N., Welling, M. (eds.) ECCV 2016. LNCS, vol. 9908, pp. 3–19. Springer, Cham (2016). https://doi.org/10.1007/978-3-319-46493-0_1
13. Bau, D., et al.: Gan dissection: Visualizing and understanding generative adversarial networks. arXiv preprint arXiv:10597 (2018)
14. Ribeiro, M.T., Singh, S., Guestrin, C.: Why should i trust you? explaining the predictions of any classifier. In: Proceedings of the 22nd ACM SIGKDD International Conference on Knowledge Discovery and Data Mining, pp. 1135–1144. ACM (2016)
15. Ribeiro, M.T., Singh, S., Guestrin, C.: Model-agnostic interpretability of machine learning. In: 2016 ICML Workshop on Human Interpretability in Machine Learning, New York, USA (2016)
16. Ribeiro, M.T., Singh, S., Guestrin, C.: Anchors: high-precision model-agnostic explanations. In: Thirty-Second AAAI Conference on Artificial Intelligence (2018)
17. Ustun, B., Rudin, C.: Supersparse linear integer models for optimized medical scoring systems. Mach. Learn. **102**(3), 349–391 (2016)
18. Singh, S., Ribeiro, M.T., Guestrin, C.: Programs as black-box explanations. In: 30th Conference on Neural Information Processing Systems, Barcelona, Spain (2016)

Cross-lingual Neural Vector Conceptualization

Lisa Raithel[1,2(✉)] and Robert Schwarzenberg[1]

[1] German Research Center for Artificial Intelligence (DFKI), Berlin, Germany
[2] Giance Technologies GmbH, Berlin, Germany
lisa.raithel@giance.ai

Abstract. Recently, Neural Vector Conceptualization (NVC) was proposed as a means to interpret samples from a word vector space. For NVC, a neural model activates higher order concepts it recognizes in a word vector instance. To this end, the model first needs to be trained with a sufficiently large instance-to-concept ground truth, which only exists for a few languages. In this work, we tackle this lack of resources with word vector space alignment techniques: We train the NVC model on a high resource language and test it with vectors from an aligned word vector space of another language, without retraining or fine-tuning. A quantitative and qualitative analysis shows that the NVC model indeed activates meaningful concepts for unseen vectors from the aligned vector space. NVC thus becomes available for low resource languages for which no appropriate concept ground truth exists.

Keywords: Interpretability · Explainability · Word vector space

1 Introduction

Neural Vector Conceptualization [14] is an interpretability method that allows to illuminate continuous, distributed word vector spaces with higher order concepts. To this end, NVC maps samples from a word vector space into a concept space, with the help of a neural network. This neural mapping is learned in advance, in a supervised manner, using a pre-trained embedding space to draw training instances from and an instance-to-concept graph to retrieve appropriate target concepts. For example, we expect the instance "Confucius" to activate the concept "philosopher." Unfortunately, the need for a sufficiently large concept graph impedes the deployment of NVC in low resource languages.

It has been shown, however, that continuous word vector spaces of different languages share structural properties, which is a feature that word vector alignment methods make use of [4,12]. A word vector alignment aims to minimize the distance between word vectors of parallel words in a source and a target

L. Raithel and R. Schwarzenberg—Shared first authorship.

J. Tang et al. (Eds.): NLPCC 2019, LNAI 11839, pp. 645–652, 2019.
https://doi.org/10.1007/978-3-030-32236-6_59

language. To this end, a transformation from the source to the target space is learned such that $W \in R^{d \times d}$ minimizes a distance δ according to

$$\frac{1}{n}\sum_{i=1}^{n}\delta(Wx_i, y_i) \tag{1}$$

where $\{(x_1, y_1), \ldots, (x_n, y_n)\}$ is a seed dictionary of parallel d-dimensional word vectors from the source and target language X and Y, respectively [9]. In this work, we train the NVC model with a high resource language Y and test it with aligned vectors from language X, aiming to make the methods accessible for low resource languages through vector space alignments.

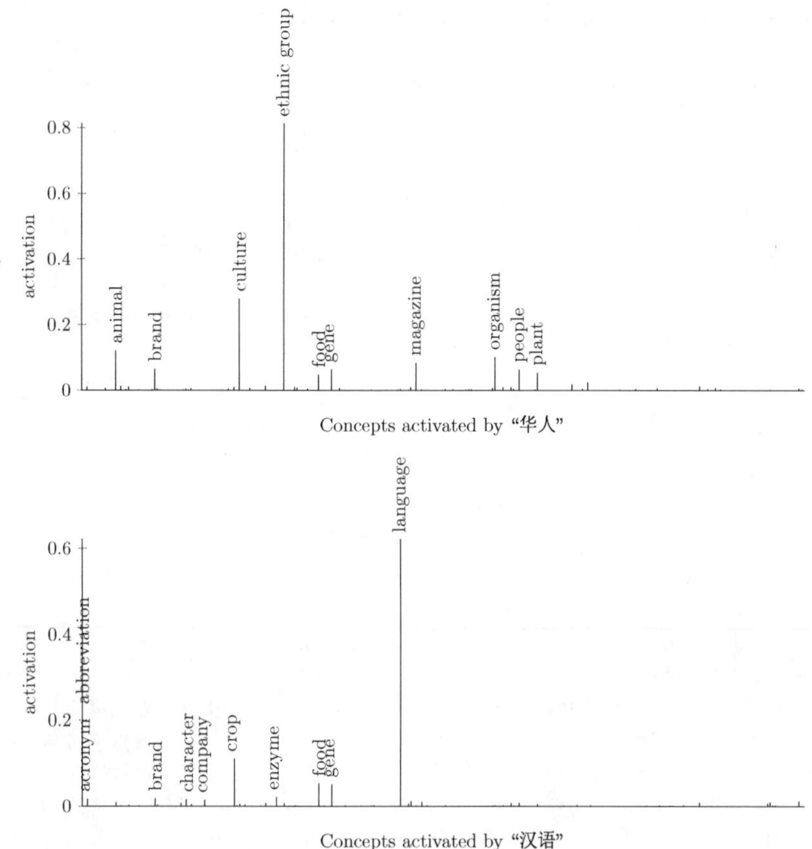

Fig. 1. Neural Vector Conceptualizations. Top: NVC of the word vector of the Chinese translation for "Chinese people." Bottom: NVC of the word vector of the Chinese translation for "Chinese language." Both word vectors were retrieved from a fastText word vector space that has been aligned with the English fastText word vector space the NVC model was trained on. The model was not retrained or fine-tuned on the aligned vector space. Consequently, both vectors were not seen during training.

2 Methods and Experiments

Following [14], for NVC, we trained a neural multi-layer feed-forward net to recognize concepts in word vectors. We drew the target concepts for each word vector training instance from the Microsoft Concept Graph (MCG) [15], using the same preprocessing steps and preprocessing hyperparameters as the authors of NVC. Preprocessing involved filtering concepts in the MCG that have a sufficient number of instances in the word vector space.

After preprocessing, 32768 instances and 275 associated concepts remained for training the NVC model (+ 8192 for validating, + 4553 for testing). We optimized with the Adam optimizer [10] with a learning rate of 0.001 and stopped training early with a patience of four epochs. The best model was determined in a five-fold cross validation procedure.

Our choice for a class membership threshold deviated from the experiments of [14]. We did not use a strict class membership threshold of 0.5 but instead optimized the threshold on the dev split after training. This step was motivated by the observation that for some word vectors the top k concept activations were meaningful but below the 0.5 threshold.

Contrary to [14], instead of with word2vec [11], we trained with English fastText vectors [1], since for these, alignments already exist in more than 40 languages.[1] For the alignments, the Relaxed Cross-Domain Similarity Scaling (RCSLS) method, which mitigates issues with high degree neighborhoods in the word vector space, was used. Here, we omit details and instead refer the interested reader to the original paper [9].

After training, the best model was used to conceptualize Chinese word vectors from an aligned fastText space. It is noteworthy that the model had never seen a vector from that space during training. To statistically validate that NVC works across language boundaries for aligned word vector spaces, without retraining, we determined the concept classification performance of the model on the unseen Chinese vectors. To this end, we treated the target concepts of parallel English words as the ground truth.

Parallel English and Chinese tokens were retrieved[2] from the 10k most frequent tokens in the Sinica Corpus [3] and then intersected with the above mentioned 45513 instances. The intersection contained 1,288 instances. In the next section, we report on the F scores our model achieved in the English and Chinese task and we also present NVCs of selected word vectors. Our experiments are publicly available under https://github.com/dfki-nlp/cross-nvc.

3 Results and Discussion

The results of our classification experiments on the English test set are summarized in Table 1. We optimized the class membership threshold on the dev set,

[1] Word vectors retrieved from https://fasttext.cc/docs/en/aligned-vectors.html on 2019/07/16.

[2] Retrieved from https://en.wiktionary.org/wiki/Appendix:Mandarin_Frequency_lists on 2019/07/30.

which yielded a threshold of 0.18. A stricter threshold of 0.5 resulted in a weighted F score of only 0.29 which is closer to the F score of 0.22, reported by [14].

[14], however, trained with over 600 concepts while we trained with only 275 concepts because the intersection of word vector vocabulary and MCG was smaller in our case. We can assume that a lower-dimensional concept space facilitates the task which should be one reason why our model performs better, in terms of F measure.

Table 1. Results on a held-out test set of 4553 English instances with 275 concepts. There are on average 1.14 concepts per instance.

	Weighted	Macro	Micro
Precision	0.365	0.327	0.393
Recall	0.375	0.334	0.375
F1	0.351	0.309	0.384

The low, optimized threshold supports the authors' suspicion that a conservative 0.5 threshold is too strict for the task since apparently, the top k activations for some vectors contain meaningful concepts below this threshold. Furthermore, we note that our F score is considerably above chance. We take this as evidence that NVC works with fastText vectors, too.

Table 2. Results on test set of 1,288 Chinese word vectors with 275 concepts.

	Weighted	Macro	Micro
Precision	0.132	0.048	0.092
Recall	0.180	0.060	0.180
F1	0.096	0.038	0.122

To determine whether NVC also works across language boundaries if aligned word vector spaces are used, we repeated the concept classification experiment with aligned Chinese word vectors that we retrieved as described above. The performance of our model, which we did not retrain, is summarized in Table 2.

We observe that unsurprisingly, the model performs worse when tested with Chinese word vectors but that its performance is again above chance with a considerable margin. We take this as evidence that NVC indeed works across language boundaries. For the loss in accuracy several reasons can be cited:

Firstly, errors and ambiguities in the dictionary we used to retrieve aligned word vectors worsen performance. In fact, inaccuracies in this step lead to the retrieval of unaligned vectors which should not activate the concepts of their supposed parallel counter parts in the English language.

Secondly, the alignment of the two vector spaces we drew samples from did not happen without loss. We can thus expect noise in aligned word vectors even if their meanings in the corpora they origin from were culturally and semantically identical. Our model never learned to filter this noise.

Lastly, even if we retrieved the most accurate translation for an instance from our dictionary, we cannot expect it to have the exact same meaning, as assumed above. Some concepts will be lost in translation, others will be activated.

Consider, for example, a culture in which people consume soups for breakfast but not for supper and another one in which it is vice versa. This could be reflected in the NVCs of the instance `soup`: While the one vector may activate `breakfast`, it may be deactivated (correctly) in the other, whereas `supper` may become activated (correctly). Cultural differences of course worsen performance. In the example above, concepts correctly activated by the translation may not be reflected in the original instance-to-concept knowledge base. Nevertheless, arguably, this could be considered a feature rather than a bug.

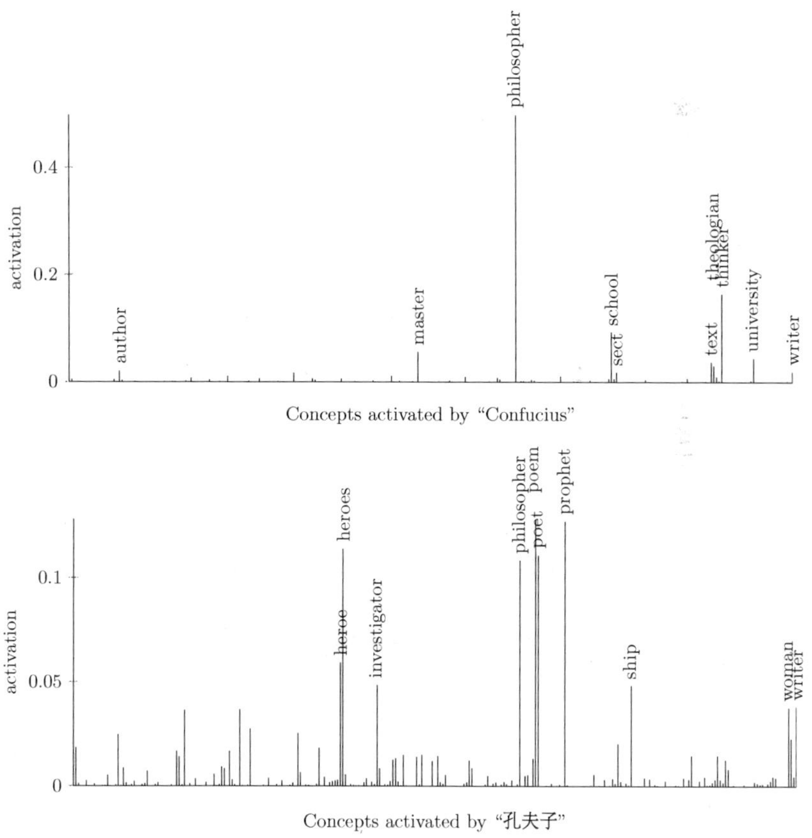

Fig. 2. Neural Vector Conceptualizations. Top: NVC of the English word vector (unseen during training) for "Confucius" from the fastText space the NVC model was trained on. Bottom: NVC of the word vector of the Chinese translation from an aligned word vector space from which no sample was drawn during training.

We now conduct qualitative analysis. Figures 1 and 2 show selected NVCs of Chinese and English word vectors. In Fig. 1 we present the NVCs of the Chinese word vectors for the terms `Chinese people` and `Chinese language`, both of which were sampled from the aligned Chinese fastText space, unseen during training. `ethnic group` and `people` are activated in the former NVC, while in the latter `language` is the top activation. We believe these to be meaningful concepts which supports our claim that NVC produces worthwhile activation profiles across language boundaries, if alignment techniques are used.

Cultural differences in word vectors might be reflected in Fig. 2. The English word vector for `Confucius` strongly activates `philosopher` while the top concept activated by the aligned vector of the Chinese translation is `poem`. We also find `poet` and `writer` under the top concepts activated by the Chinese vector with no such strong artistic connotation in the English NVC. One reason for these differences in the NVCs may be that Chinese corpora emphasize the artistic side of Confucius stronger than western corpora.

4 Related Work

In addition to related work already discussed in [14], we would like to point out the recent work by [6]. Similar to us and [14], they also use concepts for interpretation, which they automatically extract from images.

Regarding the cross-lingual capacities of NVC which we focus on here, there are several other branches of related work on multilingualism worth mentioning. [7], for instance, provide an extensive overview of cross-lingual embedding techniques and propose several measures on how to evaluate them. They argue that projection-based cross-lingual embeddings, like those of [9], are usually only evaluated on bilingual lexicon induction and offer additional downstream evaluation tasks, for example cross-lingual information retrieval. NVC can be regarded as yet another evaluation downstream task.

[8] evaluate cross-lingual word vectors on an ontology alignment task, aiming to identify overlapping concepts in multi-lingual ontologies. Cross-lingual NVC might be used for an alternative embedding evaluation and may be also useful for ontology alignment.

We additionally can relate our method to research that is concerned with biases in word embeddings. There exists a plethora of work concerned with identifying and removing biases in embeddings, see for example [2,5,13].

5 Conclusion and Future Directions

In this work, we made Neural Vector Conceptualization available to low resource languages, for which no sufficiently large instance-to-concept ground truth exists. To this end, we trained the NVC model with a word vector space of a high resource language (English) and tested it with an aligned vector space of another language (Chinese).

Quantitative experimental results strongly suggest that NVC indeed works across language boundaries, if aligned vector spaces are used. A qualitative analysis revealed that meaningful concepts were activated for unseen vectors from the aligned vector space and that we might even be able to identify cultural differences in aligned vectors with NVC.

The fastText vectors used in this work were sampled from two vector spaces, belonging to a set of over 40 aligned spaces. In the future, one should validate cross-lingual NVC for more languages and further explore how (and if) cultural differences can be identified with NVC.

Acknowledgements. This research was partially supported by the German Federal Ministry of Education and Research through the project DEEPLEE (01IW17001) and by Giance Technologies GmbH.

References

1. Bojanowski, P., Grave, E., Joulin, A., Mikolov, T.: Enriching word vectors with subword information. Trans. Assoc. Comput. Linguist. **5**, 135–146 (2017)
2. Brunet, M.E., Alkalay-Houlihan, C., Anderson, A., Zemel, R.: Understanding the origins of bias in word embeddings. In: Chaudhuri, K., Salakhutdinov, R. (eds.) Proceedings of the 36th International Conference on Machine Learning. Proceedings of Machine Learning Research, vol. 97, pp. 803–811. PMLR, Long Beach, California, USA 09–15 June 2019
3. Chen, K.J., Huang, C.R., Chang, L.P., Hsu, H.L.: Sinica corpus: design methodology for balanced corpora. In: Proceedings of the 11th Pacific Asia Conference on Language, Information and Computation, pp. 167–176 (1996)
4. Conneau, A., Lample, G., Ranzato, M., Denoyer, L., Jégou, H.: Word translation without parallel data. arXiv preprint arXiv:1710.04087 (2017)
5. Dev, S., Phillips, J.: Attenuating bias in word vectors. In: Chaudhuri, K., Sugiyama, M. (eds.) Proceedings of Machine Learning Research, vol. 89, pp. 879–887. PMLR, 16–18 April 2019
6. Ghorbani, A., Wexler, J., Zou, J., Kim, B.: Towards automatic concept-based explanations. Preprint at https://arxiv.org/abs/1902.03129 (2019)
7. Glavas, G., Litschko, R., Ruder, S., Vulic, I.: How to (properly) evaluate cross-lingual word embeddings: on strong baselines, comparative analyses, and some misconceptions. In: Proceedings of the 57th Conference of the Association for Computational Linguistics, ACL 2019, Florence, Italy, July 28- August 2, 2019, Volume 1: Long Papers, pp. 710–721 (2019)
8. Gromann, D., Declerck, T.: Comparing pretrained multilingual word embeddings on an ontology alignment task. In: Proceedings of the Eleventh International Conference on Language Resources and Evaluation (LREC-2018). European Languages Resources Association (ELRA), Miyazaki, Japan, May 2018
9. Joulin, A., Bojanowski, P., Mikolov, T., Jégou, H., Grave, E.: Loss in translation: learning bilingual word mapping with a retrieval criterion. In: Proceedings of the 2018 Conference on Empirical Methods in Natural Language Processing, pp. 2979–2984 (2018)
10. Kingma, D.P., Ba, J.: Adam: a method for stochastic optimization. In: International Conference on Learning Representations (ICLR) (2015)

11. Mikolov, T., Chen, K., Corrado, G., Dean, J.: Efficient estimation of word representations in vector space. arXiv:1301.3781 (2013)
12. Mikolov, T., Le, Q.V., Sutskever, I.: Exploiting similarities among languages for machine translation. arXiv preprint arXiv:1309.4168 (2013)
13. Prost, F., Thain, N., Bolukbasi, T.: Debiasing embeddings for reduced gender bias in text classification. In: Proceedings of the First Workshop on Gender Bias in Natural Language Processing, pp. 69–75 (2019)
14. Schwarzenberg, R., Raithel, L., Harbecke, D.: Neural vector conceptualization for word vector space interpretation. In: NAACL HLT 2019 (2019)
15. Wang, Z., Wang, H., Wen, J.R., Xiao, Y.: An inference approach to basic level of categorization. In: Proceedings of the 24th ACM International on Conference on Information and Knowledge Management - CIKM 2015, pp. 653–662. ACM Press, New York City (2015)

Student Workshop

A Dynamic Word Representation Model Based on Deep Context

Xiao Yuan[1], Xi Xiong[2(✉)], Shenggen Ju[1], Zhengwen Xie[1], and Jiawei Wang[1]

[1] College of Computer Science, Sichuan University, Chengdu 610065, China
[2] School of Cybersecurity, Chengdu University of Information Technology, Chengdu 610225, China
flyxiongxi@gmail.com

Abstract. The currently used word embedding techniques use fixed vectors to represent words without the concept of context and dynamics. This paper proposes a deep neural network CoDyWor to model the context of words so that words in different contexts have different vector representations of words. First of all, each layer of the model captures contextual information for each word of the input statement from different angles, such as grammatical information and semantic information, et al. Afterwards, different weights are assigned to each layer of the model through a multi-layered attention mechanism. At last, the information of each layer is integrated to form a dynamic word with contextual information to represent the vector. By comparing different models on the public dataset, it is found that the model's accuracy in the task of logical reasoning has increased by 2.0%, F1 value in the task of named entity recognition has increased by 0.47%, and F1 value in the task of reading comprehension has increased by 2.96%. The experimental results demonstrate that this technology of word representation enhances the effect of the existing word representation.

Keywords: Word representation · Attention mechanism · Logical reasoning · Named-entity recognition · Reading understanding

1 Introduction

The NLP (natural language processing) system available based on deep learning usually first converts the text input into a vectorized word representation [1–4], i.e. the word embedding vector for further processing. Researchers have proposed a large number of embedding methods to encode words and sentences into dense fixed vectors, which tremendously enhance the ability of neural networks to process textual data. The most commonly used word embedding methods include word2vec [5], FastText [6] and GloVe [7] and so. Studies have demonstrated that these word embedding methods can significantly improve and simplify a great number of text processing applications [8, 9].

However, at present, the commonly used word embedding techniques consider no of context and dynamics, which all regard words as fixed atomic units, and represent words by using the indices of word lists or fixed values in the pre-trained word vector matrix. Although the embedding methods that assign fixed values to represent words

J. Tang et al. (Eds.): NLPCC 2019, LNAI 11839, pp. 655–664, 2019.
https://doi.org/10.1007/978-3-030-32236-6_60

are simple, yet they limit their effectiveness in many tasks [10]. In complex natural language processing tasks such as sentiment analysis, text categorization, speech recognition, machine translation and reasoning, et al., dynamic word representations with contextual meaning are needed, namely the same word has different representation vectors in different contexts. For instance, in the sentences: "A plant absorbs water from the soil by its roots" and "There is a big amount of water in what he has said", the meanings of "water" are different. If a pre-trained word vector is used, the word "water" in both sentences can solely be represented by the same word vector. In order to solve the above problem, this paper proposes a dynamic word representation model based on deep context, which is a multi-layer deep neural network. Each layer captures the contextual information for each word of the input statement from different views [10], including grammatical information and semantic information, et cetera and then assigns different weights to each layer of the neural network through a multi-layered attention mechanism, and finally integrates the information of each layer to form a vectorized representation of the word.

2 Related Work

A word embedding model based on the shallow Neural Network Language Model (NNLM) can convert words into continuous vectors [11, 12]. At present, the mainstream word embedding models include CBOW, Skip-Gram, FastText and GloVe models, of which CBOW and Skip-Gram belong to the renowned word2vector framework. The leading improvement of FastText compared with the original word2vec is that it has introduced n-grams. GloVe is a word representation model based on overall word frequency statistics, which makes up for the lack of word2vec that doesn't consider the overall co-occurrence information of words. Experiments have proven that the word vector generated by GloVe model is better under quite a few scenarios [7]. However, both the word2vec model and the GloVe model are too simple and are limited by the representational capacity of the shallow model used (typically 3 layers).

The word representation model MT-LSTM [13] that is based on machine-translation model utilizes the Encoder-Decoder framework to pre-train the corpus for machine translation and extract the Embedding layer and the Encoder layer of the model. And then it designs a model based on the new task, and uses the output of the trained Embedding layer and Encoder layer as the input of this new task model, and lastly does the training under the new task scenario. However, this machine translation model needs a large amount of supervised data, meanwhile, the Encoder-Decoder structure limits the model to capture some semantic information.

The word representation model based on depth NNLM is generally better than shallow NNLM. Peters et al. [10] proposed a renowned model ELMo, which used the internal state of multi-layer BiLSTM (Bi-directional Long Short-Term Memory) to generate word vectors. Compared to N-gram models, word2vec models, and GloVe [10, 14], it has a better effect. However, ELMo is limited by BiLSTM's serial computer system and feature extraction capabilities, which limits its application under a good number of scenarios.

The method in this paper adopts the deep NNLM, meanwhile, it takes the idea of generating the word vector from the internal state of NNLM in ELMo, and replaces the BiLSTM encoder in the model with the Transformer encoder with concurrent computing and contextual coding capability, and introduces a multi-layer attention mechanism, blending word representation information of different levels in neural network, and generating the word vector with contextual meanings.

3 Proposed Approach

See Fig. 1.

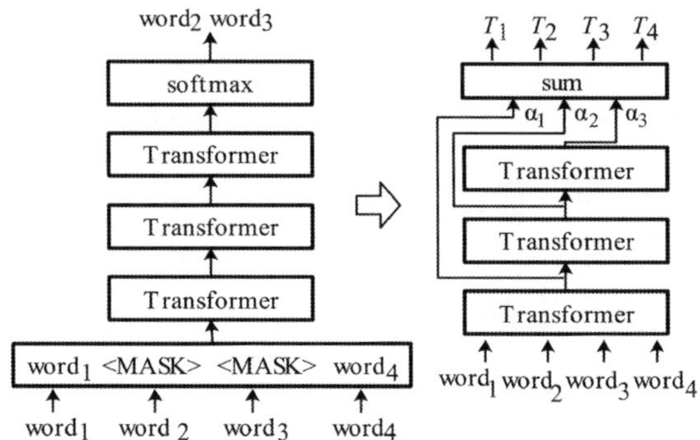

Fig. 1. Overall framework

3.1 Overall Framework

The overall framework of the dynamic context representation model proposed in this paper is illustrated in Fig. 1. It consists of two main processes: (1) the masked language model on the left of Fig. 1 (see Sect. 3.2 for details); (2) the Transformer layer in the pre-trained masked language model is extracted and a new output layer is added to form the model of this paper—the deep contextual dynamic word representation model (on the right side of Fig. 1), which blends multiple outputs of Transformer layer through a multi-layered attention mechanism, generating a deep dynamic word representation vector (see Sect. 3.3 for details). The Transformer layer of the main structure in the framework is made up of a Transformer encoder, which is a two-way contextual information extractor (see Sect. 3.4 for details).

3.2 Masked Language Model

The language model encodes the sequence of words by means of a distributed representation. The objective function of a general language model is a log-likelihood function of the probability of occurrence of all word sequences in the corpus, such as the popular CBOW, Skip-Gram, FastText, and GloVe models, et cetera. In this paper, we utilize the masked language model composed of Transformer encoder that can capture the contextual information of words in sentences to extract textual information

[16]. Unlike the general language models, the objective function of the masked language model is the log-likelihood function of the probability of occurrence of all masked words in the corpus, which is:

$$L(C) = \frac{1}{n}\sum_{i=1}^{n}\sum_{w_k \in Mask_i} \log P(w_k|context_i - Mask_i) \tag{1}$$

In it, *Mask* is a set made up of words that are masked in a word sequence *context*. *n* is the number of word sequences in the corpus. The model predicts *Mask* to the best of its ability in accordance with the remaining words. The whole process of prediction is similar to an English cloze test. As shown on the left side of Fig. 1, in the masked language model, the input word sequence *context* is first represented as a vector made up of the word sequence: $c = [word_1, word_2, \ldots, word_t]$, and then some words are blocked in the input word sequence *context* to obtain the word sequence that is partly masked: $u = [word_1, <MASK>, \ldots, word_t]$. Then, the information of the input word sequence is extracted by the multi-layer Transformer encoder, and lastly the $P(w_k|context_i - Mask_i)$ value is calculated using the normalized exponential function. The entire calculation process is shown in Eq. (2):

$$\begin{aligned} &u = MASK(c) \\ &h_0 = uW \\ &h_i = Transformer(h_{h-1}), \forall i \in [1, L] \\ &P(w_k|context_i - mask_i) = softmax(h_L M) \end{aligned} \tag{2}$$

In it, *MASK(c)* represents the masked operation for some words in the word sequence *c*, *W* and *M* denote the weight matrix, Transformer indicates that the Transformer encoder extracts the information of the input word sequence, and *L* means the number of layers of the Transformer encoder. Softmax is a normalized exponential function, which converts the input into a probability distribution.

3.3 Multi-layered Attention Mechanism

The right side of Fig. 1 is the model structure chart of deep contextualized dynamic word representations (CoDyWor). In the figure, *word* denotes the input words, Transformer is the encoder, α is the weight of different layers, and *sum* demonstrates the summation of information captured by Transformer of different layers. *T* is the generated word representation. CoDyWor is stacked by the Transformer encoder with a multi-layered attention mechanism. The model merely retains the Transformer layer of masked language model (keeping the knowledge that the masked model acquires on the dataset) and then adds a new output layer.

A CoDyWor with an L-layer Transformer generates *L* types of word representations for each input *word*: $\{h_1, h_2, \ldots, h_L\}$. Under the simplest scenario, CoDyWor directly uses the output of the last layer of Transformer as words' contextualized word representation, ie, $CoDyWor(word) = h_L$. Since different levels of Transformer can capture different types of information [17], multiple layers of attention mechanism can be used to give different layers of Transformer different weights $\alpha_1, \alpha_2, \ldots \alpha_T$. The formula for the CoDyWor word representation is as follows:

$$CoDyWor(word) = \beta \sum_{j=1}^{L} \alpha_j h_j, where \begin{cases} \alpha_1 + a_2 + \ldots + a_L = 1 \\ a_j \geq 0 \end{cases}, \beta \neq 0 \quad (3)$$

In it, h_j and a_j are respectively the output vector and the corresponding weight of the Transformer encoder of the j layer, β is a scaling parameter, and both α and β are automatically adjusted by the stochastic gradient descent algorithm. α is guaranteed by the Softmax layer to satisfy the probability distribution. Adding the β parameter mainly adjusts the norm of word representation vector generated by the model to represent the norm of the vector [10], which is convenient for model training.

3.4 Transformer Encoder

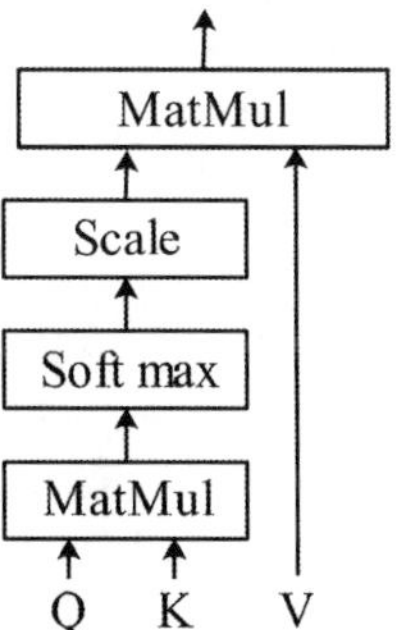

Fig. 2. Multi-head dot-product attention mechanism

The calculation diagram of Transformer encoder's multi-head scaling dot-product attention mechanism is shown in Fig. 2, in which MatMul represents matrix multiplication, *Softmax* represents normalized exponential operation, and Scale denotes scaling vector operation. The Transformer encoder duplicates the input three times, which means that the three input contents are the same. Here, Q, K, and V respectively denote of query, key, and value. First, through the query of the key, it is calculated that different keys should be given different weights, and then the values corresponding to the keys are taken out and the values are added based on the weights to form an output, the times of repeating this process is called the number of Transformer headers. The query q, the key k, and the value v are all d-dimensional. The Transformer multi-head scaling dot-product attention mechanism calculates as follows: (1) calculate the dot-product result of q and k, and then divide the result by a constant $\sqrt{d}$; (2) softmax function converts the result into probability value; (3) use probability value dot product v to obtain scaling dot-product attention operational input. In order to improve the computational efficiency, a set of queries q are put together into a matrix Q, and then the attention function is applied to a set of queries at the same time, and likewise, the key k and the corresponding value v are also placed in the matrices K and V respectively. The multi-head scaling dot-product attention formula in the entire Transformer encoder is as follows:

$$Attention(Q, K, V) = softmax(\frac{QK^T}{\sqrt{d}})V \tag{4}$$

4 Experiments

We evaluate the proposed CoDyWor model on three public datasets, MultiNLI, CoNLL03 and SQuAD.

4.1 Datasets and Experimental Settings

The datasets of natural language inference, named entity recognition and reading comprehension tasks are multi-domain logical reasoning dataset MultiNLI [18] with more than 430,000 pieces of data, named entity dataset CoNLL03 [19] containing more than 10,000 pieces of data, and Stanford reading comprehension dataset SQuAD [20] with more than 100,000 pieces of data. In order to evaluate the effect of word representational learning, the accuracy is used as the evaluative metric in the logical reasoning task, and the F1 value is used as the evaluative criteria in the named entity recognition and reading comprehension tasks. The higher the accuracy rate or the F1 score is, the better the model's effect is. The hyperparameters of the model are set as follows: the length of maximum input sentence is 128, the number of training batches is 32, the learning rate is 2e-5, and the number of epochs is 6. In addition, in order to ensure the stability of the results, the experiment is to be repeated 10 times, and the average value is adopted as the final predicted result of the model.

4.2 Logical Reasoning

In this section an experiment was carried out on the public MultiNLI dataset. MultiNLI is one of the largest corpora in logical reasoning tasks. The fields of corpus include speeches, letters, novels, and government reports, et cetera. In the logical reasoning task, MultiNLI-A is used to indicate that the data of both the training set and the test set are from the same domain, and MultiNLI-B is used to show that the data of both the training set and the test set are from the different domains. The requirement of the MultiNLI dataset is to predict a given pair of (premise, hypothesis) sentences to determine whether the hypothesis sentence is implicit, contradictory, or neutral in relation to the premise sentence.

The experimental results are shown in Table 1. The model CoDyWor proposed in this paper is apparently better than the enhanced sequence reasoning model GloVe_ESIM using GloVe word representation and the CoVe_BiLSTM and ELMo_BiLSTM models using CoVe and ELMo word representation, indicating that the word representation with contextual meaning can improve the accuracy of logical reasoning tasks. Compared to the model GPT_Transformer [15] using the one-way Transformer, the accuracy of CoDyWor (using the two-way Transformer encoder) has increased by 2.0% (on the MultiNLI-A test set) and 2.3% (on the MultiNLI-B test set). It means that the contextual text information obtained from both directions at the same time is richer than the text information obtained from one direction, which is more conducive to the model to further comprehend the meaning of the text.

Table 1. Comparison of accuracy in logical reasoning (MultiNLI datasets, %)

Method	MultiNLI-A	MultiNLi-B
GloVe_ESIM	72.3	72.1
CoVe_BiLSTM [22]	71.6	71.5
ELMo_BiLSTM [10]	76.9	76.7
GPT_Transformer [15]	82.1	81.4
CoDyWor	84.1	83.7

4.3 Named Entity Recognition

The experiment was carried out on the famous named entity identification dataset CoNLL03 in this section. The task of the CoNLL03 dataset is to identify four named entities in the sentence: people, places, organizations, and miscellaneous items (not belonging to the first three entities).

The experimental results are shown in Table 2. The F1 value of the model CoDyWor proposed in this paper is 92.69%, which is 1.48% and 0.99% respectively higher than the GloVe_BiLSTM model and the CoVe_BiLSTM model using the popular GloVe and CoVe word representation. Compared with the ELMo_BiLSTM model using ELMo word representation, it has increased by 0.47%, which reveals that the use of deep contextual dynamic word representation can enhance the F1 value of the named entity recognition task.

4.4 Reading Comprehension

In this section the experiment was carried out on the famous Stanford reading comprehension dataset SQuAD. Given a question and a paragraph from Wikipedia that contains the answer to this question, SQuAD's task is to find out the range where the answer to the question lies in the paragraph.

The experimental results are shown in Table 3. The F1 value of the model CoDyWor proposed in this paper is 88.76%, which is 2.96% higher than the ELMo_BiLSTM model using the ELMo word representation. Meanwhile, it is also superior to GloVe_BiLSTM, which uses GloVe word embedding and uses a special model structure (simulating multi-step reasoning in machine reading comprehension), indicating that using the word representation with contextual meanings can simply achieve fairly good results without designing a special model structure targeted on reading comprehension task.

Table 2. Comparison of F1 values in named entity recognition (CoNLL03 dataset, %)

Method	F1
GloVe_BiLSTM	91.21
CoVe_BiLSTMt	91.70
ESIM [3]	92.22
ELMo_BiLSTM [10]	92.69
CoDyWor	79.6

Table 3. Comparison of F1 value in reading comprehension (SQuAD dataset, %)

Method	F1
GloVe_BiLSTM	81.10
CoVe_BiLSTM	82.56
ELMo_BiLSTM [10]	85.80
CoDyWor	88.76

5 Ablation Research

In this section ablation experiments were performed on CoDyWor's multi-layered attention mechanism and Transformer encoder to analyze the effects of these two modules in the CoDyWor model.

Table 4. Effect of multi-layered attention mechanism (SQuAD dataset, %)

Layers	T1:F1	T2:F1
First layer	77.63	77.44
Last layer (twelfth layer)	77.96	77.79
Three layers (ahead)	85.15	84.96
Three layers (behind)	85.25	85.08
Six layers (ahead)	88.56	88.37
Six layers (behind)	88.64	88.47
All layers	88.76	88.56

Table 5. Effect of the size of Transformer (MultiNLI-A dataset, %)

Layers	Head	Acc
3	3	76.4
3	12	77.6
6	3	80.3
6	12	81.6
12	12	84.1
12	16	84.4

5.1 Effect of Multi-layered Attention Mechanism

Experiments were performed on the SQuAD dataset to analyze the effects caused by the number of layers (Transformer number) of the multi-layered attention mechanism of the CoDyWor model, the position of the attention layer, and the regularization parameter β. The results are illustrated in Table 4, in which the first column "Layers" indicates that the multi-layered attention mechanism is applied to different layers, the second column T1 represents the use of regularization parameter β, and the third column T2 indicates that the regularization parameters are not used. "Ahead" indicates the output of the first layer of the multi-layered neural network, and "behind" demonstrates the output of the last layer of the neural network. Three rules can be found: (1) The effect of the model is significantly improved with the increase of the number of layers of attention; (2) When the number of layers is the same, the words output from the lower layer Transformer represent better vector effects, especially when the number of layers is small, the differences are obvious; (3) The regularization parameter β can be used to increase the model's F1 value by around 0.19%.

5.2 Effect of the Size of Transformer

Experiments were carried out on the MultiNLI dataset to analyze the impact of the number of different Transformer layers and the number of self-attention heads in the Transformer adopted by the CoDyWor model on the inference accuracy. The experimental results are shown in Table 5. It can be found that increasing the number of layers of Transformer within a certain range or increasing the number of self-attention heads in Transformer can both improve the inference accuracy of the model.

6 Conclusion

This paper proposes an efficient, simply-structured deep contextual dynamic word representation model CoDyWor that can be widely used in natural language processing tasks. The contextual dynamic word representation generated by the model can be used for natural language processing tasks such as logical reasoning, named entity recognition and reading comprehension and so forth, and may be universally utilized to a certain extent. The contextual dynamic word representation generated by the CoDyWor model in the above tasks performs better than the current mainstream static word representations.

Acknowledgements. The work was partially supported by the China Postdoctoral Science Foundation under Grant No. 2019M653400; the Sichuan Science and Technology Program under Grant Nos. 2018GZ0253, 2019YFS0236, 2018GZ0182, 2018GZ0093 and 2018GZDZX0039.

References

1. Hashimoto, K., Xiong, C., Tsuruoka, Y., et al.: A joint many-task model: growing a neural network for multiple NLP tasks. In: Proceedings of the 2017 Conference on Empirical Methods in Natural Language Processing, pp. 1923–1933. Association for Computational Linguistics, Copenhagen (2017)
2. Bowman, S.R., Potts, C., Manning, C.D.: Recursive neural networks can learn logical semantics. In: Proceedings of the 3rd Workshop on Continuous Vector Space Models and their Compositionality, pp. 12–21. Association for Computational Linguistics, Beijing (2015)
3. Nallapati, R., Zhou, B., Gulcehre, C., et al.: Abstractive Text Summarization Using Sequence-To-Sequence RNNs and Beyond, pp. 280–290. Association for Computational Linguistics (2016)
4. Xiong, C., Merity, S., Socher, R.: Dynamic memory networks for visual and textual question answering. In: International Conference on Machine Learning, pp. 2397–2406 (2016)
5. Mikolov, T., Chen, K., Corrado, G., et al.: Efficient estimation of word representations in vector space. CoRR, abs/1301.3781 (2013)
6. Bojanowski, P., Grave, E., Joulin, A., et al.: Enriching word vectors with subword information. Trans. Assoc. Comput. Linguist. **5**, 135–146 (2017)
7. Pennington, J., Socher, R., Manning, C.: GloVe: global vectors for word representation. In: Proceedings of the 2014 Conference on Empirical Methods in Natural Language Processing (EMNLP), pp. 1532–1543 (2014)

8. Turian, J., Ratinov, L., Bengio, Y.: Word representations: a simple and general method for semi-supervised learning. In: Proceedings of the 48th Annual Meeting of the Association for Computational Linguistics, pp. 384–394. Association for Computational Linguistics (2010)
9. Collobert, R., Weston, J., Bottou, L., et al.: Natural language processing (almost) from scratch. J. Mach. Learn. Res. **12**(Aug), 2493–2537 (2011)
10. Peters, M.E., Neumann, M., Iyyer, M., et al.: Deep contextualized word representations. In: Proceedings of the 2018 Conference of the North American Chapter of the Association for Computational Linguistics: Human Language Technologies, Volume 1 (Long Papers), pp. 2227–2237. Association for Computational Linguistics, Stroudsburg (2018)
11. Elman, J.L.: Finding structure in time. Cogn. Sci. **14**(2), 179–211 (1990)
12. Rumelhart, D.E., Hinton, G.E., Williams, R.J.: Learning representations by back-propagating errors. Nature **323**(6088), 533–536 (1986)
13. McCann, B., Bradbury, J., Xiong, C., et al.: Learned in translation: contextualized word vectors. In: Advances in Neural Information Processing Systems, pp. 6294–6305 (2017)
14. Devlin, J., Chang, M.W., Lee, K., et al.: Bert: pre-training of deep bidirectional transformers for language understanding. CoRR, abs/1810.04805 (2018)
15. Radford, A., Narasimhan, K., Salimans, T., et al.: Improving language understanding by generative pre-training (2018). https://s3-us-west-2.amazonaws.com/openai-assets/research-covers/languageunsupervised/languageunderstandingpaper.pdf
16. Vaswani, A., Shazeer, N., Parmar, N., et al.: Attention is all you need. In: Advances in Neural Information Processing Systems, pp. 5998–6008 (2017)
17. Yosinski, J., Clune, J., Bengio, Y., et al.: How transferable are features in deep neural networks?. In: Advances in Neural Information Processing Systems, pp. 3320–3328 (2014)
18. Williams, A., Nangia, N., Bowman, S.R.: A broad-coverage challenge corpus for sentence understanding through inference. In: Proceedings of the 2018 Conference of the North American Chapter of the Association for Computational Linguistics: Human Language Technologies, Volume 1 (Long Papers), pp. 1112–1122. Association for Computational Linguistics, New Orleans (2018)
19. Sang, E.F., De Meulder, F.: Introduction to the CoNLL-2003 Shared Task: Language-independent Named Entity Recognition, pp. 142–147. Association for Computational Linguistics (2003)
20. Rajpurkar, P., Zhang, J., Lopyrev, K., et al.: Squad: 100,000+ Questions for Machine Comprehension of Text, pp. 2383–2392. Association for Computational Linguistics (2016)

A Category Detection Method for Evidence-Based Medicine

Jingyan Wang[1], Shenggen Ju[1(✉)], Xi Xiong[2], Rui Zhang[1], and Ningning Liu[1]

[1] Sichuan University, Chengdu 610065, China
jsg@scu.edu.cn
[2] Chengdu University of Information Technology, Chengdu 610225, China

Abstract. Evidence-Based Medicine (EBM) gathers evidence by analyzing large databases of medical literatures and retrieving relevant clinical thematic texts. However, the abstracts of medical articles generally show the themes of clinical practice, populations, research methods and experimental results of the thesis in an unstructurized manner, rendering inefficient retrieval of medical evidence. Abstract sentences contain contextual information, and there are complex semantic and grammatical correlations between them, making its classification different from that of independent sentences. This paper proposes a category detection algorithm based on Hierarchical Multi-connected Network (HMcN), regarding the category detection of EBM as a matter of classification of sequential sentences. The algorithm contains multiple structures: (1) The underlying layer produces a sentence vector by combining the pre-trained language model with Bi-directional Long Short Term Memory Network (Bi-LSTM), and applies a multi-layered self-attention structure to the sentence vector so as to work out the internal dependencies of the sentences. (2) The upper layer uses the multi-connected Bi-LSTMs model to directly read the original input sequence to add the contextual information for the sentence vector in the abstract. (3) The top layer optimizes the tag sequence by means of the conditional random field (CRF) model. The extensive experiments on public datasets have demonstrated that the performance of the HMcN model in medical category detection is superior to that of the state-of-the-art text classification method, and the F1 value has increased by 0.4%–0.9%.

Keywords: Evidence-based medicine · Category detection · Hierarchical multi-connected network · Self-attention · Language model

1 Introduce

Evidence-Based Medicine (EBM) is a method of clinical practice, which obtains evidence by analyzing large databases of medical literatures such as PubMeb[1] and by retrieving relevant clinical thematic texts. EBM begins with a thesis and

[1] https://www.ncbi.nlm.nih.gov/pubmeb.

J. Tang et al. (Eds.): NLPCC 2019, LNAI 11839, pp. 665–675, 2019.
https://doi.org/10.1007/978-3-030-32236-6_61

continues with human judgement by further extracting the evidential basis of specific problems. The definition of clinical practice in the field of EBM usually follows the PICO principle, which is Population(P), Intervention(I), Comparison(C), Outcome(O) [1].

In order to convert articles to medical evidence, the abstracts of articles can be exploited thoroughly since abstracts are short statements without annotations or comments. The abstracts of biomedical articles generally show the themes of clinical practice in thesis research, populations, research methods and experimental results, et al. Due to the lack of effective automatic identification techniques, it has become inefficient for doctors to retrieve medical evidence. When the content of the abstract appears in a structurized form, reading the abstract can be simpler, more convenient and more efficient.

The category detection of the medical abstract can be converted into a classification task of the sentence sequence in abstracts. The sentences of the abstract contain contextual information. In addition, there are complex semantic and grammatical correlations between sentences, which makes the classification of a medical abstract different from that of its independent sentences. This paper focuses on the representation of abstract textual information and processing of sentence characteristics. The goal is to build an automatic labeling method for medical abstracts. In particular the paper proposes a Hierarchical Multi-connected Network (HMcN)-based category detection algorithm, which includes the following mechanisms: (1) The underlying layer produces a sentence vector by combining the pre-trained language model with Bi-directional Long Short Term Memory Network (Bi-LSTM), and applies a multi-layered self-attention structure to the sentence vector so as to work out the internal dependencies of the sentences. (2) The upper layer uses to multi-connected Bi-LSTMs model to directly read the original input sequence to add the contextual information for the sentence vector in the abstract. (3) The last layer optimizes the tag sequence by means of the conditional random field (CRF) model. Experiments on public datasets demonstrates that the performance of the proposed HMcN model in medical category detection is superior to that of the mainstream text classification methods, and the F1 value increases by 0.4%–0.9%. Simulation code and pre-training results can be accessed through https://github.com/pumpkinduo/HMcN. This paper contains five chapters. The second chapter introduces relevant works, the third chapter describes the category labeling method of medical articles' abstracts, the fourth chapter compares the relevant models through experiments, and the fifth chapter discusses the research results and the prospect for future work.

2 Related Works

Traditional machine learning methods used in sentence classification of clinical medical sequences mainly include naive Bayes, support vector machine [2], and conditional random field [3] and so forth. However, these methods often require a huge number of manually built features, such as features of grammar, semantics and structure, et cetera.

Deep neural text classification, mainly perform the feature extraction through convolutional neural network (CNN) and then do the classification via recurrent neural network (RNN) [4–6]. The self-attention mechanism [7] directly calculates words' dependency, and learns the internal structure of the sentence. The pre-training language model based on ELMo [8] and BERT [9] can fine-tune the generated word vector for specific tasks and achieve the best results in multiple natural language processing tasks. However, none of the above models have been directly applied to the medical domain. Jin et al. [10] use deep learning for category detection task in evidence-based medicine for the first time, revealing that the deep learning model can tremendously improve the effect on the classification task of sequential sentences, but the model overlooks the connection between sentences within the abstract when generating the sentence vector.

When the existing work is used for the category detection of clinical medicine, the sentences are often classified separately, and the dependency between words and sentences is considered on the level of textual expression, which will lead to the poor effect on classification. Song et al. [11] splice the entire contextual encoding of the sentence with the sentence vectors to be classified for drug classification, lacking internal reliance of the sentence. When Lee and Dernoncourt et al. [12] classifying multiple rounds of dialogues, the statements in the preceding text are used for classification of the current sentence, incorporating contextual information. Bidirectional artificial neural networks (Bi-ANN) [13] are used with character information for sentence classification of biomedical abstracts and the classification results are optimized via CRFs.

3 Proposed Model

The HMcN model is comprised of three parts: single-sentence encoding, text information embedding, and tag optimization. As shown in Fig. 1, each sentence in the abstract is processed by ELMo and Bi-LSTM [14] in the single-sentence encoding layer to obtain the internal semantic information of the sentence. The obtained sentence vector is fed into the text information embedding layer in units of abstract, and the dependent relationship between the sentence vectors is extracted through the multi-connected Bi-LSTMs network. Finally, the label optimization layer uses a CRF model to deal with the categories.

In this paper, lowercase letters are used to denote scalars, such as x_1;lowercase letters with arrows indicare vectors, such as $\overrightarrow{s}_1$; bold uppercase letters demonstrate matrices, such as $\mathbf{H}$; The scalar sequences such as $\{x_1, x_2, \ldots, x_j\}$ and the vector sequence $\{\overrightarrow{s}_1, \overrightarrow{s}_2, \ldots, \overrightarrow{s}_j\}$ are represented by $x_{1:j}$ and $\overrightarrow{s}_{1:j}$ respectively.

3.1 Single Sentence Encoding

Each sentence is processed differently by ELMo and Bi-LSTM to obtain a sentence vector. Then the sentence vector is used as the input. These two processing methods can be described as:

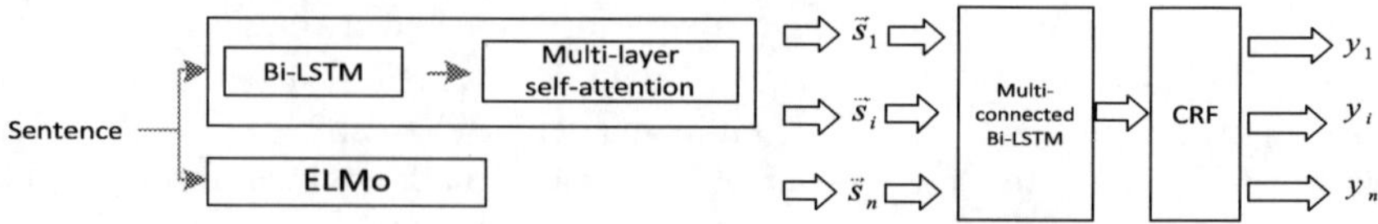

Fig. 1. Hierarchical Multi-connected Network structure.

(1) In order to address the polysemy issue, the sequence is input into ELMo, a pre-training language model. The final sentence vector $\overrightarrow{s}_i^e$ is obtained by ELMo and an average pooling layer for the sequence $\{w_1, w_2, \ldots, w_t\}$, where t is the length of the sentence.

(2) We also use a pre-trained word vector matrix obtained by joint training of texts from Wikipedia, PubMeb and PMC [16], which contains information of medical entities. A Bi-LSTM model is then built upon the pre-trained word vectors. Using the sentence vector to calculate the self-attention value can discover the internal dependency of the sentence, and the multiple calculation of the self-attention value allows the model to learn the relevant knowledge in different subspaces. Concatenating multiple results can obtain a sentence vector $\overrightarrow{s}_i^a$:

$$\overrightarrow{a} = soft\max(\overrightarrow{v}_2 \tanh(W_1 H_s^T)) \tag{1}$$

$$\overrightarrow{s}_i^a = concat(\overrightarrow{a}_1 H_s, \overrightarrow{a}_2 H_s, \ldots, \overrightarrow{a}_{l_{att}} H_s) \tag{2}$$

Equation (1) represents one self-attention head, where $\mathbf{H}_s^T$ represents the transpose of hidden layer vector matrix of the sentence, $\overrightarrow{v}_2 \in R^{1\times da}$, where the hyperparameter da is the self-attention hidden size, $\mathbf{W}_1 \in R^{da\times 2u}$ and u is the dimension of the hidden layer. Each obtained attention weights are multiplied by the hidden layer representation matrix, and l_{att} is the number of self-attention heads, $\overrightarrow{s}_i^e$ is the concatenation of all heads. At last, each sentence vector $\overrightarrow{s}_i$ is the concatenation of $\overrightarrow{s}_i^e$ and $\overrightarrow{s}_i^a$.

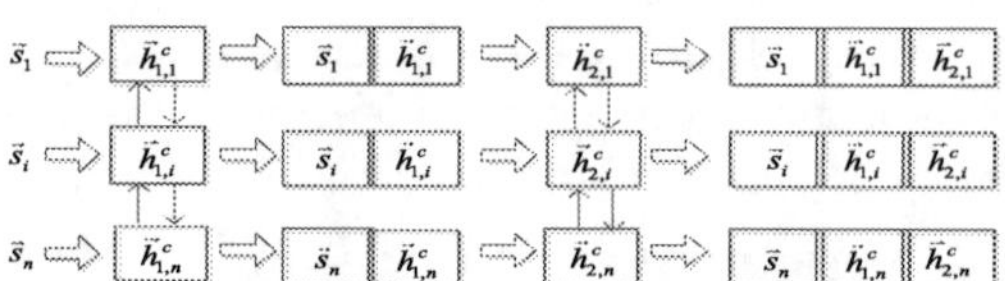

Fig. 2. Multi-connected Bi-LSTMs model.

3.2 Textual Information Embedding

The textual information embedding layer encodes the abstract's content to a representation vector.

The single-sentence encoding layer produces the sentence vectors $\mathrm{S} = \{\overrightarrow{s}_1, \overrightarrow{s}_2, \ldots, \overrightarrow{s}_n\}$ for n independent sentence in a given abstract, S is the used as the input to the multi-connected Bi-LSTMs. The multi-connected Bi-LSTMs module in HMcN is built on the basis of DC-Bi-LSTM architecture [17]. The structure is shown in Fig. 2, the input of all the layers is the concatenation of the output of the previous layers to form a multi-connected Bi-LSTMs network. It outputs a series of new sentence encoding vectors, which contain contextual information. The output of last muti-connected Bi-LSTM layer is averaged out through an average pooling layer. The above processing method can be represented by equation (3)–(4):

$$\overrightarrow{h}_{l,i}^{c} = lstm(\overrightarrow{h}_{l,i-1}^{c}, M_{l-1,i}^{c}), \overleftarrow{h}_{l,i}^{c} = lstm(\overleftarrow{h}_{l,i+1}^{c}, M_{l-1,i}^{c}) \tag{3}$$

$$M_{l-1,i}^{c} = concat(h_{0,i}^{c}, h_{1,i}^{c}, \ldots, h_{l-1,i}^{c}), h_{0,i}^{c} = s_i \tag{4}$$

In the Eq. (4) $M_{l-1,i}^{c}$ is the concatenation of the vector representation $h_{l,i}^{c}$, which is obtained by concatenating the forward hidden layer vector $\overrightarrow{h}_{l,i}^{c}$ and the reverse hidden layer vector $\overleftarrow{h}_{l,i}^{c}$ in Eq. (3). These vectors are input into a single-layer feed forward neural network, and each sentence vector $\overrightarrow{r}_i \in R^d$ output represents the probability that the sentence belongs to each label, where d is the number of labels.

Compared with the traditional Recurrent Neural Networks (RNNs) or deep RNNs, for each RNN layer, the multi-connected Bi-LSTMs network can directly read the original input sequence, namely the ELMo and Bi-LSTM encoded sentence vectors in this paper's technique, which doesn't need to pass all the useful information through the network. This paper employs very few numbers of network neurons to avoid excessive complexity of the module.

3.3 Tag Optimization

The CRF model can improve the performance of sentence sequence classification. The sentence to be classified and the sentence label respectively serve as the observation sequence and the state sequence of the CRF model. The labeling probability of a given sentence is acquired by the sentence related feature extracted by the lower layer network.

Suppose that the sentence vector sequence $\overrightarrow{r}_{1:n}$ output by texual information embedding layer is known. This layer outputs a tag sequence $y_{1:n}$, where y_i represents the prediction tag assigned to the i-th sentence. **T**[i:j] is defined as the probability with the sentence with the label i which is followed by the sentence with the label j. The score of $y_{1:n}$ is defined as the sum of the predicted probability of the label and the transition probability [13]:

$$score(y_{1:n}) = \sum_{i=1}^{n} r_i\left[y_i\right] + \sum_{i=2}^{n} T\left[y_{i-1}, y_i\right] \tag{5}$$

The correct tag sequence probability can be acquired by the *softmax* function, and the tag sequence earning the highest score through the Viterbi algorithm serves as the predicted outcome.

4 Experiments

4.1 Experimental Settings

Datasets. In order to quantitatively analyze the detection performance of the HMcN model on the sentence category detection in the medical abstract, we perform classification experiments on two standard medical abstract datasets. The datasets are described separately as follows:

NICTA-PIBOSO dataset [19] (*NP* dataset): This dataset is shared on the ALTA 2012 Shared Task, and its main purpose is to apply the biomedical abstract sentence classification task to evidence-based medicine. The label include "Population", "Intervention", "Outcome", "Study Design","Background", and "Other".

PubMeb 20k RCT dataset [20] (*PubMeb* dataset): The data is derived from PubMeb-the largest database of biomedical articles. The class labels include "Objectives", "Background","Methods", "Results" and "Conclusions".

The specific information of the dataset is shown in Table 1:

Table 1. Statistics of experimental dataset.

Dataset	$\|C\|$	$\|V\|$	Train	Validation	Test
NICTA-PIBOSO	6	17k	720(8k)	80(0.9k)	80(2k)
PubMeb 20k PCT	5	68k	15k(195k)	2.5k(20k)	2.5k(19k)

In Table 1, $|C|$ and $|V|$represent the total number of class labels and the vocabulary size respectively. For training datasets, validation datasets, and test datasets, the numbers outside the parentheses show the number of abstracts, and the numbers in parentheses indicate the number of sentences. Each abstracted sentence has merely one unique label.

Parameter Settings. The sentence vector is obtained using the open source pre-training model ELMo, and the hidden layer dimension of sentence vector is 1024. The parameters including the Bi-LSTM network and the multi-layer self-attention module are updated by Adam [21]. At each level, Dropout [22] is used to solve the overfitting problem, and L2 regularization [23] is utilized to further narrow the gap between the results of training dataset and validation dataset. The parameter settings are as follow: the self-attention hidden size da is set to 150, single sentence encoding layer hidden size u is set to 150 and 200, multi-connected Bi-LSTMs last layer dimension u_l^a as 50 and 100, multi-connected

Bi-LSTMs other layer dimension u_o^a is set to 13, the number of tags R^d is set to 6 and 5, the number of the multi-connected Bi-LSTMs layer l is set to 6, learning rate lr is set to 0.001, dropout do is set to 0.5, batch size bz is set to 30 and 40, and the number of the multi-layer self-attention layer l_{att} is set to 3.

Comparison Algorithm LR [13]**.** Logistic regression classifier, which utilizes the n-gram feature extracted from the current sentence without using any information from surrounding sentences. CRF [3]: The conditional random field classifier, as the input of the classification sentence vector, each output variable corresponds to the label of a sentence, and the sentence sequence considered by the CRF is the entire abstract. Therefore, when classifying the current sentence, the CRF baseline uses the preceding and following sentences at the same time. Best Published: A method proposed by Lui in 2012 [24], based on a variety of feature sets, introduces feature stacking and performs best on NP dataset. Bi-ANN: An annotated model proposed by Dernoncourt et al. in 2017 [13] which optimizes classification results by CRF and character vectors.

4.2 Experimental Results

Comparison of the Entire Results. The experimental results are measured by Precision, Recall and F1 values. The experimental results are shown in Table 2.

Table 2. Main results.

Model	NICTA-PIBOSO			PubMeb 20k RCT		
	Precision(%)	Recall(%)	F1(%)	Precision(%)	Recall(%)	F1(%)
LR	73.8	69.5	71.6	82.7	82.5	82.6
CRF	83.0	79.5	80.0	86.1	84.5	85.3
Best Published	–	–	82.0	–	–	–
Bi-ANN	–	–	82.7	–	–	90.0
HMcN	82.4	83.8	83.1	91.2	91.0	90.9

As displayed in Table 2, the F1 value of the HMcN model increases by 0.4%-8.3% respectively compared with the other models. The LR method performs better on the PubMed dataset than on the NP dataset, which reveals that the dependencies between the tags in the NP dataset are closer. The indicators of HMcN model are all superior to the CRF model, demonstrating that the model optimizes sentence-level features. HMcN outperforms the Best Published method in the NP dataset, indicating that the HMcN model can acquire deeper feature information. HMcN model is better than that Bi-ANN, which shows that HMcN incorporates multi-granularity information of words, sentences and paragraphs for textual representation, taking note of the internal dependence of the sentence while sentences are being encoded, which helps optimize the category detection results.

Comparison of Single-Label Predicted Effects. Table 3 and Table 4 respectively demonstrate the confusion matrix [25] and predicted effects [26,27] while running single-label prediction on the PubMeb dataset. The columns in Table 3 reveal real tags and the rows represent predicted tags. For instance, 476 sentences labeled as "Background" are predicted as "Objectives". It can be told that differentiating between "Background" and "Objectives" tags is the most tremendous problem the classifier encountered. The main reason is that there is confusion in "Background" as well as "Objectives" per se, furthermore, when the sentences tagged as "Objectives" tags are compared with those of other categories in the abstract, their semantics and characteristics are not obvious.

Table 3. Confusion matrix.

	Background	Conclusions	Methods	Objectives	Results
Background	2964	30	147	476	0
Conclusions	2	2437	25	0	190
Methods	39	13	5580	21	110
Objectives	600	0	47	706	0
Results	0	60	244	0	5432

Table 4. Single category detection results.

Label	Precision(%)	Recall(%)	F1(%)	Count
Background	69.4	86.7	77.1	3627
Conclusions	97.1	91.8	94.4	2654
Methods	93.9	97.1	95.5	5744
Objectives	79.9	52.8	63.1	1353
Results	94.8	94.7	94.7	5736
Total	91.2	91.0	90.9	19114

Comparison of Ablation Experiments. In order to verify the effect of each step in the model, HMcN-multiLSTM, HMcN-attention, HMcN-multiattention, HMcN-ELMo, and HMcN-CRF, which respectively represent the ablation model of removing the multi-connected Bi-LSTMs architecture, removing the multi-layer self-attention mechanism, replacing multi-layer self-attention with single-layer self-attention, removing ELMo and removing the CRF layer. Table 5 demonstrates the experimental results on the PubMeb dataset. It can be seen that each module is conducive to the effect of category detection, and the multi-connected Bi-LSTMs architecture is the most important component of the HMcN model.

Table 5. Ablation study of HMcN.

Model	F1(%)
HMcN-multiLSTM	87.5
HMcN-attention	90.3
HMcN-multiattention	90.6
HMcN-ELMo	90.0
HMcN-CRF	89.1
Full	90.9

Table 6. Parameter quantity of multi-connected Bi-LSTMs and the ordinary LSTMs.

l	u_l^a	u_o^a	Parameter	F1(%)
2	200	5	$1.40*10^6$	88.9
6	100	13	$1.31*10^6$	90.9

In order to verify that the multi-connected LSTMs model can achieve better results with less parameter quantity in comparison with the ordinary LSTMs, this paper carries out an analytical and comparative experiment on the parameter size. In Table 6 the first row is ordinary LSTM, and the second one is our model. Compared with the second model, the increase on PubMeb dataset are 1%, with the parameters decreased.

5 Conclusion

This paper constructs a hierarchical multi-connected network model for abstract's category detection in evidence-based medicine. The model uses the multi-connected Bi-LSTMs network to better capture complete dependencies and contextual information between sentences. Combined with a multi-layer self-attention mechanism, this model promotes the overall quality of sentence encoding, and achieves good results in the public datasets of medical abstracts. For further study, the HMcN model can be applied to tackle specific problems relevant to evidence-based medicine, such as the exploration of medical texts, document retrieval and so forth, to achieve the goal of assisting in medical treatment.

Acknowledgements. The work was partially supported by the China Postdoctoral Science Foundation under Grant No. 2019M653400; the Sichuan Science and Technology Program under Grant Nos. 2018GZ0253, 2019YFS0236, 2018GZ0182, 2018GZ0093 and 2018GZDZX0039.

References

1. Richardson, W.S., Wilson, M.C., Nishikawa, J., Hayward, R.S.: The well-built clinical question: a key to evidence-based decisions. ACP J. **123**(3), A12 (1995)
2. Wang, S., Manning, C D.: Baselines and bigrams: simple, good sentiment and topic classification. ACL: ACM, pp. 90–94 (2012)
3. Hassanzadeh, H., et al.: Identifying scientific artefacts in biomedical literature: the evidence based medicine use case. J. Biomed. Inform. **49**, 159–170 (2014)
4. Kim, Y.: Convolutional neural networks for sentence classification. In: EMNLP (2014)
5. Conneau, A., Schwenk, H., Barrault, L., Lecun, Y.: Very deep convolutional networks for text classification. In: EACL, Volume 1, Long Papers, pp. 1107–1116 (2017)
6. Lai, S., Xu, L., Liu, K., Zhao, J.: Recurrent convolutional neural networks for text classification. AAAI **333**, 2267–2273 (2015)
7. Lin, Z., et al.: A structured self-attentive sentence embedding. arXiv preprint arXiv:1703.03130 (2017)
8. Peters, M., et al.: Deep contextualized word representations. In: NAACL (2018)
9. Devlin, J., Chang, M.W., Lee, K., Toutanova, K.: BERT: Pre-training of Deep Bidirectional Transformers for Language Understanding. arXiv: 1810.04805 (2018)
10. Jin, D., Szolovits, P.: Pico element detection in medical text via long short-term memory neural networks. In: BioNLP, pp. 67–75 (2018)
11. Song, X., Petra, J., Roberts, A.: A Deep Neural Network Sentence Level Classification Method with Context Information. arXiv:1809.00934v (2018)
12. Lee, J.Y., Dernoncourt, F.: Sequential short-text classification with recurrent and convolutional neural networks. arXiv preprint arXiv:1603.03827. (2016)
13. Dernoncourt, F., Lee, J.Y., Szolovits, P.: Neural networks for joint sentence classification in medical paper abstracts. EACL **2**, 694–700 (2017)
14. Graves, A., Schmidhuber, J.: Framewise phoneme classification with bidirectional LSTM and other neural network architectures. Neural Netw **18**(5), 602–610 (2005)
15. Gu, J., Lu, Z., Li H: Incorporating copying mechanism in sequence-to-sequence learning. arXiv preprint arXiv:1603.06393 (2016)
16. Moen, S., Ananiadou, T.S.S.: Distributional semantics resources for biomedical text processing. In: LBM, Tokyo, Japan, pp. 39–43 (2013)
17. Ding, Z., Xia, R., Yu, J., et al.: Densely connected bidirectional LSTM with applications to sentence classification. In: NLPCC (2018)
18. Pennington, J., Socher, R., Manning, C.: Glove: global vectors for word representation. In: EMNLP, pp. 1532–1543 (2014)
19. Amini, I., Martinez, D., Molla, D., et al.: Overview of the alta 2012 shared task (2012)
20. Dernoncourt, F., Lee, J.Y.: Pubmed 200k rct: a dataset for sequential sentence classification in medical abstracts. arXiv preprint arXiv:1710.06071 (2017)
21. Kingma, D.P., JimmyBa, J.: Adam: a method for stochastic optimization. arXiv preprint arXiv:1412.6980 (2014)

22. Srivastava, N., et al.: Dropout: a simple way to prevent neural networks from overfifitting. J. Mach. Learn. Res. **15**(1), 1929–1958 (2014)
23. Ma, X., Gao, Y., Hu, Z., Yu, Y., Deng, Y., Hovy, E.: Dropout with expectation-linear regularization. arXiv preprint arXiv:1609.08017 (2016)
24. Liu, M.: Feature Stacking for Sentence Classification in Evidence-Based Medicine. Australasian Language Technology Association Workshop, pp. 134–138 (2012)
25. Xiong, X., et al.: ADPDF: a hybrid attribute discrimination method for psychometric data with fuzziness. IEEE Trans. SMC: Syst. **49**, 265–278 (2019)
26. Xiong, X., Li, Y., Qiao, S.: An emotional contagion model for heterogeneous social media with multiple behaviors. Physica A **490**, 185–202 (2018)
27. Xiong, X., et al.: Affective impression: sentiment-awareness POI suggestion via embedding in heterogeneous LBSNs. IEEE Trans. Affect. Comput. 1–1, (2019)

Gender Prediction Based on Chinese Name

Jizheng Jia(✉) and Qiyang Zhao(✉)

Beihang University, Beijing, China
zy1706128@buaa.edu.cn, zhaoqy@buaa.edu.cn

Abstract. Much work has been done on the problem of gender prediction about English using the idea of probability models or traditional machine learning methods. Different from English or other alphabetic languages, Chinese characters are logosyllabic. Previous approaches work quite well for Indo-European languages in general and English in particular, however, their performance deteriorate in Asian languages such as Chinese, Japanese and Korean. In our work, we focus on Simplified Chinese characters and present a novel approach incorporating phonetic information (Pinyin) to enhance Chinese word embedding trained on BERT model. We compared our method with several previous methods, namely Naive Bayes, GBDT, and Random forest with word embedding via fastText as features. Quantitative and qualitative experiments demonstrate the superior of our model. The results show that we can achieve 93.45% test accuracy using our method. In addition, we have released two large-scale gender-labeled datasets (one with over one million first names and the other with over six million full names) used as a part of this study for the community.

Keywords: Gender inference of names · Pinyin representation · BERT-based model

1 Introduction

In recent years, the problem of classifying gender has occupied an important place in academia and industry. For many research questions, demographic information about individuals (such as names, gender, or ethnic background) is highly beneficial but it often particularly difficult to obtain [1,2].

The industry can also benefit from gender data and they can gain additional information about the customers, which would be used for targeted marketing or personalized advertisements [1,3]. Also, it can be used for name translation and automated gender selection in online form filling, making the software more convenient for users. Most Internet companies in China can access to National Identification Card (People's Republic of China) database, with an odd/even number indicating male/female with 100% accuracy. However, with increasing awareness of privacy data protection, more and more Internet users are reluctant to provide their personal data.

It has long been known that the appearance of a person is not independent of the name. Parents spend extraordinary time and effort to select the perfect name for an expected child. The name of a child conveys much more information including gender both in western countries and China. As we all know, names can be divided into three

J. Tang et al. (Eds.): NLPCC 2019, LNAI 11839, pp. 676–683, 2019.
https://doi.org/10.1007/978-3-030-32236-6_62

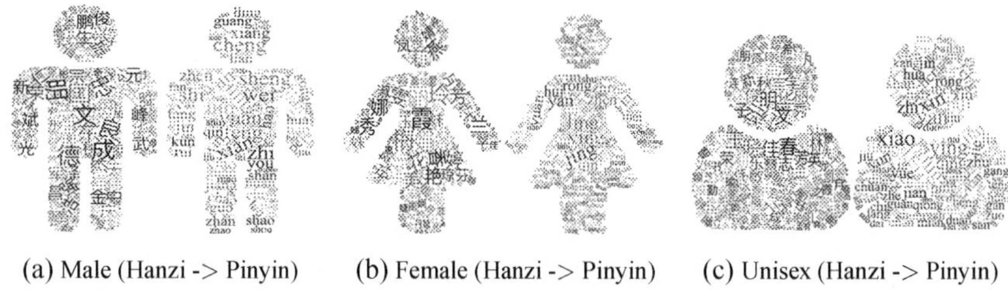

(a) Male (Hanzi -> Pinyin) (b) Female (Hanzi -> Pinyin) (c) Unisex (Hanzi -> Pinyin)

Fig. 1. The Chinese character (Hanzi) of name can indicate some information of gender, in the same way, Pinyin is gender-specific. The characters of two figures (Hanzi and Pinyin) do not completely match because different characters that have the same pronunciation are reduced to the same Pinyin representation. For instance, in the Fig. 1a, "中" and "忠" have the same Pinyin representation "zhong".

parts: first, middle, and last name, which don't have equal effects on gender. In mainland China, most people's name consist of first name and last name. According to a report [19] on Chinese names from the Ministry of Public Security, there were 23 last names that claim more than 10 million users and the number of Chinese people bearing the last names Wang and Li has surpassed 100 million for both, which indicates million of people have the same last name. Maybe we can easily get the conclusion from the report that last name has little indication about gender information. In order to verify our inference, we provide two versions of name-gender datasets so as to compare the difference between the full name and first name in terms of gender prediction.

There have been several approaches proposed for gender estimation using first names. Most previous work were rules-based [4,5] or focused on probabilistic prediction using a large corpus of known names [6]. However, rule-based methods have drawbacks that the coverage of rules was limited and they are language dependent. Thus, it seems absurd to attempt to hard code every possible pattern when we have deep learning. What's more, many previous work focused on alphabetic writing systems, their performances on Chinese deteriorated. So far, there are few studies on the Chinese language.

We intend to fill this gap by presenting a benchmark and comparison of several gender inference methods in the area of the Chinese language. There are many distinctions between Chinese and English languages. For example, Chinese sentences are not separated by spaces [7]. But the main distinction is that written Chinese is logosyllabic. A Chinese character has its own meaning or as a part of the polysyllabic word, making Chinese sentence segmentation a non-trivial task. In addition to the difficulty of sentence segmentation [8], most previous studies computed the semantic meaning of Chinese characters using the corpus from Baidu Baike[1] or Chinese Wikipedia[2]. This kind of method ignored the importance of pronunciations features. The work found that phonology also contributed to character recognition [9], which was ignored by most previous work.

[1] https://baike.baidu.com.

[2] https://en.wikipedia.org/wiki/Main_Page.

Thus, in our work, the Chinese word representations can be roughly divided into two components: semantic component and phonetic component. The semantic component indicates the meaning of a character while the latter indicates the sound of a character. Pinyin is the official phonetic representation for Chinese word, which converts Chinese character to Roman letters depending on the pronunciation of Mandarin Chinese [10]. For example, "qing" and "qin" are the phonetic component of characters "青" (seafoam) and "琴" (Qin, a Chinese musical instrument). In this case, they both contain female cues. Figure 1 shows that Pinyin is also gender inclination like Chinese characters (Hanzi). For example, in Fig. 1a, "国" /guo/ and "德" /de/ are male inclined and in Fig. 1c, we call "明" /ming/ and "晓" /xiao/ are unisex.

Then we used two representations: the simplified Chinese string and responding Pinyin representation. Our idea is that we can use phonetic features to enhance the original Chinese embeddings. Finally, we used the state-of-art model BERT [11] for gender classification based on the features we have described.

To summarize, the key contributions of this work are as follows: (1) This work fills the gap of integrating Pinyin information with traditional word embedding via BERT-Base model. (2) We compare several previous gender inference architectures with our model and the effectiveness of our idea is empirically well demonstrated. (3) To our best knowledge, this is the first large gender-labeled Chinese name dataset available for the community.

2 Related Work

Early work on gender prediction includes gender-guesser [15], Gender API [16] and Ngender [17]. The gender-guesser guesses gender from first English name using a dictionary. Sometimes, you get the "Unknown Token" if the input doesn't exist in the dictionary. Gender API infers the likely gender of a name but it is a commercial application and not free for the community. Ngender also uses a predefined dictionary. The drawback is obvious: the dictionary is too limited when it comes to new words although this work[3] uses Laplacian smoothing technique addressing low-frequency words or OOV (out-of-vocabulary) problem.

More Recent studies pay more attention to traditional machine learning such as SVM [6,12] or boosted decision trees [4]. This work finds out a set of characteristics such as number of syllables, number of vowels and ending character, extracted from first name and then use these characteristics as feature to an SVM model [1].

In recent years, some effective methods to understand Chinese names have been proposed. This work provided a tool for both English and Chinese names simultaneously but only in STEM fields when they find no free gender forecasting software to predict global gender disparity [13]. [14] proposed a framework exploring both internal character information and external context of words to explore subword-level information of Chinese characters, however, in this paper, we propose to use Pinyin to enhance the traditional Chinese word embeddings.

[3] http://sofasofa.io/tutorials/naive_bayes_classifier/.

In this paper, we'd like to use BERT model instead of traditional machine learning methods, which need manual feature extraction and selection. Moreover, we introduce Pinyin as raw training data to original embedding hoping to enhance the ability of word embedding.

3 The Approaches and Data

3.1 Four Approaches

There are mainly four types of gender prediction models in our experiment: (1) a rule-based approach, which was omitted by its limitation in specific language or region [3], (2) probabilistic model like Naive Bayes, (3) two types of machine learning algorithms such as GBDT and Random forest, (4) BERT-Base model with character-Pinyin data.

Naive Bayes Classifier. We firstly choose Naive Bayes for its simplicity since there is almost no hyper-parameter tuning needed. The Naive Bayes classifier uses Bayes Theorem to predict the probability of gender given name information [13]. The formula of Naive Bayes algorithm for gender prediction:

$$P(\frac{gender}{name}) = \frac{P(gender) \times P(\frac{gender}{name})}{P(name)}$$

In this formula, $P(gender|name)$ is the posterior probability of gender, given names; $P(name|gender)$ is the likelihood which is the probability of predictor, given gender; $P(name)$ is the prior probability of predictor.

We also apply Laplace smoothing when a frequency-based probability is zero, which is a practical technique used to deal with unknown words (names).

$$g(x) = \frac{n_x + \alpha}{l + \alpha c}$$

where n_x is the number of occurrences of the word x, l is the length of the sentence, c is the number of different words in the sentence, and α is the smooth coefficient of Laplacian smoothness, which is a hyper-parameter.

GBDT with Simple Features. GBDT, however, is chosen as "simple version" of neural network and its decent performance in many machine learning competitions. The features are term frequency of every single Chinese character from the name.

Random Forest with Various Types of Features. This model takes three types of features: the first name, the unigram of first name and a vector of size one hundred extracted from Skip-gram model via fastText trained separately using a corpus collected from Baidu Baike.

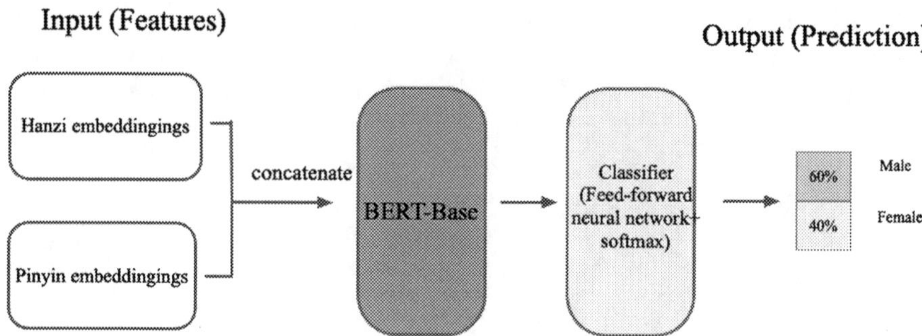

Fig. 2. BERT has achieved state-of-the-art results in wide variety of NLP language task. We load BERT-Base model, attach an additional layer for classification, and fine-tune BERT model for gender classification.

Table 1. The statistical information of our datasets. The difference between firstname dataset and fullname dataset is that the former has no first name. For example, "杨振宁" is a Chinese name that is officially displayed as Chenning Yang. And, in the fullname dataset, it's showed as "yang chen ning" where chracters are separated by space and converted into lower case. But in the firstname dataset, it is represented as "chen ning".

Data Type	Number	Percent
firstname (female)	718,400	63.70%
firstname (male)	409,411	36.30%
fullname (female)	4,366,278	66.25%
fullname (male)	2,223,964	33.75%

BERT-Base Model with Character-Pinyin Data The architecture of our model could be found in Fig. 2. We mainly have to train the binary classifier, with some changes like the dictionary to the BERT-Base model during training process. The training process is also called Fine-Tuning.

3.2 Gender-Labeled Data

The gender-labeled data can be vital to gender classification. However, to the best of our knowledge, there is no suitable gender-labeled dataset for deep network training.

In our work, data was collected with reliable gender labels collected from several public sources. After cleaning and removing repetitive names, the final data lists consist of 6,590,242 names and 1,127,811 first names, respectively. We used pypinyin [18] and Google translator to translate those Chinese names into Pinyin format. Table 1 shows more details about our gender-labeled datasets.

There are two types of datasets: The first one is Simplified Chinese character which we call "hanzi". Since each Chinese character corresponds to a Pinyin, we take each Pinyin as a token corresponding to the Chinese character. Then we call the second type dataset as "character-pinyin".

4 Experiments

We explore four different classifier types described above. We choose Naive Bayes as baseline and GBDT using TF (term frequency) as the "simpler version" of neural network. The third model is based on Random forest using the word embedding trained by fastText. Finally, our model is trained on BERT using simplified Chinese words and corresponding Pinyin data.

Comparison Experiments were done on our first name dataset without Pinyin information. For fastText, we used Skip-gram to learn word embeddings, we set the minimum length of character n-grams to be 2 and the maximum length of character n-grams to be 4. We tuned the hyper-parameters using grid search and cross-validation with 90% in the training set, 5% in the dev set. The test data (5%) was held out for final comparison. The experimental results could be found in Table 2. The high accuracy in test set indicated the effiency of our proposed model.

To analyze the effect of Pinyin representation, we also did a second type of experiment applying different merging strategies of the data training on our model. The first type of dataset was first name data of Pinyin format; the second one was first name data of Simplified Chinese (Hanzi) format; the third one was first name data from both Pinyin and Simplified Chinese format, we called this as character-Pinyin first name (Hanzi-Pinyin-first); the final one used full name data from both Pinyin and Simplified Chinese format (Hanzi-Pinyin-full). Table 3 showed the detail information of our experiment results. You could find our codes and open-source datasets here[4] sooner.

5 Conclusion

Our experiments showed the efficiency of incorporating Pinyin information to enhance previous word embedding compared with using Chinese words only. We hold that this idea can also expand to other NLP tasks or downstream tasks.

Pinyin did not do as well as the Simplified Chinese characters, but combined with Simplified Chinese words, it can get better results compared to using Simplified Chinese words alone. Also, we face problem such as unisex names, which could be the direction for future work.

Table 2. Experiment results came from Chinese characters data without incorporating Pinyin information. We reported the mean and standard deviation (SD) of results from ten repeated experiments on each model with different random seed.

	Naive Bayes	GBDT	RF	Our Model
ACC (mean)	80.67%	85.59%	84.87%	**90.89%**
ACC (SD)	2.03	1.85	1.58	1.02

[4] https://github.com/jijeng/gender-prediction.

Table 3. These experiments were trained on different combinations of our two datasets. Like last experiment, we used mean and SD of ACC to get unbiased result. ACC from "Hanzi-Pinyin-first" and "Hanzi-Pinyin-full" got better results than the others. And "Hanzi (only)" got better accuracy than "Pinyin (only)" when working alone.

	Pinyin (only)	Hanzi (only)	Hanzi-Pinyin-first	Hanzi-Pinyin-full
ACC (mean)	69.64%	90.89%	**92.33%**	**93.45%**
ACC (SD)	1.78	0.96	1.02	1.52

References

1. Mueller, J., Stumme, G.: Gender inference using statistical name characteristics in twitter. In: Proceedings of the The 3rd Multidisciplinary International Social Networks Conference on SocialInformatics 2016, Data Science 2016, p. 47. ACM (2016)
2. Karimi, F., Wagner, C., Lemmerich, F., Jadidi, M., Strohmaier, M.: Inferring gender from names on the web: a comparative evaluation of gender detection methods. In: Proceedings of the 25th International Conference Companion on World Wide Web, WWW 2016 Companion, Republic and Canton of Geneva, Switzerland, pp. 53–54. International World Wide Web Conferences Steering Committee (2016)
3. Khachane, M.Y.: Gender estimation from first name: a rule based approach. Int. J. Adv. Res. Comput. Sci. **9**(2), 609 (2018)
4. Liu, W., Ruths, D.: What's in a name? using first names as features for gender inference in twitter. In: 2013 AAAI Spring Symposium Series (2013)
5. Gu, C., Tian, X.-P., Yu, J.-D.: Automatic recognition of chinese personal name using conditional random fields and knowledge base. Mathematical Problems in Engineering (2015)
6. Burger, J.D., Henderson, J., Kim, G., Zarrella, G.: Discriminating gender on twitter. In: Proceedings of the Conference on Empirical Methods in Natural Language Processing, EMNLP 2011, Stroudsburg, PA, USA, pp. 1301–1309. Association for Computational Linguistics (2011)
7. Liu, M., Rus, V., Liao, Q., Liu, L.: Encoding and ranking similar chinese characters. J. Inf. Sci. Eng. **33**(5), 1195–1211 (2017)
8. Huang, S., Wu, J.: A pragmatic approach for classical chinese word segmentation. In: Proceedings of the Eleventh International Conference on Language Resources and Evaluation (LREC-2018) 2018
9. Peng, N., Yu, M., Dredze, M.: An empirical study of chinese name matching and applications. In: Proceedings of the 53rd Annual Meeting of the Association for Computational Linguistics and the 7th International Joint Conference on Natural Language Processing (Volume 2: Short Papers), vol. 2, pp. 377–383 (2015)
10. Huang, Y., Zhao, H.: Chinese pinyin aided IME, input what you have not keystroked yet. In: Proceedings of the 2018 Conference on Empirical Methods in Natural Language Processing, Brussels, Belgium, pp. 2923–2929. Association for Computational Linguistics, October-November 2018
11. Devlin, J., Chang, M.-W., Lee, K., Toutanova, K.: BERT: pre-training of deep bidirectional transformers for language understanding. arXiv e-prints, page arXiv:1810.04805, October 2018
12. Chen, H., Gallagher, A.C., Girod, B.: What's in a name? first names as facial attributes. In: The IEEE Conference on Computer Vision and Pattern Recognition (CVPR), June 2013

13. Zhao, H., Kamareddine, F.: Advance gender prediction tool of first names and its use in analysing gender disparity in computer science in the uk, malaysia and china. In: 2017 International Conference on Computational Science and Computational Intelligence (CSCI), pp. 222–227, December 2017
14. Jin, H., et al.: Incorporating Chinese Characters of Words for Lexical Sememe Prediction. arXiv e-prints, page arXiv:1806.06349, June 2018
15. Gender Guesser. https://test.pypi.org/project/gender-guesser/. Accessed 4 May 2019
16. Namsor Gender API. https://gender-api.com/. Accessed 4 May 2019
17. Ngender. https://github.com/observerss/ngender/. Accessed 4 May 2019
18. pypinyin. https://pypi.org/project/pypinyin/. Accessed 4 May 2019
19. Most common surnames revealed. http://www.chinadaily.com.cn/a/201901/31/WS5c528e7ea3106c65c34e78cb.html. Accessed 4 May 2019

Explanation Chains Model Based on the Fine-Grained Data

Fu-Yuan Ma[1], Wen-Qi Chen[1], Min-Hao Xiao[1], Xin Wang[2,3], and Ying Wang[1,2,4(✉)]

[1] College of Computer Science and Technology, Jilin University, Changchun 130012, China
wangying2010@jlu.edu.cn

[2] Key Laboratory of Symbol Computation and Knowledge Engineering, Jilin University, Ministry of Education, Changchun 130012, China

[3] Changchun Institute of Technology, Changchun 130012, China

[4] College of Software, Jilin University, Changchun 130012, China

Abstract. With the development of information society, Recommendation System has been an import tool to help users filter information and create more economic value for enterprises. However, it is difficult for traditional recommendation systems to interpret recommendation results. In order to improve users' trust in recommendation results, interpretable recommendation models have attracted more and more attention. In this paper, we present the Explanation Chains Model based on the Fine-grained Data (F-ECM) to enhance the effectiveness of recommendation while achieving the interpretability of recommendation. First, we generate parsing trees from user comments and extract three key sentence structure information (i.e., aspects, features and sentiment tendency) from those generated parsing tree. The fine-grained similarity is computed based on the aspects and features of the products to be recommended, and users' product satisfaction is predicted by combining sentiment tendency. Then the recommendation chain will be constructed according to the satisfaction degree in the recommendation list. Finally, we calculate recommendation chain scores of all the items to be recommended to the target user, generate the recommendation results and personal explanation for the user by the recommendation chains. Experiments in the Amazon data set show that the Explanation Chains Model based on the Fine-grained Data achieve better interpretability and performance of product recommendation systems.

Keywords: Recommendation system · Interpretation · Explanation Chain · Fine-grained Data set

This work was supported by the National Natural Science Foundation of China (61872161, 61602057), the Science and Technology Development Plan Project of Jilin Province (2018101328JC), the Science and Technology Department Excellent Youth Talent Foundation of Jilin Province (20170520059JH), the Project of Technical Tackle-Key-Problem of Jilin Province (20190302029GX), and the Project of Development and Reform of Jilin Province (2019C053-8).

J. Tang et al. (Eds.): NLPCC 2019, LNAI 11839, pp. 684–698, 2019.
https://doi.org/10.1007/978-3-030-32236-6_63

1 Introduction

With the advent of the information age, the amount of information on the Internet has increased explosively [1]. In order to deal with the problem of "information overload" and filter data quickly and effectively, recommendation system has been widely used as an effective method [2]. Currently, existing recommendation systems focus on end-to-end optimization using evaluation indicators. For example, root mean square error is used to predict user ratings of products and differences between real ratings. However, user's decision is related to many factors. End-to-end recommendation model only implicitly utilizes these factors, which can't explain explicitly which factors have an impact on recommendation results. Although many algorithms have improved the performance of indicators [3–5], when the algorithm produces poor recommendation results, it will directly lead to a decline in user acceptance of the recommendation system. In order to improve the persuasiveness of recommendation, the algorithm should explain to users why recommendation occurs, even if deviation does not unduly affect users' trust.

User's comments contain abundant information, such as product description and customer sentiment. These fine-grained data at the product level are of great significance for both of user analysis and product evaluation. A summarization system based on user evaluation can perceive the descriptors of the product that user is interested in and the satisfaction degree with the descriptors of the product and summarize all the comments on a product. In this way, it can perceive the various aspects of a particular product descriptor and its corresponding popularity. Therefore, we use fine-grained data to construct user and product descriptors, and our recommendation is based on users' sentiment tendency. The recommendation effect may be improved by utilizing the popularity of the various aspects of a particular product descriptor so as to enhance the interpretation of the recommendation system. And the recommendation system is able to recommend the products based the similarity of the descriptor aspects, meanwhile it may provide a more reasonable and convincing recommendation results. We proposes an Explanation Chains Model based on the Fine-grained Data to the interpretability of the recommendation system. The main contributions are threefold:

1. We extract the syntactic structure rules and use an unified structure to represent the user comments.
2. We propose a method for extracting key aspects from the unified structure representation and obtain fine-grained data of the user's comments on product.
3. We propose the F-ECM, and make full use of the multiple dimensions of fine-grained data to recommend, which not only improves the recommendation effect, but also provides users with readable product characteristics of the recommendation reason.

Section 2 presents related work, Sect. 3 is description of the problem, Sect. 4 is the Explanation Chains Model based on the Fine-grained Data.

2 Related Work

2.1 Interpretability of Recommendation System

With the in-depth study of recommendation system, the validity and accuracy of recommendation results are gradually improved. However, the traditional recommendation system does not provide a reasonable explanation of the recommendation results, which affects the user's acceptance of the recommendation results.

The research on the transparency of the recommendation system [6] and the explanatory research on the commonly used collaborative filtering algorithm [7] have achieved certain results. The early recommendation system provides explanatory by using the product's content tag, it can be used both for recommendation prediction and for explaining to the user [8]. Zhang et al. [9] formally defined interpretability in 2014: explaining how the system works and/or why a product is recommended, the system becomes more transparent and has the potential to allow users to tell when the system is wrong (scrutability), increase users' confidence or trust in the system, help users make better (effectiveness) and faster (efficiency) decisions, convince users to try or buy (persuasiveness), or increase the ease of the user enjoyment (satisfaction). In recent years, the explainable of recommendation systems has been systematically classified and summarized [10]. Explainable recommendation system can be classified into matrix factorization, topic modeling, graph-based, and deep learning, etc.

2.2 Explainable Recommendation Model

The topic modeling-based explainable recommendation model mainly obtains recommendation results and explanations by analyzing and combining the content topics of the text. McAuley and Leskovec [11] proposed a method to obtain the recommended interpretation by aligning the implicit aspect descriptors of the recommended decomposition with the implicit topics of the Latent Dirichlet allocation (LDA). Lin et al. [12] proposed DTMF+model, which established a positive mapping relationship between the potential topic vectors of the user comment set and the product review set and the user potential factor vector and product potential factor vector of the traditional matrix factorization, respectively, and further guided scoring prediction by adding potential topics. Tan et al. [13] proposed the concept of "recommendability" of products. Based on boosting method, the characteristic distribution of the product recommendability is linked to the user's preference distribution in the same space. At the same time, users' ratings and comments are used for collaborative recommendation.

There are connections between users and users, products and products, users and products. It is easy to construct a graph structure, especially in the social recommendation task, using the graph structure to make the user and product modeling more intuitive. He et al. [14] obtained the Top@K recommendation model by introducing the ternary relationship of the three-dimensional graph modeling (user-product-side). Wang et al. [15] proposed a tree-enhanced embedded model to obtain explainable recommendations, combining the generalization ability of the embedded model with the interpretability of the tree model. The Explanation Chains algorithm proposed by Arpit [16] is an interpretation-based recommendation algorithm that calculates recommendations by generating and sorting explanation chains which are generated by modeling the recommendation problem as a question of finding a path unifies recommendations and explanations in a productsimilarity chart.

Matrix factorization algorithm and its variants have achieved great success in recommendation tasks, including classical latent factor model LFM [17], singular value decomposition model (SVD) [18, 19], non-negative matrix factorization model NMF [20]. The recommended prediction results of these models have higher accuracy, but the factor obtained by the factorization is an implicit description. It is difficult to explain the reasons for the recommendation to the user, and the user needs a certain degree of trust in the recommendation system.

In recent years, deep learning and presentation learning have received widespread attention, and an explainable recommendation system using deep learning techniques has gradually emerged. Combined with CNN [21], RNN [22], attention mechanism [23], etc., a variety of recommendation interpretation modes are generated, for example, automatic generation of interpretation text without the template [24], visualization of interpretation based on user's attention on images without interpretation template [25], etc.

3 Problem Describe

Given a user comment data set D, first, extracting one or more sets of fine-grained triples $(a, f, s)_{ij}$ from every comment text in D which indicates that user i uses descriptor f for aspect a of item j and showing an emotional tendency s. Then, using the fine-grained data triple of the user's comment on the product, the user is represented by the evaluation content of the product evaluated by each user to establish the user data U, wherein, for the i-th user, the number set of the product evaluated by the user is represented by item-i, then $U_i = \{(a, f, s) \mid (a, f, s)_{ij}, j \in \text{item-i}\}$; the product is represented by the specific content received from a plurality of users of the product, wherein, for the j-th product, the number set of the user who has evaluated the product is represented by user-j, then $I_j = \{(a, f, s) \mid (a, f, s)_{ij}, i \in \text{user-j}\}$. Next, U and I are used to establish a recommendation chain C_{ik} for the product k that the user i has not touched, and the product k is swam in the product evaluated by the user i, meanwhile, the recommendation chain is established by using the predicted satisfaction (ps). The recommendation chain is a list. Its head is the product to be recommended, and the other items are composed of the product evaluation content in U_i. Finally, the recommended chain is evaluated to produce the recommended product and the recommended explanation (Table 1).

Table 1. Symbol table.

Symbol	Meaning
D	User-to-product review data set
(a, f, s)	Fine-grained reviews of triples (aspects, aspect descriptors, sentimental tendencies)
f_f	Aspect frequency of occurrence
U	User data set
item-i	Number set of the product evaluated by the user i
U_i	Specific composition of user i in U: $U_i = \{(a, f, s) \mid (a, f, s) \in review_{ij}, j \in$ item-r-by-i$\}$
I	product data set
user-j	Number set of the user who has evaluated the item j
I_j	Specific composition of item j in I: $I_j = \{(a, f, s) \mid (a, f, s) \in review_{ij}, i \in$ user-r-j$\}$
C_{ik}	Recommendation chain built for product k that user i has not touched
$ps(j,k)$	The predicted satisfaction of the product k calculated based on the product j evaluated by the target user

4 Explanation Chains Model Based on the Fine-Grained Data

By processing the user text to obtain the product description words and corresponding sentiment trends discussed by the user in the comments, a fine-grained data set is established. The recommendation chain model is improved by making full use of various dimensions of the fine-grained data, so it provides a more informative and accurate recommendation for recommended products.

The model we built is shown in Fig. 1:

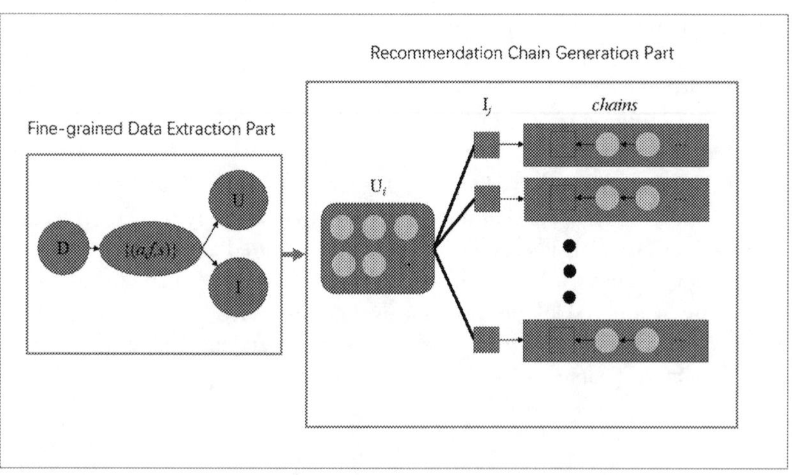

Fig. 1. Explanation chains model based on the Fine-grained data

4.1 Fine-Grained Data Extraction

The quality of fine-grained data directly affects the effect of the algorithm. We extract fine-grained data based on the principle of retaining as much information as possible. Although the expression of natural language is very flexible, some euphemistic expressions or discourses in special situations are very difficult to conduct structured analysis, so it is difficult for the machine to obtain accurate user expression. But in the specific context of product reviews, the user's expression often has a good structure, which is convenient for research and analysis.

As shown in Fig. 1, the fine-grained data extraction part is mainly completed in the following steps.

Step1. Text preprocessing to remove irrelevant expressions in text;
Step2. Syntactic structure parsing, using the parse tree to represent the comment text;
Step3. Extracting key information in the sentence by the common structural rules in the parsing tree to obtain a unified structured representation of comment text;
Step4. Extracting a three-tuple set (aspect, aspect descriptor, sentiment tendencies) from a unified structured representation of the review text.

Step1 standardizes the comment text, removes the non-utf-8 encoded characters that may exist in the text, converts the ordinary text into a uniform lowercase, restores the irregular word spelling and restores the English abbreviations. Step2 uses Stanford University's English parsing tool [26] to parse the comment text and get the parsing tree.

Step3 regards aspects of goods, aspect descriptors and emotional tendencies as key information of fine-grained data. Aspect is a property of a product, and often presented as a noun or pronoun in a sentence. Aspect descriptors are supplements to a description of a particular aspect of a product, usually appears around the aspect words as adjectives or adverbs for modification. The user's emotional tendency has two sources, one is the aspect descriptors that the user used to describe the aspect of the product, and the second is the verb used in the user description, such as: "like", "hate", "repent" and other words. In the process of extraction, in order to preserve the key information of the text as much as possible, we select a certain number of example sentences to analyze the relevant conclusions about the sentence composition in the parse tree, and proves the conclusion by statistical analysis of the data set. These conclusions propose ways to unify the expression of the text. The conclusions reached are as follows:

Conclusion 1: A sentence consists of two main components: noun phrase (NP) and verb phrase (VP)

Conclusion 2: Noun phrases are mainly composed of the following part of speech: pronoun/noun/qualifier/adjective

Conclusion 3: The verb phrase is mainly composed of the following components: verb/noun phrase/preposition phrase/adverb phrase/sentence/adjective phrase

Based on the above conclusions, we provide a unified and standardized representation of the review texts in order to extract the aspects, features and emotional tendency of the product mentioned by user. According to the conclusion 1, a sentence has two main parts—the noun phrase and the verb phrase. Therefore, according to the expression habit, we recognize the two as the subject and the predicate, and the main structure is obtained: [subject noun phrase], [predicate verb phrase].

According to the conclusion 2, the composition of the noun phrase part is formatted, the three main parts of the noun phrase are pronoun, noun, adjective. Pronouns and nouns represent real things, so they are treated as the same nature and placed in the same position. The expression nature of adjectives is different from nouns and it is of great significance to the expression of features in various aspects. So we store it together with nouns in noun phrases. Therefore, the structure of the final noun phrase is reserved as [adjective, noun/pronoun].

According to the conclusion 3, there are two kinds of different words in the verb phrase, one is the verb that expresses the user action and even the emotion, the other is the simplification and retention of the noun phrase as the action object. Verbs retain themselves, meanwhile, considering adverbs and adjectives that have a high proportion in verb phrases and play an important role in emotional expression, we finally decide to retain the verb phrase components as [[adverb, verb], adjective] format. The noun phrase appearing in the verb phrase is the same as the form of conclusion 2 as [adjective, noun/pronoun].

Finally, the sentence is uniformly normalized as the following structure: {[adjective, subject (noun/pronoun)], [[adverb, predicate (verb), adjective], [adjective, object (noun/pronoun)]}, in the sentence the components of the aspect/aspect descriptor/emotional expression potential are retained as much as possible. For the compound sentence structure, it is divided into multiple simple sentences and saved one by one, which does not affect the components of the sentence that express the key information.

Step 4 extracts all the (aspects, aspects, and emotions) triples in the structure from the results of Step 3 for subsequent use and extraction of key information. First, the core of a unified normalized structure is the predicate part, which connects the action subject and the object. First, the predicate part in the unified normalized structure is retained as the possible emotional expression in the emotional part of the second unified normalized structure. Then, extract all existing aspect descriptors–the aspect from the residual structure, that is, the adjective-noun combination, and ignore the content in the subject or object when it is a personal pronoun. If it is another pronoun, use the category of the product instead. At this time, if the adjective part is not empty, the two are combined into one aspect and aspect description, otherwise it is skipped; if the noun part is a specific noun, it is directly retained as a product, and if the adjective part is not empty, retain the description words for this aspect. For an adverb or adjective around a predicate verb, if it is not empty, it is combined with the noun in the subject to produce an aspect—aspect descriptor combination. If the noun is empty, the product category is used as a noun part. Finally, for a sentence, the predicate is combined with all aspect-side descriptors to form a triplet (verb, adjective, noun).

4.2 Recommendation Chain Generation Combined with Fine-Grained Data

As shown in the recommendation chain generation part in Fig. 1, given a target user U_i, a project to be recommended I_j Firstly, F-ECM will build a recommendation chain from the project, and then calculate the target user's prediction satisfaction with the item based on the product evaluated by the target user. And select the target user's evaluated product to make the project's prediction satisfaction highest, if the predicted satisfaction calculated by the project is greater than the set threshold, then it will be added to the recommendation chain, saying that the newly added item is a precursor item and is represented by the product data set I; otherwise, the recommendation chain is established. Then, according to the products that the target user has evaluated and not in the current recommendation chain, the user's predicted satisfaction with the predecessor items is calculated in turn, and the item with the highest satisfaction degree is selected. If the predicted satisfaction is greater than the threshold, the recommendation chain is added and the newly added project is regarded as a precursor project, otherwise the recommendation chain is established; the above process is repeated until the recommendation chain is established.

As shown in Fig. 2, the target user U_i is represented by the product it evaluated. When establishing the recommendation chain for I_j, the target user's predictive satisfaction with I_j is calculated according to I_k, I_l and other products representing U_i (which are represented by the triple representation extracted from the target user's evaluation text). After calculating, I_k in Fig. 2 which has the highest predictive satisfaction is selected and added to the recommendation chain and I_k as the precursor product. At this time, I_k as the precursor product is represented by the product data set, i.e., the triple representation in the evaluation text of the product by all users. Then, according to the items that constitute U_i and are not in the chain, the predicted satisfaction of the current precursor product I_k is calculated in turn according to the items that constitute U_i and are not in the chain. After the calculation is completed, the I_l in Fig. 2, the product with the highest satisfaction, is selected to continue the above process as a new precursor product. If all the products representing users are in the chain or the highest satisfaction calculated for the precursor product fails to reach the threshold value, stop the process and complete the recommendation chain.

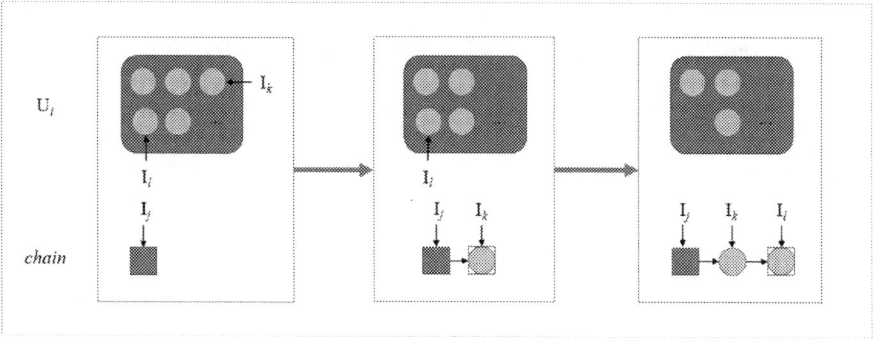

Fig. 2. Establishment of the recommendation chain

When building recommendation chain, we use similarity between goods as a criterion to select items added to the chain. Its intention is to use similarity between goods to provide an explanation for recommendation. In the fine-grained data that we used, the user's emotional inclination to aspects is mined, which can generate more accurate recommendation interpretation for users at the user's preference level. User's previous evaluation records refer to the products that the user cares about. All evaluations received by a product in some way can be used as a word of mouth for a product in this respect. When recommending a product to users, users can be predicted by analyzing the specific performance of the product to be recommended in terms of users' likes or dislikes. To quantify the satisfaction degree of products is to predict the satisfaction degree, based on fine-grained data, we propose ps_{ij} to predict the satisfaction degree of recommended product i according to user's historical product j.

In order to calculate ps_{ij}, firstly, considering the similarity of two products in aspect, then calculating the similarity between aspect descriptors based on aspect similarity. Finally, combining the user's emotional tendency towards aspect descriptors and the word-of-mouth of products on aspect descriptors, the prediction satisfaction is calculated. The specific methods are as follows:

There is a one-to-many relationship between aspects and aspect descriptors in fine-grained data. We organize product aspects, aspect descriptors, and emotional tendencies in the following ways:

$$\{a_1 : \{[f_1, f_{f_1}, s_1], [f_2, f_{f_2}, s_2], \ldots]\}, a_2 : \{\ldots\}, \ldots\}$$

That is, the product aspect is used as a first-level element describing the product, and in each product aspect, there are a plurality of aspect descriptors for the aspect as the secondary element.

Therefore, when calculating the predicted satisfaction of the recommended product based on the product (historical product) evaluated by a target user, first, calculating the similarity of all aspects of the predicted product and the user's reference in the historical product, retaining the combination of aspects the similarity of which beyond threshold. Then, for each of the remaining combinations of merchandise, calculating the similarity between the descriptors of all aspects in these two aspects. When calculating, consider the Frequency of occurrence of each historical product to indicate the user's Attention level of the descriptor, the frequency of the aspect descriptors on the aspect of each recommended item indicates the degree of recognition of the descriptor. Therefore, the proportion of the frequency of the description words in the corresponding aspects of the historical product indicates that the user cares about the description of the aspect, the frequency of occurrence of the descriptors of the recommended items indicates the degree of recognition of the descriptors, and the above factors are used to obtain the similarity of the two products in terms of aspects. Finally, combining l sentimental tendency and word-of-mouth to predict satisfaction, this paper divides sentimental tendency into three levels: positive, neutral, and negative, and uses 1, 0, −1 to express them respectively. While calculating, considering the following: If there are two items whose sentimental tendency of the aspect descriptor are consistent in a similar aspect, then the user's possible satisfaction of this similar aspect is consistent with the tendency of descriptors in this aspect.

If the emotional tendency of the two items in a similar aspect is inconsistent, then using the difference between the comprehensive sentimental tendency of the product to be recommended and the emotional tendency of the descriptor of the historical product to indicate the user's possible satisfaction, if the emotional expression of the historical product is negative, and the overall emotional sentiment of the product to be recommended is positive. In this respect, the good-to-recommended goods will be more attractive. Conversely, the descriptor of this aspect is a positive tendency, and the overall sentimental tendency of the product to be recommended is a negative tendency, then the aspect descriptor which is not good in this aspect will have more negative effects on the user who refers to the descriptor. Therefore, this paper uses the difference between the comprehensive sentimental tendency of the product to be recommended and the sentimental tendency of the descriptor in the historical product to achieve the emotion-related calculation in the forecasting satisfaction.

Finally, the user's historical product is defined as the predicted satisfaction of the recommended product ps(*j*,*i*) for:

$$\mathrm{ps}(j,i) = \sum_{a_i \in item_i} \sum_{a_j \in item_j} (sim(a_i, a_j) * \sum_{f_m \in a_i} \sum_{f_n \in a_j} (sim(f_m, f_n) * sentidifi(f_m, f_n) * w_{f_n} * f_{f_m})) \tag{1}$$

Among them, $item_i$ represents the product evaluated by the users, $item_j$ represents the product to be recommended, ai is the aspect of $item_i$, a_j is the aspect of $item_j$, f_m is the descriptor of a_i, f_n is a descriptor of a_j, w_{f_n} is the proportion of the descriptor of the item aspect f_n in the descriptor of aspect a_j, f_{f_m} the frequency of occurrence of the user-side descriptor f_m in the descriptor of aspect a_i, and sim(a_i, a_j) represents the similarity between aspects a_i and a_j, sim(f_m, fn) indicates the similarity between the aspects f_m and f_n, and the computing method of $sentidifi(f_1, f_2)$ is:

$$sentifi(f_1, f_2) = \begin{cases} senti(f_2) - senti(f_1) \ if \ senti(f_1)! = senti(f_2) \\ senti(f_1) \ if \ senti(f_1) = senti(f_2) \end{cases} \tag{2}$$

Among them, $senti(f_1)$ represents the sentimental of the user in the aspect descriptor f_1.

4.3 Recommendation Chain Generation Combined with Fine-Grained Data

The assessment recommendation chain adopts the same method as the assessment interpretation chain. After establishing the recommendation chain for all the items to be recommended for the target users, using the non-chain products in the chain to calculate the predicted satisfaction of the products to be recommended, and calculate the average to express the score of recommendation chain, select the n recommended chains with higher scores for top-n recommendation. Define score (<C, i>, C*) to describe and calculate the score of the recommendation chain with i as the chain header, where i is the item to be recommended, C is the recommendation chain with i as the chain header, and C* is the selected recommendation chain:

$$score(<C, i>, C^*) = \frac{\sum_{j \in C} ps(j, i)}{|C| + 1} + \frac{C \backslash \cup \bigcup_{j' \in C^*} j'}{|C| + 1} \quad (3)$$

Among them: the previous part represents the mean of the values of *ps* and *i* among all items in the chain, and the latter part of the pnalty chain has appeared in the recommendation chain in the final recommendation chain, while making the final recommended results cover the user's historical information as much as possible. The latter part diversifies the results while also reducing the impact of popular paranoia by not considering the items covered in the chain that have been selected in the formula.

5 Experiments and Results Analysis

5.1 Experimental Data

The experimental data in this article uses the Amazon product data: Cell Phones and Accessories. The final data set is summarized as follows:

Table 2. Data set properties

Properties	Number
Comment	12531
User	1117
Product	1232
Aspect	14573
Aspect descriptor	8452
Simplified expression triplet	220211

Note: Simplified expression of the triplet is the final result of the comment processing: (verb, adjective, noun)

As can be seen from Table 2, a total of 220,211 triples were extracted from 12,531 user comments, with an average of 17 triples in each comment. It indicates that the method of extracting key information has kept the content of the user's comment text as much as possible.

5.2 Experimental Data

The example sentence is processed according to the method used in this paper to obtain a fine-grained data set:

Example: These are awesome and make my phone look so stylish! (Fig. 3)

Parsing Tree:

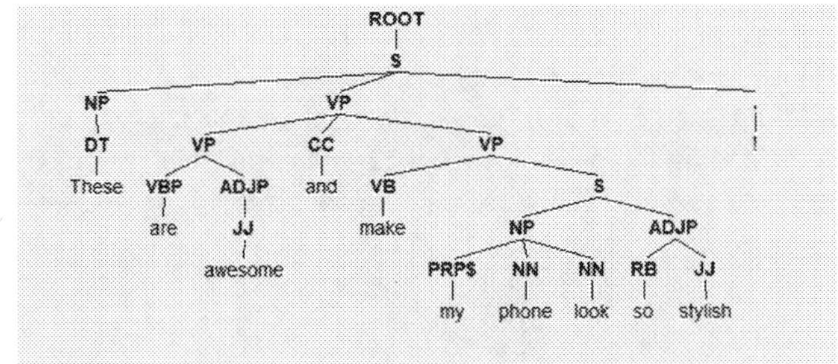

Fig. 3. An example of a parse tree

From the results of parsing, a unified normalized structure is obtained:

[[(‘ ’, ‘battery charger cases’), [[‘ ’, ‘are’], ‘awesome’], (‘ ’, ‘ ’)], [(‘ ’, ‘battery charger cases’), [[‘ ’, ‘make’], ‘stylish’], (‘stylish’, ‘phone look’)]]

Extract brief information from the unified normalized structure:

[(‘make’, ‘stylish’, ‘phone look’), (‘are’, ‘awesome’, ‘battery charger cases’), (‘make’, ‘stylish’, ‘battery charger cases’)]

It can be seen from the above example that the simplified structure preserved after parsing is relatively complete for sentence information preservation, and the simplification and extraction effect of key information based on part of speech is also reasonable.

5.3 Experimental Data

Table 3 is the experimental results of using the MAE and RMSE indicators for 5-fold cross-validation on the Amazon data set. Comparison algorithm includes KNNBasic, KNNWithMeans, NMF, biasSVD, SVD++ and NormalPredictor. The F-ECM model has the best value on the MAE index, indicating that it has a good recommendation effect, but the performance on the RMSE indicator is general, indicating a large fluctuation in the recommended effect. The main reason is that F-ECM relies heavily on users’ comments, while users’ comments are arbitrary. The amount of content involved will directly affect the effect of recommendation to users. The richer the content of comments, the more accurate the recommendation to users will be.

Table 3. Comparison of recommendation algorithms

MAE					5-fold cross-validation on the Amazon data set			RMSE				
Models	1	2	3	4	5	AVG	1	2	3	4	5	AVG
KNNBasic	0.6397	0.6352	0.6451	0.6484	0.6343	**0.6405**	0.9496	0.9272	0.9523	0.9437	0.9339	**0.9413**
KNNWithMeans	0.6545	0.6491	0.6753	0.6285	0.6476	**0.6510**	0.9637	0.9514	0.9882	0.9281	0.9578	**0.9578**
NMF	0.7412	0.7625	0.7373	0.7393	0.7394	**0.7439**	0.9951	1.0204	0.9969	0.9913	0.9949	**0.9997**
biasSVD	0.6293	0.6232	0.6170	0.6201	0.6136	**0.6206**	0.8831	0.8569	0.8565	0.8696	0.8369	**0.8606**
SVD ++	0.6059	0.6183	0.6176	0.6167	0.6011	**0.6119**	0.8475	0.8671	0.8792	0.8598	0.8459	**0.8599**
NormalPredictor	0.9488	0.9547	0.9592	0.9322	0.9472	**0.9484**	1.2674	1.2787	1.2720	1.2488	1.2630	**1.2660**
F-ECM	0.5402	0.5499	0.3646	0.4271	0.4756	**0.4915**	1.0384	1.0558	0.8593	0.6578	1.0861	**0.9395**

5.4 Experimental Data

F-ECM can generate fine-grained recommendation reasons with user characteristics for any recommended product in the data set. It can be used as a supplementary model of interpretability in recommendation system.

For example, for users whose ID is "A2P68VRKQMYBDE":

When recommending the product with the product number "B00KGU9UHS", the effect of using radar image to show users intuitively is as follows:

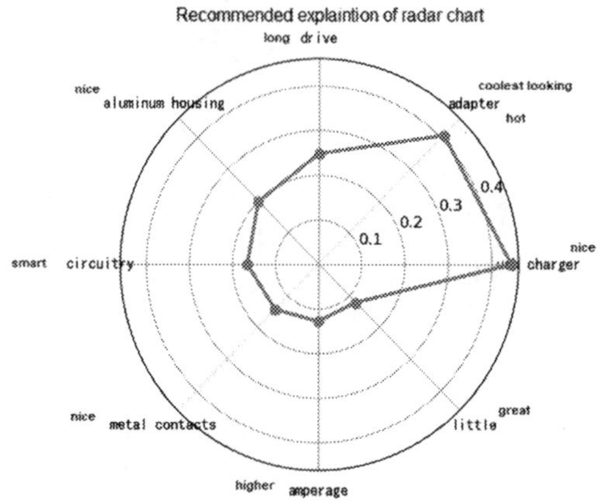

Fig. 4. Example of F-ECM

It can be seen from Fig. 4 that the item to be recommended – charger, Most of the reasons for recommendation are highly relevant to the product: usb charger, adapter, drive, aluminum housing, circuitry, metal contacts, amperage. F-ECM provides users with a reference based on the aspect of the product, the aspect descriptor combined with the performance of the product in this aspect, the user's past preferences and the frequencies mentioned in all comments.

6 Conclusion

Through the natural language analysis of user comment texts, this paper obtains the fine-grained data set from the user's text expression, and realizes the interpretability of user recommendation by establishing the F-ECM. This model not only makes it easy for users to produce interpretable recommendations for goods, but can also be used as an explanatory complement to other recommendation systems.

Since the F-ECM mainly emphasizes the interpretable effect, there is a large demand for the users in the data set, and there are some limitations in the application process. The next research will mainly consider synthesizing fine-grained data and other data to produce interpretable recommendation results, and improve the generality and recommendation efficiency of interpretable models.

References

1. Marz, N., Warren, J.: Big Data: Principles and Best Practices of Scalable Realtime Data Systems. Greenwich. Manning Publications Co, Shelter Island (2015)
2. Adomavicius, G., Tuzhilin, A.: Toward the next generation ofrecommender systems: a survey of the state- of-the-art and possible extensions. IEEE Trans. Knowl. Data Eng. **17**(6), 734–749 (2005)
3. Sangeeta, Duhan, N.: Collaborative filtering-based recommender system. In: Saini, A., Nayak, A., Vyas, R. (eds) ICT Based Innovations. Advances in Intelligent Systems and Computing, vol 653, pp. 195–202. Springer, Singapore (2018). https://doi.org/10.1007/978-981-10-6602-3_19
4. Sarwar, B., et al.: Item-based collaborative filtering recommendation. In: WWW 2001 Proceedings of 10th Internatiional Conference World Wide Web, pp. 285–295 (2001)
5. Baltrunas, L., Ludwig, B., Ricci, F.: Matrix factorization techniques for context aware recommendation. In: Proceedings of the fifth ACM conference on Recommender systems - RecSys 2011, pp. 301 (2011)
6. Koizumi, K., et al.: The role of presenilin 1 during somite segmentation. Development **128** (8), 1391–1402 (2001)
7. Herlocker, J.L., Konstan, J.A., Riedl, J.: Explaining collaborative filtering recommendations. In: Proceedings of the 2000 ACM conference on Computer supported cooperative work - CSCW 2000, pp. 241–250 (2000)
8. Ferwerda, B., Swelsen, K., Yang, E.: Explaining Content-Based Recommendations, New York, pp. 1–24 (2018)
9. Zhang, Y., Lai, G., Zhang, M., Zhang, Y., Liu, Y., Ma, S.: Explicit factor models for explainable recommendation based on phrase-level sentiment analysis. In: Proceedings of the 37th International ACM SIGIR Conference on Research & Development in Information Retrieval - SIGIR 2014, pp. 83–92 (2014)
10. Zhang, Y., Chen, X.: Explainable Recommendation: A Survey and New Perspectives. CoRR abs/1804.11192, April (2018)
11. McAuley, J., Leskovec, J.: Hidden factors and hidden topics: understanding rating dimensions with review text. In: Proceedings of the 7th ACM Conference on Recommender Systems - RecSys 2013, pp. 165–172 (2013)
12. Lin, L., Jin-Hang, L., Xiang-Fu, M., et al.: Recommendation Models by Exploiting Rating Matrix and Review Text. Chinese J. Comput. 41, 427(07), 131–145 (2018). (in Chinese)
13. Tan, Y., Zhang, M., Liu, Y., Ma, S.: Rating-boosted latent topics: understanding users and items with ratings and reviews. In: IJCAI International Joint Conference on Artificial Intelligence, pp. 2640–2646, January 2016
14. He, X., Chen, T., Kan, M.Y., et al.: TriRank: review-aware explainable recommendation by modeling aspects. In: The 24th ACM International. ACM (2015)
15. Wang, X., He, X., Feng, F., Nie, L., Chua, T.-S.: TEM: tree-enhanced embedding model for explainable recommendation. In: Proceedings of the 2018 World Wide Web Conference on World Wide Web - WWW 2018, pp. 1543–1552 (2018)
16. Rana, A., Bridge, D.: Explanation chains: recommendation by explanation. In: RecSys 2017 Poster Proceedings, Como, Italy, pp. 2, August 27–31 2017
17. Koren, Y., Bell, R., Volinsky, C.: Matrix factorization techniques for recommender systems. Computer (Long. Beach. Calif.) **42**(8), 30–37 (2009)
18. Koren, Y.: Factorization meets the neighborhood. In: Proceeding of the 14th ACM SIGKDD International Conference on Knowledge Discovery and Data Mining - KDD 08, p. 426 (2008)

19. Lee, D.D., Seung, H.S.: Learning the parts of objects by non-negative matrix factorization. Nature **401**(6755), 788–791 (1999)
20. Salakhutdinov, R., Mnih, A.: Probabilistic matrix factorization. In: Advances in Neural Information Processing Systems (NIPS), pp. 1257–1264 (2008)
21. Seo, S., Huang, J., Yang, H., Liu, Y.: Interpretable convolutional neural networks with dual local and global attention for review rating prediction. In: Proceedings of the Eleventh ACM Conference on Recommender Systems -RecSys 2017, pp. 297–305 (2017)
22. Donkers, T., Loepp, B., Ziegler, J.: Sequential user-based recurrent neural network recommendations. In: Proceedings of the Eleventh ACM Conference on Recommender Systems - RecSys 2017, pp. 152–160 (2017)
23. Chen, C., Zhang, M., Liu, Y., Ma, S.: Neural attentional rating regression with review-level explanations. In: Proceedings of the 2018 World Wide Web Conference on World Wide Web - WWW 2018, pp. 1583–1592 (2018)
24. Costa, F., Ouyang, S., Dolog, P., Lawlor, A.: Automatic Generation of Natural Language Explanations. CoRR abs/1707.01561, July 2017
25. Chen, X., Zhang, Y., Xu, H., Cao, Y., Qin, Z., Zha, H.: Visually Explainable Recommendation. CoRR abs/1801.10288, January 2018
26. Manning, C.D., Surdeanu, M., Bauer, J., Finkel, J., Bethard, S., McClosky, D.: The stanford CoreNLP natural language processing toolkit. In Proceedings of the 52nd Annual Meeting of the Association for Computational Linguistics: System Demonstrations, pp. 55–60 (2014)

Evaluation Workshop

Goal-Oriented Knowledge-Driven Neural Dialog Generation System

Ao Luo, Chen Su, and Shengfeng Pan(✉)

Zhuiyi Technology, Shenzhen, China
{frankluo,chensu,nickpan}@wezhuiyi.com

Abstract. In this paper, we propose a goal-oriented knowledge-driven neural dialog generation system, which leads the conversation based on a knowledge graph. During the conversation, the system has to actively integrate appropriate knowledge conditioned on current dialog state, and then generate coherent, fluent and meaningful responses. We use ERNIE as our backbone model, proposing a fine-tuning scheme to first pre-train on knowledge graph and dialog sequence, and then fine-tune to generate the next response. We extend multi-task learning in multi-turn dialog generation to improve consistency. We show that with well-designed transfer learning, ERNIE shows competitive performance on a knowledge-grounded dialog generation task. In the Baidu knowledge-driven dialog competition, our best single model achieved 4th in the automatic evaluation stage with 47.03 f1 score and 0.417/0.281 BLEU1/BLEU2 score, and ranked 1st in the final human evaluation stage, with descent topic completion performance(1.81/3) and highest coherence score(2.59/3).

Keywords: Knowledge-grounded dialog generation · Transfer learning

1 Introduction

Non-goal-oriented multi-turn dialog systems usually suffer from inconsistency [7] and the tendency to produce non-specific meaningless answers [6]. Recently, several datasets and models are proposed to integrate personality [3,18] or external knowledge [4,8] into dialog generation, to produce the response with richer meaning and better consistency. Based on that, Baidu steps forward and releases a dataset DuConv [16], encouraging models to proactively plan over the knowledge graph and lead in a conversation (introduce a new topic or maintain current topic), instead of only generating responses to answer questions.

Transfer learning has gained huge success in many tasks of natural language processing, thanks to the pre-trained language models [1,2,10–12], which learn rich deep contexture representations in the pre-training phase that could be transferred to downstream tasks. There are two existing strategies for applying pre-trained language representations to down-stream tasks: feature-based and

J. Tang et al. (Eds.): NLPCC 2019, LNAI 11839, pp. 701–712, 2019.
https://doi.org/10.1007/978-3-030-32236-6_64

fine-tuning, whose performance depends on the similarity of pretraining and target tasks [9].

We propose to apply transfer learning on the latest knowledge-based dialog generation datasets. Recently, a fine-tuned OpenAI GPT model TransferTransfo [15] shows strong improvements over the current state-of-the-art like memory augmented seq2seq and information-retrieval models [18] on the PERSONA-CHAT dataset, which shows the advantages of combining transfer learning with OpenAI GPT on personality-based dialog system. However, TransferTransfo might fail to generalize to a knowledge-grounded dataset like DuConv, since

1. GPT is a unidirectional auto-regressive language model. It could encode consecutive sequences such as persona in the PERSONA-CHAT dataset, but it might not make much sense to encode a knowledge graph in the DuConv, where a bidirectional encoder might be superior.
2. GPT's attention mask on the pre-training phase constraints the dependency of a sequence, which leaves us no space to optimize the structure of the input sequence.

BERT [2], however, using a bidirectional transformer encoder, could encode more complex dependency and is better in semantic representation. Thus, we want to investigate the performance of BERT in the knowledge-grounded dataset. In this work, we propose a simple variant of the ERNIE model [13], which is a Chinese version of BERT with knowledge masking training strategy, and propose a corresponding adaptation scheme, on goal-oriented knowledge-grounded dialog generation task. Our fine-tuned model shows competitive performance in both goal completion and coherence.

2 Task Data and Evaluation

Baidu's knowledge-driven dialogue competition aims to investigate machines' ability to conduct human-like conversations, in a proactive way [16]. Generally, given a set of topic-related background knowledge and dialog history, the model is expected to generate the next response which keeps the conversation coherent and informative under the guidance of the provided goal. Most importantly, the model is required to proactively shift topic from one to another in the conversation. The dataset includes 30 k sessions, about 120 k dialogue turns, of which 100k are training set, 10 k are development set and 10 k are test set.

We describe one session (Fig. 1) in detail. A goal is represented as a path {start, topic_a, topic_b} plus key spo(s), such as {topic_a, relation, topic_b} or a pair of {topic_a, property, value} and {topic_b, property, value}, which connect the two topics. It instructs the model to first introduce topic_a, and then shift to topic_b using the key spo(s). The background knowledge is organized in the form of {entity, property, value}, where entity here is either topic_a or topic_b. The number of background knowledge for each topic is usually 7 or 8, including both factoid knowledge and non-factoid knowledge such as comments. Agent is

```
{"goal":
 [["START", "阳光灿烂的日子", "王朔"],
 ["王朔", "代表作", "阳光灿烂的日子"]],
"knowledge": [["阳光灿烂的日子", "时光网 短评", "70 年代 少年 人 的 成长 经历 ， 太 过 真实 ， 再回首 至于 刺眼 的 日光 灼 目"],
 ["阳光灿烂的日子", "主演", "宁静"],
 ["阳光灿烂的日子", "上映 时间", "1994年9月9日"],
 ["阳光灿烂的日子", "类型", "剧情"],
 ["阳光灿烂的日子", "领域", "电影"],
 ["王朔", "评论", "才华横溢 ！ "],
 ["王朔", "毕业 院校", "北京四十四中学"],
 ["王朔", "主要 成就", "第53届洛迦诺国际电影节 主 竞赛 单元 - 金豹奖"],
 ["王朔", "性别", "男"],
 ["王朔", "职业", "编剧"],
 ["王朔", "领域", "明星"],
 ["阳光灿烂的日子", "是否 上映", "已 上映"],
 ["阳光灿烂的日子", "时光网 短评", "有点 西西里 的 感觉 。"],
 ["阳光灿烂的日子", "时光网 评分", "8.5"],
 ["阳光灿烂的日子", "导演", "姜文"]],
"conversation":
 ["我 发现 姜文 的 电影 产量 不 高 ， 但是 质量 都 挺 高 的 。",
  "同感 ， 那 你 觉得 你 印象 最深 的 一部 姜文 的 作品 是 什么 ？ ",
  "阳光灿烂的日子 吧 ， 有点 西西里 的 感觉 。",
  "我 也 觉得 这部 电影 不错 ！ ",
  "嗯 呀 ， 它 是 一个 年代 的 缩影 吧 。",
  "对 呀 ， 可能 姜文 只是 把 他 自己 经历 的 给 拍 了 出来 吧 。",
  "但是 里面 那位 主演 真 的 是 才华横溢 。",
  "你 说 的 是 哪 一位 ？ "
  "王朔 啊 ， 是 北京四十四中学 毕业 的 那位 。"]}
```


Fig. 1. Data

assumed to speak first, generating response on $h_0, h_2, h_4 \ldots$; person is assumed to follow agent, generating response on $h_1, h_3, h_5 \ldots$.

The automatic evaluation involves three metrics, including (1) char-based F1-score of output responses against golden responses; (2) word-based precision of output responses against golden responses; (3) diversity of the output responses. The F1 and BLEU are main metrics and DISTINCT is the auxiliary metric.

Human evaluation is based on criteria of coherence and goal completion. The coherence measures the overall fluency of the whole dialog and the goal completion measures how good the given competition goal is finished. The details could be found in [16]. This is consistent with the current main dialog challenges [3].

3 Model

Our model is adapted from Baidu ERNIE [13], which pre-train BERT base (12 layers, 12 attention heads, 768 hidden dimensions) on mixed corpus Chinese Wikipedia, Baidu Baike, Baidu news, and Baidu Tieba, using entity-level and phrase-level masking. In the DuConv task, we did the following modification:

Input. Similar to TransferTransfo [15], we prefer to concatenate dialog history and the next response as a sequence; conditioned on the dialog history, model extends the history to generate the next response, like what GPT-2 does in generating conditional synthetic text [12]. In training, we use target dialog history; during inference, we use the concatenated sequence of generated response and person's response as dialog history. As in Fig. 2, we also concatenate goal and the knowledge as a sequence, appending in the front of the conversation. Notice, we always use goal and full knowledge for every agent response generation in a dialog session. We expand the segment types of ERNIE, let segments as tags to differentiate each component in a knowledge conversation sequence. We finally acquire a token sequence and a corresponding segment type sequence. The input embedding is the summation of word embedding, segment embedding, and positional embedding.

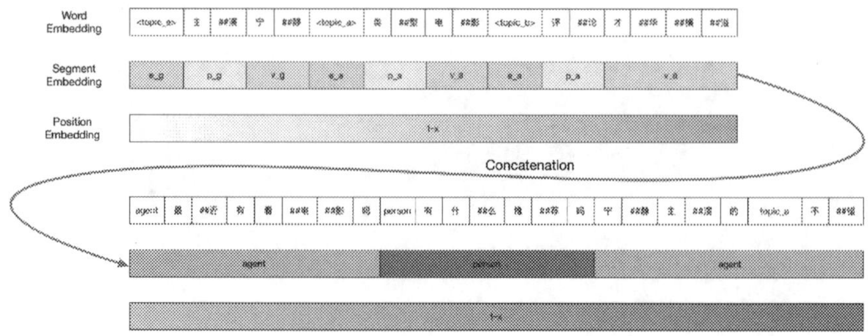

Fig. 2. Input embedding ($E_{input} = E_{word} + E_{segment} + E_{position}$)

Attention Mask. Similar to transformer decoder [11,14], we apply a future mask on conversation sequence, to allow token in conversation sequence only attend on previous tokens in self-attention. In addition, we adjust the attention mask on goal and knowledge sequence, to mimic the structure of the knowledge graph, as illustrated in Fig. 3. This new attention mask maintains bidirectional attention inside each knowledge and mutual attention between directly connected knowledge, in the meantime time, stops the mutual attention between knowledge that don't directly connect. A goal is allowed to connect with knowledge.

Primal and a variant. In primal setting (left in Fig. 4), a single model is used to encode a knowledge sequence and decode history and next response. In a variant setting (right in Fig. 4), we consider using different weights on knowledge sequence and conversation sequences, since the difference between knowledge sequence and conversation in structure, but we maintain the model architecture unchanged. It's basically equal to that a ERNIE base as an encoder to encode knowledge graph, and another ERNIE base as a conversation decoder to decode the next response; they are connected through attention mechanism in the 12 layers of transformer, as in the Eq. 1.

$$\begin{aligned} q^l &= W_q(h_{dialog}) \\ k^l &= [k_{knowledge}; W_k(h_{dialog})] \\ v^l &= [v_{knowledge}; W_v(h_{dialog})] \\ h^{l+1} &= MultiheadAttention(k^l, v^l, q^l) \end{aligned} \tag{1}$$

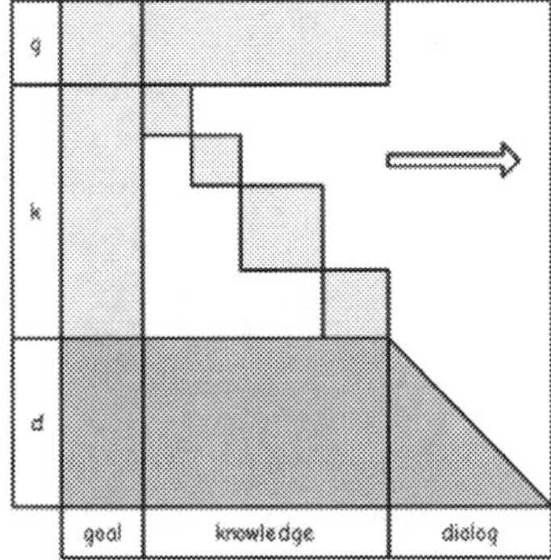

Fig. 3. Attention mask

Notice [*; *] means concatenation on the sequence length dimension.

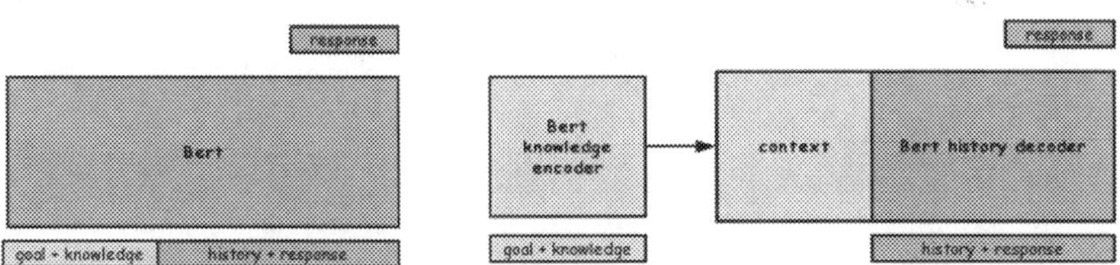

Fig. 4. Model Primal & A variant left is primal, which is a single ERNIE; right is ERNIE variant, which is still ERNIE but with different weights on knowledge and conversation

Generation. We pick the last token in the final layer of ERNIE, and project into vocab size dimension using a linear projection, and finally a log-softmax layer. The next prediction is the token that maximizes the log probability. This linear projection shares the same weights as word embedding.

4 Training

4.1 Input Features

We describe our inputs from Word, Segment type, and Concatenation.

Word. We use generalization token topic_a, topic_b to replace the original entity in knowledge and dialog, and replace back in the post-processing. In the DuConv dataset, words are segmented in both knowledge and conversation, and the BLEU metrics are based on the word level, probably because of its downstream application. To retain the word segmentation, we use WordPiece segmentation from ERNIE and first split by space. Specifically, we utilize the subword starting with "##" in ERNIE, to represent the current character is part of the front word. For example, "ABCDEF GH E" will be split into "A", "##B", "##C", "##D", "##E", "F", "G", "##H", "E". In the post-processing, the subword starting with "##" will be merged into the front word.

Segment type. We tag each token in an input sequence using a set of pre-defined segment types, based on which component it belongs to in a dialog session. The segment helps the model reconstruct the knowledge graph and conversation flow in a concatenated sequence. The basic components in goal and knowledge are {entity, property, value}, and we want to differentiate them in goal and knowledge from each topic. Thus the segment types for goal and knowledges are {*entity_goal, property_goal, value_goal*} and {*entity_a, property_a, value_a, entity_b, property_b, value_b*}. We decompose the conversation into two types $\{agent, person\}$, according to whether this response comes from agent or person; we could also decompose the conversation based on the absolute position in a conversation, $\{h_0, h_1, h_2 \ldots, h_max\}$, where h_i is the ith response in the whole conversation. In a goal-oriented multi-turn dialog generation task, the model is required to complete the goal in a limited number of turns. Thus, the position signal could be used as an auxiliary signal to dialog state. In the general case, we could sum these two sets of segments embeddings.

Concatenation. Intuitively, knowledge is positional invariant in a concatenated sequence, but positional variant within itself. Thus, we shuffle the knowledge for each topic in each time, and then concatenate them together. This also improves the generalization of the model. As we describe above, goal, knowledge, and conversation are concatenated as $\{goal, knowledge\_a, knowledge\_b, dialoghistory, nextresponse\}$.

4.2 Pre-training

We initialized the model from ERNIE, and first pre-train on knowledge, and then pre-train on whole conversation, finally finetune on response from agent. We first introduce our pre-training scheme.

Knowledge Pre-training. Since the knowledge sequence, concatenated from the knowledge graph, is different from the original corpus ERNIE pre-trained on, we first pre-train our model on knowledge sequences using masked LM task similar to ERNIE. The objective is equivalent to the Eq. 2. Based on the structure of the knowledge graph, we do not mask entity token since it's too easy; also, for each knowledge, we do not mask property and value at the same time because it's too difficult. This process helps the model adapt to the knowledge sequence.

$$\mathcal{L}_{knowledge\_pre-train} = -\log p_\theta(\bar{x}|\hat{x}) \approx -\sum_{i=1}^{|\bar{x}|} \log p_\theta(\bar{x}_i|\hat{x}) \tag{2}$$

where $\bar{x}$ represents the tokens masked, where $\hat{x}$ represents the tokens are not masked.

Sequence Pre-training. To fully use the conversation data and improve the efficiency of training, we concatenate the whole conversation into one sequence, and apply auto-regressive sequence loss on the concatenated conversation, including the response from agent and person, which shortens the training time. In addition, we randomly choose two question-answer pairs in the conversation and exchange their position in 50% of the time, and append a [CLS] token at the end of the conversation. The final hidden vector in the [CLS] position is chosen and passes through a linear classifier to do a binary classification, to differentiate whether there is a position exchange. The final loss is the weighted sum of sequence loss and classification loss, as in Eq. 3, and α is a hyperparameter. We propose it helps (1) let model focused on the last question, improving generalization (2) classification helps model figure out the inconsistency in multi-turn conversation, and then generate response more logic reasonable. Notice, when doing the exchange, we only exchange tokens and segment types are decided by the position after exchange. In this task, we only exchange the pair, in which the question is from person and the answer is from agent.

$$\begin{gathered}\mathcal{L}_{sequence\_pre-train} = \alpha\mathcal{L}_{seq} + \mathcal{L}_{cls} \\ \mathcal{L}_{seq} = -\sum_{i=0}^{|\mathbf{H}|}\sum_{t=0}^{|\mathbf{h}_i|} \log p_\theta(x_t|goal, knowledge, \mathbf{h}_{<i}, \mathbf{x}_{<t})\end{gathered} \tag{3}$$

where $\mathbf{h}_{<i}$ represents dialog history before current response $\mathbf{h}_i$, and $\mathbf{x}_{<j}$ represents previous generated tokens in current response $\mathbf{h}_i$.

4.3 Finetuning

In this phase, we train the model to generate the next response from agent, which is our final objective, with a classification task to classify the next sentence. We only concatenate history and the next response from the agent and apply NLL loss on the response, instead of the whole conversation as in sequence loss. The final loss is the weighted summation of response loss and classification loss, as in Eq. 4, and β is a hyperparameter. We extend the next sentence classification task in the original BERT to a multi-turn dialog setting. Instead of only predicting whether the next sentence is the ground truth sentence, we do a 3-way classification on (1) ground truth (2) random sampled from the large dialog corpus (3) random sampled from the current session except for the ground truth. Binary classification is too simple for a knowledge-grounded task since any response carrying knowledge different from the current dialog session will be wrong in very high probability. Therefore, the third class we added, could force the model to learn what is the appropriate sentence considering the dialog history and the last question.

$$\begin{gathered}\mathcal{L}_{finetune} = \beta\mathcal{L}_{response} + \mathcal{L}_{cls} \\ \mathcal{L}_{response} = -\sum_{j=0}^{|\mathbf{h}_i|} \log p_\theta(x_j|goal, knowledge, \mathbf{h}_{<i}, \mathbf{x}_{<j})\end{gathered} \tag{4}$$

where $\mathbf{h}_i$ is the current generated response, and $\mathbf{x}_{<j}$ represents the previous generated tokens in current response $\mathbf{h}_i$.

4.4 Decoding

We utilize a very simple decoding strategy. To improve the diversity, we split the beam size into several groups; in each group, we do a normal beam search with length penalty, with the beam size as $beam\_size/groups$. We use rules to improve choosing strategy: (1) penalize the candidates that include topic b while topic a not in the dialog history (2) penalize the sentences that include topic a, while the topic a already in the dialog history.

4.5 Ensemble

Here, we describe a very simple ensemble strategy. When we do the next sentence classification in response finetuning, we get a next sentence classifier. We use the label score from this classifier to choose final next response from several models.

4.6 Implement Details

We train the model in the order described above. We don't use other corpus in this competition, but we are exploring that and find it beneficial. In the variant model we mentioned in Sect. 3, we experiment using the weights from primal model to initialize the weights for both knowledge encoder and conversation decoder.

Pre-training. In the knowledge pre-training, we set batch_size to be 512, learning rate to be 6.25×10^{-5}, use normal BertAdam with 10% warmup and learning rate decreasing linearly. We train for 2 epochs until the knowledge loss drops slowly. We randomly mask 15% words; in 80% we use [MASK] to replace masked words, in 10% we use random tokens, in 10% we use original word token. In the sequence pre-training, we use a similar learning schedule as knowledge pre-train, except we set batch size as 32, and train about 8 epochs, with scale α set as 2. It takes about 200 min on a 20G Nvidia Tesla P40, about 25 min per epoch with 625 batches. In pre-training, we only update segmentation embedding in the first few batches, and then unfreeze all weights to update.

Finetuning. In the response fine-tuning, we set the batch size to be 64, learning rate 1.25×10^{-5}, same as above optimization schedule, with classification scale β as 2. Finetuning will continue 1 epoch. This process will take about 4 h on a 20G Nvidia Tesla P40.

Decoding. In the decoding phase, since the generated tokens do not change the representations from the knowledge and previous dialog history. We could reuse the intermediate key and value results, which improves efficiency.

4.7 Other Baselines

We also implement other models as a comparison:

1. GPT. Similar to our ERNIE adaptation in input embedding and pre-train scheme, except that we replace ERNIE with an OpenAI GPT which we trained mainly on Baidu Baike, and use a normal future mask [11,14].
2. Wiki model, from Wizzard of wiki [4]. Same with the original paper, we use a two steps transformer encoder and decoder. The encoder encodes the knowledge and dialog history independently and the decoder decode the response conditioned on encoded contexts; an additional attention mechanism is used to choose the knowledge based on encoded representation.
3. DeepCopy [17]. DeepCopy is the extension of CopyNet, which can copy from multiple sources. We use stacked long-short-term-memory as encoder and decoder, enhanced by residual connection and highway layer. We initialize the LSTM layers randomly and word embedding using Glove.

5 Results

5.1 Compare to Other Models, GPT, WIKI, DeepCopy

Table 1 is the comparison of single models on automatic metrics on the dev set. Models with only word embedding initialized like baseline, wiki and DeepCopy perform worse than models initialized from pre-trained language models like GPT and ERNIE primal and variant. In addition, the response coherence of finetuned models are obviously better than models trained from scratch; we don't compare their scores, but the final human evaluation in the competition proves that. The primal ERNIE is competitive with GPT and the variant ERNIE slightly outperforms GPT. The advantage of ERNIE is stronger in word-level metrics BLEU1 and BLEU2, probably because ERNIE vocab could easily encode and reconstruct word segmentation, while GPT needs well-designed post-processing. Table 2 is the comparison of single models and ensemble models on automatic metrics and human metrics. Ensemble models are stronger than single models in automatic metrics. However, on human evaluation, ensemble models don't achieve better results. It could be explained by the not perfect ensemble strategy, or it's because ensemble models favorite safer and non-diverse responses. Overall, it shows that (1) pre-trained language models outperform other models in a knowledge-grounded dialog generation task, especially in the coherence from the human point of view. (2) ERNIE model with appropriate adaptation and pre-training can achieve competitive or even better results over GPT in the knowledge-grounded dialog generation task. (3) Single models might be better than ensemble models in human evaluation.

In this Baidu knowledge-driven dialog competition, we do not use other corpus to pre-train BERT on a generation setting, which constraints the BERT's ability to generate sentences. A very recent paper [5] proposes that using auto-regressive, partial auto-regressive and bidirectional language objectives to pre-train on BERT (unified language pretraining) could improve BERT's ability to

Table 1. Single model comparison on automatic metircs. baseline from DuConv [16]; Wiki, DeepCopy and GPT are introduced in Sect. 4.7; primal is the single ERNIE, variant is the ERNIE with different weights on knowledge and conversation, or could be viewed as two ERNIE like model for encoder and decoder respectively; variant-2 has the same structure as variant, except that we initialize the (knowledge) encoder and (conversation) decoder with weights from single ERNIE after pre-training. It is worth mention that variant is not the same as primal. Although the encoder and decoder are initialized with the same weights, they do not share the same weights during training.

Model	F1	BLEU1/BLEU2	DISTINCT 1&2
baseline	36.21	0.320/0.169	0.072/0.156
Wiki	42.17	0.365/0.241	0.087/0.230
DeepCopy	43.10	0.365/0.234	0.107/0.287
GPT	44.30	0.385/0.256	0.112/0.301
primal	44.30	0.388/0.266	0.120/0.322
variant	44.21	0.395/0.268	0.114/0.308
variant-2	**44.80**	**0.400/0.270**	0.112/0.302

Table 2. Comparison single model and ensemble. these human evaluation is conducted by ourself using 200 examples in dev set. Our final human evaluation in the competition is 1.81 in goal completion and 2.59 in coherence using single variant-2 model.

	Automatic		Human*	(0,1,2,3)
Model	F1/BLEU1/BLEU2	DIST1/DIST2	Completion	Coherence
GPT	44.30/0.385/0.256	0.112/0.301	1.71	2.63
primal	44.30/0.388/0.266	0.120/0.322	1.80	2.51
variant-2	44.80/0.400/0.270	0.112/0.302	1.82	2.62
ensemble-GPT	45.20/0.390/0.262	0.109/0.296	1.81	2.52
ensemble-primal	45.05/0.399/0.269	0.110/0.302	1.83	2.49
ensemble-variant-2	**45.25/0.403/0.271**	0.115/0.318	1.86	2.58

generate, and BERT generative model achieves the state-of-the-art on CoQA dataset over other generative models by a large margin. We believe that with pre-training on other corpus, our BERT model could further improve.

5.2 Contribution of Different Parts

We further investigate our best single ERNIE model by comparing the contribution of each adaptation in Table 3. It shows that segment embedding and sequence pre-train are especially important in our model. It's reasonable because (1) segment embedding helps model recognize different components of knowledge and structure of dialog history easily, (2) sequence pre-train expand the data by incorporating the responses from an agent, which improves the ERNIE's ability on generation. Knowledge pre-train and attention mask designed for knowledge graph also improves performance decently, which mainly improves the model on encoding knowledge. In addition, multi-task helps improve on both automatic metrics and human evaluation scores, which mainly helps in maintaining a better consistent conversation.

Table 3. Ablation Analysis. we use variant-2 as the base, to modify each component independently, including remove segment embedding, remove knowledge pre-train, remove sequence pre-train, remove risk minimization, modify attention mask to simple bidirectional, and remove multi-task.

Model	F1/BLEU1/BLEU2
variant-2	**44.80/0.400/0.270**
- segment embedding	42.25/0.370/0.253
- knowledge pre-train	44.03/0.382/0.258
- sequence pre-train	42.65/0.372/0.256
+ simple attention mask	44.01/0.380/0.258
- multi-task	42.32/0.371/0.255

6 Conclusion

In this work, we experiment applying ERNIE in a goal-oriented knowledge-based dialog generation dataset DuConv. Although BERT outperforms other language models on natural language understanding tasks, few people use it in natural language generation tasks, since its bidirectional encoding setting. Our results prove that with proper adaptation on pre-training, modifying attention mask, and expanding segment embeddings, BERT could also shine in the knowledge-grounded dialog generation. In addition, we extend the multi-task in multi-turn dialog setting that helps improve the consistence of conversation. Our best single ERNIE base model helps us win the first place in the Baidu knowledge-driven dialog competition.

References

1. Dai, Z., Yang, Z., Yang, Y., Cohen, W.W., Carbonell, J., Le, Q.V., Salakhutdinov, R.: Transformer-xl: Attentive language models beyond a fixed-length context. arXiv preprint arXiv:1901.02860 (2019)
2. Devlin, J., Chang, M.W., Lee, K., Toutanova, K.: Bert: Pre-training of deep bidirectional transformers for language understanding. arXiv preprint arXiv:1810.04805 (2018)

3. Dinan, E., et al.: The second conversational intelligence challenge (convai2). arXiv preprint arXiv:1902.00098 (2019)
4. Dinan, E., Roller, S., Shuster, K., Fan, A., Auli, M., Weston, J.: Wizard of wikipedia: Knowledge-powered conversational agents. arXiv preprint arXiv:1811.01241 (2018)
5. Dong, L., et al.: Unified language model pre-training for natural language understanding and generation. arXiv preprint arXiv:1905.03197 (2019)
6. Li, J., Galley, M., Brockett, C., Gao, J., Dolan, B.: A diversity-promoting objective function for neural conversation models. arXiv preprint arXiv:1510.03055 (2015)
7. Li, J., Galley, M., Brockett, C., Spithourakis, G.P., Gao, J., Dolan, B.: A persona-based neural conversation model. arXiv preprint arXiv:1603.06155 (2016)
8. Liu, S., Chen, H., Ren, Z., Feng, Y., Liu, Q., Yin, D.: Knowledge diffusion for neural dialogue generation. In: Proceedings of the 56th Annual Meeting of the Association for Computational Linguistics (Volume 1: Long Papers), pp. 1489–1498 (2018)
9. Peters, M., Ruder, S., Smith, N.A.: To tune or not to tune? adapting pretrained representations to diverse tasks. arXiv preprint arXiv:1903.05987 (2019)
10. Peters, M.E., et al.: Deep contextualized word representations. arXiv preprint arXiv:1802.05365 (2018)
11. Radford, A., Narasimhan, K., Salimans, T., Sutskever, I.: Improving language understanding by generative pre-training. https://s3-us-west-2.amazonaws.com/openai-assets/research-covers/languageunsupervised/languageunderstandingpaper.pdf (2018)
12. Radford, A., Wu, J., Child, R., Luan, D., Amodei, D., Sutskever, I.: Language-models are unsupervised multitask learners. OpenAI Blog **1**(8) (2019)
13. Sun, Y., et al.: Ernie: Enhanced representation through knowledge integration. arXiv preprint arXiv:1904.09223 (2019)
14. Vaswani, A., et al.: Attention is all you need. In: Advances in neural information processing systems, pp. 5998–6008 (2017)
15. Wolf, T., Sanh, V., Chaumond, J., Delangue, C.: Transfertransfo: a transfer learning approach for neural network based conversational agents. arXiv preprint arXiv:1901.08149 (2019)
16. Wu, W., et al.: Proactive human-machine conversation with explicit conversation goals. arXiv preprint arXiv:1906.05572 (2019)
17. Yavuz, S., Rastogi, A., Chao, G.l., Hakkani-Tür, D., AI, A.A.: Deepcopy: grounded response generation with hierarchical pointer networks. In: NIPS (2018)
18. Zhang, S., Dinan, E., Urbanek, J., Szlam, A., Kiela, D., Weston, J.: Personalizing dialogue agents: i have a dog, do you have pets too? arXiv preprint arXiv:1801.07243 (2018)

BERT-Based Multi-head Selection for Joint Entity-Relation Extraction

Weipeng Huang(✉), Xingyi Cheng, Taifeng Wang, and Wei Chu

Ant Financial Services Group, Hangzhou, China
{weipeng.hwp,fanyin.cxy,taifeng.wang,weichu.cw}@antfin.com

Abstract. In this paper, we report our method for the Information Extraction task in 2019 Language and Intelligence Challenge. We incorporate BERT into the multi-head selection framework for joint entity-relation extraction. This model extends existing approaches from three perspectives. First, BERT is adopted as a feature extraction layer at the bottom of the multi-head selection framework. We further optimize BERT by introducing a semantic-enhanced task during BERT pre-training. Second, we introduce a large-scale Baidu Baike corpus for entity recognition pre-training, which is of weekly supervised learning since there is no actual named entity label. Third, soft label embedding is proposed to effectively transmit information between entity recognition and relation extraction. Combining these three contributions, we enhance the information extracting ability of the multi-head selection model and achieve F1-score 0.876 on testset-1 with a single model. By ensembling four variants of our model, we finally achieve F1 score 0.892 (1st place) on testset-1 and F1 score 0.8924 (2nd place) on testset-2.

Keywords: BERT · Multi-head selection · Soft label embedding · Weekly supervised learning

1 Problem Definition

Given a sentence and a list of pre-defined schemas which define the relation P and the classes of its corresponding subject S and object O, for example, (S_TYPE: Person, P: wife, O_TYPE: Person), (S_TYPE: Company, P: founder, O_TYPE: Person), a participating information extraction (IE) system is expected to output all correct triples [(S1, P1, O1), (S2, P2, O2) ...] mentioned in the sentence under the constraints of given schemas. A largest schema-based Chinese information extraction dataset is released in this competition. Precision, Recall and F1 score are used as the basic evaluation metrics to measure the performance of participating systems.

From the example shown in Fig. 1, we can notice that one entity can be involved in multiple triplets and entity spans have overlaps, which is the difficulties of this task.

J. Tang et al. (Eds.): NLPCC 2019, LNAI 11839, pp. 713–723, 2019.
https://doi.org/10.1007/978-3-030-32236-6_65

Text: 《蓝鸿文自选集》是2007年中国人民大学出版社出版的图书
SPO: (蓝鸿文自选集，作者，蓝鸿文)，(蓝鸿文自选集，出版社，中国人民大学出版社)

Fig. 1. An example in the dataset.

2 Related Work

Recent years, great efforts have been made on extracting relational fact from unstructured raw texts to build large structural knowledge bases. A relational fact is often represented as a triplet which consists of two entities (subject and object) and semantic relation between them. Early works [2–4] mainly focused on the task of relation classification which assumes the entity pair are identified beforehand. This limits their practical application since they neglect the extraction of entities. To extract both entities and their relation, existing methods can be divided into two categories: the pipelined framework, which first uses sequence labeling models to extract entities, and then uses relation classification models to identify the relation between each entity pair; and the joint approach, which combines the entity model and the relation model through different strategies, such as constraints or parameters sharing.

Pipelined Framework. Many earlier entity-relation extraction systems [5–7] adopt pipelined framework: they first conduct entity extraction and then predict the relations between each entity pair. The pipelined framework has the flexibility of integrating different data sources and learning algorithms, but their disadvantages are obvious. First, they suffer significantly from error propagation, the error of the entity extraction stage will be propagated to the relation classification stage. Second, they ignore the relevance of entity extraction and relation classification. As shown in Fig. 2, entity contained in book title marks can be a song or book, its relation to a person can be singer or writer. Once the relationship has been confirmed, the entity type can be easily identified, and vice versa. For example, if we know the relationship is singer, then the entity type should be a song. Entity extraction and relation classification can benefit from each other so it will harm the performance if we consider them separately. Third, the pipelined framework results in low computational efficiency. After the entity extraction stage, each entity pair should be passed to the relation classification model to identify their relation. Since most entity pairs have no relation, this two-stage manner is inefficient.

《*》 —— Writer? Singer? —— Person

Text1: 《细说光武帝》是2006年上海人民出版社出版的图书，作者是顾晨华
Text2: 《土耳其冰淇淋》是周杰伦演唱的歌曲，将在2016年6月8日开启预售，6月24日正式发行

Fig. 2. Examples: entity contained in book title marks can be song or book, its relation to a person can be singer or writer.

Joint Model. To overcome the aforementioned disadvantages of the pipelined framework, joint learning models have been proposed. Early works [8–10] need a complicated process of feature engineering and heavily depends on NLP tools for feature extraction. Yu and Lam (2010) [8] proposed the approach to connect the two models through global probabilistic graphical models. Li and Ji (2014) [10] extract entity mentions and relations using structured perceptron with efficient beam search, which is significantly more efficient and less time-consuming than constraint-based approaches. Gupta et al. (2016) [11] proposed the table-filling approach, which provides an opportunity to incorporate more sophisticated features and algorithms into the model, such as search orders in decoding and global features.

Neural network models have been widely used in the literature as well. Zheng et al. (2017) [12] propose a novel tagging scheme that can convert the joint extraction task to a tagging problem. This tagging based method is better than most of the existing pipelined methods, but its flexibility is limited and can not tackle the situations when (1) one entity belongs to multiple triplets (2) multiple entities have overlaps. Zeng et al. (2018) [13] propose an end2end neural model based on sequence-to-sequence learning with copy mechanism to extract relational facts from sentences, where the entities and relations could be jointly extracted. The performance of this method is limited by the word segmentation accuracy because it can not extract entities beyond the word segmentation results. Li et al. [14] (2019) cast the task as a multi-turn question answering problem, i.e., the extraction of entities and relations is transformed to the task of identifying answer spans from the context. This framework provides an elegant way to capture the hierarchical dependency of tags. However, it is also of low computational efficiency since it needs to scan all entity template questions and corresponding relation template questions for a single sentence. Bekoulis et al. (2017) [15] propose a joint neural model which performs entity recognition and relation extraction simultaneously, without the need of any manually extracted features or the use of any external tool. They model the entity recognition task using a CRF (Conditional Random Fields) layer and the relation extraction task as a multi-head selection problem since one entity can have multiple relations. The model adopted BiLSTM to extract contextual feature and propose a label embedding layer to connect the entity recognition branch and the relation classification branch. Our model is based on this framework and make three improvements:

(1) BERT [1] is introduced as a feature extraction layer in place of BiLSTM. We also optimize the pre-training process of BERT by introducing a semantic-enhanced task.
(2) A large-scale Baidu Baike corpus is introduced for entity recognition pre-training, which is of weekly supervised learning since there is no actual named entity label.
(3) Soft label embedding is proposed to effectively transmit information between entity recognition and relation extraction.

3 Model Description

3.1 Overall Framwork

Figure 3 summarizes the proposed model architecture. The model takes character sequence as input and captures contextual features using BERT. A CRF layer is applied to extract entities from the sentence. To effectively transmit information between entity recognition and relation extraction, soft label embedding is built on the top of CRF logits. To solve the problem that one entity belongs to multiple triplets, a multi-sigmoid layer is applied. We find that adding an auxiliary global relation prediction task also improve the performance.

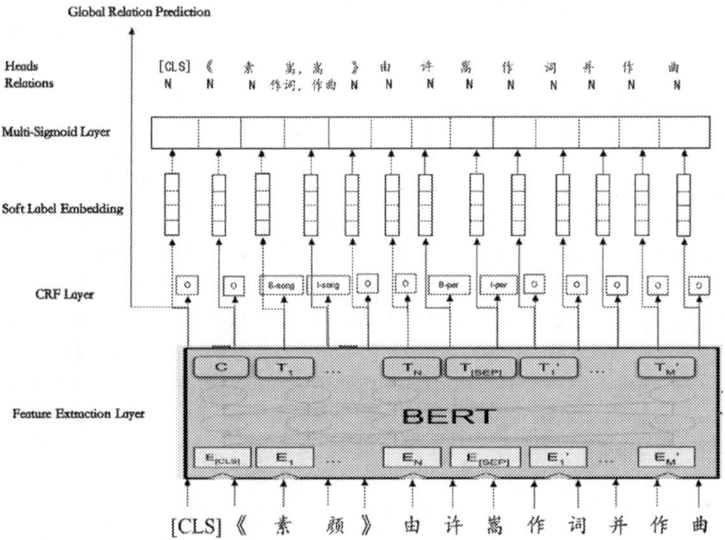

Fig. 3. Overall framwork: BERT-based multi-head selection

3.2 BERT for Feature Extraction

BERT (Bidirectional Encoder Representations from Transformers) [1] is a new language representation model, which uses bidirectional transformers to pre-train a large unlabeled corpus, and fine-tunes the pre-trained model on other tasks. BERT has been widely used and shows great improvement on various natural language processing tasks, e.g., word segmentation, named entity recognition, sentiment analysis, and question answering. We use BERT to extract contextual feature for each character instead of BiLSTM in the original work [15]. To further improve the performance, we optimize the pre-training process of BERT by introducing a semantic-enhanced task.

Enhanced BERT. Original google BERT is pre-trained using two unsupervised tasks, masked language model (MLM) and next sentence prediction (NSP). MLM task enables the model to capture the discriminative contextual feature. NSP task makes it possible to understand the relationship between sentence pairs, which is not directly captured by language modeling. We further design a semantic-enhanced task to enhance the performance of BERT. It incorporate previous sentence prediction and document level prediction. We pre-train BERT by combining MLM, NSP and the semantic-enhanced task together.

3.3 Named Entity Recognition

NER (Named Entity Recognition) is the first task in the joint multi-head selection model. It is usually formulated as a sequence labeling problem using the BIO (Beginning, Inside, Outside) encoding scheme. Since there are different entity types, the tags are extended to B-type, I-type and O. Linear-chain CRF [16] is widely used for sequence labeling in deep models. In our method, CRF is built on the top of BERT. Supposed $y \in \{B - type, I - type, O\}$ is the label, score function $s(X, i)_{y_i}$ is the output of BERT at i_{th} character and $b_{y_{i-1} y_i}$ is trainable parameters, the probability of a possible label sequence is formalized as:

$$P(Y|X) = \frac{\prod_{i=2}^{n} exp(s(X,i)_{y_i} + b_{y_{i-1}y_i})))}{\sum_{y'} \prod_{i=2}^{n} exp(s(X,i)_{y'_i} + b_{y'_{i-1}y'_i})))} \tag{1}$$

By solving Eq. 2 we can obtain the optimal sequence tags:

$$Y^* = argmaxP(Y|X) \tag{2}$$

title	content
万建国	万建国，生于甘肃平凉，毕业于西安音乐学院作曲系，指挥作曲双专业。师从指挥家刘大冬教授，作曲家饶余燕教授...
三九手机	三九手机网是集手机销售，维修售后为一体的专业化公司。是云南电子商务领域最受消费者欢迎...
《早发白帝城》	《早发白帝城》赏析是诗人李白在东下江陵途中所作，表现了诗人重获自由时欢畅轻快的心情。

Fig. 4. Crawled corpus from Baidu Baike.

Extra Corpus for NER Pretraining. Previous works show that introducing extra data for distant supervised learning usually boost the model performance. For this task, we collect a large-scale Baidu Baike corpus (about 6 million sentences) for NER pre-training. As shown in Fig. 4, each sample contains the content and its title. These samples are auto-crawled so there is no actual entity label. We consider the title of each sample as a pseudo label and conduct NER pre-training using these data. Experimental results show that it improves performance.

3.4 Soft Label Embedding

Miwa et al. (2016) [17] and Bekoulis et al. (2018) [15] use the entity tags as input to relation classification layer by learning label embeddings. As reported in their experiments, an improvement of 1~2% F1 is achieved with the use of label embeddings. Their mechanism is hard label embedding because they use the CRF decoding results, which have two disadvantages. On one hand, the entity recognition results are not absolutely correct since they are predicted by the model during inference. The error from the entity tags may propagate to the relation classification branch and hurt the performance. On the other hand, CRF decoding process is based on the Viterbi Algorithm, which contains an argmax operation which is not differentiable. To solve this problem, we proposed soft label embedding, which takes the logits as input to preserve probability of each entity type. Suppose N is the logits dimension, i.e., the number of entity type, $\mathbf{M}$ is the label embedding matrix, then soft label embedding for i_{th} character can be formalized as Eq. 3:

$$h_i = \frac{\sum softmax(s(X,i)) \cdot \mathbf{M}}{N} \tag{3}$$

3.5 Relation Classification as Multi-head Selection

We formulated the relation classification task as a multi-head selection problem, since each token in the sentence has multiple heads, i.e., multiple relations with other tokens. Soft label embedding of the i_{th} token h_i is feed into two separate fully connected layers to get the subject representation h_i^s and object representation h_i^o. Given the i_{th} token (h_i^s, h_i^o) and the j_{th} token (h_j^s, h_j^o) , our task is to predict their relation:

$$r_{i,j} = f(h_i^s, h_j^o), r_{j,i} = f(h_j^s, h_i^o) \tag{4}$$

where $f(\cdot)$ means neural network, $r_{i,j}$ is the relation when the i_{th} token is subject and the j_{th} token is object, $r_{j,i}$ is the relation when the j_{th} token is subject and the i_{th} token is object. Since the same entity pair have multiple relations, we adopt multi-sigmoid layer for the relation prediction. We minimize the cross-entropy loss L_{rel} during training:

$$L_{rel} = \sum_{i=0}^{K} \sum_{j=0}^{K} NLL(r_{i,j}, y_{i,j}) \tag{5}$$

where K is the sequence length and $y_{i,j}$ is ground truth relation label.

Global Relation Prediction. Relation classification is of entity pairs level in the original multi-head selection framework. We introduce an auxiliary sentence-level relation classification prediction task to guide the feature learning process. As shown in Fig. 3, the final hidden state of the first token $[CLS]$ is taken to obtain a fixed-dimensional pooled representation of the input sequence. The hidden state is then feed into a multi-sigmoid layer for classification. In conclusion, our model is trained using the combined loss:

$$L = L_{ner} + L_{rel} + L_{global\_rel} \tag{6}$$

3.6 Model Ensemble

Ensemble learning is an effective method to further improve performance. It is widely used in data mining and machine learning competitions. The basic idea is to combine the decisions from multiple models to improve the overall performance. In this work, we combine four variant multi-head selection models by learning an XGBoost [18] binary classification model on the development set. Each triplet generated by the base model is treated as a sample. We then carefully design 200-dimensional features for each sample. Take several important features for example:

- the probability distribution of the entity pair
- the probability distribution of sentence level
- whether the triplet appear in the training set
- the number of predicted entities, triples, relations of the given sentence
- whether the entity boundary is consistent with the word segmentation results
- semantic feature. We contact the sentence and the triplet to train an NLI model, hard negative triplets are constructed to help NLI model capture semantic feature.

4 Experiments

4.1 Experimental Settings

All experiments are implemented on the hardware with Intel(R) Xeon(R) CPU E5-2682 v4 @ 2.50GHz and NVIDIA Tesla P100.

Dataset and Evaluation Metrics. We evaluate our method on the SKE dataset used in this competition, which is the largest schema-based Chinese information extraction dataset in the industry, containing more than 430,000 SPO triples in over 210,000 real-world Chinese sentences, bounded by a pre-specified schema with 50 types of predicates. All sentences in SKE Dataset are extracted from Baidu Baike and Baidu News Feeds. The dataset is divided into a training set (170 k sentences), a development set (20 k sentences) and a testing set (20 k sentences). The training set and the development set are to be used for training and are available for free download. The test set is divided into two parts, the test set 1 is available for self-verification, the test set 2 is released one week before the end of the competition and used for the final evaluation.

Hyperparameters. The max sequence length is set to 128, the number of fully connected layer of relation classification branch is set to 2, and that of global relation branch is set to 1. During training, we use Adam with the learning rate of 2e-5, dropout probability of 0.1. This model converges in 3 epoch.

Preprocessing. All uppercase letters are converted to lowercase letters. We use max sequence length 128 so sentences longer than 128 are split by punctuation. According to FAQ, entities in book title mark should be completely extracted. Because the annotation criteria in trainset are diverse, we revise the incomplete entities. To keep consistence, book title marks around the entities are removed.

Postprocessing. Our postprocessing mechanism is mainly based on the FAQ evaluation rules. After model prediction, we remove triplets whose entity-relation types are against the given schemas. For entities contained in book title mark, we complement them if they are incomplete. Date type entities are also complemented to the finest grain. These are implemented by regular expression matching.

Note that entity related preprocessing and postprocessing are also performed on the development set to keep consistency with the test set, thus the change of development metric is reliable.

4.2 Main Results

Results on SKE dataset are presented in Table 1. The baseline model is based on the Google BERT, use hard label embedding and train on only SKE dataset without NER pretraining. As shown in Table 1, the F1 score increase from 0.864 to 0.871 when combined with our enhanced BERT. NER pretraining using the extra corpus, soft label embedding and auxiliary sentence-level relation classification prediction also improve the F1 score. Combined all of these contributions, we achieve F1-score 0.876 with the single model on test set 1.

Table 1. Performance of variant multi-head selection model on SKE dataset.

Model	dev-P	dev-R	dev-F1	test1-P	test1-R	test1-F1
Baseline	0.796	0.845	0.819	0.902	0.828	0.864
Baseline+Enhanced BERT	0.809	0.854	0.830	0.872	0.870	0.871
Baseline+NER Pretraining	0.803	0.852	0.827	0.883	0.854	0.868
Baseline+Soft label embedding	0.814	0.832	0.823	0.868	0.866	0.867
Baseline+Global Predicate Prediction	0.806	0.838	0.822	0.891	0.842	0.866
Baseline+all	0.821	0.855	0.837	0.873	0.879	0.876

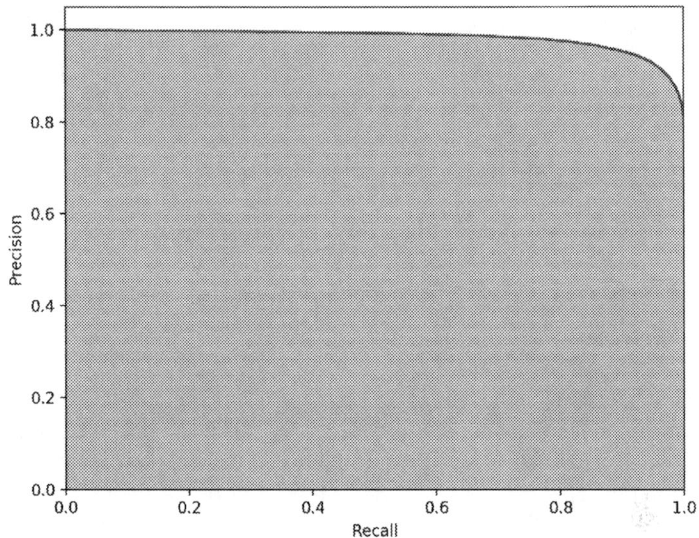

Fig. 5. Precision-recall curve

4.3 Model Ensemble

We select the following four variant model to further conduct model ensembling. The ensemble model is XGBoost binary classifier, which is very fast during training. Since the base models are trained on the training set, we perform cross-validation on development set, Fig. 5 shows the PR curve of the ensemble model. By model ensembling the F1 score increase from 0.876 to 0.892.

- Google BERT + Soft Label Embedding + Global Relation Prediction
- Enhanced BERT + Soft Label Embedding + Global Relation Prediction
- Google BERT + Soft Label Embedding + Global Relation Prediction + NER Pretraining
- Enhance BERT + Soft Label Embedding + Global Relation Prediction + NER Pretraining

4.4 Case Study

Two examples of our model fail to predict are shown in Fig. 6. For example 1, the triplet can not be drawn from the given sentence. However, the triplet is actually in the trainset. Our model may overfit to the trainset in this situation. For example 2, there is complicate family relationships mentioned in the sentence, which is too hard for the model to capture. To solve this problem, a more robust model should be proposed and we leave this as future work.

Example 1:
Text: 《隋唐英雄5》由长城影视股份有限公司出品，李翰韬执导，是《隋唐英雄4》的续作，由余少群、孙耀琦、惠英红、赵文瑄、张晓晨、黄海冰、于荣光、蒋林静、李永林等主演

Error Prediction: (隋唐英雄4，主演，黄海冰)

Example 2:
Text: 何甘棠非荷兰裔犹太人何仕文与施娣所生的儿子，而是施娣与中国男子郭兴贤所生的儿子，何甘棠是李小龙母亲何爱瑜的养父

Missing Prediction: (何甘棠，母亲，施娣)

Fig. 6. Examples the model fails to predict.

5 Conclusion

In this paper, we report our solution to the information extraction task in 2019 Language and Intelligence Challenge. We first analyze the problem and find that most entities are involved in multiple triplets. To solve this problem, we incorporate BERT into the multi-head selection framework for joint entity-relation extraction. Enhanced BERT pre-training, soft label embedding and NER pre-training are three main technologies we introduce to further improve the performance. Experimental results show that our method achieves competitive performance: F1 score 0.892 (1st place) on the test set 1 and F1 score 0.8924 (2nd place) on the test set 2.

References

1. Devlin, J., et al.: Bert: Pre-training of deep bidirectional transformers for language understanding. arXiv preprint arXiv:1810.04805 (2018)
2. Hendrickx, I., et al.: Semeval-2010 task 8: multi-way classification of semantic relations between pairs of nominals. In: Proceedings of the Workshop on Semantic Evaluations: Recent Achievements and Future Directions. Association for Computational Linguistics (2009)
3. Zeng, D., Liu, K., Lai, S., et al.: Relation classification via convolutional deep neural network (2014)
4. Xu, K., Feng, Y., Huang, S., et al.: Semantic relation classification via convolutional neural networks with simple negative sampling. arXiv preprint arXiv:1506.07650 (2015)

5. Zelenko, D., Aone, C., Richardella, A.: Kernel methods for relation extraction. J. Mach. Learn. Res. **3**(Feb), 1083–1106 (2003)
6. Miwa, M., et al.: A rich feature vector for protein-protein interaction extraction from multiple corpora. In: Proceedings of the 2009 Conference on Empirical Methods in Natural Language Processing: Volume 1-Volume 1. Association for Computational Linguistics (2009)
7. Chan, Y.S., Roth, D.: Exploiting syntactico-semantic structures for relation extraction. In: Proceedings of the 49th Annual Meeting of the Association for Computational Linguistics: Human Language Technologies-Volume 1. Association for Computational Linguistics (2011)
8. Yu, X., Lam, W.: Jointly identifying entities and extracting relations in encyclopedia text via a graphical model approach. In: Proceedings of the 23rd International Conference on Computational Linguistics: Posters. Association for Computational Linguistics (2010)
9. Miwa, M., Sasaki, Y.: Modeling joint entity and relation extraction with table representation. In: Proceedings of the 2014 Conference on Empirical Methods in Natural Language Processing (EMNLP) (2014)
10. Li, Q., Ji, H.: Incremental joint extraction of entity mentions and relations. In: Proceedings of the 52nd Annual Meeting of the Association for Computational Linguistics (Volume 1: Long Papers), vol. 1 (2014)
11. Gupta, P., Schutze, H., Andrassy, B.: Table filling multi-task recurrent neural network for joint entity and relation extraction. In: Proceedings of COLING 2016, The 26th International Conference on Computational Linguistics: Technical Papers (2016)
12. Zheng, S., et al.: Joint extraction of entities and relations based on a novel tagging scheme. In: Proceedings of the 55th Annual Meeting of the Association for Computational Linguistics (Volume 1: Long Papers) (2017)
13. Zeng, X., et al.: Extracting relational facts by an end-to-end neural model with copy mechanism. In: Proceedings of the 56th Annual Meeting of the Association for Computational Linguistics (Volume 1: Long Papers) (2018)
14. Li, X., et al.: Entity-Relation Extraction as Multi-Turn Question Answering. arXiv preprint arXiv:1905.05529 (2019)
15. Bekoulis, G., et al.: Joint entity recognition and relation extraction as a multi-head selection problem. Expert Syst. Appl. **114**, 34–45 (2018)
16. Lafferty, J., McCallum, A., Fernando CN Pereira: Conditional random fields: Probabilistic models for segmenting and labeling sequence data (2001)
17. Miwa, M., Bansal, M.: End-to-end relation extraction using LSTMs on sequences and tree structures. arXiv preprint arXiv:1601.00770 (2016)
18. Chen, T., Guestrin, C.: XGBoost: a scalable tree boosting system. In: Proceedings of the 22nd ACM SIGKDD International Conference on Knowledge Discovery and Data Mining. ACM (2016)

Proactive Knowledge-Goals Dialogue System Based on Pointer Network

Han Zhou[1], Chong Chen[1(✉)], Hao Liu[1], Fei Qin[2], and Huaqing Liang[1]

[1] State Key Laboratory of Petroleum Resources and Prospecting, College of Information Science and Engineering, China University of Petroleum, Beijing, China
chenchong@cup.edu.cn
[2] BeiHang University, Beijing, China

Abstract. Human-machine dialogue is the hot spot of current research. In this paper, we proposed an end-to-end dialogue system based on external knowledge, which realized active guidance and topic transfer in multiple rounds of dialogue. Our system is built on the pointer generator model so that the output token in the response can be generated or copied from the conversation history or background knowledge according to a trainable action probability distribution. At the same time, with the data processing and optimization of the model structure, the designed system is capable of generating high quality responses. In the 2019 NLP Language and Intelligence Challenge, our proposed dialogue system ranked third in the automatic evaluation, and ranked fifth in the manual evaluation.

Keywords: Pointer network · Attention mechanism · Background knowledge · Proactive dialogue

1 Introduction

Human-machine dialogue is a basic challenge to artificial intelligence. It involves key technologies such as language understanding, dialogue management and language generation, and has received extensive attention on academia and industry. The current human-machine dialogue technology is still in its infancy, and most of the machines are in the form of passive dialogue, that is, the machine's reply is only used to respond to the user's input, and it is impossible to conduct multiple rounds of dialogue interaction like a human. Many scholars hope to introduce knowledge graph information into human-machine dialogue, so that machines can obtain more valuable reply information, or further use background knowledge information to actively guide users to communicate. Recently, the 2019 Language and Intelligent Technology Challenge (LIC2019) which was jointly organized by the China Computer Federation (CCF), the

This work was supported by the Science Foundation of China University of Petroleum-Beijing under grant No. 2462018YJRC007.

J. Tang et al. (Eds.): NLPCC 2019, LNAI 11839, pp. 724–735, 2019.
https://doi.org/10.1007/978-3-030-32236-6_66

Chinese Information Processing Society of China (CIPSC) and Baidu Inc. have released a large-scale, high-quality proactive conversation dataset DuConv based on knowledge graph [1]. This will greatly promote the development of Chinese human-machine dialogue.

Recently, neural networks of dialogue generation have attracted attention, and a lot of works have focused on how to use context to generate fluent, consistent responses [2–5]. There are also works to introduce large-scale knowledge graph as background information on the dialogue process, giving the dialogue system the ability to expand thinking. The corresponding evaluation dataset includes the bAbI dialogue and Stanford multi-domain dialogue (SMD), etc. [6, 7]. In practical applications, a simple reply-type dialogue system cannot capture the interests in communicators. Giving the dialogue system the ability of actively chat can make it smarter.

In this evaluation task, the DuConv provided by the organizer has a total of 30,000 sessions, about 120,000 rounds of dialogue, including 100,000 training sets, 10,000 development sets, and 10,000 test sets. Each of these dialogues includes knowledge background information, context history, and dialogue goals. The data comes from the knowledge of chat value in the field of movies and entertainment characters, such as box office, director, evaluation, etc., organized in the form of triad *SPO*. The topic in the dialogue target is movie or entertainment character entity. The task of the evaluation is to give the dialogue targets G and related knowledge information $K = f_1, f_2, \ldots, f_n$, and ask the dialog system to output the machine response u_t applicable to the current conversation sequence $H = u_1, u_2, \ldots, u_{t-1}$, makes the conversation natural, informative and consistent with the goals of the dialogue. During the conversation, the machine is active, guiding users to talk from one topic to another. This task is extremely challenging We design the overall dialogue system through data preprocessing, model construction, model precision tuning and optimization, and data post-processing. Experiments show that the model we designed can effectively complete the evaluation task. In the 2019 Language and Intelligent Technology Competition evaluation, our system obtained 0.464, 0.422 and 0.289 in the machine evaluation, F1, BLEU1 and BLEU2 respectively. At the same time, in the manual evaluation, the task completion score of 1.79 and the consistency score of 2.3 were obtained.

In this paper, we present an end-to-end deep learning model to solve this problem. We introduce our work from the aspects of data preprocessing, model structure, model implementation details, experimental results, etc., and summarize the article in the last part.

2 Related Works

2.1 Dialogue Systems

Machine learning based dialogue systems are mainly explored by following two different approaches: modularized and end-to-end. For the modularized systems [8], a set of modules for natural language understanding [9, 10], dialogue state tracking [11], dialogue management, and natural language generation are used. These approaches achieve good stability via combining domain-specific knowledge and slot-filling techniques, but additional human labels are needed. On the other hand, end-to-end approaches have shown promising results recently. Some works view the task as a next utterance retrieval problem. Sequence-to-sequence model [12] has been a popular approach to many domains including neural response generation, to name just a few. Attention mechanism has been crucial in a lot of NLP tasks such as machine translation [13], machine reading comprehension [14] and natural language inference [15].

2.2 Pointer Network

Vinyals et al. uses attention as a pointer to select a member of the input source as the output [16]. Such copy mechanisms have also been used in other natural language processing tasks, such as question answering, neural machine translation, language modeling, and text summarization [17]. In task-oriented dialogue tasks, Eric & Manning first demonstrated the potential for the copy augmented Seq 2Seq model, which shows that generation based methods with simple copy strategy can surpass retrieval-based ones. Later, Eric et al. augmented the vocabulary distribution by concatenating KB attention, which at the same time increases the output dimension [7]. To integrate external knowledge [18], employed memory network for encoding facts with great progress. Madotto et al. applied memory network to store dialog history and structured knowledge base and used pointer generator to copy token from dialog history or knowledge base token for task-oriented dialog systems [19].

2.3 Baselines

The evaluation task provides two baseline systems [1]. For the search and generation formulas, the search method needs to construct candidate sets, and then use the transformer model to rank the sentence. The generative model is a reference to the work from Rongzhong Lian et al. [20], and the posterior knowledge distribution is used to guide knowledge selection.

3 Data Processing

3.1 Dataset

In this paper, except for the official dataset, we only use the pre-trained Chinese word vector, and no other external data was used. Official dataset is divided into training set, validation set, and test set. The training set and the validation set are organized in the form of session. Each session includes Dialogue Goal, Background Knowledge and Conversation. In the test set, Each sample includes Dialogue Goal, Background Knowledge and History, the participating model is required to lead the conversation according to the current dialogue history, that is, it only needs to simulate the actions of the agent. The various parts of the data are described below. And Fig. 1 presents an example from training/test sets respectively.

- Dialogue Goal (goal): It contains two lines: the first contains the given dialogue path i.e., ["Start", TOPIC_A, TOPIC_B]. The second line contains the relationship of TOPIC_A and TOPIC_B.
- Knowledge: Background knowledge related to TOPIC_A and TOPIC_B.
- Conversation: 4 to 8 turns of conversation.
- Dialogue History: Conversation sequences before the current utterance, empty if the current utterance is in the start of the conversion.

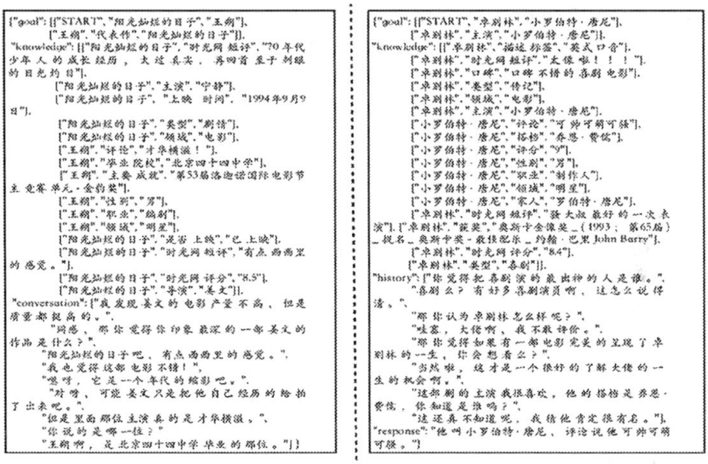

Fig. 1. Examples in the dataset

3.2 Data Preprocessing

For each session in the dataset, we split it into multiple sets of conversations as training data. Each group of conversations includes GOAL, KNOWLEDGE, HISTORY, and RESPONSE. Among them, HISTORY and RESPONSE are from the data set CONVERSATION, in which the machine's reply is RESPONSE, and the previous conversation history information is HISTORY. We analyzed all the samples in training set. We learned that the background information contains a total of 44 types of relationships, such as domain, type, time network short comment, career, starring and so on. Since the dataset contains a large number of English translation nouns and some proper nouns, they are broken up after the word segmentation, and cannot be used as a complete word to table lookup and other operations, which affects the system accuracy. At the same time, the dataset contains a large number of names of people and movies, resulting in a too large vocabulary or some words out of vocabulary problems.

Therefore, we processed the data as follows. And in Fig. 2, the processed data sample is shown:

- For the two topic words in GOAL, we use "video_topic_a" or "person_topic_a" and "video_topic_b" or "person_topic_b" instead.
- For the background information in KNOWLEDGE, we have selected eight types of relationships, including ['Representatives', 'Stars', 'Friends', 'Directors', 'Partners', 'Husband', 'Wife', 'Family'], the substitution of entity words for these types of triples, using specific characters instead of corresponding entity words.
- The words that are substituted in each set of dialog data are stored in a dictionary, and the final generated result is inversely replaced. For the HISTORY and RESPONSE sections, we use the alternative word dictionary for replacement.
- Context-sensitive entity tag. If the entity word in the background knowledge appears in the last round of conversation in HISTORY, it is marked as 'A', and if not, marked as 'O'.

Raw session	{"goal": [["START", "儿童法案", "理查德·艾尔"], ["儿童法案", "导演", "理查德·艾尔"]], "knowledge": [["儿童法案", "类型", "剧情"], ["儿童法案", "口碑", "口碑很差"], ["儿童法案", "上映时间", "2018年8月24日"], ["儿童法案", "领域", "电影"], ["儿童法案", "导演", "理查德·艾尔"], ["理查德·艾尔", "评论", "电影的诗歌"], ["理查德·艾尔", "星座", "白羊座"], ["理查德·艾尔", "出生日期", "1943-3-28"], ["理查德·艾尔", "性别", "男"], ["理查德·艾尔", "职业", "导演"], ["理查德·艾尔", "领域", "明星"]], "conversation": ["我们老师让我们看了一部电影，是今年8月上映的。", "那算是蛮新的了，是哪部？", "叫做儿童法案。", "我好像了解过。口碑很差诶。", "嗯，也不太好看。", "就是啊，好看也不会口碑差吧。", "不会，导演可是白羊座的。", "导演是谁啊？", "1943年3月28日出生的理查德·艾尔。", "你一说我想起来了。"]}
One processed data	**Input information:** GOAL [0] video_topic_a [0] 导演 [0] person_topic_b [0] video_topic_a [0] 类型 [0] 剧情 [0] 口碑 [0] 口碑 [0] 很 [0] 差 [0] 上映 时间 [A] 2018年8月24日 [A] 领域 [0] 电影 [A] person_topic_b [0] 评论 [0] 电影 [A] 的 [0] 诗歌 [0] 星座 [0] 白羊座 [0] 出生 日期 [0] $出生日期longB$ [0] 性别 [0] 男 [0] 职业 [0] 导演 [0] 领域 [0] 明星 [0] HISTORY [0] 我们 [0] 老师 [0] 让 [0] 我们 [0] 看 [0] 了 [0] 一部 [0] 电影 [0] ， [0] 是 [0] 今年 [0] 8月 [0] 上映 [0] 的 [0] 。 [0] 那 [0] 算是 [0] 蛮 [0] 新 [0] 的 [0] 了 [0] ， [0] 是 [0] 哪 [0] 部 [0] ？ [0] **Response:** 叫做 video_topic_a 。
Topic list	{"video_topic_a": "儿童法案", "person_topic_b": "理查德·艾尔", "$出生日期longB$": "1943年3月28日"}

Fig. 2. Sample data preprocessing

3.3 Answer Processing

This process is used to correct the answers which are directly generated by the model to make it closer to the real response. It mainly includes the following two procedures:

- Replace the replacement words contained in the answer according to the entity vocabulary.
- The statistical machine recovery length average is 12.37, 70% of the sentence length is concentrated between 8 and 16, so we set the minimum length of the sentence in the decoding process to 8, to ensure that the response contains enough information.

4 Model Structure

We use G, K and H to represent Goal, Background knowledge and Dialogue History respectively, and R to represent the response. The task is to find $\bar{R}$ that:

$$\bar{R} = \arg\max_{R} \Pr ob(R|G, K, H) \tag{1}$$

Words generated in $\bar{R}$ are either from G, K H or from a vocabulary V. Figure 2 shows the basic structure of the model we designed.

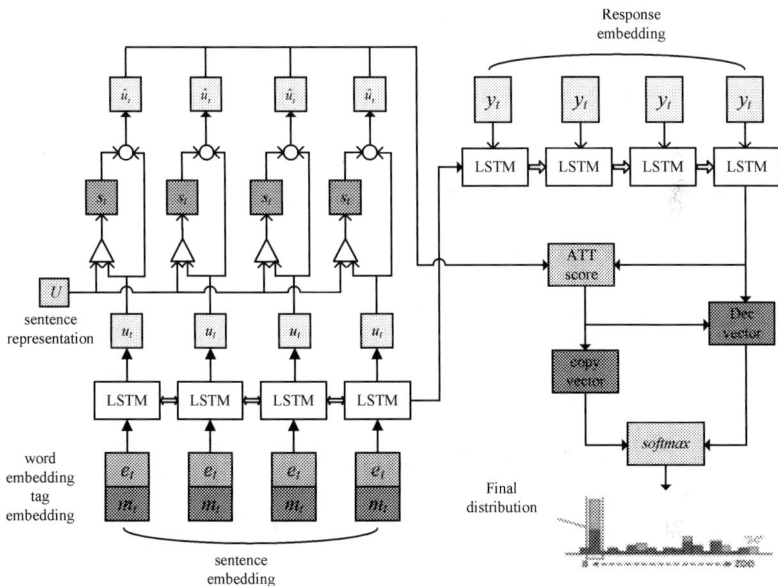

Fig. 3. End-to-end dialog system for the model with context choosing, gated self-attention and pointer network

4.1 Goal, Knowledge and History Encoding

Context choosing. We used bi-directional LSTM to present the encoding process. In Eq. 2, u_t represents the LSTM hidden state at time step t, U is the concatenated representation of the forward and backward passes.

$$U = \{[\overrightarrow{\mathrm{u_t}}, \overleftarrow{\mathrm{u_t}}]\}_{t=1}^{M} \tag{2}$$

$$u_t = LSTM^E(u_{t-1}, [e_t, m_t]) \tag{3}$$

In Eq. 3, e_t is the word embedding representation of word x_t concatenated by G, K and H. m_t is the meta-word representation of whether word x_t is in or outside the last sentence of H. $[a,b]$ represents the concatenation of vector a and b. We call this approach context choosing which is similar to the techniques in Zhao's work [21]. For applications, it is essential to be able to generate response that is coherent to a context.

Gated Self-attention. Our gated self-attention mechanism is designed to aggregate information from the whole background knowledge and embed vector, to refine the encoded knowledge-context representation at every time step. The first step is taking encoded U as input and conducting matching against itself to compute self matching representation. The specific calculation method is embodied in Eqs. 4 and 5. W_s is a trainable weight matrix, a_t is the weighted sum of all words' encoded representation in passage based on their corresponding matching strength to current word. s_t is the final self matching representation. Secondly, combining the input with self matching representation using a feature fusion gate. The self matching representation s_t is combined with original knowledge-context representation u_t as the new self matching enhanced representation f_t, Eq. 6. A learnable gate vector g_t, Eq. 7, chooses the information between the original representation and the new self matching enhanced representation to form the final encoded knowledge-context representation $\hat{u}_t$.

$$a_t = softmax(U^T W u_t) \tag{4}$$

$$s_t = U * a_t \tag{5}$$

$$f_t = \tanh(W_f[u_t, s_t]) \tag{6}$$

$$g_t = sigmoid(W_g[u_t, s_t]) \tag{7}$$

$$\hat{u}_t = g_t \cdot f_t + (1 - g_t) \cdot u_t \tag{8}$$

Through the context keyword choosing mechanism and the gated self-attention mechanism, we obtain a more effective background knowledge-context encoding vector.

4.2 Decoding with Attention Mechanism and Pointer Network

In the decoding process, we also use LSTM neural network as a decoder. It generates each word in order, with the result of each generation depending on the output of the encoder and the state of the decoder at the previous moment.

$$d_t = LSTM^D(d_{t-1}, e_{t-1}) \tag{9}$$

$$p(y_t|\{y_{<t}\}) = softmax(W \cdot d_t) \tag{10}$$

In Eq. 9, d_t represents the hidden state of the LSTM at time t, where d_0 is passed from the final hidden state of the encoder. y_t stands for the word generated at time t, and e_t is used to represent the word embedding of y_t. In Eq. 10, projects d_t to a space with vocabulary-size dimensions, then a softmax layer computes a probability distribution over all words in a vocabulary *V*.

Attention Mechanism. At each time step *t*, the decoder focuses on different parts of encoder inputs via the attention mechanism. We use Luong attention mechanism to compute raw attention scores at shown in Eq. 11. An attention layer, Eq. 13 is applied above the concatenation of decoder state d_t and the attention context vector c_t, its output is used as the new decoder state. W_a and W_b is a trainable weight matrix.

$$a_t = softmax(U^T W_a d_t) \tag{11}$$

$$c_t = U \cdot a_t \tag{12}$$

$$\hat{d}_t = \tanh(W_b[d_t, c_t]) \tag{13}$$

Pointer Network. Pointer network was introduced to allow both copying words from input via pointing, and generating words from a predefined vocabulary during decoding. Our pointer mechanism leverages raw attention scores, over the input sequence which has a vocabulary of *X*. In the vocabulary *V*, the score of the irrelevant word is set to negative infinity, which will be masked by the downstream *softmax* function. The final score on one word is calculated as the sum of all scores (*V* and *X*) pointing to the same word.

No_repeated Beam Search. Since we use the attention mechanism in the decoder, the model may focus more on background knowledge or words that have been previously generated in the context of the conversation. To improve fluency, hypotheses with repeated bi-grams are removed from further consideration during beam search. To improve fluency, hypotheses with repeated bi-grams are removed from further consideration during beam search [22].

5 Experiments

The experiment environment was as follows: Ubuntu 18.04 64-bit operating system, Intel(R) Xeon(R) Silver 4110 processor, 2.10 GHz frequency, 32 GB memory, Nvidia-RTX2080ti.

5.1 Model Parameter

During training, we set the minimum count of 8 to select the top 15000 words as vocabulary for generation. We used the pretrained 300-dimension Chinese word2vec embedding to initialize word embedding and kept fixed [23]. Embeddings for OOV tokens, if found in word2vec, were used. Otherwise, their embeddings were randomly initialized. For optimization, we used SGD with momentum. Learning rate was initially set to 0.3 and halved since epoch 8 at every 2 epochs afterwards. Models were totally trained with 20 epochs. Other hyper-parameters are shown in Table 1.

Table 1. Hyper-parameter settings

Name	Value
Vocabulary size	15000
Word embedding size	300
LSTM layers size	2
LSTM hidden size	256
Batch size	64
Beam size	6
N-gram repeat	2
Learning rate for SGD	0.3
Maximum gradient norm	5.0
dropout	0.3
Min decode step	8
Max decode step	35

5.2 Evaluation Results and Discussion

We began to optimize the model from the baseline system. In Table 2, we show the improvement of the effect of each part of the optimization. The result is the performance of the online test set automatic evaluation, which is evaluated by three indicators: F1, BLEU1 and BLEU2.

Table 2. The impact of various parts of the model on the system

Model	Total	Δ	F1	BLEU1	BLEU2
Baseline_retrieval	0.764	/	31.72	0.291	0.156
Baseline_generation	0.795	/	32.65	0.300	0.168
Pointer network base	0.933	+0.138	38.27	0.345	0.205
+raw dataset processing	0.962	+0.031	39.16	0.351	0.219
+result processing	1.052	+0.090	41.90	0.386	0.247
+Gated Self-attention	1.065	+0.013	42.64	0.386	0.253
+Context choosing	1.086	+0.021	43.78	0.392	0.256
+topical words replacement	1.108	+0.022	44.29	0.412	0.254
+Partial knowledge replacement	1.138	+0.024	45.07	0.418	0.270
+No_repeat beam search	1.175	+0.037	46.40	0.422	0.289

As indicated from the above experimental results, our data processing methods and model structure improvements have positive effects on the online evaluation results. Among them, at the very beginning, we used the pointer network innovatively to generate external knowledge-driven dialogue, which has achieved great improvement compared with the baseline method. From the perspective of model structure, improvements such as gated self-attention mechanism, context keyword tagging, and de-duplication of beam search decoding are effective for this task. In terms of data processing, the substitution of subject words and knowledge background entity words, and the length control of generated sentences have greatly improved the results. Our final result on leaderboard is from the single model introduced above. After the game, we have model ensemble, and the overall result of the offline valid dataset evaluation can be improved by about 0.02 compared with the single model.

Manual evaluation mainly evaluates the system from two aspects: target completion and dialogue consistency. The submitted model ranked fifth in the manual evaluation stage, and the results are shown in the Table 3.

Table 3. Manual evaluation of the system

Model	Score	Goal completion (0,1,2)	Coherence (0,1,2,3)
Single model	1.662	1.79	2.30

5.3 Sample Analysis

In Fig. 3, we selected a piece of data from the test set for analysis. Through the multiple rounds of dialogue with the dialogue system, it can be seen that the designed model can achieve the transfer of the dialogue goal, while having a certain context coherence. However, it can be found that the dialogue process is very different from the process set in the original sample, but both modes of dialogue can complete the set tasks, and the model has good generalization performance (Fig. 4).

```
Goal and Knowledge
{"goal":
  [["START", "星球大战前传二：克隆人的进攻", "阿凡达"],
  ["星球大战前传二：克隆人的进攻", "国家", "美国"],
  ["阿凡达", "国家", "美国"]]
"knowledge":
  [["星球大战前传二：克隆人的进攻", "幕后花絮", "本片片长142分钟，是最长的星战电影。"],
  ["星球大战前传二：克隆人的进攻", "获奖", "青少年选择奖_（2002；第4届）_获奖_青少年选择奖－最佳剧情/动作冒险电影女演员_娜塔莉·波特曼 Natalie Portman"],
  ["星球大战前传二：克隆人的进攻", "上映时间", "2002年7月12日"],
  ["星球大战前传 二：克隆人的进攻", "类型", "奇幻"],
  ["星球大战前传二：克隆人的进攻", "领域", "电影"],
  ["星球大战前传二：克隆人的进攻", "国家", "美国"],
  ["阿凡达", "类型", "奇幻"],
  ["阿凡达", "时光网短评", "电影就是机械造的梦"],
  ["阿凡达", "发布日期信息", "5年前上映"],
  ["阿凡达", "领域", "电影"],
  ["阿凡达", "国家", "美国"],
  ["星球大战前传二：克隆人的进攻", "票房", "4500.0万"],
  ["星球大战前传二：克隆人的进攻", "口碑", "口碑一般"],
  ["星球大战前传二：克隆人的进攻", "类型", "动作"]]}
```

```
our model conversation:
  Chatbot: 你喜欢看什么类型的电影？
  Person: 我喜欢看美国电影。
  Chatbot: 给你推荐一部美国的动作电影《星球大战前传二：克隆人的进攻》。
  Person: "这部电影怎么样。"
  Chatbot: "本片片长142分钟，是最长的星战电影。"
  Person: "那确实挺长的。"
  Chatbot: "再给你推荐部美国电影吧。"
  Person: "好的，什么电影。"
  Chatbot: "阿凡达，是一部奇幻类型的电影。"
  Person: "好的，有时间我一定去看看。"
  Chatbot: "我觉得你会喜欢的。"
raw conversation:
  Person1: "这个美国电影真的很一般。"
  Person2: "美国电影一般是大制作啊。"
  Person1: "真是不怎么好，《星球大战前传二：克隆人的进攻》票房也不高"
  Person2: "有原因的吧。"
  Person1: "口碑不好，看的人少吧。"
  Person2: "口碑对一部电影来说很重要了。"
  Person1: "还有一部美国电影叫阿凡达，很好看的哦！"
  Person2: "我还没看过这个电影呢。"
  Person1: "这是一部奇幻类型的电影，相信你会喜欢呢！"
  Person2: "好啊，有时间我一定去看看。"]}
```

Fig. 4. Sample model generation result

6 Conclusion

The LIC2019's knowledge-driven dialogue challenge provides high-quality multiple rounds conversation dataset based on background information. We improved the pointer generator model by adding a gated self-attention mechanism and a context choosing method that replicates OOV words in session context and background knowledge, and produces diverse and coherent responses through optimized decoding strategies. After the data processing, precision tuning and other optimization methods, we achieved 0.464/0.422/0.289 in the automatic evaluation index F1/BLEU1/BLEU2, and also achieved the task completion score of 1.79 and the consistency score of 2.3 in the manual evaluation.

References

1. Wu, W., Guo, Z., Zhou, X.: Proactive human-machine conversation with explicit conversation goals. In ACL (2019)
2. Vinyals, O., Le, Q.V.: A neural conversational model. In ICML (2015)
3. Shang, L., Lu, Z., Li, H.: Neural responding machine for short-text conversation. In: Proceedings of ACL (2015)
4. Sordoni, A., et al.: A neural network approach to context-sensitive generation of conversational responses. In: Proceedings of NAACL-HLT (2015)
5. Wen, T.-H., et al.: Conditional generation and snapshot learning in neural dialogue systems. In: Proceedings of the Conference on Empirical Methods in Natural Language Processing (EMNLP) (2016)
6. Bordes, A., Weston, J.: Learning end-to-end goal-oriented dialog. In: International Conference on Learning Representations, abs/1605.07683 (2017)
7. Eric, M., Manning, C.: A copy-augmented sequence-to-sequence architecture gives good performance on task-oriented dialogue. In: Proceedings of the 15th Conference of the European Chapter of the Association for Computational Linguistics: Volume 2, Short Papers, Valencia, Spain, pp. 468–473, April 2017. Association for Computational Linguistics. http://www.aclweb.org/anthology/E17-2075
8. Williams, J.D., Young, S.: Partially observable markov decision processes for spoken dialog systems. Comput. Speech Lang. **21**(2), 393–422 (2007)
9. Young, S., Gasic, M., Thomson, B., Williams, J.D.: Pomdp-based statistical spoken dialog systems: a review. Proc. IEEE **101**(5), 1160–1179 (2013)
10. Chen, Y.-N., Hakkani-Tur, D., Gao, J., Deng, L.: End-to-end memory networks with knowledge carryover for multi-turn spoken language understanding (2016)
11. Wu, C.-S., Madotto, A., Winata, G., Fung, P.: End-to-end dynamic query memory network for entity-value independent task-oriented dialog. In: 2018 IEEE International Conference on Acoustics, Speech and Signal Processing (ICASSP), pp. 6154–6158, April 2018
12. Sutskever, I., Vinyals, O., Le, Q.V.: Sequence to sequence learning with neural networks. In Advances in Neural Information Processing Systems (2014)
13. Bahdanau, D., Cho, K., Bengio, Y.: Neural machine translation by jointly learning to align and translate. In: Proceedings of the International Conference on Learning Representations (2015)

14. Seo, M., Kembhavi, A., Farhadi, A., Hajishirzi, H.: Bidirectional attention flow for machine comprehension. In: Proceedings of ICLR (2017)
15. Wang, S., Jiang, J.: Machine comprehension using match-lstm and answer pointer. In: Proceedings of ICLR (2017)
16. Vinyals, O., Fortunato, M., Jaitly, N.: Pointer networks. In: Neural Information Processing Systems (2015)
17. See, A., Liu, P.J., Manning, C.D.: Get to the point: Summarization with pointer-generator networks. arXiv preprint arXiv:1704.04368 (2017)
18. Ghazvininejad, M., et al.: A knowledge grounded neural conversation model. In: AAAI (2018)
19. Madotto, A., Wu, C.-S., Fung, P.: Mem2Seq: effectively incorporating knowledge bases into end-to-end task-oriented dialog systems. In: Proceedings of the 56th Annual Meeting of the Association for Computational Linguistics, pp. 1468–1478. Association for Computational Linguistics (2018)
20. Wang, F., Peng, J., Wu, H., Lian, R., Xie, M.: Learning to select knowledge for response generation in dialog systems. arXiv preprint arXiv:1902.04911 (2019)
21. Zhao, Y., Ni, X.: Paragraph-level neural question generation with maxout pointer and gated self-attention networks. In EMNLP (2018)
22. Tam, Y.-C., Ding, J.: Cluster-based beam search for pointer-generator chatbot grounded by knowledge. In AAAI (2019)
23. Li, S., Zhao, Z., Hu, R., Li, W., Liu, T., Du, X.: Analogical reasoning on chinese morphological and semantic relations. In: ACL (2018)

Multiple Perspective Answer Reranking for Multi-passage Reading Comprehension

Mucheng Ren, Heyan Huang(✉), Ran Wei, Hongyu Liu, Yu Bai, Yang Wang, and Yang Gao

Beijing Institue of Technology, Beijing 100081, China
rdoctmc@gmail.com, weiranbit@gmail.com, liuhongyu12138@gmail.com, Wnwhiteby@gmail.com, wangyangbit1@gmail.com, {hhy63,gyang}@bit.edu.cn

Abstract. This study focuses on multi-passage Machine Reading Comprehension (MRC) task. Prior work has shown that retriever, reader pipeline model could improve overall performance. However, the pipeline model relies heavily on retriever component since inferior retrieved documents would significantly degrade the performance. In this study, we proposed a new multi-perspective answer reranking technique that considers all documents to verify the confidence of candidate answers; such nuanced technique can carefully distinguish candidate answers to improve performance. Specifically, we rearrange the order of traditional pipeline model and make a posterior answer reranking instead of prior passage reranking. In addition, new proposed pre-trained language model BERT is also introduced here. Experiments with Chinese multi-passage dataset DuReader show that our model achieves competitive performance.

Keywords: Machine Reading Comprehension · Answer reranking · BERT

1 Introduction

Question Answering, as a sub-task of Natural Language Processing, has been a long-standing problem. In recent years, Machine Reading Comprehension (MRC), a task that empowers computers to find useful information and response correct answers from giving questions and related documents in natural language, has drawn a considerable amount of attention. In the beginning, MRC task only focused on cloze style test [5,8], later followed by single document datasets [15,16] and complicated open domain datasets [12,17,18].

Lots of progress have been achieved over these MRC datasets. Particularly, on benchmark single-passage dataset SQuAD [15], various deep neural network models based on Recurrent Neural Network (RNN) and attention mechanism have been proposed [13,21]. Some work has already surpassed the performance of human annotators, which can be assumed as a big milestone in MRC filed [6].

J. Tang et al. (Eds.): NLPCC 2019, LNAI 11839, pp. 736–747, 2019.
https://doi.org/10.1007/978-3-030-32236-6_67

However, SQuAD dataset already provides a single passage for each question so that answers can be definitely found in the given passage. Moreover, the length of each given paragraph is relatively short so that there exists a huge gap between this dataset and real-world scenarios since people usually need to find answer from multiple documents or webpages. Even though SQuAD 2.0 [16] which contains unanswerable questions had been built last year, it is still limited by practical difficulties. Therefore, several studies [12,17,18] start to build a more realistic MRC dataset: Read multiple related documents to answer one question which is called as multi-passage datasets.

Compared with single-passage datasets, the most critical problem in multi-passage MRC is noisy input data: for each question, all given passages are related but not essential which means every document describes a common topic but in different ways. Therefore, too much related information may confuse the model significantly. In general, multi-passage MRC task is usually done by two categories of approaches: (1) The pipeline approach usually separates whole MRC task into two subtask: passage selection and extractive reading comprehension like SQuAD. Given a question and multiple related documents, the most important document should be chosen by passage reranking techniques, then send it into MRC model to figure out the answer [11,22], our work follows this approach; (2) Joint learning approach integrates these two subtasks so that they can be trained simultaneously [3,9,14,23].

Be different from the previous pipeline method, our pipeline did not follow the traditional processing order, we discard passage selection component. Instead, we firstly do answer prediction for each passage to get a set of answer candidates, then an answer reranking component will be applied to determine confidence for each predicted answer and answer with the highest confidence is the final output answer. This multi-perspective technique allows meticulous sorting for candidate answers so that overall performance can be improved. In addition, we abandon traditional neural network entirely and choose Bidirectional Encoder Representations from Transformers (BERT) [6] pretrained language model as basic computational units. BERT is a newly proposed pretrained language model, it consists of numerous transformers [2] whose working principle is multi-head attention which can ensure each word can be greatly represented according to its context. Since it is a pretrained language model, it can be simply adopted into different NLP tasks by finetuning it, so far BERT already monopolized almost every MRC test datasets [15–17].

Our contribution is two-fold:

1. Firstly, we designed a novel pipeline model in a reversed order and proposed a multi-perspective answer reranking technique to verify the confidence of answer candidates. With confidence verification, superior answers can be explicitly distinguished with inferior ones.
2. Secondly, we explored the possibility that is applying pretrained language model BERT into multi-passage MRC task. More importantly, we chose to adopt different BERTs in whole pipeline and demonstrated the effectiveness of pretrained language model.

We conduct extensive experiments on DuReader [18] dataset. The results show that our BERT based pipeline model outperforms the baseline models by a large margin and confidence verification works well. Our project code is available[1].

2 Related Work

Multi-passage MRC
In recent year, multi-passage MRC research has drawn great attention [3,9,11, 12,14,17,18,22,23]. Be different from single passage datasets, multi-passage MRC needs model becomes more robust to noisy data. The most straightforward approach is to concatenate all passages and find the answer from the integrated one [24]. Generally, there are two categories of approaches explored in multi-passage MRC: pipeline model and joint training model. For pipeline model, most models firstly filter out the most relevant passage by using a TF-IDF based ranker or a neural network based ranker, then pass it into a neural reader [4,10,20,22]. However, the performance of the pipeline approach suffers from the document ranking model, since posterior reading comprehension component can not extract correct answer if filtered documents are incorrect. For joint learning approach [3,9,14,23], it considers all the passages and selects the best answer by comparing confidence scores. Wang [23] propose a cross-passage answer verification for more accurate prediction. Tan [3] propose an extraction-then-synthesis framework to synthesize answers from extraction result. Ming [14] further consider a proper trade-off between the pipeline method and joint learning method, it uses cascade learning to eliminate useless passages in advance and identify the best answer on remaining passage. Our model follows the pipeline model approach which trains each component separately, however we consider all passages like joint learning method does and propose a new answer confidence verification method.

Pretrained LM
Devlin [6] propose Bidirectional Encoder Representations from Transformers (BERT), a new language representation model that obtains state-of-the-art results on eleven natural language processing tasks. Nowadays, BERT has been widely adopted in various fields. For example, Hu [20] proposed a RE3QA that adopted BERT into Retrieval and Reader components for multi-document MRC, Yang [19] used BERT as new document reader in open domain question answering. Most papers have demonstrated BERT based model with simple fine-tune modification can significantly surpass the performance of traditional neural models in different fields.

3 Proposed Model

The overall pipeline of our model can be seen in Fig. 1. In the DuReader dataset, each question is given with several documents, we firstly preprocess the dataset by using several statistical tricks, then feed each question and several question-related passages into Answer Prediction module to get answers for each passage,

[1] https://github.com/trib-plan/TriB-QA.

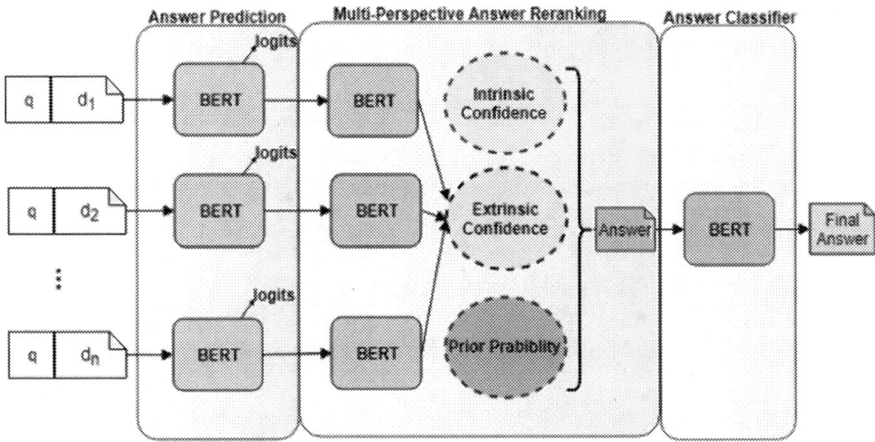

Fig. 1. Overall architecture. Given documents will be concatenated with query which are then fed into the model. Each document will generate an answer candidate. Then multi-perspective answer ranking will verify answer confidence by considering three parts: Intrinsic confidence, Extrinsic confidence and Prior document probability. The answer candidate with the highest confidence will be selected as the answer and another answer classifier will be applied if question type is Yes/No. The whole pipeline model is trained independently.

then generated answers and query will be further sent into Answer Reranking module to compare the confidence scores between each answer, and answer with highest confidence will be selected as final output answer. In addition, if the query type is Yes/No type, another Yes/No/Depends Classifier module will be applied at the end to determine the polarity of the output answer.

Particularly, during the training process, each module is trained separately. In the answer prediction part, we firstly preprocess the given documents for one question to ensure the input documents must contain the correct given answer span, therefore this part can be trained like SQuAD dataset. In the answer reranking module, we design a multi-perspective ranking technique and use self-made labels to rank generate answers. At the last, in the Yes/No/Depend classifier module, only yes/no type questions in datasets would be selected and given labels would be used here for training purpose.

3.1 Answer Prediction

Given a query $\boldsymbol{q}$ and multiple corresponding pre-processed documents $\boldsymbol{C} = \{\boldsymbol{c}_1, ..., \boldsymbol{c}_n\}$ where n is 5 at most, the Answer Prediction component aims to generate one set of answer candidates $\boldsymbol{A} = \{\boldsymbol{a}_1, ..., \boldsymbol{a}_n\}$. This can be achieved by following procedures. Firstly, we encode query with every document together by using pretrained Transformer blocks [6]. Particularly we concatenate query and document as $\{[CLS]; \mathbf{q}; [SEP]; \mathbf{c}; [SEP]\}$ where $[CLS]$ is a token for classification token and $[SEP]$ is another token for separating different sentences.

Next, the final hidden states from BERT for the $\boldsymbol{i_{th}}$ input token can be denoted as $\boldsymbol{T_i}$. In order to predict answer span with highest probability, we calculated the probability of whether $\boldsymbol{i_{th}}$ input token is start token or end token separately. Particularly, the probability of word i being the start of the answer span can be computed as a dot product between T_i and S followed by a SoftMax layer, where S is the learnable matrix that we should train. Similarly, the probability of word i being the end of the answer span can be calculated by training matrix T. At last, the answer span from word i and word j with highest probability will be selected as final answer.

$$T_i = BERT(q, c) \tag{1}$$

$$P_{Si} = softmax(start\_logits(i)) = \frac{e^{S \times T_i}}{\sum_j e^{S \times T_j}} \tag{2}$$

$$P_{Ei} = softmax(end\_logits(i)) = \frac{e^{E \times T_i}}{\sum_j e^{E \times T_j}} \tag{3}$$

Finally, the training objective for answer prediction component is the loglikelihood of the given answer span labels.

$$L_{AP} = -log(P_S) - log(P_E) \tag{4}$$

3.2 Multi-perspective Answer Reranking

After the answer candidates $\boldsymbol{A} = \{\boldsymbol{a_1}, ..., \boldsymbol{a_n}\}$ for query $\boldsymbol{q}$ are generated in the answer prediction part, we then input $\boldsymbol{q}$ and $\boldsymbol{A}$ into the multi-perspective answer reranking module. In this part, we combine the intrinsic confidence ($\boldsymbol{IC}$), extrinsic confidence ($\boldsymbol{EC}$) and statistical distribution for documents ($\boldsymbol{\alpha}$) to calculate the final answer confidence.

Statistical Distribution for Documents. The first perspective is the statistical distribution of documents. Since the Dureader dataset is constructed based on real application scenario, all questions are real questions raised by users in Baidu search engine and documents are the results retrieved from it. Therefore, the documents for one query is already sorted in order and it can be argued that the documents that are retrieved by search engine in higher order tend to have better context similarity between query and context, better user acceptance and entity matching. Therefore, we make a statistical analysis of preprocessed dataset and explore the order of documents that contains correct answers. In this way, we define a list of prior probability $\boldsymbol{\alpha} = \{\boldsymbol{\alpha_1}, ..., \boldsymbol{\alpha_n}\}$ in descending order for multiple documents corresponding to one query.

Intrinsic Confidence. The second perspective is to determine the quality of generated answer. As mentioned in Sect. 3.1, answer prediction module would transform i_{th} token hidden state into start/end logits. Then token with higher logits will be selected start/end word for an answer span. Be inspired by this, we can assume that the magnitude of logits can represent the intrinsic confidence of generated answer spans in a way. Therefore, we directly sum the start logit and end logit for an answer as intrinsic confidence.

$$ICa_i = start\_logits(a_i) + end\_logits(a_i) \quad (5)$$

Extrinsic Confidence. The third perspective aims to analyse the confidence difference between answers generated from different documents. Dureader dataset provides a series of labels that tell us whether this document contains the reference answer. However, such labels are usually misleading because for most cases, document which is labelled as false still contain reliable answers. Therefore, we decide to build a classifier to determine whether the document is trustable or not.

In order to achieve this, we use BERT cascaded with one fine-tune linear layer as classifier, we extract 60 K questions (around 200 K documents) from train datasets and build prediction labels by following the rules: if the generated answer has good ROUGE-L values compared with given answer (top 30% among all examples), we label the document as 1, otherwise 0 (last 30%). Such self-made labels could ease the misleading label issue. In this way, the extrinsic confidence for a given answer would be final values on $[CLS]$ token.

$$EC_{a_i} = Linear(BERT(q, a_i)) \quad (6)$$

After observing answer from three perspectives, final answer confidence $\boldsymbol{C}$ can be represented as follow.

$$C_{a_i} = ECa_i * softmax(IC_{a_i} * \alpha_i) \quad (7)$$

3.3 Yes or No Discrimination

For sentence classification, a BERT classifier model is applied. The model takes the representation of the answer's $[CLS]$ in and outputs its polarity.

$$P_{a_i} = Linear(BERT(a_i)) \quad (8)$$

Furthermore, we employ an advanced method which binds the answer and the corresponding question together. With the adding question information, our model can makes its decision more wisely. Meanwhile, we change the pretrained model to ERNIE [25] to achieve better performance.

$$P'_{a_i} = Linear(ERNIE(q, a_i)) \quad (9)$$

We then fine-tune the pretrained model to make it suitable for our task. The whole model is trained to minimize the cross-entropy loss.

4 Experiment Setup

In this section, we introduce the setup of our experiment which includes datasets, model settings, data preprocessing and evaluation metrics in detail.

4.1 Datasets

We experiment our model on Chinese multi-passage dataset Dureader [18]. Statistics for official dataset can be found in Tables 1 and 2. Particularly, test 1 and test 2 datasets contain mixed data so that the real numbers of evaluated questions are 3398 and 6561 respectively.

4.2 Model Settings

We initialize our model using publicly available pytorch version of BERT in Chinese[2]. For simplicity, we adopted same parameters described in [6] except:

For answer prediction component, we set *doc_stride* as 350, *max_seq_length* and *max_answer_length* as 512, *batch_size* as 20, *epoch_number* as 2. For answer reranking component, we set *batch_size* as 10, *epoch_number* as 2 or 3, *max_seq_length* as 400. For answer classifier component, we set *batch_size* as 32, *epoch_number* as 4.

We trained our answer prediction model on one NVIDIA RTX 2080Ti GPU and train rest components on one Titan XP GPU.

4.3 Data Preprocessing

The answers for every question in the dataset are summarized by the annotators. Because the current dominant models are extractive, i.e. the answer is a text span from the documents, the dataset provides us with fake answers and the corresponding text spans which have the largest F1 score with true answers for training. First we filtered out the samples where the answer is punctuation or the largest F1 score is less than 0.5. Then we calculated the ROUGE-L score between fake answers and true answers and filtered out the samples that ROUGE-L are less than 50. After sample pruning, we calculated the F1 scores of the question at paragraph-level for each document, and rearrange the top-N paragraphs into a new pruned document in the order of the original document. Finally, the pruned documents are passed to the model for training and testing.

4.4 Evaluation Metrics

In terms of answer evaluation, we adopted the ROUGE and BLEU automatic evaluation method in [1]. The method is improved for machine reading comprehension task. The Evaluation score bases on the score ROUGE-L and BLEU-4. The automatic evaluation method is improved for questions inquiring yes-no

[2] https://github.com/huggingface/pytorch-pretrained-BERT.

opinions and entity lists. If the model correctly answers the yes-no type question or correctly matches entity lists it will receive a score bonus. To some extent, it makes up for the deficiency of traditional ROUGE-L and BLEU-4. To better correlate n-gram overlap with the human judgment for answers to these two question types.

Table 1. Dureader data distribution

	Train	Dev	Test1	Test2
Zhidao	135366	1060	30000	30000
Search	136208	1179	30000	30000
Total	271574	2239	60000	60000

Table 2. Question type distribution

	Fact	Opinion	Total
Entity	14.4%	13.8%	28.2%
Description	42.8%	21.0%	63.8%
YesNo	2.9%	5.1%	8.0%
Total	60.1%	39.9%	100%

Table 3. Performance of our model and competing models on the DuReader

Model	ROUGE-L	BLEU-4
BiDAF [13]	39.00	31.80
Match-LSTM [21]	39.20	31.90
PR+BiDAF [23]	41.81	37.55
V-NET [23]	44.18	40.97
R-NET [24]	47.71	44.88
Deep Cascade [14]	50.71	49.39
MRT [7]	51.09	43.76
Our model	**55.51**	**55.71**
Human performance	68.68	69.60

5 Results and Analysis

5.1 Overall Results

Table 3 summarize all the results on the test set of Dureader dataset. It is worth noting that our model and all other models train on the same train set, but test on different test sets due to competition rules[3]. More specifically, the test dataset evaluated by our model is more complicated than others, because this year's test dataset only contains questions that were answered incorrectly last year. As we can see, our best model achieves 55.51 Rouge-L and 55.71 Bleu-4, clearly outperforming previous methods.

[3] http://lic2019.ccf.org.cn/read.

5.2 Model Analysis

In this section, we describe **(1)** the detailed procedure to achieve final result; **(2)** the insufficiency exists in our model.

Building Procedure of Model. Table 4 states detailed building procedure for our model. For the first try, we use traditional pipeline method: select most related document and send it directly into answer prediction model to get answer. Clearly, the result demonstrates traditional pipeline model relies heavily on the quality of document. Therefore, we decide to improve the quality of documents by adopting data pre-processing described in Sect. 4.3. It can be seen that the ROUGE-L value is increased by 7.4 points which verifies the above mentioned quality-matter concept. Meanwhile, we observe that the length of our generated answers is relatively short compared with reference answer so that the BLEU-4 score is far behind ROUGE-L. Hence, we find answers in a larger span and increase the answer length.

Table 4. The building procedures for our model

Model	ROUGE-L	BLEU-4
Original pipeline	**37.15**	**23.41**
+ Data preprocess	44.54	27.60
+ Increase answer length	48.13	46.70
+ Prior probability α	50.46	52.37
+ Extrinsic confidence	52.50	54.30
+ Intrinsic confidence	54.12	55.82
+ Human constraints	55.30	56.09
Final results	**55.51**	**55.71**

Next, we start considering all documents since every document corresponding to one query in the dataset is similar with each other which suggests that these documents should not be filtered out at the beginning. Thus, we adopt prior document probability to verify the answer confidence. The result demonstrates our thought is correct. In order to improve performance of answer reranking, we introduce two more variables: intrinsic confidence and extrinsic confidence. As we can see, it can significantly improve overall performance, suggesting our proposed multi-perspective answer reranking technique is necessary for our model.

At last, in order to make results more competitive, we add some human constraints over the model, including hyperparameter finetuning, punctuation replacement, substitute BERT with ERNIE etc.

Insufficiency Exist in Model. There exist two main critical problems in our model:

- **Answer Length:** Even though we already increase the answer length, some generated answers are still short. This is because BERT can only accept maximum 512 tokens-long documents so that answer span will not exceed this threshold. However, in multi-passage datasets, many documents are much longer than 512 tokens and answers are hundreds of tokens as well. This could be solved by replacing BERT with other neural network like RNN, CNN etc., because the latter one can accept much longer sequence length without consuming too much training sources.
- **Discontinuous answer:** Our model current can only output continuous answers which are directly extracted from documents. However, some question requires abstractive answers or discontinuous answers. Such answers require model to jump around looking for them, i.e. finding the keywords in the documents. This issue can probably solved by teaching mode to focus on essential terms.

Question	初学波比跳每天多少组	Prior probability	Intrinsic confidence	Extrinsic confidence	Final confidence
Doc_1 Answer	Burpee(波比)是一种高强度, 短时间燃烧脂肪, 令人心跳率飙升的自重阻力训练动作之一。Burpee结合了深蹲(Squat)、伏地挺身(Push-Ups)及跳跃(Jump)一连串的动作, 在短时间内会将心跳率拉升到将近人体最大值。	0.503	-0.36696	0.11551	0.00652
Doc_2 Answer	在你能力范围内可做3~4组波比跳, 每组8~20个。	0.2314	8.16496	0.78477	**0.60819**
Doc_3 Answer	波比运动每天做多少个。	0.1414	-3.48146	0.02304	5.47419e-14
Doc_4 Answer	在40秒里, 做尽量多的波比, 休息20秒, 为一组; 做20个波比, 休息30秒, 为一组; 不休息, 一直做波比, 直到力竭为止, 为一组; 不休息, 做多个波比(数量根据自己体能调整), 为一组。具体的循环数量, 也可以依据自己的训练经验和体能进行调整。	0.1031	8.80785	0.88716	**0.25771**
Doc_5 Answer	一般一天做90个, 15个一组, 6组, 每组间隔30秒。	0.0411	8.93052	0.75435	0.12756
Reference Answers	• 在能力范围内可做3~4组波比跳，每组8~20个，跳多少组，每组多少个看体力。 • 在40秒里，做尽量多的波比，休息20秒，为一组;做20个波比，休息30秒，为一组;不休息，一直做波比，直到力竭为止，为一组;不休息，做多个波比(数量根据自己体能调整)，为一组。				

Fig. 2. A sampled case from Dureader dev set. Our answer prediction module selects answers from each passage. The multi-perspective answer reranking module calculates confidence scores, correct answers with high confidence scores would be selected.

5.3 Case Study

To demonstrate powerfulness of our model, we conduct a case study sampled from our model on Dureader development set. For a given query, we present predicted answer candidate for each document with its prior probability, intrinsic confidence and extrinsic confidence. As can be seen in Fig. 2, we can make two conclusions.

Firstly, it can be argued that considering all documents is necessary. As can be seen from the figure, either doc2 or doc4 can give us a reasonable answer and doc1 which is labelled as best document does not contain answer. Therefore, if we implement document reranking at first like traditional pipeline model, it has large probability to choose a document that does not contain any answer and other document that may contains answers will be ignored. If we consider all documents, this issue can be avoided.

Secondly, multi-perspective answer reranking technique works as expected. If we only consider prior document probability, doc1 answer will be selected which is wrong. However, after considering intrinsic confidence, we can see that module could identify the quality of answer correctly. Particularly, doc1 and doc3 answers which are wrong answers are given negative scores. Then during extrinsic confidence verification step, our model can compare confidence between all answer candidate so that superior answers (doc2, doc4, doc5) has larger values in contrast to inferior answers (doc1, doc3). After combining prior probability, intrinsic confidence and extrinsic confidence, the answer with highest final confidence can be correctly selected. Therefore, it can be concluded that these three perspectives are compensated with each other, such multi-perspective answer reranking technique can indeed improve overall performance.

6 Conclusion

In this study, we proposed a new multi-perspective answer reranking technique. Our refined pipeline model can verify the confidence of candidate answers such that superior answers can be distinctly distinguished with inferior answers. Specifically, we make a posterior answer reranking instead of prior passage reranking. Besides, the recently proposed pre-trained language model BERT is also applied to improve the performance of our model. Experiments with Chinese multi-passage dataset DuReader show that our model achieved competitive performance.

Acknowledgments. This work is supported by National Natural Science Foundation of China No. 61751201, Research Foundation of Beijing Municipal Science and Technology Commission No. Z181100008918002. And we are grateful to Baidu Inc. and China Computer Federation for hosting competition and sharing data resources. We would also like to thank the anonymous reviewers for their insightful suggestions.

References

1. Yang, A., et al.: Adaptations of ROUGE and BLEU to better evaluate machine reading comprehension task. arXiv preprint arXiv:1806.03578 (2018)
2. Vaswani, A., et al.: Attention is all you need. In: Advances in Neural Information Processing Systems (2017)
3. Tan, C., et al.: S-Net: from answer extraction to answer generation for machine reading comprehension. arXiv preprint arXiv:1706.04815 (2017)

4. Clark, C., Gardner, M.: Simple and effective multi-paragraph reading comprehension. arXiv preprint arXiv:1710.10723 (2017)
5. Hill, F., et al.: The goldilocks principle: reading children's books with explicit memory representations. arXiv preprint arXiv:1511.02301 (2015)
6. Devlin, J., et al.: Bert: pre-training of deep bidirectional transformers for language understanding. arXiv preprint arXiv:1810.04805 (2018)
7. Liu, J., et al.: A multi-answer multi-task framework for real-world machine reading comprehension. In: Proceedings of the 2018 Conference on Empirical Methods in Natural Language Processing, pp. 2109–2118 (2018)
8. Hermann, K.M., et al.: Teaching machines to read and comprehend. In: Advances in Neural Information Processing Systems (2015)
9. Nishida, K., et al.: Multi-style generative reading comprehension. arXiv preprint arXiv:1901.02262 (2019)
10. Nishida, K., et al.: Retrieve-and-read: multi-task learning of information retrieval and reading comprehension. In: Proceedings of the 27th ACM International Conference on Information and Knowledge Management. ACM (2018)
11. Joshi, M., et al.: TriviaQA: a large scale distantly supervised challenge dataset for reading comprehension. arXiv preprint arXiv:1705.03551 (2017)
12. Dunn, M., et al.: SearchQA: a new Q&A dataset augmented with context from a search engine. arXiv preprint arXiv:1704.05179 (2017)
13. Seo, M., et al.: Bidirectional attention flow for machine comprehension. arXiv preprint arXiv:1611.01603 (2016)
14. Yan, M., et al.: A deep cascade model for multi-document reading comprehension. arXiv preprint arXiv:1811.11374 (2018)
15. Rajpurkar, P., et al.: SQuAD: 100,000+ questions for machine comprehension of text. arXiv preprint arXiv:1606.05250 (2016)
16. Rajpurkar, P., Jia, R., Liang, P.: Know what you don't know: unanswerable questions for SQuAD. arXiv preprint arXiv:1806.03822 (2018)
17. Nguyen, T., et al.: MS MARCO: a human generated machine reading comprehension dataset. arXiv preprint arXiv:1611.09268 (2016)
18. He, W., et al.: DuReader: a Chinese machine reading comprehension dataset from real-world applications. In: Proceedings of the Workshop on Machine Reading for Question Answering (2018)
19. Yang, W., et al.: End-to-end open-domain question answering with BERTserini. arXiv preprint arXiv:1902.01718 (2019)
20. Hu, M., et al.: Retrieve, read, rerank: towards end-to-end multi-document reading comprehension. arXiv preprint arXiv:1906.04618 (2019)
21. Wang, S., Jiang, J.: Machine comprehension using match-LSTM and answer pointer. arXiv preprint arXiv:1608.07905 (2016)
22. Wang, S., et al.: R 3: reinforced ranker-reader for open-domain question answering. In: Thirty-Second AAAI Conference on Artificial Intelligence (2018)
23. Wang, Y., et al.: Multi-passage machine reading comprehension with cross-passage answer verification. arXiv preprint arXiv:1805.02220 (2018)
24. Wang, W., et al.: Gated self-matching networks for reading comprehension and question answering. In: Proceedings of the 55th Annual Meeting of the Association for Computational Linguistics (Volume 1: Long Papers) (2017)
25. Sun, Y., et al.: ERNIE: enhanced representation through knowledge integration. arXiv preprint arXiv:1904.09223 (2019)

A Sketch-Based System for Semantic Parsing

Zechang Li[1,2], Yuxuan Lai[1], Yuxi Xie[1], Yansong Feng[1(✉)], and Dongyan Zhao[1,2]

[1] Wangxuan Institute of Computer Technology, Peking University, Beijing, China
{zcli18,erutan,xieyuxi,fengyansong,zhaody}@pku.edu.cn
[2] Center for Data Science, Peking University, Beijing, China

Abstract. This paper presents our semantic parsing system for the evaluation task of open domain semantic parsing in NLPCC 2019. Many previous works formulate semantic parsing as a sequence-to-sequence(seq2seq) problem. Instead, we treat the task as a sketch-based problem in a coarse-to-fine(coarse2fine) fashion. The sketch is a high-level structure of the logical form exclusive of low-level details such as entities and predicates. In this way, we are able to optimize each part individually. Specifically, we decompose the process into three stages: the sketch classification determines the high-level structure while the entity labeling and the matching network fill in missing details. Moreover, we adopt the seq2seq method to evaluate logical form candidates from an overall perspective. The co-occurrence relationship between predicates and entities contribute to the reranking as well. Our submitted system achieves the exactly matching accuracy of 82.53% on full test set and 47.83% on hard test subset, which is the 3rd place in NLPCC 2019 Shared Task 2. After optimizations for parameters, network structure and sampling, the accuracy reaches 84.47% on full test set and 63.08% on hard test subset (Our code and data are available at https://github.com/zechagl/NLPCC2019-Semantic-Parsing).

Keywords: Semantic parsing · Sketch-based · Multi-task model · Matching network

1 Introduction

Open domain semantic parsing aims to map natural language utterances to structured meaning representations. Recently, seq2seq based approaches have achieved promising performance by structure-aware networks, such as sequence-to-action [3] and STAMP [18].

However, this kind of approach mixes up low-level entities, predicates and high-level structures together, which loses precision at each level to some extent. So the sketch-based method may be an another choice for disentangling high-level structures from low-level details. In this work, we conduct our sketch-based

J. Tang et al. (Eds.): NLPCC 2019, LNAI 11839, pp. 748–759, 2019.
https://doi.org/10.1007/978-3-030-32236-6_68

approach on MSParS, a large hand-annotated semantic dataset mapping questions to logical forms. We argue there are at least two advantages to sketch-based method. Firstly, basic attention based seq2seq network [1,13] does not perform well in semantic parsing because logical forms are structured sequences and it fails to incorporate structure information of logical forms. Then sequence-to-tree(seq2tree) [6] proposes a structure-aware decoder to utilize the information. But its architecture also becomes much more complex. Instead of using intricate decoders, we can extract high-level sketches for logical forms and classify samples into several sketch classes. Logical forms of a certain sketch class have a fixed pattern which is shown in Table 1. So the structure problem is finally simplified to a classification task. Secondly, logical forms often need to copy a span of questions. Although Copynet [8] and Pointer [16] implement the copy mechanism, it is still difficult to achieve the expected effect. But for the sketch-based method, this problem becomes an individual entity labeling task which is easier than generating entities. Generally speaking, the seq2seq way decodes the entire meaning representation in one go while we deal with different parts at different levels of granularity just like coarse2fine [7]. Although we increase the number of stages, the network architecture of each stage is much simpler without sacrificing the accuracy. In this way, we are able to locate the errors and optimize according parts.

Table 1. Examples demonstrating sketches of logical forms. P represents predicate and E represents entity. Subscripts are applied to distinguish different ones.

Class	Sketch of logical form
aggregation	count (lambda ?x (P_1 E_1 ?x))
cvt	(lambda ?x exist ?y (and (P_1 E_1 ?y) (P_2 ?y E_2) (P_3 ?y ?x)))
multi-turn-entity	(lambda ?x (P_1 E_1 ?x)) ||| (lambda ?x (P_2 E_1 ?x))
multi-turn-answer	(lambda ?x (P_1 E_1 ?x)) ||| (lambda ?x exist ?y (and (P_1 E_1 ?y) (P_2 ?y ?x)))
single-relation	(lambda ?x (P_1 E_1 ?x))
yesno	(P_1 E_1 E_2)

We propose to decompose the process into three stages. In the first stage, we deal with a sketch classification task. Then, we find the entities in the questions through an entity labeling task. Actually, we combine the two stages through the multi-task model for both accuracy and efficiency [4]. The last stage is the most difficult part since the knowledge base of MSParS is not available. We define question pattern-logical form pattern pair and use the matching network to rank all these pairs. Seq2seq based approach is one of the two methods we adopted here to help rescore on the whole. We also incorporate state-of-art pre-trained work, Bert [5], in above tasks to incorporate more priori knowledge.

The error rate of our multi-task model is lower than 2%, which ensures the right sketch and entities. So the last stage actually determines the accuracy to a large extent. Our accuracy achieves 77.42% after above three stages. Seq2seq based approach and co-occurrence relationship improve the accuracy to 86.86% in validation set. Our final accuracy in full test set reaches 84.47%. And the accuracy on hard test subset has been promoted to 63.08% finally which is higher than the best model on the submission list by 5.65%.

In the rest of our paper, we first analyze the special features of MSParS for this task in Sect. 2. Afterwords, we discuss our system in detail in Sect. 3. Then in Sect. 4, we demonstrate our experimental setup, results and analyzation. Related works are mentioned in Sect. 5. At last, we make a conclusion of the whole paper and propose our future work.

2 Data Analyzation

The dataset MSParS is published by NLPCC 2019 evaluation task. The whole dataset consists of 81,826 samples annotated by native English speakers. 80% of them are used as training set. 10% of them are used as validation set while the rest is used as test set. 3000 hard samples are selected from the test set. Metric for this dataset is the exactly matching accuracy on both full test set and hard test subset. Each sample is composed of the question, the logical form, the parameters(entity/value/type) and question type as the Table 2 demonstrates.

Table 2. An sample of MSParS.

question	what is birth date for chris pine
logical form	(lambda ?x (mso:people.person.date_of_birth chris_pine ?x))
parameters	chris_pine (entity) [5,6]
question type	single-relation

Samples are classified to 12 classes originally at a coarse level while we reclassify them at a finer level, which is the basis of our sketch-based method. We replace the predicate in the triple as P_i, the entity in the triple as E_i and distinguish different ones with subscripts. The number in superlative class and comparative class is replaced as V while the type in the triple begin with special predicate "isa" is replaced as T as well. In this way, we get the sketch of the logical form. Finally, we produce 15 classes of sketches.

We believe the features of questions highly correlate with the sketch of logical forms. For instance, the sketch must begin with "argmore" or "argless" if there are comparative words such as "higher", "more" and "before" in questions. Therefore, we take questions as input to classify samples to different sketch classes.

As the Table 2 suggests, entities are concatenated tokens from the question. So we implement entity labeling to label every token in the questions.

Nonetheless, cases are tough when there are more than one entities in the logical form. Suppose that we have labeled E_1 and E_2 from the question. We do not know which one we should choose to fill in the first entity slot in the sketch. We solve this problem and pick out the suitable predicate simultaneously. The entities in the questions are replaced by label "entity" with subscripts suggesting the order they appear in questions to get question patterns. When it comes to logical form patterns, the entities in logical forms are substituted as well while predicates are split to small tokens. Table 3 gives an example of these two patterns. In this way, we combine the entity collocations with predicates successfully. Another reason for label "entity" used here is generalization. For instance, "what is birth date for barack obama" shares the same question pattern "what is birth date for entity1" with "what is birth date for donald trump". The predicate used in these logical forms is "mso:people.person.date_of_birth". So we can draw the conclusion that the predicate for this question pattern is likely to be "mso:people.person.date_of_birth". If "what is birth date for george bush" appears in the test set, we are able to find the right predicate even if we do not see "george bush" before. Without the impact of specific entities, our model learns the mapping from question patterns to logical form patterns more accurately. Since we do not have a knowledge base, we can only extract logical form patterns in training set. And we find 90.34% of logical form patterns in validation set are covered by that in training set, which ensures the feasibility of our method.

Table 3. An example for question pattern and logical form pattern.

question	travels in the interior districts of africa has how many pages? ||| when is the date of publication of the book edition?
question pattern	entity1 has how many pages? ||| when is the date of publication of the book edition?
logical form	(lambda ?x (mso:book.edition.number_of_pages travels_in_the_interior_districts_of_africa ?x)) ||| (lambda ?x (mso:book.edition.publication_date travels_in_the_interior_districts_of_africa ?x))
logical form pattern	book edition number of pages entity1 ?x ||| book edition publication date entity1 ?x

We take question patterns paired with logical form patterns as input. Then, we get logical form candidates through combining sketches and entities with logical form patterns. The ones with higher scores are more likely to be right.

3 Proposed Approach

3.1 Sketch Classification

The single sentence classification fine-tuned task in Bert is applied in this stage. A special classification embedding ([CLS]) is added to the beginning. We use the final hidden state corresponding to this token as the aggregate sequence representation for classification task denoted as $C_s \in \mathbb{R}^h$, so the probability of class c_i can be computed as:

$$p(c_i|x) = softmax_i(W_s C_s + b_s) \tag{1}$$

where $W_s \in \mathbb{R}^{k_s \times h}$ and $b_s \in \mathbb{R}^{k_s}$, k_s is the number of sketch classes here. W_s, b_s and all the parameters of Bert are fine-tuned jointly to maximize the log likelihood probability of the correct label.

3.2 Entity Labeling

We use the single sentence tagging fine-tuned task in Bert here to label every token in the question whether it is an entity token that appears in the logical form as well. To simplify the problem, we use 3 labels for the tokens in the questions. Label "b" represents the first token in an entity while label "i" for the rest ones. And label "o" represents those tokens which are not in any entities. Because of the lexical rules in Bert, we also label the special token ([CLS]) at the beginning of the sentence and the special token ([SEP]) at the ending of the sentence as "o". The last label "p" is for all the padding tokens added to reach max_length. Besides, some tokens in the questions are split into several smaller tokens by Bert. For the split ones, they are labeled as "i" if they are in the entities and "o" otherwise. In this stage, we use all the final hidden states denoted as $D \in \mathbb{R}^{h \times m}$ where m is the max_length of the input tokens we set. The hidden state is mapped into dimension k_e via $E = W_e D + b_e$ where $W_e \in \mathbb{R}^{k_e \times h}$ and $b_e \in \mathbb{R}^{k_e \times m}$, k_e is the number of labels here. We employ the CRF on the top of the network taking E as input representations. The objective is to minimize the loss of CRF layer.

3.3 Multi-Task Model

We combine sketch classification and entity labeling to share information together, which means sketches of samples can help label entities while the labeled entities can help sketch classification conversely. The architecture of our model is shown in Fig. 1 where the parameters of Bert model is fine-tuned together for two tasks. Since the scale of dataset is large, we can save lots of time through multi-task model instead of training two different models. Finally, it contributes to both accuracy and efficiency. In this way, our loss to minimize is the weighted sum of the cross-entropy loss in sketch classification task and the CRF loss in entity labeling task.

3.4 Pattern Pair Matching Network

Besides the single sentence tasks, Bert provides sentence pair classification tasks as well. We implement the matching network taking question patterns and logical form patterns as input. The right pattern pairs are regarded as positive samples. We select negative samples only from the logical form patterns in the same sketch class for fixed question patterns. The sketch mentioned is from the multi-task model. Just like sketch classification, we denote the final hidden state corresponding to token ([CLS]) as $C_p \in \mathbb{R}^h$, so the probability can be computed as:

$$p(c_j|x) = softmax_j(W_p C_p + b_p) \tag{2}$$

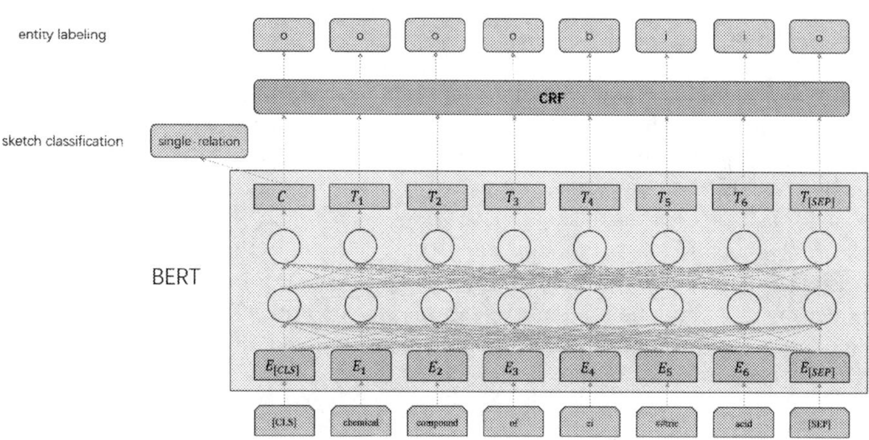

Fig. 1. An overview of multi-task model proposed. The original input question is "chemical compound of citric acid". It becomes "chemical compound of ci ##tric acid" after the tokenization of Bert.

where $W_p \in \mathbb{R}^{2\times h}$, $b_p \in \mathbb{R}^2$ and $c_j \in \{0, 1\}$. W_p, b_p and all the parameters of bert are fine-tuned jointly to maximize the log likelihood probability of the correct class.

In the prediction stage, the candidates for a question pattern are from logical form patterns in the same sketch class as well. The probabilities of class "1" are scores we get for these pattern pairs. From logical form patterns, we get not only right predicates, but right orders as well in which entities should appear. So with the sketch and entities we acquire in the multi-task model, we can already generate complete logical form candidates with scores between 0 and 1.

3.5 Predicate-Entity Pair Matching Network

To alleviate the absence of knowledge base, we incorporate the co-occurrence relationship between predicates and entities to evaluate the candidates. We create the second matching network based on Bert as well. This time, the pairs we take as input are predicate-entity ones. We label the predicate-entity pair as "1" if they have ever appeared in one triple in training set. For a certain entity, we select predicates that never appear with this entity as negative samples. In the prediction stage, we score the predicate-entity pairs in logical form candidates. However, this network does not take questions into account. The predicate for a certain entity can differ a lot according to various questions. For instance, the predicate for "what is birth date for barack obama" is apparently different from that for "what is birth place for barack obama". But the entity "barack obama" has only one predicate with highest score. Although this matching network only considers the co-occurrence relationship regardless of the information from questions, scores produced by it do work as an auxiliary.

3.6 Pointer Network

Although it is not easy for a complex network to generate the whole logical form, such networks do reflect the mapping from an overall perspective. So we adopt Pointer [16] here to rerank. We take the questions as input. For logical forms, entities and predicates are composed of words concatenated by "_" or ".". In order to utilize the information of words, we split all entities and predicates and take split logical form candidates as output. For a fixed question, we calculate cross-entropy losses of different pairs with split logical forms. Then every loss is divided by the max one and subtracted by 1 to be normalized between 0 and 1. The higher the score is, the more the logical form candidate is likely to be true.

3.7 Ranking

A linear combination of the three intermediate scores from pattern pair matching network, predicate-entity pair matching network and Pointer is used to rerank logical form candidates. Weights are roughly adjusted in validation set.

4 Experiment

The number of sketch classes is 15 and the number of labels is 4 in the multi-task model. The Bert model we applied is "BERT-Base, Uncased" with 12-layer, 768-hidden, 12-heads and 110M parameters[1]. All the parameters are fine-tuned in validation set. In the multi-task model, we train the model for 10 epoches. We set batch size to 32 and learning rate to 2e-5. The weight of the loss in sketch classification is 1 while that in entity labeling is 2. We train 3 models in pattern pair matching network with different epoches. As for predicate-entity pair matching network, the number of epoch we use is 3. In Pointer, word embeddings were initialized by Glove [15]. The hidden dim of LSTM is set to 256. More details will be released in our source codes later.

[1] https://github.com/google-research/bert.

Because of the instability of the performance of neural network over training epoches, ensemble learning is incorporated both in pattern pair matching network and Pointer. Scores of Pointer is the simple average of scores from 3 models with different epoches. When it comes to pattern pair matching net, it is a little complex. We make a prediction for training set with our "best" model. We apply ranking sampling here. From those labeled as "0" but with probabilities larger than 0.0001, we select 20 of them while 5 of those whose probabilities are smaller than 0.0001 as new negative samples. We train new models with new training data resampled before every epoch based on one "best" model and base model of Bert. After several epoches, we average the probabilities of new models and original models for ensemble.

We demonstrate the detailed performance in Table 4. All samples are classified into 15 classes. We show the results for every class and the overall weighted average performance in validation set. Because the complete test set is not open yet, we only provide the overall results in test set returned after submission.

Table 4. Performances of our best model. $F1_s$ represents the $F1$ score of sketch classification in multi-task model. We compute Err_s by $1 - F1_s$. Err_e represents the error rate of entity labeling part in multi-task model(an sample is regarded as right only when all of its entities are labeled correctly). Err_m represents the error rate of the whole multi-task model(an sample is regarded as right only when both sketch classification subtask and entity labeling subtask are correct). Acc_l is the exactly matching accuracy of logical forms. We compute Err_l by $1 - Acc_l$.

Dataset		Err_s	Err_e	Err_m	Err_l
Dev	aggregation	0.22%	1.99%	2.10%	23.84%
	comparative	0.00%	0.00%	0.00%	0.00%
	cvt	0.57%	4.04%	4.04%	13.41%
	multi-choice	0.37%	6.72%	7.46%	52.24%
	multi-constraint	0.17%	1.71%	1.71%	6.83%
	multi-hop	0.26%	1.28%	1.54%	3.85%
	multi-turn-answer	4.50%	0.00%	0.00%	5.66%
	multi-turn-entity	0.51%	1.37%	2.29%	16.59%
	multi-turn-predicate	0.50%	2.00%	2.00%	12.00%
	single-relation	0.27%	1.18%	1.31%	9.26%
	superlative0	0.40%	3.04%	3.04%	24.21%
	superlative1	0.00%	0.00%	0.00%	6.90%
	superlative2	0.00%	0.00%	0.00%	0.00%
	superlative3	0.00%	0.00%	0.00%	0.00%
	yesno	0.17%	1.33%	1.33%	9.67%
	Overall	0.36%	1.72%	1.93%	13.14%
Test(full)		-	-	-	15.53%
Test(hard)		-	-	-	36.92%

It can be seen the overall error rate of our multi-task model is only 1.93% which means this task is successful. In sketch classification, Err_s scores of all classes are lower than 1% except multi-turn-answer. Its recall is 100.00% while its precision is 91.38%. 0.92% of samples in multi-turn-entity are misclassified to multi-turn-answer in validation set. We find there are separator "|||" in logical forms from three classes of multi-turn questions. Multi-turn-predicate questions have two different entities while both multi-turn-entity and multi-turn-answer questions have only one. This kind of entity information is passed to sketch classification through shared parameters. So our system makes some mistakes while distinguishing multi-turn-entity samples from multi-turn-answer samples. As for entity labeling, the overall error rate is 1.72%. We check the wrong samples and find our model is not so good at recognizing entity boundaries especially while encountering some special tokens such as articles, genitive "s" and quotation mark. Actually, it is not easy for human to define an entity in these cases as well.

At last, Err_f of our best model is 13.14% in validation set, 15.53% in full test set and 36.92% in hard test subset. We inspect the output of our model in order to identify the causes of errors. The entity error takes up 20.43% not only because of wrong entities but also right entities in wrong order. 79.57% of incorrect samples have wrong predicates although their entities are right. Our accuracy is extremely low for multi-choice. We look into this class and find 50.72% of errors are because of right entities with wrong order. Actually, there are three different entities in sketch of multi-choice class and two of them are semantically exchangeable in the form $(or(equal\ ?x\ E_1)(equal\ ?x\ E_2))$. So it is not easy for our pattern pair matching network to deal with this problem. In the meantime, our model achieves error rate of 0% for 3 classes in validation set.

Table 5. Performance comparison. Metric is exactly matching accuracy of logical forms. "Cover" represents our covered words supplementary. "Point" represents the application of Pointer losses. "Pep" represents the predicate-entity pair matching network.

System	Acc		
	Dev	Test(full)	Test(hard)
Soochow_SP(1*st*)	-	**85.68%**	57.43%
NP-Parser(2*nd*)	-	83.73%	51.93%
WLIS(*Ours*)(3*rd*)	82.86%	82.53%	47.83%
BBD(4*th*)	-	68.82%	35.41%
$WLIS_{NEW}$(*Our New Baseline*)	77.42%	-	-
$WLIS_{NEW} + point$	84.02%	-	-
$WLIS_{NEW} + pep$	85.99%	-	-
$WLIS_{NEW} + point + pep$	**86.86%**	84.47%	**63.08%**

Our system is compared with that of other teams in NLPCC 2019 Shared Task 2. The top 4 results are shown in Table 5. Our system on the submission list is *WLIS* which achieves the 3rd place. After some optimizations for parameters, seq2seq network structure and sampling, the performance of our new system has been improved a lot. The accuracy of our new baseline reaches 77.42%. By incorporating two auxiliary scores, the accuracy is improved to 86.86% in validation set. Accuracy achieves 84.47% in full test set and 63.08% in hard test subset. Our accuracy in full test set surpasses the 2nd place but is still lower than the 1st place by 1.21% while the accuracy on hard subset is higher than that of the 1st place by 5.65%.

5 Related Work

Semantic parsing is a long-standing problem in NLP mapping natural language utterances to logical forms [2,10,12,14,21,24]. Since it is not easy for semantic parsing to label data manually, reinforcement learning [11] and transfer [20,22] are applied when data is not enough. But in most cases, we are studying how to improve the results when enough data is available for supervised learning. Basic seq2seq network [19] enables the model to be trained in an end-to-end mode. Later, structure-aware models are designed to generate logical forms more elaborately. Seq2tree [6] is equipped with a tree-structured decoder to parse hierarchical logical forms while STAMP [18] adopts a switching gate in the decoder to control the generation of SQL. The models mentioned above all generate the whole logical form in one go.

There are also some works that applied sketch-based approach to solve the problem. It has already been explored in the field of program synthesis [17]. Coarse2fine [7] decomposes the decoding process to 2 stages. Sketches are generated in the first stage while model in the second stage fills in missing details. SQL generating is especially suitable for this method because of its easy sketches. Sqlnet [23] divides the task into 6 subtasks to generate different part of SQL. SQLova [9] also inherits this idea and incorporate Bert [5] in his model. The idea of our system is similar to that of SQLova. We do not use complex decoders to make our network structure-aware. The architectures of models are easy in every stage. We first determine sketches as the high-level structure. Low-level details are added in later stages. The losses of seq2seq network is applied here to rerank from an overall perspective. So we actually combine both seq2seq method and sketch-based method to some extent.

6 Conclusion

In this paper, we presented a sketch-based system for semantic parsing which disentangles high-level structures from low-level details. Due to the absence of knowledge base, we propose to collect question patterns and logical form patterns to capture the implicit relationship between questions and predicates, which can then be used to perform reranking in a Pointer network within a seq2seq framework. Our previous submitted system achieves the 3rd place while our new system outperforms the 1st place for accuracy in hard test subset. Since the knowledge base will be released later, in future work we would like to incorporate new knowledge to improve our system. We will extend our system to other semantic parsing tasks as well.

Acknowledgements. This work is supported in part by the NSFC (Grant No.61672057, 61672058, 61872294), the National Hi-Tech R&D Program of China (No. 2018YFB1005100). For any correspondence, please contact Yansong Feng.

References

1. Bahdanau, D., Cho, K., Bengio, Y.: Neural machine translation by jointly learning to align and translate. arXiv preprint arXiv:1409.0473 (2014)
2. Berant, J., Liang, P.: Semantic parsing via paraphrasing. In: Proceedings of the 52nd Annual Meeting of the Association for Computational Linguistics (Volume 1: Long Papers), vol. 1, pp. 1415–1425 (2014)
3. Chen, B., Sun, L., Han, X.: Sequence-to-action: end-to-end semantic graph generation for semantic parsing. In: Proceedings of the 56th Annual Meeting of the Association for Computational Linguistics (Volume 1: Long Papers), pp. 766–777 (2018)
4. Chen, Q., Zhuo, Z., Wang, W.: Bert for joint intent classification and slot filling. arXiv preprint arXiv:1902.10909 (2019)
5. Devlin, J., Chang, M.W., Lee, K., Toutanova, K.: BERT: pre-training of deep bidirectional transformers for language understanding. In: Proceedings of the 2019 Conference of the North American Chapter of the Association for Computational Linguistics: Human Language Technologies, Volume 1 (Long and Short Papers), pp. 4171–4186. Association for Computational Linguistics, Minneapolis, June 2019. https://www.aclweb.org/anthology/N19-1423
6. Dong, L., Lapata, M.: Language to logical form with neural attention. In: Proceedings of the 54th Annual Meeting of the Association for Computational Linguistics (Volume 1: Long Papers), vol. 1, pp. 33–43 (2016)
7. Dong, L., Lapata, M.: Coarse-to-fine decoding for neural semantic parsing. In: Proceedings of the 56th Annual Meeting of the Association for Computational Linguistics (Volume 1: Long Papers), pp. 731–742 (2018)
8. Gu, J., Lu, Z., Li, H., Li, V.O.: Incorporating copying mechanism in sequence-to-sequence learning. In: Proceedings of the 54th Annual Meeting of the Association for Computational Linguistics (Volume 1: Long Papers), vol. 1, pp. 1631–1640 (2016)
9. Hwang, W., Yim, J., Park, S., Seo, M.: A comprehensive exploration on WikiSQL with table-aware word contextualization. arXiv preprint arXiv:1902.01069 (2019)
10. Kwiatkowski, T., Zettlemoyer, L., Goldwater, S., Steedman, M.: Lexical generalization in CCG grammar induction for semantic parsing. In: Proceedings of the Conference on Empirical Methods in Natural Language Processing, pp. 1512–1523. Association for Computational Linguistics (2011)
11. Liang, C., Norouzi, M., Berant, J., Le, Q.V., Lao, N.: Memory augmented policy optimization for program synthesis and semantic parsing. In: Advances in Neural Information Processing Systems, pp. 9994–10006 (2018)

12. Liang, P., Jordan, M.I., Klein, D.: Learning dependency-based compositional semantics. Comput. Linguist. **39**(2), 389–446 (2013)
13. Luong, T., Pham, H., Manning, C.D.: Effective approaches to attention-based neural machine translation. In: Proceedings of the 2015 Conference on Empirical Methods in Natural Language Processing, pp. 1412–1421 (2015)
14. Pasupat, P., Liang, P.: Inferring logical forms from denotations. In: Proceedings of the 54th Annual Meeting of the Association for Computational Linguistics (Volume 1: Long Papers), vol. 1, pp. 23–32 (2016)
15. Pennington, J., Socher, R., Manning, C.: Glove: global vectors for word representation. In: Proceedings of the 2014 Conference on Empirical Methods in Natural Language Processing (EMNLP), pp. 1532–1543 (2014)
16. See, A., Liu, P.J., Manning, C.D.: Get to the point: summarization with pointer-generator networks. In: Proceedings of the 55th Annual Meeting of the Association for Computational Linguistics (Volume 1: Long Papers), pp. 1073–1083 (2017)
17. Solar-Lezama, A., Bodik, R.: Program synthesis by sketching. Citeseer (2008)
18. Sun, Y., et al.: Semantic parsing with syntax-and table-aware SQL generation. In: Proceedings of the 56th Annual Meeting of the Association for Computational Linguistics (Volume 1: Long Papers), pp. 361–372 (2018)
19. Sutskever, I., Vinyals, O., Le, Q.V.: Sequence to sequence learning with neural networks. In: Ghahramani, Z., Welling, M., Cortes, C., Lawrence, N.D., Weinberger, K.Q. (eds.) Advances in Neural Information Processing Systems, vol. 27, pp. 3104–3112. Curran Associates, Inc. (2014). http://papers.nips.cc/paper/5346-sequence-to-sequence-learning-with-neural-networks.pdf
20. Wang, H., Hu, Y., Dong, L., Jiang, F., Nie, Z.: Multi-Task Learning for Semantic Parsing with Cross-domain Sketch (2018)
21. Wong, Y.W., Mooney, R.: Learning synchronous grammars for semantic parsing with lambda calculus. In: Proceedings of the 45th Annual Meeting of the Association of Computational Linguistics, pp. 960–967 (2007)
22. Xiong, H., Sun, R.: Transferable natural language interface to structured queries aided by adversarial generation. In: 2019 IEEE 13th International Conference on Semantic Computing (ICSC), pp. 255–262. IEEE (2019)
23. Xu, X., Liu, C., Song, D.: SQLNet: generating structured queries from natural language without reinforcement learning. arXiv preprint arXiv:1711.04436 (2017)
24. Zettlemoyer, L.S., Collins, M.: Learning to map sentences to logical form: structured classification with probabilistic categorial grammars. In: Proceedings of the Twenty-First Conference on Uncertainty in Artificial Intelligence, pp. 658–666. AUAI Press (2005)

Overview of the NLPCC 2019 Shared Task: Cross-Domain Dependency Parsing

Xue Peng[1], Zhenghua Li[1(✉)], Min Zhang[1], Rui Wang[2], Yue Zhang[2], and Luo Si[2]

[1] School of Computer Science and Technology, Soochow University, Suzhou, China
20175227031@stu.suda.edu.cn, {zhli13,minzhang}@suda.edu.cn
[2] Alibaba Group, Hangzhou, China
{masi.wr,shiyu.zy,luo.si}@alibaba-inc.com

Abstract. This paper presents an overview of the NLPCC 2019 shared task on cross-domain dependency parsing, including (1) the data annotation process, (2) task settings, (3) methods, results, and analysis of submitted systems and our recent work (Li+19), (4) discussions on related works and future directions. Considering that unsupervised domain adaptation is very difficult and has made limited progress in the past decades, we for the first time setup semi-supervised subtasks that allow to use a few thousand target-domain labeled sentences for training. We provide about 17 K labeled sentences from a balanced corpus as the source domain (BC), and as three target domains 10 K sentences from product comments (PC), 8 K sentences from product blogs (PB), and 3 K sentences from the web fiction named "Zhuxian" (ZX). All information about this task can be found at http://hlt.suda.edu.cn/index.php/Nlpcc-2019-shared-task, including the data sharing agreement.

1 Introduction

With the surge of web data (or user generated content), cross-domain parsing has become the major challenge for applying syntactic analysis in realistic NLP systems. To meet the challenge of the lack of labeled data, we have manually annotated large-scale high-quality domain-aware datasets with a lot of effort in the past few years.[1] Figure 1 shows an example dependency tree.

For this shared task, we provide about 17 K sentences from a balanced corpus as the source domain (BC), and as three target domains 10 K sentences from product comments (PC), 8 K sentences from product blogs (PB), and 3 K sentences from the web fiction named "Zhuxian" (ZX). We setup four subtasks with two cross-domain scenarios, i.e., unsupervised domain adaptation (no target-domain training data) and semi-supervised (with target-domain training data), and two settings, i.e., closed and open.

[1] Webpage for our treebank annotation: http://hlt.suda.edu.cn/index.php/SUCDT.

Supported by National Natural Science Foundation of China (Grant No. 61876116, 61525205).

J. Tang et al. (Eds.): NLPCC 2019, LNAI 11839, pp. 760–771, 2019.
https://doi.org/10.1007/978-3-030-32236-6_69

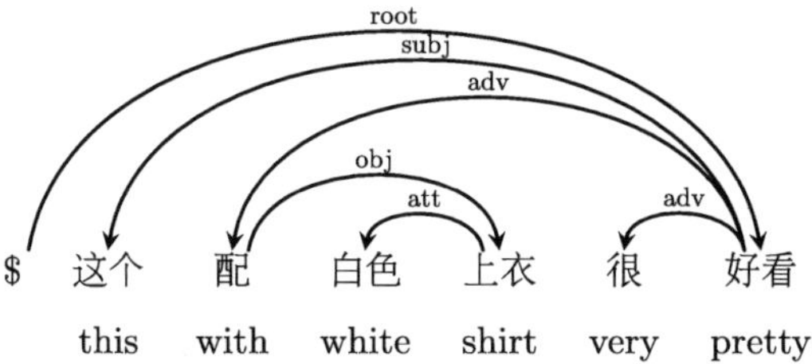

Fig. 1. An example from the PC domain. The English translation is "This looks very pretty with a white shirt."

Please kindly note that *semi-supervised in our domain adaptation scenario means that the model is also provided with labeled training data for the target domain.* In contrast, *traditional semi-supervised learning refers to approaches that make use of large-scale unlabeled data beside labeled data.* Using target-domain unlabeled data is usually considered a must for domain adaptation, and thus we use *semi-supervised* to distinguish whether using target-domain labeled data, not unlabeled data.

There are totally 16 teams that sign in this shared task, and 2 other teams that only want to use the data for study. Finally, 7 teams submit their results, among which one team misunderstands the task settings and recalls their submission.

One team (SJ_SuperLZ) submits results for all four subtasks, and wins the first place in the semi-open subtask 4 among two submissions. Another 3 teams submit results for both closed (un/semi) subtasks, and SyntaxError wins the first place on both tracks. One team focuses on the semi-closed subtask 2 and another team focuses on the semi-open subtask 4. Only two teams participate in the open (un or semi) tracks, and the use of contextualized word representations such as ELMo [15] and BERT [4] is not common. Only SJ_SuperLZ builds their system upon BERT via fine-tuning.

In order to gain more insights on the state-of-the-art progress, we also experiment with the approaches with the same codes in our recent work (Li et al. 2019, abbr. as Li+19) [10] and compare with those submitted systems.

2 Related Shared Tasks

Due to space limitation, we only give a brief and incomplete introduction on previous shared tasks on dependency parsing, especially domain adaptations. Please refer to Li+19 for discussions on methods previously proposed for cross-domain dependency parsing.

As the first CoNLL shared task on dependency parsing, **CoNLL-2006** on multi-Lingual dependency parsing releases benchmark datasets for 13 languages [1].

CoNLL-2007 focuses on both multilingual dependency parsing on 10 languages and domain adaptation on English [13]. For English, they release two non-WSJ out-of-domain datasets, i.e., PCHEM (biomedical or chemical research abstracts) and CHILDES (the EVE corpus, only unlabeled dependency tress) datasets. They provide a combined development dataset for parameter selection and two separate test datasets for final evaluation. Although the organizers put a lot of effort to make the out-of-domain datasets be the consistent with the WSJ data in annotation schemes, the annotated trees still contains a lot of consistencies between source- and target-domains, which may be the reason behind the failure of many adaptation methods, as discussed in Dredze et al. [5].

CoNLL-2008 proposes the tasks of joint parsing of syntactic and semantic dependencies for English, with the aim of encouraging joint modeling of two related tasks, i.e., dependency parsing and word-based SRL [19]. They convert span-based SRL into word-based semantic dependencies based on head-finding rules.

CoNLL-2009 extends the previous-year task from monolingual English to multilingual, covering 7 languages [7]. For English, German, and Czech, they also prepare out-of-domain test datasets for final evaluation. However, the focus is not on domain adaptation without providing the dev data, though initial results are obtained on the outside domains.

CoNLL-2017/2018 proposes multilingual parsing from raw text to universal dependencies for many languages [23,24], thanks to the development of the University Dependencies project [14]. Participants need to process raw text without gold-standard tokenization (or word segmentation) and morphological features such as part-of-speech tags. CoNLL-2018 covers 82 UD treebanks in 57 languages.

SANCL-2012. Petrov and McDonald [16] organized the "parsing the web" shared task and the first workshop on syntactic analysis of non-canonical language (SANCL), based on their newly-constructed Google English Web Treebank consisting of web texts of five sources, i.e., email, answers, weblogs, newsgroups, and reviews. Each source has 1–2 K test sentences manually annotated with constituent trees. The goal is to adapt WSJ-trained parsers (constituent- or dependency-based) to these new domains.

3 Data Annotation

Due to space limitation, we only introduce our data annotation process very briefly. Please refer to Li et al. [10] for more details.

Annotation Guideline. During the past few years, we have been developing and updating a detailed annotation guideline that on the one hand aims to fully capture Chinese syntax, and on the other hand tries to guarantee inter-annotator consistency and facilitate model learning. The current guideline has about 80 pages and contains 21 dependency labels. Please refer to the SUCDT webpage for the newest version.

Annotation Process. All sentences are labeled by two persons (*annotation phase*), and inconsistent submissions are discussed by senior annotators to determine the final answer (*review phase*). Annotators are required to re-do the incorrect submissions according to the answer given in the annotation platform, so that they can gradually improve their annotation ability (*study phase*). However, they can also decide to make complaints in the annotation system if they are sure that the provided answer is wrong, so that more senior annotators can re-check the answer (*complaint phase*).

Partial Annotation. In order to reduce annotation cost, we adopt the active learning procedure based on partial annotation, where sentences that are most difficult for the model are first chosen, and then a certain percentage of most difficult words are then selected for manual annotation. Most sentences in our labeled data are partially annotated. However, since training with partial trees is not popular in parsing community, we automatically complete all partial trees into high-quality full trees [26] based on our CRF-enhanced biaffine parser [9] trained on the combination of all our labeled data.[2]

Table 1 shows data statistics for this shared task. The source domain is balanced corpus (BC), composed of 8K sentences from HIT-CDT [2] and 8K from Penn CTB [21], annotated according to our guideline.[3] The first domain is product comments (PC) from Taobao. The product blog (PB) texts are crawled from the Taobao headline website, which contains articles written by users mainly on description and comparison of different commercial products. The third target domain is "Zhuxian" (ZX, also known as "Jade dynasty"), a web fiction previously annotated and used for cross-domain word segmentation [25].

The datasets are annotated by many different annotators, and the averaged sentence lengths and annotated words numbers per sentence also vary for different domains. Therefore, the consistency ratios can only give a rough idea on the annotation difficulty for texts of different domains.

All labeled datasets are shared by Soochow University and the PC/PB unlabeled datasets are provided by Alibaba Group. Participants need to sign corresponding data sharing agreements to obtain the data.

Table 1. Data statistics. K means thousand in sentence number.

	BC	PC	PB	ZX
train/dev/test (K)	16.3/1/2	6.6/1.3/2.6	5.1/1.3/2.6	1.6/0.5/1.1
consensus ratio (sent-wise)	45.88	39.20	35.88	46.20
consensus ratio (token-wise)	82.25	68.23	69.38	79.21
aver. sent len	13.82	13.95	12.12	21.25
aver. num of annotated words	3.80	3.33	5.09	5.07
unlabeled (K)	0	350	300	30

[2] The parser can be tried at http://hlt-la.suda.edu.cn.

[3] Our major purpose for annotating these datasets is to support supervised treebank conversion.

4 Task Settings

- Subtask 1 (un-closed): unsupervised domain adaptation (closed)
- Subtask 2 (semi-closed): semi-supervised domain adaptation (closed)
- Subtask 3 (un-open): unsupervised domain adaptation (open)
- Subtask 4 (semi-open): semi-supervised domain adaptation (open)

Unsupervised domain adaptation assumes that there is no labeled training data for the target domain. For example, when the target domain is PC, in the unsupervised domain adaptation scenario, you cannot use PC-Train. However, PC-Dev/Unlabeled are allowed to use.

Semi-supervised domain adaptation means that there exists a labeled training dataset for the target domain. For example, when the target domain is PC, PC-Train/Dev/Unlabeled all can be used in semi-supervised domain adaptation scenario.

Closed means that (1) you can only use our provided data and information, including the our provided word segmentation, automatic part-of-speech (POS) tags, pre-trained word embeddings;[4] (2) it is not allowed to use other resources such as dictionaries, labeled or unlabeled data for related tasks; (3) it is not allowed to use other tools to produce new information such as ELMo/BERT, POS tagger, etc.

Open has no restriction, and you can use any resource. However, it is strongly recommended that participants of this shared task and future researchers clearly describe in their system reports and papers what external resources are used and how parsing performance is affected.

Multi-source domain adaptation? NO. It is not allowed to use training data from other target domains. For example, when the target domain is PC, PB-Train and ZX-Train cannot be used in all four subtasks. However, after this shared task, researchers may explore this research line with our data.

Train with dev data? NO. It is not allowed to add dev data into training data. Dev data can only be used for parameter and model selection.

Evaluation Metrics. We use the standard unlabeled/labeled attachment score (UAS/LAS, percent of words that receive correct heads [and labels]). We do not complete partial trees into full ones for the dev and test datasets. It is straightforward to perform evaluation against partial trees by simply omitting the words without gold-standard heads. For any subtask, a participant team must submit results on all three target domains, so that we can obtain three LAS values. We average the three LAS directly to determine the final ranking.

5 Methods

5.1 Submitted Systems

We delete the detailed descriptions of the methods of the submitted systems, which are in the order of task registration **SJ_superLZ** (Shanghai Jiao Tong

[4] The word embeddings are obtained by training word2vec on the Chinese Gigaword 3 and all the target-domain unlabeled data.

University, Li et al. [11]), **14yhl9days** (University of South China), **Syntax-Error** (Heilongjiang University, Yu et al. [22]), **AntNLP** (East China Normal University), **BLCU_Parser** (Beijing Language and Culture University), **NNU** (Nanjing Normal University, Xia et al. [20]). *Please refer to the long version of this paper at Zhenghua' homepage.*

5.2 Summaries of the Systems from Different Aspects

Basic Parsers. Three teams (i.e., SJ_superLZ, SyntaxError, BLCU_Parser) adopt the biaffine parser, or a similar graph-based framework, due to its simplicity and state-of-the-art performance. AntNLP employs the transition-based L2RPTR parser [6] and their recently proposed graph-based GNN parser [8], as two different views for the co-training procedure. NNU adopts the transition-based STACKPTR parser [12], and 14yhl9days uses the basic transition-based parser [3] extended with a BiLSTM encoder.

Our preliminary experiments with the biaffine parser show that using charLSTM-based word representation besides word embeddings, also mentioned by BLCU_Parser, leads to better performance than using POS tag embeddings.

Handling Partially Annotated Data. To control the influence of noisy arcs in the completed trees, SyntaxError finds that it is helpful to simply removing arcs with marginal probability less than 0.7 for both the auto-completed full trees in the labeled training data and the auto-parsed 1-best trees in the unlabeled data during loss computation.

After reading their system report, we also run experiments based on the biaffine parser (w/ local loss) to verify this issue. We find that compared with using all dependencies, LAS of the CONCAT method (semi-supervised) decreases by about 4 points if using only manually labeled dependencies (probability being 1 in the provided data) on ZX-dev, and LAS increases by about 0.4 points if only using dependencies of probability higher than 0.7.

Our results show that (1) the completed full trees are actually of high-quality, considering we use a CRF-enhanced biaffine parser trained on about 100 thousand labeled sentences for the completion task; (2) filtering low-probability dependencies is helpful, but not so very helpful on the labeled training data (maybe more useful for unlabeled data).

Our previous work demonstrates that using probabilistic CRF-based parser can more effectively learn from partial trees (manually annotated or after filtering) [26].

Combination of Source- and Target-Domain Labeled Data. For the semi subtasks 2 and 4, it is a very important to combine and balance the source- and target-domain labeled training data. Four different strategies are investigated.

(1) The fine-tuning method first trains the model on the source-domain training and then fine-tunes the model with the target-domain training data.

This idea is used by SJ_superLZ, BLCU_Parser and NNU. This method may suffer from the limited use of the source-domain training data.

(2) The MTL method, used by BLCU_Parser, treats the source- and target-domain parsing as two independent tasks under the MTL framework. Since only the encoder parameters are shared, the contribution of the source-domain training data is limited, considering the two domains have the same annotation guideline.

(3) The concatenation (CONCAT) method directly merges the two training datasets together without corpus weighting. This method is intuitively more effective than the above two, and is adopted by SyntaxError and AntNLP.

(4) The domain embedding (DOEMB) method is similar to the CONCAT method but distinguishes whether the input sentence comes from the source or target domains by appending a domain id embedding for each word. This method is investigated in Li+19 and is shown to be more effective than the CONCAT method.

The corpus weighting strategy, as described in Li+19, may be useful for balancing the contributions of the source- and target-domain training data, especially when the scales of the two datasets have large gap.

Utilizing Unlabeled Data. It is very attractive to utilize the large-scale and easy-to-collect unlabeled target-domain data in the research area of domain adaptation. Self/co/tri-training are widely used as typical approaches in traditional semi-supervised learning.[5] The basic idea is first using the current parser(s) to automatically parse the unlabeled data, and selecting high-confidence parse trees as extra training data, and re-training the parser(s), and so on, in a bootstrapping fashion. Both SyntaxError and SJ_superLZ use tri-training, and AntNLP adopts co-training.

Recently, the emergence of contextualized word representations, such as ELMo and Bert, has greatly advanced NLP research. The use of very-large-scale unlabeled data via language model loss, allows very deep neural networks to effectively learn extensively useful word and sentence representations. The improvement from using such representations is surprisingly large for a variety of NLP tasks, sometimes surpassing the total amount of improvement from research during the past decade. In some sense, it seems not enough to classify ELMo/BERT-enhanced approaches as traditional semi-supervised learning approaches. In fact, some researchers even base on ELMo and BERT as a new transferring learning (broader than domain adaptation) methodology [17].

In the open subtasks 3 and 4, the use of ELMo/BERT is rare so far, with the exception of SJ_superLZ. With many different ways to use ELMo/BERT for domain adaptation, we believe that it is very helpful to fine-tune ELMo/BERT on the unlabeled data of both the source and target domains. This simple method can build connections between the open-domain very-large-scale unlabeled texts

[5] Please notice again that semi-supervised in our domain adaptation scenario is about whether using target-domain labeled training data.

for pre-training ELMo/BERT and the data for our tasks in hands, and between the source and target domains.

Model Ensemble. Model ensemble has been used as an extremely useful and popular technique in many shared tasks. Both SyntaxError and 14yhl9days use model ensemble. For traditional discrete-feature based parsing, it is usually needed to use several divergent models trained on the same training data or a homogeneous model trained on random subsets of the whole training data. For neural network based parsing, different models can usually be obtained by using different random seeds for parameter initialization, which is adopted by SyntaxError.

The arc/label probabilities of different models are averaged for finding the optimal tree via Viterbi decoding, as SyntaxError does. Another popular way is to use the vote counts of the 1-best output parses of different models as the arc/label score for Viterbi decoding [18].

6 Results and Analysis

6.1 Re-running Our Li+19 Codes

To understand the effectiveness of approaches investigated in Li+19, we run the same codes[6] on the datasets of this shared task.

The data settings differ in two major aspects between this shared task and Li+19. First, an extra PC domain is used in this shared task. Second, the BC training data in Li+19 contains about 52 K sentences from HIT-CDT, including about 8 K manually labeled sentences and 44 K sentences (noisy full trees) being converted from the HIT-CDT guideline through supervised treebank conversion [9]. Therefore, the BC training data in Li+19 is larger but more noisy.

We delete the results and discussions on the effect of **corpus weighting.** *Please refer to the long version of this paper at Zhenghua's homepage.*

Main results on the dev data. Table 2 shows the results on the dev data for the methods investigated in Li+19, i.e., CONCAT, DOEMB, ELMo, and fine-tuned ELMo. Most observations are consistent with Li+19, though the BC training data differs. In the following, we briefly examine and discuss the results from different perspectives.

Domain differences. Training on BC-train produces best performance on ZX, and worst performance on PC, indicating that BC is most similar with ZX and most dissimilar with PC. Compared with training with BC-train, training on the corresponding target-domain training data greatly boosts parsing performance, especially for PC.

CONCAT vs. DOEMB. The results clearly show that for the semi-supervised scenario, DOEMB is consistently superior to CONCAT for combining the source- and target-domain data, increasing LAS by 1.5-2.2.

[6] https://github.com/SUDA-LA/ACL2019-dp-cross-domain.

Table 2. Final results on the dev data. FT-ELMo means fine-tuned ELMo.

	PC		PB		ZX	
	UAS	LAS	UAS	LAS	UAS	LAS
Trained on the source-domain data (unsupervised)						
BC-train	40.26	25.64	67.40	60.60	71.22	63.73
BC-train + ELMo	44.31	30.46	70.91	64.70	73.95	66.17
BC-train + FT-ELMo	**52.33**	**39.13**	**77.76**	**71.77**	**76.27**	**69.70**
Trained on the target-domain data (semi-supervised)						
PC-train	**68.03**	**59.68**	62.90	55.98	54.67	44.69
PB-train	42.14	30.13	**78.11**	**72.68**	60.24	49.34
ZX-train	34.71	20.40	58.36	50.75	**75.99**	**70.70**
PC-train + FT-ELMo	**72.34**	**63.82**	73.46	67.24	63.33	53.27
PB-train + FT-ELMo	54.89	43.03	**82.18**	**77.10**	71.34	61.20
ZX-train + FT-ELMo	44.94	29.68	70.39	62.95	**80.92**	**75.83**
Trained on source- and target-domain data (semi-supervised)						
CONCAT	68.31	59.42	78.11	72.80	79.44	74.35
DOEMB	69.37	60.94	80.03	75.00	80.76	76.23
DOEMB + ELMo	*69.20*	*60.48*	80.31	75.43	81.24	*75.99*
DOEMB + FT-ELMo	**72.01**	**63.86**	**83.10**	**78.87**	**83.21**	**78.84**

Effect of un-fine-tuned ELMo. We use the same ELMo with Li+19, which is trained on the general-purpose Chinese Gigaword 3 corpus. We have added un-fine-tuned ELMo for unsupervised "BC-train + ELMo" and semi-supervised "DOEMB + ELMo", leading to opposite effect. In the unsupervised scenario, using ELMo representations as extra input boosts parsing accuracy by large margin (2.4–4.8 in LAS). In contrast, in the semi-supervised case, un-fine-tuned ELMo has little effects, maybe due to the high baseline (DOEMB) performance using the target-domain training data. We do not conduct experiments using un-fine-tuned ELMo on other scenarios to save computation resource.

Effect of fine-tuned ELMo. Similar to Li+19, we fine-tune ELMo on the combined corpus of BC-train and (PC/PB/ZX)-(train/unlabeled). It is very clear that fine-tuned ELMo can effectively further boost parsing accuracy over un-fine-tuned cases, i.e., "BC-train + ELMo" by 2.5–8.7, and "DOEMB + ELMo" by 2.9–3.4. When training with only the target-domain data in the second major row (comparing the diagonals), fine-tuned ELMo can improve LAS by 4.1–5.1.

Comparing the performance of "PC-train + FT-ELMo" and "DOEMB + FT-ELMo" on PC-dev, we can see that the source-domain BC-train provides little help, indicating again that BC and PC diverges too much to be helpful for the latter. We leave the investigation of the deeper reason behind this for future.

Overall, it is clear that the major conclusions drawn in Li+19 still stand on the datasets of this shared task. First, the domain embedding approach with

Table 3. Final results on the test data. SJ_superLZ reruns the experiments and updates their results at the posterior evaluation stage, due to incidental experimental mistakes for un-open subtask 3.

	PC		PB		ZX		Averaged	
	UAS	LAS	UAS	LAS	UAS	LAS	UAS	LAS
Un-closed Subtask 1								
SyntaxError	**49.82**	**36.86**	**71.48**	**65.43**	**73.90**	**66.54**	**65.07**	**56.28**
AntNLP	43.64	30.47	70.50	63.83	72.88	65.07	62.34	53.12
Ours (Biaffine)	38.80	25.87	66.83	60.28	69.27	61.37	58.30	49.17
SJ_superLZ	35.63	21.33	62.55	54.35	50.04	38.31	49.40	38.00
14yhl9days	26.72	10.92	41.50	27.38	40.45	26.44	36.22	21.58
Semi-closed Subtask 2								
SyntaxError	72.18	**64.12**	82.57	**77.83**	**80.53**	**75.84**	**78.43**	**72.60**
AntNLP	**72.23**	63.96	**82.94**	77.27	79.89	74.80	78.35	72.01
Ours (DOEMB)	68.88	59.96	79.22	74.40	79.60	74.50	75.90	69.62
BLCU_Parser	70.89	61.72	79.30	74.25	77.84	72.58	76.01	69.51
SJ_superLZ	69.88	59.43	77.52	71.33	77.84	71.55	75.08	67.44
14yhl9days	47.38	26.26	47.26	32.88	45.40	32.00	46.68	30.38
Un-open Subtask 3								
SJ_superLZ (BERT, Post-Eval)	**60.50**	**49.49**	**81.61**	**76.77**	**79.74**	**74.32**	**73.95**	**66.86**
Ours (+FT-ELMo)	53.04	39.48	77.15	71.54	74.68	67.51	68.29	59.51
Semi-open Subtask 4								
SJ_superLZ (BERT, Post-Eval)	**75.25**	**67.77**	**85.53**	**81.51**	**86.14**	**81.65**	**82.30**	**76.98**
Ours (DOEMB+FT-ELMo)	73.16	64.33	83.05	78.57	82.09	77.08	79.43	73.33
SJ_superLZ (BERT)	72.40	64.37	80.79	76.13	83.15	78.61	78.78	73.04
NNU	70.97	61.82	80.59	75.85	79.33	74.35	76.96	70.68

corpus weighting is the most effective way to combine the source- and target-domain training data in the semi-supervised scenario (maybe adversarial training can further improve). Second, fine-tuning ELMo on the target-domain unlabeled data is extremely helpful due to the effect of bridging the knowledge between general open-domain texts and target-domain texts.

6.2 Final Results on the Test Data

Table 3 shows the final results on the test datasets. SyntaxError dominates the un-closed subtask 1. Our Li+19 baseline biaffine parser ranks the third place. We guess we can further improve our result by (1) using charLSTM word representations; (2) performing model ensemble; (3) utilizing unlabeled data.

For the semi-closed subtask 2, though still being the best, SyntaxError outperforms AntNLP by a small margin. We do not know why the gap between them becomes much smaller than for the un-closed subtask 1. They used different techniques to handle the target-domain training data. SyntaxError uses CONCAT and adversarial training, whereas AntNLP directly combine source- and target-domain data (CONCAT).

For the un-open subtask 3, SJ_superLZ is the only submission and their posterior evaluation results outperform our Li+19 best method by 7.4 in LAS.

For the semi-open subtask 4, SJ_superLZ outperforms NNU. However, the DOEMB method with fine-tuned ELMo in Li+19 slightly outperforms SJ_superLZ, which is very interesting because BERT-based systems usually achieve much higher performance than ELMo-based ones. After retraining their models at the posterior evaluation stage, their averaged LAS increases by nearly 4 points.

7 Conclusions and Future Works

Overall, we feel that the attention so far is far from extensive for our first-year organization of the shared task on cross-domain dependency parsing. However, we have strong confidence on the future, and plan to organize more shared tasks by gradually releasing more labeled data covering more genres. We require all organizations that use our data in their experiments to release their full codes when publishing papers, in order to promote replicability.

References

1. Buchholz, S., Marsi, E.: CoNLL-X shared task on multilingual dependency parsing. In: In Proceedings of CoNLL, pp. 149–164 (2006)
2. Che, W., Li, Z., Liu, T.: Chinese dependency treebank 1.0 (Ldc2012t05). In: Philadelphia: Linguistic Data Consortium (2012)
3. Chen, D., Manning, C.: A fast and accurate dependency parser using neural networks. In: Proceedings of EMNLP, pp. 740–750 (2014)
4. Devlin, J., Chang, M.W., Lee, K., Toutanova, K.: BERT: pre-training of deep bidirectional transformers for language understanding. In: Proceedings of NAACL, pp. 4171–4186 (2019)
5. Dredze, M., Blitzer, J., Pratim Talukdar, P., Ganchev, K., Graca, J.a., Pereira, F.: Frustratingly hard domain adaptation for dependency parsing. In: Proceedings of the CoNLL Shared Task Session of EMNLP-CoNLL 2007, pp. 1051–1055 (2007)
6. Fernández-González, D., Gómez-Rodríguez, C.: Left-to-right dependency parsing with pointer networks. In: Proceedings of NAACL, pp. 710–716 (2019)
7. Hajič, J., et al.: The CoNLL-2009 shared task: syntactic and semantic dependencies in multiple languages. In: Proceedings of CoNLL (2009)
8. Ji, T., Wu, Y., Lan, M.: Graph-based dependency parsing with graph neural networks. In: Proceedings of ACL (2019)
9. Jiang, X., Li, Z., Zhang, B., Zhang, M., Li, S., Si, L.: Supervised treebank conversion: data and approaches. In: Proceedings of ACL, pp. 2706–2716 (2018)
10. Li, Z., Xue, P., Zhang, M., Wang, R., Si, L.: Semi-supervised domain adaptation for dependency parsing. In: Proceedings of ACL (2019)
11. Li, Z., Zhou, J., Zhao, H., Wang, R.: Cross-domain transfer learning for dependency parsing (2019)
12. Ma, X., Hu, Z., Liu, J., Peng, N., Graham, N., Eduard, H.: Stack-pointer networks for dependency parsing. In: Proceedings of ACL, pp. 1403–1414 (2018)

13. Nivre, J., Hall, J., Kübler, S., McDonald, R., Nilsson, J., Riedel, S., Yuret, D.: The coNLL 2007 shared task on dependency parsing. In: Proceedings of the CoNLL Shared Task Session of EMNLP-CoNLL 2007, pp. 915–932 (2007)
14. Nivre, J., et al.: Universal dependencies v1: a multilingual treebank collection. In: Proceedings of the Tenth International Conference on Language Resources and Evaluation (LREC 2016) (2016)
15. Peters, M.E., et al.: Deep contextualized word representations. In: Proceedings of NAACL-HLT, pp. 2227–2237 (2018)
16. Petrov, S., McDonald, R.: Overview of the 2012 shared task on parsing the web. In: Notes of the First Workshop on Syntactic Analysis of Non-Canonical Language (SANCL) (2012)
17. Ruder, S., Peters, M.E., Swayamdipta, S., Wolf, T.: Transfer learning in natural language processing. In: Proceedings of NAACL: Tutorials, pp. 15–18 (2019)
18. Sagae, K., Lavie, A.: Parser combination by reparsing. In: Proceedings of NAACL, pp. 129–132 (2006)
19. Surdeanu, M., Johansson, R., Meyers, A., Màrquez, L., Nivre, J.: The CoNLL-2008 shared task on joint parsing of syntactic and semantic dependencies. In: CoNLL-2008 (2008)
20. Xia, Z., Wang, L., Qu, W., Zhou, J., Gu, Y.: Neural network based deep transfer learning for cross-domain dependency parsing. arXiv (2019)
21. Xue, N., Xia, F., Chiou, F.D., Palmer, M.: The Penn Chinese treebank: phrase structure annotation of a large corpus. Nat. Lang. Eng. **11**(02), 207–238 (2005)
22. Yu, N., Liu, Z., Zhen, R., Liu, T., Zhang, M., Fu, G.: Domain information enhanced dependency parser (2019)
23. Zeman, D., et al.: CoNLL 2018 shared task: multilingual parsing from raw text to universal dependencies. In: Proceedings of the CoNLL 2018 Shared Task: Multilingual Parsing from Raw Text to Universal Dependencies, pp. 1–21 (2018)
24. Zeman, D., et al.: CoNLL 2017 shared task: multilingual parsing from raw text to universal dependencies. In: Proceedings of the CoNLL 2017 Shared Task: Multilingual Parsing from Raw Text to Universal Dependencies, pp. 1–19, August 2017
25. Zhang, M., Zhang, Y., Che, W., Liu, T.: Type-supervised domain adaptation for joint segmentation and pos-tagging. In: Proceedings of EACL, pp. 588–597 (2014)
26. Zhang, Y., Li, Z., Lang, J., Xia, Q., Zhang, M.: Dependency parsing with partial annotations: an empirical comparison. In: Proceedings of IJCNLP, pp. 49–58 (2019)

A Transformer-Based Semantic Parser for NLPCC-2019 Shared Task 2

Donglai Ge[1], Junhui Li[1(✉)], and Muhua Zhu[2]

[1] School of Computer Science and Technology, Soochow University, Suzhou, China
20175227014@stu.suda.edu.cn, lijunhui@suda.edu.cn
[2] Alibaba Group, Hangzhou, China
muhua.zmh@alibaba-inc.com

Abstract. Sequence-to-Sequence (seq2seq) approaches formalize semantic parsing as a translation task from a source sentence to its corresponding logical form. However, in the absence of large-scale annotated dataset, even the state-of-the-art seq2seq model, i.e., the *Transformer* may suffer from the data sparsity issue. In order to address this issue, this paper explores three techniques which are widely used in neural machine translation to better adapt seq2seq models for semantic parsing. First, we use byte pair encoding (BPE) to segment words into subwords to transfer rare words into frequent subwords. Second, we share word vocabulary on both the source and the target sides. Finally, we define heuristic rules to generate synthetic instances to increase the coverage of training dataset. Experimental results on the NLPCC 2019 shared task 2 show that our approach achieves state-of-the-art performance and gets the first place in the task from the current rankings.

Keywords: Semantic parsing · Sequence-to-sequence · Synthetic instances

1 Introduction

The task of semantic parsing, which aims to map natural language utterances into their corresponding meaning representations, has received a significant amount of attention with various approaches over the past few years. The languages of meaning representation mainly fall into two categories: logic based formalisms and graph-based formalisms. The former includes *first order logic*, *lambda calculus*, and *lambda dependency based compositional semantics*, while the latter includes *abstract meaning representation* and *universal conceptual cognitive annotation*. Traditional approaches are mostly based on the principle of compositional semantics, which compose the semantics of utterances from lexical semantics by using a set of predefined grammars. The widely used grammars

Supported by the National Natural Science Foundation of China (Grant No., 61876120).

J. Tang et al. (Eds.): NLPCC 2019, LNAI 11839, pp. 772–781, 2019.
https://doi.org/10.1007/978-3-030-32236-6_70

include SCFG [11,16], CCG [4,10], DCS [3,12], etc. One of the main shortcomings of grammar-based approaches is that they rely on high-quality lexicons, hand-crafted features, and manually-built grammars. In recent years, one promising direction in semantic parsing is to represent the semantics of texts as graphs. This way, semantic parsing can be formalized as a process of graph generation. In this direction, Ge et al. [6] propose to obtain semantic graphs through transformation from syntactic trees. Reddy et al. [13] use Freebase-based semantic graph representation and convert sentences into semantic graphs by using CCGs or dependency trees. Bast et al. [2] identify the structure of a semantic query through three predefined patterns. Yih et al. [18] generate semantic graphs using a staged heuristic search algorithm. All these approaches are based on manually-designed and heuristic generation process, which may suffer from syntactic parsing errors and structure mismatching, especially the case for complex sentences.

An alternative to the aforementioned approaches to semantic graph generation is to utilize the sequence-to-sequence (seq2seq) framework, which has been adopted for a variety of natural language processing tasks [1,7], semantic parsing included [5,17]. Now the task at hand translates to building seq2seq models in order to map word sequences into corresponding sequences that represent semantic graphs. To train such models, it is important to have enough training data of high quality. Generally, the performance of seq2seq models is highly dependent on the quality and quantity of available training data. However, most of the datasets for semantic parsing are curated by human, which is labor intensive and time consuming. Consequently, annotated corpora are generally limited in size and training of seq2seq models tends to suffer from the scarcity of annotated training data.

The NLPCC-2019 shared task 2 is a competition for open domain semantic parsing, which is defined to predict the meaning representation in lambda-calculus for an input question on the base of a given knowledge graph. Each question in the shared task data is annotated with entities, the question type, and the corresponding logical form. The dataset is called Multi-perspective Semantic ParSing (MSParS) and includes more than 80,000 human-generated instances. In MSParS, there is a total of 9 question types, including single-relation, multi-hop, multi-constraint, multi-choice, aggregation, comparison, yes/no, superlative, and multi-turn. Table 1 presents an illustrating example of a question accompanied by its logical form, entities, and question type: the first row is the question that we need to parse, the second row presents the logical form of the question, the third row shows the entities and their positions in the logical form, and the last row gives the question type. Participating systems are evaluated on the prediction of logical forms given input questions

In the competition of shared task 2, we build our semantic parsing system on the base of the Transformer, a state-of-the-art seq2seq model that is originally proposed for neural machine translation and syntactic parsing [15]. Furthermore, to enhance the performance of our system, we apply the following three techniques: using byte pair encoding (BPE) to segment words into subwords, sharing word vocabulary on both the source and target sides, and enlarging training data

Table 1. An example from the dataset for open domain semantic parsing.

<question id=1>	who is film art directors of "i see you" from avatar
<logical form id=1>	(lambda ?x (mso:film.film.art_director "_i_see_you_" _from_avatar ?x))
<parameters id=1>	"_i_see_you_"_from_avatar (entity) [6,12]
<question type id=1>	single-relation

by automatically generating synthetic training instances. In the NLPCC 2019 Shared Task 2, our system win the first place among all the participating systems and the proposed techniques achieve remarkable improvements over the Transformer baseline.

2 Semantic Parsing as Neural Seq2Seq Learning

In this section, we describe in detail our approach to semantic parsing. The model is built on *Transformer*, a state-of-the-art seq2seq model that is originally proposed for neural machine translation and syntactic parsing [15].

2.1 Preparing Data

Each instance in the MSParS dataset is a tuple of four elements, including a question, its logical form, parameters, and question type. In this paper we only use questions and their corresponding logical forms to train our parsing model but ignore parameters and question type because they are not evaluated. Questions are fed into the encoder as source sequences and their corresponding logical forms are viewed as target sequences.

Note that in the logical form, an entity is presented as a string which consists of multiple words concatenated by '_'. In pre-processing, we split an entity string into its corresponding multiple words and symbols of '_'. For example, the logical form in Table 1 is processed as:

(lambda ?x (mso:film.film.art_director " _ i _ see _ you _" _ from _ avatar ?x))

In post-processing, we resume entity strings by simply replacing ' _ ' with '_' in output sequences.

We have also tried to split the strings of entity types into multiple pieces. For example, *mso:film.film.art_director* in Table 1 is split into *mso : film . film . art_ director*. However, our preliminary experiments showed that it slightly hurts the performance.

2.2 Sequence-to-Sequence Modeling

As mentioned, we use Transformer seq2seq model for semantic parsing. The encoder in Transformer consists of a stack of multiple identical layers, each of which has two sub-layers, one for multi-head self-attention mechanism, and the other is a position-wise fully connected feed-forward network. The decoder is also composed of a stack of multiple identical layers. Each layer in the decoder consists of the same sub-layers as in the encoder layers as well as an additional sub-layer that performs multi-head attention to the output of the encoder stack. Experiments on the tasks of machine translation and syntactic parsing show that Transformer outperforms RNN-based seq2seq models [1]. Figure 1 shows the structure of Transformer seq2seq model.

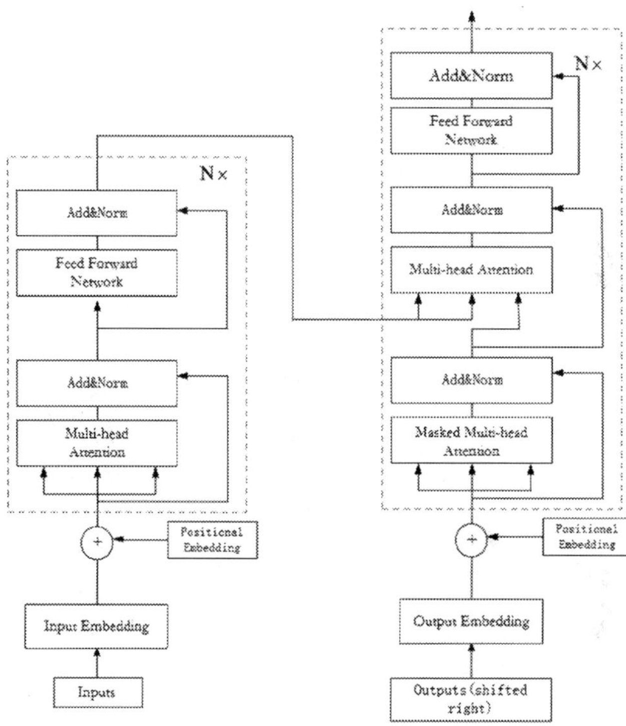

Fig. 1. Transformer seq2seq model.

The self-attention in Transformer uses Scaled Dot-Product Attention which operates on an input sequence, $x = (x_1, \cdots, x_n)$ of n elements where $x_i \in \mathbb{R}^{d_x}$ and computes a new sequence $z = (z_1, \cdots, z_n)$ with the same length:

$$z = Attention\,(x) \tag{1}$$

where $z \in \mathbb{R}^{n \times d_z}$. Each output element z_i is calculated as a weighted sum of a linearly transformed input elements:

$$z_i = \sum_{j=1}^{n} \alpha_{ij} \left(x_j W^V \right) \tag{2}$$

where $W^V \in \mathbb{R}^{d_x \times d_z}$ is a parameter matrix, and

$$\alpha_{ij} = \frac{exp(e_{ij})}{\sum_{k=1}^{n} exp(e_{ik})} \tag{3}$$

$$e_{ij} = \frac{\left(x_i W^Q\right)\left(x_j W^K\right)^T}{\sqrt{d_z}} \tag{4}$$

where the weight vector $\alpha_i = (\alpha_{i1}, \cdots, \alpha_{in})$ over input vectors is obtained by self-attention model, which captures the correspondences between element x_i and others, and e_{ij} is an alignment model which scores how well the input elements x_i and x_j match. Here $W^Q, W^K \in \mathbb{R}^{d_x \times d_z}$ are parameter matrices.

2.3 Generation of Synthetic Training Instances

Supervised machine learning algorithms tend to suffer from data imbalance problems. In the dataset of MSParS, we find entity types contain quite skewed distributions. For example, the entity type $mso : film.actor.film$ contains the most entity instances 1832 while the entity type $mso : baseball.batting\_statistics.slugging\_pct$ only has 1 entity instances. Seq2seq models trained on such a kind of dataset may be overwhelmed by training instances of big entity types while parameters for small entity types are not well learned. The resulting models are apt to achieve relatively poor performance on test set due to limited generalization ability.

To attack the data imbalance problem, we generate synthetic training instances from the following two perspectives:

- Entity-based: Given a sentence and its logical form from the original training set, we choose one entity in the sentence and replace it with another random entity which has the same entity type. Figure 2(a) shows examples of an original pair and its synthetic pair.
- Label-based: Given a sentence and its logic from the original training set, we choose one entity who has multiple entity types and replace its entity type with another valid type. As shown in Fig. 2(b), since the entity of *"_i_see_you_"_from_avatar* has multiple entity types, we randomly select another entity type but *film.film.art_director*, and generate a synthetic pair.

3 Experimentation

In this section, we first introduce the dataset we used. Then we describe the settings of our model for the experiments. After that, we present a comparative study on our system and other participating systems.

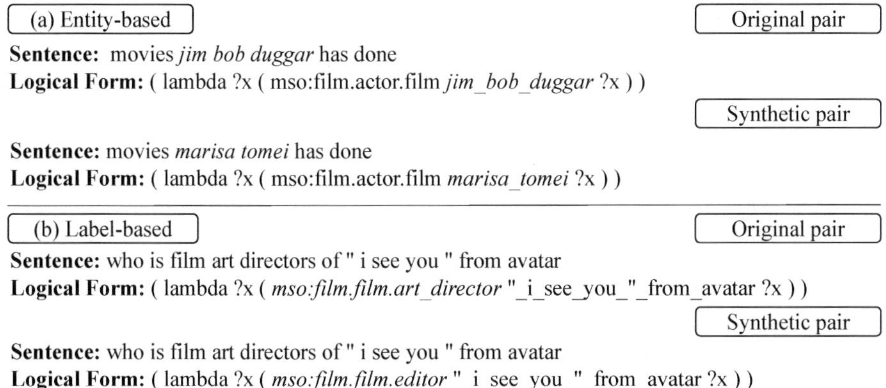

Fig. 2. Examples of automatically generated synthetic instances

3.1 Experimental Settings

Dataset. We take our evaluation on the Multi-perspective Semantic ParSing (or MSParS) released by NLPCC-2019 Shared Task 2. The dataset includes more than 80,000 human-generated questions, where each question is annotated with entities, a question type, and corresponding logical form. The organizers split MSParS into a training set, a development set, and a test set. Both the training and development sets are provided to participating teams, while the test set is not. The training set has 63,826 instances and development set has 9,000 instances. Note that the organizers divide the test set to select a hard subset according to certain criteria, so each team has two final results: full set score and hard subset score.

Evaluation. The evaluation uses accuracy (ACC), i.e. the percentage of predicted logical forms which exactly match the golden ones.

Settings. We use openNMT [9] as the implementation of the Transformer seq2seq model. In the parameter setting, we set the number of layers in both the encoder and decoder to 6. For optimization we use Adam [8] with $\beta 1 = 0.1$. The number of heads is set to 8. In addition, we set the hidden size to 512 and the batch token-size to 8192. In all experiments, we train the models for 250K steps on a single K40 GPU and save the models at every 5K steps. To overcome the data sparsity issue, in all experiments we follow Ge et al. [5] and share vocabulary for the input and the output. To address the translation of rare words, we segment words into word pieces by byte pair encoding (BPE [14]) with 8K operations. We average the last 20 models' parameters to improve the performance.

Table 2. Ablation results of our baseline system on the development set.

Model	ACC
Baseline	85.93
-BPE	54.90
-Sharing Vocab	84.00
-Both	52.47

3.2 Experimental Results

We first show the performance of our baseline system. As mentioned earlier, BPE and sharing vocabulary are two techniques we applied to relieving data sparsity. Table 2 presents the results of the ablation test on the development set by either removing BPE, or vocabulary sharing, or both of them from the baseline system. From the results we can see that BPE and vocabulary sharing are critical to building our baseline system (an improvement from 52.47 to 85.93 in accuracy), revealing that they are two effective ways to address the issue of data sparsity for semantic parsing.

Generation of synthetic training instances substantially increases the number of instances in our training set. As shown in Table 3, both the two methods of generating synthetic training instances roughly double the number of training instances and achieve similar improvements over the model trained on the original training set (e.g., 0.85 and 1.01), suggesting that our two methods are effective in increasing the coverage of training instances. However, there exists overlap in coverage of the two methods. In the presence of one method, the other method achieves limited or no improvement.

We also compare our final system with systems from other participants in Table 4. From the results we can see that our final system achieves the highest performance, especially on the hard subset. This illustrates the feasibility and effectiveness of our seq2seq-based semantic parsing.

Table 3. ACC (%) of our semantic parsing models on the development set.

Training set	# Instances	ACC
Original	63,826	85.93
+Entity-based	137,198	86.78
+Label-based	140,485	86.94
+Both (our final model)	213,857	86.96

3.3 Error Analysis

To find the reasons for improper parsing, we analyze 50 bad cases selected randomly from the development set. The mistakes mainly fall into four categories.

Table 4. Comparison of our final parser with other parsers

Model	ACC on full set	ACC on hard subset
Soochow_SP (this paper)	85.68	57.43
NP-Parser	83.73	51.93
WLIS	82.53	47.83
Binbin Deng	68.82	35.41
kg_nlpca_ai_lr	30.79	14.89
TriJ	26.77	14.49

First, entity type is incorrectly predicted when the entity has multiple types. As shown in Fig. 3(a), entity *chris pine* has 5 types in the training set and our model incorrectly predict its type as *biology.organism* in this example. 16 wrong cases out of the 50 ones are caused by this error category. Second, it is hard to correctly predict entity type if an entity occurs only once in the training set. As shown in Fig. 3(b), *langlois bridge at arles* occurs once in the training set and our model incorrectly predicts its type as *visual_art.artwork*. 7 wrong cases belong to this error category. Third, for those entities that even do not appear in the training set, our model tends to make incorrect prediction. As shown in Fig. 3, though our model successfully recognizes *body and soul* as an entity, it fails to identify its entity type. 18 wrong cases are in this error category. Finally, in few cases our model sometimes fails to recognize entities. As shown in Fig. 3(d), our model fails to recognize entity *varsity*.

(a) Sentence: what is birth date for chris pine
Logical Form: (lambda ?x (mso:people.person.date_of_birth chris_pine ?x))
Our Model: (lambda ?x (mso:biology.organism.date_of_birth chris_pine ?x))

(b) Sentence: who is langlois bridge at arles 's creator
Logical Form: (lambda ?x (mso:visual_art.art_series.artist langlois_bridge_at_arles ?x))
Our Model: (lambda ?x (mso:visual_art.artwork.artist langlois_bridge_at_arles ?x))

(c) Sentence: body and soul 's completion date
Logical Form: (lambda ?x (mso:music.composition.date_completed body_and_soul ?x))
Our Model: (lambda ?x (mso:visual_art.artwork.date_completed body_and_soul ?x))

(d) Sentence: colleges of varsity
Logical Form: (lambda ?x (mso:education.school_newspaper.school varsity ?x))
Our Model: (lambda ?x (mso:education.school_newspaper.school varges ?x))

Fig. 3. Examples of error types

4 Conclusion

In this paper, we present our seq2seq model that parses natural language utterances to logical forms. To overcome the data sparsity issue, we use BPE to segment rare words into frequent subwords, and we share vocabulary on the source and the target side, considering the fact that many words are common on both sides. Finally, to increase the coverage of training instances, we use heuristic rules to generate synthetic instances from the original ones. Experiments on the NLPCC-2019 shared task 2 show that our approach achieves state-of-the-art performance and ranks the first among the participating systems.

Detailed analysis shows that misjudgement of entity types is one of the major error sources. In future work, we will focus on joint learning of entity recognition and semantic parsing.

References

1. Bahdanau, D., Cho, K., Bengio, Y.: Neural machine translation by jointly learning to align and translate. In: Proceedings of ICLR (2015)
2. Bast, H., Haussmann, E.: More accurate question answering on freebase. In: Proceedings of CIKM, pp. 1431–1440 (2015)
3. Berant, J., Chou, A., Frostig, R., Liang, P.: Semantic parsing on freebase from question-answer pairs. In: Proceedings of EMNLP, pp. 1533–1544 (2013)
4. Cai, Q., Yates, A.: Large-scale semantic parsing via schema matching and lexicon extension. In: Proceedings of ACL, pp. 423–433 (2013)
5. Ge, D., Li, J., Zhu, M., Li, S.: Modeling source syntax and semantics for neural AMR parsing. In: Proceedings of IJCAI, pp. 4975–4981 (2019)
6. Ge, R., Mooney, R.J.: Learning a compositional semantic parser using an existing syntactic parser. In: Proceedings of ACL, pp. 611–619 (2009)
7. Ilya, S., Oriol, V., Le, Q.V.: Sequence to sequence learning with neural networks. In: Proceedings of NIPS, pp. 3104–3112 (2014)
8. Kingma, D.P., Ba, J.: Adam: a method for stochastic optimization. In: Proceedings of ICLR (2015)
9. Klein, G., Kim, Y., Deng, Y., Senellart, J., Rush, A.M.: OpenNMT: open-source toolkit for neural machine translation. In: Proceedings of ACL, System Demonstrations, pp. 67–72 (2017)
10. Kwiatkowski, T., Zettlemoyer, L., Goldwater, S., Steedman, M.: Lexical generalization in CCG grammar induction for semantic parsing. In: Proceedings of EMNLP, pp. 1512–1523 (2011)
11. Li, J., Zhu, M., Lu, W., Zhou, G.: Improving semantic parsing with enriched synchronous context-free grammar. In: Proceedings of EMNLP, pp. 1455–1465 (2015)
12. Liang, P., Jordan, M.I., Klein, D.: Learning dependency-based compositional semantics. In: Proceedings of ACL, pp. 590–599 (2011)
13. Reddy, S., Lapata, M., Steedman, M.: Large-scale semantic parsing without question-answer pairs. Trans. Assoc. Comput. Linguist. **2**, 377–392 (2014)
14. Sennrich, R., Haddow, B., Birch, A.: Neural machine translation of rare words with subword units. In: Proceedings of ACL, pp. 1715–1725 (2016)
15. Vaswani, A., et al.: Attention is all you need. In: Proceedings of NIPS, pp. 5998–6008 (2017)

16. Wong, Y.W., Mooney, R.J.: Learning synchronous grammars for semantic parsing with lambda calculus. In: Proceedings of ACL, pp. 960–967 (2007)
17. Xiao, C., Dymetman, M., Gardent, C.: Sequence-based structured prediction for semantic parsing. In: Proceedings of ACL, pp. 1341–1350 (2016)
18. Yih, W.T., Chang, M.W., He, X., Gao, J.: Semantic parsing via staged query graph generation: question answering with knowledge base. In: Proceedings of ACL, pp. 1321–1331 (2015)

A Relation Proposal Network for End-to-End Information Extraction

Zhenhua Liu(✉), Tianyi Wang, Wei Dai, Zehui Dai, and Guangpeng Zhang

NLP Group, Gridsum, Beijing, China
{liuzhenhua,daiwei,daizehui,zhangguangpeng}@gridsum.com, wangtianyiftd@gmail.com

Abstract. Information extraction is an important task in natural language processing. In this paper, we introduce our solution on NLPCC 2019 shared task 3 Information Extraction which has provided with the largest industry Schema based Knowledge Extraction (SKE) data-set. Our proposed method is an end-to-end framework which first catches the relation hints in raw text with a relation proposal layer, then follows by an entity tagging design which is targeted to decode the corresponding triplet entities with the given relation proposal. Compared with previous works, our method is efficient and can well handle overlapping and multiple triplets in one sentence. With a simple model ensemble, our solution achieves 0.8903 F1-Score on final leaderboard which ranks forth among all participants.

Keywords: Information extraction · Relation proposal · Entity tagging

1 Introduction

Information extraction is targeted to extract entities and their relations from unstructured natural language text. It is important to many Artificial Intelligence (AI) applications, such as Information Retrieval (IR), Intelligent Question and Answering (QA), and Intelligence Chat-bots (IC). The task involves entity recognition, anaphora resolution and relation classification.

In the NLPCC 2019 Information extraction competition, there are over 173 k train data which is firstly annotated with distant supervising, then human corrected on crowd-sourcing platform. It contains over 364 k triplets of 49 relations and 28 entity types. The key challenges of this task are summarized as follows:

- **Overlapping Entities**: Overlapping entities of different triplets is a common issue in information extraction that affects the extraction performance. [7] first divide the triplets into three categories, namely No Overlap (Normal), Single Entity Overlap (SEO), and Entity Pair Overlap (EPO). They find that previous methods mainly focus on Normal class and fail to extract relational

J. Tang et al. (Eds.): NLPCC 2019, LNAI 11839, pp. 782–790, 2019.
https://doi.org/10.1007/978-3-030-32236-6_71

triplets precisely. We also observe a plenty of overlapping triplets in train set, so it is of great importance for our solution to handle overlapping entities properly.

- **Multiple Triplets**: There are on average 2.10 triplets per sentence. What's more, 3.72% sentences contain five or more triplets, and these account for 19.83% of total target which can not be ignored in the competition. As mentioned by [6] and also observed in our experiments, methods which are unable to deal with multiple triplets properly will trend to recall fraction of all triplets in one sentence.
- **Categories Imbalance**: Categories of the data in this competition are extremely imbalanced. Among all 49 relation types, the top five number of relation categories account for 45.21% of the total triplets. However, the bottom five relation categories account for only 0.13%.
- **Data-set Inconsistent**: Another serious problem is that the offline train data has lower precision compared with the online test data. The sponsor of the competition has officially announced that the online test data has been double checked with more efforts, which make the offline validation result becomes unreliable. And the defection in train data may also lead to a model bias, which makes the data distill and rule amendment necessary in data pre-processing and post-processing.
- **Entity Position Uncertainty**: Even though the data-set in this competition is of high quality, there still exist problems. 11.53% of the triplets in train data contain entities which repeat more than once in one sentence, but no exact position information is given. As the same entity of different position can contain different semantics, elaborate enumerate or random choose will induce errors into the model.

To solve the aforementioned challenges, we first make a brief review of academic and industrial solutions on information extraction task. There are mainly two pipelines that solve the problem. One recognizes entities firstly and then follows with an entity pair relation classification, these methods suffer from error propagation problems [2]. The other one is to extract entities and relations in an end-to-end way. However, these methods still have problems. [5] propose the HRL which is so far the state-of-the-art, but the reinforcement learning paradigm makes it run extremely slow. [7] propose copyR can only deal with triplets that entities contain one word only. [8] propose the tagging schema that fails to deal with overlapping triplets. [1] transfer the task into a table filling problem, and their method suffers a positive and negative sample imbalance problem.

Our solution is partially inspired by Faster R-CNN [3], a two stage object detection network in computer vision which separates the different target object into parallel pipelines with region proposal layer. It works in similar logic and uses the relation proposal layer which aims to propose the target relation at each token position. With the given proposal relation and token, different triplets are decoded in parallel by entity tagging network which only decodes one triplet for one proposal.

This paper is organized as follows. Section 2 contains the data-set analysis and pre-processing. Section 3 introduces details of our solution. Section 4 presents the experimental results and analysis. Section 5 includes the conclusion and future works.

2 Data-Set Analysis and Pre-processing

2.1 Data-Set Analysis

The sponsor of competition provides us 173 k train data, and 21.7 k validation data. The online test data-set has the similar size with offline validation, but is mixed with irrelevant sentences. The Fig. 1 summarizes the triplet types in train data.

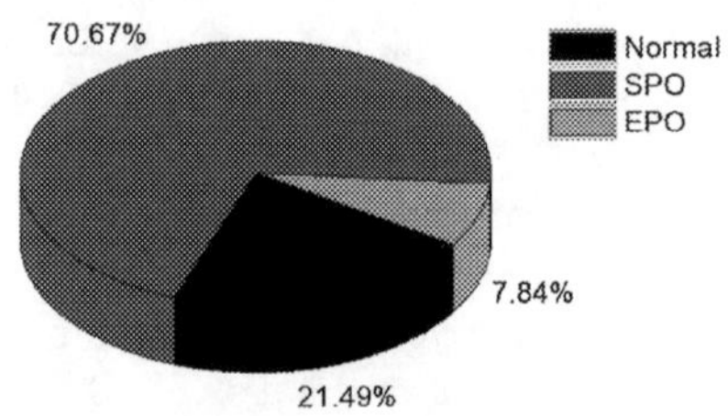

Fig. 1. The triplet types in train data, and we follow the definition by [7]

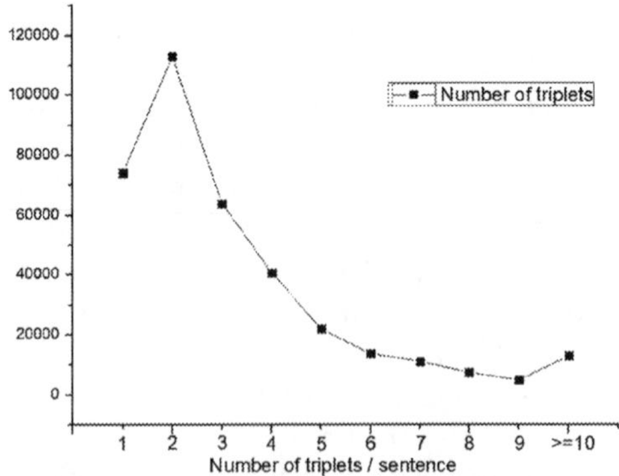

Fig. 2. Number of triplets in one sentence

Obviously, Normal triplet consists 21.49% of the total triplets which indicates the importance to deal with overlapping triplet in this task. The SPO dominates train data-set with 70.67% which is very high. And there are also a fraction of SEO triplets.

From the Fig. 2, we can find most of the sentence contains multiple triplets. There are 19.83% triplets source from the sentence which contains no less than 5 different triplets. And the number of triplets in one sentence can grow up to 25! The multiple triplets case is so common in this task which requires us to pay a special attention to ensure the recall.

The relation distribution is extremely imbalanced. Of all 49 relation types, the *actor*, *writer*, and *singer* are most highest three relations, account for 32.77% triplets of all. However, the bottom three relation types *length of schooling*, *postcode*, and *specialityid* accounts for only 0.02% of total sample (Fig. 3).

《品牌先生|专辑》是司空雷|歌手的2016年专辑，共收录2
首歌曲《一生中爱过|歌曲》《品牌先生|歌曲》

Fig. 3. Case of one entity matches multiple positions in one sentence.

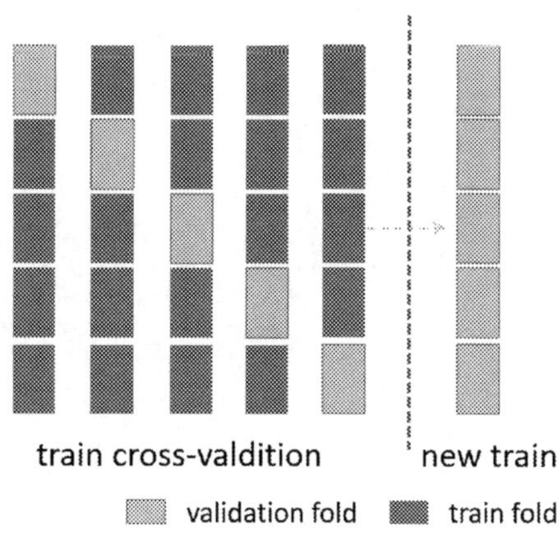
train cross-valdition
new train
validation fold
train fold

Fig. 4. Data distill. We first split the train data into 5 folds randomly. Each time we train with 4 folds and valid with the rest one fold. Finally, we get the validation on all train samples and use them as new train data for further experiments.

Besides, the data-set do not contain the entity position information, and we can not infer their right position through a regular expression matching when multiple positions are matched. As shown in Fig. 4, the *album* (专辑) entity

品牌先生 at the beginning of sentence can also match the *song* (歌曲) entity 品牌先生 at the end. Missing triplets entity position introduces noise into the model. We solve it within training process by dynamic matching.

2.2 Pre-processing

The pre-processing we use is primarily targeted to solve categories imbalance, data-set inconsistent, and the entity position uncertainty problems. Because the number of sample in different relation types is extremely imbalanced and some relation types have only a fraction of labeled data, we randomly over-sample each relation categories to 2500 sample size if it has number of labeled data below it.

As to the data-set inconsistent problem, we find the mislabeling in train-set does affect the model performance when testing online. We reduce the gaps between offline train and online test by removing errors and adding unmarked triplets in the train data. It can be done by annotating the train-set manually, however the cost would be huge. So, we distill the data with cross validations. See detail in Fig. 4.

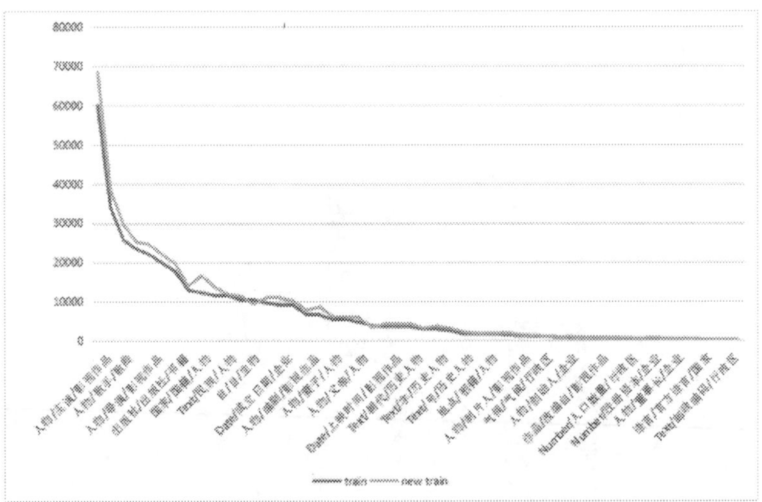

Fig. 5. Difference comparison before and after data distill. The figure contains all relation types from left to right with descending in number of labeled data.

The data distill process has changed the train data-set a lot. And the number of marked triplets increases 13.7% from 364 k to 414 k. The online test shows that this change has improved the recall a lot and the precision is less affected. The detail that number of changes in each relation types is presented in Fig. 5.

Furthermore, we find it hard to align the triplets with right position when facing with multiple occurrences situation. So we first enumerate all possible combination of multiple position entities, and then choose the best fitted one during the training process. This is done because we can infer the entity token probability in relation proposal layer and triplet CRF log-likelihood in decoding stage during the train. And we will always choose the position with highest proposal probability or triplet decoding log-likelihood.

3 Our Solution

Our solution is basically based on a relation proposal network for end-to-end information extraction. We use model ensemble and apply post-processing to get the final results.

3.1 The Model

The model we use contains three parts: (1) An encoder to encode the input sentences. It is a Bi-LSTM layer at first when we test the model structure, then we replace it with BERT encoder, and it can also be any other predefined generalized language models. (2) A relation proposal layer to propose the relation at each token position. It is a fully connected layer that output the relation

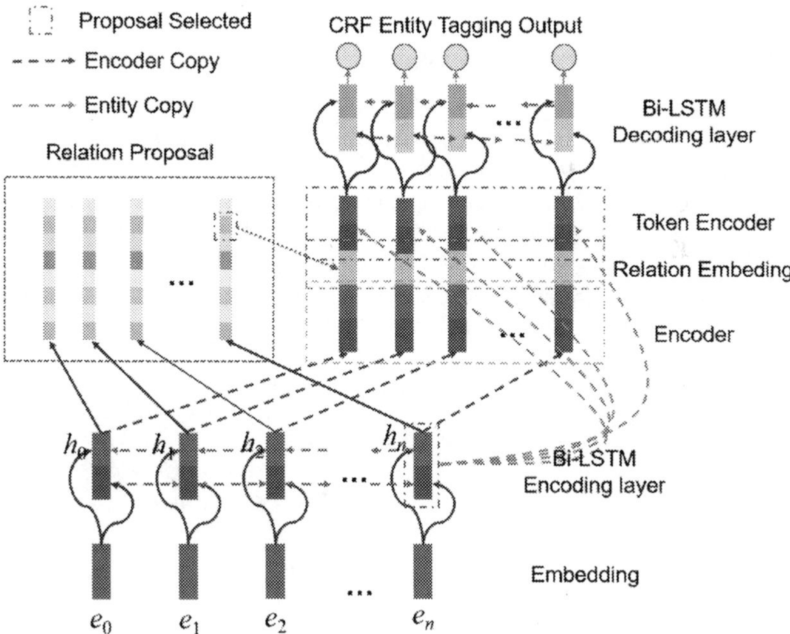

Fig. 6. The relation proposal based end-to-end neural network structure. An encoder(like Bi-LSTM) is used to encode source sentence embedding, then followed by the relation proposal. With the given relation and token, a copy mechanism is used to construct the input for decoder which is used to decode the triplet entities.

proposal probability $p_{i,r}$, where i is the token position index, and r is the rth relation type. (3) A decoder to output the triplets. It is a typical sequence tagging network, and the decoder is designed to decode one triplet for one relation proposal. The model structure is presented in Fig. 6.

The key to solve the overlapping problem is the one-triplet-one-sequence decoding design. During the train, the relation proposal layer is targeted to propose the relation for each triplet at the entity token position. Except for a very special case that two SEO triplets are of the same relation type, each valid proposal must belong to one target triplet only. Thus the decoding layer can only decode one-triplet for one-proposal. As to the special case where one proposal can match multiple triplets for the entity that two triplets share, we choose to discard it during the train. It does not matter much since we can decode the triplet from entity which two triplets do not share. The decoder layer works in one-triplet-one-sequence manner, so there is not existing triplets overlapping problem.

The multiple triplet problem is solved with a train strategy for relation proposal layer. We force the proposal layer to propose the relation for every triplet at all token position to which the entities belong. It produces the entities token number of proposal for each triplet. And any one among these potential proposal can successfully decode the target triplet. This train strategy makes the model performance well on multiple triplet cases.

3.2 Ensemble and Post-processing

Besides, we also adopt ensemble and some post-processing methods. We choose all relation proposal probability $p > 0.4$, and CRF triplet decoding log-likelihood $l > -1$ as the valid output of the model. Then we ensemble the model with a simple n in m strategy, which means we output triplets which have at least recognized by n times in m models, $n = 7$ and $m = 10$ in our final submission.

We also use rule based post-processing strategies to gain a better result, and these rules are focused to reduce the apparent mistakes resulted by inconsistent annotations, and contradiction triplet outputs. They are:

Fig. 7. The example of the post-processing.

- **Normalization** Normalization targets to correct the entities with a clear pattern. This is partial resulted by annotation mistakes. For example, the entity *book title* should be all content in 《》. However, this is not true in annotation data which needs a correction.
- **Deduplication** The model can output two triplets of the same type that partial of the entities are overlapping. It is clear that one output is wrong. Under this circumstance, we will choose the entity with longer length. Figure 7 shows the example.

4 Experimental Results

Our experiment is first conducted with Bi-LSTM as encoder at word level, and we use the Tencent word embedding [4]. This baseline model has achieved a good result at the beginning of the competition. When we stabilize the model structure, the Bi-LSTM encoder is replaced with BERT which leads to a significant improvement on precision and recall. We further apply data distill, which has improved the recall of our model a lot. With the post-processing and ensemble, our solution finally reach 0.8903 F1-score. Table 1 presents the detail.

Table 1. Experiment results.

	Precision	Recall	F1-score
Bi-LSTM Encoder	0.8736	0.8108	0.841
BERT Encoder	0.8752	0.8494	0.8621
BERT + data distill	0.8811	0.8639	0.8724
BERT + data distill + post-processing	0.8803	0.8886	0.8844
4 in 5	0.8955	0.8842	0.8898
7 in 10 Final	0.8948	0.8858	0.8903

We find the most important improvement in our experiments are: (1) A better encoder leads to a better performance. Compared with the origin Bi-LSTM encoder, the BERT based model achieves the biggest improvement of 0.0211 F1-score online. It implicates the importance of a better encoder in information extraction task. (2) Data distill is important in noisy data-set. We apply data distill on train data-set because it is apparently more noisy compared with the validation online. Noisy in train data-set is so common in real world applications as the triplets annotation is extremely hard. The implement of data distill here can also be meaningful to further applications.

5 Conclusion and Future Works

We analyze the data-set of NLPCC 2019 information extraction task, and propose the relation proposal based end-to-end information extraction method. This method successfully solves overlapping and multiple triplets problems, which are typically issues in academic researches and industry applications. Our experiments reveal the importance of better encoder in NLP tasks and data distill in noisy data, and it's meaningful to further study.

During the competition, we have only tested the Bi-LSTM and origin BERT encoder, and the Bi-LSTM decoder in our experiments with limited time. It's meaningful to have other more explorations on different encoder and decoder structures, especially in different language settings.

References

1. Bekoulis, G., Deleu, J., Demeester, T., Develder, C.: Joint entity recognition and relation extraction as a multi-head selection problem. CoRR abs/1804.07847 (2018). http://arxiv.org/abs/1804.07847
2. Li, Q., Ji, H.: Incremental joint extraction of entity mentions and relations. In: Proceedings of the 52nd Annual Meeting of the Association for Computational Linguistics (Volume 1: Long Papers), vol. 1, pp. 402–412 (2014)
3. Ren, S., He, K., Girshick, R., Sun, J.: Faster R-CNN: towards real-time object detection with region proposal networks. In: Advances in Neural Information Processing Systems, pp. 91–99 (2015)
4. Song, Y., Shi, S., Li, J., Zhang, H.: Directional skip-gram: explicitly distinguishing left and right context for word embeddings. In: Proceedings of the 2018 Conference of the North American Chapter of the Association for Computational Linguistics: Human Language Technologies, Volume 2 (Short Papers), pp. 175–180. Association for Computational Linguistics, New Orleans, June 2018. https://doi.org/10.18653/v1/N18-2028, https://www.aclweb.org/anthology/N18-2028
5. Takanobu, R., Zhang, T., Liu, J., Huang, M.: A hierarchical framework for relation extraction with reinforcement learning. In: AAAI (2019)
6. Tan, Z., Zhao, X., Wang, W., Xiao, W.: Jointly Extracting Multiple Triplets With Multilayer Translation Constraints (2019)
7. Zeng, X., Zeng, D., He, S., Liu, K., Zhao, J.: Extracting relational facts by an end-to-end neural model with copy mechanism. In: Proceedings of the 56th Annual Meeting of the Association for Computational Linguistics (Volume 1: Long Papers), pp. 506–514 (2018)
8. Zheng, S., Wang, F., Bao, H., Hao, Y., Zhou, P., Xu, B.: Joint extraction of entities and relations based on a novel tagging scheme. In: Proceedings of the 55th Annual Meeting of the Association for Computational Linguistics (Volume 1: Long Papers), pp. 1227–1236. Association for Computational Linguistics, Vancouver, July 2017. https://doi.org/10.18653/v1/P17-1113, https://www.aclweb.org/anthology/P17-1113

DuIE: A Large-Scale Chinese Dataset for Information Extraction

Shuangjie Li, Wei He(✉), Yabing Shi, Wenbin Jiang, Haijin Liang, Ye Jiang, Yang Zhang, Yajuan Lyu, and Yong Zhu

Baidu Inc., Beijing 100193, China
{lishuangjie, hewei23, shiyanbing01, jiangwenbin, lianghaijin, jiangye, zhangyang08, lvyajuan, zhuyong}@baidu.com

Abstract. Information extraction is an important foundation for knowledge graph construction, as well as many natural language understanding applications. Similar to many other artificial intelligence tasks, high quality annotated datasets are essential to train a high-performance information extraction system. Existing datasets, however, are mostly built for English. To promote research in Chinese information extraction and evaluate the performance of related systems, we build a large-scale high-quality dataset, named DuIE, and make it publicly available. We design an efficient coarse-to-fine procedure including candidate generation and crowdsourcing annotation, in order to achieve high data quality at a large data scale. DuIE contains 210,000 sentences and 450,000 instances covering 49 types of commonly used relations, reflecting the real-world scenario. We also hosted an open competition based on DuIE, which attracted 1,896 participants. The competition results demonstrated the potential of this dataset in promoting information extraction research.

Keywords: Information extraction · Dataset · Performance evaluation

1 Introduction

Information extraction (IE) aims to extract structured information from unstructured or semi-structured text. Representative structured information includes entities, their attributes and relations, carrying important semantic information conveyed by the text. IE enables machines to understand the semantics of text and acts as the foundation of many important applications, such as knowledge graph construction, semantic information retrieval and intelligent question answering etc. Many efforts focus on the task of IE and achieve significant progress, especially with deep learning techniques [1–8].

Similar to most artificial intelligence applications, high-performance IE systems require supervised learning and adequate annotated datasets. However, existing datasets for IE are mainly built for English. To the best of our knowledge, there is no large-scale dataset for Chinese IE. In fact, even the existing English datasets are subjected to limited scale or poor quality. For example, NYT dataset [9] is automatically constructed without manual annotation, and suffers from the poor data quality problem. SemEval-2010 dataset [10] and FewRel dataset [11] achieve relatively higher quality by introducing manual annotations, but their data scales are still not sufficient.

J. Tang et al. (Eds.): NLPCC 2019, LNAI 11839, pp. 791–800, 2019.
https://doi.org/10.1007/978-3-030-32236-6_72

To better evaluate the performance of Chinese IE techniques, we build a large-scale good quality dataset, DuIE, and make it publicly available for research use. We design an effective coarse-to-fine procedure including candidate generation and crowdsourcing annotation in order to achieve large data scale and high data quality.

To the best of our knowledge, DuIE is the first large-scale, high-quality dataset for Chinese IE. Specifically, it contains 450,000 instances, with 49 commonly used relation types, 340,000 unique Subject-Predicate-Object (SPO) triples and 210,000 sentences. The text in DuIE covers a variety of domains in real-world applications, such as news, entertainment, user-generated contents. The annotations contain single-valued and multi-valued triples, reflecting the real-world scenario. Table 1 gives an example of annotated sentences in DuIE.

Table 1. A sample data in DuIE dataset

Sentence	SPO list
《**给最开心的人**》是**梁咏琪**于2004年12月15日发行的音乐专辑《**娱乐大家**》中的歌曲。 *To the Happiest People* is a song in *Gigi Leung*'s music album *The Great Entertainer,* which was released on December 15, 2004.	S：给最开心的人，P：歌手，O：梁咏琪 S: *To the Happiest People,* P: singer, O: *Gigi Leung* S:给最开心的人，P:所属专辑，O:娱乐大家 S: *To the Happiest People,* P: fromAlbum, O: *The Great Entertainer*

We hosted an open competition based on DuIE dataset as a part of 2019 Language and Intelligence Challenge[1], which is jointly organized by China Computer Federation (CCF), Chinese Information Processing Society of China (CIPS) and Baidu Inc. As one of the three tasks in this challenge, the IE task attracted 1,836 teams from around the world. During the competition, 324 teams submitted 3,367 results in total. The performance of these results shows the effectiveness of DuIE on the evaluation of the IE techniques.

The rest of this paper is organized as follows. We first briefly describe the preparation of data and the schema for dataset construction. After that, we describe in details the coarse-to-fine dataset construction procedure, including candidate generation and crowdsourcing annotation. Then, we give the statistical analysis of the dataset and the competition on it. Finally, we conclude the paper and discuss future directions.

2 Construction of DuIE

This section describes the procedure of constructing DuIE dataset. In general, we design an effective coarse-to-fine method combining automatic distant supervision and human annotation, which is the key to achieve high data quality in large data scale.

[1] http://lic2019.ccf.org.cn/.

As shown in Fig. 1, our construction procedure is composed of the following three steps: (1) preparing all kinds of required data, including the schema, related SPO triples and a large-scale real-world corpus. (2) generating candidates by distant supervision methods on both SPO level and schema level to ensure high recall and precision. (3) using crowdsourcing to label the correct triples among all candidates according to sentence contexts.

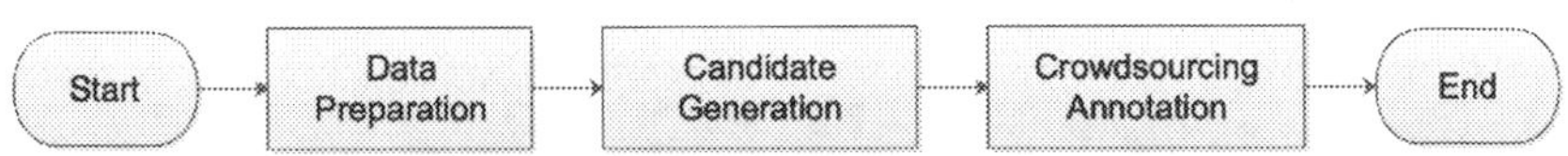

Fig. 1. Procedures of DuIE construction

2.1 Data Preparation

We design a schema to guide the dataset construction. A schema is a set of triple templates, each of which is composed of a head entity type, a relation and a tail entity type:

$$\text{Schema} = \{(Subject\, type, Predicate, Object\, type)\}$$

By analyzing Baidu information retrieval and recommendation logs, we include 49 most frequently used predicate types. Table 2 shows some examples of our schema.

According to the schema, we select related subject-predicate-object triples from the structured info-boxes of Baidu Baike[2]. In details, the predicate in a triple should be semantically equivalent to a predicate in the schema, and the subject/object should be an instance of corresponding subject/object type respectively, as specified in the schema. These triples are used to annotate large amounts of raw sentences in order to produce IE instances. The raw sentences are extracted from Baidu Baike and Baidu News Feeds[3], covering major domains in real-world information requirement, including entity descriptions, entertainment news, user-generated articles and so on.

2.2 Candidate Generation

We use two types of distant supervision methods, namely SPO-level distant supervision and schema-level distant supervision, to ensure candidate quality.

SPO-Level Distant Supervision. SPO-level distant supervision is a popular distant supervision method, which was widely used in existing dataset construction work. It is based on the closed-world assumption, i.e., entity information in the knowledge base is complete. In other words, if there was a relation between two entities, the triple found in the knowledge base and sentences that mention these two entities should express that relation. According to this assumption, we obtained all candidate instances in the form

[2] https://baike.baidu.com/.

[3] https://baijiahao.baidu.com.

of $(e_1, p_1, e_2, sentence_1)$ if (e_1, p_1, e_2) and $sentence_1$ are in triple and text candidates we got in the previous step separately, and both entity e_1 and entity e_2 appeared in sentence $sentence_1$.

Table 2. Schema examples in DuIE dataset

Subject type	Predicate	Object type	SPO example
人物 (Person)	毕业院校 (almaMater)	学校 (Educational institutions)	S: 杜道生, P: 学校, O: 北京大学 S: *Du Daosheng,* P: almaMater, O: *Peking University*
影视作品 (Film and TV works)	导演 (directedBy)	人物 (Person)	S: 逆光之恋, P: 导演, O: 任海曜 S: *The Backlight of Love,* P: directedBy, O: *Kenne Yam*
图书作品 (Book)	作者 (author)	人物 (Person)	S: 呐喊, P: 作者, O: 鲁迅 S: *Call to Arms,* P: author, O: *Lu Xun*

Schema-Level Distant Supervision. In our method, schema-level distant supervision was utilized to compensate for the data incompletion problem of SPO-level distant supervision. Although information extraction datasets could be built by the SPO-level distant supervision method without any human intervention, the quality of such datasets is often limited. One crucial reason is that the closed-world assumption is not always hold. In reality, no knowledge base could include the entire set of knowledge in the world. Therefore, some correct triples mentioned a sentence could be missed in the previous step.

In order to compensate for the data incompletion problem, we proposed a schema-level distant supervision method. Firstly, for each candidate sentence, named entities with our target types were labeled by Named Entity Recognition (NER) algorithms. Secondly, entity pairs are recalled if their types matched one of the triple patterns specified in the schema. For example, in the sentence given in Table 1, (*To the Happiest People, from Album, The Great Entertainer*) would be recalled as a candidate triple in that sentence, if we know that *To the Happiest People* is a song and *The Great Entertainer* is an album, which matches the target subject and object types of predicate *fromAlbum*, even though this triple is missing in the knowledge base.

2.3 Crowdsourcing Annotation

Finally, to filter out noise instances and improve dataset accuracy, we invited some annotators to judge whether or not every candidate instance was correct on a crowdsourcing platform. For the convenience and efficiency of human annotating, we presented instances in a special question pattern. Given one instance to be labeled as $(sentence, S, P, O)$, we converted it to a judgment question:

Is this correct? <*P*> of <*S*> (*Subject type*) is <*O*> (*Object type*) according to the *sentence*.

An annotation candidate example is shown in Fig. 2. Annotators had to judge whether the annotation questions were correct according to the following three criteria: (1) Clues should be found from and only from the sentence provided. There is no need to consider whether the triple is true in the real world. (2) Subjects and objects should match the given types, which are pre-defined in the schema. (3) Predicates do not need to appear explicitly in the sentence.

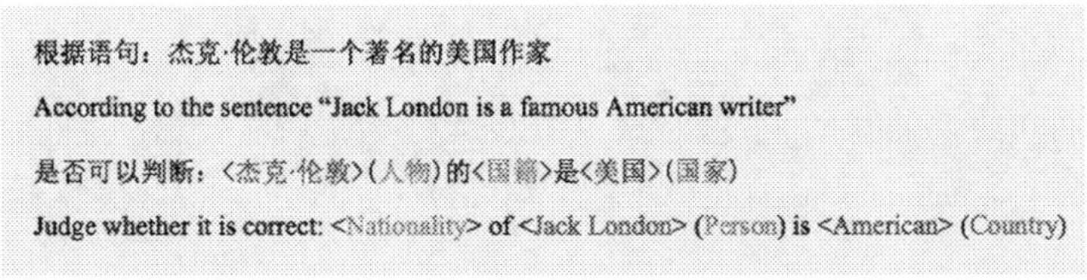

根据语句：杰克·伦敦是一个著名的美国作家

According to the sentence "Jack London is a famous American writer"

是否可以判断：<杰克·伦敦>(人物)的<国籍>是<美国>(国家)

Judge whether it is correct: <Nationality> of <Jack London> (Person) is <American> (Country)

Fig. 2. An example of annotated data

While annotating test dataset, to ensure the labeling quality, each instance was first assigned to two annotators. Instances with inconsistent answers from the both annotators would be sent to a third annotator. During the entire annotation step, about 10 crowdsourced users were involved to work on about 640,000 candidate instances. Finally, we gathered all correct instances as the final dataset.

3 Data Statistics

Based on the above construction procedure, we build the largest Chinese information extraction dataset, DuIE, which contains 458,184 instances with 49 different predicate types, 239,663 entities, 347,250 triples, and 214,739 real-world Chinese sentences, as shown in Table 3. The average length of all sentences is 54.58, and there are 8,490 unique tokens in total. In final dataset, 78% instances are from SPO-level method, while 22% instances are from schema-level method. This shows the effectiveness of our two-level distant supervision approaches.

Table 3. Statistics of DuIE dataset in detail

#Instance	#Entity	#Relation types	#Triple	#Sentence
458,184	239,663	49	347,250	214,739

Table 4. Comparison of DuIE Dataset with existing IE dataset

Dataset	#Relation types	#Instance
NYT-10	57	143,391
SemEval-2010 Task 8	10	10,717
FewRel	100	70,000
DuIE	49	458,184

Table 4 provides a comparison of our DuIE dataset to the existing popular IE datasets, including NYT-10, SemEval 2010 Task 8 dataset, and FewRel. It shows that DuIE is significantly larger than existing IE datasets.

DuIE dataset is split into three parts, a training set, a development set and a testing set, as show in Table 5, and there is no overlap among sentences among these three sets. Currently, the training set and development set are available to download[4].

Table 5. Statistics of DuIE training, dev, testing sets

Dataset	Training set	Dev set	Testing set
#Sentence	173,108	21,639	19,992
#Instance	364,218	45,577	48,389

We further analyze the data distribution in several aspects. As we can see from Fig. 3, 63% sentences are from Baidu Baike encyclopedia corpus, while 37% sentences are from Baidu Feed news. In Fig. 4, distribution on different entity types is given. The most common types in DuIE are Person, Film and TV works, Song, and Book, which are is consistent with the set of top entity type found in Baidu search logs.

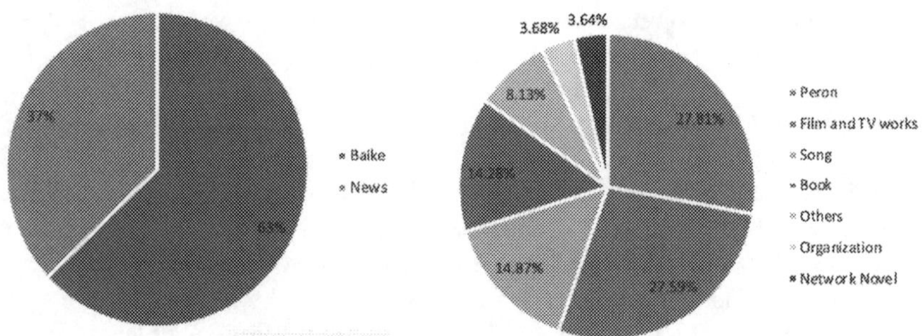

Fig. 3. Distribution on text source types

Fig. 4. Distribution on entity types

4 Evaluation on Information Extraction Task

This section provides details on the information extraction competition using the DuIE dataset, including competition task description, evaluation results and detailed analysis.

4.1 Competition Task

We hosted an IE task in 2019 Language and Intelligence Challenge (See Footnote 3), whose objective is to extract all correct triples according to the given sentences and a pre-defined schema. Specifically, a triple predicted by a participant system is

4 http://ai.baidu.com/broad/download.

considered as correct when its relation and two corresponding entities are matched with the triple annotated on the testing set. Considering that some entities are mentioned in sentences using aliases, we use a dictionary of alias in Baidu Knowledge Graph in the evaluation. Standard *Precision*, *Recall* and *F1* scores are used as metrics to evaluate the performance of participating systems. The final results are ranked according to the F1 value. During the period of competition, IE task have attracted 1,836 teams from both academia and industry, and 324 teams submitted 3,367 results in total.

Table 6. Evaluation results of the top 10 systems

System no.	Precision	Recall	F1	System no.	Precision	Recall	F1
S1	89.8%	88.9%	89.3%	S6	89.5%	87.0%	88.2%
S2	89.6%	88.9%	89.2%	S7	89.4%	86.8%	88.1%
S3	89.8%	88.5%	89.1%	S8	88.3%	86.9%	87.6%
S4	89.5%	88.6%	89.0%	S9	86.2%	87.9%	87.1%
S5	89.2%	88.2%	88.7%	S10	89.3%	84.8%	87.0%

4.2 Evaluation Results

The overall competition results are published in the competition website (See Footnote 1). Table 6 shows the list of top participant systems with their performance metric, ordered by their F1 values. We found that some techniques widely adopted by our participants, such as pre-trained models like BERT [12], lexical features, ensemble techniques, rule-based post-processing. In addition, some teams use parameter sharing, self-attention mechanism and manual-designed features to further improve performances.

4.3 Result Analysis

For comprehensive understanding for our dataset and related IE technologies, we performed a detailed analysis on the performance results of top participants.

Overall Error Analysis. We sampled incorrect triples in the top ten systems and manually labeled their error types. The top error types are shown in Table 7 "relation error", which means that an incorrect relation is extracted for an entity pair, is the most common error type and accounts for 38% of all errors. This indicates that the extraction model still has room for improvement in identifying relations between entity pairs.

The second common error type is "non-relation error", which accounted for 22% of all errors. This error type means that there is no semantic relation between the extracted subject and object in the sentence. This often happens when there are multiple entities of the same type in the given sentence. We further break down this category by source text types. An interesting observation is that "non-relation error" happens much more frequently on News text (30%) than on Baike text (17%). This indicates that it is more challenging to identify relations on more complex text styles.

The "entity boundary error" means that target entities could be found but the boundary recognition is not accurate enough which accounts for 21% of the total errors. In addition, 11% of the errors are due to the fact that entities in the triples do not conform to the types provided in schema constraint. This indicates that participants do not make full use of labels of entity types when training models or extracting triples. There are also 8% other dispersed errors such as inference knowledge error which means that the SPO cannot be extracted without the background knowledge.

Table 7. Major error types

Error type	Error description	Example	Ratio
Relation error	The relation between subject and object is wrong.	《人龙传说》是 1999 年香港电视广播有限公司出品的古装神话剧，由罗永贤监制，陈浩民、袁洁莹主演。 Error: S:人龙传说，P: 导演，O: 罗永贤	38%
Non-relation error	There is no semantic relation between extracted subject and object in the sentence.	余思经典长篇代表作《细雨湿流光》作为青春成长的经典长篇代表作，曾得到《中国式离婚》《新结婚时代》编剧王海鸰和青春文学代表人物饶雪漫的携手力推。 Error: S: 细雨湿流光，P: 编剧，O: 王海鸰	22%
Entity boundary error	Entity recognition is incomplete or redundant.	唐寅《溪山渔隐图》（下为全卷 引首"渔隐"为乾隆御笔） 唐寅（1470-1524），字伯虎，后改字子畏，号六如居士、桃花庵主等，明代画家、书法家、诗人 Error: S: 唐寅，P: 号，O: 桃花庵主等	21%
Entity type error	Entity types do not conform to schema constraint.	《电子电路与电子技术入门》是新电气编辑部所著，科学出版社出版的图书。 Error: S: 电子电路与电子技术入门，P: 作者，O: 新电气编辑部	11%
Other errors	Other dispersed errors	杨渺，男，汉族，1970 年 9 月出生于甘肃临夏，中国甘肃国际技术合作公司副总经理。 Error: S: 杨渺，P: 国籍，O:中国	8%

Effects of Source Text Types. Table 8 shows the average performance metrics of the top 5 systems and the top 10 systems on Baike and news texts respectively. The results show that compared with news text, the average F1 value of top 10 extraction systems on Baike text is 11.9% higher. One possible reason is that, Baike texts are usually edited by domain experts in a rather fixed format, while news texts is more complex in style and often involved with diversified linguistic patterns. Therefore, information extraction on news texts is much more difficult.

Table 8. Performance results in different sources of text

System	Baike			News		
	Precision	Recall	F1	Precision	Recall	F1
Avg-top5	92.6%	92.3%	92.4%	82.4%	80.1%	81.2%
Avg-top10	92.2%	91.5%	91.9%	81.5%	78.6%	80.0%

Single-valued v.s. Multi-valued Triples. We evaluated the recall of single-valued and multi-valued triples. Multi-valued triple means that a single S-P pair corresponds to multiple O values or a single P-O pair corresponds to multiple S values in the given sentence. The performance results of top five average and top 10 average systems in multi-valued and single-valued triples are shown in Table 9 respectively. It can be seen that in top 10 systems, the average recall of the single-valued triples is 6.4% higher than that of the multi-valued triples, which indicates that it is more challenging to extract all the multi-valued triples.

Table 9. Evaluation of results in multi-valued and single-valued sentences

System	Multi-valued triples recall	Single-valued triples recall
Avg-top5	84.5%	90.3%
Avg-top10	83.1%	89.5%

We sampled some unrecalled multi-valued triples and found there were two types. As shown in Table 10, the first type is that multiple entities are adjacent or simply concatenated by a separator, while the second type is that multiple entities are not adjacent in text. It can be seen that sentence characteristics of multi-valued triples are significant, and researches need to be carried on how to model such cases in the future.

Table 10. Two types of unrecalled multi-valued triples

Multi-valued type	**Instance examples**
Multiple entities are adjacent	《**新六指琴魔**》是由**海润影视制作有限公司**、**耳东影业（北京）有限公司**、**华视网聚**、**横店影视制作有限公司**联合出品，香港导演王晶担任总监制、总导演。 S: 新六指琴魔, P: 出品公司 Multi-valued O: 海润影视制作有限公司, 耳东影业（北京）有限公司, 华视网聚, 横店影视制作有限公司
Multiple entities are not adjacent to the text	但在学习过程中她却爱上了主持这个行当，从1997年的《**五星奖**》，1998 年《**正大综艺**》，2001年《**猜猜谁会来**》，一直到的《**家庭演播室**》、《**娱乐星天地**》，**吉雪萍**主持的节目留给了人们很深刻的印象，她的名字在上海可谓家喻户晓。 Multi-valued S: 五星奖, 正大综艺, 猜猜谁会来, 家庭演播室, 娱乐星天地 P: 主持人 O: 吉雪萍

5 Conclusion

In this paper, we present DuIE dataset, the largest high-quality Chinese information extraction dataset, which was built in a coarse-to-fine procedure combining of distant supervision and crowdsourcing annotation. To validate the dataset, we conduct a technical evaluation and analyze the errors in top systems. We found that the most common errors in information extraction systems are relation error and entity error, and current models still have rooms for improvement in these areas. For texts from different source types, the error distributions are quite different. In addition, further research is needed for small sample sizes and multi-valued triples. DuIE could help in evaluating and advancing information extraction techniques in future research.

References

1. Zeng, D., Liu, K., Lai, S., et al.: Relation classification via convolutional deep neural network (2014)
2. Jiang, X., Wang, Q., Li, P., et al.: Relation extraction with multi-instance multi-label convolutional neural networks. In: Proceedings of COLING 2016, the 26th International Conference on Computational Linguistics: Technical Papers, pp. 1471–1480 (2016)
3. Zeng, X., He, S., Liu, K., et al.: Large scaled relation extraction with reinforcement learning. In: Thirty-Second AAAI Conference on Artificial Intelligence (2018)
4. Miwa, M., Bansal, M.: End-to-end relation extraction using LSTMs on sequences and tree structures. arXiv preprint: arXiv:1601.00770 (2016)
5. Dai, D., Xiao, X., Lyu, Y., Dou, S., She, Q., Wang, H.: Joint extraction of entities and overlapping relations using position-attentive sequence labeling. In: AAAI (2019)
6. Takanobu, R., Zhang, T., Liu, J., et al.: A hierarchical framework for relation extraction with reinforcement learning. arXiv preprint: arXiv:1811.03925 (2018)
7. Zheng, S., Wang, F., Bao, H., Hao, Y., Zhou, P., Xu, B.: Joint extraction of entities and relations based on a novel tagging scheme. In: ACL (2017)
8. Zeng, X., Zeng, D., He, S., et al.: Extracting relational facts by an end-to-end neural model with copy mechanism. In: Proceedings of the 56th Annual Meeting of the Association for Computational Linguistics. Long Papers, vol. 1, pp. 148–163 (2018)
9. Riedel, S., Yao, L., McCallum, A.: Modeling relations and their mentions without labeled text. In: Balcázar, J.L., Bonchi, F., Gionis, A., Sebag, M. (eds.) ECML PKDD 2010, Part III. LNCS (LNAI), vol. 6323, pp. 148–163. Springer, Heidelberg (2010). https://doi.org/10.1007/978-3-642-15939-8_10
10. Hendrickx, I., Kim, S.N., Kozareva, Z., et al.: SemEval-2010 task 8: Multi-way classification of semantic relations between pairs of nominals. In: Proceedings of the Workshop on Semantic Evaluations: Recent Achievements and Future Directions, pp. 94–99. Association for Computational Linguistics (2009)
11. Han, X., Zhu, H., Yu, P., et al.: FewRel: a large-scale supervised few-shot relation classification dataset with state-of-the-art evaluation. arXiv preprint: arXiv:1810.10147 (2018)
12. Devlin, J., et al.: Bert: pre-training of deep bidirectional transformers for language understanding. arXiv preprint: arXiv:1810.04805 (2018)

Domain Information Enhanced Dependency Parser

Nan Yu[1], Zonglin Liu[2], Ranran Zhen[2], Tao Liu[2], Meishan Zhang[3], and Guohong Fu[4(✉)]

[1] School of Computer Science and Technology, Soochow University, Suzhou, China
nyu@stu.suda.edu.cn

[2] School of Computer Science and Technology, Heilongjiang University, Harbin, China
liuzonglin1993@gmail.com, zenrran@gmail.com, taoooo1009@gmail.com

[3] School of New Media and Communication, Tianjin University, Tianjin, China
mason.zms@gmail.com

[4] Institute of Artificial Intelligence, Soochow University, Suzhou, China
ghfu@suda.edu.cn

Abstract. Dependency parsing has been an important task in the natural language processing (NLP) community. Supervised methods have achieved great success these years. However, these models can suffer significant performance loss when test domain differs from the training domain. In this paper, we adopt the Bi-Affine parser as our baseline. To explore domain-specific information and domain-independent information for cross-domain dependency parsing, we apply an ensemble-style self-training and adversarial learning, respectively. We finally combine the two strategies to enhance our baseline model and our final system was ranked the first of at NLPCC2019 shared task on cross-domain dependency parsing.

Keywords: Cross-domain · Dependency parsing · Self-training · Adversarial learning · Ensemble

1 Introduction

Dependency parsing is a fundamental task in NLP research, which aims to parse the syntax structure of sentences by establishing the relationships between words. It has received great attention [3,8–10,18,26] these years, and most of them focus on the supervised methods for dependency parsing [3,8,10,17].

There are several algorithms for dependency parsing, like graph-based [8,21, 27] and transition-based [1,3,10,31]. Given a sentence, the graph-based parsers compute the scores of all arcs and labels, and find the highest scoring dependency tree, while the transition-based parsers establish a dependency tree by a sequence of shift-reduce operations. Recently, the neural features have achieved great success in NLP tasks [5,6]. Many supervised dependency parsers adopt

J. Tang et al. (Eds.): NLPCC 2019, LNAI 11839, pp. 801–810, 2019.
https://doi.org/10.1007/978-3-030-32236-6_73

the neural features and achieved high performances in news domain [3,8,10,32] (above 90%). Among these neural dependency parsers, the Bi-Affine parser [8] can achieve the top performance.

However, supervised methods have a deficiency on cross-domain dependency parsing, because of the data distribution difference between training data and test data. When these supervised models trained by the news domain training data, and then use them to predict new domain test data (like web fiction, production comments, etc.), the performances of them dropped drastically [11, 18,23].

Self-training is an effective semi-supervised method, which can improve the original model performance by utilizing the data distribution information from unlabeled data. But when we apply self-training to dependency parsing, it relies on high-quality additional training data heavily [4,13,16]. Several inappropriate methods for obtaining additional training data even have a negative influence on cross-domain dependency parsing [2,24].

Ensemble has been a simple but effective method to obtain the high-quality automatic trees [20,23,28]. [7] combines the self-training and ensemble, proposing an ensemble-style self-training for cross-domain citation classification. Inspired by [7], we use ensemble models to predict the unlabeled data and obtain 1-best automatic trees. Then we sample the automatic trees randomly to obtain the high-quantity additional training data. Finally, the original parsers can learn the target domain-specific information by several re-training iterations with the additional training data.

Domain-independent information is another effective resource for cross-domain tasks. Domain adversarial training can extract domain-independent information by the adversarial domain classifier, which have been demonstrated helpful in dependency parsing [25]. Inspired by [25], we apply the adversarial learning to enhanced our baseline.

In this paper, we investigate two kinds of domain information for cross-domain dependency parsing. We follow [8], reimplementing the Bi-Affine parser as our baseline. Then, we enhance the Bi-Affine parser with target domain-specific information and the domain-independent information, which is complementary. On the one hand, we apply the ensemble-style self-training method to extract the domain specific information from unlabeled target domain data. On the other hand, we follow [25], extending our baseline with the adversarial learning to extract the domain-independent information. Our codes will be released for public at http://github.com/yunan4nlp/cross_domain_parser.

We conduct the experiments on the NLPCC2019 shared task corpus, and our final models rank the first in all teams [22]. We perform several development experiments to analyze the adversarial training and ensemble-style self-training, and the results show these two methods are both effective methods for cross-domain dependency parsing.

2 Related Work

2.1 Dependency Parsing

There are two mainly algorithms for dependency parsing, the graph-based [8,21,27] and the transition-based [1,3,10,14,31,32].

The graph-based parsers compute the scores of all arcs and labels, and search the highest scoring dependency trees as output. And the transition-based parsers convert the dependency tree predictions into a sequence of action predictions. Both two kinds of parsers focus on the statistical models by using manually-designed features in early time [19,19,29,31].

Recently, the neural features have been widely investigated in dependency parsing [3,8,10,17,21]. Among these neural dependency parsers, the Bi-Affine parser [8] has achieved state-of-the-art performance. Thus, we reimplement the Bi-Affine parser as baseline, which is popular in dependency parsing [9,15,30].

2.2 Domain Adaption

Self-training methods have been demonstrated useful for dependency parsing by a number of studies [2,4,13,16,24]. The majority methods focus on complex additional training data sample methods to achieve this goal [4,13,16]. Ensemble is a simple but effective method for dependency parsing to improve the performance [20,23,28]. [7] propose an ensemble-style self-training method for citation classification, which can offer the high-quality additional training data for self-training. Inspired by [7], we extend the Bi-Affine parser with ensemble-style self-training.

Adversarial training has been proposed for cross-domain adaption, bringing significantly better performances for dependency parsing [25]. Our adversarial domain classifier is mainly borrowed by [12].

3 Our Methods

3.1 The Bi-Affine Parser

Our baseline model is borrowed from the Bi-Affine parser [8], which is the state-of-the-art dependency parsing model and has achieved the top performances.

The mainly structure of the Bi-Affine parser is consisted of five parts: (1) a embedding layers; Given a sentence, we input the word forms $\{\mathbf{w}_1, \mathbf{w}_2, ..., \mathbf{w}_n\}$ and part-of-speech (POS) tags $\{\mathbf{t}_1, \mathbf{t}_2, ..., \mathbf{t}_n\}$ of each word to get their neural embeddings respectively, and then concatenate them. (2) three bi-directional long short term memory (Bi-LSTM$^{\times 3}$) layers; (3) a multi-layer perceptron (MLP) layer; (4) a Bi-Affine layer, we input the hidden layers of MLP and output the scores of arcs and labels. (5) an arg max decoder. We introduce the Bi-Affine parser briefly, and for more details, one can read their original paper.

3.2 Adversarial Training

We mix two different domain training data and feed into the Bi-Affine parser [8]. The baseline parser can extract the rich information from both two domain training data, including syntax, domain information etc. Intuitively, the target domain-independent information is useful for the cross-domain adaption. We follow [12], building an adversarial domain classifier with gradient reversal layer (GRL) to reduce the source domain-specific information and learn target domain-independent information.

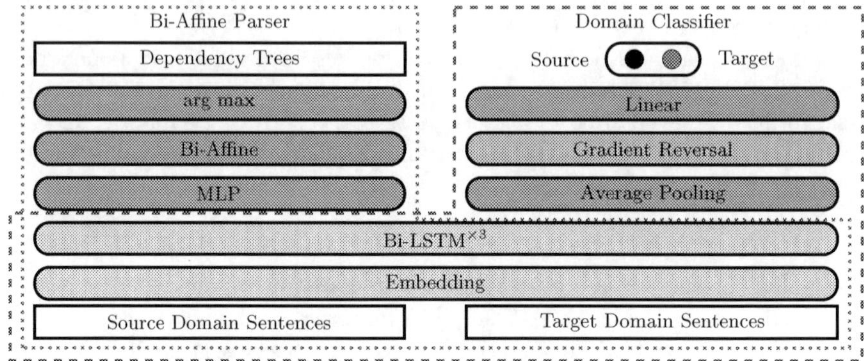

Fig. 1. The structure of adversarial learning based Bi-Affine parser

Figure 1 shows the structure of the Bi-Affine parser extended by adversarial learning, including a Bi-Affine parser and an adversarial domain classifier. In the adversarial domain classifier, the model parameters of the embedding layer and the Bi-LSTM layer are shared with the Bi-Affine parser. We use the Bi-LSTM hidden representations $\{\mathbf{h}_r^1, \mathbf{h}_r^2, ..., \mathbf{h}_r^n\}$ to calculate the sentence representation $\mathbf{h}_s$ by average pooling:

$$\mathbf{h}_s = \frac{1}{n}\sum_{1}^{n}\mathbf{h}_r^i \tag{1}$$

The essential part of the adversarial domain classifier is the GRL, and we apply it directly as follow:

$$\mathbf{h}_s = \mathrm{R}_\lambda(\mathbf{h}_s), \varDelta\mathbf{h}_s = -\lambda\frac{d\mathrm{R}_\lambda(\mathbf{h}_s)}{d\mathbf{h}_s} = -\lambda\mathbf{I} \tag{2}$$

where the $\varDelta\mathbf{h}_s$ is the gradient of the h_s, the λ is a constant factor, and the $\mathbf{I}$ is an identity matrix.

Finally, we use linear layer to compute the domain scores:

$$\mathbf{o} = \mathbf{W}\cdot\mathbf{h}_s \tag{3}$$

3.3 Ensemble-Style Self-training

In this work, we follow [7], extending the baseline models with the ensemble-style self-training. Then we apply a random sample method to obtain additional training data, which add to original training data to re-train the basic models. Ensemble-style self-training is very similar to tri-training [33], which also trains three basic models and utilizes the unlabeled data to improve basic models. In previous work, the tri-training shows no improvement in dependency parsing [28].

First, we train three Bi-Affine parser models $\{\theta_1, \theta_2, \theta_3\}$ with same original training data $G = \{g_1, g_2, ..., g_x\}$ and different random seeds as our basic models. The performances of those models are almost same. We apply the ensemble method to those models, and predict the unlabeled data $U = \{u_1, u_2, ..., u_x\}$ to obtain the automatic dependency trees $U' = \{u'_1, u'_2, ..., u'_x\}$. We get the scores of arcs and labels, and apply softmax method to get the probabilities of arcs. We average the probabilities of arcs and labels, which is given by Eq. 4, and we select 1-best dependency trees as candidates.

$$\begin{cases} p^a = \frac{exp(\mathbf{s}^a)}{\sum_{a' \in A} exp(\mathbf{s}^{a'})}, p^l = \frac{exp(\mathbf{s}^l)}{\sum_{l' \in L} exp(\mathbf{s}^{l'})} \\ p^a_{avg} = \sum_1^3 p^a_i, p^l_{avg} = \sum_1^3 p^l_i \end{cases} \tag{4}$$

We sample 100 k automatic dependency trees SU' randomly according to development experiment results and add those data into original training data. Then we use the new training data $G' = \{g_1, g_2, ..., g_x, u'_1, u'_2, ..., u'_r\}$ to re-train the three basic models. Our self-training iteration would be repeated for several time, and the additional training data SU' used only once. Finally, we use the ensemble models to predict the dependency trees of test data T to get the dependency trees T'. Algorithm 1 shows the pseudo codes of ensemble-style self-training algorithm.

Algorithm 1. Ensemble-style self-training algorithim

for $i = 1 \rightarrow 3$ **do**
  $\theta_i^1 \leftarrow Train(\theta_i^0, G)$
for $j = 1 \rightarrow k$ **do**
  $U' \leftarrow Ensemble(\{\theta_1^j, \theta_2^j, \theta_3^j\}, U)$
  $SU' \leftarrow Sample(U')$
  $G' \leftarrow SU' + G$
  for $i = 1 \rightarrow 3$ **do**
    $\theta_i^{j+1} \leftarrow Train(\theta_i^j, G')$
$T' = Ensemble(\{\theta_1^k, \theta_2^k, \theta_3^k\}, T)$

3.4 Training

We reimplement the Bi-Affine parser [8] and apply the cross-entropy plus with an l_2 regularization as the loss function of our models:

$$L(\theta) = \begin{cases} p^*_g = \frac{exp(\mathbf{s}^*_g)}{\sum exp(\mathbf{s}^{*'})} \\ -log(p^*_g) + \frac{\beta}{2}||\theta||^2 \end{cases} \tag{5}$$

where p^*_g means the probabilities of gold arcs, labels and domain, respectively; θ represents the model parameters of parser.

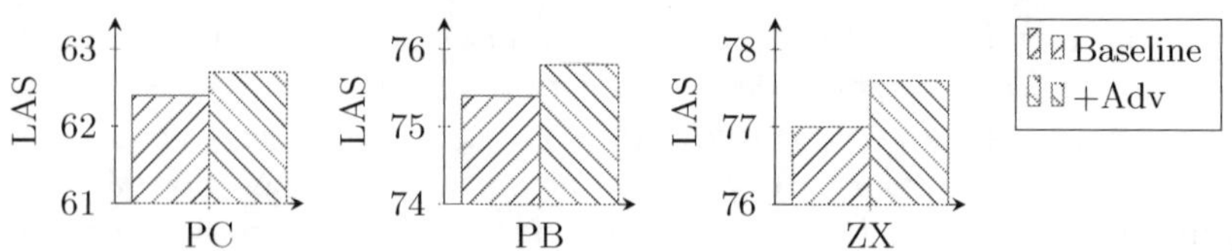

Fig. 2. The influence of adversarial learning.

4 Experiments

4.1 Settings

Data. We conduct our experiments on NLPCC2019 shared task corpus [22], which has four domains: Balanced Corpus (BC, text selected from HLT-CDT and PennCTB treebanks), Products Comments (PC, from Taobao), Product Blogs (PB, from Taobao headlines), and the web fiction "Zhuxian(ZX)". The BC is the source domain, and others are target domains.

Evaluation. We apply two standard evaluation methods to test our models, including unlabeled attachment scores (UAS) and labeled attachment scores (LAS). The UAS is the precision of the arcs without labels, and the LAS is the precision of the arcs with relation labels.

4.2 Results

There are two subtasks in the NLPCC2019 shared task: un-supervised and semi-supervised domain adaptation. The difference of two subtasks is whether can use the target domain training data. For example, when the target domain is PC, un-supervised task can only use the BC training data and PC unlabeled data to train the models. The semi-supervised task can add PC training data to original training data. Both two subtasks can only use PC development to fine-tune the models. In this section, we show three several factors of our models by conducting several sets of experiments in semi-supervised domain adaptation settings only.

Adversarial Training. First, we apply the adversarial training to enhance our baseline model according to Eq. 2. We exploit constant factor $\lambda = 10^{-5}$ according to development experiments. Figure 2 shows the influence of the adversarial learning. When adversarial learning is exploited, our model achieves at 77.7 on LAS in ZX domains. And resulting overall improvements $77.7 - 77.0 = 0.7$ LAS. The PC and PB domains have similar tendencies as well.

Ensemble. Then, we train three basic parsers for every domain by same original training data and a different random seed. And we apply the ensemble to average the arc and label probabilities from three basic models according to Eq. 4. The results are shown in Table 1, we can see the ensemble is the effective method for dependency parsing.

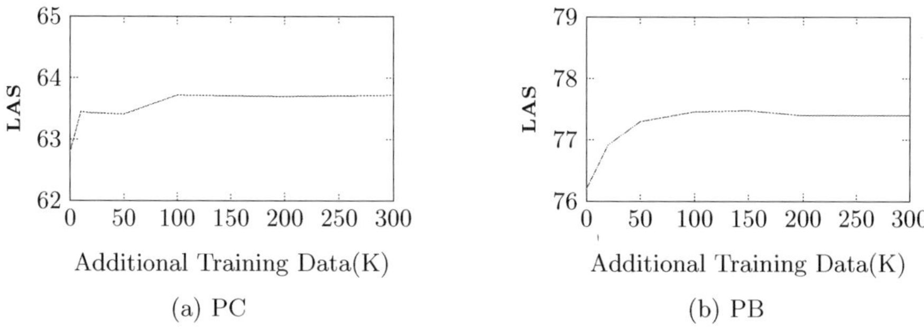

Fig. 3. The influence of different quantities of additional training data.

Ensemble-Style Self-training. Then we examine the strategy of ensemble-style self-training. The amount of additional training data is a key factor for it. In Fig. 3, the performances are relatively stable surrounding 100 k additional training data, where all domains under both settings are close to their peak values. Thus we random select 100k additional training data as the final setting. The ZX domain has only 30k additional training, so we use all of them in self-training.

Table 1. The performances of ensemble. The Baseline$_*$ means the performances of baseline models, the Ensemble means the performances of ensemble method.

	PC(UAS/LAS)	PB(UAS/LAS)	ZX(UAS/LAS)
Baseline$_1$	70.0/62.0	80.5/75.4	81.4/77.0
Baseline$_2$	70.3/62.4	80.4/75.4	81.2/77.0
Baseline$_3$	70.4/62.2	80.1/75.2	81.8/77.0
Ensemble	**70.5/62.9**	**80.8/75.9**	**82.6/78.2**

Final Model. We combine the adversarial learning and the ensemble-style self-training to enhance the baseline models. The experiment results are shown in Table 2. We find both two methods can improve the baseline models. In ZX domain, the baseline model achieves 81.4 on UAS and 77.0 on LAS. When we apply the adversarial learning, and baseline can improve by $82.2 - 81.4 = 0.8$ UAS and $77.7 - 77.0 = 0.7$ LAS, when we use the ensemble-style self-training to utilize the data distribution information from unlabeled target domain data. Baseline can improve by $82.8 - 81.4 = 1.4$ UAS and $78.5 - 77.0 = 1.5$ LAS. Finally, when we combine both two methods to baseline models, we find that the baseline model can be improved by $83.2 - 81.4 = 1.8$ UAS and $79.0 - 77.0 = 2$ LAS. Both PC and PB domains have similar tendencies as well.

Table 2. The influence of adversarial learning and ensemble-style self-training in semi-supervised adaptation. +A means apply adversarial learning to baseline. +S means apply ensemble-style self-training to baseline. +A+S means combine the adversarial learning and ensemble-style self-training to baseline.

	PC(UAS/LAS)	PB(UAS/LAS)	ZX(UAS/LAS)
Baseline	70.6/62.4	80.1/75.4	81.4/77.0
+Adv	70.6/62.7	80.6/75.8	82.2/77.7
+S	**71.5/63.7**	81.8/77.3	82.8/78.5
+A+S	71.2/63.4	**82.6/78.2**	**83.2/79.0**

5 Conclusion

We described our models submitted in the NLPCC2019 shared task on cross-domain dependency parsing. First, we borrowed the Bi-Affine parser [8] as our baseline, and exploited the ensemble-style self-training method with a simple random data sample method. Second, we enhanced them with adversarial training. Final results show that our models are very competitive and achieve the top performances in all teams [22].

Acknowledgments. We thank our anonymous reviewers for their helpful comments. This work was supported by National Natural Science Foundation of China (Grant No. 61672211, U1836222).

References

1. Ballesteros, M., Dyer, C., Goldberg, Y., Smith, N.A.: Greedy transition-based dependency parsing with stack LSTMs. Comput. Linguist. **43**(2), 311–347 (2017)
2. Cerisara, C.: Semi-supervised experiments at LORIA for the SPMRL 2014 shared task. In: Proceedings of the Shared Task on Statistical Parsing of Morphologically Rich Languages (2014)
3. Chen, D., Manning, C.: A fast and accurate dependency parser using neural networks. In: Proceedings of the 2014 Conference on Empirical Methods in Natural Language Processing (EMNLP), pp. 740–750 (2014)
4. Chen, W., Wu, Y., Isahara, H.: Learning reliable information for dependency parsing adaptation. In: Proceedings of the 22nd International Conference on Computational Linguistics, vol. 1, pp. 113–120. Association for Computational Linguistics (2008)
5. Collobert, R., Weston, J., Bottou, L., Karlen, M., Kavukcuoglu, K., Kuksa, P.: Natural language processing (almost) from scratch. J. Mach. Learn. Res. **12**, 2493–2537 (2011)
6. Devlin, J., Zbib, R., Huang, Z., Lamar, T., Schwartz, R., Makhoul, J.: Fast and robust neural network joint models for statistical machine translation. In: Proceedings of the 52nd Annual Meeting of the Association for Computational Linguistics. Long Papers, vol. 1, pp. 1370–1380 (2014)

7. Dong, C., Schäfer, U.: Ensemble-style self-training on citation classification. In: Proceedings of 5th International Joint Conference on Natural Language Processing, pp. 623–631 (2011)
8. Dozat, T., Manning, C.D.: Deep biaffine attention for neural dependency parsing. arXiv preprint: arXiv:1611.01734 (2016)
9. Dozat, T., Qi, P., Manning, C.D.: Stanford's graph-based neural dependency parser at the CoNLL 2017 shared task. In: Proceedings of the CoNLL 2017 Shared Task: Multilingual Parsing from Raw Text to Universal Dependencies, pp. 20–30 (2017)
10. Dyer, C., Ballesteros, M., Ling, W., Matthews, A., Smith, N.A.: Transition-based dependency parsing with stack long short-term memory. arXiv preprint: arXiv:1505.08075 (2015)
11. Foster, J., et al.: # hardtoparse: pos tagging and parsing the twitterverse. In: Workshops at the Twenty-Fifth AAAI Conference on Artificial Intelligence (2011)
12. Ganin, Y., Lempitsky, V.: Unsupervised domain adaptation by backpropagation. arXiv preprint: arXiv:1409.7495 (2014)
13. Goutam, R., Ambati, B.R.: Exploring self training for Hindi dependency parsing. In: Proceedings of 5th International Joint Conference on Natural Language Processing, pp. 1452–1456 (2011)
14. Honnibal, M., Johnson, M.: An improved non-monotonic transition system for dependency parsing. In: Proceedings of the 2015 Conference on Empirical Methods in Natural Language Processing, pp. 1373–1378 (2015)
15. Jiang, X., Li, Z., Zhang, B., Zhang, M., Li, S., Si, L.: Supervised treebank conversion: data and approaches. In: Proceedings of the 56th Annual Meeting of the Association for Computational Linguistics. Long Papers, vol. 1, pp. 2706–2716 (2018)
16. Kawahara, D., Uchimoto, K.: Learning reliability of parses for domain adaptation of dependency parsing. In: Proceedings of the Third International Joint Conference on Natural Language Processing, vol. II (2008)
17. Kiperwasser, E., Goldberg, Y.: Simple and accurate dependency parsing using bidirectional LSTM feature representations. Trans. Assoc. Comput. Linguist. **4**, 313–327 (2016)
18. Kong, L., Schneider, N., Swayamdipta, S., Bhatia, A., Dyer, C., Smith, N.A.: A dependency parser for tweets. In: Proceedings of the 2014 Conference on Empirical Methods in Natural Language Processing (EMNLP), pp. 1001–1012 (2014)
19. Koo, T., Collins, M.: Efficient third-order dependency parsers. In: Proceedings of the 48th Annual Meeting of the Association for Computational Linguistics, pp. 1–11. Association for Computational Linguistics (2010)
20. Le Roux, J., Foster, J., Wagner, J., Kaljahi, R., Bryl, A.: DCU-Paris13 systems for the SANCL 2012 shared task (2012)
21. Pei, W., Ge, T., Chang, B.: An effective neural network model for graph-based dependency parsing. In: Proceedings of the 53rd Annual Meeting of the Association for Computational Linguistics and the 7th International Joint Conference on Natural Language Processing. Long Papers, vol. 1, pp. 313–322 (2015)
22. Peng, X., Li, Z., Zhang, M., Wang, R., Zhang, Y., Si, L.: Overview of the NLPCC 2019 shared task: cross-domain dependency parsing. In: Proceedings of The 8th CCF International Conference on Natural Language Processing and Chinese Computing (NLPCC 2019) (2019)
23. Petrov, S., McDonald, R.: Overview of the 2012 shared task on parsing the web (2012)

24. Plank, B., Søgaard, A.: Experiments in newswire-to-law adaptation of graph-based dependency parsers. In: Magnini, B., Cutugno, F., Falcone, M., Pianta, E. (eds.) EVALITA 2012. LNCS (LNAI), vol. 7689, pp. 70–76. Springer, Heidelberg (2013). https://doi.org/10.1007/978-3-642-35828-9_8
25. Sato, M., Manabe, H., Noji, H., Matsumoto, Y.: Adversarial training for cross-domain universal dependency parsing. In: Proceedings of the CoNLL 2017 Shared Task: Multilingual Parsing from Raw Text to Universal Dependencies, pp. 71–79 (2017)
26. Shareghi, E., Li, Y., Zhu, Y., Reichart, R., Korhonen, A.: Bayesian learning for neural dependency parsing. In: Proceedings of the 2019 Conference of the North American Chapter of the Association for Computational Linguistics: Human Language Technologies. Long and Short Papers, vol. 1, pp. 3509–3519 (2019)
27. Wang, W., Chang, B.: Graph-based dependency parsing with bidirectional LSTM. In: Proceedings of the 54th Annual Meeting of the Association for Computational Linguistics. Long Papers, vol. 1, pp. 2306–2315 (2016)
28. Zhang, M., Che, W., Liu, Y., Li, Z., Liu, T.: Hit dependency parsing: bootstrap aggregating heterogeneous parsers. In: Notes of the First Workshop on Syntactic Analysis of Non-Canonical Language (SANCL) (2012)
29. Zhang, Y., Clark, S.: A tale of two parsers: investigating and combining graph-based and transition-based dependency parsing using beam-search. In: Proceedings of the Conference on Empirical Methods in Natural Language Processing, pp. 562–571. Association for Computational Linguistics (2008)
30. Zhang, Y., Li, Z., Lang, J., Xia, Q., Zhang, M.: Dependency parsing with partial annotations: an empirical comparison. In: Proceedings of the Eighth International Joint Conference on Natural Language Processing. Long Papers, vol. 1, pp. 49–58 (2017)
31. Zhang, Y., Nivre, J.: Transition-based dependency parsing with rich non-local features. In: Proceedings of the 49th Annual Meeting of the Association for Computational Linguistics: Human Language Technologies. Short Papers, vol. 2, pp. 188–193. Association for Computational Linguistics (2011)
32. Zhou, H., Zhang, Y., Huang, S., Chen, J.: A neural probabilistic structured-prediction model for transition-based dependency parsing. In: Proceedings of the 53rd Annual Meeting of the Association for Computational Linguistics and the 7th International Joint Conference on Natural Language Processing. Long Papers, vol. 1, pp. 1213–1222 (2015)
33. Zhou, Z.H., Li, M.: Tri-training: exploiting unlabeled data using three classifiers. IEEE Trans. Knowl. Data Eng. **11**, 1529–1541 (2005)

Overview of the NLPCC 2019 Shared Task: Open Domain Semantic Parsing

Nan Duan(✉)

Microsoft Research Asia, Beijing, China
nanduan@microsoft.com

Abstract. Semantic Parsing is a key problem for many artificial intelligence tasks, such as information retrieval, question answering and dialogue system. In this paper, we give the overview of the open domain semantic parsing shared task in NLPCC 2019. We first review existing semantic parsing datasets. Then, we describe open domain semantic parsing shared task in this year's NLPCC, especially focusing on the dataset construction. The evaluation results of submissions from participating teams are presented in the experimental part.

Keywords: Semantic parsing · Natural language understanding · MSParS

1 Background

Semantic parsing aims to transform a natural language utterance into a machine executable meaning representation. It is one of the core technologies for building human-machine interaction engines, such as search, question answering and dialogue systems.

A number of semantic parsing datasets have been released in last decades, such as ATIS [1], JOBS [2], Geoquery [3], Free917 [4], WebQuestions [5], SimpleQuestions [6], and LC-QuAD [7]. However, these datasets are either limited by sizes and specific domains or biased on simple questions. ComplexWebQuestions [8] is a recently released semantic parsing dataset, which contains 34,689 questions with logical forms and focuses on 4 question types (multi-hop, multi-constraint, superlative and comparative). But as it uses WebQuestionsSP [9] as the seed for complex question generation, this dataset only covers 462 unique knowledge base (KB) predicates. WikiSQL [10] contains 80,654 <question, logical form> pairs, where each question is annotated based on one of 24,241 web tables. MSParS differs from WikiSQL in two ways: (i) MSParS is labeled based on a knowledge graph, while WikiSQL is labeled based on web tables. This leads to inference on MSParS posing a significant challenge as a knowledge graph is much more complicated than a single table; (ii) most questions in WikiSQL are multi-constraint ones, while MSParS contains more question types. In summary, the community lacks of a comprehensive semantic parsing dataset to evaluate semantic parsers from different perspectives.

J. Tang et al. (Eds.): NLPCC 2019, LNAI 11839, pp. 811–817, 2019.
https://doi.org/10.1007/978-3-030-32236-6_74

2 Dataset Description

Motivated by the situation discussed above, we propose MSParS, a Multi-perspective Semantic ParSing dataset, for the NLPCC 2019 open domain semantic parsing shared task.

MSParS covers 9 types of single-turn questions: single-relation, CVT, multi-hop, multi-constraint, Yes/No, multi-choice, superlative, aggregation, and comparative. Considering the additional 3 types of multi-turn questions (multi-turn-entity, multi-turn-predicate, multi-turn-answer), the total number of the question types is 12. For each question, MSParS provides three kinds of annotations: the logical form of the question, the question type, and the parameters, i.e., the entities, types or values mentioned in the question while occurred in the logical form. Each logical form in MSParS is in form of untyped lambda-calculus and built based on a knowledge base and some predefined functions. We construct MSParS by crowd sourcing with pre-defined logical form patterns. Figure 1 shows those patterns and question examples of 9 single-turn types and 3 multi-turn types.

Type	Question Example & Logical Form Pattern
single-relation	when was James Cameron born $\lambda x.p(e,x)$
multi-hop	what company produced film with director James Cameron $\lambda x.\exists y_0 \cdots y_n.p_0(e,y_0) \wedge \cdots \wedge p_i(y_i,y_{i+1}) \wedge \cdots \wedge p_n(y_n,x)$
multi-constraint	which movie directed by James Cameron and starred by Zoe Saldana $\lambda x.p_1(e_1,x) \wedge \cdots \wedge p_n(e_n,x)$
CVT	Redskins had how many losses in 1997 NFL season $\lambda x.\exists y.p_0(e_0,y) \wedge p_1(y,e_1) \wedge \cdots \wedge p_n(y,e_n) \wedge p_{n+1}(y,x)$
Yes/No	is the Kalindula a kind of guitar instrument $p(e_1,e_2)$
multi-choice	was it Bill Gates or Steve Jobs that created Microsoft $\lambda x.p(e,x) \wedge ((x == e_1) \vee \cdots \vee (x == e_n))$
superlative	largest lake in the world $f_{max}(\lambda x.p_1(x,e_1) \wedge \cdots \wedge p_n(x,e_n), \lambda x.\lambda y.p(x,y), v)$
comparative	rocket engine with height taller than 2.6 $f_{comp}(\lambda x.p_1(x,e_1) \wedge \cdots \wedge p_n(x,e_n), \lambda x.\lambda y.p(x,y), v)$
aggregation	how many movie has James Cameron directed $f_{sum}(\lambda x.p(e,x))$
multi-turn-entity	when was James Cameron born ### which movie he directed $\lambda x_1.p_1(e,x_1)$ ### $\lambda x_2.p_2(e,x_2)$
multi-turn-predicate	when was James Cameron born ### how about Bill Gates $\lambda x_1.p(e_1,x_1)$ ### $\lambda x_2.p(e_2,x_2)$
multi-turn-answer	when was James Cameron born ### which movie released on that day $\lambda x_1.p_1(e,x_1)$ ### $\lambda x_2.p_2(x_1,x_2) \wedge \lambda x_1.p_1(e,x_1)$

Fig. 1. Examples for each question type, including natural language question and its logical form pattern.

Next, we will introduce how single-turn questions and multi-turn questions are annotated respectively.

Single-Turn Data Construction

Given a specific question type and a corresponding logical form template, we generate the <question, logical form> pairs through 4 steps including

(1) KB subgraph sampling,
(2) seed question annotation/generation,
(3) question paraphrasing/composition,
(4) logical form generation.

Figure 2 use an example to show how we annotate multi-hop questions. Other types of questions are annotated in a similar way.

The logical form of a multi-hop question q has the following format:

$$\lambda x.\exists y_0 \ldots y_n . p_0(e, y_0) \wedge \ldots \wedge p_i(y_i, y_{i+1}) \wedge \ldots \wedge p_n(y_n, x)$$

where e is an entity mentioned by q, $p_0, \ldots, p_n$ are predicates expressed by q, $y_0, \ldots, y_n$ are hidden variables, and x is the answer variable.

For example, *when is the birthday of Google's founder* is a multi-hop question, whose logical form is $\lambda x.\exists y.organization\_founder(Google, y) \wedge person\_birthday(y, x)$.

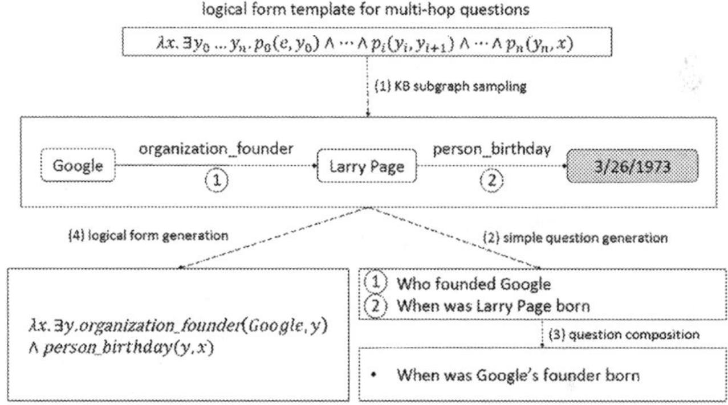

Fig. 2. Multi-hop question build workflow.

In the KB subgraph sampling step, we select valid multi-hop subgraphs from KB automatically. Each subgraph consists of two KB triples, where the object entity of the first triple is the subject entity of the second triple. Then, a template-based question generation component is used to generate two natural language questions for these two triples in the subgraph, where the answer of each generated question is the corresponding object entity. Note we annotate the seed questions for some other types by human expert instead of the QG component. In the third step, crowd sourcing annotators compose these two questions to form a multi-hop question. The annotators are also asked to paraphrase the questions to increase the diversity. Finally we translate the sampled KB subgraph into a semantic equivalent logical form, i.e., untyped lambda-calculus, and combine it with the annotated questions to compose the final <question, logical form> pairs.

Multi-turn Data Construction

In multi-turn semantic parsing task, translating a question q_i into logical form l_i relies on the former question q_{i-1} and logical form l_{i-1}. Specifically, $l_i = \{x_1, x_2, \ldots, x_{|l|}\}$ contains a sub-sequence x_{ij} where $x_{ij} \in l_{i-1}$ and x_{ij} can not be obtained from q_i directly.

In MSParS, we construct 3 types of multi-turn data according to the role of the "lending" item x_{ij}, i.e., the entity, predicate and answer. Figure 3 shows the build workflow of multi-turn-entity data. In the KB subgraph sampling step, we select two triples t_1, t_2 shared a same entity "Titanic". The two triples support two turn of semantic parsing separately. In the question annotation step an expert annotate two seed questions according to t_1 and t_2. Note that the shared entity "Titanic" can not be used when generating the second turn question. After that, the crowd sourcing workers are asked to rewrite the seed questions, i.e., question paraphrasing. Finally, the two triples are translated into two logical forms. We combine them with the annotated questions to compose the final <q_1&q_2, l_1&l_2> pairs.

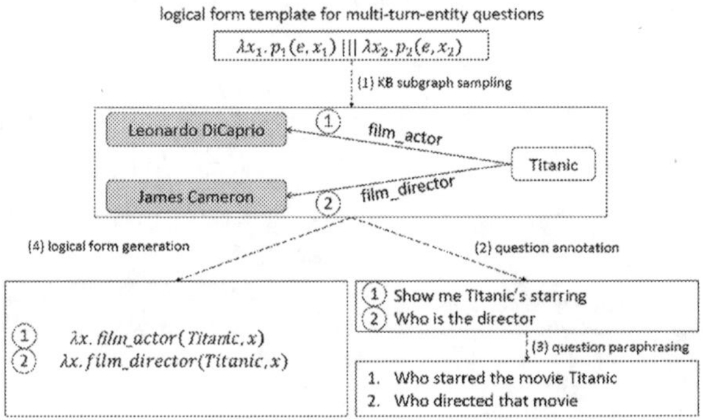

Fig. 3. Multi-turn-entity question build workflow.

Data Statistic

Figure 4 gives the statistics of MSParS, from which several characteristics can be seen. First, 41.9% questions in MSParS are single-relation questions. This is by-design, as most KB-answerable complex questions can be decomposed into a set of single-relation questions. By providing enough training data to single-relation questions, both simple questions and complex questions benefit. Second, all 81,826 questions in MSParS come from 48,917 unique question patterns based on 9,150 unique logical form patterns. It indicates that the diversity of this dataset is good, and the trained semantic parser could be robust to the paraphrases of identical meaning representations. Third, the entities occurring in MSParS are very rich as well. It makes MSParS a very challenging semantic parsing dataset. It also can be considered a new dataset for entity mention detection.

Question Type	Statistics						Train/Dev/Test Distribution		
	# Q	# E	# LFP	# QP	AvgLen Q	AvgLen LF	# train	# Dev	# Test
single-relation	34,316	18,038	1,256	25,741	7.4	9	26,955	3,727	3,634
multi-hop	7,452	1,936	690	2,043	10.6	19	5,938	780	734
multi-constraint	2,601	2,960	415	833	12.9	17	2,029	293	279
cvt	5,115	4,027	724	1,710	11.4	24	3,849	619	647
yesno	2,688	2,386	564	1,257	12	5	2,086	300	302
multi-choice	1,344	2,376	876	1,317	17	25	1,071	134	139
aggregation	7,710	6,601	256	1,649	9	10	5,871	906	933
superlative	8,429	6,506	222	2,625	6.3	26	6,623	898	908
comparative	357	254	48	168	8.2	24	268	46	43
multi-turn-entity	9,617	6,317	3,790	9,405	14.6	19	7,362	1,091	1,164
multi-turn-predicate	893	1,734	169	873	13.9	18	706	100	87
multi-turn-answer	1,304	1,287	140	1,296	13.3	29	1,068	106	130
Overall	81,826	46,733	9,150	48,917	9.5	14.7	63,826	9,000	9,000

Fig. 4. Statistics and train/dev/test distribution of MSParS.

We split MSParS into three parts: train set, dev set, and test set. Generally, data in this three sets are unbiased. The distributions of question types are listed in Fig. 4. The ratios of each question type are almost the same in three different datasets. Similarly, we keep the predicate frequencies of each dataset are balanced. In other words, we try to make sure that each predicate or logical form pattern is occurred in all the three datasets. The unbiased distributions benefits to verify the performance utilizing dev set when training the models on the train set. This data splitting is based on the following two rules: (1) questions sharing the same question patterns will NOT spread over different datasets. This is important as we do not want the semantic parsing to output correct results just by remembering the question patterns; and (2) if a logical form has less than three question patterns, then we will put them into train and dev sets only, instead of a test set. By doing so, every logical form pattern in the test set must occur in both train and dev sets, which makes semantic parsing evaluation reasonable.

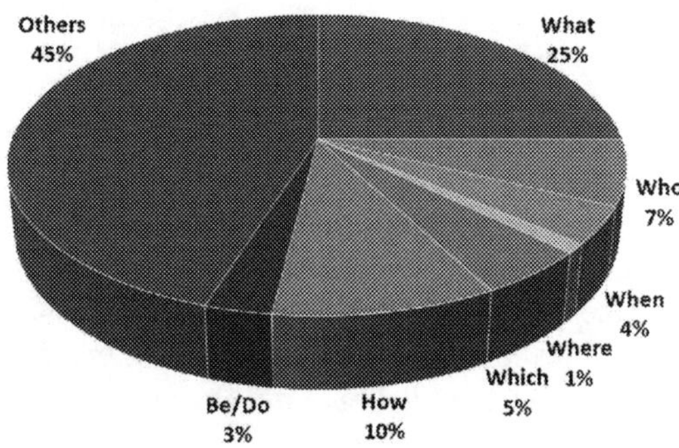

Fig. 5. Question distribution of MSParS.

Figure 5 gives the question distribution based on interrogative words. Be/Do denotes the questions starting from *is*, *are*, *was*, *were*, *do*, *does*, and *did*. Others denotes questions starting from none of these interrogative words listed in the figure, which are usually keyword queries. We randomly sample 100 examples to evaluate the quality of MSParS. Quality evaluation results show that all the questions are answerable since the logical forms are all executable, while 3% of the labeled questions contain some typo errors or spelling mistakes.

3 Evaluation Result

There are totally 25 teams registered for the open domain semantic parsing task, and 6 teams submitted final results. As we provide enough annotations in training data, most participating teams can fully leverage such information and achieved good results on the full test set. Therefore, we also select a hard subset for the full test set to further check the performances of different semantic parsers. Table 1 lists the rankings and scores of these 6 teams:

Table 1. Final submissions.

Team ID	Organization	ACC (full set)	ACC (hard subset)
Soochow_SP	苏州大学	0.8568	0.5743
NP-Parser	School of Electronics Engineering and Computer Science, PKU	0.8373	0.5193
WLIS	PIE Group, 北京大学计算机科学技术研究所	0.8253	0.4783
Binbin Deng	Fudan University	0.6882	0.3541
kg_nlpca_ai_lr	AI lab, Lenovo Research Institute	0.3079	0.1489
TriJ	大连理工大学计算机科学与技术学院,信息检索实验室	0.2677	0.1449

We also check the technique reports of the first two systems. The Soochow_SP team achieves the 1st place in the open domain semantic parsing task. A transformer-based encoder-decoder framework is used for LF generation, where the number of layers in both encoder and decoder is 6. To alleviate the in-balanced question type issue, the authors proposed a synthetic training method, where new questions are generated by either replacing an entity of an original question with a new one with the same type, or replacing the type of a given entity with another valid one. The NP-Parser team uses a sketch-based method. First, LF template is selected based on each input question. Then, missing entities are filled into the LF template to form a complete an LF. Last, a seq-to-seq model is used to re-rank different LF candidates. This paper achieves the best result on the hard subset of the test set, although after the shared task deadline.

4 Conclusion

This paper briefly introduces the overview of this year's Open Domain Semantic Parsing shared task. We see promising results and different techniques used. We are looking forward more organizations can take part in this yearly activity, and more benchmark data sets and techniques will be delivered to the community.

References

1. Hemphill, C.T., Godfrey, J.J., Doddington, G.R.: The ATIS spoken language systems pilot corpus. In: Speech and Natural Language: Proceedings of a Workshop Held at Hidden Valley, Pennsylvania, 24–27 June 1990
2. Tang, L.R., Mooney, R.J.: Using multiple clause constructors in inductive logic programming for semantic parsing. In: Machine Learning: EMCL 2001, Proceedings of the 12th European Conference on Machine Learning, Freiburg, 5–7 September 2001, pp. 466–477 (2001)
3. Zelle, J.M., Mooney, R.J.: Learning to parse database queries using inductive logic programming. In: Proceedings of the Thirteenth National Conference on Artificial Intelligence and Eighth Innovative Applications of Artificial Intelligence Conference, AAAI 1996, IAAI 1996, Portland, 4–8 August 1996, vol. 2, pp. 1050–1055 (1996)
4. Cai, Q., Yates, A.: Large-scale semantic parsing via schema matching and lexicon extension. In: Proceedings of the 51st Annual Meeting of the Association for Computational Linguistics, ACL 2013, 4–9 August 2013, Sofia, Volume 1: Long Papers, pp. 423–433 (2013)
5. Berant, J., Chou, A., Frostig, R., Liang, P.: Semantic parsing on freebase from question-answer pairs. In: Proceedings of the 2013 Conference on Empirical Methods in Natural Language Processing, EMNLP 2013, 18–21 October 2013, Grand Hyatt Seattle, A meeting of SIGDAT, a Special Interest Group of the ACL, pp. 1533–1544 (2013)
6. Bordes, A., Usunier, N., Chopra, S., Weston, J.: Large-scale simple question answering with memory networks. CoRR, abs/1506.02075 (2015)
7. Trivedi, P., Maheshwari, G., Dubey, M., Lehmann, J.: LC-QuAD: a corpus for complex question answering over knowledge graphs. In: The Semantic Web - ISWC 2017 - Proceedings of the 16th International Semantic Web Conference, Part II, Vienna, 21–25 October 2017, pp. 210–218 (2017)
8. Talmor, A., Berant, J.: The web as a knowledge-base for answering complex questions. In: Proceedings of the 2018 Conference of the North American Chapter of the Association for Computational Linguistics: Human Language Technologies, NAACL-HLT 2018, New Orleans, 1–6 June 2018, vol. 1 (Long Papers), pp. 641–651 (2018)
9. Yih, W.-t., Richardson, M., Meek, C., Chang, M.-W., Suh, J.: The value of semantic parse labeling for knowledge base question answering. In: Proceedings of the 54th Annual Meeting of the Association for Computational Linguistics, ACL 2016, 7–12 August 2016, Berlin, Volume 2: Short Papers (2016)
10. Zhong, V., Xiong, C., Socher, R.: Seq2SQL: generating structured queries from natural language using reinforcement learning. CoRR, abs/1709.00103 (2017)

An Overview of the 2019 Language and Intelligence Challenge

Quan Wang(✉), Wenquan Wu, Yabing Shi, Hongyu Li, Zhen Guo, Wei He, Hongyu Liu, Ying Chen, Yajuan Lyu, and Hua Wu

Baidu Inc., Beijing, China
{wangquan05,wuwenquan01,shiyabing01,lihongyu04,guozhenguozhen,hewei23, liuhongyu02,chenying04,lvyajuan,wu_hua}@baidu.com

Abstract. This paper provides an overview of the 2019 Language and Intelligence Challenge (LIC 2019), which assesses the ability of machines to understand language and use language to interact with humans. The challenge comprised three tasks: information extraction (IE), knowledge-driven dialogue, and machine reading comprehension (MRC), all providing large-scale Chinese datasets and open-source baseline systems. There were 2,376 teams that took part in the challenge, with a total of 6,212 system runs submitted. The participating systems performed quite well, offering a 21.65% increase over the baseline in IE, a 37.40% increase in the dialogue task, and a 34.09% increase in MRC.

Keywords: Language understanding and interaction · Information extraction · Knowledge-driven dialogue · Machine reading comprehension

1 Introduction

Language is the most important medium for communication in human life. Building machines that could understand language and use it to interact with humans is a central goal of artificial intelligence. Towards this goal, the China Computer Federation (CCF), Chinese Information Processing Society of China (CIPS), and Baidu Inc. jointly organized the 2019 Language and Intelligence Challenge (LIC 2019). The challenge assesses the ability of machines to understand natural language text, automatically extract knowledge from it, and use the learned knowledge to answer questions or hold conversations with humans.

LIC 2019 was set up with three tasks: (i) *Information Extraction* that requires systems to automatically extract structured knowledge from natural language text; (ii) *Knowledge-driven Dialogue* that requires systems to have conversations with humans based upon a given knowledge graph; and (iii) *Machine Reading Comprehension* that requires systems to read natural language text and answer questions about the given text. All the three tasks provided large-scale Chinese datasets, as well as baseline systems implemented in PaddlePaddle.[1]

[1] http://paddlepaddle.org.

J. Tang et al. (Eds.): NLPCC 2019, LNAI 11839, pp. 818–828, 2019.
https://doi.org/10.1007/978-3-030-32236-6_75

There were 2,376 teams that took part in the challenge, with a total of 6,212 system runs submitted. About 60% of the participants came from universities and research institutes at home and abroad, and the other 40% came from over 300 enterprises. The results of participating systems are promising. Compared against the baselines, the top-1 system performs 21.65% better in the information extraction task, 37.40% better in the knowledge-driven dialogue task, and 34.09% better in the machine reading comprehension task.

LIC 2019 has greatly advanced the technical development of natural language understanding and interaction. The infrastructure, including the datasets, baseline systems, and evaluation mechanisms, has been made publicly available to provide a good basis for future research in related areas.[2,3,4]

2 Tasks

LIC 2019 comprised three tasks: Information Extraction (IE), Knowledge-driven Dialogue, and Machine Reading Comprehension (MRC), detailed as follows.

2.1 Information Extraction

Information Extraction is to let machines automatically extract structured knowledge such as entities, attributes and relations from unstructured or semi-structured text. It is an important foundation for artificial intelligent application such as information retrieval, intelligent question answering, and intelligent dialogue, and has been widely concerned by the industry. The task provided a large-scale high-quality manually annotated information extraction dataset, DuIE, which aims to promote the development of information extraction technology.

Task Definition. Given a sentence *sent* and a list of pre-defined schemas which define relation P and its corresponding classes of subject S and object O. The participant system is required to output all correct triples mentioned in *sent* under the constraints of given schemas.

Dataset. DuIE dataset is the largest open-domain Chinese information extraction dataset, containing more than 450,000 instances in over 210,000 real-world Chinese sentences, bounded by a pre-specified schema with 49 predicates.

DuIE is generated by Baidu Baike and Baidu News Feeds as corpus to align with Baidu Baike Infobox as KB. Each sample in DuIE contains one sentence and a set of associated triples mentioned in the sentence. The dataset is divided into a training set (170 k sentences), a development set (20 k sentences) and a testing set (20 k sentences). The training set and the development set were used

[2] http://ai.baidu.com/broad/subordinate?dataset=sked.
[3] https://ai.baidu.com/broad/introduction?dataset=duconv.
[4] https://ai.baidu.com//broad/introduction?dataset=dureader.

for training and validating the model, the testing set was used for participants to submit the prediction result and used as the final evaluation for ranking. We further added 80k sentences as pseudo noises to rule out tuning against the test set. Table 1 provides the statistics of the dataset in detail.

Table 1. Statistics of the information extraction dataset.

Dataset	Total amount	Training set	Dev set	Testing set
#Sentence	214,739	173,108	21,639	19,992
#Instance	458,184	364,218	45,577	48,389

Baseline System. This task provided participants with an open source baseline system implemented in PaddlePaddle.[5] Baseline system separates this task into a pipelined architecture with relation classification and subject-object labeling, which significantly improved the performance of the extraction model.

Evaluation Metrics. Standard *Precision*, *Recall* and $F1$ score were adopted as the basic evaluation metrics to evaluate the performance of participating systems, while the final grade is ranked according to the F1 value. A triple predicted by participant systems will be regarded as correct when its relation and two corresponding entities are both exactly matched with the true triple annotated on the testing set. In addition, considering the cases of alias in sentences, we used a dictionary of entity alias in Baidu Knowledge Graph in the evaluation.

2.2 Knowledge-Driven Dialogue

Human-machine conversation is an important topic in AI and has received much attention in recent years. Currently dialogue system is still in its infancy, which usually converses passively and utters their words more as a matter of response rather than on their own initiatives, which is different from human-human conversation. Thus we set up a new conversation task, named knowledge-driven dialogue, where machines converse with humans based on a built knowledge graph (KG). It aims at testing machines' ability to conduct human-like conversations.

Task Definition. Given a dialogue goal G and a set of topic-related background knowledge $M = f_1, f_2, \cdots, f_n$, a participating system is expected to output an utterance u_t for the current conversation $H = u_1, u_2, \cdots, u_{t-1}$, which keeps the conversation coherent and informative under the guidance of the given goal. During the dialogue, a participating system is required to proactively lead the conversation from one topic to another. The dialog goal G is given like this: "*[start]* → *topic_a* → *topic_b*", which means the machine should lead the conversation from any start state to "*topic_a*" and then to "*topic_b*". The given

[5] https://github.com/baidu/information-extraction.

background knowledge includes knowledge related to "*topic_a*" and "*topic_b*", and the relations between these two topics.

Dataset. We created a new dataset named DuConv [7]. The background knowledge provided in the dataset was collected from MTime.com[6], which records the information of films and stars, such as box offices, directors, reviews, etc. We constructed a KG with collected knowledge organized as triplets {Subject, Predicate, Object}, where objects can be factoid facts and non-factoid sentences such as comments and synopsis. Table 2(a) lists the statistics of our KG.

Given the KG, we sampled some knowledge paths, used as conversation goals. Specifically, we focused on the simple but challenging scenario: naturally shifting the topics twice, i.e., from "*[start]*" state to "*topic_a*" then finally to "*topic_b*". We sampled two linked entities in our KG as '*topic_a*" and "*topic_b*" to construct the knowledge path. About 30k different knowledge paths were sampled and used as conversation goals for knowledge-driven conversation crowdsourcing.

Table 2. Overview of DuConv.

(a) Statistics of Knowledge

# entities	143627
# movies	91874
# person names	51753
# properties	45
# spo	3598246
average # spo per entity	25

(b) Statistics of Dialogues

# dialogs	29858
# utterances	270399
average # utterances per dialog	9.1
average # words per utterance	10.6
average # words per dialog	96.2
average # knowledge per dialog	17.1

Unlike using self-play in dataset construction [1], we collected lots of crowdsourced workers to generate the dialogues in DuConv[7]. For each given conversation goal, we assigned two workers different roles: (1) the conversation leader and (2) the follower. The leader was provided with the conversation goal and its related background knowledge in our knowledge graph, and then asked to naturally shift the conversation topic following the given conversation goal. The follower was provided with nothing but the dialogue history and only had to respond to the leader. The dialogue will not stop until the leader achieves the conversation goal. We recorded conversation utterances together with the related knowledge triplets and the knowledge path, to construct the whole dataset of DuConv. Table 2(b) summarizes the main information about DuConv. The data was divided into training, development, and test sets by 80%, 10%, 10%.

---

[6] http://www.mtime.com.

[7] The workers were collected from a Chinese crowdsourcing platform http://test.baidu.com/. The workers were paid 2.5 Chinese Yuan per conversation.

Baseline System. This task provided participants with two open-sourced baseline systems[8]: retrieval-based and generation-based systems, implemented by PaddlePaddle. To enable dialogue systems to converse with external background knowledge, the baseline systems were incorporated an external memory module for storing all related knowledge, making the models select appropriate knowledge to enable proactive conversations [7]. Our baseline systems can make full use of related knowledge to generate more diverse multi-turn conversations.

Evaluation Metrics. The participating systems were tested under two settings: (1) automatic evaluation and (2) human evaluation. For automatic evaluation, in addition to BLEU1/2 and DISTINCT1/2 which measure the relevance and diversity, we also used F1 to measure the char-based F-score of output utterance against reference utterance. The total score of F1 and BLEU1/2 was used for ranking participating systems. DISTINCT1/2 were used as auxiliary metrics.

The top 10 systems in automatic evaluation phrase were further evaluated by human on dialogue-level goal completion and coherence. Firstly, each system was required to converse with human to generate multi-turn dialogue given a conversation goal and the related knowledge. For each system, 100 dialogues were generated. Then the generated dialogues were manually evaluated to measure the goal completion and coherence. Goal completion has three grades: "0" means that the goal is not achieved, "1" the goal is achieved by making minor use of knowledge, and "2" the goal is achieved with full use of knowledge. Coherence has four grades: bad(0), fair(1), good(2) and perfect(3). The total score of normalized goal completion and coherence was used for the final ranking.

2.3 Machine Reading Comprehension

This task requires machines to read natural language text and answer questions about the given text. It is a crucial task in language understanding and also an important component of human-machine interaction. Last year, CCF, CIPS, and Baidu Inc. jointly organized the 2018 NLP Challenge on MRC, and the winning systems could answer more than 75% of the questions correctly [4]. LIC 2019 continued to set up the task, focusing on difficult questions that current systems fail to answer correctly.

Task Definition. Given a question Q and a set of documents $\mathcal{D} = \{d_1, d_2, \cdots, d_n\}$, the participating system is required to output an answer A that best answers Q based on knowledge from $\mathcal{D}$.

Dataset. The data was collected from DuReader [2], a large-scale, open-domain Chinese MRC dataset. In DuReader, all questions are sampled from anonymized user queries submitted to Baidu Search. Each question gets five documents collected from search results of Baidu Search and Baidu Zhidao, from which answers

[8] https://github.com/baidu/knowledge-driven-dialogue.

are manually generated. Questions are further divided into three types: *Description*, *Entity*, and *YesNo*. Entity answers (a single entity or a list of entities) and opinion answers (affirmation or negation) are further provided for Entity and YesNo questions, respectively. See [2] for a detailed description of DuReader.

The data was divided into training, development, and test sets. The training set, consisting of all training examples from DuReader, is the same as that used in the 2018 contest. The development and test sets consist of difficult questions that the winning systems in the 2018 contest failed to answer correctly. Specifically, for each question, we compared the quality of its system answers against human answers. Questions on which the ROUGE-L [3] score of the former lags behind that of the latter by 10 points or more were taken as difficult ones. For questions in the test set, we computed the average ROUGE-L of the top 6 winning systems in last year's contest. For questions in the development set where answers of the top 6 winning systems were not available, we picked an internal system used at Baidu which could rank among the top 3 in last year's contest and computed its ROUGE-L. In this way, we selected 3,311 questions from the original DuReader development set, and 8,996 questions from the original test set.

We further used manual annotation to judge whether the selected questions fit the bill, i.e., answerable by humans but difficult for machines. Given a question selected, we provided to an annotator a human answer and a system answer at the same time. The system answer was the one with the lowest ROUGE-L among the top 6 winning systems on the test set, and the one generated by the internal system on the development set. The annotator was then asked to judge whether there is a gap between the quality of the two answers, and to return one of the following labels: (i) the human answer is better; (ii) the system answer is better; and (iii) there is no gap between their quality. Each question was annotated by five annotators, and the majority was regarded as the final label. We selected questions with label "the human answer is better", resulting in 2,239 questions in the development set and 6,851 in the test set. We further added pseudo data to the test set to avoid exhaustive tuning. Table 3 lists the statistics of the data.

Table 3. Statistics of the machine reading comprehension dataset.

	Train	Dev	Test	Pseudo	Released test
Baidu Search	135,000	1,179	3,959	56,041	60,000
Baidu Zhidao	135,000	1,060	2,892	57,108	60,000
Total	270,000	2,239	6,851	113,149	120,000

Baseline System. This task provided participants with an open source baseline system based on BiDAF [6], implemented in PaddlePaddle.[9] BiDAF is a MRC model that achieved promising results on a variety of benchmarks.

[9] https://github.com/baidu/DuReader.

Evaluation Metrics. ROUGE-L [3] and BLEU-4 [5] were adopted as evaluation metrics, with the former used for ranking participating systems. We further made minor adaptations to the original metrics [8]. For Entity questions, correct entities mentioned in answers would receive additional reward. For YesNo questions, participants were expected to further predict the opinion of corresponding answers, and would receive additional bonus for correct predictions.

3 Organization and Participation

LIC 2019 took place between February and May 2019. The detailed schedule is:

- **Feb 25:** Registration opened, (partial) training and dev sets available;
- **Mar 31:** Registration closed, whole training and dev sets available, partial test set available, online evaluation opened;
- **May 13:** Whole test set available;
- **May 20:** Deadline of result submission, offline evaluation opened;
- **May 25:** Deadline of code submission for top 10 systems (only required for the knowledge-driven dialogue task);
- **May 31:** Notification of final rankings.

For all the tasks, test sets were released in two parts. The first part was released right after the registration deadline, used for online evaluation and ranking. The second part was released a week before the submission deadline. Performance on whole test sets was evaluated offline and used for final ranking. For the dialogue task, the top 10 systems were further required to submit their code for manual evaluation, by which final rankings and winners of this task were determined.

Overall, there were 2,376 teams that took part in the challenge, among which 1,836 participated in the IE task, 1,536 the dialogue task, and 1,553 the MRC task. About 60% of the participants came from universities, including 93 Project 211 universities at home and 28 universities abroad. The other 40% came from over 300 enterprises, e.g., NetEase, Kingsoft, and Samsung, etc.

During the evaluation phase (online and offline) 635 teams made valid submissions, with a total of 6,212 system runs submitted. The IE task got 3,367 submissions from 324 teams, the dialogue task 1,688 submissions from 178 teams, and the MRC task 1,157 submissions from 133 teams. Compared against the official baselines, the best performing system obtained an improvement of 21.65%, 37.40%, and 34.09% respectively on each task.

4 System Performance

LIC 2019 awarded one first prize, two second prizes and two third prizes for each task. This section presents the performance of these winning systems. Results of all participating systems are available on the official website.[10]

[10] http://lic2019.ccf.org.cn/.

Information Extraction. The overall evaluation results of the top 5 winning systems (S1–S5) are shown in Table 4. It can be seen that overall performances have been greatly improved, and the development of information technology has been promoted. With the F1 value, the top 1 system performance has a 21.65% (from 73.41% to 89.3%) improvement compared to the official baseline.

We further analyzed the evaluation results in different types of text sources. Table 5 presents the performance of the top 5 average and the top 10 average systems on encyclopedia and feed news separately. It can be seen that the performance of almost all participating systems on the encyclopedic text is better than the news text and the average F1 value of top 10 extraction systems on the encyclopedia text is 11.9% higher than that of the feed news. This shows that it is more difficult to extract news texts involved with diverse linguistic pattern.

Table 4. Evaluation results of the top 5 systems on information extraction.

System No.	Precision	Recall	F1
S1	89.75%	88.86%	89.3%
S2	89.62%	88.86%	89.24%
S3	89.76%	88.52%	89.14%
S4	89.48%	88.58%	89.03%
S5	89.24%	88.2%	88.72%
Baseline	**77.52%**	**69.72%**	**73.41%**

Table 5. Evaluation results in different sources of text.

	Encyclopedia			Feed News		
	Precision	Recall	F1	Precision	Recall	F1
Avg-top5	92.6%	92.3%	92.4%	82.4%	80.1%	81.2%
Avg-top10	92.2%	91.5%	91.9%	81.5%	78.6%	80.0%

Knowledge-Driven Dialogue. Tables 6 and 7 list the automatic evaluation and human evaluation results of the top 10 systems. From the results, we can see that the performance on proactive conversation has been effectively improved. The score increases by 36.99% from 0.919 to 1.259 for automatic evaluation metrics, and 37.40% from 1.287 to 1.768 for human evaluation metrics.

Table 7 shows that the conversation goals have been completed very well, with an average score of 1.85, close to the maximum score 2.0. However the conversation coherence is far from perfect, whose score is only 2.59 (the maximum score is 4). It indicates that the systems could complete the given goal in most case, but with some sacrifice of multi-turn coherence.

Table 6. Automatic evaluation results of top 10 systems on the dialogue task.

Rank	Team	Score	F1 (%)	BLEU1/2	DISTINCT1/2
1	DLUT&Dicalab	**1.259**	**49.22**	**0.449/0.318**	0.118/0.299
2	iDeepWise	1.204	47.76	0.430/0.296	0.110/0.275
3	CUP_NLP	1.175	46.40	0.422/0.289	0.118/0.303
4	bangda	1.169	47.03	0.417/0.281	0.113/0.290
5	DH-Pretender	1.159	46.01	0.420/0.279	0.118/0.307
6	fxnlp	1.149	46.03	0.417/0.271	**0.129/0.318**
7	wholly	1.148	45.74	0.420/0.271	0.096/0.248
8	travel	1.143	44.84	0.412/0.283	0.119/0.293
9	DG	1.134	45.48	0.414/0.266	0.095/0.229
10	AI 小奶娃	1.132	45.25	0.411/0.268	0.122/0.308
Baseline		0.919	37.69	0.347/0.198	0.057/0.155

Table 7. Human evaluation results of top 10 systems on the dialogue task.

Rank	Team	Score	Goal completion	Coherence
1	bangda	**1.768**	1.81	**2.59**
2	DLUT&Dicalab	1.732	**1.85**	2.42
3	fxnlp	1.720	1.80	2.46
4	iDeepWise	1.715	1.73	2.55
5	CUP_NLP	1.662	1.79	2.30
6	travel	1.602	1.73	2.21
7	wholly	1.587	1.76	2.12
8	DG	1.515	1.53	2.25
9	DH-Pretender	1.513	1.66	2.05
10	AI 小奶娃	1.503	1.72	1.93
Baseline		1.287	1.22	2.03

Machine Reading Comprehension Table 8 lists the performance of the top 5 winning systems (S1–S5), where Baidu Search and Baidu Zhidao indicate the results on questions whose documents were collected from the two channels, and Total the results on the whole test set. We can see that all the winning systems perform substantially better than the official baseline, with the ROUGE-L score pushed from 47.08% to 63.13%, i.e., a relative improvement of 34.09%. Despite this significant improvement, there is still a big gap between system and human answers. Building machines that can conduct in-depth language understanding and answer difficult questions is still a challenge.

Table 8. Results of top 5 winning systems on machine reading comprehension (%).

	Baidu Search		Baidu Zhidao		Total	
	ROUGE-L	BLEU-4	ROUGE-L	BLEU-4	ROUGE-L	BLEU-4
Human	**89.95**	**88.50**	**88.33**	**85.72**	**89.26**	**87.27**
S1	60.34	56.99	66.96	63.10	63.13	59.34
S2	56.54	58.01	64.31	61.15	59.82	59.34
S3	54.91	53.33	61.75	58.82	57.80	55.55
S4	53.84	54.89	61.32	61.08	57.00	57.30
S5	52.45	53.20	59.69	59.44	55.51	55.71
Baseline	**42.46**	**42.15**	**53.42**	**49.52**	**47.08**	**46.01**

Table 9. Results of top 5 winning systems on different query types (%).

	Description		Entity		YesNo	
	ROUGE-L	BLEU-4	ROUGE-L	BLEU-4	ROUGE-L	BLEU-4
Human	**91.50**	**89.65**	**84.75**	**76.83**	**87.26**	**87.89**
S1	64.08	61.34	62.97	51.68	56.87	56.59
S2	61.14	61.97	59.31	50.52	52.01	49.50
S3	58.78	58.47	58.25	46.31	49.46	47.42
S4	58.46	59.83	56.71	48.57	47.52	47.23
S5	56.37	58.42	56.25	47.74	47.11	45.78
Baseline	**47.85**	**47.87**	**47.18**	**37.40**	**41.30**	**30.80**

Table 9 further presents the performance of the winning systems on different query types. The results show that YesNo questions are more difficult for machines, while Entity questions are more difficult for humans.

5 Conclusion

The CCF, CIPS, and Baidu Inc. jointly organized the 2019 Language and Intelligence Challenge (LIC 2019), which comprised three tasks: Information Extraction, Knowledge-driven Dialogue, and Machine Reading Comprehension. There were 2,376 teams that participated in the challenge, with a total of 6,212 system runs submitted. The winning systems offered a 21.65% increase over the official baseline in information extraction, a 37.40% increase in knowledge-driven dialogue, and a 34.09% increase in machine reading comprehension. Although LIC 2019 has greatly advanced the technical development of natural language understanding and interaction, there are still many unsolved challenges, e.g., how to extract structured knowledge from news texts with diverse linguistic patterns, how to effectively evaluate the performance of a dialogue system, and how to conduct in-depth language understanding so as to answer difficult questions.

References

1. Ghazvininejad, M., Brockett, C., Chang, M.W., Dolan, B., Gao, J., Yih, W.t., Galley, M.: A knowledge-grounded neural conversation model. In: Thirty-Second AAAI Conference on Artificial Intelligence (2018)
2. He, W., et al.: DuReader: a Chinese machine reading comprehension dataset from real-world applications. In: Proceedings of the Workshop on Machine Reading for Question Answering, pp. 37–46 (2018)
3. Lin, C.Y.: ROUGE: a package for automatic evaluation of summaries. Text Summarization Branches Out (2004)
4. Liu, K., Liu, L., Liu, J., Lyu, Y., She, Q., Zhang, Q., Shi, Y.: Overview of 2018 NLP challenge on machine reading comprehension. J. Chin. Inf. Process. **32**(10), 118–129 (2018). (in Chinese)
5. Papineni, K., Roukos, S., Ward, T., Zhu, W.J.: BLEU: a method for automatic evaluation of machine translation. In: Proceedings of the 40th Annual Meeting on Association for Computational Linguistics, pp. 311–318 (2002)
6. Seo, M., Kembhavi, A., Farhadi, A., Hajishirzi, H.: Bidirectional attention flow for machine comprehension. In: International Conference on Learning Representations (2017)
7. Wu, W., et al.: Proactive human-machine conversation with explicit conversation goals. In: Proceedings of the 57th Annual Meeting of the Association for Computational Linguistics (Volume 1: Long Papers) (2019)
8. Yang, A., Liu, K., Liu, J., Yajuan, L., Li, S.: Adaptations of ROUGE and BLEU to better evaluate machine reading comprehension task. In: Proceedings of the Workshop on Machine Reading for Question Answering, pp. 98–104 (2018)

Overview of the NLPCC 2019 Shared Task: Open Domain Conversation Evaluation

Ying Shan, Anqi Cui(✉), Luchen Tan, and Kun Xiong

RSVP.ai, Waterloo, ON, Canada
{yshan,caq,lctan,kun}@rsvp.ai

Abstract. This paper presents an overview of the Open Domain Conversation Evaluation task in NLPCC 2019. The evaluation consists of two sub-tasks: Single-turn conversation and Multi-turn conversation. Each of the reply is judged from four to five dimensions, from syntax, contents to deep semantics. We illustrate the detailed problem definition, evaluation metrics, scoring strategy as well as datasets. We have built our dataset from commercial chatbot logs and public Internet. It covers a variety of 16 topical domains and two non-topical domains. We prepared to annotate all the data by human annotators, however, no teams submit their systems. This may due to the complexity of such conversation systems. Our baseline system achieves a single-round score of 55 out of 100 and a multi-round score of 292 out of 400. This indicates the system is more of an answering system rather than a chatting system. We would expect more participation in the succeeding years.

Keywords: Chatbot · Conversation systems · Conversation evaluation

1 Introduction

Natural language conversation as an advanced user interface has created a wide range of applications. Researchers have been working on different approaches to generate natural replies, including retrieval-based, end-to-end generation, question-answering and recommendation systems. We have already seen chatbots all around us, from smart home devices to smart phone assistants, from customer service to chatting. However, there is no standard to evaluate conversations. The quality of conversations varies from different applications and goals, and is sometimes very subjective.

This open problem has addressed much attention among researchers. Typically, conversation evaluation is treated from two sides: automatic scoring and human evaluations. While many are still exploring metrics to reflect conversation quality comprehensively, automatic models and algorithms are also studied in recent years [10].

Supported by China's National Key R&D Program of China 2018YFB1003202.

J. Tang et al. (Eds.): NLPCC 2019, LNAI 11839, pp. 829–834, 2019.
https://doi.org/10.1007/978-3-030-32236-6_76

Inspired from machine translation and summarization, metrics such as BLEU [9], METEOR [1] and ROUGE [5] are usually considered as baselines for conversations. However, they are still less informative and precise to reflect conversation quality both qualitatively and quantitatively [6,7]. Therefore, researchers begin to learn end-to-end scores to evaluate conversations' validity [2], topic coherency and diversity [3].

On the other hand, human annotations are still important and suitable for conversation evaluation. To reduce human subjectivity, the problem is usually narrowed down to either task-oriented or open domain [10]. Crowd-sourcing is also suitable to label a large amount of corpus [4], however, it is still difficult to collect standard annotations across different datasets (movie subtitles [2,8], switchboard corpus, tweets [7] or chatbot logs [3]).

In NLPCC 2019, we setup a task to evaluate human-computer conversations. All participating systems will be talking with human annotators, live user-in-the-loop. In the task, understanding natural language inputs (which can be questions or statements) is crucial, as well as providing smooth responses. The responses are evaluated from five aspects. We also provide human-annotated real data for researchers, to contribute to the community.

2 Task Description

We consider two scenarios:

2.1 Single-Turn Conversation

In this scenario, a set of natural language sentences is given to the participating systems. The systems should provide corresponding relies for each sentence just as human conversation.

2.2 Multi-turn Conversation

In this scenario, we begin with an initial sentence. Human testers will interact with participating systems manually.

3 Evaluation

Both the scenario tasks are designed to be evaluated by human assessors.

3.1 Single-Turn Conversation

We define five aspects used in the evaluation of participating systems:

1. Syntax: Correctness and smoothness of syntax.

2. Content Expression: Clear content without ambiguity. Appropriate amount of information. Esp. no inappropriate (violence, sexual, sensitive) content is allowed.
3. Emotional Expression: Subjective attitude or obvious moods. Causes mood changes (becoming glad or sad).
4. Topic Divergence: Mentioning new topics or entities, causing successive turns.
5. Contextual Association: Following the same topic from context, content or entities.

Some examples are illustrated in Table 1.

Table 1. Single-turn conversation evaluation aspects and examples.

<table>
<tr><th>Aspects</th><th>Good Cases</th><th>Bad Cases</th></tr>
<tr><td rowspan="2">Syntax</td><td>今天天气不错</td><td>今天天气错不</td></tr>
<tr><td>挺好的</td><td>好的挺</td></tr>
<tr><td rowspan="2">Content Expression</td><td rowspan="2">老虎有四条腿</td><td>嗯嗯（言之无物）</td></tr>
<tr><td>跳楼吧，像你这样我早就跳楼了（内容消极）</td></tr>
<tr><td rowspan="4">Emotional Expression</td><td>我好开心。</td><td>今天天气不错。</td></tr>
<tr><td>天哪，好疼啊！</td><td>好疼。</td></tr>
<tr><td colspan="2">问：你喜欢我吗？</td></tr>
<tr><td>答：我最喜欢你啦，么么哒～</td><td>答：嗯。</td></tr>
<tr><td rowspan="4">Topic Divergence</td><td colspan="2">问：今天好冷啊！</td></tr>
<tr><td>答：咱们去吃火锅吧。</td><td>答：是啊，好冷。</td></tr>
<tr><td colspan="2">问：你叫什么啊？</td></tr>
<tr><td>答：我叫张三，那你呢？</td><td>答：我叫张三。</td></tr>
<tr><td rowspan="4">Contextual Association</td><td colspan="2">问：你喜欢什么颜色？</td></tr>
<tr><td>答：红色。</td><td>答：苹果（不关联）</td></tr>
<tr><td colspan="2">问：你连上网了吗？</td></tr>
<tr><td>答：着啥急？</td><td>答：然后呢？（不自然）</td></tr>
</table>

Each aspect is judged by asking human assessors yes/no questions, scoring 1/0 respectively. Each reply will be judged by three human annotators separately.

For example, the Emotional Expression aspect has two evaluation metrics: (1) If the response has subjective attitude or obvious moods, earns one point. (2) If it causes changing of moods, earns one point. For a total of 200 test cases, with three annotators, the full score of Emotional Expression is $200 \times (1+1) \times 3 = 1200$ points. The participant's actual score (ranged between 0 and 1200) is then linearly converted to a max score of 100.

The overall score is the sum of scores from five aspects, a max of 500. We will rank the participants according to this score. In addition, we will also rank individual aspects, since different applications may focus on only a part of these aspects.

3.2 Multi-turn Conversation

The evaluation of multi-turn conversations consists of two categories. Each category contains two factors (with their scores shown below):

1. Single Turn Evaluation:
   (a) Logical Association (max 2 per turn): The association between question and response. Please refer to "Contextual Association" in Table 1.
   (b) Conversation Trigger (max 2 per turn): Whether or not the response could trigger another turn. Please refer to "Topic Divergence" in Table 1.
2. Multi-turn Evaluation:
   (a) Total Turns (2 per turn): Number of turns of this conversation (a question-answer pair is defined as one turn).
   (b) Total Topical Turns (2 per turn): Number of turns that have the same topic with the initial sentence.

During the testing, human testers will interact with participating systems. When the conversation ends (e.g. responding "OK.") or after the fifth turn has finished, the testers will stop. Annotators will label the whole conversations.

The overall score is the sum of all four aspects, at most $2 \times 4 \times 5 = 40$ points per topic.

4 Dataset

The dataset is adopted from commercial chatbot logs and public Internet social media conversations.

We classified them into 16 topical domains and two non-topical domains. For each topical domain, we selected 100 sentences and for the two non-topical domains, we selected 100 sentences altogether. In total, there are 1,700 sentences.

Before the evaluation, a sample conversation set (200 sentences and replies) is provided. The dataset contains the following columns:

- Column A: Input question (sentence).
- Column B: Sample reply.
- Column D: Number of annotators.
- Columns E – O: How many annotators agree on that metric for this reply.
- The last two lines (rows) of the file is an overall statistics on this dataset (200×3). Similarly, we will also evaluate participants' systems with this method.

The replies are provided by a baseline conversation system by *rsvp.ai*. Along with the sentence/reply pairs, human annotations of the replies are provided as well. When the evaluation begins, 500 sentences are used as our testing dataset. For the multi-turn evaluation, we only test with 20 (initial) sentences. The remaining sentences are posted for research purpose at the end of this evaluation, downloadable at https://github.com/RSVP-Technologies/nlpcc2019-conversation.

Considering the difficulty of open domain conversations, participants can use external resources to train or build their own conversation systems.

5 Evaluation Results

At the beginning of this task, a total of 18 teams registered for subtask Single-turn conversation and 19 teams for subtask Multi-turn conversation. About 15% teams are from companies and the rest are from colleges or institutions.

Unfortunately, none of the teams submit their system (API) at the end of the evaluation. Instead of showing the results of participants, here we list the scores from our baseline system:

5.1 Single-Turn Conversation

1. Syntax: To achieve a high Syntax score, the reply should not contain any offensive words. It also needs to be clear without ambiguity. The baseline system earns a point of $997/1200 = 83\%$.
2. Content Expression: We examine the reply with natural (not too formal) and appropriate amount of information (not too much nor too little). Our system has a point of $690/1200 = 58\%$.
3. Emotional Expression: Reply with obvious emotional expression, and leads reader to be happy/sad, for our system, $288/1200 = 24\%$.
4. Topic Divergence: The reply could motivate readers with more entities or more rounds of conversations: $538/1200 = 45\%$.
5. Contextual Association: The topic or entities continue in the reply. Our system has a point of $761/1200 = 63\%$.

Total: $83 + 58 + 24 + 45 + 63 = 273$ out of 500: 55%.

5.2 Multi-turn Conversation

We ask three experts to annotate our baseline system. Out of 20 initial sentences, our system generally interacts with people about 2.6 turns per seed, mostly under the same topic. The highest score of the interaction is 34/40. In total, the baseline system has an average score of 292 out of $40 \times 20 = 800$.

6 Conclusion

This paper briefly presents an overview of the Open Domain Conversation Evaluation task in NLPCC 2019. Detailed problem definition and evaluation design are introduced with samples. Although no participants submit their final results, we see this a pivot organization in conversation evaluations.

References

1. Banerjee, S., Lavie, A.: METEOR: an automatic metric for MT evaluation with improved correlation with human judgments. In: Proceedings of the ACL Workshop on Intrinsic and Extrinsic Evaluation Measures for Machine Translation and/or Summarization, pp. 65–72 (2005)

2. Bruni, E., Fernandez, R.: Adversarial evaluation for open-domain dialogue generation. In: Proceedings of the 18th Annual SIGdial Meeting on Discourse and Dialogue, pp. 284–288 (2017)
3. Guo, F., Metallinou, A., Khatri, C., Raju, A., Venkatesh, A., Ram, A.: Topic-based evaluation for conversational bots. arXiv preprint: arXiv:1801.03622 (2018)
4. Jurčíček, F., et al.: Real user evaluation of spoken dialogue systems using Amazon mechanical Turk. In: Twelfth Annual Conference of the International Speech Communication Association (2011)
5. Lin, C.Y.: Rouge: a package for automatic evaluation of summaries. In: Text Summarization Branches Out, pp. 74–81 (2004)
6. Liu, C.W., Lowe, R., Serban, I., Noseworthy, M., Charlin, L., Pineau, J.: How not to evaluate your dialogue system: an empirical study of unsupervised evaluation metrics for dialogue response generation. In: Proceedings of the 2016 Conference on Empirical Methods in Natural Language Processing, pp. 2122–2132 (2016)
7. Lowe, R., Noseworthy, M., Serban, I.V., Angelard-Gontier, N., Bengio, Y., Pineau, J.: Towards an automatic turing test: learning to evaluate dialogue responses. In: Proceedings of the 55th Annual Meeting of the Association for Computational Linguistics. Long Papers, vol. 1, pp. 1116–1126 (2017)
8. Lowe, R., Serban, I.V., Noseworthy, M., Charlin, L., Pineau, J.: On the evaluation of dialogue systems with next utterance classification. In: Proceedings of the 17th Annual Meeting of the Special Interest Group on Discourse and Dialogue, pp. 264–269 (2016)
9. Papineni, K., Roukos, S., Ward, T., Zhu, W.J.: BLEU: a method for automatic evaluation of machine translation. In: Proceedings of the 40th Annual Meeting on Association for Computational Linguistics, pp. 311–318. Association for Computational Linguistics (2002)
10. 张伟男, 张杨子, 刘挺: 对话系统评价方法综述. Chin. Sci. Bull. **57**, 3409 (2012)

Cross-Domain Transfer Learning for Dependency Parsing

Zuchao Li[1,2,3], Junru Zhou[1,2,3], Hai Zhao[1,2,3](✉), and Rui Wang[4]

[1] Department of Computer Science and Engineering, Shanghai Jiao Tong University, Shanghai, China
{charlee,zhoujunru}@sjtu.edu.cn, zhaohai@cs.sjtu.edu.cn

[2] Key Laboratory of Shanghai Education Commission for Intelligent Interaction and Cognitive Engineering, Shanghai Jiao Tong University, Shanghai, China

[3] MoE Key Lab of Artificial Intelligence, AI Institute, Shanghai Jiao Tong University, Shanghai, China

[4] National Institute of Information and Communications Technology (NICT), Kyoto, Japan
wangrui@nict.go.jp

Abstract. In recent years, the research of dependency parsing focuses on improving the accuracy of in-domain data and has made remarkable progress. However, the real world is different from a single scenario dataset, filled with countless scenarios that are not covered by the dataset, namely, out-of-domain. As a result, parsers that perform well on the in-domain data often suffer significant performance degradation on the out-of-domain data. Therefore, in order to adapt the existing in-domain parsers with substantial performance to the new domain scenario, cross-domain transfer learning techniques are essential to solve the domain problem in parsing. In this paper, we examine two scenarios for cross-domain transfer learning: semi-supervised and unsupervised cross-domain transfer learning. Specifically, we adopt a pretrained language model BERT for training on the source domain (in-domain) data at subword level and introduce two tri-training variant methods for the two scenarios so as to achieve the goal of cross-domain transfer learning. The system based on this paper participated in NLPCC-2019-shared-task on cross-domain dependency parsing and won the first place on the "subtask3-un-open" and "subtask4-semi-open" subtasks, indicating the effectiveness of the approaches adopted.

Keywords: Cross-domain · Transfer learning · Dependency parsing

1 Introduction

Dependency parsing is a critical task for understanding textual content which is to reveal the syntactic structure of linguistic components by analyzing their

This paper was partially supported by National Key Research and Development Program of China (No. 2017YFB0304100) and Key Projects of National Natural Science Foundation of China (U1836222 and 61733011).

J. Tang et al. (Eds.): NLPCC 2019, LNAI 11839, pp. 835–844, 2019.
https://doi.org/10.1007/978-3-030-32236-6_77

dependencies whose results can help the downstream task model better understand the input text [2–4,12]. Since dependency syntax is an artificially defined language structure, making high-quality labeled data relies on human analysis, and it is very time-consuming and painful. While most dependency parsers demonstrate very good performance currently [1,5,7,13], the existing labeled dependency parsing data are very limited in domain aspects, this means that parser, which currently performs well, has very few domains to work with. If the model trained from existing domain data is directly applied to the new domain, the performance will be greatly downgraded [19]. He et al. [9] shows that high-precision dependency syntax can be helpful for downstream tasks, while low-precision syntax is not only unhelpful but even harmful to the performance. Therefore, cross-domain dependency parsing has become the major challenge for applying syntactic analysis results in realistic downstream natural language processing (NLP) systems.

Transfer learning refers to the use of source domain $\mathcal{D}_S$ and source task $\mathcal{T}_S$ to improve the effect of target domain $\mathcal{D}_T$ and target task $\mathcal{T}_T$, that is, the information of $\mathcal{D}_S$ and $\mathcal{T}_S$ is transferred to $\mathcal{D}_T$ and $\mathcal{T}_T$. Among them, domain adaptation is a type of isomorphic transfer learning where $\mathcal{T}_S = \mathcal{T}_T$. In this paper, we focus on cross-domain transfer learning, namely domain adaptation. According to whether the target task or target domain has labeled data or not, transfer learning can be divided into three categories: supervised, semi-supervised and unsupervised transfer learning (domain adaptation).

With recent advances in transfer learning of NLP, there are two typical approaches that have shown to be very effective: pretrained language model and tri-training. Pretrained language models [6,14] have been shown to be very useful features for several NLP tasks like POS Tagging, name entity recognition (NER), constituent parsing, dependency parsing, and machine reading comprehension (MRC). Using large-scale unsupervised (unlabeled) text corpus data to train a language model, and then using supervised target task data (labeled) to finetune the language model and train the target model at the same time, so as to make the finetuned language model more emphasize the language information contained in specific tasks. Tri-training [21] aims to pick up some high-quality auto-labeled training instances from unlabeled data using bootstrapping methods. Ruder and Plank [15] found that the classical bootstrapping algorithms: tri-training, provide a stronger baseline for unsupervised transfer learning with results which are even better than the current state-of-the-art systems trained in the same domain.

In this paper, we report our system participating in NLPCC-2019-shared-task [16]. Our system[1] performs dependency parsing training at the subword level, using pre-trained language model BERT as our encoder, Biaffine attention as the scorer of dependency arcs and relations, and using the graph-based dependency tree search algorithm with the token mask to obtain the final dependency tree at the word level. Among them, we use the pre-trained language model BERT to transfer learn the language features from large-scale of the unlabeled

[1] Our code will be available at https://github.com/bcmi220/cddp.

corpus (Wikipedias, etc.). The tri-training variant method is adopted to use the unlabeled in-domain data for iterative training, and the provided development set is used for model selection during model iteration. For unsupervised sub-task, we only use the in-domain unlabeled data for tri-training, while for semi-supervised sub-task, in-domain training data and auto-parsed data were mixed for tri-training. In summary, our contributions can be concluded as follows:

- For Chinese dependency parsing, we need to do word segmentation (CWS) in the first step. Because of the different new word collections of different domains, the dictionary differences of different domains are relatively large, which affects the effect of domain transfer learning. In order to reduce this problem, we perform dependency parsing at Chinese subword level and propose a dependency tree search algorithm for subword level based on token mask, which can restore the dependency tree structure at the word level.
- Tri-training variant methods are proposed, and the results show that they are more effective than the original one for the dependency parsing task.
- The official evaluation results showed that our system achieved the state-of-the-art results on "subtask3-un-open" and "subtask4-semi-open" subtasks, which proved the effectiveness of our method[2].

2 Related Work

2.1 Token Level Dependency Parsing

Traditional dependency parsing is usually defined on word level (as shown in the top part of Fig. 1). For Chinese and similar languages, the word segmentation (WS) is the preliminary pre-processing step for dependency parsing. However, the pipeline parsing way for Chinese and other similar languages will suffer from some limitations such as error propagation and out-of-vocabulary (OOV) problems. Therefore, some researchers have studied the dependency parsing based on more fine-grained lexical units (tokens) like subwords, characters, etc. (The bottom of Fig. 1 is an example of dependency parsing at subword level).

Hatori et al. [8] first propose a transition-based model for Chinese word segmentation, POS tagging, and dependency parsing by introducing a pseudo inter-character arc inside the word. Zhang et al. [18] further expands the model of [8], and regards the internal relation between characters of a word as a real existed dependency arc, thus dividing the dependency into inter-word dependencies and intra-word dependencies. Kurita et al. [11] is the first neural approaches for fully joint Chinese analysis that is known to prevent the error propagation

[2] Subtasks "subtask1-un-closed" and "subtask2-semi-closed" are not our focus. Since our baseline parsing framework is based on BERT and subtasks 1 and 2 prohibit the use of BERT and other external resources, we only use the transformer structure of BERT, without using BERT pretrained weights for initialization. The transformer network of BERT is very deep and the currently offered training dataset is too small to train the deep network well, so we only reached comparable results to other participants. This illustrates the deep neural network need enough data for training.

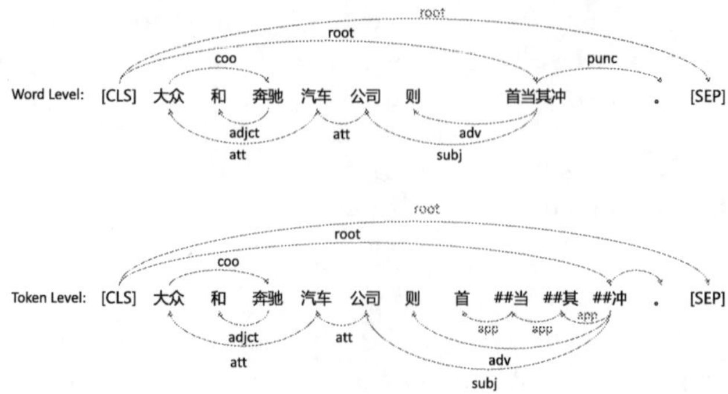

Fig. 1. Dependency tree in word and subword (token) level.

problem of pipeline models. Yan et al. [17] propose a unified model for joint Chinese word segmentation and dependency parsing at the character level which integrates these two tasks in one Biaffine graph-based parsing model by adding a real inter-character dependency like [18].

3 Proposed System

3.1 Overview

Figure 2 illustrates the architecture of our subword-level dependency parsing system which participated in the NLPCC-2019-shared-task. Our system is based on graph-based biaffine dependency parser [7], which consists of three parts: encoder, biaffine scorer and parsing inferencer. We make a few modifications to the graph-based architectures of [7]:

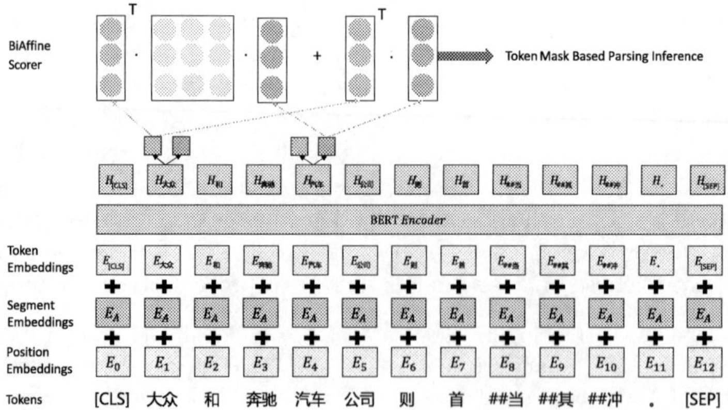

Fig. 2. The system architecture which participated in the shared task.

- For the encoder, we use the Transformer encoder with BERT pretrained weights and subword embeddings for initialization instead of the randomly initialized BiLSTM with pretrained word embeddings as input; In order to prevent error propagation, we do not use any other information such as POS tag except subword, which reduces the dependency of the model.
- For the detailed task definition in our system, we use "**[CLS]**" defined in the BERT model as the virtual "**ROOT**" node for dependency parsing and use "**[SEP]**" as the end tag of the sequence, and create a new dependent arc with "root" relation, pointing from "**[CLS]**" ("**ROOT**") to "**[SEP]**". Besides, we follow [18] to add an "**app**" dependency relation to represent the dependencies within the word (inter-character) and we take the subword end of a word as the node (if a word has no subwords, we define the subword end is the word itself) where the word generates its dependency with other words, as shown in Fig. 1.
- For the parsing inferencer: in the original word-level dependency parser, the MST algorithm is used as the search (inference) algorithm to ensure the dependency tree is well-formed at test time. Since the subword-level has an intra-word (inter-character) dependency arc, and in order to guarantee the original segmentation of the task (that is, the final dependency tree is restored to the original word-level), we propose a token mask based MST search algorithm.
- For the training objective in supervised tri-training phase: In the supervised tri-training phase, since we need to mix golden labeled data with auto-parsed data, we set different confidences on the data to control the loss of training.

3.2 Token Mask Based Parsing Inference

Due to changes in the granularity (from word to subword) of task definitions, the tree search algorithm in the test phase also needs to be changed accordingly. If the original word-level MST algorithm is used to search the dependency tree for subword-level dependency graphs, it may generate incorrect intra-word (inter-character) dependencies and inter-word dependencies, resulting in failure to restore a well-defined dependency tree at the word level[3]. Therefore, it is necessary to make some hard constraints on the score (weight) of the graph edges.

Since we have the original word segmentation information, we can use the word segmentation information to obtain the token range within the word and between the words, so that so that the mask is used to remove the illegal head. Figure 3 is a typical example to illustrate three important types of masks:

- Words with no subwords: its valid choice is the subword end of all words except itself, like "大众 (*Volkswagen*)" in the example.

[3] For the training phase, there is no need to consider this issue at all. As with other graph-based models, the predicted tree at training time is the one where each word is a dependent of its highest scoring head including intra-word and inter-word dependencies.

	[CLS]	大众	...	首	##当	##其	##冲	...	[SEP]
[CLS]	0	0	0	0	0	0	0	0	0
大众	1	0	1	0	0	0	1	1	0
...									
首	0	0	0	0	1	0	0	0	0
##当	0	0	0	0	0	1	0	0	0
##其	0	0	0	0	0	0	1	0	0
##冲	1	1	1	0	0	0	0	1	0
...									
[SEP]	1	0	0	0	0	0	0	0	0

Fig. 3. An example of token mask for parsing inference.

- Subwords that are not subword end of a word: the dependency of such subwords must be its successor subword, like "首 (*first*)", "##当 (*suffer*)", "##其 (*such*)".
- Subword ends: subword ends are the same as words with no subwords, like "##冲 (*attack*)".

Therefore, we multiply the scoring matrix predicted by the model by the mask matrix to ensure a word-level well-defined dependency tree.

3.3 Training Objective in Tri-training

The model is trained to optimize the probability of the dependency tree y when given a sentence x: $P_\theta(y|x)$, which can be factorized as:

$$P_\theta(y|x) = \prod_{i=1}^{l} P_\theta(y_i^{arc}, y_i^{rel}|x_i),$$

where θ represents learnable parameters, l denotes the length of the processing sentence, and y_i^{arc}, y_i^{rel} denote the highest scoring head and dependency relation for node x_i. It is implemented as the negative likelihood loss $\mathcal{L}$:

$$\mathcal{L} = (-\log P_\theta(y^{arc}|x)) + (-\log P_\theta(y^{rel}|x)).$$

Training with the combined labeled and auto-parsed data in supervised tri-training, the objective is to maximize the mixed likelihood (minimize the negative likelihood loss):

$$\mathcal{L} = \mathcal{L}_g + \alpha \cdot \mathcal{L}_a,$$

where α is the confidence for auto-parsed data at token level which is variable according to the number of tri-training iterations.

4 Task and Training Details

"NLPCC-2019 Shared Task on Cross-domain Dependency Parsing" [10,20] provides one source domain (BC) and three target domain (PB, PC, ZX) and setup four subtasks with two cross-domain scenarios, i.e., unsupervised domain adaptation (no target-domain training data) and semi-supervised (with target-domain training data), and two settings, i.e., closed and open.

According to the task requirements, the participant system in the closed task cannot use any external resources. As mentioned earlier, subtask 1 and 2 are not our focus, so the training details here are only for subtask 3 and 4. For the hyper-parameter of models trained on the source domain, The encoder initialized by the pre-trained language model: Chinese simplified and traditional BERT with 12-layer, 768-hidden, 12-heads, 110M parameters. When not otherwise specified, our model uses: 100-dimensional arc space and 128-dimensional relation space. We follow the downstream task finetune settings in [6], with learning rate $lr = 5e^{-5}$. The maximum number of epochs of training is set to 30. While for the models in the tri-training finetune process, the learning rate is reduced to $2e^{-3}$ and the finetune epochs is set to 3.

Algorithm 1. An variant tri-training method for unsupervised DA

```
for i ∈ {1..3} do
    m_i ← train_model(t_s, d_s, random_i)
end for
for i ∈ {4..N} do
    a_k ← parse(m_{i-3}, m_{i-2}, u_k)
    h_k ← merge(a_k, t_s)
    m_i ← finetune_model(m_{i-1}, h_k, d_k)
end for
```

Algorithm 2. An variant tri-training method for semi-supervised DA

```
for i ∈ {1..3} do
    m_i ← train_model(t_s, d_s, random_i)
end for
m_4 ← finetune_model(m_3, t_k, d_k)
for i ∈ {5..N} do
    a_k ← parse(m_{i-3}, m_{i-2}, u_k)
    h_k ← merge(a_k, t_k, t_s)
    m_i ← finetune_model(m_{i-1}, h_k, d_k)
end for
```

For unsupervised and semi-supervised domain adaptation (DA), we used slightly different tri-training variants as presented in Algorithm 1 and 2. Unlike traditional tri-training methods, we do not select data from auto-parsed data, but instead merge all auto-parsed data with source domain data and target domain data (semi-supervised domain adaptation). The golden data and auto-parsed data are assigned different weights (confidence) to achieve the goal of domain adaptation[4]. In the algorithm, we use $t_{s;k}$ to represent the golden labeled training dataset, $d_{s;k}$ denotes the development dataset on the corresponding domain, s represents the source domain (BC), and k represents the target domain ($k \in \{PB, PC, ZX\}$). u_k indicates unlabeled data on the target domain, and a_k indicates auto-parse data and h_k represents the mixed data on the target domain, and m_i represents the model of the i-th iteration training with random seed $random_i$.

We set the number of iteration tri-training steps N = 20. In each model training or finetune process, we use the labeled attachment (LAS) score on the development dataset to select the model, and only save the model with a higher score on the development dataset of the corresponding target domain for subsequent use[5]. When the iteration step $i < 10$, we set the confidence of auto-parse data to $\alpha = 0.2$, and $\alpha = 0.5$ at $i >= 10$.

Table 1. Official evaluation results of test dataset on subtask 3 and 4.

Systems	Subtask3-un-open				Subtask4-semi-open			
	PC	PB	ZX	AVG	PC	PB	ZX	AVG
PRIS_DP	39.8193	67.3118	69.5582		69.3003	77.3738	74.3534	
	26.2705	60.4097	61.5122	49.3975	60.3548	72.1046	68.2830	66.9141
Nanjing Normal	–	–	–	–	70.9653	80.5866	79.3283	
University	–	–	–	–	61.8239	75.8542	74.3534	70.6772
Ours	60.50	81.61	79.74		75.25	85.53	86.14	
	49.49	76.77	74.32	**66.86**	67.77	81.51	81.65	**76.9767**

5 Main Results

Table 1 shows the official evaluation results of test dataset on subtask 3 and 4, the results show that we have obtained the state-of-the-art cross-domain parsing results, among which the advantages of unsupervised domain adaptation are particularly obvious.

[4] Due to the tri-training iterative training process, the unlabeled data will be much larger than the golden annotation data. In order to balance the training process of the model, we repeat the golden data to achieve the same amount of data as the unlabeled data, and then perform data shuffle during training.

[5] The initial score for each model run is set to 0, so at least one model will be saved for each training session.

6 Ablation Study

To verify the effect of tri-training, we record the LAS results on tri-training process based on the setting of subtask3, and the results are shown in Fig. 4. It can be seen from the trend that the tri-training adopted by us is indeed effective.

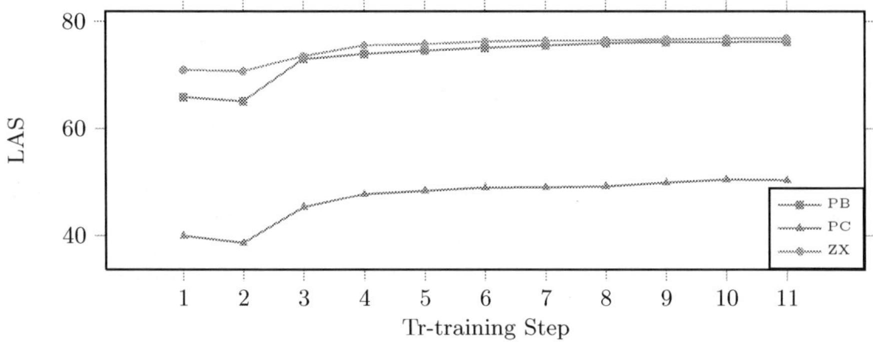

Fig. 4. Performances on dev dataset with settings of subtask3.

In order to demonstrate the role of subword in the parsing domain adaptation, we also performed an extra experimental performance comparison based on subword and word levels as show in Table 2. From the comparison results, subword can play an effect in the field migration, but for some areas, the effect may not be very obvious, especially under semi-supervised settings.

Table 2. Word and subword level evaluation results on dev dataset with setting of subtask 3 and 4.

System	Subtask3-un-open			Subtask4-semi-open		
	PC	PB	ZX	PC	PB	ZX
Word	51.70	76.37	71.34	73.54	80.73	83.35
	39.35	70.10	65.28	66.38	76.16	79.23
Subword	52.24	76.47	71.93	73.6	80.78	83.82
	39.93	70.9	65.85	66.49	76.11	79.62

7 Conclusion

This paper presents our system that participant in the NLPCC2019-shared task. The official evaluation results show that our proposed approaches can yield significantly improved results over cross-domain dependency parsing.

References

1. Andor, D., et al.: Globally normalized transition-based neural networks. In: Proceedings of ACL (2016)
2. Angeli, G., Premkumar, M.J.J., Manning, C.D.: Leveraging linguistic structure for open domain information extraction. In: Proceedings of ACL-IJCNLP (2015)
3. Bowman, S.R., Gauthier, J., Rastogi, A., Gupta, R., Manning, C.D., Potts, C.: A fast unified model for parsing and sentence understanding. In: Proceedings of ACL (2016)
4. Chen, K., et al.: Neural machine translation with source dependency representation. In: Proceedings of EMNLP (2017)
5. Clark, K., Luong, M.T., Manning, C.D., Le, Q.: Semi-supervised sequence modeling with cross-view training. In: Proceedings of EMNLP (2018)
6. Devlin, J., Chang, M.W., Lee, K., Toutanova, K.: BERT: pre-training of deep bidirectional transformers for language understanding. arXiv preprint arXiv:1810.04805 (2018)
7. Dozat, T., Manning, C.D.: Deep biaffine attention for neural dependency parsing. arXiv preprint arXiv:1611.01734 (2016)
8. Hatori, J., Matsuzaki, T., Miyao, Y., Tsujii, J.: Incremental joint approach to word segmentation, POS tagging, and dependency parsing in Chinese. In: Proceedings of ACL (2012)
9. He, S., Li, Z., Zhao, H., Bai, H.: Syntax for semantic role labeling, to be, or not to be. In: Proceedings of ACL (2018)
10. Jiang, X., Li, Z., Zhang, B., Zhang, M., Li, S., Si, L.: Supervised treebank conversion: data and approaches. In: Proceedings of ACL (2018)
11. Kurita, S., Kawahara, D., Kurohashi, S.: Neural joint model for transition-based Chinese syntactic analysis. In: Proceedings of ACL (2017)
12. Levy, O., Goldberg, Y.: Dependency-based word embeddings. In: Proceedings of ACL (2014)
13. Li, Z., Cai, J., He, S., Zhao, H.: Seq2seq dependency parsing. In: Proceedings of COLING, pp. 3203–3214 (2018)
14. Peters, M., et al.: Deep contextualized word representations. In: Proceedings of NAACL-HLT, pp. 2227–2237 (2018)
15. Ruder, S., Plank, B.: Strong baselines for neural semi-supervised learning under domain shift. In: Proceedings of ACL (2018)
16. Peng, X., Li, Z., Zhang, M., Wang, R., Si, L.: Overview of the NLPCC 2019 shared task: cross-domain dependency parsing. In: Proceedings of NLPCC (2019)
17. Yan, H., Qiu, X., Huang, X.: A unified model for joint Chinese word segmentation and dependency parsing. arXiv preprint arXiv:1904.04697 (2019)
18. Zhang, M., Zhang, Y., Che, W., Liu, T.: Character-level Chinese dependency parsing. In: Proceedings of ACL (2014)
19. Zhang, Y., Wang, R.: Cross-domain dependency parsing using a deep linguistic grammar. In: Proceedings of ACL-AFNLP (2009)
20. Zhang, Y., Li, Z., Lang, J., Xia, Q., Zhang, M.: Dependency parsing with partial annotations: an empirical comparison. In: Proceedings of IJCNLP (2017)
21. Zhou, Z.H., Li, M.: Tri-training: exploiting unlabeled data using three classifiers. IEEE TKDE **17**(11), 1529–1541 (2005)

Author Index

Printed in the United States
By Bookmasters